Colonial Crucible

"Columbia's Easter Bonnet." *Puck,* April 6, 1901. (General Research Division, New York Public Library, Astor, Lenox and Tilden Foundations)

Colonial Crucible

*Empire in the Making of the
Modern American State*

Edited by

Alfred W. McCoy and Francisco A. Scarano

THE UNIVERSITY OF WISCONSIN PRESS

Publication of this volume has been made possible, in part, through generous
support from the Evjue Foundation, Inc., the charitable arm of *The Capital Times* and,
at University of Wisconsin–Madison, the Anonymous Fund of the College of Letters
and Sciences, the George L. Mosse Program in the Department of History, and the
Robert Turell Fund of the Department of Medical History and Bioethics.

The University of Wisconsin Press
1930 Monroe Street, 3rd Floor
Madison, Wisconsin 53711-2059

www.wisc.edu/wisconsinpress/

3 Henrietta Street
London WC2E 8LU, England

Copyright © 2009
The Board of Regents of the University of Wisconsin System
All rights reserved. No part of this publication may be reproduced, stored in a
retrieval system, or transmitted, in any format or by any means, digital, electronic,
mechanical, photocopying, recording, or otherwise, or conveyed via the Internet or
a Web site without written permission of the University of Wisconsin Press, except
in the case of brief quotations embedded in critical articles and reviews.

1   3   5   4   2

Printed in the United States of America

Library of Congress Cataloging-in-Publication Data

Colonial crucible : empire in the making of the modern American
state / edited by Alfred W. McCoy and Francisco A. Scarano.
p. cm.
Includes bibliographical references and index.
ISBN 978-0-299-23104-0 (pbk. : alk. paper)
ISBN 978-0-299-23103-3 (e-book)
1. Imperialism—United States. 2. United States—Foreign relations—1897–1901.
3. United States—Foreign relations—1901–1909. 4. United States—Territorial expansion.
I. McCoy, Alfred W. II. Scarano, Francisco A. (Francisco Antonio)
E713.C68 2009
973.88—dc22
2008043120

For

WILLIAM APPLEMAN WILLIAMS (1921–1990)

and his colleagues in the
Wisconsin School of U.S. Diplomatic History

CONTENTS

ILLUSTRATIONS   xi

PREFACE   xiii

PART 1. EXPLORING IMPERIAL TRANSITIONS

On the Tropic of Cancer: Transitions and Transformations in the
U.S. Imperial State   ALFRED W. MCCOY, FRANCISCO A. SCARANO,   3
AND COURTNEY JOHNSON

Reading Imperial Transitions: Spanish Contraction, British Expansion,
and American Irruption   JOSEP M. FRADERA   34

From Old Empire to New: The Changing Dynamics and Tactics of
American Empire   THOMAS MCCORMICK   63

PART 2. POLICE, PRISONS, AND LAW ENFORCEMENT

INTRODUCTION   ALFRED W. MCCOY   83

American Penal Forms and Colonial Spanish Custodial-Regulatory
Practices in Fin de Siècle Puerto Rico   KELVIN SANTIAGO-VALLES   87

Prohibiting Opium in the Philippines and the United States:
The Creation of an Interventionist State   ANNE L. FOSTER   95

Policing the Imperial Periphery: Philippine Pacification and the
Rise of the U.S. National Security State   ALFRED W. MCCOY   106

"The Prison That Makes Men Free": The Iwahig Penal Colony and the
Simulacra of the American State in the Philippines   MICHAEL SALMAN   116

Part 3. Education

INTRODUCTION ADAM NELSON	131
Negotiating Colonialism: "Race," Class, and Education in Early-Twentieth-Century Puerto Rico SOLSIRÉE DEL MORAL	135
Enlightened Tolerance or Cultural Capitulation? Contesting Notions of American Identity AMÍLCAR ANTONIO BARRETO	145
The Business of Education in the Colonial Philippines, 1909–30 GLENN ANTHONY MAY	151
The Imperial Enterprise and Educational Policies in Colonial Puerto Rico PABLO NAVARRO-RIVERA	163
Understanding the American Empire: Colonialism, Latin Americanism, and Professional Social Science, 1898–1920 COURTNEY JOHNSON	175

Part 4. Race and Imperial Identities

INTRODUCTION CLARE CORBOULD	193
Race, Empire, and Transnational History PAUL A. KRAMER	199
Censuses in the Transition to Modern Colonialism: Spain and the United States in Puerto Rico FRANCISCO A. SCARANO	210
Race and the Suffrage Controversy in Cuba, 1898–1901 ALEJANDRO DE LA FUENTE AND MATTHEW CASEY	220
From Columbus to Ponce de León: Puerto Rican Commemorations between Empires, 1893–1908 CHRISTOPHER SCHMIDT-NOWARA	230
A Critical-Historical Genealogy of *Koko* (Blood), *'Aina* (Land), Hawaiian Identity, and Western Law and Governance RONA TAMIKO HALUALANI	238
Buying into Empire: American Consumption at the Turn of the Twentieth Century KRISTIN HOGANSON	248
Confabulating American Colonial Knowledge of the Philippines: What the Social Life of Jose E. Marco's Forgeries and Ahmed Chalabi Can Tell Us about the Epistemology of Empire MICHAEL SALMAN	260

Part 5. Imperial Medicine and Public Health

INTRODUCTION NANCY TOMES	273
Pacific Crossings: Imperial Logics in United States' Public Health Programs WARWICK ANDERSON	277

A Fever for Empire: U.S. Disease Eradication in Cuba as Colonial
Public Health   MARIOLA ESPINOSA   288

Mapping Regional and Imperial Geographies: Tropical Disease in the
U.S. South   NATALIE J. RING   297

The Conquest of Molecules: Wild Yams and American Scientists in
Mexican Jungles   GABRIELA SOTO LAVEAGA   309

Tropical Conquest and the Rise of the Environmental Management State:
The Case of U.S. Sanitary Efforts in Panama   PAUL S. SUTTER   317

PART 6. POLITY, LAW, AND CONSTITUTION

INTRODUCTION   JOHN OHNESORGE   329

Empire and the Transformation of Citizenship   332
CHRISTINA DUFFY BURNETT

The Afterlife of Empire: Sovereignty and Revolution in the
Philippines   VICENTE L. RAFAEL   342

The U.S. Constitution and Philippine Colonialism: An Enduring
and Unfortunate Legacy   OWEN J. LYNCH   353

Spanish Structure, American Theory: The Legal Foundations of a
Tropical New Deal in the Philippine Islands, 1898–1935
ANNA LEAH FIDELIS T. CASTAÑEDA   365

The Hazards of Jeffersonianism: Challenges of State Building in the
United States and Its Empire   PAUL D. HUTCHCROFT   375

PART 7. U.S. MILITARY

INTRODUCTION: THE MILITARY AND THE U.S. IMPERIAL STATE   393
CHRISTOPHER CAPOZZOLA

"Mohammedan Religion Made It Necessary to Fire": Massacres on the
American Imperial Frontier from South Dakota to the
Southern Philippines   JOSHUA GEDACHT   397

The U.S. Army as an Occupying Force in Muslim Mindanao, 1899–1913
PATRICIO N. ABINALES   410

Minutemen for the World: Empire, Citizenship, and the National Guard,
1903–1924   CHRISTOPHER CAPOZZOLA   421

From Winship to Leahy: Crisis, War, and Transition in Puerto Rico   431
JORGE RODRÍGUEZ BERUFF

French and American Imperial Accommodation in the Caribbean during World War II: The Experience of Guyane and the Subaltern Roles of Puerto Ricans   HUMBERTO GARCÍA-MUÑIZ AND REBECA CAMPO   441

Guantánamo and the Case of Kid Chicle: Private Contract Labor and the Development of the U.S. Military   JANA K. LIPMAN   452

The Impact of the Philippine Wars (1898–1913) on the U.S. Army
BRIAN MCALLISTER LINN   460

PART 8. ENVIRONMENTAL MANAGEMENT

INTRODUCTION: ENVIRONMENTAL AND ECONOMIC MANAGEMENT
J. R. MCNEILL   475

Conservation and Colonialism: Gifford Pinchot and the Birth of Tropical Forestry in the Philippines   GREG BANKOFF   479

Manila's Imperial Makeover: Security, Health, and Symbolism
DANIEL F. DOEPPERS   489

"'The World Was My Garden'": Tropical Botany and Cosmopolitanism in American Science, 1898–1935   STUART MCCOOK   499

Scientific Superman: Father José Algué, Jesuit Meteorology, and the Philippines under American Rule, 1897–1924   JAMES FRANCIS WARREN   508

PART 9. THE ELUSIVE CHARACTER OF AMERICAN GLOBAL POWER

The Limits of American Empire: Democracy and Militarism in the Twentieth and Twenty-first Centuries   JEREMI SURI   523

Crucibles, Capillaries, and Pentimenti: Reflections on Imperial Transformations   NANCY TOMES   532

Empire in American History   IAN TYRRELL   541

NOTES   557

CONTRIBUTORS   645

INDEX   649

ILLUSTRATIONS

Maps

The U.S. island empire, along the Tropic of Cancer, circa 1898	22
Submarine warfare in the North Atlantic, 1941–42	443
Gifford Pinchot's travels in the Philippines, 1902	481

Figures

"Columbia's Easter Bonnet"	ii
"The Great American Durbar"	xvi
President Roosevelt addresses the crew of USS *Connecticut*, February 22, 1909	2
"It ought to be a happy new year: Uncle Sam and his English cousin have the world between them"	36
First Company, Philippines Constabulary, Pampanga Province, 1908	82
Opium den in Manila, 1924	100
Class in lace making, Cabanatuan, Nueva Ecija, Philippines, 1912	130
Carlisle Industrial School, 1904 graduating class	168
William H. Taft and Elihu Root, circa 1904	182
"Educational Value of the Constabulary"	192
"Troubles which May Follow an Imperial Policy"	203
"There's plenty of room at the table. Why not ask the hungry little fellow to sit down?"	225
"The May Sale of Philippine Lingerie"	253
"Line-Pail Brigade, Manila, during Cholera Epidemic, circa 1902–4"	272
"The First Mountain to Be Removed"	322
William H. Taft on water buffalo, circa 1901	328

Apolinario Mabini, at Anda police station, Intramuros, Manila, 1900   347
"A Problem for the Lawyer: How to Get Around These"   359
War propaganda poster above Calle Comercio in Ponce, Puerto Rico,
    circa 1942   392
"The Harvest in the Philippines"   399
"Those pious Yankees can't throw stones at us anymore"   405
"The Gibraltar of the Caribbean." Air power over Old San Juan,
    Puerto Rico   435
Captain Juan Meléndez-Utset, during World War II   447
American colonial seated in a rubber tree, circa 1907   474
Battleship USS *Missouri* in the Miraflores Locks, Panama Canal   522

PREFACE

This volume is the culmination of a five-year collaborative effort by a community of scholars at the University of Wisconsin–Madison and some forty academics at other universities scattered across four continents. Through conversations, correspondence, and seminars at a variety of venues from Leiden to Sydney, we merged a diverse array of scholarly expertise into a singular endeavor to explore the ascent of the United States to global power. As a first step back in 2003, Victor Bascara and Courtney Johnson launched this project with a two-year colloquium through Madison's Center for the Humanities that drew a dozen scholars, local and visiting, to present working papers on the transition from Spanish to American rule in the Philippines. A year later a second strand in this inquiry started as a series of wide-ranging discussions at the VII International Philippines Studies Association Conference at Leiden, Netherlands, reflecting on the mutual transformations, colonial and metropolitan, that accompanied the U.S. conquest and colonization of the Philippines. From these early discussions emerged a wide-ranging project to explore these imperial transitions and transformations, not just in the Philippines but along an arc of islands stretching halfway around the world from Puerto Rico to the Philippines that became America's insular empire after 1898.

By joining together dozens of academics from around the globe who study the half-dozen island nations and territories that once made up this early U.S. empire, this project tried to achieve the sheer geographical and cultural range necessary for such an ambitious inquiry. To engage both transitions and transformations within this sprawling island empire, we framed a volume that pairs broad, historiographic reflections with specific inquiries into discrete arenas of colonial nation building. Consequently, this project probed a wide range of topics—policing, environmental management, economic development, race, public health, education, and military mobilization—to discover how U.S. colonial states across the globe shed their Gilded Age, laissez-faire reticence about intervention into "natural" realms and refined new tactics for the relentless imposition of rationality and order, adding, through these ad hoc experiments in colonial governance, unimagined capacities to the American practice of statecraft. From these close-grained empirical studies, often the result of years, sometimes decades of study by individual scholars, we then struggled to craft a new whole from the sum of these parts, exploring what ways, if any, the U.S. state was formed or even transformed from these experiences gained at its colonial periphery.

In this large and uncommonly costly inquiry, we drew upon almost every available source of support for the humanities at the University of Wisconsin–Madison, including the Anonymous Fund, the Brittingham Fund, the Center for the Humanities, the Harvey Goldberg Center, the George W. Mosse Fund, the A. W. Mellon Interdisciplinary Workshops in the Humanities, and the Robert Turell Fund of the Department of Medical History and Bioethics. Several administrative units also provided considerable help in managing the three-day seminar in November 2006 for a first reading of the papers in this volume, notably the History Department, the Center for Southeast Asian Studies, and the Latin American, Caribbean, and Iberian Studies Program (LACIS)

In a university run by shared faculty governance, these committees work through the efforts of individual scholars whose time, support, and advice have been essential to the publication of this volume. Throughout the first five years of this empires project, the director of the Center for the Humanities, Susanne Wofford, was a generous patron, providing strategic advice about intellectual direction and crafting an innovative frame for dialogue among scholars on all sides of this imperial divide. Within the History Department, a number of colleagues lent advice and support, including Ned Blackhawk, John M. Cooper, David McDonald, Stephen Kantrowitz, Florencia Mallon, Steve J. Stern, and Thongchai Winichakul. Much of the project's administrative support was provided by staff at the Center for Southeast Asian Studies, including Michael Cullinane, Mary Jo Wilson, and, above all, Joshua Gedacht, who managed many of the countless details that made this transnational collaboration possible. Moreover, LACIS staff, notably Aldà Blanco and Alberto Vargas, provided valuable support at key stages. At the International Institute, Dean Gilles Bousquet, Associate Dean Guido Podestá, and program director Kris Olds provided support through the World Universities Network (WUN) that facilitated collaboration with universities in Australia and Europe.

Through scholarly collaboration under this same WUN imprimatur, the University of Sydney hosted a stimulating, two-day seminar on comparative imperial transitions facilitated by the gracious cooperation of Robert Aldrich,

Warwick Anderson, Clare Corbould, and Duncan Ivison. Scholars at the Universidad de Puerto Rico were generous in their support of this common endeavor, notably Jorge Rodríguez Beruff and Humberto García Muñiz, who contributed essays. Elsewhere, Josep Maria Fradera of the Universitat Pompeu Fabra in Barcelona has lent his expertise about Spanish imperial history to this project.

Once the volume moved into production, we have enjoyed the generous support from staff at all levels at the University of Wisconsin Press. Among the many who helped we are particularly grateful to press director Shelia Leary, managing editor Adam Mehring, assistant production manager Carla Aspelmeier, our assiduous copy editor Jan Opdyke, and, above all, to our acquisitions editor Gwen Walker, who helped shape a mass of disparate conference papers into a coherent edited volume.

To make this book accessible to students, we are grateful for generous publication subventions from the Evjue Foundation, Inc., the charitable arm of The Capital Times and, at University of Wisconsin–Madison, the Anonymous Fund of the College of Letters and Sciences, the George L. Mosse Program in the Department of History, and the Robert Turell Fund of the Department of Medical History and Bioethics.

On a personal note, we are grateful for the patience and understanding of Mary McCoy and Olga Scarano, whose support allowed us, midst many competing demands, to invest our energies in this project. As some recompense for this time taken from family life, we offer our loving thanks.

We are also mindful of our intellectual debts to earlier generations of historians who have preceded us in this intellectual inquiry. Although its proponents have long retired or moved on, the intellectual influence of the famed Wisconsin school of diplomatic history still lingers about these corridors, its independent spirit still inspiring a critical perspective on the U.S. ascent to global power, sparing us the triumphal inclination that sometimes accompanies the study of this topic elsewhere in America. Among those who write in this tradition, we are grateful to Tom McCormick for contributing an essay and to both Lloyd Gardner and Walter LaFeber for their generous assessments that appear elsewhere in this volume. To acknowledge our intellectual debt to the founder of this school and its spirit of critical inquiry, we dedicate this volume to William Appleman Williams and his Wisconsin school of U.S. diplomatic history.

"The Great American Durbar" satirizes President Theodore Roosevelt's inauguration in 1905, mocking an imperial grandeur that seems to mime the grand parade of elephant-riding Indian maharajas during the Coronation Durbar at Delhi in 1903 proclaiming England's King Edward VII the Emperor of India. *Harper's Weekly*, March 4, 1905. (General Research Division, New York Public Library, Astor, Lenox and Tilden Foundations)

PART 1

Exploring Imperial Transitions

President Theodore Roosevelt addresses the crew of USS *Connecticut* in Hampton Roads, Virginia, upon return from the Atlantic Fleet's cruise around the world as the "Great White Fleet," February 22, 1909. (Collection of Lieutenant Commander Richard Wainwright, Jr., USN, U.S. Naval Historical Center)

On the Tropic of Cancer

Transitions and Transformations in the U.S. Imperial State

ALFRED W. MCCOY, FRANCISCO A. SCARANO,
AND COURTNEY JOHNSON

AMONG THE COLONIAL EMPIRES that once ruled the globe, the United States was an elusive, even paradoxical power. All the usual imperial labels that attach so readily to Great Britain or France seem to require qualification when applied to America. By 1900, Britain's empire covered a quarter of the earth's entire surface; America's skipped along a string of small islands dotting the Tropic of Cancer from the Caribbean to the Western Pacific. Europe's empires expanded relentlessly for five centuries to rule a full third of humanity; the United States held most of its larger colonies for just a few decades and governed only a few million people. Yet empire left an indelible imprint on the United States.[1] Colonialism was a crucible that plunged Washington's raw bureaucracy into the white heat of nationalist revolution and great power rivalry, forging new, heretofore unimagined state capacities. Indeed, the ramifications of this early American empire were far wider than anyone has yet imagined: a marked expansion in the role of the federal government for more activist domestic administration, and the formation of an agile, transnational imperial state for more effective global governance. From the perspective of the present, the American experience of empire is not only the least understood but arguably the most significant legacy of the high imperial age—creating a void that this volume seeks to fill.

Challenging America's post-imperial denial, this volume probes the central paradox surrounding the U.S. imperial experience. How could a fragmentary empire of island colonies have had such a profound impact upon this large continental nation? We seek to answer this question by assaying the ways that innovations in discrete areas of American colonial governance—from police and prisons to education and environmental management—migrated homeward to influence U.S. state formation in the early decades of the twentieth century. To examine the twin processes of colonial governance and imperial information transfer, these essays offer empirically based, analytically informed case studies that explore the deeper dynamics at work across this broad range of institutions governing the relationship between state and society. Tracing these now established elements of foreign and domestic policy to their inception in an imperial praxis, this volume represents a first step toward exploring the pervasive, persistent effects of the early-twentieth-century American empire—not only on the social fabric of its island colonies, or even on geopolitical relations among imperial rivals, but, crucially, on American strategies of international influence and, indeed, on the practice of statecraft in the United States itself. The transformative processes engendered by American colonial rule in the Caribbean and Pacific after 1898 gradually radiated far beyond these small islands at the edge of empire. Over time, these changes, articulated through a distinctive alliance of public and private sectors, percolated homeward through the invisible "capillaries of empire," ultimately shaping the metropolitan American state and its society in subtle yet profound ways. To be sure, empire was only one of several important factors in the formation of the modern American state. But it is one whose considerable, even catalytic role remains obscured by the current literature's focus on domestic, endogenous factors.

In discussing the United States as an imperial power, we need to make it clear at the outset that empire is not an epithet. It is a form of global governance in which a dominant power exercises control over the destiny of others through direct territorial rule (e.g., colonies) or indirect influence (e.g., military, economic, or cultural leverage). Whether we use the word *empire, bloc, alliance, commonwealth,* or *world order,* such dominion has persisted for much of the past four thousand years and is likely to continue, in some form, into the foreseeable future. Many have been brutal, some beneficent, and most a mix of both, but empires are an undeniable, unremitting fact of human history. After counting seventy empires in world history, Niall Ferguson notes wryly, "To those who would still insist on American 'exceptionalism,' the historian of empires can only retort: as exceptional as all the other sixty-nine empires."[2]

Most empires over the past two millennia have grown, as Hannah Arendt famously observed, via continental or overseas expansion. Continental empires (Hapsburg Europe, Mughal India, China, Russia, and pre-1867 United States) spread by conquest of contiguous territories that usually, though not always, centralized imperial governance within a unitary state. By contrast, overseas or maritime empires (ancient Rome, Great Britain, Spain, post-Napoleonic France, and post-1898 United States) necessarily decentralized their rule through surrogate states called, variously, colonies, protectorates, dominions, mandates, trust territories, military occupations, or even allies.[3] Muddling this too tidy typology, all empires engage in complex diplomacy with autonomous states, whose power relationship ranges from ally to vassal, to forge alliances and coalitions against both rival empires and rebels that threaten their world order.

In that fusion of power and policy called statecraft, each empire is distinct. With that qualifier, calling a nation that now controls half the world's military force and a third of its wealth an empire is nothing more than fitting an analytical frame to an array of such facts—an exercise devoid, in this post-cold-war world, of normative content or pejorative connotation.[4] Thus, we begin with the shared, self-evident premise that the United States acquired an overseas empire after 1898. Through each of these essays, we move on to explore the distinctive character of statecraft within what we call, somewhat more boldly, the American imperial state. By sparing ourselves concern for the underlying causality of imperial expansion, the old Marxist question, or the need to deny the existence of an American empire, its anticommunist antidote, we free ourselves to examine the nature of the state that Washington developed, at the dawn of the twentieth century, to rule an empire of islands that reached halfway around the globe.

Implicit within an approach that seems at first glance to sweep expansively across vast oceans and diverse cultures, there are, in fact, some significant limitations on the ambit of this inquiry. Simultaneous with its emergence as a colonial power, the United States was, of course, completing its continental expansion and flexing its influence as a rising global player via a less formal hegemony known as "dollar diplomacy." Thus, in the late nineteenth and early twentieth centuries, metropolitan state formation in the United States was, arguably, influenced by multiple processes of expansion—including the conquest of the western plains, the subjugation of Native Americans, and the exercise of global commercial influence as a second-tier imperial power quite apart from the acquisition of a formal empire of island colonies. In a complex reciprocal process, the practice of military domination in the overseas colonies drew, in part, from the experience of the Indian wars of the 1870s to 1880s, just as policies of Americanization via the school and health clinic drew on experience with "unassimilables" such as African-Americans, Native Americans, and many European immigrants. Indeed, for most of the imperial age Washington generally avoided the pitfalls of conquest and operated globally through episodic military incursions and economic influence. Direct colonial rule thus represented something of an aberration within a distinctively indirect American hegemony.

Yet there is a unique quality in the processes of formal conquest and control over overseas territories that leaves a palpable impress on a metropolitan state, lending extraordinary import to this fragment of the American experience. Several scholars have argued that Europe used its colonies as "laboratories of modernity" for "experiments in social engineering." But none has presumed to suggest that this same model might, in some way, apply to the modernization of the mighty American state.[5] Surprisingly few have responded to the provocative observation by John Lewis Gaddis that many American diplomatic historians, including some the most critical, have long assumed that "influence in international affairs flows in only one direction: outward from the United States," fostering the illusory sense that "other nations and people seldom affect what happens to Americans." According to Gaddis, comparative imperial history reveals that influence often flows "from areas of 'weakness' to those of 'strength'" or from peripheries "back to the 'metropole'"—an asymmetry of impact that means those "on the receiving end of imperialism" can, in fact, "force modifications in the behavior of even the most powerful imperial state."[6]

To cite a contemporary example that illustrates this process, the United States was arguably the world's sole superpower for nearly two decades before its recent occupation of Iraq and Afghanistan. Although hegemony and occupation are inextricably intertwined at many levels, there are some discernible differences between the generalized exercise of global power and the specific burdens of military conquest that will almost surely cause Afghanistan and Iraq to leave a lasting stamp on the American state. "An empire . . . is not just a state that subjugates other peoples or states," writes the Harvard historian Charles S. Maier most insistently. "It is a system of rule that transforms society at home even as it stabilizes inequality transnationally by replicating it geographically, in the core and on the periphery."[7]

Indeed, intense interactions with subjugated populations during these overseas occupations often stretch the capacities of an occupying power's statecraft to the breaking point, providing both the need and the opportunity for new state forms and capabilities. By thrusting the United States suddenly into an alien tropical terrain that spanned half the globe, colonial rule presented a host of unprecedented challenges—devastating storms, virulent diseases, and armed revolutionaries. Yet empire also allowed American expatriates unparalleled freedom to experiment with new ways to control both man and nature, producing innovations with the potential for a profound impact on the metropole.

Instead of engaging empire in all its variety and complexity, this collection focuses on an extreme form, colonialism, which one scholar has called "the most spectacular mode of imperialism's many and mutable states."[8] To move beyond the obvious limitations of leaving this task to specialists in U.S. history, the volume introduces the novel approach of making these consequences evident through the historiographies of the periphery instead of the core. In effect, the historians of the Philippines, Puerto Rico, and other colonies represented here are using their work, first, to capture the nuances of structure and agency within societies subjected to this form of imperial power and, then, to expose the mutually transformative nature of American colonial rule. Building on the influential work of Amy Kaplan and her colleagues, who made imperialism generally visible in American history, we are taking the next step, adding a fine-grained, empirical texture to the study of its empire and then analyzing the specific consequences of colonial rule, particularly for U.S. state formation.[9]

Weaving empire's influence deep into the warp of the American national narrative, this collection argues that Washington, through its global expansion after 1898, created a unique imperial state that exercised colonial rule with a comparatively light bureaucratic presence both at home and abroad. In contrast to the ponderous administration and visible grandeur of the great European empires, the United States ruled its disparate arc of islands through a nimble nexus of public-private alliances that relied on secondment or subcontracting for expertise and a local administration only loosely articulated, in both an institutional and a constitutional sense, within the U.S. system. Free from the gaze of far-off Washington, the more ambitious colonial officials and their private-sector partners conducted bold social experiments, which would have been difficult within domestic constraints, that later migrated homeward to contribute to a more activist federal government across a broad spectrum of administration. Innovations forged in the crucible of colonial rule contributed in significant ways to the transformation of the U.S. government from a small bureaucracy with weak domestic capacities and limited hemispheric reach into an expanded, empowered apparatus launched on a path to global power.

Often obscured and even underestimated in the wider debate about empire, colonial rule emerges from these essays as a resilient force for historical continuity, profoundly implicating all those caught in its grip whether core or periphery, colonizer or colonized. No matter how limited in scale or duration, colonialism left a lasting imprint on all states and societies somehow entangled in a powerfully Promethean experience that was, for colonizer and colonized, separately empowering and eviscerating yet mutually traumatic and transformative. Thus, in a chain of continuity spun out over the span of a century, Spain's scattered island colonies shaped the American experience of empire; dominion over these territories, in turn, unleashed catalytic forces that influenced federal state formation during the Progressive era; and traces of this lasting institutional imprint have been evident, in the aftermath of 9/11, during Washington's recent misadventures in the Middle East.

Reading Empire

Most fundamentally, the contributors to this volume share an enthusiasm for correcting what might be styled the insularity of U.S. history by placing the question of empire at the heart of metropolitan historiography. Most contributors are scholars not of the United States but of the Caribbean or Southeast Asia; they have reversed their usual optic to look not outward at Cubans or Filipinos but inward at the American colonials who conquered and colonized this early

American empire. The result is a revealing synthesis of successive historiographies that moved, over the span of decades, from the obsessive focus on the good works of white men in the tropics during the imperial age through an equally exclusive fascination with the indigenous in the postcolonial era to a more holistic approach that today joins both colonials and colonized in analysis of the modern, mutually interdependent world that took form at the ebb tide of empires.

Within the vast literature on imperialism, this volume seeks to break new ground by pursuing a path at the intersection of these established approaches. But, like most modern historiography, no matter how innovative, this endeavor builds on the work, both critical and conventional, of at least two generations of historians. During the cold war decade of the 1950s, when pressure for affirmation of America was strong, William Appleman Williams and his colleagues in the famed "Wisconsin school" of U.S. diplomatic history offered an unorthodox perspective on Washington's rise to world power. Amid this ideological clash with communism, an influential group of "consensus" historians revived the doctrine of "American exceptionalism," that is, the patriotic view that the United States had avoided Europe's class conflicts, authoritarian governments, and empires to become "an example of liberty for others to emulate."[10] In his dissenting treatise *The Tragedy of American Diplomacy*, Williams, by contrast, argued that America's "great debate of 1898–1901 over the proper strategy and tactics of ... expansion" had culminated in the triumph of a political coalition that "opposed traditional colonialism and advocated instead a policy of an open door through which America's preponderant economic strength would ... dominate all underdeveloped areas of the world." In effect, this "classic strategy of non-colonial imperial expansion," exemplified by Washington's declarations of an open door for free trade with China in 1899–1900, "became the strategy of American foreign policy for the next half-century," launching Washington on a relentless extension of its informal commercial empire.[11] Such expansion often begat aggression, most importantly against the Soviet Union at the end of World War II when, Williams argued, Washington's concerns over access to Eastern Europe and its markets sparked the cold war.[12]

As this revisionist view won a devoted audience during the Vietnam War, the Wisconsin school drew hostile fire. Its cold war revisionism was bitterly attacked in the early 1970s while its open door thesis of U.S. expansion was damned by Arthur M. Schlesinger Jr. in 1986 as "ludicrous" and dismissed by Ernest R. May in 1991 as "an artifact of the past."[13] Amid this rolling storm of controversy, few noted that Williams and his colleagues were, at least methodologically, rather conventional diplomatic historians, using U.S. sources to focus almost exclusively on American actors with little concern for foreign context whether in Europe, Latin America, or Asia.[14] The Wisconsin school was, moreover, focused on the "open door" as both precursor to and metaphor for an indirect empire of commerce and commodities, so its followers generally, though not entirely, ignored the more complex interactions of direct colonial rule that came with the U.S. conquests of 1898. To summarize such a large body of scholarship requires qualification, most importantly to note that Walter LaFeber's seminal study of late-nineteenth-century expansion, *The New Empire,* did indeed engage not only the social and economic motives for extracontinental conquest but also its colonial outcomes in the Caribbean and Pacific. Yet even this unconventional work relies entirely, in its exploration of the Caribbean context, on conventional U.S. diplomatic sources.[15]

Correcting these oversights, a succeeding generation of scholars trained in foreign area studies probed imperial interactions from an indigenous perspective, producing multifocal accounts of both imperial conquest and governance. Through an immersion in local sources, this scholarship produced new insights into the nuances of American colonial rule, particularly the dynamics of colonial warfare and dyadic ties between imperial officials and local elites.[16] The confluence of the Wisconsin school's critical perspective on U.S. global power and a succeeding generation's work in non-Western histories has laid the conceptual foundations for a renewed, even reinvigorated engagement with the problem of empire.

Drawing on these and other trends, such as dependency theory and world systems theory, more recent scholarship has laid to rest the assumption that empire and imperialism are somehow inappropriate subjects of inquiry for U.S. history, moving these topics from the dissident margins to the epicenter of contemporary scholarly concerns.[17] With the end of the cold war, which tainted the concepts of "empire" and "imperialism" in a subversively Marxist hue and made any such discussion what Andrew Bacevich calls "tantamount . . . to aiding and abetting the enemy," there has been an explosion of interest in the problem of empire.[18] Continuing, in a general sense, the critical spirit of earlier revisionist historians such as Williams, this growing literature argues, in sum, that it is vitally important to understand various phases of U.S. history, from the occupation of the western plains in the mid-nineteenth century to the invasion of Iraq in the early twenty-first, as episodes of imperial expansion and colonial subjugation.

Although the critical assessment of America's global power was generally dismissed during the cold war, its resonances have influenced the internationalization of U.S. history that has so invigorated the field over the past generation. In a 2001 roundtable published in the *Journal of American History,* Ann Stoler writes of "the profusion of new insights about 'becoming colonial' that students of North American history and colonial studies increasingly share"—a sharing quite fruitful for students of both comparative imperialism and American history.[19] Elsewhere, Christopher Capozzola focuses on studies of "America's burst of territorial acquisition after 1898" to conclude that "[a]n intellectual backwater has turned into one of the most dynamic fields in the historical profession."[20]

We do not have space in these introductory remarks to speculate on why it has taken American historians so long to discover empire in its various forms. Suffice it to say that the nation's conversion into the world's only superpower after the disintegration of the Soviet empire in 1991 has raised questions about the historical antecedents of this hegemony. The first post-cold-war decade of the 1990s also witnessed two moments of reflection about empire configured around commemorations—the quincentennial in 1992 of the irruption of Europeans into the Western Hemisphere and the Centennial of the Spanish-American War in 1998—that stirred interest in the subjects of imperialism, racialized rule, hegemony, and counterhegemony.

The parallel maturation of postcolonial studies, gender studies, New Labor History, and American studies as fields within American universities also helped erode the notion of the United States as an exception to great power imperialism. Examples of the opportunities offered by these domains for the production of new knowledge about American imperialism can be found in a volume generally regarded as pivotal, *Cultures of United States Imperialism*, edited by Amy Kaplan and Donald E. Pease. Attempting to fuse the questions, concerns, and conceptual frameworks of diplomatic historians with those of cultural studies, the editors collected essays that helped uncover "interanimations of U.S. cultures and U.S. imperialism."[21] In subsequent years, a spate of studies demonstrated how gender, race, and class open up fundamental perspectives for understanding U.S. foreign relations—particularly the creation of an island empire after 1898.

As the subject of the American empire emerged from the shadows and the historical literature grew conceptually more sophisticated, we became accustomed to scholarship that stretches the cultural boundaries of empire and nuances the practices of imperialism, usually in relation to gender, race, class, and intimacy—trends exemplified by Kaplan's *The Anarchy of Empire* and Stoler's anthology *Haunted by Empire*.[22] In Kaplan's view, imperial contacts of various sorts profoundly influenced American culture and society between the 1840s and the 1920s. Their effect was predicated on a blurring of boundaries between what or who was inside and outside of a nation or a national identity—a dimming of once important distinctions between colonizers and colonized, between foreign and domestic space. Kaplan shows the importance of understanding empire as a set of contingent, untidy, reciprocal relations rather than the accumulation of actions that, once taken at the metropolitan center, affect the colonial peripheries alone.

In Stoler's collection, such imperial reciprocities are a condition of possibility for deciphering the realm of intimate relationships within larger colonial relations, "a social and cultural space," she adds, "where racial classifications were defined and defied."[23] With intimacy as its analytical axis, Stoler's anthology lays down a crucial connector between scholarly debates in two spheres that previously had little contact—postcolonial studies on a worldwide scale and this growing literature on American imperialism. The most significant of these studies, including Mary Renda's on Haiti, Eileen Findlay's on Puerto Rico, and Eric Love's on racism in American imperialism *and* anti-imperialism, make us aware that the focus on political and military dimensions of overseas expansion, which had preoccupied much previous scholarship, did little to prepare us to grasp the reciprocal influences involved in American imperial endeavors.[24]

There is little doubt that over the past quarter century putting empire back into American history has been the single greatest achievement of a historiography no longer content with writing solely about U.S. foreign relations. The acknowledgment of empire not just as a system of political and economic domination but as a locus of production and reproduction of state, society, and culture on both sides of the imperial divide has also been an important advance in the literature on both U.S. history and American studies. Taking this self-corrective impulse as a beginning point, the present volume aims to explore its possibilities through close analysis of concrete moments in U.S. imperial history that illustrate the influence of colonial rule on specific aspects of American state formation back home in the metropole.

Imperial Transition

This "imperial turn" within American humanities has, almost inevitably, sparked renewed interest in the American conquest of a colonial empire that, for a full decade after 1898, became Washington's main national project. Through its sudden seizure of Spain's scattered island colonies, the United States was thrust into problems of pacification, colonization, and global defense for which it was generally unprepared. While westward expansion across the continent had mixed low-budget exploration and low-manpower military operations, overseas conquest was a much more demanding enterprise—a plunge into a volatile world of rival empires and revolutionary nationalism that strained the cultural, military, and diplomatic resources of the nascent American state to its limits.

As a late, largely untutored imperial power, the United States was suddenly confronted with the complexities of colonial rule in an era that witnessed both intensified imperial expansion and a resurgence of nationalist resistance. Instead of the pliable populations of earlier centuries, American officials had to deal with native elites determined to realize their own nationalist agendas for change either by confronting or collaborating with the new colonials. Lacking policies beyond Washington's broad-brush instructions on the most pressing issues, American colonizers initially defaulted to Spanish precedents or deferred to native aspirations. In the transition from Spanish to American rule in the Caribbean and Pacific, there was, therefore, an ironic dissonance between rhetoric and reality. As the U.S. Army expelled Spain from its former colonies after 1898, American empire builders espoused a rhetoric of imperial renewal, styling themselves reformers who would sweep away an antiquated, corrupt, Iberian colonialism and replace it with a modern, vigorous, Anglo-Saxon administration.

In reality, however, American imperialists were inheriting a series of late Spanish imperial states that were in the midst of their own liberal renovation. Applying the methods of science and doctrines of efficiency, the Spanish empire had created a series of centralized, modernizing colonial states markedly more effective and expansive than government in Spain itself, which was still weakened by the historic autonomy of provinces and cities, or for that matter Washington, D.C., where federalism and patronage restrained state capacities. Despite their rhetoric of uplift, American colonials in Cuba, Puerto Rico, and the Philippines were unwitting, even unwilling heirs to many of these Spanish colonial innovations—a model census, modern Benthamite prisons, centralized police, and empowered executives.

Through its immersion in these island conquests, Washington was exposed to the influence of the Spanish imperial state with its formidable central controls, powerful executive, and authoritarian police. Despite their dismissive rhetoric, accidental American colonials framed policies that thus bore the indelible traces of the resilient Spanish empire—its fusion of classical imperial controls grounded in Roman law and its liberal application of science to state modernization in the decades just before the U.S. occupation. As the former Philippine official David Barrows told an audience at the Panama-Pacific Exposition in 1915, Manila's extraordinarily powerful American governor-general reflected "the historic continuity of the office under Spain" that soon overcame an ingrained "American prejudice . . . against conferring centralized administrative control upon a single executive head."[25]

Structure of the Inquiry

To explore this elusive empire, this volume pairs broad, historiographic reflections with specific inquiries into discrete arenas of colonial nation building. The introductory essays offer broad reflections on the way the Spanish empire inscribed its cultural imprint on the succeeding U.S. imperial venture, creating a commonality and comparability across this vast swath of islands that reaches halfway around the globe. In an introductory essay, Josep Fradera places the United States' irruption as a colonial power in long gestation processes of imperial succession. By the end of the nineteenth century, all European empires were torn by a contradiction between rising expectations of liberty and inequitable colonial structures, and as Fradera notes, "all became exhausted, sooner or later, in the fight against the unstoppable leveling tide"—making the United States, with its paradoxical pairing of empire and liberty, a natural successor first to Spain and later to Great Britain. Carrying the story forward into the twentieth century, Thomas McCormick argues in this volume that, although the United

States had long been an empire through its continental expansion and episodic Caribbean adventures, it "mutated in the 1890s and thereafter as the result of structural shifts both in the American political economy and in the world system itself," becoming "arguably a new empire, a second empire." Throughout the twentieth century, the United States exercised its rising global influence through a mix of colonies, semiformal spheres, and an informal economic empire.

To lay the foundations for these expansive statements, this volume's empirical essays explore both specific U.S. colonial policies and their migration, over time, homeward to the American metropole. These seemingly distinct topics—ranging from the coercive realms of prisons and police to softer social policies of census and education—are instead analytic threads carefully selected to weave a tapestry of activist American colonial states intruding into local social or natural realms and developing a new, coercive paradigm for transforming a resilient nature and resistant native populations. If we can divine some logic within the mass of earlier scholarship on American imperial rule, much of it seemed to proceed by surveying the full spectrum of metropolitan policies applied to the colonial periphery, whether successfully or unsuccessfully. By contrast, in compiling the essays for this volume we selected a narrower range of administrative areas with particularly rich resonances between colony and metropole.

Analyzed through these areas of reciprocal influence, American colonial states across the globe shed their Gilded Age, laissez-faire reticence about intervention into "natural" realms. They refined new tactics for the relentless imposition of rationality and order, contributing, through these ad hoc experiments in colonial governance, to a marked expansion in the reach and range of domestic statecraft. In some areas, notably prison reform and public education, the United States had already developed powerful domestic mechanisms for social transformation, making their impact on the colonized the more significant aspect of this imperial interaction. But in other key areas—policing, drug prohibition, public health, and state sponsorship of natural science—American colonizers found themselves forging innovative administrative capacities that later had a significant influence on governance in the United States. On the eve of empire in 1898, this nation was what one landmark study called a "patchwork" or weak state with a loosely structured administrative apparatus, leaving ample room for the innovation and modernization that came, with stunning speed, in these imperial decades.[26]

More broadly, these essays reveal a three-tiered process of synergistic state formation: first, the growth of empowered American colonial states; next, an expanded federal government that modernized its apparatus, civil and military, as a response, in part, to the direct and indirect challenges of overseas rule; and, finally, a transnational apparatus comprising the United States, its colonial states, and their collaborators, all encompassed within an expanded defense perimeter that we call the American imperial state. In sum, these essays point toward a view of modern U.S. state formation as a three-phase imperial synthesis: first, the activist inclination of domestic progressivism was exported to these new colonies; then, its command qualities were heightened in the colonial context; and, ultimately, a new fusion for empowered governance took form as these amplified state capacities were repatriated, through personnel and precedents, back to the United States.

By trying to compress a sprawling American empire that spanned two oceans into the finite space between two covers, each contribution risks an omission and each emphasis entails an absence. Our focus on state formation at home and abroad thus precludes other approaches to empire's intersection with American culture, race relations, ethnic assimilation, and economic development. In this volume's exploration of colonial influences on the U.S. metropole, for example, Kristin Hoganson shows how the importation of tropical products wove empire, quite literally, deep into the fabric of American consumer culture. Clearly, this topic merits multifaceted elaboration, exemplified by Victoria de Grazia's recent study of the role of American-style consumption in exerting cultural influence across twentieth-century Europe.[27] Similarly, our emphasis on overseas territories such as the Philippines and Puerto Rico, the largest and most closely held of the American colonies respectively, has led to a comparatively light treatment of Cuba, Hawaii, and Panama and the outright omission of Haiti, Dominican Republic, Guam, and Samoa.[28] Yet this concentration on just two exemplary cases also affords readers a sharper sense of empire's cumulative and comparative impact—that is, the cumulative influence of multiple imperial policies on single colonies as well as a case-to-case comparison between colonies, both likely to be lost in more comprehensive coverage.

Varieties of Imperial Influence

As we sort through the ramifications of American empire, it seems that the more coercive aspects of colonial rule had a direct, discernible impact on the federal government at home, particularly in the realms of public health, policing, the military, and environmental management. By contrast, the influence of softer aspects of colonial governance, such as education and prison reform, did not seem to a make the same homeward migration. To this rough division we must add an additional filter for colonial impact—the U.S. separation of powers between federal, state, and local authorities. Federal and state governments played an important role in public health, allowing the colonial experience a ready point of entry. By contrast, education remained almost entirely a local responsibility, too diffuse for sudden, significant influence from any single source. Although policing, too, had long been a largely municipal function, the federal government began building a national security apparatus between 1908 and 1917, creating another opportunity for overseas empire to influence domestic affairs.

To begin with the basics, American colonials had an extraordinary freedom for bold social experimentation frequently barred by legal or political challenges at home. Often empire was a mere canvas on which imperious egos painted the landscape with ill-conceived disasters reminiscent of Joseph Conrad's rusting steel carcasses in that "heart of darkness" called Congo—notably, the egregiously expensive, carefully engineered Kennon Road to the Philippine highlands regularly washed away by tropical torrents or the costly San Jose sugar mill bankrupted by Mindoro's endemic malaria. But sometimes such freedom produced innovation with significant import for the colony and, to a lesser degree, for the metropole. The colonial secretary for commerce and police, the Boston Brahmin W. Cameron Forbes, successfully implemented a bold experiment in self-policing inside Philippine prisons that later proved politically impossible in the United States. Similarly, the famed architect and urban planner Daniel Burnham imposed some of his grand axial boulevards on Manila's maze and built his only complete city farther north at Baguio, a signal success he rarely achieved in America. The famed forester Gifford Pinchot steamed through the Philippine archipelago to outline a surprisingly influential master plan for management of its vast tropical forests in 1902, three years before he gained comparable authority as the founding chief of the U.S. Forest Service. Not only did junior U.S. Army officers suppress Filipino resistance with innovative forms of pacification and policing, but they repatriated this extraordinary experience during the United States' mass mobilization for World War I.

Within the vast array of U.S. colonial programs, policing was arguably the most successful in situ and the most significant in its metropolitan resonance. Confronted with intractable Filipino resistance, which persisted for over a decade, the U.S. colonial regime fused the centralized Spanish imperial police with America's advanced information systems to create an Argus-eyed colonial force, the Philippines Constabulary. Its unprecedented capacity for mass surveillance proved a bellwether for parallel domestic developments. During World War I, these colonial innovations in coercion percolated homeward, providing both personnel and procedures for the creation of a national security apparatus. Through a similar imperial dialectic, Philippine precedents also served as a blueprint for the U.S. prohibition of drugs. Between 1906 and 1908, the colonial regime prohibited opium smoking in the islands, launching a social experiment that Congress later mimed with passage of the Harrison Narcotics Act in 1914—the start of U.S. drug prohibition and, significantly, the first federal law controlling individual rights over the human body.

For a laissez-faire society with a weak federal government, empire also provided a unique opportunity for the application of state power to environmental management, serving both public health and efficient resource extraction. At both the symbolic and substantive levels, public health was central to empire. For

Americans denied the conquest of continents or the discovery of monumental ruins such as Angkor Wat and Borobodur, the defeat of tropical disease was their greatest imperial glory, legitimating colonial conquests that seemed, at first, anathema to America's democratic tradition. By expanding the American environmental experience beyond the temperate zone into the tropics, empire also had a strong influence on the development of U.S. medical and natural science—creating the field of tropical medicine, expanding the range of botany, making entomology a science, and, above all, fostering a coercive model of public health. Without aggressive control of tropical disease, Euro-American armies and empire builders could not long survive in colonial cities that were, for visitors without acquired immunities, dens of pestilence.

In the age of empire, moreover, the American conquest of cholera, malaria, and yellow fever, succeeding where Europeans had seemingly failed, created a new kind of national hero. The great American archetypes of the imperial age were men such as Walter Reed, who identified mosquitoes as the means of yellow fever transmission in Havana, William C. Gorgas, who conquered the same scourge in Cuba and Panama, Bailey K. Ashford, who discovered a treatment for hookworm in Puerto Rico, and Victor Heiser, who purged cholera from Manila. Indeed, General Leonard Wood's transformation of Santiago de Cuba from "its reeking filth, its starvation, its utter prostration" into a "clean, healthy, orderly city" created a mystique that catapulted this army surgeon from a provincial command to the governor-generalship of Cuba and the prospect of the U.S. presidency.[29]

Yet beneath these triumphal American narratives of unilateral change lurked the reality of mutual transformation of both colonizer and colonized. For while Walter Reed was credited with finding the key to defeating yellow fever in Havana, his success rested to a surprising degree on courageous, path-breaking work by a Cuban physician, Carlos Juan Finlay, who had identified the *Aedes aegypti* mosquito as the disease carrier in an 1881 scientific paper and ran an active program of experimental inoculations for years before the arrival of the Americans.[30]

In these tropical colonies, environmental management entailed the unprecedented application of science and state power not only for public health but also for resource extraction. Just as humans crowded into colonial cities were susceptible to epidemic disease, so crops concentrated in plantations were vulnerable to pests and fungi—making botanists, entomologists, veterinarians, and civil engineers all soldiers in the service of empire. In contrast to earlier explorations of the American West, overseas empire, operating in an alien tropical ecosystem with devastating storms and dangerous diseases, required the creation of new government institutions for civil engineering, public health, and scientific research.

To cut a canal across the Isthmus of Panama, for example, the United States had to create, inside the Canal Zone, an "environmental management state" for what soon became the world's most expensive civil engineering project, moving mountain-sized excavations four times those for the Suez Canal and eradicating almost every one of the omnipresent mosquito breeding areas left by torrential tropical rains. Illustrating the fluidity of careers and boundaries within the U.S. imperium, the expertise created in Panama helped sanitize military bases in the American South and contributed to the later formation of the U.S. Centers for Disease Control.

The sum of these changes in the realm of policing, drug prohibition, public health, and environmental management gave the federal government an unprecedented ability to impose coercive social controls, producing a radical change in the American social contract between the state and the individual. Once a distant, largely symbolic presence with almost no means of intruding into civil society, Washington, only two decades after the acquisition of an overseas empire, was conducting mass surveillance of citizen loyalties through new security agencies and imposing a national eugenics regime via public health, restrictive immigration, and drug prohibition.

Empire also had a profound, though more differentiated, impact on national defense. At an institutional level, the long-term impact of colonial service on the U.S. Army was mingled. Amphibious operations spanning half the globe and a protracted pacification campaign in the Philippines, unequalled in both duration and duress, had a lasting impact on the army's overall organization and command. From the Republic's founding, convention and constitution had vested the states and their militias with much of the responsibility for national defense. But the conquest of a sprawling overseas empire had pushed this volunteer force beyond its limits. In response, Secretary of War Elihu Root reformed the army's antiquated structure between 1901 and 1903, creating a centralized general staff, a modern war college, and expanded professional training for officers at every echelon. Consequently, a modern imperial army, shorn of its traditional mission of domestic defense, took form during the Spanish-American War and its bloody sequel in the Philippines.

The impact of this colonial experience on conventional combat operations seems more ambiguous. During World War I, U.S. commander General John J. Pershing and key subordinates were Philippine veterans who initially dismissed the bloody, stalemated European trench warfare and instead opted for an "open warfare" reminiscent of their earlier colonial campaigns. But the precise practice of open warfare remains unclear, its colonial origins are uncertain, and it soon gave way to conventional tactics with massive artillery barrages and massed infantry charges. For military intelligence, by contrast, the Philippine pacification was a seminal experience, forcing the army to develop its first field intelligence unit, the Division of Military Information, and staff the U.S. colonial police, the famed Philippines Constabulary, gaining thereby invaluable experience in counterintelligence. When the United States became entangled in that war of empires called World War I, the contradiction between America's far-flung global empire and its poor military preparedness snapped, sparking Washington's sudden concerns about subversion and a parallel eruption of popular xenophobia. In the midst of frantic war preparations, Washington staffed its new military intelligence service with colonial veterans and, using methods similar to those that had defeated Filipino radicals and revolutionaries, orchestrated a mass surveillance of suspected subversives, particularly German-Americans. In Europe, colonial veterans played a similarly seminal role in the establishment of the U.S. Army's Military Police and a field intelligence apparatus for combat forces along the Western Front. Along with other influences, foreign and domestic, experimentation in the Philippine colonial laboratory thus contributed both programs and personnel for modernization of the nation's domestic security apparatus and, more broadly, creation of the federal government's earliest covert operational capacity.

Empire also challenged the basic design of national defense, pushing America's frontiers far beyond the costly coastal fortifications, complete with masonry battlements and heavy artillery, that had been its front line of security for over a century. Even the navy's modernization of the 1890s produced a traditional fleet of "sea-going coastline battleships" and "short-range torpedo boats."[31] Without anything akin to Britain's navy or Prussia's army, Washington's conquest of Spain's scattered island colonies in 1898 created a far-flung, ultimately indefensible empire, fomenting deep strains in U.S. defense strategy. Starting in 1907, Washington used scarce funds to fortify Pearl Harbor, Hawaii, instead of Subic Bay, Philippines, the start of a long-term retreat to an Alaska-Hawaii-Caribbean defensive perimeter. Even the high drama of dispatching the U.S. Navy's "Great White Fleet" on its famed circumnavigation of the globe from 1907 to 1909 could not belie this imperial retreat. Just two years after the Panama Canal opened in 1914, Woodrow Wilson continued this withdrawal from the western Pacific by putting the Philippines on the path to eventual independence. Simultaneously, however, Wilson tried to secure the country's vulnerable southern flank by launching an escalating tempo of military interventions in the Caribbean and Central America—at Veracruz in 1914, Haiti from 1915 to 1934, and the Dominican Republic from 1916 to 1924. In a political complement to the same strategy, during this period Washington also imposed U.S. citizenship on those born in Puerto Rico.

Beyond periodic Marine interventions in the Caribbean Basin, the succeeding interlude between the two world wars saw the formation of a distinctive U.S. southern frontier of long-term bases and regular navy patrols. Anchored in the east by Guantánamo Bay, which had been wrested from Cuba in 1903, and in the west by the Panama Canal, which opened in 1914, defenses along the navy's porous southern perimeter stiffened slowly until the advent of World War II when they suddenly hardened into the gray steel of continuous patrols. Complemented politically by the Good Neighbor policy toward Latin America in 1934, Washington's shift away from periodic Marine interventions to a permanent naval presence required a substantial expansion of U.S. Navy facilities across the Caribbean. After a lethal German submarine campaign punctured U.S. defenses in the Caribbean during the first months of World War II, Washington scrambled to negotiate bases in both British and French territories, subcontracted much of its air base construction to Pan American World Airways, and staffed these defenses largely with Puerto Rican troops—a hybridized, subcontracting form of overseas rule typical of the U.S. imperial policy.

From this revisionist perspective, the overseas conquests of 1898 were thus pivotal for the United States in a transition from the old territorial empire of colonies and bases to a new form of global power that separates military defense from economic investments. In this sense the Hawaii-Panama-Caribbean line was an inviolable defensive perimeter that still allowed wider global investments and periodic military forays when key interests were threatened.

Moving beyond these coercive realms of law enforcement and military operations, empire's influence seems less decisive and direct. Indeed, the softer areas of social policy were more amorphous, even ambiguous, in their metropolitan impact. Though clearly an area of concern for national policy, matters of race, identity, education, and language were rooted in popular culture and diffused in myriad local governments, rendering them less susceptible to cohesive state action.

These ambiguities are particularly evident in issues of race and national identity. At the very time that the United States was fortifying domestic racial divisions by using firepower against Native Americans and the force of law against African-Americans, Washington suddenly seized an empire of islands extraordinary for its racial and cultural diversity. The result was a collision of cultures, credos, and identities, almost recombinant in its ever-changing complexity, that ramified, intersected, complemented, and conflicted within both colonies and metropole.

After 1898, empire crystallized a U.S. national consensus about the centrality of race to nationhood and a parallel sense of Euro-American superiority. Simultaneously, it produced more diverse iterations of race and identity in island colonies from the Caribbean to the Pacific. At the imperial periphery in the Philippines, more subtly shaded colonial distinctions of majority/minority, Christian/Non-Christian, however elaborately displayed at the massive Saint Louis World's Fair of 1904, were soon lost in the colored binary of domestic racial politics, contributing to the later exclusion of Filipino immigrants from the United States.

In Cuba, this imperial collision produced not division but a heightened sense of national purpose. In the years before 1898, Cuban separatists had achieved a consensus for adoption of universal manhood suffrage and abolition of discrimination against Afro-Cubans while American politicians were moving simultaneously in the opposite direction, agreeing, in state after state, to strip African-Americans of their civil rights and then affirming this segregation in an 1896 ruling by the Supreme Court in *Plessy v. Ferguson*. During the U.S. occupation from 1898 to 1902, Cuban politicians successfully resisted American attempts to impose its discriminatory racial binary in drafts of the island's constitution.

In the United States, race science, given a scientific basis by massive intelligence quotient (IQ) testing during World War I, provided affirming statistical evidence for immigration legislation shaped by a confluence of colonial and national influences. As a first step, the U.S. Congress translated this pseudoscience into a national eugenics policy by means of laws that put the Filipinos, deemed unalterably Asian, on the path to eventual independence in the Jones Act of 1916. When Congress enacted another version of the Jones Act for Puerto Rico just a year later, it deemed Puerto Ricans sufficiently "white" and imposed U.S. citizenship on the island's entire population. Using a similar racial template in the Immigration Act that same year, legislators banned anarchists, epileptics, "idiots," polygamists, and all residents of a vast "Asiatic Barred Zone" that stretched from Turkey to Southeast Asia, just short of the Philippines.

Just a few years later, Congress elaborated these exclusions into a comprehensive racial vision for America, passing the Emergency Quota Act (1921) and the omnibus Immigration Act of 1924, which included both the National Origins Act and the Asian Exclusion Act. Signed into law by President Coolidge with empire's hero General John Pershing at his side, the latter legislation tried to wind the clock of U.S. ethnic composition back to 1890 by encouraging northern European immigration and banning East Asian. Although obscured and partially negated by the 1924 Immigration Act, the sum of these diverse imperial influences contributed, albeit inadvertently, to a more pluralist foundation in the long-term evolution of American identity—a complex topic worthy of further exploration, beyond this volume, into the ways that empire transformed majority-minority relations in the United States.

While race science could be distilled in a single piece of legislation, the crafting of imperial identities was a more diffuse process manifest in monument, mythology, and historiography. Across the span of two oceans, American empire builders engaged in separate yet similar reconstructions of the past to produce powerful legitimating symbols that would inspire compliance by both rulers and ruled. In Puerto Rico, an attempt to inculcate a new identity sympathetic to the U.S. presence crashed headlong into the island's subtle yet resilient intertwining of culture, language, and history. To weaken Puerto Rico's historical ties to Spain, the U.S. colonial regime shifted public commemorations away from Christopher Columbus, who had long personified pathways westward from Spain to the Caribbean. Instead, the island's American governor focused on Juan Ponce de León, whose dual role as colonizer of Puerto Rico and discoverer of Florida intimated instead a bridge northward to the United States. Half a world away in Manila, the U.S. regime, in a parallel effort to manipulate the symbols of national identity, built a towering monument at the city's symbolic center to honor the politically moderate national martyr José Rizal rather than the radical revolutionary Andres Bonifacio. In Washington itself, President William McKinley, ignoring three hundred years of Catholic missionary work, told a Methodist delegation in 1899 that he had decided, after weeks of sleepless nights and fervid prayer, on the conquest of the Philippines "to educate the Filipinos, and uplift and civilize and Christianize them."[32]

Unlike the centralized state institutions that controlled knowledge production in European empires, American colonial knowledge was accumulated in a diffuse way that left ample room for manipulations and even fabrications. In compiling that massive, fifty-five-volume documentary reconstruction of the Spanish colonial past titled *The Philippine Islands* (1903–9), editors Emma Blair and James Robertson, the latter best known to historians as the founding editor of the *Hispanic American Historical Review,* included selections and mistranslations that no doubt met the preconceptions of their Gilded Age subscribers. At the level of political symbolism, this defining compendium of U.S. colonial knowledge seems an exercise in appropriation and displacement—displacing the Spaniards by showing their incompetence and appropriating their past to move yet another colony within the American imperial orbit.[33]

In a parallel exercise of cultural appropriation vis-à-vis the precolonial Philippine past, this same James Robertson, while later serving as director of the Philippine National Library, purchased a crude forgery titled the "Code of Kalantiaw" and celebrated what he styled an ancient Filipino legal code in a scholarly paper delivered at the 1915 Panama-Pacific International Exposition convened to celebrate the opening of the Panama Canal. While the Spanish had destroyed ancient Filipino documents and degraded their society, the Americans, Robertson reported, would now protect Filipinos from their historic inclination toward "ineffectiveness and indirection of government" and a proclivity to engage in "feud and warfare."[34]

For empires, the past is just another overseas territory ripe for reconstruction, even reinvention. Yet within this general inclination toward appropriation there is something distinctive about the way the American empire felt a strong need to assuage its angst as an arriviste power by framing and legitimating policy by means of the past—even if that past was revised to the point of fabrication or fiction.

Education was another critical arena for the self-conscious formation of new identities, both national and imperial. Few ideas were more vigorously propagated throughout the American insular empire than the ambivalent notion of *Americanization*—a category of purpose and policy that, for all its imprecision, sought to transform colonial cultures, usually via the schoolhouse, into reflections of a putatively superior Anglo-Saxon culture. In an attempt to teach insular populations certain notions of American democracy, it became vitally important not only to recast the colonial subjects' understanding of history but to regenerate their bodies and, in some cases, eviscerate the native language while forcibly teaching them English and *in* English. Regardless of where the emphasis lay, no other governmental effort became more important in the campaign to Americanize the new colonials than the diffusion of elementary education through highly centralized systems coordinated by American officials.

As soon as circumstances permitted after the conquest, these American colonial states launched a large-scale and largely successful school expansion program with a dramatic increase in the numbers of schools, teachers, and pupils. Qualitative achievements were another matter, however. Americanization policies

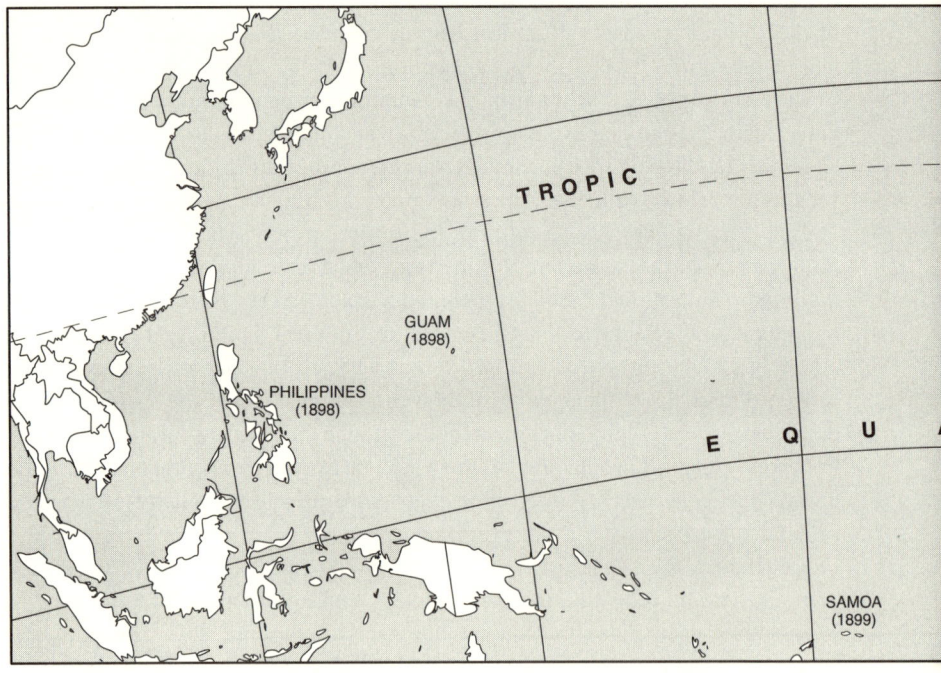

The U.S. island empire, along the Tropic of Cancer, circa 1898. (Cartography Laboratory, University of Wisconsin–Madison.

comprised a hodgepodge of half-baked, poorly articulated, and easily altered notions about pupils' behavior and schooling outcomes. In places such as Puerto Rico, Americanization policies often stressed erasing the memory of Spanish rule and, to the greatest extent possible, using English as the medium of instruction in the vain hope that it would eventually become the people's vernacular. In the Philippines, by contrast, emerging elites and middle classes used access to secondary and university education to make English their own while the children of poor peasants and workers left school after the compulsory four years with little functional ability in this foreign language.

Many of these efforts in the colonies were deeply imbued with Progressive era ideas about educational reform and its potential for both easing social tensions and augmenting participation in a democratic polity. The task of "educating the natives in self-government" evidently entailed targeted approaches to schooling, which colonial officials saw as both a means of political education and a mechanism of social control.[35] It is not surprising, then, that Americanization policies in the colonial periphery drew much of their inspiration from debates in the United States about how to assimilate immigrants and "uplift" Native

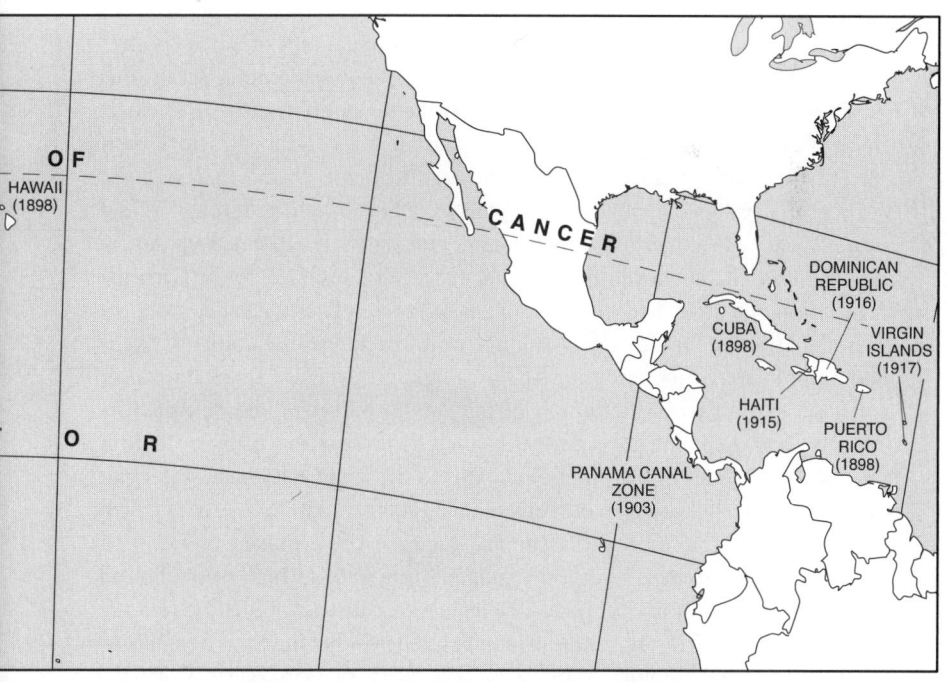

Americans, African-Americans, and other targeted minorities. In the Philippines, Puerto Rico, and elsewhere in the empire, colonial educators found a fertile terrain in which to practice these Progressive era educational reforms. However, the cadre of teachers and administrators on whom these colonial educators relied for implementation often adjusted these policies to their own needs and social philosophies. In some cases, as Solsirée del Moral reveals in her work on Puerto Rico, these teachers and administrators saw progress in local terms and were largely unconcerned about the U.S. framework for these reformist policies.

The American Imperial State

The essays in this volume represent, in their totality, the search for some term that can encompass an elusory yet powerful entity, presiding over far-flung island territories, that we might call, for want of better words, the American imperial state. To better understand this complex phenomenon, we need to move beyond formalistic models that valorize sheer size and formal hierarchy, epitomized by the work of the American diplomatic historian Richard Leopold. Instead, we should view the United States, in its overseas operations, as an agile state whose diffuse, delegated power has been the source of a surprising resilience.[36]

At the broadest level, we need to set aside narrow definitions of the "state" as a simple bureaucratic apparatus for a more inclusive concept of, say, a "polity" that is capable of encompassing modern complexities—enfolding, within this transnational imperial state, the U.S. government, its domestic power elites, colonial regimes, their collaborating elites, and legions of subcontractors, both civil and paramilitary. Instead of a closed circuit of cabinet and civil servants, Washington developed a more open process of policy formation through a fluid nexus of politicians, financiers, and academics mediated by a distinctively American creation—the nongovernmental policy forum exemplified by the Carnegie Corporation and reiterated in the Council on Foreign Relations and, more recently, the Heritage Foundation. Without a centralized colonial ministry, Washington administered its overseas territories lightly through a small Bureau of Insular Affairs buried in the bowels of the War Department and delegated its authority to subordinate governments in each of these island colonies. Within these surrogate states in the Philippines, Puerto Rico, and elsewhere, American colonial governors, lacking an empowered bureaucracy akin to the Indian Civil Service or the Dutch Indies *beamtenstaat,* maneuvered constantly to achieve a viable political consensus with local collaborating elites, which were allowed considerable agency or at least political wiggle room. Instead of lifetime colonial careers, an amazing array of American empire builders—botanists, civil engineers, entomologists, epidemiologists, foresters, governors, meteorologists, Christian missionaries, policemen, public health officers, soldiers, and teachers—circulated between colony and metropole on limited term contracts.

Lacking detailed directives from the metropole, these colonial states were thus open to diverse global and local influences, making them veritable hothouses for the creation of new, hybridized forms of governance. Such a diffuse colonialism—with rule by emissaries, surrogates, subcontractors, and local collaborators—may have seemed fragmented, weak, and even ephemeral compared to the grandeur of, say, British India's majestic Delhi *durbar* or the populous Dutch expatriate community rooted for centuries on Java. But, lest we forget, the United States' global reach has persisted far beyond the eclipse of these more centralized European empires.

Admittedly, other empires had some of these same attributes. As Christopher Bayly has argued, in its last century Britain's Asian empire "concealed a variety of administrative anomalies" that encompassed "government by the seat-of-the-pants in many small units." Yet these colonial fragments orbited about the British India state and its powerful imperial army, and this vast Asian empire was encompassed by the mighty British Navy. At its apex, this entire apparatus was given coherence and direction by centralized ministries in London. The sum of these factors was an ultimately centralized array antithetical to the American system.[37] More broadly, the British and American empires shared, in varying degrees, direct colonial rule and indirect controls, altruism and self-interest, and plans for retention and self-rule. But the United States was distinctive in the speed with which it distilled altruism, self-rule, and indirect empire into a supple global system that, by replacing colonial rule with a diffuse global hegemony in the years surrounding World War I, has far outlasted more than a dozen modern empires since swept away by war and revolution.

The omnipresent yet invisible architect of this unique American imperial state was Elihu Root, a New York lawyer who served successively as secretary of war and secretary of state from 1899 to 1909. As the prototype of the "wise man" who shuttles between corporate law in New York and government service in Washington, Root formalized this system of ad hoc imperial rule by reorganizing key elements of the U.S. government and establishing a complex of public-private linkages as president of the Carnegie Endowment for International Peace (1910–25) and founder of the Council on Foreign Relations (1921). This system of foreign policy formation was still evident at the end of the twentieth century, when one scholar described the United States as "an empire without an emperor" that reached consensus through "the impact of other participants in the political free-for-all—parties, interest groups, entrenched bureaucracies, and the media."[38] In perhaps his most lasting contribution, Root moved the United States by degrees beyond the antiquated array of colonial conquest and gunboat diplomacy to a new system of hegemonic global power grounded in international law—a contribution recognized when Root received the Nobel Peace Prize in 1912.

This novel hegemonic strategy had many advantages for the newly imperial United States. It defused the powder keg of international resentment sparked by formal colonial rule; it established the United States as powerful global broker in the resolution of international disputes; it provided a powerful veneer of international legitimacy to the hemispheric claims of the Monroe Doctrine; it effectively rebranded continuous U.S. military interventions in the circum-Caribbean as efforts to safeguard the sovereignty of vulnerable nations; and, finally, it co-opted foreign elites in advancing American interests. To manage this hegemonic system, the United States avoided the verticality of other imperial administrations in favor of a decentered yet integrated foreign policy network known in the late twentieth century as the "national security state" and originating in Elihu Root's tireless efforts to manage America's empire of islands.

The Postcolonial Debate

All of this analysis leads logically to an important question that lies, largely but not entirely, beyond the scope of this volume: what legacy did this early experience of overseas empire leave for America's emergence, just a half century later, as the world's preeminent power? If questions about U.S. expansion circa 1898 are difficult, those surrounding its current superpower status are daunting indeed. Scholars of this colonial past, says Ann Stoler, have rather little to say about the "current nature of empire because our models, unlike our objects of inquiry, have become brittle, unyielding to the range of practices, and to the blurred genres of rule and rhetoric that mark imperial relations."[39] Indeed, how can we connect the dots from past to present if we are uncertain about the shape of this present and, indeed, even that past?

In the aftermath of the Spanish-American War, the nation, though bitterly divided over the policy, was united in its terminology: proponents embraced *empire* and opponents were *anti-imperialists*.[40] Today analysts of American power are conflicted, even confused in applying a historical artifact, language and its conceptual categories, to a global behemoth whose sheer size and complexity transcend past human experience. Those who make the attempt, whether critics or advocates of U.S. global power, often apply models that derive from the Roman term *imperium*, meaning "dominion enforced by a single power." Others prefer the Greek-inflected *hegemony*, meaning a world order that "rests on consent and cooperation, not exclusively on force and domination," much as ancient Athens once led its coalition of city-state allies.[41] In sum, contemporary American scholarship separates into, first, an imperium school that sees Washington as a latter-day Rome, the command center of a centralized empire; next, a hegemonic interpretation that views America as Athens, leading a coalition of willing allies; and, finally, a conservative coterie that reads history to argue that the United

States, like the United Kingdom in its day, should use its awesome military power to defend freedom and civilization.

On the imperium side, the critic Chalmers Johnson argues that "our militarized empire is a physical reality" evident in the global deployment of U.S. armed forces and "a network of economic and political interests."[42] In his history of U.S. foreign policy since the cold war, Andrew J. Bacevich argues that Washington seeks "to expand an American imperium" through the "creation of an open and integrated international order based on the principles of democratic capitalism, with the United States as the ultimate guarantor of order." Stripped of their rhetoric, both the cold war and the war on terror are, Bacevich argues, manifestations of "the American project of creating an open and integrated world."[43] Similarly but more sympathetically, the Yale historian Paul Kennedy, after surveying the rise and fall of empires over the past five hundred years, has warned that the United States' future as "*the* global superpower" is threatened by a growing imbalance between its global military commitments and its domestic economic resources.[44]

By contrast, Marxist critics Michael Hardt and Antonio Negri argue, in a somewhat hegemonic vein, that contemporary empire, embedded in a borderless globalizing economy, simultaneously transcends any "territorial center of power" or "fixed boundaries."[45] Using the same frame to celebrate rather than critique, the imperial historian Niall Ferguson styles the United States the Anglophone successor to Great Britain's "liberal empire," which once used military power to maintain a hegemonic system of free trade and civilized standards.[46] "If the United States retreats from global hegemony," Ferguson warns darkly, the world might well plunge into "an anarchic new Dark Age; an era of waning empires and religious fanaticism; of endemic plunder and pillage in the world's forgotten regions; of economic stagnation and civilization's retreat into a few fortified enclaves."[47] In an article splashed across the cover of the *New York Times Magazine* on the eve of the Iraq invasion, foreign policy commentator Michael Ignatieff called the American iteration of this British model "an empire lite, a global hegemony whose grace notes are free markets, human rights and democracy, enforced by the most awesome military power the world has ever known."[48] After defining empire in hegemonic terms as "a particular form of state organization in which the elites of differing ethnic or national units defer to . . . the political leadership of the dominant power," the international historian Charles S. Maier makes a similar argument that "America has exercised an imperial hold . . . not merely through armed power or the CIA, but also through such institutions as the Council on Foreign Relations . . . and its frequent convocations of opinion leaders." Looking back on the twentieth century and forward into the twenty-first, Maier also admits, somewhat ruefully, that "if there are to be two or more imperial contenders, then I believe it valuable to have the United States remain one of them."⁴⁹

Between hegemony and imperium lies a more pragmatic, quintessentially conservative school that accepts, even embraces the unadorned reality of Washington's global dominion. "U.S. imperialism has been the greatest force for good in the world during the past century," writes the military historian Max Boot. "It has defeated the monstrous evils of communism and Nazism and lesser evils such as the Taliban and Serbian ethnic cleansing."⁵⁰ In the aftermath of 9/11, Boot published a book reviewing some of the literally hundreds of U.S. foreign interventions since 1800 to reach to a rather Hobbesian rendering of "the lessons of history." To protect the "inner core of its empire," which is "a family of democratic, capitalist nations," Washington, he argues, must prepare for countless future wars along a volatile imperial periphery "teeming with failed states, criminal states, or simply a state of nature."⁵¹ Similarly, Eliot Cohen, the neoconservative counselor to George W. Bush's State Department, argues that the "age of empire" is over but "an age of American hegemony has begun," requiring that "U.S. statesmen today cannot ignore the lessons and analogies of imperial history" if they are to manage the coalitions required for successful global governance.⁵²

Perhaps more important than any of these differences, a broad spectrum of contemporary analysts, including staunch supporters of unbridled U.S. power, agree that empire, with all its historical resonances, is the most appropriate descriptor for America's current superpower status. In the depths of the cold war, the radical historian William Appleman Williams once remarked wryly about what he called this country's "grand illusion," the "charming belief that the United States could reap the rewards of empire without paying the costs of empire and without admitting that it was an empire."⁵³ But by the close of the cold war even Arthur M. Schlesinger Jr., counselor to presidents and liberal U.S. historian par excellence, conceded, "who can doubt that there is an American empire?—an 'informal' empire, not colonial in polity, but still richly equipped with imperial paraphernalia: troops, ships, planes, bases, proconsuls, local collaborators, all spread around the luckless planet."⁵⁴ From Boot on the right to Bacevich on the left, a surprising yet still fragile consensus among scholars of U.S. foreign policy has formed: the question is no longer whether the United States has become an empire but what sort of empire it might be and how Washington can best exercise its global power.⁵⁵

In this volume's conclusion, two specialists in U.S. history explore a closely related question: was the American experience of overseas expansion after 1898 a significant chapter in this nation's history that somehow shaped its domestic governance or contributed to its later emergence as a world power? For the diplomatic historian Jeremi Suri the answer is a definitive "no," while U.S. international historian Ian Tyrrell offers a nuanced, carefully considered "yes"—a position endorsed by cultural historian Nancy Tomes. Their differences, as we will see, lie at the intersection of scholarly perspective and cultural politics.

By juxtaposing the exercise of U.S. power at the dawn and close of the twentieth century, Suri reaches generally negative conclusions about the applicability of the term *empire* to America. From the 1830s onward, the United States was home to "democratic institutions and habits that would eventually revolutionize the conduct of politics across the globe." Even at the high tide of empire after 1898, Americans were what Suri calls "revolutionary imperialists" who spread subversive ideals of freedom from China to Latin America. Even though American society is today riven by a contradiction between "democracy and militarism," he insists that the persistence of such idealism means that the United States "was and is too self-limiting to ever become a real empire."

To treat Suri's argument with the seriousness it demands, we must engage its core thesis that a fundamental contradiction, embedded deep in the American polity, between democratic ideals and military realpolitik has produced a foreign policy too complex and contradictory for "a real empire"—which, in his view, means long-term occupation and self-interested "exploitation of foreign societies." Read closely, Suri's central contention is that an uneasy dialectic between democracy and military expansion produced contradictions whose synthesis has been—from the Philippines in 1898 to Iraq in 2003—horrifically destructive conquest followed by humane nation building. This democratic aspiration for "a world of free societies associated with the United States" barred both "creation of any serious high-level 'colonial office'" and "any serious advocacy of a permanent American empire, especially after World War I." Although he chides the authors in this volume for oversimplifying "the ambivalent and very tenuous quality of foreign policy that emanated from Washington, D.C.," that is, for misinterpreting the larger, multifaceted U.S. global presence, he does not challenge their main argument that the most extreme form of empire, direct colonial rule, had a marked impact on formation of the metropolitan American state.

At the broadest level, Suri's analysis reflects a belief in American "exceptionalism"—its unique exemption from the curse of empire—once strongly and almost universally held in his field of U.S. diplomatic history. In an earlier cold war generation, Richard W. Leopold, then dean of diplomatic historians, argued that empire had little impact on the United States because (a) there was no expansion beyond these small islands acquired in 1898, (b) the absence of a cabinet-level department for these overseas territories lent an aura of impermanence, and (c) there was no increase in military spending to defend these otherwise indefensible islands.[56] Though separated by several academic generations, both Leopold and Suri make strikingly similar arguments that the absence of certain formalistic criteria, protracted occupation and creation of a cabinet-level colonial office, somehow exempts the United States from the status of empire.

In sharp, almost diametric contrast, international historian Ian Tyrrell argues that the "American amnesic relationship" to its imperial past masks an undeniable reality that the "United States is manifestly an empire because it has exerted power over other people." Rather than holding America up to a "mythical European model" of empire for a simple binary assessment, yea or nay, "historians must approach empire as a historically changing social formation rather than an ideal type." The question is not whether America has been an empire but what kind of empire it has been. In his own attempt to grapple with the U.S. empire's "complexities and distinctiveness," Tyrrell finds, like the other contributors to this volume, that America's ad hoc "colonial administration was often held together not by a strong civil service but by the army and navy . . . aided in considerable measure by a strong voluntarist ethic in the nongovernmental sector in which services were contracted out to missionaries, the YMCA, and other nongovernmental organizations." As another component in the supple private-public character of the country's overseas expansion, the number of American missionaries abroad surged from just nine hundred in 1890 to fourteen thousand by 1920, creating a "growing sense of the United States as a missionary nation engaged in a humanitarian endeavor" and launching a series of disaster relief missions during the 1890s, culminating in Protestant involvement in Cuba in 1897–98. Once Washington acquired overseas territories after 1898, these missionaries argued that "American empire should be moralized and turned into a moral state" through policies such as opium prohibition and venereal disease control. Apart from serving as social-welfare subcontractors for the U.S. colonial state in the Philippines, the missionaries also used the anti-opium policy to "assert American hegemony in East Asia to undermine the moral authority of the British and to aid the processes of modernization in China." Not only did missionaries make moral reform "part of the glue of American empire," they "also presaged a growing accommodation of the moral reformers and the American state"—arguably another significant domestic legacy of America's experience of empire, both formal and informal. For Suri the moral influence of the missionaries is a key factor for denial of empire; for Tyrrell this same missionary moralism was a powerful force for extending a unique form of American global hegemony.

In response to this debate, Nancy Tomes feels that Suri "engages very little with the specific issues raised here, such as education, economics, public health, and the like" and instead insists on a denial of empire grounded in the U.S. history profession's "entrenched habit of taking a single Eurocentric model of empire, and more specifically the British experience, as the template against which all others should be judged." Setting aside her profession's paralysis over this question, Tomes feels that the catalytic effect of empire "was directly and critically important to forming key aspects of the twentieth-century American state" and argues that this volume "provides many illuminating examples of how to think about the deep structures and cultural legacies of colonial rule."

In a larger sense, this debate both reflects and refracts a key issue suffused throughout the volume—the search for not only the structure but the ideology of the American imperial state. In the ideological vanguard, American presidents have sounded the ideal of the United States as the architect of human freedom—from Theodore Roosevelt's "orderly liberty,"[57] through Franklin Roosevelt's "four freedoms," to George W. Bush's "freedom is on the march."[58] And in the rear guard follow the pundits and political scientists who give weight to these words, affirming the rightness of the nation's wars, no matter how ill advised, and lending their expertise to the state's expansion.[59]

The demands on historians are both simpler and more subtle. As acolytes of the American nation-state, mainstream U.S. historians are constrained to sounds and silences as they subtly weave these simple ideological tenets into their national narratives. Every state system, imperial or national, has its unifying credo with affirmations and denials, sounds and silences. First, there are the necessary silences about the suffering of others. Empires from Ottoman to Dutch and American have insisted, says Ann Stoler, that "their violences were temporary, and that their humanitarian visions excused or distinguished their interventions as ad hoc measures, not sustained excesses."[60] Next come the sounds of affirmation. In marked contrast to the blood lust of, say, the Belgians in the Congo or the French in the *terres rouges* of Cochin China, there was, as Suri rightly argues, an undeniable idealism among Americans abroad, whether Christian missionaries or colonial governors, that often fused development, altruism, and democratic ideals in imperial arenas from China to Cuba. And he could have added that the U.S. dominion, through its emphasis on democratic nation building, was an improvement, sometimes slight, sometimes immeasurable, on the six empires that it erased or supplanted in its rise to world power throughout twentieth century—first Spain's colonies and Britain's economic empire, then the Third Reich and Imperial Japan, next French Indochina, and finally the Soviet Union.

Yet this democratic idealism, for all its power and appeal, does not necessarily represent a denial of global dominion and could well be another complementary attribute, along with its supple state apparatus, that distinguishes America's global reign from the often brutal regimes it supplanted. "American claims of benign intentions to spread democracy," writes Eliot Cohen in *Foreign Affairs*, "are surely no less and no more sincere than the *missions civilisatrices* of imperial powers in the past."[61] Viewed globally, such developmental idealism has, no doubt, tempered the excesses of most modern empires, whether those of the French in Africa, the British in Asia, or the Americans in the Philippines and Iraq. But if Suri is correct, this tension between democratic ideals and imperial realpolitik is even more pronounced in the American case, thus reducing the length of occupation and forcing nation building to the fore. If so, this distinctive fusion of moralism and imperialism is quite likely, as Tyrrell argues, a legacy of the extraordinary influence that Christian missionaries had upon U.S. overseas expansion from 1890 to 1920, producing a distinctive form of U.S. hegemony that ultimately complements rather than contradicts this volume's larger search for the elusive character of a distinctive American imperial state.

Indeed, the United States has long intertwined liberty's progress with its own expanding global influence, both the soft power of trade, culture, and Christian morality as well as the hard power of covert and conventional military operations. In the span of a single century, the U.S. armed forces have grown into a global leviathan. In 1898, the U.S. military was little more than a few strings of frontier forts and harbor fortifications manned by small territorial forces and defended by a largely coastal navy. By 2004, the United States held half the world's armaments and 725 overseas bases in some 130 countries staffed by over 300,000 personnel and stiffened by lethal armadas of air, sea, and space.[62] "Nothing has ever existed like this disparity of power; nothing," remarked historian Paul Kennedy in 2002. "I have returned to all of the comparative defence spending and military personnel statistics over the past 500 years that I compiled in *The Rise and Fall of the Great Powers*, and no other nation comes close." History, he says, confirms this conclusion: "The Pax Britannica was run on the cheap. . . . Charlemagne's empire was merely western European in its reach. The Roman empire stretched farther afield, but there was another great empire in Persia, and a larger one in China. There is, therefore, no comparison."[63] In sum, the United States commands a concentration of wealth and power not seen for more than two millennia. When arrayed on the field of battle, this awesome force has been deployed not just to defeat but to utterly destroy enemies who, as Suri argues, "appear to imperil the core foundations of American democracy" and then to rebuild these former enemies by "creating functioning, if limited, democracies in societies under occupation," producing "the remarkable coexistence of brutalizing means and idealistic ends in American military discourse."

Amid these sounds and silences of ideological hegemony, facts, historical or statistical, do not matter for scholars wedded to the ideals and ideology of American exceptionalism. The creative labor of two generations of revisionist diplomatic historians—William Appleman Williams, Walter LaFeber, Thomas McCormick, and others—is dismissed, by Suri and the many who share his view, as a testament to America's tolerance of dissident views not a trenchant critique of conventional historiography. Nearly two decades of work by scholars of cultural and postcolonial studies is often unapproachably discursive for even this impact, creating an opening for the documented, empirical studies of the early American empire that this volume hopes to offer.

Conclusion

In sum, we are ambitious. Through this single volume, compressing years, sometimes decades of scholarship into each essay, we hope to elevate this empire of islands from the obscure margins of American historiography to its bright epicenter. Instead of a few lines in Howard Zinn's *A People's History of the United States* or a clause, at best, in college history textbooks, we hope that in years to come this volume will help make the study of the United States' imperial interactions with its colonial periphery central to understanding the rise of the modern U.S. state and the formation of an American national identity.[64]

Beyond these basic aims, our attempt to reverse the usual optic and view America from its imperial periphery will offer, hopefully, a new perspective on the formation and fundamental nature of the modern American state. From their vantage points along the colonized periphery, these scholars of islands that once made up this early American empire have reached four significant conclusions noteworthy for even the most insular of American historians. First, and most fundamentally, the American colonial empire, these authors all agree, needs to be made visible in the skein of twentieth-century American history if we are to understand matters of elemental import such as state formation or conceptions of race and national identity. Second, and significantly, it appears that ruling this empire of islands scattered halfway around the globe strained the resources of the American state in directions unimagined and perhaps unrealized absent such expansion, making colonialism a crucible for forging numerous innovations in American statecraft, whether subcontracting-cum-secondment for imperial governance or bold social experimentation for mass control. Third, a new, unanticipated historical actor emerges from these pages—an agile transnational apparatus we call the American imperial state, which fused, in these formative colonial decades, public and private institutions, foreign and domestic elites, realpolitik and Christian moralism, and hard and soft power to become a uniquely adaptable array for global governance. Fourth, and finally, these essays invite a new, deeper understanding of the underlying character of colonial empire as an extraordinary form of governance, a veritable crucible of historical change that plunged both colonizer and colonized into the searing heat of a Promethean fire that consumes older cultures and kingdoms as it creates new nations, state forms, and geopolitical systems.

From this offshore perch along the Tropic of Cancer, the conventional analytic division between center and periphery, colony and metropole, nation and empire seems increasingly myopic, blocking the broad optic needed to grasp the growing inequities of power in a globalizing age. With the publication of this collection, hopefully we will never again have cause to rue, as Amy Kaplan did some fifteen years ago, the "absence of empire" in American history.[65]

Reading Imperial Transitions

Spanish Contraction, British Expansion, and American Irruption

JOSEP M. FRADERA

THE HISTORY OF THOSE POLITICAL ARTIFACTS known as empires still has some very obscure areas. In the past, the study of empires was understood, in general and with notable exceptions, as the culmination of national histories. This limitation, which seems evident to us now, more than justifies the construction of alternative, intellectually more sophisticated, interpretative frameworks. However, this possibility could be undermined in terms of its results, through the adoption of excessively generic cultural perspectives. The study of the rhetoric and cultures of empires, which in the last few years has been thrust into the center of the historiographic debate, should not allow us to forget other perspectives that were central to historiography in the recent past such as the organization of power and the influence of social and economic fundamentals. The substitution of the concept "colonial" in favor of "imperial," displacing the center of interest from topics such as the organization of work and social relationships to the terrain of ideas, languages, and propaganda, is symptomatic of these recent changes. Fortunately, the perspectives opened up by "Atlantic history," "transnational history," and "world history" doubtless helped us avoid the parochialism that is inherent to national/imperial histories and facilitate comparative approaches.[1] In these pages, therefore, I will examine some relevant features of the Spanish, British, and American cases between the second half of the eighteenth century and the "imperial turn" at the beginning of the twentieth.

One problem that has been raised repeatedly in the historiography of empires is implicit in the very definition of *imperial transition*. By this I mean the many empires—power structures that are by definition heterogeneous—that succeed each other continually throughout history. This perspective originated in the conception of empire itself forged by the eighteenth-century Enlightenment, in particular by thinkers such as Charles Louis de Secondat, Baron de Montesquieu, and Edward Gibbon.[2] In their rise and fall, empires represented institutions and culture of the times; they corresponded to the spirit of the age. For this reason, empires that adapted best to such demands succeeded those that were exhausted. But empires sometimes coexisted for centuries, and for this reason they can be compared.[3]

Taking the challenge of comparison seriously, this text addresses the crucial question of imperial political regimes. Indeed, if something distinguishes modern empires it is the construction of special regimes in their far-off possessions. In relation to rules that prevailed in the metropoles, nineteenth-century empires repeatedly created and applied exceptional political systems, exceptional taxation policies, and exceptional social principles. The reasons for this were inherent to imperial developments after the Atlantic revolutions (1770–1820s), and, while easy to understand, they were always treated by contemporary writers and later scholars as reflective of national idiosyncrasies. For the British, it was the demonstration of the celebrated Anglo-British empiricism, a quality that radically differentiated them from the systematic delusions of France and other continental powers. For the Spanish and the French, colonial and imperial policy oscillated continually between a double possibility: colonies were assimilated into or excluded from the liberal—and occasionally republican—frameworks of the metropoles or they were condemned to a special "colonial" status. For the Americans, this problem apparently did not present itself until 1901 when the so-called insular cases decided the constitutional status of the old Spanish colonies of Cuba, Puerto Rico, and the Philippines.

Following the importance attributed to this feature, the aim of this essay is to advance a thesis, somewhat different from the usual one, about the coexistence of, rivalry among, and exchanges between three experiences of empire building that evolved in parallel for a period that is too long to be properly explained by the concept of "imperial transition." I will explore three main areas: first, I will try to clarify our shared knowledge about imperial succession; second, I will discuss in some depth the colonial experiences that were common to the three empires under scrutiny; and, last, I will try to compare the ways in which these empires resolved the fundamental political questions of how to organize a suitable institutional framework for ruling other societies.

Intersecting Histories

The Spanish and Portuguese empires controlled a vast colonial space from the end of the sixteenth century to the beginning of the nineteenth. These empires did not arise simply from the Iberians' pioneering nature, or from their having conquered places not previously controlled by outside powers. Certainly these two societies solved, before others, technical issues regarding navigation and war. But, more important, they effectively used the discoveries of others to bring vast

"It ought to be a happy new year: Uncle Sam and his English cousin have the world between them." *Judge,* January 7, 1899. (U.S. Library of Congress)

spaces under control.⁴ The Portuguese pioneers forged a world empire, while the Spanish, without ever renouncing the idea of universal control, invested the greater part of their efforts organizing their empire in the Americas in addition to the Philippine appendage, which allowed them to have a long-term commercial partnership with Ming China. This capacity to build up such enormous possessions and also maintain the necessary connections between them cannot be understood as a merely technical matter. To begin with, it implied knowledge of the fundamental model of commercial and maritime influence, what the Portuguese called *feitoria*—an enclave from which to trade, the marketplace where the Phoenicians and the Greeks gave birth to the very idea of colonial expansion toward remote places. It also demanded something much more complex and decisive: the ability to construct stable frameworks of control over societies that were very diverse and, on occasion, as complex as the expansive peoples of southern Europe. Its essential precondition was the ability to subdue extensive populations in ever more distant territories, a new ability for Europeans, though one with important precedents in the expansion of the Christian monarchies in the Iberian Peninsula and adjacent archipelagos (the Balearic Islands and the Canaries).⁵ This is the factor that was genuinely new and decisive about this history, one that signaled a point of no return in the history of European expansion toward other continents.

The Spanish and Portuguese effectively resolved the double challenge of promoting trade and organizing the exploitation of new economic resources. At the risk of oversimplification, it can be argued that the Spanish empire rested, from the last decades of the sixteenth century, on the intensive exploitation of mineral resources (silver in particular). For their part, the Portuguese were very effective in long-distance trade and the exploitation of new agricultural products, particularly vegetable colorants and sugar.⁶ The Spaniards' emphasis on metal extraction was a completely rational choice based on maximizing profits under conditions in which the labor supply was decreasing daily as a result of epidemics, violence, cultural eradication, and mindless exploitation.⁷ Under these conditions, and at a great physical distance from the metropolitan centers, this was the most logical option. It was not the case of an archaic passion for precious metals among backward Catholics but rather of a spectacular capacity to produce merchandise in high demand both in Europe and in Asia, for which the Spanish empire enjoyed a significant and perceptible advantage.⁸ From this point of view, the main asset was the relative abundance of indigenous workers, who were forced to labor in the mines under conditions and at a price unimaginable in other contexts.

The Iberian empires provided a second line of colonial organization whose spread would be decisive in the formation of the modern world. I am referring to the ability to make enslaved Africans and Amerindians into a servile workforce perfectly adapted to very different productive ends while also making them a vital piece of the colonial apparatus.[9] In this sense, just as the Spanish empire possessed the most sophisticated machinery of control over the native populations of America and the Philippine archipelago, the Portuguese empire would be the great stage for the development of modern slavery, the necessary bridge between Europe, Africa, and the Americas.[10] Once the merits of the slave-based *fazenda*—large agricultural units producing sugar from São Salvador de Bahia to Pernambuco—became evident, the formula was successfully transferred to other crops and places.[11] In particular, it spread toward the Dutch, English, and French possessions of the Caribbean and the North American possessions of the English, as is well known to historians. Only on the foundations of the plantation economy run with slaves from Africa could the northern European rivals of the Catholic empires successfully establish themselves in the Caribbean and North America in areas without comparable resources of native manpower and, in the latter case, under much less favorable ecological conditions.[12]

The Seven Years' War (1756–63) meant the first open challenge to the Spanish empire in the context of a struggle between empires with crucial consequences in North America, the Antilles, and Asia. Nevertheless, the Spanish and Portuguese continued to dominate the South Atlantic and the Pacific until the beginning of the nineteenth century. So great was their control that the emerging empire of the British was forced to carry out an enormous logistical and financial effort to form two colonies—the Falklands/Malvinas and New South Wales—in order to support their presence and make it irreversible in both oceans. On the other hand, the first great Atlantic crisis ended French pretensions to control a huge area of the Americas with consequences that were felt until the era of the French Revolution and the Napoleonic empire.[13] Spain, the power that, for dynastic reasons, was allied with France, undertook a complex process of reforming its empire with the principal aim of guaranteeing its survival against such powerful rivals.[14] With this priority, the financial and administrative reforms carried out increased the income of the Spanish monarchy in the Americas, most noticeably in the last decades of the eighteenth century.[15] Part of this income was destined for the defense of the American possessions while another, smaller part was transferred directly to the coffers of the metropolitan treasury. Heightened fiscal demands resulted in a correlative increase in the degree of conflict on the continent, and produced an intense struggle between the Creole ruling groups and the metropole for control of the Americas. With the Napoleonic invasion of the Iberian Peninsula in 1808, tensions became unacceptable within the administrative and political framework the French inherited.[16] Paradoxically, however, the empire continued to expand its territories, colonizing new areas toward the south, Amazonia and the north of Mexico, in the midst of the crises that led to its final collapse.[17]

Between the Seven Years' War and the Napoleonic wars, the European empires in the Atlantic collapsed. In a Spain occupied by Napoleon, the patriotic resistance attempted to enlist the American subjects of the empire but at the cost of endless discussions about the contents of the new liberal Constitution and the power sharing that it proposed. The Portuguese monarchy preferred to move, under British protection, to Rio de Janeiro, to a Brazil that had already witnessed many republican conspiracies against the Portuguese.[18] Meanwhile, Great Britain, which had not been able to control the thirteen North American colonies after the Seven Years' War, withdrew in the Americas to coastal enclaves and began an about-face during these years toward Asian horizons, doing so by means of the East India Company's operations in Bengal and the north of India.[19] This emerging empire, despite the setbacks against the Americans and their French allies, maintained important possessions in the Caribbean and British North America while it enormously increased its political and economic influence in territories recently freed from the Spanish empire and in Dom Pedro's Brazil.[20] This influence would continue to increase throughout the nineteenth century. The French withdrew completely from North America after 1763, though Spain would later cede Louisiana to Napoleon. In 1803 they sealed, with the sale of Louisiana to the American Republic, their full withdrawal to those possessions preserved in the Caribbean after their failure to recover Saint-Domingue a year earlier. In this setting of imperial adjustments, the Republic of Haiti was the only effective decolonization by ex-slaves in the whole continent.

Imperial developments in the Americas after the two great Atlantic crises, in 1757–63 and during the Napoleonic wars (which include the war of American independence against Great Britain), were foreseeable in many ways. The former trading empire of the British in North America became oriented, after the separation, in two directions: the coastal cities linked to international trade looked outward while many of the states' hinterlands looked toward the interior. The Republic of Washington and Jefferson was very conspicuously imperial in the double sense of not accepting any tutelage from the preceding powers and in its desire to incorporate adjacent territories without recognizing the hypothetical rights of their owners, whether native peoples or the French and Spanish empires and their successors.[21] The trading empire thus turned into a land-based empire bound to push the frontier into Indian territories. The latter vocation was implicit, partly, in the very conditions of the separation from Great Britain, partly in the colonies' Lockean cultural matrix, and partly in the colonizing dynamics beyond the Appalachians.[22] Neither the limitations imposed by British policies (the "proclamation line" of 1763, whatever its origin) nor those imposed by the policies of states' dealings with Native Americans, could suppress those tendencies toward westward expansion.[23] This colonizing focus materialized in two politico-constitutional milestones that marked the process for the future. The first was the Northwest Ordinance of 1787, with its clamorous ambiguity regarding the extension of rights to those territories that aspired to constitute themselves as states of the Union.[24] The second was Supreme Court justice John Marshall's famous decision in *Cherokee Nation v. Georgia* (1831) in which, with the intent of recognizing Cherokee cultural identity, the constitutional doctrine was established that Indian peoples were subordinate entities under federal tutelage.[25] In this respect, it is important to stress how this aggressive policy was bound to stop important transformations within the so-called Indian nations.[26] As important as these constitutional developments were, equally so were the parallel and unstoppable process of expulsion, "removal," and the opening of a frontier in permanent motion toward the west.[27] In short, those colonial policies underlay the Jeffersonian perspective of an empire of liberty and prosperity of property-owning farmers.[28]

It was a still greater paradox that the empire of liberty and citizenship, the empire that had broken the yoke of political servitude tying it to the monarchy, became a haven for slavery.[29] It was a paradox but not, again, a surprise given the revealing silence of the founding text, whose only reference to unfree labor, as is well known, established the voting conditions for the southern states ("numbers").[30] The weight of real historical processes was again crucial in deciding the general lines of development for U.S. society. Against the idealized vision of North America as a society of small independent farmers, Jack P. Greene has shown that the greatest dynamism during the colonial period resided, as in the British West Indies, in slave areas.[31] The Revolution and independence did not stop this process, although they imposed serious and awkward corrections. The first of these was the prohibition on slave importations (one of the great assets of the trading empire of the New England ports). The second was the planned end to slavery in the northern states of the Union. Meanwhile, the slave world would be considered, in Jefferson's view, as one imposed without palliatives in the South—a "captive nation" without rights or political initiative.[32] Notwithstanding these serious limitations, the technical revolution in the ginning of cotton and the insatiable demand for this raw material in the industrial districts of the English Midlands made the development of slavery in the southern states unstoppable.

The interesting thing about this history of dispossession and slavery is its frightful symmetry with the British and Spanish possessions of the nineteenth century. Slavery and unfree labor were to be a cornerstone of the Second British Empire, Imperial Brazil, and the colonies preserved by the Spanish and French in the Caribbean. Despite the post-1770s debate about the morality of the transatlantic slave traffic, the slave plantation was a long way from exhausting its productive capacities. The history of cotton, coffee and sugar in the nineteenth-century Americas fully demonstrates this assertion. Stanley Engerman and many other international historians have shown how slavery as an institution and slave labor as such were sufficiently flexible to adapt themselves to the growing European demand for tropical agricultural products.[33] They have also shown how agricultural operations of a certain scale, whether in the Americas or British, Dutch or Spanish Asia, excluded work by independent peasants. In short, the plantation and its attendant ways of organizing coerced labor spread throughout those parts of the world controlled by the European empires. In view of this trend, what was unseemly was voluntary British abolition at a time when its own colonies had not yet reached their economic peak.[34] It is not surprising, then, that the figures show conclusively how the expansion of slavery in the first half of the nineteenth century could not be short-circuited by English abolitionist policy once Great Britain abolished the slave trade for its possessions and their inhabitants in 1807. When slavery entered an inexorable decline between 1833 and 1848, with the definitive British and French abolitions, slaveowners in some places, such as Spain, Brazil and the U.S. South resisted its abolition. They also resisted the spread of Asian and African indentured labor while delaying the adoption of wage-earning work and the consolidation of independent peasants.[35] In this context, the unexpected and economically unjustified abolition of slavery by the British Empire in 1833 (the "mighty experiment" as Seymour Drescher termed it) was a sort of counterpoint to a historical process of plantation expansion all over the world and, with it, the spread of slavery and indentured labor.[36]

These observations regarding slavery and unfree labor are important if we are to understand properly both the continuity of the Spanish presence in the Americas after the loss of the greater Spanish empire and the United States' particular political and social development in the nineteenth century. In the first case, the three insular colonies that remained in the Antilles and the Philippines went through a radical change in their internal structures and the ties that bound them to their metropoles.[37] Without looking into the matter of work organization we would be hard-pressed to understand either of these. Cuba was a laboratory for the changes that were to come about in the latter stages of the greater empire, changes that would continue in the enclaves preserved after the breakup of the imperial system as a whole. After the Seven Years' War, Spanish administrators tried out a formula in Cuba that would prove to be overwhelmingly effective: negotiating the loyalty of the Creole elite in exchange for the freedom to develop large-scale sugar agriculture, a formula that required abundant slave labor while presuming greater commercial freedom.[38] An abundant labor supply clashed with restrictions on the free importation of slaves, something the empire had never allowed its subjects to do; while commercial freedom implied altering existing mercantile relations between Spain and its colonial possessions. Both mercantilist restrictions were reformed in the negotiations between the metropolitan power and the local island elites, in particular with the emerging sugar plantation owners and the stock-raising old nobility.[39] These changes in the empire's old fiscal and commercial policies, decided on a global scale but carried out on a local scale, allowed the island's quick adaptation to the changed circumstances of the nineteenth century. In the first two decades of this century, as the rest of the empire collapsed, Spanish Cuba became one of the wealthiest sugar economies in the world.[40] Nothing speaks more eloquently to the changing circumstances than this transformation. At the end of the eighteenth century, the island continued to receive subsidies in vast quantities from the public finances of New Spain, the so-called *situados*. That flow of silver from the New Spanish viceroyalty paid the enormous costs of the fortification of Havana, as well as those of Puerto Rico and the Philippines; meanwhile, a military effort was sustained in Spanish Pensacola and Louisiana (until 1802, when Lousiana was returned to France). After 1825, Cuba transferred a large volume of net resources to the metropolis while it sustained the major military effort against the Bolivarians and an already independent Mexico. The tables had turned. Between one situation and the other, the sugar economy of the island had been transformed. Behind this process was, without doubt, the massive rise in the slave population on a scale never before seen in the Spanish Caribbean.

None of these colonial developments had any parallel in the Philippines. An almost marginal colony in terms of the greater empire, the possession of the archipelago was vital for the defensive strategy of the whole. Its conservation ensured an effective defense of the imperial rear guard and the Pacific. Certainly this was not yet the "Spanish lake" described by O. H. K. Spate, but, as the previously mentioned efforts of the British showed, the Philippines was the most secure outpost for the defense of the Pacific coasts against the emerging imperial powers.[41] These reasons sufficiently explain why the Spanish did not undertake the effective colonization of the interior of Luzon and the Visayas until the end of the colonial period to say nothing of their nominal presence in Mindanao. This tenuous internal colonization of the South China Sea possession was complemented by an equally feeble model of economic exploitation. Only after the crisis of 1762, when Manila was occupied by the British, did the Spanish decide to exchange the colonial model for another, more intensive one.[42] Their priority was, as with the Antilles and the rest of the empire, to guarantee the financial resources required for more effective military and social control of the possession. After some wavering, the key to the new strategy became the fiscal monopolies, particularly that of tobacco. Between 1782 and 1882, the tobacco monopoly ensured a much higher income than anything the Spanish authorities could have expected, as Edilberto de Jesus has shown in an excellent monograph.[43] A fiscal monopoly like that over tobacco had great virtues from the point of view of the continuity of Spanish dominion. It provided, first as we have said, hitherto unknown levels of income from the Philippines, despite the high costs of collecting the tax on tobacco, with these costs reflecting the greater implication of the state in the archipelago's economy (leaf production and cigarette manufacture). Second, it allowed other sectors of export agriculture (e.g., Manila hemp, sugar, and coffee) to be freed of excessive tax burdens, easing their integration into international trade circuits and, with this, allowing the emergence of a native bourgeoisie.[44] Third, the tobacco monopoly "internalized" a significant part of the costs of colonization and territorial control as collection costs within the tax system as a whole. In this way, thanks to the forced work of thousands of peasants in the Cagayan Valley and other areas, an effectively Spanish Philippines was forged. Spanish administrators in Manila often made this claim in their debates with liberal reformers back in Madrid, who did not hesitate to compare what was happening in the archipelago with the Dutch systems in Java or those of the British in the penal colony of Australia. In this way, the Philippines, an imperial periphery, as were Cuba and Puerto Rico in the Gulf of Mexico and the Caribbean, became part of a Spanish colonial cycle that was prolonged until 1898.

The Spanish and Portuguese contraction had its counterpoint in the growth and hegemony of the Second British Empire.[45] British superiority would be based on two parallel processes: the expansion of the space it directly controlled and the affirmation of its commercial and diplomatic superiority over formerly independent world areas.[46] Although scholarly debates about this second type of dominion, conventionally known as "informal," was exhausted with few results in the 1970s, the question is important in the context that we are discussing, particularly in areas that previously formed part of the Iberian empires.[47] Nevertheless, it was certainly the turn toward the great Asian societies that gave the second empire its particular character.[48] As is well known, the key factor was the transformation of a chartered company, the East India Company (EIC)—founded to carry out trade with Asia—into a real territorial power. This process began in 1757 and culminated with the wars against the Marathas in central India in the 1810s. This was, once again, a case of the conversion of a trading empire (a private one, moreover, in this case) into a territorial power, a structure for controlling very complex peasant societies.[49] To access the main source of the tax revenues of the Asian states—the agrarian income—was certainly the final aim of John Company, from Clive to Cornwallis, although political considerations influenced this decision, in particular the fear of a sudden attack by the French on the subcontinent.[50] Fear of the French also justified the British military deployment toward Dutch Java in 1811, an occupation that had lasting effects on the old Dutch base in Southeast Asia. The results of such a complex immersion in Asia are well known: the ascension of military proconsuls to the first rank of political hierarchies and the elaboration of a tax policy whose consequences for the model of British control in India would be felt for a century.[51]

The British turnaround after the North American crisis led to a still greater diversification within its imperial space. For one thing, the center of gravity would shift, as has been said, toward the Asian axis of the empire. With its dominion over immense peasant societies, British India was located at its center; its heart was the agricultural and taxation systems that so occupied the minds of the British economists and jurists during the nineteenth century. From this axis, an extensive chain (famously linked to the opium and tea trades) of British interests was created with landmark events such as the occupation of Java by Sir Thomas Stamford Raffles, the founding of Singapore and later Hong Kong, and a string of interests that branched out to Borneo and the Philippines in the south and China in the north.[52] The projection from the Chinese ports in South and Southeast Asia toward the Pacific would come together at some point with the expansion of commercial and whaling interests in Australia, New Zealand from the 1830s, and the Pacific. Furthermore, the Crown had increased its dominions in Africa after taking the Dutch colony of the Cape and some enclaves on the West African coast, with Sierra Leone as a center for the forces repressing the slave trade and a place of experimentation for the good deeds of Protestant abolitionism.[53] On the other coast, that of the Indian Ocean, Great Britain had taken over an old French possession captured at the beginning of the nineteenth century, Mauritius, vital as a laboratory for the transformation of slave-based sugar cultivation with the massive adoption of the indentured labor of Indians and Africans. The British still held important possessions in the Americas, although these were very different from each other. In the Caribbean, the "sugar islands," once the empire's center of gravity, would undergo in the nineteenth century an arduous and painful conversion into enclaves with indentured labor amid large peasant majorities.[54] The second half of the nineteenth century was to be a critical period, politically and economically, for the West Indies beset by social problems and the decline of sugar in international markets.[55] The ensuing drama in Jamaica, and indeed in many other possessions, was to force the first imperial policies of financial assistance to the colonies.

In British North America, the future Canada, different situations characterized the interior.[56] Between the 1830s and 1867 it would resolve the internal problems while becoming a testing ground of empire for power sharing in the "white settlement" areas.[57] Together with Australia and New Zealand, it was to make up a block of new countries with a high degree of autonomy within the empire and acceptable levels of prosperity in the second half of the nineteenth century (though not for their aboriginal inhabitants or indentured immigrants from other parts of the empire or the Pacific). These territories would be allowed public policies of social reform that were completely new outside Europe. Political and economic heterogeneity was the mark of the Victorian empire, the wise achievement of the vaunted English empiricism.[58] However, a subtle racial line divided the empire along its length with a very unequal share of prosperity and rights between its populations.

The Exception as the Rule

If we accept that political and social exception was the norm of empires, this exceptionality must be acknowledged with conceptual rigor. Until the crisis of the second half of the eighteenth century, the Atlantic empires were preliberal formations in the most literal sense of the term.[59] It was generally accepted that the king's subjects would not be governed by the same institutions and in the same way in distant possessions as in the metropole.[60] It is certain that the First British Empire spread forms of representation in its Atlantic dominions (many of these founded in their initial stages by chartered companies) that were different from what was common practice elsewhere.[61] However, this singularity must immediately be qualified in two ways. In the first place, it is necessary to highlight the hierarchy of representation present in the so-called Westminster system. Indeed, the existence of Caribbean or North American assemblies meant that the exercise of the individual's right to representation did not expire with the move from the mother country, although the subordinate position of the American political bodies within the imperial framework was accepted. This hierarchy would be maintained until the imperial crisis in the middle of the twentieth century. At this point in the analysis we must consider the development of North American policy in the eighteenth century as exceptional for it introduced a logic different from that of previous periods. It would not be correct either to allege that the colonies of other European countries lacked forms of representation, albeit not of the same style as the British examples.[62] In the Spanish, Portuguese, and French empires, colonial representation was generally restricted to the framework of municipal corporations. It is fair to remember that, even before the French Revolution, the monarchy had accepted that colonial assemblies (*conseils coloniaux*) would be formed in its prosperous slave colonies in the Caribbean.[63] As would happen in the Spanish empire two decades later, the demands for equality and representation were placed at the center of the debate and the political struggle during the revolutionary cycle that began in 1789.

Despite these precedents, the consolidation of liberal constitutions and of the idea of citizens' rights was accompanied by the formation of exceptional imperial regimes. Political rights and equality before the law, in many cases promised to all the inhabitants of a single political entity, could not be guaranteed in overseas possessions. Neither could the metropolitan tax regulations, increasingly formalized and systematic as they were, be extended to the colonies. Furthermore, the social and racial distinctions that existed in the colonial world—between free and unfree individuals, those who were marked by the experience of servitude, or between those who shared religion and culture and others who were alien—tended to distance it from the principle of political equality for increasingly uniform populations that were being established in the metropoles. Or, put another way, it was the cultural and political principles that applied in the metropoles that were becoming remote from the prevailing situation in the imperial peripheries. Consequently, the real differences between the inhabitants of the empires did not stop growing, at least in relative terms, despite the fact that the substratum of common political culture and experience could not be isolated in a world where commodities, ships, and emigrants brought colony and metropole increasingly together. As a result, the struggles over rights ended up recognizing differences between metropoles and colonies despite the subtle and less than subtle barriers of special regimes and racial borders that were often invoked. This was an inherent and inescapable contradiction of empire building, the contradiction from which arose oppositional forces in the periphery, including anticolonial nationalisms.

The construction of a political regime for the three insular colonies kept by Spain after the breakdown of the greater continental empire rigorously observed the rule of strict exceptionalism. This development became much clearer when the first liberal Constitution, approved in 1812, was articulated around the idea of absolute equality between the inhabitants of the Iberian Peninsula and those of the Americas and the Philippines.[64] Sadly, equality in principle was immediately qualified with some facts that meant inequality in practice. The decisive intellectual instrument for the creation of practical inequality that liberal Spaniards judged to be necessary for the smooth running of empire was the notion of the "heterogeneity" of colonial societies. Because of slavery's growing weight in the Spanish Caribbean, as well as in other parts of the empire, such heterogeneity could be easily proven. This idea led to the exclusion of the so-called *castas pardas* (colored castes)—free descendents of African slaves, approximately a third of the American population—from Spanish citizenship.[65] In this way, the peninsular liberals hoped to reduce the Spanish Americans' parliamentary representation. In 1837, the same principle of "heterogeneity" served to expel the remaining colonies' liberal representatives from the Cortes.

The second intellectual instrument was the denigration of "federalism," in other words, the clear rejection of a system of representational assemblies in the Americas in the style of the thirteen North American colonies or British Jamaica. American Creoles intended these assemblies to protect their interests vis-à-vis the monarchy.[66] With the definitive consolidation of liberalism in Spain, the argument for colonial heterogeneity would serve to make Cuba, Puerto Rico, and the Philippines the paradise of exceptionalism—colonial societies waiting patiently for "special laws" that would never be enacted.[67] In this way, the forced political assimilation of the first liberalism, which feared losing the American dominions, transmuted into the exclusion of the colonies from enjoyment of the liberal institutions that ruled in Spain.

Unlike the situation during the ancien régime, the liberal states could not create inequality other than as an exceptional regime. In the Spanish case during the nineteenth century, the exclusion of Cubans, Puerto Ricans, and Filipinos from the constitutional framework determined the particular political development of the three insular enclaves.[68] This could be defined, rather synthetically, by the following characteristics: the absolute command of the captain-general and governor; the fusion of civil and military authority; the exclusion of colonials from the political process and, with them, of *peninsulares* resident in the islands; the full use of racial barriers—"racial balance," as Spanish authorities in mid-nineteenth-century Cuba called it; and differentiated taxation systems (and, in the Philippine case, of social differentiation of groups defined by this tax system). These political rules were partially maintained until the last stage of the Spanish political regime despite the fact that in Puerto Rico (1873), first, and after the first Ten Years' War in Cuba (1878–82) as well, the Spanish governments would reinsert the colonials into the general political framework.[69] The extraordinary dynamism of Spanish policy in the Antilles (whatever its obvious shortcomings) was the immediate precursor of the complex process of adapting Cuba and Puerto Rico to the sphere of U.S. interests, an adaptation that proved, in many ways, to be a regression in constitutional and social terms.[70] While this occurred, the Philippines would be brutally separated from this political dynamic of "dominion." There a true nineteenth-century colonial society would be created, that is, a society excluded from the metropolitan liberal framework. These peculiarities of Spain's final mastery over the Philippines, and its insistence on presenting its people as an interminable mosaic of tribes and groups, would also condition the forms of U.S. domination there from the beginning.[71]

More so than in the remains of the Spanish empire, it is in the British Empire of the Victorian era were one finds the best example of differing rights in a single political zone. Political differences between the various parts of this empire had their roots in easily comprehensible historical circumstances. While the metropole at first tolerated (before and after the well-known Durham Report for Canada of 1838) and later encouraged practices of self-government in those colonies with white populations, it discouraged a similar development in contexts where the population was overwhelmingly nonwhite.[72] Great Britain covered up that difference with pious names such as Crown colonies and protectorates, which it applied to dominions where constitutional developments like those of Canada, New Zealand, Australia, and later South Africa were not foreseen.[73] This distinction allowed Great Britain to consider sharing power with local populations, to discuss the costs of sustaining its military (a decisive question in the framework of Gladstonian "retrenchment"), and to negotiate the tax policies by which such costs were to be borne.[74] While this was happening in the white settlements, the metropole denied the same rights to the rest of the empire.[75] In the Crown colonies, the power continued to reside in the hands of the governors appointed by the metropole while the colonies were governed by and from the Colonial Office.

For its part, India was governed under a special colonial statute, a consideration that derived from its establishment as a British possession by the East India Company. Until the Great Mutiny (1857), the developmental logic applied there was the conversion of company possessions into the legitimate continuation of the Mughal Empire and the development of an intricate system of parliamentary control over that odd Asian construct managed by Europeans. The proclamation of the Raj in 1857 allowed very different logics to be accommodated within it. A genuine colonial logic of *divide et impera*—the use and abuse of registered castes, the maintenance of privileges of old, assimilated political entities, continuation of different tax structures, and the adoption of practices of liberal reformism after the 1880s—was a way to co-opt the local and regional ruling classes in order to govern such a vast world.[76]

When considering empires in a global perspective we must reject the idea of an ascending staircase of politically varied situations. Instead, we can conceive of a host of situations of different origins and contrasting possibilities for development.[77] For this reason, the partition of Africa would offer the possibility of revising the policies of subordination, exclusion, and heterogeneity characteristic of imperial practice in the nineteenth century. Once again, the self-righteous mantel of the so-called dual mandates and indirect rule would give credibility to the creation, now more anthropologically informed, of special regimes and situations.[78] Moreover, because the exception was the rule for imperial development it was easy to reproduce the mechanisms of social and political heterogeneity, in the Indian style, within the framework of individually considered possessions.[79] This was the case of South Africa at the end of the nineteenth century where the institutionalization of British home rule was carried out in parallel with the segregation of tribal territories and the ex-slave and native populations from the sphere of liberal rights.[80] Such was the case of English Canada, too, with its implacable subordination of the population of French origin and the Indian nations.[81] The classic example of constitutional regression was the Jamaican political crisis provoked by the Morant Bay Rebellion of 1865.[82] A revolt of impoverished ex-slaves led to fierce repression and the dissolution of the Colonial Assembly, considered unmanageable because the presence of a party representing the free mulattoes and blacks from the cities. The island was reduced to a Crown colony and, as such, would be administrated henceforth by the Colonial Office.[83] Unfortunately, the combined lessons from the Jamaican crisis and the Indian events of 1857, together with the emergence of scientific racism in the second half of the nineteenth century, helped to moderate the idea of reforms throughout the empire while strengthening the unwritten rule of exceptionality.[84]

It is not difficult to establish analogies between what happened in the old European empires and fundamental processes evident in the formation of the United States as a nation. The American Constitution and, more important, the constitutional culture and political practice on which it was based, contained aspects not unlike those of exclusion and exceptionality discussed above. The only thing is that in a land-based imperialism these developments were carried out within the "interior" territorial framework of the nation. The call for territorial expansion repeatedly invoked by Franklin, Washington, and Jefferson, may be read as a dream of controlling the whole continental space as far as an unknown South Sea or Panama. Later territorial acquisition realized the revolutionary generation's dream: the Louisiana Purchase, the purchase of Oregon and California, the incorporation of Texas, Gadsden's picturesque purchase, and the purchase of Alaska. In parallel with this process of territorial expansion, the United States penned treaties with Great Britain that helped define the border with Canada in 1818 and declared the Monroe Doctrine five years later to ward off the ambitions of the old colonial powers.[85]

What were the underlying mechanisms of this expansion? The national formation of the United States included, at its core, two genuinely imperial processes as we have defined them. The first refers to the affirmation of rights of possession over territories previously inhabited by other groups with consolidated cultural and historical rights. It was, consequently, a plan of "internal" supremacy, one that was victorious in the long term. However, this same quality of being internal, as opposed to other countries' forms of imperial construction, must be immediately calibrated, reduced to its appropriate dimensions. First, the territories to the west of the Appalachians (some three million square miles with the exception of Alaska) were not at all internal territories but rather possessions of other empires or the natural spaces of populations of European origin or Indian nations. The great Jeffersonian argument of possession by purchase, that is to say, of the exploitation of interimperial or tribal weaknesses, does not grant an a priori different character to this question because once under American sovereignty a genuine colonial process was necessary to effectively incorporate the new territories into the Union.[86] The idea of a frontier society, free of restrictions to carry this process to its logical conclusion, is a romanticized version of that historical process. Full of colonial connotations, this process implied a drastic redefinition (and subjection as a rule) of other historical subjects.[87] It was indispensable, in the first place, to erase any appearance of doubt about the previous rights of the territories' inhabitants whether they be the Native American population, members of the old empires, or citizens of new countries.[88] This double dispossession occurred in the immense territory of the old French Louisiana and in Florida, Texas, New Mexico, and Southern California.[89] George Dargo once called the occupation and forced assimilation of Louisiana after the purchase from Napoleonic France a "clash of legal cultures."[90] Undoubtedly it was. The same history of formerly French and Spanish territory shows very well, however, that cultural conflict went far beyond a mere clash of legal systems. In a recent work, the historian Rebecca J. Scott explains, regarding the well-known legal case *Plessy v. Ferguson* (1892–98), that beneath the interpretation of the law there was continued resistance in the Creole mulatto and black communities of Louisiana to their degradation in society.[91]

Such changes in peoples' inherited situation were most dramatic in the case of the Indian tribes and nations. This process constituted over the long term an arena of colonial experience and the most immediate antecedent to the practices of racial discrimination and segregation incorporated into American expansionist adventures after 1898. As we have noted, the bases of exclusion had been laid down early, during the British colonial period. They undoubtedly became more pronounced with the harsh criticism of the British Crown's ambiguous policy toward Indian tribes.[92] Taking this a step further, the American Constitution, in its only explicit mention of their existence, made Indians "nontaxpayers," that is to say, persons excluded from the system of rights and duties. The colonial framework advanced relentlessly, however, as a result of the conflicts originated by the states' westward expansion with dramatic episodes during the dynamic stage of Andrew Jackson's presidency.[93] In Supreme Court rulings, such as justice John Marshall's famed *Cherokee Nation v. Georgia,* Indians were defined as "a domestic dependent nation,"[94] in other words, as a national group that could never constitute itself into a subject of international law and aspire to independence and would always be in a "state of pupilage." In 1886, this doctrine of warding and pupilage was reinforced and enhanced by the Supreme Court's doctrine of "federal plenary powers."[95] It is significant that an expansionist such as Henry Cabot Lodge considered the old Marshall ruling to be the resolution of constitutional questions for the Philippines.[96] This was to be the foundation of a long tradition of dealing with the "native races" not very different from the rest of the experiences mentioned above. However, the fundamental thing was not so much a constitutional culture "rooted in prejudice" as the social culture that gave it meaning and, even more so, the practices of colonial order from which it was born.[97] All this constituted a genuine regime of exceptionality in the framework of republican culture. In this sense, it had little to envy those constructed by the European empires on other continents.

Still more important as an exceptional situation, a laboratory of differentiating ideas and practices, was the North-South division of the country, especially with regard to slavery and the destiny of the population of African origin after abolition. In this case, as with the previous example, we find all the conditions for the formation of a classic colonial situation of exceptionality: divergent social relations, a culture of differentiation within the general republican framework, and supporting Supreme Court jurisprudence. The development of slavery and proslavery policies prior to 1865, as well as the development of racial distinctions after the period of so-called Reconstruction, became a critical part of comprehensively colonial practices within republican culture.[98] At the beginning of the twentieth century, at a time of very intense national debate, the jurist Gilbert Thomas Stephenson summarized, with great farsightedness, the culmination of more than thirty years of segregation policy.[99] With regard to the "suffrage clauses" adopted in six southern states, which obstructed the Afro-American population's exercise of the voting franchise, he precisely distinguished discrimination by custom from discrimination by law, showing how the laws regarding suffrage were "only links of a chain." Discrimination by custom or law was the result of the country's previous history. The very fact that of the 4 million slaves counted in a census in 1860 2.1 million were in the slave states incorporated after independence cannot be regarded as an anomaly but rather must be understood in terms of national construction and colonial conception. For this reason, the Civil War represented at the same time a great constitutional crisis, in the lucid interpretation of Arthur Bestor, and also a moment of refounding of the country itself.[100] It meant the end of three decades of powerful southern nationalism and of different conceptions of national formation in the North and the South.[101]

There were also two different understandings of how the nation's expansion, its national formation, and its imperial vocation should be. For this reason, the expansion of the southern states had been synonymous with the growth of slave societies. Between the ambiguous Northwest Ordinance and the Civil War, the idea of excluding slavery in the expansion toward the West could be neither avoided nor applied. Consequently, the growing importance of that genuinely colonial line became a two-dimensional process. On one hand, the federal state emphatically prohibited the entry of new African slaves and promoted their repatriation to the West African coast whenever possible. On the other hand, it obstructed, just as firmly, the migration of slaves from southern states to the North (the "Freedom Trail").[102] The most decisive factor, however, was the protection of the massive and planned exodus of slaves from the old south to the new, expanding slave states, the most dramatic point of this story.[103] These developments were protected by the constitutional doctrine pronounced by Supreme Court justices John Marshall and Henry Clay in a series of well-known cases of republican jurisprudence. The Missouri Compromise of 1820 and the Illinois Convention of 1823–24 demonstrated, if there was still any doubt, that the application of the 1789 Northwest Ordinance for the formation of new states could not impede some from becoming slave states.[104] Between this last event and the Civil War, the call of the southerners to so-called popular sovereignty (finally presented as a doctrine defined by Stephen Douglas in a debate with Abraham Lincoln in 1858) legitimized the expansion of slavery toward the old French Louisiana, Missouri, and, when it was incorporated, Texas. The constitutional debate at two later moments, the Kansas-Nebraska Act of 1854 and the ominous

Dred Scott Decision three years later, signaled the apogee and also the beginning of the end of the southern initiative.[105] Ideas of national formation, such as the expansion of a social system considered to be ideal, were very popular in the southern world, particularly in the part of that world that dreamed about annexing Spanish slaveholding Cuba and the formation of a Caribbean empire.[106] From this point of view, then, the history of American national formation was marked, simultaneously, by the growth of slavery, a colonial institution par excellence, and by certain social features that paralleled the European empires in the Caribbean and monarchical Brazil.

The distinctions holding back the impulse toward political homogeneity would persist and deepen in the period after Reconstruction.[107] The very meaning of the Fourteenth Amendment—the moment at which the idea of equality finally entered constitutional doctrine—was to be questioned by the southern states, and its meaning was to be limited, at the same time, by constitutional doctrine.[108] The failure of the Civil Rights Act of 1875 confirmed this difficulty, as the act was only effective in the northern states. The following decades saw the birth of a varied set of exclusionary practices. These included the separation of electoral censuses, the growing segregation of social life in the South through the so-called Jim Crow laws, and the culture of "white supremacy" in its different versions, which legitimized this state of affairs.[109] After 1877, all of this led to what has been called an authentic southern "home rule."[110] This independent form of national development, once again a whole area of sui generis colonial relations, enjoyed excellent health at the end of the century.[111] Open or attenuated segregation was very notable, for example, among the progressivist intellectual media, which would be so central to the intellectual preparation and definition of expansionism in 1898. These distant foundations eased the adoption of very consistent exclusionary policies with relation to newly arrived immigrants, in particular Asians arriving on the West Coast.[112]

Unrecognized Loans

When the United States began its territorial expansion with the annexation of first Hawai'i and then Cuba, Puerto Rico, and the Philippines, the country's framers of public opinion were perfectly aware of the complex challenges of constructing a controlled space far from the continent. Without doubt, the fundamental ingredients of an effective colonial policy derived from the experiences in developing exceptional situations in the "interior" context during the preceding period.[113] The lessons arose from those areas of colonial experience we have already discussed, which we can sum up as follows: formation of "territories" as forerunners of new states combined with a set of practices that effectively segregated those who did not correspond to the ideal of the free, self-sufficient, property-owning individual. The most significant change lies, then, in the will to carry the founding project of the Republic as an empire beyond the continental limits. As a result, the colonial logic of westward expansion, which was subordinated to the realization of the dream of the free individual in the interior, would now occupy the forefront of the state's action in the new, distant possessions. In the future, both logics (with their respective ideologies) would compete and mingle in a highly contradictory manner in U.S. imperial policy between the two world wars.

It is important to emphasize the logic of exceptionality that ensured the expansionist purpose and impulse. The American irruption into the Caribbean and the Pacific immediately provoked a reassessment of the very idea of the Republic. The problem was very simple: once the United States found itself, through its own decisions, involved in governing territories ceded by Spain through the Treaty of Paris of 1898 what would be the relationship between government and the Constitution in these territories? The conundrum had a juridical dimension and also a practical one since it fully affected the direction of military operations, the problematic assertion of civil power, the organization of an ad hoc tax system, and, finally, the adoption of more or less explicit racial policies not necessarily equivalent to those in force on the continent. At this juncture, the lessons derived from the past and the observation of overseas experiences came together.

During the colonial transition itself, the United States tackled with precision the problem of how to govern the recently acquired territories. I will look at some interesting examples. The first, replete with doctrinal rigor and clarity of purpose, is a text published in the *Political Science Quarterly* by one of the fathers of political science in the United States, J. W. Burgess.[114] For this author, the challenge was very clear: either to govern the territories acquired by extending to them constitution principles or to postpone this naturalization while awaiting "an act of the Congress commanding and proclaiming the same," that is, to allow for special situations, which would likely occur in a legal limbo. This second perspective appeared to Burgess as contradicting the very constitutional logic of the Republic. If the Constitution could not be ignored, it was necessary to establish which of its parts (if not the whole) should prevail. In fact, the Constitution distinguished perfectly between two different situations, "a constitution of government for war and a constitution of government for peace," and beyond that "a constitution of federal government for a certain portion of the country, that portion which has State local government and a constitution of centralized government for another portion of the country, that portion not possessing State local government."[115] From this starting point, the direction for creating the colonial policy that the country needed was quite clear, but for this it was necessary to choose from among the possibilities offered by the Constitution itself, allowing an act of sovereignty by Congress, the only body that was qualified to set the conditions. According to these principles, the legislature had three options in a hierarchy that, at this stage, needs little comment: martial law, centralized republican civil government, and the republican civil system of a federal type characteristic of the states that make up the republican polity. In principle, all the constitutional guarantees—civil liberties, liberty of conscience, fiscal equality, guarantees against the executive—should be valid both in the states of the Union and in the incorporated "territories" regardless of the conditions of its administration. The term *territory* is, in fact, the one Burgess and many others used to refer to the recently acquired spaces based on the so-called territorial clause of the third section of Article IV of the Constitution. Its distinction within the republican framework did not directly open the door to liberal dictatorship, but it did permit the state to elaborate, outside its territory, the type of constitutional distinctions on which the imperial practices of other countries were based. But, according to this principle, how to acquire far-off territories without creating "colonies"? This possibility, rejected by the liberal cultures of European tradition, had to be resolved—and it would be resolved by means of different formulas erected on a common platform of exceptional practices.

How was the country, under these assumptions, to organize power in the new territories and how was it to make a tax system work when that system could hardly be identical to that of the nation? These were questions that could not be resolved by a literal reading of constitutional rights despite the immediate precedents of the "organized territories" exemplified by the Organic Act Providing a Civil Government for Alaska, a territory ceded by czarist Russia in 1884, and by that of Hawai'i in 1898.[116] Burgess had already warned, like many others, that the organic law for Puerto Rico (the Foraker Act of 1900), whose central purpose was to guarantee a U.S. presence and "tutelage" on the island, did not initially fulfill the precept of fiscal uniformity throughout national territory.[117] For instance, from the point of view of the Puerto Ricans themselves, what it really meant was a kind of regression in their previous rights, at least under the terms in which Spanish colonial policy had developed between 1873 and the *in extremis* concession of autonomy in 1897. That political and constitutional regression, overcome by the weight of the new imperial power, has recently been eloquently summarized in a few words: the loss of equal citizenship, the loss of representation in the Spanish legislature, and the loss of universal suffrage and a series of newly won rights.[118] On these grounds and other matters of a similar nature, all the jurisprudence of the "insular cases" was to be formed while a legion of administrators and scholars of colonial politics would prepare themselves for the study of their own and others' experiences.[119] The Philippine Organic Act of 1902 must be looked at similarly. The act was the result of the transformation of William Howard Taft's appointment as "governor-general," terminology of British origin and very close to nineteenth-century Spanish terminology, approved within the context of a military situation that had not yet been stabilized. The fact that the brilliant governor had at his side a nonelective commission was also similar to the British regime in contexts without self-government. Similar, too, were the functions of the resident commissioner in Washington, an office almost identical in its conception to that of the commissioners of the British dominions in London. This position did not exist and would have been unnecessary in the Spanish context at the end of the nineteenth century since the Cubans and Puerto Ricans were represented in the Spanish parliament.

It is in the Supreme Court decisions around the so-called insular cases that one clearly finds the confluence of accumulated colonial tradition and previous expansionism. In these cases, a new constitutional theory was justified, occasionally in a rather nebulous manner, a theory developed in parallel with a very aggressive colonial practice in the three overseas provinces ceded by the defeated Spain. Stated with maximum brevity, this was the distinction between "incorporated" and "unincorporated" territories with the first of these being the ones that make up part of the territory of the Union and the others being those owned by, and destined never to be a part of, the Union.[120] In these latter territories, the Congress of the United States would enjoy "plenary powers" or exclusive powers in line with the argument put forward by Burgess. To be precise: these powers were not absolute or dictatorial (like those the government had in the territories inhabited by the Native Americans or in relation to immigration). Rather, these powers were in agreement with the constitutionally established guarantees for individual subjects recognized in the juridical tradition of the new metropole. Of course, this definition of possible rights excluded the social or "territorial" rights of the inhabitants of the new dominions. By this we understand questions of national or public identity that would not be recognized in the U.S., except for the practices of exclusion from suffrage and collective rights for the Afro-American population, mainly in the South. In this way, the colonial practices found the right juridical space in which to develop a "murky zone" in the words of Joseph A. Fallon.[121] In this ambiguous space, the United States was to create a set of varied political situations throughout the twentieth century. Among these we can recognize the "commonwealth" (the Philippines between 1935 and 1946), "free association," "unincorporated and organized territories," and "unincorporated and unorganized territories," as well as extraordinary protectorates in Cuba (independence with the Platt Amendment by the treaty of May 22, 1903), Haiti, and Japan and Germany after World War II. These varied and vague forms of exclusion and incorporation were evident in the string of occupations by U.S. forces after the war against Spain, the occupation of Panama, and the two great wars of the twentieth century. Compared with the unitary rigidity of the territorial context of the metropole—at least in principle—these situations represented the apotheosis of the exception. Beyond this were the "areas of influence," among which the Open Door policy for China was the most important test case, and, further, the inevitable dilemmas and problems of the "informal" empire that was opening up in the rest of the world.

It is frequently affirmed that the jurisprudence elaborated since 1901 around the "insular cases" (*Bowden v. Bidwell, Armstrong v. United States, Dooley v. United States,* and *DeLima v. Bidwell*) was a response to the legal vacuum of the American tradition.[122] The aforementioned arguments show that it was not, in any case, an arbitrary response unaware of legal precedent. The policy in relation to American Indian peoples—"local dependent communities" said the Supreme Court as of 1885—was invoked as the immediate precedent. Certainly, the military administration of the "territories" within the framework of the national government itself, the explicit limitation of rights, and the concept of "warding" are the most immediate antecedents to the administrative arbitrariness applicable to extraterritorial possessions and in the very notion of imperial tutelage. In the short term, however, the force that inexorably pushed in the direction of an ever greater involvement, the factor that raised new issues to be dealt with, was the actual practice of governance. Military involvement in the Philippines between 1900 and 1902, with a repressive escalation that was not very different from those of the Spanish in Cuba and the British in South Africa, both of which inflamed public opinion in the United States, is an example of the factors that made a precise and well-developed colonial policy both indispensable and urgent.[123]

It is ironic that these complications led from the first moments in a frighteningly similar direction to that of the old colonizers, although the tune the Americans initially played was not the same. Such aggravating circumstances led to colonial policies not unlike those of other European powers: almost absolute power in the hands of the governor appointed from Washington, powerful commissions, the rapid creation of a civil administration (although in the Philippines military influence lasted longer), the preeminence of Congress over the elements of political representation in the colonies, and a tax policy that was completely different from the one in force in the metropole. All of this was punctuated, finally, by clever manipulations of the color line. Many of these policies were similar to those applied in the Spanish colonial world throughout the nineteenth century (except, of course, for direct representation in Parliament from 1873 for Puerto Rico and 1882 for Cuba) or in India and the British Crown colonies.

But this is not about carrying out an exercise in sterile formalism. Every colonial space advanced according to a sophisticated alchemy that involved metropolitan priorities and local dynamics, and these depended in the last analysis on an array of political, social, and cultural factors. The complex and diverse factors that pushed toward a more complex articulation of colonial policy included, then, the problems of an unexpected war in the Philippines, the racial problems encountered everywhere, the forceful nationalism that confronted the occupation of a Cuba battered by two and a half years of a bloody independence war, the intricacies of relationships established with local ruling groups, and an accumulation of administrative problems.[124]

At the beginning of the twentieth century, intellectuals tried to clarify how the United States could develop special regimes, politically and fiscally, amid the new conditions of extracontinental expansion. Through the opinion media and other influential organizations, intellectuals engaged in a serious effort to solve this dilemma.[125] At first sight, it is surprising to observe the short distance that separated the academic community (a crucial part of the celebrated American "civil society") from official policy and policy makers in their attempt to affirm an external area of influence. This was, probably, the fruit of the interventionist and moralizing enthusiasm of intellectual progressivism that was so well received at the turn of the century.[126] In this regard, it is important to remember that both the *Harvard Law Review* and the *Yale Review* published numerous articles about the recently acquired territories and the world of colonies in general. In an exchange with a marked academic tone, for example, the first of these journals paved the way for the jurisprudence that would take shape during the "insular cases."[127]

While the best brains in political science were concerned with resolving the contradictions of U.S. expansion, the economists were facing up to the challenge with admirable determination. As they would quickly notice, the difficulty of fitting the incorporated territories into the American Constitution was even clearer in terms of taxation. Since, according to the eighth section of the first article of the Constitution, "all Duties, Imposts and Excises shall be uniform throughout the United States," it was necessary to create regimes of exception in the new possessions. The maintenance of existing taxation systems was equally inevitable, for practical reasons, since it was impossible to organize a new tax formula able to sustain local institutions while facilitating the new rulers' administrative capacities.

At its eleventh annual meeting, the American Economic Association decided to intervene openly in this complicated problem. Some of the best-prepared minds in this field, key figures in the reformist politics of progressivism, compiled a foundational collection of works on the fiscal policies of other countries with consolidated colonial spaces. The book was edited by a committee presided over by Jeremiah Jenks on behalf of the promoting organization, which included such important figures as Edwin R. A. Seligman, Albert Shaw, E. H. Strobel, and Charles S. Hamlin.[128] It must be borne in mind here that Jenks was not by any means an irrelevant character. At the time, he held the position of "special commissioner of the United States War Department on Colonial Administration" within the Bureau of Insular Affairs, a position from which he published an influential "Report on Certain Economic Questions of the English and Dutch

Colonies in the Orient," a dense compendium of factual information and analysis of public economies and policies throughout Southeast Asia.[129] Seligman, for his part, was considered to be the greatest authority on the country's public finances and their history, with a solid reputation from a broad range of prestigious research projects and publications, many of which were required reading well into the twentieth century.[130]

The publication date of the American Economic Association's compilation is, in itself, relevant. It shows that those materials had been prepared rapidly, as circumstances unfolded, or indeed foreseeing those very circumstances. The editors recognized, without any qualms, the speed involved in the editorial operation. In fact, the essays had been previously published in the association's magazine, the prestigious *American Economic Review*, before being definitively compiled and presented without disguise as a contribution to the political needs of the moment. "It seemed wise to the committee"—it stated in the report that precedes the material compiled—"to secure information regarding the fiscal methods and economic conditions of typical modern colonies and to endeavor, on the basis of this information, to suggest tentatively some general principles which might be applicable to the government of the new dependencies of the United States."[131] In line with this desire for intervention in the formulation of colonial policy, the case studies were preceded by a brief and dense report, which gave precise instructions on how to organize the finances of the recently acquired possessions. This is not the place for a close consideration of the report nor of the work that made up the book,[132] although, in the context of the matters that are discussed in this text, it is worth quoting explicitly the second point stated in it: "No uniform system of detailed fiscal management for a number of colonies in different parts of the world can be established. Each colony must be considered by itself and its system must be adapted to its conditions."[133] In other words, the colonies should be considered colonies, with all their idiosyncrasies and backwardness, something that was not said so crudely but was implicit throughout the report.

Going a step further, the viability of taxation regimes that were enacted depended on their framers' capacity to adapt to local conditions, that is to say, to be included within the compass of special regimes. This approach pervaded, for example, J. H. Hollander's analysis of the public finances of Puerto Rico shortly after the new authorities took possession of it.[134] The work had an academic appearance, although it was clearly angled toward the stabilization of American dominion over the island and the apologia for the new administrators. At the time, other authors expressed skepticism about the technical viability of the proposed reforms.[135] The problem was rooted in the fact that the American Constitution did not allow for formulas of exception unless the precise conditions of that exceptionality were laid down. In short, colonies could be constructed even if this were done over the ashes of previous colonial orders and even if they were to be called territories.

The contradictions to which the most outstanding minds of American progressivism fell victim were quickly grasped by their contemporaries. The New Zealander William Pember Reeves immediately highlighted, for example, the contradictions intrinsic to the work of the brilliant American economists.[136] Reeves was not just anybody. A commissioner of his dominion in London and the author of interesting material on imperial development in Oceania, he spent his life linked to Fabianism. He was a personal friend of Sidney and Beatrice Webb as well as founder and president for some time of the London School of Economics.[137] The reasoning of the New Zealander was very lucid: to study fiscal policy only in colonies where the majority of the population was presumed to be nonwhite, or was considered backward, without bearing in mind the reformist and liberal policies by which the British Empire was attempting to resolve lawsuits in the dominions or in the Indian conflicts was to lack foresight.[138] It was, he concluded, a poor way of preparing for the inevitable conflict of interests between the emerging metropole and the nationalisms that, sooner or later, would stir in its possessions.

On the American side, W. M. Daniels put his finger squarely on the problem with an argument that perfectly concludes the reflections contained in these pages. Daniels warned that no colonial system could be constructed at the margins of the metropolitan system and this was even more the case in liberal political systems. The Germans had resolved the problem by leaving authority over the colonies in the emperor's hands, though allowing the Bundestag to intervene in financial matters; the British had forged a paradise of exceptions, maintaining only the supremacy of the Parliament of Westminster as the rule. The United States, a nation born in an anticolonial revolution, was limited by constitutional rules in its capacity to incorporate new territories since strictly speaking it could neither create colonies nor cede them by an arbitrary act of the executive. Thus, Daniels concluded, "if the report of the committee is open to criticism, it is right there, that it embodies in its recommendations provisions which possibly are irreconcilable with the supreme law of the land."[139]

Dangerous Symmetries

Unlike the empires of the sixteenth through the eighteenth centuries, in which uniformity among subjects was not an aim in itself, the great Atlantic crisis was to alter radically the very conception of constitutional equality between the inhabitants of the metropoles and their possessions. The development of these aspirations of equality was not, however, to be linear.[140] In fact, a number of great conflicts with implications for the future, among which should be considered the separation of the thirteen North American colonies, the Saint-Domingue/Haiti crisis, and the dissolution of the Spanish and Portuguese empires, were to make the idea of uniformity in the imperial spaces an aim that was scarcely, or not at all, desirable. As a result, the political entities that arose from the ashes of ancien régime empires reconstructed their colonial foundations and, with this, the idea of inequality among the inhabitants and between the territories they occupied. However, to the extent that the liberal culture of the late eighteenth and the nineteenth centuries became increasingly associated with equality before the law, equal taxation, and the slow but steady expansion of electoral franchise, the inherited or emergent colonial logics increasingly took the form of exceptional situations with regard to metropolitan rule. These differences were interpreted and codified in a different way in each particular experience within the framework of distinct juridical traditions. One of the tasks of the comparative history of empires (and of their specific social structures) should be to establish the particular ways of delimiting and articulating these crucial distinctions between the metropolitan spaces and those of distant territories, of the center and periphery if one wants to appeal to a well-established terminology.

The fundamental problem that impeded legal parity between metropoles and colonies lay in the almost total impossibility of maintaining forms of colonial control over territories whose populations enjoyed equal rights (not only of representation, but also taxation and social life). Moreover, it was impossible to maintain the legitimacy of the institutions that allowed the social and economic development of distant territories under the same terms that the Europeans had established up to the eighteenth century and would continue developing until well into the next century. Under these circumstances, the continued colonial status of Spain's insular possessions, the unending expansion of the British Empire, and the presence of different European and non-European rivals and competitors—including the Americans—were resolved by forging empires as spaces of inevitable heterogeneity. Social heterogeneity was to be achieved first in those empires where certain institutions and practices could be maintained over very long periods without being questioned as different or dysfunctional compared to what was established in the metropole. There were also spaces with political heterogeneity to the extent that it was necessary to channel those differences within the framework of unequal rules. Under these conditions, the contradiction inherent in the imperial developments of the nineteenth century could be easily perceived: the universality of liberal principles ("all men are born free and equal," the inclusive character of rights and duties within the national framework) generalized the claims of political equality within the spaces controlled by them. The contradiction was clearer in places where those ideas had taken root most deeply: most obviously where the presence of populations of European origin were dominant or were becoming so. In general, European emigrants tried to make themselves fully equal to the inhabitants of the metropolis that they had left behind, generally without achieving it. At the same time, they attempted in many cases to limit the advantages of political equality and representation (when they existed) to their peers, excluding, via rules of exception, the "natives" or the nonwhite populations, by co-opting some into the spheres of equality by means of religion or education. However, the contradictions of imperial logic were equally evident where the language and culture of liberalism in their different versions had penetrated other strata of the population. This was very clearly the case in territories where slave populations understood this language as a harbinger for their upcoming liberation; events in Haiti were the most outstanding manifestation of this process.[141] This was also the case in places where the language of political equality reached even Amerindian populations, a reality that was perfectly proved by the crisis of the continental Spanish empire and in its successor republics.

In the majority of cases these multiple responses provoked the imposition of formulas of exceptionality and isolation on the metropole's institutions and political practices. The difference was affirmed because maintaining colonies implied, by their very raison d'être and for these added reasons, a considerable use of violence. For this reason, Spanish liberals in the Americas retreated from the abstract sphere of rights recognized in the Constitution of 1812 in order to fall back on more ambiguous and controllable situations. For this reason, too, the regression of the French revolutionary dynamic inevitably involved the collapse of the idea of a common native land as a space of identical rights regardless of location. In any case, the metropolitan governments learned to impose gradations and calibrate skillfully the sphere of political equality invoked in their constitutions and codes. This dynamism led to apparently contradictory results. In 1878, after the first Cuban war of independence, the successive Spanish governments understood that it was impossible (at least in theory) to maintain a regime of exception among the white populations of Cuba and Puerto Rico, which were well-off and learned, but in contrast confirmed the colonial limbo in the Philippines. Great Britain aimed toward a sophisticated set of rules of colonial elevation for its white dominions while it maintained other colonies in a state of clear exclusion, and in some cases, as happened in Jamaica after the Morant Bay massacre, to an increasing degree. France maintained Algeria under military governments for decades, while Martinique and Guadeloupe were ruled as regimes of exception until the consolidation of the Third Republic in the 1880s converted the former into a French *département* and the latter two into overseas territories following the 1794 and 1848 precedents.[142] However, in Algeria, Paris maintained two separate regimes, one for French colonials and another for the Arab and Berber populations under a system of exclusion from citizenship and inequality before the law (the *code d'indigenat*) and taxation (*impôt arabes*) that would later be extended to French Indochina.[143]

This contradiction between the expectations raised at the dawn of the modern era by the culture of political equality of foundational liberalism and the reality of social and legal constructions is one of the essential legacies of the nineteenth century. In the metropolitan spaces this contradiction was resolved slowly and with difficulty by the spread of the rights rhetorically espoused, as suffrage limitations and other exclusions by sex or age would continue to show until the twentieth century. In the colonial world, which was not a world all that distant, after all, from that metropolitan political culture, it was resolved that the struggle for the dissolution of formulas of social exclusion within the framework of political exceptionality was the norm. All the empires played at this, and all became exhausted, sooner or later, in their struggle against the unstoppable leveling tide.

From Old Empire to New

The Changing Dynamics and Tactics of American Empire

THOMAS McCORMICK

EVERY NATION FANCIES ITSELF EXCEPTIONAL—unique and superior to others. Each nation creates its own traditions and narratives, infused with more than a dollop of fiction, to lend the weight of history to its sense of exceptionalism. Nowhere has this been more evident than in the United States, a New World, where the sins of moribund, decadent Europe, the Old World, were said to be absent. And among those sins—allegedly missing in the country's unfolding— was Europe's half millennium of imperialism and its accompanying wars.

That popular myth begins with an apparent self-evident truth—that the American Republic was itself the product of an anticolonial, revolutionary war against empire and thus anti-imperialism was an inherent part of its national DNA from its very birthing. True to its origins, the subsequent expansion of America westward and southward across the North American continent was a natural, organic, inevitable process—simply a case of the flag following demography as American pioneers poured into lands either unoccupied or sparsely peopled by indigenes making nonproductive use of the land. It was an Empire for Liberty, if an empire at all, carrying with it democracy and the commercial revolution in agriculture.

To be sure, the end of that continental expansion—the end of that life-giving frontier in the 1890s—spawned a copycat overseas expansionism that seemed to ape the New Imperialism that had gripped Europe in the late nineteenth century. Even that expansionism, however, was not the result of systemic imperatives or conscious choice but rather the almost accidental consequence of a "splendid little war"—an anticolonial one at that—which freed Cuba from the yoke of Spanish empire. The resulting American empire in Puerto Rico, the Philippines, Wake Island, and Guam was miniscule compared to the European empires in Africa and Southeast Asia. Indeed, no sooner had it been acquired than the United States began to consider ways to be rid of it. In sum, American imperialism was a venal sin but not a mortal one. In the words of the late historian Samuel Flagg Bemis, American imperialism had been merely a "Great Aberration."[1] This compelling moral fable of a little sin and a great redemption enabled later historians to picture subsequent American wars, both hot and cold, as confrontations fought with clean hands by an exceptional nation, untainted by ulterior motives of aggression and aggrandizement, seeking merely to defend and promote democracy and civilization against Old World pathologies.

Continental Empire

A more persuasive telling, while less satisfying to the national psyche, paints a far more complex and dynamic historical portrait. It argues that the United States has always been an empire but one that dramatically mutated in the 1890s and thereafter as the result of structural shifts both in the American political economy and in the world system itself—arguably a new empire, a second empire.

The first empire had focused primarily on the landed colonization of North America by American farmers and entrepreneurs and the related acquisition of seaports such as New Orleans, San Francisco, and Seattle to transport their produce and primary commodities to the commercial markets of Europe and Asia. That first empire started with the American Revolution itself, which was not only a war against empire but a war for empire and a grandiose one at that. Indeed, in the American revolutionary crosshairs were the trans-Appalachian West, Canada, Florida, and the British West Indies. In the end, the United States acquired only the first item on that imperial shopping list, laying the groundwork for American dominance of the Ohio and Mississippi valleys. But even the French foreign minister, America's wartime ally, feared that America's demography, geography, and natural resources would eventually lead Americans to dominate the Caribbean. "And they would not stop here," he added, "but would in the process of time advance to the Southern Continent of America and either subdue the inhabitants or carry them along with them, and in the end not leave a single foot of the Hemisphere in the possession of any European power."[2]

Similarly, nineteenth-century American expansionism was more than a simple narrative of a booming population obeying nature's command to leave no vacuum unfilled. First, it was also the product of conscious foreign policy choices often made well in advance of American settlement. Thomas Jefferson had sought to include Texas in the Louisiana Purchase in 1803 two decades before the first wave of American migration; John Quincy Adams, buoyed with Spanish claims (the Transcontinental Treaty of 1819) had secured joint occupancy with Britain of the Pacific Northwest (the Oregon Convention of 1819) two decades before "Oregon Fever" inflamed the land hunger of midwestern farmers; and James K. Polk made California his principal objective in the Mexican-American

War in 1846 not because of the miniscule American presence in California but because the American navy had determined a decade earlier that San Francisco Bay and San Diego Bay (along with Puget Sound) were the "windows to the Orient" that held the key to America's future in Asia.³

Second, the overarching aim of this grand strategy was to roll back and then absorb the Spanish empire either formally or informally. Jefferson's "Large Policy" of 1808 suggested as much, and the Monroe Doctrine of 1823 made it explicit. Indeed, the latter might more properly have been termed the Monroe Manifesto of Empire, one that proscribed European colonization and institutions in the hemisphere while the absence of any self-denying ordinance left the United States free to interject its hegemony into the void. In the event, that meant any and all means necessary. Covert action, the War of 1812, armed incursion, and coercive diplomacy all led Spain to part with West and East Florida and its claims to the Oregon Territory. Mexico's independence in the 1820s and the birth of a sister republic did nothing to stay the course of empire. Managed revolution and annexation detached Texas while the War of the Northern Invasion (the Mexican War), ripped off the northern tier of Mexico that constitutes the present American Southwest and capped it with California and its "windows to the Orient." Only the logistical difficulties of governing a large, alien, and distant population prevented pressure from America's "All Mexico" movement to mark an end to Mexico's brief independence altogether.⁴ No such considerations stayed the American hand in Cuba, long considered a natural appendage of North America. In the 1820s and 1830s, the United States played a waiting game. It discouraged any Latin American efforts to liberate Cuba, preferring to bide its time until a weakened Spanish rule inevitably dropped Cuba into the American lap like a ripe apple. By the 1840s and 1850s, no longer content to wait for nature to take its course, successive administrations tried unsuccessfully to acquire Cuba, alternating carrot-and-stick tactics between repeated attempts to purchase the island from Spain and clandestine support for armed, private mercenaries (filibustering expeditions) to destabilize Spanish rule.⁵

Third, and inextricably coupled with this drive to roll back the Spanish borderlands, was a concerted effort to subvert and replace British hegemony in the Caribbean Basin. While northern Whigs preferred negotiated engagement and southern Democrats favored aggressive confrontation, all agreed on the general end of making the Caribbean an American lake, mare nostrum—"our sea." While this Anglo-American contest for dominance played itself out in multiple places, it was Central America, especially Nicaragua, that was the prime focal point between the mid-1840s and the British acquiescence in American pretensions six decades later. At stake was the right to build, fortify, and control a future isthmian canal as a commercial and military shortcut to the American West Coast and the Asian East Coast—a necessary prerequisite for the United

States to become not merely a hemispheric power but a Pacific power as well. It was a battle that Britain seemed to be losing in the 1850s in the face of aggressive American diplomacy and Democratic Party endorsements of filibustering expeditions such as William Walker's temporary takeover of Nicaragua in 1856 and his abortive effort to reintroduce slavery.[6]

At first glance, the American Civil War offered Britain a perfect chance to halt its retreat in the Caribbean. After all, a Confederate victory would weaken the diminished Union and permit the British to play balance of power diplomacy in North America. Britain, however, pursued that strategy in only a halfhearted way—enough to irritate the Union but not enough to be of decisive help to the South. And, while many factors explain that hesitant approach, perhaps the most overlooked was Britain's fear of Confederate imperialism in the Caribbean should it emerge as an independent nation. Effectively shut out of access to the western lands of North America, the South dreamed of an empire to the south in Central America, the Caribbean islands, and even parts of Mexico, and acquiring that empire was one of the postwar goals of the proslavery Confederacy.[7]

Overseas Empire

The three decades that followed the Civil War wrote finis to the first stage of American empire and prepared the way for the second stage, at once similar and yet so different from its predecessor.[8] The process of landed, continental expansion northward essentially ended in 1867, when dominion status blunted U.S. hopes to annex Canada, and southward in 1877 when northern financial interests, more interested in investment than landed conquests, persuaded the government to resist pressure to incite another land-grabbing conflict with Mexico from a coalition of Texas cattle and railroad interests backed by elements of the U.S. Army.[9]

There was, however, another aspect to early American expansion, one that would form the core of a new empire that would come to pass in 1898 and forever after. It rested on a grand strategic vision that had already begun to capture the imagination of national leaders such as William H. Seward and Stephen A. Douglas even before the Civil War. Its medium-term goal was to make the Monroe Doctrine not a long-term hope but an operational reality. Its longer term goal was to make America the dominant power in the Pacific Basin, a dream implicit in Commodore Perry's forced opening of Japan before the Civil War and the manner in which the United States hitchhiked on British efforts to coerce the opening of China through the Opium Wars and unequal treaties, ironically dubbed the Open Door policy.[10] And its shorter term goal—the transformation of the Caribbean into an American lake—was to facilitate both broader goals. An American-controlled isthmian canal would be the drawbridge between the Americas and Asia and U.S. control of the key Caribbean islands would protect the Windward and Mona passages that funneled trade in and out of that future canal.

Between the U.S. Civil War and the Spanish-Cuban-Philippine-America War, U.S. foreign policy makers repeatedly tried to act out this grand strategy, though only rarely with much success. In the Caribbean Basin, the United States threatened to intervene in the Cuban Revolution of 1868, sought to annex the Dominican Republic, tried to secure a naval base in Haiti, attempted to purchase the Virgin Islands from Denmark in 1867, negotiated an 1877 treaty with Nicaragua for exclusive U.S. canal rights in blatant disregard of the Clayton-Bulwer Treaty with Britain, and intervened several times to help Colombia put down Panamanian revolts. In Latin America as a whole, Secretary of State James G. Blaine embraced a proto–Good Neighbor policy in 1890 by convening an International American Conference to consider his vision of a U.S.–Latin American customs union and a common currency ("the annexation of trade" he candidly termed it). And while he failed to achieve those maximum goals he did secure a series of reciprocity treaties with Latin American countries, the first in U.S. history.[11] Finally, in the Pacific Basin the United States sought to secure the strategic Kiska-Honolulu axis, purchasing the Aleutian Islands on the northern pincer as part of the Alaskan deal and on the southern flank acquiring Midway Island and effectively absorbing the Hawaiian Islands by bringing them under the umbrella of the Monroe Doctrine, by acquiring rights to a Pearl Harbor naval base, by tacitly supporting an American settler revolt against the indigenous regime, and by ultimately negotiating a treaty of annexation. Moreover, in Asia itself, the United States led the world in opening Korea to Western trade and diplomatic exchange while enhancing its position in Japan through trade agreements and the dispatch of American experts to advise Japan on education and frontier development.[12]

Despite such initiatives by American policy makers, the United States lacked the necessary and sufficient preconditions to bring many of them to successful fruition in the quarter century after the Civil War. Consumed with the political and psychological consequences of that long and horrific ordeal, its economic focus was also largely inward looking as it completed the national rail network and integrated the last internal frontiers in the Far West and the defeated Deep South into the national common market. To be sure, exports were important to the economy, but they consisted largely of primary commodities such as grains, cotton, and raw materials and low-value, labor-intensive finished products. As a harbinger of better days, however, the balance of trade did shift in United States favor starting in 1877, the first such time in American history.[13]

That national portrait radically altered in the decade of the 1890s, perhaps the most pivotal in American history, ushering in changes that both transformed elite visions of American empire and created the circumstances that enabled their fulfillment. Some of those changes were external ones that were transforming the world system. Most prominent were the decline of British global hegemony, the global competition for empire, and the emergence of a German-British rivalry that threatened to outstrip the British economy, dominate the European continent, and compete with British interests in Asia, Africa, and Latin America. Partly in response, the British began to move away from free trade, enlarged their army and navy, and showed a greater inclination to use force in such defining episodes as the Boer War. But the British did something else just as significant. They reconsidered and ultimately reshaped their relationship with the United States. Until the mid-1890s, the British had continued to contain the expansion of American influence in Latin America. Illustrative was the Anglo-American conflict over the Brazilian Revolution of 1893–94 and the Venezuelan Crisis of 1895. Britain in decline, however, could not afford to make adversaries out of both Germany and the United States, and it was the former that threatened more fundamental British interests. So, in a series of stunning moves, the British accepted U.S. hegemony in the Western Hemisphere. In the Hay-Pauncefote Treaty, it surrendered its prior rights to joint control over any future isthmian canal, acknowledging the American right to build, own, fortify, and operate any such canal unilaterally. It explicitly accepted the Monroe Doctrine and even its Roosevelt Corollary, which stipulated that European grievances over unpaid debts could only be addressed through America's good offices since it alone had the right to exercise police power in Latin America. And to dramatize that acceptance the British essentially withdrew their fleet from the Caribbean in 1905, indicating their confidence that the United States would protect their interests for them.[14]

More important changes, however, occurred in America itself. Prominent among them were a radical restructuring of the American economy, a related revolution in economic theory, and, finally, an elite consensus on the nature of American empire and the tactics required to make it so. First, the radical changes in the U.S. political economy made American expansionism abroad far more feasible than ever before. At the start of its Civil War, the United States had been largely a breadbasket economy barely two decades into the Industrial Revolution. Within forty years, it had obtained (in the parlance of the day) "American economic supremacy," surpassing the dominant British economy in almost all major industrial indices and possessing a productivity rate likely to widen the gap indefinitely. European politicians and newspapers acknowledged this supremacy, speaking often of an "American invasion" of Europe or the replacement of the "Yellow Peril" with an "American Peril" and even prophetically musing about the need for a European customs union to deflect the U.S. threat. Possessing a unique common market and unmatched economies of scale, conceivably American big business not only could challenge its other industrial rivals in Latin America and Asia but could "carry coals to Newcastle" as well.[15]

The second key change in the 1890s was a revolution in economic theory, which argued that economic expansion was not merely *possible* but absolutely *essential* for the survival of liberal capitalism in America. That paradigm shift, in turn, resulted from the need to explain why America's economic boom was continually undermined by economic crises. Between the Civil War and the events of 1898, the United States suffered through the so-called Long Depression—three major financial panics in 1873, 1884, and 1893, each of them followed by industrial depressions.[16] Those crises, in turn, spawned unprecedented labor violence and agrarian radicalism, producing a widespread elite fear (as the *New York Tribune* put it) that "social restlessness is arraying class against class and filling the land with a nondescript Socialism as dangerous and revolutionary as it is imbecile and grotesque."[17] How, then, to address this double-edged threat of a volatility that was at once economic and social in nature?

The elite answer, a consensus by the mid-1890s, was nothing short of an economic heresy that overturned the classic law of supply and demand. Articulated mainly by large manufacturers, trade associations, and probusiness economists, it argued that America suffered from industrial overproduction, a structural surplus of supply over demand that depressed the rate of profit and could only be alleviated by a systematic quest for foreign markets. The real causes of that persistent surplus were underconsumption, born of income redistribution upward, and the related fact that "capital . . . has accumulated faster than it can be profitably invested."[18] Some American capitalists, however, found it safer to put the blame on new technologies and increased mechanization that produced more bang for the buck. Andrew Carnegie's *Law of Surplus,* for example, argued that the high fixed cost of modern industry meant that "it cost the manufacturer less to run at a loss . . . than to check his production."[19] Others blamed it on the closing of America's last frontier and the end of the railroad boom, both long crucial as investment opportunities. Whatever the causes, acceptance of the overproduction theory by 1897 was such that it is almost impossible to find any prominent trade journal, business leader, or state policy maker that did not publicly embrace both it and its corollary—that only large-scale, systematic expansion into foreign markets could stabilize a volatile economy and pacify a chaotic society. Otherwise America might well have to face the eventual necessity of redistributive policies to restore a balance between consumption and production. Elihu Root, America's leading corporate lawyer and, as secretary of war, the prime architect of American empire, put it thus: "If you once begin to limit [wealth], you can never stop short of a general division," that is, socialism.[20]

The final change in the 1890s was the consensus resolution of a hotly contested debate over a crucial question of tactics. Did commercial expansion into global markets require an empire in order to be successful? And if it did what kind of empire did it need? Did the flag have to precede trade, extending formal political sovereignty and administrative colonialism akin to the British actions in India? Or could imperial control take other forms, which might serve the same purpose without the burdens of formal rule? The contest over these issues, usually pictured as a two-sided "Great Debate" between imperialists and anti-imperialists, was actually a triangular battle of wills, power, and ideas ultimately won by a third group one might dub imperial pragmatists. While all three differed over the form of American expansion, all of them favored commercial expansion abroad; all of them tended to be racists, though racism was used both as an argument for and, more especially, against colonies; and all resorted to gendered language and values to validate their positions, although this was most true of more martial, macho imperialists.[21]

Anti-imperial expansionists made an unequivocal case that formal colonies were both undesirable and unnecessary. Among policy makers, President Grover Cleveland and his first secretary of state, Walter Q. Gresham, best epitomized this view. They and their ilk saw colonialism as undesirable for five reasons. First, their commitment to democratic dogma led them to believe that it was hypocritical to free people from Spanish rule only to subject them to American rule. Second, in ironic contradiction, their racism made them fear that the Constitution might follow flag, ultimately conferring citizenship and immigration rights on non-white, non-Anglo races, which they viewed as inferior and incapable of fulfilling the civic responsibilities of a free people. (Had they anticipated that the Supreme Court would later rule in the "insular cases" that the Constitution did not follow the flag they might have been less hostile to formal colonies.) Third, in prophetic shades of Eisenhower's military-industrial complex address, they feared that the protection and administration of a formal empire would require a large navy and a standing army in times of peace—a development feared since the days of American independence as a threat to civilian rule, the only guarantor of democracy in the United States itself. Fourth, they believed that colonialism was self-defeating, always breeding the seeds of its own destruction. Some pointed to India's resistance to British colonialism in brutal events such as the Sepoy Mutiny; others looked closer to home to America's own southern Reconstruction, which they saw as a form of internal colonialism doomed from the beginning by a southern white backlash. Fifth, and finally, as laissez-faire liberals, they opposed an activist role for the state in market expansion abroad just as they opposed any such role in a free enterprise market at home. Instead, they thought the state should limit its role to lowering the American tariff in the direction of free trade, arguing that the size and attractiveness of the giant American market would encourage other great commercial nations to follow suit. If so, they confidently believed, American economic supremacy would give the United States all the markets that its glutted economy required without the material and spiritual burdens of colonialism, the imperialism of free trade, or informal empire, to borrow oft-used British terms.

Imperial expansionists made a strong countercase that colonialism, formal empire, was both desirable and necessary. Historians often point to policy makers such as Albert Beveridge, Henry Cabot Lodge, Alfred Thayer Mahan, and the young Theodore Roosevelt as reflecting this tendency. Setting great store on national honor, personal valor, and the white man's burden, they stressed several arguments. First, since commercial expansion required political stability as a prerequisite, it could only be obtained in underdeveloped countries by the imposition of external power. Their views strongly colored by racism, they believed nonwhite societies were incapable of rising above tribalism to create true nations; thus, they would always be prone to political chaos and social upheaval. Cuba was said to be a case in point as "there are only too strong reasons to fear that, once Spain were withdrawn from the island, the sole bond of union between different factions would disappear; that a war of races would be precipitated."[22] Second, they argued that free trade, at least for the foreseeable future, could not meet America's needs for market expansion. Like the tango, free trade could not be a solo dance. But the rest of the industrial world showed little inclination to sign that dance card. The drift, instead, was all in the other direction toward protectionism, preferential trading systems, closed empires, and semiclosed spheres of influence. In that context, there seemed to be no alternative to joining in that struggle for empire, a choice that had the added benefit of demonstrating that the United States had arrived as a great power that the world would have to take into account. Third, unlike laissez-faire liberals, they believed in the use of state power to promote expansion, including the use of military force. Indeed, they welcomed the opportunity. Fearful that urbanized, industrial America was becoming too crass and materialistic, perhaps even too soft and effeminate, they hoped that the martial competition for empire would resurrect the lost frontier values of manliness and national honor.

Pragmatic expansionists approached the issues of empire in a nonideological, cost-accounting manner. Centered in the big business wing of the Republican Party, policy makers such as William McKinley, Mark Hanna, and Elihu Root sought "imperialism on the cheap" to borrow a British phrase. This entailed taking elements from both their adversaries in the three-cornered debate over tactics. On one hand, they agreed with imperialists that expansionism might well require the threat or use of military force, hence their fervent support of the big navy begun in 1890, a navy focused not on traditional defensive coastal vessels but on wide-ranging battleships and cruisers designed for offensive operations in distant seas. Similarly, they also concurred that immediate, unilateral free trade was impractical while still holding it out as a long-term historical objective, hence their compromise policy of gradually lowering American protective tariffs through bilateral reciprocity agreements (a policy more fully realized by Franklin D. Roosevelt in the 1930s). On the other hand, they saw merit in the basic anti-imperialist opposition to large-scale formal colonialism, though less out of ideological objections than concern for the high costs of colonies. Either colonies cost more to administer and defend than any profits they might produce or they risked alienating a public opinion weaned on the exceptionalist notion that empire building was a European phenomenon alien to the American tradition. Despite these concerns, however, pragmatic expansionists were willing to acquire colonies or protectorates if practical circumstances seemed to require it. One might do so partly to preempt a strategic rival, if the local situation was either so hostile or unstable that U.S. interests could not be protected, or if an area's geographic location was vital to keeping the main trade routes open to major markets—for example, potential isthmian canal routes in Central America, Caribbean islands standing guard over the leeward and windward approaches to such routes, and well-spaced coaling, cable, and naval stations in the Pacific en route to the fabled China market. In short, pragmatic expansionists abided by the old British dictum: "Informal empire where possible, [more] formal empire where necessary."

By late 1900, the so-called Great Debate over empire was essentially over, even fading in the last days of the presidential campaign. Pragmatists won it quite handily for two kinds of reasons. First, they were more integrated into the dominant corporate order of the day—an order less under attack from agrarian and urban dissidents once the 1890s depression waned in 1897–98. So they simply had more clout of all kinds at their disposal. Second, reality had forced both imperialists and anti-imperialists to modify their principled positions and move toward a pragmatic, centrist common ground. The latter, for example, had discovered that protection of commercial interests sometimes required them to abandon their aversion to the use of force. The second Cleveland administration in the mid-1890s confronted such circumstances in dealing with the Brazilian Revolution of 1893–94 and the Venezuelan Crisis of 1895—episodes that led the anti-imperial administration to tell the British that "To-day the United States is practically sovereign on this continent and its fiat is law." In effect, Secretary of State Richard Olney's corollary to the Monroe Doctrine made explicit the imperial implications of that manifesto and in so doing anticipated the Roosevelt Corollary after century's turn. At the same time, however, imperialists began to confront the reality that colonialism could be both dehumanizing and costly as they did in fighting their first colonial war in the Philippines and in confronting the real possibility of a similar war developing in Cuba should America backslide on the Teller Amendment promise of Cuban independence.[23]

Between the Spanish-American War and World War I, U.S. expansionism predictably targeted the Caribbean and North Pacific basins, seen by American policy makers as simply two halves of one megaregion connected by the drawbridge of the Panama Canal. The modes of expansionism employed varied from formal to semiformal and informal empire, depending on timing as well as the location, size, and economic development of the object countries. More formal means of control befell the periphery nations of the Caribbean and the North Pacific clustered roughly along the twentieth parallel—Puerto Rico, the Dominican Republic, Haiti, Cuba, Hawai'i, Wake Island, Guam, and Luzon. Smaller in size and market potential than major areas such as China and Mexico, their economies were less important to policy makers than their strategic locations.[24]

In the initial years between 1898 and 1903, formal empire was the chief instrument employed—that is, formal claims of U.S. sovereignty, military occupation, the imposition of a de facto colonial bureaucracy, control over basic economic and social arrangements, and the exclusion or severe limitation of any indigenous participation. In fundamentals, it was akin to the colonialism of the British in India, the French in Indochina, or the Dutch in Indonesia. Indeed, their civil governmental forms were modeled after the British "Crown colony" system. Nonetheless, policy makers tried to hide that reality from potential public hostility by choosing not to use the formal term *Colonial Office* to describe that system, perhaps trying to suggest that U.S. holdings were more akin to semiautonomous territories than outright colonies.[25]

Strategic considerations, albeit born of commercial need, dictated that this first stage be mainly colonial in nature. Disadvantaged by Europe's Suez Canal, the United States needed its own cost-saving shortcut to Asian markets—hence the interference in Colombian affairs, the encouragement of a Panamanian Revolution, and the creation of the Canal Zone as a de facto colony in 1903. As subsequent builders of that canal, it needed Caribbean pickets to guard the sea approaches to it—hence Guantánamo Bay in Cuba and the colonization of Puerto Rico. As newcomers to the global game of market competition, the United States needed along its trade routes secure coaling stations, naval bases, and cable relay points, hence Hawai'i, Wake Island, Guam, and the Philippines. Being good pragmatists, American policy makers took only what they needed. For example, they declined the Spanish offer to negotiate for all of the Caroline and Mariana Islands, settling simply for the island of Guam. Similarly, President William McKinley and Mark Hanna tried to limit their Philippine acquisition to a "naval base and coaling station" (a "hitching post" at Manila as one cabinet member put it) to project American influence into Asia and took the whole archipelago chiefly out of fear of German and Japanese designs on the islands. In effect, the early 1898–1903 period consisted of an eclectic dose of insular and isthmian imperialism—a formal infrastructure or ground floor on which later, less formal expansion could be built. Sufficient to meet national interest needs, it had the added advantage of making the overseas conquests appear to the American public (and later historians) to be too small to count as a true empire.[26]

Informal Empire

After 1903, semiformal empire became the main mode that filled in any remaining infrastructural gaps, especially in the Caribbean Basin—that is, arrangements commonly termed protectorates, satellites, puppets, client states, and the like. Stung by the experience of colonial war in the Philippines and still concerned about U.S. public opinion, American leaders embraced a safe house halfway between colonialism and independence, though closer to the former. The targeted countries retained nominal, legal independence but one fatally compromised by limitations imposed through American military coercion ("gunboat diplomacy") or financial pressure ("dollar diplomacy"). Those limitations were both financial and political-military in nature. The former usually involved American bankers buying out and refunding a nation's foreign debt so that it was owed solely to an American consortium; imposing forced loans that added to that financial leverage; taking over the collection of customs duties, the major revenue source in such commodity export economies; and requiring the appointment of an American financial adviser or fiscal agent (FA) to both make and implement the national budget, usually making debt repayment to American bankers a top priority. The political-military limitations typically involved long-term naval bases, organization and control of the National Guard, the right of unilateral intervention in case of internal chaos or external threats, and treaty and/or constitutional guarantees of "special relationships" with the United States. The model for such semiformal control was Cuba under the Platt Amendment, imposed in 1902 at the point of a bayonet. With clever variations attuned to local circumstances, similar arrangements were made in the Antilles with Haiti and the Dominican Republic and in Central America with Nicaragua and Honduras. Most of those semicolonial relationships remained operative for decades until the 1930s Good Neighbor policy modified or ended them. Most were used as well to legitimize periodic American interventions, often multiple ones such as the three in Cuba in 1906, 1912, and 1917, and often long-term ones such as the nineteen-year occupation of Haiti. Before 1917, some used an alleged German strategic threat as justification, but interventions continued apace after World War I simply substituting implicitly race-based rationales such as the paternalistic "Moral Uplift" program in Haiti.[27]

Colonies and protectorates, however, were principally important as means to a more important end—the economic penetration of heavily populated, emerging market areas such as Mexico and China. While still economically weak, such countries had the potential to become major profit makers for goods and capital if their politics could be stabilized in the hands of propertied regimes hospitable to foreign capital, if a modern railroad system could be built that would produce an integrated national market rather than fragmented local ones, if their agriculture could be commercialized and their mining mechanized so they could export and earn enough to pay for increased imports of foreign goods, and if, in like vein, they could develop cruder forms of labor-intensive manufacturing whose semifinished exports could not only earn foreign exchange but be fabricated into higher value products in core country factories.

The mode of expansion into such emerging markets was informal empire—what some have called "open door imperialism" or "the imperialism of free trade." In this mode, the major means of control are largely economic and the chief actors are not the state but private American traders and investors, albeit backed by government influence and military power if need be. Informal empire is a tricky concept that has to be used with some care. Trade and investment, after all, are not inherently exploitative or imperial in nature. So certain conditions must obtain for it is a plausible concept. For example, the exports of the developing country must be sold largely into the market of a single, core, developed country and the terms of trade must favor the latter (e.g., it takes the export of more and more primary commodities to purchase the same amount of finished products from the core country). Similarly, core country capitalists must control the industries that service that trade (banking, insurance, and shipping), the infrastructure of the developing country (its railroads and gas, electric, and telephone services), and, finally, the plantations and mines that produce the primary commodities for export.[28]

Until revolution made a surprise appearance after 1910, Mexico had seemed to be the perfect embodiment of informal empire. Since 1876, the dictator Porfirio Díaz had imposed stability through both co-optation and repression. Moreover, he and his positivist advisers had embraced an ambitious scheme of modernization but one based on the assumption that only foreign capital, technology, and entrepreneurship could bring Mexico into the twentieth century. This open door for all things foreign, coupled with U.S. proximity and power, was to transform Mexico into an American economic dependency as subordinate to the United States as it had been to Spain in the eighteenth century or Great Britain in the nineteenth. Its trade flowed overwhelmingly to and from the United States. Its peso was pegged to the American dollar, a vulnerability for which it paid dearly in the Panic of 1907. Its railroads, built and consolidated by railroad tycoons such as E. H. Harriman, ran north and south between Mexican mines and the American market, breaking promises to build a true a national grid east and west as well. The mines themselves passed under the control of the Guggenheims, Dodges, and other mining magnates, who repatriated both the profits and the products back to the United States. Mexico's infant oil industry, soon to be the second largest in the world behind America's own, came to be dominated by John D. Rockefeller, Andrew Mellon, John Gates, William F. Buckley Sr., and other American capitalists, who outmuscled British rivals for control. Finally, Mexico financed its ambitious development schemes through American bank loans, encountering the country's first, though hardly last, debt trap. As early as 1900, the two billion dollars in foreign capital exceeded total indigenous capital in Mexico, and half of that was American, more than the British, German, Spanish, and French combined.[29]

Informal empire, like globalization today, carried a high price tag for both Mexico and the United States. For Mexico, it came in the form of business cycle volatility, increasing income inequality between classes and regions, massive movements of people displaced by both market forces and government fiat, and racial tensions exacerbated by an elite government imbued with a social Darwinists mind-set. All played causative roles in the Mexican Revolution. And that was the price the United States paid. While the dynamics of that Revolution no doubt emanated largely from Mexican society itself, it was powerfully fueled by xenophobic antiforeignism, especially anti-Americanism.

That price came in two installments. Between 1910 and 1917, it came in the form of a great power threat to U.S. hegemony in Mexico. As Frederich Katz described it, it was a "secret war" among the United States, Germany, and Great Britain as each supplied arms and money to various revolutionary factions, attempting to use them as proxies to reshape post-Porfirian Mexico in ways that would benefit their national interests. Germany was America's major concern, but even Great Britain, heavily dependent on Mexican fuel oil for its Royal Navy, found that its interests did not always jibe with those of the United States. On occasion, it was a not very secret war as the U.S. occupation of Veracruz and the later Pershing expedition were to demonstrate.[30]

World War I ended the foreign threat to American dominance, but Mexico itself became a threat after 1917 when its new Constitution seemed to herald a radical turn to the left by the Revolution. Especially troubling was Article XXVII of that Constitution, which posited that subsoil mineral rights belonged exclusively to the Mexican people and could only be exploited by capitalists, foreign and domestic, on such terms as the people's representative, the Mexican state, might choose to allow. Directed primarily at American oil interests and using the threat of nationalization as a lever, Mexico attempted to restructure American investments in ways that would ensure the Mexican government a greater say in production policies and a greater share of profits. Tame by today's standards, the effort generated fierce resistance from the U.S. government and the powerful industry lobby, the American Petroleum Producers in Mexico (APPM). The battle would be waged for a two decades, until 1938, when Mexico won a symbolic but shallow victory, finally nationalizing an aging oil industry that held less promise for U.S. oil interests than did reserve lands elsewhere in the world. By the post–World War II era, however, the dominant party, the Partido Revolucionario Institucional (PRI), had institutionalized the Mexican Revolution into a PRI-controlled corporatism, and this fact, coupled with American's unrivaled global power, would mark a return to informal empire status. As before, it would prove to be a problematic status for both parties, as several debt crises, the uneven operation of the North American Free Trade Agreement (NAFTA), and the explosive issue of immigration would demonstrate.[31]

If informal empire was a recurring reality in Mexico, it appeared to be simply an obsessive hope in China—and an unlikely one at that. After all, China's imperial dynasty wobbled on its last legs, offering none of the political stability necessary for market development. China's tragic experiences with outside powers (e.g., the Opium Wars, the unequal treaties, race-based immigration exclusions, the Sino-Japanese War of 1894–95, and the great power partitioning that followed in 1897) hardly made it hospitable to their presence and influence. And the obstacles to economic development were staggering, especially the absence of an integrated railroad network, the neglect of river and harbor infrastructure, and a system of internal tariffs that discouraged the movement of goods from province to province or region to region. Those barriers notwithstanding, American leaders remained mesmerized by the sheer numbers in the world's most populous country; by the success that some American exports, such as kerosene, cigarettes, and textiles, already enjoyed; and by the belief that the United States enjoyed a special relationship with China not only because of private American initiatives there by missionaries, social reformers, and academics but because American diplomatic opposition to the partitioning of China seemed to stand in sharp relief to European and Japanese imperialism.[32] The resulting optimism, however guarded, was shared not only by state policy makers but by the big business interests that often prodded them (e.g., the National Association of Manufacturers, investors in the American China Development Company, the Cramp Shipyards, Standard Oil, the British American Tobacco Company, and a host of railroad builders and speculators).

To translate the dream of the China market into reality, the United States had to overcome one fundamental liability: it was a latecomer to the power struggle already in progress. By 1897, Germany, France, Russia, and Japan had begun to carve China's coastal provinces into de facto colonies, exercising exclusive rights in commerce, railroads, mining, and banking. Even Great Britain, the traditional champion of an open door for trade and investment, began to backslide on its commitment. To overcome this weakness, the United States had to do three things. First, it had to find a way to project American military force into the western Pacific to lend greater weight to its policies. Conquering the Philippines with seventy thousand troops and building on the old Spanish naval base at Subic Bay sought to do exactly that. The Philippines were to be the American Hong Kong, both an entrepôt to the China market and a staging ground for the American military—a fact that seemed to be validated by the ability of the United States to dispatch five thousand troops to North China (with ten thousand more at the ready) to help suppress the 1901 Boxer Rebellion while simultaneously acting as a check on the ambitions of other great powers. Second, the United States had to find ways to make its goods more cost competitive in the China market. Lowering transportation costs by using the new Panama Canal was the most obvious way, but from time to time there were also imaginative efforts to tie the American heartland to Northeast Asia more directly, chiefly by connecting America's northern transcontinental railroads to the new Manchurian railroads via packet shipping lines out of Seattle. Finally, the United States had to persuade the other great powers that partitioning and colonizing were counterproductive and informal empire, collectively pursued, was a far superior way to develop and profit from the China market.[33]

Formal and semiformal control, argued the Americans, would further exacerbate Chinese sensibilities and fuel a Chinese nationalism heavily laden with xenophobia. The result would be yet greater political instability. Moreover, it would tend to perpetuate the status quo of a China fragmented into many local and regional markets, retarding China's modernization and the overall size of its market potential. Finally, imperial rivalry among the great powers would encourage China to play one power against another, heightening the possibility that the scramble for spheres of influence in China might lead to Armageddon—the great war between the powers that many feared would begin not in the Balkans but in Asia.

The American substitute for this great power scramble was an updated version of Britain's old Open Door policy for China. Rather that divvying up China into colonies or spheres of influence, the Chinese state and territorial integrity would be kept intact both to assuage nationalist feelings and enhance China's purchasing power through integration of a truly national market. Rather than opting for exclusive trading privileges in spatially constrained spheres, the great powers would compete on an equal playing field where all would pay the same trade tariffs and railroad rates. What would ultimately distinguish the American Open Door policy from Britain's was the effort to expand it from a commercial concept to a financial one as well—an open door for investment in railroads, mines, bank loans, and the like. In practical terms, that meant funneling investment and loans into China through some sort of international clearinghouse—for example, the first China Consortium of international bankers in 1912 and the second China Consortium in 1919. In other words, informal empire, as a means of penetrating China, would be done collectively by the United States, Europe, and Japan—a kind of G-7 approach. The social Democratic theorist Karl Kautsky would refer to it as "ultra-imperialism"—the "cartelization" of foreign policy through a "holy alliance of imperialists."[34]

This venture in collectivized informal empire never materialized despite some innovative American efforts to make it happen. Like Mexico (and Russia, another emerging market economy), China had its own revolution, one in which antiforeignism and anti-imperialism again played a key role. Coupled with the distractions of two world wars and the Great Depression, interspersed with rounds of Japanese imperialism in the second decade of the century and again in the 1930s, revolutionary China was never stable or attractive enough to encourage systematic Western initiatives, cooperative or otherwise.

Conclusion

Nonetheless, this failed experiment in China provided the intellectual framework for much of the American expansionism of the twentieth century. Woodrow Wilson's internationalism was, in essence, an attempt to globalize this Open Door approach. And, while the preconditions for its realization were not yet sufficient in the post–World War I period, they would come to pass in the cold war that followed World War II. No longer challenged by any great capitalist power, and blessed with a convenient threat in the Soviet empire, hegemonic America now possessed the power "to begin the world again" and bring into being a new wave of globalization to replace the British-led one that had died at the turn of the century. Multilateralism was to be the order of the day backed by American military might, if need be, to enforce the rules of the game in Korea, Cuba, the Dominican Republic, Vietnam, Panama, Iraq, and the like. It was an order, however, dependent on the perverse stability of the cold war. And when that war ended and the manifest shortcomings of globalization produced their own backlash, it would ironically be the United States itself that abandoned informal empire and reverted to war, military occupation, permanent bases, and, most likely, long-term protectorates. As a consequence, the U.S. presence in Afghanistan and Iraq had, by 2007, begun to look less like the post–World War II occupation of Germany and Japan, as the U.S. president claimed, than it did the post-1898 occupation of Cuba and the Philippines. Perhaps it also suggested more generally that great powers in decline, like great powers on the make, are rarely happy with the status quo and much inclined to use whatever means are necessary to alter it in their favor.

PART 2

Police, Prisons, and Law Enforcement

First Company, Philippines Constabulary, Pampanga Province, 1908. (Library of Congress.)

INTRODUCTION

ALFRED W. MCCOY

As WE ASSESS, OR REASSESS, the legacy of America's early empire, the more coercive aspects of colonial rule may have had the most profound impact back home in the metropole. For a laissez-faire society with a weak central government, empire provided a unique opportunity for experiments in the application of state power. Within this intrusive imperial regime, however, it was the formally coercive areas of policing, prisons, and law enforcement that allowed the colonial state unchecked power. Not surprisingly, colonial governments that were quintessentially coercive made breakthroughs in the uses of coercion so innovative, so seductive that they became models for their respective metropoles. In these tropical hothouses of governance, it was the aggressive varieties, with sharp thorns and suffocating tendrils, that grew fast and alluring.

On eve of empire in 1898, the United States had fostered a national government with a surprisingly limited capacity to shape its society. Restrained by courts and Constitution, Washington's role in national life was restricted to enumerating a census, collecting import duties, checking the health of immigrants, awarding citizenship, titling open lands, and maintaining a small army. From the perspective of even a half century later, Washington's reach, circa 1898, was still limited and its grip on citizens' lives still light. At the dawn of the twentieth century, the federal government, unlike its European counterparts, did not tax, conscript, investigate, regulate, arrest, hospitalize, or otherwise control its citizenry. From the perspective of the modern liberal state's growing panoply of powers, Washington was still a tabula rasa on which empire could inscribe its writ.

The surrogate colonial states that Washington created so suddenly in Manila and San Juan after 1898 were the antithesis of its own minimalist governance. While citizenship assured Americans liberty from government interference, colonial rule subjected Filipinos and Puerto Ricans, until the latter won U.S. citizenship in 1917, to an activist state determined to rend their culture and reweave the fabric of their daily lives. Indeed, the entire logic of colonial rule and its "social engineering" was, at base, coercive. There were, in theory, few effective limits to the colonial state's interference in individual lives. After all, both Filipinos and Puerto Ricans were not citizens but subjects with formally circumscribed civil liberties. But, in reality, colonial regimes only had finite resources for costly social controls and generally chose to apply them to policing, prisons, and law enforcement. Not surprisingly, it was these radical social experiments in total control, pursued most aggressively in the Philippines, that ultimately proved most influential as government expanded its powers back in the metropole.

The imperial transition from Spain to the United States provided American officials with new, unexpected methods for their experiments in activist statecraft. Despite rhetoric about degenerate Iberian rule, American colonials were heirs to several late Spanish imperial states at Manila and San Juan that had participated directly in Europe's liberal application of science to governance. "It may be truthfully said that every act of every inhabitant of the island was under the critical surveillance of these guardians of the peace," the military governor of Puerto Rico, General George W. Davis, testified about the Spanish colonial police. "No man could say at what moment he might be arrested and thrown into jail, there to languish until the authorities saw fit." Such vigilance was the work of a two-thousand-strong, three-tiered, Spanish police force led by the Guardia Civil, whose members were "old and experienced soldiers" entrusted with "the power to make summary arrests on their own initiative."[1] By its conquest of these insular autocracies, Washington was exposed to the influence of Spanish imperial states with their intrusive law enforcement, modernized prisons, and centralized police.

As both metaphor and method, colonial prisons open windows of understanding about empire. Indeed, Michael Salman's study of the Iwahig penal colony in the southern Philippines reveals the extraordinary freedom that American colonials had to conduct bold social experiments that were, in fact, blocked by countervailing social and political forces back home in the United States. So all-encompassing was this coercive fusion of colonial society and prison farm that American officials could compel Filipino convicts not merely to submit to the prison's external, physical regime of visible rules but to internalize its expansive moral code.

In his parallel study of Puerto Rico, Kelvin Santiago-Valles explores the complex genealogy of police and prison reform within the transatlantic imperium. With Spain and the northeastern United States playing metropoles to their respective peripheries in the American South and Hispanic Caribbean, the Atlantic became an avenue for a crisscrossing of carceral innovations in the era of high imperialism. As formal slavery waned in the wider Caribbean Basin by midcentury, these expanded prisons, along with convict chain gangs, provided cheap, corvée labor to construct infrastructure for plantations in both the Caribbean and the American South. To press-gang labor for this coercive regime, Spain exported the liberal European model of the national rural police, mounted and armed with short-barrel carbines—called Gendarmerie Nationale in France (established in 1793), the Carabinieri in Italy (1814), and the Guardia Civil in Spain itself (1844). Without anything akin to such national police, the United States first encountered this instrument of the European liberal state in the Philippines and Puerto Rico and soon created constabularies modeled on Spanish antecedents.

In Manila, American colonials, confronted with intractable resistance, married the technologies of their own antecedent information revolution to the centralized structure of Spanish police to produce a powerful hybrid, the Philippines Constabulary, which slowly crushed armed resistance and elite political dissidence. Through a small cadre of constabulary veterans, described in Alfred W. McCoy's essay, this innovative security apparatus migrated homeward during the crisis surrounding World War I to serve as a model for a nascent U.S. domestic security apparatus.

Through this same imperial dialectic, Philippine precedents also served as a blueprint for the American prohibition of drugs. After a half century of rising domestic opiate abuse, the United States landed at Manila to find itself caught up in the ongoing struggle, led by Western missionaries, to curb China's epidemic of opium addiction. When the U.S. government seemed content to continue the lucrative Spanish licensing system, which sold smoking opium largely to the colony's Chinese, American missionaries lobbied successfully for prohibition. Between 1905 and 1909, as Anne L. Foster explains, the U.S. colonial regime banned opium smoking in the Philippines, pressed neighboring colonies to restrict smuggling, and convened an international antinarcotics conference at Shanghai, creating strong pressures on Washington for a parallel domestic prohibition. Thus, Congress restricted American opium imports in 1909 and five years later passed the Harrison Narcotics Act—the start of U.S. drug prohibition.

The sum of these changes in law enforcement, in tandem with other, less intrusive aspects of U.S. colonial policy, were something of a revolution in the relationship between the individual and the state. In contrast to the minimal U.S. government before 1898, the Philippine colonial state claimed prerogatives of controlling public discourse, penetrating households with covert surveillance, enveloping individual bodies with intrusive health regulations, and imposing internalized compliance with the prison's moral ethos.

These experiments in law enforcement at this remote periphery of empire had a discernible impact on the U.S. government, serving as catalysts for changes that have persisted to the present. "The need to promote regional, then worldwide prohibition to inhibit smuggling in the Philippines," Foster explains, "and then the measures against smuggling in both Asia and North America, changed U.S. laws . . . , setting the United States on a path of unwavering support for the prohibition of narcotics. . . . The war on drugs thus traces at least part of its heritage to a nearly forgotten policy justified for its protection of America's colonial subjects in the Philippines." Today, a century later, this colonial legacy is evident in an American drug war that consumed, as of 2005–6, some $46 billion in state and federal revenues and accounted for over half the nation's soaring prison population of 2.2 million.[2]

Although the policy lineage is less direct, colonial policing helped lay the foundations for a U.S. domestic security apparatus. Less than twenty years after an American colonial governor established the Philippines Constabulary with sweeping powers for domestic espionage, Washington, drawing on these colonial procedures, launched the world's largest mass surveillance effort, monitoring millions of Americans suspected of subversion during World War I. Clearly, the sum of these experiments in colonial coercion had a direct, discernible impact on the quality of domestic law enforcement.

American Penal Forms and Colonial Spanish Custodial-Regulatory Practices in Fin de Siècle Puerto Rico

KELVIN SANTIAGO-VALLES

THE CHARACTER OF THE AMERICAN IMPERIAL STATE and its impact on an Atlantic colonial periphery, which simultaneously impacted that same state throughout the period 1873–1914, cannot be fully understood outside this country's shifting position within a world-system still hegemonized by Great Britain.[1] One key to understanding this process is determining how American interactions with Spain's Caribbean enabled this shift during the definitive phase, 1873 to 1898. But another key is understanding how structures of governmentality, such as penal forms and policing, began to overlap and more closely mirror each other during this same pivotal phase within the rising American and declining Spanish empires.

The 1873–1914 period was marked by a complex of intersecting forces that include an advancing U.S. politico-military-economic influence within the Caribbean Basin and Pacific Rim, the British Empire's greatest expansion within the interstate system, and the global labor force's most massive ethno-racialized polarization—the "problem of the color line" on a world scale. The entire global-racial regime of the 1873–1945 period was, in essence, characterized by two intertwined structures that buttressed a world-system being targeted by subaltern and/or labor resistance.[2] One set of these world-systemic structural supports was, by the late nineteenth century, the social Darwinism (1876–1900) and eugenics (1901–45), which grounded positivist criminology's custodial-punitive discourses and practices.[3]

The other face of this global-racial regime included a reduction of legal slavery but a continuation of ethno-racially subordinate labor in plantations, mines, rural peonage, and sharecropping. Such regulatory measures likewise brought factory Taylorism and Fordism to core populations—with a corollary of formal, political, and trade union rights versus an uneven continuation of social-civil restrictions for subaltern populations, including formal, direct political rule.[4] This global-racial regime also comprised the asymmetrical long-term decline of "levying violence" for the allegedly reformable sectors of core populations located within what Foucault called the "principle of 'mildness-production-profit'" (whereby disciplinary institutions instilled efficient behavior and lucrative obedience among the laboring classes),[5] which coexisted with a harsh rule, for racially depreciated/peripheral populations, of persistent penal servitude, spectacular punishments, and generalized surveillance.[6]

During the ascendant phase of British hegemony from 1815 to 1873, military expansionism by the globally weak and decentralized American imperial state was mainly continental and driven by the needs (land, timber, and food) of the southern plantations then supplying the leading sector of the British Industrial Revolution with its vital raw material for textiles. American capital operated as the junior partner of London's free trade policies, allowing British and American businesses to economically penetrate the colonies of rival empires (e.g., from the 1830s to 1898, the United States outstripped Spain in agricultural imports from Puerto Rico and Cuba while surpassing Spanish exports of manufactured goods to these two Iberian territories.)[7] However, wars within Europe, East Asia, and North America from the 1840s to the 1860s and the world depression of 1873–96 enabled the rise of the first serious contenders to British world-systemic hegemony, that is, Germany, the United States, and Japan. Along with its fellow contenders, the American imperial state underwent a decisive transformation from the 1870s to 1920, which included administrative, economic, and military centralization; increasing protectionism; the end of internal territorial expansion; and the rise of overseas military imperialism. In the United States, such shifts were now being driven by northeastern and midwestern industries' need for cheap raw materials, new markets, low-cost labor, and regulation of a highly mobile and increasingly polarized labor force both locally and overseas.[8]

American and Spanish Penal Forms and Modern Police

By the mid-nineteenth century, the utilitarian, world-renowned Philadelphia and Auburn prison models went into crisis, derided for failing to meet their stated objectives, hence the rise of social Darwinist/positivist paradigms across the Western Hemisphere. Still based on cellular compartmentalization, the new models understood "civilized" societies as composed of self-controlled citizens who needed to be defended from "savage" elements through the learned intervention of the government and trained specialists. From the 1870s to the 1890s, the paragon of this approach was the Elmira Reformatory for Men and Boys, created in 1876 to promote the positivist-scientific demarcation between the "rehabilitation of the salvable" and "eternal damnation for the rest." Elmira fostered what came to be called penology, or "prison science," and criminology in general throughout Western countries during the period 1883–99. Yet by the 1890s, despite some improvements in inmates' conditions, many of these model prisons were publicly criticized for their persistently degrading regimens, especially as applied to African Americans and Eastern and Southern Europeans.[9]

Between the Civil War and the Spanish-Cuban-Philippine-American War of 1898, American incarceration rates increased dramatically, particularly for blacks in northern jurisdictions. There was also a shift from mostly white convicts in the antebellum South to a mostly black prison population after the Civil War, combined with extrajudicial terror and politico-economic coercion, expanding—beyond the penal system—the disciplinary confinement of African American populations below the Mason-Dixon Line at this time.[10] Mortality rates under the convict lease system were impressive; for example, during the 1880s average death rates in southern prisons were almost three times as high as they were in their northern analogs.[11] These prison reform models primarily materialized across core-based northern jurisdictions while racially depreciated elements within southern colonial-peripheral plantations and mines incarnated the abject figure of errant individual choices or atavistic behavior haunting utilitarian and positivist imaginaries. Southern convicts were subject to straightforward penal servitude—criminal surety techniques, the convict lease system, and chain gangs—coupled with widespread and methodical corporal punishment. The gender and age separation (as well as separation of the infirm) that had characterized northern prisons since the early nineteenth century only reached southern prisons in the late 1880s.[12]

Although modern American policing formally originated in the 1830s and 1840s in response to urban rioting and social unrest, uniformed paramilitary policemen—with badges and guns—only proliferated from the 1850s to the 1890s as large cities responded to massive demographic changes and socioeconomic shifts. Hardly a professionalized institution, this emerging police force lacked formal training and consistent supervision, which led to rampant politicization and corruption.[13]

Analogous transformations also affected the Spanish empire, where the core-metropole counterpart of the northern United States was Spain itself. Most of the social polarization in the Atlantic—typifying the 1873–98 period within the larger 1873–1945 global-racial regime—materialized as a bifurcation between the socioregulatory mechanisms within the Iberian core and those on Spain's Antillean, Philippine, and African peripheries.

Formally speaking, Benthamite utilitarianism had already made inroads in Spain as early as 1819 when the social philosopher Villanueva y Jordá published texts on panopticism and prison organization. Likewise, a Universidad de Salamanca professor, Toribio Nuñez, had translated Bentham's "Principles of Civil and Penal Legislation" in 1820 and written *Ciencia social según los principios de*

Jeremías Bentham, which was published by the Royal Press in 1835 by order of the Spanish government. Benthamite elements were also present in Spanish prison codes throughout this century, particularly the Ordenanza General de Presidios del Reino of 1834 and the Código Narváez of 1848.[14]

During the second half of the nineteenth century, the influence of American penal prototypes materialized in Spain in several ways, beginning with the construction of the Vitoria prison in 1859 based on the quasi-Benthamite architectural cellular models drawn up in Ramón de la Sagra's 1843 *Atlas carcelario.* This atlas was a compilation of penal architectural plans stemming from Sagra's 1835 tour of the principal utilitarian model prisons in the United States, as well as some material from Western Europe.[15] The uneven ascent of political liberalism in Spain in 1868–75 paved the way for a number of social reforms,[16] with exemplary prisons featured prominently and emulating a cellular configuration clearly visible in the new prisons of Vergara in 1870 and Bilbao in 1873.[17]

The 1875–1902 Restoration—which ended the First Republic (1873–75) and restored the Bourbons via the reign of the child Alfonso XII under the regency of María Cristina—resulted in further agrarian crises, demographic dislocations, and the massive public outlays and social costs of the second major Cuban campaign, the Filipino insurgency, and the Moroccan Rif War. Not coincidentally, there was a direct correlation between impoverished peasants flocking to towns and cities and the creation of new prisons and modern law enforcement corps.[18] One American penal influence was the adoption of the Auburn "mixed" model as the partial basis for Spain's 1870 penal code, which established parameters of carceral reform that continued up to 1900. Likewise, the Elmira Reformatory became the basis for the 1889 reorganization of Spain's North African presidio in Ceuta. Nevertheless, as in the United States, much of this penal social engineering fell short of its formal goals; most of Spain's penal institutions remained overcrowded and relatively small with 83 percent holding fewer than twenty inmates. During the 1880s and 1890s, convicts in 94 percent of these prisons still bunked together in large halls (*galeras*) containing 76 percent of the country's confined population.[19]

Spain also saw the emergence of criminological and penological trends that were social Darwinist/positivist *avant la lettre*. From the 1830s to the 1850s, the biologistic concept of the "born criminal" was already circulating in Spain within the works of Mariano Cubí (1801–75), an early advocate of Franz Josef Gall's theories of craniometry. Similar to the work of Gall and other phrenologists, Cubí, too, found the cephalic configuration of "born criminals" atavistically identical to that of certain Carib and Algerian tribes. Although he anticipated the work of Lombroso in this regard, Cubí held onto certain utilitarian correctionalist principles that, for him, were embodied in some of the prisons he visited in the United States (New Orleans, Philadelphia), as well as in Coronel Manuel

Montesinos's model presidio in Valencia, Spain.[20] In the 1830s and 1840s, Valencia's model prison had begun experimenting with techniques that the Elmira Reformatory would later make globally famous: probation, parole, "good time" credits, and indeterminate sentences.[21]

The Guardia Civil, established in 1845, was the largest Spanish law enforcement corps for the remainder of that century, but the Restoration of 1875–1902 attempted to demilitarize the defense of law and order, particularly in large cities such as Madrid and Barcelona. Spain's modern police force responded to crime waves and riots comparable to those plaguing "respectable society" in the urban(e) United Kingdom and United States, whose policing models Spain tried to replicate. Like their American counterparts, the members of this Spanish law enforcement body were usually underpaid and susceptible to bribery and political manipulation.[22]

Spain's Penal and Policing (Re)forms in Puerto Rico

Under Spanish colonial rule throughout the nineteenth century, provisional detention preceding judicial inspection transpired either within the municipal jails run by the town governments or within larger district prisons (eleven in the 1870s–90s).[23] With the introduction of the 1850 prison regulations and the 1879 extension of Spain's revised 1870 penal code to Cuba and Puerto Rico, the latter's convicts reflected aspects of utilitarian and positivist regimentation with identification numbers, shaved heads, and distinctive clothing. However, in this century penal servitude prevailed with some of the worst carceral conditions on the Spanish empire's Atlantic flank—cumbersome chains, routine floggings, near starvation, disease-ridden quarters, and higher mortality levels—long after these had begun declining in Spain. As indicated above, this racialized differentiation was a colonial-peripheral feature also common in the American South during the period 1873–1900.[24]

From 1837 to 1898, one of the main sites of penal servitude in Puerto Rico was the La Princesa presidio (Cárcel de la Princesa-Presidio de San Juan) where convicts served out hard-labor sentences (two to ten years or more) doing upkeep work on the city's fortifications, road building and repair, and so on. Initially housing 240 felons, La Princesa was expanded in 1879 to hold 672 inmates within a single, notoriously filthy and dark *galera* three meters long by twelve meters wide. Since 1818, the La Puntilla presidio at the capital's naval arsenal had been the second principal establishment for those sentenced to hard labor—usually for vagrancy—from six months to two years. Part of the convict labor thus mobilized worked under military guard in the naval yard, in the munitions depot, and on related public works projects—for example, from 1874 to 1889 constructing the military road across the central mountain range connecting San Juan with Ponce, the island's second-largest city and a major site of sugar production on the southern coast. After 1842, the percentage of convicts sentenced to hard labor on public works projects rose to approximately two-thirds of all prisoners in Puerto Rico, and their numbers continued to expand, spurred by deteriorating social conditions during the socioeconomic crisis of the 1870s–90s. The city's entire carceral archipelago was further extended when a hospital building, first proposed in 1877, was refashioned ten years later into another large prison for felons sentenced to hard labor, the Cárcel Provincial or Penitenciaría Insular y Presidio, which held 240 inmates.[25]

The closest an island-based institution ever came to fulfilling the utilitarian goals of a house of correction and/or the positivist conception of a reformatory was San Juan's Casa de Reclusión y Asilo de Beneficiencia. From 1846 to 1872, the Casa de Beneficiencia's inmate population oscillated between two hundred and three hundred, primarily those loosely defined as "mentally deficient," "lawless," and/or "orphans" and with practically no gender or age segregation. But district jails also indiscriminately confined both common criminals and "madmen" in nineteenth-century Puerto Rico.[26] From 1863 to 1898, nuns administered the Casa de Beneficiencia, attempting to introduce inmate segregation by gender, age, and condition. This later period saw the utilitarian-positivist expansion of the workshops devoted to craft education and labor discipline. Yet the Casa de Beneficiencia continued to resemble other carceral institutions in Puerto Rico in its extremely harsh physical restraints and punishments: manacles, iron fetters, whips for flogging, and booths with streams of high-pressure water at extreme temperatures.[27] Although it was formally abolished in Spain in 1814, official torture continued to be extensively utilized by colonial governments in Puerto Rico against those accused of a wide spectrum of crimes, in particular sedition. A leading example of this form of official punishment was the infamous Año Terrible del '87 (1887) when the Spanish colonial administration unleashed a massive terror campaign (called *compontes*) against "native" suspects of all social classes who were beaten, arrested, and/or physically tormented for alleged anti-government activities.[28]

As independent production and subsistence activities were further encroached upon, property itself became increasingly contested: officially, thefts in Puerto Rico increased more than fourfold from 1837 to 1864 and then more than doubled from 1864 to 1880. These figures partially responded to an expanding criminal justice system in the colony, increasing the number and scope of interventions and the illegalization of growing areas of everyday life among this island's laboring classes (gambling, cockfights, and consensual marriages).[29] Within this context, several new law enforcement measures appeared such as the creation of the Guardia Rural in 1861 as a special force assigned to the countryside where most of the population lived. This was followed, in 1869–70, by the dissolution of the existing militia corps (Milicias Urbanas and Milicias Disciplinadas), which were replaced primarily by a version of Spain's salaried, professional, paramilitary constabulary (Guardia Civil) whose "respectable" members (mostly white Creoles and Spaniards) were fully armed and quartered in all the island's districts and principal municipalities.[30]

As we already saw, by the 1870s dominant Western cultures in general were replete with narratives of sociobiological, sociocultural regression, a social disorder both prefigured and embodied by colonial-peripheral, racially depreciated populations still subject to plantation peonage, sharecropping, and other forms of coerced labor. Similar cultural cartographies continued to set the parameters for much elite textual production in Puerto Rico until the 1890s, even in the writings of prominent Creole intellectuals such as Francisco del Valle Atiles and Salvador Brau, both of them politically liberal leaders and critics of Spanish colonialism.[31]

Despite the abrogation of the 1838–76 contract-regimen laws imposed on day laborers (Leyes de Reglamentación del Trabajo), regulating vagrancy persisted as a leading custodial-punitive form during the last quarter of the nineteenth century. In effect, antivagrancy statutes continued to be linked to the procurement of labor for sugar planters, other large landowners of mostly coffee and tobacco estates (*hacendados*), and merchants in Puerto Rico. However, by this time vagrancy had changed from a specific crime as such to an all-encompassing, aggravating condition understood to confirm the probable culpability of anyone accused of a wide array of infractions.[32] Similarly, the criminalization of growing areas of everyday life among this island's laboring classes—gambling, cockfights, and consensual marriages being cases in point—illustrates just how wide the punitive/discursive net was being cast.[33] As early as 1855, for instance, colonial governor García Camba applied vagrancy penalties to couples found "living in sin."[34] Puerto Rico's laboring classes socially resisted such harsh social regulation practices via additional means, namely, social violence that went beyond rioting and the banditry of isolated debt-bound peons and landless peasants.[35] This rubric also included the vandalism and physical attacks of ex-slaves, peasants, and artisans against *hacendados,* overseers, usurer merchants, government officials, and/or their family members.[36]

1898–1930s: *Plus ça Change* . . .

Following the U.S. occupation of 1898 and formation of the civil-colonial administration two years later, most judicial district jails continued operating as before with local jails remaining under municipal jurisdiction. Indeed, San Juan's Penitenciaría Insular y Presidio and La Princesa remained the island's principal colonial penitentiaries until 1933. Penal servitude in the form of hard labor on public works projects—particularly sanitation and road construction and repair—continued as standard practice under American rule. Within the island's district jails and penitentiary, overcrowding, elevated mortality rates (due to epidemic contagion), floggings, and dungeon seclusion also persisted without substantial modifications until the 1940s.[37]

Dismantled in 1899, the local Guardia Civil provisionally gave way to two police corps, islandwide and municipal. But by 1902 these two were consolidated again into a militarized constabulary with one precinct per municipality and jurisdiction over all of Puerto Rico. Until the 1930s, this constabulary was still subordinated to a foreign-appointed governor and a foreign military commander in San Juan, controlled by the overseas metropole—the United States in this case—who were generally inexperienced in running a civilian police force. Rank-and-file policemen were now recruited from the "native" laboring classes, but European and Euro-Creole propertied and educated sectors remained the middle- and upper-echelon officers.[38]

Conclusion

This essay has briefly illustrated and documented two basic arguments. First, the Atlantic colonial periphery in question—both demographically and spatially—encompassed not only Puerto Rico (and Cuba) but also the American South. From a structural (not formal juridical) standpoint, the global division of labor's Atlantic expanse from 1873 to 1898 brought together, on the one hand, Spain and the American North as intertwined regions where mostly core populations resided and, on the other hand, Spain's Caribbean colonies and much of the American South as imbricated spaces concentrating most of each imperial state's peripheral populations.

Moreover, this structural imbrication regionally embodied the existing global-racial regime, thus partially explaining the continuity between, and impact of, (a) many of the Spanish penal forms and policing practices in Puerto Rico during 1873–98 on (b) American forms and practices during 1898–1933 despite the formal juridical break in the imperial metropole following the Spanish-Cuban-Philippine-American War. Such continuity provides important clues to the character of what the American imperial state was, or was not, able to accomplish once it assumed direct control over Puerto Rico after 1898.

Prohibiting Opium in the Philippines and the United States

The Creation of an Interventionist State

ANNE L. FOSTER

SINCE THE FOUNDING OF THE UNITED STATES, American officials have faced decisions about how to govern newly acquired territories. Until the 1890s, these decisions were intended to be temporary, merely in force until the territories could be admitted to the United States as states. In 1898, however, American officials faced a new type of decision: how to govern territories that were never intended to become states. Until recently, scholars assumed that models developed in the metropole for education, health care, and governance were meant to be exported to the colonies. Scholarship on the Philippines has primarily explored the ways in which American institutions were transplanted, sometimes in lesser forms, sometimes changed in the process, but originating in the metropole.

More recently, scholars have begun to perceive that policy development was a two-way rather than a one-way street.[1] What happened "out" in the colony had the potential to, and often did, affect what happened "in" the metropole. This observation, which motivates the present volume, is changing perceptions of the interrelated nature of the development of state capacities, democratic institutions, immigration law, and educational systems to name the most frequently studied examples. These, however, are institutions that already have received abundant scholarly attention. The new approaches serve primarily to deepen our understanding of institutions that are relatively well known. The development of a U.S. policy to prohibit opium during the early twentieth century, initially in the Philippines and consequently in the United States, has been comparatively neglected. Finding motivations for American decisions to prohibit opium in the United States, however, requires examination of policies developed for the Philippines. Opium prohibition in the Philippines, by no means an inevitable consequence of U.S. rule, prompted American leadership of the international anti-opium movement, which in turn was a key factor in passage of the first prohibitionist law against narcotics in the United States. At the turn of the twentieth century, anti-opium activists perceived colony and metropole as merely two different parts of one space needing reform.

Missionaries and Reform

Interestingly, given the vibrancy of scholarship about prohibition in the United States, American drug and alcohol policies in the Philippines have attracted little attention. David Courtwright's classic *Dark Paradise: A History of Opiate Addiction in America* outlines the basic story about U.S. policy in the Philippines in a single page: opium was legal and subject to the farm system in 1898, and Americans initially adopted a simple import tax, leading to increased consumption. American missionaries protested against the legal opium trade in part because they were worried about opium consumption in China. They began an opium prohibition campaign in the Philippines, which succeeded in 1905; prohibition was in force by 1908. At the same time, these missionaries began to push for an anti-opium conference in Shanghai. Planning began in 1906; it occurred in 1909. The American promoters of this conference, embarrassed by the legal status of opium in the United States, pushed the first major restriction on American opium imports through Congress one week after the conference began.[2]

Even in this brief account, interrelationships between "domestic" and "imperial" suggest themselves. The missionaries claim our attention first. By the turn of the twentieth century, many American missionaries viewed their mission in part as spreading ideas of Americanism: raising the status of women in Japan, introducing John Dewey's educational ideals in China, and teaching English to Filipinos. The missionaries themselves debated how to balance these cultural reforms with the more traditional mission of saving souls. American missionaries were often a group apart in the Asian missions, but in other ways they were part of a transnational movement to promote morals, in this case advocating against opium. Many were from denominations that promoted prohibition, often also of alcohol, in the United States. These American missionaries could simultaneously view themselves as promoting an American vision of a Christian life and a Christian vision of a good life.[3]

American missionaries saw an opportunity in the acquisition of the Philippines to promote the prohibition of opium there, in China, and in the United States. They perceived no hard-and-fast line dividing "domestic" from "foreign" or "colonial." The initial efforts, in 1899, to draw the attention of the U.S. government to prohibition of opium came from American missionaries in China, who had long advocated against opium. Officials in Washington were initially reluctant to tamper with the steady revenue stream opium provided, especially since opium at this time remained a legal and taxed product in the United States. These officials also saw no reason to have a different policy for the colony than was in effect in the metropole.[4] This linkage was maintained throughout the successful missionary effort to prohibit opium in the Philippines, then to call an international conference to gain adherence to anti-opium efforts in China, and as part of that effort to pass the initial laws restricting opium use in the United States.

Opium and Ethnic Chinese

The association of China and the Chinese with opium was strong in the minds of anti-opium advocates at the beginning of the twentieth century. The initial concerns about opium in the Philippines were prompted by American missionaries who had lived in China before they experienced the Philippines. As both American missionaries and American officials became more aware of the opium situation in the Philippines, the prevalence of ethnic Chinese smokers provided them with additional justification to prohibit opium. Throughout Southeast Asia, ethnic Chinese were more likely to smoke opium than were indigenous peoples, but in the Philippines the distinction had been more sharply maintained by the Spanish law permitting opium to be purchased and smoked only by ethnic Chinese. The law appears to have been effective in preventing Filipinos from acquiring the habit, although historian Carl A. Trocki argues that poverty also inhibited addiction.[5]

Anti-opium advocates employed this association of ethnic Chinese with opium consumption effectively in both the United States and the Philippines. First, if only ethnic Chinese smoked opium then prohibiting opium would affect only people who did not "belong" to the nation. Ethnic Chinese were portrayed as outsiders in the Philippines and the United States, with the opium habit both signifying that alien status and allowing their continued exclusion. David Courtwright has demonstrated that opium was consumed by all ethnic groups in the United States at the beginning of the twentieth century, but primarily ethnic Chinese were associated with opium smoking and opium dens.[6] Anti-opium advocates portrayed opium dens as mysterious places, traps in which to keep Chinese immigrants poor and embedded in Chinese rather than American culture or entice innocent, young white women to try the drug and become sexual slaves to Chinese men.[7] Similarly, in the Philippines opium smoking was a sign of Chinese status and therefore of not being a real Filipino.

In metropole and colony, anti-opium activists believed ridding the nation of opium had the potential side benefit of ridding the nation of ethnic Chinese. In 1903, a U.S. commission traveled throughout Asia to study opium policies and recommend a policy for the Philippines. The report of this commission reflected the commissioners' belief that opium smoking was a problem of China-born Chinese and concluded that extension of the "Chinese exclusion act" to the Philippines would in itself lead to a diminished opium problem there. This report also noted, approvingly, that Japan's policy of restricting opium on Taiwan had encouraged ethnic Chinese opium addicts to return to China.[8]

Constructing the opium addict as an "outsider" to both metropole and colony had distinct advantages for anti-opium advocates as well as for the progressive reformers working to civilize the Philippines and the unruly urban United States in the early twentieth century. In a practical sense, if opium addicts were outsiders, foreigners, then prohibiting opium should prompt them to go back "home." American colonial officials believed prohibition would be easier to implement in the Philippines than it would be in other regional colonies for precisely this reason.[9] The same logic applied to the United States. Additionally, if the vice of opium was not indigenous to either the United States or the Philippines, then to purify each of outside influences (opium) and outsiders (Chinese) was a necessary step in their development toward good governance, democracy, and civilization.[10] The same reform actions had to occur in both metropole and colony to provide the framework for developmental projects.

Transition from Deserving Addict to Criminal Element

Not all observers, in either the United States or the Philippines, were convinced that prohibiting opium would encourage the Chinese to leave. Rather, they worried that ethnic Chinese addicts would stay and become a criminal as well as a socially detrimental force in American and Philippine society. Medical cures for opium addiction offered a solution. Metropole and colonial reformers placed increasing faith in the medical profession's ability to treat addicts. The relatively small body of scholarship on the history of addiction treatment in this period focuses more on the gendered than the racial or ethnic discourse surrounding addicts and treatment. Apparently, though, in the United States ethnic Chinese opium smokers initially switched from smoking opium to other forms of opiates. Only when those also became difficult to obtain did they seek the treatment that governments (local, state, and even federal) offered after 1914.[11] The United States implemented a model similar to that in the Philippines after 1905: addicts there, whether of their own volition or after an arrest for possession, had the option of medical treatment for addiction.

In the Philippines, treatment was free to those who could not afford to pay, funded by proceeds from the sale of seized illicit opium. Colonial officials privately expressed concern about the treatment's efficacy: some people repeated the cure multiple times, and opium sometimes was smuggled into hospitals, apparently for those under treatment. Generally these officials, however, were publicly optimistic. They believed government-funded treatment signified the U.S. colonial government's dedication to care for citizens of the Philippines and help them again become productive members of society.[12] The view colonial officials had of these addicts was crucial: when prohibition was implemented in the Philippines in 1908, opium users rarely were viewed as hardened, incorrigible criminals. Reformers believed treatment opportunities allowed the upright citizens to distinguish themselves by their efforts to free themselves from addiction. Those who failed to take advantage of treatment or blatantly flouted the law demonstrated that they did not deserve more assistance.

In the United States by 1914, when nonmedicinal opiates were completely prohibited, the image of the addict had begun to change. Many physicians and public health officials continued to believe addicts had a disease and should receive treatment. Addicts pursuing a cure should no more be judged than someone with a disease such as whooping cough. Other physicians, public health officials, and especially those in the justice system believed opium addiction was a vice, the addict was a criminal, and prison was the proper response. Medical measures to end addiction might be offered to the prisoner.[13] Scholars have made much of this distinction in exploring policies regarding mandatory prison sentences, analysis of treatment programs, and discourse surrounding addiction and narcotics.[14] The division of the addict population into those deserving of treatment and those deserving of prison reflected ideas about who in society was worth attempting to save. Not surprisingly, the government was more willing to spend money treating middle-class, white, and educated addicts. Ethnic minorities and members of the working class were seen as posing a threat and should be removed from society rather than helped to reenter it.

Paths to Prohibition

Debates about the efficacy and desirability of treatment for addicts rather than prison sentences and heavy fines followed in the wake of decisions for prohibition in both the United States and the Philippines. In neither place, however, was prohibition foreordained. In 1898, opium was a legal product in the United States regulated primarily by means of an import tax. It was consumed in a variety of forms by people from most socioeconomic classes and many ethnic groups. In the Philippines under Spanish rule, the government awarded a monopoly over the sale of opium to the highest bidder, a system known as the opium farm. In both cases, opium taxes were lucrative, amounting to approximately U.S.$250,000 in the Philippines and approximately U.S.$1.5 million in the United States.[15] The United States moved quickly to bring Philippine opium policy into conformance with U.S. law by abolishing the opium farm and replacing it with an import tax. The change stemmed from opposition to monopolies, especially government-granted ones, not opposition to opium.

By 1900, as U.S. officials began the transition in the Philippines from a military to a civilian government, opium was still deemed a legitimate tax source. Officials planned to continue the policy of a high import tax as the only regulation of opium sales. American missionaries pressured authorities in the Philippines

Opium den in Manila, 1924, showing availability to single men, likely ethnic Chinese, long after the U.S. colonial regime prohibited opium for nonmedical use. (U.S. Library of Congress)

and Washington by mounting a large-scale direct mail campaign supporting prohibition. This campaign was energized by the proposal in 1903 to return to the opium farm system. Additionally, American colonial officials observed that the existing high import tax apparently had resulted in an increase in opium consumption, particularly by groups other than the ethnic Chinese.[16]

Officials, including Commissioner Henry C. Ide, advocated a return to the farm system because it tracked the amounts and purchasers of opium, information the benevolent colonial government could use to help Filipinos. The firestorm of opposition from missionaries in the Philippines and proponents of all types of prohibition in the United States prompted the Philippine Commission to drop this proposal, at the order of Washington, and instead launch an investigation of opium regimes in the region. The leader of the investigation, the Episcopal bishop of the Philippines, Charles H. Brent, began the study tour as an advocate of the opium farm. He returned several months later an advocate of gradual prohibition.[17] The Opium Commission report appeared in 1905, coincident with Congress passing a law that prohibited opium in the Philippines starting in 1908.

The United States thus became the first Southeast Asian colonial power to ban opium in its colony, but law in the United States itself remained unchanged. Indeed, there was little agitation for narcotics prohibition during the first few years of the twentieth century. Reformers emphasized regulation, using pure food laws, so that patent medicines containing opium (or cocaine or heroin) would be properly labeled. Bishop Brent realized, however, that it would be difficult to enforce prohibition for the Philippines while it remained legal to trade and consume opium in the surrounding colonies and nations. He wrote to President Theodore Roosevelt, whom he knew, in 1906 to propose that the United States lead an international movement to prohibit opium throughout Asia by initiating an international conference among all nations "oriental either by nature or through the possession of dependencies in the Orient."[18] Roosevelt was persuaded, and the State Department sent invitations for a conference in Shanghai in 1909.

European colonial powers did not wish to discuss their colonial opium policies, but they did want to contain the growing opium problem in China. They found the invitation difficult to refuse.[19] In preparation for the meeting, all participating nations agreed to investigate the narcotics situation in both colonies and metropole. The U.S. Department of State hired Hamilton Wright, who became another leading American in the international anti-opium movement, to conduct this investigation, which he did with a vengeance. He found hundreds of thousands of opium addicts in the United States and decried the fact that opium was legal there while the government promoted prohibition in Asia.[20] The media publicized the embarrassing predicament that the American delegation at

Shanghai would find itself in if opium remained legal. Bishop Brent cabled the *Outlook,* a magazine with close ties to the Roosevelt administration, just before the conference began, complaining that "every other nation of the twelve participating nations will be in a better light ... than is our own." The U.S. Congress responded to the pressure and just as the conference opened passed a law prohibiting imports of opium prepared for smoking.[21] This law, the first to prohibit imports of any substance, set the stage for extending prohibition to all narcotics in 1914 with passage of the Harrison Narcotics Act. In the debate on that bill, Francis Harrison, soon to be the governor-general of the Philippines, claimed that the U.S. decision to prohibit opium in the Philippines had prompted the United States to "start this series of international commissions and conventions," which promoted prohibition generally. Harrison urged passage of the 1914 law in order to maintain the high standing of the United States on this issue.[22]

Smuggling and State Power

American promotion of uniform prohibition laws worldwide stemmed from Bishop Brent's perceptive prediction that licit opium would soon find its way into the illicit market. Even though countries increasingly cooperated in tracking, regulating, and gradually prohibiting narcotics, smuggling did not diminish. Officials charged with implementing opium prohibition were not naive; they realized that even worldwide prohibition and accessible treatment could not solve the opium problem. From inception, they understood that the drug would be smuggled and state power would have to be employed to stop the smuggling. In the Philippines, many officials bluntly predicted that smuggling would be so extensive as to make prohibition ineffective. Before 1905, some American officials advocated that opium remain legal and taxed because the Chinese were "expert smugglers" and the "peculiarities and extent of the Coast line of the Philippines" facilitated smuggling.[23] Even Bishop Brent, who actively worked for prohibition, acknowledged that the problem of smuggling was nearly insoluble.[24]

The coastline of the United States is as favorable to smugglers as that of the Philippines. Concerns about smuggling were raised in both 1909 and 1914 as Congress debated restrictions on narcotics. With passage of the Harrison Narcotics Act, the smuggling problem had to be addressed, however. The officials involved with this effort believed in the power of the state to solve social problems and had few fears about increasing police and border control authority as necessary to inhibit if not completely prevent smuggling.[25]

The historian Eric Tagliacozzo has explored the issue of smuggling in Southeast Asia during these years and argues persuasively that smuggling to some extent is in the eye of the beholder. Colonial states believed that their ability to control trade, in both licit and illicit goods, across borders they had drawn provided an important demonstration of their power. Tagliacozzo paints a compelling picture of state power undermined, evaded, and extended.[26] I would like to frame the same issues slightly differently and note the implications for state power and control in the linked project American officials pursued of policing opium smuggling into both the Philippines and the United States.

It is impossible to know the extent of smuggling; the most successful of smugglers rarely come to the scholar's attention. Usually we learn only about the smugglers who fail, those who are caught. Government officials have reason both to exaggerate the extent of smuggling (in arguing for increased resources to combat the smugglers) and to exaggerate the success of their antismuggling efforts (to demonstrate the ability of the state to protect and administer). As with other threats to nations that cannot be fully delineated, the threat posed by smugglers is one government officials can deploy in ways useful to them as they pursue a variety of projects. Smuggling poses a real threat to nation-states, but it is a malleable threat. Measures taken to combat smuggling can serve other purposes.

Moreover, smuggling is always an issue of foreign relations in that goods are smuggled across at least one international border. Policing of smuggling occurs at borders or outside them. The police or military of one country may be operating against smugglers (of unknown nationality) in international or other sovereign territory. Policing smuggling takes place in this international context in which nations have choices about whether to cooperate, look the other way, or resist the antismuggling efforts of their neighbors.

When the United States took on the task of preventing opium smuggling into the Philippines, and shortly thereafter into the United States, these issues loomed large. American officials acknowledged that they did not have sufficient policing power to patrol the coastline of the Philippines or the United States. In response, they attempted to encourage regional Southeast Asian powers to also prohibit opium so that combating smuggling would be a regional effort. Most Southeast Asia colonies permitted opium sales prior to World War II but increasingly regulated and restricted those sales. The United States continued to push this agenda in international conferences, convincing colonial counterparts to work together against smuggling. American authorities most wanted cooperation from the British, since U.S. observers believed, and stated publicly, that most opium smuggled into the Philippines came from British North Borneo and Hong Kong.[27]

The British found this complaint exasperating and had their own criticisms about the effects of American attempts to police opium smugglers. The British in North Borneo believed that the U.S. revenue cutters patrolled too aggressively, disturbing innocent fishermen and local traders, and often patrolled within Borneo's territorial waters. The British were reluctant to make an official complaint, even when Philippine vessels operated extremely close to the shore. Indeed, British officials gave orders not to interfere with the revenue cutters whether or not they were in territorial waters. Additionally, the British ended the opium farm on

North Borneo, raised taxes, and otherwise moved to restrict opium sales. They thought they had done quite a lot and were irritated by American complaints that blamed the continued illicit traffic on lax enforcement by North Borneo. British authorities noted that they had discouraged opium exports, so Philippine authorities had to take responsibility for preventing imports. North Borneo, they declared, "is not justified in establishing a preventive service for the protection of American interests."[28]

The United States increasingly was willing to establish its own preventive service, as demonstrated by the often aggressive efforts of Philippine revenue cutters in the waters around North Borneo, which, as the British always noted, were manned by Filipinos. American observers seemed torn between a belief that their efforts to promote treatment for addicts during the three-year transition period had been effective and a conviction that the smuggling situation was serious. In the years immediately after prohibition, observers had been optimistic, but after a few years, they viewed smuggling as an entrenched problem and were developing the institutions to deal with it. This policing was done by at least three different organizations. In Manila, the city police took the lead, for example, arresting more than 500 people for opium violations in 1920. Across the country, the Philippines Constabulary also conducted raids against opium dens during 1920, conducting nearly three hundred of them, which led to 474 arrests and seizures worth almost 1.5 million pesos. The Customs Service led the effort against smugglers and during 1920 confiscated opium worth about 1.2 million pesos along with 158 smugglers. To those worried that these numbers were too small, the chief of the constabulary, Rafael Crame, had a ready answer: more funding. He reported that the constabulary had the primary responsibility to stop smuggling and yet received only 37,000 pesos annually in funding, one-eighth the amount he claimed he needed to "run down the wily Moros from the Sulu Archipelago, the principal importers of the drug from Borneo and the Strait Settlements, with fast launches and aeroplanes."[29]

After 1920, the government did commit to "constantly patrolling the coasts" with "several fast coast guard cutters." The amount of opium seized and people arrested fluctuated little, however.[30] Still, authorities in the Philippines believed they were making progress. The collector of customs reported in 1927 that opium had not been smuggled from Sandakan for two years following the installation at "a strategic island" of a "supervising customs secret service agent." When officials in Washington conveyed the good news about Sandakan to the British embassy, they removed the information about the secret agent.[31]

Conclusion

From the beginning of their efforts to prohibit narcotics, American officials believed the drug problem would best be solved if drugs were kept out of the

Philippines and the United States. They were willing to spend some money, to stretch the limits of appropriate behavior in the territorial waters of other countries, and even possibly to covertly place secret government agents in friendly nations. As the infrastructure grew in Asia to prevent opium from reaching the Philippines by whatever means, it grew in the United States as well.

Forces for prohibition, especially of alcohol, had been strong in the United States at the turn of the century. As opiates increasingly began to be seen as drugs rather than medicines, the movement to restrict their sale in the same way that some state and local governments prevented the sale of alcohol was already beginning in the early twentieth century. But there was not a common path to prohibition for narcotics and alcohol. It would be logical but wrong to assume that the divergent paths can be traced to the more seriously addictive nature of narcotics.

Instead, both the example of prohibition in the Philippines and the implications of its passage prompted passage of a federal law to prohibit narcotics within the United States as well. The need to promote regional then worldwide prohibition to inhibit smuggling in the Philippines and then the measures against smuggling in both Asia and North America changed U.S. laws and policies, setting the United States on a path of unwavering support for the prohibition of narcotics, enforced primarily through stringent measures against traffickers and dealers. The war on drugs thus traces at least part of its heritage to a nearly forgotten policy justified for its protection of America's colonial subjects in the Philippines.

Policing the Imperial Periphery

Philippine Pacification and the Rise of the U.S. National Security State

ALFRED W. MCCOY

AT THE DAWN OF THE TWENTIETH CENTURY, Commodore George Dewey of the U.S. Navy arrayed his squadron of steel-hulled warships at the edge of Asia. Steaming across Manila Bay at first light on May 1, 1898, his squadron's rapid-fire guns destroyed an antiquated Spanish fleet in a dramatic naval victory. After troops arrived from San Francisco a few months later, U.S. Army volunteers surged through Manila's massive stone battlements to capture a city that Spain had ruled for 350 years. At the cost of just 121 casualties in one day of sporadic fighting, the United States had become, for the first time in its history, an imperial power.[1]

Yet even in this hour of glory, the U.S. Army faced a bloody pacification that would drag on fitfully for another fifteen years. Only hours after occupying the city, the army's Provost Guard was thus charged with maintaining order in what its commander called "this revolutionary and insurrectionary city of . . . 250,000 inhabitants of the most diverse nationality and . . . an unusually large proportion of the criminal classes . . . of the unemployed and dissolute, gamblers and speculators, toughs and the blackguards."[2]

Some hundred years later, at the dawn of the twenty-first century, Chief Superintendent Florencio Fianza of the Philippine National Police arrayed his squads of helmeted riot police before the gates of Manila's presidential palace. Fighting desperately from first light on May 1, 2001, the police fired shotguns and water cannons to scatter a mob of some fifty thousand urban poor, their bodies marked by gang tattoos and fortified by drugs. At the cost of just 117 civilian casualties in six hours of street fighting, Philippine police saved the presidency of Gloria Arroyo.

Yet even at its hour of victory, the Arroyo administration faced volatile political instability. Millions of urban poor filled fetid slums that ringed Manila ready to spill into the streets in anger over miserable lives marked by disease and unemployment. Armed with special powers, Arroyo's police would struggle to prevent a recurrence of mass violence led by "hoodlums and criminals" embedded in the slums of a city swollen to some twenty million inhabitants.[3]

As indicated by the juxtaposition of these two battles, the Philippines has been the site of a protracted social experiment in the use of police as an instrument of state power. Indeed, America's ad hoc experiment with colonial policing was mutually transformative, central in both the transformation of the Philippine polity and the formation of the U.S. national security state. At this periphery of empire, freed from the constraints of courts and Constitution, the American colonial regime fused new information technologies with military intelligence to create what was arguably the world's first "surveillance state." Significantly, the colony's police, called Philippines Constabulary, became the first U.S. federal agency with a fully developed covert operational capacity.

America's Information Revolution

At the broadest theoretical level, this study of the Philippine police challenges the most venerable hypothesis about the modern state. In Max Weber's famed dictum, a state is defined by its "monopoly of the legitimate use of physical force within a given territory."[4] By emphasizing the static fact of physical force, Weber failed to understand that the modern state uses coercion not to enforce compliance but to penetrate privacy for the expropriation of information, both societal and individual.

By contrast, James C. Scott has proposed an alternative way to see the state, not looking downward from the castle's lofty keep, like Weber, but upward from its encircling forests and furrows. Viewed from below, the modern state's defining attribute is its imposition of "legibility" on man and nature. Just as cadastral maps, first adopted by the Netherlands in 1807, made a peasant patchworks into a quantified array of arable land, so Napoleon decreed in 1808 that all French citizens would have permanent patronymics, distinctive last names, to inscribe them inescapably for tax, census, and conscription.[5] But all this information was, in effect, passive, statistically even socially useful but not politically actionable. The bureaucracy was still, in a critical sense, "blind," unable to read deeply into its endless lists of property and people, discerning deviants, identifying individual subversives, and preempting threats to the social order.

By the time this initial European rationalization was played out in the mid-nineteenth century, the United States had become the site of an accelerating information revolution whose synergies were a second, significant phase in the perfection of state power. Through an extraordinary burst of ingenuity in the 1870s and 1880s, American inventors created new products and processes for the efficient collection, transmission, storage, and retrieval of information. Among its many applications, this American data management regime invested the state with its essential modern attribute, that is, the potential for mass surveillance, allowing, for the first time, an advance beyond punishment of the few to control over the many. On the eve of its imperial expansion in 1898, America's information revolution had created the potential for a state security that could identify every individual with a unique number, allowing accurate encoding, filing, and retrieval of data on countless millions, whether citizens or colonial subjects.

For nearly a quarter century, however, courts, Constitution, and civil society barred any application of these innovations to the federal government, making law enforcement an entirely local matter. Indeed, the treasury secretary reported, after President McKinley's assassination in 1901, that "no provision exists for the investigation of the secret organizations which are maintained in all centers of industrial activity."[6] Consequently, in 1908 the Justice Department established the Bureau of Investigation as a fledgling federal agency with limited policing powers. In effect, a full ten years after the American colonial regime in Manila began building a police panopticon, Washington lacked even the most rudimentary capacity for domestic investigation or surveillance.

Colonial Laboratory

The American conquest of the Philippines unleashed the potential of this information technology. Freed from the Constitution's protection of civil liberties, the American regime in Manila drew together theories and technologies that had been building for decades in the United States into a colonial praxis of coercion and information—fostering innovations, data management, and shoe-leather surveillance whose confluence created a modern surveillance state.

After 1898, the U.S. Army integrated Manila into a nationwide communications grid that allowed rapid dispatch of military forces and instantaneous transmission of intelligence. In just five years, its Signal Corps of some four hundred men had laid 5,355 miles of landlines and 1,615 miles of undersea cable that, in 1903 alone, connected 297 signal stations by telegraph or telephone and carried 3.1 million messages totaling 100 million words.[7] This fusion of information and coercion telescoped time for the Philippines, carrying the archipelago, in the space of just a decade, 1899–1909, through two centuries of technological change from the eighteenth's cruel exemplary punishment forward to the twentieth's systematic surveillance.

The U.S. Army carried the germ of this new information technology, which would soon shape the character of the American colonial state. In the decade before the Spanish-American War, the U.S. Army had established a Military Information Division (MID) that quickly developed a data set of three hundred thousand cards, a collection of six thousand maps, a military monograph series, and a photographic unit. During its first three years in the Philippines, 1898–1901, the army combined combat operations, policing, and civil reforms to crush a national revolution—creating an occupation government that it bequeathed to its civilian successor, thereby casting the new colonial state in its coercive mold. Significantly, the Spanish-American War of 1898 was the first military conflict with both real-time battlefield communication by telegraph and war planning through MID's systematic but still-limited intelligence.[8]

The four years of counterguerrilla warfare that followed would make accurate intelligence an imperative, forcing a marked expansion of the military's limited capacities, particularly in the area of operational field intelligence.[9] Landing without maps, language skills, or local knowledge, the army soon became, as one officer put it, "a blind giant" in its fight against Filipino guerrillas that was "more than able to annihilate, to completely smash anything brought against them" but found it "impossible to get any information" about where or when to unleash this lethal force. Accustomed to operating under omnipresent Spanish repression, Filipino officers, despite considerable failings in conventional military operations, were surprisingly skilled in intelligence, using codes to conceal their identities and disinformation to implicate natives disloyal to their cause.[10]

In one of history's accidents, the Filipino flair for guerrilla operations and the American appetite for limitless information combined to create a new form of military espionage that fused combat intelligence, counterintelligence, and political surveillance. Reflecting America's ongoing information revolution, the army created a complex of security forces—the modernized Manila Metropolitan Police, the paramilitary Philippines Constabulary, and its own combat intelligence unit, the Division of Military Information—that employed smart-numbered files, photographic identification, and the telegraphic transfer of combat intelligence.[11]

During its three-year pacification of Manila, 1898–1901, the U.S. Army also created a modern metropolitan police force that applied military intelligence and data management to the problem of political espionage—developing covert techniques of surveillance and penetration to fight a dirty war in the city's slums and back alleys. To these military systems, Manila's civilian police added, between 1901 and 1906, the most advanced American crime-control technology, including a centralized telephone network, the Gamewell system of police and fire alarms, electric street lights, Bertillon photo identification, and, finally, fingerprinting. Within twenty years, this "all embracing index" of police files would amass two hundred thousand alphabetized file cards covering a full 70 percent of Manila's population.[12] In an age when American metropolitan police still relied on foot patrols, wallowed in patronage, and practiced what New York City's police commissioner called "systematic and organized blackmail . . . and extortion," Manila's Metropolitans had, by 1906, a cadre of clerks trained in the use of numbered files and photographic identification, multilingual patrolmen who circulated the city with omnipresent regularity, and detectives skilled in undercover operations.[13]

After 1901, the American civil regime used its police powers to censor public discourse, infiltrate civil society, penetrate households, monitor private mail, and envelope individuals in an incessant surveillance. Through policing, intelligence, surveillance, and communications, the colonial government soon knitted a grid of coercive controls across the archipelago. Inside the colonial capital, five separate secret services—army, constabulary, police, customs, and internal revenue—deployed spies and agents in a ceaseless surveillance of Filipino politics and private lives. Within five years of its founding in 1901, the Philippines Constabulary had developed a comprehensive covert capacity with secret surveillance, media monitoring, psychological profiling, disinformation, deep penetration, and political manipulation.

Through clandestine penetration, close surveillance, and centralized intelligence in capital and countryside, the U.S. colonial police penetrated private social space to collect incriminating information on the country's political elite—whether radical or conservative, revolutionary or collaborator—thereby mediating a colonial politics of scandal. To control political discourse, the American regime initially imposed harsh punishments for both subversion and the libel of all public officials, enforced by the local courts with long imprisonments and heavy fines. Through constabulary surveillance and skillful co-optation that turned prominent Filipino activists into American spies, the radical nationalist movement imploded by 1912 amid suspicion and betrayal, leaving conservative electoral politicians, their discourse constrained within colonial bounds, in control of public space through patronage politics.

This centralized information apparatus was dedicated first to the suppression of subversion and later to the political and moral reformation of Filipino society. After the first civil governor, William Taft, imposed a rough colonial order through draconian laws and harsh repression, his successors collaborated with both American Protestant reformers and the Filipino political elite in using law and police to prohibit the personal vices, gambling and drug use, which were deemed a threat to the eugenics of the colonial body social—an element of what one historian has called American "social engineering."[14]

Information Division

By applying military methods to domestic espionage, the constabulary's Information Division quickly developed, after its founding in 1901, the means to collect, file, retrieve, analyze, and operationalize a vast amount of intelligence. With its network of some two hundred Filipino spies, the Information Division drew data through intensive surveillance, covert penetration, and careful monitoring of both press and public discourse.

All this intelligence flowed into the Information Division's centralized office where it was translated, typed, numbered, and filed in dossiers for ready retrieval.

Using filing systems such as those devised by Melville Dewey and Charles A. Cutter in the 1870s, the constabulary numbered each report to indicate both topic and sequence. These numbered files also allowed agile juxtaposition of related intelligence for psychological profiling, order-of-battle rosters, and longitudinal studies of entire movements—creating a colonial frame for analysis and action.

The combination of strict surveillance and draconian libel laws fostered a politics of scandal in Manila in which everyone, Americans and Filipinos, collected damaging gossip about everyone—secreting damning documents in private safes and holding them as insurance against political reprisals or as currency in future political maneuvers. Within this school for scandal, the constabulary was systematic in its collection of incriminating information and selective in its release—suppressing scandal to protect its allies and releasing scurrilous information to destroy its enemies.

After the first decade of repression curbed political dissent and crushed peasant resistance, Governor Taft's successors moved on to use their police apparatus to create a morals regime in an effort, supported by the Philippine elites, to uplift the Filipino national character through the prohibition of gambling, narcotics, and prostitution. This antivice campaign, as we will see, created conditions for a succession of scandals that pitted Filipino nationalists against American colonials in a protracted political confrontation.

Rule by Scandal

The greatest political controversy in forty years of American colonial rule, the Conley case, began with a minor instance of police corruption but soon spun into a serious legitimation crisis that was ultimately resolved through scandal. The progenitor of this political crisis was Detective Ray Conley, an accidental American colonial from Hicksville, Ohio, transformed by his command of Manila's vice squad into a powerful player in the intrigues swirling about Governor-General Leonard Wood.[15]

With his street smarts, fluent Tagalog, and control over the city's vice trades, Detective Conley was a formidable force in Manila's underworld—tipping the colonial balance by arresting prominent of Filipinos for gambling and protecting Americans from scandal. Through a series of sensational raids in mid-1922, Conley's squads closed eighteen opium dens and fourteen gambling joints that were "running almost openly." In a raid on the Nacionalista Party's social club, the detective arrested, as the city's police chief put it, "a large number of prominent persons including ex-representatives, attorneys, physicians, property owners and, of course, members of both political parties."[16] Conley also tangled with Mayor Ramon Fernandez, a wealthy Spanish mestizo and crony of Senator Manuel Quezon, challenging the mayor's crew of ex-detectives, who were planting drugs on Manila's Chinese to extort protection money.[17]

In March 1923, Mayor Fernandez used two of his nephews, one a police officer and the other a gambling racketeer, to stage a sting operation that led to Conley's suspension on charges of taking 1,000 pesos in "hush money" from the gambling syndicate.[18] A week later, the city prosecutor indicted Conley for accepting 7,200 pesos in bribes from two gamblers who maintain "in the city of Manila ... houses where *monte* and other games of chance were played." On May 19, after seventeen days of trial, Judge Imperial, trying to mediate the city's deep racial divide, issued a convoluted decision that simultaneously exonerated Conley and questioned his integrity.

When Mayor Fernandez and Interior Secretary Jose Laurel demanded punishment, Governor-General Wood countered, on July 16, by allowing Conley to retire on full a pension. At 10:30 p.m. the next day, Senator Quezon led five Filipino cabinet secretaries up the grand staircase into Malacañang Palace to present their resignations to the governor—precipitating a political crisis that dragged on for four years until Wood's death on an operating table in Boston.

Throughout the Conley crisis both sides used slander, but Governor Wood had a decisive edge in scandalous information through allies in command of the Manila Police and Philippines Constabulary. So shielded from the panopticon of police surveillance, Wood could challenge powerful Filipinos knowing that he had sufficient information and coercive authority to survive any confrontation. Though just a patrolman, Conley's mastery of Manila's underworld allowed him to suppress a scandal involving the governor's son and aide-de-camp, Lieutenant Osborne Wood, protecting him from the consequences of certain derelictions, sexual and financial, and thus preserving his public image as a dashing young officer who had married a genteel American woman in a grand Malacañang Palace wedding.[19] In November 1923, just a few months after Conley's resignation removed this protection, a *New York Times* Washington correspondent, Richard Oulahan, followed rumors of corruption to Manila where he reported that Lieutenant Wood had somehow made an incredible $800,000 through financial speculation—a sensational story that made Osborne into a Gatsby-like character in Jazz Age tabloids.[20] Indeed, Governor Wood's private diary reveals that Osborne had succumbed to Manila's corruptions, somehow amassing, on an army lieutenant's annual income of just $2,000, an incredible $490,000 in his Manila bank accounts, the equivalent of 245 years of his own pay or 30 years of his father's salary as governor-general.[21]

Senator Quezon himself was a master of intrigue and scandal and a worthy adversary for General Wood. On July 21, 1923, just five days after Conley retired with a full pension, the Manila daily *El Debate* hit the streets with a banner headline, "Gan Yong, Arrested, Denounces Conley," and a sensational story that constabulary captain Silvino Gallardo had arrested this "famous Chinese trafficker" who now claimed that he had paid Conley five hundred pesos a month for four years to protect his gambling and opium dens in Binondo's Chinatown.[22]

At first glance, the Gan Yong story seems to have sprung from a sequence of incredible coincidences. First, a drug dealer from Conley's dirty past suddenly reappears from far-off China. Then, in a stunning bit of police work, a constabulary captain somehow plucks this particular Chinese from hiding in a suburban lumberyard. Next, an intrepid reporter, manages to stride past police guards and conduct an interview inside a high-security prison. Surprisingly, this hardened Chinese criminal decides to make a clean breast of his crimes, confessing to felonious drug dealing. And, finally, a major newspaper splashes the story across page one.

On closer examination, this coverage shows Quezon's deft use of scandal in his war on Governor Wood. *El Debate* itself was owned by Quezon's close ally, ex-mayor Fernandez.[23] Less obviously, the arresting officer, Captain Gallardo, was a corrupt constable who was clawing his way up the constabulary hierarchy by doing confidential police work for Quezon.[24] With these two adversaries, Governor Wood and Senator Quezon, so evenly matched, theirs would be a political duel to the death with their weapon of choice—scandal.

Within a year, this protracted power struggle shifted to the Board of Control, a joint legislative-executive body that Wood's liberal predecessor had created to manage the many government corporations launched under his rule. Governor Wood took office determined to privatize these corporations but was blocked by boards that were appointed by Quezon and his ally, Manuel Roxas. In late 1926, Quezon and Roxas defied the governor's authority by convening a meeting of the National Coal Company to select its new board of directors. Wood countered by firing the two directors and filing a case in the Philippine Supreme Court where, for different reasons, both sides could be confident of the outcome.[25]

With the nine-man court balanced to give American justices a one-vote majority, Quezon believed he could count on four Filipino justices and a deciding vote from his longtime friend George Malcolm—a young Wilson appointee known for his liberal, pro-Filipino sympathies. Indeed, Malcolm and Quezon were longtime political allies who had recently celebrated their "pact of friendship" at a public banquet.[26]

But Wood had leverage in this case that went beyond merit, politics, or personal loyalty. In February 1926, just a year before the National Coal case, an older, decidedly conservative justice, E. Finley Johnson, had filed a morals charge against his junior colleague, Justice Malcolm. With an assiduousness usually reserved for Filipino derelictions, Wood ordered Manila detectives to conduct a thorough investigation of the alleged concubinage, particularly Malcolm's illegitimate children, "one of whom is supposed to be alive in one of the convents here."[27] As

Justice Johnson, armed with this damning police dossier, steamed across the Pacific to press President Coolidge for Malcolm's ouster, Wood interceded by telegramming the White House to preempt any dismissal and then summoning the justice to show him this exculpatory cable.[28]

In April 1927, just 364 days after Wood had saved his career, Justice Malcolm, writing for the majority, handed down a decision that surprised observers and stunned Quezon. Malcolm ruled decisively for Wood, ordering dismissal of Quezon's appointees to National Coal's board and finding the law allowing such appointments "unconstitutional and void."[29] In effect, Malcolm declared Wood the victor over Quezon in the four-year battle that had started with the Conley controversy.[30] From both text and context, it seems unlikely that a liberal justice like Malcolm would have written so decisively in favor of Wood, and against his friend Quezon, had he not been subject to sexual blackmail.

Through its policing, U.S. colonial rule thus created an interlocking regime of vice prohibition and paramilitary policing whose imprint on the Philippine state is still evident a full half century after independence. In the Philippines, like many postcolonial societies, policing remains a potent source of legitimacy, and regimes that fail to maintain order suffer a sharp loss of public support—as happened with the Republic in the early 1960s and the succeeding Marcos regime in the early 1980s. Similarly, the colonial prohibition of personal vice has persisted for nearly a century, fostering vast illicit industries that corrupted both the Philippine police and Filipino politicians—a phenomenon manifest in scandals over an illegal lottery called *jueteng* that toppled President Estrada in 2001 and tarnished President Arroyo's administration four years later.

Imperial Praxis

In their desperate search for security amid revolution, American colonials drew untested security techniques from the United States and perfected their practice through an imperial praxis, developing both innovative procedures and skilled personnel. For the United States, the Philippines was, viewed conservatively, the first manifestation of the repressive potential of its new information technology. Interpreted more boldly, it could be said that colonial conquest accelerated these changes, making the Philippines a social laboratory for the perfection of American state power.

Advances in policing on this periphery of empire thus served as both blueprint and bellwether for a later metropolitan transformation during the mobilization for world war—a bellwether for wartime surveillance of American citizens and a blueprint for the formation of Washington's first national security units. Honed and hardened in information warfare, a young generation of colonial officers—exemplified by Harry Bandholtz, Dennis E. Nolan, and Ralph H. Van Deman—returned home to regular duties with the U.S. Army and established, during

World War I, both its Military Intelligence and its Military Police. The sum of this colonial experience, both programs and personnel, thus played a seminal role in building Washington's domestic counterintelligence apparatus and, more broadly, its earliest covert capacity.[31] In the tumultuous aftermath of war, senior U.S. Army commanders applied lessons learned while repressing Filipino radical movements to crush a militant miners' revolt in the West Virginia coalfields—the only armed uprising against the American state in the twentieth century.

Through the prism of this small yet significant problem, American colonial policing, we can see how colonial rule embedded a formidable security apparatus within the Philippine polity and a decade later transformed the American state. The conquest and colonization of the Philippines thus proved to be an ambitious venture that strained the coercive capacities of a fledgling federal government, fostering both the formation of a domestic surveillance apparatus and, of equal import, the inclination to apply it.

"The Prison That Makes Men Free"
The Iwahig Penal Colony and the Simulacra of the American State in the Philippines

MICHAEL SALMAN

IN 1904 THE AMERICAN COLONIAL REGIME opened the Iwahig Penal Colony on a tract of swamp and forestland across the bay from Puerto Princesa, the provincial capital of remote Palawan Island, to relieve severe and dangerous overcrowding at Bilibid Prison, the central penitentiary in Manila. On this inhospitable island, so racked by endemic malaria that banishment there during Spanish rule often became a capital sentence, the Americans launched an experiment in penal reform that its advocates were not yet ready to try with adult convicts at home. When American reformers followed the Iwahig experiment with a similar effort at New York's notorious Sing Sing Prison, they found themselves constrained by powerful political pressures in the United States. Both the apparent success of the Iwahig Penal Colony and the ignominious demise of a parallel experiment with inmate self-government at Sing Sing depended on the powers of the state, powers that became more capricious despite dressing in the garb of self-government and democracy.

As in the manner of classical laboratory experiments, Iwahig was a test in miniature carried out under tightly controlled conditions using carefully preselected materials. The theory that inspired the Iwahig experiment traveled to the Philippines as a colonial import from the United States before traveling back to the United States to be employed in the experiment at Sing Sing. Iwahig and its inmates were miniatures of the colonial imagination, scaled-down simulacra of the Philippine colony as a whole, which itself was sometimes conceived as a scaled-down simulacra of American democracy and liberal capitalism, always fated, in the American colonial imagination, to be a junior republic undergoing endless tutelage and reformation through the ministrations of its American supervisors.

Origins in War, Disease, and Death

Disease and violence marked the beginning of the Iwahig Penal Colony much as they did the initial American colonization of the Philippines. The first group of 61 convicts from Bilibid began to clear land for the new penal colony in November 1904. By the end of June 1905, 313 prisoners had been delivered to the new penal settlement. Forty-eight of them died in that same period, mostly victims of beri beri, dysentery, and malaria.[1] The following year another 332 prisoners arrived, and 46 more reportedly died of disease.[2] There were several escape attempts during the penal colony's first two years of operation, including an "organized outbreak" by about 100 prisoners on September 20, 1905. Thirty-three prisoners escaped in that uprising, but most were soon killed or recaptured by the contingent of Philippine Scouts stationed across the bay at Puerto Princesa.[3]

Many of the convicts at Iwahig embodied another connection between the founding of the penal colony and the establishment of American colonial rule in the Philippines. As of June 30, 1908, there were 446 prisoners in the colony, 155 of whom had been convicted of crimes (*bandolerismo* [group banditry or brigandage] 106, assassination 18, sedition 16, insurrection, 13, treason 2) that were frequently political in nature.[4] In 1909, the first Filipino attorney general, Ignacio Villamor, explained the statistical correlation between the American conquest, the invention of *bandolerismo* as a crime by the colonial state, and the evident rise of "criminality" during the period 1903–5, when more people were tried for *bandolerismo* than any other crime, and several provinces' populations were herded into concentration camps to prosecute counterinsurgency wars to suppress this "brigandage."[5]

That the Iwahig Penal Colony and the larger American colonial state in the Philippines shared a confluence of goals, organization, representations, and techniques of power is perhaps, in one sense, not surprising for they emerged from the same source. Just like American colonialism writ large, the Iwahig Penal Colony was designed to produce citizens, laborers, and commodities in a colony that could be represented as democratic. Beginning in 1906, Iwahig was supposed to function as a self-governing, self-sufficient, and self-policed "republic" of convicts under the supervision of a colonial superintendent but constructed out of the inmates' own labor and, insofar as possible, made profitable for the state. It was during the first decade of Iwahig's operation as a republic that the American colonial regime opened the Philippine Assembly, began the process of "Filipinizing" the civil service, and implemented the provisions of the Jones Bill, which granted the colony more autonomy and promised future independence. A colony within a colony, Iwahig provides in miniature an elaboration of the ironies, contradictions, and fantasies of American colonial rule and, indeed, of American society itself.

Junior Republics

The Iwahig Penal Colony incorporated some of the most progressive trends in American penology. Its model was the George Junior Republic, a reformatory and training school for "dependent" and "delinquent" children founded in 1895 by William Reuben George in a New York town with the improbable name of Freeville. The Junior Republic evolved from George's operation of a fresh air camp for young street toughs from New York City. In the words of a historian of the Junior Republic movement, George believed these boys, mostly immigrant children, "had no concept of right or wrong, self-control or cleanliness."[6] George soon realized that his charges were more interested in the camp's material patronage than its moral instruction and feared that its gifts of food, clothing, and other goods would only "pauperize" the children and their parents rather than civilize them as he wanted.[7] To revive the reformative mission George put the campers to work. He turned charitable gifts into commodities to be purchased and converted labor into time recompensed by wages. Now, as he put it, he would "make them work for their food."[8]

From wage labor and private property, George constructed a reformatory program that replicated in miniature the larger society's institutions of discipline and governance. He replaced his daily practice of corporal punishment with "trial by jury" to make the children reflect on the matter of crime and punishment. Applying the same principle of internalizing responsibility through self-government, he fixed on the idea of a constituent "law-making body" and a police force.[9] Delinquent children could be educated in the discipline of self-control by combining self-interest and self-government through a miniaturization of the social, economic, and political processes of liberal capitalism, scaling them downward in terms of both size and age of citizenship. George believed his program worked because "[u]nderneath the whole plan ran the economic system of the big Republic... Our Glorious Republic in miniature—a Junior Republic."[10]

The renowned prison reformer Thomas Mott Osborne, a great-nephew of the abolitionist Lucretia Mott, developed his most innovative ideas from his work on the Board of Trustees for the Junior Republic at Freeville. Osborne's major contribution to prison reform was his program for convict self-government, which he instituted while warden of Sing Sing in 1914. This experiment fulfilled the desire he first expressed in 1904, the year of Iwahig's founding, to try the Junior Republic's principle of inmate self-government with adult prisoners in the United States. Before Osborne's experiment at Sing Sing, the Junior Republic's system of inmate self-government was first tried among the adult convicts at Iwahig.[11]

As early as 1900, George and Osborne began to discuss the possibility of extending their reformatory techniques to the governance and training of the United States' new colonial subjects in the Philippines. As Osborne explained to one of the Junior Republic's trustees, "We who are trying to free the children from the application of the idea of a beneficial tyranny ought to be the first to recognize that Imperialism is only the reform school principle on a larger scale."[12] In fact, there was mutual recognition between the architects of American empire and those of the "reform school principle," as well as some overlap of personnel.

Theodore Roosevelt had encouraged George in his reform endeavor from the beginning, since the days when Roosevelt served as police commissioner of New York City in 1895–97. In early 1912 Roosevelt wrote of a visit to the children at Freeville, "The Junior Republic is just exactly what . . . Thomas Mott Osborne has called it. It is a laboratory experiment in democracy."[13] During his 1912 campaign for president, Woodrow Wilson published a letter in the Junior Republic newspaper advising the citizens that in government self-control and self-government were more important than the government of others.[14] Similarly, Filipinos, Wilson wrote in a 1902 essay, could become independent and self-governing, but "discipline must precede it—if necessary, the discipline of being under masters." In the meantime, Wilson advised, "they must obey as those who are in tutelage. They are children and we are men in these deep matters of government and justice."[15] Evidently sharing this sense of a civilizing mission, Roosevelt declared in a 1908 message to Congress, "We must be wise and generous; we must help the Filipinos to master the difficult art of self-control, which is simply another name for self-government."[16]

The subminiature version of this reformatory endeavor attempted at Iwahig began as the pet project of William Cameron Forbes, who held the revealingly titled colonial cabinet post of secretary of commerce and police from 1904 to 1909, when he became governor-general. Hailing from an old abolitionist family, Forbes and his brother Alexander served with Thomas Mott Osborne on the Board of Trustees of the George Junior Republic. When Forbes first arrived in the Philippines, he was faced with severe overcrowding, raging mortality, and riots in Bilibid Prison. To relieve these conditions, Forbes sent convicts out to labor on road construction, and he began to plan the new penal colony on Palawan along the lines of the Junior Republic.

Founding Iwahig, the Colony's Colony

The first official reports on Iwahig describe the inmates as Bilibid prisoners with long sentences, often nearing release. Their status at Iwahig was likened to parole. They were sent to live without armed guards, to learn a trade, and to "receive training for the duties and responsibilities of good citizenship." With a minimal supervisory staff, usually no more than the superintendent and a few assistants, Iwahig depended on internalized discipline to provide order as well as reformation. Behind this order stood the ever-present threat of return to Bilibid or, if matters at Iwahig should become uncontrollable, recourse to the military detachment across the bay at Puerto Princesa. Ultimately, according to Forbes, "The plan is to give these prisoners an opportunity to cultivate little lots of land for themselves, and they can send for their families and eventually obtain pardon by good conduct and industry." In the meantime, the Bureau of Prisons arranged for "plantation work" to build discipline and make the colony self-supporting.[17]

Disease and rebellion effectively disrupted Forbes's plans for Iwahig through the better part of 1906, but his analysis of this initial failure traced all blame to the selection of an inappropriate superintendent, thus tracking the narcissistic narrative of imperial order. Forbes was certain that "local self-government among the prisoners, their own police force, their own court of justice," and the rest of the Junior Republic's "general plan . . . will obviate the recurrence of all the difficulties which have arisen."[18]

Affairs at Iwahig changed after Major John R. White of the Philippines Constabulary became the superintendent in September 1906, just months after his participation in the massacre of Moros at Bud Dajo on Jolo Island. White arrived at Iwahig in the company of Forbes, the director of the Bureau of Health Dr. Victor Heiser, and a surprising third visitor, the ex-president of the Philippine Republic Emilio Aguinaldo. After touring the penal colony, Aguinaldo addressed the inmates, stating that, "if he had by force of circumstances been himself a colonist, he would . . . ask nothing better than to have a plot of land given to him there and be allowed to remain on it."[19]

Convinced that he had the right man in White, Forbes instructed the Bureau of Prisons to give the prisoners "a form of self-government in the colony" by the beginning of 1907, the year the new Philippine Assembly was due to open, extending self-government in the colonial Philippines to include an elected legislature. The penal colony's government would follow the Junior Republic model with an elected "council," under the superintendent's "absolute veto power" over all acts, elections, and appointments. Forbes advised sparing use of this power on the Junior Republic theory that inmates would be "more inclined to observe and enforce the rules if they are allowed to make them themselves." Forbes had a deep faith in the practicality of "self-government" for the convicts. It had worked in schools and colleges, and, he assured White, "The George Junior Republic is a living example of this and of results attained from the most unpromising material."[20]

Iwahig employed a calculus of incentives to correct behavior in connection with its political psychology of involvement and responsibility. Like the Junior Republic, Forbes's plan called for sorting Iwahig colonists into three classes, each subdivided into three grades with corresponding privileges to awaken the "ambition to progress." New arrivals living in the Barrack Zone were to be called convicts, wear the striped uniforms of Bilibid, and do the most strenuous work, typically on a road gang. The middling class would live in the Home Zone and be called yeomen and citizens with access to a two-hectare plot and seeds. They could build houses and, if they were economically self-supporting, their families would be allowed to join them. The top class would live in the Free Zone, each with a grant of two hectares of land. They would be called freeholders if they had received conditional pardons. If they had full pardons, they would be called freemen.[21]

Material conditions improved considerably under White. The mortality rate dropped, partly because of continuous settlement but also due to the progressive clearing of land, the drainage work of "mosquito brigades," improved sanitation, and a more varied diet. Colonists constructed new barracks, an administration building, roads, and a parade ground. They put land to the tiller for a variety of foods and cash crops, including the beginnings of what would become an extensive planting of coconut trees. But the plans for self-government were implemented more slowly in part because alternative institutions of self-government had been developed by the colonists themselves before White's arrival.[22]

In the dense foliage behind the barracks the inmates constructed huts screened from sight. The boundaries of the colony blurred beyond the surveillance of the superintendent. Women from neighboring areas visited convicts there, enabling them to subvert both the penal isolation and strict sexual regulation of the colony. Not only did colonists thus elide the discipline of the colony, but in doing so several accumulated power in the underground economy. White reported that the "most influential prisoners" had the best huts and access to women. Those "with sufficient confidence or 'pull'" also secured the cooperation of their fellows to evade work details. This inmate subculture was not the kind of self-government Forbes and White meant to cultivate. Like the larger colonial promise of training for self-government and freedom, the reformatory logic of Iwahig first required the destruction of another kind of independent governance.[23]

A prisoner named Singson, an Ilocano Chinese mestizo serving a life sentence for murder and brigandage, had the best hut in the quasi-autonomous region behind the barracks. White determined that Singson led a "gang of the worst men," a group he would have to disband to establish complete "control of the colony." Desirous that discipline be "maintained by moral rather than physical force," White did not call for troops from Puerto Princesa. The severely strained living conditions in the colony already taxed the colonists' endurance. To White, the extra-institutional settlement seemed as much an accommodation to dreadful circumstances as a threat to his authority. So, instead of a frontal assault on the semiautonomous region behind the barracks, White opted for a gradual strategy to demonstrate his power. Together with the colony's chief of police, a Tagalog named Andres Ascue who was serving a life sentence for assassination, White handcuffed Singson during an inspection lineup for his return to Bilibid in full view of the assembled convicts. White conceived this as a "'grandstand' play" to impress the colony.[24]

Deportations accomplished two mutually reinforcing objectives. White returned several dozen convicts to Bilibid for disciplinary purposes during his first fiscal year at Iwahig, although the records do not furnish an exact number. The following year only nine were returned for disciplinary reasons.[25] Removal to Bilibid also functioned as an element within the process of inmate classification intended to select convicts suitable for reformatory treatment at Iwahig or, to put it another way, to determine which convicts were fit to live in a self-governing colony. In effect, deportation reclassified convicts as incorrigible.[26]

When White left Iwahig on August 31, 1908, the colony still did not operate on all the principles of self-government prescribed by Forbes. There were no representative institutions among the colonists, but there was considerable movement toward "self-government" of other kinds. The almost five hundred convicts lived under what White called "moral restraints" and "interior discipline maintained without guards." He urged his successor to continue "the feature of controlling Filipinos through Filipino assistants . . . and prisoner foremen." Some years later, when White proposed applying Iwahig's principle of self-government to convict laborers in Benguet Province, he entitled the proposal a "Plan for Using Prisoners on Road Work at Baguio and Making Them Their Own Warders."[27]

Discipline and Labor

Discipline at Iwahig often devolved to the question of labor. The section of White's annual report under the subhead "Conduct of the Colonists and Discipline" discussed labor and work supervision after a brief account of rules violations. Together with the colonists' police force, a hierarchy of foreman and assistant foremen supervised the work squads, forming a chain of observation and responsibility that extended from the group up to the superintendent. More broadly, the "principles" of administration were the "absolute and unquestioned authority of the superintendent," paternalism in the form of "considerate and sympathetic treatment of the Filipino employees and prisoners," and the practice of "controlling the bulk of the prisoners" through Filipino assistants and foremen.[28]

Labor at Iwahig continued to attract special attention in the following years. On the subject of "Discipline and Work," White's successor, Carroll H. Lamb, wrote, "The two are so closely allied that they are treated together." The discipline of work produced self-government, the only alternative to the discipline of "fear and force." Proudly, Lamb declared that the Iwahig convict "works as God ordained man should work, and not as a slave under armed guard or the lash."[29]

Stripped of its more grandiose claims, Iwahig still seems an extraordinary penal institution. Once soundly established, it was certainly a marked and humane improvement over Bilibid. There were no prison guards at Iwahig. There was reputedly no direct physical coercion of the inmates. While the colony had a small nipa hut for detention, it had no jail. Colonists received small cash allowances while prisoner foremen and assistants received additional pay. Those in the higher classes could work for their own economic benefit and travel around the colony without special passes. By June 1908, Iwahig had twenty families in residence, something unique in modern penology and no mean feat to accomplish since the authorities found "in most cases the sentence of a husband to imprisonment of any length is looked upon by the wife as equivalent to a divorce."[30] Official reports claimed that there was no incidence of recidivism among former Iwahig colonists during this time. As White put it, "Observation has shown that time-expired men leave here thoroughly rehabilitated and ready to take up the duties of citizenship once more."[31]

Self-Government under a "Czar"

But, for all the inventiveness and liberality of Iwahig as a penal institution, techniques of power were always the determinants and delimiters of self-government and democratic practice. As White later recollected, "Certainly, I was a little Czar at Iwahig as the power I possessed to recommend a man for pardon or to return him to Bilibid Prison was almost that of life and death."[32] Before he left Iwahig, White offered an apology to Forbes for not fully implementing his plan for self-government and a colonist population of two thousand. "Under the ideal conditions," he wrote, "the Superintendent of this Colony could handle 2000 or more men and might organize them on an autonomical basis." He thought Forbes should understand the limitations on self-government at Iwahig because, he explained, "the problem at the colony is not unlike that of the general Philippine government; the chief difficulty being to adjust the relations between the Filipino assistants or prisoners and the American officials so that a working basis of efficiency is established without distrust and suspicion on either side."[33]

Whereas White's authority for his job at Iwahig was formed in one imperial way, by killing Filipinos, Carroll H. Lamb had preparatory experience as a civil engineer directing Caribbean laborers building the Panama Canal, another exercise of empire. Lamb received additional training as an assistant under White before he became superintendent on September 1, 1908. Forbes's plan for self-government came to fruition during Lamb's three-year tenure at Iwahig. In April 1909, Iwahig opened a "petty court" of colonists much like the system of trial by jury in the Junior Republics. Over the next year, this developed into a full-fledged judicial system, with Justice of the Peace Courts and a Court of Last Resort for appeals. In 1910, the first-class colonists were given a "suffrage which permits the election of one-half of the minor officials, police, and petty officers." By 1911, the number of colonists at Iwahig had risen above one thousand. For the first time, wrote Forbes, "the colonists were allowed to govern themselves—elect their own president and council, or legislature, from among the men who by good conduct and industry had earned promotion to the highest grades."[34]

Ironically, while Iwahig boasted of its perfect record in rehabilitating "citizens" with no incidence of recidivism, Lamb resigned from his position at the colony under the cloud of a criminal scandal at the start of 1912. On April 22, 1912, the Court of First Instance at Puerto Princesa convicted Lamb of misappropriation of public funds in fraudulent cattle purchases.[35]

The Iwahig colony, like the colonial Philippines, seems to present a series of striking contradictions. A segregated reformatory community for criminals from a colonized society, Iwahig eschewed the coercive penal institutions required by the larger society. If Iwahig had a social life like "ordinary communities," it also promised a realm of political and economic freedoms denied to the unincarcerated populace. The colonial government of the Philippines then included an American governor-general, an executive Philippine Commission and Supreme Court of mixed Filipino–North American composition, and elected Filipino officeholders in the Philippine Assembly and local governments. Lamb described the organization of Iwahig "as a Republic over which the Superintendent has almost absolute power which is delegated in various ways thereby making the Colony a mild Despotism, republic in form."[36] Sometimes portrayed as approximating the outside society, other times held up as a better model for the outside society to emulate, Iwahig was simultaneously representative and unique.

The colonists at Iwahig were certainly not a representative cross-section of the Philippine population. They were a select group, filtrated by the colonial criminal justice system's project of identification, classification, and division. They had been convicted by courts, separated from society in prison, then graded for behavior at Bilibid. As a reformatory, Iwahig defined its subjects as corrigible. The division of convicts into categories of corrigible and incorrigible both paralleled and fell within the larger colonial dichotomies of the civilized and uncivilized, those deemed capable of civilization and those incapable. In a colonial society suffused by doubt over the extent of civilization and the capacity for its development, the colonial regime constituted Iwahig as a highly controlled community of the corrigible, just as the ideology of American colonial rule insisted that the majority of Filipinos would be, eventually, capable of progress. Iwahig would produce citizens, just as American colonial rule promised to produce citizens in the Philippines.

Laboratory Experiments with the Power of Incarceration

If the George Junior Republic was a "laboratory experiment in democracy," then Iwahig was the same for colonialism. The primary issues of colonial politics revolved around the matters of independence, self-government, and Filipino "fitness." Colonialism actively denied and disparaged Filipino assertions of rights and status. Iwahig could be self-governing in this setting precisely because it was highly controlled, segregated from the rest of society, a colony within a colony, populated by inmates who had experienced the terrors of Bilibid. Woodrow Wilson saw the essence of independence and self-government in self-discipline, in the ability to control the self. Carroll H. Lamb explained an "absolute, proven fact" at Iwahig, although it seemed "at the first glance paradoxical," and this was that "the greater the measure of self-government allowed, the higher the class of superintendence required." Woodrow Wilson wrote that nations were made by subjection to kings, that those who could not govern themselves must have a king, a master, who would teach them the self-control underlying self-government. At Iwahig, Carroll H. Lamb discovered "That a mild despotism brings out the best in the Filipino," and this was exactly what all colonial manifestos about Filipino progress under American tutelage also claimed.[37]

The claims made for Iwahig were truly extraordinary. In 1914, Bishop Charles Henry Brent, a leader of missionary and educational enterprises among the non-Christian population of northern Luzon, visited Iwahig as part of a tour of the southern Philippines. Iwahig, he told his home office, was the most "successful experiment in the treatment of criminals in the world, so far as I know. Any school we attempt ought to be built on the principles which make Iwahig what it is." In the same missive he described a copra plantation on Cagayan de Sulu. The American planter was, Brent wrote, "an aid to the natives while promoting his own commercial interests. These people of Malay origin need above all else just leadership. In one way they are quite childlike, though in other respects full of guile." In Brent's colonial view of Philippine progress, the plantation, the mission school, and the penal colony worked to the same end.[38]

Similarly, in 1917, a *New York Times* interview with the director of the Bureau of Prisons discussed convict self-government under the title "Doing the Filipino Good by Jailing Him."[39] Lyman Beecher Stowe, a grandson of Harriet Beecher Stowe and an official of the National Association of Junior Republics, called Iwahig "A Prison That Makes Men Free." He lauded Iwahig as proof that Junior Republic methods could succeed among adults. "Though the success of the colony as a maker of dollars is still to be demonstrated," Stowe found that "the experiment of giving adult Filipinos, guilty of the worst crimes, a chance to develop the best that is in them under conditions approximating those under which they must live when released has proved a complete success."[40] The irony of Stowe's assessment was surely unintended. Did Iwahig resemble a Philippine village or a Philippine plantation? Did Iwahig approximate an exterior society of free citizens or did the exterior society approximate a penal reformatory? If Iwahig was "a prison that makes men free" among a people that Woodrow Wilson thought required "the discipline of being under masters," then should not the entire population be incarcerated for the creation of their freedom?[41]

In dream and design, the institutions of American colonial rule in the Philippines approached a realization of what Michel Foucault called "the carceral continuum."[42] Following the model of progressive penology, Iwahig applied techniques of reformation to convicts that were to be applied to all Filipinos. "The object of the prison," wrote Thomas Mott Osborne, "should be to produce not good prisoners but good citizens"; therefore, it was necessary "to apply the great underlying principles of democracy to all social problems: the family, the school and college, the factory—and even the prison."[43]

Democratic forms became part of a disciplinary apparatus, alongside and within institutions of punishment, paternalism, instruction, and labor. If the best penal reformatories re-created society in miniature, if they concentrated all of the means of discipline and training utilized in the larger society—self-government, private property, labor, schooling, military drill, the family, and even the prison as a space of punishment exterior to itself (in the way that Iwahig depended on Bilibid)—then where did the reformatory end and society begin? This is not to say there were no meaningful distinctions between being in prison and being free; every attempt at escape testified to that difference just as every disjuncture between Filipino life and the idealizations of American colonial rule testified to its phantasmagoric claims. Yet, to the extent that American rule incarcerated Filipinos in colonialism as a reformative asylum, we find a continuum of techniques of power that traversed, reduplicated, and reinscribed a series of concentric boundaries between groups defined as "civilized" and "uncivilized" from the prison to the special provinces to the colony as a whole.

Until 1935, the United States repeatedly declared its paternalistic intention to prepare Filipinos for self-government without fixing a date for independence. The early versions of the Jones Bill included minimum and maximum time spans for independence, but the version signed into law in 1916 did not specify any schedule at all. It only pledged the United States to recognize Philippine independence as soon as a stable government could be established. In structural terms this was the equivalent of the indeterminate sentence favored by progressive penology for its correlation of prison term with rehabilitation rather than with some quantity of time per given offense. It replicated a technique of power familiar to every master who promised his slave manumission in the future after years or a lifetime (the master's lifetime) of faithful service. Thomas Mott Osborne—a descendent of abolitionists, advocate of prison democracy, and one of the anti-imperialists' nominees for the post of colonial governor-general in 1913 when the Jones Bill seemed likely to bring independence near—believed the indeterminate sentence was essential to rational, humane, and effective penal reform.[44]

Paradoxes of Democracy and Progressive Reform

The capricious power of the state boomeranged on Osborne when he attempted penal reforms on Iwahig's scale in his native New York. After a steady climb through state politics to the chairmanship of the Commission on Prison Reform in 1913, Osborne won instant celebrity by spending a week as Prisoner No. 33,333 at Auburn Penitentiary, emerging to denounce "the prison system as singularly unintelligent, ineffective, and cruel," indeed, "the foulest blot on our social system."[45] Appointed warden of Sing Sing Prison in December 1914, Osborne, after dismissing the guards, stood alone in the chapel before more than a thousand prisoners to announce a system of self-policing. Under a regime similar to Iwahig's, prisoners would work for wages and be judged by their peers for any infractions of the rules.[46]

But these reforms soon plunged him into political wrangling with the governor, the state prison commissioner, and his own staff. As a grand jury collected evidence against him from some of Sing Sing's toughest criminals, Osborne, speaking to fifteen hundred supporters at Columbia University, blamed politics and his insistence that appropriations be spent on prisoners "not as graft into the pockets of contractors."[47] In December 1915, Osborne was indicted on charges of mismanagement and sodomy with inmates, producing a sensational trial that ended with his acquittal and a brief, triumphal return to Sing Sing.[48]

Osborne's ability to effect further reforms in New York was destroyed, however, and he soon resigned from Sing Sing. Thereafter, his experiment in inmate self-governance remained celebrated but unreplicated. The United States' growing prison complex soon turned increasingly punitive (rather than rehabilitative) in its design, became increasingly racialized, and now has outlived and surpassed its former rivals in the former Soviet Union and old apartheid South Africa as the world's largest.

Iwahig, however, continued to practice inmate self-governance under a succession of Filipino superintendents, although some of these administrators, such as Ramon Mitra Sr., also stood trial for graft and corruption.[49] In 1931, the American criminologist John R. Gillin published an international study on innovations in prison reform funded by the Social Science Research Council. After visiting prisons and penal colonies in the United States, British India and Ceylon, Japan, Switzerland, Belgium, England, and the Philippines, he found Iwahig to be the most remarkable and promising experiment in penal reform then in existence.[50]

At the edge of empire in far-off Palawan, colonial officials such as W. Cameron Forbes, John R. White, and Carroll H. Lamb could conduct social experiments relatively unchecked and largely unmindful of political constraints, playing confidently with Filipino adults in a way that their contemporaries back in the United

States would only do with American children. For their Filipino successors, the experiment at Iwahig was an object of national pride and further proof of the nation's fitness for self-government and independence.

But when the United States' most eminent prison reformer of the era, Thomas Mott Osborne, attempted similar domestic experiments the outcome foundered on the ability of entrenched interests to corrupt and cajole the administration of justice in New York State. At home, the reformer who would give the state full powers of discretion to determine prisoners' sentences on the basis of fitness was brought down by the same sovereign power he favored and depended on. The circulation of capricious power characterizes imperial America, as do the simulacra of democracy and freedom.

PART 3

EDUCATION

Class in lace making, Cabanatuan, Nueva Ecija, Philippines, 1912. (U.S. National Archives)

INTRODUCTION

ADAM NELSON

As MOST EDUCATORS WILL READILY ATTEST, it is often difficult to tell whether lessons taught in school are, in fact, learned or whether the explicit or implicit aims of education have their desired effect. In an imperial context, questions about the "effects" of education become more complex, mediated as they are by differences of political, economic, and military power as well as differences of race, language, and cultural identity.

The essays in this section shed light on the role that education—and specifically schools—played in structuring, negotiating, and setting the discursive terms of the United States' colonial project in Puerto Rico and the Philippines in the opening decades of the twentieth century. Taken together, these chapters demonstrate not only the ways in which schools in the United States set a course for policies carried out in the colonies but also the ways in which the colonies sometimes served as "crucibles" for educational policies in the United States. Thus education, broadly construed, became a two-way process of both teaching and learning in the American imperial state.

To start, Solsirée del Moral examines how teachers in Puerto Rico, anticipating the possibility of Puerto Rican independence, or in some cases the crafting of a Puerto Rican national space within the context of the American empire, reframed colonial schools' Americanization programs to promote "an alternate nationalist project." Elite teachers cast themselves as "the primary actors who would lead the island through a process of physical and intellectual evolution, racial regeneration, and national progress." Yet, as intermediaries between Puerto Rican families and colonial authorities, elite teachers' primary goal was not "to liberate the working class and rural poor" but rather "to consolidate their authority and status within the colonial social hierarchy." Del Moral's research brings to light not only the impact that U.S. colonialism had on subsequent

Puerto Rican education but also the role that educators played in creating an anticolonial, that is, nationalist or autonomist, movement.

The role of educators in the construction of Puerto Rican nationalism is a central theme in Amílcar Antonio Barreto's essay, which confirms that Americanization policies ultimately produced a countermovement in the form of Puerto Rican cultural nationalism. "In time," Barreto notes, "Americanization fueled resentment—particularly on the part of teachers hired to implement this policy." By the 1930s and 1940s, these teachers formed the heart of a nationalist movement built on an oppositional narrative of cultural identity. Teachers' role in this nationalist movement is intriguing if, as Barreto argues, many Catholic schoolteachers in Puerto Rico participated "eagerly" in Americanization programs, including English-language instruction; meanwhile, on the U.S. mainland, Catholic schools that had challenged Americanization programs for immigrants at the turn of the twentieth century had come to embrace such efforts in the changed geopolitical context of the 1930s and 1940s. Barreto's analysis raises important questions about the church's changing role in education in Puerto Rico (and elsewhere) over time.

Of course, the meaning of education is always "negotiated" between teachers and students, and Glenn May's essay on industrial education in the Philippines offers a case in point. Industrial education was not unique to the colonies nor was it always limited to marginalized populations. In the early twentieth century, so-called progressive educators in the United States believed that "hands-on learning" could benefit students of all social backgrounds even if it was targeted most often at racial minorities and the poor. What distinguished manual education in the Philippines from contemporary efforts on the mainland was the sheer scale of the colonial enterprise: more than a *million* students in the Philippines participated in farming, gardening, embroidery, and other industrial education programs during the period of American imperial rule.

The ostensible goal of these industrial programs was to make money. The education bureau chief in the Philippines hoped "to operate every trade school and every school farm on a business basis." Booker T. Washington had described his Tuskegee Institute in similar terms, but the "business" of manual training in the Philippines operated on a much larger scale.[1] May calculates that most industrial education programs in the colonial Philippines were spectacularly *unprofitable,* but in both colonial and metropolitan settings these programs served other purposes beyond profit. For example, the Philippines "corn campaigns," with their corn-growing and corn-cooking contests, had roots in mainland efforts such as 4-H clubs and the founding in 1928 of the Future Farmers of America, both of which sought to stem the migration of farmers off the land in the 1920s. Proving that lessons taught were not always learned, however, the Philippine corn campaign, intended to encourage the cultivation of a drought-resistant crop, failed to convince inhabitants of the archipelago that corn was fit for human consumption.

Each essay in this section reveals how educational ideas moved back and forth between the United States and the colonies. Pablo Navarro-Rivera, for his part, explores the consequences of Puerto Rican students' movement to the Carlisle Industrial School in Pennsylvania. Using a series of student letters, Navarro-Rivera examines the mixed feelings that Puerto Ricans had toward the education they received. Many expected Carlisle to offer professional education in fields such as business and law, only to discover a curriculum focused on manual training and cultural assimilation. Of the sixty Puerto Ricans who attended Carlisle between 1898 and 1918, eleven returned home and five ran away from the school. Only seven graduated. More research is needed to explain why some students returned to Puerto Rico and others did not. Did returnees differ in terms of social class, religious background, or perhaps the subjects they studied? What about those who chose to attend mainland universities; how did their experience of acculturation differ? Like the other chapters in this section, Navarro-Rivera's work raises key questions about the reciprocal influences of educational programs in the colonies and the metropole.

In the section's final essay, Courtney Johnson considers the link between the United States' experience with colonialism and the evolution of professional social science in the early twentieth century. Pointing to Secretary of War Elihu Root and a trio of contemporary political scientists—Leo Rowe of the University of Pennsylvania, Bernard Moses of the University of California, and Paul Reinsch of the University of Wisconsin—Johnson traces the gradual transformation of academic disciplines, such as international relations and international law, as they were redirected to support a "new," "soft," and "understanding" form of imperial power intended (ostensibly) to "advance global stability, safeguard the sovereignty of vulnerable nations, and wisely arbitrate international disputes."

These changes were not without their antecedents. The roots of these disciplines stretch back to the antebellum era in the work of such political economists as James Kent, Francis Lieber, and later Theodore Dwight Woolsey (each of whom grappled with the diplomatic implications of the Monroe Doctrine), and the sites of American imperial intervention in both the Caribbean and the Pacific had long been objects of academic inquiry (among natural scientists and missionary-scholars as well as early linguists and "ethnologists"). But at the turn of the twentieth century there were, as Johnson highlights, significant new links that emerged between university-based political scientists and Washington-based policy makers—a growing cadre of technocrats who, facing the perplexities of colonial administration and seeking empirically grounded theories of statecraft, took up the dual task of "imperial management abroad and social engineering at home."[2]

Of course, the idea of institutionalizing "colonial studies" in the American university was not entirely new in this period. In 1904, when Henry C. Morris proposed a "colonial institute" for the American Political Science Association, he echoed a proposal made to Thomas Jefferson more than a century earlier: in 1800, in a plan for a national university, Jefferson's friend Pierre Samuel du Pont de Nemours had sketched a "school of social science" in which future leaders could study not only "internal administration and political relations" but also "the law of nations, statistics, [and] colonization." In this plan, *colonization* was defined as "the art of persuading, explaining, [and] conquering by kindness; to establish, by means of honesty and by carefully planned labor increasing happiness, uprightness and success for the [United States' expanding territories]."[3] Parallels between du Pont's school and Morris's institute, separated by a century, are striking, indicating that empire, in this instance, may have allowed the implementation of ideas with a long domestic gestation.

All five essays in this section show how lessons from the colonies informed policies and practices in the metropole and vice versa. These connections make sense. After all, in the realm of education exchanges between the island periphery and the metropolitan state preceded formal empire by several decades. The well-known example of Samuel Chapman Armstrong is worth citing. Born to missionary parents in Hawai'i in the 1830s, Armstrong recalled his experience in Honolulu's mission schools when, after service in the Union Army and the Freedmen's Bureau, he founded the Hampton Institute in Virginia in 1870.[4] Hampton, in turn, served as a model for both Tuskegee and the Carlisle Indian School, lessons from which later flowed back—in circular fashion—to schools in Hawai'i as well as colonial Puerto Rico and the Philippines.

Education, whether in the form of Americanization policies, industrial training programs, or institutionalized social science, played a key role in the United States' imperial project. These essays reveal the myriad ways in which the colonies served as crucibles for educational policy making in the metropolitan state.

Negotiating Colonialism
"Race," Class, and Education in Early-Twentieth-Century Puerto Rico

SOLSIRÉE DEL MORAL

EARLY-TWENTIETH-CENTURY PUERTO RICAN HISTORY provides scholars of the Caribbean, Latin America, and American empire with a variety of examples to choose from when making the argument that local actors consistently challenged U.S. colonialism. The historical process of creating a colonial public school system in Puerto Rico, in particular, suggests that the "successful" implementation and practice of American "benevolent imperialism" on the island was profoundly dependent on the interests and motivations of local actors.[1] My historical analysis of "elite" Puerto Rican teachers in the early American colonial period (1898–1930s) is guided by the theories, methods, and arguments that emerge from comparative colonial examples.[2] The research questions and perspectives with which historians of the American colonies and territories approach their case studies necessarily challenge the traditional interpretations produced through dependence on colonial government documents as primary sources. Looking beyond government documents provides an opportunity to locate the voices and perspectives of local teachers and to center these actors in the broader study of U.S. colonialism. In this brief essay, I examine the implications of locating local actors at the center of our research agendas for reevaluating the consolidation of American empire in the colonies.

Placing the story of Puerto Rican teachers at the center of early colonial education narratives reveals the limits of the American empire. Americanization and the creation of "tropical Yankees" were essential aspects of the U.S. benevolent imperialism project.[3] Public school teachers responsible for daily implementation of the United States' goals of transforming colonial subjects into second-class U.S. citizens did not always share the colonial administrators' vision. Teachers, occupying an intermediate role in the colonial social hierarchy, negotiated school practices with their own agendas and ambitions. They mediated the imperial goals of consolidating colonialism through the schools with the contemporary debates on the island. Political, economic, and cultural leaders in the early twentieth century debated the political trajectory the island would potentially follow (annexation or autonomy) in the coming years. Although teachers were practicing within a colonial school system, the citizenship-building venture they carried out in the classroom was based on a fundamental belief that the island would emerge from its current, but temporary, colonial relationship with the United States. When we examine the teachers' perspectives and interjections into the practice of colonial education on the island, we are better able to attest to the challenges and limits they posed to the full implementation of Americanization policies.

Recognizing how Puerto Rican teachers navigated the imposition of Americanization policies also brings to light the contradictions and ironies of the colonial school project. Elite teachers proposed an alternative citizenship-building project that imagined the "racial" regeneration of the working-class student body through the teaching and practice of modern education. The racialized citizenship-building project was also constructed around class. Existing Puerto Rican racial ideologies and class hierarchies informed the teachers' emerging middle-class, Hispanic identity as well as their characterizations of and relationships with students. Elite teachers were able to promote their project within a colonial school system because its racial and class implications resonated, though uncomfortably, with the broader intentions of Americanization policies.

"Elite" Teachers, Citizenship, and Colonialism

On December 8, 1920, the acting principal of schools for the Puerto Rican municipality of Coamo, Manuel Ortiz de la Renta, proudly submitted to the island governor an announcement for a school conference organized by local teachers. The governor of Puerto Rico, Arthur Yager, designated December 5–11 as "School Week" for the purpose of highlighting in local communities the progress of public education on the island, as well as bringing to light the improvements and expansion still required and forthcoming with public support.[4] The Coamo organizing committee called on its "fellow citizens" to take an interest in public instruction for it was a critical "factor in the progressive action of the people of Puerto Rico."[5] Progress seemed inevitable now that both Puerto Rican educators and American colonial officials had designated public schools as the critical institution for progress and teachers as the primary actors who would transform the island's children and their families through education.

Puerto Rico's governor received a similar update from the western city of Mayagüez. The interim director of the Boys Reform School, E. San Millán, submitted to the governor a report of the activities carried out by teachers and students at the correctional institution, as well as newspaper clippings documenting and celebrating their School Week participation. One of the primary events included having the *asilados,* or "inmates," parade throughout the city on two separate days, carrying banners that read "A people who does not educate its children, creates its own misfortune" and "Schools signify progress; illiteracy, misfortune."[6] The newspaper clipping San Millán submitted with his report was titled "Hacer Patria" or "To Build the Nation."

> The practice of making *patria* is entrusted, in part, to the mentors of our youth. Making *patria*, developing patriots, is the noblest of missions that the guides and shepherds of peoples can have. . . . And you make *patria,* creating a youth that is vigorous, strong, dedicated, enterprising, lover of progress, idolatrous of the virtue of citizenship, and defender of its land and its home.[7]

The key to forming a community of citizens committed to contributing to the nation-building process was education, a responsibility that fell primarily on teachers' shoulders. The reporter concluded his congratulatory summary of the reform school's activities by exclaiming, "Let us build *patria* through the school . . . let us make patriots through instruction."[8]

It is significant that these reports on the part of teachers, local principals, and newspaper reporters failed to make explicit reference to the practice of Americanization at the local level. Instead, they reflected a sense of urgency for participating in the wave of progress, evolution, and transformation that seemed to be sweeping through the island. Local actors were calling for the formation of citizens and participation in nation-building processes while locating teachers and public schools as the people and institutions that would lead the student body through the progression. The goal was not the creation of Americanized second-class citizens supportive of U.S. colonialism on the island but rather first-class Puerto Rican citizens ready to contribute to the emerging island nation.

Although Puerto Rico was a colony, different actors debated its future political status. Whether the island would develop a relationship as an integral member of the United States through annexation or, in the near future, emerge from its colonial relationship and undertake the process of nation building, creating healthy, moral, and modern citizens was a precursor to either political position. The teachers' flyer suggested that, although the people of Puerto Rico did not yet meet the intellectual, physical, and moral requirements of citizenship, with the help of public instruction they could be transformed into a healthy, moral, and intelligent community of citizens that would compose the future Puerto Rican nation. Teachers were going to help their students evolve from colonial subjects into national citizens, from illiterates into intellectuals capable of comprehending and practicing their civic duties. Teachers and educators would reach into the island's most distant and isolated, rural, and traditional communities and incorporate them into a modern, progressive, and democratic nation. The teachers' flyer and the Mayagüez newspaper report both suggested teachers and educators imagined an alternative citizenship-building project to the U.S. colonial educational policy of Americanization. This is one of many examples of the way teachers promoted their own political vision for Puerto Rico. Significantly, because this vision fell outside the Americanization project it has received scant attention in the historical literature on Puerto Rico.

The flyer and newspaper report also generated many questions. Why were Puerto Rican teachers assuming that rural folk were illiterate, backward, and traditional and urban workers potentially immoral and physically degenerate? Coamo teachers and the Mayagüez reporter asked their communities to take advantage of the opportunity to embark on the modern evolutionary path provided through schools. The "Puerto Rican race," they suggested, was in a state of degeneracy, and they further argued that teachers were *the* primary actors who would lead the island through the process of physical and intellectual evolution, racial regeneration, and national progress. The teachers' flyer and newspaper report hinted at the multiple contradictions within the teachers' colonial school project in the early twentieth century. Puerto Rican teachers and educators may have rejected Americanization policies; however, their goal was not to liberate the working class and rural poor from their alleged traditions, isolation, and resulting illiteracy. While they promoted their visions of citizenship and nation building, teachers and educators would attempt to consolidate their authority and status within the colonial social hierarchy by reinforcing the island's conservative racial, class, and gender relationships.

These examples suggest a reconsideration of the emphasis on Americanization policies within Puerto Rican historiography. Historical narratives about colonial education have carefully adhered to the initial interpretation presented in the seminal work of Aida Negrón de Montilla.[9] Negrón de Montilla surveyed the educational policies promoted by individual commissioners of education in order to achieve the effective Americanization of Puerto Rican colonial subjects. These included emphasizing English-language instruction, celebrating American patriots through school plays and public parades, replacing locally produced textbooks with approved versions, organizing the school system according to American models, and replacing local teachers with American instructors. New evidence uncovered on the role of teachers and educators in the early school system necessitates a reconsideration of the dominant role assigned to American educators and Americanization policies within historical narratives based primarily on government documents written by elite commissioners of education appointed by American presidents. While a central part of American-style benevolent imperialism was the establishment of a public school system that attended to the educational needs of the island's allegedly neglected population, government-appointed commissioners were not the only actors engaged in the process of constructing educational policy.

Instead of focusing primarily on the annual reports of the commissioner of education, scholars should also examine the variety of documentation produced by Puerto Rican actors engaged in the colonial education project.[10] Local schoolteachers, the leadership of the Asociación de Maestros de Puerto Rico (AMPR), and other island educators produced a variety of textual materials that spoke to the challenges of establishing and negotiating the goals of colonial schools.[11] In examining these sources in order to better understand how ideas about science, race, and nation were debated through the lens of schools and public education, I have sought to foreground the competing perspectives presented by a range of teachers, local and regional educators (principals, school inspectors, local school boards, parent-teacher organizations), and an assortment of Puerto Rican and American education administrators within the Department of Education. Reexamining the everyday processes of "nation building within the colony" from the perspective of different local actors encourages us to deconstruct and challenge the traditional narratives based on elite, American colonial voices.

Since Puerto Rico's colonial status and its relationship with the United States were not fully consolidated, teachers were functioning within the ambiguity of the island's colonial status and the acquisition of U.S. citizenship. Their intention was to prepare their students to assume the responsibilities of citizenship, either in the United States or Puerto Rico. They imagined this would be clearly defined in the near future.[12] A revisionist interpretation of the role of public education in early-twentieth-century Puerto Rican nation-building processes, asks that we turn our attention away from the traditional focus on English-language instruction and Americanization practices and consider alternative expressions of race, citizenship, and colonialism. By examining the rich documentation produced by teachers, educators, and administrators, it is clear that colonial Americanization policies were rarely, if ever, the teachers' primary concern.

Instead, teachers and educators were more concerned with crafting a nation-building project that advocated the racial regeneration of the Puerto Rican citizenry. The teachers' regeneration project was built on both local appropriations of the theory of "modern education" and the particular way they viewed "racial degeneracy" among the student population. American educators initially introduced the modern education concept, a post–World War I concept that promoted a three-pronged approach to the formation of well-rounded citizens through the teaching of moral, intellectual, and physical education. Puerto Rican teachers adapted this approach to preexisting local concerns over the physical defects or "racial degeneracy" of the Puerto Rican people. The racial degeneracy concept argued that the Puerto Rican "race" could be eugenically improved. Diseases, such as tuberculosis, malaria, and hookworm, and the "racial poisons" children experienced in the home and on the streets, such as alcoholism, gambling, and prostitution, combined to produce a degenerate version of the island's allegedly founding "Iberian race." These factors, in combination with the presumed illiteracy, backward traditions, and isolation of rural folk, meant that Puerto Rican individuals and family units were degenerate or abnormal. It was this "racial" degeneracy that teachers sought to combat directly through public instruction. Teachers were engaging the socially constructed concept of race to refer to the national citizenry. According to Nancy Leys Stepan, neo-Lamarckian eugenic philosophy argued that "racial poisons" exposed future generations to environmental damages that could reproduce physical, intellectual, and moral weaknesses in the race or the national body.[13] I contend that schoolteachers combined the application of modern education theory with a neo-Lamarckian belief in the possibility of racial regeneration in order to combat what they saw as the triple plague of illiteracy, delinquency, and disease in Puerto Rico.

Specifically, modern education and racial regeneration ideologies came together in discussions over the potential regenerative benefits of teaching home economics, modern agriculture, and physical education. Teachers were optimistic that they could regenerate and whiten the Puerto Rican national body through the teaching of health, hygiene, and sanitation. They would transform the allegedly physically weak and submissive Puerto Rican girls into modern and progressive homemakers by teaching domestic science in the schools and by bringing that science directly into homes through extension work. They would transform the ignorant rural *jíbaros,* or "peasants," into efficient farmers by teaching modern scientific methods of agriculture in rural schools. They would regenerate the weakened national race through the teaching of science, health, hygiene, and physical education. They would also teach literacy, civics, and academic courses that would transform their illiterate students into well-rounded citizens in the service of a potential Puerto Rican nation. Local teachers believed that by introducing the modern science that informed these school topics to the students, and by extension their parents, they could directly address the problems of the home, health, and labor of island families and instill in them modern strategies for regeneration. It was this goal, the racial regeneration of the citizenry, instead of Americanization that Puerto Rican teachers advocated throughout the early twentieth century.

In light of this we must reevaluate the traditional definition of *Americanization* in Puerto Rico, the United States, and other colonies. As local teachers and government officials on the island and mainland engaged Americanization, its goals went beyond creating English-speaking, pro-American, second-class citizens. Americanization also created the space for imagining the racial regeneration of the new citizens. Historical narratives have characterized Americanization as a clearly defined political project meant to incorporate Puerto Ricans into the U.S. colonial hierarchy, to de-Latinize and de-Africanize the social and cultural heritage of the island, and to turn Puerto Ricans into acceptable political, social, and cultural representations of U.S. colonial subjectivity. Centering Puerto Rican teachers in the debate requires a reconsideration of the traditional conceptualization of Americanization policy within Puerto Rican historiography while suggesting that local actors, both Puerto Rican teachers and American colonial administrators, were engaging a broader definition of Americanization that incorporated the goal of the racial regeneration of nonwhite peoples within the American empire. An expansive definition of Americanization allowed teachers to promote their regeneration agenda through the colonial education hierarchy without directly challenging the top-down political policy of Americanization. However, teachers chose not to use the language of Americanization and instead employed a discourse of national and racial regeneration. The teachers' project suggests an alternative to traditional visions of Americanization while simultaneously engaging in the redefinition of Americanization on the mainland vis-à-vis immigrants and in the colonies vis-à-vis new colonial subjects.

Race, Class, and Intermediate Categories

My work on the Puerto Rican teachers' national regeneration project also forms part of broader discussions within Latin American and Caribbean scholarship about race and nation in the late nineteenth and early twentieth centuries. The postrevisionist scholarship on race in Latin America has reached the consensus that "race is a contingent social and historical construct; racial identities are not simply determined by ancestry or phenotype.... Other factors, such as economic class, social context, and political mobilization contribute to shaping how people identify racially (though we do not always agree which factors have been the most important)."[14] I examine the multiple uses of the concept of race, as well as the process of racialization, defined as "the process of marking human differences according to hierarchical discourses grounded in colonial encounters and their national legacies," through the lens of colonial education.[15] The racial self-identity of the teaching force, tied to its middle-class professional image, and its racialization of the student body were informed by a combination of historical factors. Preexisting island social hierarchies, a product of Spanish colonialism and local negotiations, were further complicated by the American occupation of Puerto Rico in the early twentieth century and the way American definitions of race and racial hierarchies conflicted and complemented the ones already in place. The elite teachers' project of citizenship building was primarily a project of racial regeneration, which was based on a popular eugenic and scientific understanding of the concept of biological race in combination with social and cultural processes of racialization. Puerto Rican teachers' deployment of the categories of race and nation was part of the process of "popular and elite expressions of race and national identity in post independence Latin America." My case study lends support to the argument that "national identities have been constructed in racial terms and that definitions of race have been shaped by processes of nation building."[16]

The critical roles that intermediate, urban, and middle-class groups played in local, regional, and national politics have increasingly become central research questions in Latin American and Caribbean scholarship. In particular, the work of Greg Grandin for Guatemala and Marisol de la Cadena for Peru provides a critical lens for understanding how intermediate groups negotiated their racial and class identity with elites and differentiated themselves from the subaltern.[17] Both Grandin and De la Cadena assert the central role of education, schooling, and literacy in the construction of a middle-class identity as validation of the potential in the practice of regeneration and as a requirement for fulfilling citizenship responsibilities and contributing to nation-building processes. This "power of education to transform race" was a central part of the discourse employed by Puerto Rican teachers and educators.[18] According to the elite intellectual tradition in Puerto Rico at the turn of the century, the island was imagined to be inhabited by descendants of Iberian Latin heritage who had degenerated due to their isolation and traditional practices.[19] However, under the new colonial system, it would be public school teachers who were empowered with the resources to help regenerate students into modern citizens through the teaching of literacy, hygiene, and morality. At a moment when the island's racial Latin identity was being forged as a tool to contest Anglo-Saxon cultural values, the potential for internal racial regeneration through education became a powerful contribution to the nation-building process of which teachers demanded to be a part.

Elite teachers also constructed a middle-class professional identity by creating distance from the highly politicized working class of the 1920s and 1930s. Teachers' literacy, their positions of authority over the student body, their mobility throughout the island, and their right to "associate" as a class and to negotiate their interests defined their middle-class status and their location within the colonial hierarchy. As emerging middle-class actors, elite teachers claimed a white, Hispanic heritage and argued that it was (and they were) not inferior to the Anglo-Saxon race despite the fact that some were of racially mixed or African descent. As racial, and therefore national, regeneration became the central goal of their educational project, elite teachers increasingly constructed a negative image of "Latin" (i.e., Latin American or Hispanic) degeneracy in the student body and simultaneously silenced expressions of blackness.[20] This was part of the process by which elite teachers constructed their own class and racial identity as a professional, middle-class, respectable group.

The teaching class occupied an intermediate role within the island's colonial hierarchy. Their writings suggest that they considered themselves to be socially, economically, and culturally superior to the working class. In addition, some aspired to affiliate themselves with the professional and social standing of the island's elite. In turn, the island's elite would have traditionally rejected teachers' claims to social mobility outside their intermediate status. Meanwhile, hierarchies existed within the teaching class itself. Their writings suggest the enforcement and redefinition of generational, gender, and class hierarchies within the teaching force throughout the early twentieth century.

Elite teachers from the 1910s through the 1930s also comprised a varied group of social reformers that imagined the evolution, regeneration, and uplift of the Puerto Rican citizenry. The arguments and visions presented by elite teachers in relation to physical education, home economics, and rural agriculture were mediated by significant historical events and social movements that shaped early-twentieth-century Puerto Rico such as World War I, the Jones Act, U.S. citizenship, the Great Depression, hurricanes, and labor militancy. Their vision for rural regeneration, while informed by the late-nineteenth-century Puerto Rican intellectual arguments traditionally presented by members of the medical profession, was mediated by the historical experience of the early twentieth century and by the teachers' intermediate location within the colonial hierarchy. Additionally, elite teachers represented a reform program on which the 1930s nativist technocrats and the 1940s populists would build. The historically significant 1934 Chardón Plan tested its policies of promoting native industry and local farming with the help of agricultural instruction and rural schools. In addition, the elite teacher discourse of rescuing the rural peasantry would resonate with the discursive strategies of Luis Muñoz Marín and the Popular Democratic Party throughout the 1940s.

Local Negotiations of Empire

The elite teachers' national and racial regeneration project and the teaching force itself were fraught with contradictions and ironies. It is at precisely these moments that we can better understand the racial and class hierarchies created and reproduced within the colonial school system. In organizing a school project with the goal of creating Puerto Rican rather than American citizens, local teachers and educators rejected Americanization practices. They promoted their project within the colonial school system, however. While they did not directly challenge colonialism, they negotiated the implementation of their own project within the limits of colonialism. Their goal may have been to regenerate the citizenry, but in the process they reified the paternalism that elites reserved for the working class. As an example of the negative depictions of race and class among the student body, some elite teachers and educators portrayed an image of the student body that characterized these potential Puerto Rican citizens no differently than American colonial officials had—as poor, ignorant, traditional, backward, dirty, and black. On closer examination, then, in addition to providing an alternative to colonial Americanization efforts, elite teachers reinforced existing social hierarchies that defined the limits and boundaries of citizenship for the imagined Puerto Rican nation.

The Puerto Rican case study suggests that elite teachers and American colonial officials shared ideologies about race and education that facilitated the consolidation of everyday forms of colonialism. Clearly, there were points of contention and disagreement between local teachers and colonial administrators around the definitions and goals of U.S. citizenship within a colonial space, the relationship between language and cultural identity, the perspective presented in textbooks authorized by the United States, and the activities incorporated into pro-American patriotic school activities. Around these issues, we often found teachers and colonial administrators at opposite ends of the spectrum, though opinions varied within both camps. Nevertheless, beyond the traditional divisions between these two sets of actors and the dominant debates over language and political status, we can identify other locations of contestation, negotiation, and accommodation that led to the consolidation of a colonial school system. Elite teachers and American colonial officials hesitantly forged a space in which they negotiated goals of regenerating the citizenry.

While elite Puerto Rican teachers and American officials interpreted the "racial" heritage of the student body through different lenses and definitions of *race*, both sets of actors maintained negative and derogatory characterizations. They agreed that what they witnessed in the classrooms and throughout public spaces on the island were examples of "Latin degeneracy." Meanwhile, both groups maintained faith in the transformative power of public instruction. They shared the belief that modern education provided the majority of the student body with the science and knowledge required for social uplift and regeneration. Teachers and colonial officials disagreed over the definition of *citizen*, which was to be created through the public schools, but never wavered on the progressive relationship between public education and citizenship building. These shared ideologies in the power of modern education and the state of racial degeneracy brought teachers and colonial officials to the table and created the discourse and vision for negotiating everyday practices of colonialism through the schools. This case study suggests that the American empire was daily reproduced within Puerto Rican public schools because it was malleable enough to incorporate those interests, demands, visions, and projects local actors already maintained and defended.

Enlightened Tolerance or Cultural Capitulation?

Contesting Notions of American Identity

AMÍLCAR ANTONIO BARRETO

AFTER THE CANNONS COOLED Spain reluctantly relinquished Cuba, Guam, the Philippines, and Puerto Rico. Until the late nineteenth century American expansion followed a fairly simple pattern. Indigenous peoples were rounded up, corralled into reservations, or simply massacred, allowing citizens back East to colonize the West. But the new territories from the 1898 war were far from the Union's constituent states. Geographic and demographic impediments challenged the traditional methods of amalgamating new territories. If it was impractical to settle these colonies with old-stock Americans federal authorities determined to give them what they considered the next best thing—American culture and norms. What these policy makers could not have imagined was the unanticipated consequences of Americanization. This policy's extension overseas would spark a chain of events that would eventually challenge the role played by ethnicity and ideology in the American national narrative.

Americanization, which first targeted the country's German-speaking minority, began in the late eighteenth century.[1] "Americanization policies, like the *Manifest Destiny* notions that sustained it, not only served the dominant Anglo-Protestant sectors in supporting the expansionist policy of the United States, but also as a political and cultural resource for the production of American nationalism and, with it, U.S. national development, integration and identity."[2] Western expansion followed by statehood was intended to reabsorb old-stock Americans who moved westward and not incorporate new peoples into the national family.[3] Those who were not American had to *become* American. In 1789 Noah Webster claimed, "It must be considered further, that the English is the common root or stock from which our national language will be derived. All others will gradually waste away—and within a century and a half, North America will be peopled with a hundred millions of men, *all speaking the same language.*"[4] Thus, those retaining their previous vernaculars and cultural identities were branded as suspicious and possibly subversive.[5]

While American society largely disregarded immigrants—exception for celebrating national holidays—immigrant children were another matter.[6] Schools exposed them to a new language and traditions: "Immigrants were disparaged for their cultural peculiarities, and the implied message was, 'You will become like us whether you want to or not.' When it came to racial minorities, however, the unspoken dictum was 'No matter how much like us you are, you will remain apart.'"[7] State-run educational bureaucracies are far from neutral purveyors of information. Regimes design schools as training grounds to generate forthcoming generations of obedient citizens.[8] American public schools prepared native-born and immigrant children to accept roles as loyal citizens. They would prepare the country's new colonial wards in the same way—via government-run schools.

Shortly after the Spanish-Cuban-Philippine-American War President McKinley commissioned a study of the new Puerto Rican colony. Its author, Henry Carroll, boasted, "They will learn our customs and usages, in so far as they are better than their own, as they learn our language."[9] Prior to World War I Theodore Roosevelt emphasized, "We have room for but one language here and that is the English language."[10] In a letter appointing José Gallardo Puerto Rico's education commissioner in 1937 President Franklin Roosevelt wrote that Puerto Ricans had to learn English—the only medium through which islanders could learn "American ideals and principles."[11] Belying an official creed of liberty and equality was a belief in the ethnic and racial superiority of Anglo-Protestants. Such notions justified rejecting calls for greater Puerto Rican autonomy.[12] As Edward Said contended, this presumption of "greatness" endures in American foreign policy and popular attitudes.[13]

Policy optimization depended on staffing schools with Americans teachers.[14] Puerto Rico's distance from the U.S. mainland made that preference impractical. When available, American teachers were favored over locals for high-level administrative posts.[15] Indeed, the island's education commissioners were presidential appointees eager to carry out Washington's dictates to the fullest extent possible.[16] Americanization was also enforced by various nongovernmental organizations, including an array of new Protestant churches whose proselytizing included providing social services, such as hospitals, in a society where the Spanish state had invested paltry resources.[17] The Catholic Church also heeded Americanization's call once its Spanish prelates were replaced with Americans. Both Catholic and Protestant churches established private schools, eagerly promoting Americanization beyond encouraging language shift.[18] Both church and state assumed that Anglo-American cultural norms and practices were imperative.

Nationalism Begets Counternationalism

Among the few Puerto Ricans who espoused Americanization were statehood advocates who saw English-language acquisition as a prerequisite for admission into the Union.[19] In time Americanization fueled resentment—particularly on the part of teachers hired to implement this policy:[20] "Far from destroying Puerto Rico's national identity, the import of U.S. culture has strengthened the sense of Puerto Ricanness by providing a counterexample of what Puerto Ricanness is not."[21] Unforeseen by its Washington promoters this government-sanctioned American nationalism fueled a Puerto Rican counterpart.[22] Federal officials failed to understand that cultural assimilation is more likely to occur as an "accidental by-product" than by design.[23]

As a state-sponsored directive Americanization was enforced in Puerto Rico from 1899 until 1949. By the early 1950s American policy makers had granted islanders a modest degree of local autonomy, all the while holding ultimate military, economic, and political control. The 1952 Commonwealth Constitution was not designed to free Puerto Ricans from the *territorial clause* of the federal Constitution. Still, one of the first policies implemented by the first locally elected government was establishing Spanish as the medium of public school instruction.[24] Private schools retained their own language policies. The half-century-long conflict over language and education policy was central to the political struggle over the island's autonomy.[25] Interestingly, the bureaucrats implementing Americanization never operated under any federal statute establishing English as the official language. They functioned under a "covert" language policy.[26] In societies dominated by one ethnic community the lines separating loyalty to the state and its dominant ethnic group are often blurred.[27]

We need to clarify that nationalists aspire to correspond ethnic and political boundaries. Territorial-political ambitions differentiate ethnic aspirations from their nationalist counterparts.[28] In the case of Puerto Rico, most nationalists are autonomists.[29] Luis Muñoz Marín, the champion of commonwealth status, amply employed a moderate nationalism.[30] This soft-core nationalism has even found a cozy home in the island's statehood movement under the aegis of cultural autonomy within a larger political federation.[31] Local intellectuals led the campaign against Americanization.[32] This nationalist swell continued until the 1950s when support for independence decayed thanks to significant improvements in the local standard of living combined with state-sanctioned intimidation of independence supporters.[33] This separatist intelligentsia was shepherded largely by descendants of the hacienda-owning classes, who saw their economic fortunes and social privileges deteriorate with the advent of American rule.[34]

Generally speaking, ethnic mythmakers pen their nationalist saga out of preexisting narratives.[35] Puerto Rican intellectuals reinterpreted Spanish rule, glorifying

Iberian customs, Roman Catholicism, and the Spanish language.[36] Thus, for Vicente Géigel Polanco, "Our historic formation derives from the age of America's discovery."[37] In the 1930s Antonio Pedreira insisted that "Culturally we are and continue being a Hispanic colony."[38] For the revolutionary, Pedro Albizu Campos, "The motherland, Spain, [was the] noble founder of the modern world civilization" and its common faith, Catholicism, was responsible for the evaporation of any deep racial divisions within the Puerto Rican nation.[39] Such Hispanocentric perspectives were institutionalized in the Puerto Rican government's Institute of Culture.[40] These interpretations fit within a larger framework of Arielism—an intellectual current popular among Latin American intellectuals in the 1930s.[41] José E. Rodó's *Ariel* juxtaposed the soulless utilitarianism of Anglo North American society with a rich and spiritual heritage common to Spanish America.[42]

Nationalist mythmakers are at liberty to fabricate when others do not notice if precise information about the past is not accessible and where the adversary is too weak.[43] Thus, mythmakers have the greatest flexibility in the early stages of national consciousness—before most have already embraced one particular narrative.[44] Ethnic entrepreneurs—whether from a minority or the majority—simplify their organizational labors by exploiting a small set of group characteristics.[45] Logically, while Washington defined Americans as Anglo-Protestants, some early-twentieth-century Puerto Rican nationalist mythmakers penned a Spanish-speaking and Catholic counternarrative.

Beginning in the 1940s mass migration to and from the island created a condition whereby half of all Puerto Ricans now reside on the U.S. mainland. Ships and later airplanes became new symbols of this itinerant reality.[46] On the mainland Puerto Ricans, like other Latinos, are exposed to many of its subaltern forms of national identification, particularly in urban and African American communities.[47] Their daily cultural milieu may be quite varied. Still, the basic line separating Anglo-American from Puerto Rican endures even for English-dominant *puertorriqueños*.[48]

Institutionalized Duplicity

Although it was never declared a fundamental policy change, the decision to abandon Americanization constituted a major milestone. Washington operated under the assumption that one cultural norm had to be disseminated or imposed throughout the country and its dependencies.[49] Rexford Tugwell, one of Puerto Rico's last appointed governors, said of Franklin Roosevelt, "He just never did think Puerto Ricans were the equal of continental Americans."[50] This was reinforced by reports from Tugwell's predecessors—Governors Blanton Winship and William D. Leahy—who portrayed Puerto Ricans as "unruly and anti-American."[51] With the ascent of separatist and autonomist political parties in the 1940s Roosevelt had to recalibrate his apprehensions about the Nazi threat to the

Caribbean with rising resentment in Puerto Rico.[52] In 1943 Roosevelt agreed to move toward increasing Puerto Rican self-government, asking Congress to allow islanders to elect their own governor even while emphasizing Puerto Rico's importance to U.S. strategic interests in the region.[53]

American willingness to augment Puerto Rican autonomy was not unconditional. Under the Jones Act (in effect from 1917 to 1952) presidents could dismiss the act of a territorial legislature even if the measure was passed superseding a veto by Puerto Rico's governor. Roosevelt's successor, Harry S. Truman, exercised that authority twice in 1946—once when the Puerto Rican legislature voted to organize a plebiscite on the island's status and once when the insular administration voted to establish Spanish as the language of instruction in the public school system.[54] By 1948 Truman was willing to accede to the popular will of the island's people even if their preferred status was independence, emphasizing that he had always opposed colonialism.[55] In a speech delivered in San Juan, Truman said, "Differing languages and differing cultural backgrounds are not an obstacle to democratic unity. Such differences can provide the basis for a richer and stronger democracy."[56] He made it clear that granting Puerto Ricans the right to elect their governors would serve as a template for greater self-rule in Hawai'i and Alaska.[57] But cultural assimilation was still the goal on the U.S. mainland, as exemplified in Truman's policy toward Indian reservations.[58] In his days in the Senate, Truman had a very positive voting record on civil rights issues, although this commitment was driven more by electoral expediency than a deep philosophical devotion to the cause.[59]

Taking the first steps toward tolerance in the 1950s and 1960s was more in line with putting up with cultural heterogeneity than with embracing nondominant sociocultural forms and expressions. Forging Americanization in an overseas territory was not the same as forgoing it in a state.[60] Historically, statehood applicants had to demonstrate a commitment to advancing the English language.[61] Contemporary discussions of linguistic diversity center less on admitting non-Anglophone territories into the Union than on growing non-Anglophone, particularly Latino, communities.[62]

The debate over cultural diversity has unmasked a deep-seated paradox in popular perceptions of the nature of American national identity. Documents such as Declaration of Independence extol a common ideology. Seymour M. Lipset went so far as to describe an American ideology built atop four pillars: antistatism, individualism, populism, and egalitarianism.[63] Such a designation is open to any and all willing to embrace the same fundamental philosophical tenets.[64] Yet intertwined with an ideologically defined identity was an exclusionary variant. As John Jay wrote two centuries ago, "With equal pleasure I have as often taken notice that Providence has been pleased to give this one connected country to one united people—a people descended from the same ancestors, speaking the same language, professing the same religion, attached to the same principles of government, very similar in their manners and customs."[65]

More recent mythmakers insist that the American identity is Anglo-Protestant at its core.[66] The very reason for the country's existence, Samuel Huntington insisted, was to set up a Protestant state akin to Israel's role as Jewish sanctuary or Pakistan's raison d'être as a Muslim homeland in British India.[67] Multiculturalism, he insisted, endangers the United States and other Western societies, and thus Latin American immigration is proclaimed the most significant threat to the country's integrity.[68] Such ethnocentric comments underscore the fact that for many "all true Americans" should be able trace their ancestry to the British Isles despite the simultaneous propagation of a parallel, if not schizophrenic, national creed emphasizing liberal ideology over ethnicity.[69] American identity frequently has been restricted by race, thus challenging the official ideological national identity.[70]

Articulating national identities relies on distinguishing *us* versus *them*. Latin American nationalists glorified the racially mixed mestizo as the paradigmatic national.[71] Lauding their mestizo heritage also allowed Creole mythmakers to conveniently appropriate elements from the precolonial past even as they sidelined their living indigenous populations.[72] Americans had a harder time separating themselves from their British kin. Therefore, they turned to ideology, becoming *liberty-loving* Anglo-Saxons in North America. While ethnicity distinguished Americans from German immigrants, indigenous peoples, and slaves, it was philosophy that set Americans apart from the British. This dual, if not schizophrenic, identity endured until the culture clashes of the second half of the twentieth century.

Conclusion

Puerto Rico was by no means responsible for the cultural explosions of the 1960s. Nonetheless, this was the first major case in which federal policy makers abandoned Americanization. This was the case that *got the ball rolling*. Accepting cultural difference also helped to expose the inherent contradictions in a national identity publicly presented in ideological form while confidentially embracing cultural exclusivism. Dropping the insistence of cultural uniformity overseas made it easier to accept the same principles on the U.S. mainland. This is not to say that Anglocentric norms will fade any time soon. But in time the articulation of an Anglocentrist American identity may be more prevalent among rural and lower status whites than among their urban and wealthier counterparts.[73] What policy makers could not count on back in 1898 was the implementation of the omnipresent law of unanticipated consequences.

The Business of Education in the Colonial Philippines, 1909–30

GLENN ANTHONY MAY

THE PHOTOGRAPHS, OR ONES LIKE THEM, are familiar to some of us. In one of them, about thirty young Filipino schoolboys, all neatly dressed, are seated in a classroom. Unfinished handwoven hats are resting on their laps. Some of the boys are looking at their handiwork, but most are distracted by the presence of the camera. In a similar picture, half a dozen young Filipinas wearing white dresses are seated at their desks busily working on lace designs. Pictures of such public school activities—hat making, lace making, sewing, cooking, embroidery, and gardening—filled colonial government reports during American rule. Despite a certain innocent charm, they are, in fact, quintessential images of empire. They record an asymmetric, dyadic relationship in which only one-half of the dyad is physically present: the Filipino children, seated and posed, producing the handicraft items they have been instructed to produce. Not present are the American rulers who have issued the instructions and staged the Kodak moments.

From 1909 to 1930, American educational policy makers in the colony prioritized "industrial education"—a term used to describe both manual training classes given in the lower grades and vocational training provided in the higher grades. The program developed by these American administrators was huge, and the number of students involved was staggering. In 1910, there were slightly more than 350,000 pupils engaged in industrial work in Philippine primary schools alone. By 1924, at the apogee of the industrial education movement, the number had risen to approximately 900,000.[1]

In the course of my examination of this educational program, I offer evidence on three recurrent themes: that many of the policies introduced in the colonial periphery were variants of policies already tried and tested in the imperial metropolis; that, once launched, these policy initiatives sometimes went well beyond their U.S. models; and, finally, that, as was the case in most modern empires, such attempts at social engineering in the American colonies only infrequently achieved the policy makers' stated objectives.

The Emergence of a Program

In the late nineteenth and early twentieth centuries, industrial education was very much in vogue in the United States and much of Europe.[2] Its advocates argued that it developed the work ethic, taught pupils things of intellectual value (technical skills, facility with tools, and the like), and prepared them for specific vocations. By the 1890s, industrial work had become an important part of the curriculum in school districts around the United States. In addition, industrial education received especially strong support from American educators involved in the teaching of African Americans, Native Americans, and other non-Caucasians, who were thought by such educators to be poorly suited for purely academic instruction.

Given the belief that industrial education was valuable in the instruction of "backward races," it was hardly surprising that American colonial administrators agreed that the Philippine school curriculum should include a healthy component of industrial work. But those administrators disagreed, sometimes acrimoniously, about exactly how much emphasis should be placed on that work. One policy maker in particular, David Barrows, the head of the Bureau of Education from 1903 to 1909, favored a traditional academic curriculum emphasizing the "three R's," reading, writing, and arithmetic. During Barrows's tenure, a debate raged within the bureau about the place of industrial education in the curriculum. The matter was not settled until Barrows left the Philippines in 1909 and was replaced by Frank White, an eight-year veteran of the Philippine educational system who was a champion of industrial education.[3]

Soon after assuming the directorship, White laid out the basic program of industrial instruction that the bureau was to follow for the next decade and a half. It had three key elements. First, while White wanted the schools to continue developing the intellectual capacities of Filipinos through "literary" instruction (English language, civics, and the like), he now placed added emphasis on the direct "material" benefits of industrial classes. The schools, he wrote toward the beginning of his tenure, would aim to contribute to the "material welfare of the country."[4] Three years later he expressed satisfaction that "even in the lowest grades and more particularly in the higher ones, the pupils are taught to do and make useful things."[5]

Complementing and reinforcing the schools' growing emphasis on the material and the practical, the bureau under White "commercialized" the industrial work done in the classroom. In one of his first circulars to the teaching force, White announced, "Instruction . . . will have in view the training of the pupil to make always a serviceable and salable article. It will be our purpose to operate every trade school and every school farm on a business basis."[6] A third key element of the industrial program was "standardization." From its dealings with the merchant community, the bureau was aware that the items produced by students in the schools—and later by ex-students working in their homes—would find a market only if they were of high (and ideally uniform) quality. Hence, the bureau issued detailed instructions to teachers intended to make certain that standards were strictly adhered to. The objective was, as White explained in an annual report, "to secure prompt and effective adoption of the accepted standards throughout the field."[7] In the second and third decades of the twentieth century, "standardization" became the mantra of the Philippine Bureau of Education, and nonadherence to the standards became a punishable offense. Students who met the standards received passing grades; those whose work did not meet the standards were failed.[8]

Having adopted commercialization as a major goal and standardization as its mantra, the Philippine educational system in this period took on many of the characteristics of a mammoth business operation. At the top, in Manila, were a group of administrators-managers intent on improving the commercial value of the items manufactured in the schools. At the bottom, in the schools-cum-handicraft factories scattered around the archipelago, were tens of thousands of local teacher-supervisors who received an endless stream of circulars and bulletins from the managers and ultimately close to a million pupil-workers, who were required to follow the orders of their supervisors and copy the prescribed patterns.

Of course, it has often been remarked that schools all around the world bear a resemblance to factories, with students sitting at their individual worktables following the directions of their teachers, who are likened to foremen. Furthermore, it would be hard to make the case that the Philippine educational system was unique in its commercialized industrial work. In the schools of Gary, Indiana, most of the industrial education classes were also designed to be self-supporting. The girls engaged in domestic science work ran the school cafeteria, and their profits were used to pay some staff salaries.[9]

Still, there was one important difference between the Philippine industrial education program after 1909 and those in most other places: the extent to which the strictly economic function of industrial education was emphasized in the Philippines. In many urban school districts in the United States, pupils worked in school gardens not because they were being trained to be future farmers but rather because educators (including John Dewey) felt that gardening complemented curriculum units in "nature study" and hence contributed to the social and intellectual development of the person.[10] In the Philippine schools, however, industrial work had the quasi-vocational objective of teaching pupils handicrafts, farming techniques, and other things that would add to their future earning power.

Evolution of the System

For roughly sixteen years, from White's directorship until a major policy change in 1925, there was enthusiastic consensus within the Philippine Bureau of Education about the essentials of the new approach toward industrial education. The challenge facing White and his successors—Frank Crone, Walter W. Marquardt, and Luther Bewley—was how to achieve the agreed-upon goals. The basic approach taken was to systematize and centralize, as much as possible, industrial instruction in the schools. While regional differences and local conditions were taken into account—which is to say, under normal circumstances the bureau would permit, and even encourage, individual school divisions to focus on producing things they could readily manufacture and grow—all the work done would have to meet the standards fixed by managers in central administration, and the items made would have to be salable.

In developing this system, White and his staff built on American models. Just as the growth and appeal of industrial education programs in the United States affected decisions about the curriculum in the Philippine schools, certain developments in U.S. public education also helped to shape the administrative structure of the insular school system. Starting in the late nineteenth century, as David Tyack tells us, an "organizational revolution" was centralizing U.S. schooling "on the corporate model." Superintendents were taking on some of the characteristics of corporation presidents, a new bureaucratic structure featuring a greatly expanded supervisory force was being introduced, and new school administrators were relying increasingly on the systematic collection of survey data.[11]

The industrial education system introduced by White contained all these features, reflecting the centralizing tendencies of the U.S. schools. But it differed from the others in one important respect: its scale. Popular though industrial education was in the United States, it was not uniformly so since major decisions about education in the mother country were made by local authorities. In the Philippines, by contrast, policy makers such as White made educational policy for every child who attended public schools in the archipelago. Hence, the industrial education program in the colony dwarfed in size any then existing in the United States. The only U.S. school district that had remotely comparable student numbers was New York City, which had about 700,000 pupils in the early 1920s versus more than a million in the Philippines.[12]

The first step taken by White to systematize the industrial work of the schools was to create a new bureaucratic apparatus. In December 1909, he established an "industrial department" within the bureau's general office in Manila charged with organizing, promoting, and supervising industrial training in all Philippine schools.[13] Immediately following that, the bureau appointed a "corps" of industrial supervisors and inspectors whose principal responsibility was to visit all the schools in all the provinces "for the purpose of instructing, advising, and assisting teachers."[14]

At about the same time, the bureau launched an ambitious fact-finding project throughout the archipelago. In a series of circulars directed to all division superintendents, White required them to provide a separate detailed report about industrial instruction and economic conditions in *every* municipality in the division. As a result, a positively astounding amount of information was collected on industrial instruction and local economies.[15] With all that information, the bureau moved on to develop new curricula, new teaching materials, and new supervisory techniques. A new curriculum for primary schools called for a significant increase in the amount of time devoted to industrial work, starting with one hour (out of a school day that lasted four and a half hours) in grade one and increasing to ninety minutes (out of a total of five hours) in grade four. That classroom work was to proceed from hand weaving and gardening in grades one and two up to the production of marketable items (baskets, hats, mats, and the like) by grades three and four. In the 1911–12 school year, 91 percent of primary school pupils were taking industrial classes; in the following year, the figure grew to 93 percent.[16]

A series of bulletins and manuals were generated by the bureau for topics covered in the industrial classes—school gardening, hat making, embroidery, lace making, and so on. The bulletins served the function of conveying clearly to the supervisors and the teaching force exactly what it expected in every branch of industrial work. Moreover, the bulletins included constant reminders to the teachers that deviations from the bureau-mandated norms would not be tolerated.[17]

From 1912 to 1917, the bureau published a glossy, illustration-filled monthly magazine called the *Philippine Craftsman,* which was intended to keep teachers abreast of the progress of industrial education. Each issue included at least half a dozen substantive articles relevant to the work being done in the classrooms—studies of individual handicrafts in different regions of the Philippines, discussions of gardening techniques and furniture making, and countless pieces about the importance of adhering to the bureau's standards.

To carry out its industrial program, the bureau was acutely aware of the need to provide better training in industrial subjects to the teaching force. The curriculum of the Insular Normal School was changed to increase significantly the attention given to industrial education.[18] Guidance to thousands of teachers was provided at "vacation assemblies" and "division normal institutes," which were devoted increasingly to industrial instruction. In the case of the vacation assemblies, which usually took place in Manila or Baguio, teachers spent as much as a month in the classroom attempting to learn techniques that they were expected to impart to their students.[19]

In the Philippine schools during this era, some of the most important competitions and awards were related to industrial instruction. Within each school division, contests were held to identify and reward outstanding work done in the industrial courses with the winning pupils receiving certificates and other prizes for their industry and, of course, their adherence to the bureau's standards. At "garden days," certificates and ribbons were given for the best melons and tomatoes. At provincial industrial exhibits, the best baskets, hats, mats, pottery, embroidery, and lace were displayed. Once a year, moreover, the best of the best were sent to Manila where they were displayed (and sometimes sold) at the Manila Carnival.[20]

Within the bureau's industrial division, a General Sales Department was established in 1916, and in the separate school divisions provincial sales departments were set up.[21] But the sales of items made in the schools never amounted to much. In 1916, sales totaled about 45,000 pesos, rose to 196,000 in 1917, but then fell to 180,000 in 1918, the last year in which sales figures were mentioned in the bureau's annual reports.[22] By now, the directors of the educational system had discovered that sales could be fickle and unpredictable, being dependent on a host of variables entirely out of the bureau's control, such as whether a world war was raging. So in 1918 the bureau fastened on another quantitative measure—industrial production. Rather than count the pesos paid for things sold, it came up with figures for the "value of output" of industrial work. It then summarized those data in formidable tables, which were included among the appendixes in the director's annual report. How the totals were generated is something of a mystery. But a hint can perhaps be found in the bureau's annual report for 1921 where the phrase "value of output" was replaced in the tables with a new one: "estimated value of output."[23]

One thing that was immediately clear about the production figures is that they were considerably higher than the sales totals, which is to say they conveyed the impression that the schools made more headway along industrial lines than the sales figures suggested. By the school year 1920–21, the total output of all industrial classes, including agricultural ones, had reached almost 2.5 million pesos, and it remained at approximately the same level through 1924.[24]

If we assume these data are accurate, what do they tell us about the progress of the Philippine school system along industrial lines? On the one hand, the "output" from the schools was not inconsequential. Two and a half million pesos was hardly a small sum in the early 1920s. On the other hand, if we consider that close to 900,000 pupils were responsible for that output the totals seem much less impressive. By my calculation, for the school years 1920–21 through 1923–24 pupils enrolled in the industrial classes of the archipelago's schools produced or grew things valued at, on average, 2.94 pesos.[25] While the bureau had done much to systematize and standardize industrial instruction in the archipelago, it had failed to achieve its stated goal of operating its industrial education programs on "a business basis."

In 1925, a commission of distinguished educators, led by Paul Monroe of Columbia Teachers College, traveled to the Philippines for the purpose of conducting a "comprehensive study and survey" of the entire Philippine educational system. After visiting many schools around the archipelago, hearing hundreds of recitations, and testing more than thirty-three thousand teachers and pupils, the Monroe Commission produced a voluminous report that was, on balance, an indictment of the U.S. educational effort. Virtually nothing in the schools escaped criticism, including industrial education. Observing that neither the students nor the teachers were enthusiastic about the industrial work, that the students did not use the acquired skills after leaving school, and that there was an "inadequate return, both economically and educationally," for the time spent in industrial classes, the commission recommended "a curtailment of the type of industrial work now found in the schools." Specifically, it called for a greater focus on educational goals and the elimination of the bureau's General Sales Department.[26]

Soon after the publication of the report of the Monroe Commission, both of the recommended changes were implemented. Thereafter the stated policy of the bureau was to raise industrial instruction in the schools to a "much higher, less mechanical, and more pedagogical plane." In a circular to division superintendents, Director Luther Bewley elaborated on the change in approach, arguing that in directing a class in industrial work the teacher should be more concerned about the pupils to be taught than about the object to be made. In other words, it should be a problem of instruction not production.[27]

Despite these changes, Bewley, who stayed on as director until the establishment of the Commonwealth in 1935, continued to assert that the bureau remained committed to industrial education.[28] But, in fact, the bureau's published data belied the director's claims, telling instead a tale of relentless retrenchment. By the late 1920s, only about half of the pupils in Philippine public schools were receiving industrial instruction.[29]

Corn and Baskets

Such, then, in general terms, is the story of the U.S. experiment with industrial education in the colonial Philippines. Being general, though, it provides little sense of the particularities of the historical experience. At this juncture, I turn from the general to the specific by focusing on two initiatives. The first, the bureau's corn campaign, was briefly a priority. The second, the bureau's efforts to teach basketry in the schools, was a central component of its commercialization program.

According to the Philippine census of 1903, approximately 108,000 hectares of agricultural land were devoted to the cultivation of corn, making it the country's fourth-largest crop. While this fact might suggest that corn was an important secondary staple crop in the early-twentieth-century Philippines, such was not the case in most of the colony, as a majority of Filipinos considered the crop unfit for human consumption and fed it to animals. As one bureau specialist on school gardens remarked, "In many localities the use of corn is thought to indicate the poverty of the family."[30] To Americans, who considered corn to be an acceptable human food, the Filipinos' distaste for it was puzzling. A 1911 drought that led to a major shortfall in rice production spurred the Bureau of Education to act. In 1912, it launched a campaign to reduce the archipelago's dependence on rice by expanding its production of corn and educating the populace about its advantages.[31]

This was not the first time that the American leaders of the Philippine school system had attempted to change the Filipino diet, nor would it be the last. Even before White became director in 1909, the bureau's school gardening efforts had focused on the cultivation of vegetables—a type of comestible that traditionally did not play a large role in the Filipino diet. Under White's regime, the effort to promote vegetables became even more pronounced.[32]

The corn campaign in the Philippines was modeled to some extent on a movement then flourishing in the United States. In the early years of the twentieth century, educators in rural America, concerned that the schools were not doing a satisfactory job in the area of agricultural education, began organizing agricultural clubs that were the first seeds of the 4-H movement. Focusing initially on improving corn production, the clubs drew attention to their efforts by sponsoring corn-growing contests.[33]

A major part of the Philippine corn campaign was conducted within the schools.[34] Schoolboys were taught how to select seed, prepare the soil, and increase yields. In addition, schoolgirls learned how to "prepare palatable corn dishes with such ingredients and cooking utensils as are common in the average Filipino home." As was the case in the United States, there were regular corn-growing contests. The winners generally received certificates, but on a few occasions their names and even their pictures appeared in the pages of the *Philippine Craftsman*. In 1913, according to the bureau's figures, a total of 43,561 boys participated in corn-growing contests and 8,835 girls were taught how to prepare corn dishes.

But the schoolchildren were not the sole intended targets of the corn campaign. The bureau's larger aim was to convey its messages to the general public. In virtually every municipality of the Philippines, lectures "in the local dialect" were given to adult members of the community about the proper techniques of corn cultivation, attracting 373,185 people in 1913. The bureau also scheduled hundreds of "corn demonstrations" at which information was conveyed about seed selection and storage and the people in attendance were taught how to prepare simple corn dishes.

The bureau's assessments of the corn campaign were invariably self-congratulatory. "The economic importance of the corn demonstrations is unquestioned," Frank Crone, White's successor as director of education, wrote in 1913. But an examination of the bureau's statistics reveals that by the third year of the campaign public interest in it was already flagging and the growth in hectarage devoted to corn production was slowing.

In June 1916, acknowledging the reality that the school system could spend its time more profitably by devoting its resources and energy to other things, the new bureau chief, Walter Marquardt, announced that the corn campaign was to be discontinued because "the results striven for had been attained." Only a single vestigial component—the corn-growing contests—was retained.

Although Filipinos had a long history of making baskets, basketry had never been a significant source of income during the three centuries of Spanish rule.[35] After White became director in 1909 and the bureau's industrial work was systematized, basketry was elevated to a privileged place in the curriculum. The chief impetus was the belief shared by American educational administrators that the handicraft had considerable "commercial" potential. The preconditions for success appeared to exist: bamboo, rattan, and other basket materials were plentiful in the Philippines; and Filipinos were thought to be skilled in producing baskets. All that was lacking was for the bureau to develop a line of "salable articles of utility and beauty."[36]

After examining countless examples of the handicraft work done in the Philippines, however, the general office reached the disappointing conclusion that "the commercial and artistic value of industrial work has been reduced by lack of utility and artistic merit." Among all the baskets produced in the archipelago, there were, in the bureau's view, only a small number that had any artistic value, and most of those had been made by non-Christian peoples.[37]

Having reached that conclusion, the bureau made a conscious decision not to teach the students how to make the types of baskets commonly produced in their communities.[38] Instead, the basketry courses offered in the schools focused on the production of one or more bureau-approved baskets, many of them based on Native American, West Indian, and African designs. The number of approved designs grew steadily, reaching 431 by 1917. The bureau then developed instructional materials for the insular teaching force, which was charged with overseeing the schools' production efforts. For reasons never explained, the central office did not prepare a separate bulletin for basketry as it did for embroidery, hat making, and several other industrial lines. Instead it relied on the *Philippine Craftsman* to provide the kind of information and guidance normally found in the bulletins.[39]

At the outset, there was optimism within the bureau about the possibility of selling large numbers of Philippine baskets and developing a viable basketry industry. In 1911, Gabriel O'Reilly, a colonial official investigating the potential market for Philippine school articles in the United States, wrote to Frank White reporting that there was "unlimited demand" for Philippine basketry. As basket production began in earnest, the bureau attempted to drum up business by planting favorable stories about Philippine basketry in U.S. publications.[40] But basket exports remained virtually nonexistent, a situation O'Reilly attributed to the fact that the baskets turned out by the schools were "not fully standard."[41]

In 1915, the bureau turned optimistic again when baskets produced by students in the insular school system were featured prominently at the Panama-Pacific International Exposition in San Francisco and many items were sold. There was speculation that large orders from American customers would follow. But, as before, the anticipated demand did not materialize. Over the next two years, the bureau's General Sales Department only sold baskets valued at about fifty thousand pesos.[42]

After World War I, the Philippine educational system continued to devote an enormous amount of time and energy to basketry. In the school year 1923–24, for instance, a total of slightly more than 110,000 pupils were enrolled in basketry classes with estimated production amounting to about two hundred thousand pesos.[43] But, in fact, such production figures were anything but impressive. The average "output" of students in basketry classes amounted to less than two pesos a year.

In light of this unimpressive record, it was understandable that when the Monroe Commission of 1925 discussed the Philippine school system's industrial education program it singled out for criticism the basketry work done in the schools. In the commission's view, the basketry classes were a waste of time. Philippine schoolboys typically took more than fifty hours to make baskets with a market value of only twenty centavos.[44] In the years following the publication of the Monroe Commission's report, the basketry work of the bureau entered a period of steady decline, mirroring that of the entire industrial education program.[45] Meanwhile, with the abolition of the General Sales Department in 1926, the bureau discontinued its efforts to sell the baskets made in the schools. When in subsequent years foreign merchants interested in purchasing Philippine baskets approached the insular government to inquire about possible suppliers, government officials could offer little assistance. In the late 1920s, Philippine basketry was still forty years away from becoming a significant export industry.[46]

Qualified Success with Embroidery

While these two case studies provide abundant evidence about the failings of Philippine industrial education, it would be misleading to leave the impression that all components of that program were equally unsuccessful. One industrial line that appeared to make substantial headway was embroidery. Every year the bureau's General Sales Department sold more embroidery than any other handicraft made in the schools. More important, outside the schools a nascent, seemingly vibrant embroidery industry was taking off, a trend attributed largely to the impetus provided by the embroidery instruction given in the schools.[47] In 1920, embroideries valued at more than $7.8 million were exported by the Philippines, almost all of them going to the United States, and embroideries occupied fifth place among all exports of the archipelago.[48]

Yet even the bureau's one celebrated success was a bit deceptive. Embroidery exports to the United States grew at such a fast pace principally because they were admitted free of duty. But in order for Philippine goods to receive duty-free treatment at least 80 percent of the material in them had to be made in either the Philippines or the United States. The principal effect of that regulation was to force producers of Philippine embroideries to use cotton or linen fabrics manufactured in the United States since Philippine textile production was virtually nonexistent. As a result, the "value-added contribution" of embroideries to the Philippine economy was a good deal less impressive than the export statistics would suggest. American textile producers received most of the profits; Philippine embroidery workers earned about two pesos a day.[49]

Final Thoughts

If we are to judge people by their words, their actions, and the photographs they take, American educational policy makers in the Philippines clearly considered their industrial education experiment to be very important. But if they did how can we explain the fact that the experiment failed so miserably?

Various explanations can be offered, but let me focus on one: ambition. More students received instruction in Philippine schools than in any school system in the United States. The long-term objectives of the educational policy makers were also ambitious. Among other things, they hoped to bring about an important change in the colonial economy. Although they expected that the Philippines would long remain a place in which the two principal economic activities were farming and domestic service (as was the case in most of the world at the time), the bureau's leaders wanted, through the medium of instruction in the schools, to foster the growth of cottage industries and to gain market share for the Philippines in certain niche handicraft markets. They believed that such developments would provide many Filipinos with an alternate career path and at least as many others with a source of supplementary income.[50]

One problem with ambitious plans is that they are inherently risky. They must be both well thought out and well executed, and even then success is not guaranteed. In the case of the Philippine industrial education experiment, there were, predictably, significant failures in execution; the sheer scope of the operation guaranteed lots of those. More serious, though, was a failure of planning. The bureau's leaders gave far too little attention to the single consideration that mattered most if the Philippines was ultimately to develop its handicraft sector: the size of the market for the items produced in the schools. Instead, they adopted a *Field of Dreams* approach to handicraft production: the students would make the items, and the buyers would magically come. But most of the time the imagined stream of buyers did not come of its own accord, and the bureau's efforts to create demand (through industrial exhibits in Manila, displays at international expositions, and the promotional work of its sales department) were unsuccessful.

In the end, the bureau's industrial education program was more about activity than accomplishment. There were many Kodak moments and too few sales of Philippine hats, baskets, and lace. Rather than a successful business enterprise, the bureau's industrial operations turned out to be a mammoth experiment in busywork.

The Imperial Enterprise and Educational Policies in Colonial Puerto Rico

PABLO NAVARRO-RIVERA

EDUCATIONAL POLICIES AND PRACTICES in Puerto Rico, as a colony of both Spain (1493–1898) and the United States (since 1898), were formulated to serve the needs of the imperial enterprise. Education under Spain was one of limited schooling and a task charged to the Catholic Church. The United States, on the other hand, viewed state education as the most effective and efficient entity through which to undertake the colonization of Puerto Rico. Immediately after wresting Puerto Rico from Spain in 1898, the United States began opening schools throughout the country and importing teachers from different U.S. states. Puerto Rican teachers were trained in the educational ways of the conquering nation. Teacher-training programs were instituted and scholarships were approved by the colonial legislature to send Puerto Ricans to educational institutions in the continental United States.[1]

The wave of U.S. expansionism in the nineteenth century closely followed the pattern set previously by the British Empire. Economic and military interests that drove the expansion were supported by theories of natural superiority and divine mandates or Manifest Destiny. However, the U.S. government did not adopt the general British practice of indirect government. The model of colonial governance instituted in Puerto Rico was closer to what the British would define as "Crown colonies." In fact, the United States did not formally recognize that it had colonies, preferring to use the term *territories*.

The expansion to the Pacific and the Caribbean in 1898 signaled the emergence of the United States as an empire in the making. According to principal leadership elements in the United States, Puerto Rico was an economically and militarily important country but was inhabited by inferior beings who needed to be "civilized" in order to maximize the potential benefits of the conquest. This was the same evaluation that they made of Indians and blacks in the United

States, as well as Cubans and Filipinos.[2] In the words of Charles Eliot, president of Harvard University at the time of the 1898 colonial war, "I am inclined to the belief that we shall be able to do Cuba and Porto Rico some good; though to do so we shall have to better very much our previous and existing practices in dealing with inferior peoples."[3]

Notwithstanding these sentiments, to some Puerto Ricans the new colonial power offered possibilities for social justice and a democratic political system unimaginable under Spain. These people regarded the 1898 invasion with optimism. Their idealization of the United States, however, would not be borne out. After nineteen months of military rule, on May 1, 1900, under the Foraker Act, the occupation forces established a highly centralized civilian government under the direct control of the U.S. federal government. With the exception of a brief period with local school boards, the educational system would become a similarly centralized structure led by a commissioner of education appointed by the president of the United States until 1948. The authority of the commissioner extended to the Normal School, established in 1900, and the University of Puerto Rico, founded in 1903.[4] Thus, contrary to its tradition of decentralized governance, the U.S. state coming out of the 1898 war opted instead to govern its new colonies in the centralized manner in which it governed the affairs of its Native American societies.

In the wake of its military victory in 1898, the U.S. government initiated what the dominant discourse called a "civilizing," "Americanizing," or "assimilationist" mission. A crucial step in this mission was to grind down or "pulverize" the constituent elements of the conquered peoples' cultural identities. In 1902 Samuel McCune Lindsay, the commissioner of education of Puerto Rico, noted, "Colonization carried forward by the armies of war is vastly more costly than that carried forward by the armies of peace, whose outpost and garrisons are the public schools of the advancing nation."[5]

The process of reacculturation went hand in hand with the steps taken to destroy the cultural identity of the conquered peoples. The Puerto Rican poet and political activist Juan Antonio Corretjer (1908–89) described those who were subjected to the educational policies and practices of the early years of occupation and conquest as "the most tortured generation."[6] To this end, the United States established a public system of "American" schools and an "American" curriculum in Puerto Rico in 1898, which included the stated goal of having English as the primary language of teaching and learning, a policy that lasted until 1948.[7] A year later, in 1899, the colonial government established a series of scholarships for vocational and university study in the United States. In 1900 a Normal School for teacher education was founded, following the model already in use in the United States for the education of Indians and African Americans.[8] On March 12, 1903, the United States founded the University of Puerto Rico, in which English was the official language of instruction until 1942.[9]

Teacher training became one of the main priorities of government officials in Washington and San Juan in this period. One hundred and twenty English teachers from the United States were sent to Puerto Rico to assist in the establishment of English as the language of instruction on the island. The Department of Education organized summer institutes for the education of teachers following the model used for similar programs at the Hampton Institute in Virginia and the Tuskegee Normal and Industrial School in Alabama. In addition, as it did in 1900, when 1,273 public school teachers from Cuba were sent to Harvard University for a summer of training in the English language and for the study of educational theories and practices, 540 public school teachers from Puerto Rico were sent to Harvard and Cornell University in 1904 to participate in a similar summer program. The magnitude of the summer programs at Harvard and Cornell in 1900 and 1904 is evidenced by the fact that 1,273 teachers in 1900 represented more than 40 percent of the Cuban teaching corps and the 540 Puerto Rican teachers represented 47 percent of the teachers in service in 1904.[10]

THE CARLISLE INDIAN INDUSTRIAL SCHOOL

When Juan José Osuna arrived at the Carlisle Indian Industrial School (CIIS) in Carlisle, Pennsylvania, at six o'clock on the morning of May 2, 1901, he was fifteen years old, stood four feet six inches in height, and weighed just eighty pounds. Osuna, who would become a noted Puerto Rican educator, wrote of his arrival at Carlisle:

> We looked at the windows of the buildings, and very peculiar-looking faces peered out at us. We had never seen such people before. The buildings seemed full of them. Behold, we had arrived at the Carlisle Indian School! The United States of America, our new rulers, thought that the people of Puerto Rico were Indians; hence they should be sent to an Indian school, and Carlisle happened to be the nearest.[11]

By the time the school was closed in 1918, almost eleven thousand human beings had been subjected to one of the most ambitious experiments in the destruction of cultural identity and forced acculturation in U.S. history.[12] Of these, sixty had been sent by Puerto Rico's colonial government.

Carlisle's mission was close to the central purpose of U.S. education in Puerto Rico from the beginning. The first to be put in charge of the island's education system after 1898 was General John Eaton, who was a friend and sympathizer of CIIS. In January 1899, the same month in which General Eaton was appointed to his post on the island, CIIS's periodical, the *Indian Helper,* noted the adequacy of his role.

> It is eminently fitting that the school teacher should follow the soldier into Porto Rico. If there is anyone who can successfully light the lamp of learning in the island

it should be General Eaton, who started so successfully the same work among the freedmen of the south at the close of the civil war.[13]

Soon thereafter, Eaton initiated the process by which young Puerto Ricans would be sent to Carlisle.

Colonial officials bought into this logic from the beginning. Martin G. Brumbaugh, commissioner of education in Puerto Rico in 1900 and 1901, indicated in his 1900 annual report that the island had neither good schools nor institutions of higher education and lacked the resources to establish them. On this basis he recommended that the colonial legislature establish scholarships for forty-five students to study in the United States each year. Twenty-five males would be sent to preparatory schools and universities and a second group of twenty males and females would receive scholarships of $250 each per year to study at places such as Carlisle, Tuskegee, and Hampton.[14] Brumbaugh would later write black educator Booker T. Washington, whose work was highly regarded by federal officials considering what to do about the education of Cubans and Puerto Ricans, saying, "It has occurred to me that in order to break up their Spanish language we might scatter some of them into similar institutions; upon this subject, however, I am not clear and I write to you in perfect frankness for your advise [*sic*]."[15]

In her study of Carlisle, Genevieve Bell offers a perspective on the school that was absent from previous studies. Calling CIIS "the flagship of the American Assimilation era's education program,"[16] Bell observes that through such schools and institutes the federal government tried to "detribalize" Indians and incorporate them "as individual citizens into the American nation." Students sent there "were learning to be Indian," and, as Bell points out, "within this context 'Indian' and thus 'Indianness' are the products of ongoing colonial encounters between indigenous peoples and the American Nation-State."[17]

Just as the "Negro problem" in the United States had led to the founding of the Hampton and Tuskegee Institutes, the "Indian problem" led to the founding of the Carlisle Indian Industrial School in 1879. The conquest of new peoples in 1898 added yet another such problem, and vocational schools, as well as institutions of higher education, were useful in devising methods for their training and acculturation.

Located in the town of Carlisle in central Pennsylvania, CIIS was the first Indian school to be founded by the federal government off a reservation.[18] The guiding policy of founder Richard Henry Pratt's "civilizing mission" was called "acculturation under duress."[19] The rationale for this policy was the supposition that once they were "thoroughly subjugated" Indians would have no means by which to resist their forced acculturation in institutions such as Carlisle. Writing to Frances E. Willard in 1888, Pratt explained the logic of such forced acculturation, observing that it was more practical than the alternative of having Indian children socialized by white people, although he saw that as an ultimate solution. "There are about two hundred sixty thousand Indians in the United States, and there are twenty-seven hundred counties," he noted. "I would divide them up, in the proportion of about nine Indians to a county, and find them homes and work among our people; that would solve the knotty problem in three years' time, and there would be no more an 'Indian Question.'"[20]

If forced acculturation was the goal, it is little wonder that Carlisle operated like a military institute. On arriving there, students would get a bath, a haircut, "civilized" clothing, and a Christian name. The use of vernacular languages was forbidden; English was the only language permitted both day and night.[21] The day there began early and ended late. As Pratt indicated, "We keep them moving and they have no time for homesickness—none for mischief—none for regret."[22] The power that Carlisle had over its students, and the manner in which that power was wielded as an instrument of control, had a great impact on the students, including the Puerto Ricans. As an agency of the federal government, the school utilized its enormous power to facilitate or hinder the employment of its Native American students. Federal power over Indian individuals was enhanced by the fact that Indians were not granted U.S. citizenship until 1924, six years after Carlisle closed.[23] This legal inferiority and political disenfranchisement also affected the Puerto Rican students at Carlisle, as Puerto Rico was a colony at the time they attended. The United States would not grant citizenship to Puerto Ricans until 1917, just one year before the school closed.

I have not found information regarding the proportion of Carlisle students, including Puerto Ricans, who later returned to their communities of origin. This obstacle makes it difficult to analyze the phenomenon of return. We do know, however, that a significant number of Puerto Ricans who left the island to go to Carlisle either stayed in the United States or migrated frequently between the two countries. The fact that at least 1,850 students fled Carlisle, including five Puerto Ricans, is not given much attention in official reports.[24]

Carlisle generated a great deal of interest in both the United States and other countries. People from many parts of the world, including Cuba, Panama, Mexico, Argentina, and Japan, visited the school.[25] Carlisle was also visited by representatives of educational institutions interested in Pratt's "civilizing" and "assimilationist" experiment. In his campaign to portray the school as a successful experiment in civilization, one that could play a role in solving the Indian problem, Pratt encouraged such visits.

In viewing the role that race played in efforts (such as Carlisle's) of forced assimilation, one important factor that merits further examination is the racial and ethnic discourse common in the United States in the late nineteenth and early twentieth centuries, the manner in which the residents of new U.S. colonies were characterized within that discourse, and how this was reflected at institutions

Carlisle Indian Industrial School, 1904 graduating class, with Zoraida Valdezate, first Puerto Rican to graduate, fourth from left in the third row. (Cumberland County Historical Society, Carlisle, Pennsylvania)

such as Tuskegee, Hampton, and Carlisle.[26] On the list of tribes represented at Carlisle, for example, there is one by the name of "Porto Rico." The staff at Carlisle wrote "Porto Rico" on the records of Puerto Rican students in the space indicated for tribe of origin. Jorge Duany likewise found that officials of the Smithsonian Institution referred to Puerto Ricans as Indians during this period.[27] Others, however, such as education secretary Brumbaugh and his correspondent, Washington, preferred to put Puerto Ricans and Cubans in the categories of "colored" or "black." As Duany has suggested, such alternative labels underscore ambivalence in the use of ethnic and racial categories. It is important to note that Puerto Rican students invariably crossed off the terms *Indian* and *tribe*, replacing them with *Puerto Rico* or *Puerto Rican*.

The Puerto Rican Experience at Carlisle

The first Puerto Ricans to study at CIIS were brought to the mainland by soldiers returning to their country after serving in the war of 1898. These young Puerto Ricans were sent to Carlisle upon arrival in the United States.[28] Between 1898 and 1900, ten Puerto Ricans went to study at Carlisle. Of these ten students, only Zoraida Valdezate graduated, in 1904. In 1901, 43 Puerto Ricans arrived at Carlisle from cities and towns around the island. Only five Puerto Rican students were admitted to Carlisle after 1901.

None of the sources consulted up to this point has revealed very much of what was known in Puerto Rico about Carlisle or why the parents and guardians of young people eleven to nineteen years old would have decided to send them there. Carlisle was one of several educational institutions allotted scholarships by a colonial government that awarded such scholarships to students with connections to the U.S. government in Puerto Rico.[29] Nevertheless, it is clear from the documents encountered so far that at least until the middle of 1901 neither the young people nor their parents or guardians had much information about the institution to which the government was sending them. In their view, Carlisle was simply one of the schools in the United States for which the colonial government had approved scholarships. One may suppose, however, that both students and adults thought they would be attending an institution where they would learn English and other subjects prerequisite to professional studies.

According to Osuna, who was interviewed by Brumbaugh regarding the educational scholarships, he was informed that the colonial government was providing Puerto Rican youths with scholarships for professional studies in the United States. He had traveled to Carlisle with the impression that he would receive an education that would prepare him for the field of law.

In other applications to Carlisle, however, potential students mentioned their interest in learning English and receiving a vocational or business education.[30] Some students, such as Providencia Martínez of Ponce, are said to have been unaware that Carlisle was a school for Indians. The limited correspondence available regarding Puerto Rican students is filed among the school's student records and is almost exclusively between students or their families and school officials. This correspondence might not be a representative sample of the Puerto Rican experience at Carlisle since most of the island students chose not to maintain contact with the school.

Although we do not have letters or applications from the Puerto Ricans who attended Carlisle between 1898 and 1900, the documents we have found, particularly those pertaining to the group of forty-three students who arrived there in 1901, do not paint a positive picture of the Puerto Rican experience there. Complaints by students and parents that Carlisle was not what they had been promised led to a 1901 visit by the Puerto Rican journalist and politician Luis Muñoz Rivera, who concluded that the colonial government had not misled parents or students about the programs of study offered there.[31] A number of Puerto Ricans escaped, and others made use of their stay at the institution to enter business schools or universities. Eleven students returned to Puerto Rico on orders from their parents and only seven out of the sixty students graduated.

Sixteen letters by students have been found. Many contain numerous orthographic and grammatical errors. The ones included here appear as they were written so that the reader will have the opportunity to examine them in their original form. In a letter to the then superintendent of Carlisle, M. Friedman, Providencia Martínez revealed:

> Some time I begin to talk about the Indian school and I think it is a dream. Really, we did not know that the school was a regular school for Indians when we went there, because Miss. Weekly never told us the real truth.[32]

Martínez also commented on her father's view of Carlisle.

> After I came to P. R. lots and lots of time I talk to my dear papa about the Indian school and the poor father he used to cry thinking that that place was not a place where we could be happy. You can imagine why he thought so. Down here we do not know anything about good Indians but of those that you read in books that are regular animals.

Matilde Garnier, of Ponce, arrived at the school in 1900. She felt that it represented an opportunity that she would not have had in Puerto Rico. In response to a questionnaire sent out by Carlisle in June of 1911, Garnier indicated:

> I have nothing of interest to tell you but I will tell you that the education in Porto Rico has improved a great deal since the Americans came up here. We have at the

present time great many public schools all over the Island even in the far away countries where the teachers have to go on Mondays at horse back and returned home on Friday afternoon.³³

Records were kept for some of the students, but for others there is only a registration card containing very little information. Only a few of the photographs in the archives identify students as Puerto Rican.³⁴ José Prado, for example, complained in 1917 because he was assigned kitchen work at Carlisle. Prado, who studied there from November 1913 to August 1918, asserted that since his family was paying his tuition he should be allowed to choose the kind of work he would do. A Carlisle official replied, "As long as he was a member of our school, we would plan for him just as we would for the Indian boys who do not pay tuition."³⁵

Osuna was not happy at Carlisle. In his article "An Indian in Spite of Myself," he described the education there as "not exactly in keeping with my preconceived ideas of the 'land of promise.'"³⁶ At this time he learned about Carlisle's "outing" program, described by Pratt as the "supreme americanizer." Under this program, the students lived, usually during the summer, in private homes in places such as Pennsylvania, New Jersey, and New York. As part of the program, the students worked for their host families in return for room and board and a small salary. In March 1902, Osuna was placed with a family in Orangeville, Pennsylvania, where he was submitted to a "strict, puritanic life." In reference to Carlisle, Osuna wrote:

> Instead of returning in the fall of 1902 to Carlisle, I remained with my employer and went to a rural school. I did not want to return to Carlisle. Frankly, I did not like the place. I never thought it was the school for me. I was not an Indian; I was a Puerto Rican of Spanish descent.³⁷

Osuna did not return to Carlisle until 1905 to attend his graduation. This was, in his view, his way of escaping from Carlisle.

Dolores Nieves, of Caguas, was fourteen years old when she arrived at Carlisle in May 1901. After leaving the school in the spring of 1905, she worked in Pennsylvania for a few months and returned to Puerto Rico toward the end of that year.³⁸ From Caguas, Nieves contacted Carlisle, hoping to gain admission to the school for the adolescent boy being raised by her mother or to get help in placing him with a family. Nieves wrote to CIIS superintendent Friedman that

> both his parents are dead, he is such a smart boy in everything, he is in the eighth grade in school, he is also in the band here, yet he is not more than sixteen years old, and my mother would like him to get a good education and learn the English well, but as he can not do that here, she would like him to go to the States and make a man of him.

In the same letter, Nieves also wrote:

> I have told him [the boy] everything that he will have to do, and how he shall have to behave and everything, in fact, I have anticipated him of the rough times that he shall [have] to put up with. I know that we had it hard sometimes in the home that we used to go to, we used to think that such places were hard, at the time, but we didn't know then that in order to taste the sweet, we first must taste the bitter, as the saying is in this country. Today I thank God for the hardest time that I had at any country homes and at Carlisle.[39]

Carlisle responded that the boy would have to pay tuition of $167 per year and could only be admitted if the federal Office of Indian Affairs so authorized. Friedman turned Nieves down. Toward the end of 1915, Nieves was again living in Kirkwood, New Jersey, where she wrote to Friedman asking him to admit her seven-year-old son to Carlisle. In her letter to Friedman, Nieves said that it was impossible for her to both care for her son and work a sufficient number of hours to make even a bare living. On December 8, 1915, the superintendent informed Nieves that Carlisle was not then accepting students of her son's age. That letter is the last document in Nieves's file.

Conclusion

According to representatives of the U.S. government, Puerto Ricans, Cubans, North American Indians, African Americans, and other colonized peoples such as Filipinos and Hawaiians all needed to be "civilized." To make this civilization possible, according to Pratt, it was critical to "light the lamp of learning."[40] The journey to civilization would take some Puerto Ricans to elite preparatory schools and universities and others to vocational schools such as Carlisle and Tuskegee.

The process of civilization, which included the grinding down of salient cultural features, would transform "inferior peoples" into "colored scholars." Through schooling, according to educators such as Eaton, Brumbaugh, and Pratt, this process would result in the adaptation of the conquered peoples to the dominant society. The underlying educational principle adopted for the "civilizing mission" was "acculturation under duress." The United States established a number of institutional structures for this purpose, of which Carlisle was but one. The same strategy was followed in Cuba and Puerto Rico, where the educational system itself acted as a broadly conceived colonizing mechanism.

To implement their educational policies in Puerto Rico, the United States established a highly centralized system of governance similar to the government organized for the Philippines. This form of governance was not dissimilar to the manner in which the United States governed native groups, including their education. This practice was exceptional for a society otherwise characterized by a decentralized approach to the government of cities, towns, and schools. In the case of Puerto Rico, education was initially under the authority of the U.S. military from 1898 to 1900. Toward the end of the military government local school boards were established. These had the authority to hire teachers. But according to Osuna, the effort to decentralize the school system failed.

Osuna does not explain the nature of the opposition to decentralization, nor does he, other than a reference to conflicts between political parties, examine in any detail the "political and social conditions" that contributed to the failure of this initiative. Although he affirms that centralization was necessary "due to the failure of the local boards to perform their duties" he offers no explanation to support his claim.[41] Furthermore, Osuna does not elaborate on his claim that the law providing for local school boards was "too democratic." The law was short-lived and was followed by an increasing degree of centralization.

Language is one of the evident preoccupations encountered in the relevant documentary sources. More than one hundred years after the founding of Carlisle, words such as *Americanization* and *assimilation* continue to have currency. We still hear the word *American* used to mean "from or having to do with the United States." These words and definitions, which were used by Brumbaugh, Pratt, and many others, were repeated by Ryan in 1962 and Bell in 1998, among other scholars, without reflection on or criticism of their meaning, contextual effect, or descriptive imprecision. The words and concepts used in historical reflection and discussion remain those brought to prominence by the architects of colonial wars like that of 1898 and of identity-crushing grindstones like Carlisle.

The impact the CIIS had on its Puerto Rican students is one of the areas that warrant further study. We know that most did not like CIIS. We also know from CIIS documents and other source materials that connections to government officials played a decisive role in the awarding of scholarships. The same documents show that former CIIS students found good jobs in both the public and private sectors on their return to the island. Several occupied positions of authority in the colonial government, be it in the central government, public education, or the U.S. postal or armed services. In a period when loyalty to the United States was a requirement for government-controlled employment, the apparent social and economic accomplishments of the recipients of scholarships could suggest that the "acculturation under duress" policies instituted in Puerto Rico after 1898 and in institutions such as CIIS resulted in success for the imperial enterprise.[42]

Carlisle's influence and ideology extended beyond the school's grounds in central Pennsylvania. As previously stated, the outing program was Carlisle's "supreme Americanizer." Based on an examination of the letters and other communications between officials at Carlisle and former students, this program was certainly of much significance. In this correspondence we find positive evaluations of the experience some students had at the school. Other former students reproached the officials of Carlisle for the way they had been treated. Dolores Nieves rebuked Carlisle for its role in the difficult times she had to endure under its auspices, particularly in the outing program. Osuna, who apparently did not stay in touch with Carlisle, wrote in "An Indian in Spite of Myself" that his overall experience there was negative.

Although Osuna left the CIIS campus in Carlisle, he spent years in Orangeville, Pennsylvania, under the outing program. Orangeville was a puritanical town, the ideal environment that Pratt and the federal government sought for the reacculturation of Carlisle students. In this sense, Osuna did not leave Carlisle as long as he was part of the outing program. Orangeville was an extension of Carlisle or, to an even greater extent, Carlisle was an extension of Orangeville.

Understanding the American Empire
Colonialism, Latin Americanism, and Professional Social Science, 1898–1920

COURTNEY JOHNSON

"I WENT TO PERFORM A LAWYER'S DUTY," Elihu Root said modestly of his service as secretary of war under President William McKinley. In the summer of 1899, when Root received a telephone call at his New York law office from Washington offering him this cabinet post, he protested that he had no knowledge of war or the army. But the White House aide is said to have replied, "President McKinley directs me to say that he is not looking for anyone who knows anything about war or for anyone who knows anything about the army; he has got to have a lawyer to direct the government of these Spanish islands, and you are the lawyer he wants."[1] Indeed, few would play a more decisive and lasting role in setting the course for the United States' particular brand of empire than this New York corporate lawyer.

In the story of twentieth-century American imperialism, Elihu Root, perhaps more than any other figure of comparable significance, has been overlooked. Amid the bluster of popular debates between jingoes and anti-imperialists, the discreet and resourceful Root worked behind the scenes to do the institutional heavy lifting necessary to realize the imperial designs of his more visible clients. Cultivating networks that brought leaders in finance and government into dialogue with those in academe, he helped to create the conditions whereby certain branches of the social sciences, in what later became known as "area studies," would come to inform and be informed by matters of foreign policy—a development with profound implications for the institutional architecture of the imperium.

Understanding the new style of imperial state that Root was so instrumental in constructing requires expanding received notions about the role of imperialism in the conduct of U.S. statecraft. If the history of the so-called American century has taught us anything, it is surely that American imperialism has by no means been limited to the "unwilling" or anomalous acquisition of direct-rule island colonies. Nor does the lack of a cabinet post dedicated to coordinating the nation's imperial affairs mean that Washington was anything other than serious about its imperial interests. The costly and often bitterly divisive experience of colonial rule in the Caribbean and the Pacific did not shake American faith in its global destiny but instead ushered in a dramatic tactical shift away from direct dominion and toward a more subtle, indirect regime of international hegemony by championing the sovereign territorial rights of the existing states within the United States' Latin American and Asian spheres of influence through diplomatic agreements, multilateral arbitration, and supranational institutions.

In support of the innovative hegemonic strategy that came to define the American imperial state, Root enlisted the emerging professions of the social sciences, particularly political science. Marshaling the area-specific expertise of his scholarly associates, he charted a course that furthered U.S. commercial and geopolitical goals by anticipating and proactively defusing the objections of an international community increasingly wary of overt territorial acquisition. As the United States began to craft an image of itself as a new kind of world leader— one that eschewed the traditional privileges of empire to advance global stability, safeguard the sovereignty of vulnerable nations, and wisely arbitrate international disputes—it turned to these and others in the academy in undertaking what was in essence an emphatically imperial project.

The roots of this project, and the new national identity it aimed to articulate, should be sought in the first two decades of this century, when a surreptitious foreign policy apparatus began to take shape behind the scenes as a network linking public and private sectors of American power to the management of the country's global affairs. This network orbited the power centers of Washington and New York, but as it reached critical mass after World War I, it actively drew within its gravitational field the decisive sectors of power across the entire nation. Among the earliest and most eager satellites in this constellation of imperial management was a new wave of professional social scientists and aspiring technocrats working on university campuses across the nation. As individual scholars were tapped for imperial service, a number of professional academic disciplines— including political science, international law, and Latin American studies—developed symbiotically with the increasingly complex task of imperial management abroad and social engineering at home.

Although political scientists played but an auxiliary role in the formation of this internationalist network, their work helped to add a vital veneer of scientific objectivity and disinterested expertise to the pursuit of U.S. global designs. [2] As Ido Oren has argued, U.S. national security interests "impinged on the state of the discipline by . . . stimulating scholarly interest in regions of the world that might not have been studied otherwise, by favoring and funding the development of research methods that promised help in prosecuting America's wars, and by directly or indirectly disadvantaging scholarship of an oppositional or radical character."[3] As with many social engineering projects undertaken in the Progressive period, the technocratic aims of this foreign policy apparatus included a powerful public relations component aimed, above all, at normalizing American imperialism and marginalizing anti-imperial alternatives among the American metropolitan populace.

Networking the Empire

Elihu Root, as both a consummate insider and a prodigious managerial troubleshooter, was uniquely positioned to forge linkages between the principal sectors of this nascent form of imperial management. Working from his base at the epicenter of Anglo-American corporate, social, and political power, Root seemed ubiquitously active in networking the primary functional units of what C. Wright Mills has called the national "power elite." Moving seamlessly among the captains of corporate, political, juridical, military, bureaucratic, academic, scientific, and press power, Root facilitated the emergence of a consolidated foreign policy consensus that reflected a deep Anglo-American geostrategic orientation at the heart of U.S. imperial power.

With every step in his inexorable accumulation of influence, Root wove networks that added layer upon layer of functionality to an ambitious, expansionist program. He began his career in New York City as a corporate lawyer and there built a clientele that included the most important industrial barons of the Gilded Age, notably, J. P. Morgan, Andrew Carnegie, and Cornelius Vanderbilt. In this capacity, Root had a direct hand in the radical reorganization of American industry as his prominent clients created vast corporate monopolies such as United States Steel, the Havermeyer Sugar Trust, and the Duke Tobacco Trust. On becoming secretary of war under McKinley and then Theodore Roosevelt, Root presided over the transformation of a ruthless war of colonial conquest in the Philippines. First, he shepherded the colonial government through the thorny transition from military to civilian rule by framing legal principles consonant with a Constitution that had heretofore seemed to preclude empire. More fundamentally, he reformed the armed forces by creating a modern standing army and navy with joint force coordination. Then, in his subsequent role as secretary of state under presidents Roosevelt and Taft from 1905 to 1909, he conducted the diplomacy that made the United States a player in great power politics, reshaped U.S. policy toward Latin America, and launched a lifetime project of making law the foundation for international relations.

Throughout his multifaceted career, Root was the principal force behind an array of privately funded public policy organizations—the Carnegie Institution, Council on Foreign Relations, and others—that knitted American academics into a relationship with the most powerful circles of Wall Street and Washington.

Using his membership in important social clubs to create a seamless network of friends, corporate clients, technocrats, and political allies, Root in effect contributed to the finely spun brand of imperialism developed by the United States in response to an increasingly strident public disavowal of direct imperial control. Within this wide-ranging network, the tasks of imperial management could be distributed and debated. But its primary raison d'être was the integration of sectors with divergent views and interests related to questions of U.S. foreign policy. Yet, what bound all of the participants in this network was a commitment to expanding U.S. geopolitical and economic power.

If Root was singularly responsible for the creation of a public-private institutional network that became the hallmark of a new form of imperial administration pioneered by the United States, the new spheres of influence in the Pacific and Latin America became the proving ground for its implementation. Following a pattern set out in John Hay's Open Door policy, which aimed to preserve the territorial integrity of China against imperial partitions after the Boxer Rebellion, Root guided the United States as it turned decisively against the further acquisition of direct-rule colonies and toward a policy of international arbitration to maintain the global status quo. These efforts did not go unrewarded as both Roosevelt (1906) and Root himself (1912) won the Nobel Prize for Peace. But perhaps more important, Root successfully pioneered a regional strategy for co-opting local elites in Latin America with promises of international recognition and reciprocity that greatly reduced the cost of managing the resistance kindled by the imposition of U.S. sovereignty over subject populations.

This new form of imperial hegemony required much more sophistication than the blunt instrument of gunboats enforcing the collection Wall Street loans. It required the thoroughgoing development of what is now called "soft power" or "global leadership." As any student of Latin American history before World War I knows, the United States was not shy about asserting its harder forms of military and economic suasion over the region. Yet, even as the cruel campaign of "pacification" ground on in the Philippines, Root set about rebranding American empire through these soft power strategies. Through his construction of networks of private-public partnerships among elites at home and abroad, Root was the principal architect of a new and more "understanding" form of imperial state. Through his commingling of the public and private via policy organizations such as the Carnegie Institution and Council on Foreign Relations, Root was primarily responsible for the intellectual and institutional infrastructure of the internationalist strain of American foreign policy.

Tracing Imperialists

Within the broad social tapestry that Root wove across continents and oceans, let us tug at a single thread to trace the role of academic social science in the creation of a social infrastructure for American internationalism-cum-imperialism. In tracking the intertwined changes in the field of professional political science, the practice of foreign policy making, and the rise of Latin Americanism, I will underscore the personal role played by particular academics—Leo S. Rowe of the University of Pennsylvania, Bernard Moses of the University of California, and Paul S. Reinsch of the University of Wisconsin—in an otherwise impersonal tale of institutional transformations. These three political scientists were not alone in their eagerness to put their scientific expertise in the service of an ambitious imperial project. Nor were they necessarily the most conspicuous members of their profession. But each had a direct link to Root and his project of institutionalizing the superstructure of an understanding form of imperialism across the archipelagic bedrock of its insular colonies. Furthermore, they participated directly in the institutionalization of this new professional field of international relations through important phases of its integration into the imperial state.

In the first phases of professional activity, Root dispatched both Leo Rowe and Bernard Moses to participate in the formation of colonial administrations in Puerto Rico and the Philippines. Although Paul S. Reinsch was never a colonial official, he was an early scholar of U.S. colonial government and, together with Rowe and Moses, played a seminal role in the institutionalization of their academic profession by establishing the American Political Science Association (APSA) and related scholarly societies. In a parallel effort, these same men also played key roles in the reanimation of an American-led Pan-American movement that drove the rapid professionalization of Latin American studies in the United States. Finally, as Root's ambitious project of creating a fully integrated foreign policy apparatus began to flourish with the steady infusion of funds provided by a constellation of powerful philanthropic foundations from Root's Wall Street and industrialist clients, academics such as Rowe, Reinsch, and their political science colleagues began to staff key technocratic positions outside the university—including the foundations themselves, the State Department, the Pan American Union, and the Council on Foreign Relations. In their efforts to build from Root's blueprints, Rowe, Moses, and Reinsch represent the new cadre of scholarly experts needed to negotiate relations with this sensitive region and rebrand the American imperial project along cooperative lines.

Professor Rowe's Imperial Understanding

In 1900, Secretary Root commissioned Professor Rowe to go to Puerto Rico on a study mission, redirecting his career in ways that would make him a founding member of APSA in 1903 and, in later years, the dean of the country's growing corps of Latin American area specialists—a status affirmed by his selection in 1919 as director-general of the Pan American Union. When Rowe was initially tapped by the McKinley administration for imperial service, first as a member of the Commission to Revise and Compile the Laws of Porto Rico and later as chairman of the Porto Rican Code Commission, he was a professor of political science at the University of Pennsylvania. At century's turn, political science was in its infancy as a professional discipline and Rowe was one of the few specialists in the field of municipal administration and law. This expertise proved useful for the commissions on which he served, implementing the provisions of the Foraker Act of 1900, which outlined the organic structure of civil government in this new American colony of Puerto Rico.

Like many Americans who traveled to these new colonies, Rowe produced a book based on his experiences in Puerto Rico. But within this veritable deluge of books, pamphlets, and magazine articles presenting the nation's "new island possessions" to an avid metropolitan readership, his book, *The United States and Porto Rico* (1904), is strikingly free of the usual ethnographic photographs, patriotic garlands, and shimmering battleships. Rather, his is a sober work of political science aimed at communicating the practical difficulties of colonial governance to an audience trained to grasp the constitutional ramifications of *Downes v. Bidwell* or the theoretical subtleties of municipal management. After more than five years of American direct rule and three years of civilian government in Puerto Rico, Rowe was decidedly pessimistic about the possibility that Puerto Ricans would ever assimilate the liberal habits of U.S. republicanism. Although he was seemingly chastened by his administrative experience in Puerto Rico, Rowe's book was not a declaration of imperial retreat but rather a call for scientific understanding of the "problems arising out our contact with the Spanish-American civilization" in Puerto Rico to better meet the challenges of continuously expanding U.S. hegemony in the Americas. Understanding these problems, Rowe argued, could provide a scientific template that experts could use to work out the formulas for future U.S. contacts with Latin America. Only through "a careful analysis of the conditions under which Spanish-American civilization has developed," he concluded, could the United States "meet the complex questions which our relations with these countries present."[4]

This, Rowe makes clear, is a problem to be solved by professionals through scientific study rather than military acumen or charismatic political leadership. While the bulk of his book is devoted to a technical analysis of the difficulties faced by colonial officials in extending American political rule to Puerto Rico, Rowe suggests that the consequences of imperial contact are not restricted to the colonial periphery but are transcultural—that is, mutually transformative—in nature. Thus, for the political scientist the task of understanding empire meant not only careful study of the imperial periphery but also coming to grips with the transformation of political culture within the United States as it adapted to its new imperial role. "The establishment of civil rule in Porto Rico and in the Philippines," Rowe avers, "possesses a significance far deeper than the immediate legislative and administrative problems involved. The acquisition of these islands is only one phase of a larger movement which is profoundly influencing our national life, and which will ultimately affect the operation, if not the form, of our institutions."[5]

Looking back, Rowe's intuition that overseas expansion would profoundly change the "national life" of the metropole makes intuitive sense. Yet what is remarkable about this call to his political science colleagues to understand these changes is that, while the professional discipline of political science has flourished in the United States more than in virtually any other country, little work has been devoted to understanding the changes that Rowe predicted over a century ago. In short, we are still faced with Rowe's unanswered question: in what ways did this foray into colonial governance transform the American state?[6]

In its extensive discussion of the Supreme Court decisions in the so-called insular cases, Rowe's book makes it clear that the wholesale transfer of American political institutions to its new colonies created detrimental resistance in the colonial society and undermined the constitutional foundations of the metropole. Indeed, this "greater elasticity" demanded by the conditions of contact between north and south seemed to militate against additional formal colonies if the United States were to accomplish its hemispheric goals. "The Monroe Doctrine carries with it obligations as well as rights," Rowe argued. "The feeling of distrust toward the United States which was so evident during the recent war must be made to disappear through the assurance that the hegemony of the United States on the [Latin] American continent does not involve the destruction of the domestic institutions of the Southern Republics."[7]

EMPIRE AND THE AMERICAN POLITICAL SCIENCE ASSOCIATION

Within the framework of this discussion, the formal organization of the American Political Science Association in 1903–4 represents a milestone in the rapid institutionalization of a professional policy network in the United States. In the case of political science, the extension of sovereignty over a new island empire supplied an urgent "problem" and a foundational test around which institutional and intellectual scaffolding of the emerging discipline was quickly erected to make way for the bricks and mortar of a nascent network of expertise.

Indeed, nearly half of the presentations at APSA's inaugural conference addressed, in some way, the rising frustrations with the problems of colonial administration in the Caribbean and Pacific. Indicative of this focus were the papers given by Rowe, Moses, and Reinsch, each of whom discussed the difficulties of the American colonial experiment and developed both remedies and historical/theoretical frames for understanding the uniqueness of the American colonial "problem." As we saw in Rowe's book, the dominant theme of these three presentations was the naïveté of initial American efforts in Cuba, Puerto

Rico, and the Philippines. In its stead, all three made varying pleas for sensitivity to and respect for local conditions as well as a healthy respect for the staying power of local political social traditions. In his paper, titled "Colonial Autonomy," for example, Paul Reinsch argued that American colonial officials had failed to "respond to the social and economic needs of the Philippine people . . . of whose social and economic life we as a people know next to nothing." Instead, he explained, these officials had "approached the difficult problems of colonial administration with a finished program based upon a vague belief in Destiny

William H. Taft and Elihu Root, circa 1904. (U.S. Library of Congress)

and in the universal applicability of our institutions . . . which we admire, and concerning the usefulness of which we have no doubt."[8]

In his formal response to the conference papers presented by Reinsch and Moses, Henry C. Morris suggested that the problem of American colonialism deserved the establishment of a special section within APSA—an idea that seems to have been rejected or ignored. But if we look past the formal nature of his proposal to organize a colonial institute and a new colonial section of APSA and substitute the idea of "foreign affairs" or "Latin American policy," the proposal reveals in broad outline the professional ambitions of the first generation of American political scientists. Morris's ideas bear quoting at some length. In response to the presentations by Moses and Reinsch about the difficulties faced in the Philippines, Morris not only agreed, but went on to suggest that these difficulties represented a signal opportunity for the fledgling APSA.

> The need of the times in the elaboration and improvement of colonial government, administration and services seems emphatically to be an opportunity to become familiar with the experience of other nations under similar conditions. It is comparatively easy to criticize, but far more difficult to formulate plans and procedure. To the representatives of such an organization as the American Political Science Association, the task of aiding and assisting in this undertaking would seem to be peculiarly fitting. While not perhaps advocating at this moment the establishment of any distinct organization, it would appear that one of the most helpful steps that might be taken, would be the inauguration of some association in the nature of a colonial institute, the purpose of which should pre-eminently be the study of problems connected with colonization and colonial policy. . . . Gradually it might expand and develop the field of its operations until it became not only a permanent adjunct in the colonial system but also a potent force for good, in the development of an interest at home in colonial affairs as well as in the preservation of the colonies themselves from the evils of a harmful policy and the effects of maladministration.[9]

The fact that Morris's ideas were never formally taken up represents, I feel, an increasing awareness of the political costs associated with a direct-rule model of empire and a pragmatic move toward institutions of international cooperation as a more efficient means to manage the country's hegemonic interests.

The founding of APSA thus marked a watershed moment in the professionalization of the social sciences and illustrates the "sociocratic" ambitions of the academic community that characterized the Progressive period. Reflecting a rising technocratic ethos, the goals of the association were to provide practical expert guidance to the state, prepare a new generation of technocrats for civil service, and educate the public to better align itself with the goals of the state.

Root's Pan-Americanism and Latin American Studies

By linking colonialism and imperialism genealogically to the institutionalization of political science as a formal academic discipline, I hope to suggest not just that resolution of the theoretical and practical difficulties posed by American imperialism was central to the raison d'être of the new discipline but also that enlistment of this first generation of professional political scientists as agents of U.S. power profoundly shaped the core work of the discipline and, perhaps more important, facilitated the emergence of an increasingly surreptitious style of imperial management.

Nowhere is this process more clear than in the participation of leading political scientists such as Professor Rowe in the dramatic rebranding of American regional hegemony through the Pan-American movement. Originally the brainchild of Secretary of State James G. Blaine, the largely dormant Pan-American movement was personally reinvigorated in 1906 by Secretary of State Root's visit to the Third Pan-American Congress in Rio de Janeiro and his subsequent diplomatic tour of Latin American capitals aboard the USS *Charleston*.

In taking this unprecedented tour Root had two principal goals. First, he wished to forestall the firestorm of political ill will raging through Latin American societies as a consequence of U.S. military predations in the Caribbean following the war with Spain, thereby preparing the way for the microinterventions of U.S. soft power. Second, he hoped to capture the diplomatic goodwill of Latin American nations in preparation for the International Peace Congress in the Hague the following year. His preparations for this effort began in Washington where he broke with protocol by including Latin American ambassadors in the exclusive engagements on the capital's social calendar. As Philip C. Jessup notes, these preparatory efforts by Secretary Root ran against the grain of Washington society, but they had a remarkable effect on the *rapprochement* Root then desired.

> On the social side, Root worked assiduously, making every effort to accept all invitations he possibly could from the Latin American diplomats and extending to them invitations in return. He and [Brazilian Ambassador Joaquim] Nabuco planned a dinner, given by the Ambassador, to a list of guests which he asked Root to draw up for him. There was still a tendency to refuse a South American's dinner invitation and Root carefully rounded up guests, pressing on the Lodges the importance of their attending and writing frankly to Admiral Dewey: "Is there any chance of your reconsidering the Brazilian Ambassador's invitation for dinner on the 23rd of January? The dinner has an important bearing upon the new *rapprochement* we are endeavoring to bring about between the United States and Brazil and the United States and South America generally (with a few exceptions). We are to have

the Third Pan-American Congress at Rio next summer and I am going to attend, probably going down officially in one of our warships, and we are making a good deal of fuss about it." Dewey reconsidered.[10]

Using the financial backing of the Carnegie Corporation, of which he was the principal architect and a founding trustee, Root organized a peace conference in Washington in December of 1907 and there founded the Central American Court of Justice, an important forerunner of the Permanent Court of International Justice in the Hague. The effort paid off handsomely on all counts as Root was universally hailed in South American banquet halls and theaters, and subsequently he was able to lead a large contingent of diplomats from nearly all of the American republics to the celebration of the International Peace Conference in 1907. In this way, the Monroe Doctrine was forcefully upheld as a sound principle of international understanding at the Hague despite its extralegal status in the formal canons of international law negotiated there.

Much as Napoleon's conquest of Egypt launched French orientalism, so, on a more modest scale, Secretary Root's triumphal 1906 tour of Rio and other Latin American capitals, in the company of these academics, precipitated a reciprocal process of integrating area studies within the American academy and area specialists within his internationalist networks. Again, Root's favored Latin American specialist, Leo Rowe, provides an apt illustration of the official aspect of this process. Through a metamorphosis from academic generalist to professional point man for U.S.–Latin American relations, each step in Rowe's rapid ascent—from membership in an initial investigative mission to Puerto Rico (1900) to assistant secretary of the treasury (1917), chief of the Latin American Division at the State Department (1919), and director-general of the Pan American Union—reveals the contours of an emerging internationalist policy network and the role of American academics within it.

Like Rowe, Professor Bernard Moses was one of several academic figures who had been tapped by the McKinley administration to initiate a civilian-run administration in the newly acquired colonies. After the outbreak of hostilities with Filipino forces preempted the work of a first, largely investigative Philippine Commission, which included the president of Cornell University, Jacob Schurmann, and University of Michigan zoologist Dean C. Worcester, a second commission, which included William Howard Taft and Moses, sailed for the Philippines in 1900. Moses had taken a leave of absence from his teaching duties at the University of California to serve on the commission. He was one of the few scholars in the United States who spoke Spanish and was familiar with Spain's colonial administration in the Americas. Indeed, in 1895 he had taught the first university course in the United States devoted to a Spanish American topic and was thus one of the few with any academic expertise to qualify him for colonial service. During his later diplomatic missions to Pan-American conferences at Buenos Aires and Santiago de Chile, Moses's presence was memorable, as one fellow colonial recalled, for "the delight of those distinguished audiences to find themselves addressed by an American in cultivated and eloquent phrases of their own sonorous and beautiful language."[11]

After their official assignments ended, Rowe and Moses continued to integrate the Latin American subfield within U.S. social science. As the first to give a graduate-level course in Latin American history at a U.S. university, Moses had been an early promoter of the field, paving the way at the University of California for a first generation of area specialists that included Herbert Bolton and Charles Chapman. In a seamless intertwining of his academic and diplomatic roles, Moses used his later diplomatic missions "to add greatly to his own acquisitions of historical and political collections on South America—materials employed by him, after his retirement as Professor of Political Science in 1911, to enrich our understanding of the intellectual and political history of that continent."[12] Reinsch did not become a Latin Americanist, but at the University of Wisconsin he was instrumental in promoting academic scholarship in another area of immense interest to the United States, China and East Asia, and he ultimately secured an ambassadorship to China under President Woodrow Wilson.[13]

What were the intellectual and disciplinary consequences of colonial service for scholars such as Moses and Rowe? Intellectually, the short answer to this question is that their experience produced a robust pragmatism in their scholarly work and introduced a new imperative toward cultural understanding placed within the greater service of empire. As Rowe warned in his 1904 study of Puerto Rico, this small island held large lessons for the United States as it continued its southern expansion.

> If, in our contact with foreign civilizations in the West Indies, we show a harsh, unbending spirit, this feeling of distrust will develop into an abiding hatred, which will block effectually the fulfillment of our mission on the American continent. Although the problem of government in these islands does not present great territorial importance, it involves all those political lessons which we must learn in order to meet our political duties and obligations as the leading nation of the Western Hemisphere. The real significance of the extension of American dominion in the West Indies lies not so much in the fact of territorial aggrandizement as in the adaptation of our political ideas and standards which this expansion involves.[14]

Indeed, Rowe adds, these Caribbean conquests represented nothing less than the ultimate test, on the international stage, of the quality of America's civilization and statecraft.

It is this new necessity for adaptation that marks the real turning-point in our history. We are being put to a test to which France failed to respond and which England and Germany have met with but partial success. Nothing we can do, save an ignominious retreat, can avoid the issue. The situation adds a new responsibility to the ever-increasing demands of American statesmanship and upon American citizenship; an ability to appreciate the value of institutions which, while different from our own, fulfill the same ends of justice; a conservatism born of this comprehension, and with it all, a firm determination to bring the new peoples with whom we may be brought into close and intimate contact, by means of the slow process of education, to a free and willing acceptance of all that is best in our system of law and government.[15]

Fusing the language of instruction with the language of empire—the "lessons" and "tests" presented by Puerto Rico with the "duties," "obligations," "responsibilities," "and "mission" of the United States—Rowe never questions "our" role as "the leading nation of the Western Hemisphere." Rather, he elaborates the need for a more restrained and responsive approach for the very reason that this new strategy of "adaptation" would ultimately prove more effective in expanding America's influence in the region.

In effect, the United States could, through an imperialism of understanding-cum-suasion, draw on its experience in this small island colony to develop policies for the transformation of all Latin America. "The lessons that we are learning will be of service to us in the larger tasks that are before us," Rowe wrote. "Future generations will look upon the experience acquired in the administration of civil affairs in Porto Rico as a period of training and preparation for the problems involved in our relations with the Spanish-speaking peoples of the [Latin] American continent."[16] On a similar note, Root, in his essay "The Real Monroe Doctrine," essentially echoes this sentiment in framing a new internationalist approach to Latin America. Indeed, the principal platform of Root's interpretation of U.S. hegemony was respect for the sovereignty of subject populations and legal reciprocity through international legal agreements.[17]

Professors Rowe, Reinsch, and Moses were not architects of American imperial policies, nor did they, either single-handedly or collectively, drive the political science profession to focus its attention on imperial concerns. Even within the fields of political science and Latin American studies, there is little evidence of their legacy as founding professionals. Their importance in this study, however, lies in their participation in the creation of a unique institutional nexus that began to develop in the United States about the time of Root's Latin American tour. They represent the process whereby academic professionals were integrated into the project of preparing the U.S. government, its institutions, and its population for an international role.

Thus, it seems no accident that the development of social science scholarship coincided with the formal establishment of an American colonial empire, and many of the leading figures in the professionalization of the social sciences, especially political science, were also involved in the management of this new imperial apparatus. Reflecting a new "pragmatism" in social science scholarship, the difficulties that political scientists such as Rowe and Moses faced in this initial (colonial) phase of imperial administration led them to develop a healthy respect for the difficulty of the task and to largely abandon the theoretical principles that first framed the endeavor in favor of a more "understanding" approach to American internationalism.

More broadly, the impetus for this shift from colonial conquest and direct rule to a collaborative international system can be seen as a reaction to the uproar caused by the "secession" of Panama, the controversies over Caribbean rule, and the international skepticism over Taft's emergency governorship of Cuba's "independent" government in 1905. In presiding over this larger, long-term transition from colonial rule to imperial influence, Root saw the problem as principally a matter of diplomatic relations and public opinion and thus set about systematically cultivating the goodwill of the Latin American diplomatic corps. For Root, the most important "solution" to the "problem" faced by the United States in pursuing its hegemonic designs was the reanimation of a thoroughgoing Pan-Americanism whereby U.S. representatives could enlist Latin American elites in the formulation of a hemispheric treaty regime for trade, arbitration, extradition, and other aspects of international law. Although American hegemony would soon shift from colonial rule to international cooperation and co-optation, the domestic policy apparatus, with its layers of interlocking elites, would survive to become a resilient and recurring feature within this unique imperial state.

Conclusions

In this essay I have attempted to sketch lines of continuity between the acquisition of formal overseas colonies and the rise of the United States to its present hegemonic position in global affairs. Although the tactical procedures and rhetorical framework for American imperialism underwent a profound transformation in the years immediately following the extension of U.S. sovereignty to its island colonies, its "foreign relations" retained their imperial character throughout the twentieth century. A patient and persistent campaign was undertaken by key members of the national power elite to make American hegemony agreeable to the domestic (i.e., metropolitan) populace, acceptable to the other imperial powers, and palatable to the regions subject to American intervention and control. This campaign has been remarkably successful on all counts. At home, the "foreign policy establishment" that Elihu Root worked tirelessly to organize has effectively dominated the state apparatus, as well as public debate, whether in the press, on university campuses, or on party platforms. This has been accomplished through a process of institutional capture and a strident campaign of social engineering funded through the major philanthropic foundations, echoed by the major instruments of the national media, and reproduced on college campuses.

I have presented here only the barest outline of what I take to be the "larger movement" of imperial transformation predicted in 1904 by Leo S. Rowe. The true scope and remarkable ambition of this "understanding empire" is beyond the scope of this essay and, indeed, beyond the capacity of any single scholar. By focusing on the figure of Elihu Root, my intention has been to suggest that a discernible program of creating a foreign policy consensus in the United States was afoot in the early twentieth century and, further, that specific agents in that program can be identified. Indeed, a network of individuals from all sectors of the national power elite participated actively in this program, and they also can be identified by careful study of their respective fields of activity. What is more, this project was a natural outgrowth of the shared economic, political, and institutional interests of American finance capital that effectively dominated national politics, industry, and education through networks like the one created by Elihu Root in the field of foreign policy making. More broadly, the missionary impulse that has dominated the ethos of American relations with the rest of the world has meant that the social engineering methods developed to shape the national life of the United States have been vigorously exported and a similar logic of institutional capture has worked its effect across the globe through the exercise of a robust soft power backed by an equally vigorous economic and military hegemony.

If our aim in this volume is to come to grips with the true scope of American imperialism and to trace its effects both at home and abroad, new tools of information gathering and analysis must be sought and shared. In short, a network, not unlike that built by Root and staffed by academic professionals such as Rowe, must be built across the disciplines and geographic scenes of U.S. imperial activity. One preliminary step toward this goal of understanding the American empire would be to create a collaborative, searchable database of information to map, cross-tabulate, and analyze linkages that bind these individual agencies and agents of early imperialism. Each of the contributions to this volume is attentive in its own way to the role of certain colonial personnel, but no single resource now exists to lay bare their relations to the larger imperial apparatus. To take but one example, if the American imperial state is indeed, at its essence, an empire of subcontractors—one of our contentions in this volume—does this not beg the question of who, then, is letting those contracts?

If, as I have suggested, the perverse genius of American imperialism has been its creation and reproduction of an understanding empire under the rhetorical cover of "foreign relations" and "national security," the layers of this complex network of imperial management, like so many layers of an onion, must be peeled away if we are to understand its true structure and methods of operation. In the deeply stratified history of the American empire, it is only through close analysis of these personal and institutional networks that we can move beyond the obfuscations of American exceptionalism or the easy moralizing of high-minded resentment to demonstrate the full empirical basis for our claims.

PART 4

RACE AND IMPERIAL IDENTITIES

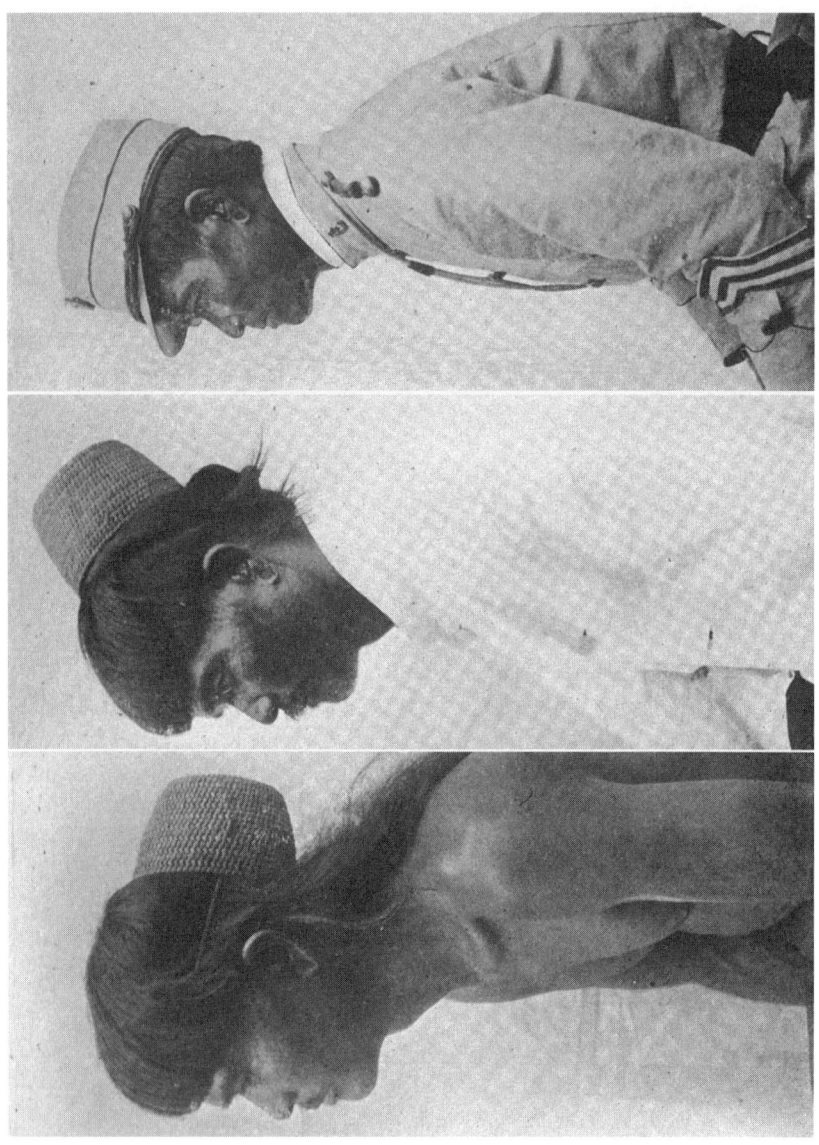

"Educational Value of the Constabulary. (1) Bontoc Igorot on entering the service, 1901. (2) After a year's service, 1902. (3) After two years' service, 1903." (Frederick Chamberlin, *The Philippine Problem 1898–1913* [Boston: Little, Brown & Co., 1913], p. 160)

INTRODUCTION

CLARE CORBOULD

Is the United States an empire? Has it ever been? Some say no; aside from a brief moment around the beginning of the twentieth century there was no annexation of land, taken to be the hallmark of empire. Naysayers point to the scrappy nature of American foreign policy as if to say, well, it was never complete or fully intended, and it had consensus among neither policymakers nor the general populace. It is, of course, a myth that other empires were any better organized; empires are always in a state of becoming, not least because they always face resistance of one sort or another. When this question is addressed from another perspective, that is, from the point of view of those who have come under the yoke of American dominion, the reply is often more straightforward, albeit equally charged with politics.

The essays in this section are all concerned in some way with meanings of race as produced in circuits of empire among the United States, Hawai'i, Cuba, the Philippines, and Puerto Rico. People formed their ideas about race in multiple contexts beyond even these complicated routes, including other empires, most obviously the Spanish and British. "Race" was not something exported out of the United States to the colonial periphery; rather, race was made by empire just as empire was made by race. Ideas about race filtered back to the "metropole" and circulated around various colonial locales, changing and being changed all the while. These ideas influenced the apparatuses of the American imperial state, and the reverse was true, too. Such technologies of rule included censuses, the franchise, education, lawmaking, commemoration, and land distribution—all things considered here. Two authors in this section also explore meanings of race outside "the state," as such, which then fed back into state institutions.

Essays by Paul A. Kramer and Alejandro de la Fuente and Matthew Casey provide a model for writing the history of racial politics during the American empire's brief "classical" (or territorial) period. Kramer reflects on his recent book, *The Blood of Government,* to propose a taxonomy of transnational history.[1] More than a manifesto, he gives flesh to the bones of the frequently made observation that race is historically contingent and in this case transnational. By examining the experiences of specific American and Filipino actors in the colonial Philippines, Kramer moves readers beyond a simple parallel between white racism in the United States and American racism in the Philippines. Race and racism in both places were calibrated by American imperialism (and vice versa), but were not totally determined by it. People in the Philippines, of course, had their own ideas about race. Kramer concludes that American white supremacy and divisions in Filipino society were shaped as much by the legacy of Spanish colonialism as by subsequent American imperial power.

De la Fuente and Casey investigate the effects in Cuba of the tendency of many white North Americans to see race in binary terms. Drawing on conditions of segregation in the United States and an unreliable memory of the havoc of the Reconstruction "experiment," white Americans anticipated that if black Cubans were allowed to vote chaos would ensue. Their attitudes ensured that the Constitutional Convention of 1900 enacted universal manhood suffrage at the birth of the Cuban Republic, even though no black delegates were present. Prior to the American intervention, representatives of the Spanish colonial order had been won over to broad-based suffrage, for which activists had campaigned since the 1860s. White Americans, blinded by their own ideas and experiences—in this instance regarding race—failed in their efforts to limit the suffrage. The authors' findings do much to demonstrate that the American imperial state was by no means efficient. In effect, the Cubans mobilized their favorable political memories of the Spanish colonial regime to cast a sharply critical light on American imperial ambitions. Their recollections of the past had a deliberate political point to make, one that Puerto Ricans also made through public rituals.

By charting the changing priorities in Puerto Ricans' public commemorations, Christopher Schmidt-Nowara explores the resistance to imperial succession from Spanish to American. Columbus had featured heavily in historical commemorations from the mid- to late nineteenth century. Yet at the quadricentenary of the island's conquest in 1908, Ponce de León took his place as Puerto Ricans began to revere rather than revile their conqueror. Why? Schmidt-Nowara shows that in the wake of the straitening U.S. colonial regime, with its personnel making it clear that they regarded Puerto Ricans as inferior, those Puerto Ricans began to emphasize the relatively positive aspects of Spanish colonialism. At the very least, they stressed, the Spanish regarded them as "Spaniards" and were prepared to include them in their own history. Americans, by contrast, behaved as though they were the ones doing the Puerto Ricans a favor by placing them under an American tutelage designed to drag them up, rung by rung, on the so-called ladder of civilization. Public commemorations emphasizing the Spanish roots of Puerto Rico—and, implicitly, the Indian roots prior to conquest—were a way for Puerto Ricans to differentiate themselves from their new conquerors.

Puerto Rican census data collected in 1910 and 1920 reveal more evidence of resistance to American imperial rule. Francisco A. Scarano and Katherine Curtis White analyze, in a conference paper not included here, the strategies that colonized people used to adapt to new systems of rule. Census data on household composition show that Afro–Puerto Ricans preferred increasingly to live in the city and in nonnuclear families. In these formations, Puerto Rico's poorest people were best able to avoid the effects of the rapid and dramatic upheaval that American capitalism wrought, especially on agrarian workers. Censuses, in other words, provide not only rich evidence of the development of an American imperial state but also of the efforts to resist its rule and the means to do so.[2]

As Francisco A. Scarano shows in this section, the censuses conducted by the new imperial regime adopted a state apparatus bequeathed it by Spain's modernizing empire. Census data collection early in the American administration of Puerto Rico mobilized Spanish technology and produced results that were much like those of a recent Spanish census. Before these data were collected, however, American officials used Spanish census tallies to argue at home that the Puerto Rican population was gradually "whitening." They discarded definitions of race dominant in the United States, whereby blackness was supposedly so pungent that a single colored ancestor made one black, and instead adopted the more calibrated attitudes of local Latin American elites. Through such adaptation, American officials argued for a tutelary colonialism, hoping that in the long term the island would be assimilated into the United States. Well beyond the scope of Scarano's essay, but an avenue worth pursuing, is the relationship between these ideas about race and contemporaneous assertions by sociologists in the United States, E. A. Ross most prominently, that the darker races were dying out.

Americans' overseas ventures during the 1890s may have felt novel to them, but the implementation of various imperial technologies would have struck Hawaiians as more familiar. Rona Halualani charts the transition from 'aina, a set of social relations in which land was sacred and goods produced on it a blessing, to social structures that rested on Western concepts of landownership and capitalist modes of production. Reproduction was key to the latter, with foreigners assuming they would pass on to their sons any land they developed. After some years of resistance, with westerners inhabiting and using land in exchange for the skilled work they contributed to their communities, eventually the transition was complete. Native Hawaiians were by and large excluded from landownership because legislation, enacted after the United States annexed the islands in 1898, deemed them to have insufficient "blood" of the islands' so-called original races.

In a conference paper not included in this collection, Kehaulani Kauanui shows that legislation and other efforts to regulate the Hawaiian population in the mid-nineteenth century were repeated several decades later in policies targeting Native Americans. The reasons for this lie partly in personnel: Samuel Chapman Armstrong—founder of the famous Hampton Institute, which taught Indian and African American pupils—was the son of Hawaiian missionaries. His father, Richard Armstrong, had been an important figure in the design and implementation of the policies and laws that ultimately dispossessed Hawaiians of their land. The most significant of these, the Mahele (1848), could well have been the model, Kauanui suggests, for the much better known General Allotment Act (the "Dawes Act") of 1887, which deprived Native Americans of some 90 million acres of treaty land, much of it on the Great Plains. The circulation of ideas, as well as people, accounts for the similarities in different times and places. Hampton itself, for example, was predated by the Foreign Mission School in Cornwall, Connecticut, founded in 1816. Among its first intake of "Heathen Youths" were Hawaiian students.[3]

By considering the island and the continental United States, both Halualani and Kauanui extend the usual template of the geography and chronology of the American empire. The language of Manifest Destiny and nation building continues to blind many to the imperial character of continental expansion, while noncontiguous Hawai'i so often falls off the map. Their study of circuits that produced imperial policy before the so-called imperial surge of the 1890s shows the need for more care in the way we divide the past into neat periods.

Michael Salman's and Kristin Hoganson's essays focus on the way ideas about race were produced—and consumed—in circuits that went beyond the state, then looped back in, either directly or indirectly. Salman's essay details the fact that historians of the Philippines were fooled for decades by a 1913 forgery of the "Code of Kalantiaw," said to have been written by a Filipino chief in 1433, over a century before Spain colonized the archipelago. The code was extraordinarily harsh, thus playing into American pretensions about bringing civilization to a nation of savages, who, even after four hundred years of Spanish rule, were considered backward and in need of help (and proving, too, the inadequacies of Spanish rule). Ideas about race, specifically the racial inferiority of Filipino people, structured not only the colonial state but also the acquisition and dissemination of knowledge that took place in libraries, museums, and universities. Commercial transaction—the literal purchase of items such as this purported fifteenth-century code—rested on false assumptions about people's nature. Those exchanges subsequently contributed to the creation and expansion of archives and the translation of seemingly key documents in Filipino history into widely read printed anthologies. These, in turn, became intrinsic to what Americans thought they knew about their colonial territory and ultimately shaped colonial policy.

Kristin Hoganson traces the beginning of globalized mass consumption of the modern kind, probing evidence to discover what it meant to American consumers, especially women, to purchase goods that came from other parts of the world, including those territories over which their country was now exercising control. By the close of the nineteenth century, cosmopolitanism had become a highly valued attribute in women, so wealthy and middle-class women consumed exotic goods to demonstrate their knowledge and appreciation of foreign goods and people. Consumption produced knowledge about empire because the foreignness of the goods became a selling point much vaunted by vendors. If descriptions were rarely precise as to the place of origin or the conditions under which objects were made, that was because it was through consumption of difference (it made little difference whether an "oriental" rug was Turkish, Persian, or Chinese) that women achieved a desirable class status and an affinity with sophisticated European women. People of "civilized" races consumed while the uncivilized were imagined to benefit from Americans' desire to purchase their goods, just as the U.S. state extended its benevolent rule over them. In so consuming, Americans transformed themselves into metropolitan citizens of empire.

Racism, and ideas about race, shaped American foreign policy and the experience of assorted armed servicemen and women, diplomats, advisers, public servants, and individuals employed by private organizations and agencies. These essays demonstrate, however, that it is simplistic to assert that racism within the United States led to the acquisition of or patterns of administration for these overseas territories. For a start, racism within the United States was hardly undifferentiated, so we cannot assume that so varied a phenomenon at home could be readily replicated abroad. Any effort to export dominant binary ideas about race were resisted by many, as the Hawaiian, Puerto Rican, and Cuban examples show. These same local conditions, moreover, often changed the ideas of those Americans sent beyond the borders of the United States, and they brought their altered attitudes home with them.

The most concrete consequence within the United States of these transnational processes of race making came in attitudes toward immigration. Debates about restricting entry into the United States from its relatively open status in the nineteenth century simmered away for some years, hardening between 1917 and 1924 into rigid racial engineering by way of federal legislation and Supreme Court decisions on the status of individuals who came before the courts. Now only specific numbers of certain "types" of people would be allowed entry each year with the aim of maintaining the idealized racial composition supposedly achieved decades earlier, which had been threatened by the large number of immigrants from Southern and Eastern Europe who entered the United States a few decades prior to the legislation's enactment.[4] The American imperial experience was not the only factor contributing to the 1924 legislation, yet such anxiety and the response to it were typical results of imperial race formation. Concern about the impact of Irish and Jewish migrants to England had likewise prompted the British Parliament to enact the Aliens Act, restricting immigration, in 1905. As in the United States, concern about the suitability of these newcomers was articulated through studies of urban slums, which were seen as an expression of the newcomers' racial inferiority rather than a result of poverty and poor governance.

Changing ideas about race in colonial circuits also affected the status of people already in the United States. Colonial policy decreed a new status for people in the unincorporated territories the United States had seized. Neither citizen nor alien, they were declared U.S. nationals. Puerto Ricans became citizens, of a sort, in 1917. By altering what it meant to belong to the United States, colonial lawmaking also gave legitimacy to domestic racism against black Americans. Their citizenship, granted after the Civil War by a constitutional amendment, had always been tenuous, but new ways of thinking about the racial composition of the nation shored up the pervasive sense among white Americans that black people did not really belong in the United States.

Although racism was a feature in all of these colonial settings, it was never monolithic. For those who deny the existence of an American empire, this might seem heartening; there was, after all, no mastermind bent on world domination. For others still, the mutability of racism in different arenas does not discount the existence of an American empire but rather shows how the "imperial state"— a tapestry of players and modes of rule—was both adaptable and diverse.

Race, Empire, and Transnational History

PAUL A. KRAMER

AT THE END OF THREE MONTHS in command of U.S. forces in Lanao in 1901, David J. Gilmer, captain in the 49th U.S. Volunteer Infantry in the Philippines, issued a proclamation. The traditional historiography of race and American colonialism would lead us to expect that this proclamation would thickly apply a language of civilization, social Darwinism, and the white man's burden. Perhaps American racial formations at home, such as racist references to Filipinos as Indians or African Americans, would be "exported" or "projected" in it.

But two factors in particular turned Gilmer's statement in quite different directions. Specifically, he felt compelled to respond to Filipino fears that American white supremacy, about which rumors circulated widely in the Philippines, would "invade" the islands under American colonialism. Second, Gilmer was African American, a fact that he decided to use as an object lesson to make a larger point about the character of the United States as a society and a colonial power. Speaking from "the visible Negro blood that flows in the veins of my body," Gilmer praised the United States as a "true democracy." It was true that in the United States there was a "rabble" that ran "riot at times," but Gilmer assured his audiences that they "need not have any fear of that class of Americans, for they cannot reach you." Against the notion that "all white men are unfair to the Negro races," he urged the people of Lanao to "judge men according to the deeds of the individual and not by the color of his skin."[1]

This small episode illustrates a broader historiographic point about the way historians approach race and empire. Scholars have often connected histories of race and empire in the early twentieth century by asserting either that race was a powerful, causal impetus for imperialism or that prior American racial formations directed against African Americans or Native Americans fundamentally shaped colonial policy.[2] Both of these approaches, however, view race in a static,

199

ahistorical, and decontextualized manner while reducing American imperialism to its metropolitan actors and dynamics. Speaking in Lanao, David Gilmer was not an "exporter" of Anglo-Saxonism; indeed, to pacify the town's elites, he had made himself into the ambassador of an empire "without" race.

Writing a transnational history of imperial race making will mean paying close attention to precisely these kinds of immediate contexts and the way they shaped, and were shaped by, the politics of race. In the present setting, this will mean opening the frame of analysis so as to fully integrate histories unfolding on both sides of the Pacific that involve both Filipinos and Americans as agents and have stakes for both American and Philippine historiographies.

The Racial Politics of Empire

This essay, and the larger work whose arguments it reviews, is, on the one hand, a history of the racial politics of empire, of the way hierarchies of difference were generated and mobilized in order to legitimate and organize invasion, conquest, and colonial administration.[3] Where many prior accounts have emphasized the functionality of race to empire, often as "colonial discourse," my work highlights race as a dynamic, contextual, contested, and contingent field of power. It is, on the other hand, a history of the imperial politics of race, of the way empire building interacted with, and transformed, the process of racial formation. Where historians have often seen colonial racial formations as exports or projections of prior, domestic ones, the present work argues for the necessity of examining metropole and colony in a single, densely interactive field in which colonial dynamics are not strictly derivative of, dependent on, or respondent to metropolitan forces. The work argues, moreover, that these two histories—of the racial remaking of empire and the imperial remaking of race—are not separable. It was not simply that difference made empire possible: empire remade difference in the process.

My analysis of the racial politics of Philippine-American colonialism hopes to point the way more generally toward a more thoroughly "transnational" history of the American empire. It begins from the assumption that transnational history is not a what but a how, not a subject, and something less rigorous than a unitary method, but rather a set of overlapping reorientations and reframings that can be applied, in virtually infinite variety (and with widely varying degrees of usefulness) to any historical subject.[4] In particular, I emphasize four dimensions that I believe distinguish transnational from conventional, nation-based approaches to history-writing.[5] First, transnational histories are suspicious of periodizations that emerge from a single, nationally defined context, seeking out chronological boundaries and plotlines that correspond to the rhythms of transnational dynamics themselves.[6] Second, transnational histories are cautious of what might be called false cognates, presumed connections across national divides on the basis of perceived homologies in the absence of evidence of actual interaction in discursive, practical, or institutional domains.[7] Third is the question of power: while transnational history has often been represented as the history of liberated and liberating transborder currents obstructed only by the institutional power of nation-states, my sense is that transnational history ought to concern itself fundamentally with the way power flows across borders.[8] Fourth, rather than proceeding reflexively, exploring the transnational simply to illuminate or enrich national pasts or to respond to questions originating from a single nation-based historiography, transnational history ideally speaks to—and has the potential to transform—inquiries posed by multiple nation-based historiographies.

My project here attempts to carry out a transnational history of race making in Philippine-American colonial histories of the early twentieth century. In doing so, it participates in a rich, emerging literature on racial and gendered difference and the American empire in this period.[9] But it also seeks to push beyond perspectives that focus only on the perceptions and agency of U.S.-based actors, or that comprehend U.S. colonial racial formations as involving either the export of domestic racial discourses, practices, and institutions or the installation of generic colonial discourses that emerge organically from the colonial situation itself.[10] It aspires instead to a transnational perspective attuned to dynamics unfolding in both the United States and the Philippines, to the syncopated timelines of Philippine and U.S. histories as they collided and interwove, and to Filipino and American perceptions, voices, and actions. In historiographic terms, it hopes to address the impact—necessarily asymmetrical—of Philippine-American colonialism on both American and Philippine nationalisms.[11]

In advancing these objectives, I approach colonial race making as intimately tied up in a broader politics of recognition, a struggle over the terms by which sovereignty would be determined in Philippine-American history. In colonial situations, I argue, this politics of recognition began where the capacity of violence to determine behavior ended. It was formally inclusionary, inviting its subjects to participate actively in colonial state building to the extent that hegemonic authorities recognized their capacities for discipline, political rationality, and self-government. In this way, it stabilized colonialism by providing a flexible ideological basis for a calibrated mixture of empowerment and disenfranchisement. In polities with strong anti-imperialist elements, it delivered the highly useful illusion of impermanence through a politics of benchmarks: moments when recognition of the capacities of the colonized would (in theory) translate into counterimperial transfers of sovereignty. It also oriented the politics of colonized elites toward the fulfillment of the colonizers' criteria and away from critiques of the colonizers' evaluative authority itself. But the politics of recognition also left colonial subjects with discursive resources, especially where the colonizing powers, held to their own criteria, proved unrecognizable.

Transnational Encounters

By the late nineteenth century, the Philippines was an exception among Spain's remaining colonies, the only one whose inhabitants were denied representation in the metropolitan legislature.[12] As the Philippines became more fully integrated into the world economy, especially through commercialized, export agriculture, the islands' urban elite, known as *ilustrados* (enlightened), mobilized, through the Propaganda movement, in pursuit of greater rights within the Spanish colonial structure and ultimately through a revolution on behalf of independent statehood.[13] First, they challenged the logic of Spanish racist exclusions. Where, for example, Spaniards attributed features of indolence and superstition to the Philippine Islands' peoples due to "race," *ilustrados* traveling to Europe observed with satisfaction that Spanish workers and peasants themselves possessed many of these characteristics.

Moreover, the movement sought recognition of the *ilustrados*' "civilization," measured in educational and artistic achievement, Spanish-language ability, and bourgeois sophistication. In their attempt to deracialize civilization, the propaganda activists succeeded in mitigating among themselves racial divisions between *criollos* (persons born in the Islands of two Spanish parents); *mestizos* (persons with one native parent) and *indios* (persons with two native parents).[14] Especially among *ilustrados* living in Europe, a new term—*Filipino*—was used to cut across these racial divisions. But by defining the borders of "civilization" in terms of Spanish evangelization—even as they secularized it—the *ilustrados* also drew boundary lines around a still prospective "Filipino" nation that closely followed the edges of Spain's power, with Muslims and animists—unconquered and unconverted by Spain—outside of the emerging, imagined polity and society.[15] In 1887, for example, when Spanish colonial officials organized an elaborate Philippine Exposition in Madrid, failing to invite or involve overseas *ilustrados* while showcasing animists before Spanish audiences, it prompted some *ilustrados* toward sympathy for their exploited compatriots, but for most it represented Spain's deliberate misrepresentation of the Philippine populace.[16] This approach to Philippine society comprises what I have called nationalist colonialism: assertions of national capacity on the basis of either self-homogenization (the minimizing or erasing of "internal" differences) or the right and duty to rule over internal others.

When the Philippine Revolution under Emilio Aguinaldo succeeded in defeating Spanish land forces in spring 1898 and Aguinaldo declared an independent Philippines in June, he did so in the name of Filipino "civilization."[17] Up until this period, the United States had played a relatively small role in *ilustrado* imaginaries relative to the gravitational pull of European civilization. When the propagandist and physician José Rizal traveled eastward toward Europe in 1888, for example, he had seen the United States as a sort of vast geographic obstacle to be overcome. On his train ride across on the continent, Rizal's jottings and letters home included pointed references to Chinese exclusion and Americans' lack of civil liberties, evidenced in antimiscegenation laws. But they also included—as would Propaganda journals such as *La Solidaridad*—references to the United States as a brash, powerful, and modern republic that the Philippines might emulate. This latter perspective surged in prominence with the arrival of the U.S. Navy's Asiatic Squadron at Manila Bay in May 1898 to confront the Spanish navy. Returning from Hong Kong to the Philippines on a U.S. vessel, Emilio Aguinaldo proclaimed Philippine independence, publicly declared Americans the Philippines' "liberators," and urged Filipinos to take up their customs and practices.

"Troubles which May Follow an Imperial Policy" conveys anti-imperialist anxieties over the ongoing conquest of the Philippine Islands by depicting a possible future "Representative from the Philippines" in the U.S. Congress as a savage warrior. *New York Herald*, July 3, 1898.

The outbreak of fighting in February 1899 abruptly and dramatically tipped the balance in favor of Filipino and American suspicion and hostility. The Americans were faced with new questions. What kind of enemy were the Filipinos? And what kind of world power was the United States to have earned the right to conquer them?[18] In answer to these questions, the war's defenders developed a novel, two-sided racial formation attuned to the need for an annexationist argument. Its first side racialized Americans as Anglo-Saxons and, by racial-historicist means, annexed them to the British Empire and the inherent rights, duties, and capacities to conquer and colonize. Where an emerging anti-imperialist movement opposed the American invasion on the grounds of republican continentalism—that American tradition established oceans and white settlers as the empire's outer limits—Anglo-Saxonism made overseas empire part of U.S. history by rooting it in deeper, "racial" history.[19] Its second half racialized Filipinos as a "tribal" society. Social-evolutionary theory of the time held that societies evolved from tribal fragmentation to civilized nationality. Derecognizing the Philippine Republic meant making it something other than a nation: the administration's defenders, especially the Philippine Commission sent to investigate the islands, recast the Philippine population as composed of an impossible "eighty-four tribes" and Aguinaldo's government as merely the hegemony of a "single tribe" of Tagalogs over the others, which were in need of "liberation."[20]

Filipino nationalists actively contested these new racial formations, with the logistical support of U.S.-based anti-imperialists.[21] In doing so, they deployed many of the same rhetorical strategies that propaganda activists had deployed against Spanish racists, appealing to metropolitan audiences with demands for recognition. Sixto Lopez, for example, challenged the Philippine Commission's depiction of the Philippine "tribes," ridiculing its report as shoddy, inaccurate, and deliberately misleading. But while he undermined some U.S. criteria for "nationhood," Lopez also shared in others. He held the United States to its own standards of nationhood—especially political unity and linguistic homogeneity—and on the basis of the United States' own polyglot immigrant world and its decentralized federalist politics denied it Filipino recognition. Not unlike the propaganda movement had in the nineteenth century, he also minimized the significance of non-Christians to the Philippine population.

Race Making and Colonial Violence

If the defense of the war before anti-imperialists required the derecognition of the Philippine Republic and promoted the U.S. racialization of both Americans and Filipinos, an even more decisive factor in these developments was the decision, made by reluctant Filipino commanders, to adopt guerrilla tactics in November 1899. Filipino and American leaders, perhaps ironically, shared a common military vocabulary, which cast conventional wars as civilized and guerrilla wars as savage.

Despite disastrous defeats at civilized warfare, Filipino commanders had hesitated to adopt guerrilla tactics for fear that, even were they to win on the battlefield, they would lose the war for international recognition on the basis of their army's perceived savagery. The next two years would prove them right. While guerrilla warfare did prevent the Americans from consolidating their control, it was increasingly perceived by American soldiers, commanders, and the American public as a sign that whatever recognition they had advanced Filipinos—even as an opposing army—had been misplaced. The savagery of Filipino combat—measured in its concealment and strategies of deception—indexed Filipinos' own supposed savagery as a race. Furthermore, assistance to the guerrillas by Filipino peasants suggested to Americans that the United States was not at war with an opposing army but with an entire population, one that was increasingly comprehended by American soldiers in racial terms.[22] While soldiers' letters and diaries reveal the novel application of such terms as *nigger* to Filipinos, soldiers also invented the term *goo-goo* to characterize their new enemy. Following McKinley's reelection in November 1900, the American generals authorized a broadening of the "enemy" to include perceived supporters of the "insurrection"; the result was an increase in American atrocities, which spiraled together with the racialization of the population.

As Filipino resistance collapsed and American civilians and collaborating elites took over in "pacified" areas, however, the limits of this racial formation became apparent. The American authorities had managed to end the war—or come close to it—through a combination of brutal violence against the rural population, political recognition of the rural elite, or *principalía*, and the establishment of local governments through the auspices of the newly invented Federalista Party.[23] As civilian authorities pointed out, racializing the entire Philippine population as a savage foe was unsuited to the more subtle arts of feint and manipulation that would necessarily characterize power sharing between Filipinos and Americans. This was especially true, they believed, given the Filipino elites' sensitivities to racism as it was experienced under the Spanish colonial regime. American military commanders, still at war with the Philippine population, had little interest in placating Filipino sensibilities. As a result, a "postwar" collaboration-based racial formation would initially find its greatest obstacle in a stubborn race war that American officers in many cases refused to end.[24]

The Colonial Racial State

With the consolidation of civilian control, however, a new racial formation would develop, organized around the claim of nonracialism—the empire of David Gilmer, with which I began.[25] This was an inclusionary racism that invited Filipino participation in the colonial state but also delimited and qualified it. At the border between Filipino power and U.S. exclusion, American authorities produced new Filipino deficiencies that justified their incomplete "self-government." The

Filipino masses—the *tao*—were passive, backward, and superstitious; Filipino "*cacique*" elites—the American regime's interlocutors—were corrupt and exploitative.[26] But both would be transformed over a long, indeed an indefinite, period under U.S. rule. Metaphors of tutelage, assimilation, evolution, and maturation established a calibrated colonialism in which Filipinos would be progressively granted power in the state as Americans recognized their developing "capacity" for self-government.[27] The phrase "little brown brother," attributed to Governor-General William Howard Taft, was not a generic expression of paternalism but a formulation cut to meet the demands of partial, qualified recognition.

This framework hoped to accommodate to formal colonialism racist anti-imperialists in the United States who had feared that were Filipinos annexed to the country's body politic they would corrupt American institutions; inclusionary racism promised that colonialism would be a one-way valve, that Americans could assimilate Filipinos without Filipinos assimilating Americans.[28] Calibrated colonialism also held out the assurance that, while protracted, U.S. colonialism would be processual and self-liquidating, permanently temporary.

The new inclusionary formation also needed to accommodate Filipino elites' desire for power and recognition. Much of what the new American authorities learned, and institutionalized, about Philippine society came precisely from their dialogues and collaborations with Filipino elites. The American authorities, for example, identified as their initial Filipino counterparts figures such as T. H. Pardo de Tavera, an intellectual who proved willing to see in U.S. colonialism the fulfillment of Filipino hopes: whereas *ilustrados* had once gone to Europe in search of civilization, he maintained, it had now come to them in the form of American schoolteachers.[29] It was in the context of these Filipino-American interchanges that one of the most significant dimensions of the new colonial state emerged: its bifurcation of the Philippine population into "Christian" and "non-Christian" segments. While other categories of difference—especially in terms of nativity and *mestizaje* (racial mixture)—had been mitigated by the emergence of "Filipino" reform and revolution, Filipinos and Americans in the early twentieth century would together reinforce and institutionalize a civilizational boundary between the Hispanicized world and its "outsides."[30]

The Philippine-American colonial state would establish a racially bifurcated system of rule: Christians would be granted partial, local self-government while non-Christians would be governed exclusively by American politico-military commanders. After 1905, this distinction would be territorialized, in the form of "special provinces": the Mountain Province for Luzon's animists and the Moro Province for Muslims of the southern archipelago.[31] The central territorial-political axis of the Philippine-American colonial state, then, would not be drawn along traditional, U.S.-based lines of difference but along lines of difference whose origins stretched far back into the Spanish colonial past.

The collaborationist means and bifurcated racial ends of the Philippine-American colonial state were put vividly on display for the consumption of U.S. audiences in 1904 when the regime succeeded in mounting an enormous, forty-seven-acre display of its accomplishments at the Louisiana Purchase Exposition at Saint Louis. This "Philippine Exposition," the largest single display at Saint Louis, was not, however, merely the result of metropolitan elites' efforts to persuade domestic audiences of their visions of race, nation, and empire. It was, rather, the by-product of a distinct moment in the history of Philippine-American colonial politics. Its semantic architecture was intended to convey to U.S. audiences highly specific messages: suppressing memories of the Philippine-American War, advertising the "assimilability" of Filipinos, and promoting the United States as an exceptional and exemplary world power.[32]

But if the exposition's origins and shape can be read from the exigencies of colonial politics, the manner in which it was experienced and interpreted by U.S. audiences emerged from other mandates. To the horror of many American officials, spectators largely ignored the displays of "civilized," Hispanicized peoples and gravitated instead to sensationalized displays of "savage" Igorots. To the shock of *ilustrado* collaborators, U.S. audiences came to understand the islands' "civilized" peoples as those fragments of the Philippine population that the United States had managed to civilize over the previous five years. Coming less than two decades after Spaniards had deliberately displayed Igorots at Madrid as representative of the Philippines—a significant moment in the history of *ilustrado* alienation from Spain—the Philippine Exposition at Saint Louis left elite, Hispanicized Filipinos with a powerful sense of the need to police the representations of the Philippines and, specifically, to minimize the presence of non-Christians.[33] It also greatly estranged many of the regime's *ilustrado* interlocutors within the Federalista Party.

Despite debacles such as the Philippine Exposition, the framework of calibrated colonialism, inclusionary racism, and the bifurcated state proved remarkably durable over the decades to follow. This was in part because the system proved relatively open to the aspirations and demands of Filipino elites. The colonial state, for example, inaugurated a Philippine Assembly, elected by a highly restricted suffrage, in 1907.[34] Even the largest perceived crisis of the regime—the 1912 election of Woodrow Wilson and subsequent "Filipinization" of the state under Democratic rule—arguably stabilized rather than undermined U.S. colonialism.

While it promised and delivered recognition and progressively greater power for Hispanicized Filipino elites, this system also provided American authorities with rich resources for a politics of divide and rule. Operating within a bifurcated state, the American authorities claimed exclusive control over nearly half of the islands' territory, and often compared their administration (in highly favorable ways) to government in regions partially under Christian control, as arguments for Christians' continuing incapacity for complete self-government. Furthermore, such bifurcation facilitated narratives of internal "race war": the islands' Christians and non-Christians, the American authorities argued, were inherently antagonist toward each other and left to themselves would either exploit each other through deceit, land seizure, or enslavement or wage interminable warfare.[35] These narratives sometimes made the "civilized" Christians the aggressors in such conflicts, and on other occasions the non-Christians were cast as the villains, but in either case the American presence was cast as protection, the only way to keep the Philippines united as a single entity. Hispanicized Filipino politicians objected to such divide-and-rule politics but often did so in nationalist-colonialist terms; it was not that the Americans were dividing the nation against itself but that they denied Hispanicized Filipinos the right to rule their "own" others. They would prove their capacity for self-government to the Americans in part through the elaboration of internal empire with respect to Muslims and animists.[36]

Exclusion and Decolonization

Ultimately, the greatest challenge to the stability of the Philippine-American colonial racial formation came not from Philippine nationalism but from American nativism. It was triggered by the politics of Filipino migration. Recognized as U.S. "nationals," Filipinos had (with the exception of Chinese Filipinos) been granted the right to migrate to American territory.[37] The impact of Philippine-American colonialism on metropolitan formations became clearest as American nativists assembled new legal barriers to immigration in the second and third decades of the twentieth century: when the boundaries of the expansive Asiatic Barred Zone were drawn in the exclusionary Immigration Act of 1917 and Johnson-Reed Act of 1924, they were carefully gerrymandered around the Philippines, whose inhabitants were, for purposes of exclusion, other than Asiatic, at least at first. Here the inclusionary racism of the colonial state, which permitted Filipino migration, fundamentally shaped, and qualified, exclusionary racial nativism.

A rising demand for labor and newly exclusionary laws left Filipinos, with Mexicans, the only available source of migrant labor for West Coast agricultural industries in the United States.[38] Often through initial migrations to the sugar plantations of Hawai'i, Filipino workers—disproportionately young and male—migrated in large numbers to agricultural and industrial labor markets in California and the Pacific Northwest.[39] They soon inherited the racist-nativist politics that had targeted earlier waves of Asian migrants.[40] But white supremacists faced a quite distinct challenge with respect to Filipinos; because, in a sense, the United States occupied the Philippines, Filipinos retained a right to occupy the United States. Beginning in 1930, in the wake of white supremacist mob violence against Filipinos, racist-nativists promoted legislation banning Filipino migration within the colonial framework, in part by redefining them as Asiatics like the earlier, excluded, Chinese and Japanese migrants.[41]

Whereas José Rizal had failed to recognize the United States as a fully free republic on the grounds of Chinese exclusion in 1888, Filipinos would, four decades later, be incorporated into this more expansively exclusionary racial state. This exclusionist politics directly challenged the inclusionary racism of the colonial state; rejecting its promises of assimilation, it derecognized Filipinos as especially unassimilable. Filipino nationalists were affronted by these racist charges but also tried to use their momentum to argue for Philippine independence; the United States could exclude Filipinos, they argued, only if they gave the Philippines the right to exclude Americans. When the racial nativists failed to achieve exclusion within empire, they joined the coalition of interests—including protectionist agricultural interests that feared the competition of Philippine imports—in support of Philippine independence. The partially recognized little brown brother had been transformed into the excluded Asiatic. Decolonization would be racial exclusion by other means.[42]

It is not, perhaps, incorrect to see in racist-nativist mob violence against Filipino migrants in the early 1930s the realization of those fears that David Gilmer had presumed his Filipino audiences possessed three decades earlier at Lanao: that were the United States to colonize the Philippines, its racist "rabble" would eventually make Filipinos their next object of attention. But it would be an error to see in this violence an automatic, unmediated export or projection of U.S. racial formations. Indeed, Filipinos were in the United States in the first place because for over thirty years the United States had failed to fully export Asiatic exclusion to the Philippines. Instead, in a global world of deepening transregional connection, the Philippines had exported its workers to the United States, forcing a confrontation between inclusionary colonial and exclusionist nativist racial politics in which the latter had ultimately triumphed.

The racial politics of colonialism belonged to both Philippine and U.S. histories, having unfolded simultaneously on both sides of the Pacific, in struggles between American imperialists and anti-imperialists, between military and civilian American authorities, between American and Filipino colonial elites, and, ultimately, between American colonialists and racists-nativists in the United States. They were the result of decades of struggle, dialogue, and collaboration between diverse groups of Americans and Filipinos, had been shaped by processes as diverse as racial-exterminist warfare and colonial state building and immigration, and had left deep traces in Philippine and U.S. histories, histories that they also played a profound role in entangling. Studying race making in a transnational context will mean more than studying the outward export or projection of difference; it will mean remaining open to the difference that empire made.

Censuses in the Transition to Modern Colonialism

Spain and the United States in Puerto Rico

FRANCISCO A. SCARANO

BY MOST ACCOUNTS, THE UNITED STATES' OCCUPATION of Puerto Rico was a resounding success. Unlike the situation in Cuba, where expectations of independence after a long anticolonial struggle frustrated a complete U.S. takeover, or the Philippines, where a bloody resistance war ensued, the American takeover of Puerto Rico encountered few practical obstacles. For a short time, peasant insurgents threatened widespread unrest. The violence was directed mostly against Spanish merchants and landowners, however, and the U.S. Army and a revamped police force were able to subdue the soot-faced rebels (*tiznados*) within months. Elite reaction was, on the whole, much more favorable to the U.S. presence. Except for isolated cases, influential groups initially aligned themselves decisively in favor of annexation and eventual statehood, only to be frustrated later with the colonial framework created by the Foraker Act of 1900. But before this happened a honeymoon period would first run its course. In keeping with a military campaign that the Associated Press had called a "picnic," the immediate aftermath of the U.S. invasion of Puerto Rico went rather swiftly for the new colonial rulers.

In this essay I argue for an understanding of the transition that takes full account of the United States' appropriation of institutions, modalities, and technologies of rule from the preceding Spanish colonial state. I wish to claim specifically that one of the most important mechanisms of colonial control passed on by the Spaniards was the practice of carrying out regular and, by nineteenth-century standards, modern population censuses. As Benedict Anderson reminds us, in the nineteenth-century colonial world censuses and census taking were "institutions of power" that, along with maps and museums, "profoundly shaped the way in which the colonial state imagined its dominion—the nature of the human beings it ruled, the geography of its domain, and the legitimacy of its ancestry."[1] The tallies taken in Puerto Rico in the nineteenth century had allowed the Spanish state, especially in its more liberal incarnation from the 1870s onward, to count, classify, and etch onto mapped space its colonial subalterns, placing them in a position of inequality vis-à-vis a peninsular Spanish population (*peninsulares*) deemed more entitled to the blessings of liberal citizenship. Approaching the chronological apogee of scientific racism, these censuses produced bodies of quantitative data that lent demographic and economic data collection an air of scientific validity. When the Americans arrived and began to assume tutelage over the new colonials, the much practiced and deeply engrained practice of census taking helped provide an idiom of racial difference from the continental citizenry. In a critical way, this idiom supported the colonial project of exclusion and what Josep Fradera calls colonial "exceptionality."[2] In another way, however, it also was read by important American officials as a means of resolving the critical questions of the day: would the Puerto Ricans be entitled to ultimate assimilation; and, if so, what would the path leading them there look like?

The Colonial Transition

In accounting for the relatively smooth transition from Spanish to U.S. colonialism in Puerto Rico, few topics have been more overlooked than the ease with which the new metropole appropriated the institutions, including the apparatus of rule, of the old. Instead of focusing on imperial continuities, historians have preferred to focus on innovation and change. This emphasis is, for the most part, warranted. The onset of American rule precipitated dizzying changes in all spheres of life. To the Puerto Ricans, it felt *discontinuous* with that of the former imperial power—for a people accustomed to (and born out of) an aged Spanish colonialism as different, no doubt, as the culture and language of the new metropolitan actors. The old metropole had proven unable to propel its Caribbean colonies quickly enough toward a modernity intensely desired by liberal elites. The United States, by contrast, moved promptly to open up conditions for economic and social modernization. Within a decade of the establishment of civil government in 1900, highly profitable sugar and tobacco industries had been founded; schools, including a university, were inaugurated; novel, and for the most part efficacious, health campaigns were launched; and laws to recognize workers' and women's rights were adopted. Thus, by 1910, in the new "American Porto Rico," many key milestones on the road to modernity seemed within reach. At the same time, however, to those who had expected this modernity to also mean freedom it was disappointing that the relationship with the new metropole had turned out to be starkly colonial—indeed, in some respects, even more so than under Spain.

The case for continuity across the imperial divide cannot be dismissed so readily, however. As Fernando Picó has argued, 1898 was less of a watershed moment than the historiography has made it out to be.[3] The street celebrations that greeted the invading troops followed several decades of elite and subaltern disillusionment with, and resistance to, Spanish rule. Thus, the transition from Spanish to American rule provided a framework for the people's expression of their disenchantment with the old colonial order. As Eileen Findlay and others have revealed, the Americans, whose own internal struggles in the nineteenth century had resulted in progressive social legislation in some areas (workers' and women's rights, for example), used such progress to set themselves apart from Spain. American officials and ideologues back home made sure that the people of the "new possessions" knew about this difference. They portrayed the former metropole as a retrograde ("medieval"), Catholic, monarchical, and decaying power unable to usher in progressive laws and institutions to satisfy the longings of Puerto Rican liberal elites.[4]

In viewing the transition from Spain to the United States as a prolongation rather than a break, a key criterion is the latter's ability to latch its own institutions of rule onto an existing Spanish colonial state. At the end of the Spanish period, the colonial state in Puerto Rico was hinged atop an intrusive, multilayered, and deeply embedded apparatus of surveillance and punishment whose presence in the daily lives of the people had few counterparts anywhere in the colonial periphery. The growth of this apparatus of the state dated back to the late eighteenth century. Its expansion had basically followed a steep ascent ever since. In the nineteenth century, as it became increasingly fearful of the growing African slave population and the possibility of a pro-independence insurgency, the colonial government stepped up its surveillance and military presence on the island. Further, in order to provide colonial jobs for *peninsulares*, who expected to reap the rewards of their origins, even government at the local level had greatly increased in size and intrusiveness. To American leaders "on the ground," this fact did not go unnoticed. General George W. Davis, whose military regime was chiefly responsible for the transition to civilian rule between the 1898 war and the Foraker Act, put it succinctly when he tallied up the size of the police force at the end of the Spanish period, finding that it numbered one thousand men. "Anglo-Saxon countries do not tolerate the existence of such a police force," he remarked, "but all Latin countries are accustomed to maintain a similar body."[5]

The interlocking, interdependent nature of church and state guaranteed that institutions of social control (the police, the judiciary, prisons, local bureaucracies, etc.) would be etched on a political and moral canvas. Spanish Puerto Rico was a place in which church and state combined to keep close tabs on individuals and groups. Even in remote areas of this mountainous island, the combination of police forces, parish priests, urban and rural *alcaldes* (mayors), and private hacienda guards made it difficult for persons to escape the watchful eye of the more powerful. Numerous attempts to criminalize vagrancy, which culminated in the draconian Reglamento de Jornaleros (1849–73), a comprehensive program intended to extract labor from a reluctant peasantry, were steps in the direction of greater state involvement in people's lives. Picó has noted that in the highland valley of Cayey the cholera epidemic of 1855–56 revealed the presence in town of numerous individuals whose existence the authorities had not yet reckoned with. While he considers this a sign of a certain fluidity in island society that underscores the inaccuracy of the government's claims that it exercised iron-fisted control, one could also take a different view of the matter: that only in an emergency, such as a deadly epidemic, could one perceive the extent to which the colonial state was not in *total* control.[6] Under normal conditions, the presumption most people made was that no one escaped the double whammy of state-church vigilance. That people perceived the government to be intrusive was in itself an important measure of social control.

Acknowledging the utility of this preexisting state for U.S. hegemonic designs was part of the governance plans drawn by colonial policy makers. General George W. Davis (military governor, 1899–1900) and special commissioners Henry K. Carroll and Henry S. Rowe, on whose work "on the ground" the United States laid the foundation of its (re)colonization of Puerto Rico, all acknowledged this. As Courtney Johnson notes in his contribution to this volume, most enlightened American envoys, such as Rowe, recognized the efficacy of the legal and institutional means by which Spain had governed in Puerto Rico, especially over the three decades preceding the invasion.[7] Spain, they argued, had built a solid foundation of colonial governance. The United States only needed to adapt it to a vague set of "American traditions" and "American institutions" to make it work on behalf of the new colonial project.

Indeed, the Puerto Rican case highlighted how deeply embedded in civilian life, even (or perhaps *especially*) at the local level, a colonial state could be. It was clearly more so there than in Cuba, where thirty years of war had damaged, at least in many areas, the Spanish government's capacity to inject itself into peoples' lives, except under conditions of martial law, or in the Philippines, where Spain had governed much more indirectly than in its Caribbean colonies, relying instead on the authority of landowners and powerful regional chieftains, especially in areas of this enormous archipelago where the state's presence was virtually nonexistent.[8] In Puerto Rico, power was so centralized in the hands of peninsula-born bureaucrats and their conservative cohorts that when liberal Creoles spoke insistently of their desire for "local autonomy," they essentially referred to a regime in which they were liberated from such intrusive power.

Censuses as Adaptable Instruments of Colonial Rule

For more than a century, the Spanish colonial state's knowledge of the colonial population—of its size, characteristics, and distribution—informed and justified its ability to control it. John L. Lombardi has noted that the "pragmatic and rationalist" Spanish colonial administration required an extensive and accurate population-reporting system, one that could be trusted to reveal, on short notice, "what population aggregates could be deployed at various tasks throughout the empire."[9] Resources available for defensive mobilization were among the most important of these aggregates and thus some of the best reported. In the eighteenth-century Caribbean, the Crown assumed that a revamped system of colonial militias would provide the defensive manpower that the thinly stretched regular army could not.[10] When taking stock of valuable resources, the number of men ready for militia service was a key consideration.

The Seven Years' War (1756–63) enhanced the strategic value of Puerto Rico for the Spanish Crown. Afterward, colonial governance hinged, more than before, on knowledge about the colony's population. As Spain rebuilt its military fortresses in San Juan and reorganized the local militias, officials saw it as an obligation of the first order to collect population statistics and keep these data constantly updated. It is no wonder that the colony's late-eighteenth-century *padrones* or aggregate population tallies—*censuses* would not be an accurate term—are among the most complete sets of population statistics ever uncovered for the Spanish empire.[11] Between a count taken in 1765 during Alejandro O'Reilly's *visita*, a high-level fact-finding mission prompted by Spanish fears of another Havana-style takeover, and a compilation ordered by *intendant* Alejandro Ramírez in 1815, historians have identified at least thirty-five *padrones* and other surveys, mostly of agricultural wealth and production.[12] It appears that in the beginning parish priests were the ones mobilized to produce this knowledge. In time, however, as local governments became more complex, civil officials began to compile crucial population and resource statistics. This evolution involved a shift from aggregate to more detailed data. Not surprisingly, the turning point appears to have been the 1812 constitutionally sanctioned local governments, the first experiment with a decentralized local administration, with considerable input by Creole patricians. The constitutional *ayuntamientos* (city governments) produced very detailed population data, surviving examples of which are the earliest individual-level censuses of which we know. After 1812, while reports to the central government in San Juan continued to give only aggregate numbers of men, women, and children in each *partido*, or district, with each of these groups divided by racial and free or slave status, individual-level data seem to have been collected regularly.

Politics and census-taking operations continued to go hand in hand throughout the remainder of the nineteenth century. As Fradera and others have argued, in 1837 Spanish liberals transformed the country's relationship with its remaining colonies, tightening the economic and administrative embrace while distancing the native-born insular residents ever more from rights obtained by their peninsular counterparts. Both operations required increasingly accurate information about the population, economy, and society, particularly in the Caribbean, where the metropole's hold on the territory and population was quite thorough—and its economic stake, already significant (in Cuba especially), was expanding rapidly.

For Puerto Rico, the story of census taking accurately reflects the broader political context. There, in addition to the early-nineteenth-century tallies, Spain conducted major population censuses in 1845, 1860, 1877, 1887, and 1897. These initiatives inaugurated the modern study of the island's population. It is also no exaggeration to say that they are among the most thorough population surveys undertaken in any colonial context before the advent of the twentieth century. The nation's inaugural Statistical Commission of the Kingdom (later known simply as the Statistical Commission), founded in 1856 and operating under relatively modern census-taking guidelines, guaranteed the high quality of colonial population statistics when it decided to include the Caribbean colonies in its ambitious 1860 census of Spain (the Philippines was excluded this time). The commission's successor, the Geographical and Statistical Institute (GSI, founded in 1870), continued the practice until the waning years of Spanish rule. By 1897 it even included the Philippines in the national census, an undertaking that presented enormous logistical challenges. Again, because of the exceptional conditions in which these two larger colonies found themselves, it is fair to say that the Spanish censuses of Puerto Rico produced the most reliable statistics of the three.

Insights culled from the last three Spanish colonial censuses were to be a key component of the Americans' understanding of Puerto Rico. Unlike the situation in the Philippines, where the United States had to construct the enormously complex Filipino ethnic and racial picture largely on its own, in Puerto Rico and Cuba it relied on constructions inherited from the Spanish.[13] The nineteenth-century Caribbean statistics comprised a knowledge baseline on which the colonizers would attach, discursively and in praxis, their novel colonial project. Aware of the manner in which racial categories operated in this society, the Spanish GSI had used variants of the classic three-tiered racial classification system (whites, mulattoes, and blacks) throughout the second half of the nineteenth century. Until the 1877 census, the population was also divided into slave and free; emancipation in 1873–76 made this unnecessary in later counts. Altogether, this simple scheme proved useful in documenting several crucial aspects of the new colony. As the data in table 1 make plain, since the mid-nineteenth century the Spanish censuses had classified a growing proportion of Puerto Ricans as "white," the number having risen steadily from 49 percent in 1846 to 64 percent in 1897. This racial breakdown was consonant with but less dramatic than the situation in Cuba, where over a similar period the "white" element had grown from 42 percent to 68 percent.[14] In the Caribbean colonies that most interested Americans at the turn of the century, the second half of the nineteenth century had seen a substantial increase in the proportion of "whites" in the population.

Thus, even before the Americans launched the first intensive data collection exercise of their own (the military census of November 10, 1899, which mirrored the one taken in Cuba just weeks before) they would be reassured that in their Caribbean "new possessions," racial statistics covering several generations pointed to a population that was considerably lighter skinned and European descended than in the other colonies acquired by Europeans at the time and in the Pacific colonies similarly acquired from Spain. The Spanish censuses of the early statistical era (taken after 1860) all underscored this notable feature.

Even when the census schedules were not available for consultation, the Americans clearly based many of their initial impressions on general figures publicized by the former metropole. In the 1899 census report it is noted that the American census administration had not been able to use the (Spanish) 1897 one for comparison. This must mean that the full schedules, which had been sent to Spain for tabulation, were not available, and that the American census takers perhaps only saw overall summaries. Earlier that year, the well-known physician, historian, and high public official Cayetano Coll y Toste had published a book summarizing all the pertinent 1897 statistics on population, agriculture, and industry.[15] American deliberations on Puerto Rico's future and all the opinion pieces, published in books and journals, that declared its people more assimilable on account of their relative (and increasing) "whiteness," depended on the population data offered by the Spanish censuses, including the one for 1897.[16] It is significant that the first U.S. tally, taken two years later, would not be officially transmitted to the secretary of war until November 7, 1900. By then, the Foraker Act was in force and a civil government had been in operation for six months.[17] All of the major decisions about Puerto Rico's future had been sealed beforehand, very likely on the basis of the latest Spanish results.

TABLE 1. Puerto Rico's Population by Color and Status, 1846–97

	Whites	Free Blacks and Mulattoes	Slaves	Total
1846	216,083	175,791	51,265	443,139
1860	300,406	241,037	41,738	583,308
1877	411,712	319,936	NA	731,648
1887	474,933	323,632	NA	798,565
1897	570,187	315,632	NA	894,302

Source: José L. Vázquez Calzada, *La población de Puerto Rico y su trayectoria histórica* (San Juan: n.p., 1988), p. 8.

There is some evidence to suggest that American officials used Spanish data to support their contention that Puerto Rico's "whiter" population deserved a form of tutelary colonialism of the sort outlined in the Foraker Act. In January of 1900, months before the military census's data became publicly available, and as Congress was deliberating the Foraker bill outlining the constitutional and legal framework for Puerto Rico, military governor Davis had gone before the Committee on Pacific Islands and Porto Rico to pronounce that "the inhabitants are mostly of Spanish origin—emigrants from Spain during the last 400 years and their descendants." He figured that for every million inhabitants there were "about 300,000 negroes and mulattoes, approximately a little more than that number."[18] While the figure of "one million" appears to be the result of rounding, the racial breakdown offered conforms almost exactly to the 1897 Spanish count (315,632 nonwhites). These data showed Puerto Rico to be overwhelmingly white, at least in the local usage of the term. As such, Davis pleaded with Congress to legislate for it a sort of tutelary colonialism, which the general had defended in correspondence with Secretary of War Elihu Root. In Davis's view, it would be acceptable, in the long run, to slant the Puerto Ricans toward U.S. citizenship (a grant of which was contained in the Jones Act of 1917) even if the island itself were kept in a state of constitutional exception. As Christina Duffy-Burnett explains in this collection, in the famous insular cases, beginning with *Downes v. Bidwell* in 1901, the Supreme Court would rule that the Constitution did not apply to its full extent in the territories recently captured from Spain. Furthermore, for such territories, unlike the case for the "incorporated" ones, there was no expectation of future statehood.[19] Scholars now regard these decisions, unambiguously, as the constitutional justification for empire.[20]

Addressing a congressional audience eager to know more intimately the people for whom they were creating milestone legislation, General Davis had already pointed out in his writings that not only the last Spanish census but the trend over many of the latter counts made by the old metropole pointed to a *whitening* of the Puerto Rican population over time. While he acknowledged that many people categorized as white were actually mulatto, and as such would fall under the category of "colored" in the United States, he also pointed with glee to the progressive disappearance of the "pure negroes." The 1887 statistics "[show] plainly that the pure negroes are marrying with the mixed bloods and whites, the progeny being classed as colored," Davis wrote. "This diminution is certain to continue, and the pure negro type will disappear, unless there should be an immigration of blacks."[21] Davis's statement underscores the fact that key architects of the colonial projects shared the belief with contemporary Latin American elites that the "pure" population of African (or Indian) descent would melt into in a much hoped for racial amalgam. The belief that in this new colony a racial shift was actually taking place would figure quite prominently in American perceptions of the islanders and was to play a significant role in Puerto Rican attempts to combat American racism later.[22]

At this point one might justifiably ask why Davis and others relied on data collected by a "medieval" and "backward" country to usher in the policies of the new metropole. In using their predecessors' work, however, they were quite justified. The final Spanish and first American censuses generated data that were compatible across the board. The American census-taking enterprise was, to be sure, more robust in conception and methods. As such, it allowed observers to draw a more detailed demographic and economic profile of Puerto Rican society than any prior census initiative had permitted. The American authorities knew this would be the case, and they used the census to showcase the enlightened intentions of the U.S. government. The demographer José L. Vázquez Calzada notes, however, that the two bodies of data were not that different—that they were, in demographers' terms, "internally consistent." After performing a mathematical operation to test for intercensus reliability, he concludes that "the last Spanish censuses were as trustworthy as the first American census."[23]

Conclusion

Modern colonialisms, including the variety practiced by the United States in the Caribbean and Pacific after 1898, depended critically on forms and institutions of governmental control that ranged from bureaucracies to police forces, judicial systems, prisons, missionaries and churches, schools, and a variety of other means of intellectual classification and labeling. These institutions helped imperial countries to "naturalize" their exercise of raw power and convert it into an attempt to bring rationality and order to chaotic societies and corrupt polities. Often overlooked among such institutions and practices, albeit less so today than a few decades ago, is the institution of the modern census. A means by which metropoles created "grids" or mental images of their colonial subjects, census taking as an enterprise commensurate with empire took off in the latter part of the nineteenth and early decades of the twentieth centuries. While fixing those mental images in colonial censuses, hierarchies of rule were erected and historical tendencies apprised. Given the importance of "race" to all modern colonial enterprises, it is not surprising that some of the most profound and long-lasting images forged in the census-taking enterprise were precisely constructions of racial difference and hierarchy.

In assessing the transition from the Spanish to the American empire, in the Caribbean most particularly, it is worth considering how grids, which long predated the onset of American rule, bridged the exercise of power by the two metropoles. I have argued in this essay that those grids were most critical in a colony such as Puerto Rico where the Spanish state was deeply grafted onto the social body via multiple applications of power, many of which included coercion and some of which involved local consent. As in its bigger sister colony, Cuba, by the time the American troops invaded there was in Puerto Rico a tradition of census taking made more necessary in the late 1700s and early 1800s by military-strategic considerations and the revival of African slavery. The island's incorporation into metropolitan statistical initiatives made it the subject of several flawed but nonetheless modern censuses of population, agriculture, and industry, all of them infused with the same liberal, modernizing purpose that inspired similar exercises in Spain.

American officials used these statistics repeatedly to understand the island and its people and gauge the potential for profit by American capitalists. They adopted the Spaniards' racial grids but tried to fit them into American preconceptions of race and class. As in Cuba, the Puerto Rican census results pointed to a population that was, according to local constructs of race, whiter, and thus more assimilable, to the United States than perhaps any other Caribbean society at the time—and certainly more so than the majority of colonial spaces opened up by European rivals in the latter part of the nineteenth century. That the population censuses showed a sharp and unbroken diminution in the "pure negro" population surely made a difference in the way important figures such as George W. Davis and Elihu Root conceived of "American Porto Rico" as a long-term prospect for territorial assimilation even if it took a period of colonial tutelage in order to get there. That a Supreme Court majority and many others in the new metropolitan nation did not see it the same way, and largely on racial grounds banished the new colony to a limbo of territorial unincorporation, is a story whose outlines and implications we are now seeing more clearly and, as the colonial relationship enters its 109th year, lamenting it more intently than ever before.

Race and the Suffrage Controversy in Cuba, 1898–1901

ALEJANDRO DE LA FUENTE AND MATTHEW CASEY

THE NEWSPAPER *LA LUCHA* put it bluntly in 1899: "In Washington they believe that in order to devise a political constitution and an election law for Cuba, it is unavoidable to have a precise knowledge of the ethnic elements that form its population."[1] That a Cuban newspaper with a fairly large circulation chose to comment on this particular issue and on Washington's "beliefs" was of course not fortuitous. This was one of those areas in which Cubans and Americans were more or less clearly delineated in two separate, antagonistic blocs. When it came to issues of race and politics, of elections and definitions of the suffrage, differences between Cubans and Americans were significant: an easy target for journalists and politicians. There was not a single unified view on these important matters on either side of the divide, but the editorialist of *La Lucha* knew quite well that this diversity was politically inconsequential. What truly mattered were the differences between Cubans and Americans regardless of gradations: "in Washington *they* believe."

Implicit in the text was the notion that Cubans, in turn, had a very different set of beliefs on issues of race, electoral politics, and the future constitution of the Republic. This, of course, was not true. Planters, merchants, and property owners had supported colonialism to the bitter end precisely because they feared the rule of popular sectors. The prospect of humble Cubans—the stuff the Liberation Army was made of—controlling government and public affairs terrified them. When it appeared that Spain would no longer be able to defend their properties and interests, they deserted the old metropolis and called on a new one for protection and support, petitioning for annexation to the U.S. government after 1896. They did not have to wait for any census count to know that the Cuban population was utterly incapable of building a responsive and prosperous republic in which their interests and properties would be protected.

But this group found itself isolated, as even its long-term allies, the Spanish colonial authorities, moved to accept the notion of universal manhood suffrage. Cuba's peculiar political history during the late nineteenth century forced political actors of various persuasions and ideological preferences to agree, however reluctantly, on two basic premises: first, that despite their undeniable importance, racial differences should not be codified in law and should not preclude participation in civic life. From this it followed that all male citizens, regardless of race, social status, and even literacy, were entitled to participation in civic rituals, particularly in elections. By 1898, when American troops landed in eastern Cuba, this was one of the few areas in which the insurgents of Cuba Libre and at least some of the defenders of the colonial compact agreed: all adult males were entitled to vote.

It is then possible to think about the American occupation of the island, as the editorial in *La Lucha* somehow suggested, as a cultural clash in which two different worldviews, informed by different experiences, expectations, and bodies of knowledge, collided. In many other areas there was significant overlap and agreement between the occupation forces and some sectors of the population on the island. In the area of electoral rights, however, the contrast seems to have been particularly crisp and sharp. This is not to suggest, of course, that propertied Cubans did not think it was a good idea to limit the suffrage. It is to indicate that in this area the experiences and expectations of the North Americans and the Cubans, including those who supported independence or the colonial status, differed considerably.

These conditions, in turn, limited considerably what the occupying forces could do. As North American economic, political, and military actors moved into foreign territories such as Cuba and began to build a modern empire, they discovered that their power was not without limits. Imperial agents were forced to negotiate with local actors who had their own interests and networks of influence. As the controversy over universal manhood suffrage in Cuba shows, the building of the empire was a contested and negotiated process.

Race and Suffrage by 1898

The principle of universal manhood suffrage was incorporated into the legal documents of Cuba Libre as early as the late 1860s. As the leadership of the revolutionary movement accepted, somewhat reluctantly, the notion of the legal equality of all adult Cuban males regardless or race, origin, social status, and literacy, the legal definition of citizenship became at least nominally egalitarian and inclusive. The first constitution of Cuba Libre—Guáimaro, 1869—did not regulate electoral rights but did proclaim the equality of all Cubans and that all male citizens of the Republic were to be considered soldiers in the Liberation Army.[2] A complementary law issued by the revolutionary legislative authority a few months later endorsed universal suffrage by noting that all "citizens" older than twenty years of age could vote and be elected to any position.[3]

This principle was reproduced in subsequent legal documents. The 1897 Constitution of La Yaya, which was theoretically the law of the land in the territories of Cuba Libre by the time the North Americans entered the war, gave the government the power to regulate "electoral rights" but noted that the executive would do so "on the basis of universal suffrage." The criminal code approved by the insurgent government on January 1, 1898 characterized any attempt by either military chiefs or civilian authorities to restrict or intimidate voters as a crime and condemned as illegal any meddling in the electoral process.[4]

This does not mean that all revolutionaries subscribed to the intertwined principles of inclusive citizenship, racial equality, and universal suffrage. As was the case with many other aspects of the revolutionary program, these principles reflected "an imperfect consensus," to borrow Louis A. Pérez's expression.[5] But divergences centered on rivalries between the civilian and military authorities rather than on how to constitute the electorate and on who should participate in the civic life of Cuba Libre. When General Máximo Gómez referred sarcastically to those who "speak of constitutions and laws, when in my judgment we have desired only to present a simple basis of government for higher political ends abroad, and nothing more," he was not questioning the extent of the franchise but noting that in times of war legal niceties would have to take a back seat to military imperatives. By 1898 universal manhood suffrage had become entrenched in the imaginary of Cuba Libre—"a key separatist ideal."[6]

Meanwhile, developments on the other side of the political divide contributed as well to the gradual enlargement of the franchise and ultimately to the acceptance of universal manhood suffrage. On the one hand, the experience of the Ten Years' War (1868–78) showed conclusively that political peace would be only possible if Spain gained the upper hand in the competition for the sympathies and support of the large Afro-Cuban population. The colonial government was fully aware, of course, that this process entailed significant dangers, for the most resolute defenders of colonialism—planters and property owners—would resent any concession to their social inferiors. Step-by-step, however, the colonial government sought to eliminate some of the legal barriers that prevented the so-called *gente de color* from participating in different areas of social life. Immediately after the war, an 1878 decree authorized Afro-Cuban youths to attend secondary schools and the university. One year later, the captain general issued a circular in which he ordered municipalities to create educational opportunities for children of color. Several decrees and circulars stipulated in the 1880s that public spaces could not be segregated and were to be open to all regardless of race. In 1893, at the urging of Afro-Cuban activists and organizations, municipal schools were desegregated and Afro-Cubans acquired the legal right to use the honorific titles don and doña.[7]

If, on the one hand, the colonial state sought to gain the support of the black population, on the other hand it introduced limited political reforms to diffuse the appeal of insurgency. The reforms introduced after the Ten Years' War allowed for the creation of political parties, freedom of the press, and the election of representatives to the Spanish Parliament. The electoral law approved for Cuba established a limited suffrage, with stringent income requirements and other discriminatory provisions that favored *peninsulares,* Spanish voters resident in the island. It has been estimated that less than 3 percent of the population could vote under this law. But it was a first step toward the establishment of some sort of electoral regime, which would be enlarged subsequently. As the war of 1895 progressed and the colonial army proved unable to control the insurrection and defeat the Liberation Army, Spain granted full autonomy to the island, including voting rights for all adult males. On January 1, 1898, the Autonomist regime was put in place. The new government called for elections for representatives to the insular Parliament, which took place in April 1898. Although the elected insular Parliament was short-lived and barely had time to constitute itself due to the intervention of the North American forces in the war, this was the first time in Spanish Cuba that a collective body was elected under universal manhood suffrage. The electoral principle that Cuba Libre had been promoting since the late 1860s was finally embraced by representatives of the colonial order. The North American forces had landed on an island with two competing governments, but both governments had come to endorse similar electoral regimes.[8]

North American Assumptions

Most North Americans, however, arrived on the island with a very different set of ideas about politics, race, and suffrage. According to the mainstream press, these ideas revolved around three different issues. First, the demographic composition of the island did not bode well for its political future. To complicate things further, blacks and other "low elements" seemed to be well represented in the Liberation Army, a point that several journalists stressed even before the Americans entered the war. Second, to many journalists the experience of other Spanish American republics seemed relevant to the Cuban case. That experience was assessed in universally negative terms. Last, but certainly not least, in their analysis of Cuba's future, some writers and journalists invoked the experience of Reconstruction in the United States—that is, the failure of Reconstruction—to argue that the island would mirror the chaos and lawlessness that had allegedly characterized the South since the end of the Civil War.

Preoccupations with the racial composition of the Cuban population and its capacity for self-government were voiced even before the U.S. government declared war on Spain. Well before the census results were known, numerous observers of the Cuban situation had concluded that the island had too many blacks to be politically viable. The *Nation* lamented in early 1898 the potential difficulty of "administering in some fashion a territory ... containing a population of 1,500,000, one third being colored, and all unused to self-government."[9] The "best" elements of Cuban society—white property owners—could not be expected to submit to the control of the low social elements that formed the Liberation Army, so chaos would surely ensue.[10]

Americans also arrived at conclusions about Cuban difficulties with self-government by drawing on their observations of political events in the other independent republics of Latin America. The *Nation* opined, "Judging from the example of the other Spanish-American colonies, half a century of intestine [*sic*] strife and bloodshed" would follow Cuban independence.[11] In a *Harper's Weekly* article, the author argued against American involvement in Cuba by invoking the constant "wars of factions" in South America, which he blamed on the region's "tropical conditions" and "Indian admixture." Cuba, a country with a similar climate and "a strong Negro element," would suffer an equivalent fate.[12]

Others saw in Cuba a reenactment of Reconstruction and predicted that, as in the American South, extending suffrage to former slaves and their descendants would inevitably lead to "carpet-baggers, Negro suffrage, and a chaos of institutions." As an editorial in the *New York Times* put it, it was "inexcusable for us to subject Cuba to an experiment from the failure of which we have ourselves so severely suffered." Universal manhood suffrage would be "fatal to the political, industrial, and moral development of the Cuban population."[13]

The one dissenting voice on these issues coming from the United States was articulated by the African American press. Black newspapers had been following the war of independence in Cuba and had commented on the transformative potential of the anticolonial movement with great enthusiasm. In a lengthy letter to the *Richmond Planet*, for instance, a reader described the Cuban struggle for independence as "an Afro-Cuban Socialist uprising." The intervention of the United States, however, turned that "holy cause" into "a bloody farce" for the intervention's "chief object" was "to fasten the chains of ... color-line barbarism and race despotism in the name of stable government, on the necks of those brave Afro-Cubans."[14]

As other black newspapers noted, to do this it was indispensable to transform the Cuban insurgents from brave honorable patriots into savages incapable of self-government: "The Cuban soldiers that maintained the war with Spain for three years were brave and sturdy patriots until we found ourselves in a position to seize the island, when they suddenly became ... a lot of ragtags too ignorant and indolent to govern themselves."[15]

This transformation was analogous to the aftermath of Reconstruction, when

"There's plenty of room at the table. Why not ask the hungry little fellow to sit down?" *Judge*, February 3, 1906. (General Research Division, New York Public Library, Astor, Lenox and Tilden Foundations)

African Americans were deprived of the basic rights of citizenship. "It is the same old story," noted the *Richmond Planet* with pessimism. "The dark-skinned inhabitants of the island will be the victims of race prejudice, and this combined with Spanish contempt will make their wretched lives miserable."[16] Although these predictions were basically correct, the newspaper underestimated the degree of mobilization of black Cubans and how much the notion of universal manhood suffrage had come to inform the expectations of many poor Cubans, black and white.

The Suffrage Controversy in Cuba

As Ada Ferrer states, in the contest between racism and antiracism we know "with certainty" that American officers and bureaucrats would champion policies and views resulting in the exclusion and subordination of blacks.[17] American authorities shared the views sustained by most mainstream newspapers in the United States about the capacity of Cubans to establish a responsible government. They also concurred that the problem did not concern the population as a whole but what military governor Leonard Wood called "the illiterate mass of people," many of whom were the "sons and daughters of Africans imported into the island as slaves," who were clearly unable to become responsible citizens.[18]

Many of these "sons of Africans" were members of the Liberation Army, so the issue of what to do with the insurgents became "the ugliest factor" in the controversies surrounding suffrage, as the *Nation* anticipated in 1898.[19] Although most elite white Cubans agreed with Governor Wood that it was desirable to restrict the vote to literates, they deemed it unthinkable to deprive members of the Liberation Army of electoral rights. Although this extended the franchise to a large numbers of blacks and lower class whites, Governor Wood came to accept this compromise as an unavoidable evil. "Giving a vote to the ex-soldiers has removed the only element which would be in any way dangerous," he acknowledged. On the other hand, Wood successfully negotiated the introduction of income and literacy requirements for other Cubans, effectively disenfranchising most poor natives.[20]

The electoral law was not published until April, but by February the qualifications for suffrage were generally known. They were greeted with opposition, and this opposition was framed as a struggle between Cubans, on the one hand, and the North Americans forces of occupation on the other. As *La Discusión* put it as early as January 1900, the Cuban people would not tolerate being "deprived of a right that was recognized by the governments of the Revolution and by the very government of Spain."[21]

Numerous expressions of protest and resistance further reinforced divisions along national lines. Even the most conservative papers, such as the *Diario de la Marina,* reported on meetings, gatherings, and pronouncements against the American authorities' attempt to exclude members of the civilian branch of the

Liberation Army from the provision that gave electoral rights to the *mambises* (soldiers in the Liberation Army).[22] Town councils sent messages to Wood demanding universal (male) suffrage, a petition endorsed by the influential Club of Veterans.[23] Furthermore, at least some of the emerging political parties organized street marches in Havana.[24]

The suffrage limitations imposed by the U.S. forces of occupation allowed some of the conservative pro-Spanish papers to sing the praises of Spanish civilization and to reinforce the line separating Cubans and Spaniards—conveniently regrouped under a "Latin race" label—from the people from the north. "We Catholics are more democratic," explained *Diario de la Marina*.[25] The daily joined other newspapers in calling for unity among Cubans and Spaniards, warning that otherwise it would be impossible to resist the progressive Americanization of the island. These calls for unity did not exclude blacks. "We believe much more on the virtues than on the vices of the colored race, so frequently insulted," editorialized *Diario de la Marina*. The archconservative *Unión Española* concurred: "The Cuban negro is intelligent, industrious, polite, and tractable. And he is many." The occupation of the island threatened the very existence of "the Cuban people as part of the race to which we belong" and the linguistic, religious, moral, and legal institutions created by Spain in Cuba. Among those institutions was universal suffrage: "Before they are deprived of a right that was recognized by the governments of the Revolution and by the government of Spain," all residents of the island would mobilize to defend "the democratic principles that sustain the institutions of the truly free peoples."[26] The North American opposition to universal suffrage and the Americans' crude and undisguised racism had given the pro-Spanish press the opportunity to align Spanish colonialism with democracy and freedom.

Curiously, as the suffrage controversy unfolded in Cuba, some voices within the United States supported the notion that all Cuban males should vote. To begin with, some newspapers acknowledged that, given the fact that even Spain had enlarged the franchise in 1898, it would be difficult for the Americans to restrict it: "No doubt the immediate future of Cuba would be safer under a limited suffrage. But, on the other hand, the autonomist suffrage promised by Spain was not limited to the literate, and it might well seem not only ungenerous if we should be more strict than Spain, but also that our ulterior purpose was to secure annexation."[27]

Support for universal manhood suffrage came from the most unlikely corner of the American political spectrum: annexationists. They recognized that most Cubans, who they described as the "illiterate and mercurial classes," opposed annexation and were "hot for a republic of their own . . . with all the spoils."[28] But this was precisely where they placed their hopes. These lower class Cubans would create such turmoil that better class Cubans would run to hide under the

American flag. "The theory underlying this ... policy ... toward Cuba is the belief that if the Cubans are given the necessary rope they will hang themselves, or in other words, they will quickly prove that an American control is necessary."[29] As Cubans mobilized in early 1900 against suffrage restriction, the annexationists rejoiced, noting that whites would "organize an annexation party rather than to accept Negro domination."[30] The conflict that would ensue would be of such magnitude that even the insurgents would "no longer pretend that they could set up a government in Cuba."[31]

Within the island, pressures to overturn the limitations on the suffrage were effective enough that the government of occupation felt the need to respond somehow. In order to give the impression that he was seeking the input of Cubans, Governor Wood created a commission to study the electoral question and even appointed a well-known "black" politician, Martín Morúa Delgado, as a member. The commission, however, was for publicity purposes. Its functions were merely deliberative and lacked the power to redefine the franchise. As these limitations became obvious, Morúa Delgado resigned.[32]

Governor Wood tried to minimize the importance of this resistance and explained to his superiors that universal suffrage would result in the ruin of the island. He had to concede, however, that the electoral limitations introduced by his government did not enjoy universal approval even among those who could otherwise be considered their allies. "The limitation on suffrage . . . met the approval of practically all the best people here," he informed the secretary of war. He advised against yielding to the growing popular protest for "Any change . . . would be taken as an indication of decided weakness . . . [and] universal suffrage would be fatal to the interests of Cuba."[33]

Both the municipal elections and the election of representatives to write the new constitution were carried out under the electoral law approved by the government of occupation. According to newspaper accounts, even these local elections, carried out with a limited suffrage, were regarded with apprehension by the American public. The *New York Times* warned that "the clash of native parties for provincial offices will be to decide whether the Negroes, farm hands and bushwhackers who composed the bulk of the army, or the merchants, professional, and other educated men of the elites shall rule Cuba."[34] The same sense of anticipation was conveyed by a group of U.S. senators who visited the island in March 1900 and claimed that "much [would] depend upon the result of these [municipal] elections."[35] An editorial in the *New York Times* concurred: "We are just trying an experiment in establishing local self-government in the Cuban communities. . . . It is quite too early to say that that experiment is successful."[36]

At least in the eyes of some North American observers, the experiment failed. The "Revolutionists [national party] secured control everywhere," the *Independent* noted with despair, and "the war party is composed of men least fitted to conduct a civil government." The electoral results were so negative, in fact, that the newspaper described the situation as "beyond redemption."[37] To make matters worse, the *mambises* were also well represented in the convention charged with drafting the constitution of the future republic.

These fears were not groundless. Although there was some debate on the question of suffrage, no delegate to the Constitutional Convention dared to openly question the principle of universal manhood suffrage, which was presented by various delegates as an "acquired right" that had been previously recognized in the constitutions of Cuba Libre and in the Autonomist Constitution approved by Spain in 1898. As a result, the overwhelming majority of delegates approved the inclusion of universal suffrage in the constitutional text.[38] Those who later advocated restrictions on the franchise were attacked as traitors to the motherland. For instance, when several conservative political leaders "condemned" the convention's results and promised a future "revision" of the Constitution they were labeled "enemies of independence" by *El Mundo*.[39] When some delegates to the convention later tried to restrict the franchise by introducing the notion of the "plural vote," which gave privileged rights to literate voters, they were quickly overturned.[40] As a politician linked to the forces of Cuba Libre put it later, in Cuba it was "not possible, without grave and serious consequences, to restrict suffrage," which had become "the right of every citizen."[41]

North American observers had trouble understanding that the views of what they had repeatedly described as "the Negro party" could triumph in the convention in the virtual absence, in fact, of black delegates.[42] They did not grasp the extent to which cross-racial cooperation had permeated the military and political activities of the insurgents. Their classification of the population as white property owners, on the one hand, and Negroes, on the other, reflected prevalent views of race, suffrage, and politics in the United States rather than Cuba's own racial imaginary or the peculiar political trajectory of the island. This division ignored the depth of the nationalist antiracist discourse, which, in certain scenarios, explicitly sought to challenge the very line that according to North American newspapers divided the Cubans. Furthermore, by insisting on those lines, the forces of occupation may have in fact contributed to legitimizing further the principle of universal suffrage and allowing the formers foes of independence to find common ground and a shared agenda with the forces of Cuba Libre. The Cuban Republic would be born with universal manhood suffrage despite the North American agents of empire and in no small degree thanks to them.

From Columbus to Ponce de León

Puerto Rican Commemorations between Empires, 1893–1908

CHRISTOPHER SCHMIDT-NOWARA

THE NORTH AMERICAN RULERS OF PUERTO RICO stockpiled knowledge of the island's history and people. The government transferred the Spanish colonial archives from San Juan to Washington. The Saint Louis World's Fair (1904) displayed Puerto Rico and Puerto Ricans to the American public. Museums and foundations such as the Smithsonian dispatched anthropologists to the island to explore the historical roots of Puerto Rican culture and to gather collections for exhibit and study.[1]

Despite claims of American exceptionalism, the U.S. government was comparable to the European colonial empires of the era in its use of anthropology, history, and other scholarly disciplines to consolidate control of Puerto Rico.[2] Moreover, gathering knowledge about recently annexed territorial possessions was not new to the United States in 1898. These techniques were honed in another region once ruled by Spain, the American Southwest, in the decades preceding the occupation of Puerto Rico. To take but one example, the Smithsonian ethnohistorian Jesse Walter Fewkes began his career by studying the Hopi Indians of Arizona. After 1898, he moved to Puerto Rico where he carried out research on the history of the Taíno.[3] He joined the numerous scholars and soldiers who made that peregrination.

How Puerto Ricans responded to American efforts to comprehend and interpret their history is the subject of this essay. I will show that in opposing American visions of history, and the political regime legitimated by these historical perspectives, Puerto Rican political and intellectual leaders called on forms of public historical commemoration developed under Spanish rule in the late nineteenth century. I will also argue that, while there was continuity in the public use and representation of history, conflict over the justice of American rule forced Puerto Ricans to reconsider the nation's historical origins. Finally, I will suggest that Puerto Rican affirmations of the nation's origins and past forced subtle changes in how the American imperial state represented its own origins and lineage.

Commemorating Puerto Rico's Past before 1898

In the aftermath of the Spanish American revolutions of the first two decades of the nineteenth century, which led to the independence of most of the colonies, Spain struggled to reconstruct its authority in its few remaining overseas possessions, including Puerto Rico. These efforts involved forging national historical narratives that emphasized the essential unity of Spain and Puerto Rico. The island, in the metropolitan view, was not a colony or nation with a separate history but a piece of Spanish national territory bound not by force but by the historic ties of shared language, religion, law, and, in some renderings, racial mixture. To signify this unity, Spaniards dug deep into archives in Madrid and Seville, penned historical studies, republished old colonial chronicles, raised monuments, and planned public commemorations of major figures and events from the era of overseas expansion. The response in the colony rarely met metropolitan expectations. Puerto Rican patriots carried out their own research, looking for their national origins in the indigenous victims of conquest and those who rebelled against the first conquistadors.[4]

This divergence was apparent in the attempts to resurrect the memory of Juan Ponce de León, who conquered Puerto Rico in 1508. In 1863, Ponce de León's remains were exhumed with little ceremony in the San José church, close to the cathedral in the heart of San Juan. In 1882, the municipal government raised a statue to the conqueror in the Plaza de Santiago with financial assistance from the metropole, including the monarch, Alfonso XII. The material for the statue was charged with meaning, at least for some: it was melted down from the cannon taken from the English during the successful defense of San Juan in 1797. This patriotic amalgam apparently failed to capture the local imagination. Later that year, the periodical of the conservative pro-Spanish party, the *Boletín Mercantil*, complained of the indignity done to the memory of the conqueror by surrounding his monument with a shoddy wooden fence.[5]

Puerto Ricans reaffirmed their low regard for Ponce de León during the celebration of the four hundredth anniversary of Christopher Columbus's first voyage to the island in 1493. Local elites showed little enthusiasm for the metropolitan festivities of 1892 but in 1893 rallied to a key date in Puerto Rican history. Several municipalities, including Aguada, Guayanilla, and Mayagüez vied for the honor of being recognized as the site of Columbus's first landing. Ultimately, the commission responsible for the celebration settled on Aguada where the monument to the event was eventually placed. The stone cross at Aguada was not the only marker of the occasion. A statue of Columbus was erected on a towering pedestal and column, also in San Juan's Plaza de Santiago, now renamed the Plaza de Colón.

This placement of the monument to the discoverer of Puerto Rico displaced the monument to the conqueror of the island. Ponce de León's statue was moved to the much smaller Plaza de San José, abutting the church where his remains lay in comparative obscurity. The soaring monument to Columbus, the Admiral of the Ocean Sea, not only displaced that to Ponce de León but also accentuated through its scale the squatness of the conquistador's statue.

The treatment of the two figures associated with exploration and conquest revealed the limits of the metropolis's capacity to shape remembrance of the past. Puerto Rico shared in the Columbian centennial with enthusiasm. For Spanish officials, the appropriation of Columbus in Puerto Rico was glad news given the controversies stirred by his memory, not least those provoked by Spaniards such as Cesáreo Fernández Duro who preferred to commemorate more unquestionably Spanish figures from the early empire such as Martín Alonso Pinzón. Also troubling was Cuban unwillingness to share in the pomp of the centennial or to defend Havana as the legitimate resting place of the admiral's remains.[6]

Nonetheless, while participating in Spanish efforts to promote a historical narrative that emphasized the spirit of unity, Puerto Rican municipalities and historians crafted their own version of the admiral, one that called attention to the peculiarities of Puerto Rican history instead of celebrating the glories of the Spanish past. Subtly inflecting the metropolitan version of discovery and conquest by shifting the commemoration to 1893 indicated a desire to differentiate the chronologies of Puerto Rican and Spanish history. It also reflected the profound ambivalence of Puerto Rican patriots regarding the meaning of conquest. They acknowledged Columbus because he inscribed Puerto Rico in the mainstream of Western history, a move desirable for elites preoccupied with progress and modernization. However, the arrival of Columbus signaled the beginning of the end of the people historians such as Agustín Stahl considered the first Puerto Ricans, the prehistoric Indians of Boriquén, who continued to dwell at the center of the nineteenth-century patriotic imagination.[7] Hence, Ponce de León was at the limit of Puerto Ricans' willingness to compromise with metropolitan history. If Columbus could be rendered as a figure of universal significance, Ponce de León bore more chauvinistic and sanguinary associations particularly troublesome in the colony.

Similar strategies were at work during festivities in 1897 on the eve of the North American invasion. The occasion was the centennial of the defense of San Juan against a British invasion. Monuments were erected and polished. The first stone of a monument to the Spanish commander in 1797, General Ramón de Castro, was laid in the Plaza de la Lealtad (Plaza of Loyalty), while plans were made to restore an older monument on the campo del Morro dedicated to the defeat of Dutch invaders in 1625. The very date was resonant: May 2 was the day of the Madrid uprising against French occupying forces in 1808, a national holiday, though a beleaguered one, back in the metropolis. A special issue of the government's newspaper was published to mark the event, bearing the news that the Spanish monarchy had bestowed on Puerto Rico the appellation *siempre fiel*, "always loyal."[8]

Spanish perspectives dominated the official events: 1797 represented Spanish military prowess, Puerto Rican loyalty, and the convergence of colonial and metropolitan interests against a common enemy, a bond that officials hoped to renew in the event of another foreign invasion, this time from the United States. Puerto Rican commentators chose another tack. They muted the talk of loyalty and instead celebrated the valor of the Puerto Rican people. For them, 1797 became a chapter of national, not imperial, history.

Salvador Brau's contribution to the commemorations, a poem entitled "El Dos de Mayo de 1797," demonstrates this divergence from the imperial historical narrative of loyalty and harmony. Brau was a prominent leader of Puerto Rico's Autonomist Party, which sought greater local control over political and economic affairs in the face of Spain's historical commitment to tight control from Madrid. He was also an eminent man of letters who authored numerous works on Puerto Rican history.

His poem trod the line between loyalty and autonomy, linking the heroic feats of May 2, 1797, and 1808: "Una misma fé vehemente / ambos pueblos vivifica: / una fé, que no se explica, / más cuyo imperio se siente" ("The same vehement faith / gave life to both peoples: / a faith that cannot be explained / but whose dominion one feels"). Brau also nodded toward the peculiarities of the Puerto Rican people. He described the Puerto Rican peasants, the *jíbaros*, flocking to battle against the English in 1797, drawing on stereotypical features such as their hats, bare feet, machetes, and idiomatic Spanish: "Al aire el pecho velludo, / amplio pañuelo a la ceja, / el *empleita* hacia la oreja, / y el calloso pie desnudo" ("Hirsute chest exposed, / wide kerchief on the brow, / *empleita* drawn toward the ear, / and the callused foot bare"). These rude and valiant warriors who resisted English forces were as heroic as their more celebrated *madrileño* counterparts who had risen against the French in 1808. Indeed, Brau concluded by hinting that the patriotic valor commemorated on May 2 had its origins not in Spain but in Puerto Rico, which he tellingly referred to by its preconquest name, Boriquén: "Que el sol fúlgido que adora / el español adalid, / si fué espléndido en Madrid, / radió en Boriquén su aurora" ("The brilliant sun that shines on / the Spanish champion, / if it were resplendent in Madrid, / its dawn radiated in Boriquén").[9]

Calling Puerto Rico Boriquén was a subtle yet eloquent act of distinction. Puerto Rican patriots dwelled on the Indian past, evoking it in poetry, plays, novels, and paintings and contemplating the methods needed to write its history.

They crafted it as the original time and place of the Puerto Rican nation, distinct from the world created by the Spanish conquests of the sixteenth century. Brau's poem, written officially to commemorate the glory of Spanish arms, shared this patriotic Puerto Rican vision of the past, inscribing within an act of affiliation the desire for differentiation.

Conquest(s) Vindicated

The North American invasion in 1898 and takeover of the island forced Puerto Ricans to reconsider these attitudes toward Spanish triumphalism. Opposing the new regime called for new histories. The United States invaded Puerto Rico in the summer of 1898 and then annexed the island through the provisions of the Treaty of Paris, which ended the Spanish-American War. Puerto Ricans and Americans confronted each other with competing and contradictory expectations. The Americans believed that the Puerto Rican people were in dire need of tutelage and uplift after almost four centuries of Spanish rule. To that end, the government imposed a highly centralized administration through the Foraker Act of 1900. It placed virtually all power in the office of the governor, a presidential appointee and always an American until the mid-twentieth century. The governor's appointees, most of whom were also Americans, controlled the island's key administrative units. Puerto Rican representation was limited to a consultative elected body that had no binding power on the governor and his cabinet.

The American certainty of Puerto Rican incompetence derived from two potent ideological strains. On the one hand, the Black Legend of Spanish cruelty and backwardness remained alive in the United States throughout the nineteenth century. This narrative of Spanish and Spanish American history derived from the reception of the polemical works of the friar Bartolomé de las Casas, who in his defense of the native population against the conquistadors in the sixteenth century called attention to the brutality of the conquest in graphic terms.[10] Popular outrage over Spanish atrocities during the Cuban insurgency (1895–98) only strengthened this stereotype. As subjects of a backward power, Puerto Ricans must be incapable of self-government. On the other hand, advocates of Anglo-Saxon superiority viewed Latin peoples and racial mixtures with deep suspicion and distrust. Not only history impeded the Puerto Ricans in this view but also their very makeup.

The centralized regime created by the Foraker Act and premised on American superiority came as a rude shock to the people of Puerto Rico. Contrary to American preconceptions, Puerto Rico before 1898 was a highly mobilized society. There were political parties, an active press, and a broad range of trade and professional associations. On the verge of the American invasion, Puerto Rican political leaders had achieved a goal for which they had fought for decades: effective self-government devolved from Madrid. The first elections for the local governor and assembly took place just months before the arrival of the U.S. military. The new regime, then, could be seen locally only as a great setback, depriving Puerto Ricans of hard-earned rights.[11]

Political marginalization went hand in hand with new forms of colonial knowledge that were also at odds with the Spanish period. Under Spanish rule, Puerto Ricans had crafted a distinctive sense of history and identity in contention with metropolitan efforts to defend Spanish sovereignty by casting colonial subjects as actors in the drama of Spanish history. The dynamics of conflict changed radically under the United States. The North American regime perceived its new subjects as racially, religiously, and culturally distinct peoples degraded by centuries of despotic colonialism, Catholicism, and miscegenation. Puerto Ricans suddenly found themselves treated as savages and curiosities in need of U.S. guidance.[12]

In these altered political circumstances, the sense of historical lineage changed. The island's conqueror acquired new luster. In 1908, four centuries after Ponce de León conquered Puerto Rico and became the island's first Spanish governor, a procession of Puerto Rican and Spanish admirers interred his remains in the San Juan cathedral. The procession included political, business, and ecclesiastical dignitaries and a young man dressed as the conqueror. A plaque with an inscription penned by Salvador Brau signaled the new resting place.

Puerto Rico's Cámara de Delegados, the limited representative body created by the Foraker Act, took the initiative in proposing the holiday and commemoration in January of 1908. The governor, Regis H. Post, appointed by Washington, named a commission of local officials and dignitaries to plan the commemoration of the conqueror. The commission's meetings took place in the Casino Español, indicating a telling collaboration between Puerto Ricans and Spanish immigrants who were still prominent in the island's economy. The Puerto Rican historian Cayetano Coll y Toste carried out research in Spain's Archivo General de Indias to ascertain the exact date of Ponce de Leon's arrival. He pinpointed August 12. Post declared the day a holiday, one marking the establishment of the "first civilized government in the Island of Puerto Rico."[13]

The return of Ponce de León in 1908 occurred during a time a heightened tension between Post and political parties in Puerto Rico, especially the Unión Puertorriqueña, which brought together advocates of independence and self-government. As we see in other essays in this volume, the American imperial state faced opposition in many quarters after 1898. In Puerto Rico, there was conflict over education, language, the relation between church and state, the applicability of the U.S. Constitution, tariffs, and public health. History also became a site of conflict as Puerto Ricans agitated against the restricted nature of the Foraker regime. Against a government that insisted that they were uncivilized and unprepared for self-government after centuries of Spanish colonialism, Puerto

Rican political and intellectual leaders crafted a historical narrative that placed the island at the center of Western historical development.

Governor Post's comments regarding "civilized government" hint at why Puerto Ricans were more willing to commemorate Ponce de León after 1898. Ponce, along with Columbus, symbolized Puerto Rico's historical origins in European civilization. Puerto Ricans were Spaniards, descendants of an illustrious people with a history that Americans understood. Spanish origins, no matter how problematic for the new conquerors, enabled Puerto Rican elites to demand reforms, or in some cases independence, from the new regime as fellow Creoles with origins in the cradle of Western civilization.[14]

The American takeover thus transformed visions and appropriations of the past in Puerto Rico. However, important strategies and symbols were still at work. As under the Spanish regime, Puerto Rican patriots were willing to meet the colonial rulers only partway in their renderings of the past. Under American rule, they rejected the characterization of Puerto Rico as uncivilized and in need of tutelage. By championing Ponce de León and other European forebears, they insisted on the comparability of Puerto Rico's history with that of the United States. But while seeking compromise with the North Americans through claims to European origins Puerto Ricans nonetheless maintained their distance. Most important, Spanish remained the language of Puerto Rican civilization under American rule, an act of distinction that ironically harkened back to the earlier colonial regime.

Embracing the Spanish past was important; defending the mix of races and cultures so despised by the Americans was also crucial. By the mid-twentieth century, powerful scholars such as the anthropologist Ricardo Alegría had enshrined in schools and museums the belief in the "three roots" of Puerto Rican identity: European, Indian, and African. This vision of Puerto Rican history, coupled with strict adherence to the Spanish language, further differentiated the colony from the North American metropole, making a virtue of racial and cultural mixing.[15]

The idea of the three roots had its own roots in the patriotic histories of the nineteenth century; the silences inscribed in that historical rendering also recurred under the new regime. The third root of Puerto Rican history, the African, was the least visible. Making Puerto Rico Spanish and European, or Indian, downplayed the African origins of Puerto Rican culture, a silencing with its own history but one reinforced by the preoccupations and prejudices of the occupying power. The preferred counterpoint to the European past was still the Indian, the symbol of preconquest simplicity.[16]

Conclusion

The use of history in Puerto Rico to defy the vision of the colonial power had an impact on the American imperial state. As American officials encountered the tenacity of interests and ideas in the colonies, they had to reconsider their goal of effacing local history and culture through Americanization. They soon learned that they could not expect Puerto Ricans to accept the simple vision of Spanish colonial history encapsulated in the Black Legend, the complacent telling of U.S. national history laden with assumptions of Anglo-Saxon racial superiority, or the political regime that these narratives justified.

This reconsideration was more than a concession to Puerto Rican elites' own claims to civility. The Spanish imperial past became a rich source of images, heroes, and narratives from which Americans could draw their own imperial lineage and justify their colonizing and civilizing mission. Beyond the new insular possessions, the American imperial state in the early twentieth century was exerting its influence in Mexico and throughout the Caribbean and Central America. Even before the imperial transition of 1898, the United States had incorporated to varying degrees huge swaths of the former Spanish empire, especially the Mexican territories annexed through the Guadalupe-Hidalgo Treaty and the Gadsden Purchase. While the Black Legend and Anglo-Saxonism remained alive and well during this era of expansion, identification with the Spanish conquistadors, friars, and governors also thrived in those territories where the United States built its empire on Spanish ruins: Kino in southern Arizona, Coronado and Oñate in New Mexico, and Cabrillo and Serrá in California became precursors to American rule. In Puerto Rico, Governor Post ultimately found his own predecessor in the island's first European governor: Ponce de León.[17]

A Critical-Historical Genealogy of *Koko* (Blood), *'Aina* (Land), Hawaiian Identity, and Western Law and Governance

RONA TAMIKO HALUALANI

AT FIRST GLANCE, THE TRAVELING OF IDENTITY through time seems naturally consistent, effortless, and without consequence. Its movement and collisional encounters guised, identity just "is." Stuart Hall interrupts this seamlessness by provoking us to look again, this time with a watchful eye and a tracing finger.[1] That is, we must analyze with an eye for articulated stability and a penchant for silent historical implosions of identity within and without Western colonized indigenous worlds. Beneath the face of identity, according to Hall, lies its historical production, an aspect that has already challenged cultural studies scholars to dig deeper. We hold this notion tight, that we can never understand identity expressions without looking to the social-political conditions within which they were produced, overtaken, and rehauled.

Thus, in this critical-historical genealogy, I move where Hawaiian identity once did; from its early establishment to the Western upheaval of "Cook time" and its gradual incorporation into Western law and governance. In this essay, I engage several sovereignty and critically bent Hawaiian land histories and analyze the historically specific identity practices and structured identifications for "Hawaiians."[2] As such, I present this analysis as a historical genealogy with the following question in mind. How did the construction of Hawaiianness change by and through Western colonialism?

I argue that Western formal policy, law, and governance—from the late 1700s to early 1900s—disintegrates an indigenous Hawaiian system and subjectivity.[3] This becomes a pressured confrontation that writes out the Kanaka (Hawaiian) language through the structural exclusion of "prehumanity," a soon to be blooded group constructed as existing outside of Western moral-political jurisdiction with its discursive tools of excision: the doctrine of discovery, the sovereign resident position, the legal principles of ultimate land use and alienation, and the incorporation of land commissions. Tools such as these, structurally normalize "rightful" *haole* (foreigner) citizenry and install a legacy of (mis)recognized identity for Hawaiians. This misrecognition of Hawaiians continues and is further imprinted in the colonial rule over the islands when Hawai'i was illegally overthrown in 1893 and made a U.S. territory on a path to statehood.

Understanding the historicization of the (mis)recognition of Hawaiians—the shift from a Hawaiian kinship relation to a Western technology of blood and from a Hawaiian social structure grounded in land use (*'aina*) to Western governance based on landownership/citizenship—reveals the complicated nature of the (mis)-recognition of Hawaiians and the encoded stakes in current political struggles. Our analytical movements should note the dominant framings of Hawaiian identity and uncover the cultural material useful for identity remakings.

A Blood-y History

Before the misleading marker of "original Hawaiian history"—1778—the indicator of the popular memory surrounding Captain Cook, there *already* existed a moving cultural world of Hawaiian subjectivity. This world embodied and breathed the philosophy of *'aina* (land) and land communion.[4] *'Aina* was not a mere physical space; it translates in Hawaiian as the act of living through land. *'Aina* was a way of life, a spiritual understanding of land as the natural, deified force of Lono, the god of fertility and love, or Kane, the god of agricultural growth. Land was therefore the physical manifestation of a greater, nonmaterial power.[5] You couldn't "own" it; land was a sacred presence in your life. Through the land, these *akua*, or gods, among others, watched over and cared for Hawaiians, bestowing rich soil and conditions for the bountiful production of food for a thriving Kanaka (Hawaiian) population, one estimated by the historian David Stannard to be at least eight hundred thousand to a million at the time of contact, although it declined drastically, to less than forty thousand, by 1890.[6]

Collectively, within their own inherited social positions, Hawaiians were culturally summoned both to live through and work the land in specialized labor. Assigned different duties, the overall goal was to carefully tend the land so that it would bear enough food for all people.[7] The gods ruled over and emanated from the land, which is why Hawaiians culturally never understood or expressed the principle of ownership.[8] "Trustees" were those deemed to be of divine blood kinship, meaning that particular relations were honored and elevated because they were closer to the gods in birthright and thus held great *mana* (power, status). They were our *ali'i nui* (Hawaiian leaders/royalty).

For example, in critical detail, Lilikala Kame'eleihiwa explains how a select few kinship relations were considered sacred.[9] King Kamehameha I, Hawai'i's skilled political warrior who unified all of the islands, increased the power of his lineage by mating with Keopuolani who through her family line surely proved to be an *akua*. Thus, the mating between Kamehameha and Keopuolani, which produced three children—Liholiho, Kauikeaouli, and Nahi'ena'ena—was of divine distinction; the children's divine ancestry (their links to higher status and evidence of ascending generation gaps) was higher than that of their parents. They stood closer to the *akua*.[10] Traditional Hawaiian genealogies, in this context, demonstrated the "rightfulness" of certain *ali'i nui* to care for the Hawaiian people. Higher, close-to-*akua* status was established through a lived blood metaphor, meaning that blood was signified less as biological substance and percentage amount than as a performative indicator/producer of the collective honor, and the *mana* (power, status) of a family. This would mark the difference between an indigenous practice of blood and an imposed state policy of blood.

While claims to the purity of a family line appear in traditional Hawaiian texts, genealogies help to bring into being an identity of "who one is" through those before and after her or him.[11] As a metaphor, blood is double sided, seemingly positioning genealogies as purely factual and indisputable tables of parentage while symbolically encoding them as to-be-performed relations via *ni'aupi'o* matings (chiefly incest) and chantings. Genealogies were not givens (ends in themselves), guaranteed, or even valued for their accuracy as fixed truths. These relations were to be, within a certain social class, re-created and reconstituted time and time again.[12] As performative political practices, blood relations and genealogical chants reproduced and maintained a hierarchical structure of power in Hawaiian society.[13]

With a genealogically divine status, the *mo'i* (king) was granted responsibility for a *moku*, a large land division equivalent to the size of an island, which typically was an independent kingdom. A leader who provided for his people was considered a "favorite" of the *akua*. Lower in the social hierarchy were the *maka'ainana* (people of the land, commoners) who worked and cultivated *ahupua'a*, which were land units that extended from mountaintop to coast, encompassing terrains for wet- and dryland farming and inshore fishing (allowing for the gathering of taro, breadfruit, sweet potato, and fish). On these land units, the commoners were entitled to use all the food and water resources of the land. Use was a privilege granted by the *akua*. Hawaiians religiously made sense of this status hierarchy; they believed that each Hawaiian, in different social roles, worked and lived in interdependence. Although the social hierarchy structurally formed disproportionate power relations between the chiefs and *maka'ainana*, there was a perpetual give and take.[14]

In a cultural frame different from a market-driven society, 'aina was *not* a capitalist-centered system with commercially valued land. Instead, productivity was always a spiritually infused offering by the *akua*. Land productivity therefore meant the amount of food cultivated to feed a bustling population and the social and cultural use of land by the larger Hawaiian community. They would make use of and work the land. Land use was ensured as long as proper respect was given to the gods and social groups performed their designated labor. The archives, though cryptic in nature, describe the land base at this time—a time marked by the greatest amount of warfare in the islands—as richly fertile and expansive, thus affirming the deep structure and organization of Hawaiian 'aina. But Hawaiian life was not perfect. There were limits within this organized social system; only the mo'i and ali'i nui could materially attain and control land through conquest or inheritance (especially in the case of ruling chiefs with distinguished lineages). The maka'ainana would be able to live on land but never materially make claim to it.[15]

In a non-Western culture motivated by deeply held religious and cultural practices, religiosity constituted the lived relations of Hawaiian society. It stood as the primary force in reproducing a secure, fully functioning, social formation. Scholars such as Elizabeth Buck highlight the difference between capitalist and noncapitalist formations; religion ideologically united an indigenous culture.[16] The hegemony of the early Hawaiian everyday would be politically transformed and historically subsumed under a larger struggle for existence only when it was thrown "into crisis" by the Western contact and colonization of the eighteenth century.[17]

National Loyalties, Property Ownership, and "Primitivized" 'Aina Use

In the eighteenth century, European "discoverers"—the Spanish and then the British—set out for the New World and its exploitable wealth. Sometime around "1778" (and perhaps even earlier), secondary Western cultural contact was established through several coaligned forms. The first contact took place—at home—through the religious doctrine explicating the noble mission of the Christian nation and the untamed New World and its peoples who had yet to find the Word of God.[18] From the initial intercultural meetings of discoverer and "native" on the decks to the sexual affairs down below between Cook's men, sailors, and Hawaiian men and women (which led to the spread of venereal disease and the swift collapse of the Hawaiian population), the "native" body called for the suspension of Western virtue for exoticized sexuality—the intriguing native male, to be politically contained, and the native female whose nonthreatening yet alluring appeal pleasurably exceeded colonial domesticity and social conduct. Underneath the large banyan trees, American Congregationalist and French Catholic missionaries eloquently promised physical and eternal life to the "heathenist" Hawaiians who only saw death and disease all around them. Jehovah or Christ could indeed save them from mass extinction. Near the shipping docks, those points on the culturalizing maps, traders from Great Britain, Spain, Russia, and the United States traded Western objects of metal, iron, guns, and ammunition to *ali'i nui* for Hawaiian sandalwood. On stretches of Hawaiian land (still cultural worlds apart from *'aina*), European and American business interests and political figures questioned the Hawaiian kingdom's strange form of governance and land tenure system, urging for the formalized institution of property rights for all residents. Through the melding of discovery, sexual desire, transgression through Christ, trade and commerce, and formal policy, the Hawaiians would, in all ways, surely be visited upon.[19]

As foreigners flocked to Hawaiian shores, King Kamehameha, a leader who was always wise to the ways of modern nations, allowed *haoles* to live on land parcels, but only through an agreement that somewhat paralleled traditional Hawaiian land tenure forms: the exchange of Western services for land use.[20] For their skilled work in circulating Western goods and practices, carpenters, shipbuilders, masons, blacksmiths, and physicians could reside in the islands and enjoy (in Hawaiian terms) free use of land. Ownership or land title was never formally granted to these first lessees. Thus, the exchange of Western goods and services was absorbed into the still predominantly noncapitalist, traditional Hawaiian formation (a point Marshall Sahlins argues).[21] Within the extant, ideologically bound hierarchy, Western goods represented a new way to elevate one's social position and *mana*.[22] The strange and shiny mirrors, metal pieces, nails, and iron buckets—these, to Hawaiians, clearly paved the divine path to power from the *akua*.

The *ali'i*, enamored with the items first brought by Cook and his men, often exerted the *maka'ainana* to cultivate produce and sandalwood and even offer the favors of Hawaiian women, which could be traded for iron, guns, and fur. Such a cycle took its toll as the *maka'ainana* could not keep up with the demands of their *ali'i* as well as their debts to traders and foreign interests.

After the Hawaiian Islands were unified into one kingdom in 1810 by King Kamehameha, the land tenure system was changed to ensure political stability.[23] Tactically, to retain the loyalty of those around him and establish Hawai'i as a *lahui* (Hawaiian nation) capable of strong foreign relations with national powers, Kamehameha granted land parcels to lower *ali'i* and foreigners who served as political advisers.[24] These *haoles* presumed that they had a natural right to land and were entitled—*before* any formal institution of Hawaiian law and *through* sovereign ideologies at home—to pass land on to their heirs and families. This would become a prevailing mode of identity logic throughout the 1800s, informed by the popular gallery's doctrine of discovery, discourses of travel (which nativized the discoverer and rendered the "native" foreign), and the geographic gaze.

King Kamehameha was determined to maintain the Hawaiian kingdom in the face of great change. Thus, in 1814 he expelled all foreigners without land tenure.[25] However, Kamehameha's unique style of leadership, in which he recognized the value of modern items (iron, metal, guns, and ammunition) while maintaining cultural tradition, would end with his death in 1819. Hawai'i would never be the same.

Immediately after his father's death, Liholiho (Kamehameha II) assumed the throne as *haole* residents and *ali'i* continued to push for the formalization of land inheritance within the Hawaiian land tenure system. And soon it became law. In 1825, a young Liholiho and the Council of Chiefs, heavily influenced by Britain's Lord Byron, adopted a formal policy—the Law of 1825—allowing *ali'i* to transfer retained lands (upon the king's death) to their heirs.[26] As mentioned earlier, this right had *already* been ideologically assumed (though not yet formally recognized by Hawaiian leaders) ten years earlier by foreign-born residents. *Haoles* from Britain, France, Russia, and America believed they "naturally" had individual rights to property and ownership of the land they occupied. In fact, even in the face of expulsion from Hawai'i, many *haoles* blatantly conducted business with one another, leasing, selling, and buying titles to land that was formally held by *ali'i*.[27] Thus, residency, for Westerners, ideologically exceeded the mere use and leasing of land. It encompassed a superior right to the New World (and its perpetually producing resources) based on the natural order of humanity. Through the reigning mandates of their imperial homelands, *haole* residents called invoked intermingling natural rights and discovery discourses together with their national identities to claim privatized rights *before, outside of,* and thereby *over* indigenous structures.

Living without contradiction, European settlers and American residents after 1820, represented Hawaiians as "uncivilized" and "lazy" in that these Hawaiians did not own or control land and lacked proper modes of governance (capitalistic individualism and self-reliance) and citizenship. Hawaiians, it seemed, could not sustain their society.[28] Hiram Bingham, an American Calvinist missionary and instigator of the 1893 overthrow of the last Hawaiian monarch, Queen Lili'uokalani, described Hawaiians as "naked savages" whose "appearance of destitution, degradation, and barbarism . . . was appalling. Some of our number were ready to exclaim, 'Can these be human beings! . . . Can they be Christianized?'"[29]

It was primarily within this locus—a combination of religious doctrine, backed by the law of nations or the justification for New World discovery and conquest, and the citizenship ideal of "capitalist virtue" (the fusion of moral living and economic production)—that the "Hawaiian" was excised out of temporal existence, residing only in the popular imagination as "before time" or "pre-European/Cook time."[30]

In the 1830s, *haole* residents pressed the *ali'i* to incorporate a land law embodying this principle of ultimate use. Hawaiians accordingly would receive five times as much land as they cultivated. As a result, any undeveloped land would be placed on the market.[31] This circumscribed a means of attaining a majority of Hawaiian lands while also setting into place a commercial economy based on the practice of private ownership and market competition among individual farmers. Formal Western law therefore installed a normative white citizen position while differentially marking Hawaiians as outside Christian principles and the societal good. Their tribal rituals and lack of land production and economic sustenance placed them outside of legal citizenry, their identities and practices (mis)recognized through Western colonialism and the enacted land law.

A New World order and its accompanying natural rights discourse therefore collapsed into, collided into, and racially restructured a Hawaiian social formation. After 1820, residents clamored for the necessary transition from usufruct (the granted *use* of land held in title by the *ali'i*, who could revoke land tenure at any time) to the Western ideal of fee simple ownership (the absolute, unrestricted ownership of land). *Haoles* engaged in practices that partly dissolved the local native structure such as intermarriage between *haole* men and Hawaiian women, as well as the invocation of the doctrine of discovery and national identities.[32] During this time, private residents (British, French, and American) amplified their identity rights and privileges in Hawai'i by invoking the doctrine of discovery and the authority of their national governments (their homelands).

Writing Over 'Aina as an Individual, Private Right

The coarticulated forces of Western law, policy, and commerce overwhelmed Hawaiian society. In 1845, pressured by influential foreigners and interested in empowering Hawaiians, King Kamehameha III agreed to establish a land commission to approve privatized land claims by Hawaiians and residents. He strongly reminded all vested interests that Hawaiian land tenure would still formally guide this commission. Soon after, in 1848, the Mahele (Division), mandated the equal division of Hawaiian kingdom lands among the king, chiefs, government, and Hawaiian people. The king claimed and divided approximately 2.5 million acres of all Hawaiian lands, 1.5 million of which were designated as government lands "set apart forever to the chiefs and people."[33] The leftover million acres of the king's allotments were set aside as his private set of lands for his heirs and their families; these were the "king's lands" (or Crown lands).[34] After the king's share was allotted, the *ali'i* were assigned the remaining 1.5 million acres of the kingdom; portions of these lands (and cash payments made for titles) would revert to the government. Hawaiians were framed here as private tenants who when occupying any of the lands (government, king's, or chiefs') possessed ownership rights and thus were formally obligated to individually cultivate these lands. This concept was strange to Hawaiians. The new structure conflicted with their *akua*-centered communal land structure, which was based on specialized labor and reciprocity. As new native tenants Hawaiians could assert their rights only by applying to a land commission board for a fee simple title claim through the Kuleana Act.

Immediately before the passage of the Kuleana Act, in July of 1850, as pressure mounted, the Hawaiian government granted allodial (fee simple) ownership to foreign residents regardless of citizenship as long as political intervention on the part of their governments was not practiced. As defined in the Kuleana Act, native tenants could be awarded fee simple titles to individual, richly fertile plots of land (*kuleanas*), which were to be taken out of the king's, government, or chiefs' lands. Formally designed to provide for *maka'ainana*, the Kuleana Act minimally benefited Hawaiians, as only 26 percent (7,500 *maka'ainana* males) of the total native male population actually received claimed lands; "only 28,600 acres (less than one percent of the total land)" were transferred in title to Hawaiian commoners.[35]

The Kuleana Act foretold the legal future of Hawaiians: containment under the procedural hands of the law. For example, the notion of a land commission for native tenants presumed that tenant identity and land rights existed only *through* and *after* legal recognition. The act itself, while posing as an equitable procedure of law, had to be completed in order for a Hawaiian (male) to gain the right to land.[36] Completion seemed to be a difficult (almost unlikely) feat for potential tenants first had to understand English, the often ambiguous and all too specific letter of the law, and the complex nature of an entirely new land system through which use was reframed as an individual entitlement given certain conditions and duties. Most Hawaiians did not know English nor could they comprehend these massive changes; they dismissed the Kuleana grant as a form of betrayal against their *ali'i nui*, who they feared would punish them for accepting the new policy. This refusal shows how difficult it was for Hawaiians to break from an interdependent, albeit imperfect, hegemonic order in which food and basic needs were for the most part guaranteed to one tiered by relatively autonomous yet cooperating power outlets. Suddenly, sustenance, a responsibility that in Kanaka eyes called for interdependent, organized labor, was based, in the Western way, on individual ability and competition. To Hawaiians, the prospects seemed dismal.[37]

Complicating the supposedly neutral procedurality of law, native applicants were required to present surveys of the land plots being claimed. However, surveys were conducted mostly by *haole* missionaries for only they could read and write in English. Surveyors and census enumerators held the advantage of English in record keeping, which would later haunt Hawaiians in their search for seemingly accurate documents. The surveys were also expensive and again reflected the dominant ultimate-use land law under which many surveyors only reported the amount of land cultivated and not the totality held.[38] Moreover, all land applications were to be filed and documented (proven) within the brief period of four years, substantially less time than it took for Hawaiians to understand the whirlwind of legal technicalities, save enough money to pay for a survey, and find a fair surveyor for a *kuleana* plot.

Thus, the incorporation of Western policy transformed and forever changed—in terms of formal practices—the relationship between Hawaiians and 'aina. From the 1893 illegal overthrow of Hawai'i through its 1898 acquisition and beyond, Western law and policy officially ushered in a racially homogeneous (soon to be American) citizenship and legal membership in which *haole* residents were made "native citizens" and Hawaiians were rendered foreign and racialized out of its boundaries.

The Hawaiian Homes Commission Act and Blood Quantum

In 1898, not long after (but deeply reminiscent of) the 1893 illegal overthrow of Queen Lili'uokalani's rule, the United States declared Hawai'i a territory. As such, it held complete authority over the island territory and on July 9, 1921, signed into law the Hawaiian Homes Commission Act (HHCA), which was "designed to rehabilitate the Native Hawaiians." In the 1920s, as a result of the HHCA, government homesteading programs were created to "rehabilitate a population-in-need" and place Hawaiians on land parcels. The HHCA initially defined a Native Hawaiian as a descendant "of not less than one-thirty-second part of the blood of the original races which inhabited the islands at the time of their discovery by Captain Cook."[39] A later amendment further restricted the quantum to "½ part of the blood."

Before the bill's passage, the thriving sugar and ranching interests, which leased richly fertile Crown lands for their plantations, were facing a hard blow. Their contracts would likely be terminated. As it turned out, the official lease expiration date came just as Congress began debating the HHCA.[40] The implications were serious as all leased plantation lands could revert to general homesteading purposes for Native Hawaiians.

Several commercially vested senators began to propose resolutions that would allow sugar planters and ranchers to maintain their leaseholds. One was House Resolution 13500, which linked commerce to "federal rehabilitation" by exempting sugarcane lands from homesteading. Thus, dominant sugar and rancher leases could continue, and Hawaiians could be "reformed" through land. The money made from the leases would subsidize the government administration of Hawaiian homesteads.[41] After the revised version of the HHCA was approved in 1921, about two hundred thousand acres of land were set aside specifically for homesteading by Native Hawaiians.[42] If a Native Hawaiian male qualified, he could obtain a ninety-nine-year lease for one dollar per year for residential, pastoral, and agricultural lots.[43]

With the construction of a dying or long-lost pure Hawaiian race, the formal creation of Native Hawaiians by the HHCA was suspect. The 1921 amendment's definition of a Native Hawaiian as a person ½ part of the blood "of the races inhabiting the Hawaiian Islands" is curious.[44] In the officially approved write-up of the HHCA, it was estimated that the full-blood population had decreased from 142,650 in 1826 to about 22,600 in 1919.⁴⁵ Yet, in drafting the HHCA of 1921, U.S. legislators still inscribed a rigid 50 percent blood requirement that most Hawaiians could never meet.

The approval of the HHCA in 1921 thus perpetuated a previously (mis)-recognized Hawaiian identity and further compounded it at the hands of the U.S. federal government and the state of Hawai'i. The definition of Native Hawaiians as possessing ½ Hawaiian blood (the result of pressure from plantation owners and ranchers), created two distinct legal identities for Hawaiians: Native Hawaiians (at least 50 percent Hawaiian blood) and Hawaiians (less than 50 percent Hawaiian blood). Later, after statehood in 1959, section 204 of the HHCA was amended to allow the commission to "dispose of such (homestead) lands by lease or license to the general public." Thus, non-Hawaiians were able to lease designated Hawaiian homestead areas. This amendment was in clear violation of the letter of the HHCA.⁴⁶

Blood quantam, a hegemonic tool of classification, ultimately highlights the sheer flexibility of U.S. federal power, illustrating how the essential binaries (black-white) of race, its gradations (Native Hawaiianness as pure or mixed-blood quantum), and the liberality of assigned whiteness can still bolster a racially homogeneous (or white) American polity. In this light, the blood-quantumed racial characterization of Hawaiians safeguards the national capital by securing its possession of Hawaiian lands—legislatively writing out purebloods through administrative extinction, excluding mixed Hawaiian progeny as potential citizens, and specifying who has the discursive authority to claim Hawaiianess. All the while, the nation-state, head held high and myths in place, refashions itself as the legal-moral adjudicator of justice and rehabilitation.

Buying into Empire

American Consumption at the Turn of the Twentieth Century

KRISTIN HOGANSON

MILITARY INTERVENTIONS AND STATE POWER are only part of the story of American imperialism at the end of the nineteenth century and beginning of the twentieth. Historians have long recognized that in addition to its formal political empire the United States had an informal economic empire. More recently, historians have come to appreciate the social and cultural dimensions of American imperialism as well. The emerging scholarship on the cultures of U.S. imperialism has demonstrated that we do not need to look overseas to find evidence of empire, that the domestic realm of the United States has itself been an arena of imperial contact and contestation. This becomes particularly clear if we consider consumption. Looking back to the decades around 1898, we can see that consumer culture not only shaped imperial worldviews but also was fully imbricated in the imperial politics of the time. As imperial networks opened up new terrains of consumer possibility, consumption became a significant form of imperial engagement. The world of consumption linked the formal empire of U.S. state power to the informal empire of U.S. commercial power and the secondhand empire of European power, in the process deepening American consumers' material and emotional investments in all these imperial projects.

Historians of the late nineteenth and early twentieth centuries, like historians of other time periods, have tended to focus on domestic aspects of U.S. consumption. But the post–Civil War period was an era of rising imports. After falling by more than half during the Civil War, ocean shipping rebounded in the postwar years. Although domestic manufacturers supplied the majority of household goods, an unprecedented amount of imports entered the country.[1] In 1865, for example, the United States imported around $55.7 million worth of food; in 1900, it imported over $226 million, a fourfold rise. By 1920, the figure was about $1.84 billion, an eightfold increase over the 1900 amount.

The increase in imports reflects the growing commercial prowess of the United States after the Civil War. The richer the United States became, the more it could afford to import. Yet causality went two ways: as economic expansion helped globalize consumption, consumer appetites drove economic expansion. As they filled their houses with imported objects, stuck ostrich plumes on their hats, and shopped for tropical produce, a growing number of Americans developed materially rooted imperial sensibilities. They came to see themselves as having needs that could no longer be satisfied and stature that could no longer be sustained merely by home production. Rather than buying strictly domestic items, countless American consumers—women prominent among them—bought into the global order that enabled their high standard of consumption, and this order was, at the turn of the twentieth century, thoroughly imperial.

By imperial buy-in, I mean popular participation in, if not support for, informal (commercial), formal (political and military), and secondhand (European) empire. Historians have already addressed various aspects of buy-in without using this expression. We understand why many exporters and investors eagerly supported expansion and why fervid evangelicals, self-professed humanitarians, and would-be bodybuilders might have too.[2] But there is another aspect of buy-in that has not received much attention, the literal aspect. To be an imperial power involved more than making a mark on the world; it meant consuming the fruits of empire.[3] The story of imperial buy-in may seem particularly important for women's, cultural, and economic history, but it is also important for U.S. political history. Besides being political players in their own right, women consumers helped shape the worldviews of their male associates and those of their children, some of whom exercised power well into the "American century."

This is not to say that consumers were the sole determinants of what consumption meant. To the contrary, producers, importers, retailers, advertisers, advice purveyors, conspicuous style setters, and others contributed to the discourses that surrounded particular material objects, lending them meaning. Yet in the end it was up to individuals to choose what to buy. In contrast to those who regard consumption as a trivial pursuit, with no significance beyond individual impulses, I see consumers' choices as politically fraught. Consumption helped mark the bounds of inclusion and exclusion that differentiated classes, races, ethnicities, nationalities, and civilizations, and it constituted a key terrain in which particular groups struggled over the kind of world in which they wished to live. Ample evidence for this point can be found at the turn of the twentieth century in debates over what constituted appropriate consumption. The white, well-to-do, native-born Americans who favored relatively cosmopolitan forms of consumption found themselves at odds with their social peers who insisted that they should buy American and shun foreign styles. Rather than treat consumption as politically inconsequential, the participants in these debates understood it to be highly meaningful.[4]

So how do we parse the political significance of, say, a Persian carpet or silk stockings? Despite our ability to quantify trade statistics, the absence of opinion polls pertaining to the matter makes it difficult to trace how consumers regarded their tablecloths and teapots. Did the women who filled their houses with Asian imports look sympathetically on the U.S. military presence in the Philippines and China? Did wearing a kimono around the house signify any particular stance toward Japan? How often did banana eaters think about the United Fruit Company's dealings in Central America, if at all?

One way to answer these questions would be to correlate the household inventories and personal account books of particular consumers with their political outlooks. This would make it possible to determine if women who favored Baghdad curtains really regarded world affairs differently from those who stuck to the colonial revival. But archival considerations would make this a difficult project. Few householders left complete records of their purchasing and consumption habits. It would be even harder to locate a collection combining inventories with insights into what individual householders thought about cashmere shawls and curry powder and how they related to the imperial politics of the era.

Given these archival constraints, how can we make the jump from trade data to worldviews and political inclinations? One way is to consider geographies of consumption. By this, I mean the various ideas in public circulation that attempted to explain and contextualize particular goods. Even if there were as many attitudes about consumption as there were consumers, exploring the geographies of consumption that swirled around imports can help us get at various constellations of views. It can help us understand the contexts in which consumers positioned their own particular preferences.

In addition to surveying geographies of consumption, we can interpret practice. What did fashionable women wear in the boudoir and what did they choose for the streets? When and where did white Americans try curry, chili, and chop suey? By helping us to understand how consumers wove imports and ostensibly foreign cultural production into the fabric of daily life, evidence of consumption practices can help us understand whether consumers got the lessons expounded by sources of geographic knowledge such as the popular press and commercial establishments. Though not a fully transparent window into *mentalité*, evidence of practice nonetheless can help us to appreciate how consumers regarded imports. It can help us determine whether anyone really knew where their stuff came from and how it ended up in their hands and whether material life affected worldviews and political commitments.

Geographies of Consumption

It is possible to buy a button or a banana with no clue as to its origins, but turn of the century retailers did not hesitate to expound on the provenance of their wares. A sampling of fashion advertisements illustrates this point. The 1902 Sears catalogue hawked Chinese, Japanese, and French silks. John Forsythe, a New York establishment with a catalogue department, sold waists with "fine Mexican hand embroidery and drawn work." The furrier Revillon Frères advertised that its pelts originated in northern Siberia, Bukhara, and Chile, to list just a few places. To help consumers visualize the world of production, one import shop ran ads with maps showing where its dress goods originated—including China, Southeast Asia, Japan, India, Morocco, and Egypt.[5]

Retailers were not the only ones to trumpet origins. Cookbooks, decorating columns, domestic manuals, fashion pages, fiction, and other printed materials made a point of identifying where things came from. Instead of rattan, advice purveyors referred to Chinese rattan; instead of rugs, they referred to "Oriental rugs" or, more specifically, Turkish, Persian, Bukhara, Caucasian, and other geographically identified rugs. Although its accuracy could be questioned, the consumerist literature of the post–Civil War period acknowledged the increasingly expansive system of production that supplied Americans' wants.[6] Because of such domestic writings, imported objects did not stand without signification. To the contrary, they came with place markers attached.

Just as domestic writings taught geographic lessons, geographic writings taught domestic ones, for they, too, traced the trajectories of particular consumer goods. In 1916, for example, *National Geographic* ran an article, "How the World Is Fed," that investigated the origins of the U.S. food supply. "Where once all roads led to Rome," it remarked, "now they come directly to our dinner tables." The article invited readers to contemplate how those roads converged on a dinner menu. Many of the components of the elaborate feast had U.S. origins, but other items came from farther afield: the pepper from Africa, the rice from China, the cherries from Sicily, the olive oil from Spain, the sugar from Cuba, the vanilla from Ecuador, the chocolate from Mexico. "When it comes to coffee," the article observed, "if we are fastidious we will have issued a draft on both Turkish Arabia and Dutch Java, or if we are only folk of every-day taste we will content ourselves with the Brazilian product."[7] By tracking down the far-flung origins of the American diet, this article mapped the expansive geographies that supplied American consumers' desires.

Print sources were not the only ones that supplied knowledge of provenance. The increasing numbers of tourists who traveled overseas and the influx of immigrants who landed in the United States also contributed to consumerist geographies. So did the numerous commercial, entertainment, and educational venues that displayed imported objects in settings intended to reveal something about their origins. These living dioramas ranged from ethnographic circus displays to museum collections, manufacturing exhibits, arts and crafts of the homelands events, and department store ensembles. World's fairs played a particularly important role in helping consumers to locate imports geographically. Besides gazing on the goods collected in glass cases, fairgoers could see curiosities in use in purportedly authentic settings, and they could purchase the items arrayed in midway bazaars.[8]

According to printed materials and exotic exhibits alike, imports could do more than add color and novelty to daily life: they could convey geographic knowledge. It may seem that the only kind of geography lessons that consumer goods could teach would pertain to the geography of pleasure: where did the good things of life hail from? But the geography of consumption was a thoroughly political geography. Along with teaching consumers where things originated, it taught them how various goods came to the United States. The answer, in countless cases, was via imperial conduits. Foremost among them were those of the British Empire.

That British imperial rule played a crucial role in bringing non-European goods to the attention of Americans can be seen, for example, in an *Atlanta Constitution* column that identified London as "the place to buy East India things cheap."[9] Food writers joined with shopping experts in attributing novel consumer choices to British imperialism. One article, for example, explained the transmission of Indian condiments as follows: "The Englishman resident in India takes very readily to the peppery chutneys and sauces so much in vogue in that sun-parched land, and when he returns home he usually brings with him some treasured formula for concocting at least . . . one of its varied relishes." The British labels pasted on the curry jars found in American groceries underscored their imperial origins.[10] According to the written texts and three-dimensional displays that introduced American consumers to such things as Indian brassware and Worcestershire sauce, European imperialism benefited Americans by facilitating their access to global production.

Europeans were not the only imperialists on the block, however. Geographies of consumption also taught lessons about U.S. power. Cooking writers, for instance, pointed out that chili owed its presence in the U.S. culinary lexicon to U.S. continental expansion in the mid-nineteenth century. They waxed equally enthusiastic about the culinary repercussions of later U.S. interventions in the Caribbean and East Asia. As a 1910 *Good Housekeeping* piece noted, peppers had "become more common since the Spanish war, as they are used in our new territories so much that Americans are beginning to use them as the English learned curry from India."[11] Several months later *Good Housekeeping* ran another article rife with imperial imagery: "Uncle Sam is literally ransacking every corner of the

"The May Sale of Philippine Lingerie." *Vogue*, May 1, 1917. (Courtesy of the Winterthur Library)

globe for dainty and novel foods.... The Bureau of Plant Industry is sending agricultural experts to the uttermost ends of the earth to bring to us foods that the people of other countries find excellent."[12]

The expanding American power alluded to in consumerist writings stretched far beyond that of the federal government. Consumer geographies made it clear that Uncle Sam and his officials had plenty of company on the banana steamers that plied the Caribbean. The *New York Tribune*, for example, credited the "enterprising American canner who had planted his foot in Cuba and other Southern countries" with introducing guavas to U.S. markets.[13] On reading such accounts, an American housewife could conclude that the curry-eating British were not the only ones with an imperial cuisine, that the United States was busy producing its own by both formal and informal means.

Although writings on tropical produce focused attention on U.S. economic, political, and military expansion in the Caribbean, geographies of consumption taught that American power was increasingly global. As the decorator Harriet Prescott Spofford wrote in 1877, American shoppers could obtain finer goods than ever before due to "our better acquaintance with the Eastern countries, the farther depth to which we have penetrated them."[14] Much of this penetration was understood to be commercial in nature, but formal imperial endeavors also led to payoffs for American consumers. The Philippine-American War resulted, among other things, in the establishment of a significant lingerie trade with the islands. By 1920, clothing imports from the Philippines topped seven million dollars—much of it underwear. The Bonwit Teller department store ads that stressed the Philippine origins of its lingerie presented its merchandise as a direct result of imperial endeavors.[15]

The tendency to regard international exchanges in imperial terms extended far beyond the goods imported from U.S. colonies. Consumer geographies commonly drew on militaristic language. They claimed that the markets of the East had been "ransacked" for products; they referred to foreign goods as "plunder" and "trophies of travel." "It is not unusual for a buyer to invade the dwelling of a Persian gentleman and bid for his dishes or the rugs on his floors and walls," claimed an article in *House and Garden*.[16] Such word choices vividly linked consumer opportunity to aggressive commercial dealings.

It is one thing to recognize that all but the most obtuse American consumers had a sense of where their stuff hailed from and how it came to the United States, and it is another to say that their knowledge of imperial geographic networks led them to particular political conclusions. I am not arguing that everyone who craved curry became a jingo or that everyone who opposed U.S. incursions in the Caribbean foreswore bananas, sugar, and coffee. Consumer preferences did not determine policy choices. But that does not mean they were irrelevant to imperial politics because consumption itself is a political act. Furthermore, the fact that no widespread consumer movement arose to protest imperial consumption (along the lines of the mid-nineteenth-century abolitionist boycotts of slave-made goods) suggests that Americans generally did not see their taste for imports as problematic.

Although shoppers did encounter reports of grim overseas working conditions, geographies of consumption were more likely to turn a blind eye to the upheavals caused by export-oriented production. Instead of elaborating on the unsavory aspects of international trade, they tended to strike a blither tone, one more conducive to commerce. As a catalogue of Mexican handicrafts that touted the pleasant, home-based manufacturing conditions of its workers exclaimed: "Here are no sweatshop methods!"[17] The result of such rosy accounts was to make the U.S. position within the world marketplace seem benign. By ignoring conflict and obscuring unsavory working conditions, such accounts made the inequitable international distribution of wealth and power seem unexceptionable. They thus helped forestall critiques of imperialism based on evidence of exploitation.

Indeed, it appears that many Americans had grounds to regard their consumption practices as acts of benevolence, a charitable transfer of wealth to the needy. Claimed an article on Mexican drawn work, "Save a meager livelihood through the natural products of the soil, with many Mexican families the sale of this work furnishes the only means of subsistence."[18] Seen from this perspective, international trade was a win-win endeavor that provided for foreign workers and American consumers alike. The housewife could purchase foreign sundries with a clear conscience. Better yet, every time she bought an exotic curio or tropical fruit she could feel invested in the project of philanthropic uplift.

The tendency among geographies of consumption to depict imperial expansion as beneficial to both American consumers and foreign producers contributed to imperial buy-in. But it is possible to enjoy material goods, especially luxuries, without considering them to be essential. It is possible to purchase things without feeling deeply invested in the political economy that made them available. Buy-in connotes a sense of commitment, not just the absence of protest.

Consumer Investments

So where can we find evidence of commitment? The aggregate trade data referred to earlier provides some hints. Further clues to commitment levels can be found by returning to consumer geographies, for in addition to explaining where things came from and how they happened to reach the United States, they helped attach meanings to particular objects and entire consumption regimes. Consumer geographies insisted that imports paved the path to social distinction.[19]

This distinction had multiple levels. The first was local. The many writings that extolled cosmopolitan tastes as markers of education, class, and good breeding encouraged consumers to look down on their neighbors with more parochial preferences. By preparing foreign dishes a housewife could, in the words of the *General Federation Bulletin* (the mouthpiece of the segregated General Federation of Women's Clubs), "give to her table a truly cosmopolitan distinction."[20] That is, she could differentiate herself from less cultivated hostesses or from those who lacked the wherewithal to throw exotic entertainments. By buying the best the world had to offer, white, middle-class, American women could show that their frame of reference extended far beyond the local.

Second, writings on imports contributed to a sense of national superiority. They taught American consumers that their nationality conferred on them a position of privilege in the global scheme of things. Thanks to their nation's international standing, they could relish everything from Argentine lamp shade covers to Puerto Rican drawn work, Russian caviar, Singapore malacca, and Zulu baskets.[21] By insisting that American consumers had unparalleled access to global production, geographies of consumption encouraged shoppers to view their forays into the marketplace as the result of national mastery. In reading the John Wanamaker catalogue's exultant "Nowhere in all the world is there another such variety of furniture," they could count their blessings. Indeed, enthusiastic nationalists often told American women to regard consumption as a sign of national strength, to thank their lucky stars that they had been born into a country where women were "spenders" not "earners."[22]

In addition to casting consumption as a marker of national standing, geographies of consumption presented it as a marker of civilizational attainment. They made it clear that cosmopolitan consumption served as a way for American consumers to associate themselves with the global elite, whose members they understood to be primarily white, wealthy, and Western. Through their consumer choices, Americans could experience the pleasures of European imperialism, if only secondhand. Furthermore, by contrasting the cosmopolitan tastes of the imperial elite with the circumscribed consumption regimes of poor, colored, and colonized peoples, consumer geographies implied that buying only local items meant adhering to the material regimes of the have-nots in the global scheme of things.

The sensory pleasures offered by luxury goods can generate feelings of physical stakeholding in whatever regime provides them. But *emotional* stakeholding can lead to an even deeper sense of investment. Geographies of consumption prodded consumers to buy more fully into the imperial world system by teaching them that they owed not only their enviable material position but also their lofty social status to empire. Among the writings that taught American consumers to feel fortunate in the existing global scheme of things was the *National Geographic* article on food provisioning mentioned earlier. A subtitle read, "The World Our Servant."[23] By claiming that a dinner was not just a meal but a manifestation of social and political relations, geographies of consumption turned imports into a means of enacting entitlement and privilege.

Prescription is one thing, of course, and practice another. Did consumers actually pay any heed to the geographies that accompanied imports? Did they appreciate the imperial webs behind the American cornucopia? Did they feel emotionally invested in their acquisitions? Did they, in sum, buy into empire? Looking at consumption practices suggests that many did.

One place to find evidence of imperial buy-in is the orientalist niches that took off in the 1870s and 1880s. Middle-class decorators who shared the eclectic tastes but not the budgets of superrich decorators often settled for a "cosey corner." These typically consisted of an upholstered divan, a profusion of cushions, a rug, a Turkish coffee table, a few decorative objects such as screens, fans, lanterns, and pottery, and lush draperies to frame the entire ensemble. Some cosey corners struck viewers as essentially Japanese or Chinese, but most looked primarily to the Middle East for inspiration. It is difficult to gauge the exact extent of their appeal, but they did spring up across the country in places such as New York City, Chicago, Houston, and Denver.[24]

Constructing a cosey corner meant more than mimicking the wealthy within the United States: like the rich who hired decorators to compose lavish oriental retreats, the middle-class American women who piled pillows in the corner demonstrated a sense of European sophistication through their exhibitions of oriental exoticism. American women did not get their orientalist ideas straight from Turks or Egyptians. They got them via Europe, which had a long history of orientalist design with aristocratic cachet.[25] Even cosey corners had European connections for the 1892 Exhibition of Rooms at London's Crystal Palace had one on display.[26]

The American housewives who constructed orientalist cosey corners showed that they got the messages of consumer geographies. Besides demonstrating a decorator's ability to assemble Eastern products, cosey corners demonstrated geographic knowledge. True, their creators might not have known exactly where their carpets and coffee tables came from, but they surely knew that they were foreign, from somewhere in the vast swath of the globe deemed oriental. Given white, middle-class, American women's reluctance to fake blackness, it seems clear that their intent in producing orientalist spectacles in their parlors was not to produce an unmediated Eastern decor. Rather, it was to produce a colonial decor that was as much European as oriental.[27]

Culinary practices also reveal enthusiastic engagements with empire. Yes, a housewife might eat a curried egg for lunch without associating it with anything other than a neighbor's recipe. But the popularity of "foreign" entertainments around the turn of the twentieth century suggests that menu planners and hostesses regarded novel foods as a way to convey and experience foreignness. Rather than simply domesticating foreign dishes, they also relied on seemingly foreign fare to evoke difference. At Japanese tea parties, guests drank tea. Guests at a tea *à la Russ* ate black bread. At a "Chinese frolic," they ate rice and chop suey.[28]

Perhaps the most spectacular efforts to feign foreignness can be found in the fundraising fairs that turned churches into bazaars of all nations. These bazaars used objects for both atmosphere and inventory. The Paris booth might have fans, perfumes, handkerchiefs and gloves. At Constantinople shoppers could procure Turkish coffee. The maidens of Tokyo or Shanghai sold china cups, straw baskets, embroideries, umbrellas, prints, tea, rice wafers, crystallized fruits, and nuts. Coming at last to Manila, fairgoers might find oranges and bananas, shells, beads made into strings and bags, pictures of the islands, soldier dolls, and "little brown dolls representing savages."[29] Such entertainments reveal that American consumers appreciated the exoticism of their bottled sauces and spices no less than that of their Turkish coffee tables. The women who produced around-the-world events treated food as a means to experience foreignness—and to enact privilege.

The celebration of hierarchy became particularly clear in the fund-raising events in which "foreign" women served much of the food and American women ate it. These bazaars underscored the idea of buying as an act of benevolence, as something that advanced mission work and other charitable causes. These bazaars also show a sense of identification with European power: it was always Dutch booths that purveyed chocolate, not Javanese ones. Like the world's fairs they echoed, around-the-world fetes linked material abundance to an imperial world order. The shoppers who surveyed the world and then plunked their money down on pictures of the Philippines and little savage dolls went home that much more invested in empire.

Imperial Buy-In

Taken together, consumerist geographies and practice reveal several things: the importance of material objects as conduits for geographic knowledge; the imperial dimensions of that knowledge; the ties between consumption and social positioning on local, national, and global scales; and, ultimately, the significance of consumption for imperial buy-in. Consumers participated in the formal empire of U.S. political control, the informal empire of U.S. commercial power, and the secondhand empire of European imperialism through trifles and savories. They spun elaborate webs of meaning around imported household objects, fashions, and foods that highlighted their foreignness, and they celebrated their ability to obtain such delights. Regarding empire from the perspective of stockholders rather than workers made it possible to ignore the costs of production incurred by distant, unseen peoples. In contrast to those who experienced imperialism as a more menacing development entailing exploitation, impoverishment, and bloodshed, the American consumers who purchased imports experienced it as a collection of goods.

In buying foreign goods and creating ostensibly foreign experiences, these consumers recognized that the much-vaunted American standard of living depended on foreign production. They accepted, often tacitly but sometimes explicitly, the relations of power that brought imported products to their doorsteps. As beneficiaries of an imperial economic and political order, they flaunted their purchases as markers of privilege. And what was the point of the nation, the point of empire, if not to preserve that privilege? Cosmopolitan consumption produced as well as reflected international relations for wide-ranging tastes added impetus to commercial expansion, military incursions, and political control. But cosmopolitan consumption was far more than a cause or result of imperialism; it was part and parcel of it. Exporters, investors, missionaries, and militarists were not the only groups with an interest in empire: countless middle-class Americans had quite a lot at stake as well.

Confabulating American Colonial Knowledge of the Philippines

What the Social Life of Jose E. Marco's Forgeries and Ahmed Chalabi Can Tell Us about the Epistemology of Empire

MICHAEL SALMAN

AMERICAN COLONIAL RULE OVER THE PHILIPPINES was one of the conditions of possibility that enabled the formulation of knowledge about and over the Philippines. The will to colonial power elicited a desire for knowledge and incited discourse about the Philippines. How was this colonial power exercised, institutionally speaking? Surely the will to American colonial power in the Philippines was first given collective representation and emblematized by the U.S. military invasion, conquest, and occupation that began in 1898. And that will to power was just as surely concretized, extended, and maintained by the ensuing elaboration of a colonial state, the history of which is a fundamental theme of this volume. But is the epistemology of empire fundamentally a product of the colonial state?

The colonial state based in Manila often played a central role in the formulation of American imperial knowledge about the Philippines. It directed ethnographic surveys and the census, sponsored expeditions and tours throughout the Philippines, published its own voluminous reports and journals, served as a clearinghouse for the shipment of these and other texts and various exhibits to the United States, and, last but not least, was also one of the principal consumers of knowledge about the Philippines. Not surprisingly, it is easy to see the colonial state at the center of American knowledge production about the Philippines. Our line of sight is drawn to that conclusion by the visibility of the colonial state through its large archive, simultaneously centralized by the United States National Archives and widely dispersed through the distribution to libraries of voluminous public documents such as the reports of the Philippine Commission and the Philippine census. There is much validity and value to such an approach. Nevertheless, any depiction of one-way knowledge relations with the colonial state playing the central role would be far too simplistic, untenable in light of the sociology of knowledge, empirically wrong, and it might rob Filipinos of all agency, creativity, and originality. The epistemology of American empire, despite its own manifestly hierarchical and dualistic tendency to establish American rule over the Philippines and Filipinos, has a genealogy that is complex, transnational, and rhizomatic.[1]

American world power at the end of the nineteenth century was not primarily military or territorial but commercial, built on the foundation of industry, agriculture, and finance capital. The same was true of emerging American institutions of knowledge production—for example, libraries, museums, and universities. Along with the mass media, these institutions worked to construct colonial knowledge in a dispersed way that departed from the centralized direction and focus of the colonial state. Perhaps the ultimate message often remained the same as that disseminated by the colonial state, but the specific relations that produced knowledge differed, and therefore offered differential opportunities for resistance, evasion, participation, and subversion. Contrary to what one might expect from a focus on the colonial state, most Philippiniana in the United States was acquired privately by individuals or nonstate corporations, stored in privately funded museums, published with private funds, and research on these materials and the Philippines itself was financed by nonstate foundations and the commercial media. American colonial knowledge about the Philippines had a social life that fed it, sustained it, and consumed it.[2]

Marketplaces of Colonial Artifacts

The most influential Philippiniana collections assembled in the United States have been the Newberry Library's in Chicago and the monumental, fifty-five-volume compilation of documents edited by Emma H. Blair and James Alexander Robertson, *The Philippine Islands, 1493–1898*.[3] These two collections were related to each other. Edward E. Ayer, the wealthy industrialist who donated his collection on the Philippines, Hawai'i, and American Indians to the Newberry, also played a leading role in supporting Blair's and Roberston's endeavor. In return, Blair and Robertson aided him in acquiring rare manuscripts and books, and once they completed their massive compilation they sold their collection of transcriptions to Ayer, who transferred them to the Newberry. Robertson went on to direct the Philippine National Library from 1910 to 1916, an eventful time in the collection of Philippiniana.

One could trace succeeding generations of authors using the Blair and Robertson collection, and soon the linked texts would encompass most of the last hundred years' scholarly and not so scholarly output. Robertson's career at the Philippine National Library also bequeathed a legacy, however questionable, to Philippine historiography and mythology, a legacy dispersed over as many texts and institutional sites as there are references to the Code of Raja Kalantiaw of

1433, a supposed precolonial legal code of uncharacteristic harshness. We know that the inventor of the Code of Kalantiaw and the forger of several other artifacts and narratives touted by Robertson as great acquisitions for the National Library was none other than Jose E. Marco, a dealer in antiquities, manuscripts, and stamps, and a sometime historian who lived in the town of Pontevedra, Negros Occidental, on the major sugar-producing island of Negros in the Central Visayas, from the late nineteenth century to the 1960s.[4]

Marco sold several manuscripts to the National Library under Robertson's auspices. Half a century later, Marco's manuscripts and the legacy of Robertson's contributions to the collecting of empire became a preoccupation of the University of Chicago's Philippine Studies Program, funded by grants from the Rockefeller, Carnegie, and Ford foundations. Under the direction of Fred Eggan and E. D. Hester, the Chicago program spent roughly a decade publishing new translations of Robertson's treasured acquisitions and another set of manuscripts the program obtained from Marco in the 1950s. To bring matters into a tight little circle around Chicago, the University's Philippine Studies Program was partnered with the Newberry Library and also the Field Museum of Natural History, the latter endowed by the commercial magnate Marshall Field and also the possessor of a large ethnological and natural history collection from the Philippines.

These collectors, both individuals and institutions, depended on relationships with informants, dealers, translators, and various other kinds of middlemen. Colonial exchange relations have been studied as patron-client relations of power and benevolence, a mode of reciprocity that is familiar from colonial sources and the behavioralist literature that dominated Philippine studies a generation back. Perhaps too little attention has been given to the commercial nature of many transactions. The marketplace for objects and information was like all marketplaces, an arena in which the buyer must beware for things that are sold are not always what they appear to be.

Truth, Knowledge, and the Social Life of Fakes

The historiography of the Philippines is unusually given over to debates about fraud and fabrication.[5] It would be interesting to theorize why this is so. I suspect one key to understanding this unnerving characteristic is to be found in the self-conscious way the first generation of nationalists in the Philippines imagined their nation into existence in the late nineteenth century and the way their effort continued in the face of first Spanish and then American denigration. It would be useful to remember that it was literature from the Philippines and Indonesia, especially novels, that inspired and informed Benedict Anderson's theorization of nations as "imagined communities."[6]

While Anderson correctly insisted that the imagination of a new reality should neither be mistaken for nor cynically reduced to falsity, it is nevertheless the case that all such invaluable imaginative acts must also be potential inducements to fraud—to fabricating, conveying, and promoting what people want to hear about their ancient nationality and the goodness of their nation. Furthermore, Philippine history is not just punctuated with lacunae, as are all national histories; it is also periodized by the near total absence of precolonial monuments and surviving precolonial indigenous written sources. Whereas other nations of Southeast Asia point, however fancifully, to the monuments of ancient dynastic and religious centers as evidence of their past (Angkor, Borobudur, Ayutthaya), Filipinos have not inherited similar court traditions and stone remains. Consequently, as Reynaldo Ileto has elegantly argued, the Philippine Revolution, begun against Spain in 1896 and continued against the United States after 1898, became a principal foundation for nationalist discourse.[7] But this modernist understanding of the nation has long been accompanied by a desire for primordial roots.[8] The resultant imperatives and incentives to invent a past for this intensively imagined nation provided richly fertile grounds for dubious sources. Coincidentally, the same vacuum drew in American colonial officials and scholars, who could fashion themselves as the fathers of Philippine prehistory and thus as the godparents, if you will, of the Philippines itself.

Glenn Anthony May and the late William Henry Scott wrote entire books critiquing the authenticity of source materials central to the two most powerful meaning-creating periods in Philippine historical narratives: the Revolution of 1896 and the precolonial past before Magellan's ill-fated arrival in 1521. Published in 1997, May's *Inventing a Hero: The Posthumous Re-creation of Andres Bonifacio* provoked a virulently critical reception.[9] In contrast, Scott's 1968 study, *A Critical Study of the Prehispanic Source Materials for the Study of Philippine History*, has not been challenged in any large way.[10] But in the silent assent to Scott's findings and in much of the criticism piled on May, I think there has been a missed opportunity, as Vince Rafael suggested in his review of May's volume.[11] The opportunity missed by Scott and May lingers because history cannot be about truth and the authentic past without also being about fraud and fabrications, as well as about myth and meaning, which are somewhat different. We historians often operate as if we are prospectors, digging in the ground for gold and tossing away all of the dust and detritus. But the debris that historians toss away is not a natural layer of sediment. That rubbish is composed of human artifacts that we think are insignificant, unintelligible, or, in the kind of case I have in mind, fake. However, these fakes are human history, too, perhaps not traces of the history they were purported to represent but certainly traces of another history, one that we can and should know.

As Ackbar Abbas proposes for the analysis of fake branded commercial goods in contemporary Chinese cities, "[T]he fake [is] a symptom that enables us to address, rather than dismiss, some of the discrepancies of a rapidly developing and seemingly ineluctable global order. We can think of the fake then . . . as a social, cultural and economic response, at a local and apparently trivial level, to the processes of globalization, and the uneven and often unequal relations that globalization has engendered."[12] Whereas Abbas is concerned with fake consumer goods, I am interested in the exchange of texts, manuscripts, artifacts, and information—some genuine, some copied, some faked—that were processed into colonial knowledge, itself a suspect body of work.

Imperial Knowledge in the Industrial Age

One lineage feeding into the network that would give social life to Jose E. Marco's forgeries began with Edward E. Ayer, the Chicago-based merchant and industrialist who made his fortune selling wooden ties and other railroad construction materials in the American West and Mexico.[13] Ayer matched his endeavor in building the crucial infrastructure of American territorial and economic expansion in the late nineteenth century with a reverse process of collecting rare books and manuscripts related to American expansion. His initial interest was in European colonization of the Americas and the native peoples thereby displaced. Then, while in Europe at the outbreak of the Spanish-American War in May 1898, he contacted his network of booksellers and purchasing agents to request that they locate rare books and manuscripts on the Philippines, the United States' newest imperial target.[14] A flood of responses awaited him on his return to Chicago, and his rapid acquisition of early imprints and manuscripts began.

Ayer's collecting of Philippiniana constituted a colonial project of power and knowledge.[15] As a matter of politics and ideology, there was no discernible difference between Ayer and the colonial administrations put in place by presidents McKinley, Roosevelt, and Taft. Indeed, Ayer maintained sympathetic correspondence with several colonial officials, including the master of colonial ethnology, the irascible colonial secretary of the interior Dean C. Worcester.[16] But, while Ayer shared the politics and ideology of the colonial state, his endeavors were enacted not so much in and through the offices of the state as in exchanges, networks, and institutional sites in the so-called private realm of civil society.[17] First and foremost, his collecting was commercial, made possible by his fortune. Ayer went out to the market in Europe, the Philippines, and South America, most frequently through agents who effected his transactions, conveyed intelligence about the whereabouts of collectibles, and frequently provided instrumental advice on what to acquire. In this manner Ayer purchased rare editions of Antonio Pigafetta's chronicle of Magellan's 1521 voyage and hundreds more rare books, manuscripts, and documents.[18] Ayer became such a force in the field that he did not always have to go to the market. The market came to him. The Jesuit Father Pablo Pastells, the ethnologist A. B. Meyer, the propagandist Eduardo de Lete, and others contacted Ayer to sell him manuscripts, books, and artifacts, thereby converting their lives' labor and some of their most cherished possessions, including letters and artifacts from the martyred national hero Jose Rizal, into cold, hard, soulless American cash.[19]

Ayer's personal collection and his association with the Newberry Library proved a boon for Emma H. Blair and James A. Robertson as they embarked on their ambitious project to make the documentary history of the Philippines known to its new colonizers. Blair did most of her editing work from the Newberry, and Ayer's collection provided her and Robertson access to many rare volumes and manuscripts. Like Ayer's collecting, the Blair and Robertson enterprise was a colonial power and knowledge project and was explicitly cast as such in its introductory and historical essays. Blair and Robertson opened their preface to the first volume by declaring that "the establishment of American authority in the Philippine archipelago . . . render the history of those islands and their numerous peoples a topic of engrossing interest and importance to the reading public. . . . The present work . . . is offered to the public with the intention and hope of casting light on the great problems which confront the American people in the Philippines."[20]

Blair and Robertson recast the history of the Philippines in a familiar American idiom. They did this quite literally by translating and mistranslating documents from the original Spanish into American English and more generally by presenting the Philippines' "tribal" indigenous background and indulgently backward Spanish past as a backdrop against which American assumptions of superiority, benevolence, and secular Protestantism would seem to glow. The first volume of *The Philippine Islands* included a "Historical Introduction" by Edward Gaylord Bourne, a professor of Latin American history at Yale University, which emphasized the sleepiness and isolation of "the old regime" of rule by Catholic missionaries in the Philippines. Bourne began his brief synopsis of the history and effects of Spain's evangelization in the Philippines by first identifying the heart of the "great problems" alluded to by Blair and Robertson. "The American people," he wrote, "are confronted with two race problems, one within their own confines . . . the other, new, remote, unknown, and even more imperatively demanding intelligent and unremitting effort for its mastery." Indeed, in Bourne's way of thinking it was mastery that distinguished African Americans from Filipinos—the former "disciplined to labor, raised to civilized life, [and] Christianized" by slavery and the latter "moulded through the . . . self-sacrificing devotion of the missionaries into a whole unlike any similar body elsewhere in the world."[21] It would be difficult to formulate a more eager statement of a seamlessly interwoven will to power and will to knowledge, ready to appropriate the Spanish past as the prelude to American rule, and then to displace its backwardness and indigenous incivility with a program of wholesale reformation through civilizing mastery.

The Blair and Robertson volumes were fully congruent with the ideology and historiography of the American colonial state, but, just as in the case of Ayer's avocation, Blair and Robertson were not engaged in a state project. The fifty-five volumes of *The Philippine Islands* were commissioned by its commercial publisher, the A. H. Clarke Company of Cleveland, to be sold individually and by subscription in order to turn a profit. In this respect, among others, the massive document collection was deemed a failure in its day. Subscriptions were poor, the publishers lost more than twenty thousand dollars on the project by 1909, and leading colonial scholar-administrators such as James A. LeRoy and David Prescott Barrows were harshly critical of the series in personal correspondence.[22]

Although it was a failure in commercial and scholarly terms, Blair and Robertson have had a remarkably long shelf life, lasting to the present day and now newly enhanced by the technologies of CD-ROM, the Internet, and relational database search engines. The debate over the merits and demerits of Blair and Robertson is dwarfed by the use of the volumes in debates about other things. The series became a standard reference and substitute archive for students and scholars who could not travel to see original texts or read their original Spanish, and it also supplied cudgels for political debates on both sides of the independence question.

The Blair and Robertson series left behind several additional legacies. Foremost among them, the massive series opened professional doors for James Alexander Robertson. Despite their critical assessments of the series, Barrows, LeRoy, and others promoted Robertson's candidacy to become the first director of the newly established Philippine National Library, a position he took up in 1910 and held until 1916. He then returned to the United States and enjoyed a career as a professor of Latin American history at the University of Florida, a career memorialized by an annual national prize in the field that bears his name. In relation to the Philippines, however, Robertson should be best remembered for his acquisition, while director of the National Library, of a series of reputedly ancient manuscripts from a certain antiquities dealer in Negros Occidental, Jose E. Marco.

William Henry Scott's memorable chapter "The Contributions of Jose E. Marco to Philippine Historiography" takes the conniving dealer to task for his frauds and baleful influence on succeeding generations of scholars, students, and Philippine statesmen.[23] Marco did make such contributions but only because there was a willing market and audience. Looked at from this angle, it is more proper to speak of Robertson's contributions to Philippine historiography than Marco's. It was Robertson who purchased for the Philippine National Library the first set of Marco manuscripts: the purported 1572 parchment manuscript titled *Historia de la Isla de Negros* (History of Negros Island) and an accompanying map, ostensibly by the *encomendero* (tribute collector) Diego Lope Povedano;

two leather-bound manuscripts of 1838 and 1839 titled *Las antiguas leyendas de la Isla de Negros* (The Ancient Legends of Negros Island), ostensibly by the parish priest Father José María Pavón; and three bark-cloth documents with the old syllabary brushed in cuttlefish ink, purportedly precolonial in origin. It was Robertson who endowed these documents with authority, hailing the Povedano and Pavón manuscripts in his 1914 director's report and calling Marco a "good friend" to the library.[24] It was Robertson who sent a facsimile of one of the bark-cloth documents to the 1915 Panama-Pacific International Exposition in San Francisco, along with an official letter stating that the documents were "the greatest literary treasure of the native culture of the Philippine Islands, and their discovery was the greatest literary discovery ever made in the archipelago."[25] And it was Robertson who publicized the draconian "Code of Calantiao" from Pavon's *Ancient Legends* in an essay he wrote on early Philippine social structure and law for H. Morse Stephens and Herbert E. Bolton's influential *The Pacific Ocean in History* (1917).[26] Marco was an agent in his own history and that of the Filipino nation, but it was Robertson who was at the center of authority, able to authorize Marco's texts as authentic and put them into circulation.[27] Robertson was also in control of a budget to support the collection of a national/colonial archive, and we should remember that Marco was out for the money as well as a certain oddly romantic and draconian portrait of the nation's ancient past.

Robertson's brilliant additions to the National Library became a cornerstone of precolonial historiography that lasted for fifty years, and school textbooks with discussions of the Code of Kalantiaw still circulate. His role in breathing social life into Marco's forgeries is largely forgotten, although his name crosses Philippinists' lips as often as we still cite and debate the meaning of documents from his compilation with Emma H. Blair. Jose E. Marco, on the other hand, is best remembered now only for the sarcastic drubbing he received at the hands of William Henry Scott. But I think it is time for us to rewrite the story so that Jose E. Marco enjoys the last laugh.

Postcolonial Confabulations

As noted earlier, in the 1950s and 1960s, the University of Chicago maintained a Philippine Studies Program, with support from the Carnegie, Rockefeller and Ford foundations, which had close ties to the Newberry Library and the Field Museum. The program was fundamentally research oriented, providing postdoctoral fellowships to several of the leading Philippinists of the time so that they could conduct research in Spain and at the Newberry, and similarly aiding some of the university's graduate students in anthropology and sociology, including E. Arsenio Manuel and F. Landa Jocano, the most prominent Filipino social scientists of their generation, and the Americans Robert Fox and Fr. Frank Lynch, SJ, who became directors of major research institutes in the Philippines.

The Philippine Studies Program's largest and most sustained enterprises were two publication series, one composed of recent ethnographic studies and the second a mimeographed series of historical documents, including the Povedano and Pavón manuscripts acquired by Robertson in 1913 and several more manuscripts purveyed by Jose E. Marco in the 1950s.

Eggan and Hester spent an enormous amount of time seeking help from experts and people in the field to verify the authenticity of these documents, checking ethnographic data in remote villages on Negros and tracking down historical records in Spain.[28] Their correspondence about the Marco manuscripts is simply incredible to read for it reveals a stubborn conviction about the authenticity and importance of the early Povedano and Pavón manuscripts, the kind of unshakable faith in a seemingly obvious falsehood that would make George W. Bush proud. Nevertheless, not all of the pieces fit into the puzzle.

The first person to challenge and lay out a case against all the Marco fabrications was the Filipino bibliophile and scholarly editor Mauro Garcia, who had been raising doubts about them for years. At the seventy-fourth meeting of the Bibliographical Society of the Philippines, held in 1959, Garcia presented devastating internal evidence that all of the Povedano manuscripts were frauds and that Marco dealt in other fraudulent items, especially stamps. But Garcia was not at the center of authority, so he concluded his paper meekly, suggesting that the manuscripts' "authenticity should be determined once and for all" and warning that "unless this is done, there is the possibility of their being accepted as genuine source materials on their subject."[29]

As early as 1956, Garcia had begun to convince one of Eggan's star students, Robert Fox, that he should be "extremely suspicious" of Marco.[30] Fox had spent much time verifying ethnographic data in the manuscripts. He had recently produced a substantial essay, "The Negros-Bisayan Syllabary Recorded by Povedano," in which he declared the 1572 Povedano manuscript the first recorded full account of a Philippine syllabary and the source of "valuable data."[31] However, under Garcia's growing persuasion, in February 1956 Fox told Hester that, although the data looked good, he thought Hester and Eggan should consider the possibility that "Marco is a kind of genius who is fabricating the manuscripts in their entirety."[32] Hester would not buy it.[33]

Although Hester and Eggan grew suspicious of Marco's current offerings in the late 1950s, they continued to insist after 1960 that the Povedano manuscript of 1572 must be authentic. In the early 1960s, William Henry Scott began research for his doctoral dissertation on sources for the study of the pre-Hispanic Philippines. He explained in the preface to the 1984 edition of his book that the topic had been suggested to him "by the late Mauro Garcia with the persuasive argument that since no Filipino historian had shown any interest in pursuing this subject, I could make a contribution to Philippine historiography by doing so myself."³⁴ He corresponded with Eggan and Hester and reported to them his findings that all of the materials from Marco were fraudulent. It is Scott's 1967 dissertation and subsequent book that are credited with debunking Marco. Scott's book is read in historiography seminars in the United States, the Philippines, and elsewhere, not Mauro Garcia's earlier and quite erudite, though brief, indictment.

In a postscript to the 1984 edition of *Prehispanic Source Materials,* Scott related that he had only learned since Garcia's death that the old bibliophile had "personal reasons" for leading Scott to his dissertation topic, stemming from Garcia's early postwar acquisition from Marco of several documents supposedly in the hand and under the signature of Father Jose Burgos, the great Filipino martyr of 1872. Scott thought that Garcia had done him a "scholarly service" by keeping these "more blatant forgeries" from his notice so that he could "examine the earlier Marco contributions without prejudice."³⁵ It seems Scott did not know that Garcia had been making the case for ten years that all of Marco's ancient manuscripts were forgeries. Garcia did not need an unprejudiced opinion to tell him that the Povedano and Pavón texts were frauds, but perhaps he needed the authority of a mature American earning a doctorate at the University of Santo Tomas in order to persuade others.

In his treatment of Jose E. Marco, Scott gets all his facts right about the Marco manuscripts but makes the mistake of dismissing Marco and making only a simple diatribe against the fake. "The full display of Jose E. Marco's contributions to Philippine historiography," concluded Scott, "would present an almost ludicrous appearance but for their sobering implications for many aspects of prehispanic Philippine historiography."³⁶

Life, Laughter, and Death in the Chalabian Moment

What are we to make of this folly born of market circulation and indigenous informants in a colonial situation? I am reminded of the recent affair my country has carried on with Ahmad Chalabi, the leader of the Iraqi National Congress, convicted embezzler, and erstwhile supplier of informants about weapons of mass destruction. Later he became a critic of American empire in Iraq, and so his house was ransacked. Then he became minister for oil production and, for a while, deputy prime minister. One former analyst with the Central Intelligence Agency turned critic quipped, "With Chalabi, we paid to fool ourselves. It's horrible. In other times it might be funny. But a lot of people are dead as a result of this." And a former ambassador opined, "It's not [Chalabi's] fault that his strategy succeeded. It's not his fault that the Bush Administration believed everything he said."³⁷

In this moment I think of the prescient words of Niccolo Machiavelli. Machiavelli warned his prince, "Each councilor will consult his own interests; and the prince will not know how to correct or understand them. Things cannot be otherwise, since men will always do badly by you unless they are forced to be virtuous. So the conclusion is that good advice, whomever it comes from, depends on the shrewdness of the prince who seeks it, and not the shrewdness of the prince on good advice."[38]

The historian J.G.A. Pocock wrote of the "Machiavellian Moment," a recurring frame of time in republican political discourse in which people fear for the demise of the republic. The cause and circumstances of the feared decline vary historically, but Pocock argued that the political language has been similar for centuries, locked, as it were, in a moment of time.[39] Thinking about James Alexander Robertson's and George W. Bush's contributions to the discourse and practice of American empire, I think it is clear that we are locked in another kind of moment, which for mellifluousness I will call the Chalabian Moment, the recurring moment in which the empire hears what it wants to hear from its colonial informants. All nations live in their own fictions and mythic histories, but empires also appropriate, invent, and live in someone else's.[40]

William Henry Scott, rest his dear soul, got it wrong when he sardonically titled his chapter "The Contributions of Jose E. Marco to Philippine Historiography." It wasn't Marco's fault that Robertson was such a sucker, and we have only begun to try to analyze, rather than dismiss, Marco's contributions. Will we dismiss the story of Ahmed Chalabi now that we know it was not "true"? Or turn to see in the story other truths, perhaps truths about how Americans' own set of falsehoods readied them to believe anything attributed to Saddam Hussein, or about the political ingenuity of postcolonial Iraqis, ranging from Saddam Hussein to Chalabi and Muqtada al-Sadr?

As Akbar Abbas suggested, "[T]he Fake is a symptom that enables us to address, rather than dismiss, some of the discrepancies of a rapidly developing and ineluctable global order." The epistemology of empire is, after all, a lie, and on that foundation great monuments of truth are built. Jose E. Marco's monument, consecrated by James Alexander Robertson and the University of Chicago's scholars, should make us laugh. George W. Bush tries to consecrate monuments, too, but in his case these are tombs filled with dead bodies resting on falsehoods that seem likely to disturb the world into the future.

PART 5

Imperial Medicine and Public Health

Bodies as Subjects

"Line-Pail Brigade, Manila, during Cholera Epidemic, circa 1902–4." (NARA, RG 350-P-#44.2I/2)

INTRODUCTION

NANCY TOMES

As HISTORIANS OF EMPIRE have long understood, the control of disease was essential to the colonizing effort. As nations expanded outward, their armies had to be protected, their trade routes kept free of contagion, and their contact with potentially unhealthy natives carefully managed. Setting up viable colonial governments required negotiating the terms of "biomedical citizenship," in Warwick Anderson's term, that is, the physical boundaries between rulers and subjects. Imperial powers that failed to meet these objectives could not hope to succeed in the larger goals of empire.

Thus, it would seem obvious that medicine, public health, and disease control should feature prominently in any history of the American imperial state. Yet such has definitely not been the case. Indeed, no field better illustrates Amy Kaplan's lament about the "absence of empire" in American history than the study of medicine and public health. While historians of other parts of the world began writing about medicine and empire over a decade ago, Americanists have remained remarkably uninterested in the subject until very recently. Ironically, it has largely been through the scholarship of an Australian, Warwick Anderson, that the health dimensions of the American empire have finally begun to get their due. Thus, perhaps more than any other set of essays in this volume, the ones in this section represent a major historiographic break with the past by redressing the absence of empire in the history of American medicine and public health.[1]

From different perspectives, these five essays explore how the experience of overseas empire transformed public health in both the United States and its colonies. Although comparatively small in size, at least compared to the British Empire, the territories, colonies, and zones of influence acquired over the course of the late nineteenth century—Hawai'i, Cuba, the Philippines, the Panama Canal Zone, Puerto Rico, and Guam—became public health laboratories for an activist

American state. Read together, these essays provide a wide-ranging, provocative examination of imperial bodies as subjects.

A central theme running through these works is how the "imperial periphery" worked to produce "metropolitan transformations." To appreciate this theme fully, we need to start with the realization that American medicine and public health were forged in the context of the two centuries of continental expansion that occurred before the acquisition of an overseas empire. The creation of the modern United States constituted a continental imperialism that involved removing other colonial powers, as well as controlling native peoples, so that Anglo-Americans could migrate westward. In addition, the internal imperial project required responding to the waves of immigrants in the nineteenth century—a focal point not only for late-nineteenth-century public health but for the growth of government power more generally. By the time it acquired an overseas empire in the late nineteenth century, the U.S. government could draw on a long tradition in American medicine and public health of safeguarding settlers' health in unfamiliar climates and managing alien others deemed deficient in hygienic virtue. Tactics developed during the process of internal colonization were quickly transplanted to overseas colonies.

These colonial experiences were particularly important to the United States, I would suggest, because of the deep-seated sense of inferiority that American doctors and public health officials had so long felt in relation to Europe's scientific achievements. This long-standing preoccupation with Europe may help explain why American historians have spent so little time thinking about empire, at least until recently. Instead they have been deeply engaged with trying to prove—or disprove—that American developments were merely inferior copies of European achievements. This insight points to an important point: unlike European colonial powers, the United States had been a colony itself, a periphery to the English metropole, and suffered the predictable pangs of inferiority as a result, nowhere more apparent than in medicine. This fact helps explain the special pride expressed in American narratives about their ability to succeed where European powers had failed. This theme appears clearly in the Cuban yellow fever campaign, described by Mariola Espinosa, and also in the Panama Canal's completion, as described by Paul S. Sutter.

In fact, the American style of colonial public health exemplified one area where its scientific elite *had* excelled prior to 1900, namely, administration. Americans may have come up with few laboratory discoveries in the nineteenth century, but, as their European contemporaries acknowledged, they excelled at the practical application of laboratory knowledge, as in Herman Biggs's remaking of the New York City Department of Public Health. In ways similar to other domains discussed in this volume, such as military intelligence and education, America's overseas possessions provided public health officials new opportunities to develop this administrative style without the political resistance they so often encountered in the United States. In the homeland, growing powers of surveillance and control ran counter to American traditions of democracy and autonomy, which immigrant groups tried to turn to their own advantage by hiring lawyers and organizing community resistance.[2]

In comparison, colonial subjects, who lacked the full rights of American citizens, could, at least theoretically, be managed with less difficulty. Technologies of control hardened and perfected on colonial peoples of color could be exported back to the United States as part of the early-twentieth-century activist state. Transplanted to the Philippines, American public health's style evolved into a surveillance-oriented emphasis on isolating the sick rather than tackling the "filth" in which they lived. Anderson argues that the Philippines was the testing ground for this new approach, which was exported back to the United States after 1910 as the "new public health." Whereas previous historians have portrayed the rise of the new public health solely as a response to domestic developments, Anderson shows that it had a distinctly imperial cast.

All of these essays suggest that American health imperialism featured a peculiar combination of detachment and harshness. American colonizers seem to have disliked the "geographies of intimacy," to use Ann Laura Stoler's phrase, even more than their European counterparts.[3] The native-born Americans of English Protestant ancestry who became colonial administrators inherited a profoundly racialized set of democratic traditions. Their fear of and contempt for alien peoples reflected decades of wrestling with the health sins of millions of foreign "Others," from enslaved Africans to turn of the century "new immigrants." Underlying their administrative style was a deep-seated ambivalence toward its object. The "rotten, grotesque" bodies of the alien Other could never be made clean enough. The "wily native" resisted, sometimes by outright revolt, sometimes by sly mimicry. Thus, all too often the colonial experience recapitulated the frustrations that public health experts in the homeland had experienced with the new immigrants. American colonizers seem to have been particularly attracted to large-scale bureaucratic interventions of the sort Paul S. Sutter describes so well in his essay. In many ways, the "environmental management state" envisioned for Panama represented the ideal colonial project: the natives could be safely walled off in their own zone while American tourists floated by on cruise ships.

The essays by Mariola Espinosa and Gabriela Soto Laveaga remind us of how that harshness was experienced by the people subjected to it. Espinosa's critique of the famous yellow fever campaign in Cuba shows that this showpiece of American benevolence primarily served the needs of the American colonizers. Likewise, Soto Laveaga's account of the peasant labor involved in harvesting wild yams to make cortisone products reveals the high price paid locally for expanding trade relations. The fact that the oral contraceptives eventually derived from the yam trade would be tested first on Puerto Rican women, to make sure they were safe for white Americans, forms a fitting conclusion to this unequal circuit of exchange.[4]

Finally, Natalie J. Ring's essay suggests another important connection between overseas and homeland developments. As she shows, imperial experiences fueled a "southern neo-orientalism" in post-1898 public health discourse in which both white and black southerners were viewed as pseudo-tropical peoples beyond sanitary reclamation. This insight helps explain the peculiar obsession American eugenicists had with poor southerners, blacks and whites alike. Ring's work suggests a useful context for understanding not only the horrific Tuskegee syphilis experiment but also the successful campaigns to sterilize poor white women in states such as Virginia—most famously in the case of Carrie Buck, who was sterilized after the U.S. Supreme Court ruled in 1924, in the infamous words of Justice Oliver Wendell Holmes Jr., that "three generations of imbeciles are enough."[5]

If Ring's essay emphasizes the flow of ideas between empire and metropole, so Sutter suggests that imperialism was a necessary first step in the birth of the Caribbean vacation. These are fertile areas for further research; I would suggest that one promising line of analysis would be to focus on prostitution and sexually transmitted diseases in American colonies. Philippa Levine's work has shown how important the regulation of sexuality was to British colonizers; Paul Kramer has begun doing likewise for the Philippines. Likely the same was true of other American possessions. We may well find in this earlier era the genesis of the so-called sex tourism that would later develop between the United States and the Caribbean as white Americans headed south of the border to indulge their "dark side."[6]

Another such flow might be the connection between empire and the American obsession with cleanliness, so strikingly absent in the early nineteenth century and so intensely evident by the 1920s. Pervasive fears of unwelcome assimilation, both at home and abroad, surely contributed to the growing commitment to hypercleanliness. As suggested by my own and others' work, Americans took the cleanliness fetish of British colonizers, so well documented by Anne McClintock, to new extremes. Hypercleanliness worked well to resolve both domestic and imperial anxieties about unclean "barbarians."[7]

As this brief introduction makes evident, these five essays illustrate well the larger theme of this volume: how the "imperial periphery" has been linked to "metropolitan transformations." They ensure that empire is no longer absent from the history of American medicine and public health and in so doing provide important new insights into the history of the American imperial state.

Pacific Crossings
Imperial Logics in United States' Public Health Programs

WARWICK ANDERSON

For W. E. B. DuBois the most significant national event at the end of the nineteenth century was the annexation of the Philippines and Puerto Rico, which doubled the colored population under the United States' protection. "This is for us and the nation," he wrote in 1900, "the greatest event since the Civil War.... What is to be our action toward these new lands and toward the masses of dark men and women who inhabit them?" DuBois went on to declare that the problem of the twentieth century would be "the problem of the color line."[1] With sharp anticipation and some apprehension, he predicted that this fateful line would trace imperial contours. Unlike most subsequent historians of American life and character, DuBois was a confident internationalist convinced that one could not know the nation without heeding its colonial entanglements.

In this essay, I want to explore the imperial logics of U.S. public health both in the colonial Philippines and at home. Elsewhere I have described the colonial assemblage of medicine and hygiene in the early-twentieth-century Philippines; here I will focus instead on various Pacific crossings, transfers of persons, ideas, models and practices between the continental United States and its island possessions in Southeast Asia.[2] Traffic on these busy routes across the Pacific traveled in both directions, influencing rationalities of rule and structures of feeling at each destination. In particular, public health authorities transferred to the Philippines and adapted there—under conditions of colonial warfare—some military modes of population management and hygiene. Later, several health officers brought back to a few American urban centers these transformed techniques of state intervention in ordinary lives, retuning and adding impetus to the domestic new public health in a variety of settings. Neither site was a mere palimpsest for imperial discourse, but these foreign perceptions and models did nonetheless make some behaviors legible, shift local trajectories, intensify certain styles of intervention, and reshape social life. Such patterns will appear only when historians make empire visible again in U.S. public health.

My approach is largely genealogical, tracing experts and their practices as they moved across the Pacific and around the Caribbean. The logic of a career as an American colonial official could connect the new eastern medical schools and research universities, the Public Health Service, the Army Medical Department, the public health departments of the Philippines and Puerto Rico, and state and city health units at home. The medical doctors and bureaucrats I write about were itinerants with an imperial (if not global) view of things that historians, so preoccupied with the local and constrained by nation or region, are only now coming to appreciate. In a generally uncritical way, these colonial technicians were prepared to find the modern in the colony, the colonial in the metropole. José David Saldívar, among others, has urged us to look at the borderlands between the United States and Mexico as "the spaces where the nation begins and ends."[3] But we should remember that the colonial laboratories of the Philippines, Puerto Rico and Hawai'i also were borderlands where many experts were experimenting with various national bodies, including their own.[4]

An alternative study might seek to compare unconnected sites in the United States and the Philippines, perhaps to identify the frameworks of a trans-Pacific taxonomy of racial hygiene. I have tried this taxonomic gaze before, hoping to discern the patterns and logics of separate colonial sites.[5] But it seemed to me a distancing, imperial optic and one that obscured agency in order to illuminate structure. Here I will merely follow a few colonial experts around as they make their careers in the American empire.

Biomedical Citizenship

I want to focus on an argument I made in *Colonial Pathologies* about biomedical citizenship and see how this medicalized regime of "graduated sovereignty" traveled. I argued then that racial hygiene was, to use Ann Laura Stoler's formulation, one of the colonial state's "scaled genres of rule that produce and count on different degrees of sovereignty and graduations of rights."[6] Therefore, colonial public health gives us opportunity to discuss the linkage of bodily states, diagnostic or prognostic, to estimates of civic virtue. It also directs attention to how benevolence figures in state projects and imperial visions.

In *Colonial Pathologies*, I described an American poetics of pollution in the Philippines, a racializing of germ theories that conventionally contrasted a clean American body with a polluting Filipino body. From the early twentieth century on, public health officers argued that Filipinos, evolving with local pathogens, would surely have been natural reservoirs of disease organisms, containers that racial customs kept filled to the brim. Filipinos, then, were cast along with other local fauna as disease dealers, and even apparently healthy Filipinos might secretly carry the invisible pathogens from which supposedly pure bourgeois Americans were typically exempt and to which they seemed more vulnerable. "Natives" would thus appear as meretriciously healthy carriers and transmitters of local diseases while those Americans who fastidiously restricted local contact were represented as innocent victims. As the American "lower bodily stratum" was erased in tropical hygiene, the poorer class of Filipino, like other natives, became the chief source of contamination and danger.

In other words, the new tropical hygiene that developed at the end of the nineteenth century led to an anthropomorphic mobilization of disease agency in the tropics, as elsewhere, giving pathological depth to older racial and class stereotypes. I call this a "poetics" in order to emphasize the way in which colonial public health officers attempted to close the structure of medical metaphor and omit any relations between these imputative texts and political practice. The closed system of equivalence and opposition erased any historical or social context for disease patterns, substituting instead contrasting natural typologies, a poetics of purity and danger.[7]

The Manichean opposition in the medical text—the contrast of a white bourgeois American body with a Filipino grotesque body—proved in practice excitingly assailable and perhaps necessarily unsustainable. American self-possession was always fragile, and, no matter how repressed, a secret rottenness kept surfacing in even the most apparently abstracted of bodies, thus disturbing and reconstituting American identity. American males repeatedly broke down in the tropics, going native or becoming neurasthenic or nostalgic. On the other hand, a few select Filipinos seemed ever more reformable, perhaps able through training to transcend their lower bodily stratum and eventually become eligible for social citizenship. Positioned at the polluting pole of a binary typology, Filipinos were to confess their failings, announce their desire for "civilization" or modernity, and make themselves available for reformation.

Medical and civic discourses were thus overlaid on each other. The American civil authorities treated Filipinos as infants in need of, and capable of responding to, bodily training and guidance in proper behavior, that is, subject to a "benevolent assimilation" into a sort of American adulthood. In heeding the gospel of hygiene, some Filipinos—with needy lepers in the vanguard—might therefore be given limited civic rights, becoming probationary citizen subjects. As Woodrow Wilson, the U.S. president, remarked in relation to American duties in the Philippines: "[S]elf-government is a form of character and it follows upon the discipline which gives a people self-possession. . . . No people can be 'given' the self-control of maturity. Only a long apprenticeship of obedience can secure them this precious possession."[8]

Unlike most other colonial powers at the time, and unlike the earlier Spanish authorities, the American regime thus began to supplement a project of native homogenization with limited individuation and developmentalism. The newly recognized individual's moral reform was linked symbiotically to bodily reform, but the satisfactory achievement of both normalizations could be endlessly deferred. Native imitations of white American citizenship appealed to the narcissistic demands of colonial officials, but these performances usually appeared immature and unfaithful—that is, in need of further surveillance and discipline.[9]

What did this mean in practice? In developing a distinctive "new public health" that would modify Filipino habits—whether through education or regulation—the Philippine Bureau of Health was attempting to imbue a distrust of the body, a dread of personal contact, and a respect for American sanitary authority. Health authorities targeted toilet practices, food handling, dietary customs, and housing design; they rebuilt the markets, using more hygienic concrete, and suppressed the unsanitary fiestas; and they assumed the power to examine Filipinos at random and to disinfect, fumigate, and medicate at will.[10]

Strict enforcement of the rules of personal and domestic hygiene promised multiple benefits: local populations would work more efficiently and be less likely to carry disease organisms. They would present fewer dangers to Europeans, whose own disease-carrying capacity generally was ignored. In this sense, the new tropical public health was principally a militarized form of industrial hygiene, especially for the laboring colonized. And the policy of education and supervision had other advantages. Its goal of nurturing self-control among Filipinos offered to absolve the authorities from major environmental and social alteration, including segregation, thus promising the financial savings never far from a colonial administrator's thoughts. Moreover, the reform of personal and domestic hygiene accorded in the most progressive style with the new science of disease causation, transmission, and acquisition.

I have referred to this as a colonial "civilizing" project, for that is the goal to which American bureaucrats in the Philippines aspired, but in the 1940s this task would come to be called "development." This story may therefore be read as an account of a colonial precursor of the development discourse that proliferated after World War II.[11] This early effort to produce development knowledge would prove immensely influential, shaping later Rockefeller Foundation policies and stimulating other international agencies to conduct similar projects. Although the term *development* was soon taken up by local elites and used as nationalist rhetoric, it continued to offer recolonizing possibilities. Indeed, one might argue that the notion of development never quite discarded colonial legacies; it often seemed to repeat the older dichotomies of modernity and tradition, science and ignorance, global and local, purity and danger, only to characterize the subjects of development as arrested at stages between these opposites. Much development remained, at heart, a civilizing mission, disempowering local communities and demanding that the "native" or the "underdeveloped" person follow a single track toward a Western modernity, not really expecting that this distant prospect, the light on the hill, would ever be reached.

It is perhaps worth thinking some more about the origins of this peculiar form of colonial public health, predicated on racial hygiene, before considering its influence in the continental United States.

Peculiarities of Colonial Public Health

In *Colonial Pathologies* I emphasized the impact of the shift in Filipino resistance to guerrilla warfare in 1899 on the U.S. military medical officer's perceptions of risk and containment. New doctrines of colonial warfare demanded the intense surveillance and disciplining of local populations: it was supposed that reform of the social and moral terrain, a policy of attraction and transformation, would turn "savages" into docile, disciplined subjects. It was no longer enough to protect a colonial garrison or enclave militarily and medically; the goal was now to occupy and organize a territory and a people, cultivating new forms of life within "protection zones." This did not mean coddling local populations: the notion of "attraction" in colonial warfare did not connote enticement; rather, it implied an involuntary, magnetic force. Just as raw recruits to the army were trained and transformed into disciplined soldiers, so might the medical officer attempt to reeducate Filipinos, to make them proper, retentive colonial subjects. Through the discipline of hygiene, Filipinos might eventually become properly self-governing. Of course, there was little expectation that Filipinos possessed the capacity for hygiene that even the most ignorant rural American troops could demonstrate; hence full hygienic citizenship would be deferred in practice and colonial supervision would continue indefinitely.

Colonial warfare was not the only influence on the emergence of American public health in the Philippines, but it was a powerful adjuvant, promoting the growth of features that might otherwise have turned vestigial. Since the 1870s, interest in social pathology had developed in North America and Europe at the expense of older concerns with geographic or climatic determinants of disease.[12] In the Philippines, colonial warfare would further focus attention on mobile human agency. Similarly, the interventionism of the military surgeon at the end of the nineteenth century should not be separated from the rise of progressivism in the United States during this period.[13] But the medical officer's self-confidence and assertiveness would give impetus to these more general and diffuse reformist trends. The increasingly widespread recourse to business models for administrative efficiency also was mirrored in the transformation of the military bureaucracy, but in the Philippines it was the military that became the sole direct means whereby these organizational changes generated a health service.[14] The idea of "the gospel of hygiene," the plan to evangelize a Catholic or heathen population, must have struck a chord with American colonial officials, most of whom were

Protestant, but it was colonial warfare that made proselytization a military and medical necessity.

Colonial health officers in the Philippines were thus among the first advocates of what came to be known in the United States as the new public health. In 1902, on his return from Havana, Charles V. Chapin, MD—the influential superintendent of health in Providence, Rhode Island—deplored the fact that in the United States so "little stress was laid on *personal* uncleanliness" and too much still on "filth."[15] A few years later, in the "Fetich of Disinfection," he pointed to the danger of the "healthy carriers" of disease, who ramified further the risk of contact between infected and uninfected. "It is our duty," he wrote, "to teach that hygienic salvation can only be attained through the good works of personal cleanliness."[16] Similarly, Charles-Edward Amory Winslow, another votary of the new public health, warned in 1914 that "it is people, primarily, and not things, that we must guard against."[17] But this was old news in Manila. Gradually, in the continental United States, too, the emphasis of local health work would shift from sanitation to a focus on the individual and management of the population. The discovery of "Typhoid Mary" in 1907 served to amplify concerns about the role of healthy carriers in the spread of disease.[18] But in the Philippines the public health service had been—almost from the beginning—predicated on the identification and control of dangerous individuals and the regulation of social contact.

The new public health that emerged at the edge of empire initially was considerably more racialized in character, and military in inspiration and style, than the versions developing at a slower pace along the northeastern seaboard of the United States. The colonial Bureau of Health had absorbed the Army Medical Department's commitment to drill, discipline, and bodily reform—and its disregard of the existing civic structures and sources of power. In the Philippines, the public health officer could generally work out an interventionist program with fewer constraints than in the urban centers of the United States. Moreover, in the colony the interventionist health officer would always be as sensitive as any physician in the American South to the boundaries of race as he campaigned against personal uncleanliness and sought to regulate social contact.

Race was also a salient in the North American war against infectious disease, yet it rarely seems to have been as pervasive as it was in colonial skirmishes. In San Francisco, certainly, since the late nineteenth century, epidemics of smallpox and bubonic plague, and fears of venereal disease and leprosy, had caused the public health department to focus on the dangers of Chinatown and later on the personal pathogenicity of Chinese bodies.[19] Some physicians, especially those in the South, also worried that African Americans might be fearsome vectors of disease. In 1903, for example, William Lee Howard, a Baltimore physician, argued that "there is every prospect of checking and reducing these [infectious] diseases in the white race, if the race is socially ... quarantined from the African."[20] Also, during the first decade of the twentieth century, U.S. immigration authorities became ever more likely to view the bodies of poor, non-Anglo immigrants as potentially diseased or potential carriers of disease.[21] But in the Philippines the race card had trumped all others—even class was secondary. In the United States, the patterns of disease carriage would often appear more complex and for some time yet also more readily circumscribed by older methods of isolation and quarantine.

Colonial Public Health

As president of the United States, William Howard Taft liked to attribute the origin of reformist American sanitary science to the stimuli of the Spanish-American War and the need to pacify and purify the Philippines. Advances in the tropics "brought to the attention of the whole country the necessity for widespread reform in our provisions for the maintenance of health and the prevention of disease at home."[22] Having to deal with disease-carrying natives, the former Philippine governor-general told an international congress on hygiene in 1912, had made clear the need for "an additional branch of general education in the matter of the hygiene of the home." Initially, the purpose was simply to make the region "habitable for white people." But now colonial medical authorities were "engaged in the work of developing the tropical races into a strength of body and freedom from disease" even though the Filipinos' "natural laziness and resentment at discipline makes the enforcement most difficult."[23] Hygiene reform in the Philippines was nonetheless a model for what might yet be achieved in North America.

We should think seriously about the extent to which urban health services in America that targeted immigrants and minorities were legacies of empire. Colonial influences could be symbolic and direct. After 1910, few health departments in the United States were able to resist referring to American sanitary achievements in Panama and aligning their own efforts with those of Colonel William C. Gorgas, MD, and other heroes of tropical medicine. As late as 1918, the director of the Illinois Department of Public Health was repeating Hermann Biggs's truism that "public health is purchasable," a fact that "can be illustrated no better than in the construction of the Panama canal."[24]

In the early twentieth century, the logic of some medical careers had connected American metropolitan health more directly with colonial engagements. Military surgeons in the Spanish-American War, once demobilized, often applied their energies and new skills to public health rather than the retail aspects of the profession. A decade or so later, many colonial bureaucrats who had been repatriated as the result of Filipinization moved into senior positions in city and state health departments. In 1912, the U.S. Public Health Service chose Dr. Rupert Blue as surgeon general over Dr. Victor G. Heiser, the director of health in the

Philippines (1905–15), but within a few years the colonial reject refused an offer to direct the New York City Department of Public Health. Instead, his old friend Dr. Haven Emerson set about reforming administrative procedures in New York while enduring Heiser's insistent advice and reiteration of Philippine lessons.[25] Dr. William E. Musgrave, the director of the Philippines General Hospital, fled to San Francisco in 1917 after nurses poisoned him and became a leading hospital administrator and professor of tropical medicine at the University of California, where he, too, constantly proffered advice to local health authorities.[26] In the Milwaukee public health department from 1913 to 1914, Dr. Louis Schapiro applied lessons from his time in Bontoc to further improve the personal hygiene, and vaccination rates, of the inhabitants of "the healthiest city." But he longed for the tropics and soon left Wisconsin for Costa Rica, where he directed the Rockefeller hookworm campaigns.[27] Such examples of professional mobility could be further multiplied.

The influence of the colonial Philippines on the new public health in the United States varied considerably: it might be negligible, as in Chicago; filtered and mediated but still detectable, as in San Francisco; or profound, as in Boston.[28] In general, the medical experience of empire served to amplify existing features of domestic public health work and to reshape structures and policies already in place rather than introducing wholly new procedures and goals. In particular, it tended to focus more attention on the fault lines of race and force recognition of the need to intervene more vigorously to reform the personal and domestic hygiene of those on the margins of society.

The career of Dr. Allan J. McLaughlin epitomizes the metropolitan reach of the colonial bureaucrat. As deputy director of health in the Philippines, McLaughlin had demonstrated the importance of cholera carriers in spreading the disease and warned against promiscuous defecation by inferior races. After his appointment as commissioner of health for Massachusetts in 1914, this evangelist of personal hygiene "set the pace and direction for reorganization" of the public health department.[29] McLaughlin recruited district health officers, created a division of hygiene, and improved operational efficiency.[30] He wanted the public health department to run like a "well-regulated business," as it had, unimpeded, in the Philippines, and to ensure this he introduced formal administrative procedures and organizational charts. Colonial experience had made him aware of the need for a "wider application of the principles of personal hygiene by the individual citizen himself" and sensitive to opportunities to carry sanitary instruction into the home, especially those of immigrants and minorities.[31] McLaughlin appointed visiting nurses and arranged for a physical and mental survey of every schoolchild in the state. The hygiene division delivered health lectures, set up exhibitions, and published educational pamphlets. Its first, revealingly, was on mosquitoes and malaria despite the fact that, while the insect was a summer nuisance, the disease was rare in New England. By 1918, when he resigned to take up the position of an assistant surgeon general of the U.S. Public Health Service, McLaughlin had more or less adapted the Philippine Health Service to Massachusetts. To be sure, class mattered more than it had in the colony, and the main target of preventive medicine was now the urban white child. But, whether in Manila or Boston, McLaughlin tried earnestly to convince all his charges—Filipino, American born, and immigrant—that "there is more romance in the achievements of right living than in all the other episodes of glamorous lives."[32]

Public health, military medicine, and industrial hygiene all could be—at least in part—surrogates of colonial health services in the United States. Despite the efforts of old Philippine hands such as Dr. Richard P. Strong and Dr. Andrew W. Sellards at Harvard and Colonel Charles F. Craig, MD, at Tulane, tropical medicine itself did not flourish in North America. The military legacy, of course, is not surprising: the links between the army and colonial medicine were lasting. For example, Craig and Weston P. Chamberlain became commandants of the Army Medical School after their colonial rotation, Edward L. Munson alternated instruction in military hygiene at the Army Service Schools in Fort Leavenworth with advice to the Philippine government and ended his career as commandant of the Medical Field Service School at Carlisle Barracks, P. C. Fauntleroy taught hygiene at the Army Medical School, and P. E. Garrison directed the Naval Medical School. The training camp and the colony had come to resemble each other; raw recruits and natives displayed a striking affinity, even if they were credited with disparate capacities for discipline and improvement. Military hygiene had become a transferable skill and a widely available mechanism of modern government.

The logic of the colonial medical officer's career could bridge fields that now seem separate from military and colonial medicine. Struggling to make a living in tropical medicine in the United States, some repatriated physicians instead contributed to the further development of the new specialty of industrial hygiene. Munson had drawn attention to military hygiene as a resource for managing the domestic workforce, and many colonial bureaucrats, once in the United States, recognized the sense of his precepts. Dr. John R. McDill, the first president of the Philippine Islands Medical Association, became a professor of surgery at the Medical College of Wisconsin but by the 1920s was advising the Federal Board for Vocational Education in Washington, D.C.

More strikingly, in 1938, the National Association of Manufacturers (NAM) made Heiser its consultant on "healthful working conditions." After his forced retirement from the International Health Division of the Rockefeller Foundation, Heiser had written *An American Doctor's Odyssey*, which sold half a million copies.[33] As a celebrity physician, Heiser urged workers to take personal responsibility for preventing injury and sickness in American industry. On behalf of the

NAM, he organized clinics for local manufacturers' groups where he extolled the benefits of vitamin supplementation, regular exercise, and personal hygiene. Heiser's goal was to help management use its personnel to greatest advantage in production. He believed that the physician's mission in the factory was "as bold and as adventurous as in any of nature's jungles."[34] Later, during World War II, the aging colonial medico turned his attention to improving stamina on the home front, addressing radio audiences and writing pamphlets urging white Americans to enhance their diets and "toughen up" to meet the Nazi challenge.[35] Throughout this period he continued to express disdain for African American capacities.[36]

The focus on Pacific crossings—from the United States to the Philippines and its reverse—should not obscure widespread efforts to translate American colonial medical practices elsewhere in Asia and the Western Hemisphere. A complex circulation and repatterning of practices of public health emerged, flexibly coupled with ideas of race and development, and as these models passed from place to place they would be readjusted before moving on. Out of this play of assertion and caution came alterations in the style and form of the hygienic management of populations.

While serving as director for the East of the Rockefeller International Health Board, Heiser attempted to reshape health services in more than forty countries, supporting more efficient and interventionist bureaucracies, directing attention to racial hygiene and health instruction, and developing medical and nursing education. Other Philippine medical officers followed his example. After working in Manila and the Culion Leper Colony, Dr. John E. Snodgrass took over the Rockefeller hookworm scheme in Ceylon, seeking through latrine building to improve the productivity of plantation laborers."[37] Dr. John D. Long, Heiser's successor in the Philippines, shuffled between Manila and San Francisco, where he repeatedly led the Public Health Service's response to disease outbreaks, before joining the Pan-American Sanitary Bureau in the 1920s. Making analogies between colonial discipline and urban health in Asia and the Americas, he drafted the Pan-American Sanitary Code in 1923–24 and later wrote national health codes for Chile, Panama, and Uruguay based on a Philippine model.[38] Dr. Paul F. Russell, as a leading malariologist, concentrated on manipulating the nonhuman elements of disease ecology by fighting mosquitoes. His Philippine experiences directed him to specific disease eradication campaigns, which necessarily became global in scope, abrogating colonial and national boundaries.

Conclusion

I have not addressed here, apart from that last passage, those trans-Pacific and inter-Caribbean circuits of personnel, scientific knowledge, and medical technologies related to hookworm, malaria, and leprosy control and treatment. Instead

I concentrated on the transfer of racialized estimates of civic virtue and stipulations of personal conduct or hygiene. Mostly I provided a rough sketch of how the colonial state impelled some persons, ideas, and techniques to travel in both directions across the Pacific. I wanted to argue that the national bodies that medicos hoped to forge in Manila and Boston were at least partly envisioned through an imperial lens. Of course, they were always more than that—and multiply contested—but I believe the imperial dimensions of national embodiment in the United States deserve special emphasis now to make up for their having been forgotten for so long. Still, this essay does not quite accomplish that objective.

In *Colonial Pathologies* I tried to describe more fully what might be called a biomedical or biopolitical "assemblage" in the Philippines. Recently, Stephen Collier and Aihwa Ong have written of global forms that are "territorialized in assemblages," in "ensembles of heterogeneous elements." Global forms—such as biomedicine—are "able to assimilate themselves to new environments, to code heterogeneous contexts and objects in terms that are amenable to control and valuation."[39]

To make stronger claims about the colonial impact on U.S. domestic public health and government of problem populations, one would need to examine such biomedical and biopolitical assemblages back "home" in the United States, giving them as much critical and cosmopolitan scrutiny as we do colonial sites. That is, we should more carefully reexamine public health at various sites in the United States in order to make empire visible again at the level of bodies, behavior, and everyday life. That way we may finally be able to relocate the imperial contours of the U.S. color line and perhaps respond more pertinently to the question DuBois couched so long ago when he called the acquisition of a colored empire "the greatest event since the Civil War" and wondered how the expansionist nation might treat its "masses of dark men and women."

A Fever for Empire

U.S. Disease Eradication in Cuba as Colonial Public Health

MARIOLA ESPINOSA

IN THE YEARS FOLLOWING THE 1898 U.S. INTERVENTION in the Cuban war with Spain, the American forces occupying Cuba worked ceaselessly to control the dreaded yellow fever in Havana and the rest of the island. But, like the public health campaigns of other colonial powers, these efforts were not an expression of medical beneficence. As elsewhere, public health in Cuba served the needs of the colonizer rather than the colonized: to protect commerce, maintain the labor force, safeguard troops and colonial administrators, and justify colonial rule. The eradication of yellow fever in Cuba—an unprecedented success of colonial public health—achieved for the United States nearly all of these goals. American public health efforts in Cuba were a colonial enterprise that provided economic and political benefits to important supporters of the American imperial state, demonstrated that American imperialism could succeed where European powers had failed, and so inspired further American colonial expansion in the region.

There is little conclusive evidence of when yellow fever first appeared in Havana, but by the nineteenth century it was undoubtedly continuously present. In a typical year, yellow fever claimed hundreds of lives in the city, and it was very rare that more than a few days went by without at least one new case being identified. In particularly bad years, over six hundred people could succumb to the disease within just one hot, rainy, summer month.

Yellow fever was one of the most dreaded diseases of the high imperial age. The onset of the disease was marked by a fever that lasted for several days before breaking; for many, this development meant that they could begin to slowly recover. For some, however, the fever would soon return. With it came the disease's most characteristic symptoms: jaundice and black vomit. As the liver failed, the victim's skin and eyes turned yellow. Hemorrhaging of the eyes, nose, gums, throat, stomach, and intestines was common. The internal bleeding caused most patients who reached this stage of the disease to suffer bouts of uncontrollable retching; terrifyingly, the clotted blood turned the regurgitated liquid black. Few of those who experienced the black vomit ever recovered.

Ignorance compounded fears: even those who had spent years studying yellow fever seemed to have little understanding of how it was transmitted. With the development of germ theory in the latter half of the nineteenth century, many doctors believed that a thorough cleaning would render a location safe. Yellow fever, however, continued to strike even in well-kept neighborhoods. Many pointed to the lack of circulation in Havana's harbor as the source of the disease. But ships that anchored in the middle of the harbor and kept their crews aboard were much less likely to develop cases of yellow fever than those that docked and allowed sailors to enter the city.[1]

After the American intervention in the Cuban struggle for independence from Spain, the army immediately began an intense campaign against yellow fever in Havana and other Cuban cities. Despite great exertions, the fight against the disease met with little initial success. But then a team of American military doctors charged with investigating its cause took up and confirmed an elaborate version of a much-ridiculed theory put forward by a Cuban doctor, Carlos Finlay, decades earlier: that a particular house-dwelling species of mosquito was the only means by which the disease made its way from one victim to the next. Redirecting the efforts against yellow fever toward mosquito eradication had quick results. Within months, the disease was completely eliminated in Havana. By May 1902, when the U.S. Army departed, no cases of yellow fever had occurred anywhere on the island for over half a year.

Even after withdrawing its troops, the United States closely monitored conditions in Cuba for any sign of yellow fever and demanded that the newly installed Cuban government continue and expand efforts to ensure that the disease would not recur. When, in late 1905, political disorder disrupted these efforts and yellow fever again appeared in Havana, it was not long before the U.S. Army was sent back to quell the unrest. During the next three years, the occupation government expended over one-tenth of Cuba's national income on measures to eradicate this small outbreak and eliminate conditions favorable to the disease.[2] These measures and subsequent Cuban public health policies were successful: yellow fever never reappeared on the island.

Many will conclude that this successful exercise in disease eradication was a boon for Cubans. In fact it was not. Yellow fever, though terrible and often fatal to adults, causes such mild symptoms in children that infection often goes unnoticed. Further, a single bout of the disease generates a permanent immunity. Together these two aspects made it of little concern to lifelong inhabitants of areas where yellow fever was endemic or frequently epidemic: nearly all had become immune to the disease through childhood infection.

Many other diseases were of much greater concern to Cubans but were for the most part ignored by occupying U.S. forces. Enteritis, meningitis, malaria, and pneumonia each regularly took many more Cuban lives than yellow fever yet attracted little attention. Tuberculosis was the leading cause of death, killing many times more people in Havana than yellow fever each year.[3] During the first occupation, Cuban doctors begged American public health officials to dedicate a fraction of the effort that was directed at combating yellow fever to confronting tuberculosis. But it was not until 1902, after yellow fever was eradicated, that the occupation government allowed the creation of a tuberculosis sanitarium and a modest program of testing and education.

So if not to help the Cubans why did the United States make exterminating yellow fever such a high priority? The extensive campaign against yellow fever in Cuba can only be understood as a profoundly colonial enterprise, one that had important implications for the development of the American imperial state.

The Motivations for Colonial Public Health

Efforts by foreign powers to control epidemic diseases, scholars of colonial public health have long recognized, primarily served the interests of the colonizers rather than the colonized. These interests were both economic and political. For the economy of the empire, disease posed two threats. First, it menaced the commerce that makes the domination of foreign lands profitable. Colonial public health measures therefore frequently had as their goal the protection of trade. The famed Liverpool School of Tropical Medicine, for example, was founded by the city's commercial community to prepare medical officers for the British colonies. The shipping magnate Alfred Lewis Jones made the school's purpose clear at its inception: it was "an investment, and we expect dividends from it."[4] Second, epidemics could debilitate the native workforce on which the colonial economy depended. Where labor was in short supply, as in central Africa, protecting the health of miners, farmworkers, and rubber tappers became a matter of considerable importance to the authorities.[5]

There were also two political interests that motivated colonial health efforts. The first was protecting troops and administrators from disease, which was paramount to the maintenance of colonial rule. The use of quinine by colonial troops as a prophylaxis against malaria, for example, is frequently credited with allowing the European colonization of Africa to succeed.[6] The consequences to the colonial enterprise of not protecting soldiers' health were clear. The massive French expedition sent by Napoleon to put down the Haitian Revolution in 1802 failed because twenty-five thousand of its thirty-five thousand men succumbed to yellow fever in a span of just nine months; an earlier British effort to seize the rebellious colony had been abandoned after losing three-fifths of its soldiers to disease.[7]

The second political interest was that colonial public health could provide a justification for the domination of foreign lands. Public health was an integral part of the "civilizing mission" that served as the rationalization for most imperialist ventures; moreover, advances in health were both readily observed and difficult for critics to deny. In the Belgian Congo the need to burnish a public image badly tarnished by revelations of the mistreatment of the Congolese was a principal motivation for the decision of King Leopold II in 1903 to mount an investigation into sleeping sickness, and Belgian colonial administrators continued decades later to point to their successes in controlling it as a justification for empire.[8]

Public health efforts also sought to convince subjugated peoples of their own inferiority and, therefore, the desirability of continued colonial rule. As they carved out a sphere of influence in Southwest China in the 1890s, the French established medical dispensaries to check the spread of bubonic plague and win the confidence of the locals. The resulting improvements in public health convinced many of the superiority of Western ways and "proved to be an effective way to gain the sympathy of both the elite and the common people" for French domination of the region.[9]

The relative importance of these four motivations to a particular colonial effort to combat disease depended on the specific characteristics of the malady concerned, most directly its method of infection, which determines both its propensity to spread and the identity of its most frequent victims. Contagious diseases and diseases whose vectors are well suited to travel most often triggered imperial responses aimed primarily at protecting trade. The policies adopted by both British and French colonial authorities against cholera and bubonic plague in the latter decades of the nineteenth century were expressly directed at preserving commercial intercourse while the health of the local labor force and that of the imperial presence were of only secondary concern.[10] On the other hand, diseases whose pathologies confined them to particular environments—such as sleeping sickness and malaria—instead prompted measures directed mainly at safeguarding local workers and the colonial authorities. Dangers to trade in such cases could be ignored without risk to the imperial project. Whatever the balance among these motivations in fighting a particular disease, it was the interests of the empire, not those of colonial subjects, that impelled disease control efforts.

American Interests in Eradicating Yellow Fever in Cuba

Although yellow fever was not a serious problem for Cubans or others living in places where the disease was endemic, it was a nightmare for new arrivals to such places: it was therefore known as "the strangers' disease" in those cities of the American South, such as New Orleans, that were subject to frequent epidemics.

Yellow fever also took a terrible toll when it made its way into strange lands: those living in areas that were touched by epidemics only infrequently were hit very hard when the disease did strike. The American approach to yellow fever in Cuba was shaped by the disease's potential to spread beyond its usual range as well as its predilection for new arrivals.

Safeguarding commerce was always the most important motivation for the U.S. efforts against yellow fever in Cuba. Although the manner by which yellow fever was transmitted from one victim to the next was not known at the time of the first intervention in Cuba, it was well understood that the disease could be spread from place to place aboard both ships and trains. This meant that trade between Havana and ports such as New Orleans posed a constant threat of an epidemic not only in those coastal cities but also in all the cities and towns of the interior that were linked to the ports by river and railroad traffic. The decline in frequency of yellow fever epidemics in the American South in the years after the Civil War only increased the number of their potential victims. The 1878 Mississippi Valley epidemic, for example, claimed more than 20,000 lives; over 120,000 people were stricken with the disease in more than one hundred cities and towns.[11] By disrupting business and trade, the epidemic was also disastrous to the U.S. economy: contemporary estimates of the monetary losses ranged as high as two hundred million dollars. Afterward, the mere rumor of an outbreak was often sufficient to generate panic and disrupt the operation of businesses across the South.

Public health officials quickly identified the source of the 1878 epidemic as a ship that had arrived in New Orleans from Havana, and after that they relied on quarantine to protect against again importing yellow fever from the island. But quarantine was costly to implement, a source of tension among states as well as between the states and the federal government, and a constant drag on the expansion of commercial traffic. Worse still, the quarantine periodically failed when either its administrators placed the development of their own local economies before the public's health or smugglers circumvented quarantine protections entirely. Even with the quarantine in place, major epidemics struck the South about once each decade.[12]

Technological developments worked to further reduce the desirability of relying on quarantine to protect commerce from yellow fever. Advances in shipping, particularly the widespread adoption of steam-powered vessels, had greatly reduced the time required to transport goods between Cuba and the ports of the United States by the end of the nineteenth century. A shorter voyage meant that to be effective in preventing the spread of yellow fever time spent in quarantine would have to be longer. Unless the disease was eradicated at its source in Havana, the promise of profits to be gained from the technological advances in shipping, from new U.S. investments in Cuba, and from expanding commerce with the rest of the tropics threatened either to slowly melt away alongside the docks of southern quarantine stations or to suddenly evaporate in the panic of the next yellow fever epidemic to strike the southern states. It was this concern that most motivated the U.S. campaign against yellow fever in Cuba; indeed, it had been an important reason for the entry into the war against Spain.[13]

Like any colonial enterprise, the U.S. conquest of Cuba depended on maintaining the good health of legions of soldiers and administrators. The intervention in the war with Spain involved transporting tens of thousands of people from the United States to Cuba, and keeping these people free of yellow fever was a major concern of the invasion's planners. Many considered sending an army into the homeland of yellow fever during the hot, humid Cuban summer—when the disease was at its fiercest—to be a suicidal endeavor.

The health of U.S. forces, though, was not a central motivation for the officials who oversaw the extermination of yellow fever in Cuba. The U.S. Army's experience with the disease during the Mexican-American War and afterward had demonstrated that relatively simple preventative measures served well to keep troops free of infection. Although they did not understand why, by the time of the intervention U.S. Army officers had known for decades that yellow fever could be kept at bay by keeping troops stationed outside of cities and, when possible, at higher elevations. The fate of the Spanish army, which had been ravaged by yellow fever while garrisoning the island's cities and towns, underscored this fact. As a result, although epidemics of typhoid and malaria among the ranks caused scandals during the intervention, the U.S. Army was little affected by yellow fever. Protecting the troops only declined further in importance with the passage of the Platt Amendment in 1901, which instituted indirect rule. By its terms, which were included in Cuba's Constitution under threat of continued occupation, the U.S. Army would return to the island—and so risk becoming infected with yellow fever—only in the event that the newly installed Cuban government failed to adequately safeguard U.S. interests. So long as the Cuban government faithfully served Washington's interests, American soldiers would remain safely on the opposite shore of the Gulf of Mexico.

But ensuring a healthy workforce in Cuba was not a principal motivation for the extensive efforts expended by the United States to fight yellow fever. To be sure, the condition of the rural population was a subject of considerable concern to the American authorities after 1898. During the Cuban war for independence, both the insurgents and the Spanish army sought to deprive their opponents of resources by destroying the rural economy. Beginning in 1896, the Spanish army sought to relocate the entire rural population to concentration camps where they could be easily monitored and unable to support the insurgents. These *reconcentrados* had little access to food or clean water, and the camps were soon wracked with disease. By 1897, when the reconcentration policy was abandoned, over two hundred thousand people had perished in the camps. After the United States assumed control, the devastated Cuban countryside presented attractive opportunities to American investors. But reestablishing the island's sugar industry and its other agricultural operations would require a new rural workforce—and that workforce would have to remain free of yellow fever. The Spanish immigrants the United States invited after the war to help repopulate the island's rural interior, though, were vulnerable to yellow fever only if they lingered in Havana. Therefore, the new arrivals were sent directly to camps established well outside urban areas until they settled in the countryside.[14]

If the importance of providing a healthy workforce and protecting soldiers was small and declined over the years, the need to provide a gloss of legitimacy to U.S. domination of Cuba only increased over time. Freeing Cuba from Spanish tyranny had been a popular cause among the citizens of the United States, but maintaining colonial rule clashed uncomfortably with the anti-imperialist rhetoric that had been used to gain that support. The fight against yellow fever, however, provided both a rationale for continued close U.S. supervision of Cuban affairs and a basis for arguments that such tutelage was both necessary and beneficial. These arguments resonated well with the prior U.S. public conception of the war in Cuba as a humanitarian crusade. Figures such as Major Walter Reed, whose experiments demonstrated conclusively that mosquitoes carried the disease from one victim to the next, and Private John Moran, who was among the volunteers for Reed's experiments, became national heroes celebrated for decades afterward. A particularly noteworthy example of the persistence of this national self-justification for empire is the 1938 MGM film *Yellow Jack,* which offers a fictional account of U.S. Army enlisted men volunteering to be experimented on—and nobly declining any monetary compensation—so that Cubans could be freed from the ravages of yellow fever.

Not surprisingly, the transformation of Cuba into a U.S. colony was in need of legitimization on the island as well. Although they were pleased to see the end of Spanish rule, most Cubans did not believe the U.S. intervention in their conflict with Spain was necessary. After all, Cuban insurgents had remained in the field for three years, avoiding all the Spanish efforts to crush them, and shown no signs of weakening. The conflict had destroyed the economy and converted Cuba into a singularly unprofitable colony. In the eyes of most Cubans, it was simply a matter of time before the Spanish would grant them their independence and withdraw from the island. The arrival of the United States, in their view, only hastened the war to its inevitable conclusion. It certainly did not justify the imposition of U.S. rule.[15] Claims of medical and scientific superiority in fighting yellow fever provided the United States with an additional argument with which to persuade skeptical Cubans that its continuing domination of their island was justified and desirable.

Yellow Fever in Cuba and the American Imperial State

As an exercise in colonial public health, the eradication of yellow fever in Cuba had several major implications for the development of the American imperial state. First, the defeat of yellow fever in Cuba allowed the state to deliver benefits to several of its important constituencies without asking these groups to bear the cost. By eliminating the disease in Havana, the United States allowed commercial interests to expand trade with Cuba and beyond unfettered by lengthy and expensive quarantines. Similarly, American investors were able to take advantage of opportunities in Cuba's war-ravaged agricultural sector without concern that the disease would complicate the arrival of trusted American managers or immigrating farmworkers.

These benefits to investors and merchants extended not only to Cuba but also to the U.S. South. The conquest of yellow fever freed the South from the devastating epidemics that had repeatedly debilitated the region after the Civil War, freed it to become a place to which migrating "strangers" need not fear to settle, a site for investment and economic expansion, and an entry point for goods from the Caribbean and points even farther south. It delivered these crucial benefits without making any demands on wealthy white southerners or their supporters among poor whites. Intrusive house-to-house inspections for mosquito larvae, like those conducted monthly in every residence in Havana, were unnecessary in the South. Massive government spending on public water and sewer systems—serving the homes of rich and poor, whites and blacks alike—to eliminate mosquito breeding places was not required as it had been in Cuba. No matter how little was done to eliminate the conditions that would allow yellow fever to thrive if it were ever introduced, the South was safe while Cuba remained free of the disease. As colonial subjects of the United States, Cubans were forced to bear the vast majority, if not all, of the inconvenience, indignity, and expense of the disease control effort even though yellow fever barely affected them.

Second, overcoming yellow fever in Cuba demonstrated that the United States could succeed in a colonial venture where a European power had failed. Yellow fever played a central role in the defeat of the Spanish: indeed, Cuban insurgents had for three years successfully pursued a military strategy built around the disease, withdrawing into the countryside while yellow fever dramatically reduced the effectiveness of their better trained, better equipped, and more numerous foe. Eliminating yellow fever made it clear that the U.S. Army, if and when called on to enforce Cuban obedience to Washington's dictates, would not suffer as the Spanish had.

Together, these two implications gave rise to a third: they inspired additional imperial expansion. This process was most obvious in Panama. The massive French effort to construct a waterway across the isthmus had been abandoned in

1889 not least due to the yellow fever deaths of tens of thousands of workers over the previous decade. However, the prospective returns to commercial interests and its success in eliminating yellow fever in Cuba encouraged the American imperial state to take up the challenge. In time, the experience in Panama would have its own effects on the development of the imperial state, as Paul S. Sutter documents elsewhere in this volume. Without the successful campaign against yellow fever in Cuba, however, the construction of the Panama Canal would likely not have even been attempted.

As an exercise in colonial public health, the fight against yellow fever in Cuba served the interests not of Cubans but of the United States. Eliminating Cuban yellow fever protected commerce, safeguarded American troops and administrators, ensured the recovery of the rural workforce, and provided a gloss of legitimacy to U.S. domination of the island. In so doing, it provided significant benefits to important supporters of the American imperial state and furnished evidence of its superiority to the European powers, both of which encouraged the expansion of the U.S. overseas empire.

Mapping Regional and Imperial Geographies
Tropical Disease in the U.S. South

NATALIE J. RING

IN 1915 ELLSWORTH HUNTINGTON, a well-known geographer and advocate of environmental determinism at Yale University, published a book entitled *Civilization and Climate* that illustrated how tropical and subtropical climates inhibited the development of modern civilization around the globe. Like Latin America, Mexico, India, Egypt, and South Africa, the cultural geographer noted that the southern parts of the United States suffered from "climatic handicaps." What all of the inhabitants in these areas had in common, Huntington asserted, was a certain "tropical inertia," a state of mind and physical constitution that undermined the propensity to engage in efficient labor, engendered backwardness and disease, and contributed to the degeneration of the white race.[1] Indeed, the Yale geographer's fascination with the plague of tropical inertia in the U.S. South and countries in the Caribbean and South America underlines one of the central questions guiding this volume: in what ways did the colonial periphery alter the configuration of the U.S. metropole?

Huntington's inclination to link the U.S. South with tropical and subtropical areas around the world was not an unfamiliar trope. In the late nineteenth and early twentieth centuries American social reformers, physicians, and government experts, as well as native and foreign travelers to the region, formulated an "imaginary geography," a set of discourses about the tropical South that focused on the landscape, the people, the climate, and diseases such as hookworm, yellow fever, and malaria. The discursive construction of southern "tropicality" generated a familiar set of cultural images that resonated with Western imperialist imagery and legitimated and reflected practical efforts to reform and reconstruct the domestic tropics in America's own backyard.[2] From 1898 to the end of World War I, the United States had an imperial presence in several overseas possessions that, in conjunction with expanding U.S. economic development in parts of Latin America, fueled a fascination with the "tropical." Sudden and extensive contact with the tropical world encouraged Americans to make links between domestic and foreign tropical spaces and demonstrate the remarkable fluidity of America's conceptual and geographical boundaries at the turn of the century. Indeed, a transnational circulation of colonial discourses, people, and patterns of reform encouraged American cultural imperialists to construct the U.S. South as a tropical space in need of colonial uplift, much like the tropical possessions listed above.[3]

America's vision of the tropics (both within and outside the nation's borders) had much in common with Europe's long-standing interest in tropical geography. The discovery of the tropical world coincided with the expansive tendencies of European imperialism. As far back as the fifteenth century, Portuguese explorers of equatorial Africa knew the climate was an unhealthy one. In the early part of the nineteenth century the French conquest of Algeria and the British interest in India, the West Indies, and Africa brought Europeans into contact with tropical climates and raised questions about the ability of the white man to survive in foreign environments. Between the 1840s and 1860s, European naturalists and scientists touring South America, particularly Brazil, began to categorize and classify everything that was tropical. Increasingly, the idea that some places, peoples, and plants were tropical and some were not generated a set of recognizable tropes, metaphors, and symbols designed to convey the meaning of the tropics. Even places that were not geographically located in equatorial regions were often deemed tropical.[4]

Like their European counterparts, Americans' conceptual category of the tropical fluctuated depending on the context or the people involved. Viewed from the northern industrialized hemisphere the tropics were always located south of temperate regions. From the perspective of the United States, then, the southern tropics included Mexico, Central America, and South America. By the late nineteenth century, the conceptual boundary between the temperate and tropical had shifted farther north, and the southern region of the United States was incorporated into a broader vision of the tropical "South" that included all of the Americas south of the Northeast. As Nancy Leys Stephan notes, "In this way, the 'tropical' came to constitute more than a geographical concept; it signified a place of radical otherness to the temperate world."[5]

What, then, does the historical fascination with the tropical South at the height of overseas imperialism have to tell us about the relation between region and nation, as well as that between region and empire? The fluidity of the category of the tropical suggests that we need to rethink the most recent historiography surrounding the relationship between the South and the nation-state at the turn of the century. According to most historians, the late nineteenth and early twentieth centuries was an era in which the hostilities of the Civil War and the dashed hopes of Reconstruction gave way to the powerful forces of cultural reunion. The national interest in reunification is said to have downplayed sectional grievances, supported industrial harmony, evoked a nostalgic memory of the Old South, and celebrated the idea of a white republic. The conventional narrative of sectional reconciliation also posits that imperialism and military ventures overseas, such as the Spanish-American War in 1898, had a nationalizing influence on American culture and that a shared patriotic sentiment made it easier for white Americans to forget the sectional hostilities of a previous generation.[6]

Yet an equally powerful and opposing set of representations of the South as a backward tropical region played counterpoint to the discourse of sectional reconciliation and distorted the nation-state's mythmaking efforts to construct a more benign social memory of the Civil War and its consequences. Ironically, imperialism may have bound the sections together with a shared racialized national sentiment but the expansion abroad also made it abundantly clear how much the South had in common with many foreign countries. Americans began to locate the South and some of these imperial territories as deviant geographical spaces in the broader transnational world. The prominence of the idea of the tropical South (climate, topography, and disease) suggests that rather than framing the relationship between the South and the nation on a regional and national scale we need to broaden the units of our analysis. The path of empire cannot be separated from region or nation as we step back from the simple North-South binary framework that has long dominated the field of southern history. The cultural construction of a universal and dangerous tropicality reflected a global movement of peoples, patterns of governance, colonial models of reform, and social science theories that traversed the borders of multiple nation-states. Efforts to reform and rehabilitate the tropical South might be viewed as a project of domestic imperialism.

Perception of the Paradoxical South

Depictions of the tropics typically drew on a complex of themes such as climate, race, landscape, and disease, and the discourse on tropical spaces often was unstable and marked by representational duality.[7] In his 1929 book *The Romance and Rise of the American Tropics*, Samuel Crowther stated quite precisely this paradox: "The curse of the tropics is poverty—a startling poverty existing amid splendour."[8] In addition, the tendency to paint the tropics as both pathological and paradisiacal generated what one geographer has called a "moral climatology."[9] The use of moralistic idioms, even under the guise of scientific objectivity, contributed to the construction of the tropics as the Other, a geographical entity often deemed inferior to the temperate regions of the world.[10]

Certainly the idea of southern tropicality included a host of contradictory meanings cast in both a negative and a positive light. The region was simultaneously viewed as alluring and perilous, exotic yet familiarly American.[11] In the late nineteenth and early twentieth centuries a spate of promotional books and pamphlets focusing on the salubrious climate, the Edenic landscape, and the availability of exotic fruits and vegetables welcomed tourists and real estate developers to the region.[12] Yet underneath the allure of southern tropicality there lurked a dark side, a dangerous and pestilential character that needed to be tamed.[13] John Milton Mackie, who wrote a travel diary entitled *From Cape Cod to Dixie and the Tropics,* described the "primeval aspect of things" and marveled at the fecundity of the vegetation on his tour of the broader southern tropics. Yet by the end of his tour, even though Mackie had enjoyed the paradoxical combination of spectacular beauty and decay in the South, he remarked that he was glad to leave behind the "pet nursery of fever and pestilence" and return to a more salubrious environment.[14]

Various travelers to the U.S. South likened the topography to foreign tropical locations and saw no inconsistency in touring the South and other tropical countries on one continuous trip. Mackie's journey linked "Dixie" with the "Tropics," including Cuba and the Bahamas. Other cultural geographers interested in studying the South developed parallel interests in foreign locales, too. In 1910, Albert Bushnell Hart, a historian at Harvard University, published a study based on a seven-month investigation of the "southern problem" entitled *The Southern South.*[15] Just one year later, he published a second work, entitled *The Obvious Orient,* in which he recounted his nine-month experience of "globe trotting" through Japan, China, and the Philippines.[16] In each case of exploration, Hart presented a survey of an unexamined alien tropical space. Hart described the Orient as a place marked by "mystery, distance, romance, [and] myths" and the South as a place with "temperamental peculiarities" and a "peculiar life and standards."[17] Hart's fascination with presenting a "comprehensive view" of allegedly uncharted territory cut a wide geographical swathe, linking domestic imperial tendencies with foreign imperial impulses.

The same year in which Ellsworth Huntington warned of the dangers of the tropical U.S. South, the editors of the *New Republic* urged Americans to be magnanimous and patient with the southern state of Georgia, much like they would be with Haiti and "the more primitive Balkan states." They noted that Georgia had "self-government" but was "not yet fit for it." The remaining inhabitants were "primitive," "uneducated," and "burdened with a citizenship" they were ill-equipped to handle and needed "the guidance of comparatively more advanced people."[18] The rhetoric used to invoke compassion for this southern state's problems could have easily been applied to any of the tropical colonial possessions, as the article suggested. In essence, to borrow a phrase from Wilbur J. Cash, the South was thought to be "a nation within a nation," a place that posed intricate problems warranting imperial solutions.[19]

Empire and Disease

More than anything else, the discourse of the tropics typically invoked notions of disease. In the earliest attempts to colonize the tropics Europeans noted the existence of certain "alien" diseases that appeared to be indigenous to the warm, damp climates. The development of medical geography and the topographical survey demonstrated a belief in the influence of the physical environment on disease. Physicians of colonial medicine contributed to a new body of knowledge that helped define these tropical areas as exotic alien spaces.[20] The miasmatic theory of contagion posited that disease spread through atmospheric infection and without any known connection to the infective substance, making it even more difficult to anticipate or control. The study of diseases in the tropics initially fell under the purview of the military, and medicine played a pivotal role in negotiating the relationship between colonized and the colonizers.[21] Physicians interested in tropical diseases dubbed the field tropical hygiene, medical climatology, medical topography, or medical geography.[22]

By the late nineteenth century, the continued need for healthy bodies in military combat and imperialist expeditions into the tropics generated an interest in a professional scientific field designed to facilitate these goals. While physicians recognized and treated diseases in the tropics throughout the nineteenth century, a series of closely related developments in the last two decades of the century contributed to the identification of specific tropical diseases that warranted treatment by means of a separate medical discipline.[23] Thus, tropical medicine became a scientific specialty. The germ theory of disease and research done in parasitology changed the conceptual framework for understanding the tropics by positing that microbes and parasites, not the climate, were responsible for tropical diseases. The developing power of the microscope and laboratory in the study of tropical diseases now meant that explanations for the etiology of illness were exclusively scientific and could not be based on loose observations and impressions of the environment. The new tropical medicine argued that the direct causes of disease in the tropics were germs and parasites and that a reliance on scientific solutions such as sanitation and public health would enable human beings to survive in unfamiliar topographies and environments.

European and American exploration of new regions across the globe linked the acquisition of geographical knowledge of the globe with imperialism, and the presence of disease in these newly discovered spaces irrevocably connected the subject of health with global expansion. A popular medical text by Patrick Manson entitled *Tropical Diseases: A Manual of the Diseases of the Warm Climates* was published in 1898 at the height of Western imperialism and offered doctors a new tool for interpreting foreign environments and cataloging disease. The American and European acquisition of so many new territories in the Southern and Eastern Hemispheres by the turn of the century illustrated how close the various regions of the world had become.[24] Scientific knowledge would make it possible for Western colonizers to survive the dangers of the tropics in the imperial world.

However, the new scientific paradigm of tropical medicine was unstable since the older notions of miasmatic infection and the tendency to stress the significance of climate lingered well into the twentieth century. Old ideas about the connections among disease, climate, and topography existed uneasily with new ideas about the "scientific" reasons for specific tropical diseases. Even when the scientific and popular communities came to accept the germ theory of disease, the notion of place as intrinsic to the question of disease still remained a central component of this new knowledge. While the new medical discipline emphasized the power of science in conquering germs and parasites responsible for tropical maladies, the paradigm still reinforced notions of diseased geographical spaces since certain microbes were believed to be specific to the tropics.

Moreover, in the late nineteenth century the discovery of the malarial and hookworm parasites helped draw continued attention to the indirect role topography played in disease transmission. Hookworms survived best in sandy soils, and the mosquitoes that carried malaria were far more prevalent in warm, humid climates. Discussions of the geographical distribution of insects and their vectors and the travel of secondary hosts as disseminators of disease dominated the scientific literature on such illnesses as malaria, serving to reinforce the connections among climate, place, and disease. In the South, a region long identified as a distinctive locale, the assumption that place had a strong relationship with disease not surprisingly took hold even in the face of scientific certainty that parasites and germs, not the climate per se, were responsible for tropical diseases.

The South and Tropical Pathology

As the scientific and medical communities began to focus on the connections among insects, environment, and disease in their surveys of foreign tropical locales, many began to associate the South with tropical pathology. The United States' imperial ventures overseas raised questions about the nature of infectious diseases thought to have entered North America in the bodies of American soldiers, missionaries, businessmen, sailors, or diplomats who had been traveling abroad. A number of organizations such as the Rockefeller Foundation and the United States Public Health Service relied on the tools of the new science of tropical medicine to catalogue tropical pathology in the South. Beginning in 1909, they sent scores of experts and observers into the region to diagnose both the people and the place, and the ensuing cultural and medical cartography framed the South as an infectious, primitive space. One doctor noted that southern ports in particular were potential hotbeds for diseases indigenous to the damp, hot climate of tropical regions.[25] Employing a military metaphor that resonated with the rhetoric of imperial conquest, the *Southern Medical Journal* declared that as a result "it falls to the lot of southern physicians to act as outpost sentinels, guarding the land from being unconsciously invaded by devastating diseases."[26] The opening editorial of the first issue of *The American Journal of Tropical Medicine* in 1913 warned that formerly "exotic" diseases such as yellow fever, hookworm, pellagra, and malaria had planted themselves in some sections of the United States.[27] The existence of tropical diseases in the South meant that one did not need to travel abroad to discover an "exotic" disease or experience the enervating effects of a tropical climate.[28] Physicians, reformers, and social scientists writing and talking about disease in the South did not always make the distinction between imported diseases and diseases understood to be native to the region. The tendency to blur the line between the two modes of origin and geographical manifestation in scientific and popular discourse contributed to an image of the tropical South as a place that had long harbored unusual and potentially life-threatening illnesses.

Comparisons between the U.S. South and some of the country's colonial possessions were not surprising given that many of the doctors and public health officials working in the South had previously been stationed in tropical countries. Lewellys Barker, the president of the Southern Medical Association, received his training in tropical diseases in the Philippines as a young student from Johns Hopkins University, and Charles W. Stiles, the scientist credited with discovering hookworm in the South, taught military hygiene and tropical sanitation at the Army Medical School. The Rockefeller Foundation used the activities of its Hookworm Commission of Puerto Rico as a template for later hookworm eradication campaigns in the southern United States.[29] Then, in circular fashion, the foundation's International Health Board maintained that public health work to eradicate tropical diseases in the South was valuable because it served as a training school for men "given responsible posts in foreign countries."[30]

To observers at the beginning of the twentieth century, southerners' apparent ignorance of rudimentary health measures, as well as the region's disease, dirtiness, and lassitude, looked remarkably similar to the lack of basic public hygiene found among the nonwhite peoples living in the American colonial possessions. Ellsworth Huntington explained that many southerners had "ceased to be careful about food and sanitation" and did "not feel the eager zest for work" as they did in temperate climates.[31] At times the level of filth and community indifference was so appalling that it startled sanitary engineers working in the region. The director of the Public Health Department in Tennessee, who traveled to Kingsport to make an inspection of an area owned by a local corporation, reported that "what privies there were overflowing with filth, and soil pollution was evident all over the place . . . ; flies were buzzing by the millions; the whole territory around the place was covered with a rank growth of weeds, grass, and bushes."[32] A local newspaper described an area in New Orleans as a "loathsome spot," a "disease-breeding ulcer," and a "festering mass of law-violating putrescence."[33]

The absence of privies in many homes and schools in the rural South constituted the most offensive breach of cleanliness in the minds of public health reformers. In some counties in Mississippi the percentage of homes without proper sanitary privies was as high as 94 percent.[34] Southerners lacking indoor toilets or outhouses often defecated on the ground, and the resulting "soil pollution" was the principal means of hookworm transmission. Elementary privies known as "umbrella privies," which were holes in the ground over which there was a box with no bottom, and privies situated over rivers, which washed away the waste, posed a grave danger to human health. Some farmers fertilized their fields with human excrement.[35]

Public health reformers often described southerners' sanitary practices as animal-like and argued that even cattle and hogs made the effort to stay away from their own excrement. A doctor in the U.S. Public Health Service noted that since "we house-break our pet cats and dogs" it did not "seem too much to expect of human intelligence" that people could be trained to become "yard-broke" and give up their practice of defecating on the ground in such a "dangerous and disgusting manner" so close to their water supplies and kitchens.[36] Charles Wardell Stiles caused quite a bit of consternation in a few southern communities by encouraging the local public health officers to send out letters informing parents that their children were eating human feces.[37] The suggestion that white people might even be ingesting the excrement of blacks precipitated tremendous alarm and aversion.[38]

Many victims of hookworm were known as "clay-eaters" because of the parasite's occasional tendency to precipitate bizarre eating habits (such as eating dirt), and these practices only reinforced the notion that southerners were a backward class of tropical-like people who were inclined to eat soil and human feces. Both official reports from the Rockefeller Foundation and popular magazines published sensational accounts of poor white southerners' inclination to ingest strange objects because of hookworm infection. One magazine reported that "Pebbles, sand, clay, mud, chalk, slate-pencils, shells, rotten wood, salt, raw cotton, cloth, paper, tobacco-pipes or pipe stems, mice, and young rats all have their devotees."[39]

Such accounts of "pure Anglo-Saxon stock" behaving in an unhygienic, animal-like manner usually attributed to nonwhite races shocked the American public and reinforced stereotypes that somehow the white race in the South was degenerating rapidly.[40] No doubt public health reformers and sanitary engineers, including Lewellys Barker, saw similarities between the personal hygiene practices of Filipinos and poor white southerners. Excremental customs in both tropical locales muted the distinction between white and black and American and Filipino and highlighted the tenuous boundaries between empire and region.[41]

Public Tropical Geography

The spectacle of tropical geographies most accessible to the public could be found in the art of world expositions and exhibits. The exposition proved to be the best cultural model through which imperial propagandists could showcase both the potential merits and exotic features of their colonial territories.[42] The display of tropical otherness included both the U.S. South and foreign locales. In 1915, the Rockefeller Foundation presented an exhibit on hookworm disease at the Panama-Pacific International Exposition in San Francisco, California, to raise public awareness about infection in the southern states through the use of models, life-size photographs of diseased bodies, and live demonstrations of microscopic examinations of fecal matter. The exhibit included a colored map of the world showing places where hookworm could be found and the various tropical regions targeted by the International Health Commission for public health reform. Juxtaposed next to the illustrated charts on the results of the campaign in the South, the world map reinforced the connection between the social and corporeal deficiencies of the tropical South and distant tropical countries.[43]

Popular magazines and public philanthropic literature such as pamphlets also drew national attention to the similarities between the U.S. South and foreign tropical locales. The early International Health Commission (IHC), later named the International Health Board, of the Rockefeller Foundation, established to take over the duties of the Rockefeller Sanitary Commission in the U.S. South in 1914, instituted public health work in such places as Puerto Rico, Ceylon, Central America, Mexico, and Brazil, as well as continuing its work in the southern states. One IHC pamphlet noted, in decreasing order, that the greatest number of people infected with hookworm across the globe lived in China, Brazil, the African Congo, Mexico, and the U.S. South.[44]

Walter Hines Page—journal editor, member of the board of the Rockefeller Foundation, and a leading supporter of public health and education reform in the South—published an article in his widely distributed magazine, *World's Work*, entitled "The Hookworm in Civilization," which made comparisons between the "disease belts" of the world (Puerto Rico, Ceylon, and the Philippines) and the way public health work in the U.S. South seemed likely to lead to "the reclamation of other tropical peoples." In short, Page argued that the rehabilitation of tropical and subtropical citizens, the economic mastery of tropical places, and the successful extraction of labor from tropical peoples depended on the health of individual bodies. The emphasis on curing sickness or, as Page described it, "the reclamation of tropical peoples," was a more successful strategy for establishing a productive colonial economy in the tropics than relying on the infusion of outside capital and expensive technology.[45]

Some historians have made the case that the New South developed into a colonial economy partly due to the infusion of northern capital and its isolated labor market, low wages, lack of immigration, and one-crop economy.[46] National interest in an efficient, healthy, southern workforce reflected a broader colonial effort to control economically the larger tropical "South" of which the southern states were a part. The profits derived from low-cost labor were immaterial if labor could not perform. Dr. Lewellys F. Barker insisted that all physicians consider the "economic problem" when treating rural diseases in the South. Barker's plea that public health reformers and physicians take this relationship into account reflected a broader imperial understanding of the prevalence of destitution in tropical areas. Writing in the *North American Review,* Carl F. Westerberg noted that "the great common characteristic of all tropical countries is poverty of the type which exists among our Southern mountaineers."[47] Active dialogue about the prevalence of tropical diseases and poverty in the South reflected a larger anxiety about the fate of the political economy in the region and its place in a rapidly industrializing nation. Conquering tropical poverty and its attending consequences in both domestic and imperial contexts was key to buttressing the power of the nation-state.

Race and Tropical Disease

Finally, scientific inquiry into tropical pathology could not be divorced from race, either, since one of the objectives of tropical medicine was to explain the various interactions between racial constitutions and regional environments. Theories about racial immunity and the role of racial differences in the expression of disease were not surprising given the racial designs of American and European imperialism. During the nineteenth century, many physicians, zoologists, anthropologists, and geographers turned to the study of "acclimatization," which often focused on the tropics and in part investigated the connection between race and climate.[48] Experts tried to reconcile the tension between race and place. They questioned whether the energy, initiative, and progressive drive believed to be intrinsic to the white race could overcome the debilitating effects of the tropical climate. The new scientific discipline of tropical medicine provided answers by demonstrating how attention to public health and sanitation could ensure the survival of white civilization.

Yet, in spite of some rather optimistic proclamations about the ability of science to conquer disease and reverse the decline of civilization, anxieties about the dangers of race-specific disease lingered in the popular and medical imaginations. Colonial doctors working in the tropics initially pointed to the nonwhite races' apparent immunity to certain illnesses while simultaneously implicating them in spreading those diseases. These accusations were largely based on anecdote, and further experience in the tropics demonstrated that local inhabitants were not necessarily immune to local diseases.[49] Moreover, physicians and travelers to the tropics still worried about possible expressions of white degeneration as a result of the hot, humid climate, particularly mental and moral retrogression.[50]

Apprehension about the connection among race, illness, and the tropical climate in the South continued to dominate the national imagination, too. The significant population of African Americans in the South reinforced the idea of a pathological diseased-carrying region of nonwhite people. In addition, the white race's tendency to succumb to tropical diseases and climates in spite of its supposed racial superiority was especially apparent the region because a great number of poor whites suffered from hookworm and pellagra. An increasingly conspicuous population of poor whites exhibiting tropical characteristics accentuated the unstable and uncertain place of poor whites in the racial hierarchy. Ellsworth Huntington argued that certain tropical diseases native to the southern climate had exacerbated the penchant for laziness that had caused white southerners to "fall below the level of their race" and become "'Poor Whites' or 'Crackers.'"[51] Wickliffe Rose, the secretary of the Rockefeller Sanitary Commission for the Eradication of Hookworm, noted the degeneracy of the white race during a trip to Richmond County, Virginia, in 1911. He reported that the poor whites in this community, called "Forkemites," were known for their extreme poverty, lack of thrift, "dense illiteracy," and "low moral tone" and subsequently had begun to take on the appearance of a "distinct race."[52]

The existence of what was sometimes referred to as "the new race question" or the "Caucasian problem" provoked tremendous alarm.[53] In the tropical South, a white race moving backward toward a state of barbarism rather than forward toward a state of civilization collapsed the boundaries/binaries between black and white, civilized and savage. The pathology of the tropics played a critical role in this process of racial deevolution. In an era in which the social separation of the races in the South had become codified into law, as well as a universal de facto practice, the possible existence of a degenerate white race created tremendous anxiety about the potential violation of these boundaries. More important, evidence of Anglo-Saxon regression in the region challenged the national consensus on white racial superiority that underlay much of modern American identity at the turn of the century.[54]

Just when the American imperialist project abroad was helping to contribute to the construction and celebration of a white national identity through its dominance of the nonwhite races in the tropical world, the distinctive problems of the tropical South, magnified by the new interest in tropical medicine, including the pathology of the poor white, threatened to weaken this ideology from within. The existence of a degenerate, poor, southern white population endangered white prestige and weakened imperial prerogatives in all colonial settings. Mastering disease in the tropics—whether in the U.S. South or abroad—was a crucial part of the colonial project, a step toward saving white civilization.

Conclusion

In analyzing the process by which Americans constructed the tropical U.S. South we can begin to move away from thinking about it as an anomaly in an exceptional nation. The treatment of the South as a distinctive place in need of reform was not simply reinforced by comparisons between the region and the rest of the country. Americans also located the region and other foreign countries as alien, pestilent spaces in the transnational world, blurring the boundaries between metropole and periphery in the process. A fascination with imperial difficulties encouraged some intellectuals, reformers, and social scientists to think about the South as a particular manifestation of a broader problem around the globe. The larger problem included such concerns as the perceived conflict between the white race (viewed as civilized) and the darker races (viewed as barbarous), the dangers of tropical illnesses and climates, and the obstacles to industrial development, including disease and rural poverty. Anxieties about the decline of civilization, racial degeneration, diseased bodies, and a weak labor force in the South begin to make more sense when we situate them within the context of turn of the century understandings of the tropics and the overseas colonies. Over time, a global circulation of peoples, medical theories, and reform practices linked the uplift of the South with the uplift of the colonial possessions abroad. The spatial projection of American power at the height of Western imperialism drew attention to the significance of place and infused regionalist discourse with new life.

Finally, the metropole's anxiety about the tropical U.S. South, an area within its own geographic boundaries, also underscores the relative difficulty of facilitating the integration of the region into the nation-state in the wake of the Civil War. Contrary to what many historians have argued, sectional reunification did not always occur with ease or mutual goodwill. In drawing attention to the dangers of the United States' backyard tropics—including racial degeneration, "tropical poverty," and tropical diseases—the burgeoning liberal state articulated a new but shaky path to sectional reconciliation. This involved the sustained concomitant focus on the colonial uplift of both domestic and foreign imperial territories. In short, the wider question being considered was how to incorporate a backward region or colonial possession into a modernizing nation. Paradoxically, the procedures and discourses of colonialism and empire making were used to facilitate the process of national reunification in the United States. In a curious way, the discourse of the tropical South was refracted through the lens of American imperialism and subsequently reconfigured the relationship between the South and the regulatory state.

The Conquest of Molecules
Wild Yams and American Scientists in Mexican Jungles

GABRIELA SOTO LAVEAGA

IN MAY 1951 FORTUNE MAGAZINE, under the intriguing headline "Mexican Hormones," reported that "the biggest technological boom ever heard south of the border" was that a Mexican laboratory, Syntex, had derived synthetic cortisone from Mexican wild yams.[1] Months later, in October 1951, a Mexican chemist, also working on yams out of Syntex, codiscovered the substance that would later be known simply as the "pill": oral contraceptives.[2] These discoveries transformed Mexico from, as the press described it, a "presumably backward" country into the world's premier supplier of synthetic hormones.[3] The country controlled this monopoly until the late 1960s when domestic politics and alternate sources of raw materials displaced Mexico from its synthetic-steroid-producing throne.[4]

But, while the histories of the discovery of synthetic cortisone and progesterone often featured intrepid American scientists venturing into tropical jungles or struggling to perform experiments under the weight of cultural misunderstandings, they rarely featured Mexican scientists or, for that matter, any Mexicans—a presence that, I argue, was crucial to the mass production of steroid hormones in the twentieth century.[5]

What can this omission reveal about empires in transition? Because science should represent the apolitical triumph of reason for the benefit of humankind one does not readily think of the hard sciences as being involved in imperial conquest. But it is precisely in the West's appropriation of science as a national creation in need of export to other lands that we can most easily see how the idea of empire is reinforced. Roy Macleod, in describing how colonial science was seen as removed from the continent, described how knowledge production outside of Europe "meant derivative science, done by lesser minds working on problems set by savants in Europe."[6] In creating inferior constituents colonizers reinforced the idea of superiority and justified their presence.[7] By the 1940s, the ever-shifting imperial ambition of the United States was not as overt as in the 1898 pivotal juncture. It is for this reason that to understand an empire in transition we need to focus before the period of military invasion but certainly after the events of the close of the nineteenth century.

As my contribution to this volume, I want to press the reader, and challenge those who so swiftly deny that the United States was ever an imperial player, to go beyond staid definitions of empire and seek the understated, and sometimes more lasting, forms of control and political domination, powerful forms that emerged after, or in place of, battleships, soldiers, and colonial administrators. For, as we learn, empire takes on many guises.

Empire and Scientific Discovery:

In this essay I want to first and rather briefly explore how individual scientists' memoirs reinterpreted the narrative of discovery as one that sanitized scientific discovery of local participation. Through depictions of Mexico as a "rough" and "backward" country where serious science could not take place, American and European chemists effectively removed themselves from their locality. Surrounding themselves with beakers, microscopes, and petri dishes they were able to keep a chaotic Mexico at bay while selectively using its natural resources and technicians to aid their discoveries. In effect, by demonstrating how to control molecules while also ingeniously teaching locals to mimic American technicians, foreign scientists, in their telling, transformed Mexico, at least the one contained within laboratory walls, into an awkward copy of Western laboratories. It is precisely in these tales of discovery that we also begin to acknowledge the repeated stories of dependence.

Edward Said warned that "the power to narrate, or to block other narratives from forming and emerging, is very important to culture and imperialism and constitutes one of the main connections between them."[8] So I argue that in the process of retelling their discoveries foreign scientists effectively, and possibly unconsciously, created a subclass of scientist, the Mexican chemist in laboratories run by Americans and Europeans. But, more tellingly, foreign scientists ignored and hence eliminated from historical memory the participation of another curious participant in the steroid race, Mexican peasants.

Second, I want to bring into the argument, as others have before me, the way in which by the mid-twentieth century science and technology would supplant military excursions and political saber rattling to become the proving ground for U.S. might.[9] These subtler and later forms of power were crucial in cementing the role of Americans as leaders in the sciences in the Americas, but its roots are, no doubt, in the quest for geopolitical expansion. But it is the power to narrate in order to retain premier discovery status that interests me in this short essay.

In the past century few scientific quests have involved such expectations as that for the mass production of cortisone. Carl Djerassi, the Austrian-born American chemist who joined Syntex in 1949, described the search for cortisone as a race in which "the new ways of producing cortisone come as the climax to an unrestrained, dramatic race involving a dozen of the largest American drug houses, several leading foreign pharmaceutical manufacturers, three governments, and more research personnel than have worked on any medical problem since penicillin."[10] Among those laboratories researching the problem was Syntex in Mexico. Recalling how he went to Mexico City, he wrote, "I arrived at Syntex in the late autumn of 1949, just around my twenty-sixth birthday. I have never regretted that decision, even though at that time my American colleagues considered me mad to move to a country that, although famous for mariachi music, bull fights, and pre-Columbian ruins, had only generated the barest of blips on the radar screen of international chemical journals."[11] Despite his colleagues' preconceptions, Mexico had five years earlier made a rather large international "blip" when the American chemist Russell Marker discovered that commercial quantities of progesterone could be derived from Mexican yams.[12] It was these same yams that would later be used for the synthetic production of cortisone and oral contraceptives.

It was in the late 1930s that Russell Marker, affiliated with Pennsylvania State University, grew convinced that Mexico's jungles contained dioscoreas, what are commonly referred to as yams, with enough diosgenin to synthetically produce progesterone. For that reason, in 1941 he traveled to Veracruz and with the help of local Mexicans did indeed find various yam specimens.[13] Returning to the United States, he proved that diosgenin derived from Mexican yams was the most inexpensive and effective starting material for synthetic hormone production. But Marker, even after demonstrating the process in Parke-Davis's Detroit laboratories, was greeted with the same skepticism that would follow Djerassi to Mexico years later.

Indeed, even by 1944, and despite Marker's remarkable production of more progesterone than had ever been synthesized before and the promise of enormous profits, Parke-Davis, Marker's financial backers, hesitated to fund continuing research in Mexico. For, as the president of Parke-Davis, Alexander W. Lescohier, insisted, Mexico was an inadequate place for sophisticated research let alone hormone production.[14] Instead, Lescohier countered that Parke-Davis would find it preferable to "get a thousand bulls if necessary and just collect the urine. But there's no use of thinking of going to Mexico City because it can't be done in the first place."[15]

Given that it was so difficult to derive cortisone it is quite surprising that scientists met any resistance at all. It was common to derive cortisone from material such as cattle bile and other organic matter, but it was extremely difficult to extract. In fact, Upjohn Pharmaceuticals experimented with the adrenal glands of 2.2 million hogs, but the price per gram produced was nearly eight hundred dollars.[16] The cost was high and the quantities too low to effectively treat the population of rheumatoid arthritis sufferers in the United States. Moreover, the invention of fermentation chemistry demonstrated that bacteria and molds were a cheaper and more efficient means of obtaining steroids. Despite proof of it being a more versatile source of the purest forms of synthetic hormones, *barbasco*, as the yam was called locally, would have to wait until it was sanitized of its jungle status.

Some perceived obstacles to working in Mexico on such a "precarious adventure" according to sources of the time were that the "Mexican pharmaceutical industry was virtually non-existent: there were no facilities for processing the black root, and what was more the *cabeza de negro* was hardly the most accessible of source material, for it grew in steamy hilly jungle [sic] where nobody in his senses ever went. And was Mexico politically stable? How could any large company setting up an establishment there be sure of the future?"[17]

The allusion to Mexico as a technologically backward nation whose citizens were ill-prepared to grasp the complexity of steroid chemistry would become a frequent theme and one of the reasons why Mexicans demanded the ouster of foreign laboratories in the 1970s. There were constant references in these earlier accounts to how foreign chemists, instead of working with "Ph.D. colleagues and well-educated technicians," had to manage a laboratory with "one college graduate and several charming, but giggly, *señorita*-assistants who had not finished high school."[18]

So how did some of the most significant chemical discoveries of the twentieth century emerge from a nation where serious science "could not be made"? Quite simply Djerassi and Rosenkranz had at their disposal more trained Mexican chemists than memoirs and history have acknowledged. While, in effect, there were relatively few trained organic chemists in Mexico, Syntex had a ready supply at the nearby Institute of Chemistry on the National Autonomous University campus. Among these was Luis Ernesto Miramontes who, together with Djerassi and Rosenkranz, holds the U.S. patent as the codiscoverer of the synthesis of oral contraceptives.

Indeed, it was Miramontes' lab notebook, which Djerassi quoted in Spanish in his autobiography, that contains the step-by-step account of the synthesis of the first active oral contraceptive.[19] In his recounting, Djerassi described, Miramontes as "a young Mexican chemist doing his undergraduate bachelor's thesis work at Syntex under my tutelage,"[20] and, while Miramontes acknowledged working with Djerassi at Syntex, he denied that Djerassi had any advisory capacity, which is how his collaboration has most often been described.[21] Relegating Miramontes' participation to the role of an undergraduate assistant, despite his claims to the contrary, as well as Djerassi's famous use of Miramontes' notebook as evidence of the former's participation, was consistent with the depiction of Mexicans as unable to conduct any experimental chemistry on their own. Miramontes, however, has a different version.

In his telling, Miramontes explains how he was approached by researchers at Syntex Laboratories because of his proven experience and ability to derive and isolate compounds, a prized talent in any laboratory. Miramontes was reportedly working on what he believed to be the synthesis of chemicals needed to prevent natural abortions. The chemicals he isolated, however, would become the foundation of the contraceptive pill. During a 2004 interview, Miramontes also volunteered that, despite having contributed to the discovery, he did not find out what he had contributed to until he read about it in chemical journals months after his participation.[22] Although he was excluded from future narratives, Miramontes' presence points to an obvious fact: there were students completing masters- and doctoral-level work in Mexico while Syntex was searching for viable ways to extract cortisone from Mexican yams. While this may seem an absurd fact to point out, its omission is an essential clue for understanding how Mexico today is seldom associated with the commercial production of steroid hormones.

Despite their various contributions, when Mexicans in the laboratory were portrayed it was often with a wink of the eye, as in a photo caption that describes the activities inside of Syntex, Mexico City. The photo shows two females, dressed in white uniforms, looking through microscopes while below their platform another team of identically dressed women work with beakers as nearby men unload cartloads of wild yams. To add to the implausibility of the picture the caption states, "The main Syntex plant is a former gun powder mill built upon the remains of a seventeenth-century castle. Girl operators here synthesize male hormones on the lower level, female hormones on the upper."[23] To reinforce the quaintness of this Mexico-based steroid research a second picture shows a makeshift table, teeming with bubbling beakers, on a terrace overlooking the countryside. As the captions explains, "When weather permits, which is most of the time, odorous reactions can be done outside. While few of the operators have high-school diplomas, Syntex has trained them to equal U.S.-chemical plant technicians."[24]

So, while magazines such as *Fortune* and *Life* were quick to mention the exotic nature of what was termed "jungle-root chemistry," they also showcased how adaptable science could be when comingled in a Mexican setting. For the contrasts were surely plenty. Whereas the pristine laboratories of American universities served as models for foreigners working in Mexico, scientists in the land of the Aztecs had to adjust their expectations to meet the rigors of working at a different altitude and in a "tropical" setting. But they did manage with, as Djerassi explained, "the type of high-altitude chemical cookery that most gringos working in the fancy sea-level laboratories of Harvard or Merck never even had to consider."[25] Indeed, the cunning scientist was able to triumph in Mexico for by 1959 "no laboratory in the world—academic or industrial" had published as much as Syntex in the field of steroid research.[26] As Djerassi succinctly added, "Chemistry south of the Rio Grande had finally made the grade."[27]

Representations of Mexico as a place where science could barely be conducted while scientists, who encountered more than the usual obstacles, nonetheless triumphed reinforced the idea of the intrepid westerner who, undaunted by baffling surroundings, managed to dominate in the name of progress. In attempting to control the reaction of molecules, scientists working in Mexico were unwittingly bound to the reactions of local people to their presence. For, as foreign scientists would discover, Mexico had more than good music, sweaty bulls, and competent technicians; it also had Mexicans willing to go into the jungles to dig up wild yams. We now turn from Mexico City laboratories to the crucial element rarely mentioned in scientific research, Mexican peasants.

Role of Mexican Peasants

As the search for a plentiful and ready supply of synthetic hormones continued, astounded scientific journals reported that until then insignificant Syntex in Mexico had beat out the larger and better financed research teams. *Harper's* said it best when it reported, "The cortisone production problem was solved ... [and] it should be noted that the leader in the race was a chemical manufacturer in presumably backward Mexico."[28] In the early 1950s, as more researchers began to experiment with various synthetic alternatives, the product derived from Mexican yams continued to be the purest form available. American chemists found the Syntex product between four and eight times more effective than natural progesterone when taken orally.[29] Articles in popular magazines such as *Time*, *Newsweek*, *Harper's*, and *Fortune* encouraged American readers to marvel at what had been discovered south of the border.

At the height of the steroid hormone trade more than ten tons of wild yams were removed from the jungles of Oaxaca, Veracruz, and Chiapas on a *weekly* basis. In the jungles these yams were dug up, fermented, dried, chopped, and packaged by Mexicans before arriving, as fine powder, at dozens of transnational laboratories throughout Mexico. Although other scholars have explored the intricate and often contentious relationship that developed between Syntex Laboratories and the Mexican state over control of the yam trade or examined the lives of the chemists based in Mexico City, they have rarely focused on a basic question: how did so many yams make it out of the jungles and into the hands of laboratory scientists?[30]

Between 1949 and 1975, nearly one hundred thousand Mexican families extracted *barbasco* from southeastern jungles and delivered it to collection sites that would then ship it to foreign-owned laboratories based in Mexico. Without their participation yams would never have been available for experimentation.

When, in 1975, the story was told of how foreign laboratories benefited from using Mexican yams, the rhetoric of empire was conveniently seized by a populist government. Peasant leaders, representing the interests of "all Mexicans," appropriated the nationalization of the steroid hormone industry as their own because "a Mexican product such as barbasco must benefit the Mexican peasantry."[31] For some Mexicans, chemical discoveries had become a tool of empire. As a letter to President Luis Echeverría urged, "May we fight together so that transnational companies in Mexico, which exploit not only our products but also our chemists and ourselves, be nationalized. So that we, as Mexicans, can fix the price for pharmaceutical products extracted from barbasco and not the transnational laboratories that have lived off our resources and our sweat, creating a vast capital that rightly belongs to us."[32]

As the above quote shows, by mid-twentieth century in southeastern Mexico it was not nations that were redefining political boundaries, extracting resources, and creating new colonial spaces. In this case it was transnational laboratories that had become the handmaidens of empire. Moreover, a control of the narrative of discovery was the crucial justificatory tool because, it was argued, locals simply could not understand something as complex as chemistry. But the accounts of intrepid foreign researchers were contested by unlikely participants, Mexican peasants, who understood chemistry not as something to be performed by outsiders but as a transformative tool capable of eroding rigid rural social hierarchies.

Ultimately, what these peasants wanted was that the price of fresh *barbasco* be increased to a subsistence level. However, they first listed the needs of chemists, other Mexicans, and the nation as a whole to underscore the fact that in controlling the steroid trade foreigners had stripped Mexico of any public recognition and hence in the process also divested it of any profit. While the peasants' project would ultimately fail, for a few years Mexican peasants seized control of foreign chemical laboratories and made the search for steroid hormones something uniquely Mexican and no longer an erstwhile American endeavor.

Concluding Thoughts

Histories of scientific discovery often center on the role of the scientist as the principal actor in a narrative of persistence, intuition, and cunning. When discoveries entail foreigners in "strange lands," the participation of locals is often excluded, as in the case of Mexican peasants, or downplayed, as in the case of Luis Miramontes, to the benefit of non-nationals. While the role of Mexicans was erased from the narrative of 1940s and 1950s steroid discoveries, by the 1970s Mexican peasants were freely and desperately associating themselves with erstwhile discoveries with the hope of retaining what had become an anachronistic peasant way of life. The wild yam, *barbasco*, brought together the worlds of science, politics, and modern and rural Mexico in a complex relationship that questioned the nature and definition of chemistry, traditional medicine, health, and Mexican peasants. What we find is that some peasants embraced steroid hormone production and chemical terms as a way to retain an endangered way of life. In so doing Mexican peasants openly contested the presence of transnational pharmaceutical laboratories and their power to control a domestic natural resource. While foreign chemists had dominated the narratives in the previous decades it was rural Mexicans who decades later called attention to the importance of domestic chemists and Mexican science. In bringing Mexicans into the narrative of scientific discovery one challenges traditional versions that seem to insist that science could be imported but not produced in places such as Mexico. By shifting the focus from scientists to rural Mexicans we can begin to understand how the changing face of empire was being perceived. It was American pharmaceutical companies and not invading American armies that, in the eyes of many Mexicans, posed a threat to sovereignty over their natural resources.

Tropical Conquest and the Rise of the Environmental Management State

The Case of U.S. Sanitary Efforts in Panama

PAUL S. SUTTER

IN THE DECADE OR SO AFTER THEIR COMPLETION of the Panama Canal in 1914, Americans were triumphant. They had successfully built one of the greatest engineering projects of the era, and they claimed that, through intelligent administration, they had brought order and modernity to a storied strip of postcolonial Spanish America. Moreover, and perhaps most strikingly, Americans consistently celebrated their apparent conquest of tropical nature on the isthmus, insisting that they had transformed one of the world's most debilitating and pestilential places into a veritable health resort for white outsiders. As a 1920s cruise line brochure proclaimed of the Americanized Canal Zone, "The quarters, the hospital, the docks, are all a triumphant gesture of American disdain for the tropics, the jungle, the slackness and demoralization of life near the equator. Here the humblest American will feel some of that imperial pride aroused in the citizen of ancient Rome or of modern Britain by the sight of his race carrying light to the dark places of the world."[1] This landscape of tropical conquest—what another brochure aptly referred to as "Uncle Sam's New Ten Mile Strip of Empire"—was the result of a massive and unprecedented intervention by the American imperial state.[2]

Built by the United States between 1904 and 1914 in the wake of a failed French effort two decades earlier, the Panama Canal was the largest and, at $352 million, most expensive public works project that the nation—and perhaps the world—had yet known. That it occurred beyond the borders of the United States is striking; as an external improvement, it symbolized both the growing geopolitical importance of rapid transit between the Atlantic and Pacific Oceans, a naval necessity made clear during the Spanish-American War, and the rising commercial involvement of U.S. corporate interests in Latin American and Asian Pacific agricultural and resource sectors. Canal construction also necessitated the creation of a new administrative arm of the government, the Isthmian Canal Commission (ICC), which in turn employed, housed, fed, and managed the lives of tens of thousands of workers, mostly black West Indians, during the decade of construction. All of this came in the service of building a fifty-mile-long lock canal that many lauded as an engineering masterpiece. Americans particularly celebrated the massive concrete locks that stepped ships up almost a hundred feet to the artificial Lake Gatún, which itself was created by a huge dam built to control the unruly Chagres River. Witnesses also marveled at the gargantuan Culebra Cut through the isthmian hills—the Bucyrus steam shovels that ate away at the hillsides, the intricate rail system that removed the spoil from the cut, and the Lilliputian workers who toiled amid all these modern machines. Americans excavated and moved more than 230 million cubic yards of rock and dirt to complete the canal or roughly four times the excavation required in constructing the Suez Canal. Official hospital records put the employee death toll at 5,609 (only 350 of whom were white Americans) with disease and industrial accidents as the major causes.[3] The Panama Canal, a federal mobilization of personnel, technology, and resources comparable only to war, was a signature achievement of U.S. state-sponsored imperial engineering.

But beyond the heroic engineering achievements that came to define the Panama Canal, its history suggests that one big job of the American imperial state has been to manage nature. Environmental management was at the heart of Americans' sense of accomplishment and imperial pride in Panama, a sense visible in the tourist literature of the postconstruction era. There were, moreover, strong parallels and connections between the history of the American West and Panama in terms of the rise of the American imperial state, and seeing these allows us to rethink environmental management programs as they emerged at the federal level.

Empire as Tourism

American tourists who cruised through the Panama Canal after World War I encountered a new "tropics." From the Gold Rush through the turn of the last century, Americans had represented Panama as a dangerous tropical place, exotic not only in social, racial, and civilizational terms but also because of its natural setting and the suite of tropical diseases—malaria and yellow fever in particular—that seemed to emanate from it. And Americans were not alone in their tropical thinking. By 1900, the tropics had become a global and imperial environmental problem of the first order, and imperial administrators often couched their public health efforts in terms of solving this geographical and environmental riddle.[4] But the successful completion of the Panama Canal—and the environmental management practices that had controlled tropical diseases there—helped to alter American attitudes about the promise and perils of tropical nature. One place to see this shift is cruise line brochures, which increasingly portrayed the tropics as romantic and defanged. Whereas before the completion of the canal Panama's tropical atmosphere had seemed filled with emanations that threatened white bodies and constitutions, these brochures insisted they were filled only with the exotic perfumes of tropical flowers and fruits. A cruise to Panama and through the canal thus offered a trip to the newly tamed tropics.

But it was not only that. To see the Panama Canal Zone, these brochures also insisted, was to see a part of the United States itself. "For Americans who like to take their country with them and whose favorite emotion is a swelling of the breast with patriotic pride," another brochure suggested, "Panama is equally satisfying."[5]

What did it mean for American tourists to take home with them impressions of the Panama Canal Zone as a slice not merely of a new American empire in the tropics but of a new America itself? The first lesson came in the area of "intelligent administration." New, modern, clean, planned, and manicured American settlements stood in sharp contrast not only to the unruly jungles that fringed them but also the dense and chaotic "native" cities that were their neighbors. "Here is no clean-cut racial line, but rather an almost unimaginable conglomeration of racial types," William McFee observed of Colón in a tourist booklet for the United Fruit Company steamship line. "It is as though a tide of heterogeneous humanity had surged up against the immense white concrete walls of the Canal Zone and had been flung back upon itself in a burst of chaotic color and movement."[6] The cruise companies sold the Canal Zone to affluent white tourists as a physical manifestation of everything that separated temperate America from the tropics, a separation that was social as well as environmental. At a time when American cities themselves were teeming with racial and ethnic others, the Panama Canal Zone suggested to American tourists an intriguing model for spatial segregation. As a national enclave in the tropics, the Canal Zone foreshadowed not only future American military enclaves in the developing world but also a new suburban form: the exclusive gated suburb or resort community, particularly those that came to mark the "semitropical" regions of America. An immense white wall indeed![7]

The cruise brochures also celebrated American engineering expertise and its role in the conquest of geographical disadvantage: Americans created at Panama a second nature to replace the first one that had denied them access to the West, the Pacific, and the markets of Asia. If technology was a marker of civilizational superiority for Western imperial nations, it was in Panama more than anywhere else in the early twentieth century that American heroic engineering made such civilizational claims.[8] To pass through the Canal Zone, then, was to be impressed not merely with American enterprise but with the American imperial state itself. In the decades that followed, not only would the state be a crucial wedge in opening the developing world to American enterprise, and in protecting that enterprise, but it would also muster engineering expertise to handle a set of environmental and public health challenges closer to home. The Panama Canal Zone was a model in both arenas.

Westward Bound

Many American tourists visiting the canal headed south and through Panama on their way west, continuing a decades-old pattern that offers another set of lessons about environmental management and the American imperial state. During the early years of the Gold Rush, the Panama route was the quickest route west (though also the most expensive), and tens of thousands of emigrants thus traveled through the American tropics to get to California. Indeed, the cruise industry had its origins in the initiation of federal mail service with the West Coast in 1848, which involved contracting with steamship lines to take mail to and across the isthmus. From late 1848 into the 1850s, those lines also enjoyed huge demand among Gold Rush migrants. Panama was also the site of the first American transcontinental railroad, completed in 1855 by an American company. Between 1848 and 1869, the Isthmus of Panama was a vibrant, Americanized crossroads with a boomtown mentality quite like those of other frontier gateway settlements.[9] And after 1869, when a better-known transcontinental railroad's completion diverted trans-isthmian traffic to the north, American designs on a canal meant a flurry of federal expeditions to Panama and Central America—seven alone during the Grant administration—with the attendant scientific and visual work that accompanied such state-sponsored expeditions. During the late nineteenth century the Isthmus of Panama was a territory of westward expansion.

This relationship between late-nineteenth-century Panama and the American West suggests a number of important points. First, it points not only to the continuities but also to the strong links between westward expansion and extracontinental imperialism. In this case, extracontinental expansion served rather than followed westward expansion and vice versa. Second, just as the West was an important "kindergarten of the American state," so the Canal Zone during the construction period allowed the American state to act and extend its powers unfettered by the competition and limitations of state and local politics. Over the course of the nineteenth century, much of what the American state did was to oversee territorial expansion through the Land Office, the Geological Survey, the Bureau of Indian Affairs, and even the U.S. Army. It was in the West that the federal government grew stronger, often by exercising environmental management powers. Indeed, between the creation of Yellowstone National Park in 1872 and the Taylor Grazing Act of 1934, the federal government created a public landscape and a set of conservation bureaucracies—the U.S. Forest Service, the Bureau of Reclamation, the National Park Service, and the Grazing Service (later the Bureau of Land Management)—that constituted the core of the modern environmental management state. To a great extent, this set of state capacities was forged in the crucible of American expansion.[10] As the United States entered Panama in the early 1900s, there were few places where state capacity was expanding more quickly than in the area of environmental management.

Implicit in my invocation of an environmental management state is a rejection of the exceptionalism that has shaped traditional understandings of the rise of conservation in the United States. One of the most striking lessons of the rise of the American environmental management state is just how much it was influenced by international and imperial examples. The founding figure in American conservation, George Perkins Marsh, was a diplomat and thorough internationalist who learned conservation by observing Old World examples of environmental degradation. Gifford Pinchot, the founder of professional forestry in America, trained in continental forestry methods with European foresters who had cut their teeth in imperial settings. Elwood Mead, a pioneering irrigationist, worked across the Pacific transferring water management expertise between Australia and the western United States. And Hugh Hammond Bennett brought to his tenure as the head of the Soil Conservation Service substantial experience in Latin America. Moreover, a focus on environmental management rather than conservation also allows us to see a new group of state actors—plant explorers such as David Fairchild and entomologists such as L. O. Howard—as both critical to the rise of the environmental management state and decidedly international in their outlooks. Scholars of American conservation have begun to paint a picture of that movement that is both transnational and transimperial, one that challenges exceptionalist invocations of America as "nature's nation."[11] The state-sponsored effort to control the tropics in Panama was but a variation on this theme.

Disease and Tropical Conquest

What, specifically, constituted the American sense of its conquest of nature in Panama? In the grandest sense, what Americans claimed to have conquered in Panama was geography itself. That task was made difficult by the environmental conditions on the isthmus, which Americans often described in hyperbolic terms—the stifling heat and humidity, the incessant and powerful rains, the dense and predatory jungle, and the full array of animal life that threatened comfort and safety. On top of these climatic and environmental threats to the success of the project, there were so-called tropical diseases. The United States entered Panama at a critical moment of change in scientific understandings of these diseases, with mosquito vectors replacing older miasmatic explanations of their origins. Miasmatic thinking had linked these diseases to particular medical geographies, places that allegedly produced unhealthy or poisonous emanations; it

Uncle Sam tells President Theodore Roosevelt that "The First Mountain to Be Removed" in the Panama Canal Zone should be the dreaded "Yellow Jack," or yellow fever. *Harper's Weekly,* July 22, 1905. (Wisconsin State Historical Society)

was a mode of thinking that meshed well with other environmental indictments of the tropics. Vector theory changed that thinking in important ways, but it reinforced it in others. Indeed, to the extent that tropical diseases were vector diseases—and the emerging discipline of tropical medicine focused strongly on them—environmental management remained critical to combating them, this at a time when the American medical profession, transformed by the germ theory, was focusing less on environmental management and more on discrete disease agents and human bodies. In all of these ways—in overcoming geographical obstacles, combating a hostile climate and biota, and managing disease—Americans couched their efforts in Panama as a conquest of nature, and they built state capacity to achieve that conquest.

To manage tropical nature in the name of public health required experts, and concerns about the tropics contributed to the construction of new sorts of expertise. One of the most intriguing groups of experts deployed to Panama was entomologists. The discovery that mosquitoes transmitted both malaria and yellow fever led Americans to focus their efforts on mosquito control in Panama. In choosing mosquito control as their primary public health strategy, Americans not only built on the success of William Gorgas's sanitary campaign in Havana in the wake of the Spanish-America War, but they also followed the lead of several imperial public health examples—most notably Ronald Ross's malaria work in India and Africa and Malcolm Watson's work in British Malaya.[12] But the focus on mosquito control also revealed a scientific blind spot that needed quick redress: mosquitoes remained a fauna incognita among Western scientists. As a result, targeted attacks on their breeding and adult habitats were difficult to plan. And so sanitary officials turned to entomologists to figure out which species were spreading these diseases, where and how they bred and lived, and how they might be controlled effectively and efficiently.

By serving post–Civil War American agricultural expansion, entomologists had assumed a central place within both the American scientific community and the growing federal agricultural bureaucracy. In the late nineteenth century, a series of high-profile insect threats to farms and forests prompted a significant rise in federal sponsorship of applied or "economic" entomology as the migratory nature of these pest species encouraged national and even international approaches to their control. L. O. Howard was entomology's chief institution builder and champion of its applied value during this period, and he insisted that an intricate knowledge of insect ecology was crucial to controlling vector and pest species. By the early twentieth century, then, American entomologists, no strangers to serving as careful ecological observers of and problem solvers within a colonizing mission, were well prepared to bring their ecological approach to another round of American expansion. Entomologists were, in other words, at the vanguard of the environmental management state.[13]

Entomologists entered Panama not so much as the primary proponents of mosquito control but as experts who promised to refine existing efforts and make them more efficient—primarily by cataloguing mosquito fauna, determining which species transmitted tropical fevers, and then figuring out the breeding and feeding habits of vector mosquitoes. In the case of yellow fever, the Reed Commission's work in Havana, and the work of Cuban physician Carlos Finlay before it, suggested that just a single species—*Aedes aegypti*—was responsible for transmission. *A. aegypti* is a peridomestic species that lived in and around human habitations and bred almost exclusively in artificial containers, and those habits thus made it easy to control. With this knowledge in hand, Americans not only isolated yellow fever sufferers in screened hospital wards, but they set about overhauling urban water supplies in Panama. They screened water barrels or covered their surfaces with a thin sheen of oil, which asphyxiated larvae. They policed communities to make sure that gutters, planters, and other artificial containers did not harbor *A. aegypti* larvae. And they began constructing modern plumbing systems, which had the effect of eliminating many of *A. aegypti*'s favored breeding sites. As a result of this targeted effort to limit *A. aegypti* breeding, yellow fever ceased to be a problem in Panama within a couple of years. Malaria was a different story. The species responsible for malaria transmission come from the genus *Anopheles,* and their ecology is complex and varied. After a series of field studies and experiments, entomologists and sanitarians determined that *Anopheles albimanus* was the prime culprit in spreading malaria in Panama and that it showed a decided preference for breeding in the numerous sources of standing water that resulted from the environmental disturbances rife throughout the Canal Zone. To control this particular vector, then, involved draining wet areas, oiling standing water, clearing brush around work sites and settlements that might harbor adult mosquitoes, screening worker housing, and constantly monitoring landscape changes and the creation of new *A. albimanus* breeding places.

While many American observers hailed mosquito control as a core success in the American conquest of tropical nature, the work of mosquito control experts revealed a picture somewhat at odds with the rhetoric of conquest. As in the American West, and other imperial settings worldwide, these expert environmental managers were not mere facilitators of conquest; they also could be critical observers of and commentators on the environmental implications and mechanics of conquest. How, then, does this position them as agents of empire? As state scientists who enabled an imperial mission, they support arguments made by scholars who have suggested how critical science has been to framing imperial problems and providing the techniques to solve them. But entomological workers were also careful observers of the natural world. They were not mere captives of a discourse on the tropics that made its conquest the centerpiece of the American mission. Instead, they often recognized the ways in which environmental processes in Panama did not always match American rhetoric. Indeed, their most basic conclusion implicitly challenged those who celebrated the American disdain for the tropics; the vectors for both malaria and yellow fever, they argued, were less the result of tropical nature per se than the result of the environmental transformations wrought by the massive canal-building enterprise. While many naturalized mosquito breeding as tropical, entomologists and mosquito control workers knew full well that their sanitary efforts were largely focused on mitigating environmental conditions produced by the activities of the American imperial state.[14]

Focusing on state environmental managers working on the ground in imperial contexts raises some critical questions about how they functioned as imperial actors. In the case of disease control in Panama, environmental managers were critical to Americans' success in making the Canal Zone a healthier place, particularly for whites. To a large degree, then, they support arguments that see state science as an enabler of imperial state expansion. But this case also suggests that scientists could become sources of tension, or even dissent, within the state apparatus, a theme that has emerged as an important one in the history of twentieth-century environmental politics in the United States. Indeed, state scientists would be critical actors in the rise of environmentalism as a social movement in the United States and its confrontations with the environmental management state. In some cases, state scientists themselves were forces for change. In others, activists used the expertise generated by the state to challenge the traditional prerogatives of environmental management agencies such as the Forest Service, the Bureau of Reclamation, and the Department of Agriculture. The generation of environmental expertise within the state could cut several ways.

Entomological workers in Panama never mounted a full-scale challenge to the American discourse on tropical conquest, and so in a narrow sense they might be seen mostly as enablers of U.S. imperial control. But they did contribute to a growing scientific interest in, and then concern about, tropical ecology, interest and concern that were soon lodged in the state—in this case, in the founding in 1923 of what would become the Smithsonian Tropical Research Institute (STRI), a federal research agency that is now one of the premier institutions of tropical ecological research in the world and has its home in the former Canal Zone. A federal commitment to sponsoring tropical ecological research would be a lasting legacy of the American efforts in Panama.[15]

Conclusion

How does my focus on the environmental management state and its public health intervention in Panama address larger questions about the character of American empire in the making? Let me make or reiterate several key points. First, my expansive definition of environmental management facilitates a set of clear connections between American continental colonization, its extracontinental imperial endeavors, and the rise of the American state. My arguments for connections between the conquest of tropical nature and the rise of the environmental management state are still more suggestive than conclusive, but they hint at how much a part of a broader environmental management impulse the Panama Canal project was.

While I have not made this a focus of this particular essay, I think it is important to note just how much the public health effort that began in the Canal Zone reverberated throughout the United States in terms of state public health policy and capacities. Malaria and yellow fever control methods first worked out in Havana and then Panama were imported back into the United States in the early twentieth century, and they modeled an increasingly federalized effort to manage not only these diseases but broader public health threats. To cite only one example, the Centers for Disease Control grew directly out of efforts to protect military installations in the American South from malaria, an effort that traced a direct path back to disease control in Panama.[16]

Moreover, sanitary efforts in Panama provided models for a series of public health efforts that worked outside of the American imperial state but made strong use of the expertise it generated. The Rockefeller Foundation, for instance, became deeply involved in sanitary efforts to rid South American port cities of yellow fever. And the United Fruit Company made extensive use of mosquito control techniques first developed in Panama to control malaria on its plantation lands. Indeed, the company hired former ICC sanitary personnel, including William Deeks, who directed its Sanitary Department for years after the canal was completed. These examples, while they do not directly speak to the strengthening of the American imperial state, do suggest that we need to pay attention to the porosity of state-society boundaries, particularly at a moment when some of the most far-reaching U.S. interventions in the developing world are coming at the hands of increasingly powerful corporations, foundations, and other nongovernmental organizations.

The capacities of the American imperial state would ebb and flow over the course of the twentieth century, and when they ebbed expertise often migrated to places outside the state. Indeed, one of the challenges of charting more fully the history of the imperial state will be tracing the extragovernmental capacities and alliances that were part and parcel of U.S. expansion. In the case of the rise of the environmental management state, those capacities often bled into developmentalist interventions after World War II, which, while they had lost some of their imperialist taint, still retained many of the biases of expert-driven environmental management.

PART 6

Polity, Law, and Constitution

William H. Taft on water buffalo, Philippine Islands, circa 1901. (Wm. C. Brown Collection, U.S. Military History Institute)

INTRODUCTION

JOHN OHNESORGE

THE MAINSTREAM OF AMERICAN LEGAL ACADEME has traditionally concerned itself with the study of legal doctrine—the parsing of cases, statutes, and constitutions—and with making normative arguments based more on moral philosophy than social scientific evidence. Since the age of Weber and Durkheim there have been scholars who approached law sociologically, studying how law and legal institutions actually interact with other aspects of society, but such external approaches long remained on the fringes of the legal academy. Since the 1970s, however, the "law and society" movement has become a major force in the American legal academy. Law and society is a highly eclectic movement, but at its core is a commitment to the idea that the law "on the books" and the law "in action" are two very different animals and worrying about the former without paying serious attention to the latter is to miss the real story.

In some parallels with the essays in this volume, many of the scholars who founded the law and society movement were also involved in the efforts of the 1960s to foster "modern" legal systems in poor countries around the world. While this could be just a coincidence, it seems unlikely. The experience of trying to fundamentally change third world societies by instituting top-down legal reforms, based at least on Western assumptions and often Western models as well, opened an intellectual Pandora's box. Participants in those "law and development" efforts realized that societies often do not react to changes in the formal law in predictable ways because law is just one part of any society's normative structure and not necessarily the most important part. If social engineering through top-down legal reform did not work in the third world, then it could no longer be assumed to work at home. Attempting to export Western law and legal ideals also forced Western scholars to ask whether what they were exporting represented some sort of universal good or whether they were exporting a particular combination of institutions and ideology that could be a force for ill in another society even if it were a force for good at home. Finally, their efforts forced them to consider whether what they were exporting was even a true picture of law in their own societies or whether they were propagating a myth of unity, coherence, and goodness that in fact did not exist at home. In short, confronting the complexities of implementing radical law reforms abroad helped trigger a major reevaluation at home.

The essays that follow present a set of powerful reminders that "law and development" as practiced in the 1960s was not the first time that the United States tried to use law to remake foreign societies and that the practical as well as moral problems entailed in such efforts likewise were not new. Legal technical assistance to poor but sovereign nations is not the same as colonial imposition, yet it is not entirely different, either. And as today's cadre of American lawyers travels to Iraq and Afghanistan to try to rebuild those devastated legal systems they are encountering the same basic set of issues, even if they do not realize it or wish to deny it. What the following essays also reveal, however, is why we may be wrong to expect today's law reformers to do much better than we have in the past. The essays remind us of how powerful the ideology of Western liberal legality really is to both the exporters and the importers. Western law can be a tool of oppression, but it carries with it a vocabulary and ideological apparatus with which to formulate claims for individual freedom and dignity that make it highly seductive.

For example, when Vicente L. Rafael connects authoritarianism in the Philippines to imported Western religion and notions of sovereignty, the Western lawyer can argue that the rulers of non-Christian polities such as China were also above the law and that the Western legal tradition has gone farther than others in thinking through how law might actually constrain political power. Anna Leah Fidelis T. Castañeda also demonstrates the power of Western legal ideology when she shows that American constitutional theory was flexible enough to justify Philippine court decisions that in fact diverged substantially from U.S. practice but that the imported American constitutional tradition also seemed to seriously constrain the imaginations of Filipinos when they came to draft their own constitution. In hindsight it should not be surprising that people in subjugated societies influenced the ways in which imported law and legal institutions functioned.

The essays that follow also prompt reflection on the individual lawyers involved in the spread of legal institutions whether through overt imposition or less violent means. The Puerto Rican lawyer and diplomat Federico Degetau y González and the Filipino lawyer and nationalist leader Apolinario Mabini, described by Christina Duffy Burnett and Vicente L. Rafael, respectively, display the lawyer's classic nonradical optimism as they seek positive results for their societies within the imposed framework of law and legal argument. These essays also put on display the lawyers on the other side of the exchange, such as those discussed in the essay by Owen J. Lynch, who leave us wondering whether they are actually convinced by the Byzantine arguments they weave to justify exercises of raw political power.

Finally, the story of law in America's earlier imperial adventures cries out for comparative analysis both among imperialists, England, France, Holland, or Japan versus Spain and America, for example, and longitudinally, Iraq and Afghanistan being the prime examples. Rafael's indictment of Spain in the Philippines again prompts one to ask whether former colonies of other imperial powers fared any better in their efforts to subject power to law following independence, and the same is true of Paul D. Hutchcroft's concerns over exports based on Jeffersonian biases favoring decentralization, as former colonies that suffered under centralized colonial regimes, Taiwan and Korea in particular, have had their share of political hardships since decolonization.

In sum, the following essays provide a wonderfully rich lens though which to consider a story that is different each time it is told yet which remains uncomfortably the same. And, although it is possible to trace developments within legal scholarship to hard lessons learned in law reform adventures abroad, we must ask how much has really changed in the realm of politics and power.

Empire and the Transformation of Citizenship

CHRISTINA DUFFY BURNETT

ON JANUARY 4, 1904, THE U.S. SUPREME COURT handed down its decision in *Gonzales v. Williams*, a closely watched case that was widely expected to solve the puzzle of the citizenship status of the people of Puerto Rico and the Philippines—islands that had been annexed by the United States after the war with Spain in 1898.[1] The inhabitants of earlier territories had become U.S. citizens promptly following their annexation.[2] But in legislating for the former Spanish colonies Congress had simply declared Puerto Ricans "citizens of Porto Rico" and Filipinos "citizens of the Philippines" while remaining mum with respect to the question on everyone's mind: were these people now citizens of the United States?[3]

The *Gonzales* decision delivered a crushing blow to those who had pinned their hopes for an answer on the Supreme Court. The court held that the native inhabitants of the newly annexed territories were no longer "aliens" (i.e., citizens of a foreign country), but at the same time it declined to consider the question of whether they were U.S. citizens. The court's reluctance to address the issue squarely was widely understood to mean that the inhabitants of the new territories were neither citizens nor aliens but something in between. The cryptic *Gonzales* opinion offered little by way explanation of that "something in between," but eventually the ambiguous status of Puerto Ricans and Filipinos acquired a formal legal designation: they were noncitizen "nationals," members of the U.S. polity but only partial members, subject to U.S. sovereignty but denied citizenship.

The events culminating in the *Gonzales* decision mark a watershed moment in the legal history of American citizenship. Contrary to the language of the Fourteenth Amendment, which in 1868 declared that "all persons born or naturalized in the United States, and subject to the jurisdiction thereof, are citizens of the United States," the imperial policies developed in the wake of 1898 established that not all persons born within the internationally recognized boundaries of the United States and subject to its jurisdiction enjoyed the amendment's guarantee of birthright citizenship.[4] The guarantee did not apply to persons born in places that, though completely subject to U.S. sovereignty, were "not a part of the United States."[5] Such people—the colonial subjects of the United States—were merely "nationals," occupying the lower rung in a legal hierarchy of political membership crafted to meet the needs of empire.

This essay examines the origins, emergence, and significance of the legal category of the noncitizen national in American law. As I interpret them, the events culminating in the *Gonzales* case transformed the meaning of the Fourteenth Amendment, replacing its guarantee of birthright citizenship with a two-tiered legal framework consisting of full and partial membership in the American polity. Or, to put it another way, empire created the occasion for a reconceptualization of the law of American citizenship and the Supreme Court did its part in the *Gonzales* case.[6]

"Puerto Ricans Are Now Americans"

The summer before the decision in *Gonzales* came down, the chief of the Bureau of Insular Affairs at the War Department received a letter from Federico Degetau y González, who was then serving as Puerto Rico's first "resident commissioner," or nonvoting representative, in Washington.[7] Degetau wrote with a question concerning two government reports on Puerto Rico, the Caribbean island that had recently been added to the portfolio of U.S. overseas possessions.[8] The first of these reports identified the inhabitants of the island as "American citizens." But the second, issued by the War Department, described them ("by mistake," Degetau noted hopefully) as "in suspense." Degetau had recently heard a rumor that the director of the census considered the designation *American citizens* erroneous and for that reason had decided to replace it with a note concerning the suspended citizenship status of the people of the new territories; Degetau wrote to inquire about this decision. Although he phrased the letter as a polite request for further information, his characterization of the change in designation clearly reflected his views on the matter: Puerto Ricans were American citizens. (Weren't they?)

The citizenship status of his constituents was a strange issue for Degetau to have to spend his time on: how could they be anything other than U.S. citizens? Puerto Rico had been annexed by the United States in 1898 after Spain ceded sovereignty over the island at the end of the Spanish-American War, and Congress had established a civil government on the island in 1900 (as it had done for Western territories throughout the nineteenth century), the same year that Puerto Ricans had elected Degetau. Didn't all of this mean they had to be U.S. citizens?

And, anyway, were there any doubt, how hard could it be to resolve? Either they were citizens or they were not; it ought to be easy to get this right instead of having to resort to an inconclusive label such as "in suspense."

Yet matters were rather more complicated than Degetau's letter implied. Article IX of the treaty of peace that had ended the war with Spain (known as the Treaty of Paris) had not promised U.S. citizenship to the native-born inhabitants of these new territories. Rather, it provided only that "the civil rights and political status of the native inhabitants of the territories hereby ceded to the United States *shall be determined by Congress.*"[9] Two years later, the statute creating the island's civil government—known as the Foraker Act after its main sponsor, Senator Joseph Foraker—perpetuated the uncertainty; instead of bestowing U.S. citizenship on the inhabitants of Puerto Rico, as early drafts had done, the final version of the act described them as "citizens of Porto Rico."[10] No one knew quite what this phrase meant.

Degetau kept his eyes peeled for a test case, and a promising fact pattern soon materialized in the form of Isabel González, a twenty-year-old pregnant woman detained at Ellis Island on her arrival from Puerto Rico and excluded from admission on the ground that she was an alien immigrant likely to become a public charge.[11] González sued for habeas, arguing that as a native inhabitant of Puerto Rico she was not an alien immigrant and could not be denied entry. Her case drew Degetau's attention, along with that of Frederic R. Coudert Jr. of the prominent international law firm Coudert Brothers. Coudert had argued the first round of cases involving the new territories, collectively known as the insular cases, before the Supreme Court two years earlier.[12] These cases had established that the newly annexed territories were "domestic" territory but not "part of the United States," or, in the paradoxical shorthand that nicely encapsulated the so-called doctrine of territorial incorporation, they were "foreign to the United States in a domestic sense."[13] The doctrine of territorial incorporation had not, however, addressed the citizenship status of the inhabitants of what came to be known as the "unincorporated" territories. Hoping to have a role in resolving that matter as well, Coudert became involved in González's litigation, taking the lead in appealing the case to the Supreme Court after a federal circuit court in New York rejected her petition for habeas.[14] Coudert contended that González, along with all Puerto Ricans, was a U.S. citizen; Degetau contributed an amicus curiae brief to the effort.

The court took the case and held, in *Gonzales v. Williams,* that under the federal immigration laws then in force the native inhabitants of Puerto Rico could not be considered alien immigrants and therefore could not be denied entry into (other parts of) the United States.[15] (The Court did not say whether different immigration laws would yield a different result, thus leaving open the possibility that Congress could pass a new statute barring their entry.)[16] At the same time, the court expressly declined to consider the question of whether Puerto Ricans were citizens of the United States, thus leaving unsolved the puzzle of their citizenship status.[17]

Observers were baffled. The Foraker Act had been ambiguous enough, and now *Gonzales*, which had seemed destined to clarify things, had merely underscored the uncertainty.[18] Although the court had refused to be specific about what Puerto Ricans were, resolving only what they were *not*, it had gone at least so far as to assert that a "citizen of Porto Rico" was an "American." The upshot, then, was that a person could be "an American . . . and yet not a citizen of the United States."[19]

Exceptional Citizens

But the lawyers in the case had seen it coming. Indeed they had helped to pave the way for the ambiguous outcome by attempting to shape it according to their preferences. Coudert had argued that the court should consider adopting a new label to describe persons who were neither citizens nor aliens while Solicitor General Henry M. Hoyt had insisted that no matter what label applied to them the inhabitants of the territories could still be treated as aliens.

Coudert's main contention had been that González, along with all Puerto Ricans, was a U.S. citizen. But evidently sensing that the court would find this argument unpersuasive, Coudert had made an argument in the alternative: if the court were to conclude that Puerto Ricans were neither citizens nor aliens, it should coin a formal legal designation to capture their in-between status: *nationals*.[20] The term, he explained, was in use by European countries and had been accepted by international lawyers.[21] It simply meant the same thing as *subject*, but it was an improvement over that term because it had "a less arbitrary sound."[22]

In support of his proposal, Coudert drew the court's attention to the unresolved content of the category of citizenship itself. "To call [the Puerto Rican] a citizen when we are in hopeless disagreement as to the meaning of that term will only result in creating added confusion," he observed, adding that the rights of U.S. citizens "are almost impossible of definition."[23] A review of the constitutional text itself proved him right; as he pointed out, the document confers precious few positive rights upon *citizens* in particular as opposed to *persons* in general. Indeed, the "only positive right conferred by the Constitution upon a citizen as such seems to be the right to sue in a Federal Court," he noted.[24] Beyond that, one could comb the text of the Constitution in vain in search of the rights of citizenship per se.

In the ambiguity of the concept of citizenship, Coudert saw an opportunity. The lack of a clear definition, he argued, left room for "various gradations or subdivisions of subjection."[25] Although the Founders believed that citizenship and subjecthood were identical, Coudert continued (echoing what was then a familiar assertion that a citizen was simply the subject of a republic), there were examples of such gradation or subjection in U.S. practice.[26] Drawing his examples from Supreme Court cases, Coudert pointed to the notorious *Dred Scott* case (1857), which had held that blacks, even when free, were not citizens of the United States (a holding overruled by the Fourteenth Amendment), and *Elk v. Wilkins* (1884), which had held that, even after the Fourteenth Amendment, Native Americans could not become U.S. citizens by voluntarily separating from their tribes and taking up "residence among the white citizens of a State" but only by a congressional act of naturalization (until the Indian Citizenship Act of 1924 made the issue moot by conferring citizenship on all Native Americans).[27] Of course, Coudert quickly added, one would not want to revive either of these ignominious precedents.[28] But that was precisely what was attractive about the category of the national: it was a term free (in Coudert's opinion) of all that historical baggage.

Arguing for the United States, Solicitor General Hoyt similarly discovered a just in time antipathy for the strictures of legal language—and then used it to challenge the utility of the category of the national itself. "This is an inquiry in which uncompromising insistence on mere words must be avoided," Hoyt explained. "[T]hese logical categories are neither mutually exclusive nor completely comprehensive.... All these words are *inter se* synonymous, correlative, or antithetic, but not completely so. The meanings are relative rather than absolute; they shade off into each other, and the outlines of the delimitation are not sharp, but hazy."[29] Moreover, Coudert's proposal for the adoption of the term *national* was simply "a matter of terminology, of the conventional and convenient uses of language, and the growing use of the noun *national* does not throw any light upon our investigation."[30] This was a nuanced and subtle view of the indeterminacy and porousness of legal language and also, conveniently, a view that would permit the federal government to draw the boundaries around citizenship wherever it wanted.[31]

As we have seen, Coudert had defended the term *national* on the ground that it had a "less arbitrary sound" than *subject*. Hoyt, too, carefully navigated his way around that controversial word: subjects had no place in a republic. Instead, the term *citizen* "denotes a member of republic." Meanwhile *nationals* "signifies all persons who belong to, who constitute objects of, any particular government, whether they are citizens, subjects, or in some intermediate category."[32] But the term *national*, Hoyt insisted, was not a panacea, for even if the people of the new territories had become American nationals they could still be treated as aliens.[33] This, of course, was the point of insisting, as Hoyt had done, that the terms at stake in the debate were "relative rather than absolute" and "not sharp, but hazy." They could mean whatever the court wanted them to mean.

Degetau, in his amicus brief, subjected to scrutiny yet another term that had turned out to have implications for membership in the polity, but one his colleagues had left unexamined: *natives*. As noted above, the Treaty of Paris provided that "the civil rights and political status of the *native* inhabitants of the territories hereby ceded to the United States shall be determined by Congress."[34] Relying on that language, the other lawyers and the lower court had asked whether the "native inhabitants" of Puerto Rico had become U.S. citizens when the island was annexed. But, reminding the court that the Foraker Act described them as "citizens of Porto Rico," Degetau argued that the question was not whether a "*native* of Porto Rico" was a U.S. citizen but rather whether "a *citizen* of Porto Rico is a citizen of the United States."[35] And the answer to that question, Degetau insisted, was yes.

In the process of challenging the relevance of the word *natives* to the inquiry, Degetau laid bare the prejudices toward the inhabitants of the new territories that had informed the decision to deny them citizenship—prejudices concerning their level of "civilization" and capacity for self-government.[36] Degetau tackled this issue by turning the court's attention to the sensitive topic of precisely what lay behind the distinction in the Treaty of Paris between "natives of the Peninsula" (persons born in mainland Spain who had been allowed to choose between U.S. and Spanish citizenship) and "native inhabitants of the territories" (persons born in Puerto Rico, the Philippines, and Guam, whose citizenship status had been left up to Congress to resolve).[37] The distinction seemed to be based simply on birthplace. But Degetau argued that this language should not be interpreted literally. The treaty negotiators, he argued, had intended the distinction to exclude from citizenship *not* all native-born Puerto Ricans and Filipinos but rather only "uncivilized tribes"—which, he hastened to add, could only be found in the Philippines.[38] As for Puerto Rico, Degetau went on, it should not be affected at all by the exclusion of "native inhabitants" because there were no "uncivilized tribes" on the island and there had not been any for centuries.[39]

In support of this argument, Degetau quoted a telegram dated November 29, 1898, from Secretary of State John Hay to the American representatives at the Treaty of Paris negotiations in which Hay had instructed the negotiators to follow the example of the treaty ceding Alaska to the United States.[40] The Alaska treaty had given the inhabitants of the territory a choice between returning to Russia or remaining and becoming U.S. citizens—except for the "uncivilized native tribes," whose status was up to Congress to handle.[41] The negotiators at Paris in 1898 had followed Hay's instructions, but rather than distinguishing between Spanish subjects and uncivilized native tribes they had distinguished between "natives of the Peninsula" and "native inhabitants of the territories," leaving the status of the latter up in the air. The implication was that the native-born inhabitants of Puerto Rico, the Philippines, and Guam belonged in the same category (and required the same treatment) as uncivilized native tribes. Degetau begged to differ, and thus he found himself arguing—against the plain text of the treaty—that the negotiators could not have intended to include native-born Puerto Ricans in the phrase "native inhabitants." In Puerto Rico, he insisted, everyone had been a Spanish citizen.[42] Degetau's point was clear: natives of Puerto Rico were not *that* kind of native.

The court, in its opinion in the *Gonzales* case, praised Degetau's argument as "excellent," but, as we have seen, it did not agree with his conclusions—or, indeed, with anyone else's.[43] The analysis that came closest to carrying the day was Coudert's alternative argument that even if Puerto Ricans were not U.S. citizens they were not aliens, either, but something in between. The court did not ultimately take up Coudert's suggestion that it adopt a new, specific legal designation.[44] Nevertheless, Coudert's proposal would soon catch on, and a new legal category would emerge to designate a new class of Americans: the noncitizen national.[45]

Nationals and the Reinvention of American Citizenship

In a recent essay, William J. Novak points out that the modern conception of citizenship posits the citizen as "the unified legal subject of the modern nation-state, thereby entitled to make rights claims upon that state. This modern idea of citizenship brings a presumption of universality and uniformity in the allocation of rights and duties—*all* citizens are entitled to the same bundle of state protections and privileges *qua* national citizens."[46] Like others, Novak dates the emergence of the modern conception of citizenship to the aftermath of the Civil War and, in particular, to the passage of the Fourteenth Amendment. The Fourteenth Amendment repudiated Justice Roger Taney's infamous opinion in the *Dred Scott* case excluding blacks from national citizenship and replaced it with a formal guarantee of birthright citizenship for persons born on U.S. soil, thus establishing "one supreme membership in the body politic of the United States above all others."[47] This new, universal, and equalizing status replaced the caste system endorsed by *Dred Scott* and (at least in theory) conferred legal parity on all Americans.

There were exceptions to be sure. The amendment promised citizenship to "[a]ll persons born or naturalized in the United States *and subject to the jurisdiction thereof.*"[48] The phrase "and subject to the jurisdiction thereof" served as limiting language, exempting Native Americans (as well as the children of foreign officials such as ambassadors) from the guarantee of birthright U.S. citizenship.[49] Additionally, many persons—saliently, women and blacks—continued to be denied the full enjoyment of rights despite their status as citizens. But these exceptions proved the rule. While the status of Native Americans raised difficult questions, their exclusion from citizenship, along with that of the children of foreign officials, was based on the rationale that they were not entirely subject to the jurisdiction of the United States (even when born within its territorial limits) because they were members of and owed allegiance to other nations—whether foreign sovereigns or, in the case of Native Americans, quasi-sovereign "domestic dependent nations," as Chief Justice John Marshall put it in his opinion in *Cherokee Nation v. Georgia*.[50] Whatever the persuasiveness of this legal fiction, it at least reflected the amendment's equalizing spirit: conceiving of the United States as a singular and uniform national entity, the amendment sought to preserve a singular and uniform membership in it; anyone born to the American nation would be a citizen of the American nation-state. As for citizens denied rights, while such discrimination unquestionably violated the promise of the Fourteenth Amendment, at the same time it reinforced the status of the amendment as the source of that unfulfilled promise and consequently as the cornerstone of the struggle for constitutional rights.

Thus the Fourteenth Amendment, in Novak's words, "remade the American state, and that process of re-creation began with a redefinition of national citizenship and the rights entailed therein."[51] Or, as James H. Kettner puts it in his history of American citizenship, new struggles over citizenship "most certainly would emerge after 1870," but they "would be addressed within the framework of a concept that at last was fundamentally outlined in the Constitution. And the answers would be determined by the authority of a sovereign people, a community of citizens, that formed a single and united nation."[52]

It would indeed be difficult to exaggerate the importance of the Fourteenth Amendment in reshaping law and politics in the United States.[53] Yet any assessment of the amendment's impact on the law of citizenship must contend with developments that occurred in the wake of the United States' imperial turn several decades later, in 1898. As these developments reveal, the concept of citizenship turned out to be highly uncertain and hotly contested decades after the Fourteenth Amendment redefined it. The amendment was supposed to have accomplished this feat by obliterating once and for all the distinction between citizen and subject, thereby repudiating the notion that there were American subjects who were not American citizens. Yet imperial policies at the beginning of the twentieth century opened the door for the reintroduction of precisely this distinction into the American legal system, establishing that there were persons born on domestic soil and subject to U.S. sovereignty who were consequently Americans, not aliens, and yet at the same time were not citizens of the United States.

In this respect, the United States' foray into empire undid a crucial aspect of what the Fourteenth Amendment had done: it revived a hierarchy of membership in the American polity—and what's more, it invested this hierarchy with unlimited expansive potential. No longer were the exceptions to the citizenship guarantee narrowly circumscribed. Instead, just as the first round of insular cases in 1901 had made it possible for the United States to expand its territorial domain without extending its status quo national boundaries, the new two-tiered legal framework of membership made it possible—despite the Fourteenth Amendment—for the United States to expand its territorial domain without extending its status quo citizenry. In this sense—in the context of empire—the entire citizenship clause of the Fourteenth Amendment became "limiting" language as the phrase "born in the United States" ceased to gesture toward universality, becoming instead a means of excluding those subject to U.S. sovereignty but not, constitutionally, part of the polity that comprised the United States.

The amendment's already tenuous adherence to a single and uniform national membership thus disintegrated in the context of empire. According to the imperial logic of political membership, all citizens were nationals but not all nationals were citizens: the more exclusive status of *citizen* now applied solely to the constituent parts of the American nation (in theory anyway, "a sovereign people, a community of citizens, . . . a single and united nation," to borrow Kettner's words) while the broader status of *national* encompassed all those belonging to that nation's imperial domain. As one contemporary observer summed it up, "[B]etween citizens and aliens there is in the American empire an intermediate class of American subjects or, as the newer and gentler phrase describes them, 'nationals.'"[54] It was a newer and gentler phrase for an ostensibly newer and gentler empire.

Conclusion

The category of the noncitizen national survives, although it no longer applies in Puerto Rico (which remains a territory of the United States) or the Philippines (which gained independence in 1946).[55] A little over a decade after the *Gonzales* decision, in 1916–17, Congress conferred U.S. citizenship on Puerto Ricans but not Filipinos while at the same time promising independence to the Philippines but not Puerto Rico.[56] The bifurcated citizenship histories of the Philippines and Puerto Rico shed further light on the imperial uses of the hierarchy of membership that was devised on the occasion of their annexation: retaining sole discretion over their status, Congress tweaked the membership categories to suit its new needs.

As the date of the Philippines' independence drew closer, Congress answered one of the questions the *Gonzales* case had left unresolved—whether Congress had the power to bar the entry of noncitizen nationals into the United States—by imposing a stringent quota on Filipinos and making some of those already in the country subject to deportation.[57] As for Puerto Ricans, the grant of citizenship in 1917 was an act of greater inclusion in the American polity but a highly ambiguous (and ambivalent) one. The grant came to the island, as most everything else did, by way of a unilateral exercise of congressional discretion without any serious consultation of Puerto Ricans. Birth in Puerto Rico now conferred

U.S. citizenship by virtue of a congressional statute, but this change did not alter the status of Puerto Rico itself, which remained an "unincorporated" territory.[58] As a result, Puerto Ricans became a population of American citizens subject to U.S. sovereignty but without a clear or permanent relationship to the rest of the United States—a confusing and unresolved situation that plagues island politics to this day.

Although most Puerto Ricans came to embrace American citizenship, many also developed a strong sense of a distinct Puerto Rican national identity, which grew stronger, not weaker, as the island's integration into the United States increased.[59] This situation gave rise to a curious political phenomenon: among those who accepted citizenship but rejected complete integration into the United States by way of statehood, it became fashionable to declare, "I am a U.S. citizen but not an American." This declaration turned on its head the Supreme Court's pronouncement in *Gonzales* that a person could be "an American . . . and yet not a citizen of the United States."[60] The empire, it is tempting to suggest, reaped what it sowed.

The Afterlife of Empire

Sovereignty and Revolution in the Philippines

VICENTE L. RAFAEL

LIKE MANY OTHER NATION-STATES, the Philippines is marked by an imperial inheritance. The colonial regimes of Spain and the United States have left behind a certain idea of sovereignty rooted in Christian thinking. It is an idea of sovereignty that gives the ruler the freedom to take exception to the law. Whether embodied by the king, by the state or, in its nationalist revolutionary moment, by the people, sovereignty is the power to define and decide what is exceptional, so exceptional as to warrant the breaking of laws in view of either preserving or destroying the existing order and establishing a new one altogether. In Carl Schmitt's oft-quoted definition, "Sovereign is he who decides on the exception"[1] It is the sovereign who, in founding the law, gives to himself the license to operate both inside and outside of it. The self-legislating and self-granting agency of the sovereign is precisely what allows him to decide who will live and who will die and what forms such living and dying are to take, who is the friend and who is the enemy and the terms of such friendship and enmity, and who is the citizen and who is the foreigner and the laws of citizenship that allow for the assimilation or expulsion of the foreign.

The power to *decide* on the exception—to break with the norm, rupturing the precedents and processes of deliberation and debate—gives to sovereignty an absolutist nature. Jean Bodin, writing some three and a half centuries earlier (1576), foreshadows Schmitt in saying, "Sovereignty is not limited either in power or in function.... For he is absolutely sovereign who recognizes nothing, after God, that is greater than himself."[2] Sovereignty as absolute power is thus absolutely free of any obligations and conditions. This makes it a kind of impossible power, truly exceptional because it is beholden to no one and nothing but God. However, rather than serving as a limit, God here figures as an infinite force, exceeding any attempt at codification into positive human law. Like a "pure gift," it can neither be calculated nor reciprocated. That true sovereignty is beholden only to God's laws means that the latter enables the former. The sovereign comes to be the sole agent of divine power. He thereby embodies the impossible possibility of a thoroughly nonhuman, immortal power manifesting itself in the world.[3]

It is arguably the legacy of this absolutist notion of sovereignty that constitutes the afterlife of empire. It haunts every articulation of democracy in postcolonial societies, the ghost that both enlivens and poisons the nationalist struggles for freedom and social justice. In this essay, I will ask how this paradoxical notion of sovereignty came about in the Philippines.

Emerging through the work of Spanish conquest and conversion, *las islas Filipinas* was transformed into the Republic of the Philippines by the violent and contradictory forces unleashed by the revolutionary nationalist movement of the late nineteenth century, the counterrevolutionary nationalism of the elite-led Malolos Republic, by U.S. imperial war and nation building, and by way of the imposition of and resistance to Japanese military occupation. Thus, the history of the Philippine nation-state, like that of many other formerly colonized countries, is usually understood as the negation of empire and the assertion of a new basis for human community, the nation. Rejecting the social inequality and absolutist politics of empire, the nation-state presents itself as the privileged site for the actualization of freedom, equality, and fraternity. Whereas injustice and the "reason of force" characterized the rule of empire, justice and the "force of reason," to paraphrase the Filipino revolutionary thinker Apolinario Mabini (of which more will be said), is said to guide the laws of the nation-state.[4] And where imperial sovereignty emanates from an indivisible and transcendent source ruling over human destiny, national sovereignty is thought to come from an immanent source, residing in the people whose will finds expression in the media of public opinion, free elections, and representative government.

Put another way, the nation-state succeeds empire, but it is a succession marked by an irreparable rupture, untold violence, and unaccounted deaths. We might think of the nation-state, then, as the ground on which empire is buried. But, like every burial place, it is also the site where empire is recalled and periodically reappears. During its more expansive moments, nationalism comes to resemble a kind of imperial necrophilia. Indeed, in negating empire the nation-state holds fast to the former's remains only to find itself visited by its many ghosts. One such ghost, I'd like to suggest, is the specter of sovereignty, which is often confused with freedom and always associated with power. What do I mean by this? How is it possible to see in Philippine history, at least through the late and early twentieth century, the return of various apparitions of imperial sovereignty?

We can begin with the Spanish regime.[5] At the cornerstone of Spanish imperialism was the institution of the Patronato Real or Royal Patronage of the

Catholic Church. Emblematic of the vanguard role of the Spanish Crown in the Counter-Reformation, the Patronato Real obligated the monarch to supply the material and military needs of the Church and further its planetary project of evangelization. Evangelization, in turn, legitimized conquest as a supremely moral undertaking designed to liberate the very subjects it subjugated, filling them with the Word of God, which resonated with the will of the Spanish king. In a similar vein, the *Laws of the Indies* (*Recopilación de las Leyes de los Reinos de Indias*, 1681) was not only meant to address and regularize the administrative complexity of empire. It was also cast as the positive encoding of natural law, which in turn was thought to derive from divine law.[6]

We can see, then, how Spanish imperialism was sustained by a kind of political theology. State power was understood in ideal terms as the expression and extension of divine power and human law as the instrument for the actualization of natural law. In this context, sovereignty ultimately had a transcendent source. Because it rested on the nonhuman, its force was such that it could break with every human norm and custom so as to pave the way for the emergence of a new social order under God's name. Not surprisingly, such an order was constituted in and through a hierarchy that reached down from heaven to earth: God, king, colonial officials, and missionaries ruling over local elites and the mass of male and female natives.

Spanish political theology was far from seamless, however. The actual exercise of sovereignty was mired in the material complications of historical contingencies: corrupt officials, for example, or rebellious natives. Even more important was the presence of the missionary priest. The key importance of evangelization placed the Spanish missionary as an essential relay in the transmission of God's word and the king's will. Often the only representative of empire in the farthest reaches of the realm, the missionary enjoyed considerable influence and great latitude in interpreting, or more often disregarding, the laws of the king in the name of preserving and furthering God's laws. The missionary's power was further enhanced by his knowledge of native speech. It allowed him to stand as the indispensable mediator between colonizers and colonized, translating between the demands of one and the responses of the other. In this way, the clergy constituted a critical force within colonial society. Intimately, and at times oppressively, involved in the day-to-day affairs of the people, he came to possess the power to decide on the exception, for example, abusive colonial officials, accused sorcerers, heterodox ritual practices, or subversive nationalists. This capacity for deciding not only what was an exception but how to deal with it turned the clergy into a kind of sovereign power itself, often undercutting the authority of the king's colonial representatives in Manila. The missionary was thus a kind of double agent, simultaneously enacting and limiting, enabling while challenging the absolutist vocation of Spanish political theology.

Revolutionary Sovereignty

By the late nineteenth century, the contradictions of Spanish sovereignty would become stunningly apparent to an emergent colonial bourgeoisie.[7] Indeed, the emergence of nationalist thought was in part a response to the highly problematic role of the Spanish friar in at once ratifying and usurping a sovereign power whose origins were understood to lie in an extraterrestrial and suprahuman source. Resentful yet envious of the friar's proximity to this power, the first generation of Filipino nationalists, called *ilustrados* (enlightened ones), began a steady campaign to remove or at least neutralize missionary influence spurred by Enlightenment ideals of progress. With the eruption of the Revolution in August of 1896, imperial sovereignty entered into a prolonged period of crisis from which it would never fully recover.

What was the Revolution and how would it come to reappropriate Spanish sovereignty? Among the revolutionists, some of the most astute answers came from Apolinario Mabini (1864–1903), the most important theoretician of the Revolution and the most gifted adviser of Emilio Aguinaldo, the leader of the First Filipino Republic. Born in Batangas of *indio* parents of modest means, Mabini was educated in philosophy and law in Manila. Having contracted an illness that left him paralyzed from the waist down in 1896, he had to be transported by hammock during the Revolution as the revolutionary government sought to elude American forces. Popularly known as the "sublime paralytic," Mabini, unlike other prominent nationalist leaders, never traveled outside the Philippines except when he was exiled to Guam by the Americans, thus making it all the more remarkable that he articulated a robust and sophisticated formulation of revolutionary theory.[8]

Filipinos fought, Mabini claimed, to attain independence but not as an end in itself. Rather, it was to be the means to arrive at a "moral government" with which to secure the conditions for the general "well-being" and "happiness" of the country. Such conditions required, furthermore, a popularly elected and truly representative government that would "assure all Filipinos of the freedom of thought, conscience, association; privacy of their persons, houses and correspondences." While the Revolution, according to Mabini, may have started out as an act of vengeance in 1896, it had by 1898 been transformed into something else: a manifestation of the irresistible movement of reason around the world.[9]

In his writings, Mabini repeatedly situates the Philippine Revolution as a continuation of the American and French Revolutions, inspired by the same ideals and moved by the same aspirations for liberty, equality, and fraternity.[10] It is this shared history of revolutionary beginnings that Mabini reminds Americans of in the aftermath of the Treaty of Paris and in the midst of the Philippine-American War. Indeed, in fighting the Americans, Filipinos "show to the United States that they possess sufficient culture to know their rights.... They hope that the war reminds the Americans what their forefathers had to sustain in their past against the English for the emancipation of their Colonies and what is today the free states of North America."[11]

From Mabini's perspective then, the Revolution was neither a race war nor a criminal act of uncivilized people as both Spaniards and Americans had claimed. Rather, it was the most compelling evidence of the people's enlightenment, suggesting thereby an emergent historical kinship between revolutionary Filipinos and civilized Americans and Europeans. This is underlined by the fact that, as Mabini points out, the Filipino people fought to recover and protect their "natural right" to be free and in so doing joined their fate to that of all the civilized peoples of the world. For Mabini, it was never the Declaration of Independence of June 12, 1898, nor the establishment of the Malolos Republic and Constitution that proved the Filipino capacity for independence. In fact, he had repeatedly criticized these institutions as premature and saw how the *ilustrados* used them to recolonize the nation under their rule. Rather it was the very fact of risking their lives to fight injustice that filled a people with what he and Rizal before him called "virtue," that is, the ability to place the common good above one's self-interest, a capacity he felt was scandalously lacking among the elite leaders of the Republic. Founded on reason and stemming from "natural law," it was propelled by a virtuous people simultaneously enacting the very thing it sought to restore to itself: its own sovereignty.[12]

In Mabini's account of the history leading up to the Revolution, he cites a common theme in nationalist historical thinking: that a bond of friendship and mutual support characterized the initial relationship between *indios* and Spaniards sealed by the blood compact, the *pacto de sangre*. This originary social contract was betrayed by Spanish duplicity and oppression, and Filipinos responded by rebelling.[13] In breaking the social contract, the Spaniards had broken the natural law. So, too, had the Americans who, in signing the Treaty of Paris (1899), assumed sovereignty over the Philippines from Spain in exchange for the sum of $20 million. In using the instruments of positive international law, the Americans gained legal title to the Philippines but did so by violating natural law, which forbade slavery and the usurpation of another people's sovereignty.[14]

In rising up first against the Spaniards then against the Americans, Filipinos were seeking to restore what justly pertained to them. "Then and now our battle cry remains natural law, the eternal foundation and regulator of justice and of all human laws." Natural law, in turn, "recognizes no other sovereignty except that of the people.... [T]heir precepts are orders from Divine Reason dictated to the human conscience."[15] Popular sovereignty derived from natural law is thus a function of divine sovereignty and shares its absolute nature. To the extent that Mabini regards the Revolution as a providential event that reveals God's will in

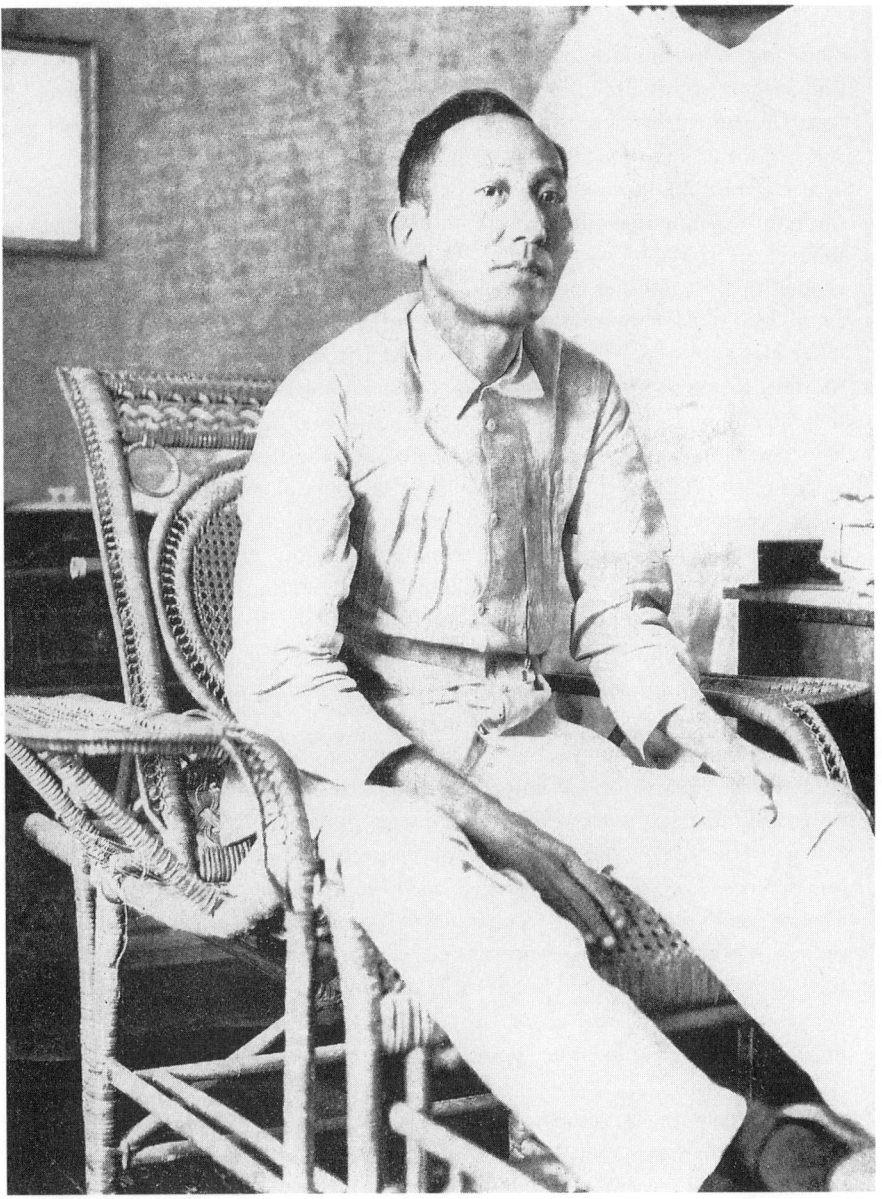

Apolinario Mabini, Filipino lawyer and primary author of the Malolos Constitution for the first Philippine Republic, at Anda police station, Intramuros, Manila, 1900. (Lopez Museum)

the recovery of a people's natural rights, he reiterates the political theology of empire, resorting to a language of rights that finds its ultimate sanction in the Christian notion of natural law.[16] Sovereignty in this case rests on the people but only insofar as they are infused with divine reason and thus become the privileged instruments of God's will. Their freedom, if it exists at all, cannot be disassociated from their subordination to and assimilation of His awesome power.

It is important, however, to stress that Mabini's texts do not merely occasion the return of imperial Christian ghosts. There is another powerful force that inhabits all of Mabini's writings, and that is, of course, the Revolution, whose eruption points to other possibilities. The Revolution comes across not simply as the medium for the restoration of absolute sovereignty in a national body; it can also appear as a radically new, profoundly unrecognizable, and therefore thoroughly inhuman force. In one essay, Mabini writes of the fear and trembling that the Philippine Revolution struck in the hearts of other European colonizers who saw it as "contagious, very contagious." For the Revolution "bears in its volcanic bosom the germ of yellow fever or the bubonic plague, which is fatal to their colonial interests. In the not so distant future, it could constitute the uncontrollable dike against their overwhelming ambitions." And in addressing the conservative *ilustrados* Pedro Paterno and Felipe Buencamino he warns of the "dangers" that another revolution would bring should the Republic negotiate with the Americans without first securing the recognition of Filipino rights. Without justice, there can be no peace, he avers, only an unending uprising beyond the Republic's—or any other regime's—control.[17]

In this and other passages, the Revolution exceeds both human and, it would seem, divine agency. Its "naturalness" leads not to the creation of new institutions, and much less to the revelation of divine reason, but to sheer destruction. Like a plague, it knows no boundaries and respects no rank, inflicting its relentless violence on everyone. In this sense, the Revolution becomes something like a "pure event" that cannot be recuperated for social uses inasmuch as it impairs the very mechanisms and agencies of social recuperation. In the name of justice, the Revolution as such could just as easily sow injustice or, more precisely—and here is the source of real terror—confuse men's minds about the difference between the two. Mabini at one point imagines the following scenario.

> We took the enemy by surprise and made them prisoners. . . . We ordered the soldiers to tie the hands of the prisoners and shoot them after stripping them of their money, clothes and jewelry They were also ordered to take the prettiest women and then burn the town. The last words of the order had barely left our lips when a thunderous voice shouted: God, humanity, progress! We looked up at the sky and it was red as blood. . . . The mountains rumbled and the ground shook beneath our feet. We then hurriedly withdrew the orders as terror and dread overcame us.[18]

Here Mabini paints a lurid account of Revolution unmoored from reason and bereft of virtue.[19] The "fever" of the Revolution infects fighters with an exaggerated pride that leads them to assume arbitrary power over their prisoners, women, and property. It leads them, that is, to take exception to all consideration of law, natural as well positive, acting with a kind of violence freed of all restraints. For them, sovereignty devolves into sheer destructive power. Side by side with the concept of the Revolution as the collective sacrifice and struggle with which to restore a people's natural rights there is thus the ongoing danger of the Revolution as the dissolution of such rights, unleashing a state of permanent violence by way of civil war. In such a case, society would be reduced to a "corpse," that is, a body without its soul. Mabini writes, "If there is no more than the reunion of men that move with neither direction, nor order nor harmony, society becomes a veritable corpse."[20]

By raising the possibility of pure violence, the Revolution turns every man against every form of authority and thus threatens to rob society of its soul. In doing so, it converts society into a spectral version of itself. It is in light of this permanent possibility of social death that authority becomes essential as a means of resurrecting social life. Furthermore, it is an authority that, as Mabini repeatedly reminds us, resides in the people.[21] At the same time, the Revolution threatens to violate not only positive human laws but putative natural laws—what today we more commonly refer to as "human rights"—giving rise to a spectral society incapable of making or preserving laws as such and thereby unable to distinguish between just and unjust acts.

Put another way, we can think of the Revolution working as a principle of deconstruction in the world. It periodically calls into question various claims of sovereignty whether based on the reason of force or the force of reason. And it excavates the irrational foundations of rational institutions, exposing the terror-filled excesses of the sacrificial economy of virtue. It is, however, important to stress that the deconstructive effect of the Revolution does not end with the sheer destruction of oppressive social orders; nor does it rest mainly on the propagation of terror and the spread of criminality. Other accounts reveal how the Revolution occasionally opened up the possibility of another experience of sovereignty, one that is predicated on an experience of freedom or what in Tagalog is called *kalayaan*, that is, freedom from the necessity of labor and the violence of law.

Sovereignty and the Experience of Freedom

In approaching these other accounts, it might help first of all to briefly consider an alternative notion of sovereignty offered by the French writer Georges Bataille (1897–1962). A librarian, novelist, anthropologist, pornographer, and philosopher, Bataille, of course, has no direct connection to the Philippines. But in the spirit of Mabini invoking analogies between the Philippine and the French Revolutions when addressing his American interlocutors, I want to broach an analogy between Bataille's thinking about a non-theological notion of sovereignty and the experience of the Revolution recorded in other Filipino accounts. For Bataille, sovereignty entails not the exercise of the absolute power to take exception but rather the joyful consumption of surplus beyond the boundaries of what is useful. "Life beyond utility," he writes, "is the domain of the sovereign."[22] In this way, sovereignty has little to do with self-government or the governing of others. Instead, sovereignty for Bataille comes from the enjoyment of that which is "savored" since "The sovereign, if he is not imaginary, truly enjoys the products of this world—beyond his needs.... Let us say that the sovereign (or sovereign life) begins when, with the necessities ensured, the possibility of life opens up without limit."[23]

This limitless opening up of life: how can we understand this?

Perhaps, one way to do so is to consider the account of Santiago Alvarez (1872–1930), one of the leaders of the Filipino Revolution. In his memoirs, written in the 1920s, Alvarez recalls life in the liberated towns of Cavite, a province south of Manila, during the initial flush of victory against the Spanish forces in September 1896. Reading it, we get a sense of the experience of sovereignty as sheer enjoyment beyond what is useful.

> During those times, the Enemy did not launch any attacks.... The people were truly happy (*totoong masaya*). Free in their enjoyment of different diversions, abundant food, everything was cheap, and there were no criminals, no thieves, or pickpockets. Each loved the other (*lahat ay may pagmamahal sa kapwa*) and from one end of the town to the other, sibling love (*pag-ibig-kapatid*) which is the teaching of the Katipunan, reigned supreme.[24]

Alongside accounts of horrific battles, heroic sacrifices, and unforgivable betrayals, Alvarez's memoirs are peppered with recollections of these moments of what he calls "mad" happiness. To be sure, these did not last long. The state of "sibling love" could neither be consolidated nor sustained in the face of Spanish attacks and the factional strife that would eventually tear the revolutionary movement apart. But it is precisely its surprising and ephemeral occurrence that Alvarez and his readers savor, lingering on the memory of moments that could neither be consolidated nor institutionalized. Rather, the pleasure of recalling the experience of liberation comes precisely from their vanishing.[25]

Alvarez's description of the sovereign experience has a vernacular context. It has to do with its invocation of the conditions historically associated with *kalayaan*, the Tagalog word usually translated as "freedom." It is important to note, however, that there is no easy correspondence between these two words.

As the historian Reynaldo Ileto has pointed out, *kalayaan* has meant both more *and* less than *freedom*, holding a range of connotations that exceed words such as *independence, autonomy,* and the political-theological implications of *sovereignty*. Pointing out the historical link between *katipunan*—the word as well as the name of the secret revolutionary organization—and *kalayaan,* Ileto writes:

> The meaning of "wholeness" or "becoming one" implied by the term *katipunan* is also contained in *kalayaan*. Prior to the rise of the separatist movement, *kalayaan* did not mean "freedom" or "independence." [It is] . . . built upon the [root] word *layaw* or *laya,* which means "satisfaction of one's needs," "pampering treatment by parents," or "freedom from strict parental control." Thus, *kalayaan* as a political term is inseparable from its connotations of the parent-child relationship. . . . As a revolutionary document put it, the "Katipunan of Man" is none other than the extension of the experience of the unity between mother and child.[26]

Ileto asks us to consider *kalayaan* in its protopolitical sense as a return to the state of *laya*—the pre-oedipal and prelapsarian moment of perfect reciprocity between mother and child. Idealized as a state of bonding without bondage, the condition of *layaw* comes from acts of giving that do not expect a return and so escape the economy of the gift, of taking without incurring a debt and so dispensing with the formation of hierarchy. Freed from the need to calculate and wait, reciprocity ceases to be reciprocal altogether. Indeed, one might even say that the state of *layaw,* as far as it centers on the relationship between mother and child, is one in which the father counts for little if at all. The latter has yet to make his presence felt much less assert his authority over the family by establishing the law regulating the relationship between mother and child.

Kalayaan, or "freedom," understood as *layaw* thus conjures a scene of sovereignty that reminds us of Bataille's vision and Alvarez's account of a liberated Cavite. It is a scene where the family as a patriarchy is yet to emerge and law as a coercive device and instrument of power over life and death is yet to be established. Unlike the violent inequalities and inequities that inhere in the colonial and republican state, the state of *kalayaan* engenders constant caring. For all these reasons, *kalayaan* delineates a utopic and therefore impossible state. Yet, as Ileto points out, it also furnished the idiomatic context for the enactment of Enlightenment, nationalist notions of "liberty, equality and fraternity."

Put differently, to say with Ileto that "*kalayaan* is *katipunan*" is to say that the impossible is at the foundation of the possible, the utopic at the foundation of the real. The incredible state of *layaw* invoked by *katipunan* as "wholeness" and "becoming one" is that which lends credibility to the possible and periodic incarnations of *kalayaan* in the Revolution. In Alvarez's account of Cavite, life attains the state of *layaw*. It is momentarily freed from the labor of fighting and the struggle for recognition. There is only consumption beyond necessity together with a general indifference to the prospect of death. In the midst of revolution, the world appears not simply upside down but wholly new. Impossible to anticipate, it arrives suddenly, always, it seems, for the first and last time. For this reason, it is perhaps not too unreasonable to ascribe to this experience of sovereignty the sense of the miraculous. Such sheer enjoyment even and especially in close proximity to death is a kind of miracle if by *miracle* we mean the impossible becoming suddenly real. Here is Bataille again: "Beyond need, the object of desire is, humanly, the miracle; it is sovereign life, beyond the necessity that suffering defines."[27] Sovereign life as the singular yet recurring condition of *kalayaan*—this, too, no doubt constitutes the afterlife of empire.

The political theology of empire asserts the possibility of the impossible: divine force as absolute power incarnated in the sovereign's body and expressed in his capacity to take exception. Revolution, as I have argued, simultaneously dismantles even as it reappropriates this enduring and terrifying fiction. But it is also capable of bringing about the impossible possibility of sovereignty as the experience of mad joy, the miraculous, if evanescent, opening of an entirely new life.

The U.S. Constitution and Philippine Colonialism
An Enduring and Unfortunate Legacy

OWEN J. LYNCH

ONCE THE UNITED STATES ASSERTED SOVEREIGNTY over the Philippine Islands in 1898, the legal framework for internal control of the colony needed to be established. Laws passed by the U.S. Congress, especially the Organic Act (Philippine Bill) of 1902, garnered most attention from both contemporary observers and later historians. The insular decisions of the U.S. Supreme Court, however, were equally, if not more, significant to the Philippines, especially the novel concept of "unincorporated territories." Among other things, this concept upheld the notion that the U.S. Constitution, including long-established jurisprudence interpreting and applying the Bill of Rights, did not follow the American flag to its new colony.[1] The legacy of these narrowed, even compromised, constitutional protections endures to this day and undergirds weakened notions of civil rights, property rights, and other legal rights in the constitutions of the postcolonial Philippine Republic.

On April 25, 1898, the United States government declared war against Spain. Ostensibly as a response to Spanish abuses being inflicted on the Cuban people, the declaration of war soon spurred developments in Spain's Philippine colony. During the morning of May 1, Commodore George Dewey led his American fleet into Manila Bay. By 12:30 p.m. the Spanish had surrendered and the United States was poised to establish and secure a sovereign claim over the entire Philippine archipelago.[2]

After learning of Dewey's success, President William McKinley was quoted as saying during a "well-authenticated interview at the White House" that he "didn't want the Philippines, and when they came to us, as a gift from the gods, I did not know what to do with them." McKinley claimed that his decision to acquire the colony came only after he had knelt for "more than one night" and prayed to "Almighty God for light and guidance."[3]

Contrary to the "tenacious myth, created and nurtured by two generations of historians," however, Dewey's alacrity was no coincidence.[4] Nor was President McKinley telling the whole story for "The order to attack Manila was . . . sanctioned by the President at a conference in the White House on Sunday, April 24, 1898."[5]

McKinley's ruse was political. It helped obfuscate his imperial ambitions while U.S. public opinion gelled in favor of acquiring the Philippine colony. Meanwhile, important Republican constituencies would work hard to generate support for the nation's metamorphosis into a colonial power.[6] It was a chaotic period of policy formation whose outcome, as we will see, was an ambiguous confluence of competing forces.

Sugar Trust and Tariffs

The McKinley administration was markedly conservative. Its most important and favored constituency was big business, and few big businesses at the time had more clout than the sugarcane industry. Cuba had long been coveted by one of President McKinley's most influential supporters, Henry O. Havermeyer, president of the American Sugar Refining Company. Havermeyer and his allies believed that if the United States were to acquire sovereignty over Cuba, Cuban sugarcane could be imported into the United States tariff free. This would have given the Sugar Trust an important economic advantage over domestic sugar beet producers.[7]

The strategy to acquire Cuba, however, was foiled by the U.S. Congress less than two weeks before Commodore Dewey's arrival in Manila Bay. On April 21, 1898, Congress attached the Teller Amendment to a pro-administration resolution demanding that Spain withdraw and relinquish its claim to Cuba.[8] The amendment's sponsor was Senator Henry Teller, an advocate of Cuban independence and an ardent supporter of the domestic sugar beet industry. As originally proposed, the administration's resolution made no reference to prospective relationships between the United States and its Caribbean neighbor. Teller's amendment, by contrast, required the U.S. government to disclaim any "intention to exercise sovereignty, jurisdiction or control of said island except for the pacification thereof." It also required that the United States assert "its determination when [pacification] is accomplished to leave the government and control of the island to its people."[9]

The Teller Amendment was not drafted with the interests of the Cuban people foremost in mind. It was meant to prevent Cuba from being situated under the U.S. tariff umbrella. Ever since the Civil War, tariffs had been "the dominant economic issue in the U.S.," and cane sugar was, by 1900, the largest commodity imported into the country.[10] By 1898 the political clout of the Sugar Trust was ebbing. Antimonopoly sentiment was growing, and much of the political ire focused on the trust. If supporters of the sugar beet industry joined forces with anti-imperialists, the trust would be vulnerable in Congress, a fact confirmed by passage of the Teller Amendment.

McKinley had little alternative but to sign the resolution, with Teller's amendment, into law. He was determined to make Spain appear the aggressor once war broke out, and a presidential veto would, among other things, expose his close ties to the trust and make him appear to hold imperial ambitions. On April 20, therefore, McKinley signed the resolution, which was tantamount to a declaration of war. According to Francisco and Fast, the passage of the Teller Amendment prompted McKinley and his advisers to reevaluate their war objectives. "If Cuba was going to be denied to the U.S.," they write, "the case for acquiring another cane-producing colony became all the more pressing."[11]

Admiral Dewey's quick success in Manila Bay paved the way for acquisition of the world's third-largest sugarcane supplier after Cuba and Java.[12] Dewey and his men, however, were only to defeat the Spanish fleet in Manila Bay and establish a military presence in the city. The first contingent of U.S. Army forces arrived over a month later, on June 30, and initially they also made no move to occupy any other part of the colony. On August 12, a protocol between Spain and the United States was signed in Washington. Article III entitled the United States "to occupy and . . . hold the city, bay and harbor of Manila pending the conclusion of a treaty of peace." More important, in Article V Spain committed itself to meet U.S. representatives in Paris by October 1 in order "to determine the control, disposition and government of the Philippines."[13] On August 13, unaware of the Washington protocol, Spanish and American officials carried out the pro forma capitulation of the Spanish army.[14]

Treaty of Paris

Pursuant to the protocol, on September 13, McKinley appointed five commissioners to represent the United States at the Paris negotiations.[15] McKinley reportedly told the commissioners that the "dictates of humanity" had prompted U.S. military action in the Philippines. The United States, McKinley claimed, "had no design to aggrandizement and no ambitions of conquest."[16] McKinley's written instructions to the commissioners indicated otherwise. They declared that the "success of our arms at Manila imposes upon us obligations which we cannot disregard." The bottom line of these obligations was that the "United States cannot accept less than the cession in full right and sovereignty of the island of Luzon."[17]

Negotiations between Spain and the United States officially commenced on October 1. After one week, Spain, pursuant to its commitments in the August 12 protocol, acceded to all U.S. demands regarding Cuba, Puerto Rico, and the Ladrones (Guam). The Philippines presented the only obstacle to a final agreement. Spain insisted that, according to previously unchallenged principles of international law, the protocol implied no change in the political status of the archipelago other than recognition of a temporary U.S. military presence in Manila.[18] McKinley and most of his advisers felt otherwise. They had concluded that the colony should not be split.[19] They also knew that public opinion in the United States, including that of the anti-imperialists, had united against any suggestion that Spanish rule be continued. On October 12, instructions were cabled to the commissioners in Paris that all of the Philippines should be taken.[20]

After the congressional elections in early November, the U.S. panel presented its "final proposition," insisting that Spain cede the islands to the United States in exchange for $20 million and do so by a deadline of November 28. Unless an agreement was reached by that date, the Spanish commissioners were informed, the United States would resume armed hostilities. Faced with a renewed outbreak of armed conflict, Spain agreed to the American demands on the day of the deadline. The treaty was signed in Paris on December 10, 1898, and submitted to the U.S. Senate on January 4.

Senate ratification was by no means certain.[21] Opposition, particularly to provisions related to the Philippines, was growing. A Republican, George Frisbie Hoar of Massachusetts, delivered what some considered "the outstanding speech in the Senate in opposition to the acquisition of the Philippines."[22] Hoar claimed that "under the Declaration of Independence you cannot govern a foreign territory, a foreign people . . . because you think you are going to give them the blessings of liberty."[23]

Technically the treaty "went no further than to give its consent to the acquisition of the Philippines. This action did not necessarily imply any commitment to hold the Islands permanently."[24] To clear up the ambiguity concerning official U.S. intentions, the Senate passed a resolution proposed by Senator Samuel D. McEnery of Louisiana. It was indefinite as to the potential duration of the colonial enterprise, but it was specific in denying Filipinos any status as American citizens. The McEnery Resolution was approved twenty-six to twenty-two with forty-two senators not voting.[25] In sum, the Treaty of Paris is "generally regarded as establishing the foundation of the constitutional system" of the Philippine Republic.[26] Once the treaty was ratified, the "opportunity for preventing imperial expansion certainly had passed."[27]

Presidential Election of 1900

Despite the Senate ratification of the Paris treaty other avenues remained open for channeling opposition to U.S. colonialism and constraining its reach. The Supreme Court offered some hope of relief. But before it rendered an opinion the 1900 presidential campaign and election intervened. The election presented the American public with an opportunity to repudiate or uphold the colonial endeavor by voting for or against President McKinley and his congressional allies.

The Democratic presidential candidate was Senator William Jennings Bryan, who declared that the "paramount issue" was imperialism. For its part, the Democratic Party platform denounced the government's Philippine policy. The rationale behind the anti-imperialism plank, however, was not only based on concerns about the inherent incompatibility between democracy and colonialism. It was also patently colorphobic and stated, "The Filipinos cannot be citizens without endangering our civilization."

Despite the Democrats' campaign hullabaloo about anti-imperialism, its Philippine plank resembled the Republicans', which pledged to grant Filipinos the "largest measure of self-government consistent with their welfare and our duties."[28]

The magnitude of the Democrats' muddled campaign and another well-financed Republican juggernaut provided the greatest Republican electoral victory since 1872. McKinley won every state he had captured four years earlier and added Wyoming, South Dakota, Washington, Kansas, and even Bryan's home state of Nebraska. Although Bryan garnered 46 percent of the popular vote, opposition to colonial expansion apparently generated few votes for the Democratic ticket.

Spooner Amendment of 1901

With the elections over, Congress resumed its deliberations on colonial issues. The general consensus was that the president's power as commander in chief "did not go beyond the use of the necessary and proper means to carry out the aim of the military operations, which was pacification of the islands." Allocating legal rights to natural resources or granting permanent franchises, therefore, "could not be said to be within the scope of the president's military power."[29]

In Manila, the U.S. Philippine Commission, headed by William H. Taft, was aware of the legal ambiguities and limitations. On October 11, 1900, the commission rebuffed several American citizens who were "asking for the privilege of purchasing, at government rates, certain tracts of land" in Palawan. The official reason given for the denial was that "under present conditions, the power of the Commission to alienate public land is in such doubt that the Commission declines to take any action."[30]

On March 2, 1901, Congress responded to the commission's predicament when it passed an amendment to an army appropriations bill. The amendment was proposed, and named after, Wisconsin senator John C. Spooner.[31] Passage of the Spooner Amendment made the Philippine government "really civil in nature, deriving its power from Congress and not from the President."[32] The amendment, however, did not create a procedure for the establishment of civilian colonial government. Rather, it merely ratified actions already taken by the president and his subordinates.

Senator Spooner had introduced an identical provision the previous year.[33] The powers he wanted Congress to delegate to the commission included the authority to alienate and otherwise allocate legal rights to forests, minerals, and "public" lands, that is, lands not privatized and documented by the Spanish colonial government. The sugar beet industry, domestic sugarcane and rice growers, and ant-imperialists in the United States opposed giving this power to the new colonial regime. Senator Spooner's proposal reinforced their fears about the McKinley administration's subservience to big business and in particular the Sugar Trust. Senate opponents waged a filibuster on the Senate floor for over two months, and Spooner's original bill never reached the Senate floor.[34]

As 1901 commenced, a revised amendment by Spooner was attached to a military appropriations bill. Senators who opposed it asserted that the sole reason for the amendment was to enable the executive branch to grant permanent franchises and dispose of lands and mines. Senator Turner explained that "those are the only objects to be accomplished by the passage of this amendment which cannot be accomplished now by the President of the United States as Commander in Chief of our armies."[35] Not surprisingly, among the foremost proponents of this view were the would-be wielders of the coveted powers, that is, the members of the Philippine Commission.[36]

As during the previous year, the prevailing sentiment in the Senate was not favorable. In response, the newly appointed secretary of war, Elihu Root, offered some crucial concessions.[37] One provided that the proviso for the establishment of a civil government could be made transitory pending final action by Congress. Another placed a severe limit on the commission's power to grant franchises. Most significant, a blanket prohibition on the disposition of "public" lands, including "the timber thereon or the mining rights therein," was appended to the amendment. With this compromise, the wording of the army appropriations bill was amended and enacted into law on March 2, 1901.

The language in the amendment pertaining to natural resource allocation was clear. Nevertheless, in an effort to evade the amendment's prohibitions, ostensibly on humanitarian grounds, the president of the commission, William H. Taft, cabled Root on March 7, noting, "If new legislation abrogates General Military Order Military Governor Ninety-two last year fixing reasonable rates and proper limitation under which any resident can cut public timber, will produce great hardship," and asking, "Is cutting public timber prohibited?"[38]

Charles E. Magoon, an attorney in the Department of War, was ordered to draft the administration's response to Taft's inquiry and finished his assignment within eight days. Relying on the Manila-based regime's mistaken understanding of the commission's actual influence in the vast colonial archipelago, Magoon concluded:

If a construction is given this Congressional enactment which cuts off the inhabitants of the islands in their hour of need from the natural supply of timber to which they have had recourse for centuries, they will be at the mercy of the owners of the small amount of timber land subject to private ownership, who will possess a monopoly capable of being more oppressive than any one of the exclusive concessions granted by the Crown of Spain.[39]

Secretary of War Root agreed. Like his subordinates, Root was eager to interpret the Spooner Amendment in a way that might allow for continued commercial exploitation of at least forest resources. But the amendment was explicit,

"A Problem for the Lawyer: How to Get Around These." *The Literary Digest*, August 12, 1899. (Wisconsin State Historical Society)

stipulating that "no sale or lease or other disposition of the public lands or the timber thereon or the mining rights therein shall be made." Root opted, therefore, to make an ambiguous reply, and on March 30 he cabled the commission, "Do not interfere with established forestry regulations provided for by Spanish law, as modified by the military governor, Order 92, dated June 27, 1900."[40] The order prohibited all cutting or harvesting "without license" of public forest products, as well as the "unauthorized clearing of public lands" for farming purposes. But, more significant, it also established a licensing procedure.[41] Indeed, in an early example of its de facto autonomy on many important issues, the commission interpreted the secretary's telegram as providing authorization—contrary to the explicit language of Congress—to continue issuing timber licenses; between July 1, 1901, and June 30, 1902, at least 1,304 licenses were issued.[42] The secretary of war remained officially ignorant of these illegal machinations.[43]

U.S. Constitution and Colonialism

The faraway commission's undetected defiance of Congress would be repeated in future responses to mandates from Congress and even the Supreme Court. Although it may not have been perceived early on, additional powers might be assumed if the commission was not bound by the same restrictions on domestic powers imposed by the Constitution on the U.S. government.

The Paris treaty failed to resolve an array of fundamental constitutional questions. The most basic was whether the United States could constitutionally acquire sovereignty over people without first securing the consent of at least a majority of the affected constituency. In popular parlance, the question was "Does the Constitution follow the flag?"

The Northwest Ordinance of 1787 had established the organizational pattern for U.S. territories. Territories organized pursuant to its provisions were eventually to be divided into states and admitted into the union with full congressional representation. It was also understood that the territories were within the purview of the Constitution.[44] Chief Justice Roger B. Taney provided a terse summary of the limits on governmental power over territories in the infamous 1857 Dred Scott decision, which upheld slavery, arguing that "there is certainly no power given by the Constitution to the Federal Government to establish or maintain colonies bordering on the United States or at a distance."[45]

The outcome of the Spanish-American War prompted a reappraisal of this long-standing constitutional doctrine. Except for the annexation of Alaska in 1867 and Hawaii in 1897, all previous territorial acquisitions had been contiguous, and, more important, a majority of their inhabitants were Caucasian migrants or their progeny. This was not true of the Philippines, which was twice as far from the U.S. mainland as Hawaii and was the ancestral abode of an estimated eight million Malay peoples.

Magoon had been appointed as a solicitor (soon after renamed law officer) of the War Department's newly reorganized Division of Customs and Insular Affairs (DCIA) on January 1, 1899. Soon after he was charged with conceptualizing the executive branch's position.[46] Six weeks later he submitted to the secretary of war a *Report on the Legal Status of the Territory and Inhabitants of the Islands . . . with Reference to the Territorial Boundaries, the Constitution, and the Laws of the United States*. It was "the most lasting, the most significant of his reports" primarily because it "anticipated the decisions of the Supreme Court in the Insular cases."[47]

Magoon considered it "incontrovertible that the unorganized territory of the United States is not bound and benefited by the Constitution and the laws of the United States until Congress has made appropriate provision therefore." The resolution, moreover, officially declared that the U.S. government did not intend to extend citizenship to the Filipino peoples or to annex the archipelago permanently into the United States. As a result, Magoon averred that the Constitution did not follow the flag. He hastened to add, however, that U.S. sovereignty did.[48]

To mitigate the harsh-sounding implications of this position, Magoon attempted to articulate a theoretical basis by which the insular populations would not be completely bereft of legal recourse should the U.S. regime prove unduly harsh. He began by asking rhetorically, "If these islands and their inhabitants are without the aegis of the Constitution, what are their protections from an oppressive government and unjust laws?" He asserted that the answer was "plain."

> Such protection is found in the character and enlightenment of the new sovereign within whose jurisdiction they now are. . . . They are a charge upon the conscience of that sovereign, and the "inalienable rights" of a people are safe in that custody even when not guaranteed by the letter of the Constitution, for they are protected by laws higher than the Constitution, being the laws of American civilization.[49]

Other than its duty to safeguard these unspecified "inalienable rights," Magoon asserted, Congress possessed general plenary power over noncontiguous territories and their peoples.

As with Magoon's analysis of the Spooner Amendment, Root agreed with his subordinate's innovative theory.[50] Magoon's theory also received a strong endorsement from the First Philippine Commission (also known as the Schurmann Commission).[51] Like Magoon and Root, the first Philippine commissioners opted to overlook the theory's fundamental contradiction. If it were officially adopted, the U.S. government would be empowered to determine unilaterally the legal rights of millions of people who had involuntarily found themselves within the territorial jurisdiction of the United States.

Insular Decisions

The last hope for preventing, or somehow mitigating, the metamorphosis of important components of the U.S. government into antidemocratic colonial institutions rested with the Supreme Court. On May 21, 1901, less than three months after passage of the Spooner Amendment, it rendered the first in a series of opinions concerning legal issues arising from the colonial acquisitions.[52] The civil rights of the peoples within the colonies, however, were of peripheral concern. Most of the court's decisions concerned commercial interests affected by the legal realignments that followed colonial expansion.

The initial controversy involved an interpretation of Article I, section 8, of the U.S. Constitution. It mandates that "all Duties, Imposts and Excises shall be uniform throughout the United States." The case, *De Lima v. Bidwell*, involved an action to recover back duties exacted and paid under protest to the Port of New York by an importer of Puerto Rican sugar. The exaction had been made during the autumn of 1899 after Puerto Rico's cession to the United States but prior to the enactment, on March 24, 1900, of the Puerto Rican Bill, which reduced the duty on sugar imports.[53]

The dispute raised "the single question whether territory acquired by the United States by cession from a foreign power remains a 'foreign country' within the meaning of the tariff laws."[54] On May 27, 1901, the court held that the answer was no. In the court's opinion, Puerto Rico ceased to be a foreign country upon ratification of the Treaty of Paris. Instead, it became a territory of the United States. The tariff duties were, therefore, deemed to have been illegally exacted from the importer and they were ordered to be returned.

In other decisions released on the same day, however, the court accepted arguments advanced by Magoon. These cases involved the importation of merchandise after Congress had passed legislation providing for a Puerto Rican tariff.[55] In the leading case, *Downes v. Bidwell*, the issue was "whether merchandise brought into the Port of New York from Puerto Rico since the passage [by Congress of a Puerto Rican tariff] is exempt from duty."[56] By a five to four majority, the court concluded that "the island of Puerto Rico is a territory appurtenant and belonging to the United States, but not a part of the United States within the revenue clauses of the Constitution." The tariff, therefore, was held to be constitutional.

For more than six months it remained uncertain whether these decisions applied to the Philippine Islands.[57] On December 2, 1901, the U.S. Supreme Court made it official that they did. The decision came in the case of the "Fourteen Diamond Rings," *Pepke v. United States*.[58] The case involved a discharged American veteran who, subsequent to the ratification and proclamation of the Treaty of Paris, had acquired fourteen diamond rings in the Philippines. The rings were brought with him on his return to the United States on September 25, 1899, but no declaration was made at the port of entry. The issue was whether the rings were imported from a foreign country. The court, relying on the reasons articulated in the Puerto Rican cases, held that the answer was no.

The insular decisions boded ill for the civil rights of those who lived in the former Spanish colonies. They confirmed that the Filipino, Puerto Rican, and Cuban peoples had become the "rarest of phenomena under the republican form of government, subjects."[59] They implied that if Congress, despite the constitutional mandate regarding uniform duties, could impose tariffs on Puerto Rican merchandise, then perhaps the Bill of Rights could likewise be abrogated within the colonial possessions.[60]

The insular decisions evoked a variety of reactions. Domestic agricultural producers were mostly delighted. An amicus curiae "Brief on Behalf of Industrial Interests in the States" had warned that if the tariffs were not upheld domestic producers of tobacco, hemp (abaca), rice, sugar, and fruit could "not compete on the unequal terms which would be forced upon them with like products grown in the ceded (tropical) possessions."[61]

Not all sugar producers were pleased, however. The decisions were a "severe blow" to the sugarcane industry, in particular the American Sugar Refining Company.[62] Duty-free importation of sugarcane from the newly acquired colonies was no longer certain; tariff fees would have to be fought out in Congress. Sugar beet growers were delighted by the prospect. The sugar beet lobby was waxing strong and confident in Congress during 1901. Farmers reported a sharp increase in the amount of land planted with sugar beets that summer, and this was soon followed by a 140 percent increase in production.[63]

Civil libertarians and anti-imperialists in the United States were outraged. The newspaper columnist and noted anti-imperialist Finley Peter Dunne (more popularly known as Mister Dooley) remarked that "whether the Constitution followed the flag or not, the Supreme Court followed the illiction returns."[64] Among Filipino elites, by contrast, there was little if any reaction. Neither they nor the masses of Philippine people were involved in the debates concerning the colony's and their futures.

Portions of the Bill of Rights, of course, were replicated in McKinley's April 1900 "Instructions to the Philippine Commission" and Congress's 1902 Organic Act. But these laws did not emanate directly from the U.S. Constitution. This fact enabled the first civilian overseers of the American colony to bend, circumscribe, dilute, and sometimes completely ignore otherwise binding constitutional jurisprudence.[65]

Perhaps the most egregious variation concerned the writ of habeas corpus. The right to the writ was guaranteed in McKinley's instructions and the Organic Act. In addition, the colony had been largely subdued, except for Muslim Mindanao, by the end of 1904. Nevertheless, there continued to be "men confined in prisons throughout the archipelago arrested without warrant and entirely ignorant why they have been detained."[66] But Secretary Root took no notice. In September 1902 he stated, "The policy of the Republican Administration has been ... to give the people of the Islands all the blessings of civil and religious liberty, of just and equal laws, of good and honest administration."[67]

Fifty years later, two respected American scholars of Philippine-American political history who rendered a generally favorable view of the colonial endeavor proffered an alternative perspective. Summing up the rationale behind the insular decisions, they opined:

> From a constitutional viewpoint, it is not altogether easy to understand how Congress, which is established under the Constitution and derives its powers from that document, could totally disregard the Constitution in governing the newly acquired territory. From practical viewpoints, however, the decisions were more rational. What advantages were there in an expanding imperialism if the Constitution and its guarantees and protections were to apply to the new territory?[68]

Spanish Structure, American Theory

The Legal Foundations of a Tropical New Deal in the Philippine Islands, 1898–1935

ANNA LEAH FIDELIS T. CASTAÑEDA

To CONSTRUCT THE PHILIPPINE COLONIAL GOVERNMENT, American military and civil officials built on the remnants of the Spanish colonial administrative structure, staffed it with American personnel, operated it using American practices, employed it to pursue American-style modernization projects, animated it with American principles, and justified its activities within the American liberal constitutional tradition. While collaborating with the colonial regime, Filipino political leaders sought to Filipinize this institution and apply it toward Filipino goals. Their experience within the relationships that this institution ordered, of the programs for which it was used, and of the manner in which its activities were legitimated within American liberal constitutionalism provided Filipino delegates to the 1935 Constitutional Convention with the design and theoretical foundations on which to build their tropical New Deal.

The 1935 Constitution, and the 1973 and 1987 charters that revised it, all strike a high-minded tone in charging the Philippine government with the task of promoting lofty goals such as social justice. To achieve such noble ends, the framers of all three charters empowered the Philippine government to take over industries and revise contract and property rights whenever this was required by the public interest. The power accorded to the Philippine government in the name of public welfare is a striking feature of the Philippine constitutions and was a point of great pride among the framers, as seen in the convention debates. Why did the Filipino framers take it for granted that this was how a government ought to operate, and what does this assumption reveal about Filipino understandings about the nature and role of public authority in the Philippine constitutional order? This essay argues that the key to answering these questions lies in the discourse and practice of American liberal constitutionalism in the context of the U.S. colonial government machinery and the projects that it undertook in the Philippine Islands.

The Americans combined the highly centralized and interventionist Spanish era administrative structure, which was dominated by the Spanish governor-general for the most part, with a separation of powers design that concentrated even more power in the American-dominated executive branch at the expense of the Filipino-controlled legislature, in order to accommodate Filipino incapacity and guarantee the colonial sovereign's preeminence. The lopsided framework and functioning of this American colonial state were facilitated and legitimized by a Philippine Supreme Court whose relatively weak position within the colonial institutional context, formalist and essentialist conception of law in general and of departmental roles in particular, and reliance on nineteenth-century American police power jurisprudence conditioned it to defer to the exercise by the political branches of their constitutionally assigned prerogatives, thereby validating these departments' broad construction of the public category. The dynamic between Spanish structure and American theory created an activist colonial leviathan that Filipino political leaders attempted to capture throughout the colonial period and eventually adopted at its conclusion. Why the framers of the 1935 charter preferred the colonial constitutional model over other alternatives is best explained by delegate Manuel Roxas of Capiz, who said, "Because it is the government with which we are familiar. It is the form of government fundamentally such as it exists today; it is the only kind of government we have found to be in consonance with our experience."[1]

The U.S. Colonial State

The American colonial project in the Philippine Islands was transformative and developmental. This reflected the character of American colonialism in the islands, which was shaped by the need to reconcile the consent that underlay American democratic ideology with the inherently coercive nature of colonialism. In his instructions to the Philippine Commission, which served as the islands' first organic act, President William McKinley exhorted the commissioners to "bear in mind that the government which they are establishing is designed not for our satisfaction or for the expression of our theoretical views, but for the happiness, peace, and prosperity of the people of the Philippine Islands."[2] To sell colonialism both in the United States and in the Philippine Islands, American policy makers asserted that U.S. colonial rule, unlike Old World imperialism, would be temporary, tutelary, and benevolent. That is, colonial government in the islands would be instituted to prepare the Filipino people for independent nationhood and carried out for their benefit.

Francis Burton Harrison, a Democratic New York congressman who served as Philippine governor-general from 1913 to 1920, characterized American developmental imperialism as a significant departure from that practiced by Europeans, who had "conveyed to the peoples of Asia little share in the benefits of European civilization."[3] While Harrison conceded the difficulty and danger of remaking local systems and acknowledged that different cultures were entitled to develop on their own, he regarded the British, Dutch, and French colonial policy of leaving local cultures unmolested as "the clearest evidence ... that European colonization has not been conducted in Asia for the benefit of the people, but for purposes of gain."[4] Rather, instead of leaving Filipino natives "to sink into sloth and ignorance,"[5] and obtaining their labor cheap in order to benefit the mother country's merchants, manufacturers, and agricultural proprietors, W. Cameron Forbes, Harrison's Republican predecessor in office, noted that Americans set about educating the people of the islands, improving their health and sanitation, and raising the standard of living among laboring men.[6] Forbes believed that it was ultimately "good business and good policy to win the good will of the governed people, and that kind treatment resulted in better trade relations and less draft on the home treasury than engaging in hostilities and quelling insurrection."[7] To be sure, the American policy was pragmatic as well as altruistic. According to the historian Peter W. Stanley, the Philippine Commission regarded economic development, along with education, as the cutting edge of pacification as well as tutelage. If Americans succeeded in improving the standard of living in the islands, then perhaps in the end Filipinos would elect to remain within the American fold.[8]

To achieve their developmental goals, American colonial policy makers, Republican and Democratic alike, relied on the colonial government to take a leading role. They did not have to construct this apparatus from scratch. Rather, in the early months of the American military occupation, American military governors Wesley Merritt, Elwell Otis, and Arthur MacArthur found that the Spanish had left behind a viable, centralized, specialized, and interventionist colonial government structure, which they commandeered, modernized, and operated. Aside from collecting taxes, preserving public order, and administering justice, the Spanish government had established, beginning in 1861, specialized bureaus to regulate commercial activity, husband agricultural and forestry resources, and attend to public health, hygiene, sanitation, and instruction.[9] Thus, the Americanized Spanish bureaucracy in the islands was relatively more developed than its state and federal counterparts on the U.S. mainland. Described by the political scientist Stephen Skowronek as a "patchwork state," the late-nineteenth-century American administrative apparatus was a loose organization whose operations were manned and harmonized by political parties and whose internal dynamic and range and scope of activities were defined and rationalized by the common law courts.[10] The Spanish governmental structure inherited by American colonizers had evolved from one that, for reasons of economy and simplicity, had concentrated civil and military functions and authority in the Spanish governor-general to one that had become more functionally specialized through the creation of separate offices, over which supervision was apportioned among the divided but competing and overlapping authority of the governor-general, the Audiencia or the highest court, and the Intendant General or the finance head. Eliminating this confusing assignment of functions, Americans clearly centralized control over the Insular Government in the colonial executive. Writing for the *American Historical Review* in 1916, David P. Barrows pointed out that by centralizing "administrative control upon a single executive head," the Philippine governor-general differed from his American state and territorial counterparts, who were neither the sole heads of state administration nor the "centre of communication between all departments of the federal and local governments."[11] By adopting and streamlining the Spanish model of government organization, the American colonial government in the Philippines "took on a bureaucratic character, and thus from the beginning Philippine administration in American hands was unified, centralized, and made responsible to the chief executive of the archipelago."[12]

The foundation laid by the military governors shaped the subsequent colonial state-building efforts of the civil authorities. Indeed, President William McKinley directed the Second Philippine Commission, as the islands' first civil government, to "continue and perfect the work of organizing and establishing civil government already commenced by the military authorities."[13] Thereafter, the Philippine Commission formalized and reconstituted the administrative offices that were already operating and established them along civil service principles. In 1902, the U.S. Congress "approved, ratified, and confirmed" these actions in the preamble of the Philippine Organic Act.[14]

American colonial authorities modified the Spanish government structure, but they did not radically transform it. The historian Frank Golay pointed out that, while they Americanized activities at various levels of colonial government and increased efficiency, American officials provided essentially the same services as those provided by the Spanish regime. And, although supremely confident of the altruism of their imperial enterprise and the superiority of their institutions and policies, Americans "found no occasion to revolutionize the colonial government inherited from Spain."[15] It was thus in this Americanized Spanish body that American ideas were incarnated. But animating the Spanish structure with the American vision of government, law, politics, and the economy led to unexpected, sometimes contradictory, outcomes that shaped the character of the Philippine colonial state as well as that of the independent republic that followed in its wake.

Separation of Powers

Among the most important modifications introduced by American colonial policy makers to the Spanish government structure was the departmental theory of government or separation of powers doctrine. The departmental theory divided and distributed the functions and powers of the central government among executive, legislative, and judicial branches. President McKinley endorsed it for the Philippines in his instructions as forming part of those "certain great principles of government which have been made the basis of our governmental system."[16] However, invoking Filipino inexperience and incapacity in democratic government and the need to ensure "the supremacy of the sovereign power," the War Department and the U.S. Congress did not adopt this design for the colonial government. Instead, they placed it on a gradual path toward more clearly demarcated boundaries between the departments. Thus, in the early years of American rule the military governors and the American-controlled Philippine Commission exercised combined executive and legislative powers, much as the Spanish governor-general, as well as the U.S. territorial governments, had done.[17] Only in 1916 did the U.S. Congress more neatly separate these two functions and vest executive power in the American governor-general and legislative power in a colonial legislature, which soon came under full Filipino control.[18] Because authority over the Philippine colonial administration was clearly located in the executive department and because the colonial administration controlled revenue collection and expenditure, government jobs and salaries, licensing and privileges, and the formulation and implementation of government policies and projects, political struggles between American and Filipino colonial officials regularly revolved around attempts to control this apparatus. Dividing the branches of the central government according to race transmuted racial conflicts into legal contests, casting them as separation of powers disputes between the executive and legislative branches.[19]

That the administrative bureaucracy formed part of the Philippine constitutional landscape from the inception of American rule in the islands and that control over it was lodged in the colonial executive defined its relationship with the colonial judiciary and shaped Philippine constitutional doctrine. Common law courts in the United States mightily resisted the transfer of control over issues that once fell within their jurisdiction to specialized regulatory agencies such as the Interstate Commerce Commission. The Philippine courts, however, deferred to administrative agencies from the beginning, invoking the language of expertise and professionalism as justification.[20] In his authoritative 1920 textbook *The Constitutional Law of the Philippine Islands,* George A. Malcolm noted that with respect to administrative bodies "the well-known principles of public officers and extraordinary remedies apply. Within these rules, which the cases cited enunciate, the judiciary can control a duty not discretionary, imposed by law on a public officer. But usually the courts will confine themselves to the enforcement of legal and equitable rights, 'leaving the administrative affairs of the government to administrative officials.'"[21] More than any single figure in the American colonial period, Malcolm shaped Philippine constitutional law.

As the founding dean of the University of the Philippines College of Law, he authored influential casebooks and textbooks and taught public law to the Filipino legal elite. The members of this elite shaped Philippine political and legal development by serving in the legislative, judicial, and executive departments as well as in the law schools of the colonial and independent Philippine states. As an associate justice of the Philippine Supreme Court, Malcolm penned landmark decisions that would permanently determine Filipino understandings of such constitutional categories as separation of powers, due process, and equal protection.

From the beginning, however, the colonial judiciary's prospects for acting as a check on the activities of the colonial government were quite dim. As the islands' first civil governor, William Howard Taft believed that establishing an American-style judiciary in the islands was indispensable to the colonial project's success. Captive to the dominant legal ideology in the United States now known as "classical legal thought," Taft felt that common law courts were the "basis of all civil right and liberty," having traditionally checked the threat of majoritarian domination in a democratic society.[22] He deemed them essential in transmitting constitutional values to a Philippine judiciary that had as yet "no adequate conception of what practical liberty is."[23] But Taft's plans were compromised when he failed to recruit enough Spanish-speaking American lawyers for Philippine courts. Compounding this problem were the lower stature of courts in the civil law system exported by Spain to the Philippines compared to those of the common law and the Philippine Supreme Court's lack of sufficient power, money, and prestige to guarantee its independence.

Modes of Legal Thought

Apart from practical and institutional factors, the Philippine Supreme Court's mode of legal thinking also inclined it to adopt what Malcolm described as a "scrupulous" approach to judicial review.[24] Indeed, Malcolm and his American colleagues on the Supreme Court had learned their law in nineteenth-century American law schools when classical legal thought was ascendant. Their decisions displayed much of the categorical thinking, formalist analysis, textualism, and essentialism associated with this style of legal thinking.

When assessing the constitutional validity of a government action, the Philippine Supreme Court during the American period tended to first classify parties or transactions into abstract and neutral legal categories, often by identifying which government branch—executive or legislative—was acting. The justices then applied the appropriate formula of principles and doctrines, which was the departmental theory of government, and located authority for the measure either by identifying the relevant constitutional or statutory text or by matching the nature of the act with the nature of the function assigned to the branch.

Once they found the right authority, the "right" legal conclusion that they consistently derived was to confer a high presumption of constitutionality for measures undertaken by coequal branches. Ultimately, this "separate spheres" method insulated the exercise of constitutional discretion by the American governor-general and the colonial legislature from judicial review by the Philippine Supreme Court.[25] In practice, the court extended similar deference even to lower order municipal and provincial government units and administrative agencies. By treating legal argument like a mathematical equation, this approach attempted to depoliticize judicial decision making, pretensions that progressive and realist scholars in the United States challenged in the early twentieth century.

The Philippine Supreme Court's deferential stance and formalist mode of reasoning had implications for substantive doctrine. Since the legislature represented "the people," it was in theory best positioned to determine what the public interest was and what measures were necessary to secure it. But interdepartmental boundaries had never been airtight, and newly emergent administrative law allowed administrative agencies controlled by the executive branch to partake in legislative power through their rule-making functions. In addition, these agencies actually identified what this public interest was in concrete, day-to-day situations in the course of executing the law. The colonial administration drew on two sources of doctrinal justification to shield its activities from judicial scrutiny, namely, the newer language of administrative expertise and the older separation of powers doctrine. As a result, both political branches participated in constituting the Philippine notion of "the public."

Another expression of the fear of majoritarian tyranny, the "public" and "private" categories are used to determine when the government can legitimately intrude on individuals through its exercise of what had emerged by the late nineteenth century as its "three great powers," namely, eminent domain, taxation, and police power. While "the private" shields the individual from this intrusion, "the public" is a powerful enabling concept. The Philippine Supreme Court effectively entrusted the determination of the public's nature and scope to a colonial government that was interested in defining it as broadly as possible in the context of its activities in the islands.

Malcolm and his colleagues on the Supreme Court drew on late-nineteenth-century police power jurisprudence to validate the political branches' expansive construction of the public. They religiously invoked cases such as *Commonwealth v. Alger* (1851) in which Massachusetts chief justice Lemuel Shaw held that property *publici juris*, or privately owned property that was "susceptible of use by the public," was subject to police power regulation, and *Munn v. Illinois* (1877), which provided what was then the broadest formulation of public purpose in the open-ended category of "business affected with public interest."[26] And, while the U.S. Supreme Court under Chief Justice Melville Weston Fuller effectively emasculated *Munn* by heavily qualifying the use of its "affectation doctrine," landmark Philippine cases tended to cite both *Munn* and *Alger* liberally.[27] Perhaps the colonial context, which rendered precarious the survival of the state and ultimately the success of the entire colonial project, more readily supplied the justification for using *Munn*'s and *Alger*'s capacious formulations.

In the Philippine context, it is important to ask not just *what* is public but *who* is the public. In other words, in whose name, or for whose benefit, were the colonial government's interventions warranted? But perhaps one should start by asking who the public was *not*. Supported by American precedents that justified differential treatment for women, children, Native Americans, aliens, and other persons deemed excluded from membership in the constitutive community, foundational cases decided by Justice Malcolm ratified the determination made by local and central government officials that the Philippine public did not include the uncivilized, such as the Mangyan tribes of Mindoro; the "scourges of society," such as prostitutes, vagrants, and lepers; and "undesirable foreigners" such as the non-U.S. national British and Chinese.[28]

In some cases, the Philippine justification for differential treatment followed the protective rationale that underlay the American rule, but it also provided Filipino legislative leaders with the means to harness public resources in order to enable Filipinos to compete with foreigners for control over the islands' political economy. Frustrated that their economy had always been monopolized by foreigners, namely, the Spanish, the British, the Chinese, and now the Americans, but lacking adequate capital to compete with them, Filipinos were lukewarm to plans encouraging the inflow of private American capital into the islands. However, they welcomed investment in the *public sphere* since they believed that these investments would be theirs when they took over the colonial government. Thus, in the Filipino mind public became equated with Filipino, that is, the Hispanicized Filipino majority. Pent-up Filipino frustrations were translated into law and public policy through Speaker Sergio Osmeña's post–World War I "economic nationalism" initiative, which called for chartering and financing government corporations with public funds to develop major industries. These frustrations were further expressed, this time with a vengeance, in the "Filipino first" strategy of the 1935 Constitution, which imposed a minimum 60 percent Filipino equity requirement for investments in key economic sectors and allowed the Philippine government to nationalize these sectors if Filipino private capital failed to step up. Thus, despite American liberal constitutionalism's deep-seated and long-standing fear of majoritarian despotism, the Philippine constitutionalism after which it was modeled developed justifications precisely to ensure that the Filipino majority's representatives could secure control over the country's resources and its political, economic, and social life, which they felt was theirs by right but of which they believed they had always been deprived by foreigners.[29]

Under its police power, or its power to adopt measures necessary for its public's health, morals, and welfare, the colonial government could do virtually anything. Through the Insular Doctrine, the U.S. Supreme Court created unincorporated territorial status that placed the new insular possessions outside the federal relationship and the operation of the U.S. Constitution. But while this doctrine mandated that the provisions of the U.S. Constitution had to be explicitly extended to the islands by Congress, the same did not hold true for the government's three great powers, which American jurists and theorists had characterized as inherent in sovereignty, indefinable, and illimitable. The Philippine Supreme Court emphasized this boundless view of police power to justify all manner of regulation such as allowing the customs collector to condition the grant of shipping licenses on transporting explosives or allowing the revenue collector to remove billboards for being "offensive to sight."[30] The court conceded the futility of restricting the reach of police power by describing the numerous attempts to limit its scope by definition as interesting only insofar as they illustrated "its rapid extension within comparatively recent years to points heretofore deemed entirely within the field of private liberty and property rights."[31]

Not only did the Philippine Supreme Court construe police power broadly, but it also evaluated the constitutionality of government measures against due process and equal protection challenges using what American lawyers today would recognize as rational basis review.[32] Described as a "brain dead" standard, rationality review is currently regarded as the easiest to meet of the three tests subsequently developed by the U.S. Supreme Court. Since virtually any purpose can be asserted as a *legitimate government purpose* and any measure shown as being *reasonably related* to said purpose, it is practically impossible to invalidate anything under this test. Only in 1924 did the Philippine Supreme Court annul legislation on substantive due process grounds, following the line of cases begun in 1905 by *Lochner v. New York*.[33] This was the case of *People of the Philippines v. Pomar*, which voided maternity leave legislation and invoked *Lochner* for the first time in a Philippine decision.[34]

Despite evidence that long working hours severely affected the health of bakers, the *Lochner* court held fast to an essentialist conception that denied that baking was an occupation that was in and of itself unhealthy, which resulted in its rejection of maximum hours legislation as an infringement on the erstwhile constitutionally protected freedom of contract.[35] And just as *Lochner* had galvanized the U.S. progressive and realist assault on the classical legal paradigm, so *Pomar* similarly inspired a landlord-dominated Constitutional Convention, threatened by growing agrarian and labor unrest, to water down what were already weak Philippine due process and equal protection clauses by mitigating their impact on parties with disadvantaged bargaining positions through the social justice principle and by shrinking their scope through constitutionalized exceptions for labor and women.[36] In light of the threat to the existing order, however, the delegates' enlightened progressivism seems like a reactionary, albeit sincere and well-meaning, attempt by the Filipino social, political, economic, and legal elite to save the status quo by constitutionalizing the paternalism that had up until then characterized Philippine social relations. Aware that progressive and realist critics of classical legal jurisprudence had long blamed its solicitousness of private property rights for thwarting U.S. social and economic reforms prior to the Depression, the Filipino framers regarded their constitutional innovations as enlightened, even socially progressive. But was it prudent to unshackle a government run by elites who equated their interests with the public good and who felt that their nationality entitled them to inherit, unaltered, inequitable foreign controls over the Philippine economy? As an empowered iteration of the preceding colonial government, the Philippine Republic's combination of vast capacities and relatively lax restraints was designed to benefit a Filipino public for whom these elite leaders presumed to speak. But those same expansive state powers also posed equivalent dangers for individual rights. It thus seems ironic that what progressives and realists had once derided as the reactionary conservatism of Classical Legal Thought just might have minimized the pernicious potential of this colonial constitutional legacy, if wielded by a cautious judiciary.

Conclusion

By animating the highly centralized colonial government structure and its far-reaching projects with the doctrines and principles of turn of the century American liberal constitutionalism, American and Filipino colonial officials created and legitimated an activist Philippine state that evoked the rhetoric and approaches of the New Deal but substantially differed from it in form and philosophy. The framers of the 1935 Philippine Constitution essentially preserved and elaborated on this colonial organization, practice, and discourse. While freeing those at the helm of the Philippine government from the structural and doctrinal strictures that hampered them from doing what they thought was much good, the framers placed in their hands tremendous potential for abuse, which has all too frequently been exploited in postcolonial Philippine history.

The Hazards of Jeffersonianism
Challenges of State Building in the United States and Its Empire

PAUL D. HUTCHCROFT

JEFFERSONIAN POLITICAL APPROACHES AND IDEALS have become, for many, indistinguishable from American political approaches and ideals. "The United States," observed Clinton Rossiter during the cold war, "is a Jeffersonian country [with] ... as powerful and uncritical an ideological commitment to Jefferson as the Communists have to Marx."[1] As the United States has moved from republic to empire to superpower in the past century, key precepts of Jeffersonianism have moved beyond American shores to influence the character of state formation—and reformation—in countries throughout the world. In this brief analysis, I will focus particular attention on two of the most fundamental components of Jeffersonian thought: its strong bias in favor of decentralized forms of governance and its "essential optimism" about the character of American political development. Both are highly attractive notions, and it is not surprising that these closely related elements of Jeffersonian thought have come to have such a major impact on academic analysis and public policy not only in the United States but also abroad.

Unfortunately, as I will demonstrate, there are major hazards associated with these understandably appealing elements of Jeffersonian thought. First, the Jeffersonian bias in favor of decentralization has often been very inappropriately exported to settings with inegalitarian social structures and high concentrations of socioeconomic and coercive resources at the local level. In the largest and most important U.S. colony, the Philippines, early colonials began the process of state formation with the observation that central government intervention in local affairs "is foreign to American practice" and decentralization was "one of the crying needs" of the archipelago. Echoing Jefferson, and with fond reference to New England, Governor-General William Howard Taft proclaimed "town government" to be "the practical way of building up general government."[2] As will be analyzed below, however, Jeffersonian ideals were generally more influential in bolstering the power of local and provincial bosses than in laying the foundations for participatory democracy.

Second, the persistence of Jeffersonian optimism hinders careful analysis of major historical challenges faced in the process of American political development; in particular, the common assertion that egalitarian social structures encouraged a comparatively smooth and untroubled process of state formation generally fails to grapple with the enormous struggles over slavery that culminated in the bloody and protracted "War between the States." Faulty analysis of the historical process of U.S. state formation, in turn, often contributes to a common tendency to underestimate the enormous challenges of state formation in other parts of the world. This was demonstrated, again, in the Philippine colonial experience, where initial U.S. optimism about the process of "political tutelage" was eventually replaced with far more cautious assessments of what might be accomplished.

In relation to the larger volume, the goal of this essay is to provide an initial inquiry into important ideological moorings of the U.S. imperial state by, first, surveying the central tenets of Jeffersonian thought, both its "sanguine temper" and belief in decentralized structures of governance; next, critiquing the common view that American state formation was relatively easy; third, examining how Jefferson's optimistic outlook and decentralist bias are most inappropriate when applied to his home region, the South; and, finally, analyzing how many of the same Jeffersonian ideals in favor of local autonomy were exported to the first overseas target of systematic American "political tutelage," the colonial Philippines.[3]

Optimism and Decentralization as Jeffersonian Impulses

Thomas Jefferson has long been considered an extraordinarily difficult person to interpret, not least since he himself adhered only loosely to the body of thought that came to bear his name. His archrival, Alexander Hamilton, found him a "contemptible hypocrite," and historians ever since have noted his many incongruities.[4] Not unlike Tocqueville's later observations of Americans in general, Jefferson seems to have been less interested in philosophy than in the actual practice of government.[5]

Through the haze of contradictions, however, it is possible to discern certain outlooks and inclinations that have come to be associated with both Jefferson and Jeffersonianism. Stanley Elkins and Eric McKitrick identify a particular Jeffersonian *approach* to politics, notably the liberal idealism that "has made him so perennially attractive a figure in American culture." Jefferson tended to favor the reform of a system on the margins rather than at the core, and he avoided complex problems that needed to be "fully thought through from top to bottom." Most important for the present analysis is their characterization of the optimistic outlook that colored Jefferson's examination of political issues.

> Failure, and the functional grounds on which failure might occur, were never actually built into his thinking.... [B]ecause of his essential optimism Jefferson seldom felt it necessary to break lances. He believed, and often in effect said, that all would come right with time. And so it may have been his sanguine temper, as well as his *a priori* mental habits and the faith he put in reason, that made so many of his schedules, his rules, his plans and sketches of the world, a reflection of how he wanted things to look rather than the way they happened to be.[6]

On the level of *ideals*, Jefferson's fervent support for decentralization and states' rights has had a pronounced impact on the subsequent character of American administrative development. "The debate over the relative powers... of the state and national governments," observed Samuel P. Huntington in 1959, "has been very largely carried on Jeffersonian terms." From the days of Tocqueville, comparative analysts have frequently remarked on the considerable degree to which the American state is territorially decentralized.[7] The federal system of government established in the Constitution reserves a great deal of authority for the states—even if the precise balance between federal and state authority has remained a matter of continuing contention in American politics for over two centuries. The dominance of decentralization in American political thought has diverse origins, but Thomas Jefferson is commonly held to be most responsible for making it the powerful and enduring legacy that it remains today. As Lynton Caldwell explains, "[H]e held it an axiom that good administration would provide for the greatest degree of decentralization possible to the successful execution of public policy."[8]

In his 1821 autobiography, Jefferson wrote that it is through the distribution of power across its territorial units "that good government is effected."[9] As part of his faith in decentralization, Jefferson idealized the notion of an agrarian democracy that would draw together a homogeneous and egalitarian community of small farmers. In his correspondence, Jefferson declared the New England townships to be "the wisest invention ever devised by the wit of man for the perfect exercise of self-government and for its preservation" and advocated a system of "ward republics" that would extend the New England genius to the rest of the country with the goal of devolving the functions of government to the local level and giving every citizen "a part in the administration of the public affairs."[10]

Not surprisingly, Jefferson's vision for implanting this system into a very different social structure—that of his native South—were notably unsuccessful.[11] Here, once again, one can observe the enormous gap between "how he wanted things to look rather than the way they happened to be." As Elkins and McKitrick explain, Jefferson expressed strong convictions about how "the yeoman farmer was the ideal citizen of an ideal republic, ... [but] [t]he controlling forces of Virginia life were concerned not for a society of small farmers but for one of large estates.... [T]he good yeoman ... was in fact ringed about by influences (a slaveholding planter elite) which contained him and made him agreeable to a man of Jefferson's benevolent views and social location." Jefferson's proposals for a New England style of public education and homesteading on the frontier were roundly defeated by his fellow members of the Virginia elite, but despite such defeats he never proceeded to think beyond piecemeal attempts to apply his grandiose ideas about social *equality* to the social *inequality* in his midst.[12] "The leisure that made possible his great writings on human liberty," Hofstadter wryly notes, "were supported by the labors of three generations of slaves."[13]

Despite the many contradictions that they contain, Jeffersonian and American political approaches and ideals have, for many analysts, become largely indistinguishable. It is significant that two of the leading Hamiltonian figures of American history, Abraham Lincoln and Franklin Delano Roosevelt, found it convenient to cloak their centralizing projects in the rhetoric of Jeffersonianism.[14] Even a leading biographer of Alexander Hamilton readily acknowledges Jefferson as the "high priest" of the America's "secular religion" of democracy.[15] As the following section demonstrates, Jefferson's "essential optimism" has deeply influenced—and often skewed—comparative analysis of American state formation.

The Challenges of American State Formation

Alexis de Tocqueville, the first major comparative analyst of the American polity, shared Jefferson's perception of an essentially homogeneous and egalitarian American society, writing that "the general equality of condition among the people ... is the fundamental fact from which all others seem to be derived."[16] Tocqueville and Jefferson also display a similarly "sanguine temper" in viewing the United States as a land in which beneficial political arrangements had seemingly fallen in place without much effort. The French observer saw in America "a democratic community in which the citizens have been equal from the first." The role for the state was correspondingly small, and decentralized patterns of governance very effectively served the common weal; as Tocqueville concluded, "society governs itself for itself."[17]

Jeffersonian and Tocquevillian insights are both readily apparent in more recent comparative historical scholarship on American political development. This body of work is remarkably sparse.[18] Many of its most influential insights can be found in the analysis written by Samuel Huntington a generation ago. Huntington faults Jefferson for basing his ideas on how American society "ought to be" rather on careful analysis of how it actually was, but he does credit Jefferson with [singling] out one important truth. American did not remain agrarian, but it did maintain and develop the *homogeneity of interest and opinion* which has been so frequently commented upon by acute social observers from de Tocqueville to the present. In this respect, Jefferson pointed to one of the most basic foundations of America society and one ... which ... most clearly distinguishes America from Europe.[19]

In addition, Huntington's analysis of the United States takes on Jefferson's "sanguine temper" and Tocqueville's admiration for the society of the New World as it portrays American state formation to be a relatively easy and straightforward process. He asserts "the absence in the American historical experience of the need to found a political order. ... America was born with a government [imported from England]. ... Hence Americans never had to worry about creating a government." Huntington further argues that because the United States was a homogeneous, egalitarian, nonaristocratic, consensual society lacking a feudal heritage it could avoid the more common patterns of state centralization found in Europe. The sum total is a "happy history" with a "pleasant conjuncture of blessings." In making this argument, Huntington's purpose is to emphasize that the "United States never had to construct [powerful, centralized] authority in order to modernize its society, and hence its experience has little to offer modernizing countries today."[20]

The observations and analysis of Tocqueville and Huntington contain extremely valuable insights; early U.S. social structures were, to be sure, notably different from those found in Europe at the time. But in suggesting the relatively untroubled and straightforward character of American political development both analysts seriously understate the daunting challenges that were in fact encountered. In other words, while it is accurate to say that the United States was free of many of the obstacles of societal modernization faced by Europe, it must at the same time be emphasized that state formation in the New World encountered its own *distinct* problems and hurdles.

The most glaring problem in their analysis is the assertion of egalitarian structures in a country where slavery was still practiced in the mid-nineteenth century and disputes over slavery rent the nation asunder. Even if the focus is on the relatively egalitarian structures within white American society, however, it is a mistake to assert that such structures contributed to a "happy history." Bernard Bailyn's analysis of prerevolutionary American politics highlights very clearly the error in presuming that egalitarian societies necessarily contribute to easy political development. The lack of a well-defined class structure, he argues, was actually the source of extraordinary conflict; indeed, Bailyn describes the political system as not merely "troubled and contentious" but even "explosive."[21]

The American Revolution was, to a significant extent, a reaction against British attempts at centralization in the 1760s and 1770s. The colonials previously enjoyed a considerable degree of self-government, and out of British efforts at reform there emerged "a strong distaste for centralized authority."[22] In later decades, the early Republic experienced pitched political battles, many having to do with the proper role of the national government and the proper balance between national and sectional interests.[23] The Constitution, which replaced the highly decentralized Articles of Confederation, was an equivocal document that created what has variously been described as "part-national, part-federal government" and "centralized federalism."[24] As James Roger Sharp explains, this "serious ambiguity" about the precise relationship between the national government and the states came "perilously *close* to causing a civil breakdown in the 1790s" and "*did* cause a bloody civil war in the 1860s." Sharp faults scholarship for minimizing both the "dissonance" that existed in American politics of the 1790s and the anxiety that existed over "the tenuousness and fragility of the union and the Constitution." Huntington, in particular, is singled out for his overly sanguine account of early American political development.[25]

Thomas Jefferson was, of course, at the center of the controversies of the time, and his antagonism with Alexander Hamilton became a "blistering public feud" by 1792. Hamilton's more centralist program was not only antithetical to Jefferson's vision of agrarian democracy but was also perceived to have a sectional bias disadvantageous to Virginia and certain other southern states. Tensions grew throughout the decade, and with them the level of political organization on both sides. The result was two "protoparties," the Federalist and the Republican, each determined to bring about the destruction of its traitorous political enemies in order "to save the country from ruination."[26] In the analysis of Samuel Eliot Morison, the two parties represented "the political expressions of a deep-lying antagonism between two great sectional interests—the planting-slaveholding interest which was mainly rural-Southern, and the mercantile-shipping-financial interest of seaport cities from Salem to Charleston."[27] Jefferson's increasingly hostility to the federal government (in which he held the office of vice president) helped him rally fellow Republicans and win the presidency in 1800—and in the process defeat the Federalists. As Jefferson later proclaimed, his election in 1800 was "as real a revolution in the principles of government as that of 1776 was in its form."[28]

Whatever the short-term consequences, it is clear that Jefferson's increasingly outspoken support for states' rights had a major impact on the character of American political discourse into the nineteenth century and beyond. It is notable that this man of libertarian rhetoric continued to espouse forcefully his states' rights ideology even after it had been clearly connected to proslavery arguments.[29] As Sharp concludes, the Republican rhetoric of this period "laid the ideological groundwork for more than a century of Southern particularism in the United States" and proved very useful in the defense of slavery and racial discrimination. During the nullification movement of 1832 in South Carolina, explain Elkins and McKitrick, Republican precepts of the 1790s were invoked "with Jefferson as its prophet." And on the eve of the Civil War leading southern politicians derived from them "a complete theory of state sovereignty accompanied by the right of peaceable secession."[30] Jeffersonian principles of states' rights lived on in the Democratic Party, which dominated from 1828 to the Civil War and was still a major force in postbellum America.[31] In short, the impact of Jefferson's hostility toward the federal government went far beyond the controversies of the late 1790s to influence the character of American political discourse for many decades to come.

Hazards of Jeffersonianism in the American South

Just as Tocqueville and Huntington give insufficient emphasis to many important difficulties faced in the process of American state formation, so also do they fail to grapple with the realities of slavery in the American South. The problems in their analysis highlight the hazards of Jeffersonianism in Jefferson's home region.

Like Jefferson, Tocqueville finds particular appeal in the New England townships. But, unlike Jefferson, he does acknowledge that the New England experience is not readily generalizable. He differentiates the egalitarian and nonaristocratic inhabitants of areas east of the Hudson from the "rich landed proprietors" and slave owners in the South. "The farther we go towards the South," he comments, "the less active does the business of the township or parish become; ... the population exercises a less immediate influence on affairs; town meetings are less frequent, and the subjects of debate less numerous." Unfortunately, Tocqueville does not integrate these caveats into his conclusions about the character of local governance in the United States, which are based primarily on one region of the country: New England.[32] In short, he fails to emphasize that the best of the American political tradition does not equal the entirety of the American political tradition. Far worse is Huntington's comparison of "political modernization" in the United States and Europe, which almost completely ignores the South, a region, alas, that has anything but a "happy history."[33]

C. Vann Woodward, on the contrary, very directly confronts the problems of bringing the South into a national narrative of freedom: "One of the simplest but most consequential generalizations ever made about the national character was Tocqueville's that American [sic] was born free.... There *are*, Americans, after all, who were not 'born free.'" The experience of human bondage in the southern United States, he further argues, brought forth a "basically pessimistic ... social outlook" at odds with "the American legend of innocence and social felicity." In sum, the distinctive heritage of the South puts this region "far more closely in line with the common lot of mankind than the national legends" more appropriately associated with the North.[34]

With the failure of Reconstruction in the 1870s, the goal of bringing freedom to the American South was abandoned and new forms of institutionalized racial oppression were put in place. This did not, however, deter the country from overseas ventures carried out in the name of democracy and freedom. Just two decades later, the U.S. venture into imperialism was justified at least in part by the need to free the remnants of the Spanish empire from the oppression of colonial rule.

The Taft Era in the Philippines

The imperial venture did not go as planned. Across the Pacific, the Spanish-American War evolved into the Philippine-American War—a widespread Filipino guerrilla struggle for independence that united much of the population and tied down some seventy-two thousand U.S. troops. Steady reports of atrocities, meanwhile, fanned anti-imperialist sentiment at home. Out of a combination of expediency and ideals, the blueprints for a new colonial state were drawn.[35]

As part of the "policy of attraction," the goal of which was to win over a cosmopolitan *ilustrado* (educated) elite, as well as local "caciques" who had given strong support to the revolutionary struggle for independence, American governor William Howard Taft and his associates drafted administrative reforms that envisaged the creation of strong local governments throughout the lowland Christian areas of the Philippines.[36] To quote David Joel Steinberg, "Taft reversed Karl von Clausewitz's maxim by making politics an extension of war by other means."[37] Expediency alone, however, does not explain the manner in which American colonials crafted a new Philippine state; distinctly American notions of governance also played a major role. Unusual in the annals of colonialism, American officials began the task of colonial state formation with a strong belief in the necessary *limitations* on governmental authority. In addition, as set forth in Secretary of War Elihu Root's instructions to Taft's Philippine Commission in 1900, a foundational goal was the rapid establishment of municipal governments "subject to the least degree of supervision and control . . . consistent with the maintenance of law, order, and loyalty." Local units were to be favored in "the distribution of powers among the governments."[38] Through a combination of expediency and ideals, therefore, the architects of American colonial rule demonstrated a strong inclination to grant substantial authority to local officials throughout most of the archipelago and thus replicate the spirit of the local self-rule practiced at home. As noted above, Jeffersonian notions of "town government" were very much at the fore. In a setting in which de facto decentralization was already far advanced (as landed elites that had emerged under Spanish rule held sway in many localities), Taft promoted the devolution of a considerable degree of decision-making authority to local officials.

Building on the units and boundaries already established under Spanish colonial rule, the Philippine Commission quickly put in place the legal framework for more systematic organization of local governments. Whereas under the Spanish opportunities for gaining political power were largely confined to the municipal level, the Americans provided new and expanded opportunities from the municipal to the provincial and national levels.[39] In 1901, at the municipal level, a sharply restricted elite electorate was given the right to vote for the positions of president (mayor), vice president, and council. In providing for the indirect election of provincial governors, in 1902, the Americans significantly expanded the political arena to a new, supralocal level. This trend was furthered after 1906, when provincial governors came to be directly elected (by the elite electorate). By 1907, as the American project of "self-government" moved beyond municipalities and provinces to the creation of an Assembly in Manila, provincial factions were in place to become a major building block of national-level maneuvering.[40]

The distinctiveness of central-local relations in the American Philippines becomes especially apparent when viewed in comparative perspective. The centralizing prefectoral models common in other colonial states were rejected in favor of a clearly articulated devotion of authority to provincial and municipal governments. Manila's supervision of local government was directed by the Executive Bureau and assisted by centrally appointed provincial treasurers (a post initially reserved for Americans). As prominent as the Executive Bureau was within the Philippine polity, its authority paled in comparison with the highly centralized interior ministries set up by most other major colonial regimes of the day. Whereas the Executive Bureau was one of many agencies with field offices throughout the country, the pattern elsewhere was for interior ministries to monopolize the dealings of the central state with lower tiers of authority, notably prefects, who were given broad responsibility for exercising control over their assigned regions. And, whereas in the Philippines the Executive Bureau sought to supervise the activities of elected officials with their own bases of power, the interior ministries in other colonies supervised the rest of the country through appointed officials and sought to curb any tendencies for them to develop their own bases of power at the local level. Compared to other colonies utilizing prefectoralism—the state-of-the-art means for regimes promoting administrative and political centralization—the American colonial regime in the Manila was simply not set up in such as way as to encourage effective central control over the hinterland.

More fundamentally, it must be emphasized that American officials gave far more attention to elections and the creation of representative institutions than to the creation of a modern bureaucratic apparatus. As Benedict Anderson explains, "[U]nlike all the other modern colonial regimes in twentieth century Southeast Asia, which operated through huge, autocratic, white-run bureaucracies, the American authorities in Manila ... created only a minimal civil service and quickly turned over most of its component positions to the natives."[41] This reflects what Huntington describes as a distinctly American tendency toward the process of state formation. The typical American, he observes, "is so fundamentally anti-government that he identifies government with restrictions on government.... Confronted with the need to design a political system which will maximize power and authority, he has no ready answer. His general formula is that governments should be based on free and fair elections."[42]

That said, Taft and his counterparts did believe in the virtues of a modern civil service and devoted significant effort to its emergence. To promote honest and efficient government at all levels, the Philippine Commission in 1901 enacted a Civil Service Act. Taft expected the law to save the colony from "the most marked evil of American politics, the spoils system," and the Commission declared that "[w]ithout this law American government in these islands is ... foredoomed to humiliated failure."[43] In trying to construct a reliable civil service, the Philippine Commission was not doing anything out of the ordinary. What makes American colonial rule distinctive is the simultaneous pursuance of policies of "political tutelage" that unwittingly promoted the rapid emergence of a patronage-infested polity. In the end, the goal of building an efficient bureaucracy was greatly overshadowed—and undermined—by American innovations in the political sphere.

The American colonials' lack of success in administrative development can be understood in large part as a function of historical timing. Drawing on the framework of Martin Shefter, one can observe that because representative institutions in the Philippines emerged prior to the creation of strong bureaucratic institutions "the depredations of patronage-seeking politicians" quite easily overwhelmed the Philippine bureaucracy. Nascent attempts at building an effective system of administration, in other words, were engulfed by another, more powerful logic: patronage. "As in the United States," explains Anderson, "civil servants frequently owed their employment to legislator patrons, and up to the end of the American period the civilian machinery of state remained weak and divided."[44]

This is an important observation regarding dynamics at the center, but it must also be emphasized how the prevalence of patronage tends to heighten local power at the expense of central authority. First, and most obvious, the prevalence of patronage undermines the coherence of the civil service and thereby undercuts the supervisory capacity of the center. When American colonials proclaimed the virtues of "town government" and denounced central control as "foreign to American practice," there seemed to be a strong faith that their system of government would produce good results and demonstrate its inherent superiority. Alas, it did not. American colonial officials soon discovered that the goal of local autonomy quite often conflicted with the goal of seeking to ensure that government was doing its job well (building roads and ports, providing law and order, dispensing good justice, fighting disease, etc.). There were also increasing concerns—as voiced by Taft himself in 1902—over "caciquism" and "feudal relations of dependence" in the countryside. Many municipal councils were appropriating funds to their own salaries, leaving roads untended and teachers unpaid. "The truth is," Taft acknowledged in 1903, "that the municipal governments have not been as satisfactory in their operations as could be wished."[45]

Concerned over abuses of government power in the countryside, American colonials sought to increase central supervision and improve the quality of local government. It soon became apparent that key bureaus in Manila often lacked the administrative capacity to do so. Hobbled by both shortages and high turnover of personnel, the Executive Bureau had to supervise municipalities through increasingly autonomous provincial governments. Supervision was also undermined by the fact that the bureaucracy constructed by the Americans was never well insulated from patronage pressures. This became a particular problem after the opening of the Philippine Assembly in 1907; in essence, the creation of legislative institutions heightened the logic of patronage at a time when bureaucratic structures had barely had a chance to consolidate their strength. In the final days before the convening of the Assembly, the Philippine Commission rushed through a range of bills with a centralizing intent; the first impulse of the new Assembly, correspondingly, was to decrease supervision and increase the powers and resources of local government. The civil service law was an early target, and in 1908 the critical position of municipal treasurer was removed from civil service protection, freed from oversight by the provincial treasurer, and transformed into a blatantly political post beholden to local forces rather than the center.

Second, the prevalence of patronage provides important informal avenues for the promotion of local interests. Just as Stephen Skowronek writes of the "broad dispersion of particularistic benefits downward to the localities" in the United States in the late nineteenth century, so, too, can one find a similar phenomenon in the American Philippines.[46] It is very unusual for colonials to actively encourage the formation of political parties, but in the Philippines Taft considered it an important element of his larger project of "political education." The first beneficiary was the pro-American Federalista Party, to which Taft gave ample opportunities to transcend its thin elite Manila political base and build a larger following throughout the provinces; this included a powerful role in making appointments to key provincial offices. After 1905, the major beneficiary was the Nacionalista Party, composed of an emerging group of provincial elites turned national politicos who very deftly channeled patronage resources for the benefit of themselves and their allies in the provinces. The party's publicly proclaimed demand for national independence became secondary to other goals, namely, the quest for increased autonomy (against belated American efforts at central supervision), expanded legislative authority (against an executive controlled by American colonials), and more extensive opportunities for patronage (to nurture the party's base in the countryside).

At a point in history when most colonial powers were building powerful bureaucracies in the capital and relying on prefectoral systems to centralize control over the countryside, therefore, the American colonial government in Manila began the task of state formation with a pronounced emphasis on local autonomy. Unlike other colonial rulers, Taft did not share the same telos of overcoming competing centers of local power and achieving larger degrees of autonomy from (and dominance over) civil society. He was, instead, acting out of distinctly American notions of what a state ought to be. There were indeed provisions for central administrative supervision, but this was countered by the fact that increasingly assertive local interests were attaining political office amid expectations of gaining an ever-widening role in government affairs. In terms of expediency, this strategy of building a state through compromise with established provincial lords was remarkably successful in enabling American colonials to defeat the Philippine struggle for independence.[47] As an effort to duplicate town government in the New England style in a distinctly contrasting socioeconomic milieu, however, the strategy was quickly revealed to be a monumental failure.

In the Philippine context, where American colonials encountered highly inequitable socioeconomic structures, the introduction of representative institutions with a highly restricted electorate served to transform the Spanish era economic elite into an American era political-economic elite. The promotion of local autonomy and representative institutions produced little democratic substance, either at the local level (where town government had more in common with Tammany Hall than New England) or at the national level (where the most ambitious of the provincial lords now enjoyed a new arena in which to exert their authority and power over the rest of the population). Taft himself was not entirely comfortable with the overall results of his strategy, and as early as 1908 he expressed concern that the effect of U.S. colonial policy might merely be "to await the organization of a Philippine oligarchy or aristocracy competent to administer government and then turn the Islands over to it."[48] Over the longer term, however, he hoped that American ideals would shine through and undercut what he had once called "a kind of quasi slavery called caciquism."[49] More specifically, he hoped the combination of an American-style civil service and widespread public education would eventually promote "popular self-government" and enable the common people to maintain their civil rights "against a more powerful class."[50]

Without implying that William Howard Taft or any other American colonials in the Philippines are the direct descendants of Thomas Jefferson, one can note strong Jeffersonian impulses as the United States undertook a concerted program of "political tutelage." First, and most obvious, is the distrust of centralization and the strong initial bias in favor of decentralized forms of governance. Second, at a more subtle level Taft and other American colonials began their tutelage with optimism about the way in which political order in the Philippine archipelago might readily be reconstructed along American lines. There was a general suspicion of government authority along with ineffectual attempts to construct the ongoing administrative apparatus of the state—very much in line with Jefferson's distrust of "professionalized administration and complex administrative machinery."[51] American colonial officials believed instead in the capacity of elections and representational structures to transform Philippine society, only to realize later the profoundly antidemocratic character of the polity they had shaped.

Colonial state formation in the Philippines began just as what Skowronek calls a "new American state" was emerging at home; this was characterized by "new national administrative institutions . . . free from the clutches of party domination, direct court supervision, and localistic orientations."[52] Elements of contemporary American state reformation were exported to the Philippines, most notably attempts to build a professional and efficient civil service, but the agencies of the central state soon became captive to "patronage-seeking politicians" who were, in turn, strongly oriented toward local needs. Furthermore, as is richly detailed elsewhere in this volume, there are many ways in which elements of the colonial state apparatus provided a laboratory for major innovations in such specific fields as public health. In terms of the overall character of national administrative institutions, however, it was generally an older version of the American state that the colonials ended up implanting in the Philippines. Because the major builders of the colonial state were—by the standards of the day—conservatives rather than reformers or progressives, the major political and bureaucratic reform impulses of the metropole were generally not replicated in Manila.[53] Taft, himself a patronage politician from Ohio who had emerged from a system in which courts and parties still played a dominant role, explicitly set out to make the "modern lawyer-politician" the dominant figure in Philippine society.

Conclusion

As the United States moved from republic to empire at the end of the nineteenth century, the challenges of state building moved from the home front to a foreign land. The colonial experience in the Philippines was thoroughly influenced by Jeffersonian ideals in terms of both an explicit bias in favor of local (as opposed to central) government and unrealistic expectations about the process of "political tutelage."

In noting the dysfunctional consequences of American colonial policies in the Philippines, my purpose is not of course to offer implicit praise to those colonial regimes that instituted a highly centralized form of authoritarian rule. We can, however, note very different legacies that emerge from distinct forms of colonial rule. A particularly stark contrast comes forth from examination of Japanese colonial rule in South Korea. While the Americans in the Philippines transformed an economic elite into a political-economic elite capable of frustrating colonial goals, the Japanese turned the political-economic elite of the Yi Dynasty into an economic elite that was quite effectively harnessed to their colonial goals. The U.S. colonial state in the Philippines was remarkably weak and decentralized, continually plundered by the oligarchy that the Americans had fostered, while the Japanese created a highly centralized and overbearing state able to exercise a high degree of control over a weak and poorly organized society. Partly (but by no means wholly) because of their dramatically contrasting colonial legacies, the historical character of state-society relations in the Philippines and South Korea are the mirror image of each other. The modern Philippine state continues to confront highly entrenched authoritarian enclaves, where local power holders can draw on their very considerable coercive and socio-economic resources to thwart democratic goals. In the modern Korean state, by contrast, one finds no similar concentrations of local power able to challenge the implementation of policies produced through democratic deliberation. As the two countries consider possible reform in their respective structures of central-local relations, they can proceed with the following simple premise: it is an easier task, historically, to engage in the (de jure) decentralization of that which is already centralized than to centralize that which is already (de facto) decentralized.[54]

In line with the broader analysis of this volume as set forth in the introduction, the colonial Philippines can be seen as "a particularly revelatory case" for understanding subsequent patterns of "the rise of the United States to geopolitical dominance." In future work, I plan to extend the scope of the analysis to more contemporary efforts at state building within the American empire. As a broad overview, it is important to note that Jeffersonian sentiments in favor of local autonomy have been readily apparent in recent decades as private and public U.S. aid agencies have actively promoted strategies of decentralization throughout the world. One 1995 analysis by the U.S. Agency for International Development, for example, explained that "observers of many political persuasions find something very attractive about the Jeffersonian ideal of yeoman farmers managing their own local affairs, as in the frequent reverential invocation of the

New England town meeting as an institution to be emulated. Democratic decentralization is thought to be 'good for the soul'—an end in itself."[55] But, just as the doctrine of "states' rights" sanctioned great injustices in Jefferson's home region throughout much of American history, so do strategies of decentralization sometimes promote highly undemocratic outcomes in many developing countries today.

Even more recently, Jefferson's "sanguine temper" seems to be present in the current U.S.-led "war on terror," in particular an invasion of Iraq that from the start has been premised more on how the Bush administration "wanted things to look rather than [on] the way they [happen] to be." As the war began, Iraq's post-Saddam national transformation was proclaimed to be the miraculous linchpin for bringing forth a new Middle East. But those in charge of postwar reconstruction displayed an insouciant disregard for institutions, apparently thinking that what can be brought down one day can be rebuilt the next. In their rush to dismantle a regime, they proceeded to dismantle a state. In the end, the optimism that propelled the war has led to a disastrous quagmire that will probably burden the United States for years to come. American officials are once again learning, the hard way, that state formation is not an easy task.

Americans have long sought to propagate Jeffersonian outlooks and inclinations, presuming that the rest of the world will benefit from the inculcation of ideas that have been inextricably linked to American democracy and "the American way of life." Both in the United States and as part of American overseas expansion, however, Jeffersonian ideals have often undermined the democratic and developmental objectives toward which they were applied with zeal. As the American century moves ever farther into the past and U.S. power slowly declines under the weight of its own hubris, it would be wise for Americans to reflect on the hazards of Jeffersonianism. Contrary to the views of this Virginia slave owner, centralization is not always a bad thing and good political arrangements do not always fall in place with ease. After all, it took systematic action by the central government to advance the cause of civil rights and democratic change in Jefferson's home region—and this came about nearly a century and a half after his death.

PART 7

U.S. Military

War propaganda poster above Calle Comercio in Ponce, Puerto Rico, circa 1942. (Fundación Luis Muñoz Marín)

INTRODUCTION

The Military and the U.S. Imperial State

CHRISTOPHER CAPOZZOLA

WE HAVE NOT LACKED FOR EXPLANATIONS: American leaders were cunning planners who scrutinized the naval theories of Alfred Thayer Mahan and coveted the China trade. Or they were accidental imperialists who brought roads, schoolbooks, and sewers. Colonial subjects were helpless ciphers, victims of the armies of empire and their political cartoonists. Or they were resistant heroes wielding the weapons of the strong and the weak. But the fact of the matter is that historians have rarely operated with a rich understanding of what it meant to be a soldier in America's insular possessions—until now. This section's essays tell new social, political, and labor histories that demonstrate the reach of military power over the formal imperial possessions of the United States and the long shadow that 1898 continues to cast. Military institutions emerge from these essays as more conflicted, contested, and improvisational—in short, more human—than in earlier studies. And yet, of course, they were no less powerful for that fact.

As the ink dried on the Treaty of Paris, Americans suspected they had undertaken a difficult task; encountering the people they sought to colonize confirmed their fears. As Joshua Gedacht shows, wars of territorial expansion with "savage" Others were not new. But Gedacht goes beyond interpretations that simplistically assert that nineteenth-century Indian wars offered a ready-made template for conquest. Focusing on two massacres, one in 1890 at Wounded Knee in present-day South Dakota and another in 1906 atop Bud Dajo, a mountain in the southern Philippines, Gedacht reconstructs the transnational nature of a racialized violence that permeated both the American metropole and its colonial periphery. As Lakota people sought refuge in performances of the Ghost Dance and as the Moros, the Philippines' Muslim minority, retreated to mountain settlements outside Uncle Sam's reach, the army's grudging tolerance gave way to cultural misunderstanding, outright panic, and needless escalation. When rumors spread that Moro warriors were preparing suicide missions against American troops, violence ensued. Like his predecessors at Wounded Knee, Brigadier-General Leonard Wood justified the deaths of one thousand people with the claim that the "Moros one and all were fighting not as enemies but as religious fanatics." The road to massacre, Gedacht shows, is lined with history.

Pacification of the Philippines took conflicting forms, as did the colonial state that American policy makers built. Patricio N. Abinales shows that this was particularly true in the southern Philippine province of Mindanao, where the task of ruling a predominantly Muslim population puzzled American colonialists; the region remained under direct military occupation and martial law until 1913. The Mindanao occupation, Abinales argues, was for Americans "a relatively successful project of suppression, domination, and legitimation." Inspired by the "armed progressivism" of their hero Theodore Roosevelt, military elites wanted to "turn the Moro Province into a showcase" for a new state to match the one Roosevelt was building in Washington; they left as their legacy "a political landscape that bore the imprint of their autocratic, quasi-managerial, and progressive-influenced rule." But collaboration and compromise with distant power structures had long been part of Mindanao leaders' tool kits; the Moro chiefs used the Americans to protect their own distinctive culture from majority rule in Manila. The result, Abinales argues, was an "alternative pathway" from colonial state building "to that of the civilian-controlled, patronage-centered, and accommodation-driven governance" found elsewhere in Philippines.

The Moro Province governors—Leonard Wood, Tasker Bliss, and John J. Pershing—returned to Washington and West Point ready for change. Armed with charts, statistics, and friends in the White House, military reformers sought to build a twentieth-century army and do away with the old National Guard. But America's cherished militias died hard. Although historians have typically interpreted that struggle as a domestic political battle between tradition and modernity, my essay shows that it cannot be separated from international issues. The early twentieth century's debate over whether the National Guard could be deployed outside the United States reveals how "the imperial republic emerged from a startling rereading" of the Constitution driven by America's increasing international engagement between 1898 and 1918. By the end of World War I, as four million men were serving under arms (including tens of thousands of colonial subjects), it was clear that America had built its modern army. The new citizen soldiers who filled its ranks were symbols of "the complex hybrid of republic and imperial impulses that underlies the twentieth-century American state."

New challenges accompanied America's presence in the global arena of the 1930s: international communism, Japanese aggression, and a world economic crisis that weakened European empires. World War II marked a turning point in the military administration of empire. Historians of decolonization have frequently noted that the war thrust the imperial world system into uncertainty. Jorge Rodríguez Beruff reminds us that empires are always uncertain affairs, and in his essay on Puerto Rican politics in the mid-twentieth century he argues that the social crisis of the 1930s was the more fundamental juncture. In Washington, President Franklin Roosevelt, once the assistant secretary of the navy, and Hugh Johnson, a former selective service administrator and veteran of a tour of duty in the Philippines, together gave the New Deal a military air. The glint of brass shone often in 1930s Puerto Rico, too, whether in the gruff military style of Governor Blanton Winship, in the flint of gunmetal that exploded in the 1937 Ponce Massacre that left nineteen dead, or in the visits of American naval planners in the years just before Pearl Harbor. As Rodríguez Beruff shows, though, military actions exacerbated the Depression's social unrest.

World War II did not provoke a crisis, but the war made it possible—and necessary—to overcome an existing one. The introduction of emergency measures during the 1930s paved the way for the increased militarization of Puerto Rican society later. "[L]ooming war," writes Rodríguez Beruff, "dramatically increased the need for political stability," even as the switch to a more industrial war footing transformed the island. The "flexibility and adaptability, at critical junctures, of U.S. policy" gave energy to new phenomena—bases, airstrips, and amenable politicians—and helps explain the ongoing relationship between Puerto Rico and the United States.

War, it turns out, takes a lot of work. The men and women who served in the armed forces during World War II were also workers, as Humberto García-Muñiz and Rebeca Campo show in their account of U.S. and French imperial rivalries in the Caribbean during the war. The U.S. presence increased as it traded destroyers for Caribbean bases. Later, the draft brought fifty thousand Puerto Rican troops into the military. The color line ensured that they would not fight in Europe or Asia but would work closer to home; nearly 60 percent of U.S. forces in the Caribbean were Puerto Ricans, most in labor battalions. The work they did resembled the labors of some fifteen hundred Puerto Rican civilian workers who were transported to the French colony of Guyane. After it surrendered to the Free French in March 1943, American military authorities worked with a private corporation to build an airstrip. While keeping their eyes on the men and women who worked at Rochambeau Field, García-Muñiz and Campo creatively trace the instability of race in the interimperial wartime confrontation.

Jana K. Lipman likewise shows that the Cuban workers who moved in and out of the U.S. Naval Station at Guantánamo Bay understood it both as a site of armed imperial control and a place to get a job. Workers in the surrounding region had long been dependent on North American employers, and the wartime construction boom promised steadier work than United Fruit had ever delivered. As in Guyane, the navy expanded Guantánamo using a public-private hybrid that drew on older models of Caribbean imperialism and laid the foundation for a postwar network of military bases that claimed the privileges of sovereignty yet evaded its responsibilities. Lipman deftly shows the impact of this "fluidity between economic and military power" in her account of the conflict over jurisdiction surrounding the death of a Cuban worker on the base in December 1940.

That essays in this section explore the history of military concerns about Muslims' propensity for suicide tactics in war and legal jurisdiction at Guantánamo Bay should come as no surprise. In recent years, policy makers and pundits have looked back to the years after 1898 in search of precedents that could inform America today. They have found much to learn there even if the military historically has not. Despite the fact that the "United States Army devotes considerable attention to the study of history as a guide for current and future policy," the army, as Brian McAllister Linn argues, generally ignored the implications of the Philippine-American War for most of the twentieth century—not only because "the 'lessons' of the Philippines are confused, ambiguous, and controversial" but because military planners did not wish to learn from them. Leonard Wood, for one, worried that the exceptional lessons they taught would "spell disaster" when soldiers were "called upon to play the real game." In the post–Cold War era, the military operations of the imperial state now receive "more attention within the U.S. armed forces than they ever have." Historians, including the authors of this section's essays, are paying attention too.

"Mohammedan Religion Made It Necessary to Fire"

Massacres on the American Imperial Frontier from South Dakota to the Southern Philippines

JOSHUA GEDACHT

EARLY IN MARCH 1906, 790 AMERICAN SOLDIERS under the command of onetime Rough Rider Major General Leonard Wood converged on Bud Dajo, an extinct volcano at the southern, predominantly Muslim periphery of the Philippine Islands. Hoping to dislodge approximately one thousand "Moro malcontents" who were encamped beyond the reach of colonial authority in the volcano's crater, Wood issued orders to launch an assault up the mountainside. In the ensuing three-day artillery fusillade, at least six hundred of those Muslims, including hundreds of unarmed women and children, perished. The American forces suffered only twenty deaths and seventy casualties.[1]

In the aftermath, sensational headlines about Bud Dajo filled newspapers across America, and anti-imperialist congressmen accused the "Wood Brigade" of having committed a "massacre."[2] Metropolitan interest in this remote corner of empire, however, proved ephemeral. General Wood, whose career seemed briefly threatened, would instead continue his relentless rise, ascending to command the army and almost winning the Republican presidential nomination in 1920. Bud Dajo, by contrast, would soon vanish from public consciousness, and today, if mentioned at all, it is little more than a footnote to larger narratives of U.S. expansion.

This brief essay seeks to restore Bud Dajo to mainstream historiography by placing it at the forefront of a wide-ranging, albeit preliminary, inquiry into the understudied nature of "massacres" within the American imperium. From 1890 until 1913, the U.S. Army's colonial campaigns produced recurring yet distinct incidents of extreme bloodshed, including the 1890 Wounded Knee massacre in South Dakota, the 1901 Samar slaughters in the central Philippines, and the 1913 massacre at Bud Bagsak in the southern Philippines. The failure to situate such geographically and temporally disparate sites of violence in a single, transnational framework denies the possibility of exploring these sordid incidents as recurring yet ever-evolving concomitants of global imperial expansion. Inserting Bud Dajo into a comparative analysis of mass violence will thus yield a fuller picture of the dynamics that turned routine military operations into unmitigated slaughters and help explain how these acts of violence at the edge of empire were made acceptable to metropolitan audiences.

Indeed, during the era of America's imperial ascent from the 1890s to the 1920s, nearly half of all officers who rose to command the U.S. Army had been implicated in colonial massacres at critical junctures in their careers, massacres that, for all their dissimilarities, had at least one thing in common: the killing of non-Christian subject peoples.[3] In their various campaigns to subdue non-white resistance, these ambitious officers would invoke the diffuse, ambient, but strikingly potent specter of non-Christian savagery as justification, couching their "battles" in terms of the threat posed by "heathen" Sioux, the *pulahan* folk-religious "cult," and the "suicidal Mohammedan." Those few officers who failed to transpose colonial brutality onto the "savageness" of indigenous faith suffered public disgrace. In marked contrast, the heroes of empire would ride their martial exploits—cleansed of the taint of bloodshed by time and the phantasmagoria of religious fanaticism—to the military's highest echelons. From South Dakota to the southern Philippines, it was thus the volatile confluence of military careerism, territorial conquest, and religion-inflected fears that would play a decisive role in the making of these massacres.

Battle of Wounded Knee

On December 29, 1890, American troops opened fire on an encampment of Lakota Sioux on the South Dakota plains, killing between approximately 150 to 300 people, including 62 women and children. This slaughter at Wounded Knee Creek marked a fitting coda to a long history of expansion and dispossession. Almost thirteen years earlier, in the Sioux wars of 1877, the U.S. military had vanquished the Lakota Sioux, driving the surviving warriors into submission or hiding. Through the U.S. Army's Western Command and the Bureau of Indian Affairs, the army encircled the Sioux reservations with a network of military bases, developed collaborative relationships with the majority of their chiefs, and appropriated more than half the remaining Sioux land for ever-expanding railroad companies. For officials of the bureau and military officers, any lingering expression of cultural autonomy now held threatening intimations of incipient violence.[4]

In many respects, Wounded Knee stemmed from contradictions inherent to the processes of colonial pacification around the globe. Perhaps most illustrative of the contradictions that would explode at Wounded Knee was the government's education of American Indians. Pedagogues such as Richard Henry Pratt, the founder of the much heralded Carlisle Industrial School in Pennsylvania, and Merrill Gates, president of Rutgers University and member of the U.S. Board of Indian Commissioners, envisioned education as a vehicle for refashioning Indian children in the idealized mold of the so-called Anglo-Saxon American.[5] Gates typified this sentiment in his 1885 treatise *Law and Land as Agents in Educating American Indians,* couching his rhetoric in the ascendant ideology of racial hierarchy and emphasizing the salutary role of Christianity. "The years of contact with ideas and civilized men and Christian women so transform them," Gates wrote, that "the prematurely aged look of hopeless heathenism has given

"The Harvest in the Philippines." *Life,* July 6, 1899. (Wisconsin State Historical Society)

way to that dew of eternal youth which makes the difference between the savage and the man who lives in the thoughts of the future."[6]

Pedagogues such as Gates did not simply wish to educate the Indian child. They also intended to efface any lingering traces of Indian cultural identity and inculcate Christianity, individualism, and other ideas associated with Anglo-Saxon civilization. Indeed, as the fundamental fact of American dominance on the Great Plains grew more evident by 1890, educators, and especially their patrons in the U.S. government, became less tolerant of even the faintest germ of resistance in their charges. These hegemonic ambitions embodied by education rendered any expression of Sioux cultural autonomy suspect. As the government succeeded in strengthening the instruments of control at its disposal and set out on the task of molding "civilized men and Christian women," fear of any "heathen activity" metastasized.[7]

Against this backdrop of Christianizing education, it is not surprising that the ascendance of the Ghost Dance figures prominently in the prevailing explanations of Wounded Knee. This indigenous religious dance ritual promised the return of the vanished buffalo, as well as the disappearance of the white man, and it quickly spread among the Dakota Sioux tribes.[8] At first, several military officers, including Lieutenant Hugh L. Scott, who was later involved in the American colonization of Muslim areas in the Philippines, thought the dance could be "utilized for the great benefit of the Indian."[9] However, this sanguine view soon gave way before more ingrained prejudices. Media reports about the violent portents of the Ghost Dance quickly reached a fever pitch, and President Benjamin A. Harrison felt that Indians stirred by "false prophets" would shortly make "a crusade upon whites."[10] Fearful of an "outbreak," Washington ordered seven thousand troops to the Pine Ridge Reservation.

Ambition and rivalries within the military itself amplified these concerns. The commander for the Dakotas, General Nelson A. Miles, had parlayed his role in the surrender of the famed Apache chief Geronimo decades earlier into a promotion to major general.[11] For an officer of Miles's relentless ambition, the tensions surrounding the Ghost Dance presented an opportunity to win a coveted third star. Contrary to some of his earlier benign statements, the general warned that Indians "prompted by some wild, savage religious frenzy" were on the verge of "the most serious and general uprising ... in the whole history of Indian warfare."[12] Although most historians agree that Miles actually sought to avoid bloodshed, it still undoubtedly served his interests to exaggerate the peril for the consumption of Washington and the general public.[13] His calculations went awry when his tense soldiers opened up fire without provocation.

As news of the events at Wounded Knee reached the press, criticism of the army and Miles mounted. Organizations such as Herbert Welsh's influential Indian Rights Association denounced the slaughter and raised money for its victims.[14]

Several newspapers also condemned the "massacre," and the *Washington Evening Star* suggested that Miles had wanted to "create a scare and pose as the savior of the country" to improve his chances of winning a presidential nomination.[15] However, despite the initial unease over Wounded Knee, public concern dissipated and Miles continued his steady ascent. Decrying Wounded Knee as "a massacre" himself, Miles launched an investigation and succeeded in deflecting the blame onto a subordinate. As soon as 1894, the *Chicago Tribune* was lauding the "effective work under General Miles at Wounded Knee."[16] In November of that same year, he was promoted to lead the Division of the East, a key step in his appointment, a year later, to command of the U.S. Army.[17]

Into the Howling Wilderness of Samar

In 1898, General Miles, now a three-star general, encouraged the secretary of war to dispatch an expeditionary force to Manila Bay to exploit the U.S. Navy's defeat of the Spanish squadron. Simultaneously, Moorfield Storey, a lawyer and active civil rights advocate, warned the New England Anti-Imperialist League that "when we undertake to govern subject peoples separated from us by half the world, let us remember how we despoiled the Indian."[18] The juxtaposition of Miles and Storey reveals how from the very outset the conflict was entangled in deeply contentious debates over empire and its associated massacres.

By 1901, Samar Island in the central Philippines had become a uniquely vexing theater of guerrilla warfare that shared resonances with conditions that the U.S. Army had faced in South Dakota.[19] Perhaps most important, that same polarity of Christian civilization versus heathenism that had infused Nelson Miles's Dakota campaign recurred on Samar, where the insurgents were seen as members of the fanatical pagan *pulahan* religious cult.[20] As in the case of the Lakota Sioux Indians, the supposed fierceness of this small, remote Visayan Island had become the stuff of army lore. Such a volatile cocktail of perceived racial and religious disorder left soldiers primed for an engagement that would not meet the standards of "civilized warfare."[21]

The catalyst for the worst atrocities on Samar was twofold: the leadership of Brigadier General Jacob H. Smith and the outbreak of the infamous "Balangiga massacre." In a well-coordinated attack on September 28, 1901, Filipino insurgents destroyed the entire garrison at the town of Balangiga and killed some 74 American soldiers, thus eliciting widespread calls in the army and metropolitan media for revenge. General Smith, known among many troops for his racist attitudes and less than competent military performance, complied. He ordered his subordinates to "kill and burn" every male above ten and to turn Samar into a "howling wilderness." Between October and December 1901, officers under Smith's command executed 22 unarmed civilians without trial, tortured countless Samar residents, and killed or captured 759 putative insurgents.[22]

News of the excesses in Samar provoked a furor in the American metropolitan press. Headlines blared "Butcher of Samar" and "Samar to Be Made a Howling Wilderness," and the Democratic Party's standard-bearer, William Jennings Bryan, likened the heinous abuses to Adam's consumption of the apple. This commotion culminated in the court-martial of General Smith and three other officers; and, in its aftermath, it appeared that massacres couched in the discourse of race and religion, were, perhaps, a thing of the past.[23]

"The Ridiculous Little Sultan of Sulu"

In May of 1899, General Elwell Stephen Otis, commander of the U.S. forces in the Philippines, sent a relatively small contingent of soldiers to the Sulu archipelago, a remote, mostly Muslim area in the far south, starting what turned out to be the army's longest and bloodiest occupation in the Philippines. Although the military relinquished formal control of the rest of the colony to the Manila-based civilian government in 1901, it ruled over the "Moroland" province of Mindanao and Sulu until 1914, launching periodic punitive campaigns that killed three thousand Muslim Filipinos.[24]

The U.S. occupation of this troubled region, however, started rather auspiciously. In 1899, General John C. Bates signed a treaty with Sultan Hadji Mohammed Jamalul Kirim of Sulu recognizing nominal U.S. sovereignty in exchange for significant concessions, including guarantees that Americans would honor the "right and dignities of His Highness the Sultan and the datos" and a promise that "the Moros should not be interfered with on account of their religion."[25] More broadly, the decision to formally acknowledge Moro religious practice represented a departure from the past American promotion of Christianity as an instrument of pacification.

At first, General George W. Davis, who then commanded the Mindanao and Sulu Division, was cautious about repeating the army's experience in the American West. A lifelong military engineer, Davis argued in his 1902 report on "Mindanao and Neighboring Islands" that the army's record with American Indians offered a poor model for Moroland.

> Those of us who have spent the best part of our lifetime in observing the failure of the Americans to civilize . . . "our Indian Wards" not unnaturally have the feeling that the failure is due to a mistaken policy . . . for a century . . . [as] the Indians died off or were slaughtered. The result has been disastrous to the aborigines. . . . Cities have been rebuilt over the ashes of burned tepees . . . but there can scarcely be found an intelligent and well informed human being who knows the real characteristics of our Indian policy in this century of dishonor who will not acknowledge that the crusade has been as cruel and heartless as any recorded in human history.[26]

While wishing to avoid the specter of "the ashes of burned tepees," however, General Davis still supported a stronger military government and grew increasingly frustrated with the Bates Treaty.

In early 1903, metropolitan political intrigues would soon precipitate the arrival of a new, forceful leader for Mindanao and Sulu—the former U.S. governor-general of Cuba, Brigadier General Leonard Wood. As the hero of San Juan Hill and a confidante of President Theodore Roosevelt, Wood appeared destined for far loftier positions than a second-tier post on the colonial frontier. But political infighting between Wood and his bitter intraparty rival, Senator Mark Hanna of Ohio, stalled the Rough Rider's professional advancement. As a result, President Roosevelt decided to send him into exile as governor of remote "Moroland."[27]

While Wood keenly followed the ongoing contretemps in Congress from Zamboanga, he also pursued his new position with vigor. Among other things, Wood envisioned the military as the vanguard of rational "good government," financial probity, and order, and during his earlier tenure as governor-general there he had turned Cuba into "a workshop for American progressivism."[28] In short, Wood hoped to transform his Moroland colony into a successful social laboratory.[29]

Once on the job, the new governor wasted little time in confronting perceived impediments to the modernization of American rule, and foremost among those obstacles was the Bates Treaty, which, he felt, placed unjustifiable constraints on American governance in the name of "the ridiculous little Sultan of Sulu."[30] He also felt the treaty had "brought about a condition of chaos and petty wars."[31] Believing that "these Mohammedan communities have no legal organization or fixed form of government such as was represented to us when the so-called Bates Treaty was signed," Wood unilaterally revoked the agreement and established a new, more "rational," tribal ward system that would transform those sultans and *datus* into paid agents of the American government.[32]

Similarly, Wood's simultaneous resumption of armed hostilities around Lake Lanao in western Mindanao would provide a preview of just how toxic this confluence of careerism, progressive ideology, and anti-Muslim discourse could become. Distant from the coastal cities and inaccessible by road or rail, Lake Lanao stood beyond the reach of American authority, an imagined refuge, in the minds of many colonial officials, for the untamed, semi-savage, "Mohammedan" fanatics who would commit *juramentado*—a suicide attack in which a Moro rushed at Christians with a sharp *kris* sword, killing them in the name of Islam.[33] In early 1903, therefore, the army sent Captain John J. Pershing to awe the locals into submission with an overwhelming display of force. A veteran of the Indian wars who had served in South Dakota and been nearby when Wounded Knee transpired, Captain Pershing was no stranger to the project of colonizing non-Christian peoples. Although he encountered only scattered resistance in his new Moroland mission, Pershing's command killed, in one battle alone, at least 250 people. The metropolitan media, perhaps starved for stories of military success after years of controversy and scandal, hailed Pershing as a hero. In 1905, President Roosevelt ordered his promotion to the rank of brigadier general above 835 more senior officers. Despite such martial prowess and celebrity, Lake Lanao still remained beyond the grasp of colonial control, and Wood was intent on revisiting the issue.[34]

In particular, with a rivalry between Pershing and Wood growing, and rumors that it had in fact been Pershing, not Wood, who played the principal role at the Battle of San Juan Hill in Cuba, the new Moroland governor seemed eager to burnish his military credentials anew.[35] Noting that Pershing had subdued "only a small portion of the total number of forts" around Lake Lanao,"[36] Wood vowed to "completely crush . . . the Lake Lanao outfit."[37] Thus, with the promise of glory on the horizon, General Wood revived the Lake Lanao campaign in a new round of battles that would result in about fifteen hundred deaths between mid-1903 and mid-1904.[38] Wood justified these slaughters by saying "our Mohammedan friends . . . have to be thumped a little now and then."[39]

The general's plans to gain full control over the Muslims would be delayed about two years, however, until May of 1905, when a group of Tausug-speaking Muslim Filipinos on Jolo Island in the Sulu Sea attempted to escape American authority by moving to the top of a steep, densely vegetated volcano more or less inaccessible to troops. They went to Bud Dajo.

Anatomy of a Massacre

This encampment of some two hundred Muslim Filipinos at first aroused little concern among military officials. The main proponent of noninterference was the Sulu district governor, Major Hugh Scott. Also a veteran of the Indian wars, Scott had developed a reputation in the army as a prodigious linguist and ethnologist who displayed some sensitivity toward the cultures of the peoples he conquered.[40] In stark contrast to his colleague General Miles, who had fanned fears about the Ghost Dance in South Dakota, Scott had defused tensions over comparable practices in Oklahoma, averting bloodshed.

When Scott arrived on Jolo Island in 1903, he pursued a similarly levelheaded approach. Immersing himself in the culture of his new charges, the major generally avoided Wood's impetuous approach to "skirmishing" and attempted to negotiate with the enemy. This is not to deny that Scott routinely attacked his perceived Moro enemies. Indeed, the major launched two expeditions in pursuit of so-called outlaws, and low-level warfare remained an endemic feature of colonial life in Sulu under his rule.[41] However, when the Bud Dajo encampment emerged in the wake of one of Wood's "skirmishes," Major Scott felt that it posed little threat to military dominance or "good government." In a retrospective 1906 report, for example, the major stated that the people on Dajo "declared they had no intention of fighting,—ran up there only in fright, [and] had some crops planted and desired to cultivate them."⁴²

By November 1905, the encampment had swelled to approximately one thousand, arousing widespread fears in the military that infected even Major Scott, who commented that "there is some unrest among the Moros which may turn serious."⁴³ In January 1906, with Scott on leave, there remained little moderating influence within the military establishment, and the Moro Province secretary, George Langhorne, described the rebels as "a menace to the people in the lowlands" that would "probably have to be exterminated."⁴⁴ Striking a more ominous

"Those pious Yankees can't throw stones at us anymore," chants a chorus of old imperialists in the background—Britain, France, Germany, Spain, and Holland. *Life*, May 22, 1902. (Wisconsin State Historical Society)

chord, Wood also cautioned, "The Moro outbreaks are largely due to actions of fanatical Arab priests, of a class which is a disturbing element throughout the East."[45] On March 2, he ordered Colonel J. W. Duncan to prepare his Sixth Infantry to "capture or destroy the band of lawless characters on or in the vicinity of Bud Dajo Mountain."[46]

Duncan first endeavored to occupy all of the various trails to the top of the mountain, effectively blocking escape. Next he sent troops up the mountain's slope to engage in close range combat and force an opening in the Dajo *cotta*, an indigenous defensive fortification with fifteen-foot-high walls made of *nipa* and bamboo. When this was completed, those troops retreated down the mountain and the colonel ordered heavy military artillery to fire on what remained of the *cotta* from afar. This fusillade opened a gaping hole in Dajo's defenses, allowing the Americans to put a "Machine Gun . . . in position where it could sweep the crest of the mountain between us and the cotta." After the troops fired from this safe vantage point, the *cotta* was deemed secure. Of the one thousand people in the crater, according to Duncan, "no living Moro was found."[47] General Leonard Wood's order to "clean up" Dajo had been executed.

"Mohammedan Religion Made It Necessary"

On March 9, 1906, one day after the Bud Dajo massacre, the *New York Times* headline read "Women and Children Killed in Moro Battle. President Wires Congratulations to Troops."[48] Secretary of War William Howard Taft warned Wood that "it is charged there was wanton slaughter of Moros, men, women, and children, in the fight of Bud Dajo."[49] Moorfield Storey's Anti-Imperialist League published several widely disseminated tracts about the "massacre" at the "Battle of the Crater."[50] Before long, politicians in the U.S. Senate also entered the fray, criticizing the actions of Wood and his superiors.[51]

In contrast to the aftermath on Samar, however, all the principal actors involved in Bud Dajo escaped punishment or court-martial. In 1906, General Wood was promoted to command of the Philippine Division, a stepping-stone to his later command of the army. While the Samar atrocities unfolded in the twilight of a bitter, hard-fought, and unpopular war, Bud Dajo occurred almost four years later, well after both the Philippine-American War and the debates over imperialism had receded.

Moreover, the valences associated with Islam in American consciousness also likely played a role in reconciling public opinion to the atrocity. For example, the *Mindanao Herald*, an American-owned newsweekly, editorialized, "General Wood and the forces under his command have no excuses to make or pardons to beg for their work at Bud Dajo. . . . They did their plain duty, regretfully, of course, that Mohammedan religion and custom made it necessary to fire in the direction of women and children."[52] Wood himself argued that "it must be understood that the Moros one and all were fighting not as enemies but as religious fanatics, believing Paradise to be their immediate reward if killed in action with Christians."[53] Reports of fanaticism, moreover, reverberated throughout the metropolitan press. In a representative editorial, the *Washington Star* claimed that "the defiant attitudes of the outlaws and the Arab priests persuaded their followers that the government would be unable to dislodge them from their fortress within two years," thus locating the blame not with the colonial perpetrators but with Islam.[54]

Pershing and the Last Moroland Massacre

News of the Bud Dajo massacre quickly spread throughout the southern Philippines, and played a large role in the abatement of violence between 1906 and 1911. Indeed, Wood's successor, General Tasker H. Bliss, deliberately sought to reverse his predecessor's approach. Arguing that "our purpose ... is, to preserve the peace, to prevent war, [and] to make unnecessary the killing of a single Moro," Bliss focused his administrative energies on encouraging economic growth, reforming the governing structures of the province, and containing the remaining malcontents.[55]

After three years of tense peace, Tasker Bliss was succeeded as governor by John J. Pershing, who returned to the scene of his past "glories." Despite the absence of significant American casualties, Pershing regretted that "the Moro Province has long been known as a dangerous place ... where the fanatical Moro had ran amuck time and time again," and he issued orders in September 1911 to proscribe all weapons.[56] In a grim assessment of the local character, he asserted that "with a fanatical disregard of the consequences of crime and an inborn desire to fight and plunder, the Mohammedan Malay is ... at once the most virile and fearless of Orientals, as well as the most aggressive and determined."[57] By 1912, Pershing concluded that "the result" of his efforts would likely "be a general uprising or holy war."[58]

When an attack in October on Jolo Island killed one soldier, Governor Pershing wasted little time in organizing a force to scour the interior and enforce his disarmament measures. By December of 1911, approximately one thousand Muslim Filipinos had returned to Bud Dajo.[59] Acutely conscious of the calumnies heaped on his rival Leonard Wood after a "massacre" four years earlier, Pershing elected to pursue a different approach, effectively blockading food and access to the mountain without firing artillery shells into the volcano's crater. This strategy managed to avert a bloodbath, as many women and children fled with Pershing's tacit approval.

In June of 1913, however, frustrated by continuing recalcitrance, the general resolved to launch an attack at another location, Bud Bagsak, which "would surprise the outlaws so completely that they had no time to assemble their families" and thus prevent innocent deaths.⁶⁰ On June 11, American troops assaulted the volcanic crater, killing "between three and four hundred hopeless fanatics and cattle thieves" and suffering only fourteen deaths and thirteen casualties.⁶¹ This asymmetric bloodbath halted what remained of the armed resistance in the southern Philippines and effectively brought fourteen years of incipient guerrilla warfare to a definitive close.

Despite the dramatic parallels between Pershing's 1913 "battle" and the Bud Dajo incident seven years before, Bud Bagsak barely registered in the metropolitan consciousness. To the extent that they did cover the battle, journalists generally hailed Bud Bagsak as yet another laurel in Pershing's impressive career.⁶² The army even nominated the general for the Medal of Honor. Within the next three years, Pershing would lead forces against Pancho Villa on the Mexican border, and ultimately he became the commander of the Allied Expedition Forces in World War I.⁶³

The Implications of Imperial Massacres

The "battle" at Bud Bagsak signaled the end of armed conflict against Muslim Filipinos in the southern Philippines and the beginning of a new colonial normality in the region. Within a year, the U.S. authorities for the first time incorporated Mindanao and Sulu into Manila's civilian administration, collaborationist *datus* began to participate in archipelago-wide politics, and economic growth intensified.⁶⁴ Much as in South Dakota over twenty years earlier, where Lakota Sioux resistance effectively ground to a halt after a similarly asymmetric display of violence, Bud Bagsak and Bud Dajo seemed to represent critical junctures in the history of colonial control, decisive markers for populations unable to continue sustained armed resistance against imperial power.

In the context of imperial expansion, the ambient fear of a savage religion encouraged officers such as Nelson Miles, Leonard Wood, and John Pershing to perform a fundamental act of inversion, turning anxieties about control into brutal massacres. All three officers tapped into intertwined anxieties about the precariousness of American rule and the valences of non-Christian "heathens" or "Mohammedans" to create the circumstances propitious for violence. Instead of stigmas, these massacres propelled the three officers to the highest echelons of the military establishment. Criticisms of their actions were quickly shunted aside by the politics of the imperial age.

With the severity of U.S. power evident, the Sioux Indians under Big Foot, the rebels of Samar *pulahan*, and the *juramentados* of Moroland lost much of their influence. The structures of collaboration that bonded indigenous elites with colonial rulers solidified, and the phantasmagorias of religious insurrection dissipated. To note that massacres served a useful purpose from the colonial perspective, of course, does not mean that they were entirely premeditated. These episodes possessed a certain organic quality, arising from personal ambitions that merged with a deep, pervasive fear of non-Christian savagery to produce spasms of spectacular bloodshed, sometimes provoking controversy at home in the metropole.

To draw any overarching conclusions from the bloodshed at Wounded Knee and similar Philippine slaughters about the role massacres played in the making of modern empires might be premature. Nonetheless, the anxieties that accompanied the initial work of colonial conquest—combined with the ambitions of military officers and religious fears—repeatedly proved conducive to the excessive, indiscriminate use of force. It is difficult to guess whether massacres constituted a momentary aberration or a key factor in empire's consolidation, as colonial rule did not hinge exclusively on these large-scale killings. Even so, the fact that these displays of overwhelming force often ushered in periods of imperial dominion from South Dakota to the southern Philippines requires further attention by scholars of American empire.

The U.S. Army as an Occupying Force in Muslim Mindanao, 1899–1913

PATRICIO N. ABINALES

IN 1900 GENERAL WILLIAM A. KOBBE reported that his command, the Department of Mindanao and Jolo, exhibited an extraordinary "diversity of race, religion and habitat" involving pagans, Muslims, and Christian Filipinos that made it "necessary to adopt a military and civil policy varying with the locality," producing "virtually autonomous subdistricts and post commands [with] each commander [allowed] considerable flexibility." As the historian Brian McAllister Linn has explained, General Kobbe's task was complicated because his was "the largest department in area, and the smallest in terms of manpower" with just "2,600 soldiers to hold Mindanao's 36,500 square miles and the Sulu Archipelago's 160 inhabited islands."[1]

This unique paramilitary structure was necessary, army officers felt, because the peoples of Muslim Mindanao exhibited what American officials described as backward, fierce cultures prone to fanaticism and violence.[2] But if Americans knew of the "savagery" of the Muslim "tribes," why did they not expand the size of their military force in Mindanao after defeating the Filipinos in the north? And why was it that, despite the arguments of Filipino nationalists that southern resistance to American rule was "a product of Muslim ethnic pride . . . and . . . individualism which have never failed to generate strong determination to resist any forms of outside domination," governing these same Muslims actually turned out to be relatively unproblematic?[3]

I would suggest that answers to these questions lie in the manner in which the colonial state was built in the southern Philippines. While civilian rule quickly replaced local military administrations elsewhere, in "Moro Mindanao," the country's second-largest island, the U.S. Army ruled for over fourteen years. This was not entirely a novel situation as the army played a similar role in the American West and Southwest prior to the U.S. colonization of the Philippines.[4] But Moro Mindanao—so named because of the area's Muslim majority population—also had several distinguishing features. First, it became the zone that represented for colonial state building an alternative pathway to that of the civilian-controlled, patronage-centered, and accommodation-driven governance in most of the Philippine lowlands. Second, it was a relatively successful project of suppression, domination, and legitimation. Although Muslims initially resisted the Americans as they had the Spanish, by the end of the first decade of American rule the majority supported martial law.

Biases and Ambitions

The U.S. Army arrived in the Philippines with preconceived notions about who the Filipinos and Muslims were and what exactly were the United States' long-term goals for its first Asian colony. In the hope of formulating a viable policy for their new colony and its still unpacified southern islands, the Americans relied initially on information from departing Spaniards as well as preinvasion studies of other colonial empires.[5]

The Americans agreed with the Spanish portrait of the Muslims as backward and barbaric. General Leonard Wood, declared that "the Moros and other savage peoples have no laws—simply a few customs . . . many of them revolting and practically . . . utterly and absolutely undesirable from every standpoint of decency and good government," while to General Tasker Bliss subduing a savage people such as the Moros meant using force until they "accept our system in its entirety."[6] Secretary of War William Howard Taft, agreed, writing, "Force seems to be the only method of reaching them in the first instance and is the only preparation for the beginning of civilized restraints among them."[7]

Most American officers had little interest in learning about Islam and shared this impression of a senior officer that the religion was nothing but a set of "certain vague, ill-defined notions out of which [a Moro's] practice grows."[8] Wood himself referred to the Muslims as nothing but "religious and moral degenerates."[9] At least one member of the U.S. expeditionary force strongly disagreed. After a careful study of the cultural and social practices of the various Muslim groups, Najeeb Saleeby, a Lebanese-American Muslim, concluded that Muslims "possessed tribal organization, and fairly well-recognized customs that have the force and value of laws."[10] But his opinions were ignored, and Saleeby would soon leave the military for the private sector.

Nonetheless, the Americans, unlike the Spanish, never saw Islam as a serious threat. By contrast, senior American officials kept true to the principle of separating religion from politics and governance and did not interfere with Muslim religious practices—a key factor in their sudden success. As the Philippine observer Vic Hurley explained, "Bullets could not, and did not conquer the Moros. They would have fought against the United States to the last man if religious questions had been involved. Tolerance and fair treatment brought the Moros into subjection where the arquebuses of Spain had failed."[11] Islam was a problem that, in the American view, a public education system could readily resolve.[12] Bliss hoped that the spread of public schools would bring about "a natural transition from the *Pandita* school to the lowest grade of the public school system" and launch the Moros on the journey to "civilization."[13]

Finally, there was Mindanao's dense ecology, which added color to colonial images of savagery and backwardness. Wood's biographer, Herman Hagedorn, described the islands as "thirty six thousand square miles of mountains and lakes and cultivated valleys, coral reefs and mangrove swamps; rivers flowing through a trackless jungle, forests, dark and terrifying."[14]

Another writer described Mindanao as a "terra incognito, many parts never having been visited by civilized man."[15] This terrain inevitably drew comparisons with the Western frontier where "unexplored" territory was populated with small groups of "savage Indians." Indeed, the most effective Americans in this tropical frontier were the veterans of the Apache war.[16]

Unlike the Dutch and the British, who saw their superiority over colonial subjects as immutable, American arrogance was tempered by an unusual belief that, given the proper training, the Muslims could be "civilized." As Bliss put it, "If we apply our own system of government to these wild peoples we demoralize, we extirpate, and we never really civilize. We cannot compress the work of ten centuries into one."[17] But Bliss, Wood, and other U.S. officers believed that Mindanao could, if insulated from Manila's patronage politics, develop rapidly through American administrative reforms and economic initiatives.

The impulses behind this point of view may have been the army's experience with Native Americans. In a letter to a fellow officer, for example, Wood described the defiant Cotabato Datu Ali of Kudarangan as being "a good deal on the Geronimo type and by far the most capable Moro we have run into."[18] For the Americans, "civilizing the Moros" required their leaders to eventually transform themselves from *datus* into assemblymen or colonial officials.[19]

"Civilizing the Moros" eventually expanded to mean protecting them from their old nemesis, the Filipino Christians. Army officers believed that Filipino politicians now collaborating with the colonial regime in faraway Manila were more concerned about enriching themselves than honestly governing.[20] Protecting their "savage wards" from the corrupting influence of Filipino politics thus turned American racism into a shield that provided space in which to train Muslims in civilization. The administrative body that would be established to govern Moro Mindanao reflected all these biases, fears, and aspirations.

Structure, Authority, and Power

The Philippine Commission passed Act No. 787 on June 1, 1903, creating a Moro Province as "the framework within which transition from military to civilian rule in Moroland would take place *wherever and whenever the duly constituted authorities felt it was indicated.*"[21] All its officials—from the governor to the superintendent of schools—were from the army, appointed by the commission, and given "a very large measure of discretion in dealing with the Moros and in preserving as far as possible, consistent with the fundamental act, the customs of the Moros, the authority of the dattos [local Muslim leaders], and a system of justice in which Moros could take part."[22] The Moro Province was divided into five districts, which were, in turn, subdivided into municipalities and fifty-one tribal wards administered under laws enacted by the army's provincial government.[23]

With over 38,888 of the 115,860 square miles within the total Philippine landmass, the Moro Province was the largest administrative unit in the entire colony. It was also the most sparsely populated with a ratio of ten people per square mile compared to the rest of the colony's sixty-seven.[24] This was the classic frontier that the province's three governors—Leonard Wood (1903–6), Tasker Bliss (1906–9), and John J. Pershing (1909–13)—were ready to rule like "the medieval Christian knights fighting the Saracens or the Puritan reformers in Cromwell's England."[25] All demanded the same strong commitment from their subordinates. Wood insisted that his administration be manned by "young Americans" who would be willing to serve in the "remote districts among the half-civilized peoples."[26] Bliss instructed his subordinates "to acquire the knowledge and experience necessary for local popular government." He specifically ordered his district governors to learn the dialects of their districts and required examinations in these languages after eighteen months of service with dismissal as the penalty for failure.[27]

Their example rubbed off on the younger officers. Some of the notable district governors included Lieutenant Edward Bolton of Davao, the son of an Episcopal minister who studied mechanical engineering before joining the army in 1894. Bolton was the first to map and survey the Davao and Cotabato coastlines, and his technical skills made him an obvious candidate for district governor.[28] Similarly, Major John Finley of Cotabato was a good administrator who conducted "scholarly investigations" among the Muslims and non-Christian indigenous communities in his district.[29] Cornelius Smith was admired for the way he brought stability to Davao in 1906–7 and then, three years later, repeated this feat in Lanao, all while winning recognition for his translation of a Spanish priest's grammar of the Magindanao language for use by the army.[30] What was the motivation for such zeal? At base, there was the strong antipathy toward American civil officials in Manila whom the army saw as too conciliatory to Filipino interests, the longtime bête noire of all Muslims. More broadly, members of the regime exuded self-confidence not only due to their skills but also in their identification with the principles of American progressivism.[31]

Wood himself believed that the creation of federal programs that aimed for "a broader education in citizenship and the ideals of national service" could help form "a single national spirit transcending sectional, class, and nationality group differences."[32] In later years, Wood and Bliss would be involved in U.S. legislative battles against the patronage-driven spoils system, rooted in state political machines, over such issues as the creation of a national army loyal only to Washington. In the Philippines, these "armed progressives" wanted to turn the Moro Province into a showcase for their administrative talents, vowing that their leadership would reflect the "managerial reforms inspired by the progressives."[33]

Disgusted with the spread of patronage politics to the colony, these officers vowed to turn the Moro Province into the progressive antithesis of the machine-ruled Christian provinces to the north.[34] Similarly, the zeal with which they both recast the "local economy" away from "traditional" practices—slave raiding, opium consumption, and regional maritime trade—and fought to promote export agriculture reflected the progressive dedication to economic development. Indeed, a new economy was taking form, supported by expansion of provincial exports to Manila and Southeast Asia, which, in turn, led to increased customs revenues and other taxes in the first five years of army rule.[35]

By the second half of the decade, 1905–10, the signs of progress were everywhere. The growth of the hemp and timber industries in Davao made it an attractive area for migrants, including Japanese workers.[36] Hemp estates grew from nothing to over forty plantations covering 16,410 hectares, and contributing 35 percent of total Philippine production.[37] Cotabato, home of the Magindanao Muslims, also experienced "pyramiding growth" in exports, which one official gleefully described as "little short of marvelous."[38] The district's revenues rose from 21,246 pesos in 1908 to 311,043 just three years later.[39] The province's total export revenues from hemp, rubber, pearls, and coconuts totaled 3,410,712 pesos in 1910 and doubled to 6,468,587 pesos in 1913.[40]

The army had transformed Moro Mindanao from a backwater into one of the most productive provinces in the Philippines. The only thing that was lacking was a formalization of Manila's noninterference in Mindanao affairs or, better, for Washington to separate Mindanao from the colonial body politic.

Moro Resistance Reconsidered

The army was aware that Mindanao was no emptier than the U.S. frontier had been and that Muslims had engaged the Spaniards and their Filipino Christian allies in a long, drawn-out "war."[41] They also knew that the once powerful Sulu and Magindanao sultanates were now weaker due to internal divisions and the constant challenge by ambitious upstarts. Moro Mindanao had, moreover, lost importance in a Southeast Asian trade now dominated by the Dutch and British.[42] Whatever Muslim resistance remained was easily quelled by the "liberal use of ammunition," which achieved "very excellent results against the semi-savages."⁴³ Governor Wood would boast to an acquaintance in the United States that "we have had three rather large expeditions against them and have thoroughly broken the power of the three main Moro groups.... As a military proposition they never had been serious and much that has been written about them is the cheapest kind of rubbish."⁴⁴

It helped that the Americans kept the Muslims divided by co-opting their elites. Attracted by new business opportunities and a chance to regain some of their lost power, these *datus* abandoned their rebellious allies and accepted American rule.⁴⁵ Their relatively successful integration to the new order became not only an alternative and attractive pathway for many communities but also an effective delegitimizing instrument against rebellion.⁴⁶

There is, however, also one additional feature of "Moro resistance" that historians have often overlooked: the restricted geography and relative rarity of these irruptions. Contrary to nationalist and pro-Muslim separatist arguments, these incidents of "struggle against the Americans" were really feeble and few. A listing of Muslim military encounters against the Americans compiled by a Filipino historian who has been a consistent advocate of the unified Muslim insurgency shows the majority of a total of just nineteen battles was a response to American impositions, five were caused by intermittent battles between Muslim groups, and three targeted Filipinos. In effect, there was no consistent opposition to American rule. Moreover, only in a single settlement, the village of Jolo, did conflicts recur; armed encounters in other villages only happened once, never to be repeated, perhaps because of the American use of deadly firepower.⁴⁷

In fact, U.S. military expeditions spent more time trekking through dense forests than engaging *datus* in firefights. Pacification campaigns got bogged down by the absence of forest trails or stymied by mud or rain. For example, one Datu Ampuanagaus from Lake Lanao escaped an American attack on his *cotta* (fort) and retreated "into the mountains where he held out for more than a dozen years," knowing that the Americans would consider it impractical to send troops into an impenetrable area.⁴⁸ The army made sure that no resistance would recur by constructing a network road and telegraph lines "through almost the whole western and southern part of the Cotabato River valley" and Lake Lanao to ensure a much faster response.⁴⁹

With a total of only 164 kilometers of dusty roads and bridges, the infrastructure was, however, far from perfect. Roads became impassable and bridges deteriorated, all because of the torrential rains. The army compensated by setting up a network of coastal outposts, which served as "choke points" to limit the movement of rebellious *datus* and jumping-off points for mobile military units in pursuit of the rebels.⁵⁰ The hazards of geography worked both ways, however, imposing limits on the rebels as well. Datu Ali of Kudarangan, for example, fought a successful guerrilla war in the swamplands of Cotabato and "kept [the Americans] chasing after him for months."⁵¹ He could hide out in the swamplands but could not stray far from his base, where—in classic guerrilla fashion—he relied on local people for both material support and intelligence. Once he left his "stronghold" to attend to family needs, he was a dead man.⁵²

Finally, one cannot minimize the effects of American brutality on Muslim communities as a deterrent to future resistance. Reports of what happened at the massacre of Bud Dajo in 1906, where over six hundred Tausugs were killed, including a "considerable number of women and children," may have stoked Muslim anger. But they also caused serious shock and trauma not only among the survivors but also among the communities that heard about these bloodlettings.⁵³

In the thirteen years it ruled Moroland, the U.S. Army completed the destruction of the Muslim sultanates, brought recalcitrant *datus* under its control, and formally integrated southern Mindanao into the rest of the colony. So confident was the army of its triumph that it began to transfer the job of peace and security to the Philippine Constabulary, which even scaled down its forces from 800 in 1905 to 657 in 1908.⁵⁴

Center-Periphery Tensions

The fear created by the brutal pacification campaigns was soon replaced by increased Muslim loyalty as programs began to alter the economic landscape. But what drew the Muslims closer to the Americans was the latter's repeated assurances that as long as the army was in control of the Moro Province they would "never be [placed] under Filipino rule."⁵⁵ Aware that the *datus* were listening, they also sent "strong signals" to Manila, asserting the army's sole right to alter regulations as they deemed fit.⁵⁶ They broadened the powers of the tribal ward courts, which adjudicated cases involving Muslims and non-Christians, thereby creating a justice system that ran parallel to the civil courts that Manila mandated for all provinces.⁵⁷

The Americans worked hard to slow the conversion of Moroland to a "regular province." Wood convinced the Philippine Commission to exempt the province from a code for municipalities that would have hastened this shift, and his successors would invoke this policy to ward off pressures to reclassify the region and transfer it to civilian rule. And when the Filipinos, now in control of the legislative powers of the colonial state, upped the ante in 1909 by demanding that provincial officials hold municipal elections as the first step toward regularization, the army indicated its opposition by repeatedly reminding Manila of its role as the final arbiter of provincial and municipal politics.⁵⁸

The army kept Manila constantly guessing about the true state of the province, sending glowing reports about successful pacification and economic breakthroughs only to follow these up with warnings that Moro Mindanao was still unsafe. American officers warned that Muslims still regarded their old enemies, the Filipinos, with intense suspicion and would likely revolt if the latter took over.[59] To reinforce this argument, they also underscored the shortcomings of Filipinos. Wood did not hesitate to describe Filipino leaders as making "peons [of] the civilized people of the interior and compell[ing] them to dispose of their products most disadvantageously to themselves."[60]

Army officers were emboldened by the backing of powerful supporters such as William Howard Taft, who promised that a "Filipino Assembly would have no say about Moro Province affairs."[61] Other leaders, including the maverick William Jennings Bryan, likewise backed the army; Bryan went so far as to announce during a visit to the Moro Province that the only way it could prosper would be to break away from the Philippines.[62]

Filipino leaders responded by accusing the Americans of breaking up the Philippines and creating a false breach between Filipinos and Muslims.[63] They sent "political agitators, coming principally from the northern provinces," to launch movements demanding that the army "cut off the District of Zamboanga from the Moro Province and make it a part of the northern group, with representation in the [Philippine] Assembly."[64] While these "agitations" were easily contained in the province itself, the army had more difficulty dealing with these attacks in Manila.[65] Filipinos who served in such bodies as the Philippine Commission used every available means to assert their authority over the province and end the army's autonomy. For example, Gregorio Araneta, the Filipino attorney general, questioned the commission's delegation of powers "to modify, amend or repeal Acts of the Philippine Commission" concerning the Moro Province to the local legislative council.[66]

Filipino leaders likewise undermined the province's power to lease, sell, reclaim, or grant title to public lands, giving Manila a hold over such lands and a final say about their disposition.[67] They used their control over the budget to block or delay the release of funds for public education and infrastructure development to the irritation of many provincial officials. An exasperated General Pershing, for example, had to "halt the construction of new public works projects and limit public works activity to repair and maintenance only" because of such delays.[68] He and other army officers suddenly found themselves going to Manila like any other provincial official to beg for the release of funds.

Once it became clear that the fight with the Filipinos was a lost cause, the army sought desperate measures to keep the Moro Province from Filipino control. Bliss suggested that Mindanao's separation from the Philippines might be the best way to continue the army's civilizing mission. Army officers were emboldened by the support given by the white American community in the province, whose mouthpiece, the *Mindanao Herald,* warned, "[The] future of the Moro country is menaced through no more serious offence on our part than being incorporated with the Philippine Islands."[69]

This budding separatist movement never bloomed, blighted mainly by a "routine state regulation" that rotated or promoted army officers out of the province. Convincing officers to stick to their provincial postings was almost impossible as no one in his right mind would refuse promotion to a higher post, especially if it meant returning to the United States. Moreover, the province was in no position to offer greater compensation to its officials, and more money could be had once one left the military. The turnover rate of district governors for Cotabato, for example, was 1.5 times a year.[70] It did not help that the American settlers failed to sustain their initial trailblazing efforts in districts such as Davao. By the second decade of U.S. rule, American planters there faced labor and capital problems that compelled them to sell or lease their lands to an increasingly competitive Japanese community.[71]

Ironically, it was the army's own paternalistic approach toward governing the Muslims that proved to be the most serious handicap in the long run. For any attempt to portray Muslim support for separatism as "a voice of the people" easily opened up the army to the criticism that it was simply manipulating a "backward" people. Neither could army officers declare publicly that the Muslims were ready to share in the burden of governance once Mindanao separated from the Philippines for this argument ran counter to their own assessment that a "civilized" Muslim population ready for "civil government" was still in the distant future.[72]

Filipinos were quick to exploit these contradictions. Manuel Quezon, the leader of the emergent Nacionalista Party, declared that under Filipino rule Muslims would be treated as equals since "Filipinos and Moros belong to the same race as the Christian Filipinos." He promised that under a Filipino-controlled government, Muslims and other non-Christians would be granted the right to vote as suffrage could hasten the civilizing process.[73] Quezon hoped to drive a wedge between the Americans and their Muslim wards and entice the latter to join the Nacionalistas. He was only partly successful, and most Muslims continued to support the army as long as it was the power in Moro Mindanao.

The debate over whether martial rule should continue in the Moro Province was eventually resolved by fiat when President Woodrow Wilson kept his promise to prepare the Philippines for eventual independence by allowing Filipinos a larger role in running the colonial state. In 1913, army officers began to turn over their posts to their civilian counterparts while Quezon and company began extending invitations to prominent *datus* and sultans in Cotabato and Sulu to join the government.[74]

Muslims and the American settlers were adamantly opposed to this transfer of power, with Jolo *datus* demanding that Washington intervene to annex "the territory occupied by the Moros and . . . give them a permanent government by Americans."[75] Maranao *datus* signed a "Dansalan declaration" expressing a similar demand while a "Committee of Petitions and Communications" formed by a group of unknown Muslim leaders warned of "bloodshed and disorder" if Mindanao was not separated from the Philippines.[76] The reality, however, was that without arms and the U.S. Army to protect them, their opposition was hopeless. Inevitably, many of the *datus* who warned of bloodshed accepted Quezon's offer and began positioning themselves as the "spokesmen" of the Muslim people in the Philippine Assembly.[77] Such actions have been offered as proof of their elite opportunism.[78] But one could also see this switch of support as a more recent version of what their fathers and forefathers had done in the past—deftly navigating their way between powerful trading states in maritime Southeast Asia to promote their own economic and diplomatic interests.[79]

There was one last opportunity for reversing Filipinization, and this came when Leonard Wood returned to the Philippines as governor-general in 1921. Immediately, the erstwhile integrated Muslim elites switched sides, welcoming the return of "Datu Wood" who would free them from the Filipinos and keep Mindanao separate.[80] Wood whetted their appetites when he reassigned Americans to the provincial posts and acted as a buffer for the Muslims against the intrusive Filipinos.[81] In that brief moment, the Muslim's pro-Americanism returned only to be dashed when Wood died in 1927 on an operating table in faraway Boston. From then on, Moro Mindanao was completely embedded in the Philippine body politic, and it would take another fifty years for the issue of separatism to be resurrected.

Conclusion

The officers who governed the Moro Province moved on to more illustrious careers, some within the empire and others in the domestic political arena. While it is difficult to find a definitive correlation between their experiences as provincial officials and what they did after leaving the Philippines, their records seemed to attest that colonial service in Mindanao proved vital to their careers. The historian Wayne Thompson notes that Wood, Bliss, and Pershing all went on to become army chiefs of staff. While Wood would return to the Philippines in the 1920s as governor-general, Bliss would become the American military representative on the allied Supreme War Council in Paris during World War I.[82]

Pershing's pilgrimage took a more circuitous route. He returned to the Moro Province as its last military governor, preparing for the transfer to the new civil regime by launching a series of military expeditions to disarm the Muslims.[83] As expected, the Muslim communities resisted Pershing's moves. The worst violence came at Bud Bagsak in Sulu District, where the army killed over five hundred Muslim men, women, and children in a massacre that Pershing described, almost dismissively, as "the last large-scale action fought by Americans in the Moro country."[84] Untouched, Pershing turned over the Moro Province to a new civilian commissioner and the "guerrilla warrior" continued his brilliant military career—first pursuing the Mexican rebel Pancho Villa, later commanding of the American Expeditionary Forces during World War I, and finally serving as the army chief of staff in the 1920s.[85]

What Pershing and his fellow officers left behind was a political landscape that bore the imprint of their autocratic, quasi-managerial, and progressive-influenced rule. As mentioned above, Davao—once Mindanao's most backward district—had become one of the most productive sections of the province and perhaps even of the entire colony. The army also left a Moro Province whose population retained a fraught relationship with the colonial capital. Administrative successes nurtured a Muslim *umma* that simultaneously favored the U.S. Army over Filipino politicians, but it was too weak to resist Filipinization.[86] In the end, its leaders opted to subordinate their interests to Quezon and the Nacionalistas, and in turn they were invited to engage in colonial politics, albeit with little influence. Non-Muslim areas such as Davao accepted Filipinization, but their economic successes also enabled them to keep Manila at a distance. With Filipino politicians in their pockets, the Japanese planters were able to attain an autonomy that their Muslim counterparts could only dream of. In fact, one could make the argument that at the end of American colonial rule it was the Muslims who were more politically integrated into the emerging Philippine state than the settlers in the non-Muslim zones.

These complicated state-society relations and the sentiments they nurtured extended beyond life in the Moro Province. In the postcolonial era these complications would be invoked as the most powerful validation for two Muslim separatist movements. Over time, the colonial origins of this "invented tradition" would fade away to be enfolded within an argument that links modern day separatism to a mythical, century-long, Moro struggle against the Philippine state.

Minutemen for the World

Empire, Citizenship, and the National Guard, 1903–1924

CHRISTOPHER CAPOZZOLA

ON A GREEN FIELD IN CONCORD, MASSACHUSETTS, stands a statue known as the Minute Man. Sculpted in 1874, Daniel Chester French's monument to America's revolutionary soldiers also serves as an emblem of the United States National Guard. Yet, for all the nostalgia and patriotism the image embodies, it begs a simple question: why does a nation with some 750 overseas military bases and tens of thousands of nuclear warheads represent its military power with a statue of a rifle-bearing farmer? Who, in other words, are Americans trying to kid?

Americans have usually evaded that question, but sometimes they have tried to answer it. In the early twentieth century, after war with Spain and the annexation of a formal empire, Americans debated the structure, status, and manpower of the nation's military force and, in turn, reconsidered the relationship between citizenship and military service. Battles in the halls of Congress and the pages of military journals led, among other reforms, to the creation of the modern National Guard. Since 1903, the guard has been the United States' "organized militia": civilian men and women who are fully trained, part-time soldiers. The soldiers who filled the ranks of the National Guard stood at a crucial political intersection: they embodied America's older republican minuteman tradition, but in the twentieth century they increasingly marched as foot soldiers in an armed force deployed around the globe. The guard's history thus sheds light on the complex hybrid of republican and imperial impulses that underlies the twentieth-century American state.

The impassioned debate of a century ago combined, in fine American tradition, lofty rhetoric about the nation's constitutional principles and a grabby struggle for money and status. To be sure, fights over the modernization of the U.S. military reflected domestic political concerns, but fundamental constitutional conflicts accompanied more narrowly political ones. In an era that ratified amendments authorizing taxation, women's suffrage, and the direct election of senators, and another forbidding the manufacture of alcohol, the constitutional status of the military remained textually unchanged. Instead, the imperial republic emerged from a startling rereading of the existing constitutional structure that was no less significant for modern American history.

After World War I, the nation's citizen soldiers served a new authority: a state more thoroughly controlled from Washington and the executive branch, a state more able (and more willing) to intervene by force in sovereign nations without exercising formal imperial control over them, a state that mobilized colonized people into its armed forces without extending to them the privileges of citizenship. It was a state, in short, at ease with contradictions. And yet at times America's imperial citizen soldiers themselves—both colonial subjects and republican citizens—proved to be less amenable to contradiction than the imperial republic's architects. Their challenges brought the paradoxes of the American imperial state to the fore.

Aftermath of the Philippine War

The minuteman is a mythic figure: a male republican citizen, civilian in status, peaceful in disposition, yet trained in the arts of war and ready at a minute's notice to spring forth to defend the republic. It was a popular notion. During the nineteenth century, Americans summoned the memory of Lexington and Concord when they volunteered in state and local militia companies, and the concept meshed well with a political theory that premised a small federal government, active states, a weak presidency, and a small standing army. Yet the minuteman describes a myth better than a reality. In the late nineteenth century, state militias were in particularly sorry shape, ill-equipped and underfunded by their own governors and mistrusted by the working classes whose strikes they were called out to break. The forward-looking, outward-oriented professional soldiers who increasingly officered the services were even more contemptuous; they derided the patronage positions of the militias' officers and the drunken sociability and amateurish war-gaming of the enlisted men.[1]

All that changed after 1898. Military modernizers seized the opportunity to attack the militia system as an outdated relic of America's long-ago colonial past. Elihu Root, appointed secretary of war in August 1899, was their spokesman and hero. From his office in the recently constructed State, War and Navy Building, an enormous office complex near the White House, Secretary Root looked at the militias and saw inefficiency. At the mercy of state governors for funds, the nation's state militias stood at markedly different points of readiness. Both governors and the president could mobilize the militias, creating unclear lines of authority. In most states, men elected their own officers and—particularly galling in an age that equated bureaucracy with progress—they maintained their own muster rolls. In such a system, argued Root, "there will always be confusion, waste, delay and suffering." Everything that had gone wrong in the war with Spain—and much had—was attributed (often wrongly) to the militias. "The confusion, controversy, and bad feeling" arising from the militia's "uncertain status were painfully apparent at the beginning of the war with Spain," Root announced. These were the lessons of the "splendid little war."[2]

As war raged in the Philippines and Washington jingoes continued to speak in the full-throated language of empire, moves to reform the militias ensued. Some wanted to do away with them entirely. "Our militia law," Theodore Roosevelt told Congress in 1901, "is obsolete and worthless." Others sought to use carrot and stick to bring the militias more firmly under federal control. Elihu Root befriended Charles Dick, a Republican congressman from Ohio who chaired both the House Committee on the Militia and the National Guard Association, a private organization of militia supporters. Together they pushed through the Dick Act in early 1903, which established the National Guard in its modern form. In exchange for generous allocations of federal money, state forces would be increasingly subject to supervision and inspection by the army. Scholars influenced by the modernization theory of the mid-twentieth century depicted these developments as the inevitable adjustments of military institutions to the facts of modernity, a new structure to match the modern function of the American state. For military modernizers and their latter-day historians, opponents of reform were corrupt "old army" types stuck in Victorian mud.[3]

And yet at the time the march of progress appeared less certain. Reformers faced considerable obstacles. A bloc of senators opposed standing armies with the same vocal rhetoric they had marshaled against the acquisition of a formal empire, and they often linked the two innovations. Likewise, the National Guard had its own constituency on Capitol Hill. But most important, it had a place in the Constitution. Conflict emerged over the question of whether National Guard troops could be deployed overseas. To most Americans, the Constitution was perfectly clear on the subject: Article I, section 8, clearly stated that the militia was to "execute the Laws of the Union, suppress Insurrections and repel Invasions." History provided clear precedents of militia troops refusing to serve outside the United States, as when the New York Militia halted at the border with Canada during the War of 1812. The battle between modernizers and the "old army" was thus a struggle over what kind of military the Constitution could sustain—a live question for military officers, civilian policy makers, and the American public.[4]

Early reformers respected the controlling power of the militia clause. The military thinker Emory Upton, the apostle of the twentieth-century modernizers, deferred to limits on the guard's extraterritorial use. His influential plans, which circulated among army officers, called for the employment of militias "as a last resort to be used only as intended by the Constitution." Elihu Root recognized constitutional limits as well. He rejected the advice of officers who coveted Europe's large standing armies and hoped to phase out the militias altogether. Root proposed a hybrid organization instead. The secretary was no fan of militias, states' rights, or isolationism. But he was more sensitive than most War Department planners to what he called the "difficulties arising from our form of government and the habits and opinions of our people." Root knew that Americans would balk at a large standing army not only because it was expensive but because it departed from national traditions.[5]

The War Department chafed at these limits and the entrenched power of the old army types who benefited from them, and reformers soon plotted an end run around them. In the years after 1898, and particularly during the administration of President William Howard Taft from 1909 to 1913, a new guard of military planners consolidated their power in the halls of the State, War and Navy Building. These men had come of age not in the era of frontier Indian fighting—nor even in the fuss and feathers of war with Spain—but in the slow-boiling crucible of imperial domination and counterinsurgency that they called the Philippine Insurrection: men such as Secretary of War Henry Stimson, Army Chief of Staff Leonard Wood, Judge Advocate General Enoch Crowder, and President Taft himself. All had experience in the Philippines; all were committed to a flexible global army freed of the constraints of the militia clause.

First, they attempted a bold assault on the Constitution backed up by a novel theory to justify their move. Legislation passed in May 1908 provided that the president could call out the National Guard for an unlimited term of service and explicitly permitted its use "within or without the territory of the United States." For authority, the act's sponsors cited not the militia clause but a different passage of Article I, section 8, one authorizing Congress to "raise and support armies." Elihu Root, who in 1908 was serving in the U.S. Senate, amplified that line of argument. He justified extraterritorial military actions through the president's power as commander in chief, particularly when dealing with governments "too feeble or too ill-organized" to protect Americans abroad.[6]

Just two years later, the "feeble" and "ill-organized" nation on policy makers' minds was Mexico, then in the midst of a revolution that threatened to spill over its northern border into the United States. Secretary Stimson asked Enoch Crowder, the army's top lawyer, whether the National Guard might be used outside the United States—particularly (if not explicitly) in Mexico. Crowder replied that the answer was no. His opinion found its way into a February 1912 ruling by Attorney General George Wickersham advising Stimson that "the militia while in U.S. service might pursue an invading force beyond the U.S. boundary as part of repelling an invasion, but in general the militia cannot be employed outside the

United States." The War Department's 1908 assault on the militia clause appeared to have failed.[7]

Historians have generally interpreted Wickersham's ruling as an underhanded attempt by Stimson, Wickersham, and Taft—modernist reformers who wanted a professional military and disparaged the citizen soldier tradition—to destroy the National Guard by tying its hands, freeing the War Department to replace it during this moment of crisis with a larger standing army and a reserve force under direct army control. Certainly the guard saw it that way. An editorial in *National Guard* magazine called the attorney general's ruling a "monkey wrench" deliberately designed to scuttle the guard.[8]

Certainly, Crowder and Wickersham were up to something. But their persistent deference to the Constitution testifies to the magnitude of the problem that the military faced. Lawyer warriors such as Root, Stimson, Crowder, and Taft took constitutional principles seriously, and, given the contentious constitutional politics of the Progressive era, they hesitated to move quickly. These were, after all, the same men who believed that child labor laws and workmen's compensation provisions violated Americans' freedom of contract. Their solution to the military's problem, therefore, had to accord in some fashion with the Constitution.[9]

This was all the more true in the constitutional context of formal empire. The debate over the use of the National Guard outside the United States took place together with another constitutional conversation about what, precisely, made up the territorial United States. In a series of cases that followed in the wake of the American defeat of the Spanish empire, the Supreme Court ruled that the new territories were part of the United States yet not fully. They were, in the evocatively evasive words of Justice Henry Brown, "foreign . . . in a domestic sense." Territorial residents were U.S. nationals, but not U.S. citizens, and the lands they lived in were "appurtenant to" the United States but not a fundamental part of it.[10]

While none of the insular cases directly addressed the status of the National Guard or its deployment to America's appurtenances, the linkage of two constitutional discourses of territoriality is clear. Federalization of the militia was a logical consequence of owning and keeping lands that existed both inside and outside the United States. Empire would require an imperial army, and while the nation's republican traditions never disappeared—as the citizen soldiers of the National Guard showed—they would increasingly come second to the demands of global military power.

The National Guard in World War I

War in Europe soon outpaced the schemes of military planners, and a national debate on military "preparedness" ensued after guns roared in August 1914. President Woodrow Wilson's secretary of war, Lindley Garrison, wanted to replace the National Guard with a new "Continental Army," a federal reserve force of four hundred thousand trained soldiers. Representative James Hay of Virginia, chairman of the House Military Affairs Committee, denounced Garrison's plan, which he thought would "bring everlasting shame and ruin upon this great republic." Wilson, deferent to powerful southern Democrats on Capitol Hill and hostile to the imperial ambitions of his Republican predecessors, backed away from Garrison's Continental Army and supported Hay's compromise plan, which would keep the National Guard but place it more firmly under federal control. Garrison, knowing he was defeated, abruptly resigned in February 1916; that June, Wilson signed the National Defense Act. The bill's supporters justified their dramatic reforms with the "raise and support armies" clause. As armies warred in Europe, the militia clause sounded ever more anachronistic.[11]

The National Defense Act remade the relationship between American citizenship and military service. Among its many provisions, the new law required that individual members of the National Guard swear an oath of allegiance to both their states and the federal government, thereby giving either their governor or the president the authority to call them directly into federal service. The act also stipulated that all soldiers in the guard must either be United States citizens or have declared their intention to become citizens. This feature of the statute had less to do with the social contract than with international law: soldiers who fight in the armies of nations of which they are not citizens are technically mercenaries and thus lack legal protections. Coming after two decades of mass immigration, the 1916 act's terms of citizenship efficiently mobilized an ethnically diverse army of citizen soldiers to fight a global war "outside" the United States.[12]

War pressed Wilson to achieve what many Republicans had wished for but most Democrats never intended: a large standing army controlled in Washington. By 1916, America's military forces were on the road toward transformation: bigger, more flexible, more federal, a change to which the three million men drafted under the Selective Service Act could attest. But what did these armies look like on the ground, whether that ground was the "territorial" United States or its margins and dependencies? From Kansas to Hawai'i and the Philippines, soldiers challenged the army of the imperial republic, posing questions not only about where it could be sent but who would fill its ranks and on what terms of citizenship they would consent to do so.

On December 3, 1917, at Camp Funston in Kansas, a Missouri-born soldier named Robert Cox told the camp commandant—none other than Major General Leonard Wood—that he rejected the authority of the Selective Service Act, which had brought him into uniform. Cox argued that Congress's power "to call the citizens of the United States, the national militia, to compulsory service" derived from the militia clause. Thus, the Constitution forbade the use of drafted men outside the boundaries of the United States. It was hardly a surprising challenge considering the previous decade's debates. More remarkable was the Supreme Court's response.[13]

Cox turned to Hannis Taylor, a Southern patrician and part-time constitutional scholar, who brought the case all the way to the United States Supreme Court. Taylor, who had been a minister to Spain from 1893 to 1897, was an enthusiastic supporter of America's imperial turn; in his writings he had called empire a "predestined and settled element in our national life" and dismissed Thomas Jefferson's agonies over the Louisiana Purchase as "constitutional quibbles." Yet Hannis Taylor also shared much of the white South's principled commitment to states' rights and its ardent opposition to European intervention. Before the Supreme Court he railed against Woodrow Wilson's "bacchanalian revel of illegality." Should conscription come to pass, warned Taylor, "this Republic is at an end." Arguing for the United States, Solicitor General John W. Davis called Taylor's claims "a gross attack upon the government" and ridiculed Robert Cox's position. "From his home in Missouri . . . he bids defiance to the German Empire . . . and challenges them to combat—but on American soil." Justice Oliver Wendell Holmes Jr., in the middle of Taylor's oral argument, muttered to a colleague that Taylor was "a pig-headed adherent of an inadequate idea."[14]

In May 1918, the justices ruled unanimously that the "raise and support armies" clause was plenary and Congress's powers under it "knew no limit." Chief Justice Edward White went out of his way to denounce Hannis Taylor's "obviously intemperate" and "patently unwarranted" brief. Cox's failed appeal brought to an end the last serious constitutional challenge to America's global army in U.S. courts.[15]

Robert Cox, a citizen soldier, found himself in an army the minutemen of Concord would have had trouble recognizing. The wartime experience of the Philippine National Guard revealed a further contradiction, one between republican citizen soldiers and the imperial possessions they guarded. When Democrats regained control of the White House in 1913 after nearly two decades out of office, Wilson initiated a policy of Filipinization for the colonial civil service, legislature, and police, culminating in the 1916 Jones Act, which promised the territory eventual independence. "The Philippines are at present our frontier," Wilson announced, "but I hope we presently are to deprive ourselves of that frontier."[16]

As an unincorporated territory, the Philippines didn't have a National Guard, but in March 1917, as war clouds gathered, the Philippine legislature authorized the creation of one, using language that mirrored the National Defense Act of the year before. The proposed guard was the pride and joy of Governor-General Francis Burton Harrison, who believed it would act as a school for the incipient citizen soldier, trained with the "assistance given," as one military officer put it, of an "older and stronger brother—the United States." Wilson, too, reportedly expressed "unconcealed enthusiasm" for the guard. In Manila, many Filipino nationalist elites believed that Wilsonian rhetoric highlighting the morality of a war "for the rights of nations great and small" might open a door for independence. They encouraged ordinary Filipinos to enlist in the rank and file of the new guard, and they added their own names to the list of the officer corps, which would mix both American and Filipino soldiers. The Philippine Senate announced in December 1917 that twenty-five thousand men stood "ready and anxious to fight under the American flag."[17]

The U.S. military, however, balked at their use. For one thing, no one wanted to train them. In April 1917, regular officers in the Philippines made up the army's experienced core; the declaration of war prompted their transfer to the Western Front. Among men who had waited years for promotion opportunities and battlefield glory, few relished the idea of staying behind in the Pacific to train soldiers destined never to see combat. Likewise, just fifteen years after the formal end of the Philippine-American War, anticolonial resistance continued; in a corner of the territorial United States where the Second Amendment explicitly did not apply, and where colonial policy even banned the Boy Scouts, many hesitated to arm tens of thousands of Filipinos and then leave the islands in their care.[18]

Just as important as the boundary between citizens and subjects was the color line that divided Americans by race. The National Defense Act promised that federalized guard troops would carry their ranks into the U.S. Army; federalizing the Philippine National Guard would mean placing Filipino officers in command of white men. This was not easy for either Wilson or the military to swallow. Woodrow Wilson had brought to Washington an administration committed to Philippine independence; he had also insisted on the color line within the federal bureaucracy, including the offices of the State, War and Navy Building where his war planners met. Equally committed to white supremacy and global warfare and dependent on the votes of southern Democrats in Congress, the administration confronted an impossible dilemma: either leave power in Manila in the hands of an armed and trained Filipinized military unsupervised by the "older and stronger brother" of the U.S. Army or incorporate the Filipino troops. Rather than confront this dilemma, they avoided it. Civilian politicians in Washington dragged their heels, military officers in Manila dug theirs in, and only a few insistent voices joined Governor Harrison's. The Philippine National Guard, almost fifteen thousand strong, gathered at Camp Tomas Claudio near Manila for the first day of its three-month training period on November 11, 1918, a telling date. Woodrow Wilson wanted it both ways: Filipino citizen soldiers who would symbolize an enlightened imperial policy even as they remained racially unequal citizens. As military mobilization put pressure on the social contract that bound millions of men to the state, it brought forth demands for new privileges of citizenship to reward the risks they had undertaken.[19]

Not all Americans, though, were hesitant about letting Filipinos serve under arms, and a different story played out in Hawai'i. Even before the declaration of war, territorial officials recruited soldiers for the Hawaiian National Guard. Migrants from the Philippines, who numbered perhaps fifteen thousand in 1916, made up a substantial proportion of the islands' population, but the National Defense Act's provision that all guardsmen must be citizens ran up against conflicting court rulings about whether Hawai'i's Filipinos were in fact eligible for citizenship. In March 1916, after hearing the petition of Marcus Solis, U.S. District Court Judge C. F. Clemons concluded that since Filipinos owed allegiance to the United States they were eligible for citizenship and thus eligible to serve in Hawai'i's guard; the War Department began enrolling them forthwith. Filipinos made up half the enlisted men of the Hawaiian National Guard by the end of 1916.[20]

Then enlistments suddenly halted. In December 1916, U.S. District Judge H. W. Vaughan reasoned that because U.S. citizenship law barred Asians from naturalization Filipinos could not become citizens and thus—regardless of their allegiance—they could not serve in the National Guard. Frustrated, Brigadier General R. K. Evans appealed to the War Department from his headquarters on Oahu: "By denying them the privilege of joining the National Guard, we deny them the opportunity of training themselves for self defense in time of war." Evans got his way: an April 1917 amendment to the National Defense Act "provided that in the Territory of Hawaii the National Guard may include citizens of the Philippine Islands." [21]

Many in Hawai'i's Filipino community viewed this legislation as a victory, and they celebrated again a year later when the Naturalization Act of May 1918 promised full citizenship rights for alien servicemen, a statute that appeared—at least on its face—to trump racist naturalization laws. Others were less enthusiastic. Pablo Manlapit, a Filipino labor activist and guardsman, announced, "I have my own country to serve. . . . I do not want American citizenship. I am a member of the National Guard. . . . But if the Filipinos are given their independence I shall return to the islands."[22]

Just a few years later, Manlapit would lead a strike of Filipino sugarcane workers in Hanapepe on the island of Kaua'i. In September 1924, the Hawaiian National Guard intervened in the labor dispute, and sixteen strikers and four guardsmen died. Filipino soldiers were not involved since Governor Wallace Farrington deliberately had chosen non-Filipino soldiers for duty on Kaua'i. But in the months that followed the territorial attorney general ordered the immediate discharge of all 550 Filipino guardsmen. By 1935, the Hawaiian National Guard, more than 1,500 strong, counted only 12 Filipinos in its ranks.[23]

Hawai'i's Filipino guardsmen and their opponents both struggled with the terms of the 1916 National Defense Act, a law drafted in the capital of the imperial republic without considering the possibility that its army of citizen soldiers would include its imperial subjects. During World War I, perhaps as many as six thousand Filipinos joined the U.S. military outside the Philippines. After the war, federal courts reined in the Naturalization Act's expansion of citizenship to Asians, but special legislation did maintain an exception for Filipinos who had served in the U.S. armed forces. They continued to do so, particularly in the navy, where Filipinos worked as messmen, stewards, and stevedores in the interwar years. Just outside Camp Tomas Claudio, where the Philippine National Guard marched in its pointless training exercises, the navy established a recruitment station. Dust had begun to settle on the militia clause of the Constitution, but questions persisted, not about whether citizens could be sent outside the United States but whether the privileges of citizenship would reach the nation's farthest territorial borders. Soldiers proved ever more mobile, the rights of citizenship far less so.[24]

Conclusion

Today, the idea that the National Guard cannot serve outside the United States seems almost as old-fashioned as the Victorian architecture of the State, War and Navy Building. In fact, in 2007 men and women of the guard made up about 43 percent of the fighting forces in Iraq and Afghanistan. A series of post–Vietnam War reforms in the 1970s created the Total Force Policy, which requires that National Guard troops must be part of every military intervention inside or outside the United States. The republican citizen soldier is now fully integrated into international undertakings. But the roots of this policy are found in this moment of the early twentieth century and the skill with which military modernizers evaded the text of the Constitution, the tenacity with which the Supreme Court upheld their actions, and the indifferent reaction of the American public.

Cox v. Wood, it turns out, wasn't the last challenge to America's global army. In late September 2006, California gubernatorial candidate Phil Angelides pledged to use any means necessary to bring the California National Guard back from Iraq, where twenty-one of its members had died since 2003. The force with which Governor Arnold Schwarzenegger ridiculed the proposal matched that marshaled against Hannis Taylor decades before; the governor accused Angelides of "spewing political rhetoric calling for action he knows is both illegal and unconstitutional." Had Angelides pursued the case, he would surely have been as unsuccessful as Minnesota governor Rudy Perpich, who attempted in the 1980s to recall the state's troops from Central America. Before the U.S. Supreme Court, Perpich was, like Robert Cox, unanimously rebuked. The vehemence and the unanimity, from Oliver Wendell Holmes to Arnold Schwarzenegger, suggests the importance to American political culture of the imperial citizen soldier more than two centuries after the minutemen gathered in Concord.[25]

From Winship to Leahy

Crisis, War, and Transition in Puerto Rico

JORGE RODRÍGUEZ BERUFF

IN *The Age of Extremes: A History of the World, 1914–1991*, Eric Hobsbawm writes, "The large British Caribbean colonies were quietly decolonized in the 1960s, the small islands at intervals between then and 1981, the Indian and Pacific islands in the late 1960s and 1970s. In fact, by 1970 no territory of any significant size remained under direct administration by the former colonialist powers or their settler regimes, except in Central and Southern Africa—and, of course, in embattled Vietnam. The imperial era was at an end. Less than three quarters of a century earlier, it had seemed indestructible."[1]

There is no point in trying to clarify what "significant size" meant to Hobsbawm nor how he defined "direct administration." The fact is that more than a decade after this work was published, all political forces in Puerto Rico, in one way or another, seem to agree that the issue of colonial rule has not been resolved. It subsists as an apparently stable arrangement. The flexibility and adaptability, at critical junctures, of U.S. policy toward this "insular possession" must be taken into account to explain the continuity of a colonial relationship which, in the case of Puerto Rico, survived the profound crisis of the 1930s and the challenges of the war and postwar periods.

The transition from the sugar-based economy and more direct forms of rule during the first three decades of U.S. administration in Puerto Rico to the more modern economic and political arrangements under the Estado Libre Asociado, or Commonwealth of Puerto Rico as it is known in its English version, has been a topic of debate and research for many years. The transformation embraced a reform of the colonial state toward more democratic and socially inclusive forms of governance without undermining the continuity of U.S. power.

This change is normally seen to have taken place during the war years and the early 1950s, culminating in the approval of the elective governorship in 1947 and the adoption of the Constitution of Puerto Rico and the establishment of the Estado Libre Asociado, the name given to the new governmental institutions in 1952. Explanations place great emphasis on the reformist bent of the Roosevelt administration, the decision to name Rexford G. Tugwell, a radical New Dealer, as governor in 1941, and his close collaboration with Luis Muñoz Marín, the leader of the reformist Popular Democratic Party. In fact, Tugwell propounds the view that his governorship represented a rupture with previous colonial policy.[2] Also international conditions during the emerging cold war are cited as a factor in the reform of the colonial state.

In this essay, I argue that a major restructuring of American–Puerto Rican relations took place beginning in the late 1930s, specifically in the aftermath of the Ponce massacre and during the 1940s and early 1950s. In this sense, I see the transition as a prolonged process spanning three, and possibly four, gubernatorial periods: those of Admiral William D. Leahy, Guy Swope, Rexford Tugwell, and even Jesús T. Piñeiro. This restructuring included the transformation of the economic arrangement to ensure a certain economic viability, the redefinition of alliances with internal political groups, major changes in American policy-making actors (including the almost simultaneous removal of the main Washington functionary and the governor), and legal reforms and symbolic concessions that made possible a controlled redistribution of power to new Puerto Rican political actors, broadened the social base of support of the state, and served as the framework for a new style of imperial governance.

I also posit that looming, and later actual, war strongly conditioned U.S. policy toward Puerto Rico, which increasingly sought to overcome the sharp social and political conflicts of the Depression for reasons of strategy and defense. Thus, in order to understand the transition, World War II should not be seen as merely a "background" to events but as a major factor that made political, economic, and even cultural change necessary and viable. Contrary to other colonial experiences to which Hobsbawm refers, World War II did not provoke a crisis for metropolitan power in Puerto Rico; rather, it created the conditions of possibility for overcoming the profound crisis of the years of the Depression.[3]

The 1930s was a decade of great political unrest and instability in Puerto Rico, one that could be characterized as a multifaceted crisis of the colonial relationship. Economically, the crisis manifested itself in the incapacity of the sugar industry to generate employment or improve the lot of those employed. By 1938, 60 percent of the population was unemployed. Politically, the crisis led to the radicalization and increasingly violent action of the Nationalist Party. Also, the dissident Liberals under Muñoz's leadership were excluded from power and purged from government jobs. In the United States, a "liberal network" was sharply critical of colonial policies and Winship's administration. By 1939, all political parties were rent by internal strife and dissension and experienced major splits.

Harold Ickes, the secretary of the interior, metaphorically referred to Puerto Rico in the 1930s as a "powder keg."

Robert Gore, the first governor named by Roosevelt, had promptly succumbed in the whirlpool of insular politics. After Gore's demise, Roosevelt named General Blanton Winship governor in 1934, a strong-fisted military figure with colonial experience. He governed in alliance with the Coalición, formed by the Republican and the Socialist parties, the political force that won the elections in 1932 and 1936. Roosevelt continued backing Winship despite the tensions heightened by the virtual illegalization of the Nationalist Party, culminating in the Ponce massacre of 1937, which resulted in nineteen deaths and a major political commotion with ramifications in the United States.

In Washington, policy toward Puerto Rico was to a great extent managed by Ernest Gruening, who controlled both the Division of Territories and Island Possessions of the Department of Interior and the huge budget and bureaucracy of the Puerto Rico Reconstruction Administration (PRRA). The secretary of the interior, Harold Ickes, while formally in charge of Puerto Rico and the superior of Gruening, was, to his intense dislike, left with diminished authority over Puerto Rico. Gruening, with Roosevelt's blessing, became the most powerful Washington functionary in Puerto Rican policy. The Gruening-Winship-Coalición arrangement developed an increasingly repressive and authoritarian style of governance not only toward the Nationalist Party but also toward *muñocismo*, particularly after the assassination of the chief of police, Francis Elisha Riggs, in 1936. Luis Muñoz Marín represented an important pro-independence faction of the Partido Liberal that eventually followed this leader in his break with the party and the establishment of the Partido Popular Democrático. After the Ponce massacre, Harold Ickes strongly opposed this alliance and sought to undermine it. The break between Ickes and Gruening regarding Puerto Rican policy meant that the prevailing tensions also involved key Washington officials.

Winship's main claim to success was having repressed the Nationalist Party and thus "pacified" Puerto Rico. However, two events during 1938 undermined this triumphalism while underscoring the still unstable, and even violent, social and political circumstances. In January 1938, a massive and militant port strike paralyzed shipping activities for thirty-seven days. Later Winship decided, in a provocative move, to celebrate the July 25 anniversary of American rule in Puerto Rico with a military parade in Ponce. His decision was clearly designed to demonstrate the success of his "law and order" policies. Thousands attended the parade, which was broadcast by radio. The event was interrupted by gunfire from Nationalists that left thirty-six persons wounded, including several high officials. A detective was wounded when he leaped in front of the governor and a National Guard colonel, Luis Irizarry, was killed. It was a major security catastrophe. The *New York Times* poked fun at Winship's incompetence. An article published the day after the shootout was entitled "Winship's Tenure Stormy, Nationalist Uprisings and Labor Troubles Have Beset Him."[4] His troubles were further compounded in late 1938 by a major corruption scandal (the "Capitol Racket") and internal strife in both of the Coalición's parties.

During 1938, the European crisis escalated further with the Anschluss of Austria in March and the Munich Agreement of September 29, which allowed the subsequent annexation of the Sudetenland. The Munich Crisis confirmed the perception in Washington that it could no longer rely on Britain and France to contain Germany, consequently forcing the Roosevelt administration to take the initial steps toward war.

In this context a new strategic debate began in 1938 that tended to underscore U.S. military weakness and its unpreparedness for both continental and hemispheric defense. Although the Caribbean had always figured prominently in the country's strategic thinking, its crucial importance for U.S. defense plans was considerably magnified after 1938. The Caribbean became the object of analysis in a deluge of articles and books published between 1938 and 1941.[5]

Among the strategic proposals that were publicly discussed in 1938, George Fielding Eliot's book *The Ramparts We Watch: A Study of the Problems of American National Defense*—which by 1939 was in its sixth printing—had particular implications for military policy toward the Caribbean. He had also written, with R. E. Dupuy, a book published in 1937, *If War Comes*, dealing with similar issues.[6] Eliot was a former major of army intelligence. In a broad analysis of U.S. military security and strategy, he proposed a policy of "hemispheric security" based on a balanced expansion of naval and military forces but placing great emphasis on the navy's role. He also sharply criticized undue reliance on the expansion of air power.[7] It is interesting to note that the epigraph in the first chapter is a quotation from a Roosevelt speech on the deteriorating international situation while the chapter on naval policy is headed by a statement by Admiral William D. Leahy, then chief of naval operations and later to become governor of Puerto Rico (1939–40), on the importance of battleships.[8] Regarding the Caribbean, his argument closely followed known tenets of Captain Alfred Thayer Mahan's geopolitical outlook, underscoring the vital importance of the Panama Canal and the need to ensure naval control of the entire region and access to bases.[9]

Eliot placed great emphasis on the importance of the Puerto Rico–Virgin Islands area. In a map of the Caribbean region, he drew a square over the zone and named it the "Eastern Outpost." The vital Mona and Anegada passages could be controlled from these islands and air and naval power projected toward the Atlantic and the Lesser Antilles. He proposed augmenting the Puerto Rican garrison the level of fifteen hundred men and providing it with coastal artillery. With an additional base in Barbados or Trinidad and one or more auxiliary bases in the Lesser Antilles, the United States could seal all potential entry points to the Caribbean and project its naval forces toward the South Atlantic as far as the strategically important Brazilian "salient."[10] It is striking how closely actual U.S. military planning followed Eliot's recommendations.

In late October 1938, *Life* magazine published an article entitled "America Gets Ready to Fight Germany, Italy, and Japan," which included a half-page photo of Admiral Leahy standing in front of a world map. The map had a large arrow connecting the region of Dakar in Africa with the Brazilian bulge and a caption that read, "It is only two thousand miles from Africa to South America." It also included a map of the Caribbean indicating naval bases and maritime routes with the caption "Caribbean is strategic key to the Western Hemisphere" and indicated that "the region above is the part of his map which Admiral Leahy studies with most concern." It also said, "From the strategist['s] viewpoint, America's long soul-searchings over 'imperialism' in the Caribbean are sentimental twaddle. America *must* control the Caribbean or some other power may control America." The article cited Eliot's books *The Ramparts We Watch* and *If War Comes* as

"The Gibraltar of the Caribbean." Air power over Old San Juan, Puerto Rico, showing B-18A bombers, November 5, 1940. (Fundación Luis Muñoz Marín)

authoritative sources on the Caribbean, emphasizing his recommendation for additional bases in several European possessions.[11]

Military security concerns prompted the revision of defense plans beginning in 1938. New defense plans for Puerto Rico began to be drafted during that year, with the process gathering momentum in 1939. The U.S. Navy had not carried out a major study on base requirements since 1923 when the Rodman Board Report was prepared. A broad review of naval requirements began in mid-May 1938 with the creation of the Hepburn Board, which delivered its report on December 1, 1938, to Admiral William Leahy, the chief of naval operations. The board identified the Atlantic-Caribbean area as in the greatest need of base infrastructure and recommended the construction of a base in the Isla Grande area of the San Juan Harbor and further installations in the Virgin Islands. In addition, Roosevelt decided that the 1939 Fleet Maneuvers, Fleet Problem XX, would be held for the first time in the Caribbean.

Fleet Problem XX maneuvers were held in this region, with particular emphasis in the Puerto Rico–Virgin Islands zone, during February 1939. The war hypothesis included fascist subversion in South America, a German naval attack on the American continent, and a thrust against U.S. forces in Puerto Rico. The maneuvers served to lay bare the military vulnerabilities in the region and to clarify the most urgent defense measures. All the participating admirals met with Roosevelt in Culebra, Puerto Rico, to discuss the results of the exercise.

The sharply enhanced strategic importance of Puerto Rico and the entire Caribbean area made the issue of political stability a very critical one to all metropolitan countries with colonies in the region. Winship tried to argue that he could provide the required political conditions for the implementation of the ambitious defense measures in Puerto Rico. However, the events of 1938 must have seriously undermined his credibility and that of the American officials in Puerto Rico. By late 1938 and early 1939, he increasingly appeared to be an embattled administrator facing charges of repression, incompetence, corruption, and subservience to the conservative policies of his Coalición partners. Winship and the Coalición were increasingly perceived as contributing to actual or potential unrest in Puerto Rico at a time when the island's value to defense measures was being dramatically enhanced by approaching war. Acting within the context of the Fleet Problem XX maneuvers, Roosevelt decided to initiate a redefinition of policy toward Puerto Rico. On March 1, 1939, while cruising near San Juan in the USS *Houston* on his return trip to the United States, he offered the governorship of Puerto Rico to his chief of naval operations, Admiral William D. Leahy.

President Roosevelt announced during a press conference held on May 12, 1939, that he would name Admiral William D. Leahy to the governorship of Puerto Rico. The following day *El Mundo* carried the news in bold letters as the main front page story with a photograph of Leahy and a brief biographical sketch.

The story mentioned his interest in Puerto Rico's strategic value and announced that he would be taking office the following July.[12] In a brief letter to Ruby Black, Jesús T. Piñero, the president of the *colonos* (independent cane farmers), who was a follower of Muñoz Marín, claimed that the cablegram was handed to Winship while he was taking a siesta and that the Coalición interrupted a legislative caucus to "mourn" the decision with Winship at La Fortaleza.[13]

On May 14, *El Mundo* followed up on the story by reporting that the decision had been based on the "need to eliminate all sources of dissension" due to the "growing importance of Puerto Rico in national defense."[14] It also reported that more than $30 million would be devoted to defense preparations in 1940 and a total of $200 million over the next five years (1940–45). Leahy would "head and coordinate the enormous national defense projects."[15] It was claimed that the base construction program was part of a broader, ambitious plan to "industrialize" Puerto Rico, and for this purpose the staggering amount of $1 billion would be assigned over the next twenty years![16] The American press also attributed Leahy's nomination to strategic military considerations regarding defense plans for Puerto Rico and the Caribbean.[17]

As leftist U.S. congressman Vito Marcantonio argued, the surprise announcement was equivalent to destitution since Winship had not resigned despite Ickes's considerable arm-twisting.[18] Winship's letter of resignation was dated June 3 and states that he had been thinking about resigning for about a year but "for different reasons had postponed the request."[19] This letter received a polite reply from the president two days later, thanking him for his "long and distinguished career in the service of your government" and for his "most arduous task" in the governorship of Puerto Rico.[20]

Winship's close alignment with the Coalición, his reputation as a repressive colonial administrator, the insistent accusations of corruption, and his evident reluctance to follow instructions emanating from Washington, particularly from Harold Ickes, not only disqualified him as an acceptable agent for a change in policy but also transformed him into a political liability. To Ickes, who never liked him, the envoy had become too "creolized" and was acting as a "puppet" of the real strongman, Rafael Martínez Nadal, the Coalición leader. President Roosevelt was fully cognizant of the Puerto Rican political situation, which he had closely followed since his first term, and of Winship's difficulties when he offered the governorship to Admiral Leahy.

Understandably, the leadership of the Coalición interpreted Winship's removal as a major political blow engineered by the hated secretary of the interior, which could indicate a major and negative shift in Washington's policy. The mainstream Partido Liberal and the recently established Partido Popular Democrático led by Luis Muñoz Marín, on the other hand, welcomed Winship's removal. By January 1940, the initial support from Muñoz had become hyperbolic praise.[21]

José Ramírez Santibañez, Antonio R. Barcelo's successor as Liberal leader, publicly expressed satisfaction. A change in the governorship would clearly create a more favorable environment for the opposition Tripartista political formation that he was building. However, the American liberals with whom Muñoz had developed a close relationship of collaboration received the nomination of Admiral Leahy with great misgivings as they saw the move as prolonging the military administration.[22]

A few days before Leahy's inauguration, on September 11, 1939, Ernest Gruening was relieved of his duties in Puerto Rican policy making and appointed governor of Alaska. His removal meant a major triumph for Harold Ickes, who could now reconstruct his influence under the admiral and revise policy toward Puerto Rico. According to Leahy, his oral instructions from Roosevelt included taking care of the "appalling conditions" of the urban poor and keeping himself informed of defense measures in Puerto Rico and the Caribbean. He referred to the leader of the Coalición, Martinez Nadal, as a "*caudillo*" who had to be kept in check.[23] Just after the outbreak of war in Europe, Roosevelt swiftly redefined the policy-making actors with responsibility for Puerto Rico.

During Leahy's brief tenure (September 1939 to November 1940), the worst fears of the Coalición were confirmed. His administration was inimical to the majority political formation during a crucial preelectoral juncture. Among other things, he vetoed a large number of bills, named Coalición dissidents to his government, and decreed fiscal austerity precisely when the legislature wanted to increase spending in order to prepare for the elections. He also made a firm commitment to hold clean elections. Simultaneously, Leahy governed during a period when defense measures were gathering momentum, the draft was reintroduced, and the National Guard was integrated into the regular military. Germany's invasion of Poland on September 1, 1939, just a few days before Leahy's arrival in Puerto Rico, moved defense construction into high gear, with almost immediate land expropriations for the construction of Borinquen Field in Aguadilla. Leahy also would keep abreast of the impact of the war in the Caribbean region. He dealt with the Martinique crisis and the military initiatives that led to the crucial Destroyers for Bases agreement with the United Kingdom of September 2, 1940.

The political and military aspects of policy during Leahy's tenure were not unconnected. It was evident that Washington wanted to remove the ruling coalition from power and promote a new political formation, led by Miguel Angel García Méndez, known as Tripartismo. Roosevelt felt the Coalición could not ensure loyalty and political stability in Puerto Rico during a military crisis and was thus no longer an acceptable partner.

However, Tripartismo's electoral weakness in the 1940 elections and the Partido Popular Democrático's surprising electoral success created the opportunity for the Populares to implement their reformist program. Despite Nationalist claims, Muñoz was not at this time a leader anointed by Washington, but he certainly was making every effort to become acceptable through his vocal support of the Roosevelt administration and its military preparations. Roosevelt, who had previously named the repressive and conservative Winship to the governorship, now preferred to negotiate with this new reformist political force and recognize its close "victory." His approach to Puerto Rican politics indicates his flexibility and pragmatism at a time when he was simultaneously consolidating his relations with dictatorships in the Dominican Republic and Nicaragua.

Muñoz's main legislative program would be approved under the governorship of Guy Swope, Leahy's successor. It was argued at the time that reform would be an instrument through which to achieve political stability and the active support of Puerto Ricans for the war effort. Swope's governorship already embodied the new political understanding with the Popular Party. Without underestimating Rexford Tugwell's role, it should be said that by the time he took over in 1941 the new political alliances that would prevail during the war were in place. His selection possibly expressed these new alliances, as he was considered capable of administering the complex relationship with Muñoz. His nomination facilitated the continuation of reforms under war conditions and the forging of a "modern colonialism" during the 1940s.

The war operated in the dynamics of the American–Puerto Rican relationship in two ways. On the one hand, looming war dramatically increased the need for political stability in view of the large strategic role the entire Caribbean and Puerto Rico would play in U.S. defense according to prevailing strategic thinking. On the other hand, the war preparations that began in 1938, the outbreak of war in 1939, and the American entry into the war as a belligerent in 1941 had a major social and economic impact in Puerto Rico, which facilitated the transition from the prevailing colonial model to a new, more "modern" imperial arrangement. The war economy, with its huge state structure and military expenditures, permitted the transition from the declining sugar-dominated model of the first phase of American rule, to the industry-led growth of the 1950s.

The federal state, which had already grown substantially during the 1930s, mainly in the form of huge relief agencies such as the Puerto Rico Reconstruction Administration, shifted toward war preparations. Bureaucracies such as the Works Progress Administration rapidly expanded, becoming major sources of investment and employment. Military service also absorbed tens of thousands of potentially unemployable workers. More than fifty thousand Puerto Ricans were recruited. Despite a period of dire shortages and interruptions of commerce by the submarine blockade, the war years were in balance a period of rapid economic growth.

The reform of the Puerto Rican government structure under Tugwell's and Muñoz's leadership, and the increase in war-related fiscal income, also meant an enlarged local government. The war, together with the reformist program implemented under Muñoz and Tugwell, created new forms of social and political integration that enabled the United States to overcome the sharp political conflicts and unrest of the 1930s. In Puerto Rico, the Roosevelt administration pursued a policy that made possible social reform under war conditions while contributing to the removal from power of forces associated with the previous political and economic arrangement.

French and American Imperial Accommodation in the Caribbean during World War II

The Experience of Guyane and the Subaltern Roles of Puerto Rico

HUMBERTO GARCÍA-MUÑIZ AND REBECA CAMPO

IN 1943, IN THE MIDST OF WORLD WAR II, an imperial United States reached the zenith of its military power in the Caribbean Sea with bases, landing strips, or garrisoned troops in almost all the islands and territories bordering that body of water. The only ones without a U.S. military presence, the French Antilles and Guyane, came into the fold with the crumbling of the Vichy regime that year. Imperial France reached its nadir, with its colonies occupied by Axis or Allied forces and divided by a dispute between the factions of General Charles De Gaulle and General Henri Giraud.

This essay examines aspects of a French and American interimperial encounter during World War II in the Caribbean, the case of Guyane. We begin by comparing the French and American empires with regard to their expansion and defense policies. Within this context, the twofold subaltern roles played by colonials in the imperial armed forces is studied, especially that of the Puerto Ricans in different regional colonial and neocolonial scenarios, namely, the British and French territories and Panama. This is followed by a discussion of Guyane's strategic position and the participation of Pan American Airways (PAA) in the construction by Puerto Rican civil workers of an airfield for an aerial route toward French West and North Africa. Finally, short quotes from an oral history interview and photographs of Major Juan Meléndez-Utset, a Puerto Rican who served as commander of the American Rochambeau Field in Guyane, bring to life the impact of the U.S. armed forces in Puerto Rico and Guyane by illustrating several of the issues analyzed in this work.[1]

There were several similarities and differences between the French and U.S. imperial systems. France had a longer experience in the management of overseas empire. Second to Spain in acquiring and settling territory in the New World during the sixteenth and seventeenth centuries, France focused first on North

America, then on the Caribbean, and shortly afterward on South America. Cayenne, eventually the capital of Guyane, was established in 1604, one of the early *ancienne colonies* of the first French empire. Bordering Brazil and Dutch Guiana (Suriname today), Guyane, a backwater in the empire, stumbled initially as a slave-based sugar plantation society.[2] In 1803, as a result of Napoleon's plans to retreat from the Western Hemisphere due to the defeat of French forces in Saint Domingue (today's Haiti), France sold the Louisiana territory to the United States: "Louisiana was a remarkable case of expansion without conquest . . . but it was nonetheless an imperial acquisition—imperial in the sense of the aggressive encroachment of one people upon the territory of another, resulting in the subjugation of that people to alien rule."[3]

As a result, France facilitated American expansion by land and sea—opening a territorial front on the Gulf of Mexico and furthering the United States' continental expansion westward to the Pacific. Imperial France ceased to be a North American power and lingered mainly in Martinique, Guadeloupe, and Guyane, colonies whose contribution to the national economy diminished in the mid-1840s as sugar beets displaced slave-planted cane as the leading crop for sugar production, an ironic twist of history considering that France had retained Guadeloupe rather than Canada in the Seven Years' War. In the second half of the nineteenth century France failed twice to position itself geopolitically in the Western Hemisphere, first, with Maximilian's fiasco in Mexico and, second, with Ferdinand de Lesseps's debacle in attempting to build an isthmian canal. By that time, Guyane had become a penal colony (*le bagne*) infamous for *l' affaire Dreyfus*.

Successful in its continental expansion in the nineteenth century, the United States failed to expand simultaneously in the Caribbean: no free space remained for a colonial scramble. Except for independent Haiti (1804) and the Dominican Republic (1844), all Caribbean territories were in British, Danish, Dutch, French, or Spanish hands long before the United States attained its independence in 1783. The United States failed to purchase the Danish Virgin Islands (1867), to acquire the Spanish colonies of Cuba (1848) or Puerto Rico (1868), to annex the sovereign Dominican Republic (1870), or to rent land for naval bases in such places as Môle St. Nicholas in Haiti (1890).[4] As a latecomer imperial power in the region, the United States resorted to a war of conquest and annexation (1898) and territorial purchase (1917), two familiar methods already utilized on its road of expansion to the Pacific.

At the turn of the century, due in great part to Alfred Thayer Mahan's popular geopolitical writings, U.S. interests in the Caribbean centered mainly in aquapolitics, namely, the acquisition, building, and ownership of a canal and its protection by controlling the seaways leading to it. As a consequence of the Spanish-Cuban-Philippine-American War, the United States annexed Puerto Rico and established

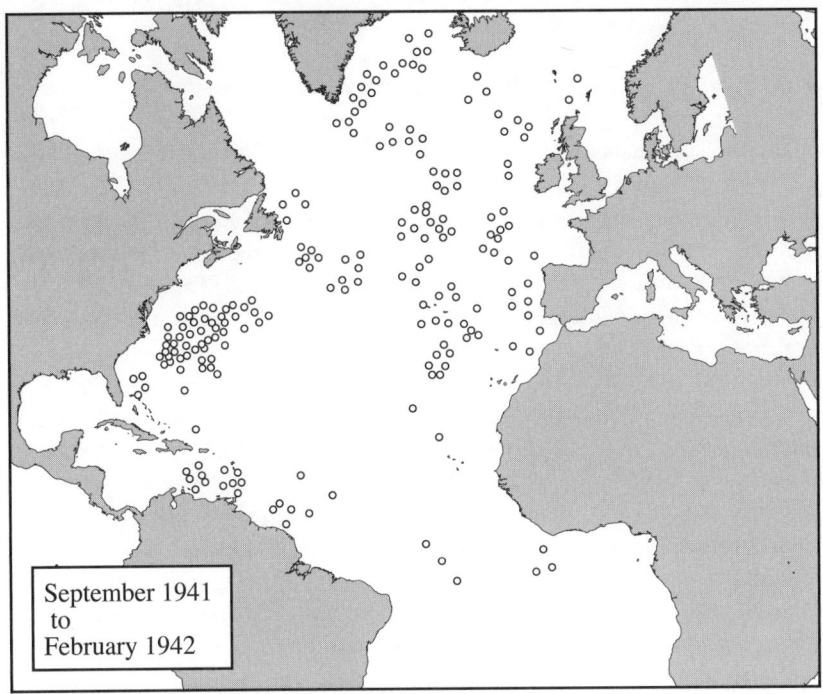

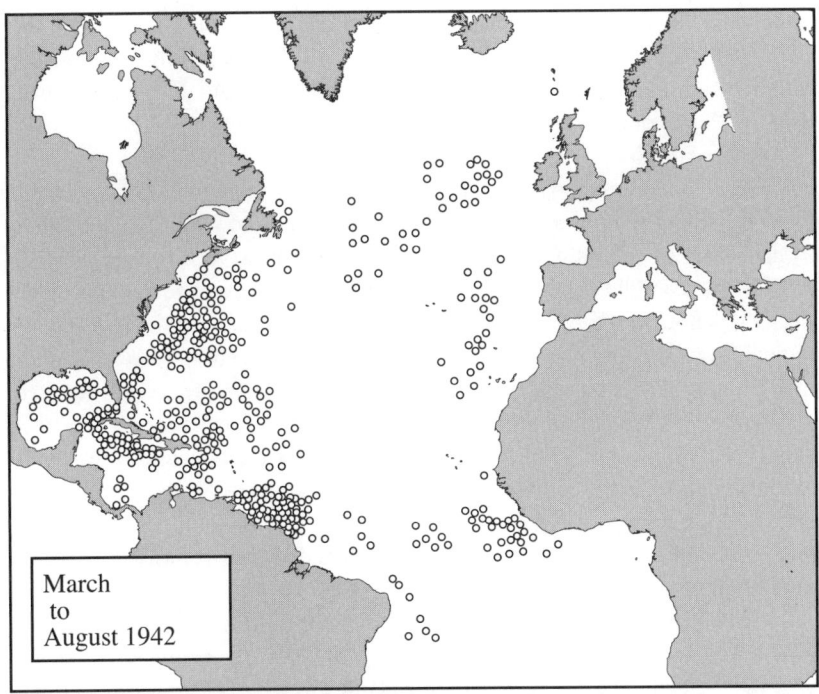

Submarine warfare in the North Atlantic, with dots showing German U-Boat attacks, 1941–42. (Cartography Laboratory, University of Wisconsin–Madison)

a naval base in Guantánamo, Cuba, controlling in that way several routes to the canal, which opened in 1914. In the discussion about the granting of U.S. citizenship to Puerto Ricans in 1917, Representative Henry A. Cooper of Wisconsin recognized the strategic value of the island in relation to the canal: "We are never to give up Porto Rico for, now that we have completed the Panama Canal, the retention of the island becomes very important to the safety of the canal, and in that way to the safety of the Nation itself. It helps to make the Gulf of Mexico an American lake."[5]

Strategic interests also led to the purchase of the Danish Virgin Islands for $25 million less than a month after of the United States' declaration of war against Germany on April 6, 1917, and its administration by the U.S. Navy (until 1931). The importance of U.S. national security in the region was evident, as occupations by the Marines were under way in Haiti since 1915 and the Dominican Republic since 1916, and gunboat diplomacy was frequent in Central America.

Notwithstanding the importance of the Panama Canal and the Caribbean seaways in the U.S. strategy of aquapolitics, the navy was unprepared during World War I for German submarine attacks, although they never occurred. So it is perplexing that on the eve of World War II the U.S. Navy again found itself unprepared for submarine warfare in the North and South Atlantic, as well in the Caribbean, with the matter complicated by the same lack of readiness among the air forces, which were not yet a separate service. As a result, German U-boats won the "Battle of the Caribbean" during most of 1942 and part of 1943.

Another French and American imperial commonality was military service by colonials. France seems to have been "the first Western nation to employ exotic races as soldiers in her wars."[6] In the 1820s France exported West African soldiers to fight wars of conquest and occupation in other possessions of its growing empire. For example, in 1831, 220 Wolof soldiers were dispatched to Guyane. Of these French African forces, the *tirailleurs sénégalais,* founded in the 1857 and recruited from West and North African French colonies, received wide acclaim for their military prowess under French officers.[7] From 1905 onward, France adopted a military doctrine calling for the use of colonial troops in every corner of its empire. Partially conscripted for imperial service since 1912, close to two hundred thousand Africans, drawn mainly from Senegal, served in World War I and suffered high death rates. The empire's defense policy centered on continental France: all military forces, French and colonial, had as their priority the defense of *la patrie.*[8]

In 1901, Puerto Ricans became the first colonials to form a regiment, though provisional and trained by American officers, under a U.S. administration.[9] By 1908 the regiment became part of the regular army, with Puerto Ricans serving in the U.S. armed forces a decade before the imposition of American citizenship on March 2, 1917, and less than a month before the United States declared war on

Germany. It also became the first regiment comprised of Puerto Rican "whites" to be placed on a war footing and sent to serve in the American overseas empire when it was transferred to the Panama Canal Zone for garrison and police duty.[10] Both empires had segregation and conscription policies during World War I and continued them during World War II.

The value of the Caribbean was not limited to aquapolitics. Aeropolitics surfaced in the building of air and naval bases on the Antillean islands and the northern coast of South America from which the Americans hoped to locate and attack German U-2 submarines. A string of airfields and bases was constructed from which the United States could reach French West Africa. Like two pincers—one running though Panama, Colombia, and Venezuela and the other through the Antilles and the Guianas—the expected routes converged on the Parnamirim Field at Natal in northeastern Brazil, the closest point in South America to Dakar, French West Africa (eight hours away by air) via Ascension Island.[11]

Two agreements enabled the United States to create this outer line of defense, which consisted of land, naval, and air bases, as well as troops stationed in the countries of the Caribbean and Central and South America. World War II historiography hails the Anglo-American destroyers-for-bases deal of September 2, 1940, by means of which the United States, with some fanfare, provided Great Britain with fifty aged destroyers in exchange for eight naval and air bases in British colonies in the Western Hemisphere, five of which were in the Caribbean: Antigua, British Guiana (Guyana today), Jamaica, Saint Lucia, and Trinidad.

Seldom noted is the impact in the Caribbean and South America of the "secret" agreement between the U.S. War Department and the PAA by which this corporation built landing fields in the Caribbean, South America, and Africa.[12] The rationale was that it would be easier for PAA than for the U.S. government to negotiate with the countries involved considering that the corporation had a network of airfields acquired on its own and through its displacement of competing airlines, among them the German-influenced Sociedad Colombo Alemana de Transporte Aéreo (SCADTA) in Colombia and Condor in Brazil. By 1944, the agreement had led to the construction of fifty-two airfields, hydroplanes bases, radio and weather stations, and fuel deposits in sixteen colonial and sovereign countries in the Caribbean, South America, and Liberia.

As the war moved away from the Caribbean at the end of 1942, a massive relocation of U.S. troops of white complexion began while those classified as blacks stayed in the region. News of this policy aroused the opposition of the British colonial administration in Trinidad and Tobago, which had been against the presence of colored troops since their arrival became known. Governor Bede Edmund Hugh Clifford claimed that "prominent Trinidadians of the African race protest that the British West Indians have nothing in common with the American negro and allege that the latter are debauching their people and disrupting their family life."[13]

These attitudes came together with the stereotyping of these forces by the U.S. military, which described them as "less efficient than continentals" and suited for a tropical climate.[14] Clifford suggested replacing these troops with Puerto Ricans, observing, "[T]hough neither would be wanted here, Puerto Ricans would be preferable to United States negroes."[15] Yet other colonial governors in the British Caribbean disagreed and strongly opposed the idea. To assuage their anxieties, American military officials promised what they could not deliver: only "white Puerto Ricans with knowledge of English and a high educational standard" would be sent.[16] One wonders about the motivations for the British opposition. Did they fear that Puerto Ricans, with their different culture and color lines, would subvert local social and racial orders?[17] By the end of 1943, all bases in the British Caribbean were manned by Puerto Rican soldiers, and by July 1945 of the 38,518 U.S. military men in the Caribbean Defense Command 22,000 were Puerto Ricans.[18]

The official role of Puerto Rican soldiers in the Caribbean theater repeated that of World War I: "garrison duty in inactive posts." High military officers such as the Wisconsin native General Thomas R. Phillips, chief of staff of the Antilles Department, held Puerto Ricans in low regard. To his Puerto Ricans friends, he said "their class was lazy, spoilt and full of pride," and as potential soldiers he rated the island's workers and farmers at "about the level of the poorer stocks in the Southern states." In the end, the army "reluctantly" recruited Puerto Ricans for "limited service," but the navy "would not take them."[19] The imperial military services lacked a consistent policy on this issue.

Within the imperial administration, Governor Rexford G. Tugwell tried to involve President Roosevelt but could only obtain a weak promise of intervention as the admirals "refused to obey" presidential directives over having the "Negroes . . . rated as anything but mess boys." Tugwell contested "Army and Navy discrimination" because this "supercilious exclusion was . . . deeply resented."[20] The highest colonial official on the island—renowned for his liberalism—was conscious of the resentment within Puerto Rican society. Resistance to racial segregation within the U.S. armed forces came from "Puerto Rican whites" due to their classification as "*non-whites*." As a result, a special classification resulted: "the *Portorican white*."[21]

By 1943, the U.S. military "occupied" all of the Caribbean with the exception of the French Antilles and Guyane. The fall of France in April and May and the signing of the armistice by Marshall Pétain on June 1940 had been unexpected developments. Admiral Georges Robert, the high commissioner to the French Caribbean and the commanding officer of the French naval and military forces in the Antilles Station, with headquarters in Martinique, sided with the Vichy government in France.[22] Very ably, Admiral Robert negotiated first a modus vivendi and later an agreement with the United States maintaining a status quo

Captain Juan Meléndez-Utset, a Puerto Rican who served as commander of the U.S. Rochembeau Field, Guyane, during World War II. (Major Juan Meléndez-Utset)

that allowed the movement of warships among the French colonies for purposes of local administration or defense. France's imperial defense in the Caribbean "basked in the relative safety of America's regional enforcement of the Monroe Doctrine."[23]

Based on this agreement, in September Admiral Robert sent 300 French marines aboard the *Quercy* to Guyane and crushed an anti-Vichy, pro-Gaullist movement. Governor Robert Chot could not rely on the 70 *tirailleurs sénégalais* assigned to him personally and the 650 local troops, especially after Captain Claude Chandon, a French reserve officer turned planter, began to organize an internal coup with British and Free French support.[24] Crucial for Chot was that, "in a back up show of gun boat diplomacy," a U.S. warship arrived on September 21 and left just two days before the *Quercy* disembarked its military contingent.[25]

By maintaining the status quo in the French Caribbean colonies, the United States advanced two of its policies. First, President Roosevelt's policy of maintaining official relations with Vichy thwarted Brazil's territorial ambitions, which had already been checked by the Havana Declaration of July 1940. In the Havana Declaration the foreign ministers of the American Republics proclaimed that, pending final disposition, European colonies in Latin America might be made collective trusteeships of the American republics to prevent unfriendly powers from establishing control over them; any of the republics could act in an emergency while awaiting concerted measures. Second, bauxite mining in neighboring Dutch Guiana (Surinam today) could continue without the fear of an Axis attack, which would affect aluminum production in the United States, indispensable for the building of planes.[26]

In April 1941, Governor Chot obtained, "by several subterfuges," Admiral Robert's authorization to build a PAA airport at Le Gallion near Cayenne.[27] Almost a year later, Chot himself approved the start of construction, which stopped when the airport was almost 90 percent complete. Pressure from the Nazi government halted the work and led to the removal of Chot. Rene Veber, a Vichy adherent, succeeded Chot in the position.[28]

The Allied landings in French North Africa in November 1942 rallied most of Vichy's overseas colonies to the Allied side. By February 1943, only the French Antilles, Guyane, and Indochina remained loyal to Vichy. At that time, the United States decided to end the status quo with Vichy in the Caribbean by employing destabilization measures, primarily withholding food. In Guyane, the American consul, George D. LaMont, played an active role in directing popular wrath against Veber.[29] On March 18, Veber placed the colony at the disposal of General Henri Giraud, asking LaMont to assist in the maintenance of order until the transfer occurred. A joint U.S.-Brazilian military team arrived in late March to ensure a peaceful *ralliement*, that is, popular adhesion to the new Allied administration.

Veber's support of Giraud thwarted the plans of Ulrich Sophie, the mayor of Cayenne and a sympathizer of Félix Éboué, to side with the Free French. As a result, a small drama developed between De Gaulle and Giraud with each trying to appoint his own military official to the governorship. With U.S. support, Giraud won this first round, and Jean Rapenne took the position, but by 1944 De Gaulle, by then in sole control of the Free French, appointed General Jules Surlemont.

While this political sideshow played itself out, the U.S. War Department rejected the Le Gallion Field because of faulty construction, bad drainage, and depressions in the runway. With Rapenne's authorization, the Caribbean Defense Command immediately began constructing another field, about twelve miles from Cayenne, which was ready for traffic in December 1943. In March 1944, the new field, which could accommodate DC-4 and DC-5 aircraft, was officially named Rochambeau Field.[30]

Because of the traditional shortage of labor in Guyane, the Antilles Command brought in fifteen hundred Puerto Rican civilian laborers to work alongside local labor. The fact that about four hundred of them remained in 1945 was the main reason advanced by Major Meléndez-Utset for his appointment as commander of Rochambeau Field.

Major Meléndez-Utset, son of the well-known writer Miguel Meléndez-Muñoz and a person of unusual sensibility, was born in Cayey, an agricultural town in the interior of Puerto Rico. A U.S. Army camp, Henry Barracks, helped familiarize Meléndez-Utset and the town itself with various aspects of American culture and the American military way of life. "[L]ife in Cayey at that time revolved around the military camp . . . [as it] provided many jobs for the people. There I ate 'Corn Flakes' for the first time in my life . . . and the famous bread that one buys today to make sandwiches, there it was for the first time in Puerto Rico."[31]

Because he "always liked the military," Major Meléndez-Utset had tried and failed to enter West Point. Instead, he earned a commission as a U.S. Army second lieutenant through the Reserve Officers' Training Corps (ROTC) while completing a bachelor's degree in agronomy at the College of Agriculture, University of Puerto Rico, in 1936.[32] Two years later he was recruited and stationed at several military installations in Puerto Rico—Buchanan, Salinas, Tortuguero, Borinquen Field, and Henry Barracks (where he served as executive officer)—with the Sixty-fifth Infantry Regiment in Diablo Heights, and as company commander at Camp Boruga, Panama.[33] Major Meléndez-Utset was one of several university graduates—teachers, agronomists, engineers, lawyers, and physicians—who completed the four-year ROTC course and attained leadership positions in Puerto Rican regiments.[34]

On his arrival at Rochambeau Field in January 1945, Major Meléndez-Utset found a detachment of Puerto Rican soldiers, the Fifty-second Wing, an air unit, and quartermaster and supply units, for a total of eight hundred men, most of them "Americanos" under Puerto Rican officers such as Bernardo Soler, post engineer.[35] Guyane served as a resupply point for planes coming from Atkinson Field in British Guiana en route to Brazil and Dakar in Africa. "The work was tremendous. It was a base with lots of movement. We had a lot of air transit there. . . . We had military planes that landed, about fifteen or twenty every day, and we had to fill them with gas."[36]

In his daily, censored letters to his wife, Rosalina Brau, from January to December 1945, Major Meléndez-Utset's life emerges as one of rigid routine and almost daily contact with Governor Surlemont.[37] He noted that Surlemont's only complaint was that the daily wage of U.S.$2.50 paid to the eighty to one hundred local males hired weekly for airport maintenance, compared to local wages of around three cents, had disrupted the colony's work routine because the men did not return to the sugarcane fields for several months.[38] France's provisional government recognized Major Meléndez-Utset's performance with the decoration of Cavalier de l'Etoile d'Anjoun, signed by General De Gaulle on December 20, 1945, three days before he left for Puerto Rico. To our knowledge, Major Meléndez-Utset was the only Puerto Rican who commanded a field station of strategic value in the Caribbean region with Puerto Rican and American detachments. The press report read: "A beaming guard of honor composed of Puerto Rican soldiers marched during the ceremony, the one in which Governor Surlemont gave the commander the traditional French kiss in both cheeks."[39]

The intersection of the French and American empires in the Caribbean during World War II, although they collided in the beginning, ended in accommodation, first with Admiral Robert and finally with General De Gaulle. While aeropolitics widened the Caribbean's geopolitical boundaries, the human drama played out by colonials in military uniform showed similar imperial racialist policies. The great majority of Puerto Rican soldiers and *tirailleurs sénégalais* remained in segregated units, their loyalty distrusted and their main duties limited to guarding the outskirts of the empire. Not only the color and ethnic discrimination of the imperial states was revealed but also that of the British Caribbean colonies, as shown by their rejection of American black soldiers and their qualified acceptance of Puerto Ricans. Tugwell, as the colonial governor of Puerto Rico, contested the racist policies of the U.S. armed forces and referred to similar problems within Puerto Rican society. Clifford, as the colonial governor of Trinidad and Tobago, objected to the presence of Negro troops and questioned the deployment of Puerto Ricans in the name of both the empire and local elites.

Subalternity acquired here a double meaning. Puerto Ricans performed the role of subaltern military men in segregated and discriminatory units assigned to garrison duty or as civilian labor working in the construction of military facilities in both the Caribbean region and surrounding territories. The U.S. armed forces even changed its traditional classification of "whites" and "blacks" to accommodate a new term: "Puertorrican white." That accommodation extended to the appointment of Major Meléndez-Utset as commander of Rochambeau Field in Guyane. It certainly was atypical for a Caribbean colonial of the American empire to be placed in charge of a U.S. military installation located in a Caribbean colony of the French empire.

Guantánamo and the Case of Kid Chicle

Private Contract Labor and the Development of the U.S. Military

JANA K. LIPMAN

In December 1940, Lino Rodríguez Grenot decided to try his luck in Guantánamo.[1] A former boxer known as "Kid Chicle," Rodríguez was twenty-seven years old, black, and unemployed. He had a checkered work history and had attempted to earn a living as a professional boxer. In search of more secure employment, he traveled from Santiago de Cuba to Guantánamo where the surge of World War II military construction had created thousands of new jobs on the U.S. military base in Guantánamo Bay (GTMO).[2]

Once he reached the bay, Rodríguez's best hope for work was with the Frederick Snare Corporation, a private company that had won the U.S. government contract to expand the base facilities. On December 17, Lieutenant Kenneth M. West, a marine, was recruiting workers for the corporation. West had previously worked for the United Fruit Company (UFC) in eastern Cuba, and the navy had placed him in charge of transporting workers for the corporation "due to his experiences in Cuba." On this day, he selected twenty-nine local workers, but not Lino Rodríguez. Ignoring the fact that he had been rejected, Rodríguez leaped unauthorized onto the launch. West did not welcome the intruder. As the launch pulled away from the dock, he allegedly struck Rodríguez with a "black-jack" and threw him out of the boat. Rodríguez fell into the bay and died within minutes.[3]

The death of Kid Chicle came to embody the complexity of the United States' neocolonial presence in Cuba and the interplay between a weak Cuban state, private capital, and the U.S. military. Since its intervention in 1898, the United States had profited from corporate investments, and the military had intervened in 1898, 1906, 1912, and 1917, arguably to defend American capitalist interests.[4] In 1933, the United States announced a new strategy of "good neighborly" relations with Latin America, and especially Cuba, whereby it shifted from a policy of military invasion to one of intervention via diplomatic and economic channels.[5]

Still, alongside the constellation of American companies in Cuba, the outpost in Guantánamo Bay remained a tangible reminder of the U.S. military presence.

During World War II, private corporations became central to the U.S. military's own development in Cuba. Base workers navigated a terrain dominated by U.S. economic and military control, often alternating between employment on sugar plantations, GTMO civil service positions, and private contract work on the base. The case of Kid Chicle underscores the transformation of the American empire; the U.S. Navy not only protected private capital, but it came to welcome the benefits of private, subcontracted labor in its own operations.

Geography and U.S. Capitalism in Eastern Cuba

In response to political coercion and martial strength, in 1902 the Cuban Constitution adopted the Platt Amendment and ceded territory to the United States for "coaling or naval stations." The subsequent 1903 leasing agreement compromised Cuba's "ultimate sovereignty" by granting the United States "complete jurisdiction" over the territory surrounding Guantánamo Bay.

The U.S. Navy established GTMO in eastern Cuba (Oriente), more than six hundred miles from Havana. Underdeveloped by the Spanish colonial regime and in close proximity to Jamaica and Haiti, eastern Cuba's economy was quite limited at the turn of the century. After 1898, U.S. financial interests invested heavily in Oriente. For example, in 1902 Cuba's eastern provinces produced only 15 percent of the island's sugar; by 1924 the proportion had increased to 54 percent, and by 1929 it was 69.5 percent.[6] American-owned sugar companies, including the Cuban American Sugar Company, the UFC, and the Guantánamo Sugar Company, dominated Oriente's economic landscape. United Fruit Company towns such as Banes and Preston, as Louis Pérez has argued, existed largely outside Cuban law as quasi-independent enclaves within eastern Cuba.[7]

Sharing the same name as the more famous bay, Guantánamo was a moderate-sized Cuban city in Oriente approximately fifty miles from Santiago de Cuba and fifteen miles from Guantánamo Bay and the base. To North Americans, and even many men and women in Havana, Guantánamo and the base were often thought of as a single place. The city of Guantánamo worked to assert its own identity but was never able to fully escape its economic reliance on and geographic definition by the U.S. occupation. In the 1930s, Guantánamo's economy was dependent on the American-owned Guantánamo Sugar Company and the commercial activity generated by the naval base. Guantánamo's elite was composed largely of North American expatriates tied directly to the sugar industry and Cuban restaurant proprietors, café owners, and alcohol distributors who profited from GTMO's proximity.

However, for Guantánamo's working class, the base offered relief from the sugar economy. For example, the Guantánamo Sugar Company hired 4,500 workers during the *zafra* (harvest) and 2,000 during the *tiempo de muerto* (dead period).[8] These jobs offered irregular, seasonal employment and were marked by their brutal physicality. With the World War II base expansion, there were thousands of new employment opportunities at GTMO. For workers accustomed to the neocolonial control of the sugar companies, the leap to employment on the U.S. military installation may not have been particularly great. It could be seen as just one more facet of the United States' political and economic control of the region. Moreover, base employment often appeared more attractive, for it offered security, steadier wages, and a level of prestige. Men and women who worked on the base were part of Guantánamo's "aristocracy of labor."[9] As a result, with the sudden increase in base employment in 1940, workers from across Cuba traveled to Guantánamo in search of these jobs. What they did not know was that the U.S. Navy had subcontracted most of the new construction work to the Frederick Snare Corporation.

The Frederick Snare Corporation

The rapid development and growth of the naval base was a joint effort of the U.S. Navy and the Frederick Snare Corporation. In 1940, the navy awarded the corporation the government contract to expand GTMO's facilities. At its peak, Snare employed nine thousand local workers and its expenditures reached $34 million. In his *History of Guantánamo Bay*, Admiral Marion Emerson Murphy wrote, "The history of contract NOy-4162 is virtually the history of the World War II buildup of Guantánamo Bay."[10] The navy maintained that Snare was a separate, private entity distinct from the military. However, when it served U.S. military purposes, the navy assisted Snare with materials, labor, and security information.

Prior to World War II, the United States had relied on private companies in Guantánamo but on a smaller scale and at least nominally under Cuban jurisdiction. For example, GTMO lacked its own water supply, and the dry, almost desert-like conditions in the region made it impossible for the base to be self-sufficient. It relied on the nearby Yateras River, which was located on the Cuban side of the military boundary. After experimenting with water delivered by train, the United States initiated a competition for an aqueduct. To minimize complications with Cuban law and governance, the United States insisted that the aqueduct could only transport water to the base; it could not service any of the surrounding Cuban communities. In fact, the United States rejected a bid from the Guantánamo municipal government, which had hoped to use the U.S. contract to improve local public health and gain access to clean drinking water. Instead, the navy granted a private contract to Henri Schueg Chassin, a business affiliate of the Bacardí Company in 1938.[11] Thus, the United States created a precedent whereby a private entity within Cuba worked solely for the U.S. Navy on Cuban soil.

With the urgent need to develop GTMO in the late 1930s, the United States again turned to a private corporation. The U.S. Navy granted GTMO's contract to the American-owned Snare Corporation largely because of its long-term operations in Cuba. Snare had completed projects in New York, Havana, Buenos Aires, and the Panama Canal. It constructed much of early Havana's infrastructure, including the national baseball stadium. Frederick Snare himself was a prominent North American actor in Havana's social scene; he designed the Havana Country Club's first golf course and served as president of the club until 1946.[12] Already based in Cuba, Snare could quickly shift its operations east and modernize the base. The American ambassador to Cuba, George S. Messersmith, described this new relationship between the U.S. Navy and Snare as "desirable." He was confident that the company's familiarity with Cuba would enable it to meet the challenge.[13]

In the expediency of war, Snare occupied a newly defined niche between private and public activities, allowing the navy to erase or emphasize these distinctions as it best served U.S. military interests. Between 1940 and 1943, Snare became a dominant force on GTMO. It built a new, self-contained Marine Corps base, new airfields on McCalla Hill and Leeward Point, ninety-two magazines, and various social and recreational facilities, including a chapel and a school. Speed was critical, and military and private materials became indistinguishable. As Admiral Murphy recorded, "Due to the speed with which construction was begun, the contractors had no opportunity to make preliminary preparation; therefore all available equipment of the [GTMO] station was turned over to the Frederick Snare Corporation for their use."[14]

In this context, the U.S. Navy had no qualms about assisting Snare in its hiring procedures or blurring the line between government and private employers. While the navy maintained that it did not have jurisdiction or control over Snare's labor practices, it was intimately involved in its employment policies. Mistrustful of Snare's ability to weed out potentially subversive workers, the United States gave direct aid and advice. For example, American officials feared that fascist Falangists (supporters of Francisco Franco in Spain) would be able to infiltrate the base, and on this premise they banned Spanish employees. The American base intelligence officer investigated employees to root out Spanish-born workers for Snare and the U.S. government alike, making no distinction between the two.[15]

For workers, however, the disparity between short-term Snare jobs and steady government employment was vast. It resulted in a two-tiered hierarchy. Navy civilian positions offered permanent employment at steady wages and were far more likely to provide a clear path to advancement. In contrast, Snare offered inferior working conditions, lower pay, and only temporary, time-sensitive work. As a result, many men and women gained employment for a brief time, only to be laid off and rehired later. Cuban workers quickly recognized that U.S. government civil service positions came with far better benefits and salaries than the contract jobs offered by Snare. To workers, the division seemed disingenuous as they recognized that their labor, whether for the government or a private employer, contributed to U.S. military strength.[16]

Moreover, Snare existed outside both the U.S. and Cuban legal systems. Snare argued that as a U.S. entity operating within the confines of the base, it did not have to follow Cuban laws. At the same time, as a private employer in Cuba, it maintained that it did not have to follow U.S. law, particularly as it applied to labor standards. Workers resented this lack of accountability and legal doubletalk. For example, in 1940, two base workers, Pedro Salgado and José Fernández, wrote to President Roosevelt, "In reality, this company [Snare] sometimes followed Cuban law and other times American law, from our perspective mocking the laws of both nations."[17] They believed Snare was acting in a hypocritical manner, insulting the rule of law and American principles.

The semantics and economics of this private-public venture in military expansionism created a great deal of confusion and unease in Guantánamo. Into this social context, the death of Lino "Kid Chicle" Rodríguez became a rallying call and a recognizable flashpoint of workers' insecurity along the military border.

Migration and the Lure of Base Employment

Workers in Guantánamo desperately wanted base jobs, and Lino Rodríguez was only one of thousands of migrants who traveled to Guantánamo in search of work in the late 1930s. Men and women from Santiago de Cuba, Holguín, Camagüey, and even Havana traveled to Guantánamo seeking work and relief from the 1930s economic crisis.

The process of obtaining a job on the base was informal, unregulated, and largely dependent on individual connections. A prospective employee needed to secure a "pass" regardless of whether he or she was hoping to obtain work with the military or a private contractor. For example, Ricardo Baylor had a fraught and anxiety-ridden time acquiring a pass and finding work at GTMO. Ricardo grew up in Preston, a UFC town. He had a cousin who worked as a domestic servant on the base, and he recalled somewhat resentfully that she was "a little indifferent" when it came to helping his family make contacts on the base. It was not easy to get a job at GTMO, Ricardo explained, because there were more willing workers than jobs. His brother went to Guantánamo first. He told Ricardo stories about the boss coming out onto the docks, and the men would then rush and jump into small, crowded launches, pushing their way through for the opportunity to work on the base. After many months, his brother acquired a pass for Ricardo. With the pass in hand, Ricardo moved to Guantánamo in 1945 and began to work on the military base.[18]

Even a self-conscious anti-imperialist could reconcile his ideology with working for the U.S. *marinos*. For example, as a young boy Alberto Torres admired his father, who was among the founders of the Cuban Communist Party in the region, and he, in turn, headed the local chapter of the Young Communist League. Despite this political education, Torres recalled working on the base, ironically enough, as a golf caddy. He obtained a permanent job in the Supply Department in 1940. "All of my brothers spent time and worked there," he recalled, "because work in Cuba was scarce. Because of this, the Americans could assert themselves. . . . The sugar harvest lasted only two months and then there was unemployment."[19] In Guantánamo, the base offered one of the clearest paths to economic security regardless of its ramifications for national sovereignty or Cuban nationalism. While the military base was a tangible reminder of U.S. dominance, for most workers, economic need far outweighed any political objections.

Workers without informal ties inside the base often felt desperate, and a black market quickly emerged. Notoriously, Francisco Ochoa, the chief of inspectors in the port, engaged in a lucrative venture, illegally using his position and selling passes to prospective employees.[20] The American neocolonial empire benefited from corrupt Cuban officials and the jockeying for jobs in the Guantánamo region. Without a pass, a worker could only wait, hope, or bribe his or her way onto the naval base.

Kid Chicle: Anger, Ambiguity, and Accommodation with the American Neocolonial State

Lino Rodríguez became emblematic of the unemployed workers who were unable to gain a pass or find employment on the base. His death demonstrated the Guantánamo community's anger at both the Snare Corporation and the U.S. military. In Guantánamo, hundreds of workers on the docks had witnessed the events, and Rodríguez's death spurred outrage and unprecedented protests against the naval base.[21] After several men fished his corpse out of the water, local unions and the Communist Party argued that a crime had been committed and Lieutenant West must be tried in Cuban territory. Rodríguez's family also came forward, and his aunt expressed her desire to see justice done under Cuban law. Workers wore black armbands in protest, locals marched to the cemetery and demanded justice, and several newspapers predicted a strike.[22]

The tragedy also underscored the collaboration between the Cuban state, American corporations, and the U.S. military, which structured the United States' neocolonial relationship with Cuba. In the Rodríguez case, the line between U.S. military aggression and economic strength was exceptionally thin. West, the main assailant, had worked for the United Fruit Company before becoming an officer in the U.S. Navy. The Guantánamo periodical *El Vigilante* called attention to his past with the UFC and concluded, "Lt. West was responsible for the premature death of the boxer Lino Rodríguez Grenot, the defenseless victim of the savage Yankee marine, who maybe thought that a man of color did not merit the same consideration or respect as a white man."[23] From a *guantanamero* perspective, the distinction between American private capital and military power had collapsed.

The national Communist Party periodical *Hoy* also emphasized that the U.S. military was gaining strength through the profits of a private corporation, declaring, "It is a problem when a foreign company . . . discriminates and pays ridiculous salaries for the benefit of military activities put in practice by the U.S. government."[24] The U.S. military owed its expansion and modern capabilities to the labor of local workers even as it denied direct responsibility for Snare and its employment practices.

This incident of brutality had the potential to become a local, national, or even international crisis, or at the very least a headache for the newly elected Batista government in Cuba. Even the generally staid, pro–North American newspaper *Diario de la Marina*, which rarely reported any news east of Havana, published a report of the incident.[25] The Cuban government responded quickly; President Fulgencio Batista commissioned Cuban investigators to visit Guantánamo almost immediately. The Cuban government needed to provide the appearance of a thorough, independent investigation, even though it had little desire to challenge the U.S. military directly. Throughout the subsequent controversy and legal debate, the U.S. Navy aimed to defend Lieutenant West, pacify local workers, and keep the case out of the Cuban court system.[26] The navy maintained that even though the alleged crime took place in Guantánamo Bay, waters that remained under Cuban jurisdiction, the event occurred in an American-owned boat. According to the navy, the launch, not the bay, governed jurisdiction. From the capital in Havana, the Cuban Ministry of Justice agreed that crimes committed onboard foreign ships remained within the jurisdiction of the foreign nation.[27] The Cuban government did not challenge U.S. military authority.

The American ambassador noted that the Cuban government "had taken a very correct attitude" and allowed the United States to handle the matter.[28] Thus, West escaped a local trial. He did face a court-martial for "involuntary manslaughter" and "conduct to the prejudice of good order and discipline," but he was found not guilty.[29] That said, the American ambassador was a bit "embarrassed" when West was acquitted of all charges. While he was pleased to learn that the United States did not have to "assume any responsibility for the loss of this man's life," he did suggest that "act of grace" of five thousand dollars be paid to Rodríguez's family.[30] As the case lingered, American officials' disdain for Rodríguez's life became palpable and less discreet. In 1942, the American consul described Rodríguez as "that worthless Cuban boxer."[31]

Private Contract Workers and Precedent

In the weeks following Lino Rodríguez's death, the Frederick Snare Corporation opened an employment office in Guantánamo to help facilitate the pass system and avoid future conflicts. And, while the U.S. Navy could not avoid some responsibility in the "Kid Chicle" case, workers who died on the job (as opposed to by the hands of a U.S. marine) could be ignored more easily. For example, in 1941 Agustín Alvarez and Venancio Hechavarría, both Snare employees, died on the base. Their families received no compensation, nor did the U.S. military investigate the causes of death. Journalist Lino Lemes chastised the U.S. government for not intervening in these cases and insisted that if "only the American flag flies" on the base, the government should be held accountable for what happens there.[32] He further condemned the Snare Corporation, writing, "We know that there can be no justice with this company."[33]

The Snare Corporation set the precedent for private contractors on GTMO. In conflicts between workers and the base, Snare offered the U.S. military more than just speed, efficiency, and lower costs. As a private employer, it had flexibility and could shield the United States from direct accountability. It had less incentive than the U.S. government to make accommodations with the Cuban government or articulate the language of good neighborliness. When the base expanded again during the Korean War, GTMO contracted with the Drake Winkleman Company for much of the work. Today the majority of GTMO's employees are overseas contract workers from Jamaica and the Philippines, and the U.S. military has embraced the model of private, subcontracted labor.

Lino "Kid Chicle" Rodríguez's death and its aftermath underscore how the American empire wed economic and military interests in neocolonial Cuba. The U.S. government could wield its military arm, but it also had a diplomatic need to recognize Cuba's independence and formal sovereignty. Private corporations did not face this pressure, as their primary goal was making a profit. Lieutenant West's affiliation with the UFC, taken together with the Frederick Snare Corporation's construction of the Havana Country Club, demonstrates the fluidity between economic and military power. In this milieu, it was the base workers who most often recognized the absence of law and the collapse of boundaries between economic and military spheres.

The Impact of the Philippine Wars (1898–1913) on the U.S. Army

BRIAN MCALLISTER LINN

THE UNITED STATES ARMY devotes considerable attention to the study of history as a guide for current and future policy. It employs hundreds of historians to study the past and sends some of its brightest officers to top universities for advanced degrees. Its fills its doctrinal manuals with historical vignettes illustrating tactics, leadership, and values; a history-based article appears in almost every issue of each branch and school professional journal. Military history also plays a significant role in professional military education, from Reserve Officers' Training Corps (ROTC) classes to the Army War College. The army's official histories of World War II, the Korean War, and the Vietnam War are extensively researched operational and institutional studies. Even academic historians, who have a philosophic bias against any practical application of their discipline, must acknowledge the service's efforts to use history as a source of intellectual self-improvement.

Yet until recently the army limited its focus on historical "lessons learned" to large-scale conventional operations, or the "Big Wars"—particularly the Civil War and World War II—and, to a lesser extent, on peacetime periods of reform or "transformation." Indicative of this emphasis, in 1993 one historical agency produced a 434-page operational history of the 1991 Gulf War, but not until 1998 did the official history program publish a comprehensive analysis of the army's counterinsurgency operations. The terms used for irregular warfare in the military lexicon—such as military operations other than war (MOOTW)—illustrate the service's conviction that this is a secondary mission. In 1994, students at the Army War College felt it necessary to inform their readers that "warfighting and MOOTW are not mutually exclusive. The leadership skills required for MOOTW are the same as those necessary for warfighting. Only the degree of skill emphasis differs."[1] The army's preference for Big War and its disinclination to study the "savage wars of peace" are readily apparent in its interpretation of the 1898–1913 imperial wars in the Philippine Islands.

Although several commentators have outlined what they believe are specific "lessons" from the Philippine conflicts—both positive and negative—that apply to Iraq, they are far less obvious to officers charged with applying these lessons.[2] In fact, perhaps even more than most wars, the "lessons" of the Philippines are confused, ambiguous, and controversial. In part this is because over the course of its active military operations from 1898 to 1913 the army was involved in at least three distinct "wars" (only one of which was formally a war), several regional "pacification campaigns," and innumerable combat incidents or "engagements." During this period soldiers fought, sometimes simultaneously, Spanish regulars, the nationalist armies of Emilio Aguinaldo, local guerrillas, religious sects, agrarian rebels, brigands, and Muslim tribes—and various combinations of these opponents. In the process, they encountered a variety of tactical challenges: assault on a fortified city (Manila), pitched battles in Central Luzon, skirmishing in virtually every type of terrain, mass bolo attacks on Samar, Moro *cottas* (fortifications) in Mindanao, and direct assaults on mountain strongholds (Jolo). Not surprisingly, the lessons that officers took from their varied combat experiences were diverse and often contradictory for what worked in one area might not in another.

The army's first, and only, declared Philippine war was an outgrowth of the conflict with Spain in 1898. To help secure Commodore George Dewey's victory at Manila Bay, President William McKinley ordered the army to dispatch an expedition to capture Manila. The first American forces arrived in late June 1898 and by August had increased to eleven thousand. With little more than token resistance from the Spanish, the Americans successfully stormed the city on August 13 and immediately turned their attention to keeping Emilio Aguinaldo's nationalist army from entering Manila. Under McKinley's directive to serve as agents of "benevolent assimilation," soldiers socially engineered the city, cleaning up sewers, rebuilding markets, opening schools, and otherwise establishing the foundations of colonial rule.

Counterguerrilla Warfare

The second war, officially termed an "insurrection," began on the evening of February 4, 1899. The ensuing conflict can be broken into two distinct phases. In 1899, the main American effort was directed toward large-unit offensives into Central Luzon to destroy the conventional forces of the Philippine Republic. With only some twenty-six thousand troops in mid-April, and most of them due to be repatriated as a result of the end of the war with Spain, the Americans lacked sufficient strength to sustain their Luzon victories or carry out sideshow operations in Negros and Panay. In October and November 1899, swelled by reinforcements to some forty thousand troops, the army delivered the final blow to Aguinaldo's crumbling army and drove him into the mountains. It then turned south, sweeping into southern Luzon, sending amphibious expeditions to capture the key ports and municipalities, and defeating the local militias.

The second phase of the war, roughly from January 1900 to July 1902, was a succession of regional struggles extending from Mindanao to Luzon. Although the nature, effectiveness, and composition of the resistance varied greatly, for the most part it was characterized by guerrilla tactics, strong efforts to discourage collaboration, and the rejection of the imposition of colonial government. The army, which at its peak strength numbered seventy thousand and usually numbered some forty-five thousand—with perhaps twenty-six thousand fit for combat duty—was deployed in small garrisons, or "stations," which expanded from 53 in September 1899 to 413 in September 1900 and 492 in January 1902.

In its first months of occupation, army policy emphasized conciliation manifested through local government, police, the suppression of crime, and social reform projects such as roads, markets, schools, and medical clinics, most of which had some military utility. While this policy of attraction quelled dissident violence in a few areas (most notably Manila), for the most part conciliation was applied with equal amounts of coercion. What some officers termed "hard war" took a variety of forms, ranging from controls on travel and food transportation to the selective destruction of crops and livestock. By mid-1901, coercive tactics in the few areas that were judged actively hostile were increasingly punitive, including the forcible relocation of civilians, indiscriminate destruction, and the torture of suspected guerrillas. By that time, Aguinaldo and virtually all the revolutionary leaders had surrendered and resistance was confined to a few provinces. The last campaigns in Batangas Province on Luzon and on Samar Island, both of which ended in early 1902, were particularly harsh and inflicted widespread suffering on the populace. President Theodore Roosevelt's declaration of peace on July 4, 1902, officially ended what the U.S. government termed the insurrection in the Philippines.

The official declaration of the end of the Philippine insurrection on July 4, 1902, did not end the violence. Indeed, in some areas, particularly in the predominantly Muslim Mindanao-Sulu region (referred to within the army as "Moroland"), armed resistance to American authority dramatically increased. This phase was even more diffuse and disconnected than had been the "war" of 1899–1902. The so-called Moro Wars were actually a series of sporadic and largely unconnected punitive campaigns against either charismatic leaders (Datu Ali), fortified *cottas* (Pandapatan and Bayan in 1902), or communities of believers (Bud Bagsak in 1913). For the most part, the Moros' failure to adapt their tactics, their faith in individual heroism, and their internal divisions precluded effective resistance.

From 1902 to 1913, the army, which by now comprised a sizable Filipino contingent of five thousand Philippine Scouts (roughly 25 to 30 percent of the total forces), supported the Philippine Commission in suppressing armed resistance to the colonial government. Although rebels in southern Luzon, such as Felizardo and Sakay, claimed to be continuing the struggle for independence, or at least a Tagalog nation, the Visayan sects (*pulahans* and *babylanes*) and the Moros sought to restore their traditional religion and customs. Outside of Moroland, American soldiers were usually called in only when the local police, the commission's Philippines Constabulary, and scouts acting under civil control had failed to control violence. In most cases, as in Cavite in 1904–5, the deployment of a few hundred Americans to garrison towns, protect supplies, and launch sweeps of the countryside, when combined with scout reinforcements and significant numbers of local militia and volunteers, was sufficient to impose order. In many respects, the post-1902 conflicts, like some of the regional struggles in the 1899–1902 conflict, were actually internecine "miniwars," episodes of communal violence that pitted factions, villages, and religious sects against each other.[3]

As many officers commented, the Philippine conflicts lacked the decisive battles and large-scale operations that characterized their idealized vision of Big War. From 1900 to 1913, only two engagements may be termed battles, and both Bud Dajo in 1906 and Bud Bagsak in 1913 resulted in such disproportionate casualties, especially among women and children, that critics termed them massacres. The rest of what the army termed its 2,811 "engagements" between February 4, 1899, and July 4, 1902, were ambushes, firefights, and skirmishes that were usually inconclusive.

Stripped of its romance, soldiering in the new empire consisted largely of guard duty and patrolling the countryside; building barracks, roads, and bridges; and assisting in a host of civil affairs projects. The pacification of the archipelago was a long war of attrition in which American military superiority and the ability to hold the major towns ultimately wore down a fragmented, localized, and divided guerrilla resistance that lacked, for the most part, extensive popular support. Occasionally a particularly able guerrilla leader such as Juan Cailles at Mabitac, Laguna, or Eugenio Daza at Balangiga, Samar, would inflict a sharp defeat on a badly led American force. But army organization, logistics, tactics, weaponry, and leadership were usually sufficient to defeat virtually any combination of opponents.

The casualties of army actions in the Philippines are still controversial. An Army War College committee concluded that from January 31, 1899, to July 4, 1902 the army suffered 795 killed in action, with 242 dead of wounds, and a total of 3,737 deaths from all causes and another 3,022 wounded. It also estimated that from May 5, 1900, to June 31, 1901, 5,041 Filipinos were killed as a direct result of combat operations and another 30,000 were captured or surrendered. But other sources, both civilian and military, dismissed such body counts as "plainly excessive."[4] Attempts since then to determine the number of Filipino deaths as a direct or indirect result of the war have been mired in methodological and ideological controversy.

American officers fighting in the Philippines viewed both popular resistance and guerrilla tactics as illegitimate, more equivalent to insurrection than war. According to Major General Arthur MacArthur, "The men who propose to lead small bodies for the purpose of guerrilla warfare must act without even the shadow of authority from a de facto government.... In other words, men who try to continue the strife by individual action become simply leaders of banditti." Captain John M. Taylor commented in his history of the conflict, "If war in certain of its aspects is a temporary reversion to barbarism, guerrilla warfare is a temporary reversion to savagery." Frederick Funston, one of the most capable guerrilla fighters in the army, grieved that a fellow officer who had survived many Civil War battles should be killed "in this bushwhacking business."[5]

The tendency of most officers to impose their own cultural preconceptions of warfare precluded an impartial interpretation of their own Philippine combat experiences. Lieutenant Colonel Charles J. Crane fulminated, apparently without irony, "If these people will only organize their forces into an army and get together in some number, and generally speaking, use modern, civilized methods of warfare, our task would be a simple one and comparatively easy." Showing similar frustration, another officer commented, "If our enemy possessed courage we would be compelled to use different tactics but if they had been courageous we should have killed or captured all of them before this."[6]

Some veterans recognized that military measures alone would not achieve the nation's goal of peacefully occupying the Philippines and improving the lives and morality of the Filipinos. In an article entitled "Some Random Notes on the Fighting in the Philippines," one officer observed, "If we give the natives peace and prosperity, they will be content; and opposition will cease."[7] Robert L. Bullard, the army's most significant imperial theorist, contributed several articles on his experiences with Moros and emphasized that peacemaking was likely to be as important as war fighting in the army's foreseeable future. But Bullard was also convinced that "Pacification . . . has depended and probably will continue to depend more upon the wisdom, tact, personality and disposition of the officials applying it than upon any defined governmental policy. It is largely personal."[8]

As Bullard's comment indicates, a significant factor inhibiting the assimilation of specific lessons from the Philippine experience was the widely held conviction that an individual's leadership skills and character were the most important determinants of success or failure. Commanding perhaps one hundred troops and responsible for thousands of Filipino civilians, the typical commander's duties required the simultaneous performance of a myriad of civil roles—mayor, police chief, accountant, road builder, and so forth—while simultaneously defeating the local guerrilla opposition and securing compliance to U.S. rule. One observer commented that this experience did "a great deal to develop in all officers that most important quality, self-reliance, for with the defective communications, junior officers and their companies were often isolated for months from their headquarters."[9] Henry T. Allen, head of the Philippines Constabulary, put it even more simply: "It is a fact that the disposition of nearly every town in the archipelago depends upon the officer or officers who have been commanding in that town."[10]

Lessons of War

The twin beliefs that individual character was crucial and Philippine combat was not real war may explain why so much of the intraservice analysis focused on very practical matters. One of the best of these was Major Hugh D. Wise's account of fighting *pulahan* sectarians on the island of Samar. Wise, a veteran of many Philippine struggles, analyzed enemy and American tactics, provided advice for logistics in the jungle, emphasized the importance of local intelligence, and urged commanders to win over the local population.[11] The army also issued questionnaires to combat officers and distributed their answers throughout the archipelago. From these, officers could learn how to ford a river or search a village. But there was no institutional effort to develop a coherent body of counterinsurgency or pacification theory or to draw on the Philippine experience to prepare for the irregular conflicts of the future.

Indeed, far from drawing inspiration from the imperial wars, there is far more concern that they had "played havoc" with officers' tactical judgment and "inculcated erroneous and regrettable ideas."[12] Major General Leonard Wood, for example, believed that in the Philippines "we were opposed by a very inferior enemy and moved as it suited us, conditions which do not exist when confronted by troops trained for war and well-handled. Lessons taught in schools of this sort are of little value."[13] Even as he was authorizing the crushing of Moros on Bud Dajo, Wood insisted that the real mission of the archipelago's garrison was to train for modern warfare against a rival great power.[14]

Wood's priorities were reflective of the army's. The service's new tactical systems, first articulated in the *Field Service Regulations* of 1905, incorporated virtually nothing from the imperial wars. There was no effort to release a manual on small wars or bush tactics, and officers in the Philippines noted that many of the tactical formations recommended in their manuals were completely impractical in jungles or rice paddies. Some individuals who might have been expected to be at the forefront of developing a small wars doctrine were conspicuously silent. The War Department ordered J. Franklin Bell, famous for the campaign that crushed resistance in Batangas, to prepare a detailed narrative of the lessons he had learned. But the only record of Bell's policies comes from a staff officer who privately printed five hundred copies of the general's telegraphic orders on the grounds that they were "classics on native warfare."[15]

The army also failed to support the most ambitious effort to capture the lessons of the war, John R. M. Taylor's five-volume *The Philippine Insurrection against the United States*. Fascinated by the dynamics of the guerrilla resistance, Taylor included over one thousand captured documents, which detailed the military structure, financial system, and strategy of the insurgents. Of equal importance, these documents showed how decentralized the guerrillas were, how divided they were by factions and personality clashes, and how they sought to ensure popular support. In sum, the work is an invaluable resource on the dynamics of agrarian insurgency as useful to officers today as it was a century ago. But Taylor's open dislike of the civil government that succeeded military rule offended a former civil servant, James A. LeRoy. LeRoy, who was writing his own history of the war, urged William Howard Taft to suppress Taylor's work completely rather than allow its revision. Taylor tried for years to reverse this decision, but the army leadership refused to support him and the book was soon forgotten. Only in 1971 was it published, ironically by a Filipino historical association.[16]

The army made almost no effort to incorporate the lessons of the Philippine experience into its professional education system. At the staff college at Fort Leavenworth and the Army War College, students studied European-based "military science" and the Civil War, the German Wars of Unification, and the Russo-Japanese War. But it is virtually impossible to find any mention in the curriculum of the lessons learned in the army's own imperial wars in the Philippines. Between 1903 and 1911, the army's strategic planning agency, the Army War College, compiled some five hundred note cards related to topics of military interest. These cards contained only one entry on the "Philippine Question" and none on guerrilla war, pacification, or counterinsurgency.[17]

In the Philippines there was only slightly more interest. With the decrease in active campaigning after 1906 and the simultaneous appearance of a tangible threat of invasion from Japan, even this effort to glean practical, utilitarian lessons ceased. Officers turned their attention from keeping order in the provinces to defending the archipelago from invasion. The Japanese-American war scare of 1907 made fortifying Manila Bay and defending Central Luzon the dominant concern for the next three and a half decades. In the first decade of the twentieth century, when fears of an anticolonial rebellion were widespread, the army made some effort to preserve its institutional memory of guerrilla war. It distributed official correspondence, circulated reports on jungle fighting, and surveyed officers on the lessons they had learned fighting Moros and *pulahans*. But the service's emphasis remained fixed on matériel and tactical issues with no in-depth analysis of guerrilla warfare.[18]

World War I

The effect of the Philippine experience on American operations in World War I deserves some consideration. Nearly all the senior leaders of the American Expeditionary Forces (AEF) were Philippine veterans, including John J. Pershing and both army commanders. It is tempting to see a direct connection among their dismissal of Allied trench warfare tactics, their advocacy of "open warfare," and earlier operations in Luzon and Mindanao. But recent research has complicated the issue. Throughout the AEF there was persistent confusion over what "open warfare" meant, with many officers interpreting it less as a training and tactical system than as a directive to pursue the offensive. Scholars have demonstrated that the AEF's best commanders adopted the firepower-intensive methods of the British and French armies. And by the time of the Armistice, American divisions were relying less on marksmanship and the bayonet than on massive artillery and machine gun barrages, extensive planning, and methodical advances. Clearly, the ideological and practical connections between the imperial wars and the Western Front deserve far more historical research.[19]

In contrast, when army officers were confronted with conditions that resembled their Philippine experience, they were quick to implement the lessons of the imperial past. Major General William S. Graves, the commander of the Siberian expedition of 1918–20, had served under Bell in the Batangas campaign and fought Moros in Mindanao. Insisting on a policy of strict neutrality, Graves opposed Allied efforts to aid the anticommunist "White" forces, in large measure because he was both militarily and morally disgusted with the Whites' counterproductive terrorism against the population. He at first pursued a conciliatory policy, but as American troops were drawn into the civil war their methods became increasingly coercive. In the Suchan Valley, they "concentrated" males of military age and conducted extensive and destructive sweeps, killing hundreds of guerrillas.[20]

Forgotten War

In the post–World War I period, the army virtually ignored its imperial military experience. Army doctrine was based entirely on the perceived lessons of the European war. Oliver Lyman Spaulding accorded the entire 1899–1902 conflict less than 1 percent of the text in his history of the U.S. Army. He dismissed the guerrilla war in four paragraphs—two of which were on Funston's capture of Aguinaldo—with the comment, "The troops ... were unceasingly active, in the most distasteful employment which ever falls to the lot of military men—interference in civil affairs."[21]

A far more significant postwar effort to extract military lessons from the Philippine experience was William T. Sexton's *Soldiers in the Sun: An Adventure in*

Imperialism.²² A military officer with extensive service in the islands, Sexton toured the battlefields of Luzon, interviewed veterans, and studied War Department and unit records. *Soldiers in the Sun* focused on the 1899 large-unit battles and campaigns, providing a detailed narrative of operations and an often sardonic critique of military foibles. Like many writers before and after him, Sexton emphasized the importance of combat leadership, small-unit tactics, and morale. His heroes were officers such as Henry W. Lawton and Frederick Funston, charismatic warriors who led from the front. He was dismissive of General Elwell S. Otis, who he considered a bureaucrat, but gave him good marks as a strategist. Yet he did recognize both the diversity of the resistance and the American response and the ultimate importance of coordinating political and military strategies and balancing coercion with conciliation. Although it would remain the best military narrative of the war for several decades, it is difficult to determine the influence of *Soldiers in the Sun* on the army. The book was published in 1939, a time when imminent Philippine independence and fascist expansion limited military attention in the lessons to be learned from earlier imperial wars.

Even among officers serving in the Philippines there was little interest in the earlier conflict. In 1936, Charles H. Gerhardt, a staff officer in the army's Philippine Department in Manila, could not find a single study of military operations during the 1899–1902 conflict. When Gerhardt wrote his own history of this period he focused entirely on the large-unit, conventional operations of 1899. The far bloodier and longer pacification and peacekeeping operations in the islands that followed he dismissed as no more than "a very extended police system."²³

Army interest in the imperial wars did not revive after World War II. Fixated on the threat posed by the Red Army in Europe, American officers initially studied guerrilla war largely as a method through which to weaken it. Their own experience in Korea, the British campaign in Malaya, and the French wars in Indochina and Algeria alerted Americans to the danger posed by communist "wars of national liberation." These conflicts were viewed as so unique that the study of past conflicts had little relevance. In the words of one War College student, "We have passed from a period of national wars to one of ideological conflicts, and war has a consequently revolutionary nature."²⁴

Officers serving in the Philippines in the 1950s were equally convinced that the emergence of communist revolutionary warfare rendered previous methods obsolescent. Colonel Edward G. Lansdale's advice to Ramon Magsaysay—that he pursue civic action projects such as schools, roads, and health care—was a response to the specific challenge posed by the Hukbalahap insurgency and not a conscious revival of "benevolent assimilation." Indeed, there is no clear evidence that Lansdale, or other advisers in the archipelago, studied the army's earlier counterinsurgency operations, much less that they sought to apply the lessons of the past.²⁵

During the Vietnam War, military interest in the lessons of the imperial wars revived, although more recent case studies still dominated the literature. An early effort was Colonel Robert N. Ginsbaugh's 1964 "Damn the Insurrectos." Despite its title, the article highlighted the importance of civil reforms, honest government, and other nonmilitary methods. Ginsbaugh concluded that although communist revolutionary war posed unique challenges, "these only serve to reinforce past experience in the necessity of combining political, military, economic, and psychological efforts in order to combat insurgency successfully."[26] An article by Lieutenant Colonel Richard W. Smith in 1968 emphasized that "The ideological nature of today's struggle in Southeast Asia makes it unique, but the lessons learned by the Philippine Constabulary are useful wherever military men and irregulars struggle for control of the jungle."[27] Among the most important of these lessons were leadership, constant patrolling, and ensuring that local troops represented and understood their own society. Perhaps reflecting the growing disenchantment with the war, Major Allan D. Marple's 1970 masters thesis contrasted the army's use of Philippine Scouts with the Kit Carson program in Vietnam and concluded, "The U.S. Army demonstrated unusual ignorance and sluggish mismanagement in Vietnam."[28]

In the decade following the Vietnam debacle, the army turned away from the study of guerrilla war and once again focused on Big War in Europe. Army counterinsurgency doctrine eschewed the direct involvement of U.S. military forces and instead emphasized political, economic, and social reforms. Counterinsurgency was officially renamed "internal defense and development," an indication of both the post-Vietnam era's aversion to using military force and Jimmy Carter's faith in softer forms of nation building. But with the late 1970s came the oil boycott, virtual civil wars in Nicaragua and El Salvador, the Iran hostage crisis, various African insurgencies, and the Soviet invasion of Afghanistan; the army began to pay increased (though still minimal) attention to what were now referred to as "low-intensity conflicts." However, as it did before Vietnam, the army school system still downplayed the importance of pre–World War II case studies.[29]

Three conspicuous exceptions to the twenty-five years of army neglect of imperial wars were Thomas F. Burdett's 1975 revisionist article on General Elwell S. Otis; Major Andrew J. Bacevich's 1981 study of the Moro Wars; and Major Edward J. Filiberti's 1988 analysis of army counterinsurgency. Perhaps reflecting the humbling experience of Vietnam, Burdett offered a dispassionate and balanced treatment of the much-maligned general, correctly identifying Otis's ability to establish the foundations of a colonial civil government. He praised Otis for balancing social reform with military action and for his emphasis on winning Filipino popular support. Less obvious was Burdett's contrast between the methodical, cautious, and most unromantic Otis and Vietnam era commanders such as William Westmoreland—flashy, movie star handsome, and singularly ineffective.[30]

Bacevich's meticulously researched study of Brigadier General Leonard Wood is far more open in its criticism. His analysis of the 1906 pacification of Sulu and the Battle of Bud Dajo denounced Woods's impatience, belligerence, and "cultural arrogance." In Bacevich's view, Woods's methods were counterproductive, resulting in unnecessary civilian casualties and tarnishing the army's reputation.[31]

Filiberti's 1988 article reflected the growing conviction among many army officers that both the service and the nation were poorly prepared for future unconventional warfare. Using J. Franklin Bell's own telegraphic correspondence, Filiberti sought to determine the concepts and methods that had guided early American counterinsurgency. Although he praised the effectiveness of the 1901–2 pacification campaign in Batangas, Filiberti was no anachronistic hero-worshiper. He lauded Bell's comprehensive strategy, which combined political, economic, cultural, and military operations in pursuit of a clearly defined objective. But Filiberti was dubious that Bell's methods would meet current American moral standards, and he questioned whether it was possible for soldiers to achieve the nation's goals with today's limited means.[32]

After the Cold War

The resurgence of army interest in its Philippine experience dates from the end of the cold war. With the collapse of the Soviet Union in 1991, the threat of Soviet-sponsored proxy wars, insurgencies, and wars of national liberation diminished. But at the same time, it was clear that in many respects the end of the Soviet-American confrontation would contribute to global instability. As Bacevich argued in two provocative books, the militarization of American foreign policy, globalization, and engagement all but ensured an active, and often-violent, American presence abroad in the 1990s.[33] The Gulf War of 1991 demonstrated the folly of any nation attempting to defeat the U.S. armed forces in conventional warfare. The absence of any opposing army that might be labeled a "peer competitor" and the experience of Somalia, the Balkans, and other unconventional conflicts, turned the army's attention once more to case studies that fell outside of recent cold war experience.[34]

Of the post-cold-war military analyses of the imperial war, the following are typical. Lieutenant Colonel Richard W. Mills's 1997 Naval War College paper sought to deduce from the conflicts in the Philippines the six principles of counterinsurgency. From these, he determined that the primary rule was the need for a clear political objective, without which unity of command, popular support, and other essentials could not be achieved.[35] Major Madelfia A. Abb's 2000 School of Advanced Military Studies (SAMS) paper examines military institutional adaptation during the Philippine conflict.[36] Major Thomas S. Bundt's 2004 article is filled with interpretive and factual errors. Among Bundt's more bizarre mistakes are his assertions that the "Philippine Insurrection" began and ended in 1899 and that the Moros were responsible for the "Balangiga Massacre." Equally suspect are his conclusions that soldiers had "learned to abide by the laws or war and set more humane boundaries for future military operations" and "the Army's 1899 Philippine Campaign led to important doctrine for irregular warfare."[37]

To date, Colonel Timothy K. Deady's 2005 article may best represent both the strengths and the weaknesses of much recent army analysis of the Philippine-American War.[38] Deady provides a short and succinct treatment of the war and concluded (correctly) that American pacification worked to a large extent because of the army's ability to balance incentives with punitive sanctions. Yet, much like his fellow officers after Vietnam, Deady does not apply the same objectivity to the army's conduct in Iraq. Unwilling to admit that mistakes have been made, he presents a relentlessly optimistic view of the army's performance there. Typical is his conclusion that "two flaws of the Philippine experience are easily avoided. Joint force commanders today can expect clearer mission guidance than General Merritt had and a better understanding of the strategic end-state. Political and military elements operations together today, while not free of friction, will be much more closely integrated than those of Taft and MacArthur."[39] In fact, Bush administration officials, most notably Secretary of Defense Donald Rumsfeld and Paul Wolfowitz, not only interfered with Iraq campaign planning but also imposed unclear and unrealistic campaign objectives. And the relations between Paul Bremer and General Ricardo Sanchez were every bit as bad, and probably far more dysfunctional, than those between Taft and MacArthur.[40]

At present, and for both good and bad, the army's military operations in the Philippines are attracting more attention within the U.S. armed forces than they ever have. The recent joint Marine Corps–Army counterinsurgency field manual draws a direct parallel between Marine Corps operations in Iraq and the Philippine experience.[41] A military history of the war is on the professional reading lists for all company grade officers in the U.S. Air Force and U.S. Army, as well as on the reading lists of the John F. Kennedy Special Warfare Center and the U.S. Marine Corps Small War Center of Excellence. The war is also the subject of seminars at West Point, the Army Command and General Staff College, the Marine Corps School of Advanced Warfighting, and other service schools. In its current analysis, as in the past, the military can be accused of being utilitarian and present minded. Yet it is worth noting that in many ways it has a far more detailed and sophisticated understanding of the imperial wars than do many academics if op-ed columns and American history textbooks are any guide.

Conclusion

The lessons that the U.S. Army might have learned from pacification and peacekeeping in the Philippine Islands during 1899–1913 would have confirmed those hard-won convictions learned on the western frontier—the importance of leadership, adaptability, and tactical skill. But the very diversity of military experience in such localized and multifaceted guerrilla campaigns militated against analysis. Indeed, the nature of the fighting raised the concern that officers were more likely to have assimilated unsound practices that would hamper their ability to fight conventional warfare. Finally, the threat of Japanese attack, which became apparent in 1905 and an urgent priority by 1907, distracted the army from assimilating the lessons of pacification prior to World War II. The cold war sparked a resurgence of interest in unconventional warfare, but officers focused on more recent, and apparently more relevant, communist insurgencies and pacification campaigns. The imperial war experience thus played a very small role during the Vietnam War and the two decades that followed. Only with the collapse of the Soviet Union and the emergence of threats by what was termed "nonstate actors"—religious fundamentalists, terrorists, criminal gangs, and warlord factions—did the army finally begin to look to the imperial wars of the distant past for answers to the questions of a new and challenging future.

PART 8

Environmental Management

American colonial seated in a rubber tree, Botanical Gardens, Manila, circa 1907. (Memorial Library, Special Collections, University of Wisconsin–Madison)

INTRODUCTION

Environmental and Economic Management

J. R. MCNEILL

IN HIS PANORAMIC STUDY OF THE SUCCESS of European imperialism, David Abernethy suggested that the key to the durability of European imperial rule lay in what he called the "Triple Assault."[1] This consisted of simultaneous military/political, commercial, and cultural assaults on the states, economies, and societies of peoples in the Americas, Africa, and Asia. The assaults were not necessarily coordinated consciously, and some of those involved in, let us say, religious conversion may have had misgivings about fellow countrymen involved in military conquest. But the effect was an imperial positive feedback loop, a whole greater than the sum of its parts.

Abernethy might have added a fourth assault: environmental science. The term was not in use in the late nineteenth and early twentieth centuries, but it is a convenient term with which to refer to botany, scientific forestry, meteorology, or sanitation—the subjects of the next four essays—as well as other allied fields of inquiry that were enlisted in the service of empire. Unlike Abernethy's assaults, all of which were directed at human communities, this fourth assault took aim at nature but with the clear intent of making both it and the people living in it easier to govern.[2]

By the end of the nineteenth century, science and scientists had acquired sufficient knowledge and power that they could hope to alter nature and make it more tractable. Foresters could manage woodlands so as to maximize timber yields over the long haul. Public health experts could check the spread of infectious diseases. Botanists could introduce economically useful plants where they had not grown before and could hope to control pests and crop diseases. And meteorologists could create early warning systems that would allow preparation (or flight) before storms hit. Scientists in the service of the state could, in short, hope to manage the environment rationally. Professionally ambitious men (no women played prominent roles in the cases that follow) could hardly resist the temptation.

Such opportunities were often easier to find in an empire than at home. In the United States, as in much of Western Europe by the end of the nineteenth century, populations at home had entrenched rights to property and their persons. This made it more difficult to impose new practices, however rational or scientific, on forests, fields, or city streets. In the colonies, the necessary intrusions were often easier to make, especially when backed by military force and the prestige of modern, rational science. As Richard Grove noted, remote imperial outposts made good stages for environmental observation and experimentation.[3] Imperial environmental science could help make empire profitable by lowering costs and in some cases, such as forestry and economic botany, raising economic productivity.

All this required something more than the intermittent expeditionary science that prevailed in overseas empires before 1860. European empires had long benefited from the fruits of expeditionary science in the tradition of Maurits, Malaspina, Humboldt, Bougainville, Cook, and dozens of others. The French in the early nineteenth century raised this form of science to a high art, notably in Egypt and Algeria, and the Americans imitated it.[4] Merriwether Lewis received crash courses in natural history so as to serve as a scientist when crossing the continent and firming up the claims of the United States to its newly acquired domains in western North America. The Wilkes Expedition (1838–42) carried this tradition to Pacific waters, gathering masses of data on every aspect of the ocean and its islands. But the transformation of nature so as to make empire financially sustainable required something more, something more permanent and ongoing. It required the institutionalization of imperial environmental science and management.

Greg Bankoff's chapter shows how American foresters responded to the challenges and opportunities presented by Philippine tropical forests. Through the influence of the apostle of scientific forestry in the United States, Gifford Pinchot, the Americans had absorbed doctrines of modern forest management from Germany. They had begun to apply these to the American West when, as it were, the Philippines fell into their lap. Spanish forest management seemed to them retrograde and unscientific, and the American colonial government after 1900 had the power to overcome resistance within Filipino society in ways that could not easily be done in Ohio or Oregon. The foresters, like the sanitarians, had almost carte blanche to follow their inclinations and training. The enormous stands of marketable timber in the Philippines represented a great economic opportunity, which, if carefully managed on a rational-scientific basis, could help make the colony financially sound while preserving the resource for the future. This, of course, required the training and maintenance of cadres of foresters, both American and Filipino. By the time of his retirement in 1914, George Ahern, the godfather of scientific forestry in the Philippines, had succeeded in this project, though never to his or anyone else's full satisfaction.

In Daniel F. Doeppers's chapter, American sanitarians tackle the challenges of public health in a crowded tropical city, Manila. Armed with new knowledge (the germ theory of disease), they seek to make the city safe for its new masters and—some of them at least—for Filipinos as well. Cholera, typhoid, dysentery, and other waterborne diseases routinely killed thousands in Manila in the nineteenth century, but the Americans arrived at a time when it was increasingly tempting to do something about it. New dams, pipes, and filtration systems, in place by 1930, made Manila a healthier place for all those with access to the new water system, a change for the better, surely, even if it was unevenly experienced. Similar things happened throughout the colonial world, keeping imperial troops and administrators alive.[5] The Americans did not stop there. Safer milk and vegetables also seemed within reach. So did an orderly, planned, esthetically pleasing cityscape of the sort recently installed on the Chicago lakefront. All of these projects lowered the cost of running the Philippines by taming parts of the microbial world and improving human health, both American and Filipino.[6]

In Stuart McCook's essay, American botanists take up the challenges posed by tropical plantations. In Cuba, Puerto Rico, Hawai'i, and the Philippines, the most likely way to make empire pay was through sugar and coffee plantations. But all monocrop agriculture invites pest infestations and plant diseases, and the American scientific establishment had limited experience combating these scourges in tropical settings before 1898. This presented a challenge, or more precisely a set of challenges, some ecological but others institutional or financial. Over the course of the next forty years or so, American botanists and their students met those challenges with considerable success despite chronic funding crises, serving the cause of empire as well as that of planters and consumers of sugar, coffee, tobacco, pineapples, and much more besides. Without the work of these botanists, could plantation agriculture have turned a profit? And without profitable agriculture, could the American empire have lasted in the Caribbean and Pacific? Perhaps it could have if the U.S. Navy's interests had prevailed over the sensibilities of accountants; but perhaps not. We shall never know.

James Francis Warren's chapter tells a different story, that of a Spanish Jesuit who found a niche within the American colonial order after 1898. Father José Algué, a meteorologist in the Philippines with years of experience and an international reputation as a scientist, weathered the storms of war and regime change deftly, emerging as the director of the Philippines Weather Bureau after 1902. Father Algué hoped to improve the art of weather prediction so as to safeguard Filipinos, and indeed all populations in monsoon Asia, from the deadly blows of tropical cyclones. With enough observation stations and telegraph lines, Algué's network might save hundreds of thousands of lives. To do this well, he needed the political and financial support of the Americans and the latest meteorological technology. He got it. His project suited the new masters of the Philippines nicely as modern science in the service of humanity was just the thing to justify empire to skeptics in America; moreover, the U.S. Navy could make good use of the information Algué's legions provided. While it would be hard to prove, it may safely be assumed that Algué's life's work made nature more manageable and saved lives by providing early warning of deadly storms.

All of these essays demonstrate the links between science and the sustainability of empire. By and large, distant colonies provided free rein for forms of environmental science and modification that in some cases proved too intrusive to be undertaken at home. American science and sanitation did make empire more practical and in many cases made life somewhat easier and longer for colonizers and colonized alike. Ironically, the Spanish empire, in which science had played a more restricted role, somehow sustained itself for more than 350 years in Cuba and the Philippines while the American empire, despite the real impact of environmental science and sanitation, came and went quickly. Or perhaps one should say it was transformed into a larger, informal empire sustained, in part, by sciences of all sorts.

Conservation and Colonialism
Gifford Pinchot and the Birth of Tropical Forestry in the Philippines

GREG BANKOFF

THE QUESTION OF THE WILDERNESS and national forest reserves that proved so divisive in late-nineteenth- and early-twentieth-century U.S. politics had its counterpart in America's erstwhile colony across the Pacific. In the Philippines, however, the colonial context somewhat simplified matters: the conservation movement was not rent apart by any semblance of the acrimonious dissension between preservationists who wished to set aside certain landscapes and those who advocated a more utilitarian or planned use of resources. Only the state stood between sawmill operators, mineral companies, and the like and their unfettered designs on the natural riches of the archipelago. The principal source of that wealth lay in the extensive forests that still covered large areas of the islands. But far from facilitating unrestricted access to all this timber by its own citizens and newly acquired subjects, the nascent colonial administration had already been captured by proponents of the creed of utilitarian conservation. It was in America's Asian colony that the Progressive era state was able to implement its reformist agenda virtually unopposed, providing a testing ground for many of the programs later enacted in the continental United States.

The Insular Bureau of Forestry was largely established along lines advocated by Gifford Pinchot, the "father" of professional forestry in the United States, and his associates, Henry Graves, dean of the new Yale Forest School, and George Ahern, founder and long-serving chief of the forestry service in the Philippines.[1] Consequently, the bureau's policies and agents sought to promote the lumber potential of the islands in such a manner that yields might be sustainable and the forest made to pay for its own maintenance. That involved both imposing limits on felling through the enforcement of a licensing system and learning how to conserve species through a study of their properties. It was a challenge that Pinchot and his colleagues welcomed, convinced as they were that Americans were engaged on "the finest piece of work ... the Anglo-Saxon people are trying to do."[2]

Forestry from the Deck of a Ship

In 1902, Gifford Pinchot took leave from his official duties as chief of the fledgling U.S. Forestry Service in Washington, D.C., and embarked for America's new colony, the Philippines.[3] His tour took place at a critical moment in the history of the forestry services in both the United States and the Philippines. Over a few short years, until 1910, Pinchot oversaw the consolidation of U.S. forest management services and the rapid expansion of its responsibilities and personnel under his direction.[4] The moment was no less auspicious in the Philippines where George Ahern, an army captain, had been charged with the task of heading the newly formed Insular Bureau of Forestry in 1900 while the war with Filipino republican forces still raged. Ahern had a long association with Pinchot, and so it was only natural that he should turn to his mentor for support and advice.[5] Pinchot arrived in Manila on October 26 and was lodged as a guest of Governor-General William Howard Taft, who even put his official yacht, the USS *General Alava*, a commodiously fitted out gunboat of fourteen hundred tons, at his disposal.[6]

The eminent Dutch historian Jacob van Leur decried Western historiography as being "observed from the deck of a ship" to denote a particular ethnocentric and littoral-minded perspective on Southeast Asia.[7] Perhaps no single episode so exemplifies what the historian had in mind than Pinchot's six-week, twenty-three-hundred-mile odyssey about the islands, steaming past partially verdant but sometimes hostile shores and landing from time to time to make excursions into the hinterland. This, indeed, was forestry from the deck of a ship, giving him "the opportunity to see a good deal of islands from the ocean"![8] And what he observed impressed him deeply. "This was my first real sight of tropical forest," he wrote his father on November 6, "and consequently it was full of the keenest interest, although somewhat bewildering to be dropped into the midst of a forest not one tree of which I knew."[9]

Sailing south from Manila, the party made its way along the western coast of Luzon, skirted around the principal islands of the Visayas to reach Mindanao, and returned by way of the Sulu archipelago, Sandakan in British North Borneo, and the east coast of Paragua (Palawan). Once back in the capital, Pinchot rested for a few days, talking all the while with officials, foresters, and lumbermen, before embarking once more on the *General Alava*. This time he turned north, following the coastline as far as the extreme northeast of Luzon before finally leaving Philippine waters altogether for Japan and home (see map).[10]

Pinchot's itinerary gave him a fairly reasonable impression of the overall state of the archipelago's forests and the extent of deforestation. It is interesting

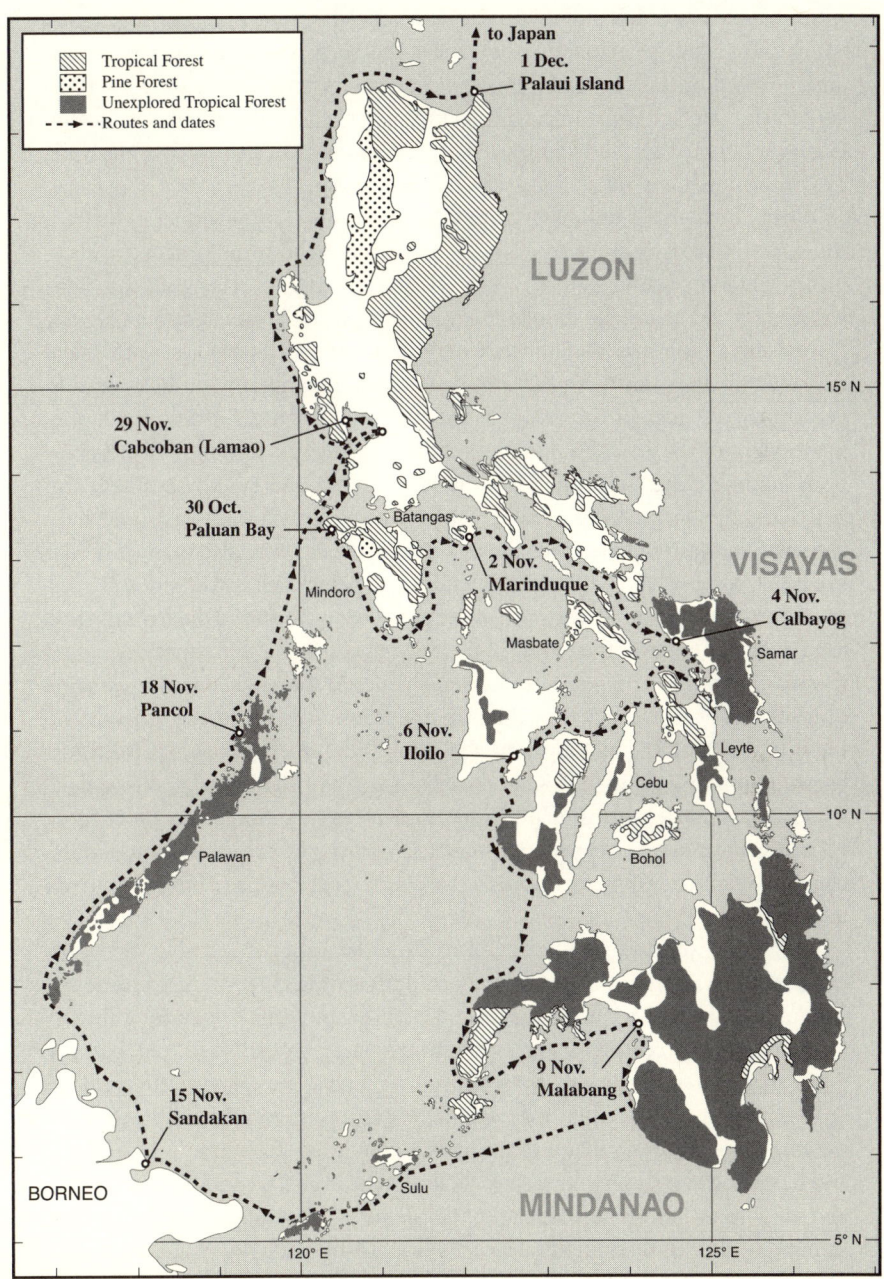

Gifford Pinchot's travels in the Philippines, 1902.

to note that Pinchot estimated that 50 percent of the forest had already been lost, a figure very much out of keeping with official American colonial statistics, which calculated the remaining cover at 65 to 70 percent.[11] Moreover, he was accompanied on his travels by those most acquainted with the state of tropical forests, who provided him with technical expertise: Ahern himself; Regino García, a botanist formerly employed by the Spanish forestry service; and various of the newly appointed American district foresters.

What Pinchot saw impressed him greatly. This was tropical forest, the real thing, and there was much to elicit his amazement and wonderment. In many places, the forest came right down to the water's edge, overhanging the high-water mark and giving the shoreline "an enormously interesting and enormously fascinating appearance."[12] The trees were of an extraordinary size with many diameters in excess of three feet, but he was too unfamiliar with the species to get any correct idea of the timber's distribution. Onshore, he was struck, too, by the vigor of the life about him.[13] As the trip proceeded, however, the observations became more "scientific." He was surprised to find the tallest, finest, and best-sized timber on the slopes and not in the valleys, where he would have expected the wash to have made the soil richer.[14] There were also many different kinds of trees, over seven hundred species already identified and described to science. The composition of the forest, moreover, changed from island to island and even from day to day.[15] Beginning at the coast, the forest passed through gradual transformations. The trees were shorter, smaller in diameter, and less valuable immediately at the water's edge than they were even slightly farther inland. The finest timber with the best logs was always on the steepest slopes, but the forest began to diminish again the higher one climbed. The great variation throughout the islands made it "very difficult in so rapid a survey ... to get any thoroughly reliable general rules."[16] However, it was clear that there were great tracts of merchantable timber despite the extensive forest clearing that had already occurred in some places.[17]

This forest world was not only one of potential riches. It was also filled with perils: strange sights, unknown species, wild upheavals, deadly fevers, and primitive peoples akin to what the historian David Arnold calls *tropicality*, a threat-laden, nineteenth-century discourse about tropical regions.[18] It started with the fabric of the forest itself, with images of species such as the balete (*Ficus elastica*), "tree-eaters" that "devoured" their fellows.[19] But it was not so much the trees as the forest undergrowth that was the principal menace, the vines, ferns, rattans, and bamboos that sprang up wherever the overhead canopy had been disturbed and grew to an immense size. Often the tangle of plant life was so dense that "a man would be practically useless off a trail, without a bolo."[20] The chief concern, however, was not the inconvenience but the effect on the forest's ability to regenerate. As the growth of "these forest weeds" was so much faster than that of the trees, they "choked out" a large proportion of the saplings.²¹ What is more, there were also predators in this forest world, not the wildlife that one senses Pinchot found slightly disappointing but *anay,* the white ants that were the real masters of this world beneath the forest canopy. So significant was their impact on the forest that only thirty to forty of the more than seven hundred varieties of trees known to grow in the islands were regularly used by indigenous people, a selection largely made according to "what trees the natives knew the white ant would eat." Over hundreds of years, the effect of felling only a few species was the "complete exhaustion in certain provinces of the best kind of timber."²²

If all this were not enough to make the forest a strange and perilous environment, one also had to contend with the land on which the trees stood and the air above its canopy. The Philippines is one of the most seismically active landmasses in the world as well as being subject to frequent typhoons.²³ Fever and disease also stalked the land, with forests, in particular, held to harbor certain diseases.²⁴ Cholera was a scourge, and in rural areas there was something worse—leprosy.²⁵ And it was not only people that were struck down by disease: Rinderpest and surra decimated the carabao (*Bubalus bubalis*), cattle, and horse herds while plagues of locusts ravaged the fields on certain islands.²⁶ To complete the somewhat apocalyptic vision he drew of this hazardous environment, Pinchot noted that the country was still at war with the United States and that often "the forests were the refuge of the disaffected." Up in the mountains, of course, there were also the inevitable headhunters.²⁷

Le Coup d'Oeil Forestier (The Forester's Eye)

Did the uncertain perils of the forest put off men such as Gifford Pinchot, George Ahern, and Henry Graves? Not in the least. "The work that we are doing out there," Pinchot told an audience at the Yale Forestry School in March 1903, shortly after his return from the Philippines, "is in many ways the finest piece of work that I have been in contact with. I have never been as proud of being an American as I was after finding out what our men are doing in the Islands." When they acquired the Philippines from Spain, Americans had placed themselves under an obligation to put these immense timberlands under "some sort of management adapting the ideas we had developed in the U.S. to the very different conditions that were to be found in the islands."²⁸

American attitudes toward Spanish forestry were ambivalent, a combination of grudging respect for its intent and outright condemnation of its practice, especially the state's apparent inability to enforce its own laws. Existing methods were inefficient, slow, destructive, wasteful, and uneconomic, and the forest had only escaped further devastation because of the difficulties the terrain posed to logging.²⁹ Trees were felled by ax, squared to the largest log size possible, floated downriver to a common rafting place, and collected by lighter and taken to

Manila, the principal market.[30] Sawn timber was not only very roughly hewn, causing much waste, but it reached the market in insufficient quantities to meet local demand and so was expensive.[31] Such logging practices were also highly destructive of the environment, and many trees were simply abandoned after felling and left to rot on the forest floor according to the whims of men or the vagaries of the market. Areas were often simply cleared of all trees, making regeneration unlikely.[32] Reflecting on a barren patch of from two to three acres, Pinchot remarked, "I have never seen a more complete slash, because it is impossible to make one. Everything was destroyed."[33]

All this, of course, was not destined to continue; it had to change and change soon. After all, that was the reason why men such as Ahern were out in the Philippines, and it was the raison d'être behind Pinchot's and later Henry Graves's trips. Both visits were pivotal in establishing the structure and purpose of American forest policy in the Philippines. Pinchot's report formed the basis of draft legislation on the rules and regulations of the Insular Bureau of Forestry that were put into practice as the Forestry Organic Law of May 7, 1904, and Graves's recommendations led to the bureau's further reorganization and fine-tuning under the act of October 25, 1905. Nor should Ahern's contribution be minimized at least in the initial legislation. He accompanied Pinchot on his inspection of the archipelago and even as far as Japan aboard the *General Alava* with the chief forester noting in his journal how "A. and I plugged away on our report" during the entire crossing.[34] Ahern had also been the instigator behind both men's visits and was the man on the ground, remaining as head of the bureau until his retirement in 1914. In large part, therefore, he was principally responsible for the implementation of these regulations.[35]

The report on which Pinchot and Ahern "plugged away" at all the way to Japan provided considerable details on how the Insular Forestry Bureau should be reorganized. Great emphasis was placed on labor-saving methods and eliminating red tape. Until such measures were implemented, Pinchot recommended limiting the number of licenses granted and varying duties collected on cut timber as a means of directing where logging took place.[36] A bill closely following these recommendations was duly presented to the Philippine Commission and formed the basis of the forestry law enacted in 1904. Through its provisions, Pinchot believed he had achieved his aims of greatly improving the position of the bureau, facilitating forestry operations, and promoting conservationist forest development.[37]

At Ahern's suggestion, Pinchot asked Henry Graves to go to the Philippines to investigate how the new laws and regulations had been implemented and to familiarize himself with tropical conditions.[38] A close friend and associate of Pinchot and the latter's successor as the nation's chief forester, he set out in early December 1904 and spent more than a month talking to central office staff and examining actual conditions in the forests. Although it was not his original intention to suggest any changes in the new law, Graves was confronted with glaring deficiencies that required prompt, systematic correction. In particular, he proposed that the existing management by correspondence system be done away with and that it be replaced with senior staff inspections of the provinces on a regular basis. Not only would the central office be kept in touch with field operatives by this means, but district foresters would have the opportunity to present their views and opinions to the chief forester or his deputy personally, providing valuable local input and doing much to improve morale in the service. Unfavorable public opinion of the bureau might also be improved if local government officials, lumbermen, and others with grievances were able to bring their complaints directly to the attention of senior forestry officials for speedy redress.[39]

In reviewing Pinchot's earlier report, Graves was less sanguine than his mentor, discovering that the draft shown him by Pinchot had been altered to accommodate the criticisms of both lumbermen and insular administrators. "Although the law has been in force only a short time," Graves wrote, "many defects and inconsistencies [have] become manifest." Instead, what impressed Graves most on his arrival in the islands was how the bureau was "becoming every day more unpopular, and the laws more distasteful."[40] His recommendations led to the supplementary Forest Law of October 25, 1905. However, the change that proved to be of greatest value in Pinchot's eyes was the transfer of revenue collection to the Bureau of Internal Revenue, leaving foresters with "more time FOR forest investigation and practical work."[41]

Conservation and Colonialism

If figures such as Gifford Pinchot, George Ahern, and Henry Graves loom large in the annals of colonial forestry in the Philippines, the reverse is hardly the case: The Philippines is barely if ever referred to in any history of modern American forestry.[42] Yet the timing is crucial here. The insular forestry service is not a pale reflection of its metropolitan counterpart suitably adapted to colonial conditions as, say, Baguio was of Daniel Burnham's City Beautiful plans for Washington, D.C.[43] Instead, it anticipated similar changes in America. The Philippine forestry laws of 1904 and 1905 predate or coincide with major U.S. reforms that led to the establishment of a nationwide professional forestry service and the transfer of forest reserves from the older Land Office.[44]

The Insular Bureau of Forestry, then, did not stem from the U.S. Forest Service but was a unique development created by particular times and circumstances. Forest conservation in the United States was a cooperative venture involving complex relationships between the federal government, states' rights, and industry.[45] Nor could it completely ignore public opinion in the form of individuals and pressure groups such as John Muir and the Sierra Club. In contrast, those in charge of the Philippine forestry service had uncontested authority over the whole enterprise with a direct channel to executive power that, at least initially, was little answerable to local interests and little restrained by the voice of industry or public opinion, which were both muted by U.S. military operations. The Philippines was a professional forester's dream come true: vast stretches of still largely "untouched" primary forest and no one to stop foresters from doing what they thought best. It was the colonial condition that provided them with the wherewithal to put into practice what they preached. The Philippines was not just a prologue to later U.S. forestry policy but a prism through which can be viewed the full vision of this founding generation of American environmentalists, undistorted by metropolitan political restraints.

But what was it that Pinchot and his associates so ardently advocated? At the end of the nineteenth century and the beginning of the twentieth, the nascent U.S. conservation movement was split between preservationists and the so-called utilitarian conservationists. Preservationists held that nature had beauty and intrinsic wealth sufficient unto itself and its protection needed no further justification. Any use other than recreational (and even that was disputable) was contrary to the notion of conserving designated reserves as wildernesses untrammeled by human activity. Its most prominent proponent was John Muir, one of the founders and first president of the Sierra Club.[46] Utilitarian conservation, with its practical philosophy of the wise management of nature for the benefit of humanity, was able to reconcile commercial activity in nature with legislation to ensure its long-term sustainability. Its chief promoter was Pinchot who actually claimed to have coined the word *conservation* while out riding one fine winter's morning in Washington's Rock Creek Park.[47] "Conservation," he wrote in his autobiography, "is the foresighted utilization, preservation, and/or renewal of forests, waters, and lands and minerals for the greatest good of the greatest number for the longest time."[48]

Under the new U.S. administration, these were to be the guiding precepts for forestry in the archipelago. All three men espoused such ideas, as did the foresters they appointed to carry out that work. Ahern spoke of the need for what he termed "rational forestry." For Graves, the problem of forestry was "how the production of high grade trees may be kept up." For Pinchot, it was all a matter of "liberalising the rules" so as to give "added impulse to forest development."[49] To make the forest pay for its own conservation and management, two courses of action required immediate implementation: silvicultural studies of the forest to discover what actually went on there and the creation of detailed local maps to make the whole enterprise scientifically and financially practical.

On one level, utilitarian conservation in the Philippines was mainly a matter of reproduction. "The time has come now," Pinchot told his audience of young foresters at Yale in March 1903, "when real forest work is going on, chiefly through studies of reproduction."[50] How long did it take valuable hardwood trees to grow to maturity and, perhaps more important, how long did it take them to grow back? Which conditions favored regrowth and which hindered it? Did clear-felling or selective-felling favor sustainable yields and what interval of time was required before a forest was harvestable again?[51] These and similar questions could only be answered by means of meticulous and laborious observation of individual species, planting them from seed and watching them grow in specially designated reserves that included every terrain and all possible elevations. Until such detailed research had been carried out and forest management under tropical conditions had become anything more than informed guesswork, logging had to be restricted "until cutting can proceed without forest destruction."[52]

What was needed was a detailed on-the-ground knowledge of Philippine forests to put this soon to be acquired data to any practical advantage. And for that maps were required. Citing the British experience in India, Graves observed how control over the subcontinent's forests was dependent "practically entirely on maps." Exercising control over cutting areas was more critical than elaborate calculations of the volume logged, supervision that was not possible without accurate maps prepared by trained foresters. Over the next few years, men under the guidance of trained foresters literally walked the length and breadth of the archipelago's forests, mapping the species and size of the trees they encountered.[53]

This was utilitarian conservation in operation, as it was conceived to be without any of the compromises, trade-offs, or acts of political sleight of hand needed to effect similar measures in the United States. Developments in the Philippines both paralleled those in American forestry and served as a forerunner of what was to yet to come. And what put insular foresters in such a fortunate position? Colonialism! It was the colonial condition that gave Pinchot, Ahern, Graves, and their subordinates the freedom to put their ideas into practice virtually unopposed by any other interest groups. As Pinchot admitted to Yale foresters that evening in March 1903, "The Philippine Government has this great advantage for the preliminary condition in which it is placed, that a majority of eight men can make any law any time they please.... The Commission is exceedingly favorable to forest work in the Islands and has done everything it could to help the Bureau of Forestry."[54]

As for Pinchot himself, what further part did he have to play, directly or indirectly, in the Philippines? As long as Ahern remained insular bureau chief, till 1914, utilitarian conservation remained the paramount methodology and even spread to Republican China, whose forestry regulations were modeled after those of the Philippines.[55] Pinchot was to remain what he termed "an interested party," an adviser but one whose principal work was done. He continued to know more about the situation of forestry in the archipelago than most others in the United States, but he was now content to be "merely an observer on the fringe of the battle."⁵⁶ More important, from his perspective, he now had a wider canvas on which to play out his ideas about forestry and conservation than the colonial Philippines. In the years between his 1902 Philippine tour and his controversial dismissal in 1910, Pinchot oversaw the transfer of more than 60 million acres of forest reserves from the Land Office to his newly formed U.S. Forest Service, their designation as national forests eventually comprising over 150 million acres, their management growing from 9 employees to 150 foresters, and their annual budget rising from twenty thousand dollars a year to nearly four hundred thousand.⁵⁷ These changes are usually regarded as laying the foundation of modern forestry in the United States, but many of them were first trialed in the Philippines.

Manila's Imperial Makeover

Security, Health, and Symbolism

DANIEL F. DOEPPERS

AT THE HIGH TIDE OF EMPIRE starting in the late nineteenth century, the grand, awe-inspiring colonial capital became central to the imperial enterprise as the site of its expatriate population, a symbol of its military power, an institutional center, and a locus of major port facilities. Even now, a full half century after the imperial age, these massive conurbations, no longer mere metropolises but now megacities, remain the most visible legacy of colonial rule. While modern cities faced myriad problems as they grew to unprecedented size and complexity across the globe, the diffusion of European urban forms to the tropics brought special problems of health, safety, and food security that seem, in retrospect, to reveal something of the character of the imperial state.

How should we think about the task of the American invaders in taking over Manila, a city of perhaps three hundred thousand people? Any outside power taking over cities heretofore run by others faces certain problems inherent both in the situation and in the management of urban places. These may vary along several dimensions of culture and social organization, previous managerial practices and institutions, the amount of infrastructure and destruction, and so on, but they will also tend to have many common elements. As Veena Talwar Oldenberg has argued about the British imperial makeover of Indian cities, the chief problems facing Americans were security, public health, and metropolitan design.[1] The first, and arguably the most fundamental, of these challenges was design, that is, the imposition of a modern urban structure on a historic city with inadequate infrastructure and a knot of streets and waterways without a unifying plan.

SYMBOLIC FORMS AND METROPOLITAN MODELS

A dual problem addressed by most imperial rulers in the late nineteenth and early twentieth centuries had to do with both the political symbolism of power and expatriate psychology in the sense of establishing urban spaces where the colonizers could feel comfortable. The more heroic dimension of this problem has to do with the establishment of symbolic architectural and landscape forms that give a plastic expression to the imperial presence, forms whose intent is to awe and impress, to create a distinctive "brand" signature.

Manila, as a capital, began with Intramuros, an orderly, well-laid-out, sixteenth- and seventeenth-century fortress city. Institutionally speaking and in political psychology, Manila's Intramuros, literally, "inside the walls," long retained its preeminence in Spanish colonial space. Even if some prominent Spaniards and affluent European merchants moved out to bucolic suburban locations, Intramuros remained the ultimate nineteenth-century institutional power center. Except for the palace of the governor-general, the buildings of government the American rulers inherited were there, as was the main cathedral. These walled city spaces can be thought of as symbolic forms.

Practically minded, American administrators leaned toward filling in the moat around Intramuros as a noxious threat to public health. They could have carted off the massive walls as well. It was a question for a time. But Intramuros was densely packed with major churches, cloisters, and schools and a great collection of old stone masonry residential buildings. Leveling the walls would not have changed the congestion of narrow streets and packed structures. Fortunately, they hesitated.

Enter the proconsul and future president, William Howard Taft, now secretary of war, in 1904 and his protégé, the eastern Brahmin W. Cameron Forbes. Young Forbes was appointed to the Philippine Commission with the portfolio for transportation and public works. What was on the imperial minds was the creation of a grand plan for a new hill station, as well as for a proper capital, one that presented well to both foreigners and local citizens—and an answer to the questions about the inherited Spanish architectural styles. Forbes had earlier met Daniel H. Burnham through family connections and backed his friend for the commission. Burnham was appointed to make an assessment and conceptual plan for Manila and a Baguio hill station. He was then perhaps the most famous American urban architect and planner after Frederick Law Olmsted Jr., who had declined this commission. Burnham was celebrated for his work on Chicago's Columbian Exposition, including the Outer Drive, lakeside parks, and museum settings that are still critical parts of Chicago's landscape, and he spent a whirlwind month on site in Manila at the end of 1904.[2] He quickly advocated the retention of the city walls and the aesthetic use of them to lend a heroic quality to the former military fire zone to the south of Intramuros. With the noxious moat filled in, the open area outside the walls and its outlying defensive demilune was now to be reimagined as the center, a beautiful "greensward" to be outlined eventually with the construction of the legislative and court buildings of the central government. It was also to be extended seaward through reclamation, creating a space for the frequent band concerts and promenades that were part of Manila life.

At a stroke, this open area became the symbolic center of the colonial space and the Filipino nation that was one day to be established. In keeping with this newfound symbolic centrality, the bones of Jose Rizal, the late (and safely dead) national hero, were interred on "the Luneta" and marked with a proper but modest monument. The Luneta's conceptual similarity to the national mall in Washington, D.C., can hardly be missed, but the centuries-old city wall gives it an even greater time depth.[3] On the long seaside of the Walled City and Luneta, Burnham proposed a great boulevard that would extend for miles to the north and south along the shore—an exact parallel to Chicago's Outer Drive. Beyond these central elements would extend great diagonal boulevards in the fashion of Washington, D.C. Outward in four directions he penciled in open space parks with looping carriage drives as well as numerous "play fields" for the positive development of urban youth.

The plan was large minded and impressive, though simple in the City Beautiful mode. The central elements were quickly established. The open, grassy Luneta highlights and draws the eye to the impressive government buildings that followed. A short segment of the envisioned seaside boulevard was built on reclaimed waterfront to the south, and likewise one of the parks with looping drives eventually materialized in Malate, also to the south, an area of concentrated, but not segregated, American residence.[4] Later, this was converted into a set of athletic facilities and used to host the Asian games in the prewar era.

But a plan is only a guide. Implementation requires a powerful supporting coalition of active interests like those that came together in Chicago. Much of the rest of the plan was not realized. What Burnham did leave behind was the architect he selected to implement elements of the plan. This was William Parsons, a graduate of both Yale and the French École de Beaux Arts. In eight years in residence, Parsons drew on Burnham's work to execute his own plans for Cebu and Zamboanga. He also designed scores of schools, provincial capitals, and other buildings, employing his own take on Burnham's enthusiasm for major elements of the Spanish era architectural heritage, including especially the red tile roofs. In Thomas S. Hines's view, Parsons "designed buildings of warmth, efficiency, and engaging simplicity. Utilizing the vocabulary of indigenous Spanish-Philippine architecture, Parsons' buildings had plain, broad surfaces of solid pastel colors and were usually topped by handsome tile roofs."[5] He eventually returned to California and took with him many of these design elements.

All of this represented an imperial imperative to create a beautiful and awe-inspiring place. But it was in no sense a clean break with the past. Rather it was a case of creative transition well rooted in the Spanish heritage but also drawing on American public models and expressing the grand conceptions and practical spirit of the new imperial regime.

Security

Within the grand imperial design of the Burnham plan, security was the most pressing concern for American colonials who had to live and move on its streets. In contrast to the extensive damage the British had inflicted on Lucknow in India, central Manila suffered comparatively limited damage when the U.S. Army wrested it from Spanish control in August 1898. The fighting of early 1899 against the forces of the Philippine Revolution resulted in extensive burning and destruction of poor residential districts that lay outside the commercial and institutional cores of the city. This did not provoke the Americans to construct a British-style cantonment.[6] Instead, a sufficiently effective police force was established that was staffed with former American soldiers and officers and included native Filipinos, not necessarily Tagalogs, almost from the first. The great majority of Americans came to live immersed in the city like the Spaniards before them. In the British system, cantonments included barracks, artillery parks, and parade grounds, but they were also centers of low-density foreign residence and administration. They were the physical places from which foreign power was projected. The Americans, coming from a racially segregated society in which many states had miscegenation laws, nevertheless did not set up a segregated and militarized zone. This was important for it implied that whatever security or public health problems were encountered they would have to be addressed for most of the urban population, not just a main group of segregated foreigners.

The point is that in Manila personal and military security did not develop as a critical problem for colonial managers. When civilian American families chose residences, they were not in gated communities or a cantonment. Commercial establishments, theaters, and band concerts were open to all. So were most Christian churches. Manila in 1900 and beyond did not devolve into Baghdad of the twenty-first century. There was no "Green Zone," and the likelihood of being murdered on the streets was small.

Public Health

When a large number of people live and interact in concentrated fashion, public health problems immediately arise. What the new imperial managers do about these has a lot to do with what the microbial assaults are and what knowledge and practices the invading group brings with it. It also has to do with the local reception of what the occupiers see as "public health" innovations. Acting on the discoveries of Pasteur, Koch, and others, public health strategies proceeded at very different rates in the metropolitan societies and even between various cities. Decades separated the public health practices and declining death rates of advanced Scandinavia from those of laggard France. Whether out of selfish fear for themselves or a more general concern for entire urban population, the colonial managers instituted various public health policies and practices, and these drew on developments at home as well as on interactive experiences with the dominated society.

In the event, American civilian scientists quickly set up laboratories and instituted the *Philippine Journal of Science* in order to discover and communicate their findings and to involve Filipinos in the effort. There were also several preexisting Spanish-language medical journals. Initially, however, as Warwick Anderson has written in *Colonial Pathologies,* American colonial public health practices rested on a military basis.[7] The topic of public health is immense, and several of its dimensions have just been definitively explored by Anderson. In this brief essay, I focus only on the water supply and the provision of food using the case of the importation and retailing of fresh vegetables.[8]

In a way that urban historians have generally failed to appreciate, the provisioning of these fundamental human needs through secure urban-rural linkages was the essential precondition for the dramatic growth of historically modest cities of a few hundred thousand or less into modern metropolises of ten to twenty million. Without such food security, great masses of humanity could not, and would not, have alienated themselves from the land and most of the essentials for human survival. In a real sense, these seemingly small, ephemeral matters of water and vegetables are essential foundations of the modern city.

The Water System

Fresh water for the use of the urban population during most of the nineteenth century came from shallow wells and cisterns that collected rainwater from the tile roofs of the more substantial homes. Considerable water for ordinary folks was taken from the Pasig River upstream from the city and from the *esteros* (tidal creeks). The water was transported in great earthen jars carried by commercial watercraft and retailed throughout the city. These practices became extremely problematic as the human density rose and the pollution of wells and incidence of waterborne disease rose concomitantly.

In this environment, cholera, a disease transferred by contaminated water, became a major periodic scourge, and a majority of the population was also preyed on by intestinal parasites. This was not limited to the city, but because of density sanitation problems were generally more acute there, resulting in higher death rates, the so-called urban penalty. Increasingly, Manila required a steady stream of new migrants to replace those who died of waterborne diseases.[9]

The problem of a sanitary water supply was long-standing. In 1743, a Spaniard, one Francisco Carriedo, left a substantial legacy to be used for the construction of a proper water system for the city. Carriedo lived in the Philippines for twenty years and served on the Manila *cabildo* (municipal board). Evidently he had become wealthy in the galleon trade. Carriedo distrusted local sources of water. Not sufficient to finance a waterworks initially, his money was left to accumulate by investment in trade. Long after the amount had reached a critical level, the trustees declined to take action. One reason may have been their use of the fund as a source of loans to themselves. Finally, in the 1880s, after an extended mano a mano between the central authorities and the city council, the council was forced to use the funds to install the city's first piped water system. In the event, the amount from the fund was almost matched by the proceeds of a specially enacted tax of 1 percent on the beef and pork cleaned in the city abattoir. Xavier Heutz de Lemps points out that along with a growing scientific appreciation of disease transmission the Spanish administration was concerned with heading off the kind of antiforeign riots that were occasioned by the first cholera epidemic in 1820 and the possibility of such mass events becoming connected to a rising concept of Filipino nationalism.[10]

In 1884, numerous public water taps and a new fountain became important fixtures of the city—with the population then at about a quarter million. The newspapers pointed to the Carriedo waterworks as one of the great accomplishments of Spanish rule. The intake for the new system was located in the next valley to the east on the Marikina River opposite Santolan. From the river, great steam engines pumped the water up to underground reservoirs. From this *deposito* (reservoir), the water moved by gravity through a large above ground pipe across the river and into the city. From Quiapo, smaller diameter distribution pipes branched out underground. The small size of the distribution pipes severely limited water pressure. By 1902, only eighteen hundred residences were connected. Still the system was useful. There were hydrants from which the public could draw water for free, and unauthorized tapping into the water main began almost at once. Many other colonial cities in the region lagged far behind. Still, the Carriedo system "did not reach all the people in Manila. As a result, the poorer classes, among whom the danger of cholera was greatest, were [still] accustomed to take water from shallow wells, ponds, esteros, or other questionable sources."[11]

Attacking this problem directly, the new American managers quickly doubled the capacity of the pumps. By that time, however, the use of water in the city was such that the *depósito* supply was only sufficient for one day's use—leaving everyone vulnerable to any mechanical failure. A further problem was the initial failure to remove amoebic dysentery from the water supply. At least one longtime resident advocated taking wine at meals rather than water in order to avoid "dyspepsia."[12] Many foreigners and other relatively affluent families learned to drink only distilled or boiled water. This was especially true following the onset of a new epidemic of Asiatic cholera in 1902.[13] At least in part, the Chinese population of the city was protected by the practice of drinking hot tea. They also took readily to distilled water. But for provincial migrants and other poor inhabitants boiling drinking water was not an accustomed behavior, and this was reflected in urban morbidity and mortality rates. Ulcerated colons and, in severe cases, liver abscesses were all too common results of amoebic dysentery in drinking water supplies.

The new colonial regime was anxious to tackle big issues and set infrastructure problems right. Further, the cholera experience of 1902 left Americans in the city with an acute sense of vulnerability. With the use of bond issues, a greatly augmented water system and a new sewer system were placed near the head of the list of projects—in both cases because the health implications of not doing so were understood by both the military and the civilian bureaucracies.[14] Further, unlike the imperial British authorities in nineteenth-century Bombay, they made a commitment to serving the entire population, not just themselves.[15] Americans were not separated in a cantonment that could be served separately. As a start, deep "artesian" wells of five hundred to a thousand feet were dug and shallow private wells ordered closed. Where water was available and the wells properly constructed, there was little need for distilled water.[16]

In addition to the immediate relief provided by the deep wells, a new surface water reservoir system commenced operations in 1908. The critical element was the construction of a dam on the Marikina River at Wawa twenty-five miles east of the urban area. This created a less compromised supply than that at Santolan. It was the sort of project at which the new managers excelled. The project overseer was James Case, one of the most competent of the colonial engineers. He was appointed city engineer in 1903 and soon became the chief engineer of city sewer and water construction. Immediately following completion of the dam, Governor-General Forbes made him director of a greatly expanded Bureau of Public Works. In the sort of career that imperial systems offered, Case went on after 1910 to become general manager of the Cuban Construction and Engineering Company, where he was responsible for building Havana's drainage works, and later went to Europe to rebuild war-damaged infrastructure.[17]

Nevertheless, there were also significant problems. The head of the Government Laboratories had warned that the new system must add a filtration facility to remove "animal parasites [amoebas] which are present in the Marikina River," but unfortunately no filtration plant was included. The watershed of the new reservoir was cleared in order to reduce the surface sources of pollution entering the system, and former soldiers were hired to guard it. But the river was subject to some contamination. Still, the reservoir behind the dam provided a cleaner water source for an enlarged piped water system, and its elevation was such that the water traveled by gravity flow rather than having to be pumped. Waterborne disease rates in the city went down as this improved system came online and the clean new wells were opened for free use.[18]

Still, the piped system did not deliver water of ideal quality. The authorities added chlorine—reducing bacterial counts by 70 percent—which was helpful but insufficient. Without effective filtration, amoebas, ciliates, and flagellates were routinely present. Health authorities found it prudent to compel food market stallholders to "sterilize the city water by thoroughly boiling it." Despite these shortcomings, a substantial apparent decline in the death rate in the city in 1913 was attributed primarily to the "decrease in water-borne diseases, owing to the radical improvement in the water supply." At least typhoid was not endemic, and 1912–13 passed without a single reported case of cholera. Still, this was a surface water system; after a heavy rain the bacterial count would greatly increase, and amoebas were always present.[19]

By 1915, growing demand had outstripped the capacity of the system to deliver sufficient water to get the city through the dry season. Water from the upriver reservoir now had to be supplemented with the Santolan pumps on the lower Marikina River. By the 1920s, the piped water system could no longer deliver consistent pressure during April and May, the peak months of the dry season, and from 1921 through 1929 this season became a public health officer's nightmare. Finally, a giant new earthen dam was constructed at Novaliches north of the urban area, and a new reservoir was filled by 1930. The water of this reservoir system was consistently of better sanitary quality than that from Montalban, but water quality really began to achieve universally acceptable standards with the opening of the filters at Balara in what is now Quezon City in 1935.[20] In all, this was a huge achievement first of the colonial engineers and later of Filipino professional leaders.

Sanitary Vegetable Supply

The American colonialists happened to arrive during the great urban public health debates generated by the scientific discoveries concerning the biological causes of spoilage and contamination brought to a head by the "muckrakers" and reformers in American literary and political life. These sorts of concerns were in the minds of colonial bureaucrats, and they informed the policies pursued in Manila. As with health and sanitation in general, Dr. Victor Heiser was the point person first as quarantine officer and then as the director of the Bureau of Health from 1905 until the end of 1914. Orphaned in the infamous Johnstown, Pennsylvania, flood of 1889, Heiser used his inheritance to earn a medical degree. Half finished with his internship, he passed the examination for appointment to the Marine Hospital Service. It was 1898, and his first duty was to treat soldiers returning from tropical service in Cuba and Puerto Rico. He was reassigned to deal with the medical screening of immigrants, was briefly involved in the federal takeover of port quarantine services, and was then posted to Naples, Italy, to advise foreign governments and steamship companies on the screening of emigrants. In

1902, he was sent to the international meetings on tropical medicine in Cairo. Heiser was, in both intellect and experience, one of the few Americans well prepared to serve the imperial enterprise as chief quarantine officer for the Philippine Islands, to which he now proceeded. Despite his autocratic, even militaristic style and his reputation as a skilled intriguer, one is impressed today with the degree of Heiser's professional commitment to high sanitation and inclusive public health goals for the entire society, not just the foreigners as in some other colonial cities.[21]

Against this background, the import trade in vegetables resulted in significant exposure to human disease. Vegetable imports alone were on the order of 1.3 to 3.7 million kilos annually during 1876 and 1894. The great majority of this produce came from the South China coast, and most was landed at Manila after making the short trip from Hong Kong and Amoy. Cantonese were provisioning Manila with fresh vegetables, but they were obtaining most of them from China rather than their extensive suburban gardens.

In the early twentieth century, the new public health authorities in Manila zeroed in on a contaminated food supply as a prominent cause of diarrhea and related diseases, including cholera, and also as a source for the introduction of plague. After news of cholera at Canton in March 1902, for example, Heiser reported that "port authorities at Manila immediately placed an embargo on low-growing vegetables" since "the Chinese were accustomed to sprinkle human excreta in liquid form on growing cabbages."[22] On this occasion, the master of the first ship to be turned back unceremoniously dumped his cargo of vegetables into Manila Bay whence they washed ashore in the poorest seaside neighborhoods.

As part of their sanitation efforts, the new authorities moved to replace most of the former public markets with airy concrete buildings that could be hosed down each day and where vegetables and other perishable foods could be inspected, disinfected, and controlled. An outbreak of cholera in January 1908, for example, led Heiser to temporarily ban the sale of a long list of vegetables, some fruits, numerous locally prepared foods, and all street peddling of food and drink. In the late nineteenth century, individual fruit vendors were a common sight in Manila. But in Heiser's day perishables could be retailed legally only through public markets.

The early gains in public market sanitation were heavily concentrated in Manila.[23] By the 1930s, however, the major public markets were said to be unsanitary and mobbed by flies. The *Critic* pointed out to Mayor Juan Posadas that the public markets of the city needed a "thorough overhauling and cleansing." The next mayor, Eulogio Rodriguez, even announced that cleaning up the public markets was one of his top priorities. The unlicensed, illegal, but convenient street markets known as *talipapas* had reemerged, but still the great majority of perishable vegetables continued to be sold through the system of public markets.

Heiser believed that this was a public health initiative that pleased nearly everyone—one of the few. "The city liked it because of the income, the dealers because of the cheap rents, the housewives because of the wide choice of foods," and the public health authorities because of the enhanced sanitary control. During the worst of the cholera epidemics, the authorities required everyone entering market buildings to disinfect their hands.[24]

Conclusion

The imposition of American imperial rule brought a roughshod urgency to tackle the larger problems of what the Americans saw as "public health." At its best, a small set of public officials was able to make a substantial difference in sanitary regulation, infrastructure development, and the training of Filipinos to participate in and carry on the work. The decision at the outset not to create a segregated American cantonment meant that most of these interventions yielded more or less beneficial results for much of urban society not just or primarily the foreigners. Experience in Manila also yielded benefits for American cities. In particular, Victor Heiser was called on during his Manila service to consult with Seattle and other American ports on the practical public health matter of rat and plague control. And, at the aesthetic level, William E. Parsons brought to California a distinctive Spanish-Philippine-American take on public and residential architecture. In Daniel Burnham's case, what the city structure gained from his cosmopolitan experience and perspective is more readily apparent than what he may have learned and later applied in the United States.

Like Heiser and Parsons, James Case found a great opportunity in the imperial enterprise to gain professional experience by taking on important problems—in his case in engineering and public works. Case moved on within imperial channels first to Havana and then to war-torn France, further applying and developing his skills. Heiser also moved on in the colonial world but in his case through the auspices of the private Rockefeller Foundation.

None of this is said with an eye to defending imperialism, since it has no defense, but is presented to show some of the connections and some of the opportunities for socially useful work, such as solving urban sanitation and provisioning problems. Without such solutions, the megacity that is modern Manila could hardly have emerged.

"The World Was My Garden"
Tropical Botany and Cosmopolitanism in American Science, 1898–1935

STUART McCOOK

IN THE SECOND HALF OF THE NINETEENTH CENTURY, the United States created a large domestic agricultural research infrastructure. Through the Morrill Land-Grant Act (1862), and the Hatch Act (1887), the federal government created and funded a national network of state agricultural colleges and experiment stations. In 1888, the U.S. Department of Agriculture (USDA) established an Office of Experiment Stations (OES) in part to act as a clearinghouse for the research conducted by the state experiment stations. In 1900, the USDA consolidated its extensive agricultural and botanical research divisions into the Bureau of Plant Industry. The U.S. National Herbarium, housed at the Smithsonian Institution, contained one of the continent's largest collections of botanical specimens.[1] Surprisingly, however, before 1898 these public research institutions conducted no significant research on tropical plants even though the United States was by that point one of the world's largest consumers of tropical crops.

This indifference to tropical research came to an abrupt end in 1898 when U.S. imperial expansion—both formal and informal—created a large demand for experts in the study of tropical plants. American officials and business people alike wanted to make sense of the complex and unfamiliar tropical landscapes newly under their control; they also wanted to make these landscapes as productive and profitable as possible. The work of tropical plant scientists in this period, therefore, fell into two major areas. One group of scientists—the botanists—were primarily concerned with collecting, classifying, and mapping tropical plants. Botanists focused mainly on wild plants in their native habitats. The second group—the agricultural scientists—devoted their attention to cultivated plants in agricultural ecosystems. The main purpose of their research was to solve agricultural problems, particularly issues of how to sustain and increase agricultural production.

After 1898, federal research agencies in Washington, D.C.—especially the USDA, the U.S. National Herbarium, and later the National Research Council—developed new research initiatives in tropical botany and agriculture. In addition, the new territories, protectorates, and nations created in the wake of American expansion established agricultural and botanical research centers. Most of these were modeled on the state or federal research centers in the United States. The federal agencies in Washington provided most of the staff for these institutions. American expansion thus created a new career path for American plant scientists. Young graduates from the state agricultural colleges would find work at a government laboratory in Washington. From Washington, they obtained jobs at one of the new research centers in the tropics. Few of them had any experience with tropical botany and agriculture, so they learned on the job. Once they had developed some experience and expertise, many moved to other institutions in the tropics, sometimes with intervals at institutions in the United States. Most ultimately returned to research or teaching positions in the United States after a decade or two in the tropics. These scientists helped consolidate tropical botany and agricultural research at home. American expansion thus transformed the plant sciences in the United States from a nationalist and parochial enterprise into one that was cosmopolitan and global.

Surveying Tropical Flora:
Plant Hunters and Agricultural Explorers

For American scientists, the newly acquired tropical territories were botanically terra incognita. American plant hunters and agricultural explorers began collecting plants across the tropics. Botanical surveys were the botanical counterparts to the censuses and surveys that the U.S. government had conducted in most of its new tropical possessions. They were designed to make unfamiliar tropical plants and landscapes legible and manageable for Americans both for scientific and for commercial purposes. The research also helped translate local vernacular botanical knowledge into more "universal" botanical Latin and English.

In the early decades of the twentieth century, the U.S. government became a leading publisher of both pure and applied botanical research in publications such as *Contributions from the U.S. National Herbarium,* the *USDA Yearbook of Agriculture,* and other USDA bulletins and circulars. Many of the earliest U.S. publications on tropical botany were written by Orator Fuller Cook, one of the few American botanists who had any experience in the tropics before 1898. A graduate of Syracuse University, Cook worked as a special agent for the State Colonization Society in Liberia, from 1891 to 1898, before joining the USDA as a "botanist for tropical agriculture" and later as a "bionomist in charge of acclimatization and adaptation investigations." A prolific researcher and writer, he wrote important botanical studies on the economic plants of the tropics. In one brief period, for example, he produced studies on shade in coffee culture (1901), the economic plants of Puerto Rico (1902), the Central American rubber tree (1903), the food plants of ancient America (1903), cotton culture in Guatemala (1904), and the nomenclature of royal palms (1904).[2]

In addition to narrow studies on particular groups of plants or areas, American botanists also published comprehensive regional floras of the tropical regions where they worked. For example, the botanist E. D. Merrill—an employee of the Philippine Bureau of Agriculture and Forestry and a former USDA agrostologist—published *Flora of Manila* in 1912. It was based in part on his extensive field researches in the Philippine archipelago. It also translated and incorporated the work of naturalists from the Spanish colonial period such as Manuel Blanco's *Flora de Filipinas* (1837).[3] In the Americas, the botanist Paul Standley—a graduate of New Mexico State College and an employee of the U.S. National Herbarium—wrote several important floras for Central America. Between 1909 and 1928, Standley spent much of his time conducting botanical research in Central America, producing many research papers and full floras of the Panama Canal Zone, Panama as a whole, and the Lancetilla Valley, Honduras (home to the United Fruit Company's agricultural research center). Later, after he left the U.S. National Herbarium, he also wrote national floras of Costa Rica and Guatemala. Like Merrill's work in the Philippines, Standley's work in Central America was partly based on extensive original research and partly on a synthesis of the work of earlier researchers.[4]

American botanists in this period were also engaged in plant hunting—exploring the globe for useful plants that could be acclimatized in the continental United States. Scientists at the USDA believed that carefully planned introductions could greatly enhance the United States' agricultural potential. This position was argued most forcefully by David Fairchild who ran the USDA's Office for Seed and Plant Introduction (OSPI) from 1903 to 1928. Fairchild practiced what he preached, and his long tenure at the USDA was interrupted by frequent and lengthy expeditions to the tropics.[5] The OSPI employed many American botanists as agricultural explorers. Perhaps the best-known was Fairchild's fellow-Kansan Wilson Popenoe, who worked for the office as an explorer from 1913 to 1925. In these years, Popenoe traveled to Brazil to study the navel orange, to Florida and Cuba to study the mango, and to Guatemala to study the avocado. Popenoe also made shorter trips to the Pacific, visiting Hawai'i, the Philippines, and several other countries. His job at the Bureau of Plant Industry had, in a few short years, taken him virtually everywhere in the formal and informal American empire in the tropics. Based on this research, Popenoe published the *Manual of Tropical and Subtropical Fruits* in 1920. This book symbolized the new pan-tropical scope of American plant sciences; it transcended any particular country or continent, taking as its subject the entire tropics. This book remained the definitive work on the topic for several decades; it was reissued as late as the 1970s.[6]

In the 1920s, however, ecological cosmopolitanism gradually fell out of favor in the United States as botanical nativists—who sought to preserve the country's native vegetation as much as possible and protect it from "foreign" invaders—gradually gained the upper hand in shaping disease legislation. In 1918, as the nation retreated from its colonial adventures, the USDA passed restrictive regulations for plant quarantines, effectively ending the era of botanical cosmopolitanism in the United States. The importance of acclimatization in botanical research declined sharply. In spite of this, the flow of dried herbarium species continued virtually unabated, and the United States remained an important enter for the description and classification of tropical plants (especially from the neotropics). It consolidated this position during World War I, when exchanges between European herbaria and the tropical world ground to a virtual standstill. While European herbaria did recover after the war, by that point American herbaria had decisively gained the upper hand.[7]

After World War I, as growing botanical nativism limited opportunities for botanical research in the USDA, the National Research Council's Division of Botany and Agriculture assumed a greater role in promoting tropical plant research. In the 1920s, academic biologists in the United States organized the Institute for Research in Tropical America to coordinate the efforts of biologists working on the American tropics. In 1922, the institute's executive committee—which included biologists from Harvard University, the Smithsonian Institution, the New York Academy of Sciences, the Philadelphia Academy of Sciences, and the University of Michigan—decided to organize a research station in Panama.[8] The station was to be managed by the institute and supported by "the museums and colleges of America," which were supposed to collaborate with small grants. The following year, a committee of American scientists convinced the Canal Zone's governor to set aside Barro Colorado Island, "a beautiful area of virgin, tropical rainforest about six miles square . . . as a forest reservation to be used in connection with a biological station." Thomas Barbour, then the curator of reptiles at Harvard's Museum of Comparative Zoology, oversaw the construction work.[9] The entomologist James Zetek, formerly an entomologist with the USDA and the Isthmian Canal Commission, was appointed the laboratory's resident custodian.[10]

The station became a popular summer destination for American academic biologists almost immediately. It helped form and define an American community of academic researchers in tropical biology, including such eminent scientists as David Fairchild (who was still formally attached to the Bureau of Plant Industry), Thomas Barbour, Frank Chapman, and Warder Allee. At Barro Colorado Island American tropical botanists began to move beyond their traditional work of collecting and classifying plants, conducting pioneering work in tropical ecology.[11] While various agencies of the U.S. government provided logistical support and support in kind for the laboratory, the government never made any significant financial contribution to the station's operating expenses. The station's finances—and its very existence—remained precarious until 1946 when it was incorporated into the Smithsonian Institution.

Exporting American Agricultural Research to the Tropics

Besides collecting and acclimatizing tropical plants, Americans also built agricultural research institutions in the tropics. These were often modeled on state and federal agricultural centers in the United States. American agricultural research in the tropics sought to "rationalize" tropical agriculture by applying American ideas and practices to tropical landscapes. Although the process of exporting American models to the tropics was fraught with difficulties, it created a global network of tropical agricultural researchers.

In 1900, the U.S. Congress authorized the establishment of federal experiment stations at Mayagüez in Puerto Rico and near Honolulu in Hawai'i; later it opened research stations in Guam and the U.S. Virgin Islands. The new national government of Cuba and the insular regime in the Philippines also created agricultural research institutions along the American model. In Cuba, the USDA helped organize the Estación Experimental Agronómica near Havana in 1904; its first director was the Louisiana sugarcane researcher Franklin Sumner Earle. The American government in the Philippines established a range of biological, medical, and agricultural research institutions after 1899; in 1905 the government consolidated them into a central Bureau of Science in Manila. In 1909, the government established a Philippine College of Agriculture at Los Baños, staffed entirely by American scientists. Private individuals and groups also sought to bring the purported benefits of American agricultural science to the tropics. The Hawaiian Sugar Planters Association (HSPA)—dominated by planters from the United States—hired its first scientist in 1895. By 1939, the HSPA experiment station had grown to a staff of fifty scientists. Similarly, the Puerto Rico Sugar Planters Association founded an experiment station at Río Piedras in 1910. While the HSPA station prospered, its Puerto Rican counterpart stagnated. In 1914, Puerto Rico's insular government acquired the station and rebaptized it the Insular Experiment Station. In Cuba, the Boston-born sugar planter Edwin F. Atkins established a botanical garden at his sugar mill near Cienfuegos, Cuba, in 1904. Somewhat later, in the 1920s, the Cuba Sugar Club established an agricultural experiment station of its own. American corporations also spread the influence of American agricultural ideals and practices beyond the United States' formal tropical territories and protectorates. In 1930, for example, the United Fruit Company founded a banana research station and botanical garden at Tela, in the Lancetilla Valley of Honduras.[12]

These tropical research institutions opened a new career path for American agricultural scientists, creating a generation of American experts in tropical agriculture. American scientists regularly moved from one part of the tropics to another, between public and private institutions, and between the tropics and the mainland. Most of them, at one point or another, passed through either the USDA or the Smithsonian Institution. The career of the scientist Otis Warren Barrett is a good example of the career trajectories opened by American expansion. After receiving his bachelor's degree from the University of Vermont in 1896, Barrett worked for the West India Improvement Company and the Mexican Comisión Geográfico-Exploradora. He then moved to the federal experiment station at Mayagüez in Puerto Rico, after which he worked as a "plant introducer" for the USDA in Washington, D.C. He left the USDA to become director of agriculture for Mozambique. Later he worked as the chief horticulturalist for the Bureau of Agriculture in the Philippines, as a horticulturist in the Panama Canal Zone, as an agricultural adviser for the Liberian government, as director of agriculture for the Department of Agriculture and Labor in Puerto Rico, and finally as a horticulturalist in Hawai'i.[13] Barrett's career was not unusual; dozens of other American agricultural scientists followed similar paths through the new centers for tropical research. Barrett illustrates the tremendous demand for experts in tropical agriculture across the tropics in the early decades of the twentieth century.

Agricultural research at most of these tropical institutions focused on the main export crops—sugar above all—destined for U.S. markets. At first, the USDA had wanted the experiment stations in Puerto Rico and Hawai'i to promote "democratic farming." In this view, the stations would conduct research that would benefit small farmers and would help diversify the islands' economies while also helping the United States become "self-sufficient" in tropical crops. Both stations conducted extensive work on coffee, pineapples, and other tropical cash crops. None of this research, however, could stem the gradual dominance of sugar on these islands. Most research in tropical agriculture in this period, then, was devoted to making the existing agricultural systems more efficient and productive. Agricultural scientists at these institutions focused on acclimatizing new varieties and hybrids of the main crops from abroad. American scientists and institutions in the tropics began to participate in a global intertropical exchange of seeds and plants. For example, experiment stations in Cuba and Puerto Rico exchanged sugarcane varieties and hybrids with research centers in the Dutch East Indies and with British and French institutions in Asia, Africa, and the Caribbean Basin.

American researchers in the tropics also had to contend with new environmental problems in their tropical crops. Ironically, many of these agricultural problems were the result of the explosive expansion of American demand for tropical commodities, which had led, in turn, to the rapid expansion of crop cultivation and the virtually unrestricted global movement of seeds and plants.[14] Soil scientists confronted the emergent problems of chronic soil exhaustion and soil erosion. Plant pathologists were mobilized to address the growing range of diseases and pests that plagued these crops. In 1903, the coffee rust fungus (*Hemileia vastatrix*) was accidentally taken from Java to Puerto Rico in a shipment of coffee plants. Fortunately, the shipment was inspected by the botanist Otis Barrett—then working at the Mayagüez experiment station—and he recognized the fungus and destroyed the infected plants before the disease could escape into the coffee farms. He narrowly averted a crisis that could have engulfed the hemisphere.[15] Other crop diseases could not be eradicated so easily. The Panama Disease of bananas swept through Central America and the Caribbean during the first two decades of the twentieth century, causing massive losses. American scientists in Cuba, Panama, Puerto Rico, Jamaica, and the USDA in Washington collaborated in identifying the pathogen that caused the disease (*Fusarium oxysporum* f. *cubense*). In 1917, a viral disease of sugar—the *matizado*, or yellow-stripe disease—was accidentally transferred from Java to Puerto Rico and caused losses of up to 100 percent on some Puerto Rican sugar farms. It soon spread to Cuba's vast sugar farms. Again, American scientists working in laboratories and the field in Puerto Rico, Cuba, and Washington, D.C., collectively identified the pathogen and developed means to limit its impact by introducing and breeding disease-resistant hybrids.[16]

The collective efforts to control the Panama Disease and the *matizado* show that, although American tropical researchers worked for a wide range of research institutions in different polities, in practice they functioned as a strikingly cohesive research network. This network was centered at the USDA in Washington, where many researchers had spent at least part of their careers. Key figures at the USDA connected these scientists. Erwin F. Smith acted as mentor to several leading tropical researchers, including John R. Johnston, who later became director of research for the United Fruit Company. The USDA biologist E. W. Brandes conducted critical lab work on banana and sugar diseases at the USDA laboratories in suburban Washington, coordinating his work with American field researchers across the tropics. Most American agricultural researchers in this network had learned about tropical agriculture while working at one or more of the agricultural experiment stations in Cuba or Puerto Rico.

Throughout the 1920s and early 1930s, the National Research Council (NRC) developed several initiatives to organize and institutionalize this network. In 1924, the NRC's Committee on Phytopathology established the Tropical Plant Research Foundation (TPRF). Its goals were explicitly practical. Under the leadership of the plant pathologist William Orton, the TPRF became an intellectual broker, providing American scientific expertise to businesses, organizations, and governments interested in promoting tropical agriculture. The foundation operated a sugar experiment station in Cuba on behalf of the Cuba Sugar Club. It did consulting work for the governments of Peru and Colombia. It also sponsored two monumental research projects, which resulted in the publication of Robert Allison and Hugh Bennett's *The Soils of Cuba* (1928) and Tom Gill's *The Tropical Forests of the Caribbean* (1931). These were both pioneering and innovative works of basic scientific research that were also of immense economic importance. As with the institute on Barro Colorado Island, however, the TPRF's financial support remained uncertain. It depended almost exclusively on contracts and contributions from outside institutions rather than on appropriations from the U.S. government. When global markets for tropical commodities crashed in the late 1920s, these outside organizations curtailed their support for the foundation. Its director, William Orton, died suddenly in 1930, and the foundation declared bankruptcy in 1931.[17]

The NRC's Division of Biology and Agriculture was also involved in organizing a graduate school of tropical agriculture in Puerto Rico. Since the early 1920s, the division had considered establishing such a school "under the stars and stripes" but had made little headway. In 1927, Carlos Chardón—a plant pathologist and director of Puerto Rico's Department of Agriculture—made plans to establish a school in Puerto Rico in collaboration with Cornell University. Cornell would have been responsible for raising most of the operating funds. After an inspection visit, the NRC decided to support the project, concluding that "a Graduate School of Tropical Agriculture in Puerto Rico will make another step toward a Pan-American University in a place of mutual sympathy." Cornell's fund-raising efforts stalled in the aftermath of the 1929 stock market crash, and plans for the graduate school were suspended indefinitely.[18]

Conclusions: Tropical Plants and American Cosmopolitanism

The rapid expansion of American tropical botany had first been sparked by formal imperial expansion—a desire on the part of Americans to understand and manage the new tropical landscapes under their control. Nonetheless, the federal government only provided limited financial and bureaucratic support for this expansion. Federal agencies such as the USDA informally coordinated a network of scientists and an array of territorial and national institutions. Only the federal experiment stations in Hawai'i and Puerto Rico were centrally controlled and financed. The federal government's main role was to mobilize an ad hoc array of private, corporate, and public support in the tropical plant sciences and to provide a central clearinghouse for the research. The expansion of the tropical plant sciences was ultimately financed—directly or indirectly—by growing demand for and rising prices of tropical commodities. When the tropical export booms slowed after World War I and ended during the Great Depression, funding for these institutions was sharply curtailed. Career paths for American researchers in the tropics were also constrained in the face of emergent ecological nativism in the United States, which limited the demand for plant hunters and agricultural explorers. An emergent sense of nationalism in the tropics also began to curtail opportunities for American researchers in the tropics. Research institutions in Cuba, Puerto Rico, and the Philippines began to employ their own nationals wherever they could. As early as 1910, the Cuban government had tried to completely Cubanize the staff of the Estación Experimental Agronómica, although it ultimately relented and allowed some American scientists to continue working there.

Nonetheless, the experience of empire in the early twentieth century had transformed the plant sciences in the United States. Many of the leading American tropical researchers returned to the United States, sometimes entering government service but also engaging in academic and corporate research. For example, when E. D. Merrill left the Philippines in 1923, he worked as director of the California Botanical Garden (1927–29), the New York Botanical Garden (1930–35), and the Arnold Arboretum at Harvard University (beginning in 1935). He played a central role in promoting tropical research at each of these institutions. In 1928, the botanist Paul Standley left the USDA for the Field Museum of Natural History in Chicago; as a result, the systematic botany of the Americas became one of the museum's specialties. After retiring from the USDA, David Fairchild moved to the outskirts of Miami, where with a friend he established a private tropical botanical garden. The Fairchild Tropical Botanic Garden is now a major center for research in tropical botany.[19] Ultimately, the experience of American scientists on the peripheries of empire transformed the institutions of the metropolis. As a result of empire, American botanical and agricultural research became cosmopolitan.

Scientific Superman

Father José Algué, Jesuit Meteorology, and the Philippines under American Rule, 1897–1924

JAMES FRANCIS WARREN

IN NOVEMBER 1898, IN MANILA BAY onboard the bridge of the flagship of the American fleet, the *Olympia*, a carefully arranged meeting between Admiral Dewey and the Jesuit meteorologist Father José Algué was to pave the way for the reorganization of the Manila Weather Observatory under American rule.[1] But this momentous meeting was to do more. Dewey had already demonstrated to the world in stunning fashion that America's most important weapon as an emergent colonial power in the eastern Pacific was its navy. He realized that the potentially devastating consequences of extreme weather in the Asian Pacific Basin was as great a nemesis as the enemy in terms of sending ships, even entire fleets, to the bottom of the sea in cyclonic storms. With this in mind, admirals of the American fleet stationed in Manila Bay had already visited the Manila Observatory and were enormously impressed by its meteorological and scientific work. The admirals recognized in Algué's character and intellect a "scientific superman" and a skillful, articulate, Spanish Jesuit administrator. The November meeting between Dewey and Algué resulted in a marriage between Jesuit science and American imperialism with powerful implications for both partners.

Algué's extraordinary, pioneering scientific account of the climate and storms of the Philippines, *Baguios ó ciclones filipinos: Estudio teórico-práctico* (Baguios or Filipino Cyclones: A Study in Theory and Practice), published the year before, "took a prominent place in the literature on cyclonology" and was a volume much prized by navigators.[2] A revised and expanded English edition of this special report was published in 1904 as *Cyclones of the Far East*. Also in 1897, Father Algué had given the public his barocyclonometer—an improvement on Father Faura's invention—by means of which storms could be foretold not only in the Philippines but throughout the entire Orient.[3]

The United States recognized that supporting Algué's work was a pragmatic policy that could help establish America's future success as a colonial power in the Philippines.[4] The greatest impetus to this development occurred when Dean Worcester and Charles Denby, two members of the Schurmann Commission, appointed in January 1899, initiated arrangements for the establishment of an independent Philippine weather service patterned after that of the United States. These commissioners recommended Algué as director, and the existing Manila Observatory House was to become the central office of the Weather Bureau. Algué was asked to draft a plan for a weather service in the Philippines and on May 22, 1901, with new equipment supplied from America, he was able to reorganize the Observatorio to encompass the Weather Bureau.[5]

In 1897, Algué had succeeded Father Federico Faura, the founder of the Manila Observatory, as director of the Jesuit institution.[6] A Spanish-born Jesuit, Algué had been sent to Washington by the order to train for this leadership position, and that cultural encounter and experience prepared him to direct the observatory during the difficult period of the changeover from Spanish to U.S. sovereignty, at which time he "won the respect of Filipinos, Spaniards and Americans." Through his handling of the negotiations he was able to effect the transfer of the observatory from Spanish to American administration without the loss of a single day's pay for his employees.[7]

After the administrative transfer there was practically no change in personnel with the exception of the gradual introduction of English-speaking staff as several American-trained Jesuits arrived from the United States. The American officials recognized that the newly constituted Weather Bureau was unique because the majority of its officers and employees were Filipino. These employees included first-, second-, third-, and fourth-class observers, calculators, clerks, draftsmen, and the highly skilled mechanics who repaired and constructed the numerous precision instruments used by the bureau.[8] Many had been recruited, trained, and assigned to postings throughout the archipelago where they were authorized to make synchronous weather predictions for their areas and to telegraph local conditions to the Manila office. Under Algué's able leadership, as telegraph and cable lines were extended throughout the archipelago, the scale of service and efficiency of the newly constituted Philippine Weather Bureau increased.

The rapid increase in real-time teletechnologies must be understood as a technological development in the name of imperialism. It had particular significance for communication, commerce, and meteorological science, which, in turn, had a profound effect on the production of colonial subjects and the creation of regional networks for the circulation of scientific knowledge.

As a successor to the Spanish colonial empire, where decision making had been hidebound in conventions associated with the Crown and the Catholic Church, the American colonial state showed itself to be an adaptable hybrid political order that appropriated diverse influences in its agile transnational movement to advance and transform the imperialist cause.

Algué and American Colonialism

In the second half of 1898, the Spanish Jesuits pragmatically switched allegiances to serve a new colonial master. Washington, rather than Madrid or Rome, was now the focus of their thoughts and actions. The U.S. Departments of War and Agriculture realized from the very moment of the annexation of the Philippines in 1899 that more accurate weather and storm forecasting would have a tremendous impact on the economic and social systems of the archipelago. An adverse climatic event—typhoon, flood, or drought—could jeopardize commodity prices for rice, sugar, tobacco, and abaca within the world capitalist system.[9]

The government's wholesale appropriation of Jesuit meteorological technologies and science was proclaimed as a significant leap forward in the field of weather prediction—a panacea to solve all the problems facing the colony. In this context, the reorganization of the Observatorio, and the birth of modern meteorology in the Philippines, sprang not only from the violence of the American annexation and a collaborative Jesuit science but also from the modernizing impulse of its indigenous elite leaders, who, by the end of the first decade of the twentieth century, were also collaborating with the United States.[10] This symbiotic regime of thought and action was fostered by the profits to be made from the predictive value of meteorological science, as well as by a colonial rhetoric about progress, development, scientific thinking, and taming the weather.[11] In an imperial and technocratic age, the Jesuits' rational explanations of meteorological calamities found a receptive audience as events once viewed as acts of divine retribution were subsumed into a more readily comprehensible realm of natural systems and forces.

While the professed objective of Algué's scientific weather research was human welfare, the Jesuit practice of modern meteorology both reinforced and upheld a colonial economic system based on exploitation, profit maximization, and accumulation.[12] So much so that the insular government quickly reported, in 1901, that the Manila Weather Bureau had continued its vigilant work on behalf of agriculture and commerce.[13] At the beginning of the twentieth century, Algué's scientific authority and control of the Manila Observatory were recognized globally, and justified locally, as the Jesuits continued their world class research, observations, and experiments, providing weather forecasting services and helping to set up a regionwide storm-warning network. American colonial rule would provide Algué with a political and financial charter for the rapid development of the science of meteorology. As the transformed Philippine Weather Bureau grew in size and stature so, too, did the worldwide reputation of Algué.[14]

Saint Louis World's Fair

Algué's role as a leading authority in his field reached its symbolic culmination at the Saint Louis World's Fair of 1904. The international exhibition and trade fair provided the Jesuit with the unique opportunity to prepare an exhibit of sweeping scope about the work of the new Weather Bureau in the Philippines and its spectacular technology. From November 20, 1903, to August 2, 1904, Algué was in the United States engaged in the preparation of the Weather Bureau exhibit.[15] The event may be seen as both defining and announcing the relationship between colonial meteorological science and "what it meant to be an American at the beginning of the twentieth century."[16]

The 1904 fair introduced American fairgoers to both the marvels of early-twentieth-century architecture and technology and to other peoples and places. The size and geographical location of the Philippines was of great commercial and strategic importance to the United States because of its geographical position in relation to China, and the development of Philippine trade, agriculture, and industry under the auspices of the Bureau of Insular Affairs was a matter of significant interest in Saint Louis at the close of 1903.[17] For nearly a year, an exposition board of the insular government endeavored to ensure that the Philippine exhibit would give the general public an idea of the value and importance of America's "insular possessions in the Orient" in relation to products, manufactures, art, and ethnology.[18] Viewed in combination with a related attraction—a Philippine "reservation" with more than eleven hundred Filipinos on display—the Weather Bureau exhibit showcased the "civilizing" and "modernizing" effects of American rule in the islands. In keeping with the goals of the exhibition as a whole, the Philippine section reinforced the opposition between past and future, primitive and modern, savage and civilized. Through these dichotomies, the two attractions effectively rationalized the U.S. occupation of the archipelago in the name of progress.

The exhibit of the Jesuit Weather Bureau consisted of three sections: a map; a building, and two towers. The first of these, a huge relief map of the Philippines, highlighted the geographical proximity of the islands to Japan, China, Borneo, and Celebes so that fairgoers would have a clear idea of the relationship between the archipelago and the "civilized and uncivilized" peoples surrounding it. The second section consisted of a building, on the roof of which various meteorological instruments were installed. Inside the building, the geographical, seismic, and meteorological exhibits represented the discrete scientific divisions within the Manila Observatory. The geographical section gave information on the religious and political variances of the archipelago, the regions inhabited by different ethnic and tribal groups, and the distribution of rainfall at certain times of the year. The individual seismic and meteorological exhibits included precision instruments used by the Jesuits to pioneer the new predictive science of meteorology.

The third section consisted of two thirty-meter-high galvanized steel towers, which flanked the front of the building. Wires, which served as antennae for the ceraunograph, were stretched between the tops of these towers.[19] Both the interior and exterior of the Philippine exhibit were brilliantly lit against the evening skyline of Saint Louis.

No other exhibit was so widely commented on in the press as the Philippine Islands Exposition. Virtually everybody who went to the fair visited the insular exhibit and, of course, the Weather Station and the "Filipine" village. They came away self-assured, full of wonder, and with new ideas regarding their recently acquired island possessions and their government's policy with regard to the future development and welfare of the Filipinos and the archipelago.[20] Juxtaposed with the "savage" and "primitive" tribes on display in the model Filipino village, the Weather Bureau exhibit impressed visitors with the meliorating role of modern science placed in the seemingly benign service of empire.

Algué's Master Plan

On his return to Manila from St. Louis in August 1904, Algué got down to business straightaway. A science based on a network of observation stations linked by cable and wireless that would be able to describe distinct meteorological patterns in space and time had first been proposed in 1901 by Algué to William Howard Taft, the civil governor of the Philippines. It was the construction of these weather stations throughout Luzon and the Visayas to which Algué turned his attention on his return from St Louis so that a continuous flow of information on climatic conditions could be achieved to better gain an understanding of the relationship between large- and medium-scale weather patterns. With new equipment sent from the United States, a network of new stations was developed on Mindanao, Cebu, Leyte, Panay, and various sites on Luzon.[21]

Systematic reporting of rainfall and temperature was a central goal of the newly reorganized meteorological service. The prosperity of the entire archipelago and its various agricultural industries—rice, sugar, tobacco, coconuts, and abaca—was bound up with the amount of rain and its seasonal distribution and timely fall. As such, the impact of short-term climatic variations on key rain-fed export commodities and major food crops was of extreme importance. Algué's reorganization plan, which included storm observation, typhoon forecasting, and increasing the number of rain-reporting stations, was both scientifically valid and economically sound for developing effective strategies to cope with climatic variability. Even so, the task of the pioneering Jesuit weather forecasters was formidable due to the lack of observation posts and the complicated local conditions during certain times of the year.[22]

There was an obvious necessity for a meteorological service that could predict weather on the basis of data sent simultaneously by telegraph at set hours every day in order to compile a daily weather map.[23] The Philippine Commission had provided for the establishment of a widespread network of seventy-two weather stations, and the number was to be increased at Algué's behest. Under his leadership telegraph and cable lines were extended to the principal islands of the archipelago and also to the Caroline Islands and the Marianas, and this extended Philippine meteorological service was totally dependent on the Central Observatory of Manila.

Algué divided the archipelago into four meteorological zones, two in the northern part and the other two in the central region. Initially, the plan called for the establishment of nine first-class stations, twenty-five second-class stations, seventeen third-class stations, and twenty rain stations, which were to cover the entire archipelago.[24] Algué also designated the instruments with which these stations would have to be provided according to the category of the station. By August 1905, the meteorological stations of the Philippine Weather Bureau were of two sorts—official and voluntary. The former were staffed by paid observers, the others by volunteers—usually officials of the insular government or the U.S. Army—who were lent meteorological instruments on the express condition that the Weather Bureau in Manila be furnished with a copy of their daily observations.[25]

In the Philippines, which soon had more than seventy well-equipped observation posts, barefoot weather observers abounded. Algué's "mass efforts" in archipelago-wide weather forecasting involved a handful of typhoon professionals, the Jesuit meteorologists, and scores of rural people trained by the Weather Bureau. Many of these unsung weather observers completed decades of outstanding work in meteorological observation based on accurate local knowledge, legible recording of the climate and weather, and care of equipment. The firsthand experience that came with years of observation and training was especially necessary in the typhoon-prone regions of the Philippines. It was often the case that from the time the Weather Bureau issued the first warning, the chief forecaster and the observers at their stations were forced to remain on duty for ten to fourteen hours per day for three to four days in succession.[26] Yet the job of the weather observer also offered deep personal satisfaction because to warn the public of the existence of an impending typhoon was *pro bono publico*—humanitarian in the best sense of the word. In areas vulnerable to storms, long hours, hard work, and extraordinary effort were sometimes required to save instruments from damage in the face of cyclonic conditions. Tilted, snapped, or flattened power and telephone posts or lines were common after the passage of a typhoon and caused the loss of electricity and communication for weeks or even months at a time.

Manufacturers of meteorological instruments such as rain gauges and the Dines tube anemometer, quickly realized the importance of manufacturing sturdy recording instruments as many high wind velocities had failed to be recorded because of the destruction of the apparatus in a remarkable typhoon. By the 1930s, new anemographs were built for the Manila Observatory that had a scale above the limits of any typhoon wind that was likely to blow over Manila. Equally important, the outdoor attachments of the instruments were also being built to withstand the most severe impacts of wind and rain.[27]

Cable and Wireless Communication

The cable and wireless communication between the islands that facilitated the reporting of the paid and voluntary observers had been planned by the U.S. government and Algué on a widespread scale, and new cables had been rapidly laid. Manila was quickly connected with Iloilo, Cebu, and other points in the Visayan Islands while the archipelago itself was connected with the Asian mainland, Europe, and America by a cable running from Manila to Hong Kong.[28] Teletechnology, in singling out those places to be admitted to the weather and communication network, played an important role in their futures.

Although the telegraph lines, trunk lines, and telegraph facilities erected during the Spanish period had practically disappeared during the Philippine-American War, by the end of the war they were already being reconstructed on a permanent basis; their locations were changed and some new ones were established.[29] However, repeated destruction of telegraph lines during the typhoon season caused problems for the bureau, and therefore the question of effective inter-island communication by means of wireless telegraphy caught the attention of both the Jesuit meteorologists and the insular authorities right from the start of the American occupation.

Algué recognized that the establishment of three wireless telegraph stations in the northern half of Luzon—at Baguio, Santa Domingo de Basco (Batanes Islands), and Manila—would be of great importance, for they would be able to send storm warnings to vessels in the China Sea and to Hong Kong and other stations on the neighboring coasts of Asia. Because the Batanes Islands lay directly in the track of many typhoons that formed to the east and south of the Philippines, weather information recorded by observers and transmitted promptly to Manila was essential. Algué stressed to the American authorities that such a station would also enable officials of the remote province to keep in close touch with the insular government, particularly in times of calamity—an impossibility without wireless.[30]

Cables, too, were an indispensable part of both the new colonial meteorology and the new imperialism. Cables helped to tie America's new island possession together in real time, and they became the lifeline of an ever-increasing flow of weather observations, typhoon warnings, and business communications that bound the United States to its colony across the Pacific. Guam's isolated location in the mid-Pacific was to prove ideal for the establishment of a new cable-relay station for typhoon forecasting and for sending market news and top secret information. Between 1902 and 1903, Algué took steps to establish a meteorological cable-wireless station on Guam.[31] The French scientific periodical *Cosmos*, noting the advantages to be derived for colonial meteorology from stations established on islands such as Guam, stressed the "completeness with which the Asiatic continent, from Cape St. James to the mouth of the Amur River, is safeguarded against surprises thanks to the meteorological services of Japan and the Philippines."[32]

By the end of 1923, there were 159 official weather stations: 7 first-class stations, including the branch observatory at Mirador, Baguio; 12 second-class stations; 30 third-class stations; and 110 rain stations.[33] There were also 90 volunteer stations by 1925. This figure, added to the 159 official meteorological stations and the two seismic and magnetic stations, where rainfall observations were also taken, made a total of 252 meteorological stations reporting daily and monthly rainfall returns for climatological and economic purposes and data to assist in typhoon forecasting.[34] As the agricultural commodity market boomed with the cessation of World War I, Algué hastened to assign trained observers to analyze local data for places and regions not previously covered. The Weather Bureau concentrated its efforts in northern and central Luzon and the Visayas and virtually completed Algué's scheme of providing the capital of every province with adequate technology and know-how to receive typhoon warnings.

By 1926, typhoon warnings were being sent regularly not only to all the Weather Bureau's first-, second-, and third-class observers throughout the Philippines but also to the naval stations at Cavite and Olongapo, the quarantine station in Mariveles, the artillery engineer in Corregidor, the surveyor of the Bureau of Customs in Manila, the superintendent of the Telegraph Division of the Bureau of Ports, Fort Santiago, and the Manila Railroad Company. In the case of extremely dangerous typhoons, warnings were also sent to the governors of the provinces where there was no established meteorological station. Regular typhoon warnings were also sent to parts of Asia beyond the Philippines: to the observatories of Tokyo, Shanghai, Taihoku, and Phulien, as well as to the American consul at Hong Kong. This regional approach of telegraphing information on impending storms to typhoon-prone countries helped establish Algué's preeminent position within meteorological circles in Asia which, at the same time, provided a greater sense of security to shipping and business circles from Singapore to Yokohama.

Thus, the Jesuit meteorologists, while helpless in the face of the damage typhoons caused to landline communication, nevertheless managed to bring about a unification of hours for the exchange of telegraphic advice relative to storm conditions within the islands and among Japan, Formosa, the Philippines, Indochina, and China—a technological advance that greatly facilitated public warnings and the making of serviceable weather maps.

Shared real-time data were to prove critical in identifying, understanding, and attempting to manage the complex environmental and social problems that faced Philippine society in times of calamity. Daily weather maps and charts proved indispensable for Jesuit meteorologists concerned with storm modeling. Most of the typhoons occurred in a belt that extended from the Marianas and Caroline Islands across the western Pacific and through the Philippines to the East Asian rim stretching from central Vietnam north along the coast of China. For the first time, a teleconnected network of meteorological observatories could simultaneously report, map, and transmit data on the track and intensity of an impending typhoon because the storm event had been identified with a distant early warning. As the Philippine Islands and neighboring colonies and nations entered a period of unprecedented economic growth and environmental change—induced by the exploitation of natural resources and rapid growth of the human population—the development of scientifically based weather maps was to play a leading role in managing the environment, trade, and strategic interests of the region.

The Manila Observatory

For a period of almost six decades the Manila Observatory remained, on a daily basis, a critical site and focus of stereoscopy, the simultaneity of virtual and real environments. It was also to remain the site of a multidisciplinary regional discourse about climate, weather, and scientific agriculture.[35] In the early decades of the twentieth century, day-to-day activity and Weather Bureau policy were bounded by two global networks—the geopolitical and the electromagnetic. The documents tell us that Algué and his staff spent much of their daily lives suspended between these two networks precisely because of the ubiquitous nature of typhoons and dangerous storms. The Jesuits fully understood the significance of the electromagnetic realm for weather prediction even as they recognized the fundamental role of geopolitical networks in influencing the fate of the colony.

In 1907, the weather map, based on electronically transmitted data, was introduced and soon proved useful in both daily forecasting and typhoon warnings.[36] Based on daily meteorological registries from China, Japan, the secondary stations of Luzon, and points further south, the Weather Bureau created a detailed weather map. Studying this map, the bureau then issued a report forecasting the weather for the next twenty-four hours.[37] This report was published in the newspaper of the capital and telegraphed to the port of Manila and the naval station at Cavite. The daily maximum and minimum temperatures were also sent to the newspaper. The captain of the Port of Manila and the chiefs of the squadron received a report via telegraph twice a day—at 10:00 a.m. and 4:00 p.m.—of the observations made of atmospheric pressure, temperature, direction and force of the wind, and state of the weather. Likewise, at 10:00 a.m. and 4:00 p.m. the same observations were transmitted to the most important stations on the coasts of China and Japan.[38]

During the typhoon season, daily weather maps were covered with isobars (lines drawn through places of equal pressure)—each whorl labeled with a date or name. As all the weather observations over a given area were plotted on the map, the Jesuit meteorologists analyzed every detail. Various types of lines such as isobars, isotherms (lines drawn through places of equal temperature), and isotachs (lines drawn through places of equal wind speed) were drawn on the weather map using different colors for each set of lines. On these weather maps a typhoon or storm was signified as a number of closed concentric lines, the outermost ones oval shaped and becoming more and more circular toward the centre of the disturbance—the vortex or eye of the storm. As each of the isobars approached the center their value in atmospheric pressure diminished, ultimately becoming zero.[39] The typhoons of the Asian Pacific Basin had been categorized into eleven types by Algué with graphic representations of the trajectory, veering, and intensity of the wind represented by means of arrows on the various weather maps and storm charts. The Jesuit storm forecasters, with the aid of simple devices such as the compass and slide rule, developed an acute sense of judgment in preparing the daily weather map.

The accuracy of this information, though primarily for the benefit of the Philippine Islands, proved of inestimable value to shipping from Singapore to Yokohama, from which places telegrams from captains of vessels were often received, asking for information about the chance of running into a typhoon in the course of their outward passage.[40] And up-to-date information on the approach of typhoons and storms was routinely telegraphed from Manila to Hong Kong, Macao, Saigon, Shanghai, and Tokyo during the typhoon season to help alleviate general uncertainty and foster public awareness of the impending arrival of a typhoon.

The Jesuit meteorological team under Algué's leadership and the administration of the insular government worked together as never before to demystify typhoons. By recording the weather on a day-to-day basis and comparing it year in and year out the Jesuits had begun to clarify the origin, structure, and movement of typhoons while a growing number of Filipinos grew to believe that destructive typhoons and storms were no longer simply a sign of the wrath of God—a punishment meted out through divine intervention.

For American colonial administrators and scientists the actual work of the modern observatory was impressive. The Manila-centered, teleconnected, meteorological network projected a daily image to American politicians and the public at large of the Jesuits scientifically ordering the geographies and cultures of an archipelago considered inherently disordered and violent.[41] The Weather Bureau under Algué became the domain in which scientific knowledge and power intersected in a politically charged colonial, hierarchical world that valued science in the service of agriculture, commerce, public safety, and global stability.[42]

Conclusion

The invitations to international expositions and scientific congresses within the context of the day-to-day activity of the Manila Observatory highlighted the growing importance of the Jesuit meteorologists in the development of modern meteorological science and American colonization. But none of the accolades would have been possible without the contribution of the more than fifty trained Filipino staff members of the Weather Bureau, most of whom remained loyal to the service until separated by death or old age. Furthermore, the telegraph operators were of immense importance for the part they played in helping the meteorologists provide accurate weather forecasts and for the continued Jesuit domination of the island's weather scene.

As far as Algué was concerned, the decade following the publication of his classic work on cyclonic storms in 1897 proved remarkable. He reorganized the Manila Observatory and created the Weather Bureau (1901). He established and administered the meteorological exhibit at the St. Louis World's Fair (1903–4) and presented papers at major conferences in Spain (1897), Russia (1899), and Austria (1905). In the course of this scientific globetrotting, Algué rubbed shoulders with the president of the United States and leading American officials, politicians, and tycoons. He also made the personal acquaintance of other Jesuit directors of meteorological services and leading research scientists in the field of meteorology from around the world. To top it off, he was elected an honorary member of the Royal Meteorological Society (London) at a meeting held on January 17, 1906.

The Philippine National Weather Bureau had its origins in the history of the Philippine Revolution and the United States coming of age as a colonial power in the Spanish-American War of 1898. When the Philippine Revolution was transformed into the Philippine-American War a new weather agency was born: a Spanish, Jesuit-inspired, American-supported institution that would dramatically affect the daily lives of the newly colonized subjects of the United States through its innovative scientific model and practice, weather forecasts, and storm warnings. Retained by the United States on short notice, the skillful, articulate Algué would pave the way for the reorganization of the Manila Observatory under new colonial masters. The range of activities performed by the Weather Bureau was perceived by the United States government to be of great importance to the agricultural and economic development of the Philippines. The birth and development of Jesuit meteorology, as practiced in Manila, was considered one of the cutting-edge interdisciplinary models of scientific endeavor that held the key to addressing many of the problems facing the country's future commercial and agricultural progress.

Algué was a scientist who chose to see meteorology as the responsibility of the colonial state. At the same time, he realized that it was a science inextricably tied to colonial politics and practice. His personal drive and extraordinary talent were crucial in building meteorological science as a major source of justification for the Philippines' economic development as well as for its continued political dominance by the United States. One early observer was quick to note the central role played by Algué with respect to the United States' newfound civilizing mission and scientific influence in the islands, writing, "Science and the Philippines have not been acquaintances very long, but there was one scientific man here on our arrival who has remained in our service. He is at the head of the Weather Bureau, and we cannot find his equal. . . . Father Algué . . . has [been] kept on under our administration and is one of the great scientists of the world."[43]

PART 9

The Elusive Character of American Global Power

Battleship USS *Missouri* in the Miraflores Locks, Panama Canal, en route from the Pacific to New York City, October 13, 1945. (U.S. National Archives)

The Limits of American Empire
Democracy and Militarism in the Twentieth and Twenty-first Centuries

JEREMI SURI

DEBATES ABOUT EMPIRE HAVE A DEFINITE PLACE in American history, but where? What do we gain—conceptually and empirically—by calling the United States an empire? The contributors to this groundbreaking collection of essays interrogate the "capillaries"—and sometimes arms and legs—of American expansion in the Caribbean and the Pacific during the early twentieth century. The essays point to the transformative effect that the experience of American overseas warfare, occupation, and control had on institutions such as the U.S. Army, the U.S. National Guard, philanthropic foundations, public health organizations, and even consumer groups. The editors of the collection describe the "elusive, even paradoxical" quality of these intersections between the foreign and the domestic, the "insiders" and the "outsiders," the empowered and the dispossessed. They analyze how American activities in the Caribbean and the Pacific changed conceptions of race, culture, and authority at home, as well as abroad. All of these "catalytic" relationships comprise what the editors provocatively call the making of "a unique American imperial state"—one that has implicitly endured into the twenty-first century.

There is surely some truth to these claims. The careers of figures such as John Hay, Theodore Roosevelt, and Elihu Root in the early twentieth century—as well as Dean Acheson, Henry Kissinger, and Condoleezza Rice decades later—highlight how the conduct of American foreign policy provided a platform for the mobilization and centralization of enormous power within particular crevices of American society. The careers of Roosevelt and Root, like those of Kissinger and Rice, are unthinkable without an expanding transnational American polity at the time. The power exercised by these figures was global in scope but personalized in practice.[1]

Roosevelt, Root, and their contemporaries carried a "big stick" overseas, as all of these essays show, but were they imperial consuls? Did they really rule or even manage an empire? Most significant, did their redefinitions of American power create a political system keyed to the exploitation of foreign societies?

I am skeptical about the "empire" label because I believe it obfuscates more than it explains. It asserts a core American similarity with historical empires that overrides too many fundamental differences. The scholars in this volume are appropriately energized by their desire to escape the frequent provincialism of scholarship on U.S. history, but they are also too quick to jump to judgment about the transformations in the American state. As I will describe below, the United States that emerged from the transformations of the early twentieth century was *both* more democratic and more militaristic—more committed to anti-imperial ideas and expansive in its reach than ever before. This explains how figures such as Roosevelt and Root could advocate sincerely for foreign wars of self-government and development. They were acting on behalf of American self-interest but also in pursuit of a strong image of anti-empire—a world of free societies associated with the United States. This image constrained American actions, prohibiting the creation of any serious high-level "colonial office" in the U.S. government. This image also constrained American debate, prohibiting any serious advocacy of a permanent American empire, especially after World War I.

If we collapse the complicated politics of the early twentieth century into a catchall empire label, we will lose the significance and enduring influence of the anti-empire thinking about democracy and war that guided the American state through this period and later decades. Anti-empire rhetoric and imaginations structured political debate within the United Sates, and they influenced how Americans acted abroad. For just one example, take the Open Door policy of 1899 and 1900 described in Thomas McCormick's excellent essay in this volume. American leaders asserted a right to trade and invest in Asia through this policy, but they also explicitly renounced the division of China or other regions of the continent into separate imperial spheres of interest—the policy pursued by the European and Japanese empires in the region. The American position on the open door matched American claims to freedom and opposition to empire. In place of empire, as traditionally constituted, a diverse range of American figures chose guaranteed access but not direct control.

Some continue to call this empire, but I do not think that helps very much. American policy, as William Appleman Williams explained, aimed to serve anti-imperial purposes.[2] Figures such as Hay, Roosevelt, and Root conceptualized it as an alternative to empire or isolation. That was not mere propaganda. Americans acted as expansionists but also serious reformers. The Open Door was an effort to reform the European and Japanese empires and also alleviate Chinese "backwardness." Those who encountered Americans in places such as China, the

Philippines, Cuba, and Puerto Rico often saw things differently, and that is the point of this volume. The dynamic and sometimes violent clash of perspectives that these encounters elicited transcends the assumptions of oppression and exploitation inscribed in any basic definition of *empire*.

To avoid the label empire is not to deny the growing presence of American influence and control in the Caribbean and Pacific, as well as in other regions. The essays in this volume offer unmistakable empirical evidence for that. Beyond this band of islands in the Caribbean and Pacific where Washington acted as a colonial power, the term *empire* cannot capture the complexities of American influence in a wider global arena encompassing China, Europe, and the Middle East, as well as other regions. American influence manifested itself in very diverse and contradictory ways across different terrains.

The shortcoming of the collected essays is conceptual. If U.S. historians neglect the depth and complexity of American interactions with other societies, the mostly non-American historians in this volume oversimplify the ambivalent and very tenuous quality of the foreign policy that emanated from Washington. We need a richer and more multivocal history of America's growing international presence at the start of the twentieth century. *Empire*, unfortunately, curtails more discussion than it enables. We need to escape old labels and focus on the richer and more complicated intersections of ideas, identities, and policies in the making of the twentieth-century world system.

Despite the claims of the contributors to this volume, many influential foreign policy figures in the United States have lamented the nation's penchant for excessive idealism, not imperialism. Henry Kissinger most famously criticized American policy makers from Woodrow Wilson to Lyndon Johnson, for articulating a vision of global change that simultaneously overextended the nation's resources and diminished its ability to act with subtlety, playing friend and foe against one another. The United States was, according to Kissinger, a "power favored by geography" and "great material superiority," but it failed to "couple the prudence, calculation, and skill of a government of experts with an act of imagination that encompasses the opportunities before us."[3] Americans threw their weight around, but they did not build a functioning empire like their predecessors in Great Britain, France, and Spain did. Quite the contrary, the mix of democracy and militarism in American history means that Washington acted in spurts of energy, oscillating between extreme engagement with particular regions and general neglect.

As its power grew, the United States pursued contradictory democratic and militaristic impulses, the combination of which limited the reality of empire. From the late nineteenth century to the end of the twentieth, Washington deployed military and nonmilitary agents around the globe—as many of the essays in this volume show—but these agents rarely had consistent control over policy.

Even such powerful figures as Hay and Root in the early twentieth century (and Acheson and Kissinger in later decades) were episodic in their influence, limited in their leverage over what was far less than an "imperial state." The essays in this volume could have grappled more seriously with the complexities of U.S. global influence, perhaps moving beyond the limiting concept of empire to craft a more flexible framework. American society promoted many complex and contradictory discourses reinforced by the experience of commerce and warfare overseas. The United States was much more than an empire and also much less.

The United States as a Revolutionary Power

Alexis de Tocqueville was certainly correct when he recognized in Jacksonian America a set of democratic institutions and habits that would eventually revolutionize the conduct of politics across the globe. Tocqueville, like many later observers, was struck by the pervasive and deep attachment to personal liberty exhibited by white American males during his visit to the "New World." The strong American emphasis on liberty created a presumption against inherited aristocracy, centralized institutions, and, most significant, restrictions on individual enterprise. African Americans, Native Americans, women, and many other groups were brutally excluded from this constellation of values, but Tocqueville had the prescience to recognize that these exclusions would not stand the test of time.[4] In the words of the historian Bernard Bailyn, the "contagion of liberty" would, despite significant resistance, extend the basic core beliefs of American democracy to a wider population.[5]

This wider population included those, like Tocqueville, living in societies far from the United States. As contacts with Europe, Latin America, Asia, and Africa grew in the late nineteenth century, American assumptions about democracy accompanied merchants, missionaries, and military men on their voyages overseas. American relations with China between 1876 and 1911 are a case in point. During this period businesses (e.g., the Singer Sewing Machine Company), religious zealots (e.g., the American Home Missionary Society), and armed forces (e.g., the American marines deployed as part of the international response to the Boxer Rebellion in 1900) worked hard to increase the influence of the United States in what many vaunted as the lucrative "China market."[6] Unlike the other powers vying for their share of riches in this area—Great Britain, Japan, France, and Russia—Americans invested more than any of their counterparts in efforts that would help the Chinese empire transform itself into a developed democratic polity. These "nation-building" endeavors (to use a late-twentieth-century term) included the construction of universities and hospitals, the creation of Western-style law, and diplomatic activity to assure the sovereignty of the Chinese state.[7]

Americans profited greatly from their growing influence in China, and they acted as imperialists in their disregard for many local customs and traditions.

Nonetheless, American imperialism was clearly distinguished in the eyes of Chinese leaders such as Li Hongzhang from the less idealistic and more rapacious behavior of other major states.[8] Li went so far as to encourage greater American activity in China as a source of domestic development and protection from other imperialists. For Li and his modernizing counterparts, the United States was a positive revolutionary force. Its ideas and actions promised a democratic alternative to aristocratic decadence. This perception carried through to the end of World War I when students protested throughout China for the implementation of Woodrow Wilson's "Fourteen Points." Young Chinese revolutionaries of all varieties adopted American ideas about self-determination and individual rights in the early twentieth century.[9]

The nature of American foreign interventions surely grew in scale and scope after the experience in late-nineteenth- and early-twentieth-century China. Many of the patterns, however, remained essentially unchanged. In Asia, as on other continents, American merchants, missionaries, and military men acted as revolutionary imperialists. Their actions liberated domestic modernizers and crippled inherited elites. This was even true in cases in which the United States worked with dictators such as Chiang Kai-shek and the Chinese Guomindang regime. For purposes of expediency, Washington often allied itself with antidemocratic "strongmen," but the presence of American institutions and ideas inevitably contributed to domestic resistance against these leaders. Asian communists such as Mao Zedong and Ho Chi Minh recognized the powerful appeal of American ideals and used them to support their own revolutionary movements. Ho, most famously, quoted from the American Declaration of Independence when he declared Vietnamese independence from colonial exploitation in September 1945.[10]

This pattern continues today. The United States might ally itself formally with the degenerate royal family that rules Saudi Arabia, but images (and sounds) of American freedom inspire resistance among local businesspeople, youths, and especially women. This is not to say that Saudi, Iranian, and Egyptian citizens are becoming American in their ways of life. Foreign ideological penetration produces much more complicated results. American democratic influence occurs at a discursive level that does not eliminate traditions but transforms the expression of inherited ideas. Recipients of American influence have access to a language of individualism, initiative, and progress that they can call on, consciously or unconsciously, to challenge old authorities.

The growth of Islamic fundamentalism in Saudi Arabia and other states is as much a reaction to the allegedly blasphemous "Americanization" of domestic society as the foreign policies of the United States. After all, citizens in faraway lands generally feel an American presence most directly through music, movies, and consumer products. Over the course of the twentieth century these extensions of American influence have contributed to an international youth culture that dresses, speaks, and thinks in much more democratic ways than any of its predecessors. This is profoundly revolutionary. It is liberating for many, and it unites estranged figures—from Osama bin Laden to the Saudi royal family—in their fear of its implications.

American influence at the dawn of the twenty-first century reflects the spread of ideas and images across the globe during the preceding hundred years. Merchants, missionaries, and military forces have acted out of self-interest and frequent disregard for the "others" that they have encountered, but they have also planted revolutionary seeds in the soil of foreign societies. Sometimes by design, often by happenstance, exported democratic sensibilities have created fertile ground for continued American profit and influence. Those who hate the United States continue to attend American movies, listen to American music, and buy American-designed products because these items speak an appealing and comprehensible language. American influence is, in fact, so revolutionary that it provides the framework for many anti-American protests.

The United States as a Military Power

Growing from a relatively small force in the late nineteenth century to its gargantuan size a hundred years later, the American military has acted as an extraordinarily violent and democratizing institution. The two qualities reinforce one another. The military historian Russell Weigley has called this the "American way of war." Unlike most of its counterparts, the United States has employed extensive force against a wide range of distant enemies with remarkable—and sometimes excessive—zeal. Brian McAllister Linn's excellent essay in this collection covers some of this ground. Calls for "unconditional surrender" in World War II, for instance, articulated a long-standing American rejection of compromise with military foes. As Weigley explains, the American military has acted across the globe not just to defeat enemies in a traditional sense but to eliminate them from any future existence. The self-proclaimed "arsenal of democracy" has proven profoundly intolerant of international political diversity.[11]

In a curious way, the extremes of the "American way of war" are profoundly democratic. The perceived adversaries of liberty—fascist, communist, and terrorist—pose more than just strategic challenges that can be neutralized through a reconfiguration of boundaries. Antiliberal threats are commonly depicted as philosophical, existential, and irredeemable. They appear to imperil the core foundations of American democracy. They do not accept the individualism necessary for self-government, and they threaten to subvert democracy by exploiting its openness for their own purposes. Liberal thinkers from Woodrow Wilson to Arthur Schlesinger Jr. have feared for the precariousness of democracy in the face of foreign threats. Although the liberalism of these figures has explicitly rejected utopianism, it has also contributed to the supposition that the safety of democracy anywhere requires safety everywhere. An open and free society is just too vulnerable to perpetrators who would turn its openness and freedom to destructive purposes. Military and political leaders have expressed these fears in the nomenclature of "credibility" and "falling dominoes." In this context, the defense of democracy has appeared to call for the violent elimination of antidemocratic foes.[12]

This historical observation explains the remarkable coexistence of brutalizing means and idealistic ends in American military discourse. The American commanders who enjoyed considerable autonomy in the conquest of western Germany and Japan during World War II did not flinch from the mass bombing of cities and eventually the use of two atomic bombs. Men such as George Marshall, Dwight Eisenhower, Douglas MacArthur, Lucius Clay, and Curtis LeMay knew that they would inflict tens of thousands of civilian casualties on target societies, crossing a recognized line in the distinction between the legitimate killing of combatants and the questionable mass murder of innocents in war. These military officials—like their predecessors in the Philippines and Cuba and their successors in Korea and Vietnam—justified their use of overwhelming force in idealistic terms. They were not just winning a war but protecting the future foundations of democracy from existential threats. The perceived profundity of the strategic and philosophical challenge elicited a pervasiveness of violence in self-defense.[13]

This teleological claim was crude and self-serving, but we must take it seriously as historians. After Marshall, Eisenhower, MacArthur, Clay, and LeMay succeeded in vanquishing Germany and Japan, they proceeded to reconstruct these societies along remarkably democratic lines. American occupation forces, operating with minimal guidance from Washington, rebuilt the local infrastructure, created a relatively free press, supervised elections to newly empowered legislatures, and, perhaps most important of all, enfranchised women politically. Scouring the archives of American government planning, one will find few blueprints for occupation policy along these lines.[14] Nonetheless, the military officers who held enemy territory after World War II instinctively fell back on the democratic assumptions that they imbibed through their civic education at institutions such as the U.S. Military Academy at West Point. The conduct of war was hardly democratic, but the Americans who fought with brutality and zeal deeply believed in what they said they were fighting for. This was true in the Philippines and Cuba a generation earlier, as well as in Germany and Japan at midcentury.[15]

Although there is much to criticize in the racist and imperialist elements of American occupation policies throughout the twentieth century—and this volume eloquently articulates many of these criticisms—one must take the democratizing impulses of American reconstruction efforts seriously. No other military force has displayed the same consistent commitment to creating functioning, if limited, democracies in societies under occupation. No other military force has taken control of distant territories with the same consistent commitment to an early departure. No other military force has rebuilt, financed, and then defended its own economic competitors.[16]

Many scholars shy away from studying the American military because of the political taboo that surrounds this institution in parts of the academy. Unfortunately, this bias diverts attention from one of the most quintessentially democratic American institutions. The military is largely comprised of working-class men and women who rise through the ranks in a generally meritocratic fashion. They are trained to kill, but they are also inculcated with a sincere belief in the simple assumptions of liberty that struck Tocqueville so profoundly. The intellectual narrowness of the American military limits its recognition of alternative points of view, and it creates a tendency toward social and political intolerance. Life in the armed forces is surely not the model for the kind of democracy we would like to construct in society at large. At the same time, the American military manifests the most consistent commitment to foreign democratizing endeavors, often through very violent means. This is an element, once again, of the interpenetration of idealism and militarism—rather than mere empire—in the American worldview.

Domestic Reverberations

Assertions about the existence of an imperial American state are not new. William Appleman Williams famously described "empire as a way of life" for Americans. By the end of the nineteenth century, Williams wrote, "All major segments of the economy came to be dominated by a tiny number of giant firms which shared an interest in controlling any new rivals, and establishing rules and procedures to control their part of the marketplace.... [T]he history of that dynamic interaction, and particularly the story of how the citizens were increasingly limited to choosing between policies formulated by the corporations or the government (or the two in collaboration), makes it apparent that all those protagonists accepted an imperial way of life."[17]

Focusing more closely on culture, knowledge, and various social, political, and military institutions, the essays in this volume expand on Williams's insight. The experience of overseas expansion and imperialism, they argue, had strong domestic reverberations. Intelligence agencies, police institutions, public health facilities, and even universities became infected with an imperial frame of mind. They became both engines and apologists for empire.

These essays tell part of the story very well. They also miss a lot. The history of the American state and society in the twentieth century shows striking democratic and anti-imperial features. Just as the discourse of power was filled with contradictions, so was the practice of domestic politics. For all the talk of "military-industrial complexes" and "garrison states," recent scholarship has pointed to the strong and consistent limitations on domestic preparations for empire. The United States, in part because of its democratic structure, pursued policies of "guns and butter." Washington mobilized Americans for war but not for permanent foreign occupations. Americans consumed more than any other modern society but not enough to undermine military preparedness. The United States never became an imperial garrison state or a free consumer market. It was always something in between.[18]

Although twentieth-century America had some imperial qualities, the phrase "imperial state" leaves too little room for antitrust, New Deal, civil rights, and other legislation that empowered individuals and communities against larger interests. The phrase neglects the fiscally conservative instincts of lawmakers and citizens who endeavored to reduce government spending, especially on foreign programs. Most jarring, the phrase implies a depth of planning and preparation for control of other societies that was never a reality. Since 1898, the United States has ended each of the major wars it fought unprepared for the management of the postwar order. American society has never been a society dominated by empire in perception or experience.[19]

A more accurate assessment of American society would turn on the tension—or perhaps the contradiction—between democracy and militarism. The United States became a democratic and military leader of the world through the course of the twentieth century. It took both roles seriously. Its citizens received the benefits and paid the costs incurred. Democracy and warfare went hand in hand, just as imperial and anti-imperial influences conditioned policy. The United States was and is too self-limiting to ever become a real empire. What other country, after all, supported so much passionate anti-imperial scholarship? The very existence of this volume—and its many predecessors—proves that empire is a somewhat misleading label for American society.

Crucibles, Capillaries, and Pentimenti

Reflections on Imperial Transformations

NANCY TOMES

THE NATURE OF "EMPIRE," particularly as embodied in the modern United States, has been a prominent topic of public discussion in recent years. The September 11 terrorist attacks, followed by the wars in Afghanistan and Iraq, have stimulated a wave of anxious reflection about America's place in the world. The historian Charles S. Maier noted in 2006 that "empire has displaced civil society as the fashionable political concept for the new decade." In recent years, the best-seller list has featured big books with imposing titles on the subject, among them *Empire, Colossus,* and *Are We Rome?* Politicians, journalists, and academics engage in lively debates about whether the United States is an empire and, if so, how it compares to empires of the past. Does the United States dominate primarily by means of hard power (military intervention, authoritarian rule) or soft power (economic power, cultural influence)? Is the American empire in decline, following the pattern of the Roman or the British empires, or is it capable of regeneration? Is it, and has it been, a "good" empire or a "bad" one?[1]

This volume also takes as its subject the American imperial state, but, unlike the big books mentioned above, *Colonial Crucible* is not the work of one or two authors trying to use history to shape contemporary foreign policy debates. Rather it is what the coeditors describe as a "multivocal" reflection, representing the work of over forty historians not just of the United States but of the other nations that share its imperial history, including Spain, the Philippines, Puerto Rico, Mexico, and Cuba. Moreover, this book is primarily a work of history, not policy debate. Although the contributors are certainly concerned about contemporary issues, their goal is to acquire a fuller sense of the nation's imperial past not its future.

To that end, this collection focuses on a pivotal era in our imperial past, namely, the turn of the last century: the early years of formal empire, when the flow of ideas and practices between the United States and its colonies first became both highly visible and deeply significant. And, while the work of many authors, those of us involved in the writing of this book had the special good fortune to be able to present our work to each other and to revise our final essays in accordance with what we heard. Thus, more so than in many edited collections, there is a real sense of dialogue in these pages because the essays gathered here were forged in conversation.

In conducting this conversation, the volume's organizers and participants took some assumptions as givens. There was virtually no discussion, at the conference or in the completed essays, of whether or not the United States *was* an imperial power. Participants started with the premise that there was an American imperial state whose evolution was worth serious analysis. In addition, they started with a commitment to look not only at the rhetorical meanings of empire but also at its concrete manifestations in the form of power relations and institutional practices. While deeply influenced by the cultural turn of the 1990s, with its attention to the *language* of empire, participants also expressed a need to foreground the material consequences of imperial expansion as well.

The central themes arrived at in this multivocal collaboration are reflected in the images of crucibles and capillaries that recur throughout the essays. Colonies served as crucibles where mainland theories and practices regarding matters as diverse as policing, constitution writing, eugenics, and agronomy could be hardened and refined. Through what Alfred W. McCoy, Francisco A. Scarano, and Courtney Johnson refer to as the "capillaries of empire," these overseas experiences filtered back to the mainland where they reacted with domestic currents of change. This "imperial dialectic," as they term it, meant that even the "little" empire acquired by the United States after 1898 produced far-reaching transformations, profoundly changing both the ruler and the ruled.

In exploring these transformations, it is fair to say that the participants, particularly the American historians, felt a sense of trepidation as well as excitement. Compared to historians of other countries, Americanists have been relative latecomers to the new imperial history and postcolonial studies, both of which have concentrated on Europe and its former colonies in Africa, South Asia, and East Asia. As a case in point, the enormously influential 1997 collection *Tensions of Empire*, edited by Frederick Cooper and Ann Laura Stoler, contained not one article on the Western Hemisphere.[2] To some extent, as Josep M. Fradera points out in his essay in this volume, Atlantic history and African diaspora studies have begun to rectify this imbalance. But to date those new approaches have focused on imperial history prior to the nineteenth century. Compared to the rich studies of late European colonialism, work on modern Latin America and the United States seems far less developed.

For American historians, the sense of being "backward" is a familiar one. As Thomas McCormick notes in his essay, we have inherited a long historiographic legacy of ambivalence toward the nation's imperial past. As schoolchildren, and even as graduate students, we learned to think of that past as "the Great Aberration," in Samuel Flagg Bemis's oft-noted phrase. The acquisition of empire after 1898 has customarily been treated as "the worst chapter in almost any book," as James Fields noted back in 1978.[3] Outside the specialist history of foreign relations, American history has long been noted for the "absence of empire," as described by Amy Kaplan in the landmark 1993 collection, *Cultures of United States Imperialism*. Although that absence has begun to be addressed over the last decade, the idea persists, and was even voiced by a few at this conference, that the "United States did not have much of an empire" and therefore its imperial ventures must have had relatively little impact on American institutions and culture.[4]

The "not much of an empire" argument reflects the entrenched habit of taking a single Eurocentric model of empire, and more specifically the British experience, as the template against which all others should be judged. By rejecting this viewpoint, the essays in *Colonial Crucible* suggest a far more interesting reading of the United States' imperial past, a reading that broadens not only the scope of American history but also the agenda of the new imperial history. By emphasizing the influence of peripheries on metropoles, and colonials on colonizers, the new imperial history has produced a vibrant rethinking of the meanings of empire. Yet to date that rethinking has largely centered on the connections among European nations and their colonial empires. The United States, as well as Latin America, have been essentially irrelevant to the new imperial history, at least so far.

To borrow an image from Dipesh Chakrabarty, the United States and its colonies have been consigned to the back row of the "waiting-room version of history" in which countries are stuck in the process of becoming like—but never achieving—models of historical evolution derived from the European past. Ironically, for all the iconoclasm of Chakrabarty's enormously influential call to "provincialize Europe," his approach illustrates the very problem he identifies in that he never considers how his critique might apply to New World empires. It remains for those of us writing and reading books like this one to make that conceptual leap by attempting to envision a more expansive imperial history that includes North and South America; the authors in *Colonial Crucible* do exactly that by connecting Atlantic and Pacific, European and American history (South and North) in new, exciting ways.[5]

Perhaps the greatest contribution of the essays presented here lies in their insistence on taking the American imperial past seriously, no matter how unlike the British model it may be. To be sure, it remains hard to imagine American historians ever seeing Americanness as inseparable from empire, as do British historians, for whom "the idea of Britishness . . . cannot be unyoked from the fact of empire," as Philippa Levine has put it. For American historians, the opposite is true: yoking Americanness to the concept of empire remains an enormous challenge, though one the essays in this volume successfully convince us to take up.[6]

Read together, the essays in this volume reveal those yokings in subtle and unexpected ways that belie the often simplistic characterizations of imperial rule. The uses of racial ideology and eugenics are a good example. In her essay, Solsirée del Moral shows how Puerto Rican teachers applied mainland theories of "Latin degeneracy" to their own students in ways that bolstered their own elite class interests. At the other end of the capillary, so to speak, Natalie J. Ring's essay documents how the experience of empire encouraged a "neosouthern orientalism" in which both white and black southerners were viewed as pseudo-tropical peoples beyond the reach of Americanization.

In addition to crucibles and capillaries, the essays in this volume suggest the importance of what Patricia Seed has termed "pentimenti": the shadows of historical experience left by prior generations of colonial rule.[7] In his introductory essay, Josep M. Fradera invited participants to stop thinking narrowly in terms of imperial transitions from one empire to another. As he points out, the Iberian, British, and American empires coexisted for long stretches of time, setting up complicated patterns of influence. Even when one empire definitely succeeded another, as happened with the Spanish-American War, those complexities remained.

For example, in part 4, "Race and Imperial Identities," the essay by Christopher Schmidt-Nowara, and another by Alejandro de la Fuente and Matthew Casey, show how nationalist groups began to reflect more favorably on their Spanish past as they became dissatisfied with the terms of American rule. A figure such as Ponce de León, once thought of as a conqueror, became rehabilitated as a national hero, as Schmidt-Nowara argues. At the other end of the capillary, Amílcar Antonio Barreto calls attention to the unintended consequences of the Americanization programs run by Puerto Rican schools, which inadvertently laid the foundation for later Puerto Rican nationalist movements.

These complex histories do not easily fit into the model of the benevolent or liberal empire set forth by Niall Ferguson. In his words, the liberal empire is the kind "that not only underwrites the free international exchange of commodities, labor and capital but also creates and upholds the conditions without which markets cannot function—peace and order, the rule of law, noncorrupt administration, stable fiscal and monetary policies—as well as provides public goods, such as transport infrastructure, hospitals, and schools, which would no otherwise exist."[8] Whether they concern the "hard power" of military conquest and authoritarian regimes or the "soft power" of economic and cultural assimilation, the essays in this collection make relatively little overt use of concepts such as "benevolence" and "liberality." Perhaps this is because so many of the essays are by scholars writing from the perspective of the colonized. For Cubans, Filipinos, or Puerto Ricans, the "hardness" of American power was quite evident.

Even in the case of public health, one area in which the interests of the colonizers would seem clearly to benefit their subjects, the results seem decidedly mixed. In his essay, J. R. McNeill emphasizes what might be seen as the benevolent or liberal aspect of the new environmental management state in that it brought about an end to recurrent cholera epidemics. Yet other essays, in particular Warwick Anderson's account of the Philippines and Mariola Espinosa's account of Cuba, underline how one-sided and self-serving American investments in public health institutions actually were. Public health experts conceived of their colonial subjects as biomedical inferiors and assessed the urgency of their health problems largely in terms of how much they threatened American interests.

Whereas few American historians are likely to question that the imperial bond left indelible marks on the colonial subjects who experienced U.S. rule, the other side of the coin—that this small island empire profoundly changed the continental United States—is likely to be more controversial. But the essays gathered here present a strong case for exactly that argument: the acquisition of formal empire, no matter how small in scope or short in duration, served to catalyze a longer, deeper history of continental expansion and commercial empire building. Imperial rule reacted with other transnational developments, including the second Industrial Revolution, massive worldwide immigration, and the rise of modern science, to produce the activist state of the Progressive era.

Would that activist state have emerged had the United States not acquired its formal empire after 1898? The answer is likely yes. We do not want to overstate the case, replacing the absence of empire with an overemphasis on empire. As McCoy, Scarano, and Johnson carefully qualify in the introduction, the rise of the modern American state was part of a "complex reciprocal process" that included "multiple processes of expansion," including westward migration, the conquest of Native Americans, and an expanding industrial economy, as well as the formal acquisition of colonies. But as the essays in this collection convincingly demonstrate, the acquisition of empire had a catalytic effect on the conception of governmentality itself. The imperial experience was directly and critically important to forming key aspects of the twentieth-century American state, namely, the national security state; the new linkages among academic, business, and governmental elites; the environmental management state; and the expansion of mass consumer culture. Let me briefly elaborate on each of these aspects.

In his essay on the Philippines, Alfred W. McCoy shows a clear connection between colonial policing and the birth of the twentieth-century national security state. Faced with insurgents of diverse types, American colonial administrators deployed new information technologies to track and control Filipino activists.

Methods of information gathering and surveillance developed in the Philippines were later exported to the United States during the turbulent World War I era. So, while traditionally the Palmer Raids, J. Edgar Hoover, and the Federal Bureau of Investigation are seen solely in relation to World War I and the Red Scare, McCoy shows how integral the experience of colonial policing was to the formation of the national security state.

The essays by Glenn Anthony May, Warwick Anderson, and Stuart McCook document the new alliances among scientists, government officials, and business interests forged in the colonies. Through this new "capillaries of empire," the scientific achievements of the Progressive era, including the germ theory of disease, plant and animal genetics, and meteorology, to name just a few, were set to imperial uses. The early American empire thus laid the foundation of what the 1960s generation would christen the "military-industrial-academic complex." One of the most important products of that complex was the environmental management state, described by Paul S. Sutter, J. R. McNeill, and Stuart McCook. Science in the service of the state provided new ways to tame overseas "nature" that maximized social order and economic productivity. That environmental management state also undergirded the connections between empire and American consumer culture, a link persuasively traced by Kristin Hoganson in her essay. As she clearly shows, "consumer choices became acts of imperial engagement," that "brought the empire home" as American women decorated their homes with Asian imports and learned to make desserts with imported tropical fruits.

By exposing the hard substrate that made possible the "softer" empire of the post-1920s period, *Colonial Crucible* fills a much needed void in the literature. It documents the backbreaking labor literally as well as figuratively required to secure the political stability, social order, and economic dominance that underlay the seemingly "effortless" expansion of the market-based liberal empire. As such, it provides a much needed prolegomenon to the "irresistible empire" described by Victoria de Grazia in her 2005 book by that title. After this collection is published, it will hopefully no longer be possible to write a book of nearly five hundred pages about the American "market empire" without a single reference to Latin America or the Philippines. (Obviously American historians are not the only ones who suffer from empire denial.) The point here is not to berate de Grazia for her Eurocentric focus but rather to argue that in future work the connections between formal and informal empire need to be more fully elaborated. Put simply, we need to think more seriously about how McCoy's surveillance state made the world safe for Victoria de Grazia's international order of Rotarians.

As the contributors to this volume would be the first to admit, there is still much work to be done. In future work, we need further to "creolize" the modern

American empire, balancing the traditional emphasis on Europe with a greater appreciation of Latin American and Pacific Rim influences. We need to continue looking for the pentimenti left by different imperial experiences. We have only begun to heed Fradera's call to explore more fully the Spanish legacies of American colonial rule and to ponder the suggestion made by McCoy, Scarano, and Johnson that "the resilient Spanish empire" helped to form the new American state of the early twentieth century. Finally, we need to ponder the relationship between the formal empire, created by military conquest and an authoritarian regime, and the other "softer" empires so closely associated with American influence, including not only the market empire associated with the expansion of American consumer capitalism and popular culture but also the "benevolent empire" created by American missionaries, an important point that Tyrrell raises in his concluding essay.[9]

As American historians well know, the history of American foreign policy is and has long been a famously contentious field. *Colonial Crucible* will surely spark yet more arguments. The concluding essays by Jeremi Suri and Ian Tyrrell anticipate the shape those arguments are likely to take. Suri takes the position of what we might term the "empire deniers": calling the United States an empire "obfuscates more than it explains." As have many historians and political scientists before him, Suri affirms the importance of an "ideal type" of empire. A "real empire" is a "political system keyed to the exploitation of foreign societies," which in his opinion the United States is not. The U.S. is better understood as a "revolutionary power," an interpretation Suri has championed in the past, and that none of the arguments in this volume about capillaries and catalysts have convinced him to modify. In contrast, Tyrrell rejects Suri's empire "essentialism" and argues for a much more fluid conception of empire as one nation exerting power over another, through warfare, occupation, and economics, a definition by which "the United States is manifestly an empire." The real crux of the historical project at hand lies properly in the "arguments over what kind of an empire it is or was."

Tyrrell's perspective is much more compatible with the articles in this volume than is Suri's position. After finishing this collection, readers will have to decide for themselves who won the argument. I suspect that the majority of American historians will find Tyrrell's interpretation more convincing, as do I. Suri seems so intent on reasserting his interpretation that he engages very little with the specific issues raised here, such as education, economics, public health, and the like. For cultural historians such as myself the idea of "bringing the empire back into" American history in general, and the Progressive era in particular, seems long overdue. Thus, for me, participating in the conference and contributing to this volume have transformed my way of looking at an American past I thought I knew well.

Colonial Crucible reflects over a decade's worth of new work among historians, many of them influenced by cultural studies, who have gone in search of American empire and found it in many unexpected places. Their work provides enlightening instances of the circulation of ideas and practices from metropole to colony back to metropole, forcing us to consider the imperial roots of developments conventionally thought to have little or no relationship to overseas developments. It provides many illuminating examples of how to think about the deep structures and cultural legacies of colonial rule, extending concepts of transnationality and the yoking of metropole and colony to include the late nineteenth and twentieth centuries.

What this volume gives us finally is a framework within which to conceive this "second empire" as a "three-tiered process of synergistic state formation," as McCoy, Scarano, and Johnson term it. The book makes a bold argument that modern U.S. state formation is best thought of as an "imperial synthesis," in which "the activist inclination of domestic progressivism [was] exported to these new colonies," where "its command qualities were heightened in the colonial context." In time, "these amplified state capacities were repatriated, through personnel and precedents, back to the United States."

Inevitably, this bold argument suggests comparisons with another academic development that began a half century ago at the University of Wisconsin–Madison when William Appleman Williams began to produce work that sent the history of American foreign relations off in new directions. I believe that in this volume we see an equivalent, though intellectually independent, transformation in the making. The idea of "schools" of history having become passé, it makes no sense to speak of a "second Wisconsin school"; a more accurate label would be "the new American imperial synthesis" or, more succinctly, "the new imperial synthesis." Whatever label it may inspire, this collection represents a much needed effort on two intellectual fronts: first, to incorporate the history of the United States and Latin America into an overly Eurocentric "new imperial history"; and, second, to incorporate the experience of empire into the formation of the modern American state.

Clearly one of the appeals of the new imperial synthesis is its relevance to contemporary events, in particular the controversial war in Iraq and the new global concern with terrorism. Faced with seemingly unprecedented challenges in the present, we instinctively seek a fuller understanding of America's imperial past. It is hard work for, as the editors observe in their introduction to the 2006 collection *The Lessons of Empire: Imperial Histories and American Power*, "the lessons of empire do not leap from the pages of history unambiguous and uncontested."[10] The debates begun in this volume are no exception.

But, apart from the arguments made here, I want to conclude by applauding the process of collaboration through which this book came to be. It represents the work of a diverse array of scholars from different nations who gathered to address a wide range of topics. This seems to be a particularly fruitful way to interrogate such a complicated past. Only from such a cross-national exchange can a truly transnational perspective on American empire be achieved. Thus, I look forward to the next installment of this "imperial transformations" project, which will hopefully take the themes developed here into transnational comparisons or later periods in modern American history. The results should be just as challenging and enlightening.

Empire in American History

IAN TYRRELL

THE MEMORY OF WAR IS DEEPLY ETCHED on American public consciousness through memorials of national significance. Witness the Vietnam Memorial, then the Marine Corps' Iwo Jima Monument, the Tomb of the Unknown Soldier, and Gettysburg. Yet the interested observer must look much harder for scattered and unobtrusive memorials of the Philippine-American conflict or even the Spanish-American War that preceded it. Not so in 1899 when Admiral George Dewey returned triumphantly from his 1898 naval victory over the Spanish in the Battle of Manila before the Philippines came under formal American control in the Treaty of Paris of December 1898. Dewey stayed in Manila assisting the American military occupation and then, in the summer of 1899, began a slow triumphal return via the Mediterranean.[1] The nation's leaders had wavered over whether to grasp the nettle of empire, but they did. Dewey arrived home the hero who had upheld the nation's honor and laid the foundation for that empire. While still governor of New York, Theodore Roosevelt proclaimed that "The thunder of Dewey's guns ... raised in a moment's time the prestige of American arms throughout the world and added a new honor to American citizenship at home and abroad."[2]

Despite Roosevelt's confident bombast, Dewey's views on empire were at first unclear. He made noises on both sides of the question, as befitted a man sizing up his chances for a presidential nomination. But he judged that the Filipino people lacked "honesty" and suitability for self-government.[3] When Secretary of the Navy John D. Long christened the Philippine "dominion" an "imperial" form of "expansion" at Dewey's tumultuous Washington reception in early October 1899, Dewey led the loud round of applause. The *New York Times* declared Dewey lost to the cause of anti-imperialism. The pomp and ceremony was that of a country entering the true world of nations because it now had colonies (in

Puerto Rico, Guam, and the Philippines) and was set on a course of "moral and physical growth."[4]

Since the spring of 1899 a New York committee had been planning a spectacular return for Dewey, and for the purpose a special arch was constructed at Madison Square modeled in part on the Arch of Titus in Rome. The Dewey Arch, as it became known, was decorated with the works of sculptors and crowned with an imposing quadriga of four seahorses drawing a ship. Inscriptions to the "West Indies" and the "East Indies" were planned in order to symbolize the joining of the Pacific and the Atlantic, thereby adding to the imperial theme. At night the arch shone with the glare of electric lightbulbs; in its showy brilliance the monument commemorated the achievements of an empire newly minted and very modern, an empire of the electric age. Yet the cost was said to be comparatively small. Representations of empire were evidently, like the empire itself, to be done on the cheap.[5]

Fireworks displays greeted the hero of Manila, and poets extolled his achievements in doggerel verse while Dewey subjected himself willingly to naval and land parades. A New York street parade was held on September 30, 1899 (filmed by the Edison Company for a short newsreel), but Dewey did not actually enter the arch. He mounted the official viewing platform just a few meters short to review the parade, thereby allegedly becoming the "first victor in military history denied the rite of passage through his triumphal arch."[6] City officials became cautious about the structural soundness of the memorial, which sculptors, not architects, had designed. If the arch had not already deteriorated it quickly did so thereafter because it was made of plaster similar to that used to build the Columbian Exposition in Chicago in 1892. Attempts to raise money to rebuild the memorial with more durable materials failed, and, a poet lamented, "into calm disdainfulness she sinks."[7] Within two years the triumphal arch had been demolished. Today the "only existing reminder . . . near the site is a bar and restaurant called Dewey's Flatiron," which features a tacky replica of part of the arch's top together with a portrait of the victorious "admiral of the navy" and his exploits.[8]

Dewey stated in his autobiography that had he died while crossing the Atlantic an "outpouring of subscriptions" would have quickly made the arch a permanent monument "in marble." Dewey's mistake was to have lived.[9] But there are other possible interpretations of the failure to commemorate his achievement securely. Traffic problems complicated the claim for a permanent location while the *New York Times* believed his clumsy attempt to become a candidate for president had not helped. Nor did the changing political situation.[10] In 1899 the rebellion of the Filipino insurgents against American rule had already begun in earnest. By 1900 the conflict had turned into a dirty guerrilla war. American critics saw the return of American soldiers in coffins as a symbol of the wantonness of war and of the mistakes made in acquiring the colony. The nation did not repudiate empire, but after the conflict was declared over in 1902 it receded from the public memory. There was no desire for commemoration. The war should be forgotten.

The detritus of Deweymania can still be seen in the United States. But commemoration of Dewey's ship, the *Olympia*, came much later when in 1957 it took up residence at Penn's Landing in Philadelphia. The Spanish-American War fared only marginally better. The masthead salvaged from the wreckage of the sunken warship *Maine* became, in accordance with an act of Congress in 1910, a memorial in Arlington National Cemetery dedicated in 1913, but that commemorated the alleged reasons for the war in Cuba, not the Philippine conflict, and cast the United States as the injured party. War memorials around the United States commemorating the American campaigns of 1898–1902, like one in Minneapolis, are both much more obscure and more overtly ideological, but they told, until recently, narratives of liberation and distorted the course of the Philippine-American War.[11]

This selective remembering is not unique to the United States. A recent trip to Lisbon reminded me how amnesic the representations of empire could be. Portugal's African empire of Mozambique and Angola is marginalized there, but the great age of Portugal's explorers is everywhere. This, and Fado, is practically all that the tourist sees as truly distinctive about Portuguese history. Time stopped with Prince Henry the Navigator and Vasco da Gama; it especially stopped during the Salazar regime from 1928 to 1968. Portugal, too, wants to forget. One has only to enter at any corner of the Jardim-Museu Agrícola Tropical (Gardens of Tropical Agriculture) near Belém to see how fleeting and decrepit are the reminders of the nation's African past and how history has been marginalized; Macau, however, is a success story, and Portugal carefully cultivates its heritage in that place. The Portuguese empire is one of quaint lemon- and salmon-painted colonial architecture with the reality of sugar and slavery almost nowhere to be seen except tucked discreetly in the odd reference in that Belém garden.

In the American case what stands out is the positive production of images of military heroism. The most recent example is St. Florian's World War II Memorial on the Mall in Washington, a monument of truly Roman proportions. It is appropriate to current circumstances and historical precedents since the American empire has been very much a military one as befitted the pomp and ceremony surrounding Admiral Dewey.[12] In the American version of empire, the colonial administration was often held together not by a strong civil service but by the army and navy either directly or indirectly, aided in considerable measure by a strong voluntarist ethic in the nongovernmental sector in which services were contracted out to missionaries, the Young Men's Christian Association (YMCA), and other nongovernmental organizations. But the pattern of voluntarism has been forgotten, too. In the United States, empire is translated into war.

How empire is remembered and forgotten needs to be a subject of analysis in its own right. That is in part why I have opened with this discussion. James Loewen, in *Lies Across America: What Our Historic Sites Get Wrong*, has taken up the issue of representations of the Philippine-American War in passing as part of a catalogue of commemorative sins but without historical depth or comparisons with European imperialism. The work of Oscar Campomanes tackles a range of visual representations, but clearly there is much more to be done.[13] Not only does the relative absence of memorials and their misleading and didactic language need analysis. The historical development of this marginalized commemoration does, too.[14]

However, the story of Dewey's Arch may be also presented as a metaphor for the American amnesic relationship with empire. At times the concept has been embraced; in the nineteenth century, *empire* was not a dirty word but rather a story of the extension of liberty: Jefferson's empire for liberty.[15] Never mind the Indians. When Europe embraced formal colonialism the United States followed suit. But the ebbs and flows of political fortune, partisan conflict, and fiscal parsimony interacted with historical traditions of anticolonialism to undermine the development of consistent imperial policies and to render the kind of empire that the United States became all but invisible to the naked eye.

The failure to confront that checkered history has continued to affect the way Americans look at their nation in regard to colonialism and imperialism. The problem of American exceptionalism stalks this issue as it does so much of American historiography. Europe has empires; the United States has an anticolonial tradition stemming from the American Revolution. A prominent interpretation that erases the extent, complexity, and duration of the formal empire has been to accept the acquisition of colonies in 1898 as something that occurred as an aberration.[16] The United States hastily acquired a real empire as a footnote to the European imperial expansion of the late nineteenth century and then worked earnestly to limit and eliminate it. It signaled its anticolonial intentions in the Jones Act of 1916. In this interpretation, that phase effectively ended in 1946 with Philippine independence, though the writing was on the wall well before this.[17]

Such an assessment is understandable in view of the changing manifestations of the processes of empire in American history. But that does not mean we cannot talk about an American empire, only that we must understand its complexities and distinctiveness. The United States is manifestly an empire because it has exerted power over other people; it has occupied other countries, changed their political regimes, and fought wars over the control of the territory of others. It has sought to influence other peoples indirectly as well. There can, of course, be arguments over what kind of an empire it is or was. But we should really be beyond debates over whether it is or is not. Unfortunately that is not the case. Ignorance of the United States' deeply entrenched imperial experiences has been common not only in the work of that well-known historian and philosopher Donald Rumsfeld but across the historical profession and in related disciplines.[18] Too often arguments about empire assume an essentialism that I would reject. Rather, American empire is best seen as an accretion of policies and traditions.

While there has been a good deal of discontinuity and complexity in American empire, comparison with other empires remains valid. When comparisons are made there is a tendency to assume a mythical European model based on formal acquisition of territory seized from tribal societies or sovereign states; the peoples in the lands so acquired are subject peoples not citizens or even potential citizens.[19] This ideal type does not work well for the wider exertion of American power in the world in the period 1880–1940, nor does it uniformly fit other empires. One can easily identify many gradations within this rather rigid framework. There are key distinctions between commercial seaborne empires and land-based ones, between white "settlement" colonies and others, and between formal control of territory and informal military and political power. One can also find a bewildering combination of these forms. For this reason an American empire must be set against a range of historical empires not an American idea of what an empire ought to be. The American experience has some features in common with the British Empire, to which it has been closely related, and some important differences. For this reason historians must approach empire as a historically changing social formation rather than an ideal type.

Alongside elements of similarity to the British Empire, however, one can detect contributions that flourished at the moment of American power; these have included an ideological distaste for formal colonialism and the presence of transnational institutions rooted, nonetheless, in American cultural, economic, or political experience.[20] The export of American culture has been thought important to American power in recent times. Political scientists have coined the term *soft power*, and Chinese scholars of American history have taken up this idea earnestly, arguing that the United States since the 1990s has squandered its soft power option and the Chinese are claiming the mantle.[21] Yet the term lacks precision, and the boundaries between soft and hard power are difficult to establish. Soft power always depends in part on military force. Moreover, soft power appears to afford little scope for agency from below or from outside the behemoth. I prefer the older and perhaps unfashionable term *cultural hegemony*, not to mean "domination" in the sense of raw power but the exercise of power under a shared moral and political order in which that power is the subject of multilateral contestation among nations as much as classes.[22] Power is also reciprocal. Effects do not simply proceed outward but inward as events, circumstances, and people abroad influence the United States. Attempted cultural hegemony (or soft power) was far from new in the 1990s and could certainly be seen in the 1890s. It was pioneered in the kinds of cultural expansion undertaken by Protestant Christian reformers and missions in that decade. Architects of American empire such as Alfred Thayer Mahan advocated a "higher form of Christianity" to underpin American civil authority in the new colonies with the "enlightened public opinion" necessary in a civilized society.[23] This did not mean that Mahan saw the soft power of religion as a substitute for the application of force. In his writings he articulated a view in which force is the necessary precondition of civilization's advance when subtler means fail and "the sword is necessary."[24]

In the light of these methodological strictures the topic of "empire in American history" could be taken two ways in line with the meanings of history itself: history as the knowledge that historians produce or history as events that happened. I have vacillated about which to stress partly because they are so closely connected. The history of American historiographical perceptions of its empire helps us to understand how and why American historians have failed to combat the amnesia surrounding empire effectively. Historians have put alternative cases that make use of some of these themes, but they did so in the twentieth century with only episodic force and in ways that reflected the complicated and multilayered nature of American empire. The formal empire of colonies was not the only empire that American historians had to confront. American empire has taken a number of forms. Interpretation of these has been hotly contested, and the relationship between them is unclear.

There is the settlement society empire of westward expansion, the colonial island empire of 1898, and the informal empire of trade and investment (the open door). Overlapping the latter is the Fordist empire of mass consumption, circa 1920–70, ably discussed by Victoria de Grazia, in which American economic power was projected outward and harnessed to a post–World War II project of American hegemony within the Western world.[25] This might be aligned with the Marshall Plan and the constellation of political and economic institutions that constituted the post-1945 great power settlement. Here, as described by the historian Geir Lundestad, an "empire by invitation" developed in which allies courted and acceded to American hegemony.[26] Most recently, there has been some discussion of a nonterritorial, networked empire in the era of new globalization since the 1970s.[27] While historians and others can hardly deny the existence of an island empire in the period after 1898, the settlement empire of the American West is often asserted to be wholly different and not appropriate to call imperial. Other, more recent phases are likewise controversial. Although there is some underlying continuity of themes in the historiography of American empire, the patterns of scholarship were constantly in flux because of, first, the rapid changes in the external environment and growth of the United States to a world power and second, the growth of the American state. Empire was very much a moving target, and historians struggled to keep up.

Historians did not initially ignore the Spanish-American War and the territorial dilemmas that followed; like the physical monument makers they rushed to make a public contribution. Historians intervened vigorously in public debates over the appropriateness and meaning of empire for the United States during the years 1898–1902. As the historian Frederick Jackson Turner observed at the time, the United States had a colonial history and policy "from the beginning of the republic," but colonial status had "been hidden under the phraseology of 'interstate migration' and 'territorial organization.'"[28] According to Albert Bushnell Hart, or "Bushy," as he was known, the United States had many "colonies" in the form of its Indian reservations. "[O]ur Indian agents have a status," the eminent Harvard historian argued, "very like that of British residents in the native states of India." He regarded the western Indian Territory as comparable to the British colonial system. But the sudden enthusiasm among scholars did not last any longer than did Dewey's Arch. Turner was always ambivalent. He suggested that the United States could either expand externally or reform internally. Which would the country choose?[29] This remained a common response of those who considered this question. Even Bushy Hart later converted his support for an American territorial empire into clamor for great power preparedness in the crisis of World War I.[30]

Support for empire turned in the aftermath of that war into support for Wilsonian idealism and the League of Nations. Hart himself came out against isolationism or unilateralism.[31] Historians quickly sensed that the American empire could not be confined to the island colonies. A range of historians in the 1920s worked on American intervention in the Caribbean precisely because this was a hot political topic. In 1928 Leland H. Jenks of Wellesley College published *Our Cuban Colony: A Study in Sugar* as part of a series on American imperialism edited by Harry Elmer Barnes.[32] Others in the series included University of California economic historian Melvin Knight's *The Americans in Santo Domingo*; and J. Fred Rippy's *The Capitalists and Columbia*.[33] These and similar works lacked a certain subtlety, and some are now described as merely "muckraking exposés," but the exposés continued to be influential for some decades.[34]

Though dismissed at the time in journals such as the *Hispanic American Historical Review* by establishment Latin Americanists, this body of work was not without effect for several reasons. Notably, it was connected to a broader public current of concern about the nation's place in the world. The focus on a nefarious economic imperialism exploiting Latin Americans with marines as policemen for American finance jelled well with the historiographical spirit of the era. American historians turned hostile to war in reaction to the outcome of World War I, an event that seemed to Barnes and others to be a testimony to imperialism's greed and calumny. The political scientist Parker T. Moon became a well-known figure in the 1920s as an exponent of an academic form of American anti-imperialism, criticizing U.S. "domination" of Latin America.[35] Furthermore, the attack on growing U.S. economic investment and military intervention in Latin America became linked to the broader interpretation of the United States as an aggrandizing state prepared to go to war in the aid of economic interests, hence the involvement not only of Barnes but also of the most formidable figure in American historiography, Charles Beard, through his 1930s studies of American militarism and the state, especially *The Devil Theory of War*.[36]

This anti-imperialist work was produced largely for a popular, or at least non-specialist, audience at a time when many American academic historians lacked university posts. It was connected to the leftist progressivism of the late 1920s, 1930s Communist and Socialist party politics, antiwar pacifism, and the activities of liberal and radical teachers in the nation's leading public schools. It was in the 1930s that the progressive education designers of American school curricula first became seriously interested in world history; an important part of this development was interest in Pan-Americanism and support for the Good Neighbor concept appropriated by official U.S. government policy under Franklin D. Roosevelt after 1934. The teacher-educators, high school teachers, and academics who wrote for *Social Studies*, the leading educational journal in the field, and those who pushed the new progressive school social studies curricula, such as Beard and his acolytes, were very much interested in Latin America and U.S. imperialism.[37]

World War II disrupted the continuity of this interpretation, and the early cold war undermined the position of the teacher groups. The broad social movement committed to intellectual assessments of the informal American empire did not completely die, but it became attenuated for a time. It lost its practical political edge and its links to a hard-nosed economic analysis. In the meantime a wider range of American historical assessments covering relations with the Caribbean and Latin American nations emerged. This work produced more sober and conservative judgments, for example, in the works of Dana G. Munro, which blunted the appeal of the more radical, anti-imperial interpretations and often favored arguments of national security as explanations for American conduct.[38]

Yet the historical work of William Appleman Williams revived in the late 1950s the older anti-imperial tradition within a broader philosophical theory of American empire.[39] Williams's work was not so much an economic interpretation of empire as one involving the central role of economic ideas. He could be criticized for the elasticity of this philosophical idealism and for his failure to connect the weltanschauung of an open door to concrete endeavors to expand American territory or execute foreign policy.[40] But another gap in his approach has received almost no attention. Although this idea of an informal empire was being simultaneously discussed within British Empire historiography and various economic historians centered their work on British "free trade imperialism" and United Kingdom investments in Latin America, there was virtually no American acknowledgment of any connection to this world of scholarship.[41] Williams and his students seemed largely oblivious to other empires and the debates over free trade empire. Their approach continued the American tradition of debating U.S. empire internally and parochially. Although Ernest May purported to analyze the American war with Spain and the conflict with the Philippines from a multiarchival perspective, he still addressed a rather insular position that the forces of American intervention were endogenous. No matter how mindful of the diplomatic and military intricacies abroad, the president and his administration were buffeted, in May's view, by the forces of an irrational, internal "public clamour" and by domestic demands for humanitarianism in war and colonial possession. McKinley had "heard the voice of the people."[42]

The interpretations outlined here have had more than purely academic significance. From the time of Hart some American historians attempted to intervene in the public debate, at first mainly supporting empire, then by the 1920s acting as a vocal intellectual chorus against American involvement in Latin America and for isolation from Europe's wars on the grounds that such involvement would ultimately create an imperial state. And so it did. Williams and his disciples drew on this tradition and opposed American intervention in Vietnam.[43]

The Williams school's open door approach of the 1960s and 1970s became one of the most recognizable and influential schools of historical interpretation in the modern era. It produced a large body of influential work (notably Walter LaFeber's *The New Empire*), and his and his students' general view of American foreign expansion in the late nineteenth century has not been completely thrown out. It has been correctly criticized for failing to take sufficient account of the culture of U.S. imperialism, but Williams's analytical framework has been revived by Andrew Bacevich as a foundation for analyzing the military empire of post-cold-war America.[44]

From this brief survey we can conclude that American historians did not, as is sometimes claimed, ignore American empire, at least not entirely. The effects on the empire at home were not totally neglected either; empire's reciprocal effects were in one way contained in earlier historiography. The price of empire was something Williams perceived, at least from the time of *The Tragedy of American Diplomacy*, and he and his followers regarded the nation as paying a high price in terms of imperialism's impact on American democracy and American credibility in the world; this followed in the tradition of Turner and the critics of the 1930s. Critics of Williams generally overlooked "the enormous tragedy endured by American society precisely because of its counterrevolutionary posture."[45] The deliberations of those who now seek to gain greater recognition for the impact of the American formal empire of 1898 fall within a broad tradition in which dissenting forces within American history attempted to alert American historians to truths about the nation's imperial and colonial past. Within public life, however, there has been little evidence of movement away from the consensus that American power must hold sway and yet that the United States is not an empire but a force for good. On the seeming hypocrisy or naïveté of politicians who lecture the world on issues of political democracy from the standpoint of American exceptionalism while meddling in that world with a combination of Wilsonian idealism and Theodore Roosevelt's penchant for the exercise of power, the arguments are telling. George W. Bush has not been walking down this path alone.[46] The idea of empire as an American tradition does not have a great deal of political traction, and one suspects it would not win support in Gallup polls.

One of the problems with these arguments about empire since the 1960s has been that they continue to be mired within quite insular American debates. In all of these interpretations one thing remains relatively constant; the emphasis on outward American expansion. There has until relatively recently been little done on the actual ruling of the formal empire and on the interconnections between the various parts of that empire: Puerto Rico, Samoa, Guam, the Philippines, and the Virgin Islands.[47] Although the effects on the empire at home were not totally neglected, we do not have much in the way of studies of the contribution of empire in terms of costs and benefits comparable to those done decades ago for the United Kingdom.[48] We have relatively little, too, on the feedback effects of colonial administrators, missionaries, and other cultural emissaries who served in the American colonies.

As globalization accelerated in the 1970s and beyond, the question of U.S. power relationships began to take on new significance, and the deployment of traditional power even in the form of informal empire seemed less relevant. Because globalization enshrines sets of rules that in theory are above the powers of any nation-state, even the United States, it became fashionable in some circles no longer to look for the exercise of a specifically American power but rather to see patterns of globalization, or alternatively to refigure empire as something entirely new, and to read this new insight back into American history. The result is work that ironically continues to focus on the United States. Seen in Michael Hardt and Antonio Negri's *Empire*, the new orientation is not only utopian in its political predictions but ahistorical in its failure to consider the complexities of the U.S. empire as a set of responses to historical circumstances not entirely of the nation's own making.[49]

At each stage historical interpretation responded to the immediate circumstances of American engagement from settlement society to formal empire, informal trading empire, economic imperialist power, and nonterritorial communications empire. These views often fail to see the United States in a wider transnational context. It is necessary to abandon this internal focus and go back and ask whether the assertion of American power on the world stage in the 1890s was something that stemmed only from the dynamic nature of American society. I shall argue that Americans embraced empire as they became more strongly engaged with the world in that period and as the result of the interaction of foreign and domestic forces. The nation was brought to the brink of imperial expansion by its growing implication in that world economically, politically, and culturally. The events of 1898 become explicable as a product of a much larger pattern.

One of the questions posed in the editors' introduction to this volume is as follows: how could the fragmentary empire of island colonies have had such a profound impact on a large continental nation? My own research can illustrate what might be done to reorient the study of American empire to a transnational story in which the reciprocal impacts of empire are more central and yet at the same time might also explain why the occlusion of empire was relatively effective. One thinks of Americans as a missionary people, but few missionaries went abroad until the 1880s; in fact in 1890 there was only a total of about 900 missionaries in the field after eighty years of missionary work. Churches prevaricated about sending missionaries while possible candidates and their families and friends grumbled about tropical heat, disease, and other dangers. But the trickle of missionaries soon turned into a torrent. By 1898, 3,468 were in the field, and by 1920s, the total number sent was over 14,000. In the course of a decade and a half from 1886 the American missionary movement was transformed quantitatively and qualitatively. It became a movement heavily influenced by nondenominationalism, innovative business methods, lay leaders, and the thorough mixture of "reform" and religion. New organizations, especially the Student Volunteer Movement for Foreign Missions (SVM), were founded and older ones, such as the YMCA, revamped and exported as models for social and moral reform elsewhere.[50]

This expansionism may or may not be imperialism. Certainly cultural imperialism may be too blunt an analytical tool, as Ryan Dunch has pointed out.[51] Yet the cultural expansion of missionaries and reformers ran parallel to the growth of the American informal economic empire and formal political empire, and the interpretation of this cultural history has typically been shaped by internalist arguments analogous to that for the empire of trade. Like the Williams school, missionary historiography has emphasized the outward thrust of American power and motives. In the 1950s Paul Varg found a national spirit of progressivism, humanitarianism, and nationalism behind the surge of American missionary activity.[52] In the early 1980s Emily Rosenberg charted, in *Spreading the American Dream,* the dynamism of the Student Volunteer Movement, which gave an important impetus to missionary activity from the late 1880s to 1914.[53]

Michael Parker's recent history of the SVM, *Kingdom of Character* (1997), credits the YMCA, revivalism, and premier nineteenth-century American evangelist Dwight Moody as being at the root of the SVM, noting that from the revivalist spirit came the huge outpouring of missionary effort in the 1890s and beyond.[54]

Rather than seeing these activities as the result of dynamic internal American development spilling beyond American borders, it was external stimuli that drew American reformers and missionaries abroad and encouraged innovative policies and organizational forms for the subsequent push. This reinterpretation centers especially on the attempts of missionaries "on the ground" in the colonies and spheres of influence of the European powers to frame Christian responses to the rise of indigenous religious or nationalistic revitalization and the impact of Western agnosticism in the colonies. Whereas most scholarly attention on the American missionary contribution has come from a focus on China, it was India that produced the initial ignition point for this expansion because it was there that the education of indigenous youths in Western schools had, in the 1880s, proceeded the farthest among elites.[55] From there the influence of the American missionary reaction spread across Asia and Latin America, influencing the way American missionaries confronted imperial and quasi-imperial contexts.

The movement is said to have begun in 1886 at the Northfield Conference organized by Dwight Moody—Bradley J. Longfield has called it a missionary "gusher" like an oil field—but the effects came from careful planning by religious leaders who were responding to the new opportunities for evangelization and was not new at all.[56] It was part of a wider attempt at Christianization addressed by missionary converts from the field, including by foreign figures from Britain. The movement was anticipated by the Cambridge Seven, led by Charles Studd, who played Test cricket for England and took a band of Christian Cambridge blues to missionary glory in China.[57] External demands were vital to the American missionaries in many ways. It was the takeover of Africa and Asia by the colonial powers that provided new opportunities and new anxieties about the failure to evangelize and produced the "evangelization of the world in this generation" as a millenarian catch cry in the 1880s. In particular, missions and mission boards at home sensed the challenge of indigenous religious revitalization in the colonies and European spheres of influence and produced the stimulus for the reorganization of American missions.

As the new missionaries spurred by these challenges moved into the field they required greater support at home. This led to the search for business involvement, and financial and organizational support, and the transformation of the missionary movement into a lay movement. The various "forward movements," especially the Layman's Missionary Movement of 1906–8, were products of the returning evangelical missionaries and YMCA workers of the 1885–1900 period.

Can this strenuous Christian agitation be connected to empire? We cannot literally prove that messianic religion was the causal factor in the annexing of an island empire, even though William McKinley was an unctuous cultivator of the evangelical reformers and reputedly prayed to God for assistance in his decision-making process. But the great religious ferment of the 1880s spurred a set of little-known humanitarian endeavors in the 1890s, particularly the Armenian refugee relief of 1895–96 and the American famine relief to India in 1897–98. In turn these experiences influenced the Cuban humanitarian relief campaign of late 1897–98. The missionary movement of the 1880s and 1890s set the context for humanitarianism. The interpretation of how the United States acquired a formal empire looks very different when seen from the perspective of these humanitarian relief debates. Whereas in the Armenian case the American effort was stymied by great power rivalries and traditions of nonintervention in Europe and the Indian famine relief was attenuated by distance and British bureaucratic control, when it came to the Spanish oppression of Cubans American hands were not tied. This is why the Protestant churches supported this manifestly political exercise. The growing sense of the United States as a missionary nation engaged in a humanitarian endeavor affected the political discourse.[58] This is not to downplay economic motives. In a similar fashion the United States had by the 1890s acquired an interest in raw materials from Latin American and Asia, as well as a thirst for markets; these were areas in which U.S. economic interests were implicated in terms of the rights and responsibilities of American citizens.

After 1898 the missionaries and their immense network of allies at home had to confront the reality of an American formal empire. They were divided over the efficacy of American action but saw opportunities to convert this potential calamity into a positive achievement by lobbying for policies to improve the American empire.[59] This intervention occurred in the politics of alcohol, sex, and opium. In each of these areas a missionary and reformist lobby arose to cleanse the American empire. Strangely, although the American colonial officials were allegedly concerned with modernization and showing how exceptionally benevolent they were, they had a much lighter touch on morals. It was the forces of the voluntarist arm of the American state that developed the idea that the American empire should be moralized and turned into a moral state. By 1905 this moral state had begun to be achieved through the policy of prohibiting the use of opium in the Philippines by 1908, and after 1906 by the appropriation of what was nongovernment advocacy into official U.S. government policy on opium, to make the United States the bearer of the anti-opium ideas of the missionaries, but for reasons of foreign policy. American policy makers sought to assert American hegemony in East Asia to undermine the moral authority of the British and to aid the processes of modernization in China.[60]

These moralist policies operated outside the idea of formal empire but told much about the emergence of U.S. hegemony. They also presaged a growing accommodation of the moral reformers and the American state. Although politicians and moral lobbyists were often at odds over the details of policy and on how far moral reform should be taken, the moral state was reflected in the professed opinions of leading politicians. From Theodore Roosevelt through William Howard Taft, secretaries of state John Hay and Elihu Root, and Woodrow Wilson, as well as in the thought of strategists such as Alfred Thayer Mahan, American leaders saw the moral reform societies and Protestant missionaries as an important part of the extension of American influence in the Philippines, East Asia generally, and globally.[61] An evangelical coalition became aligned with the formal structures of empire but encouraged informal rather than formal control. Moral reform became part of the glue of American empire. One can trace this process in the Philippines through the role of the YMCA in creating a notion of Filipino manhood through muscular Christianity and in the strong racial hierarchy of that organization in Manila before World War I. Also worthy of attention are the activities of the Episcopal bishop of Manila, Charles Henry Brent, as an informal adviser to the government and a go-between with the white business community. The same theme is also present in the way a church hospital did part of the work of the state in controlling venereal disease among prostitutes on behalf of the Philippine government after the official inspection of prostitutes by the American army was abandoned. In this way the services of the colonial state were partly subcontracted.[62]

Although opinion among moral reformers was divided over the efficacy of a formal empire, missionaries and reform organizations contributed the moral scaffolding that enabled that formal colonial empire to be sustained. They also contributed across the colonial world to the development of larger informal networks of influence that complemented the better-known informal activities of American trade and finance. The neglect of American empire has reflected partly the forgetting of these voluntarist activities and partly their highly successful effort to promote American "expansion" as different from that of European countries.

In this essay I have focused on selective remembering by looking at three themes in the conceptualization of empire in American history. One is the memorialization of colonial wars, the second the historiographical context found in an attenuated tradition of confronting the history of American empire in all of its complexity, and the third the relationship between more commonly accepted ideas about American empire and transnational reform and missionary networks. Empire is a multilateral process, not simply one of outward "expansion," although the reciprocal effects are uneven; the American empire is held together not only by the glue of trade but also by culture and morality. The question posed in this volume—how could the fragmentary empire of island colonies have had such a profound impact on a large continental nation?—can be partly answered by attending to the networks of missionaries and moral reformers that lobbied for changes in government policy in the United States on the basis of events and circumstances in the Philippines and other territories acquired in 1898. These same forces encouraged the American experience of colonialism and imperialism to be seen as benevolent expansion.[63]

Answering the question about the domestic American impacts of the island empire is complicated, however, by the activities of these missionaries and other evangelical reformers because their experience was not confined to formal or even informal colonial power. Missionaries who served in the Philippines, such as Methodist (later bishop) Homer Stuntz, also served elsewhere or had global careers. Stuntz's work in the Manila Evangelical Union against U.S. colonial drug policies in 1903 was informed by time spent as a missionary observing the British government's opium policies in India, where he had spent nine years, more time than he would spend in the Philippines.[64] Bishop Brent did not serve in other missionary stations, but, like many missionaries, he saw the Christian missionary enterprise as one that was above nation and empire. Brent's contacts were with Anglican prelates, clergy, missionaries, and colonial rulers all over the British Empire. Brent was just as likely to hobnob with Archbishop of Canterbury Randall Davidson as with Theodore Roosevelt. The world was ultimately his field, which was why he found working for the United States in 1909 as a member of the International Opium Commission in Shanghai a necessary task and why his last years were devoted to this issue on the world stage as part of the American delegations to additional opium conferences in the 1920s. Missionaries obscured the rise of American empire by directing attention to its Christian and global dimensions. But the idea that American empire is everywhere, and not limited to specific territorial bounds, is precisely the dimension that makes it distinctive today.

This essay began with a representation of American empire and ends with another that will reinforce this final point. In the summer of 1906 Methodists gathered in the annual camp meetings at Ocean Grove, New Jersey. Eight thousand people assembled on the morning of August 5 to hear the testimony of a dozen missionaries from India, China, and the Philippines. Homer Stuntz delivered a sermon in praise of American colonialism. "Since Dewey and his men won that memorable victory over the Spaniards," Stuntz rejoiced, Methodism had "made rapid strides in the Far East." Note that he did not limit the salutary benefits of the American occupation to the Philippines alone, despite the checklist of church schools, hospitals, and "native" preachers there that he recited.[65] The American entry was to the "Far East," allowing the United States to intervene on behalf of threatened missionaries and businessmen as part of the response of the "civilized world" to the Boxer Rebellion. But more than that the role of the United States would henceforth be one of a transnational arbiter of righteous power. As Stuntz put it in his 1904 book, *The Philippines and the Far East*, God had "unhinged the barred gates of these Islands" with "cannon and shell and all the horrid din of war," but the "Almighty Ruler" had thereby placed the United States in a special position. He had "made America for a mighty destiny." He had "set her in these seas not for her own aggrandizement, but that she may work out His sovereign will of righteousness among these nations."[66] Stuntz grasped the world-historical role that the United States had assumed, and he both reflected and helped to create the notion that the United States was developing of its own imperial role. He hoped that American influence would be spread not by guns but by "silently wafting the bloom of our civilization over the vast populations of the Orient" using the Philippines as a beachhead. The Methodists at Ocean Grove apparently agreed. They heard the good tidings from India and China, where the United States did not rule, and made no distinction between a formal and informal empire. These were all territories for Christ. In the afternoon, after Stuntz spoke, Sunday school students brought home the point that the American missionary field was to the whole world when they presented "an entertaining floral exercise." The feature of the service was the formation of two "human bouquets" by the students. This was the "World's Bouquet," presented in grateful honor of the worldwide mission that American Protestant Christianity had undertaken. The American empire was not to be located in a specific colony; its influence was to be felt everywhere.[67]

NOTES

MCCOY, SCARANO, AND JOHNSON—ON THE TROPIC OF CANCER

1. Angus Maddison, *The World Economy* (Paris: Development Centre of the Organization for Economic Cooperation and Development, 2006), pp. 98–99, 486–87, 540, 582–85; D. K. Fieldhouse, *The Colonial Empires: A Comparative Survey from the Eighteenth Century* (London: Macmillan, 1982), pp. 242, 303, 357.

2. Niall Ferguson, *Colossus: The Price of America's Empire* (New York: Penguin, 2004), pp. 14–15.

3. For a widely read discussion of this distinction, see Hannah Arendt, *The Origins of Totalitarianism* (New York: Meridian, 1958), pp. 222–66.

4. Eliot A. Cohen, "History and the Hyperpower," *Foreign Affairs* 83, no. 4 (July–August 2004): pp. 49–63; Stockholm International Peace Research Institute, *SIPRI Yearbook, 2006: Armament, Disarmament, and International Security* (New York: Oxford University Press, 2006), p. 301.

5. Ann Laura Stoler and Frederick Cooper, "Between Metropole and Colony: Rethinking a Research Agenda," in Frederick Cooper and Ann Laura Stoler, eds., *Tensions of Empire: Colonial Cultures in a Bourgeois World* (Berkeley: University of California Press, 1997), p. 5.

6. See John Lewis Gaddis, "New Conceptual Approaches to the Study of American Foreign Relations: Interdisciplinary Perspectives," *Diplomatic History* 14 no. 3 (1990): pp. 411–12; and Edward P. Crapol, "Coming to Terms with Empire: The Historiography of Late Nineteenth-Century American Foreign Relations," *Diplomatic History* 16, no. 4 (1992): p. 586.

7. Charles S. Maier, *Among Empires: American Ascendancy and Its Predecessors* (Cambridge: Harvard University Press, 2006), pp. 20–21.

8. Benita Parry, "Problems of Current Theories of Colonial Discourse," *Oxford Literary Review* 9, nos. 1–2 (1987): pp. 27–58, quoted in David Spurr, *Rhetoric of Empire: Colonial Discourse in Journalism, Travel Writing, and Imperial Administration* (Durham: Duke University Press, 1993), p. 5.

9. Amy Kaplan and Donald E. Pease, eds., *Cultures of United States Imperialism* (Durham: Duke University Press, 1993).

10. Ian Tyrrell, "American Exceptionalism in an Age of International History," *American Historical Review* 96, no. 4 (1991): pp. 1031–35; Julian Go, "The Provinciality of American Empire: 'Liberal Exceptionalism' and U.S. Colonial Rule, 1898–1912," *Comparative Studies in Society and History* 49, no. 1 (2007): pp. 74–108.

11. William Appleman Williams, *The Tragedy of American Diplomacy* (New York: Dell, 1962), pp. 24, 37–38, 43–45; Bradford Perkins, "The Tragedy of American Diplomacy: Twenty-Five Years After," *Reviews in American History* 12, no 1 (1984): pp. 1–3; Andrew J. Bacevich, *American Empire: The Realities and Consequences of U.S. Diplomacy* (Cambridge: Harvard University Press, 2002), pp. 23–31.

12. Williams, *The Tragedy of American Diplomacy,* pp. 232–34, 244–59; Perkins, "The Tragedy of American Diplomacy," pp. 9–11, n. 43.

13. Joseph Fry, "From Open Door to World Systems: Economic Interpretations of Late Nineteenth Century American Foreign Relations," *Pacific Historical Review* 65, no. 2 (1996): p. 278; Arthur M. Schlesinger Jr., *The Cycles of American History* (Boston: Houghton Mifflin, 1986), p. 143.

14. Schlesinger, one of the few to point out the Wisconsin school's reliance on conventional U.S. sources, noted that among the 1,700 footnotes in Williams's *The Roots of the Modern American Empire* "only 22 referred to non-American books" and among the 557 ootnotes in Walter LaFeber's *Inevitable Revolutions: The United States in Central America* "only 7 were to works in Spanish" (*The Cycles of American History,* p. 140). For some sense of the controversy over cold war revisionism, see Francis Loewenheim, "The New Left and the Origins of the Cold War," *New York Times Book Review,* June 17, 1973, pp. 6–8, 10; Robert James Maddox, *The New Left and the Origins of the Cold War* (Princeton: Princeton University Press, 1973), pp. 13–37; Perkins, "The Tragedy of American Diplomacy," pp. 9–14; Schlesinger, *The Cycles of American History,* pp. 193–216; and Paul M. Buhle and Edward Rice-Maximin, *William Appleman Williams: The Tragedy of Empire* (New York: Routledge, 1995), pp. 186–96.

15. For sources used to document the Caribbean context for U.S. expansion, see Walter LaFeber, *The New Empire: An Interpretation of American Expansion, 1860–1898* (Ithaca: Cornell University Press, 1963), pp. 127–30, 218–29, 242–83, 285–300, 333–51.

16. On the transactional political relationship between American colonials and Filipino elites, see Theodore Friend, *Between Two Empires: The Ordeal of the Philippines, 1929–1946* (New Haven: Yale University Press, 1965); Bonifacio Salamanca, *The Filipino Reaction to American Rule, 1901–1913* (Hamden, Conn.: Shoe String Press, 1968); Michael Cullinane, *Ilustrado Politics: Filipino Elite Responses to American Rule, 1898–1908* (Quezon City: Ateneo de Manila University Press, 2003); Michael Cullinane, "The Politics of Collaboration in Tayabas Province: The Early Political Career of Manuel Luis Quezon, 1903–1906," in Peter W. Stanley, ed., *Reappraising an Empire: New Perspectives on Philippine-American History* (Cambridge: Harvard University Press, 1984), pp. 69–81; and Nicholas Cullather, *Illusions of Influence: The Political Economy of United States–Philippines Relations, 1942–1960* (Stanford: Stanford University Press, 1994). On the multifocal views of Philippine colonial warfare, see, Glenn A. May, *Battle for Batangas: A Philippine Province at War* (New Haven: Yale University Press, 1991); William H Scott, *Ilocano Responses to American Aggression, 1900–1901* (Quezon City: New Day, 1986); and Resil Mojares, *The War against the Americans: Resistance and Collaboration in Cebu, 1899–1906* (Quezon City: Ateneo de Manila University Press, 1999).

For an innovative study of disease regimes with important implications for our understanding of colonial warfare and related American public health efforts, see Ken DeBevoise, *Agents of Apocalypse: Epidemic Disease in the Colonial Philippines* (Princeton: Princeton University Press, 1995). For a useful summary of the contributions and deficiencies of this literature see, Glenn A. May, "The Unfathomable Other: Historical Studies of U.S.–Philippine Relations," in Warren I. Cohen, ed., *Pacific Passage: The Study of American–East Asia Relations on the Eve of the Twentieth Century* (New York: Columbia University Press, 1996), pp. 279–312. For a discussion of sources with parallel insights into the Caribbean and Latin America, see Fry, "From Open Door to World Systems," pp. 284–86.

17. Thomas J. McCormick, "World Systems," *Journal of American History* 77, no. 1 (1990): pp. 125–32; Tyrrell, "American Exceptionalism in an Age of International History," pp. 1042–44; Fry, "From Open Door to World Systems," pp. 284–300.

18. Andrew Bacevich, "Introduction," in William Appleman Williams, *Empire as a Way of Life* (Brooklyn: Ig, 2007), p. vi; Crapol, "Coming to Terms with Empire," pp. 584–97.

19. Ann Laura Stoler, "Tense and Tender Ties: The Politics of Comparison in North American History and (Post) Colonial Studies," *Journal of American History* 88, no. 3 (2001): p. 830.

20. Christopher Capozzola, "Empire as a Way of Life: Gender, Culture, and Power in New Histories of U.S. Imperialism," *Journal of the Gilded Age and Progressive Era* 1, no. 4 (October 2002): p. 364.

21. Kaplan and Pease, *Cultures of United States Imperialism*, p. 23.

22. Amy Kaplan, *The Anarchy of Empire in the Making of U.S. Culture* (Cambridge: Harvard University Press, 2002); Ann Laura Stoler, ed., *Haunted by Empire: Geographies of Intimacy in North American History* (Durham: Duke University Press, 2006).

23. Stoler, "Tense and Tender Ties," pp. 830–31.

24. Mary A. Renda, *Taking Haiti: Military Occupation and the Culture of U.S. Imperialism, 1915–1940* (Chapel Hill: University of North Carolina Press, 2001); Eileen Findlay, *Imposing Decency: The Politics of Sexuality and Race in Puerto Rico* (Durham: Duke University Press, 1999); Eric T. L. Love, *Race over Empire: Racism and U.S. Imperialism, 1865–1900* (Chapel Hill: University of North Carolina Press, 2004).

25. David P. Barrows, "The Governor-General of the Philippines under Spain and the United States," in H. Morse Stephens and Herbert E. Bolton, eds., *The Pacific Ocean in History* (New York: Macmillan, 1917), pp. 253, 265.

26. In the twenty-five years since Stephen Skowronek's *Building a New American State* appeared, historians and political scientists have argued that the American state, though comparatively small, still compiled an impressive record of achievement by protecting intellectual property, procuring armaments, regulating trade, closing the frontier, and presiding over the construction of a massive transport and communications infrastructure. Yet even with this corrective Washington's achievements lay in the realm of regulating private sector actors, and it still lacked, circa 1898, an apparatus for active governance of its citizens. See, Stephen Skowronek, *Building a New American State: The Expansion of National Administrative Capacities, 1877–1920* (Cambridge: Cambridge University Press, 1982), pp. 26, 45–56; Daniel P. Carpenter, "The Multiple and Material Legacies of Stephen Skowronek," *Social Science History* 27, no. 3 (2003): pp. 465–74; Richard R. John, "Ruling Passions: Political Economy in Nineteenth-Century America," *Journal of Public Policy* 18, no. 1 (2006): pp. 1–20; and Richard Franklin Bensel, *Yankee Leviathan: The Origins of Central State Authority in America, 1859–1877* (Cambridge: Cambridge University Press, 1990), pp. 5–17.

27. Victoria de Grazia, *Irresistible Empire: America's Advance through Twentieth-Century Europe* (Boston: Belknap, 2005).

28. For an example of the literature on Haiti, see, for example, Renda, *Taking Haiti*.

29. Ray Stannard Baker, "General Leonard Wood. A Character Sketch," *McClure's*, February 1900, pp. 368–79.

30. "Carlos Juan Finlay (1833–1915)," Philip S. Hench Walter Reed Yellow Fever Collection, Historical Collections, University of Virginia Health Sciences Library, http://etext.virginia.edu/healthsci/reed/finlay.html (accessed January 28, 2008).

31. James A. Field Jr., "American Imperialism: The Worst Chapter in Almost Any Book," *American Historical Review* 83, no. 3 (1978): pp. 652–53.

32. Stanley Karnow, *In Our Image: America's Empire in the Philippines* (New York: Random House, 1989), pp. 127–28.

33. E. Arsenio Manuel, *Dictionary of Philippine Biography*, vol. 2 (Quezon City: Filipiniana, 1970), pp. 304–8.

34. James A. Robertson, "Social Structure and Ideas of Law among Early Philippine Peoples and a Recently Discovered Prehispanic Criminal Code of the Philippine Islands," in H. Morse Stephens and Herbert E. Bolton, eds., *The Pacific Ocean in History* (New York: Macmillan, 1917), pp. 164–65, 167, 177.

35. Truman R. Clark, "'Educating the Natives in Self-Government': Puerto Rico and the United States, 1900–1933," *Pacific Historical Review* 42, no. 2 (1973): pp. 220–33.

36. Richard W. Leopold, *The Growth of American Foreign Policy: A History* (New York: Knopf, 1962), pp. 192–201.

37. Christopher Bayly and Tim Harper, *Forgotten Armies: The Fall of British Asia, 1941–1945* (London: Allen Lane, 2004), pp. 30–36.

38. Andrew J. Bacevich, "New Rome, New Jerusalem," in Andrew J. Bacevich, ed., *The Imperial Tense: Prospects and Problems of American Empire* (Chicago: Ivan R. Dee, 2003), pp. 98–101.

39. Ann Laura Stoler with David Bond, "Refractions off Empire: Untimely Comparisons in Harsh Times," *Radical History Review* 95 (spring 2006): p. 95.

40. Go, "The Provinciality of American Empire," p. 77.

41. Alejandro Colas, *Empire* (Cambridge: Polity, 2007), pp. 5–11, 162–78.

42. Chalmers Johnson, *The Sorrows of Empire: Militarism, Secrecy, and the End of the Republic* (New York: Metropolitan Books, 2004), p. 5.

43. Basevich, *American Empire*, pp. 2–3, 232–33.

44. Paul Kennedy, *The Rise and Fall of the Great Powers: Economic Change and Military Conflict from 1500 to 2000* (New York: Vintage, 1989), pp. 528–40.

45. Michael Hardt and Antonio Negri, *Empire* (Cambridge: Harvard University Press, 2000), pp. xii–xvi, 186–90. For an application of the concept of hegemony to the United States as a world power see McCormick, "World Systems," pp. 128–32.

46. Fergusson, *Colossus*, pp. 2–19.

47. Niall Fergusson, "A World without Power," *Foreign Policy*, no. 143 (2004): pp. 32–39.

48. Michael Ignatieff, "The Burden," *New York Times Magazine*, January 5, 2003, pp. 22–23.

49. Maier, *Among Empires*, pp. 14–15, 32–33.

50. Max Boot, "American Imperialism? No Need to Run Away from Label," *U.S.A Today*, May 6, 2003; Bacevich, *The Imperial Tense*, pp. xii–xiii.

51. Max Boot, *The Savage Wars of Peace: Small Wars and the Rise of American Power* (New York: Basic Books, 2002), pp. xx, 351–52.

52. Cohen, "History and the Hyperpower," p. 56.

53. William Appleman Williams, *Empire as a Way of Life* (New York: Oxford University Press, 1980), p. 170, quoted in Basevich, *American Empire*, p. 243.

54. Arthur Schlesinger Jr., *The Cycles of American History* (Boston: Houghton Mifflin, 1986), p. 141, quoted in Basevich, *American Empire*, p. 30.

55. Basevich, *American Empire*, p. 244; Boot, "American Imperialism?"

56. Richard W. Leopold, "The Emergence of America as a World Power: Some Second Thoughts," in John Braeman, Robert H. Bremner, and Everett Walters, eds., *Change and Growth in Twentieth Century America* (New York: Harper and Row, 1966), pp. 13–14.

57. Quoted in David H. Burton, "Theodore Roosevelt's Social Darwinism and Views on Imperialism," *Journal of the History of Ideas* 26, no. 1 (1965): p. 111.

58. George W. Bush, "President's Remarks at the 2004 National Convention," http://www.whitehouse.gov/news/releases/2004/09/20040902-2.html (accessed September 12, 2007).

59. Samuel P. Huntington, "Bases of Accommodation," *Foreign Affairs* 46 (July 1968): pp. 642–56; Michael E. O'Hanlon and Kenneth M. Pollack, "A War We Just Might Win," *New York Times*, July 30, 2007, p. 17.

60. Stoler, "Refractions off Empire," p. 95.

61. Cohen, "History and the Hyperpower," p. 55.

62. Johnson, *The Sorrows of Empire*, pp. 151–85; Chalmers Johnson, "America's Empire of Bases," *TomDispatch.com*, January 15, 2004, http://www.tomdispatch.com/post/1181 (accessed September 12, 2007).

63. Paul Kennedy, "The Eagle Has Landed," *Financial Times* (London), February 2, 2002, p. 1.

64. Howard Zinn, *A People's History of the United States, 1492–Present* (New York: Harper-Perennial, 1995), pp. 305–16.

65. Amy Kaplan, "Left Alone with America: The Absence of Empire in the Study of American Culture," in Amy Kaplan and Donald E. Pease, eds., *Cultures of United States Imperialism* (Durham: Duke University Press, 1993), pp. 3–21.

FRADERA—READING IMPERIAL TRANSITIONS

1. C. A. Bayly, *The Birth of the Modern World, 1780–1914* (Oxford: Blackwell, 2004); Bernard Bailyn, *Atlantic History: Concepts and Contours* (Cambridge: Harvard University Press, 2005).

2. Anthony Pagden, *Lords of All the World: Ideologies of Empire in Spain, Britain, and France, 1500–1800* (New Haven: Yale University Press, 1995).

3. John H. Elliott, *Empires of the Atlantic World: Britain and Spain in America, 1492–1830* (New Haven: Yale University Press, 1995).

4. J. A. Hobson, *The Eastern Origins of Western Civilisation* (Cambridge: Cambridge University Press, 2004).

5. Pierre Guichard, *Al-Andalus frente a la conquista cristiana: Los musulmanes de Valencia (siglos XI–XIII)* (Valencia: Publicacions de la Universitat de València and Biblioteca Nueva, 2001).

6. A. J. R. Russell-Wood, *The Portuguese Empire, 1415–1808* (Baltimore: Johns Hopkins University Press, 1992).

7. Carlos Sempat Assadourian, "La despoblación indígena en el Perú y México durante el siglo XVI y la formación de la economía colonial," in *La formación de América Latina: La época colonial* (Mexico City: El Colegio de México, 1992), pp. 63–98.

8. Peter J. Bakewell, *Miners of the Red Mountain: Indian Labor in Potosí, 1545–1650* (Albuquerque: University of New Mexico Press, 1984).

9. Herbert S. Klein, *La esclavitud africana en América Latina y el Caribe* (Madrid: Alianza Editorial, 1986).

10. Luiz Felipe de Alencastro, *O trato dos viventes: Formaçao do Brasil no Atlântico Sul, séculos XVI e XVII* (São Paulo: Companhia das Letras, 2000).

11. Stuart Schwartz, *Sugar Plantations in the Formation of Brazilian Society: Bahia, 1550–1853* (Cambridge: Cambridge University Press, 1985).

12. David Eltis, *The Rise of African Slavery in the Americas* (Cambridge: Cambridge University Press, 2000); Stuart Schwart, ed., *Tropical Babylons: Sugar and the Making of the Atlantic World, 1450–1680* (Chapel Hill: University of North Carolina Press, 2004).

13. James Riley, *The Seven Years War and the Old Regime in France* (Princeton: Princeton University Press, 1986).

14. Stanley J. Stein and Barbara H. Stein, *Apogee of Empire: Spain and New Spain in the Age of Charles III, 1759–1789* (Baltimore: John Hopkins University Press, 2003).

15. Herbert S. Klein, *Las finanzas del imperio español en América, 1680–1809* (Mexico City: Instituto de Investigaciones José Luis Mora, 1994).

16. Carlos Marichal, *La bancarrota del virreinato: Nueva España y las finanzas del imperio español, 1780–1810* (Mexico City: Colegio de México, 1999).

17. David J. Weber, *Bárbaros: Spaniards and Their Savages in the Age of Enlightenment* (New Haven: Yale University Press, 2005).

18. Patrick Wilken, *Empire Adrift: The Portuguese Court in Rio de Janeiro, 1808–1821* (London: Bloomsbury, 2004).

19. Lawrence Stone, ed., *An Imperial State at War: Britain from 1689–1815* (London: Routledge, 1994).
20. C. A. Bayly, *Imperial Meridian: The British Empire and the World, 1780–1830* (London: Longman, 1989).
21. R. W. Alstyne, *The Rising American Empire* (Chicago: Quadrangle, 1960); Peter S. Onuf, *Jefferson's Empire: The Languages of the American Nationhood* (Charlottesville: University Press of Virginia, 2001).
22. Barbara Arneil, *John Locke and America: The Defence of English Colonialism* (Oxford: Clarendon, 1996).
23. C. A. Bayly, "The British and Indigenous Peoples: Power, Perception, and Identity," in Martin Daunton and Rick Halpern, eds., *Empire and Others: British Encounters with Indigenous Peoples, 1600–1850* (London: UCL Press, 1999), pp. 19–41.
24. Peter S. Onuf, *Statehood and Union: A History of Northwest Ordinance* (Bloomington: Indiana University Press, 1987).
25. William G. McLoughlin, *Cherokee Renascence in the New Republic* (Princeton: Princeton University Press, 1986).
26. Claudio Saunt, *A New Order of Things: Property, Power, and the Transformation of the Creek Indians, 1733–1816* (Cambridge: Cambridge University Press, 1999).
27. Stuart Banner, *How the Indians Lost Their Land: Law and Power on the Frontier* (Cambridge, Mass.: Belknap, 2005).
28. Roger G. Kennedy, *Mr. Jefferson's Lost Cause: Land, Farmers, and the Louisiana Purchase* (Oxford: Oxford University Press, 2003).
29. Edmund S. Morgan, *American Slavery and American Freedom: The Ordeal of Colonial Virginia* (New York: Norton, 1976).
30. Merrill Jensen, *The Articles of Confederation: An Interpretation of the Social-Constitutional History of the American Revolution, 1774–1781* (Madison: University of Wisconsin Press, [1940] 1970).
31. Jack P. Greene, *Pursuits of Happiness: The Social Development of Early Modern British Colonies and the Formation of American Culture* (Chapel Hill: University of North Carolina Press, 1988).
32. Onuf, *Jefferson's Empire*, p. 149.
33. Stanley L. Engerman, ed., *Terms of Labor: Slavery, Serfdom, and Free Labor* (Stanford: Stanford University Press, 1999); David Eltis, Frank D. Lewis, and Kenneth L. Sokoloff, eds., *Slavery in the Development of the Americas* (Cambridge: Cambridge University Press, 2004).
34. Seymour Drescher, *Econocide: British Slavery in the Era of Abolition* (Pittsburgh: University of Pittsburgh Press, 1977).
35. William Green, *British Slave Emancipation: The Sugar Colonies and the Great Experiment, 1830–1865* (Oxford: Clarendon, 1976); Yves Bénot and Marcel Dorigny, eds., *Les rétablissements de l'esclavage dans les colonies françaises* (Paris: Maisonneuve et Larosse, 2003); David Northrup, *Indentured Labor in the Age of Imperialism, 1834–1922* (Cambridge: Cambridge University Press, 1995).
36. Drescher, *The Mighty Experiment: Free Labor versus Slavery in British Emancipation* (Oxford: Oxford University Press, 2002).
37. J. M. Fradera, "De la periferia al centro (Cuba, Puerto Rico, y Filipinas en la crisis del Imperio español)," *Anuario de Estudios Americanos* 61, no. 1 (2004): pp. 161–99.
38. Allan J. Kuethe, *Cuba, 1753–1815: Crown, Military, and Society* (Knoxville: University of Tennessee Press, 1999).
39. Allan J. Kuethe and Douglas Ingliss, "Absolutism and Enlightened Reforms: Charles III and the Establishment of the Alcabala and Commercial Reorganization in Cuba," *Past and Present* 109 (1985): pp. 118–43.

40. Manuel Moreno Fraginals, *El Ingenio: Complejo económico social cubano del azúcar*, 3 vols. (Havana: Editorial de Ciencias Sociales, 1978); Francisco A. Scarano, *Sugar and Slavery in Puerto Rico: The Plantation Economy of Ponce, 1800–1850* (Madison: University of Wisconsin Press, 1984).

41. O. H. K. Spate, *The Spanish Lake* (London: Croom Helm, 1979).

42. J. M. Fradera, *Filipinas, la colonia más peculiar: La hacienda pública en la determinación de la política colonial, 1766–1868* (Madrid: Consejo Superior de Investigaciones Científicas, 1999).

43. Edilberto de Jesus, *The Tobacco Monopoly in the Philippines: Bureaucratic Enterprise and Social Change, 1766–1880* (Quezon City: Ateneo de Manila Press, 1980).

44. Benito Legarda Jr., *After the Galleons: Foreign Trade, Economic Change, and Entrepreneurship in the Nineteenth-Century Philippines* (Quezon City: Ateneo de Manila University Press, 1999).

45. Vincent Harlow, *The Founding of the Second British Empire*, 3 vols. (London: Longman, [1952] 1964).

46. John Darwin, "Imperialism and the Victorians: The Dynamics of Territorial Expansion," *English Historical Review* 112, no. 447 (1997): pp. 614–42.

47. Martin Lynn, "British Policy, Trade, and Informal Empire in the Mid-Nineteenth Century," in Andrew Porter, ed., *The Oxford History of the British Empire: The Nineteenth Century* (Oxford: Oxford University Press, 1999), pp. 101–23.

48. Bayly, *Imperial Meridian*.

49. C. A. Bayly, *India and the Making of the British Empire* (Cambridge: Cambridge University Press, 1988).

50. Ranajit Guha, *A Rule of Property for Bengal: An Essay on the Idea of Permanent Settlement* (Durham: Duke University Press, [1963] 1996); Burton Stein, *Thomas Munro: The Origins of the Colonial State and His Vision of Empire* (Delhi: Oxford University Press, 1989).

51. David Washbrook, "South India, 1779–1840: The Colonial Transition," *Modern Asian Studies* 38, no. 3 (2004): pp. 479–516.

52. Carl Trocki, *Opium, Empire, and the Global Political Economy: A Study of the Asian Opium Trade* (London: Routledge, 1999).

53. Robert Ross, *A Concise History of South Africa* (Cambridge: Cambridge University Press, 1999); Philip D. Curtin, *The Images of Africa: British Ideas and Action, 1780–1850*, 2 vols. (Madison: University of Wisconsin Press, 1964).

54. William A. Green, "Plantation Society and Indentured Labour: The Jamaican Case, 1834–1865," in P. C. Emmer, ed., *Colonialism and Indentured Labour before and after Slavery* (Dordrecht: Martinus Nijhoff, 1986), pp. 163–86.

55. Michael Craton, *Empire, Enslavement, and Freedom in the Caribbean* (Kingston: Ian Randle, 1997).

56. J. M. Busted, *Canadian History before Confederation: Essays and Interpretations* (Georgetown: Irwin-Dorsey, 1972).

57. Ged Martin, *Britain and the Origins of Canadian Confederation, 1837–1867* (London: Macmillan, 1994).

58. Colin Newbury, *Patrons, Clients, and Empire: Chieftaincy and Over-rule in Asia, Africa, and the Pacific* (Oxford: Oxford University Press, 2003).

59. Mark Greengrass, ed., *Conquest and Coalescence: The Shaping of the State in Early Modern Europe* (London: Edward Arnold, 1991).

60. Christine Daniels and Michael V. Kennedy, eds., *Negotiated Empires: Centers and Peripheries in the Americas, 1500–1820* (New York: Routledge, 2002).

61. Jack P. Greene, *Peripheries and Center: Constitutional Development in the Extended Polities of the British Empire and the United States, 1607–1788* (New York: Norton, 1990).

62. Noelia González Adánez, *Crisis de los imperios: Monarquía y representación política en Inglaterra y España, 1763–1812* (Madrid: Centro de Estudios Políticos y Constitucionales, 2005).

63. Jean Tarrade, "De l'apogée économique à l'effrondement du domaine colonial (1763–1830)," in *Histoire de la France Coloniale: Des origines à 1914* (Paris: Armand Colin, 1991), pp. 272–74.

64. Manuel Chust Calero, *La cuestión nacional americana en las Cortes de Cádiz* (Valencia: Fundación Historia Social, 1999).

65. J. M. Fradera, "Raza y ciudadanía: El factor racial en la delimitación de los derechos de los americanos," in *Gobernar colonias* (Barcelona: Península, 1999), pp. 51–70.

66. José M. Portillo Valdés, *Revolución de nación: Orígenes de la cultura constitucional en España, 1780–1814* (Madrid: Centro de Estudios Políticos y Constitucionales, 1998).

67. J. M Fradera, "Why Were Spain's Special Overseas' Laws Never Enacted?" in Richard L. Kagan and Geoffrey Parker, eds., *Spain, Europe, and the Atlantic World: Essays in Honour of John H. Elliott* (Cambridge: Cambridge University Press, 1995), pp. 334–49.

68. J. M. Fradera, *Colonias para después de un imperio* (Barcelona: Ediciones Bellaterra, 2005).

69. Earl R. Beck, "The Martínez Campos Government of 1879: Spain's Last Chance in Cuba," *Hispanic American Historical Review* 56, no. 2 (1976): pp. 268–89.

70. Inés Roldán de Montaud, *La Restauración en Cuba: El fracaso de un proceso reformista* (Madrid: Consejo Superior de Investigaciones Científicas, 2000).

71. Luis Ángel Sánchez, *Un imperio en la vitrina: El colonialismo español en el Pacífico y la Exposición de Filipinas de 1887* (Madrid, CSIC, 2003).

72. David Huttenback, "The Durham Report and the Establishment of Responsible Government in Canada," in *The British Imperial Experience* (New York: Harper and Row, 1966), pp. 20–37. For a critical assessment, see Ged Martin, "The Influence of the Durham Report," in Ronald Hyam and Ged Martin, eds., *Reappraisals in British Imperial History* (London: Macmillan, 1975), pp. 75–87.

73. James A. Williamson, *A Short History of the British Empire and Commonwealth* (London: Macmillan, 1953). Much more interesting, see Peter Borroughs, "Imperial Institutions and the Government of Empire," in Andrew Porter, ed., *The Oxford History of the British Empire: The Nineteenth Century* (Oxford: Oxford University Press, 1999), pp. 172–97.

74. Martin Daunton, *Trusting Leviathan: The Politics of Taxation in Britain, 1799–1914* (Cambridge: Cambridge University Press, 2001).

75. J. A. Hobson, *Imperialism: A Study* (Ann Arbor: University of Michigan Press, 1991), 223.

76. David Metcalf, *Ideologies of the Raj* (Cambridge: Cambridge University Press, 1995).

77. Hugh Cunningham, *The Challenge of Democracy: Britain, 1832–1918* (Harlow: Longman, 2001), p. 184.

78. H. F. Morris and James Read, *Indirect Rule and the Search for Justice: Essays in East African Legal History* (Oxford: Clarendon, 1972).

79. Michael H. Fisher, *Indirect Rule in India: Residents and the Residency System, 1764–1858* (Delhi: Oxford University Press, 1991).

80. Clifton C. Crais, *White Supremacy and Black Resistance in Preindustrial South Africa: The Making of the Colonial Order in the Eastern Cape, 1770–1865* (Cambridge: Cambridge University Press, 1992).

81. Jacques Monet, *The Last Cannon Shot: A Study of French-Canadian Nationalism* (Toronto: University of Toronto Press, 1969).

82. Bernard Semmel, *Governor Eyre Controversy* (London: McKibbon and Kee, 1963); Gad Heuman, *"The Killing Time": The Morant Bay Rebellion in Jamaica* (Knoxville: University of Tennessee Press, 1994); Thomas C. Holt, *The Problem of Freedom: Race, Labor, and Politics in Jamaica and Britain, 1832–1938* (Baltimore: Johns Hopkins University Press, 1992).

83. W. P. Morrell, *British Colonial Policy in the Age of Peel and Russell* (London: Frank Cass, 1966).

84. Catherine Hall, *Civilising Subjects: Metropole and Colony in the English Imagination, 1830–1867* (Cambridge: Polity, 2002).

85. Jeremy Adelman and Stephen Aron, "From Borderlands to Borders: Empires, Nation-States, and the Peoples in between in North American History," *American Historical Review* 104, no. 3 (1999): pp. 814–41.

86. Onuf, *Jefferson's Empire*, pp. 182–88.

87. Edward Countryman, "Indians, the Colonial Order, and the Social Significance of the American Revolution," *William and Mary Quarterly* 53, no. 2 (1996): pp. 342–62.

88. James E. Lewis, *The American Union and the Problem of Neighborhood: The United States and the Collapse of Spanish Empire, 1783–1829* (Chapel Hill: University of North Carolina Press, 1998).

89. Charles Montgomery, *The Spanish Redemption: Heritage, Power, and Loss on New Mexico's Upper Rio Grande* (Berkeley: University of California Press, 2000); Tomas Almaguer, *Racial Fault Lines: The Historical Origins of White Supremacy in California* (Berkeley: University of California Press, 1994); David Montejano, *Anglos and Mexicans in the Making of Texas, 1836–1896* (New York: Macmillan, 1968).

90. George Dargo, *Jefferson's Louisiana: The Clash of Legal Traditions* (Cambridge: Harvard University Press, 1975); Peter J. Castor, *The Nation's Crucible: The Louisiana Purchase and the Creation of America* (New Haven: Yale University Press, 2004).

91. Rebecca J. Scott, "Derechos y honra públicos: Louis Martinet, Plessy contra Ferguson, y el acceso a la ley en Luisiana, 1888–1917," *Debate y Perspectivas* 4 (2004): pp. 171–97.

92. R. A. Williams, *The American Indian in the Western Legal Thought* (Oxford: Oxford University Press, 1990).

93. Robert Wauchope, ed., *Handbook of the Middle American Indians*, vols. 11–14 (Austin: University of Texas Press, 1964–76).

94. Bartolomé Clavero, *Derecho indígena y cultura constitucional en América* (Madrid: Siglo Veintiuno Editores, 1994), pp. 30ff.

95. David E. Wilkins, "The U.S. Supreme Court's Explication of 'Federal Plenary Powers': An Analysis of Case Law Affecting Tribal Sovereignty, 1886–1914," *American Indian Quarterly* 18, no. 3 (1994): pp. 349–68.

96. Walter L. Williams, "United States Indian Policy and the Debate over Philippine Annexation: Implications of the Origins of American Imperialism," *Journal of American History* 66, no. 4 (1980): p. 818.

97. Irene K. Harvey, "Constitutional Law: Congressional Plenary Power over Indian Affairs. A Doctrine Rooted in Prejudice," *American Indian Law Review* 10 (1982): pp. 117–50.

98. Eric Foner, *Reconstruction: America's Unfinished Revolution, 1863–1877* (New York: Harper and Row, 1988).

99. Gilbert Thomas Stephenson, "Racial Distinctions in Southern Law," *American Political Science Review* 1, no. 1 (1906): pp. 44–61.

100. Arthur Bestor, "The American Civil War as a Constitutional Crisis," *American Historical Review* 68, no. 2 (1964): pp. 327–52.

101. J. MacCardell, *The Idea of Southern Nation: Southern Nationalists and Southern Nationalism, 1830–1860* (New York: Norton, 1979).

102. Don E. Fehrenbacher, *The Slaveholding Republic: An Account of the United States Government's Relations to Slavery* (Oxford: Oxford University Press, 2001), pp. 205–30.

103. Ira Berlin, *Generations of Captivity: A History of African-American Slaves* (Cambridge, Mass.: Belknap, 2003).

104. John Ashworth, *Slavery, Capitalism, and Politics in the Antebellum Republic*, vol. 1: *Commerce and Compromise, 1820–1850* (Cambridge: Cambridge University Press, 1995), pp.

19–80; Anders Stephanson, *Manifest Destiny: American Expansion and the Empire of Right* (New York: Hill and Wang, 1995).

105. Kenneth M. Stamp, *America in 1857: A Nation on the Brink* (New York: Oxford University Press, 1990).

106. Robert E. May, *The Southern Dream of a Caribbean Empire, 1854–1861* (Athens: University of Georgia Press, 1989).

107. Peter Kolchin, *American Slavery* (London: Penguin, [1993] 1995), pp. 229ff.

108. Stanley N. Katz, "The Strange Birth and Unlikely History of Constitutional Equality," *Journal of American History* 75, no. 3 (1988): pp. 747–62.

109. On electoral censuses, see Michael Perman, *Struggle for Mastery: Disfranchisement in the South, 1888–1919* (Chapel Hill: University of North Carolina Press, 2001). On Jim Crow laws, see C. Vann Woodward, *The Strange Career of Jim Crow* (Oxford: Oxford University Press, 1974).

110. Steve Hahn, "Class and State in Postemancipation Societies, 1863–1877: Southern Planters in Comparative Perspective," *American Historical Review* 95, no. 1 (1990): pp. 75–98; Steve Hahn, *A Nation under Our Feet: Black Political Struggles in the Rural South from Slavery to the Great Migration* (Cambridge, Mass.: Belknap, 2003).

111. Harold D. Woodman, *New South–New Law: The Legal Foundations of Credit and Labor Relations in the Postbellum Agricultural South* (Baton Rouge: Louisiana State University Press, 1995).

112. Ali Behdad, *A Forgetful Nation: On Immigration and Cultural Identity in the United States* (Durham: Duke University Press, 2005).

113. Ernest May, *American Imperialism: A Speculative Essay* (Chicago: Imprint, 1991); Julius W. Pratt, *Expansionists of 1898: The Acquisition of Hawaii and Spanish Islands* (Chicago: Quadrangle, [1936] 1964); Walter LaFeber, *The New Empire: An Interpretation of American Expansion, 1860–1898* (Ithaca: Cornell University Press, [1963] 1998); William Appleman Williams, *The Tragedy of American Diplomacy* (New York: Norton, 1959); Alberto Aquarone, *Le origini dell'imperialismo americano: Da McKinley a Taft (1898–1913)* (Bologna: Il Mulino, 1973). More recently, see Frank Ninkovich, *The United States and Imperialism* (Malden, Mass.: Blackwell, 2001).

114. J. W. Burgess, "The Relation of the Constitution of the United States to Newly Acquired Territory," *Political Science Quarterly* 15, no. 3 (1900): pp. 381–98.

115. Ibid., p. 384.

116. William R. Hunt, *Distant Justice: Policing the Alaska Frontier* (Norman: University of Oklahoma Press, 1987).

117. Efrén Rivera Ramos, "Antecedentes históricos de la autonomía política de Puerto Rico como Estado Libre Asociado: Elementos definidores de la autonomía política puertorriqueña y sus fuentes de derecho," in *El alcance de la autonomía política de Puerto Rico* (Barcelona: Publicaciones del Parlamento de Cataluña, 2005), pp. 13–25.

118. José Trías Monge, *Puerto Rico: The Trials of the Oldest Colony in the World* (New Haven: Yale University Press, 1997), p. 43.

119. Arnold H. Leibowitz, *Defining Status: A Comprehensive Analysis of United States Territorial Relations* (Dordrecht: Martinus Nijhoff, 1989).

120. Ibid., p. 23.

121. Joseph A. Fallon, "Federal Policy and U.S. Territories: The Political Restructuring of the United States of America," *Pacific Affairs* 64, no. 1 (1991): p. 23.

122. Bartholomew H. Sparrow, *The Insular Cases and the Emergence of American Empire* (Lawrence: University of Kansas Press, 2006).

123. John Tone, *War and Genocide in Cuba, 1895–1898* (Chapel Hill: University of North Carolina Press, 2006); Richard E. Welch, *Response to Imperialism: The United States and the Philippine-American War, 1899–1902* (Chapel Hill: University of North Carolina Press, [1979] 1987).

124. Daniel B. Schirmer, *Republic or Empire: American Resistance to the Philippine War* (Cambridge: Schenkman, 1972).; Norman G. Owen, *Compadre Colonialism: Philippine-American Relations, 1898–1946* (Manila: Solidaridad, 1971); Peter W. Stanley, *A Nation in the Making: The Philippines and United States, 1898–1921* (Cambridge: Harvard University Press, 1974); Stanley Karnow, *In Our Image: America's Empire in the Philippines* (New York: Random House, 1989); Kenton J. Clymer, *Protestant Missionaries in the Philippines, 1898–1916* (Urbana: University of Illinois Press, 1986); Glenn Anthony May, *Social Engineering in the Philippines: The Aims, Execution, and Impact of American Colonial Policy, 1900–1913* (Westport: Greenwood, 1980); Glenn Anthony May, *Battle for Batangas: A Philippine Province at War* (New Haven: Yale University Press, 1991); Frank Hindman Golay, *Face of Empire: United States-Philippine Relations, 1898–1946* (Quezon City: Ateneo de Manila University Press, 1997); Theodore Friend, *Between Two Empires: The Ordeal of the Philippines, 1929–1946* (New Haven: Yale University Press, 1965); Theodore Friend, *The Blue-Eyed Enemy: Japan against the West in Java and Luzon, 1942–1945* (Princeton: Princeton University Press, 1988); Michael Cullinane, *Ilustrado Politics: Filipino Elite Responses to American Rule, 1898–1908* (Quezon City: Ateneo de Manila University Press, 2003); Paul A. Kramer, *The Blood of Government: Race, Empire, the United States, and the Philippines* (Chapel Hill: University of North Carolina Press, 2006).

An important interpretative counterpoint may be found in Michael Salman, "In Our Orientalist Imagination: Historiography and the Culture of Colonialism in the United States," *Radical History Review* 50 (1991): pp. 221–32; Michael Salman, *The Embarrassment of Slavery: Controversies over Bondage and Nationalism in the American Colonial Philippines* (Berkeley: University of California Press, 2001); and Reynaldo C. Ileto, *Filipinos and Their Revolution: Event, Discourse, and Historiography* (Quezon City: Ateneo de Manila University Press, 1998).

For Cuba an important bibliography also exists. Without any intention of citing exhaustively, the following works must be consulted: Ada Ferrer, *Insurgent Cuba: Race, Nation, and Revolution* (Chapel Hill: University of North Carolina Press, 1999); Louis A. Pérez Jr., *Cuba between Empires, 1878–1902* (Pittsburgh: University of Pittsburgh Press, 1989); *The War of 1898: The United States and Cuba in History and Historiography* (Chapel Hill: University of North Carolina Press, 1998); Louis A. Pérez Jr., Ivan Musicant, *Empire by Default: The Spanish and American War and the Dawn of the American Century* (New York: Henry Holt, 1998); Alejandro de la Fuente, *A Nation for All: Race, Inequality, and Politics in Cuba, 1900–2000* (Chapel Hill: University of North Carolina Press, 2000).

For Puerto Rico, see Astrid Cubano Iguina, *El hilo en el laberinto: Claves de la lucha política en Puerto Rico (siglo XIX)* (Río Piedras: Ediciones Huracán, 1990); Astrid Cubano Iguina, *Rituals of Violence in Nineteenth-Century Puerto Rico* (Gainesville: University of Florida Press, 2006); Fernando Picó, *La guerra después de la Guerra* (Río Piedras: Ediciones Huracán, 1987); Raymond Carr, *Puerto Rico: A Colonial Experiment* (New York: Vintage, 1984); Lillian Guerra, *Popular Expression and National Identity in Puerto Rico: The Struggle for Self, Community, and Nation* (Gainesville: University of Florida Press, 1998); and Rosa E. Carrasquillo, *Our Landless Patria: Marginal Citizenship and Race in Caguas, Puerto Rico, 1880–1910* (Lawrence: University of Kansas Press, 2006).

125. Albert G. Keller, "Essays in Colonization," *Yale Review* (August 1900): pp. 175–90; (May 1901): pp. 30–52; (February 1902): pp. 390–416; (May 1902): pp. 1–26.

126. David W. Noble, "The Paradox of Progressive Thought," *American Quarterly* 5, no. 3 (1953): pp. 201–12.

127. Arnold H. Leibowitz, *Defining Status*, p. 17.

128. American Economic Association, *Essays in Colonial Finance* (New York: Macmillan, 1900).

129. Jeremiah W. Jenks, *Certain Economic Questions in the English and Dutch Colonies in the Orient* (Washington, D.C.: Government Printing Office, 1905).

130. Edwin R. A. Seligman, *Essays on Taxation* (New York: Macmillan, 1895).

131. American Economic Association, *Essays in Colonial Finance*, p. 17.

132. The careful analysis of this book and other material on colonial finances are the subject of a work in progress, which I hope to publish soon.

133. American Economic Association, *Essays in Colonial Finance*, p. 18.

134. J. H. Hollander, "The Finances of Porto Rico," *Political Science Quarterly* 16, no. 4 (1901): pp. 553–81.

135. H. E. Bourne and C. H. Hull, *Publications of the American Economic Association* 2, no. 1 (1901): pp. 131–43.

136. Keith Sinclair, *William Pember Reeves: New Zealand Fabian* (Oxford: Clarendon, 1965).

137. William Pember Reeves, *State Experiments in Australia and New Zealand*, 2 vols. (Melbourne: Macmillan, 1899–1902).

138. William Pember Reeves, *Economic Journal* 11, no. 41 (1901): p. 60.

139. W. M. Daniels, *Political Science Quarterly* 16, no. 2 (1901): p. 361.

140. Uday Sing Metha, *Liberalism and Empire: A Study in Nineteenth-Century British Liberal Thought* (Chicago: University of Chicago Press, 1999).

141. Carolyn E. Fink, *The Making of Haiti: The Saint Domingue Revolution from Below* (Knoxville: University of Tennessee Press, 1990); Laurent Dubois, *A Colony of Citizens: Revolution and Slave Emancipation in the French Caribbean, 1787–1804* (Chapel Hill: University of North Carolina Press, 2004); Laurent Dubois, *Avengers of the New World: The Story of the Haitian Revolution* (Cambridge, Mass.: Belknap, 2004); David P. Geggus, ed., *The Impact of the Haitian Revolution in the Atlantic World* (Columbia: University of South Carolina Press, 2001).

142. Nicolas Bancel, Pascal Blanchard, and Françoise Vergès, *La République coloniale* (Paris: Hachette, 2003).

143. Olivier Le Cour Grandmaison, *Coloniser, Exterminer: Sur la guerre et l'État colonial* (Paris: Fayard, 2005).

McCormick—From Old Empire to New

1. See Gaddis Smith, "The Two Worlds of Samuel Flagg Bemis," *Diplomatic History* 9 (fall 1988): p. 299.

2. Richard W. Van Alstyne, *The Rising American Empire* (New York: Norton, 1960), p. 37.

3. Ibid.

4. David M. Pletcher, *The Diplomacy of Annexation: Texas, Oregon, and the Mexican War* (Columbia: University of Missouri Press, 1973).

5. Van Alstyne, *Rising American Empire*, pp. 150–57.

6. Ibid., pp. 149, 158–60.

7. See Robert E. May, *The Southern Dream of Caribbean Empire, 1854–1861* (Athens: University of Georgia Press, 1988).

8. Walter LaFeber, *The New Empire: An Interpretation of American Expansionism, 1860–1898* (Ithaca: Cornell University Press, 1963).

9. See Richard H. Zeitlin, "Brass Buttons and Iron Rails: The U.S. Army and American Involvement in Mexico, 1869–1881," PhD diss., University of Wisconsin–Madison, 1973.

10. See Tyler Dennett, *Americans in Eastern Asia: A Critical Study of the Policy of the United States with Reference to China, Japan, and Korea in the Nineteenth Century* (New York: Barnes and Noble, 1922).

11. Walter LaFeber, *The American Age: U.S. Foreign Policy at Home and Abroad, 1750 to the Present*, 2d ed. (New York and London: Norton, 1994), p. 175.

12. Van Alstyne, *Rising American Empire*, pp. 170–84.

13. Edward C. Kirkland, *A History of American Economic Life*, 3d ed. (New York: Appleton-Century-Crofts, 1951), p. 536.

14. See Bradford Perkins, *The Great Rapprochement: England and the United States, 1895–1914* (New York: Atheneum, 1968).

15. See Brooks Adams, *American Economic Supremacy* (New York: Macmillan, 1900).

16. See Readings Fels, *American Business Cycles, 1865–1897* (Chapel Hill: University of North Carolina Press, 1959).

17. Quoted in Thomas J. McCormick, *China Market: America's Quest for Informal Empire, 1893–1901* (Chicago, Quadrangle Books, 1967), p. 25.

18. Ibid., p. 28.

19. Ibid.

20. Ibid., p. 52.

21. On racism, see Eric Love, *Race over Empire: Racism and U.S. Imperialism, 1865–1900* (Chapel Hill: University of North Carolina Press, 2004). On gender, see Kristin Hoganson, *Fighting for American Manhood: How Gender Politics Provoked the Spanish-American and Philippine-American Wars* (New Haven, Yale University Press, 1998).

22. LaFeber, *New Empire*, p. 292.

23. Olney is quoted in Lloyd Gardner, Walter LaFeber, and Thomas J. McCormick., *Creation of the American Empire* (Chicago: Rand McNally, 1975), p. 239.

24. Walter LaFeber, *The American Search for Opportunity, 1865* (New York: Cambridge University Press, 1995), pp. 183–239.

25. See Julius Pratt, *America's Colonial Experiment: How the United States Acquired, Governed, and in Part Gave Away a Colonial Empire* (New York: Prentice-Hall, 1950).

26. McCormick, *China Market*, pp. 105–26.

27. See David Healy, *Drive to Hegemony: The United States in the Caribbean, 1898–1917* (Madison: University of Wisconsin Press, 1988); Thomas Schoonover, *The United States in Central America, 1860–1911: Episodes of Social Imperialism and Imperial Rivalry in the World System* (Durham: Duke University Press, 1991).

28. McCormick, *China Market*, pp. 127–54; John Gallagher and Ronald Robinson, "The Imperialism of Free Trade," *Economic History Review* 6, 2d ser. (1953): pp. 1–15.

29. See David M. Pletcher, *Rails, Mines, and Progress: Seven American Promoters in Mexico, 1867–1911* (Ithaca: Cornell University Press, 1958).

30. See Frederich Katz, *Secret War in Mexico: Europe, the United States, and the Mexican Revolution* (Chicago: University of Chicago Press, 1981).

31. William Greider, *One World, Ready or Not: The Manic Logic of Global Capitalism* (New York: Simon and Schuster, 1997), pp. 259–76.

32. The discussion of U.S. China policy draws on McCormick, *China Market*, pp. 127–95.

33. Ibid.

34. Karl Kautsky, "Ultra-Imperialism," *Die Neue Zeit*, September 1914, reprinted in the *New Left Review* 59 (January–February 1970): pp. 41–46.

McCoy—Introduction to Part 2

1. U.S. House of Representatives, 56th Cong., 2d sess., "Report of the Military Governor of Porto Rico on Civil Affairs," in *Annual Reports of the War Department for the Fiscal Year Ended June 30, 1900* (Washington, D.C.: Government Printing Office, 1902), pt. 13, p. 35.

2. White House, *National Drug Control Strategy: FY 2006 Budget Summary* (Washington, D.C.: White House, February 2005), pp. 1, 5; *Washington Post*, December 1, 2006, p. A3.

Santiago-Valles—American Penal Forms and Colonial Spanish Custodial-Regulatory Practices

1. This concept of "periphery" follows from Fernand Braudel, *Civilization and Capitalism, 15th–18th Century*, vol. 3: *The Perspective of the World* (Berkeley: University of California Press, 1992), pp. 40, 44.

2. For me, global-racial regimes are part of Braudel's "social conjunctures." See Fernand Braudel, "History and the Social Sciences," in Peter Burke, ed., *Economy and Society in Early-Modern Europe* (New York: Harper and Row, 1972), pp. 16–18.

3. See, for example, Stephen Jay Gould, *The Mismeasure of Man* (New York: Norton, 1981), pp. 73–233; and Nancy Leys Stepan, *"The Hour of Eugenics": Race, Gender, and Nation in Latin America* (Ithaca: Cornell University Press, 1991), pp. 96–97.

4. See, for example, Michel Aglietta, *A Theory of Capitalist Regulation: The U.S. Experience* (London: New Left Books, 1979), pp. 79–85, 111–19.

5. Michel Foucault, *Discipline and Punish* (New York: Vintage, 1977), p. 219.

6. See, for example, Martha Knisely Huggins, *From Slavery to Vagrancy in Brazil* (New Brunswick, N.J.: Rutgers University Press, 1985). See also notes 10, 11, and 12, below.

7. Daniel Hodas, *The Business Career of Moses Taylor* (New York: New York University Press, 1976); Birgit Sonesson, *Puerto Rico's Commerce, 1765–1865* (Los Angeles: Latin American Center, University of California, Los Angeles, 2000).

8. See, for example, Aglietta, *A Theory of Capitalist Regulation*, pp. 78–80; and Willi Paul Adams, *Los Estados Unidos de América* (Mexico City: Siglo XXI Editores, 1979), pp. 157–65, 247–54.

9. See, for example, Pasquale Pasquino, "Criminology: The Birth of a Special Savoir," *Ideology and Consciousness 7* (autumn 1980): pp. 17–32; Pedro Trinidad Fernández, *La defensa de la sociedad: Cárcel y delincuencia en España (siglos XVIII–XX)* (Madrid: Alianza Editorial, 1991), pp. 248–82; and Lawrence M. Friedman, *Crime and Punishment in American History* (Boston: Basic Books, 1993), pp. 59–163.

10. See, for example, Martin B. Miller, "At Hard Labor: Rediscovering the 19th Century Prison," in Tony Platt and Paul Takagi, eds., *Punishment and Penal Discipline: Essays on the Prison and Prisoners' Movement* (Berkeley: Crime and Social Justice Associates, 1979), pp. 82–84.

11. Friedman, *Crime and Punishment*, p. 95.

12. See, for example, Blake McKelvey, *American Prisons: A Study in American Social History prior to 1915* (Chicago: University of Chicago Press, 1936), pp. 173–87.

13. Evelyn L. Parks, "From Constabulary to Police Society: Implications for Social Control," in William Chambliss and Milton Mankoff, eds., *Whose Law, What Order?* (New York: Wiley, 1976), pp. 130–32; Friedman, *Crime and Punishment*, pp. 67–71, 149–55.

14. Jesús María Miranda, "Bentham en España," in Jeremy Bentham, *El panóptico* (Madrid: Ediciones de La Piqueta, n.d.), p. 141.

15. Ramón de la Sagra, *Cinco meses en los Estados Unidos de la América del Norte desde el 20 de abril al 23 de septiembre de 1835: Diario del viaje* (Paris: Imprenta de Pablo Renouard, 1836), pp. 12–18, 63–76, 166–69, 205–16, 284–94, 322–47, 402–10; Pedro Fraile, *Un espacio para castigar: La cárcel y la ciencia penitenciaria en España (siglos XVIII–XIX)* (Barcelona: Ediciones del Serbal, 1987), pp. 172–75, 180–81.

16. Manuel Tuñón de Lara, *La España del siglo XIX*, 2 vols. (Barcelona: Editorial Laia, 1977), vol. 1, pp. 271–96, vol. 2, pp. 11–33.

17. Fraile, *Un espacio para castigar*, p. 187.

18. See, for example, Josep Fontana, *Cambio económico y actitudes políticas en la España del siglo XIX* (Barcelona: Editorial Ariel, 1975), pp. 184–97.

19. See, for example, Francisco Tomás y Valiente, "Las cárceles y el sistema penitenciario bajo los Borbones," *Historia* 16, vol. Extra 8 (October 1978): pp. 80, 82.

20. Ramón Carnicer, *Entre la ciencia y la magia: Mariano Cubí* (Barcelona: Editorial Seix Barral, 1969), pp. 87–107, 273, 279, 291, 296.

21. See, for example, Israel Drapkin, "Manuel Montesinos y Molina: An Almost Forgotten Precursor of Penal Reform in Spain," in Marvin E. Wolfgang, ed., *Crime and Culture: Essays in Honor of Thorsten Sellin* (New York: Wiley, 1968), pp. 315–46.

22. See, for example, Jaume Curbet, "Los orígenes del aparato policial moderno en España," in José María Rico, ed., *Policía y sociedad democrática* (Madrid: Alianza Universitaria, 1983), pp. 63–72.

23. *Boletín histórico de Puerto Rico* (*BHPR*), edited by Cayetano Coll y Toste, vol. 12 (San Juan: Tipografía Cantero Fernández, 1925), 165; *BHPR* (1926), vol. 13, p. 177. This fourteen-volume series was published between 1914 and 1928.

24. *Reglamento para el Presidio de la Plaza de Puerto Rico* (n.p.: Imprenta del Gobierno, 1850); *Código Penal para las Provincias de Cuba y Puerto Rico* (Madrid: Imprenta Nacional, 1879), pp. 26–49.

25. Archivo General de Puerto Rico (AGPR), Fondo Gobernadores Españoles (FGE), Serie Presidio de la Puntilla, Entrada no. 154, Cajas nos. 247–64; *BHPR* (1917), vol. 4, p. 254; *BHPR* (1918), vol. 5, pp. 229–30; *BHPR* (1922), vol. 9, pp. 16, 21; *BHPR* (1924), vol. 11, p. 273; María de los Angeles Castro, *La arquitectura en San Juan de Puerto Rico (siglo XIX)* (Río Piedras: Editorial Universitaria, 1980), pp. 94–98, 304, 308.

26. AGPR, FGE, Serie Casa de Beneficiencia, Entrada no. 215, Cajas nos. 300–301; Henry K. Carroll, *Report on the Island of Porto Rico* (Washington, D.C.: Government Printing Office, 1899), p. 599; *BHPR* (1924), vol. 11, p. 273; *BHPR* (1922), vol. 9, p. 16.

27. AGPR, FGE, Serie Casa de Beneficiencia, Entrada no. 215, Caja no. 300; Francisco de Goenaga, *Desarrollo histórico del Asilo de Beneficiencia y Manicomio de Puerto Rico* (San Juan: n.p., 1929), pp. 12–24, 227–231; Teresita Martínez-Vergne, *Shaping the Discourse on Space: Charity and Its Wards in Nineteenth-Century San Juan, Puerto Rico* (Austin: University of Texas Press, 1999), pp. 49, 50, 64, 77, 109.

28. Ruth Pike, *Penal Servitude in Early Modern Spain* (Madison: University of Wisconsin Press, 1983), pp. 60–61; Lidio Cruz Monclova, *Historia del año 1887* (Río Piedras: Editorial Universitaria, 1970), pp. 260–62, 278–80, 312–17.

29. Fernando Picó, *Libertad y servidumbre en el Puerto Rico del siglo XIX* (Río Piedras: Ediciones Huracán, 1979), pp. 107, 114–15.

30. Andrés Molinero y Gómez Cornejo, *Compilación de las disposiciones de la Guardia Civil de Puerto Rico* (n.p.: Establecimiento del Boletín, 1879).

31. Francisco del Valle Atiles, *El campesino puertorriqueño* (San Juan: Tipografía J. González Font., 1887), p. 131; Salvador Brau, *Ensayos (disquisiciones sociológicas)* (Río Piedras: Editorial Edil, 1972 [1882–1906]), p. 46.

32. Sandra S. García Selva, "Delincuencia y control social: Los jóvenes delincuentes de Arecibo, 1880–1890," MA thesis, University of Puerto Rico–Río Piedras, 1993, pp. 146–47, 151–52, 154–57; Astrid Cubano-Iguina, "Legal Constructions of Gender and Violence against Women in Puerto Rico under Spanish Rule, 1860–1895," *Law and History Review* 22, no. 3 (fall 2004): pp. 531–64.

33. Jesús Lalinde Abadía, *La administración española en el siglo XIX puertorriqueño* (Sevilla: Escuela de Estudios Hispano-Americanos de Sevilla, 1980), pp. 42–49, 144–66; *BHPR* (1915), vol. 2, pp. 32–44; *BHPR* (1917), vol. 4, pp. 223–25; *BHPR* (1918), vol. 5, pp. 22–23, 146–47; *BHPR* (1919), vol. 6, pp. 242–48; *BHPR* (1925), vol. 12, pp. 87–93; Picó, *Libertad y servidumbre*, pp. 107, 114–15.

34. Adolfo de Hostos, *Historia de San Juan, ciudad murada* (San Juan: Instituto de Cultura Puertorriqueña, 1966), pp. 506–7.

35. Brau, *Ensayos*, p. 56; Andrés Ramos Mattei, "La importación de trabajadores contratados para la industria azucarera puertorriqueña, 1860–1880," in Francisco Scarano, ed., *Imigración y clases sociales en el Puerto Rico del siglo XIX* (Río Piedras: Ediciones Huracán, 1981), pp. 135–39.

36. See, for example, Carlos Buitrago, *Los orígenes históricos de la sociedad precapitalista en Puerto Rico* (Río Piedras: Ediciones Huracán, 1976), pp. 39–40.

37. E. Fernández García, *El libro de Puerto Rico* (San Juan: "El Libro Azul," 1923), pp.

278–81; Fernando Picó, *El día menos pensado: Historia de los presidarios en Puerto Rico (1793–1993)* (Río Piedras: Ediciones Huracán, 1994), pp. 29, 43, 72, 99, 111.

38. William F. Willoughby, *Territories and Dependencies of the United States: Their Government Administration* (New York: Century, 1905), pp. 131–43, 163–70; José Martínez Valentín, *La presencia de la policía en la historia de Puerto Rico, 1898–1995* (San Juan: n.p., 1995), pp. 8, 20, 29, 31–32, 69.

FOSTER—PROHIBITING OPIUM IN THE PHILIPPINES AND THE UNITED STATES

1. Glenn May, *Social Engineering in the Philippines: The Aims, Execution, and Impact of American Colonial Policy, 1900–1913* (Westport: Greenwood, 1980); Julian Go and Anne L. Foster, eds., *The American Colonial State in the Philippines: Global Perspectives* (Durham: Duke University Press, 2003).

2. David T. Courtwright, *Dark Paradise: A History of Opiate Addiction in America* (Cambridge: Harvard University Press, 2001), pp. 79–80.

3. For the larger "morals" movement, see Frank Charles Laubach, *The People of the Philippines: Their Religious Progress and Preparation for Spiritual Leadership in the Far East* (New York: George H. Doran, 1925), pp. 211–14.

4. William F. Spurgin, U.S. Collector of Customs, Manila, to Secretary of War, December 21, 1899, file 1023, entry 5, Record Group (RG) 350, Records of the Bureau of Insular Affairs (BIA), U.S. National Archives (USNA), College Park, Md.; Rev. H. C. DuBose to Senator John McLaurin, September 23, 1899, file 1023-1, entry 5, RG 350, USNA.

5. Carl A. Trocki, *Empire and the Global Political Economy: A Study of the Asian Opium Trade, 1750–1950* (London: Routledge, 1999), p. 89.

6. Courtwright, *Dark Paradise*, pp. 61–77.

7. Ibid., pp. 76–77.

8. Philippine Opium Commission Committee, *Report of the Committee Appointed by the Philippine Commission to Investigate the Use of Opium and Traffic Therein* (Washington, D.C.: U.S. War Department, BIA, 1905), pp. 14–20, 45–48.

9. Rev. Homer C. Stuntz to Dr. Wilbur Crafts, May 2, 1903, file 1023-17, entry 5, RG 350, USNA; Wm. T. Nolting to Secretary of Finance and Justice, February 5, 1914, file 1023-205, entry 5, RG 350, USNA.

10. Patricio N. Abinales, "Progressive-Machine Conflict in Early-Twentieth-Century U.S. Politics and Colonial-State Building," in Go and Foster, *The American Colonial State*, pp. 148–81.

11. Courtwright, *Dark Paradise*, pp. 82–83; Caroline Jean Acker, *Creating the American Junkie: Addiction Research in the Classic Era of Narcotic Control* (Baltimore: Johns Hopkins University Press, 2002), pp. 34–42.

12. Acting Collector of Internal Revenue (Ellis Cromwell) to BIA, January 28, 1908, file 1023-164; Governor General of the Philippines (James F. Smith), Executive Order No. 24, March 6, 1908, file 1023-166; Cromwell to Government of Philippine Islands, March 14, 1908, file 1023-165; Smith to Secretary of War, cable of March 20, 1908, file 1023-163; Cromwell to Government of Philippine Islands, May 4, 1908, file 1023-167, all in entry 5, RG 350, USNA.

13. Acker, *Creating the American Junkie*, pp. 32–45.

14. Courtwright, *Dark Paradise*; Acker, *Creating the American Junkie*.

15. The Spanish era figures are estimates based on fragmentary figures available in U.S. government sources. See Foster, "Models for Governing: Opium and Colonial Policies in Southeast Asia, 1898–1910," in Go and Foster, *The American Colonial State*, pp. 95–96; and *Report of the International Opium Commission*, vol. 1: *Report of the Proceedings* (Shanghai: North-China Daily News and Herald, 1909), p. 364.

16. Foster, "Models for Governing," pp. 97–100, 109–10.

17. Brent became the leading U.S. figure in the international anti-opium movement, chairing the 1909 Shanghai Commission and the first Opium Conference at the Hague in 1911.

18. Charles H. Brent to Theodore Roosevelt, July 24, 1906, in *Foreign Relations of the United States 1906*, vol. 1 (Washington, D.C.: Government Printing Office), pp. 360–61.

19. Anne L. Foster, "Prohibition as Superiority: Policing Opium in South-East Asia, 1898–1925," *International History Review* 22, no. 2 (June 2000): pp. 260–64; William O. Walker III, *Opium and Foreign Policy: The Anglo-American Search for Order in Asia, 1912–1954* (Chapel Hill: University of North Carolina Press, 1991), pp. 14–17.

20. Appendix B to "Report to the Department of State by the American Delegation to the International Opium Commission at Shanghai," March 1, 1909, entry 47, RG 43, Records of International Conferences, Commissions, and Expositions, USNA.

21. "The Warfare against Opium-Smoking in America," *Outlook*, February 6, 1909, p. 275; "Congress Acts in the Nick of Time," *Outlook*, February 13, 1909, pp. 316–17.

22. Francis B. Harrison, Hearings in the House of Representatives, on H.R. 1967, 63d Cong., 1st sess., *Congressional Record*, 1913, pp. 2169, 2192.

23. Quoted from Collector of Customs, Philippines (Lt. Col. William Spurgin) to Secretary of War (Elihu Root), December 21, 1899, file 1023, entry 5, RG 350, USNA.

24. Charles H. Brent to Commissioner of Education (James F. Smith), July 6, 1903, file 1023-68, entry 5, RG 350, USNA.

25. Eugene R. Block, "Fighting the Opium Ring," *Overland Monthly* 58 (September 1911): pp. 184–91.

26. Eric Tagliacozzo, *Secret Trades, Porous Borders: Smuggling and States along a Southeast Asian Frontier, 1865–1915* (New Haven: Yale University Press, 2005).

27. Mrs. Hamilton Wright, widow of the anti-opium activist Hamilton Wright, repeated this well-worn claim in Mrs. Hamilton [Elizabeth] Wright to Chair, Opium Advisory Committee, June 3, 1926, document 51976, dossier 717, carton 709, League of Nations Archives, Geneva, Switzerland.

28. Smuggling in North Borneo, 1913–1921, Colonial Office file 874-914, British National Archives, Kew.

29. Rafael Crame, Chief of Constabulary, to Department of the Interior, Government of the Philippines, July 20, 1921, file 811b.114 Narcotics/3, Central Decimal File (CDF), RG 59, Records of the Department of State, USNA.

30. L. R. Sweet, Philippines Constabulary, to Governor General, Philippines, August 4, 1927, file 811b.114 Narcotics/74 and ⅓, CDF, RG 59, USNA.

31. W. Aldanese, Insular Collector of Customs, to Governor General, Philippines, September 20, 1927, file 811b.114 Narcotics/74 and ⅔; Dwight Davis, Secretary of War, to Secretary of State, November 7, 1927, file 811b.114 Narcotics/74 and ⅔; Frank B. Kellogg, Secretary of State, to Sir Esme Howard, British Ambassador to the United States, December 23, 1927, file 811b.114 Narcotics/77 and ½, all in CDF, RG 59, USNA.

McCoy—Policing the Imperial Periphery

1. James A. LeRoy, *The Americans in the Philippines*, vol. 1 (Boston: Houghton Mifflin, 1914), pp. 156–71.

2. U.S. House of Representatives, 55th Cong., 2d sess., document 2, *Annual Reports of the War Department for the Year Ended June 30, 1898: Report of the Major-General Commanding the Army* (Washington, D.C.: Government Printing Office, 1898), pp. 44–45; U.S. House of Representatives, 57th Cong., 1st sess., document 2, *Annual Reports of the War Department for the Year Ended June 30, 1901: Report of the Lieutenant-General Commanding the Army. In Five Parts* (Washington, D.C.: Government Printing Office, 1901), Pt. 5, pp. 78–79, 103–7; LeRoy, *The Americans in the Philippines*, vol. 1, pp. 238–48; Major Emanuel A. Baja, *Philippine Police*

System and Its Problems (Manila: Pobre's Press, 1933), pp. 253–54; U.S. War Department, Bureau of Insular Affairs, *Third Annual Report of the Philippine Commission, 1902*, pt. 1 (Washington, D.C.: Government Printing Office, 1903), pp. 105–7; U.S. House of Representatives, *Annual Reports of the War Department for the Year Ended June 30, 1898*, pp. 44–45.

3. *Philippine Daily Inquirer/EXTRA*, 1 May 2001, 2 May 2001, 4 May 2001, 5 May 2001, 6 May 2001, 8 May 2001, 9 May 2001; *Philippine Star*, 2 May 2001, 10 May 2001.

4. H. H. Gerth and C. Wright Mills, *From Max Weber: Essays in Sociology* (New York: Oxford University Press, 1946), pp. 77–78.

5. James C. Scott, *Seeing Like a State: How Certain Schemes to Improve the Human Condition Have Failed* (New Haven: Yale University Press, 1998), pp. 11–22, 24, 29–33, 44–45, 59–61, 64–72, 373.

6. *Annual Report of the Secretary of the Treasury on the State of the Finances for the Fiscal Year Ended June 30, 1902* (Washington, D.C.: Government Printing Office, 1902), pp. 51–52.

7. U.S. House of Representatives, *Annual Reports of the War Department for the Fiscal Year Ended June 30, 1903*, vol. 3 (Washington, D.C.: Government Printing Office, 1903), pp. 201–4.

8. Elizabeth Bethel, "The Military Information Division: Origin of the Intelligence Division," *Military Affairs* 11, no. 1 (spring 1947): pp. 17–24; Maj. Marc B. Powe, "American Military Intelligence Comes of Age," *Military Review* 55, no. 12 (December 1975): pp. 17–21.

9. Richard Brown, "General Emory Upton, the Army's Mahan," *Military Affairs* 17, no. 3 (autumn 1953): pp. 128–31.

10. Brian McAllister Linn, *The Philippine War, 1899–1902* (Manhattan: University Press of Kansas, 2000), pp. 127, 191; Brian McAllister Linn, "Intelligence and Low-Intensity Conflict in the Philippine War, 1899–1902," *Intelligence and National Security* 6, no. 1 (1991): pp. 90–96; U.S. Senate, 57th Cong., 1st sess., doc. 331, pt. 3, *Affairs in the Philippine Islands: Hearings before the Committee on the Philippines of the United States Senate* (Washington, D.C.: Government Printing House, 1902), pp. 2850–51.

11. Linn, "Intelligence and Low-Intensity Conflict in the Philippine War," pp. 100–104, 107–9; Ralph E. Weber, ed., *The Final Memoranda: Major General Ralph H. Van Deman, U.S.A. Ret., 1865–1952, Father of U.S. Military Intelligence* (Wilmington: Scholarly Resources, 1984), pp. 7–9.

12. *Khaki and Red*, September 1927, pp. 5–8; *Khaki and Red*, September 1932, p. 12; *Philippines Free Press*, 11 May 1918, p. 3.

13. General Francis V. Greene, *The Present Condition of the Police Force by Police Commissioner Greene* (New York: City Club of New York, 1903), pp. 3–8.

14. Glenn Anthony May, *Social Engineering in the Philippines: The Aims, Execution, and Impact of American Colonial Policy, 1900–1913* (Westport: Greenwood, 1980), xv–xvi.

15. Ray Conley to Chief, Bureau of Insular Affairs, 8 July 1930, Personal Name Information Files: Ray Conley; John W. Green to Richard Ely, 15 September 1938, Personal Name Information File: John W. Green, Entry 21, Bureau of Insular Affairs (BIA), Record Group (RG) 350, U.S. National Archives and Records Administration (USNA).

16. *La Vanguardia*, 10 March 1923; *Philippines Free Press*, 23 September 1922, p. 33; JWG [John W. Green], Confidential Memorandum, 24 July 1923, Personal Name Information Files: Ray Conley, entry 21, BIA, RG 350, USNA.

17. JWG [John W. Green], Confidential Memorandum, 24 July 1923, Personal Name Information Files: Ray Conley, entry 21, BIA, RG 350, USNA.

18. *La Vanguardia*, 26 April 1923; *Manila Times*, 26 April 1923, 27 April 1923; *El Debate*, 25 April 1923.

19. Leonard Wood, "Diaries, 1921–27," 2 April 1922, 19 August 1922, 20 January 1923, 7 May 1923, 11 July 1923, 9 January 1924, Manuscript Division, U.S. Library of Congress; Leonard Wood to W. Cameron Forbes, 14 April 1922, W. Cameron Forbes Papers, Houghton Library, Harvard University.

20. *New York Times,* 26 December 1923, 27 December 1923, 28 December 1923, 29 December 1923, 4 January 1924.

21. Leonard Wood, "Diaries, 1921–27," 19 August 1922, 11 July 1923, 23 September 1924, 9 October 1924, Manuscript Division, U.S. Library of Congress; Adjutant General's Office, *Official Army Register, January 1, 1923* (Washington, D.C.: Government Printing Office, 1923), pp. 1312–13.

22. *El Debate,* 18 July 1923, 21 July 1923, 26 July 1923.

23. Carlos Quirino, *Philippine Tycoon: The Biography of an Industrialist* (Manila: Madrigal Memorial Foundation, 1987), pp. 59–60, 66–67.

24. Silvino Gallardo to Manuel L. Quezon, 6 April 1929, File: Constabulary, Box 61, Series VII, Manuel L. Quezon (MLQ) Papers; Summary of All Records of Captain Silvino Gallardo (of Rizal), Headquarters Philippine Constabulary, 6 January 1936, File: Constabulary, Box 62, Series VII, MLQ Papers.

25. Leonard Wood, "Diaries, 1921–27," 10 November 1926, 11 November 1926, 17 November 1926, 15–25 February 1927, 26 May 1927, 27 May 1927, Manuscript Division, U.S. Library of Congress; House of Representatives, 70th Cong., 1st sess., *Annual Report of the Governor General of the Philippine Islands, 1926* (Washington, D.C.: Government Printing Office, 1928), p. 15.

26. Leonard Wood, "Diaries, 1921–27," 16 July 1924, 2 August 1924, 8 August 1924, 10 August 1924, 12 September 1924, 27 October 1924, 17 November 1924, 6 December 1924, 12 December 1924, Manuscript Division, U.S. Library of Congress; George A. Malcolm, *The Commonwealth of the Philippines* (New York: Appleton-Century, 1936), pp. 79–80, 182–86, 390; George A. Malcolm, *American Colonial Careerist: Half a Century of Official Life and Personal Experience in the Philippines and Puerto Rico* (Boston: Christopher, 1957), pp. 29, 84–85, 139, 143; *Manila Times,* 15 June 1917; Isagani A. Cruz and Cynthia Cruz Datu, *Res Gestae: A Brief History of the Supreme Court (from Arellano to Narvasa)* (Manila: Rex Book Store, 2000), p. 50; Supreme Court of the Philippines, "Government of the Philippine Islands v. Springer," GR no. 26979, *Reports of Cases Determined in the Supreme Court of the Philippine Islands from March 2, 1927, to October 5, 1927. Volume 50* (Manila: Bureau of Printing, 1929), pp. 296, 333.

27. Leonard Wood, "Diaries, 1921–27," 5 June 1921, 20 February 1926, 24 February 1926, 11 March 1926, 11 November 1926, Manuscript Division, U.S. Library of Congress; William H. Taft to Senator J. B. Foraker, 7 September 1903, Reel 40, William H. Taft Papers, Manuscript Division, U.S. Library of Congress; Manuel L. Quezon to George A. Malcolm, 25 August 1920, Box 43, Reel 9, Manuel L. Quezon Papers, Bentley Historical Library, University of Michigan; Malcolm, *American Colonial Careerist,* pp. 139–40; Malcolm, *The Commonwealth of the Philippines,* p. 184; *National Cyclopaedia of American Biography,* vol. 49 (New York: James T. White, 1966), pp. 456–57.

28. Leonard Wood, "Diaries, 1921–27," 18 March 1926, 25 March 1926, 26 March 1926, 28 March 1926, 29 March 1926, Manuscript Division, U.S. Library of Congress.

29. Supreme Court of the Philippines, *Government of the Philippine Islands v. Springer,* pp. 295–96.

30. *Manila Times,* 1 April 1927; Cruz and Cruz Datu, *Res Gestae,* pp. 79–81.

31. Weber, *The Final Memoranda,* pp. 7–23; Captain Michael E. Bigelow, "The First Steps: Battalion S2s in World War I," *Military Intelligence* (January–March 1992): pp. 26–28; Linn, "Intelligence and Low-Intensity Conflict in the Philippine War," pp. 108–9.

SALMAN—"THE PRISON THAT MAKES MEN FREE"

1. U.S. National Archives (NA), Record Group (RG) 350, Bureau of Insular Affairs (BIA) Library, Manuscript (MSS) Report of the Philippine Commission (RPC), 1905, vol. 3, pt. 2, p. 15 (George N. Wolfe, "Annual Report of the Bureau of Prisons").

2. NA, RG 350, BIA Library, MSS RPC, 1906, vol. 3, pt. 2, p. 12 (George N. Wolfe, "Report of the Director of Prisons").

3. NA, RG 350, BIA Library, MSS RPC, 1905, vol. 3, pt. 2, p. 38 (W. Cameron Forbes, "Annual Report of the Commissioner of Commerce and Police"); NA, RG 350, BIA Library, MSS RPC, 1906, vol. 3, pt. 2, pp. 12–13 (George N. Wolfe, "Report of the Bureau of Prisons"); White Papers, Box 6, File 300–9.1b, p. 2 (John R. White to Director of Prisons, July 22, 1908).

4. White Papers, Box 6, File 300–9.1b, pp. 7–8 (White to Director of Prisons, July 22, 1908).

5. Ignacio Villamor, *Criminality in the Philippines* (Manila: Bureau of Printing, 1909), p. 12, 48.

6. Jack M. Holl, *Juvenile Reform in the Progressive Era: William R. George and the Junior Republic Movement* (Ithaca: Cornell University Press, 1971), p. 82.

7. William Reuben George, *The Junior Republic: Its History and Ideals* (New York: D. Appleton, 1910), pp. 16–18.

8. Ibid., pp. 19–36, 55–58.

9. Ibid., pp. 47, 61–63.

10. Ibid., pp. 63–64.

11. Holl, *Juvenile Reform*, pp. 126–72, 273–84; Frank Tannenbaum, *Osborne of Sing Sing* (Chapel Hill: University of North Carolina Press, 1933); Maria C. Lanzar-Carpio, "Anti-imperialist Activities between 1900 and the Election of 1904," *Philippine Social Science Review* 4 (October 1933): p. 250.

12. Osborne to V. Everit Macy, August 1, 1900, quoted in Holl, *Juvenile Reform*, p. 205.

13. Theodore Roosevelt, "The Junior Republic," *Outlook,* January 20, 1912, p. 117.

14. Woodrow Wilson, "What Is Government and How Can a Boy Early Learn Its Value?" *Republic News,* March 1912, quoted in Holl, *Juvenile Reform*, p. 10.

15. Woodrow Wilson, "The Ideals of America," *Atlantic Monthly,* December 1902, pp. 730–31.

16. NA, RG 350, File 141-10, "U.S.-Philippine Relations—Executive, Compiled in the Bureau of Insular Affairs, War Department, by Mrs. Leila M. Pool," manuscript, 1934 ("Extracts from President Roosevelt's Annual Message to Congress, 12 December 1908").

17. Osborne, "Introduction," in George, *The Junior Republic,* p. viii; NA, RG 350, BIA Library, MSS RPC, 1905, vol. 3, pt. 2, p. 14 (George N. Wolfe, "Annual Report of the Bureau of Prisons"); NA, RG 350, BIA Library, MSS RPC, 1905, vol. 3, pt. 2, p. 38 (Forbes, "Annual Report of the Department of Commerce and Police").

18. Houghton Library, Harvard University, W. Cameron Forbes Papers, fMS Am 1366, vol. 3 (Forbes to James F. Smith, Secretary of Public Instruction, October 31, 1905).

19. W. Cameron Forbes, *The Philippine Islands* (Boston: Houghton Mifflin, 1928), vol. 1, pp. 508–9; John R. White, *Bullets and Bolos: Fifteen Years in the Philippine Islands* (New York: Century, 1928), p. 320.

20. Houghton Library, Forbes Papers, bMS Am 1364.4, Box 4 (Forbes to Director of Prisons, September 8, 1906); NA, RG 350, File 1446-4, p. 1 (Forbes to White, January 2, 1907).

21. Houghton Library, Forbes Papers, bMS Am 1364.4, Box 4 (Forbes to Director of Prisons, September 8, 1906); NA, RG 350, File 1446-4, pp. 3–9 (Forbes to White, January 2, 1907).

22. Forbes, *The Philippine Islands,* vol. 1, pp. 505–6; White, *Bullets and Bolos,* pp. 322–28; University of Oregon Library, White Papers, Box 6, File 300–9.1b, pp. 25–27 (John R. White, "Annual Report of the Iwahig Penal Colony for Fiscal Year 1908").

23. White, *Bullets and Bolos,* pp. 324–25; White Papers, Box 5, File 300-08.3, pp. 280–81 (White, "Bullets and Bolos," draft manuscript).

24. White, *Bullets and Bolos,* pp. 324–27.

25. White Papers, Box 6, File 300-9.1b, p. 5 (White, "Annual Report of the Iwahig Penal Colony for the Fiscal Year 1908"); NA, RG 350, BIA Library, MSS RPC, 1905, and MSS RPC,

1906 ("Table II: Showing Sex and Changes in Prison Population," in "Report of Bureau of Prisons").

26. White, *Bullets and Bolos,* p. 325.

27. White Papers, Box 6, File 300-9.1b, p. 44 (White, "Annual Report of the Iwahig Penal Colony for Fiscal Year 1908"); White Papers, Box 6, File 300-9.1b, p. 4 (White to Carroll H. Lamb, September 25, 1908).

28. White Papers, Box 6, File 300-9.1b, pp. 39–45 (White, "Annual Report of the Iwahig Penal Colony for Fiscal Year 1908"); White Papers, Box 5, File 300-08.3, p. 2 (White, "The Development of the Colony").

29. NA, RG 350, BIA Library, MSS RPC, 1909, vol. 4, pp. 105, 120–25 (Carroll H. Lamb, "Annual Report of the Iwahig Penal Colony for Fiscal Year 1909"); NA, RG 350, File 1446-7 (Lamb quoted in William L. Altdorfer, "Unique Penal Colony," *Sunday Star* [Washington, D.C.], July 16, 1911).

30. White Papers, Box 6, File 300-9.1b, p. 25 (White, "Annual Report of the Iwahig Penal Colony for Fiscal Year 1908").

31. Ibid., p. 43.

32. White Papers, Box 5, File 300-08.3, p. 4 ("The Development of the Colony," in "Bullets and Bolos," draft manuscript).

33. White Papers, Box 6, File 300-9.1b, pp. 1–2 (White to Forbes, June 28, 1908).

34. Forbes, *The Philippine Islands,* vol. 1, pp. 507–8; NA, RG 350, BIA Library, MSS RPC, 1909, vol. 4, pp. 137–42 (Lamb, "Annual Report of the Iwahig Penal Colony for Fiscal Year 1909"); NA, RG 350, BIA Library, MSS RPC, 1910, vol. 3, pp. 21–22 (Lamb, "Annual Report of the Iwahig Penal Colony for the Fiscal Year 1909–1910").

35. The following year the Supreme Court of the Philippines reversed the decision and acquitted Lamb.

36. NA, RG 350, BIA Library, MSS RPC, 1910, vol. 3, p. 2 (Lamb, "Annual Report of the Iwahig Penal Colony for the Fiscal Year 1909–1910").

37. Ibid., pp. 142, 171; Wilson, "The Ideals of America," pp. 729–31.

38. Episcopal Theological Seminary of the Southwest, Episcopal Church Archives, RG 76, Box 16, pp. 2, 5 (Brent to Reverend Hugh L. Burleson, November 25, 1914).

39. USNA, RG 350, File 1446-25 (*Literary Digest,* April 14, 1917, reprinted from the *New York Times*).

40. Lyman Beecher Stowe, "A Prison That Makes Men Free," *The World's Work* (April 1914): pp. 626–28.

41. Wilson, "The Ideals of America," p. 730.

42. Michel Foucault, *Discipline and Punish: The Birth of the Prison,* trans. Alan Sheridan (New York: Pantheon Books, 1977), pp. 293–308.

43. Osborne, "Introduction," in Frank Tannenbaum, *Wall Shadows: A Study in American Prisons* (New York: G. P. Putnam's Sons, 1922), p. ix; Thomas Mott Osborne, *Society and Prisons: Some Suggestions for a New Penology* (New Haven: Yale University Press, 1916), p. 233.

44. Osborne, *Society and Prisons,* pp. 66–71.

45. "Osborne Out, Hits at Convict System," *New York Times,* October 6, 1913, p. 1; "Denounces New York's Penal System of 'Revenge,'" *New York Times,* May 24, 1914, p. 47.

46. Frank Tannenbaum, *Osborne of Sing Sing* (Chapel Hill: University of North Carolina Press, 1933).

47. "'Frame-Up Charged by Warden Osborne,'" *New York Times,* June 29, 1915, p. 1.

48. Tannenbaum, *Osborne of Sing Sing.*

49. White Papers, Box 6, File 300-09.1, Philippines (John T. Clark to White, October 28, 1929).

50. John L. Gillin, *Taming the Criminal: Adventures in Penology* (New York: Macmillan, 1931).

Nelson—Introduction to Part 3

1. See Booker T. Washington, *Up from Slavery* (New York: Doubleday, 1901).
2. See, for example, James Kent, *Commentaries on American Law*, 4 vols. (New York: O. Halstead, 1826–30), especially vol. 1; Francis Lieber, *Manual of Political Ethics*, 2 vols. (Boston: Little and Brown, 1838–39); and Theodore Dwight Woolsey, *Introduction to the Study of International Law* (New York: C. Scribner, 1864), notably pp. 68–71. For another early commentary on international relations, international law, and the Monroe Doctrine, see Richard Rush, *Memoranda of a Residence at the Court of London, 1817–1825* (Philadelphia: Key and Biddle, 1833).
3. Du Pont de Nemours, *National Education in the United States of America*, trans. Bessie Gardner DuPont (Newark: University of Delaware Press, 1923), pp. 134, 136.
4. See, for example, Robert Francis Engs, *Educating the Disfranchised and Disinherited: Samuel Chapman Armstrong and Hampton Institute, 1839–1893* (Knoxville: University of Tennessee Press, 1999).

Del Moral—Negotiating Colonialism

1. Amílcar Barreto, *The Politics of Language in Puerto Rico* (Gainesville: University Press of Florida, 2001); José Manuel Navarro, *Creating Tropical Yankees: Social Science Textbooks and U.S. Ideological Control in Puerto Rico, 1898–1908* (New York: Routledge, 2002); Pablo Navarro-Rivera, *Universidad de Puerto Rico: De control político a crisis permanente, 1903–1952* (Río Piedras: Ediciones Huracán, 2000); Aida Negrón de Montilla, *La americanización en Puerto Rico y el sistema de instrucción pública, 1900–1930* (San Juan: Editorial de la Universidad de Puerto Rico, 1998).
2. Solsirée del Moral, "Race, Science, and Nation: The Cultural Politics of Schools in Colonial Puerto Rico, 1917–1938," PhD diss., University of Wisconsin–Madison, 2006.
3. Navarro, *Creating Tropical Yankees*; Eileen J. Suárez Findlay, *Imposing Decency: The Politics of Sexuality and Race in Puerto Rico, 1870–1920* (Durham: Duke University Press, 1999).
4. Arthur Yager, "Proclamation," Archivo General de Puerto Rico (AGPR), Serie Oficina del Gobernador (SOG), General file 3024, box 778.
5. Manuel Ortiz de Renta, "Letter/clippings," AGPR, SOG, General file 3024, box 778.
6. E. San Millán, "Letter/clippings," AGPR, SOG, General file 3024/1, box 778.
7. Ibid.
8. Ibid.
9. Negrón de Montilla, *La americanización en Puerto Rico*; Navarro, *Creating Tropical Yankees*; Navarro-Rivera, *Universidad de Puerto Rico*; Rubén Maldonado Jiménez, comp., *Historia y educación: Acercamiento a la historia social de la educación en Puerto Rico* (San Juan: Editorial de la Universidad de Puerto Rico, 2001).
10. Maldonado Jiménez, *¿Hasta cuándo? La lucha de los maestros por justicia salarial, antes y después de la invasión de Estados Unido a Puerto Rico, 1898–1901* (San Juan: Ediciones Nueva Provincia, 1998).
11. In the second decade of the twentieth century, teachers and the media used two interchangeable names in reference to the AMPR: Asociación de Maestros de Puerto Rico and Asociación de Maestros Puertorriqueños.
12. Although the island was officially an American colonial territory until 1952, Puerto Ricans acquired U.S. citizenship in 1917 and were required to fulfill the duties of citizenship such as military service.
13. Nancy Leys Stepan, *"The Hour of Eugenics": Race, Gender, and Nation in Latin America* (Ithaca: Cornell University Press, 1991).
14. Nancy P. Appelbaum, "Post-revisionist Scholarship on Race," *Latin American Research Review* 40, no. 3 (October 2005): pp. 206–17.

15. Nancy P. Appelbaum, Anne S. Macpherson, and Karin Alejandra Rosemblatt, eds., *Race and Nation in Modern Latin America* (Chapel Hill: University of North Carolina Press, 2003).

16. Nancy P. Appelbaum, Anne S. Macpherson, and Karin Alejandra Rosemblatt, "Introduction: Racial Nations," in Appelbaum, Macpherson, and Rosemblatt, *Race and Nation in Modern Latin America*, p. 2.

17. Greg Grandin, *The Blood of Guatemala: A History of Race and Nation* (Durham: Duke University Press, 2000); Marisol de la Cadena, *Indigenous Mestizos: The Politics of Race and Culture in Cuzco, Peru, 1919–1991* (Durham: Duke University Press, 2000).

18. De la Cadena, *Indigenous Mestizos*, p. 27.

19. Ileana M. Rodríguez-Silva, "A Conspiracy of Silence: Blackness, Class, and National Identities in Post-emancipation Puerto Rico (1850–1920)," PhD diss., University of Wisconsin–Madison, 2004, chap. 2.

20. Del Moral, "Race, Science, and Nation," chap. 2.

BARRETO—ENLIGHTENED TOLERANCE OR CULTURAL CAPITULATION?

1. Dennis Baron, *The English Only Question: An Official Language for Americans?* (New Haven: Yale University Press, 1990), pp. 64–93.

2. Roamé Torres González, *Idioma, bilingüismo y nacionalidad: La presencia del inglés en Puerto Rico* (Río Piedras: Editorial de la Universidad de Puerto Rico, 2002), p. 39.

3. Arnold H. Leibowitz, *Defining Status: A Comprehensive Analysis of the United States Territorial Relations* (Dordrecht, Netherlands: Martinus Nijhoff, 1989), p. 8.

4. James Crawford, ed., *Language Loyalties: A Source Book on the Official English Controversy* (Chicago: University of Chicago Press, 1992), p. 34 (emphasis in original).

5. Eric Hobsbawm, "Mass Producing Tradition: Europe, 1870–1914," in Eric Hobsbawm and Terence Ranger, eds., *The Invention of Tradition* (Cambridge: Cambridge University Press, 1983), p. 280 (emphasis in original).

6. Ibid., pp. 278, 280.

7. Stephen Steinberg, *The Ethnic Myth: Race, Ethnicity, and Class in America* (Boston: Beacon, 1989), p. 42.

8. Sam Kaplan, *The Pedagogical State: Education and the Politics of National Culture in Post-1980 Turkey* (Stanford: Stanford University Press, 2006), p. 9.

9. Henry K. Carroll, *Report on the Island of Porto Rico: Its Population, Civil Government, Roads, Tariff, and Currency, with Recommendations* (New York: Arno, [1899] 1975), p. 59.

10. Theodore Roosevelt, *Theodore Roosevelt: Letters and Speeches* (New York: Library of America, 2004), p. 751.

11. Franklin D. Roosevelt, *The Public Papers and Addresses of Franklin D. Roosevelt*, vol. 6: *The Constitution Prevails, 1937* (New York: Macmillan, 1941), p. 161.

12. Pedro A. Cabán, *Constructing a Colonial People: Puerto Rico and the United States, 1898–1932* (Boulder: Westview, 1999), p. 81.

13. Edward W. Said, *Culture and Imperialism* (New York: Vintage, 1994), pp. 8–9.

14. Aida Negrón de Montilla, *Americanization in Puerto Rico and the Public School System, 1900–1930* (Río Piedras: Editorial Universitaria, 1975), p. 10.

15. Juan J. Osuna, *A History of Education in Puerto Rico* (New York: Arno, [1949] 1975), p. 143.

16. Amílcar A. Barreto, *Language, Elites, and the State: Nationalism in Puerto Rico and Quebec* (Westport: Praeger, 1998), p. 95, n. 24.

17. Nélida Agosto Cintrón, *Religión y cambio social en Puerto Rico, 1898–1940* (Río Piedras: Ediciones Huracán, 1996), pp. 68–69.

18. Ibid., pp. 68, 134.

19. Edgardo Meléndez, *Movimiento anexionista en Puerto Rico* (Río Piedras: Editorial de la Universidad de Puerto Rico, 1993), p. 53.

20. Alfonso L García Martínez, *Idioma y política: El papel desempeñado por los idiomas español e inglés en la relación política Puerto Rico–Estados Unidos* (San Juan: Editorial Cordillera, 1976), pp. 99–101.
21. Nancy Morris, *Puerto Rico: Culture, Politics, and Identity* (Westport: Praeger, 1995), p. 152.
22. Barreto, *Language, Elites*, pp. 77–79.
23. Walker Connor, *Ethnonationalism: The Quest for Understanding* (Princeton: Princeton University Press, 1994), p. 139.
24. García Martínez, *Idioma y política*, p. 109.
25. Edith Algren de Gutiérrez, *The Movement against Teaching English in Schools of Puerto Rico* (Lanham, Md.: University Press of America, 1987), p. 127.
26. Harold F. Schiffman, *Linguistic Culture and Language Policy* (London: Routledge, 1996), p. 150.
27. Connor, *Ethnonationalism*, p. 196.
28. Thomas Hylland Eriksen, *Ethnicity and Nationalism: Anthropological Perspectives* (London: Pluto, 1993), 6.
29. Morris, *Puerto Rico*; Ángel I. Rivera, *Puerto Rico: Ficción y mitología en sus alternativas de status* (San Juan: Ediciones Nueva Aurora, 1996).
30. Gabriel Villaronga, *Toward a Discourse of Consent: Mass Mobilization and Colonial Politics in Puerto Rico, 1932–1948* (Westport: Praeger, 2004), p. 217.
31. Juan Duchesne, *Ciudadano insano: Ensayos bestiales sobre cultura y literatura* (San Juan: Ediciones Callejón, 2001), p. 4; Carlos Romero-Barceló, *Statehood Is for the Poor* (San Juan: Carlos Romero-Barceló, 1976), p. 9.
32. Ángel Ferrao, "Nacionalismo, hispanismo y élite intelectual en el Puerto Rico de la década de 1930," in Silvia Álvarez-Curbelo and María E. Rodríguez Castro, eds., *Del nacionalismo al populismo: Cultura y política en Puerto Rico* (Río Piedras: Ediciones Huracán, 1993), pp. 39–40.
33. Richard Weisskoff, *Factories and Food Stamps: The Puerto Rico Model of Development* (Baltimore: Johns Hopkins University Press, 1985), p. 121.
34. Ángel G. Quintero Rivera, "La ideología populista y la institucionalización universitaria de las ciencias sociales," in Silvia Álvarez-Curbelo and María E. Rodríguez Castro, eds., *Del nacionalismo al populismo: Cultura y política en Puerto Rico.* (Río Piedras: Ediciones Huracán, 1993), p. 127.
35. Alexander J. Motyl, "Inventing Invention: The Limits of National Identity Formation," in Ronald G. Suny and Michael D. Kennedy, eds., *Intellectuals and the Articulation of the Nation* (Ann Arbor: University of Michigan Press, 2001), pp. 58–61.
36. Silvia Álvarez-Curbelo, "El discurso populista de Luis Muñoz Marín: Condiciones de posibilidad y mitos fundacionales en el período, 1932–1936," in Silvia Álvarez-Curbelo and María E. Rodríguez Castro, eds., *Del nacionalismo al populismo: Cultura y política en Puerto Rico* (Río Piedras: Ediciones Huracán, 1993), p. 27; Ferrao, "Nacionalismo, hispanismo," pp. 46–47; Amílcar A. Barreto, "Constructing Identities: Ethnic Boundaries and Elite Preferences in Puerto Rico," *Nationalism and Ethnic Politics* 7 (2001): pp. 21–40.
37. Vincente Géigel Polanco, *El despertar de un pueblo* (San Juan: Biblioteca de Autores Puertorriqueños, 1942), p. 30.
38. Antonio Pedreira, *Insularismo* (Río Piedras: Editorial Edil, [1934] 1978), p. 25.
39. Pedro Albizu Campos, *La conciencia nacional puertorriqueña*, 3d ed. (Mexico City: Siglo Veintiuno, 1977), pp. 59, 88.
40. Arlene M. Dávila, *Sponsored Identities: Cultural Politics in Puerto Rico* (Philadelphia: Temple University Press, 1997), p. 63.
41. Juan Flores, *Divided Borders: Essays on Puerto Rican Identity* (Houston: Arte Público Press, 1993), pp. 37–38.

42. José E. Rodó, *Ariel*, Margaret Sayers Peden, trans. (Austin: University of Texas Press, [1900] 1988), pp. 70–77.
43. Eugeen E. Roosens, *Creating Ethnicity: The Process of Ethnogenesis* (Newbury Park, Calif.: Sage, 1989), p. 161.
44. Ronald G. Suny and Michael D. Kennedy, "Toward a Theory of National Intellectual Practice," in Ronald G. Suny and Michael D. Kennedy, eds., *Intellectuals and the Articulation of the Nation* (Ann Arbor: University of Michigan Press, 2001), p. 405.
45. Sun-Ki Chai, "A Theory of Ethnic Group Boundaries," *Nations and Nationalism* 2 (1996): p. 291.
46. Arcadio Díaz Quiñones, *El arte de bregar: Ensayos* (San Juan: Ediciones Callejón, 2000), pp. 136–37.
47. Juan Flores, *From Bomba to Hip-Hop: Puerto Rican Culture and Latino Identity* (New York: Columbia University Press, 2000), p. 163; Bonnie Urciuoli, *Exposing Prejudice: Puerto Rican Experiences of Language, Race, and Class* (Boulder: Westview, 1998), p. 78.
48. Urciuoli, *Exposing Prejudice*, pp. 78–79.
49. Efrén Rivera Ramos, *The Legal Construction of Identity: The Judicial and Social Legacy of American Colonialism in Puerto Rico* (Washington, D.C.: American Psychological Association, 2001), pp. 73–100.
50. Rexford G. Tugwell, *The Art of Politics as Practiced by Three Great Americans: Franklin Delano Roosevelt, Luis Muñoz Marín, and Fiorello H. La Guardia* (Garden City, N.Y.: Doubleday, 1958), p. 151.
51. Ibid., p. 80.
52. Ibid., p. 150. Quintero Rivera, "La ideología populista," p. 134.
53. Franklin D. Roosevelt, *The Public Papers and Addresses of Franklin D. Roosevelt*, vol. 12: *The Tide Turns, 1943* (New York: Russell and Russell, [1950] 1969), pp. 117–18, 413–14.
54. Harry S. Truman, *Public Papers of the Presidents of the United States: Harry S. Truman*. 1946 vol. 2 (Washington, D.C.: Government Printing Office, 1962), pp. 248, 466–67.
55. Margaret Truman, *Harry S. Truman* (New York: Morrow 1973), p. 486; Harry S. Truman, *Memoirs*, vol. 1: *Year of Decisions* (Garden City, N.Y.: Doubleday, 1955), p. 275.
56. Harry S. Truman, *Public Papers of the Presidents of the United States: Harry S. Truman*. 1948 vol. 4 (Washington, D.C.: Government Printing Office, 1964), p. 154.
57. Harry S. Truman, *Public Papers of the Presidents of the United States: Harry S. Truman*. 1952–53 vol. 8 (Washington, D.C.: Government Printing Office, 1966), p. 156.
58. Clayton R. Koppes "From New Deal to Termination: Liberalism and Indian Policy, 1933–1953," *Pacific Historical Review* 46 (1977): p. 544.
59. Gary M. Fink and James W. Hilty, "Prologue: The Senate Voting Record of Harry S. Truman," *Journal of Interdisciplinary History* 44 (1973): p. 220.
60. Amílcar A. Barreto, *The Politics of Language in Puerto Rico* (Gainesville: University Press of Florida, 2001).
61. Daniel P. Moynihan, *Pandaemonium: Ethnicity in International Politics* (New York: Oxford University Press, 1993), pp. 73–74.
62. Amílcar A. Barreto, "The Evolving State of Latino Politics in New England," in Andrés Torres, ed., *Latinos in New England* (Philadelphia: Temple University Press, 2006), pp. 291–309.
63. Seymour M. Lipset, *Continental Divide: The Values and Institutions of the United States and Canada* (London: Routledge, 1990), p. 26.
64. Eric P. Kaufmann, *The Rise and Fall of Anglo-America* (Cambridge: Harvard University Press, 2004), pp. 49–50.
65. Alexander Hamilton, James Madison, and John Jay, *The Federalist Papers*, Clinton Rossiter, ed. (New York: New American Library, 1961), p. 38.
66. Samuel Huntington, *Who Are We? The Challenge to America's National Identity* (New York: Simon and Schuster, 2004), p. xviii.

67. Ibid., p. 63.
68. Samuel Huntington, *The Clash of Civilizations and the Remaking of World Order* (New York: Simon and Schuster, 1996), p. 318; "The Hispanic Challenge," *Foreign Policy* 141 (2004): p. 30.
69. Connor, *Ethnonationalism*, p. 201.
70. George M. Fredrickson, *The Comparative Imagination: On the History of Racism, Nationalism, and Social Movements* (Berkeley: University of California Press, 2000), p. 63.
71. Ariel E. Dulitzky, "A Region in Denial: Racial Discrimination and Racism in Latin America," in Anani Dzidzienyo and Suzanne Oboler, eds., *Neither Enemies nor Friends: Latinos, Blacks, Afro-Latinos* (New York: Palgrave Macmillan, 2005), pp. 47–49.
72. David A. Brading, *The First America: The Spanish Monarchy, Creole Patriots, and the Liberal State, 1492–1867* (Cambridge: Cambridge University Press, 1991), p. 371.
73. Kaufmann, *Rise and Fall*, p. 263.

MAY—THE BUSINESS OF EDUCATION IN THE COLONIAL PHILIPPINES, 1909–1930

1. Glenn Anthony May, *Social Engineering in the Philippines: The Aims, Execution, and Impact of American Colonial Policy, 1900–1913* (Westport: Greenwood, 1980), p. 118; Philippine Islands, Director of Education, *Report of the Director of Education* (RDE), 1924 (Manila: Bureau of Printing, 1925), p. 28.
2. On industrial education, see Herbert M. Kliebard, *Schooled to Work: Vocationalism and the American Curriculum, 1876–1946* (New York: Teachers College Press, 1999), pp. 1–118.
3. May, *Social Engineering*, pp. 89–117.
4. RDE, 1909–10, p. 24.
5. Frank R. White, "Industrial Education in the Philippine Islands," *Vocational Education* 2 (March 1913): p. 277.
6. *Philippine Education* (PE) 6 (Jan. 1910): p. 22.
7. RDE, 1910–11, p. 36.
8. Circular no. 3, s. 1911, Jan. 11, 1911, Records Division of the Philippine Department of Education, General Office Circulars (RD).
9. John Dewey and Evelyn Dewey, *Schools of To-morrow* (New York: Dutton, 1915), pp. 261–62.
10. Ibid., pp. 90, 93, 269.
11. David B. Tyack, *The One Best System: A History of American Urban Education* (Cambridge: Harvard University Press, 1974), pp. 3, 126–98.
12. Ibid. p. 203; RDE, 1923, p. 9.
13. PE 6 (Jan. 1910): p. 22; RDE, 1909–10, p. 27.
14. PE 6 (Jan. 1910): p. 22; circular no. 111, s. 1912, Aug 9, 1912, RD. The quotation can be found in the first source.
15. PE 6 (Jan. 1910): p. 22; PE 6 (Feb. 1910): p. 9; circular no. 1, s. 1910, Jan. 3, 1910, RD; circular no. 19, s. 1910, Feb. 9, 1910, RD; *Philippine Craftsman* (PC) 1 (July 1912): p. 66.
16. May, *Social Engineering*, pp. 117–18; RDE, 1912–13, p. 37.
17. Hugo H. Miller, *Philippine Hats*, Bureau of Education Bulletin, no. 33 (Manila: Bureau of Printing, 1910); *Lace Making and Embroidery*, Bureau of Education Bulletin, no. 34 (Manila: Bureau of Printing, 1911); *Embroidery: A Manual for Use in Philippine Public Schools* (Manila: Bureau of Printing, 1916); RDE, 1914, p. 89; RDE, 1919, p. 28.
18. RDE, 1914, p. 36; RDE, 1915, p. 43.
19. Circular no. 142, s. 1912, Sept. 26, 1912, RD; RDE, 1912–13, p. 35; RDE, 1914, p. 81; PC 1 (July 1912): pp. 53–59; PC 2 (July 1913): pp. 59–62; PC 3 (July 1914): pp. 26–30; PC 3 (Nov. 1914): pp. 305–9; PC 5 (July 1916): pp. 42–51.
20. RDE, 1912–13, p. 39; RDE, 1914, pp. 81–82; PC 1 (Mar. 1913): pp. 631–57; PC 5 (July 1916): pp. 42–51; circular no. 110, s. 1911, Aug. 16, 1911, RD; circular no. 136, s. 1912, Sept. 23, 1912, RD.

21. RDE, 1915, pp. 39–40; RDE, 1916, p. 28; RDE, 1917, pp. 45–47; RDE, 1918, pp. 54–55; RDE, 1919, pp. 28–30; PC 1 (Dec. 1912): p. 510.
22. RDE, 1916, p. 28; RDE, 1917, pp. 45–47; RDE, 1918, pp. 54–55.
23. RDE, 1918, pp. 164–65; RDE, 1921, pp. 144–47.
24. RDE, 1920, pp. 34, 146–47; RDE, 1922, p. 43; RDE, 1923, p. 45; RDE, 1924, p. 28. The average output from 1920–21 through 1923–24 was 2,549,620 pesos. I calculated the average from data in the tables on the cited pages.
25. The average output per pupil was calculated by dividing total output by total enrollment in industrial classes. RDE, 1922, p. 43; RDE, 1923, p. 45; RDE, 1924, pp. 28–29.
26. Philippine Islands, Board of Educational Survey, *A Survey of the Educational System of the Philippine Islands* (Manila: Bureau of Printing, 1925), pp. 3, 7, 59–62, 275–300.
27. RDE, 1926, 48–49; circular no. 29, s. 1926, July 21, 1926, Records of the U.S. Bureau of Insular Affairs (BIA), U.S. National Archives, 3565/49.
28. RDE, 1926, p. 49; RDE, 1929, p. 12; RDE, 1930, pp. 19–20.
29. RDE, 1927, pp. 40–41; RDE, 1928, pp. 172–75; RDE, 1929, pp. 140–45, 150–51; RDE, 1930, pp. 166–69, 174–75; RDE, 1931, pp. 210–13, 218–19.
30. U.S. Bureau of the Census, *Census of the Philippine Islands, 1903*, 4 vols. (Washington, D.C.: Government Printing Office, 1905), vol. 4, pp. 325–28; Frederick L. Wernstedt and J. E. Spencer, *The Philippine Island World: A Physical, Cultural, and Regional Geography* (Berkeley: University of California Press, 1967), pp. 174, 182, 198–200, 320–22, 472–73, 678, 680, 692; PC 2 (Nov. 1913): p. 307.
31. United States Philippine Commission, *Report of the Philippine Commission, 1912* (Washington, D.C.: Government Printing Office, 1913), pp. 22–23, 237–38; RDE, 1912–13, pp. 35–36; "Corn to Take Place of Rice," *Manila Times*, Jan. 6, 1912, p. 7.
32. RDE, 1909, p. 12; Philippine Islands, *School and Home Gardening for the Primary Grades*, Bureau of Education Bulletin, no. 31 (rev.) (Manila: Bureau of Printing, 1913), pp. 7, 10, 53–68.
33. Thomas Wessell and Marilyn Wessell, *4-H: An American Idea, 1900–1980* (Chevy Chase, Md.: National 4-H Council, 1982), pp. 3–42.
34. On the campaign, see RDE, 1912–13, pp. 35–36, 115; RDE, 1913, pp. 49–51; RDE, 1914, pp. 85–86; RDE, 1915, pp. 78–79; RDE, 1916, p. 30; RDE, 1918, p. 39; PC 1 (July 1912): p. 73; PC 1 (Sept. 1912): pp. 210–15, 221–23, 231–34; PC 1 (Dec. 1912): pp. 487–92, 508–10; PC 1 (Mar. 1913): pp. 654–57, 712–15; PC 2 (Nov. 1913): pp. 297–309, 335; PC 3 (Sept. 1914): pp. 166–83.
35. William Henry Scott, *Barangay: Sixteenth-Century Philippine Culture and Society* (Quezon City: Ateneo de Manila University Press, 1994), pp. 45, 205.
36. PC 2 (Nov. 1913): pp. 310–20.
37. Ibid.
38. PC 1 (July 1912): pp. 1–47, 49–50, 69–70; PC 1 (Dec. 1912): pp. 445–65: PC 1 (Mar. 1913): pp. 641–42; PC 2 (Nov. 1913): pp. 310–20; PC 2 (Jan. 1914): pp. 484–505; PC 2 (Mar. 1914): pp. 645–56; PC 3 (July 1914): pp. 1–25; PC 5 (Nov. 1916): pp. 313–25, 341–44; RDE, 1912–13, plate 14 (after p. 38); Luther Bewley to Charles Zinn and Co., Sept. 21, 1917, BIA/26554/10.
39. PC 1 (July 1912): pp. 1–47; PC 3 (Oct. 1914): pp. 247–62. For other valuable pieces on basketry, see PC 2 (Aug. 1913): pp. 71–83; PC 3 (July 1914): pp. 1–25; PC 3 (Sept. 1914): pp. 184–90; and PC 5 (Nov. 1916): pp. 313–25. For guidance, see PC 1 (Feb. 1913): pp. 624–25; PC 2 (Jan. 1914): pp. 485–505; PC 4 (Dec. 1915): pp. 386–90; PC 4 (Jan. 1916): pp. 479–85; and PC 5 (Feb. 1917): pp. 547–59.
40. Circular no. 134, s. 1911, Oct. 10, 1911, RD; J. F. Boomer, "Philippine Progress in Basket Making," *Daily Consular and Trade Reports*, June 19, 1914, BIA/26554/4.
41. Gabriel A. O'Reilly to Charles C. Walcutt, June 25, 1914, BIA/26554/9; Gabriel A. O'Reilly to Locke and Clarke Company, Jan. 18, 1915, BIA/25116/23A.
42. RDE, 1915, 73–75; Luther Bewley to Charles Zinn and Co., Sept. 21, 1917, BIA/26554/10.

43. RDE, 1924, pp. 158–59.
44. Board of Educational Survey, *Survey of the Educational System*, p. 282.
45. RDE, 1927, pp. 190–91; RDE, 1928, pp. 174–75; RDE, 1929, p. 151.
46. Robert F. Lane, *Philippine Basketry: An Appreciation* (Makati: Bookmark, 1986), pp. 5–6.
47. W. Cameron Forbes, *The Philippine Islands*, 2 vols. (Boston: Houghton Mifflin, 1928), vol. 1, pp. 463–68.
48. Daniel F. Doeppers, *Manila, 1900–1941: Social Change in a Late Colonial Metropolis* (New Haven: Council on Southeast Asian Studies, Yale University, 1984), pp. 22–23; Filomeno V. Aguilar Jr. and Virginia A. Miralao, *Southern Tagalog Embroideries: A Case Study of a Philippine Handicraft*, Handicraft Project Paper Series, no. 5 (Manila: Ramon Magsaysay Award Foundation, 1985), p. 9.
49. Doeppers, *Manila*, pp. 22–23; Aguilar and Miralao, *Southern Tagalog Embroideries*, pp. 8–12.
50. Educational policy makers rarely hinted that the Philippines would play a significant role in the evolving industrial age except as a producer of raw materials.

NAVARRO-RIVERA—THE IMPERIAL ENTERPRISE AND
EDUCATIONAL POLICIES IN COLONIAL PUERTO RICO

1. My initial work on the Carlisle Indian Industrial School was published as "Acculturation under Duress: The Puerto Rican Experience at the Carlisle Indian Industrial School, 1898–1918," *Centro Journal* 18, no. 1 (spring 2006): pp. 222–59. This essay, while drawing much from the earlier one, examines the policy of forced acculturation in the broader context of educational policy in Puerto Rico during the early years of United States rule.
2. Warren Zimmerman, *First Great Triumph: How Five Americans Made Their Country a World Power* (New York: Farrar, Straus and Giroux, 2002).
3. Charles W. Eliot to S. L. Parrish, September 21, 1899, Harvard University Papers, C. W. Eliot, Box 92, Letter Book, C. W. Eliot, January 17, 1898, to March 23, 1903, p. 42A.
4. Pablo Navarro-Rivera, *Universidad de Puerto Rico: De control político a crisis permanente, 1903–1952* (Río Piedras: Ediciones Huracán, 2000).
5. Puerto Rico Department of Education, *Annual Report of the Commissioner of Education* (Washington, D.C.: Government Printing Office, 1902), p. 257, quoted in Aida Negrón de Montilla, *Americanization in Puerto Rico and the Public-School System, 1900–1930* (Río Piedras: Editorial Edil, 1971).
6. *Corretjer*, dir. J. Meléndez, 1989.
7. Roamé Torres González, *Idioma, bilingüismo y nacionalidad: La presencia del inglés en Puerto Rico* (Río Piedras: Editorial de la Universidad de Puerto Rico, 2002). Also see Negrón de Montilla, *Americanization in Puerto Rico*; and Amílcar Barreto, "Enlightened Tolerance or Cultural Capitulation?" in this volume.
8. Roamé Torres González, "Preámbulo histórico al establecimiento of la Escuela Normal Industrial de Fajardo: Antecedentes metropolitanos e insulares," *Revista Pedagogía* 35 (2003): pp. 6–33.
9. Pablo Navarro-Rivera, "Colonialism and the Language of Teaching and Learning at the University of Puerto Rico," *Journal of Pedagogy, Pluralism, and Practice* (fall 1999), http://www.lesley.edu/journals/jppp/4/navarro.html.
10. Puerto Rico Department of Education, *Annual Report of the Commissioner of Education* (Washington, D.C.: Government Printing Office, 1904), pp. 14–15.
11. Juan José Osuna, "An Indian in Spite of Myself," *Summer School Review* 10, no. 5 (1932): p. 3.
12. According to Barbara Landis, "Carlisle Indian Industrial School History," http://home.epix.net/~landis/histry.html, 2001, 10,702 students attended Carlisle between 1879 and 1918, including 2,090 who were not classified by tribe or nation.

13. *Indian Helper*, January 27, 1899. See also Landis, "Carlisle Indian Industrial School History."

14. Puerto Rico Department of Education, *Annual Report of the Commissioner of Education* (1904), p. 25. Members of the colonial legislature, as well as officials of the colonial government, constituted the selection committee for the scholarships, which typically went to sons and daughters of the elite and well connected.

15. Ibid., pp. 106–7.

16. Genevieve Bell, "Telling Stories Out of School: Remembering the Carlisle Indian Industrial School, 1879–1918," PhD diss., Stanford University, 1998, p. vi.

17. Ibid., p. 9.

18. See the document titled "Carlisle School," Office of Indian Affairs of the Department of the Interior, Record Group (RG) 75, Records of the Bureau of Indian Affairs, Entry 1349 C, NN 369–71, Records of Nonreservation Schools, Records of Carlisle, Miscellaneous Publications and Records, CA 1908–18, Box 1, U.S. National Archives (NA), Washington, D.C.

19. Carmelita S. Ryan, "The Carlisle Indian Industrial School," PhD diss., Georgetown University, 1962, p. 23.

20. See Frances E. Willard, "The Carlisle Indian School," RG 75, Entry 1349 C, NN 369–71, Box 2, NA.

21. Ryan, "The Carlisle Indian Industrial School"; *In the White Man's Image,* dir. C. Lesiak, Public Broadcasting Service, 1991; José Manuel Navarro, "Creating Tropical Yankees: The 'Spiritual Conquest' of Puerto Rico, 1898–1908," PhD diss., University of Chicago, 1995; Bell, "Telling Stories Out of School."

22. Bell, "Telling Stories Out of School," p. 121.

23. See the Indian Citizenship Act of 1924 (8 U.S.C. §1401). Also see Bell, "Telling Stories Out of School."

24. In "Telling Stories Out of School," Bell estimates that 66 percent of these were captured and returned to the school.

25. RG 75, Register of Visitors, 1909–1917, Box 1, NA.

26. Frank A. Guridy, "Racial Knowledge in Cuba: The Production of a Social Fact, 1912–1944," PhD diss., University of Michigan, 2002; Jorge Duany, *The Puerto Rican Nation on the Move: Identities on the Island and in the United States* (Chapel Hill: University of North Carolina Press, 2002).

27. See Guridy, "Racial Knowledge in Cuba," and Duany, *The Puerto Rican Nation on the Move.*

28. "Records of the Bureau of Indian Affairs," Records of the Carlisle Indian Industrial School (CIIS), Letters Sent, Aug. 28–Oct. 1900, Jan. 26–May 6, 1901, RG 75, Entry 1323, Box 1, PI 163, p. 372, NA.

29. Navarro-Rivera, "Acculturation under Duress."

30. "Record of Graduates and Returned Students," CIIS, RG 75, Entry 1328, HM 1996, Student Records, 1344-1404, Box 29, PI 163, NA.

31. Luis Muñoz Rivera, "Una visita al Indian School," *Puerto Rico Herald*, September 14, 1901.

32. Providencia Martínez to M. Friedman, Superintendent, CIIS, June 16, 1911, CIIS Student Records, 2835-2890, Box 57, Entry 1327, PI 163, HM 1996, NA.

33. Matilde Garnier, Record of Graduates and Returned Students, CIIS Student Records, 2835-2890, Box 57, Entry 1327, PI 163, HM 1996, NA.

34. The Cumberland County Historical Society, in Cumberland County, Pennsylvania, where Carlisle is located, houses one of the main collections of documents of the CIIS.

35. Chief Clerk in Charge (no name included), CIIS, to Father Feeser, St. Patrick's Rectory, Carlisle, PA, January 8, 1917, Carlisle Student Records, 4955-4984, Box 124, Entry 1327, PI 165, HM 1996, NA.

36. Osuna, "An Indian in Spite of Myself," p. 3.
37. Ibid.
38. CIIS, RG 75, Entry 1327, NA.
39. Country homes were the residences in which students resided for months as part of the outing program.
40. *The Indian Helper* 14, January 27, 1899.
41. Juan José Osuna, *A History of Education in Puerto Rico* (Río Piedras: Editorial de la Universidad de Puerto Rico, 1949), p. 132.
42. On government-controlled employment, see Navarro-Rivera, *Universidad de Puerto Rico*.

JOHNSON—UNDERSTANDING THE AMERICAN EMPIRE

1. Philip C. Jessup, *Elihu Root*, 2 vols. (New York: Dodd, Mead, 1937), vol. 1, p. 215.
2. Ido Oren, "The Enduring Relationship between the American (National Security) State and the State of the Discipline," *PSOnline*, www.apsanet.org, p. 53 (accessed August 10, 2007).
3. Ibid., p. 54.
4. Leo S. Rowe, *The United States and Porto Rico* (New York: Longmans, Green, 1904), p. vii.
5. Ibid., p. xi.
6. Ibid., p. 17.
7. Ibid. p. 261.
8. *Proceedings of the American Political Science Association* 1, no. 1 (1904): p. 120.
9. Henry C. Morris, "Discussion," *Proceedings of the American Political Science Association* 1, no. 1 (1904): p. 140.
10. Jessup, *Elihu Root*, vol. 1, pp. 473–74.
11. David P. Barrows, "Teacher and Public Servant," in *Addresses Delivered at the Memorial Service for Bernard Moses, April Thirteenth Nineteen Hundred and Thirty,* http://content.cdlib.org/xtf/view?docId=hb6489p0g7&brand=calisphere&doc.view=entire_text (accessed August 15, 2007).
12. Ibid.
13. Crawford Young, *Political Science at the University of Wisconsin* (Madison: Board of Regents of the University of Wisconsin, 2006), p. 27.
14. Rowe, *The United States and Porto Rico,* p. 18.
15. Ibid., pp. 18–19.
16. Ibid., p. 261.
17. Elihu Root, "The Real Monroe Doctrine," *American Journal of International Law* 8, no. 3 (1914): pp. 427–42.

CORBOULD—INTRODUCTION TO PART 4

1. Paul A. Kramer, *The Blood of Government: Race, Empire, the United States, and the Philippines* (Chapel Hill: University of North Carolina Press, 2006).
2. Francisco A. Scarano and Katherine Curtis White, "A Window into the Past: Household Composition and Distribution in Puerto Rico, 1910 and 1920," *Caribbean Studies* (forthcoming).
3. J. Kehaulani Kauanui, "Native Hawaiians, American Indians, and Assimilation: Through the Other End of the Telescope," paper presented at the conference "Transitions and Transformations in the U.S. Imperial State: The Search for New Synthesis," University of Wisconsin–Madison, November 9–11, 2006.
4. Mae M. Ngai, *Impossible Subjects: Illegal Aliens and the Making of Modern America* (Princeton: Princeton University Press, 2004).

KRAMER—RACE, EMPIRE, AND TRANSNATIONAL HISTORY

1. Statement of David J. Gilmer, *Colored American*, January 19, 1901, reprinted in Willard Gatewood, *"Smoked Yankees" and the Struggle for Empire: Letters from Negro Soldiers, 1898–1902* (Urbana: University of Illinois Press, 1971), pp. 292–93. Here Gilmer identifies his location as "Linao"; given his troops' service in Mindanao, however, I am assuming this took place in Lanao.

2. Richard Hofstader, *Social Darwinism in American Life, 1860–1915* (Philadelphia: University of Pennsylvania Press, 1944); Walter L. Williams, "United States Indian Policy and the Debate over Philippine Annexation: Implications for the Origins of American Imperialism," *Journal of American History* 66, no. 4 (1980): pp. 810–31.

3. Paul A. Kramer, *The Blood of Government: Race, Empire, the United States, and the Philippines* (Chapel Hill: University of North Carolina Press, 2006).

4. Akira Iriye, "The Internationalization of History," *American Historical Review* 94, no. 1 (1989): pp. 1–10; Ian Tyrrell, "American Exceptionalism in an Age of International History," *American Historical Review* 96, no. 4 (1991): pp. 1031–55.

5. Paul A. Kramer, "Connecting Pasts: Transnational and Imperial Histories of the Modern United States," paper presented at the conference "Bridging the World(s): Contributions of American Studies in a Time of Conflict," Nagoya, Japan, June 2006.

6. Walter Johnson, "Time and Revolution in African America: Temporality and the History of Atlantic Slavery," in Thomas Bender, ed., *Rethinking American History in a Global Age* (Berkeley: University of California Press, 2002), pp. 148–67.

7. Ann Laura Stoler, "Tense and Tender Ties: The Politics of Comparison in North American History and (Post) Colonial Studies," *Journal of American History* 88, no. 3 (December 2001), pp. 829–65.

8. David Thelen, "Of Audiences, Borderlands, and Comparisons: Toward the Internationalization of American History," *Journal of American History* 79, no. 2 (1992): pp. 432–62.

9. Kristin Hoganson, *Fighting for American Manhood: How Gender Politics Provoked the Spanish-American and Philippine-American Wars* (New Haven: Yale University Press, 1998).

10. Nicholas Thomas, *Colonialism's Culture: Anthropology, Travel, and Government* (Princeton: Princeton University Press, 1994); Lanny Thompson, "The Imperial Republic: A Comparison of the Insular Territories under U.S. Dominion after 1898," *Pacific Historical Review* 74, no. 4 (2002): pp. 535–74.

11. Joseph Fry, "Imperialism, American Style, 1890–1916," in Gordon Martel, ed., *American Foreign Relations, 1890–1993* (London and New York: Routledge, 1994), pp. 52–70; Louis A. Pérez, *The War of 1898: The United States and Cuba in History and Historiography* (Chapel Hill: University of North Carolina Press, 1998); Glenn May, "The Unfathomable Other: Historical Studies of U.S.-Philippine Relations," in Warren Cohen, ed., *Pacific Passage: The Study of American–East Asian Relations on the Eve of the Twenty-First Century* (New York: Columbia University Press, 1996), pp. 279–312.

12. Josep Maria Fradera, *Gobernar Colonias* (Barcelona: Ediciones Península, 1999).

13. Vicente L. Rafael, *The Promise of the Foreign: Nationalism and the Technics of Translation in the Spanish Philippines* (Durham: Duke University Press, 2005); Cesar Majul, "*Principales, Ilustrados*, Intellectuals, and the Original Concept of a Filipino National Community," *Asian Studies* 15 (1977): pp. 1–20.

14. Marya Camacho, "Race and Culture in Spanish and American Colonial Policies," in Hazel M. McFerson, ed., *Mixed Blessing: The Impact of the American Colonial Experience on Politics and Society in the Philippines* (Westport: Greenwood, 2002), pp. 43–74.

15. Paul A. Dumol, "Rizal contra European Racism: An Autobiography of José Rizal Embedded in Blumentritt's Obituary of Rizal," in Vyva Victoria Aguirre, ed., *European tudies: Essays by Filipino Scholars* (Quezon City: Center for Integrative and Development Studies with the Institute of International Legal Studies, University of the Philippines, 1999);

Filomeno V. Aguilar Jr., "Tracing Origins: Ilustrado Nationalism and the Racial Science of Migration Waves," *Journal of Asian Studies* 64, no. 3 (August 2005): pp. 605–37.

16. Luis-Angel Sánchez-Gómez, *Un Imperio en La Vitrina: El Colonialismo Espanol en el Pacífico y La Exposición de Filipinas de 1887* (Madrid: Consejo Superior de Investigaciones Científicas, Instituto de Historia, 2003).

17. Teodoro Agoncillo, *Malolos: The Crisis of the Republic* (Quezon City: University of the Philippines Press, 1960).

18. Richard E. Welch, *Response to Imperialism: The United States and the Philippine-American War, 1899–1902* (Chapel Hill: University of North Carolina Press, 1979); Jim Zwick, "The Anti-imperialist Movement, 1898–1921," in V. M. Bouvier, ed., *Whose America? 1898 and the Battles to Define the Nation* (Westport: Praeger, 2001), pp. 171–92.

19. Paul A. Kramer, "Empires, Exceptions, and Anglo-Saxons: Race and Rule between the British and U.S. Empires, 1880–1910," *Journal of American History* 88, no. 4 (2002): pp. 1315–53.

20. Glenn A. May, *Social Engineering in the Philippines: The Aims, Execution, and Goals of American Colonial Policy, 1900–1913* (Westport: Greenwood, 1980).

21. Jim Zwick, "The Anti-imperialist League and the Origins of Filipino-American Oppositional Solidarity," *Amerasia Journal* 24, no. 2 (1998): pp. 65–85.

22. Stuart Creighton Miller, *"Benevolent Assimilation": The American Conquest of the Philippines, 1899–1903* (New Haven: Yale University Press, 1982).

23. Paul D. Hutchcroft, "Colonial Masters, National Politicos, and Provincial Lords: Central Authority and Local Autonomy in the American Philippines, 1900–1913," *Journal of Asian Studies* 59, no. 2 (2000): pp. 277–306.

24. R. E. Minger, "Taft, MacArthur, and the Establishment of Civil Government in the Philippines," *Ohio Historical Quarterly* 70, no. 4 (1961): pp. 308–31.

25. Frank Furedi, *The Silent War: Imperialism and the Changing Perception of Race* (New Brunswick, N.J.: Rutgers University Press, 1998).

26. Reynaldo C. Ileto, "Orientalism and the Study of Philippine Politics," in *Knowing America's Colony* (Honolulu: Center for Philippine Studies, School of Hawaiian, Asian and Pacific Studies, University of Hawai'i at Manoa, 1999).

27. Kramer, *The Blood of Government*, chap. 3.

28. Eric T. L. Love, *Race over Empire: Racism and United States Imperialism, 1865–1900* (Chapel Hill: University of North Carolina Press, 2004); Christopher Lasch, "The Anti-imperialists, the Philippines, and the Inequality of Man," *Journal of Southern History* 24, no. 3 (1958): pp. 319–31.

29. Barbara Gaerlan, "The Pursuit of Modernity: Trinidad H. Pardo de Tavera and the Educational Legacy of the Philippine Revolution," *Amerasia Journal* 24, no. 2 (1998): pp. 87–108.

30. Daniel Doeppers, "Tracing the Decline of the Mestizo Category in Philippine Life in the Late 19th Century," *Philippine Quarterly of Culture and Society* 22, no. 2 (1994): pp. 80–89.

31. Mahmood Mamdani, *Citizen and Subject: Contemporary Africa and the Legacy of Colonialism* (Princeton: Princeton University Press, 1996); Patricio Abinales, "An American Colonial State: Authority and Structure in Southern Mindanao," in *Images of State Power: Essays on Philippine Politics from the Margins* (Diliman: University of the Philippines Press, 1998), 1–52; Michael Salman, *The Embarrassment of Slavery: Controversies over Bondage and Nationalism in the American Colonial Philippines* (Berkeley: University of California Press, 2001).

32. Paul A. Kramer, "Decolonizing the History of the Philippine-American War," preface to Leon Wolff, *Little Brown Brother: How the United States Purchased and Pacified the Philippine Islands at the Century's Turn*, Francis Parkman Prize, ed. (New York: History Book Club, 2006), pp. i–xviii.

33. Robert W. Rydell, *All the World's a Fair: Visions of Empire at American International Expositions, 1876–1916* (Chicago: University of Chicago Press, 1984), chap. 6; Paul A. Kramer,

"Making Concessions: Race and Empire Revisited at the Philippine Exposition, St. Louis, 1901–5," *Radical History Review* 73 (1999): pp. 74–114.

34. Michael Cullinane, "Playing the Game: The Rise of Sergio Osmeña," in Ruby Paredes, ed., *Philippine Colonial Democracy* (Quezon City: Ateneo de Manila University Press, 1989), pp. 70–113.

35. Salman, *The Embarrassment of Slavery.*

36. Kramer, *The Blood of Government*, chap. 5.

37. Irene Jensen, *The Chinese in the Philippines during the American Regime, 1898–1946* (San Francisco: R. and E. Research Associates, 1975).

38. Mae Ngai, *Impossible Subjects: Illegal Aliens and the Making of Modern America* (Princeton: Princeton University Press, 2004), chap. 1.

39. Dorothy Fujita-Rony, *American Workers, Colonial Power: Philippine Seattle in the Trans-Pacific West, 1919–1941* (Berkeley: University of California Press, 2002); Bruno Lasker, *Filipino Migration to the Continental United States and to Hawaii* (Chicago: University of Chicago Press, 1931).

40. Roger Daniels, *The Politics of Prejudice: The Anti-Japanese Movement in California, and the Struggle for Japanese Exclusion* (Berkeley: University of California Press, 1962); Alexander Saxton, *The Indispensable Enemy: Labor and the Anti-Chinese Movement in California* (Berkeley: University of California Press, 1971).

41. Josefa M. Saniel, ed., *The Filipino Exclusion Movement, 1927–1935* (Quezon City: University of the Philippines Press, 1967).

42. Kramer, *The Blood of Government*, chap. 6.

SCARANO—CENSUSES IN THE TRANSITION TO MODERN COLONIALISM

1. Benedict Anderson, *Imagined Communities: Reflections on the Origins and the Spread of Nationalism*, 2d ed. (New York: Verso, 1991), pp. 163–64.

2. Josep M. Fradera, "Reading Imperial Transitions: Spanish Contraction, British Expansion, and American Irruption," in this volume.

3. Fernando Picó, "La revolución puertorriqueña de 1898: La necesidad de un nuevo paradigma para entender el 98 puertorriqueño," *Historia y Sociedad* 10 (1998): pp. 7–22.

4. Eileen Findlay, *Imposing Decency: The Politics of Sexuality and Race in Puerto Rico* (Durham: Duke University Press, 1999).

5. U.S. House of Representatives, 56th Cong., 2d sess., "Report of the Military Governor of Porto Rico on Civil Affairs," in *Annual Reports of the War Department for the Fiscal Year Ended June 30, 1900*, pt. 13 (San Juan: Academia Puertorriqueña de la Historia, [1902] 2003), p. 99.

6. Fernando Picó, *Cayeyanos: Familias y solidaridades en la historia de Cayey* (Río Piedras: Ediciones Huracán, 2007).

7. Courtney Johnson, "Understanding the American Empire: Colonialism, Latin Americanism, and Professional Social Science, 1898–1920," in this volume.

8. Julian Go, "Chains of Empire, Projects of State: Political Education and U.S. Colonial Rule in Puerto Rico and the Philippines," *Comparative Studies in Society and History* 42, no. 2 (April 2000): pp. 333–62.

9. John V. Lombardi, "Population Reporting Systems: An Eighteenth-Century Paradigm of Spanish Imperial Organization," in David J. Robinson, ed., *Studies in Spanish American Population History* (Boulder: Westview, 1981), p. 12.

10. Altagracia Ortiz, *Eighteenth-Century Reforms in the Caribbean: Miguel de Muesas, Governor of Puerto Rico, 1769–76* (Rutherford, N.J.: Fairleigh-Dickinson University Press, 1983).

11. Nonetheless, here *padrones* is used interchangeably with *censuses*. See Sherburne Friend Cook and Woodrow Wilson Borah's relevant discussion in *Essays in Population History: Mexico and the Caribbean*, 3 vols. (Berkeley: University of California Press, 1971–79), vol. 1, pp. 41–42.

12. *Intendentes*, or "intendants," were officials introduced by the Spanish Bourbons in the 1770s who consolidated managerial and fiscal functions.
13. Vicente L. Rafael, "White Love: Census and Melodrama in the United States' Colonization of the Philippines," *History and Anthropology* 8, nos. 1–4 (1994): pp. 265–97.
14. Victor H. Olmsted and Henry Gannett, comps., *Cuba: Population, History, and Resources, 1907* (Washington, D.C.: U.S. Bureau of the Census, 1909).
15. Cayetano Coll y Toste, *Reseña del estado social, económico e industrial de la isla de Puerto-Rico al tomar posesión de ella los Estados-Unidos* (San Juan: Academia Puertorriqueña de la Historia, [1899] 2003).
16. Robert T. Hill, *Cuba and Porto Rico with the Other Islands of the West Indies* (New York: Century, 1899), p. 165.
17. Porto Rican Census Office, U.S. War Department, *Report on the Census of Porto Rico, 1899* (Washington, D.C.: Government Printing Office, 1900).
18. Cited in Javier Morillo Alicea, "Looking for Empire in the U.S. Colonial Archive: Photos and Texts," *Historia y Sociedad* 10 (1998): p. 27.
19. Christina Duffy-Burnett, "Empire and the Transformation of Citizenship," in this volume.
20. Bartholomew H. Sparrow, *The* Insular Cases *and the Emergence of the American Empire* (Lawrence: University Press of Kansas, 2006).
21. U.S. House of Representatives, 56th Cong., 2d sess., "Report of the Military Governor of Porto Rico," p. 94.
22. Mara Loveman, "The U.S. Census and the Contested Rules of Racial Classification in Early Twentieth-Century Puerto Rico (1910–1920)," *Caribbean Studies* 35, no. 2 (July–December 2007): pp. 79–113.
23. José Luis Vázquez Calzada, *La población de Puerto Rico y su trayectoria histórica* (Río Piedras: Escuela de Salud Pública, Universidad de Puerto Rico, 1988), p. 9.

De la Fuente and Casey—
Race and the Suffrage Controversy in Cuba, 1898–1901

1. "La población de Cuba," *La Lucha*, September 21, 1899.
2. Ada Ferrer, *Insurgent Cuba: Race, Nation, and Revolution, 1868–1898* (Chapel Hill: University of North Carolina Press, 1999), pp. 22–28.
3. Ley de Organización Administrativa, August 7, 1869, in Julio Carreras, *Historia del estado y el derecho en Cuba* (Havana: Ministerio de Educación Superior, 1981), pp. 245–58. See Article 5 of the law on electoral rights.
4. Constitución de la Yaya, October 29, 1897, Art. 10; Ley Penal de Cuba, January 1, 1898, Art. 65, both in Carreras, *Historia*, pp. 191, 218.
5. Louis A. Pérez, *Cuba between Empires, 1878–1902* (Pittsburgh: University of Pittsburgh Press, 1983), pp. 89–108; Ferrer, *Insurgent Cuba*, pp. 70–94.
6. Pérez, *Cuba between Empires*, pp. 101, 310.
7. Aline Helg, *Our Rightful Share: The Afro-Cuban Struggle for Equality, 1886–1912* (Chapel Hill: University of North Carolina Press, 1995), pp. 36–38.
8. There is a growing body of scholarship on postwar political reforms and the Autonomist regime. Most of this work has been produced by Spanish scholars. See, especially, Luis Miguel García Mora, "Tras la revolución, las reformas: El Partido Liberal Cubano y los proyectos reformistas tras la Paz del Zanjón," in *Cuba: La perla de las Antillas*, Consuelo Naranjo Orovio and Tomas Mallo, eds. (Aranjuez: Doce Calles, 1994), pp. 197–212; Mariano Esteban de Vega and José G. Cayuela Fernández, "Elite hispano-cubana, autonomismo y desastre del '98," *Colonial Latin American Review* 9, no. 1 (June 2000): pp. 81–112; and Inés Roldán de Montaud, *La Restauración en Cuba y el fracaso del proyecto reformista* (Madrid: Consejo Superior de Investigaciones Científicas, 2000).

9. "After Intervention—What?" *Nation,* March 17, 1898.
10. Albert Gardner Robinson, "The Real Cuban," *Independent,* December 20, 1900; Albert Gardner Robinson, "Cuban Autonomy or Independence?" *Nation,* March 10, 1898; Albert Gardener Robinson, "Multiplying Difficulties in Cuba," *Nation,* August 4, 1898.
11. Robinson, "Cuban Autonomy or Independence?"
12. Carl Schurz, "The Future of Cuba," *Harper's Weekly,* March 26, 1898. See also Henry Banga, "What Form of Government Should Cuba Libre Adopt?" *Independent,* August 9, 1900.
13. "After Interventions—What?"; "Cuba's Future," *New York Times,* April 3, 1900.
14. "Charles Gano Baylor on Cuba and Imperialism," *Richmond Planet,* July 23, 1898.
15. "Against Annexation: American Hypocrisy Scored," *Salt Lake City Broad Ax,* January 14, 1899.
16. "Gloomy Outlook for the Dark-Skinned Cubans," *Richmond Planet,* August 20, 1898.
17. Ferrer, *Insurgent Cuba,* p. 199.
18. Leonard Wood to Elihu Root, Havana, February 8, 1900, and Wood to Root, Havana, February 8, 1901, Library of Congress, Ms. Division, Wood Papers, 28 and 29. See also Pérez, *Cuba between Empires,* pp. 303–14.
19. Robinson, "Multiplying Difficulties in Cuba."
20. Root to Wood, Washington, D.C., June 20, 1900, Leonard Wood Papers, 28; "Asuntos varios. Conferencia," *Diario de la Marina,* January 25, 1900, evening ed.
21. Quoted in "La Prensa," *Diario de la Marina,* January 12, 1900, morning ed.
22. "Asuntos varios: Conferencia," *Diario de la Marina,* January 25, 1900, evening ed.; "La Prensa" (quoting *El Cubano Libre*), *Diario de la Marina,* February 17, 1900, morning ed.
23. "Asuntos varios: El sufragio universal," *Diario de la Marina,* March 21, 1900, morning ed.; *Diario de la Marina,* March 23, 1900, evening ed.; Telegram, Severino Oviedo, Mayor of Cartagena, to Wood, February 23, 1900, Leonard Wood Papers, 28. See also Pérez, *Cuba between Empires,* pp. 303–14.
24. "Asuntos varios: Manifestación," *Diario de la Marina,* March 26, 1900, evening ed.
25. "La nota del día," *Diario de la Marina,* October 21, 1901.
26. "El vínculo religioso," *Diario de la Marina,* April 15, 1900, morning ed.; *Unión Española* quoted in "Questions of the Day," *La Lucha,* October 31, 1899. See the section "La prensa" in *Diario de la Marina,* January 12, 1900, September 1, 1900, and February 12, 1902.
27. Robinson, "Multiplying Difficulties in Cuba."
28. Ibid.; "The Conditions of Cuban Suffrage," *Independent,* January 11, 1900.
29. J. W. Whelpley, "Coming Events in Cuba," *Independent,* September 20, 1900.
30. "A Contest at Santiago," *New York Times,* April 2, 1900; "Excitement at Santiago," *New York Times,* April 7, 1900.
31. "The Conditions of Cuban Suffrage"; Robinson, "Multiplying Difficulties in Cuba."
32. "La Prensa," *Diario de la Marina,* February 17, 1900, morning ed.; "Asuntos varios: La comisión electoral," *Diario de la Marina,* February 20, 1900, morning ed.
33. Wood to Root, Havana, February 23, 1900, Wood Papers, 28. Wood corrected the draft to note that limitations of suffrage had been accepted "almost" universally. See Wood to Root, April 12, 1900, Wood Papers, 28.
34. "Problem of Cuba at Close Range," *New York Times,* April 2, 1900.
35. "Cuban Commission Returns," *New York Times,* April 2, 1900.
36. "Evacuating Cuba," *New York Times,* April 27, 1900.
37. Whelpley, "Coming Events in Cuba."
38. These debates are analyzed in Alejandro de la Fuente, *"A Nation for All": Race, Inequality, and Politics in Twentieth-Century Cuba* (Chapel Hill: University of North Carolina Press, 2001), pp. 56–60.
39. "Los enemigos de la independencia," *El Mundo,* April 27, 1901.
40. "¡No hubo quórum!" *La Discusión,* July 8, 1901.

41. "Los debates del Ateneo: Discurso pronunciado por el doctor Alfredo Zayas," *La Discusión*, November 20, 1905.

42. There were only two delegates considered to be nonwhite at the convention, Morúa Delgado and the patriot and activist Juan Gualberto Gómez.

Schmidt-Nowara—From Columbus to Ponce de León

1. María de los Angeles Castro Arroyo, "La memoria en orden: Rescate, organización, y perspectiva de los archivos en Puerto Rico," *Revista del Centro de Investigaciónes Históricas* 5 (1990): pp. 105–32.

2. Ann Laura Stoler and David Bond, "Refractions Off Empire: Untimely Comparisons in Harsh Times," *Radical History Review* 95 (2006): pp. 93–107.

3. Jesse Walter Fewkes, *The Aborigines of Porto Rico and Neighboring Islands* (New York: Johnson Reprint, [1907] 1970).

4. Christopher Schmidt-Nowara, *The Conquest of History: Spanish Colonialism and National Histories in the Nineteenth Century* (Pittsburgh: University of Pittsburgh Press, 2006).

5. See Vicente Murga Sanz, *Juan Ponce de León: Fundador y primer gobernador del pueblo Puertorriqueño, descubridor de la Florida, y del Estrecho de las Bahamas*, 2d ed. (Río Piedras: Universidad de Puerto Rico, Editorial Universitaria, 1971), pp. 242–45.

6. See Schmidt-Nowara, *The Conquest of History*, pp. 53–95.

7. Agustín Stahl, *Los indios borinqueños: Estudios etnográficos* (San Juan: Imprenta y Librería de Acosta, 1889).

8. J. Aquenza, "Las fiestas del Centenario," in *1797: Lealtad y heroísmo de la isla de Puerto Rico, 1897* (San Juan: A. Lynn é hijos de Pérez-Moris, 1897), pp. 335–63; "El 2 de Mayo," *Boletín Mercantil* (San Juan), May 2, 1897.

9. Salvador Brau, "El Dos de Mayo de 1797," in *1797*, pp. 123–27.

10. On the receptions and trajectories of Las Casas's writings, see Christopher Schmidt-Nowara and John Nieto-Phillips, eds., *Interpreting Spanish Colonialism: Empires, Nations, and Legends* (Albuquerque: University of New Mexico Press, 2005).

11. See Francisco Scarano, "Liberal Pacts and Hierarchies of Rule: Approaching the Imperial Transition in Cuba and Puerto Rico," *Hispanic American Historical Review* 78 (1998): pp. 583–601.

12. Jorge Duany, *The Puerto Rican Nation on the Move: Identities on the Island and in the United States* (Chapel Hill: University of North Carolina Press, 2002).

13. "El gobernador Regis H. Post correspondiendo al Mensaje de la Cámara de Representantes, ha dado la siguente proclama," in *Gratitud y progreso: Cuarto centenario de la colonización cristiana de Puerto Rico* (San Juan: Tipografía Boletín Mercantil, 1908), p. 11.

14. See for example Arcadio Díaz Quiñones, "1898: Hispanismo y Guerra," in Walther L. Bernecker, ed., *1898: Su significado para Centroamérica y el Caribe* (Madrid: Iberoamericana, 1998), pp. 17–35.

15. See Duany, *The Puerto Rican Nation on the Move*, pp. 122–65.

16. José Luis González, *El país de cuatro pisos y otros ensayos* (Río Piedras: Ediciones Huracán, 1980); Gabriel Haslip-Viera, ed., *Taíno Revival* (New York: Centro de Estudios Puertorriqueños, 1999).

17. Carey McWilliams, *North from Mexico: The Spanish-Speaking People of the United States* (Philadelphia and New York: Lippincot, 1949).

Halualani—A Critical-Historical Genealogy of Koko, 'Aina, Hawaiian Identity, and Western Law and Governance

1. Stuart Hall, "Introduction: Who Needs 'Identity?'" in S. Hall and P. DuGay, eds., *Questions of Cultural Identity* (London: Sage, 1996), pp. 1–17.

2. Lilikala Kame'eleihiwa, *Native Land and Foreign Desires: Pehea La E Pono Ai?* (Honolulu: Bishop Museum Press, 1992); Melody Kapilialoha MacKenzie, "1893–1993: Overthrow, Annexation, and Sovereignty," *Hawaii Bar Journal* 21 (February 1993): pp. 8–11.

3. Rona Halualani, *In the Name of Hawaiians: Native Identities and Cultural Politics* (Minneapolis: University of Minnesota Press, 2002).

4. John Papa I'I, *Fragments of Hawaiian History*, trans. Mary Kawena Pukui (Honolulu: Bishop Museum Press, 1959).

5. Kame'eleihiwa, *Native Land*; Linda Parker, *Native American Estate: The Struggle over Indian and Hawaiian Lands* (Honolulu: University of Hawai'i Press, 1989); Marion Kelly, "Statement," in U.S. Senate, 98th Cong., 2d sess., *Hearings on the Report of the Native Hawaiians Study Commission before the Senate Committee on Energy and Natural Resources* (Washington, D.C.: Government Printing Office, 1984); Melody Kapilialoha MacKenzie, *Native Hawaiian Rights Handbook* (Honolulu: Native Hawaiian Legal Corporation and Office of Hawaiian Affairs, 1991).

6. David E. Stannard, *Before the Horror: The Population of Hawai'i on the Eve of Western Contact* (Honolulu: Social Science Research Institute, University of Hawai'i, 1989).

7. Kame'eleihiwa, *Native Land*; MacKenzie, *Native Hawaiian Rights Handbook*; David Malo, *Hawaiian Antiquities*, trans. Nathaniel B. Emerson (Honolulu: Bishop Museum Press, 1951); Parker, *Native American Estate*.

8. Kame'eleihiwa, *Native Land*; MacKenzie, *Native Hawaiian Rights Handbook*; Parker, *Native American Estate*.

9. Kame'eleihiwa, *Native Land*.

10. Ibid.

11. Samuel M. Kamakau, *Ruling Chiefs of Hawai'i* (Honolulu: Kamehameha Schools, 1961); Malo, *Hawaiian Antiquities*.

12. Kame'eleihiwa, *Native Land*.

13. Ibid.; Elizabeth Buck, *Paradise Remade: The Politics of Culture and History in Hawai'i* (Philadelphia: Temple University Press, 1993).

14. Kame'eleihiwa, *Native Land*; MacKenzie, *Native Hawaiian Rights Handbook*; Malo, *Hawaiian Antiquities*; Parker, *Native American Estate*.

15. Kame'eleihiwa, *Native Land*; MacKenzie, *Native Hawaiian Rights Handbook*; Parker, *Native American Estate*.

16. Buck, *Paradise Remade*.

17. Kobena Mercer, "'1968': Periodizing Politics and Identity," in K. Mercer, ed., *Welcome to the Jungle: New Positions in Black Cultural Studies* (New York: Routledge, 1994), pp. 287–308.

18. Kame'eleihiwa, *Native Land*; Parker, *Native American Estate*.

19. Buck, *Paradise Remade*; Parker, *Native American Estate*.

20. Kame'eleihiwa, *Native Land*; Parker, *Native American Estate*.

21. Marshall Sahlins, *Historical Metaphors and Mythical Realities: Structure in the Early History of the Sandwich Islands Kingdom* (Ann Arbor: University of Michigan Press, 1981).

22. Buck, *Paradise Remade*; Kame'eleihiwa, *Native Land*.

23. Kame'eleihiwa, *Native Land*; MacKenzie, *Native Hawaiian Rights Handbook*; Malo, *Hawaiian Antiquities*; Parker, *Native American Estate*.

24. Kame'eleihiwa, *Native Land*.

25. MacKenzie, *Native Hawaiian Rights Handbook*; Parker, *Native American Estate*.

26. Kame'eleihiwa, *Native Land*; MacKenzie, *Native Hawaiian Rights Handbook*; Parker, *Native American Estate*.

27. O. Kotzebue, *A Voyage of Discovery into the South Sea and Bering's Straits, for the Purpose of Exploring a North-East Passage, Undertaken in the Years 1815–1818* (London: Printed for Sir Richard Phillips and Co. Bride Court, 1821); Parker, *Native American Estate*.

28. Kame'eleihiwa, *Native Land;* MacKenzie, *Native Hawaiian Rights Handbook;* Parker, *Native American Estate;* Haunani Kay Trask, *From a Native Daughter: Colonialism and Sovereignty in Hawai'i* (Monroe, Maine: Common Courage Press, 1993).

29. Hiram Bingham, *Residence of Twenty-one Years in the Sandwich Islands; or the Civil, Religious, and Political History of Those Islands* (Hartford: Hezekiah Huntington, 1847), p. 81.

30. James Duncan, "Sites of Representation: Place, Time, and the Discourse of the Other," in *Place/Culture/Representation,* J. Duncan and D. Ley, eds. (London: Routledge, 1993), pp. 39–56.

31. Parker, *Native American Estate; Polynesian,* July 8, 1848.

32. Stuart Hall, "Race, Articulation, and Societies Structured in Dominance," in *Sociological Theories: Race and Colonialism* (Paris: United Nations Educational, Scientific, and Cultural Organization, 1979), pp. 305–45.

33. Hawaii, *Revised Laws of Hawaii, 1925* (Honolulu: Honolulu Star-Bulletin, 1925), n. 29; MacKenzie, *Native Hawaiian Rights Handbook,* p. 7.

34. Kame'eleihiwa, *Native Land;* MacKenzie, *Native Hawaiian Rights Handbook;* Parker, *Native American Estate.*

35. MacKenzie, *Native Hawaiian Rights Handbook,* p. 8.

36. Parker, *Native American Estate.*

37. MacKenzie, *Native Hawaiian Rights Handbook;* Parker, *Native American Estate.*

38. MacKenzie, *Native Hawaiian Rights Handbook;* Parker, *Native American Estate.*

39. U.S. House of Representatives, 66th Cong., 2d sess., *Rehabilitation of Native Hawaiians: Report to Accompany H.R. 13500,* report no. 839 (Washington, D.C.: Government Printing Office, 1920), p. 8.

40. MacKenzie, *Native Hawaiian Rights Handbook.*

41. Alan Murakami, "The Hawaiian Homes Commission Act," in MacKenzie, *Native Hawaiian Rights Handbook.*

42. U.S. Senate, 66th Cong., 3d sess., "Hearings before the Committee on the Territories," *A Bill to Amend an "Act to Provide a Government for the Territory of Hawaii," Approved April 30, 1900 as Amended to Establish an Hawaiian Homes Commission, and for Other Purposes,* H.R. 13500 (Washington, D.C.: Government Printing Office, 1921), p. 7.

43. Murakami, "The Hawaiian Homes Commission Act."

44. U.S. Senate, 66th Cong., 3d sess., Hawaiian Homes Commission Act, 1920, *Hearings before the Committee on Territories, United States Senate, Sixty-sixth Congress, Third Session, on H.R. 13500, a Bill to Amend an Act Entitled "An Act to Provide A Government for the Territory of Hawaii," Approved April 30, 1900, as Amended, to Establish an Hawaiian Homes Commission, and for Other Purposes* (Washington, D.C.: Government Printing Office, 1921), p. 7.

45. U.S. House of Representatives, *Rehabilitation of Native Hawaiians.*

46. Diana Hansen, *The Homestead Papers: A Critical Analysis of the Management of the Department of Hawaiian Home Lands* (Honolulu: State of Hawaii, 1971).

HOGANSON—BUYING INTO EMPIRE

1. On shipping, see Thomas C. Cochran and William Miller, *The Age of Enterprise: A Social History of Industrial America* (New York: Macmillan, 1942), p. 111. Overall U.S. imports rose from $354 million in 1860 to $1.9 billion in 1914. In the same period, exports rose from $316 million to $2.4 billion. Stuart Weems Bruchey, *Enterprise: The Dynamic Economy of a Free People* (Cambridge: Harvard University Press, 1990), pp. 296–300.

2. See, for example, Walter LaFeber, *The Cambridge History of American Foreign Relations,* vol. 2: *The American Search for Opportunity, 1865–1913* (Cambridge: Cambridge University Press, 1993).

3. Nupur Chaudhuri, "Shawls, Jewelry, Curry, and Rice in Victorian Britain," in Nupur Chaudhuri and Margaret Strobel, eds., *Western Women and Imperialism: Complicity and Resistance* (Bloomington: Indiana University Press, 1992), pp. 231–46.

4. M. G. Van Rensselaer, "The Development of American Homes," in Candace Wheeler, ed., *Household Art* (New York: Harper and Brothers, 1893), p. 37.

5. *The 1902 Edition of the Sears Roebuck Catalogue*, with an introduction by Cleveland Amory (New York: Bounty Books, 1969), p. 851; "John Forsythe," *Vogue*, April 18, 1907, p. 665; "Revillon Frères in the Orient," *Vanity Fair*, November 1918, pp. 78–79; "Where Vantine's Buy," *New York Tribune*, February 2, 1896.

6. "Oriental Rugs and Why They Are So Highly Valued," *New York Tribune*, September 22, 1912; George Leland Hunter, "Oriental Rugs for $50 and Less," *House and Garden*, December 1909, p. 204; Agnes Bailey Ormsbee, *The House Comfortable* (New York: Harper and Brothers, 1892).

7. William Joseph Showalter, "How the World Is Fed: The World Our Servant," *National Geographic*, January 1916, pp. 1–110, 104–5.

8. See, for example, Allen H. Eaton, *Immigrant Gifts to American Life: Some Experiments in Appreciation of the Contributions of Our Foreign-Born Citizens to American Culture* (New York: Russell Sage Foundation, 1932); and Robert W. Rydell, *All the World's a Fair: Visions of Empire at American International Expositions, 1876–1916* (Chicago: University of Chicago Press, 1984).

9. Maude Adams, "Maude Adams in London," *Atlanta Constitution*, July 5, 1896.

10. Flora Michaelis, "Anglo-Indian Pickles and Chutneys," *Delineator*, October 1909, p. 322. On labels, see "A Curry," *New York Tribune*, June 19, 1892. On colonialism and curry, see Chaudhuri, "Shawls, Jewelry, Curry, and Rice," p. 238; and Arjun Appadurai, "How to Make a National Cuisine: Cookbooks in Contemporary India," *Comparative Studies in Society and History* 30 (January 1988): pp. 3–24, 18.

11. Edith Bradford Gird, "Spanish-California Cookery," *Good Housekeeping*, February 1910, pp. 272–73. On later interventions, see Gail Cooper, "Love, War, and Chocolate: Gender and the American Candy Industry, 1880–1930," in Roger Horowitz and Arwen Mohun, eds., *His and Hers: Gender, Consumption, and Technology* (Charlottesville: University Press of Virginia, 1998), pp. 67–94, 76. See also Anna Barrows, "In Place of Meat, What?" *Good Housekeeping*, February 1910, pp, 268–71, 271.

12. Mary Hamilton Talbott, "'New' Fruits and Vegetables," *Good Housekeeping*, August 1910, p. 213. On overseas researchers for the U.S. Department of Agriculture, see Jeffrey Charles, "Searching for Gold in Guacamole: California Growers Market the Avocado, 1910–1914," in Warren Belasco and Philip Scranton, eds., *Food Nations: Selling Taste in Consumer Societies* (New York: Routledge, 2002), pp. 131–54, 133.

13. "Home Interests," *New York Tribune*, March 14, 1880.

14. Harriet Prescott Spofford, *Art Decoration Applied to Furniture* (New York: Harper and Brothers, 1877), p. 161.

15. "Bonwit Teller and Co.," *New York Tribune*, January 16, 1916; "Bonwit Teller and Co.," *Vogue*, May 1, 1917, p. 5.

16. On ransacking, see W. L. D. O'Grady, "Influence of Oriental Art on Modern American Decoration," *Decoration and Furnisher*, November 1884, p. 211. On plunder, see Laura B. Starr, "An Indian Room," *Decorator and Furnisher*, May 1889, p. 38. On trophies, see Mary Gay Humphreys, "House Decoration and Furnishing," in *The House and Home: A Practical Book in Two Volumes*, vol. 2 (New York: Charles Scribner's Sons, 1896), pp. 103–78, 144. John Kimberly Mumford, "Glimpses of Modern Persia," *House and Garden*, September 2, 1902, pp. 429–36, 433.

17. Francis E. Lester Co. catalogue, Mesilla Park, N.M., 1904.

18. S. A. Brock Putnam, "Mexican Drawn Work," *Decorator and Furnisher*, August 1895, p. 178.

19. On distinction, see Pierre Bourdieu, *Distinction: A Social Critique of the Judgement of Taste*, trans. Richard Nice (Cambridge: Harvard University Press, 1984).

20. "The Book Review," *General Federation Bulletin,* January 1904, p. 57.

21. "Imported Argentine Lamp Shade Covers," *Chicago Tribune,* August 1, 1920; on drawn work, see "The Shopping Guide," *House Beautiful,* January 1918, p. 69; on caviar, see Maria Parloa, *Miss Parloa's Kitchen Companion* (Boston: Estes and Lauriat, 1887), pp. 88–91, 435; on malacca, see *Fiber Rush Imported Malacca and Mission Furniture* (Chicago: J. S. Ford, Johnson, 1904), p. 173; on baskets, see "The Shopping Guide," *House Beautiful,* August 1910.

22. Laura Jean Libbey, "Praying for a Husband," *Atlanta Constitution,* November 17, 1912.

23. Showalter, "How the World Is Fed."

24. Barnard, Sumner and Putnam Co., *The Artistic Home* (Worcester, Mass.: n.p., 1903); Carrie May Ashton, "Home Workshop: Cosey Corners," *Decorator and Furnisher,* October 1891, p. 29; Marion A. McBride, "Cosy Corners," *Decorator and Furnisher,* October 1894, p. 18; Laura B. Starr, "Cosy Nooks and Corners," *Decorator and Furnisher,* November 1889, p. 43; "An Oriental Cosey Corner," *Decorator and Furnisher,* May 1896, p. 47; Joseph T,. Butler, "The Decorative Arts," in Wendell D. Garrett, Paul F. Norton, Alan Gowans, and Joseph T. Butler, *The Arts in America: The Nineteenth Century* (New York: Charles Scribner's Sons, 1969), pp. 285–384, 323; Beverly Gordon, "Cozy, Charming, and Artistic: Stitching Together the American Home," in Jessica H. Foy and Karal Ann Marlin, eds., *The Arts and the American Home, 1890–1930* (Knoxville: University of Tennessee Press, 1994), pp. 124–48, 127.

25. John M. MacKenzie, *Orientalism: History, Theory, and the Arts* (Manchester: Manchester University Press, 1995), p. 81.

26. "The Exhibition of Rooms at the Crystal Palace, London," *Decorator and Furnisher,* June 1892, p. 97.

27. Tony Bennett, "The Exhibitionary Complex," in Nicholas B. Dirks, Geoff Eley, and Sherry B. Ortner, eds., *Culture/Power/History: A Reader in Contemporary Social Theory* (Princeton: Princeton University Press, 1994), pp. 123–54; on the secondhand appeal of "Japonisme," see Julia Meech and Gabriel Weisberg, *Japonisme Comes to America: The Japanese Impact on the Graphic Arts, 1876–1925* (New York: Abrams, 1990), pp. 16, 22–26, 35–36.

28. On Japanese fare, see Ellye Howell Glover, *"Dame Curtsey's" Book of Party Pastimes for the Up-to-Date Hostess* (Chicago: McClurg, 1912), pp. 35, 192; on bread, see "Just among Ourselves," *Bay View,* February 1905, p. 301; on chop suey, see "Just among Ourselves," *Bay View,* January 1911, p. 224.

29. Beverly Gordon, *Bazaars and Fair Ladies: The History of the American Fundraising Fair* (Knoxville: University of Tennessee Press, 1998), p. 131; Caroline French Benton, *Fairs and Fetes* (Boston: Dana Estes, 1912), pp. 129–33.

SALMAN—CONFABULATING AMERICAN COLONIAL KNOWLEDGE OF THE PHILIPPINES

1. Gilles Deleuze and Félix Guattari, *A Thousand Plateaus: Capitalism and Schizophrenia,* trans. Brian Massumi (Minneapolis: University of Minnesota Press, 1987).

2. Arjun Appadurai, ed., *The Social Life of Things: Commodities in Cultural Perspective* (New York: Cambridge University Press, 1986).

3. Emma H. Blair and James Alexander Robertson, eds., *The Philippine Islands, 1493–1898,* 55 vols. (Cleveland: A. H. Clarke, 1903–9).

4. William Henry Scott, *Prehispanic Source Materials for the Study of Philippine History,* rev. ed. (Quezon City: New Day, 1984), pp. 91–140.

5. Thomas N. Headland, ed., *The Tasaday Controversy: Assessing the Evidence* (Washington, D.C.: American Anthropological Association, 1992).

6. Benedict Anderson, *Imagined Communities: Reflections on the Origin and Spread of Nationalism,* rev. ed. (London: Verso, 1991).

7. Reynaldo C. Ileto, *Filipinos and Their Revolution: Event, Discourse, Historiography* (Quezon City: Ateneo de Manila University Press, 1998).

8. Filomeno V. Aguilar Jr., "Tracing Origins: Ilustrado Nationalism and the Racial Science of Migration Waves," *Journal of Asian Studies* 64, no. 3 (August 2005): pp. 605–38.

9. Glenn Anthony May, *Inventing a Hero: The Posthumous Re-creation of Andres Bonifacio* (Madison: Center for Southeast Asian Studies, University of Wisconsin, 1996); Vicente L. Rafael, Review of *Inventing a Hero: The Posthumous Re-creation of Andres Bonifacio,* by Glenn Anthony May, *American Historical Review* 103, no. 4 (October 1998): pp. 1304–6.

10. William Henry Scott, *A Critical Study of the Prehispanic Source Materials for the Study of Philippine History* (Manila: University of Santo Tomas Press, 1968), reissued as *Prehispanic Source Materials for the Study of Philippine History,* rev. ed. (Quezon City: New Day, 1984).

11. Rafael, Review of *Inventing a Hero.*

12. Ackbar Abbas, "Theory of the Fake," in Laurent Gutierrez, Ezio Manzini, and Valérie Portefaix, eds., *HK LAB* (Hong Kong: Map Book, 2002), pp. 312–21.

13. Frank C. Lockwood, *The Life of Edward E. Ayer* (Chicago: McClurg, 1929).

14. Ibid., pp. 83–84.

15. See the works of Michel Foucault, especially *Discipline and Punish: The Birth of the Prison,* trans. Alan Sheridan (New York: Pantheon, 1977); and Edward Said, *Orientalism* (New York: Vintage, 1979).

16. Newberry Library, Ayer Collection of Philippine Photographs, 5 vols.

17. James C. Scott, *Seeing Like a State: How Certain Schemes to Improve the Human Condition Have Failed* (New Haven: Yale University Press, 1998).

18. Paul S. Lietz, ed., *Calendar of Philippine Documents in the Ayer Collection of the Newberry Library* (Chicago: Newberry Library, 1956); Ruth Lapham Butler, *Check List of Manuscripts in the Edward E. Ayer Collection* (Chicago: Newberry Library, 1937).

19. Newberry Library, Edward E. Ayer Collection, Box 2, Folder 1, Fr. Pablo Pastells, SJ, to Ayer, March 15 and April 29, 1915; Box 1, Folder 19, Eduardo de Lete to Ayer, June 24, 1914; Box 1, Folder 14, A. B. Meyer to Clara A. Smith, January 8, February 25, July 30, and October 24, 1909; A. B. Meyer to Ayer, February 25, 1909.

20. Emma H. Blair and James Alexander Robertson, "General Preface," in Blair and Robertson, *The Philippine Islands,* vol. 1, p. 13.

21. Edward Gaylord Bourne, "Historical Introduction," in Blair and Robertson, *The Philippine Islands,* vol. 1, p. 20.

22. On the collection's lack of profitability, see Newberry Library, Edward E. Ayer Papers, Box 1, Folder 14, Arthur H. Clark to Ayer, March 15, 1909. For the opinions of LeRoy and Barrows, see Duke University, Special Collections Library, Box 2, File: Letters 1902–1904, Barrows to LeRoy, March 5 and September 29, 1904.

23. Scott, *Prehispanic Source Materials,* pp. 104–35.

24. Ibid., p. 109.

25. Newberry Library, Edward E. Ayer Collection, MS 1710, Facsimiles of Old Bisayan Manuscripts, James A. Robertson annotations, November 17, 1914.

26. James Alexander Robinson, "The Social Structure of, and Ideas of Law among, Early Philippine Peoples and a Recently Discovered Pre-Hispanic Criminal Code of the Philippine Islands," in H. Morse Stephens and Herbert E. Bolton, eds., *The Pacific Ocean in History: Papers and Addresses Presented at the Panama-Pacific Historical Congress Held at San Francisco, Berkeley, and Palo Alto, California, July 19–23, 1915* (New York: Macmillan, 1917), pp. 160–91.

27. Hendrick M. J. Maier, *In the Center of Authority: The Malay Hikayat Merong Mahawangsa* (Ithaca: Southeast Asia Program, Cornell University, 1988).

28. See, for example, a list of technical comments from Harold Conklin (University of Chicago Library, Special Collections, Philippine Studies Program Papers, Box 32, Folder 10, "Notes by Harold Conklin on Povedano 1572," May 20, 1954); Timoteo S. Oracion's ecstatic report from the field in Negros (Box 32, Folder 7, Oracion to Fred and Dorothy Eggan, May

24, 1954); and John Leddy Phelan's frustrated report on his fruitless search in Spain for Povedano manuscripts or any record of the mysterious *encomendero* (Box 10, Folder 19, Phelan to Hester, November 2, 1954).

29. University of Chicago Library, Special Collections, Philippine Studies Program Papers, Box 11, Folder 15, Mauro Garcia, "A Postscript to the Povedano Manuscript," in "Minutes of the 74th Meeting of the Bibliographical Society of the Philippines," November 28, 1959, pp. 3–4.

30. University of Chicago Library, Special Collections, Philippine Studies Program Papers, Box 5, Folder 10, Fox to Hester, February 2, 1956.

31. University of Chicago Library, Special Collections, Fred Eggan Papers, Box 103, Folder 12, Robert B. Fox, "A Special Note on the Negros-Bisayan Syllabary Recorded by Povedano."

32. University of Chicago Library, Special Collections, Philippine Studies Program Papers, Box 5, Folder 10, Fox to Hester, February 2, 1956.

33. University of Chicago Library, Special Collections, Philippine Studies Program Papers, Box 5, Folder 10, Hester to Fox, May 21, 1956.

34. Scott, *Prehispanic Source Materials*, p. ix.

35. Ibid., pp. 134–35.

36. Ibid., p. 129.

37. Jane Mayer, "The Manipulator," *New Yorker*, June 7, 2004.

38. Niccolo Machiavelli, *The Prince*, trans. George Bull (New York: Penguin, 1980), pp. 3, 127.

39. J. G. A. Pocock, *The Machiavellian Moment: Florentine Political Thought and the Atlantic Republican Tradition* (Princeton: Princeton University Press, 1975).

40. Caroline Hau, *Necessary Fictions: Philippine Literature and the Nation, 1946–1980* (Manila: Ateneo de Manila University Press, 2000).

Tomes—Introduction to Part 5

1. Amy Kaplan, "Left Alone with America: The Absence of Empire in the Study of American Culture," in Amy Kaplan and Donald E. Pease, eds., *Cultures of United States Imperialism* (Durham: Duke University Press, 1993), pp. 3–21. The works cited in two recent review essays suggest the comparative absence of work on colonialism in the United States until very recently: Warwick Anderson, "The Third-World Body," in Roger Cooter and John Pickstone, eds., *Companion to Medicine in the Twentieth Century* (New York: Routledge, 2003), pp. 235–45; and Randall Packard, "Post-colonial Medicine," in the same volume, pp. 97–112.

2. For examples of this resistance, see Judith W. Leavitt, *Typhoid Mary: Captive to the People's Health* (Boston: Beacon, 1997); Howard Markel, *When Germs Travel* (New York: Pantheon, 2004); and Nayan Shah, *Contagious Divides: Epidemics and Race in San Francisco's Chinatown* (Berkeley: University of California Press, 2001).

3. Ann Laura Stoler, ed., *Haunted by Empire: Geographies of Intimacy in North American History* (Durham: Duke University Press, 2006).

4. Annette B. Ramirez and Conrad Seipp, *Colonialism, Catholicism and Contraception: A History of Birth Control in Puerto Rico* (Chapel Hill: University of North Carolina Press, 1983).

5. Stephen Jay Gould, "Carrie Buck's Daughter," in *The Flamingo's Smile* (New York: Norton, 1985), pp. 307–13.

6. Philippa Levine, *Prostitution, Race, and Politics: Policing Venereal Disease in the British Empire* (New York: Routledge, 2003); Paul A. Kramer, "The Darkness That Enters the Home: The Politics of Prostitution during the Philippine-American War," in Stoler, *Haunted by Empire*, pp. 367–404.

7. Nancy Tomes, *The Gospel of Germs: Men, Women, and the Microbe in American Life* (Cambridge: Harvard University Press, 1998); Anne McClintock, *Imperial Leather: Race, Gender, and Sexuality in the Colonial Conquest* (New York: Routledge, 1995).

ANDERSON—PACIFIC CROSSINGS

I am grateful to Duke University Press for permission to reprint some excerpts from my book, *Colonial Pathologies* (2006). I would also like to thank Alfred W. McCoy, Francisco Scarano, and Gabriela Soto Laveaga for their close readings of this essay.

1. W. E. B. DuBois, "The Present Outlook for the Dark Races of Mankind," *AME Church Review* 17 (October 1900), pp. 95–110, 95.

2. Warwick Anderson, *Colonial Pathologies: American Tropical Medicine, Race, and Hygiene in the Philippines* (Durham: Duke University Press, 2006).

3. José David Saldivar, "Looking Awry at 1898: Roosevelt, Montejo, Paredes, and Mariscal," *American Literary History* 12 (2000): pp. 386–406.

4. Julian Go, "Introduction: Global Perspectives on the U.S. Colonial State in the Philippines," in Julian Go and Anne L. Foster, eds., *The American Colonial State in the Philippines: Global Perspectives* (Durham: Duke University Press, 2003), pp. 1–42.

5. Warwick Anderson, "States of Hygiene: Race 'Improvement' and Biomedical Citizenship in Australia and the Colonial Philippines," in Ann Laura Stoler, ed., *Haunted by Empire: Geographies of Intimacy in North American History* (Durham: Duke University Press, 2006), pp. 94–115.

6. Ann Laura Stoler, "On Degrees of Imperial Sovereignty," *Public Culture* 18 (2006): pp. 125–46, 125.

7. Mary Douglas, *Purity and Danger: An Analysis of the Concepts of Pollution and Taboo* (London: Routledge and Kegan Paul, 1966).

8. Woodrow Wilson, *Constitutional Government in the United States* (New York: Columbia University Press, 1921), pp. 52–53. See also Vicente Rafael, *White Love and Other Events in Filipino History* (Durham: Duke University Press, 2000), p. 22.

9. Homi K. Bhabha, "Of Mimicry and Man: The Ambivalence of Colonial Discourse," *October* 28 (1984): pp. 125–33.

10. "Stand Off Heiser's Men at the Point of a Gun: Filipino Family in Santa Cruz Would Die Rather Than Be Disinfected," *Manila Times*, July 1, 1907, p. 1.

11. James Ferguson, *The Anti-politics Machine: Development, Depoliticization, and Bureaucratic Power in Lesotho* (Cambridge: Cambridge University Press, 1990).

12. Warwick Anderson, *The Cultivation of Whiteness: Science, Health, and Racial Destiny in Australia* (Durham: Duke University Press, 2006), chap. 2.

13. Samuel Haber, *Efficiency and Uplift: Scientific Management in the Progressive Era, 1890–1920* (Chicago: University of Chicago Press, 1964).

14. Louis Galambos, "The Emerging Organizational Synthesis in American History," *Business History Review* 44 (1970): pp. 279–90; George Rosen, "The Efficiency Criterion in Medical Care, 1900–1920: An Early Approach to the Evaluation of Health Service," *Bulletin of the History of Medicine* 50 (1976): pp. 28–44.

15. Charles V. Chapin, "Dirt, Disease, and the Health Officer," in *The Papers of Charles V. Chapin, M.D.: A Review of Public Health Realities*, Frederic P. Gorham and Clarence L. Scamman, eds. (New York: Commonwealth Fund, [1902] 1934), pp. 20–26, 21, 24; James H. Cassedy, *Charles V. Chapin and the Public Health Movement* (Cambridge: Harvard University Press, 1962).

16. Charles V. Chapin, "The Fetich of Disinfection," in *The Papers of Charles V. Chapin, M.D.: A Review of Public Health Realities*, Frederic P. Gorham and Clarence L. Scamman, eds. (New York: Commonwealth Fund, [1905] 1934), pp. 65–75, 75; Charles V. Chapin, *Sources and Modes of Infection* (New York: Wiley, 1910).

17. Charles-Edward Amory Winslow, "Man and the Microbe," *Popular Science Monthly* 85 (1914): p. 9.

18. Judith Walzer Leavitt, *Typhoid Mary: Captive to the Public's Health* (Boston: Beacon, 1996); Judith Walzer Leavitt, *The Healthiest City: Milwaukee and the Politics of Health Reform*

(Princeton: Princeton University Press, 1982); Nancy Tomes, *The Gospel of Germs: Men, Women, and the Microbe in American Life* (Cambridge: Harvard University Press, 1998).

19. For example, see Nayan Shah, *Contagious Divides: Epidemics and Race in San Francisco's Chinatown* (Berkeley: University of California Press, 2001).

20. William Lee Howard, "The Negro as a Distinct Ethnic Factor in Civilization," *Medicine* 60 (1903): pp. 418–28, 424.

21. Alan M. Kraut, *Silent Travelers: Germs, Genes, and the "Immigrant Menace"* (Baltimore: Johns Hopkins University Press, 1994).

22. William Howard Taft, "Address of President Taft at the 15th International Congress on Hygiene and Demography," *Science*, new ser., 36 (October 18, 1912): pp. 504–8, 505.

23. Ibid.

24. *First Annual Report of the Department of Public Health [Illinois], July 1, 1917, to June 30, 1918* (Springfield: State Printers, 1919), p. 19; Charles-Edward Amory Winslow, *The Life of Hermann M. Biggs, Physician and Statesman of Public Health* (Philadelphia: Lea and Febiger, 1929); Alexandra Minna Stern, *Eugenic Nation: Faults and Frontiers of Better Breeding in America* (Berkeley: University of California Press, 2005).

25. Victor G. Heiser, *An American Doctor's Odyssey: Adventures in Forty-Five Countries* (New York: Norton, 1936); John Duffy, *A History of Public Health in New York City*, 2 vols. (New York: Russell Sage Foundation, 1968), vol. 2, p. 271.

26. William Everett Musgrave Papers, Archives and Special Collections, Kalmanovitz Library, University of California at San Francisco, mss. 27-5.

27. Luis Felipe Gonzalez Flores, *Historia de la influencia extranjera en el des envolvimiento educacional y cientifico de Costa Rica* (San José: Editorial Costa Rica, 1976), p. 160; Steve Palmer, *From Popular Medicine to Medical Populism: Doctors, Healers, and Public Power in Costa Rica, 1800–1940* (Durham: Duke University Press, 2003), pp. 155–81. I am grateful to Steve Palmer for drawing this to my attention. On Milwaukee, see also Leavitt, *The Healthiest City*.

28. *Annual Report of the Department of Public Health, San Francisco, California, July 1, 1910–June 30, 1911* (San Francisco: Neal, n.d.), p. 7.

29. Barbara Gutmann Rosenkrantz, *Public Health and the State: Changing Views in Massachusetts, 1842–1936* (Cambridge: Harvard University Press, 1972), p. 142.

30. *Forty-Sixth Annual Report of the State Board of Health of Massachusetts [1914]* (Boston: Wright and Potter, 1915), p. 2.

31. *First Annual Report of the State Department of Health of Massachusetts [1915]* (Boston: Wright and Potter, 1916), pp. 8, 22–23.

32. Allan J. McLaughlin, assisted by James A. Tobey, *Personal Hygiene: The Rules of Right Living* (New York: Funk and Wagnalls, 1924), p. 63.

33. In *A Yankee Doctor in Paradise* (Boston: Little, Brown, 1941), p. 4, S. M. "Sam" Lambert wondered why Heiser's book was not entitled "Alone in the Orient."

34. Victor G. Heiser, "Conquering Industrial Diseases [c. 1940]," p. 11, Heiser Papers, American Philosophical Society, B: H357; "Industrial Health Programs Are Good Business, 1947," Heiser Papers, American Philosophical Society, B: H357, p. 6.

35. Victor Heiser, *Toughen Up America* (New York: McGraw-Hill, 1941), p. 21.

36. Victor Heiser, "Conquering Industrial Diseases [c. 1940]," p. 1.

37. Soma Hewa, *Colonialism, Tropical Disease, and Imperial Medicine: Rockefeller Philanthropy in Sri Lanka* (Lanham, Md.: University Press of America, 1995).

38. See Ralph Chester Williams, *The United States Public Health Service, 1798–1950* (Washington, D.C.: Commissioned Officers Association of the U.S. Public Health Service, 1951).

39. Stephen J. Collier and Aihwa Ong, "Global Assemblages, Anthropological Problems," in *Global Assemblages: Technology, Politics, and Ethics as Anthropological Problems*, Stephen J. Collier and Aihwa Ong, eds. (Oxford: Blackwell, 2005), pp. 3–21, 4, 4–5, 11.

Espinosa—A Fever for Empire

1. Stanford E. Chaillé, "Report to the United States National Board of Health on Yellow Fever in Havana and Cuba," in U.S. National Board of Health, *Annual Report of the National Board of Health, 1880* (Washington, D.C.: Government Printing Office, 1881).

2. Charles E. Magoon, *Republic of Cuba, Report of Provisional Administration from December 1st, 1907, to December 1st, 1908* (Havana: Rambla and Bouza, 1908), p. 143.

3. William C. Gorgas, Chief Sanitary Officer, to Brigadier General Leonard Wood, "Report of Vital Statistics of the City of Havana, Year 1900," Miscellaneous Records of Various Agencies, Department of Cuba, 1899–1902, Records of the Military Government of Cuba, Record Group 140, National Archives, College Park, Md.

4. Maryinez Lyons, "Sleeping Sickness, Colonial Medicine, and Imperialism: Some Connections in the Belgian Congo," in Roy MacLeod and Milton Lewis, eds., *Disease, Medicine, and Empire: Perspectives on Western Medicine and the Experience of European Expansion* (New York: Routledge, 1988), p. 247.

5. Maryinez Lyons, *The Colonial Disease: A Social History of Sleeping Sickness in Northern Zaire, 1900–1940* (Cambridge: Cambridge University Press, 1992).

6. Philip D. Curtin, *Death by Migration: Europe's Encounter with the Tropical World in the Nineteenth Century* (Cambridge: Cambridge University Press, 1989).

7. David Patrick Geggus, *Slavery, War, and Revolution: The British Occupation of Saint Domingue, 1793–1798* (Oxford: Clarendon, 1982), pp. 354–64.

8. Lyons, *The Colonial Disease*.

9. Florence Bretelle-Establet, "Resistance and Receptivity: French Colonial Medicine in Southwest China, 1898–1930," *Modern China* 25 (1999): p. 173.

10. Mark Harrison, *Public Health in British India: Anglo-Indian Preventative Medicine, 1859–1914* (Cambridge: Cambridge University Press, 1994).

11. See Khaled J. Bloom, *The Mississippi Valley's Great Yellow Fever Epidemic of 1878* (Baton Rouge: Louisiana State University Press, 1993).

12. John H. Ellis, *Yellow Fever and Public Health in the New South* (Lexington: University Press of Kentucky, 1992).

13. Mariola Espinosa, "The Threat from Havana: Southern Public Health, Yellow Fever, and the U.S. Intervention in the Cuban Struggle for Independence, 1878–1898," *Journal of Southern History* 72 (2006): pp. 541–68.

14. Civil Order No. 451, November 6, 1900, in Leonard Wood, *Civil Report of Major General Leonard Wood, Military Governor of Cuba (1900) for the Period from December 20th, 1899, to December 31st, 1900* (Washington, D.C.: Government Printing Office, 1901).

15. See Louis A. Pérez Jr., "Incurring a Debt of Gratitude: 1898 and the Moral Sources of United States Hegemony in Cuba," *American Historical Review* 104 (1999): pp. 356–98.

Ring—Mapping Regional and Imperial Geographies

1. Ellsworth Huntington, *Civilization and Climate* (New Haven: Yale University Press, 1915), pp. 17, 42.

2. David Arnold, *The Problem of Nature: Environment, Culture, and European Expansion* (Cambridge: Oxford University Press, 1996), pp. 141–68.

3. Felix Driver and Brenda S. A. Yeoh, "Constructing the Tropics: Introduction," *Singapore Journal of Tropical Geography* 21 (March 2000): p. 3.

4. See Stephen Frenkel, "Jungle Stories: North American Representations of Tropical Panama," *Geographical Review* 86 (July 1996): p. 318.

5. Nancy Leys Stephan, *Picturing Tropical Nature* (Ithaca: Cornell University Press, 2001), p. 17.

6. Nina Silber, *The Romance of Reunion: Northerners and the South, 1865–1900* (Chapel Hill: University of North Carolina Press, 1993); David Blight, *Race and Reunion: The Civil*

War in American Memory (Cambridge: Harvard University Press, 2000); Grace Hale, *Making Whiteness: The Culture of Segregation in the South, 1890–1940* (New York: Pantheon, 1998).

7. David Arnold, "'Illusory Riches': Representations of the Tropical World, 1840–1950," *Singapore Journal of Tropical Geography* 21, no. 1 (2000), p. 7; Frenkel, "Jungle Stories."

8. Samuel Crowther, *The Romance and Rise of the American Tropics* (New York: Arno, [ca. 1929] 1976), p. v.

9. See David N. Livingstone, "Race, Space, and Moral Climatology: Notes toward a Genealogy," *Journal of Historical Geography* 28 (2002): pp. 159–80.

10. Homi K. Bhabha, "The Other Question: Stereotype, Discrimination, and the Discourse of Colonialism," in *The Location of Culture* (New York: Routledge, 1994), pp. 66–84; Stephen Frenkel, "Geographical Representations of the 'Other': The Landscape of the Panama Canal Zone," *Journal of Historical Geography* 28 (2002): pp. 85–99.

11. See Silber, *The Romance of Reunion*, pp. 66–92.

12. See Hampton Dunn, "Florida: Jewel of the Gilded Age," *Gulf Coast Historical Review* 10 (1994): pp. 19–28.

13. Rebecca C. McIntyre, "Promoting the Gothic South," *Southern Cultures* (summer 2005): p. 33.

14. J. Milton Mackie, *From Cape Cod to Dixie and the Tropics* (New York: G. P. Putnam, 1864), pp. 153, 169.

15. Albert Bushnell Hart, *The Southern South* (New York: D. Appleton, 1910).

16. Albert Bushnell Hart, *The Obvious Orient* (New York: D. Appleton, 1911).

17. Hart, *The Obvious Orient*, 9; Hart, *The Southern South*, 2–3.

18. Editorial, *New Republic*, August 21, 1915, p. 56.

19. Wilbur J. Cash, *The Mind of the South* (Garden City, N.Y.: Doubleday, 1941), p. viii.

20. David Arnold, "Introduction," in *Warm Climates and Western Medicine: The Emergence of Tropical Medicine, 1500–1900* (Amsterdam: Rodopi, 1996), pp. 5–10.

21. David Arnold, *Colonizing the Body: State Medicine and Epidemic Disease in Nineteenth-Century India* (Berkeley: University of California Press, 1993).

22. Stephan, *Picturing Tropical Nature*, p. 156.

23. Douglas M. Haynes, *Imperial Medicine: Patrick Manson and the Conquest of Tropical Disease* (Philadelphia: University of Pennsylvania Press, 2001).

24. Earl Baldwin McKinley, *A Geography of Disease: A Preliminary Survey of the Incidence and Distribution of Tropical and Certain Other Diseases* (Washington, D.C.: George Washington University Press, 1935), p. xxiii.

25. John D. Swan, MD, "Tropical Diseases and Health in the United States," *Southern Medical Journal* 4 (July 1911): p. 499.

26. "The American Society of Tropical Medicine," editorial, *Southern Medical Journal* 4 (February 1911): pp. 175–76.

27. Editorial, *American Journal of Tropical Diseases and Preventive Medicine* 1 (July 1913): p. 1; "The Existence of Tropical Diseases in the South," editorial, *Southern Medical Journal* 1 (October 1908): p. 269.

28. R. A. Henry, "The White Man and the Tropics," International Health Board (IHB), Record Group (RG) 5, Series 2, Subseries 200, Box 64, Rockefeller Center Archives, Tarrytown, New York.

29. Warwick Anderson, *Colonial Pathologies: American Tropical Medicine, Race, and Hygiene in the Philippines* (Durham: Duke University Press, 2006), pp. 32, 195–96.

30. "Intensive Community Work for the Relief and Control of Hookworm Disease in the Southern States," IHB, RG 5, Series, 2, Box 3, Folder 20, Rockefeller Center Archives.

31. Huntington, *Civilization and Climate*, p. 24.

32. "Reports Southern States 1916," IHB, RG 5, Series 3, Box 5, Rockefeller Center Archives.

33. "A Picture of an 'Ulcer' That New Orleans Is Going to Have Cured by Summer Time," *Times-Picayune*, March 29, 1920; "Clio Dump Conditions Astound Orleanians," *Times-Picayune*, March 30, 1920, both in United States Department of Agriculture, RG 7, Southern Field-Crop Insect Investigations, General Correspondence, Box 2, National Archives, Washington, D.C.

34. W. H. Rowan to W. S. Leathers, February 1, 1912, Rockefeller Sanitary Commission for the Eradication of Hookworm (RSC), Box 9, Folder 134, Rockefeller Center Archives.

35. Charles Wardell Stiles, "The Sanitary Privy," RSC, Box 3, Folder 77, Rockefeller Center Archives.

36. L. L. Lumsden, "The Privy as a Public Health Problem," *American Journal of Public Health* 10 (January 1920): pp. 45–46.

37. Charles Wardell Stiles to U.S. Surgeon General, July 17, 1913, RSC, Box 3, Folder 75, Rockefeller Center Archives; Charles Wardell Stiles to Wickliffe Rose, January 12, 1914, RSC, Box 3, Folder 76, Rockefeller Center Archives; Charles Wardell Stiles to Wickliffe Rose, September 8, 1914, RSC, Box 3, Folder 76, Rockefeller Center Archives.

38. Charles Wardell Stiles, circular letter, April 5, 1914, RSC, Box 3, Folder 76, Rockefeller Center Archives; Charles Wardell Stiles, "Confidential Letter to the Most Prominent Citizens: Fight Flies, Filth, and Fever!!!" September 1914, RSC, Box 3, Folder 76, Rockefeller Center Archives.

39. Marion Hamilton Carter, "The Vampire of the South," *McClure's Magazine* 33 (October 1909): pp. 617–18.

40. Ibid.

41. See Anderson, *Colonial Pathologies*.

42. For example, see Paul Kramer, "Making Concessions: Race and Empire Revisited at the Philippine Exposition, St. Louis, 1901–1905," *Radical History Review* 73 (winter 1999): pp. 74–114.

43. "Countries by Groups in Which Hookworm Infection Has Been Demonstrated," International Health Commission (IHC), Pamphlet Collection, Box 4, Folder 58, Rockefeller Center Archives.

44. Ibid.

45. Walter H. Page, "The Hookworm and Civilization," *World's Work* 24 (September 1912): p. 504.

46. Gavin Wright, *Old South, New South: Revolutions in the Southern Economy since the Civil War* (New York: Basic Books, 1986); C. Vann Woodward, *Origins of the New South* (Baton Rouge: Louisiana State University Press, 1951), pp. 291–320.

47. Lewellys F. Barker, "The Wider Influence of the Physician," *Southern Medical Journal* 12 (December 1919): pp. 723–26; Carl F. Westerberg, "Revolt in the Tropics," *North American Review* 231 (January 1931): p. 257.

48. David N. Livingstone, "Human Acclimatization: Perspectives on a Contested Field of Inquiry in Science, Medicine, and Geography," *History of Science* 25 (December 1987): pp. 359–94.

49. Anderson, "Immunities of Empire," pp. 99–100.

50. Warwick Anderson, "The Trespass Speaks: White Masculinity and Colonial Breakdown," *American Historical Review* 102 (December 1997): pp. 1343–70.

51. Huntington, *Civilization and Climate*, p. 24.

52. Wickliffe Rose to Frederick T. Gates, June 28, 1911, IHB, RG 5, Series 200, Subseries 252, Box 19, Folder 113, Rockefeller Center Archives.

53. A. S. Hamilton, "The New Race Question in the South," *Arena* 27 (April 1902): pp. 352–53; Hart, *The Southern South*, pp. 68–69.

54. Hale, *Making Whiteness*; Gail Bederman, *Manliness and Civilization: A Cultural History of Gender and Race in the United States, 1880–1917* (Chicago: University of Chicago Press, 1996).

Soto Laveaga—The Conquest of Molecules

1. "Mexican Hormones," *Fortune*, May 1951, p. 161.
2. Carl Djerassi, *This Man's Pill: Reflections on the 50th Birthday of the Pill* (Oxford: Oxford University Press, 2001), p. 47.
3. Leonard Engle, "ACTH, Cortisone & Co.," *Harper's Magazine*, August 1951, pp. 25–33.
4. Gary Gereffi, *The Pharmaceutical Industry and Dependency in the Third World* (Princeton: Princeton University Press, 1983); Gabriela Soto Laveaga, "Uncommon Trajectories: Steroid Hormones, Mexican Peasants, and the Search for a Wild Yam," *Studies in History and Philosophy of Biological and Biomedical Sciences* 36, no. 4 (December 2005): pp. 743–60.
5. George Rosenkranz, "From Ruzicka's Terpenes in Zurich to Mexican Steroids via Cuba," *Steroids* 57 (August 1992): pp. 409–18; Djerassi, *This Man's Pill*; Lara Marks, *Sexual Chemistry: A History of the Contraceptive Pill* (New Haven: Yale University Press, 2001); Paul Vaughan, *The Pill on Trial* (New York: Coward-McCann, 1970); Luis Ernesto Miramontes, interview with the author, Mexico City, July 7, 2004.
6. Roy Macleod, "On Visiting the 'Moving Metropolis': Reflections on the Architecture of Imperial Science," in Nathan Reingold and Marc Rothenberg, eds., *Scientific Colonialism* (Washington, D.C.: Smithsonian Institution, 1986), p. 221.
7. Warwick Anderson, *Colonial Pathologies: American Tropical Medicine, Race, and Hygiene in the Philippines* (Durham: Duke University Press, 2006).
8. Edward W. Said, *Culture and Imperialism* (New York: Vintage, 1994), p. xiii.
9. Ashis Nandy cleverly links this to his example of the race to put a man on the moon. See "Science as Reason of State," in *Science, Hegemony and Violence: A Requiem for Modernity*, ed. Ashis Nandy (Tokyo and Delhi: The United Nations University and Oxford University Press), pp. 257–87.
10. Cited in Carl Djerassi, *Steroids Made It Possible* (Washington, D.C.: American Chemical Society, 1990), p. 34.
11. Djerassi, *This Man's Pill*, p. 38.
12. Marks, *Sexual Chemistry*, pp. 62–70; Russell E. Marker, interview with Jeffrey L. Sturchio, Pennsylvania State University, April 17, 1987, Oral History Transcript 0068, Chemical Heritage Foundation, Philadelphia, pp. 20–25.
13. Marker, interview with Sturchio, pp. 20–25.
14. Marks, *Sexual Chemistry*, p. 66; "Glands as Cause of Many Crimes," *New York Times*, December 4, 1921; "Glands Held Key to Peace in World," *New York Times*, December 3, 1937.
15. Quoted in Marker, interview with Sturchio, p. 23.
16. Margaret Kreig, *Green Medicine: The Search for Plants That Heal* . . . (Chicago: Rand McNally, 1964), p. 267.
17. Vaughan, *The Pill on Trial*, p. 13.
18. Kreig, *Green Medicine*, p. 265; Rosenkranz, "From Ruzicka's Terpenes."
19. Djerassi, *This Man's Pill*, p. 47.
20. Ibid.
21. Luis Miramontes, interview with the author, Mexico City, July 6, 2004.
22. Ibid.
23. "Cortisone from Giant Yam," *Life*, July 23, 1951, pp. 75–77.
24. Rosenkranz mentions in his article that Syntex founded Mexico's Institute of Chemistry in 1944. This is incorrect as the institute was founded four years earlier, in 1940, before the creation of Syntex. What is true is the continuous financial support that Syntex gave to the institute.
25. Djerassi, *This Man's Pill*, p. 48.
26. Ibid., p. 49.
27. Ibid., p. 39.
28. Engle, "ACTH, Cortisone, and Co.," pp. 25–33.

29. Vaughan, *The Pill on Trial*, p. 20.

30. Gereffi, *The Pharmaceutical Industry and Dependency in the Third World*; Carl Djerassi, *The Pill, Pygmy Chimps, and Degas' Horse: The Remarkable Autobiography of the Award-Winning Scientist Who Synthesized the Birth Control Pill* (New York: Basic Books, 1988); Djerassi, *This Man's Pill*; Rosenkranz, "From Ruzicka's Terpenes."

31. "Nacionalizar la Industria Farmacéutica y Asegurar el Derecho del Pueblo a la Salud," *El Día*, March 26, 1976.

32. Unión de Ejidos de Producción y Comercialización Agropecuaria Licenciado Adolfo López Mateos to Luis Echeverría Álvarez, Hidalgotitlán, Veracruz, August 14, 1976, Alejandro Villar Borja Papers, Mexico City.

Sutter—Tropical Conquest and the Rise of the Environmental Management State

1. "Go East by Sea," brochure, n.d. but post-1920, Panama Pacific Line, Folder 1, Kemble Maritime Ephemera Collection (KMEC), Henry E. Huntington Library (HEH), San Marino, California.

2. "Raymond-Whitcombe Cruises: West Indies," brochure, 1921, Folder 4, United Fruit Company, KMEC, HEH.

3. David McCullough, *The Path between the Seas: The Creation of the Panama Canal, 1870–1914* (New York: Simon and Schuster, 1977), pp. 610–11.

4. See, for instance, Benjamin Kidd, *The Control of the Tropics* (New York: Macmillan, 1898).

5. "Canal Route Becomes 'The Thing': Glamour of the Tropics and Quaint Cities Appeal," by George P. West, Folder 1, Panama Pacific Line, KMEC, HEH.

6. William McFee, "The Gates of the Caribbean: The Story of a Great White Fleet Caribbean Cruise," booklet, United Fruit Company Steamship Service, 1922, United Fruit Company, Folder 33, KMEC, HEH.

7. Stephen Frenkel, "Cultural Imperialism and the Development of the Panama Canal Zone, 1912–1960," PhD diss., Syracuse University, 1992.

8. See Michael Adas, *Machines as the Measure of Men: Science, Technology, and Ideologies of Western Dominance* (Ithaca: Cornell University Press, 1989); Adas, *Dominance By Design: Technological Imperatives and America's Civilizing Mission* (Cambridge: Harvard University Press, 2006).

9. See John Haskell Kemble, *The Panama Route, 1848–1869* (Berkeley: University of California Press, 1943); Aims McGuinness, *Path of Empire: Panama and the California Gold Rush* (Ithaca: Cornell University Press, 2008).

10. Richard White, *"It's Your Misfortune and None of My Own": A New History of the American West* (Norman: University of Oklahoma Press, 1991); Adam Rome, "What Really Matters in History? Environmental Perspectives on Modern America," *Environmental History* 7 (April 2002): pp. 303–18.

11. On this international turn, see Paul S. Sutter, "What Can U.S. Environmental Historians Learn from Non-U.S. Environmental Historiography?" *Environmental History* 8, no. 1 (January 2003): pp. 109–29.

12. See Ronald Ross, *Mosquito Brigades* (New York: Longman's, Green, 1902); Malcolm Watson, *Rural Sanitation on the Tropics: Being Notes and Observations in the Malay Archipelago, Panama, and Other Lands* (London: John Murray, 1915).

13. See A. Hunter Dupree, *Science in the Federal Government: A History of Policies and Activities to 1940* (Cambridge: Harvard University Press, 1959); Willis Conner Sorenson, *Brethren of the Net: American Entomology, 1840–1880* (Tuscaloosa: University of Alabama Press, 1995); L. O. Howard, *A History of Applied Entomology (Somewhat Anecdotal)* (Washington, D.C.: Smithsonian Institution, 1930).

14. For a detailed discussion of these issues, see Paul S. Sutter, "Nature's Agents or Agents of Empire? Entomological Workers and Environmental Change during the Construction of the Panama Canal," *Isis* 98, no. 4 (December 2007): pp. 724–54.

15. See Joel B. Hagen, "Problems in the Institutionalization of Tropical Biology: The Case of Barro Colorado Island Biological Laboratory," *History and Philosophy of the Life Sciences* 12 (1990): pp. 225–47.

16. See Margaret Humphreys, *Yellow Fever and the South* (New Brunswick, N.J.: Rutgers University Press, 1992); Humphreys, *Malaria: Poverty, Race, and Public Health in the United States* (Baltimore: Johns Hopkins University Press, 2001).

BURNETT—EMPIRE AND THE TRANSFORMATION OF CITIZENSHIP

1. 192 U.S. 1 (1904).

2. Previous treaties for the annexation of territory had promised citizenship to the affected inhabitants, and Congress had followed up with the appropriate legislation. See generally Grupo de Investigadores Puertorriqueños, *Breakthrough from Colonialism: An Interdisciplinary Study of Statehood*, vols. 1–2 (San Juan: Editorial de la Universidad de Puerto Rico, 1984).

3. See Puerto Rico Organic Act ("Foraker Act"), *U.S. Statutes at Large*, vol. 31 (1900): p. 79 (section 7); Philippine Organic Act, *U.S. Statutes at Large*, vol. 32 (1902): p. 692 (section 4). The United States officially misspelled Puerto Rico as Porto Rico until 1932. See José A. Cabranes, *Citizenship and the American Empire: Notes on the Legislative History of the United States Citizenship of Puerto Ricans* (New Haven: Yale University Press, 1978), p. 1, n. 1.

4. U.S. Constitution, Amendment 14. The amendment's "limiting" language ("and subject to the jurisdiction thereof") excluded several other groups—mainly Native Americans and the children of foreign ambassadors—on the ground that they were not fully "subject to the jurisdiction" of the United States. I address the status of Native Americans, and its relationship to the status of Puerto Ricans and Filipinos, below.

5. The quoted language comes from *Downes v. Bidwell*, 182 U.S. 244, 287 (1901).

6. Relatively few scholars have examined the *Gonzales* case. See, for example, Rogers M. Smith, *Civic Ideals: Conflicting Visions of Citizenship in U.S. History* (New Haven: Yale University Press, 1997), pp. 438–39. A recent article thoroughly examines the significance of the case. See Sam Erman, "Meanings of Citizenship in the U.S. Empire: Puerto Rico, Isabel Gonzalez, and the Supreme Court, 1898–1905," *Journal of American Ethnic History* 27 (2008): p. 5.

7. Federico Degetau to Clarence R. Edwards, June 20, 1903, Box 4, File 3, Document 222, Papers of Federico Degetau y González, Ángel Mergal Collection, Centro de Estudios Históricos, Universidad de Puerto Rico, San Juan. The statement quoted in the subheading is from the *Dallas Morning News*, January 11, 1904, p. 6.

8. These "possessions" already included Hawaii, annexed earlier in 1898, and a number of so-called guano islands. For the little-known story of the guano islands, see Jimmy M. Skaggs, *The Great Guano Rush: Entrepreneurs and American Overseas Expansion* (London: Macmillan, 1994). On the relationship of guano islands to the law of American empire, see Christina Duffy Burnett, "The Edges of Empire and the Limits of Sovereignty: American Guano Islands," in Mary Dudziak and Leti Volpp, eds., *Legal Borderlands: Law and the Construction of American Borders* (Baltimore: Johns Hopkins University Press, 2006).

9. Treaty of Peace between the United States and the Kingdom of Spain ("Treaty of Paris"), *U.S. Statutes at Large*, vol. 30 (1899): p. 1759 (article 9) (emphasis added).

10. Foraker Act, 31 *Stat.*, p. 79.

11. On the criteria for admission, see generally Mae M. Ngai, *Impossible Subjects: Illegal Aliens and the Making of Modern America* (Princeton: Princeton University Press, 2004).

12. The "insular cases" rubric covers a series of cases handed down between 1901 and 1922, including *Gonzales*. For discussions of which cases belong on the list, see Bartholomew Sparrow, *The Insular Cases and the Emergence of American Empire* (Lawrence: University

Press of Kansas, 2006), pp. 257–58; Christina Duffy Burnett and Burke Marshall, eds., *Foreign in a Domestic Sense: Puerto Rico, American Expansion, and the Constitution* (Durham: Duke University Press, 2001), pp. 389–90; and Efrén Rivera Ramos, "The Legal Construction of American Colonialism: The *Insular Cases* (1901–1922)," *Revista Jurídica de la Universidad de Puerto Rico* 65 (1996): pp. 240–42, nn. 40–42.

13. *Downes*, 182 U.S., pp. 341–42.

14. H. W. Van Dyke to Degetau, April 4, 1903, Degetau Papers, Box 4, File 2, Document 122 (on behalf of Coudert, expressing Coudert's interest in the case and his willingness to discuss it).

15. *Gonzales*, 192 U.S., p. 13.

16. Congress did eventually pass such a statute affecting the Philippines, the Philippine Independence Act of 1934, which treated Filipinos "as if they were aliens." See An Act to Provide for the Complete Independence of the Philippine Islands, Etc., *U.S. Statutes at Large*, vol. 48 (1934): p. 462 (section 8[a][1]-[2]). See generally Ngai, *Impossible Subjects*, pp. 119–20; Donald S. Leeper, "International Law: Effect of Philippine Independence on Filipino Citizens Resident in the United States," *Michigan Law Review* 50 (1951): p. 159; and Donald S. Leeper, "Effect of Philippine Independence on Filipinos Residing in the United States," *Columbia Law Review* 50 (1950): p. 371.

17. 192 U.S., p. 12.

18. *The Evening News* (San Jose, California), January 15, 1904, p. 4.

19. *Gonzales*, 192 U.S., pp. 14–15.

20. Brief for Petitioner in *Gonzales v. Williams*, No. 225 (October Term, 2003), November 3, 1903, submitted by Frederic R. Coudert Jr., Paul Fuller, and Charles E. Le Barbier, p. 11. See also the transcript of Coudert's oral argument (hereafter Argument for Petitioner), *Gonzales v. Williams*, No. 225 (October Term, 2003); and Coudert, "Our New Peoples: Citizens, Subjects, Nationals, or Aliens," *Columbia Law Review* 3 (1903): p. 13, where Coudert developed these arguments.

21. Brief for Petitioner, pp. 33–37.

22. Argument for Petitioner, p. 53.

23. Brief for Petitioner, pp. 4, 24.

24. Ibid., pp. 24–25; see also p. 27.

25. Ibid., p. 27.

26. See, for example, *Minor v. Happersett*, 88 U.S. 162, 166 (1874).

27. Brief for Petitioner, pp. 28–32. See also *Scott v. Sandford*, 60 U.S. 393 (1857); *Elk v. Wilkins*, 112 U.S. 94 (1884); and An Act to Authorize the Secretary of the Interior to Issue Certificates of Citizenship to Indians, *U.S. Statutes at Large*, vol. 43 (1924): p. 253.

28. Brief for Petitioner, p. 39.

29. Brief for the United States in *Gonzales v. Williams*, No. 225 (October Term, 2003), submitted by Solicitor General Henry M. Hoyt, pp. 5–6.

30. Brief for the United States, p. 13.

31. On boundaries and law, see Dudziak and Volpp, *Legal Borderlands*.

32. Brief for the United States, p. 13.

33. Ibid.

34. Treaty of Paris, article 9 (emphasis added).

35. Brief of Amicus Curiae, Federico Degetau y González, submitted in *Gonzales v. Williams*, No. 225 (October Term, 2003), p. 7.

36. These prejudices were doubtless informed by contemporary racial attitudes. On the history of assigning U.S. citizenship based on "ascribed characteristics" such as race, see, for example, Smith, *Civic Ideals*.

37. Treaty of Paris, article 9.

38. Brief of Amicus Curiae, p. 30.

39. Ibid., p. 33.

40. Ibid., p. 28. The president of the commission that negotiated the treaty was William R. Day, who was now a justice on the court. This put Degetau in the rather awkward position of arguing Day's intent to Day himself.

41. Treaty concerning the Cession of the Russian Possessions in North America by His Majesty the Emperor of All the Russias to the United States of America, *U.S. Statutes at Large*, vol. 15 (1867): p. 542 (article 3).

42. Brief of Amicus Curiae, p. 30.

43. *Gonzales*, 192 U.S., p. 12.

44. The court did make passing reference to the more familiar term *nationality*. See ibid., pp. 10, 15.

45. The term soon worked its way into official legal material, and by 1906 the State Department had sanctioned its use. See John Bassett Moore, *Digest of International Law*, vol. 3 (Washington, D.C.: Government Printing Office, 1906), p. 273.

46. William J. Novak, "The Legal Transformation of Citizenship in Nineteenth-Century America," in Meg Jacobs, William J. Novak, and Julian E. Zelizer, eds., *The Democratic Experiment: New Directions in American Political History* (Princeton: Princeton University Press, 2003), p. 86.

47. Ibid., p. 109.

48. U.S. Constitution, Amendment 14 (emphasis added).

49. See *Elk*, 112 U.S., p. 102.

50. 30 U.S. 1 (1831).

51. Novak, "Legal Transformation," p. 109.

52. James H. Kettner, *The Development of American Citizenship, 1608–1870* (Chapel Hill: University of North Carolina Press, 1978), p. 351.

53. Novak, "Legal Transformation," p. 109.

54. Munroe Smith, review of Frederick Van Dyne, *Citizenship of the United States* and *Das amerikanische Burgherrecht*, *Political Science Quarterly* 19 (1904): p. 329.

55. The category now covers persons born in American Samoa and Swain's Island. See *United States Code*, vol. 8, §1101(a)(3), 11(a)(21)-(22), (29), 1408.

56. See An Act to Declare the Purpose of the People of the United States as to the Future Political Status of the People of the Philippine Islands and to Provide a More Autonomous Government for Those Islands, *U.S. Statutes at Large*, vol. 39 (1916): p. 545 (Philippines); and An Act to Provide a Civil Government for Porto Rico and for Other Purposes, *U.S. Statutes at Large*, vol. 39 (1917): p. 951 (Puerto Rico).

57. See Philippine Independence Act, 48 *Stat.*, p. 462 (section 8[a][1]-[2]); and Ngai, *Impossible Subjects*, pp. 119–20.

58. *Balzac v. Porto Rico*, 258 U.S. 298, 305–6 (1922).

59. See generally Ramón Grosfoguel and Frances Negrón-Muntaner, eds., *Puerto Rican Jam: Essays on Culture and Politics* (Minneapolis: University of Minnesota Press, 1997); and Nancy Morris, *Puerto Rico: Culture, Identity, and Politics* (Westport: Praeger, 1995).

60. *Gonzales*, 192 U.S., pp. 14–15.

RAFAEL—THE AFTERLIFE OF EMPIRE

1. Carl Schmitt, *Political Theology: Four Chapters on the Concept of Sovereignty*, trans. George Schwab (Chicago: University of Chicago Press, 2005), p. 5.

2. Jean Bodin, *On Sovereignty: Four Chapters from Six Books on the Commonwealth*, ed. and trans. Julian H. Franklin (Cambridge: Cambridge University Press, 1992), p. 3.

3. Ibid., pp. 8–11.

4. Apolinario Mabini, *La Revolucion Filipina*, 2 vols. (Manila: Bureau of Printing, 1931), vol. 2, pp. 54–55.

5. Vicente L. Rafael, *Contracting Colonialism: Translation and Christian Conversion in Tagalog Society under Early Spanish Rule* (Durham: Duke University Press, 1993); *The Promise of the Foreign: Nationalism and the Technics of Translation in the Spanish Philippines* (Durham: Duke University Press, 2005).

6. *Recopilación de las Leyes de los Reinos de Indias* (1681) (Madrid: Consejo de Hispanidad, 1943).

7. Rafael, *The Promise of the Foreign*; John Schumacher, SJ, *The Propaganda Movement, 1880–1895*, rev. ed. (Quezon City: Ateneo de Manila University Press, 1997).

8. Cesar Adib Majul, *Mabini and the Philippine Revolution* (Quezon City: University of the Philippines Press, 1960).

9. Mabini, *La Revolucion Filipina*, vol. 2, pp. 56–57, 125, 134–35.

10. Ibid., pp. 57–59.

11. Ibid., p. 196.

12. Ibid., pp. 53–59, 206–9, 300–25.

13. Ibid., pp. 278–79.

14. Ibid., pp. 72–74, 131, 161–67.

15. Ibid., pp. 93, 54–55.

16. Thomas Aquinas, *Summa Theologica*, in Anton C. Pegis, ed., *Introduction to St. Thomas Aquinas* (New York: Random House, 1945), pp. 616–45.

17. Mabini, *La Revolucion Filipina*, vol. 2, pp. 48, 206, 180.

18. Ibid., pp. 66–67.

19. Milagros Guerrero, "Luzon at War: Contradictions in Philippine Society, 1898–1902," PhD diss., University of Michigan, 1977, chap. 3.

20. Mabini, *La Revolucion Filipina*, vol. 2, pp. 68–69.

21. Ibid., p. 69.

22. George Bataille, "Sovereignty," in *The Accursed Share*, trans. Richard Hurley, 3 vols. (New York: Zone, 1993). The quote is from vol. 3, p. 198.

23. Ibid.

24. Santiago V. Alvarez, *Katipunan at ang Paghihimagsik*, trans. Paula Carolina Malay as *The Katipunan and the Revolution: Memoirs of a General* (Quezon City: Ateneo de Manila University Press, 1992), p. 281. All translations from the Tagalog are mine.

25. Bataille, "Sovereignty," p. 200.

26. Reynaldo Ileto, *Pasyon and Revolution: Popular Movements in the Philippines, 1840–1910* (Quezon City: Ateneo de Manila University Press, 1979), pp. 88–89.

27. Bataille, "Sovereignty," p. 201.

LYNCH—THE U.S. CONSTITUTION AND PHILIPPINE COLONIALISM

1. See notes 52 and 53 for citations to the insular decisions.

2. George Dewey, *Autobiography of George Dewey: Admiral of the Navy* (New York: Scribner, 1913), p. 222. See generally pages 197–233.

3. Quoted in Charles S. Olcott, *The Life of William McKinley*, vol. 2 (Boston: Houghton Mifflin, 1916), pp. 109–11.

4. Stuart Creighton Miller, *"Benevolent Assimilation": The American Conquest of the Philippines, 1899–1903* (New Haven: Yale University Press, 1982), p. 13.

5. J. A. S. Grenville and George Berkeley Young, *Politics, Strategy, and American Diplomacy: Studies in Foreign Policy, 1873–1913* (New Haven: Yale University Press, 1966), p. 269.

6. Wayne H. Morgan, *William McKinley and His America* (Syracuse: Syracuse University Press, 1963), pp. 387–92.

7. Luzviminda B. Francisco and Jonathan S. Fast, *Conspiracy for Empire: Big Business, Corruption, and the Politics of Imperialism in America, 1876–1907* (Quezon City: Foundation for Nationalist Studies, 1985), pp. 150–57.

8. USSt 30:738. Francisco and Fast, *Conspiracy for Empire*, pp. 150–57.
9. *Congressional Record* (CR), 55th Cong., 2d sess., p. 3988.
10. Francisco and Fast, *Conspiracy for Empire*, p. 232, citing "Merchandise Imports, 1900," 58th Cong., 3d sess., House Doc. 3:1:166.
11. Francisco and Fast, *Conspiracy for Empire*, p. 159.
12. Ibid.
13. W. Cameron Forbes, *The Philippine Islands*, vol. 2 (Boston: Houghton Mifflin, 1928), pp. 425–28.
14. David Prescott Barrows, "The Governor General of the Philippines under Spain and the United States," in H. Morse Stephens and Herbert E. Bolton, eds., *The Pacific Ocean in History* (New York: Macmillan, 1917), p. 251.
15. Francisco and Fast, *Conspiracy for Empire*, p. 184.
16. CR, 56th Cong., 2d sess., p. 3021. See, for example, James A. LeRoy, *The Americans in the Philippines: A History of the Conquest and First Years with an Introductory Account of the Spanish Rule*, vol. 1 (New York: AMS, 1970), pp. 354–77.
17. Villanueva Conference, 107. See 55th Cong., 3d sess., Senate Doc. 62, pt. 3, for a duplicate of the map used at Paris.
18. Villanueva Conference, 105–6, 125.
19. Margaret Leech, *In the Days of McKinley* (New York: Harper and Bros., 1950), p. 327.
20. Villanueva Conference, 115.
21. Richard E. Welch, *George Frisbie Hoar and the Half-Breed Republicans* (Cambridge: Harvard University Press, 1971), pp. 221–51.
22. Garel A. Grunder and William E. Livezy, *The Philippines and the United States* (Norman: University of Oklahoma Press, 1951), p. 40.
23. CR, 55th Cong., 3d sess., p. 493. See generally pp. 493–503.
24. Grunder and Livezy, *The Philippines and the United States*, p. 70.
25. Ibid., pp. 45–46.
26. Vincente V. Mendoza, *From McKinley's Instructions to the New Constitution: Documents on the Philippine Constitutional System* (Quezon City: Central Lawbook Publishing, 1978), p. 2.
27. Grunder and Livezy, *The Philippines and the United States*, p. 48.
28. Forbes, *The Philippine Islands*, vol. 2, pp. 566–70.
29. Jose S. Reyes, *Legislative History of America's Economic Policy toward the Philippines* (New York: Columbia University Press, 1923), pp. 137–38.
30. United States, *Executive Minutes of the Philippine Commission from Sept. 1, 1903, to March 1, 1904*, vol. 2 (Manila: Philippine Commission, 1904), p. 66.
31. USSt 31:910; Forbes, *The Philippine Islands*, vol. 2, p. 448, app. 9.
32. George A. Malcolm and Maximo Kalaw, *Philippine Government: Development, Organization, and Functions* (Manila: Associated Publishers, 1923), p. 82.
33. CR, 56th Cong., 1st sess., p. 763.
34. Francisco and Fast, *Conspiracy for Empire*, p. 235.
35. CR, 56th Cong., 2d sess., p. 3067. For the congressional debate over the amendment, see pp. 2955–72, 3064–68, 3103–5, and 3331–84.
36. United States, *Report of the Philippine Commission to the President* (Washington, D.C.: Government Printing Office, 1900) pp. 5–6, 34. The report was reprinted in U.S. Philippine Commission, *Annual Report of the Philippine Commission* (Washington, D.C.: Government Printing Office, 1904), p. 27.
37. Peter Stanley, *A Nation in the Making: The Philippines and the United States, 1899–1921* (Cambridge: Harvard University Press, 1974), p. 88.
38. United States, *Executive Minutes of the Philippine Commission from Sept. 1, 1903, to March 1, 1904*, vol. 3, p. 322.

39. "Construction to Be Given to Congressional Enactment," in United States and Charles Edward Magoon, *Reports on the Law of Civil Government in Territory Subject to Military Occupation by the Military Forces of the United States* (Washington, D.C.: Government Printing Office, 1903), p. 611.

40. United States and Charles Edward Magoon, *Report on the Construction to Be Given the Congressional Enactment Approved March 2, 1901: Relating to the Public Lands and Timber in the Philippines* (Washington, D.C.: Government Printing Office, 1901), p. 611.

41. General Order No. 92, articles 73–74.

42. "Statement of Licenses Granted during the Fiscal Year Ending June 30th, 1902, and for the Months of July and August 1902," in U.S. Philippine Commission, *Annual Report of the Philippine Commission*, vol. 1 (Washington, D.C.: Government Printing Office, 1902), p. 463.

43. Elihu Root, Robert Bacon, and James B. Scott, *The Military and Colonial Policy of the United States: Addresses and Reports by Elihu Root* (Cambridge: Harvard University Press, 1916), p. 304.

44. Carman F. Randolph, "Constitutional Aspects of Annexation," *Harvard Law Review* 12, no. 5 (December 1898): p. 306.

45. *Dred Scott v. Sandford*, 60 U.S. 393 (1857), p. 446.

46. Romeo V. Cruz, *America's Colonial Desk and the Philippines, 1898–1934* (Quezon City: University of the Philippines Press, 1972), p. 34.

47. Ibid., p. 119.

48. United States and Charles Magoon, *Report on the Legal Status of the Territory and Inhabitants of the Islands Acquired by the United States during the War with Spain, Considered with Reference to the Territorial Boundaries, the Constitution, and Laws of the United States* (Washington, D.C.: Government Printing Office, 1900), pp. 16–17.

49. Ibid., p. 26.

50. United States, *Annual Report of the Secretary of War* (Washington, D.C.: Government Printing Office, 1899), vol. 1, p. 24. See also Philip C. Jessup, *Elihu Root*, vol. 1 (New York: Dodd, Mead, 1938), pp. 332–33.

51. U.S. Philippine Commission, *Report of the Philippine Commission to the President* (1900), vol. 1, pp. 111–12.

52. By the end of Taft's term as the American president there had been at least twenty-four appeals to the Supreme Court from decisions of the Philippine Supreme Court, including *Kepner v. United States*, 195 U.S. 100 (1904) (double jeopardy), and *Dorr v. O'Brien*, 195 U.S. 138 (1904) (libel). Pursuant to a resolution of the Philippine Supreme Court dated August 15, 1918, most of these decisions were also published in an appendix to volumes 40 and 41 of *Philippine Reports*.

53. USSt 31:51.

54. *De Lima v. Bidwell*, 182 U.S. 1 (1901).

55. *Goetze v. United States*, 182 U.S. 221 (1901); *Dooley v. United States*, 182 U.S. 222 (1901); *Armstrong v. United States*, 182 U.S. 243 (1901); *Downes v. Bidwell*, 182 U.S. 244 (1901); *Huus v. New York and Puerto Rico Steamship Co.*, 182 U.S. 392 (1901).

56. 182 U.S. 247 (1901).

57. Pedro E. Abelarde, *American Tariff Policy towards the Philippines, 1898–1945* (New York: King's Crown, 1947), p. 61.

58. 183 U.S. 76 (1902).

59. James C. Thomson, Peter W. Stanley, John C. Perry, *Sentimental Imperialists: The American Experience in East Asia* (New York: Harper and Row, 1981), p. 106.

60. USR 182:282–3. For additional background on the insular decisions, see United States and Albert H. Howe, *The Insular Cases, Comprising the Records, Briefs, and Arguments of Counsel in the Insular Cases of the October Term, 1900, in the Supreme Court of the United*

States, Including the Appendixes Thereto (Washington, D.C.: Government Printing Office, 1901).

61. George F. Edmunds and George S. Boutwell, *The Insular Cases* (Boston: Anti-Imperialist League, 1901), p. 239.

62. Ibid., p. 242.

63. Francisco and Fast, *Conspiracy for Empire,* pp. 243, 390, n. 12, citing 57th Cong., 1st sess., Senate Doc. 439, p. 178.

64. Grunder and Livezy, *The Philippines and the United States,* p. 79.

65. The first test of these relaxed constitutional standards to reach the U.S. Supreme Court concerned a case of double jeopardy, *Kepner v. United States,* 195 U.S. 100 (1904).

66. Henry P. Willis, *Our Philippine Problem: A Study of American Policy* (New York: Henry Holt, 1905), p. 95.

67. Elihu Root, "American Policies in the Philippines in 1900," in Robert Bacon and James Brown Scott, eds., *The Military and Colonial Policy of the United States* (Cambridge: Harvard University Press, 1916), p. 70.

68. Grunder and Livezy, *The Philippines and the United States,* p. 79.

Castañeda—Spanish Structure, American Theory

1. Jose M. Aruego, *The Philippine Constitution: Origins, Making, Meaning, and Application* (Manila: Philippine Lawyers Association, 1970), vol. 1, p. 158.

2. "The President's Instructions to the Commission," Public Laws of the Philippines 1:LXIII, LXVI (April 7, 1900).

3. Francis Burton Harrison, *The Corner-Stone of Independence: A Narrative of Seven Years* (New York: Century, 1922), p. 333.

4. Ibid.

5. Ibid.

6. W. Cameron Forbes, *The Philippine Islands* (Boston and New York: Houghton Mifflin, 1938), vol. 2, p. 392.

7. Ibid.

8. See Peter W. Stanley, *A Nation in the Making: The Philippines and the United States, 1899–1921* (Boston: Harvard University Press, 1974), pp. 109–10.

9. See Eliodoro Robles, *The Philippines in the Nineteenth Century* (Quezon City: Malaya Books, 1969), p. 3.

10. See Stephen Skowronek, *Building a New American State: The Expansion of National Administrative Capacities, 1877–1920* (Cambridge: Cambridge University Press, 1982), pp. 24–31.

11. David P. Barrows, "The Governor-General of the Philippines under Spain and the United States," *American Historical Review* 21 (January 1916): pp. 288, 301.

12. Ibid., pp. 288, 302.

13. "The President's Instructions to the Commission."

14. Philippine Organic Act of 1902, July 1, 1902, ch. 1269, 32 Stat. 691.

15. Frank Hindman Golay, *Face of Empire: United States-Philippine Relations, 1898–1946* (Quezon City: Ateneo de Manila University Press, 1997), pp. 60–62.

16. "The President's Instructions to the Commission."

17. Barrows, "The Governor-General of the Philippines under Spain and the United States," pp. 288, 300, 303; Philippine Commission, *Report of a Commission Appointed to Investigate Affairs in the Philippine Islands* (Washington, D.C.: U.S. Congress, 1900), pp. 106–11.

18. In 1902, the U.S. Congress passed the Philippine Organic Act, which vested in Filipinos control over the lower house of the colonial legislature, called the Philippine Assembly. Through the 1916 Philippine Autonomy Act, Congress created an all-Filipino legislature with a Senate and House of Representatives.

19. Anna Leah Fidelis T. Castañeda, "The Board of Control Cases: Containing Colonial Conflict in Constitutional Categories," paper presented at the annual meeting of the Organization of American Historians, March 31–April 1, 2007, Minneapolis.

20. See *Case v. Board of Health*, 24 Phil. 250 (1913).

21. George A. Malcolm, *The Constitutional Law of the Philippine Islands, Together with Studies in the Field of Comparative Constitutional Law* (Rochester, N.Y.: Lawyers' Cooperative Publishing, 1920), vol. 1, p. 248, quoting *Olsen and Co. v. Herstein*, 32 Phil. 520 (1915).

22. Other designations adopted by scholars for "classical legal thought" include "legal formalism," "the orthodox ideology," and "legal classicism."

23. William Howard Taft to Judge Howard Hollister, May 26, 1901, quoted in Bonifacio S. Salamanca, *The Filipino Reaction to American Rule, 1900–1913* (Quezon City: New Day, 1984), p. 60.

24. Malcolm, *The Constitutional Law of the Philippine Islands*, vol. 1, p. 245.

25. See *Barcelon v. Baker*, 5 Phil. 87 (1905); and *United States v. Ten Yu*, 24 Phil. 1 (1912).

26. See, for example, *United States v. Toribio*, 15 Phil. 85 (1910); and *United States v. Gomez Jesus*, 31 Phil. 218 (1915).

27. See Owen M. Fiss, *Troubled Beginnings of the Modern State, 1888–1910* (New York: Cambridge University Press, 2006), chap. 7. For one such landmark case, see *De Villata v. Stanley*, 32 Phil. 541 (1915).

28. See *Rubi v. Provincial Board of Mindoro*, 36 Phil. 660 (1919); *Villavicencio v. Lukban*, 39 Phil. 778 (1919); *Smith, Bell and Co. v. Natividad*, 40 Phil. 136 (1919); and *Yu Cong Eng v. Trinidad*, 47 Phil. 385 (1925).

29. Castañeda, "The Board of Control Cases."

30. See *Fisher v. Yangco Steamship*, G.R. No. 8095, November 5, 1914, and March 31, 1915; and *Churchill and Tait v. Rafferty*, 32 Phil. 581, 605 (1915).

31. *Churchill and Tait v. Rafferty*, 32 Phil. 581, 605 (1915).

32. See, for example, *Case v. Board of Health*, 24 Phil. 250 (1913).

33. *Lochner v. New York*, 198 U.S. 145 (1905).

34. *People of the Philippines v. Pomar*, 46 Phil. 440 (1924). See also Hans Leo J. Cacdac, "*People v. Pomar* Revisited: Substantive Due Process and the Emergence of the Afford Protection to Labor Clause," *Ateneo Law Journal* 42 (June 1998): pp. 330–80.

35. Morton J. Horwitz, *The Transformation of American Law, 1879–1960* (New York: Oxford University Press, 1992), pp. 29–33.

36. Aruego, *The Philippine Constitution*, vol. 2, p. 232.

HUTCHCROFT—THE HAZARDS OF JEFFERSONIANISM

1. Clinton Rossiter, *Alexander Hamilton and the Constitution* (New York: Harcourt, Brace and World, 1964), p. 234.

2. *Report of the Philippine Commission to the President, I, January 31, 1900*, 4 vols. (Washington, D.C.: Government Printing Office, 1900), vol. 1, quotes from pp. 91, 70; Taft quotes from Glenn Anthony May, *Social Engineering in the Philippines: The Aims, Execution, and Impact of American Colonial Policy, 1900–1913* (Westport: Greenwood, 1980), p. 41.

3. As I embark on this brief but far-reaching essay, three caveats are in order. First, while ideas are an important force in history, I do not mean to imply that they are determinative. Second, Jeffersonianism is, of course, rivaled in American political thought, and its dominance should not be treated as inevitable. In future research, I will also examine other influential elements of American thought including Hamiltonianism, the missionary zeal of American Protestantism, and Wilsonianism. Third, it is not only in the United States that one finds strong political traditions in favor of decentralization. Many other countries, as well, possess strong and deeply felt historical instincts favoring villages over the city and the local over the center; consider, for example, the "village republics" of India (Harry Blair,

Assessing Democratic Decentralization: A CDIE Concept Paper [Washington, D.C.: U.S. Agency for International Development, Center for Development Information and Evaluation, 1995], p. 13; Abdul Aziz and David D. Arnold, eds., *Decentralized Governance in Asian Countries* [New Delhi: Sage, 1996]).

4. See, e.g., Lynton K. Caldwell, *The Administrative Theories of Hamilton and Jefferson* (New York: Holmes and Meier, [1944] 1988), pp. 104, 128, 146, 234–35; Richard Hofstadter, *The American Political Tradition* (New York: Vintage, 1948), p. 23.

5. Alexis de Tocqueville, *Democracy in America*, 2 vols. (New York: Knopf, [1835] 1953), vol. 2, pp. 3, 18–19; A. Whitney Griswold, "The Agrarian Democracy of Thomas Jefferson," *American Political Science Review* 40 (August 1946): p. 669; Caldwell, *Administrative Theories*, p. 146.

6. Stanley Elkins and Eric McKitrick, *The Age of Federalism* (New York: Oxford University Press, 1993), pp. 199, 197, 205.

7. Samuel P. Huntington, "The Founding Fathers and the Division of Powers," in Arthur Maass, ed., *Area and Power: A Theory of Local Government* (Glencoe, Ill.: Free Press, 1959), p. 197; J. Rogers Hollingsworth, "The United States," in Raymond Grew, ed., *Crises of Political Development in Europe and the United States* (Princeton: Princeton University Press, 1978), p. 163.

8. Caldwell, *Administrative Theories*, p. 136.

9. Ibid.; see also Huntington, "Founding Fathers," pp. 163, 173, 175.

10. Griswold, "Agrarian Democracy," p. 660; Huntington, "Founding Fathers," pp. 176–77; quotes from Jefferson's letters in Charles Maurice Wiltse, *The Jeffersonian Tradition in American Democracy* (New York: Hill and Wang, 1960), p. 132.

11. Caldwell, *Administrative Theories*, p. 236.

12. Elkins and McKitrick, *Age of Federalism*, pp. 197–200, quotes from pp. 198, 200.

13. Hofstadter, *American Political Tradition*, p. 19. See also James Roger Sharp, *American Politics in the Early Republic: The New Nation in Crisis* (New Haven: Yale University Press, 1993), pp. 241–42; and Forrest MacDonald, *Alexander Hamilton: A Biography* (New York: Norton, 1979), p. 212.

14. Michael Lind, *Hamilton's Republic: Readings in the American Nationalist Tradition* (New York: Free Press, 1997). See also Rossiter, *Alexander Hamilton*, p. 232; and Samuel H. Beer, *To Make a Nation: The Rediscovery of American Federalism* (Cambridge: Belknap, 1993), p. 14.

15. Rossiter, *Alexander Hamilton*, pp. 227, 235.

16. Tocqueville, *Democracy*, vol. 1, p. 3. See also vol. 1, pp. 51–52, and vol. 2, p. 299.

17. Ibid., vol. 2, pp. 298–99, quote at 299; vol. 1, pp. 89–94, 57, quote at 57.

18. Theda Skocpol, ed., *Democracy, Revolution, and History* (Ithaca: Cornell University Press, 1998), p. 73.

19. Huntington, "Founding Fathers," quotes from pp. 180, 196–97 (emphasis added).

20. Samuel P. Huntington, *Political Order in Changing Societies* (New Haven: Yale University Press, 1968), pp. 5, 7, 125–26, 135, 136 (quotes at 7, 136, 5, and 135, respectively).

21. Bernard Bailyn, *The Origins of American Politics* (New York: Knopf, 1970), pp. 99–105.

22. John M. Murrin, "A Roof without Walls: The Dilemma of American National Identity," in Richard Beeman, Stephen Botein, and Edward C. Carter II, eds., *Beyond Confederation: Origins of the Constitution and American National Identity* (Chapel Hill: University of North Carolina Press, 1987), p. 346; Hollingsworth, "The United States," p. 173.

23. Sharp, *American Politics*, p. 34.

24. Richard Beeman, "Introduction," in Richard Beeman, Stephen Botein, and Edward C. Carter II, eds., *Beyond Confederation: Origins of the Constitution and American National Identity* (Chapel Hill: University of North Carolina Press, 1987), p. 17; William H. Riker, *The Development of American Federalism* (Boston: Kluwer Academic Publishers, 1987), pp. 40–41.

25. Sharp, *American Politics*, pp. 3–6, quotes from pp. 4, 5, and 6 (emphasis in original).

26. Ibid., pp. 31–66 (quote at 66).

27. Samuel Eliot Morison, *The Oxford History of the American People*, 3 vols. (New York: New American Library, 1972), vol. 2, p. 46.

28. Sharp, *American Politics*, pp. 170–71, 187, 194–201, 224; Elkins and McKitrick, *Age of Federalism*, pp. 719–23. Jefferson is quoted in Caldwell, *Administrative Theories*, p. 145.

29. Major L. Wilson, *Space, Time, and Freedom: The Quest for Nationality and the Irrepressible Conflict, 1815–1861* (Westport: Greenwood, 1974), 22–48.

30. Sharp, *American Politics*, pp. 187–88, 206 (quote at 187–88); Elkins and McKitrick, *Age of Federalism*, pp. 720–21 (quotes at 721).

31. Sharp, *American Politics*, 286; John Gerring, *Party Ideologies in America, 1828–1996* (New York: Cambridge University Press, 1998), p. 183.

32. Tocqueville, *Democracy*, vol. 1, pp. 47, 79, 61, quotes at pp. 47, 79.

33. There is one brief exception; see Huntington, *Political Order*, p. 126.

34. C. Vann Woodward, *The Burden of Southern History* (New York: New American Library, 1968), pp. 28–29, 31.

35. This section draws on Paul D. Hutchcroft, "Colonial Masters, National Politicos, and Provincial Lords: Central Authority and Local Autonomy in the American Philippines, 1900–1913," *Journal of Asian Studies* 59, no. 2 (May 2000): pp. 277–306.

36. For analysis of the term *ilustrado*, see Michael Cullinane, *Ilustrado Politics: Filipino Elite Responses to American Rule, 1898–1908* (Quezon City: Ateneo de Manila University Press, 2003), chap. 1, "'Ilustrados' and Filipino Elites in the Nineteenth Century," pp. 8–48.

37. David Joel Steinberg, *The Philippines: A Singular and a Plural Place*, 4th ed. (Boulder: Westview, 2000), p. 67.

38. Bonifacio Salamanca, *The Filipino Reaction to American Rule, 1901–1913* (Quezon City: New Day, 1984), pp. 239, 241.

39. Glenn Anthony May, "Civic Ritual and Political Reality: Municipal Elections in the Late Nineteenth Century," in Ruby R. Paredes, ed., *Philippine Colonial Democracy* (New Haven: Council on Southeast Asia Studies, Yale University, 1989), pp. 13–40.

40. See Cullinane, *Ilustrado Politics*, esp. pp. 274–85, 318–24.

41. Benedict Anderson, "Cacique Democracy and the Philippines: Origins and Dreams," *New Left Review* 169 (1988): pp. 3–33 (quote at 11). In his study of the African colonial state, Crawford Young describes the norm of the day as "[r]ational, prudent management of the colonial estates by a professional cadre of administrators applying increasingly scientific methods to their development." See Crawford Young, *The African Colonial State in Comparative Perspective* (New Haven: Yale University Press, 1994), p. 165.

42. Huntington, *Political Order*, p. 7.

43. Quoted in Joseph Ralston Hayden, *The Philippines: A Study in National Development* (New York: Macmillan, 1942), p. 91.

44. Martin Shefter, *Political Parties and the American State: The American Historical Experience* (Princeton: Princeton University Press, 1994); Anderson, "Cacique Democracy," p. 12.

45. Norman G. Owen, "Philippine Economic Development and American Policy: A Reappraisal," in Norman G. Owen, ed., *Compadre Colonialism: Studies on the Philippines under American Rule* (Ann Arbor: Center for South and Southeast Asian Studies, University of Michigan, 1971), p. 5; *Report of the Philippine Commission, 1903*, 3 vols. (Washington, D.C.: Government Printing Office, 1904), vol. 1, pp. 83–84 (quote at 84).

46. Stephen Skowronek, *Building a New American State: The Expansion of National Administrative Capacities, 1877–1920* (Cambridge: Cambridge University Press, 1982), p. 39.

47. Onofre D. Corpuz, *The Philippines* (Englewood Cliffs, N.J.: Prentice-Hall, 1965), pp. 65–66; Leopoldo Y. Yabes, "The American Administration in the Philippines," *Solidarity* 2 (1967): pp. 16–26.

48. Steinberg, *The Philippines*, p. 70.

49. Quoted in Peter W. Stanley, *A Nation in the Making: The Philippines and the United States, 1899–1921* (Cambridge: Harvard University Press, 1974), p. 67.

50. Michael Cullinane, "Implementing the 'New Order': The Structure and Supervision of Local Government during the Taft Era," in Norman G. Owen, ed., *Compadre Colonialism: Studies on the Philippines under American Rule* (Ann Arbor: Center for South and Southeast Asian Studies, University of Michigan, 1971), p. 16; Taft quotes from David Joel Steinberg, ed., *In Search of Southeast Asia: A Modern History*, rev. ed. (Honolulu: University of Hawaii Press, 1987), p. 287.

51. Caldwell, *Administrative Theories*, p. 136.

52. Skowronek, *Building a New American State*, p. 15.

53. May, *Social Engineering*, p. xviii; Frank Hindman Golay, *Face of Empire: United States Philippine Relations, 1898–1946* (Madison: Center for Southeast Asian Studies, University of Wisconsin, 1998), p. 63.

54. Paul D. Hutchcroft, "Reflections on a Reverse Image: South Korea under Park Chung-Hee and the Philippines under Ferdinand Marcos," in Byung-Kook Kim and Ezra Vogel, eds., *The Park Era, Volume One: Formation and Consolidation* (forthcoming); and Paul D. Hutchcroft, "Centralization and Decentralization in Administration and Politics: Assessing Territorial Dimensions of Authority and Power," *Governance* 14, no. 1 (January 2001): pp. 23–53.

55. Blair, *Assessing Democratic Decentralization*, p. 13.

GEDACHT—"MOHAMMEDAN RELIGION MADE IT NECESSARY TO FIRE"

1. Peter Gowing, *Mandate in Moroland: The American Government of Muslim Filipinos, 1899–1920* (Quezon City: University of the Philippines Press, 1977), p. 161.

2. "Wood's Battle Called Murder," *New York Times*, March 16, 1906.

3. William Gardner Bell, *Commanding Generals and Chiefs of Staff, 1775–1983* (Washington, D.C.: Center for Military History, United States Army, 1983), p. xi.

4. Jeffrey Ostler, *The Plains Sioux and U.S. Colonialism from Lewis and Clark to Wounded Knee* (New York: Cambridge University Press, 2004), pp. 109, 345, 359–60.

5. David Wallace Adams, *Education for Extinction: American Indians and the Boarding School Experience* (Lawrence: University of Kansas Press, 1995), pp. 18–23, 36–59.

6. Merrill Edward Gates, *Land and Law as Agents in Educating Indians*, annual report of the secretary of the interior, 1885, 783, quoted in Adams, *Education for Extinction*, p. 56.

7. Adams, *Education for Extinction*, pp. 28–59.

8. Ostler, *The Plains Sioux*, pp. 243–63.

9. Lieutenant H. L. Scott to Post Adjt., Ft. Sill, December 16, 1890, Record Group (RG) 75, Special Case 188, Roll 1, National Archives and Record Administration (NARA), quoted in Ostler, *The Plains Sioux*, p. 279.

10. Benjamin Harrison to the Secretary of War, October 31, 1890, Benjamin Harrison Papers, Roll 29, Library of Congress (LC), Washington, D.C., quoted in Ostler, *The Plains Sioux*, p. 292.

11. Ostler, *The Plains Sioux*, p. 289.

12. Nelson A. Miles, "The Future of the Indian Question," *North American Review* 152 (January 1891): 1–10, quoted in Ostler, *The Plains Sioux*, p. 305.

13. Ostler, *The Plains Sioux*, pp. 302–6.

14. Roger DiSilvestro, *In The Shadow of Wounded Knee: The Untold Final Chapter of the Indian Wars* (New York: Walker, 2005), pp. 123–30.

15. Quoted in DiSilvestro, *In The Shadow of Wounded Knee*, p. 225.

16. *Chicago Tribune*, September 17, 1894, p. 2.

17. Robert Wooster, *Nelson A. Miles and the Twilight of the Frontier Army* (Lincoln: University of Nebraska Press, 1993), pp. 195–213.

18. Quoted in Walter L. Williams, "United States Indian Policy and the Debate over

Philippine Annexation: Implications for the Origins of American Imperialism," *Journal of American History* 66 (March 1979): p. 822.

19. Stuart Creighton Miller, *"Benevolent Assimilation": The American Conquest of the Philippines, 1899–1903* (New Haven: Yale University Press, 1982), pp. 219–52.

20. Ibid., p. 199.

21. Ibid., p. 207.

22. Brian McAllister Linn, *The Philippine War, 1899–1902* (Lawrence: University of Kansas Press), pp. 306–319.

23. Miller, *"Benevolent Assimilation,"* pp. 229, 257–60.

24. Gowing, *Mandate in Moroland*, p. 164.

25. "Agreement between General John C. Bates, United States Army, and the Sultan of Sulu, Together with Certain Sulu Chiefs, Signed at Jolo, August 20, 1899," quoted in Gowing, *Mandate in Moroland*, p. 348.

26. Major General George W. Davis, "Notes on the Government of the Country Inhabited by Non-Christians in Mindanao and the Neighboring Islands," RG 350, 5075-A, NARA, quoted in George William Jornacion, "The Time of the Eagles: United States Army Officers and the Pacification of the Philippine Moros, 1899–1913," PhD diss., University of Maine, 1973, pp. 293–94.

27. Jack McCallum, *Leonard Wood: Rough Rider, Surgeon, and Architect of American Imperialism* (New York: New York University Press, 2006), pp. 206–9.

28. A. J. Bacevich, *Diplomat in Khaki: Major General Frank Ross McCoy and American Foreign Policy, 1898–1949* (Lawrence: University of Kansas Press, 1989), p. 18.

29. Patricio Abinales, "Progressive-Machine Conflict in Early Twentieth Century U.S. Politics and Colonial State Building in the Philippines," in Julian Go and Anne L. Foster, eds., *The American Colonial State in the Philippines: Global Perspectives* (Durham: Duke University Press, 2003), pp. 165–67.

30. Leonard Wood to Senator R. H. Alger, September 22, 1903, Leonard Wood Papers, LC.

31. "From Report of Civil Governor, 1903, Beginning with p. 79," RG 350, File 4865, NARA.

32. *Datu* are Muslim leaders in Mindanao and Sulu who Jeremy Beckett defines as "entitled to rule on account of his descent"; see Beckett, "Political Families and Family Politics among the Muslim Maguindanaon of Cotabata," in *An Anarchy of Families: State and Family in the Philippines*, ed. Alfred W. McCoy (Madison: University of Wisconsin, Center for Southeast Asia Studies, 1982), p. 398; Leonard Wood to President Theodore Roosevelt, September 20, 1903, Leonard Wood Papers, pp. 8–9, LC.

33. Howard M. Federspiel, "Islam and Muslims in the Southern Territories of the Philippine Islands during the American Colonial Period (1898–1946)," *Journal of Southeast Asian Studies* 29, no. 2 (spring 1998): pp. 344–45.

34. Frank E. Vandiver, *Black Jack Pershing: The Life and Times of John J. Pershing*, vol. 1 (College Station: Texas A&M Press, 1977), pp. 82–104, 261–318, 394–408.

35. McCallum, *Leonard Wood*, p. 210.

36. Leonard Wood to Theodore Roosevelt, September 20, 1903, Leonard Wood Papers, LC.

37. Leonard Wood to Colonel H. P. McCain, August 29, 1904, Leonard Wood Papers, LC.

38. McCallum, *Leonard Wood*, pp. 217–18.

39. Leonard Wood to Colonel Arthur H. Lee, January 4, 1903, Leonard Wood Papers. LC.

40. Ostler, *The Plains Sioux*, p. 279.

41. Jornacion, "The Time of the Eagles," pp. 123–39, 159–71.

42. Hugh L. Scott, "Annual Report of the District of Sulu from July 1st, 1905, to June 30, 1906," June 30, 1906, Tasker Bliss Papers, LC.

43. Hugh L. Scott to George T. Langhorne, December 5, 1905, Box 37, Leonard Wood Papers, LC.

44. George T. Langhorne to Leonard Wood, February 9, 1906, Box 37, Leonard Wood Papers, LC.

45. Leonard Wood, "Report Department of Mindanao," in *Annual Reports of the War Department for the Fiscal Year Ended June 30, 1905*, vol. 3: *Reports of Divisions and Commanders* (Washington, D.C.: Government Printing Office, 1905), p. 299.

46. J. W. Duncan, "The Fight at Bud Dajo; or, the Battle of the Lava Cone," in *Year Book: Army of the Philippines, Eighth Annual Reunion*, ed. National Society, Army of the Philippines (Kansas City, Mo.: Camp Louis A. Camp, 1907), p. 59.

47. J. W. Duncan, "Report of the Operations on Bud Dajo, Island of Jolo," March 12, 1906, sheet 8, RG 94, Adjutant General Office 1108562, NARA.

48. *New York Times*, March 9, 1906.

49. William Howard Taft to Leonard Wood, Leonard Wood Papers, LC, quoted in McCallum, *Leonard Wood*, p. 229.

50. Moorfield Storey, *The Moro Massacre: Letter* (Boston: Anti-Imperialist League, 1906).

51. Gowing, *Mandate in Moroland*, p. 162.

52. "A Plain Duty Regretfully Performed," *Mindanao Herald*, March 24, 1904, p. 4.

53. Leonard Wood to Theodore Roosevelt, "Message from the President of the United States Transmitting an Account of the Engagement on Bud Dajo between United States Forces and a Band of Moros, March 15, 1906," U.S. House of Representatives, 59th Cong., 1st sess., Doc. 622, RG 350, File 4865, NARA.

54. "Not All Were Slain," *Washington Star*, RG 350, File 4865, NARA.

55. Tasker H. Bliss, "Annual Report, Department of Mindanao," in *Annual Reports of the War Department, 1907*, vol. 3 (Washington, D.C.: Government Printing Office, 1908), p. 294, quoted in Jornacion, "The Time of the Eagles," p. 202.

56. John J. Pershing, "Annual Report of the Governor of the Moro Province for the Year Ending June 30, 1912," August 15, 1912, Box 371, John J. Pershing Papers, LC; Donald Smythe, "Pershing and the Disarmament of the Moros," *Pacific Historical Review* 31, no. 3 (August 1962): pp. 241–56.

57. Government of the Moro Province, *Annual Report of Brigadier General John J. Pershing, Governor of the Moro Province, for the Year Ending June 30, 1911* (Zamboanga: Government of the Moro Province, 1911), p. 25, quoted in Smythe, "Pershing and the Disarmament of the Moros," p. 242.

58. John J. Pershing, "Annual Report of the Governor of the Moro Province for the Year Ending June 30, 1912," August 15, 1912, Box 371, John J. Pershing Papers, LC.

59. John J. Pershing, "Memoirs," chap. 18, p. 13, Box 379, John J. Pershing Papers, LC.

60. John J. Pershing to Adjutant General, June 17, 1903, RG 350, File 4865, NARA.

61. Lt. V. L. Whitner to Major W. M. Wright, Adjutant General, June 21, 1913, and cable of Major General J. Franklin Bell to War Department, July 3, 1913, quoted in Gowing, *Mandate in Moroland*, p. 240.

62. Gowing, *Mandate in Moroland*, pp. 240–42.

63. Vandiver, *Black Jack Pershing*, pp. 571, 595–668.

64. Patricio Abinales, "From Orang Besar to Colonial Big Men: Datu Piang of the Magindanaos and the American Colonial State," in Alfred W. McCoy, ed., *Lives at the Margin: Biographies of Filipinos Obscure, Ordinary, and Heroic* (Madison: Center for Southeast Asian Studies, University of Wisconsin, 1998), pp. 193–228.

ABINALES—THE U.S. ARMY AS AN OCCUPYING FORCE
IN MUSLIM MINDANAO, 1899–1913

1. Brian McAllister Linn, *The Philippine War, 1899–1902* (Lawrence: University of Kansas Press, 2000), p. 226.

2. See Vic Hurley, *Swish of the Kris: The Story of the Moros* (New York: E. P. Dutton, 1936), pp. 14–15.

3. Samuel K. Tan, *The Filipino Muslim Armed Struggle, 1900–1912* (Manila: Filipinas Foundation, 1977), p. 25.

4. Peter G. Gowing, "Moros and Indians: Commonalities of Purpose, Policy, and Practice in American Government of Two Hostile Subject Peoples," *Philippine Quarterly of Culture and Society* 8 (1980): pp. 146–48.

5. Pio Pi, SJ, "The Moros of the Philippines," in "Department of Mindanao Annual Report," app. 6, in *Annual Report of the War Department* (ARWD), *Fiscal Year ended June 30, 1903* (Washington, D.C.: Government Printing Office, 1903), pp. 365–78; Bureau of Statistics, United States Treasury Department, *Colonial Administration, 1800–1900: Methods of Government and Development Adopted by the Principal Colonizing Nations in Their Control of Tropical and Other Colonies and Dependencies* (Washington, D.C.: Government Printing Office, 1901).

6. Leonard W. Wood, ARWD, September 1, 1904, as added to *Report of the Philippine Commission* (RPC), vol. 12, pt. 2, June 30, 1904 (Washington, D.C.: Government Printing Office, 1904), p. 577. Tasker Bliss, *Report of the Governor of the Moro Province* (RGMP), June 30, 1907 (Washington, D.C.: Government Printing Office, 1907), 391.

7. William Howard Taft, RPC, vol. 5, in ARWD, June 30, 1903, p. 81.

8. RGMP, June 30, 1907, p. 391.

9. ARWD, September 1, 1904, in RPC, vol. 12, pt. 2, June 30, 1904, p. 577.

10. Gen. William Kobbe, "Annual Report of Brig. Gen. W. Kobbe, United States Volunteer Commanding, Department of Mindanao and Sulu," in ARWD, 1900, pp. 268–69; Najeeb Saleeby, *The Moro Problem: An Academic Discussion of the History and Solution of the Problem of the Government of the Moros of the Philippine Islands* (Manila: n.p., 1913), pp. 16–31, quoted in Shinzo Hayase, *Mindanao Ethnohistory beyond Nations: Magindanao, Sangir, and Bagobo Societies in East Maritime Southeast Asia* (Quezon City: Ateneo de Manila University Press, 2007), p. 151.

11. Hurley, *Swish of the Kris*, pp. 174–75.

12. Charles Burke Elliot, *The Philippines to the End of the Commission Period: A Study in Tropical Democracy* (Indianapolis: Bobbs-Merrill, 1917), p. 246.

13. RGMP, 1908, p. 13.

14. Hermann Hagedorn, *Leonard Wood: A Biography*, vol. 2 (New York: Kraus, 1969), p. 3.

15. *Mindanao Herald*, February 20, 1904, p. 5. See also "Report of the 5th District, Philippine Constabulary," June 25, 1904, in RPC, vol. 12, p. 121.

16. Such was the case of the Apache war veteran Major Hugh L. Scott, who became governor of Sulu District. See RPC, vol. 11, pt. 1, in ARWD, June 30, 1904, p. 12; and Ernesto Corcino, "Pioneer American Entrepreneurs in Mindanao," *Mindanao Journal* 8 (1981–82): pp. 101–2.

17. Tasker Bliss, "The Government of the Moro Province and Its Problems," *Mindanao Herald*, February 3, 1909, p. 4.

18. Leonard Wood to Col. Edward Davis, August 2, 1904, quoted in Wayne Wray Thompson, "Governors of the Moro Province: Wood, Bliss, and Pershing in the Southern Philippines, 1903–1913," PhD diss., University of California, San Diego, 1975, p. 69.

19. Donna J. Amoroso, "Inheriting the 'Moro Problem': Muslim Authority and Colonial Rule in British Malaya and the Philippines," in Julian Go and Anne Foster, eds. *The American Colonial State in the Philippines: Global Perspectives* (Durham: Duke University Press, 2003), p. 118.

20. See, for example, the report of a Colonel James G. Harbord, "Report of the Officer Commanding 5th District, PC," RPC, vol. 12, pt. 3, June 30, 1904, p. 577.

21. "An Act Providing for the Organization and Government of the Moro Province," June 1, 1903, in "Acts of the Legislative Council of the Moro Province," September 7, 1903, to August 31, 1904, in RGMP, 1904, pp. 113–31. Emphasis added.

22. "The Government of the Moro Province," RPC, vol. 5, in ARWD, June 30, 1903, p. 78.

23. Legislative Council of the Moro Province, "Act No. 35, an Act to Amend Act No. 82 of the Philippine Commission entitled 'The Municipal Code,' as Amended in Its Application to the Moro Province," enacted January 27, 1904, and approved April 27, 1904, RPC, 1904, p. 613; Act No. 39 of the Moro Province's Legislative Council, February 19, 1904; T. H. Bliss, RGMP, September 10, 1907, in RPC, vol. 7, in ARWD, February 19, 1904, pp. 393–94.

24. United States Bureau of Census, *Census of the Philippine Islands*, vol. 2 (Washington, D.C.: Government Printing Office, 1903), pp. 123–27, 400–407.

25. Peter Gowing, *Mandate in Moroland: The American Government of Muslim Filipinos, 1899–1920* (Quezon City: New Day, 1983), p. 110.

26. RGMP, 1906, in RPC, 1907, p. 590.

27. *Mindanao Herald*, February 3, 1909, p. 3; Frederick Palmer, *Bliss, Peacemaker: The Life and Letters of General Tasker Bliss* (New York: Dodd, Mead, 1934), p. 94.

28. *Mindanao Herald*, June 16, 1906.

29. Among Finley's works is an ethnographic survey of a non-Muslim indigenous community. See *The Subanu: Studies of a Sub-Visayan Mountain Folk of Mindanao* (William Churchill, coauthor) (Washington, D.C.: Government Printing Office, 1913).

30. J. Juan Marti, *A Grammar of the Magindanao Tongue* (Washington, D.C.: Government Printing Office, 1906).

31. Patricio N. Abinales, "Progressive-Machine Conflicts in Early Twentieth Century American Politics and Colonial State-Building in the Philippines," in Julian Go and Anne Foster, eds., *The American Colonial State in the Philippines: Global Perspectives* (Durham: Duke University Press, 2003), pp. 148–81.

32. Samuel P. Huntington, *The Soldier and the State: The Theory and Practice of Civil-Military Relations* (Cambridge, Mass.: Belknap, 1957), p. 280.

33. Jack C. Lane, *Armed Progressive: General Leonard Wood* (San Rafael, Calif., and London: Presidio, 1978), p. 114.

34. Francis Burton Harrison, *The Cornerstone of Philippine Independence: A Narrative of Seven Years* (New York: Macmillan, 1942), p. 124.

35. Taxes from the trade were collected efficiently such that customs revenues rose from 82,240.04 pesos in 1904 and 108,719.86 pesos in 1905 to a high of 178,818.96 pesos in 1906. *Mindanao Herald*, September 15, 1906.

36. Douglas Thompson Kellie Hartley, "American Participation in the Economic Development of Mindanao and Sulu, 1899–1930," PhD diss., James Cook University, 1983, pp. 38, 44–45. On the timber industry, see *Mindanao Herald*, June 20, 1906.

37. Mariano Garchitorena, *The Philippine Abaca Industry* (Manila: Bureau of Printing, 1938).

38. W. Cameron Forbes, *The Philippine Islands*, vol. 2 (Boston and New York: Houghton Mifflin, 1928), p. 26, n. 1.

39. *Manila Times*, July 12, 1912.

40. Gowing, *Mandate in Moroland*, pp. 221–22.

41. *Correspondence Relating to the War with Spain, Including the Insurrection in the Philippine Islands and the China Relief Expedition, April 15, 1898, to July 30, 1902*, vol. 2 (Washington, D.C.: Center of Military History, 1993), pp. 1105–6. See also Horace P. Hobbs, *Kris and Krag: Adventures among the Moros of the Southern Philippine Islands* (n.p., 1962), pp. 6–7, 42–43.

42. Russell Roth, *Muddy Glory: America's "Indian Wars" in the Philippines, 1899–1935* (West Hanover, Mass.: Christopher's Publishing House, 1981), pp. 30–37, 148–54.

43. Ibid., p. 30. See also George Yarrington Coats, "The Philippine Constabulary, 1901–1927," PhD diss., Ohio State University, 1968, p. 361.

44. Leonard Wood, Letters, Special Collection, Bird Library, Syracuse University. The first quote from Wood is cited in Thompson, "Governors of the Moro Province," p. 59, while the

second is from RGMP, in RPC, 1907, p. 351. On peace and order, see RGMP, 1906, pp. 419–20; and *Philippine Free Press*, July 10, 1909. See also *Mindanao Herald*, June 16, 1905, July 21, 1905, and August 25, 1906.

45. Carl A. Trocki, *Prince of Pirates: The Temenggongs and the Development of Johor and Singapore* (Singapore: Institute of Southeast Asian Studies, 1979), pp. 40–60.

46. Patricio N. Abinales, "From Orang Besar to Colonial Big Men: Datu Piang of the Magindanaos and the American Colonial State," in Alfred W. McCoy, ed., *Lives at the Margin: Biographies of Obscure Filipinos* (Madison: Center for Southeast Asian Studies, University of Wisconsin, 1999; Quezon City: Ateneo de Manila University Press, 2000), pp. 293–338.

47. Tan, *The Filipino Muslim Armed Struggle*, pp. 161–67.

48. Thompson, "Governors of the Moro Province," p. 64. On *cotta* warfare, see Roth, *Muddy Glory*, pp. 30–37, 148–54.

49. Gowing, *Mandate in Moroland*, p. 59.

50. Ibid., pp. 138–39, 194.

51. Thompson, "Governors of the Moro Province," p. 69.

52. Ruth Cabanero-Mapanao, "Magindanao, 1890–1913: The Life and Times of Datu Ali of Kudarangan," MA thesis, University of the Philippines, 1985.

53. Thompson, "Governors of the Moro Province," p. 88.

54. "Report of the District Governor, 5th District, Bureau of Constabulary," July 15, 1908, RPC, vol. 8, pt. 2, in ARWD, 1908, pp. 416–17.

55. Harrison, *The Cornerstone of Philippine Independence*, p. 110.

56. These signals came in the shape of laws passed by the Philippine Commission upon the instigation of its Filipino members. Act No. 35, "Revisions to the Municipal Code as Applied to the Moro Province," RPC, 1904, 613–32; Act No. 39, "An Act Temporarily to Provide for the Government of the Moros and Other Non-Christian Groups," RPC, 1904, pp. 633–37.

57. RGMP, 1911, p. 24.

58. *Journal of the Philippine Commission, Being a Special Session and the First Session, October 17, 1910–February 3, 1911* (Manila: Bureau of Printing, 1911), p. 771.

59. *Mindanao Herald*, December 15, 1906.

60. RGMP, 1904, p. 21.

61. Thompson, "Governors of the Moro Province," p. 118.

62. *Mindanao Herald*, September 8, 1906.

63. *La Vida Filipina*, July 1906; *La Vanguardia*, August 31 and December 2, 1910; *El Ideal*, April 16, 1913; *La Democracia*, February 8, 1913, all cited in Gowing, *Mandate in Moroland*, pp. 205–6, 252–54.

64. RGMP, June 30, 1909, p. 31.

65. Part of the reason for the weakness of "nationalist agitations" in the Moro Province derived from the fact that the Nacionalista Party's local networks there were still in their embryonic stage. See Carlos Quirino, *Quezon: Paladin of Philippine Freedom* (Manila: Filipiniana Book Guild, 1971), p. 92.

66. *Journal of the Philippine Commission*, October 17, 1910–February 3, 1911, p. 771.

67. *Journal of the Philippine Commission*, First Session, October 16, 1912–February 3, 1913, of the Third Philippine Legislature (Manila: Bureau of Printing, 1913), p. 765.

68. Gowing, *Mandate in Moroland*, 194; *Mindanao Herald*, June 15, 1907.

69. On Bliss's proposal, see *Mindanao Herald*, December 15, 1906, and August 12, 1905.

70. On the salaries of provincial officials, see *Official Register of Officers and Employees in the Civil Service of the Philippine Islands* (Manila: Bureau of Printing, 1904), p. 89. On the turnover rate, see "Testimony of Frank W. Carpenter," U.S. House of Representatives, 64th Cong., Doc. 1378, pp. 400–401, in Garel A. Grunder and William E. Livezy, *The Philippines and the United States* (Norman: University of Oklahoma Press, 1951), p. 144.

71. Douglas Kellie Hartley, "A Preliminary Study of the Pioneer American Entrepreneurs in Mindanao and Sulu," *Mindanao Journal* 1, no. 4 (1981–82): p. 214; Shinzo Hayase, "Tribes, Settlers, and Administrators on a Frontier: Economic Development and Social Change in Davao, Southeastern Mindanao, the Philippines," PhD diss., Murdoch University, 1984, pp. 75–76; *Philippine Free Press*, April 19, 1910.

72. RGMP, June 30, 1909, pp. 3–4.

73. *The Filipino People*, October 1912, pp. 4–5.

74. Gowing, *Mandate in Moroland*, p. 172.

75. Forbes, *The Philippine Islands*, vol. 2, pp. 293–94.

76. Alunan Glang, *Muslim Secession or Integration?* (Quezon City: R. P. Garcia, 1969), pp. 16–17. On the warning issued by the Committee of Petitions and Communications, see Samuel K. Tan, *Critical Decade, 1921–1930* (Quezon City: College of Social Sciences and Philosophy, University of the Philippines, 1993), pp. 47–48.

77. Frank W. Carpenter, "Report to the Governor-General, Philippine Islands, Department of Mindanao and Sulu, 1915," in *Report of the Governor-General of the Philippine Islands to the Secretary of War* (Washington, D.C.: Government Printing Office, 1917), p. 295. On collaborating *datus* such as Hadji Butu and Hadji Gulamu Rasul of Jolo, see *Philippine Free Press*, September 1, 1914, April 29, 1916, and November 10 and 17, 1917.

78. On *datu* flip-flopping, see Maximo Kalaw, "The Moro Bugaboo," *Philippine Social Science Review* 3, no. 4 (1931): pp. 73–74.

79. Oliver Wolters, *History, Culture, and Region in Southeast Asian Perspectives* (Singapore: Institute of Southeast Asian Studies, 1982), pp. 18–19.

80. Ralph Benjamin Thomas, "Muslim but Filipinos: The Integration of the Philippine Muslims, 1917–46," PhD diss., University of Pennsylvania, 1971, pp. 85, 132; Howard T. Fry, "The Bacon Bill of 1926: New Light on an Exercise in Divide-and-Rule," *Philippine Studies* 3d quarter (1978): pp. 266–67; Forbes, *The Philippine Islands*, vol. 2, pp. 44–45; R. Joel de los Santos, "Reflections on the Moro Wars and the New Filipino," in Peter Gowing, ed., *Understanding Islam and the Muslims in the Philippines*, (Quezon City: New Day, 1988), p. 102.

81. Tan, *Critical Decade*.

82. Thompson, "Governors of the Moro Province," pp. 190–91.

83. Gowing, *Mandate in Moroland*, pp. 245–46; Thompson, "Governors of the Moro Province," pp. 190–91; *Philippine Free Press*, February 1, 1913.

84. RGMP, 1912, pp. 14–15. See also Donald Smythe, *Guerrilla Warrior: The Early Life of John J. Pershing* (New York: Scribner, 1973), pp. 166–73.

85. Frank E. Vandiver, *Black Jack: The Life and Times of John J. Pershing*, vol. 2 (College Station: Texas A&M University Press, 1977); Donald Smythe, *Pershing: General of the Armies* (Bloomington: Indiana University Press, 2007).

86. Nagasura Madale, "The Future of the Moro National Liberation Front as a Separatist Movement in the Philippines," in Lim Joo Jock and Vani S., eds., *Armed Separatism in Southeast Asia* (Singapore: Institute for Southeast Asian Studies, 1984), pp. 180–81.

Capozzola—Minutemen for the World

1. Jerry M. Cooper, *The Rise of the National Guard: The Evolution of the American Militia, 1865–1920* (Lincoln: University of Nebraska Press, 1997), pp. 108–27; Stephen Skowronek, *Building a New American State: The Expansion of National Administrative Capacities, 1877–1920* (New York: Cambridge University Press, 1982), pp. 212–47.

2. United States Department of War, *Annual Reports of the War Department for the Fiscal Year Ended June 30, 1901* (Washington, D.C.: Government Printing Office, 1902), pp. 23–24. Root is quoted in Philip C. Jessup, *Elihu Root* (New York: Dodd, Mead, 1938), vol. 1, p. 268. See also Russell F. Weigley, "The Elihu Root Reforms and the Progressive Era," in William

Geffen, ed., *Command and Commanders in Modern Warfare* (Washington, D.C.: Office of Air Force History, 1971), pp. 11–27.

3. Theodore Roosevelt is quoted in Frederick Bernays Wiener, "The Militia Clause of the Constitution," *Harvard Law Review* 54 (December 1940): p. 194. See also Cooper, *Rise of the National Guard*, p. 112. For modernization theories, see Samuel Huntington, *The Soldier and the State: The Theory and Politics of Civil-Military Relations* (Cambridge: Harvard University Press, 1957); and Weigley, "Elihu Root Reforms."

4. John Whiteclay Chambers II, *To Raise an Army: The Draft Comes to Modern America* (New York: Free Press, 1987), p. 70; Wiener, "Militia Clause," p. 189.

5. Emory Upton, *The Military Policy of the United States* (Washington, D.C.: Government Printing Office, 1904), p. xiv. Root is quoted in John McAuley Palmer, *America in Arms* (New Haven: Yale University Press, 1941), p. 133.

6. Elihu Root, "The Power of the President to Send United States Troops out of the Country," in Robert Bacon and James Brown Scott, eds., *The Military and Colonial Policy of the United States* (Cambridge: Harvard University Press, 1916), p. 158; John K. Mahon, *History of the Militia and the National Guard* (New York: Macmillan, 1983), p. 142.

7. George W. Wickersham to Henry L. Stimson, February 17, 1912, reprinted in *War Department Annual Reports, 1912* (Washington, D.C.: Government Printing Office, 1913), vol. 1, pp. 147–50; Elbridge Colby and James F. Glass, "The Legal Status of the National Guard," *Virginia Law Review* 29 (May 1943): p. 844.

8. Quoted in Cooper, *Rise of the National Guard*, p. 115.

9. Morris R. Cohen, "The Legal Calvinism of Elihu Root," in *Law and the Social Order: Essays in Legal Philosophy* (New York: Harcourt Brace, 1933), pp. 12–18.

10. *Downes v. Bidwell*, 182 U.S. 244 (1901), p. 341; Bartholomew H. Sparrow, *The Insular Cases and the Emergence of American Empire* (Lawrence: University Press of Kansas, 2006); Christina Duffy Burnett, "The Edges of Empire and the Limits of Sovereignty: American Guano Islands," *American Quarterly* 57 (September 2005): pp. 779–803.

11. Lindley M. Garrison to Woodrow Wilson, February 10, 1916, in Arthur S. Link, ed., *The Papers of Woodrow Wilson* (Princeton: Princeton University Press, 1981), vol. 36, p. 164. James Hay is quoted in George C. Herring Jr., "James Hay and the Preparedness Controversy, 1915–1916," *Journal of Southern History* 30 (November 1964): p. 385. On the National Defense Act, see John Dickinson, *The Building of an Army: A Detailed Account of Legislation, Administration, and Opinion in the United States, 1915–1920* (New York: Century, 1922), pp. 3–56; and Arthur S. Link, *Woodrow Wilson and the Progressive Era, 1910–1917* (New York: Harper and Brothers, 1954), pp. 174–96.

12. Chambers, *To Raise an Army*, pp. 113, 117.

13. *Cox v. Wood*, 247 U.S. 3 (1918), p. 4.

14. Hannis Taylor is quoted in Tennant S. McWilliams, *Hannis Taylor: The New Southerner as an American* (Tuscaloosa: University of Alabama Press, 1978), p. 70 (first quote), p. 68 (second quote). See also Hannis Taylor, *Loyalty to the Constitution the Only True Standard of Patriotism: An Appeal to the American Press and People in Behalf of the American Constitution Whose Life Is Now at Stake* (n.p., [1917?]), p. 2. John W. Davis is quoted in McWilliams, *Hannis Taylor*, p. 80 (first quote); and Wiener, "Militia Clause," p. 204 (second quote). Oliver Wendell Holmes Jr. is quoted in Alexander M. Bickel, *The Judiciary and Responsible Government, 1910–1921* (New York: Macmillan, 1984), p. 521 n. 296.

15. *Cox v. Wood*, 247 U.S. 3 (1918), pp. 6, 7; "Court Sustains Draft Statutes," *Washington Post*, May 7, 1918, p. 9.

16. Woodrow Wilson is quoted in Roy Watson Curry, *Woodrow Wilson and Far Eastern Policy, 1913–1921* (New York: Bookman Associates, 1957), p. 69.

17. Ricardo Trota Jose, "The Philippine National Guard in World War I," *Philippine Studies* 36 (3d quarter, 1988): p. 277; "Filipinos Anxious to Aid in the War," *New York Times*,

December 10, 1917, p. 11; Woodrow Wilson, "An Address to a Joint Session of Congress," April 2, 1917, in Link, *Papers of Woodrow Wilson*, vol. 41, p. 525; L. H. Thibault, "The War Affects the Philippines: Special Correspondence," *Asia* 17 (September 1917): pp. 557–58. See also Richard Bruce Meixsel, "An Army for Independence? The American Roots of the Philippine Army," PhD diss., Ohio State University, 1993; and Erez Manela, *The Wilsonian Moment: Self-Determination and the International Origins of Anticolonial Nationalism* (New York: Oxford University Press, 2007).

18. L. H. Thibault, "Notes from the Philippines: From a Manila Correspondent," *Asia* 17 (July 1917): p. 384; Maximo M. Kalaw, *Self-Government in the Philippines* (New York: Century, 1919), pp. 61–62.

19. Jose, "Philippine National Guard," pp. 286, 294–99; Kalaw, *Self-Government in the Philippines*, pp. 63–64. On African American officers, see Mark Ellis, *Race, War, and Surveillance: African Americans and the United States Government during World War I* (Bloomington: Indiana University Press, 2001), pp. 48–73.

20. "Filipinos Get Citizen Right under Rule of Judge Clemons," *Pacific Commercial Advertiser*, March 26, 1916, p. 1; Ralph S. Kuykendall, *Hawaii in the World War* (Honolulu: Historical Commission of the Territory of Hawaii, 1928), pp. 29, 30; *Biennial Report of the Adjutant General of the Territory of Hawaii, 1915–1916* (Honolulu: Adjutant General's Office, 1917), pp. 9–10.

21. "Filipinos Not Eligible Says Judge Vaughan," *Pacific Commercial Advertiser*, December 31, 1916, p. 1; Kuykendall, *Hawaii in the World War*, p. 31; R. K. Evans to Adjutant General of the Army, August 15, 1916, Lucius Pinkham Papers, Hawai'i State Archives, Honolulu; Charles Lamoreaux Warfield, "History of the Hawaii National Guard from Feudal Times to June 30, 1935," MA thesis, University of Hawai'i, 1935, pp. 71–72.

22. Pablo Manlapit is quoted in "Thinks Filipinos Not Inclined to Citizenship," *Honolulu Star-Bulletin*, March 28, 1916, p. 2. See also Lucy E. Salyer, "Baptism by Fire: Race, Military Service, and U.S. Citizenship Policy, 1918–1935," *Journal of American History* 91 (December 2004): pp. 847–76.

23. *Biennial Report of the Adjutant-General of the Territory of Hawaii, 1923–1924* (Honolulu: Adjutant General's Office, 1925), p. 9; John E. Reinecke, *The Filipino Piecemeal Sugar Strike of 1924–1925* (Honolulu: University of Hawai'i Press, 1997), pp. 35–37, 79, 83; Warfield, "History of the Hawaii National Guard," pp. 83–84; Sidney Gulick, *Mixing the Races in Hawaii: A Study of the Coming Neo-Hawaiian American Race* (Honolulu: Hawaiian Board Book Rooms, 1937), p. 95.

24. Jose, "Philippine National Guard," pp. 295 n. 63, 298; Salyer, "Baptism by Fire," pp. 856–62; Frederick S. Harrod, *Manning the New Navy: The Development of a Modern Naval Enlisted Force, 1899–1940* (Westport: Greenwood, 1978), pp. 60–61.

25. Juliet Williams, "Calif. Candidate Wants State Troops Home," *Washington Post*, September 26, 2006; *Perpich v. Department of Defense*, 496 U.S. 334 (1990).

Rodríguez Beruff—From Winship to Leahy

1. Eric Hobsbawm, *The Age of Extremes: A History of the World, 1914–1991* (New York: Vintage, 1994), p. 222.

2. Rexford G. Tugwell, *The Stricken Land: The Story of Puerto Rico* (New York: Doubleday, 1947), p. 45.

3. Hobsbawm, *The Age of Extremes*, p. 216.

4. Harwood Hull, "Puerto Ricans Fire upon Gov. Winship, Two Slain as 15 Bullets Miss Official, Reviewing Parade before 40,000 at Ponce," and "Winship's Tenure Stormy," *New York Times*, July 26, 1938, pp. 1, 11.

5. See Jorge Rodríguez Beruff, "Puerto Rico and the Caribbean in U.S. Strategic Debate on the Eve of the Second World War," *Revista Mexicana del Caribe* 1, no. 2 (1996): pp. 55–80.

6. George Fielding Eliot, *The Ramparts We Watch: A Study of the Problems of American National Defense* (New York: Reynal and Hitchcock, 1938); R. E. Dupuy and George Fielding Eliot, *If War Comes* (New York: Macmillan, 1937). See also Eliot's "Defending America," Foreign Policy Association, World Affairs Pamphlets, new series, no. 4, 1939.

7. The notion that rearmament should mainly be based on the massive development of air power was advanced by Roosevelt toward the end of 1938 and was opposed by both the navy and the army.

8. Eliot, *The Ramparts We Watch*, pp. 1, 193.

9. Ibid., pp. 154–57.

10. Ibid., pp. 148, 152–53, 154–55, 259.

11. "America Gets Ready to Fight Germany, Italy, and Japan," *Life*, October 31, 1938.

12. "Almirante Leahy Gobdor. de Pto. Rico," *El Mundo*, May 13, 1939, p. 1. See also "Nombramiento de Leahy relacionado con defensa nacional," *El Mundo*, May 13, 1939, p. 1; and "Leahy to Succeed Governor Winship," *New York Times*, May 13, 1939, p. 1.

13. Jesús T. Piñero to Ruby Black, May 15, 1939, Ruby Black Collection, Box 4, Folder 13, Document 105, Historical Research Center, Library of Congress.

14. "Nombramiento de Leahy trata de eliminar fuentes de disensión," *El Mundo*, May 14, 1939, p. 1.

15. "Emplearán en la isla más de $30,000,000 en el próximo año," *El Mundo*, May 15, 1939, p. 1.

16. "Hay planes para industrializar a Puerto Rico," *El Mundo*, May 19, 1939, p. 1.

17. William D. Leahy Papers, Manuscript Division, Library of Congress.

18. "Marcantonio insiste en que Winship fue destituído," *El Mundo*, May 12, 1939, p. 5.

19. Blanton Winship, Governor, to the President, June 3, 1939, Franklin Delano Roosevelt Library, Franklin Delano Roosevelt Papers, OF 400, Container 25, Folder P.R.

20. Franklin D. Roosevelt to Honorable Blanton Winship, Governor, June 5, 1939, Franklin Delano Roosevelt Library, Franklin Delano Roosevelt Papers, OF 400, Container 25, Folder P.R.

21. Luis Muñoz Marín to Ruby A. Black, January 8, 1940, Box 5, Folder 14, Document 2, Ruby Black Collection, Historical Research Center.

22. Robert W. Claiborne to Ruby Black, May 13, 1939, Box 4, Folder 13, Document 102, Ruby Black Collection, Historical Research Center.

23. Jorge Rodríguez Beruff, *Las memorias de Leahy* (Río Piedras: Fundación Luis Muñoz Marín, 2002), pp. 160, 164.

García-Muñiz and Campo—
French and American Imperial Accommodation in the Caribbean

1. All photographs and texts cited are from Major Meléndez-Utset's war collection.

2. Serge Mam-Lam-Fouck, *Histoire générale de Guyane française* (Cayenne: Ibis Rouge, 2002).

3. D. W. Meinig, *The Shaping of America*, vol. 2: *Continental America, 1800–1867* (New Haven: Yale University Press, 1993), p. 23.

4. In Cuba, the Atkins family, Elisha and his son, Edwin F., directors of the Union Pacific Railroad and the Sugar Trust, personified U.S. expansionism to the West as well as to the Caribbean.

5. Quoted in Efrén Rivera Ramos, *The Legal Construction of Identity: The Judicial and Social Legacy of American Colonialism in Puerto Rico* (Washington, D.C.: American Psychological Association, 2001), p. 149.

6. Alfred Vagts, *A History of Militarism, Civilian and Military*, rev. ed. (New York: Meridian, [1937] 1959), p. 251.

7. Myron Echenberg, "Slaves into Soldiers: Social Origins of the Tirailleurs Senegalais," in Paul E. Lovejoy, ed., *Africans in Bondage: Studies in Slavery and the Slave Trade* (Madison: African Studies Program, University of Wisconsin, 1986), p. 313.

8. Martin Thomas, "At the Heart of Things: French Imperial Defense Planning in the Late 1930s," *French Historical Studies* 21, no. 2 (spring 1998): pp. 325–61.

9. "Porto Rico Troops' Status," *New York Times*, October 26, 1902, p. 23.

10. María Eugenia Estades Font, *La presencia militar de los Estados Unidos en Puerto Rico, 1898–1918: Intereses estratégicos y dominación colonial* (San Juan: Ediciones Huracán, 1999), pp. 190–96.

11. Frank McCann Jr., "Aviation and Diplomacy: The United States and Brazil, 1939–1941," *Inter-American Economic Affairs* 21, no. 4 (1968): pp. 35–51.

12. "U.S. to Finance Airports in Latin America," *Washington Post*, July 10, 1940, p. 1.

13. Quoted in Annette Palmer, "The Politics of Race and War: Black American Soldiers in the Caribbean Theater during the Second World War," *Military Affairs* 47, no. 2 (April 1983): p. 59.

14. Ibid., p. 60.

15. Ibid.; Humberto García-Muñiz, *La estrategia de los Estados Unidos y la militarización del Caribe* (Río Piedras: Instituto de Estudios del Caribe, Universidad de Puerto Rico, 1988), p. 60.

16. Palmer, "The Politics of Race and War," p. 61.

17. Luis García Sánchez, interview with Humberto García-Muñiz, tape recording, Coamo, Puerto Rico, December 23, 1996.

18. Palmer, "The Politics of Race and War," p. 59.

19. Rexford G. Tugwell, *The Stricken Land: The Story of Puerto Rico* (New York: Doubleday, 1947), quotes from pp. 365, 367, and 322, respectively.

20. Ibid., p. 322.

21. Francisco M. Rivera Lizardi, *La guerra y yo* (Caguas: Editorial Raíces, 1999), p. 61 (italics in original). See also Héctor Negroni, *Historia militar de Puerto Rico* (Madrid: Sociedad Estatal Quinto Centenario, [1992?]), p. 444.

22. See "Martinique Chief Gets Vichy Powers: Admiral Robert Made Virtual Dictator over French Areas in Western World," *New York Times*, December 11, 1940, p. 1; and Georges Robert, *La France aux Antilles de 1939 à 1943* (Paris: Libraries Plon, 1950).

23. Thomas, "At the Heart of Things," p. 351.

24. Nicol Smith, *Black Martinique, Red Guiana* (Indianapolis: Bobbs-Merrill, 1942), pp. 133–42.

25. Fitzroy A. Baptiste, "The Anti-Vichyite Movement in French Guiana, June to December 1940," in Leslie A. Manigat, ed., *The Caribbean Yearbook of International Relations, 1976* (Leyden, Netherlands: A. W. Sijthoff; Trinidad and Tobago: Institute of International Relations, University of the West Indies, 1977), p. 139.

26. "Soldados P.R. ascendidos en base Surinam," *El Mundo*, November 20, 1943, p. 5.

27. Rodolphe Alexandre, *La Guyane sous Vichy* (Paris: Editions Caribéens, 1988), p. 138 (our translation).

28. See Stetson Conn and Byron Fairchild, *The Framework of Hemisphere Defense* (Honolulu: University Press of the Pacific, [1960] 2002), p. 256.

29. See Humberto García-Muñiz and José Lee Borges, "U.S. Consular Activism in the Caribbean, 1783–1903," *Revista Mexicana del Caribe* 5 (1998): pp. 32–79.

30. See "French-American Military Relations in the Caribbean Theatre in World War II," pp. 78–96, 1945, Historical Section, Caribbean Defense Command, U.S. Army, Office of the Chief of Military History, Washington, D.C.

31. Juan Meléndez-Utset, interview with Humberto García-Muñiz, tape recording, San Juan, Puerto Rico, September 10, 1998 (our translation).

32. Ibid.
33. Tugwell, *The Stricken Land*, p. 367.
34. Estades Font, *La presencia militar de los Estados Unidos en Puerto Rico*, pp. 194–95.
35. Juan Meléndez-Utset, interview with Humberto García-Muñiz, tape recording, San Juan, Puerto Rico, September 10, 1998 (our translation).
36. Ibid.
37. Rosalina Brau, interview with Rebeca Campo, tape recording, San Juan, Puerto Rico, June 24, 2004.
38. Juan Meléndez-Utset, interview with Humberto García-Muñiz, tape recording, San Juan, Puerto Rico, December 28, 1998.
39. "El Gobierno Francés premia a oficial puertorriqueño," *El Mundo*, December 28, 1945.

Lipman—Guantánamo and the Case of Kid Chicle

1. I use Guantánamo to refer to the Cuban city and the abbreviation GTMO to refer to the U.S. naval base at Guantánamo Bay.
2. "La víctima de Guantánamo," *Hoy*, December 22, 1940; "La madre de crianza de Lino Rodríguez tiene fe en nuestros tribunales," *Diario de Cuba*, December 22, 1940.
3. Rolando E. Quintero Mena, "El Caso Chicle: Un crimen del imperialismo yanqui que quedó impune," *El Managuí, Sección de Investigaciones Históricas del Comité Provincial del PCC, Guantánamo* 4, no. 9 (1989): pp. 3–12; Mary Ellene Chenevey McCoy, "Guantanamo Bay: The United States Naval Base and Its Relationship with Cuba," PhD diss., University of Akron, 1995, pp. 129–35.
4. William Appleman Williams, *The Tragedy of American Diplomacy*, new ed. (New York: Norton, 1984).
5. Robert Whitney, *State and Revolution in Cuba: Mass Mobilization and Political Change, 1920–1940* (Chapel Hill: University of North Carolina Press, 2001).
6. César J. Ayala, *American Sugar Kingdom: The Plantation Economy of the Spanish Caribbean, 1898–1934* (Chapel Hill: University of North Carolina Press, 1999), p. 202.
7. Louis A. Pérez Jr., *On Becoming Cuban: Identity, Nationality, and Culture* (New York: HarperCollins, 1999), pp. 220–38.
8. Alberto Soler Zunzarren, *Guantánamo Historia: Guía General* (1947), Guantánamo Provincial Archive, archivist's private collection.
9. Informe del equipo de la escuela de historia, Universidad de la Habana, "Guantánamo: Esquema de la historia de una ciudad," unpublished report, May 1967, José Martí Library, Havana, Cuba.
10. Marion Emerson Murphy, *The History of Guantánamo Bay* (U.S. Naval Base Guantánamo Bay: District Publications and Printing Office, Tenth Naval District, 1953), p. 31.
11. McCoy, "Guantanamo Bay," pp. 146–84.
12. Rosalie Schwartz, *Pleasure Island: Tourism and Temptation in Cuba* (Lincoln: University of Nebraska Press, 1997), p. 48.
13. George S. Messersmith, Ambassador's Memorandum, August 31, 1940, Record Group (RG) 59/811.34537/271, Box 3784, U.S. National Archives and Records Administration (NARA), College Park, Maryland.
14. Murphy, *History of Guantánamo Bay*, pp. 31–2.
15. Cpt. George Weyler to U.S. Ambassador, January 14, 1943, RG 181, GTMO World War II Files, Box 3, NARA.
16. Lino Lemes García, "Guantánamo al día," *La Voz del Pueblo*, October 14, 1940.
17. Pedro Salgado and José Fernández to Franklin Roosevelt, September 3, 1940, RG 59/811.34537/278, Box 3784, NARA.
18. Ricardo Baylor (pseud.), interview with the author, November 21, 2004, Guantánamo, Cuba (interview conducted in Spanish).

19. Alberto Torres (pseud.), interview with the author, December 5, 2004, Havana, Cuba (interview conducted in Spanish).

20. Lino Lemes García, "Guantánamo al día," *El Vigilante*, November 15, 1940; "El Caso Pomares-Ochoa," *La Voz del Pueblo*, November 18, 1940.

21. Víctor Alonso, "Golpean brutalmente y lanzan al mar a un trabajador cubano en Caimanera," *Diario de Cuba*, December 18, 1940; "El Cabo de Marina," *La Voz del Pueblo*, December 19, 1940.

22. Víctor Alonso, "Piden que se juzgado en Cuba el Teniente West," *Diario de Cuba*, December 20, 1940; "La madre de crianza de Lino Rodríguez tiene fe en nuestros tribunales," *Diario de Cuba*, December 22, 1940; "Designado juez especial," *Hoy*, December 21, 1940; "Demuestra la Autopsia que fue Asesinado el Obrero Cubano," *Información*, December 20, 1940 (*Información* clipping in RG 59/811.34537/284 PS/FF, Box 3784, NARA).

23. Lino Lemes García, "Guantánamo al día," *El Vigilante*, December 23, 1940.

24. *Hoy*, September 3, 1940 (clipping in RG 59/811.34537, Box 3784, NARA).

25. "Detenido el oficial americano que mató a un obrero cubano," *Diario de la Marina*, December 22, 1940.

26. James Forestal to Liaison Office, January 6, 1941, RG 59/ 811.34537/286 PS/FF, Box 3784, NARA.

27. "Memorando relacionado con el homicidio de Lino Rodríguez Grenot," December 26, 1940, Secretaria de la Presidencia, Ministerio de Justicia, Caja 45, Número 2, Archivos Nacional de Cuba.

28. "Excerpt of Letter Addressed to Mr. Bonsal," March 19, 1941, RG 59/811.34537, Box 3784, NARA.

29. James Forrestal, Acting Secretary of the Navy, to the Secretary of State, June 18, 1941, RG 59/811.34537, Box 3784, NARA.

30. Excerpt of Letter Addressed to Mr. Bonsal, March 19, 1941, RG 59/811.34537, Box 3784, NARA.

31. Harry Story to Harold S. Tewell, May 22, 1942, RG 84, STGO Conf., 1941–2, All Numbers, Box 4, NARA.

32. Lino Lemes García, "El lamentable suceso de ayer en la estación naval," *El Vigilante*, November 26, 1940; Lino Lemes García, "Falleció el obrero santiaguerro Agustín Alvarez que sufrió un accidente en la base naval," *El Vigilante*, November 29, 1940.

33. Lino Lemes García, "La muerte misteriosa de un trabajador de la Snare Coporation," *El Vigilante*, May 14, 1941.

LINN—THE IMPACT OF THE PHILIPPINE WARS (1898–1913) ON THE U.S. ARMY

1. Richard L. Crosby et al., "Roads to New Strength: Preparing Leaders for Military Operations Other Than War," 1994, student paper, Army War College (AWCSP), U.S. Military History Institute (MHI), Carlisle, Pennsylvania; Andrew J. Birtle, *U.S. Army Counterinsurgency and Contingency Operations Doctrine, 1860–1941* (Washington, D.C.: Center of Military History, 1998). Many of these ideas appeared in Heritage Lectures, no. 908 (November 14, 2005), www.heritage.org/research/nationalsecurityh908.cfm.

2. Max Boot, *The Savage Wars of Peace: Small Wars and the Rise of American Power* (New York: Basic Books, 2002); Fred Kaplan, "From Baghdad to Manila: Another Lousy Analogy for the Occupation of Iraq," October 21, 2003, *Slate* (http://www.slate.com/default.aspx?id=2090114, accessed May 24, 2008); Brian McAllister Linn, "Foreshadowing Postwar Iraq: The U.S. War in the Philippines, 1899–1902," in Peter B. Lane and Ronald E. Marcello, eds., *Warriors and Scholars: A Modern War Reader* (Denton: University of North Texas Press, 2005), pp. 254–73.

3. Peter Gowing, "Mandate in Moroland: The American Government of Muslim Filipinos, 1899–1920," PhD diss., Syracuse University, 1968; Brian McAllister Linn, "The Pulahan Campaign: A Study in U.S. Pacification," *War in History* 6 (January 1999): pp. 45–71.

4. Adj. Gen. to William R. Green, March 6, 1922, Philippine Insurrection File, No. 2159, Legislative and Policy Precedent Files, 1943–1975, Record Group (RG) 407, National Archives 2 (NARA2), College Park, Maryland; Samuel Reber, J. W. Craig, and F. D. Evans, "Study of the Laws Relating to the Organization of the Military and Volunteer Forces of the United States . . . ," 1905–6, Series 25, Entry 299, RG 165, NARA2.

5. Arthur MacArthur to Theodore Schwan, November 23, 1899, in *Report of the War Department, 1900* (Washington, D.C.: Government Printing Office, 1900), vol. 1, pt. 7, p. 59; John R. M. Taylor, "The Philippine Insurrection against the United States, 1898–1903: A Compilation of Documents and Introduction," 27 HS, Microfilm 9, Microcopy M719, NARA2; Frederick Funston to William A. Kobbé, March 1, 1899, Correspondence 1899 File, William A. Kobbé Papers, MHI.

6. Charles J. Crane, "Fighting Tactics of Filipinos," *Journal of the Military Service Institute* 30 (July 1902): p. 496; John Leland Jordan to Mother, April 28, 1900, John Leland Jordan Papers, MHI.

7. James Parker, "Some Random Notes on the Fighting in the Philippines," *Journal of the Military Service Institute* 27 (March 1900): p. 340.

8. Robert L. Bullard, "Military Pacification," *Journal of the Military Service Institute* 46 (January–February 1910): p. 3.

9. Archibald R. Colquhoun, *The Mastery of the Pacific* (New York: Macmillan, 1904), p. 98. See also Dean C. Worcester to Mrs. Henry W. Lawton, May 5, 1901, Box 2, Henry T. Lawton Papers, Library of Congress, Washington, D.C.

10. Henry T. Allen to [John A. Johnston?], January 21, 1902, Box 7, Henry T. Allen Papers, Library of Congress.

11. Hugh D. Wise, "Notes on Field Service in Samar," *Journal of the U.S. Infantry Association* 4 (July 1907): pp. 3–58.

12. Sand-30, "Trench, Parapet, or the Open," *Journal of the Military Service Institute* 31 (July 1902): pp. 471–86.

13. Leonard Wood to Adj. Gen., July 1, 1907, Box 40, Leonard Wood Papers, Library of Congress.

14. "Confidential Report, Maneuvers, Philippines Division," 1910, Adjutant Generals Office (AGO) 1710830, RG 94, National Archives 1 (NARA1), Washington, D.C.; "Chief Umpire's Report, Exercise No. 2, Philippine Maneuver Campaign, January 22 to February 5, 1914," Army War College 8438-5, RG 165, NARA2; A. C., Sharpe, "The Campaign at Dinaluphin," *Journal of the Military Service Institute* 47 (July–August 1910): pp. 13–24.

15. Milton F. Davis to Mathew F. Steele, January 12, 1903, Box 11, Matthew F. Steele Papers, MHI.

16. John R. M. Taylor, *The Philippine Insurrection against the United States, 1898–1903: A Compilation of Documents and Introduction*, 5 vols. (Pasay City: The Eugenio Lopez Foundation, [1906] 1971); John R. M. Taylor to Secretary, War College Division, August 24, 1914, War College Division 8699-2, Entry 296, RG 165; John M. Gates, "The Official Historian and the Well-Placed Critic: James A. Le Roy's Assessment of John R. M. Taylor's *The Philippine Insurrection against the United States*," *Public Historian* 7 (summer 1985): pp. 57–67.

17. T. W. Jones to Superintendent, U.S. Military Academy, November 5, 1905, Entry 301, RG 165; Army War College, Record Cards for Miscellaneous Correspondence, 1903–10, Entry 291, RG 165; Timothy K. Nenninger, *The Leavenworth Schools and the Old Army: Education, Professionalism, and the Officer Corps of the United States Army, 1881–1918* (Westport: Greenwood, 1978).

18. Alexander Brodie to Commanding Officers, Department of the Visayas, October 20, 1906, Entry 2712, RG 395.

19. Mark E. Grotelueschen, *The AEF Way of War: The American Army and Ground Combat* (New York: Cambridge University Press, 2006); Brian McAllister Linn, *The Echo of Battle: The Army's Way of War* (Cambridge: Harvard University Press, 2007); William O. Odom,

After the Trenches: The Transformation of U.S. Army Doctrine, 1918–1939 (College Station: Texas A&M University Press, 1999); Timothy K. Nenninger, "Tactical Dysfunction in the AEF, 1917–1918," *Military Affairs* 51 (October 1987): pp. 177–81.

20. Birtle, *U.S. Army Counterinsurgency and Contingency Operations Doctrine*, pp. 218–26.

21. Oliver Lyman Spaulding, *The United States Army in War and Peace* (New York: G. P. Putnam's Sons, 1937), pp. 339–40.

22. William T. Sexton, *Soldiers in the Sun: An Adventure in Imperialism* (Harrisburg, Pa.: Military Service Publishing, 1939).

23. C. H. Gerhardt, "An Account of the Conduct of the Armed Forces of the U.S. in the Philippine Islands, 1898–1902, from the Viewpoint of the High Command," March 1936, Pre-presidential Papers, Box 154, Philippine Island File, Dwight D. Eisenhower Presidential Library, Abilene, Kansas.

24. Robert G. MacDonnell, "Unconventional Methods of Warfare," March 1, 1952, AWCSP, MHI; Command and General Staff College, "Study of Army Attitude toward Arming Partisans," 1950, File 334, Box 21, Entry 54, RG 337, NARA2; Bruce Palmer Jr., "The Modern Role of Unconventional Warfare," March 1, 1962, AWCSP, MHI; Herman L. Purkhiser, "Unconventional Methods of Warfare," March 24, 1952, AWCSP, MHI.

25. Andrew J. Birtle, *U.S. Army Counterinsurgency and Contingency Operations Doctrine, 1942–1976* (Washington, D.C.: Center of Military History, 2007), pp. 62–64.

26. Robert N. Ginsbaugh, "Damn the Insurrectos," *Military Review* 54 (January 1964): pp. 58–70, quote from p. 70.

27. Richard W. Smith, "Philippine Constabulary," *Military Review* 58 (May 1968): pp. 73–80, quote from p. 80.

28. Allan D. Marple, "The Philippine Scouts: A Case Study in the Use of Indigenous Soldiers in Northern Luzon, the Philippine Islands, 1899," Masters of Military Art and Science thesis, U.S. Army Command and General Staff College (CGSC), Fort Leavenworth, Kansas, 1970, p. 109.

29. *Low Intensity Conflict: Counterinsurgency Case Studies (Selected Readings)*, CGSC Student Text 20-9 (Fort Leavenworth, Kans.: CGSC, 1985), p. 11.

30. Thomas F. Burdett, "A New Evaluation of General Otis's Leadership in the Philippines," *Military Review* 65 (January 1975): pp. 79–87.

31. Andrew J. Bacevich, "Disagreeable Work: Pacifying the Moros, 1903–1906," *Military Review* 71 (June 1981): pp. 49–61.

32. Edward J. Filiberti, "The Roots of U.S. Counterinsurgency Doctrine," *Military Review* 78 (January 1988): pp. 50–61.

33. Andrew J. Bacevich, *American Empire: The Realities and Consequences of U.S. Diplomacy* (Cambridge: Harvard University Press, 2002); *The New American Militarism: How Americans Are Seduced by War* (New York: Oxford University Press, 2005).

34. Alan C. Lowe, "Foreign Devils and Boxers: A Concise History of Combined Interoperability during the Boxer Rebellion," Masters of Military Art and Science thesis, U.S. Army Command and General Staff College, Fort Leavenworth, Kansas, 2000.

35. Richard W. Mills, "The Philippine Insurrection: America's First Venture into Military Operations Other Than War," June 1997, student paper, Naval War College, Newport, Rhode Island; Victor Holman, "Seminole Negro Indians, Macabebes, and Civilian Irregulars: Models for the Future Employment of Indigenous Forces," Masters of Military Art and Science thesis, U.S. Army Command and General Staff College, Fort Leavenworth, Kansas, 1995.

36. Madelfia A. Abb, "Bringing about a Military Learning Organization: The U.S. Army in the Philippine War, 1899–1902," February 18, 2000, School of Advanced Military Studies Monograph, Combined Arms Reference Library, Fort Leavenworth, Kansas.

37. Thomas S. Bundt, "An Unconventional War: The Philippine Insurrection, 1899," *Military Review* 94 (May–June 2004): pp. 9–10.

38. Timothy K. Deady, "Lessons from a Successful Counterinsurgency: The Philippines, 1899–1902," *Parameters* 35 (spring 2005): pp. 53–68.

39. Ibid., 65. On teaching Vietnam at CGSC, see Peter Maslowski, "Army Values and American Values," *Military Review* 70 (April 1990): pp. 10–23.

40. Rajiv Chandrasekaran, *Imperial Life in the Emerald City: Inside the Green Zone* (New York: Knopf, 2006); Michael R. Gordon and Bernard E. Trainor, *Cobra II: The Inside Story of the Invasion and Occupation of Iraq* (New York: Pantheon, 2006); Thomas E. Ricks, *Fiasco: The American Military Adventure in Iraq* (New York: Penguin, 2006).

41. U.S. Department of the Army, *FM 3-24: Counterinsurgency* (Washington, D.C.: Department of the Army, 2006), pp. 4–7.

McNeill—Introduction to Part 8

1. David Abernethy, *The Dynamics of Global Dominance: European Overseas Empires, 1415–1980* (New Haven: Yale University Press, 2002).

2. Sujit Sivasundaram, *Nature and the Godly Empire: Science and Evangelical Mission in the Pacific, 1795–1850* (Cambridge: Cambridge University Press, 2005).

3. Richard Grove, *Green Imperialism: Colonial Expansion, Tropical Island Edens, and the Origins of Environmentalism, 1600–1860* (New York: Cambridge University Press, 1995).

4. Marie-Noëlle Bourguet, Bernard Lepetit, Daniel Nordman, and Maroula Sinarellis, eds., *L'invention scientifique de la Méditerranée* (Paris: Ecole des Hautes Etudes en Sciences Sociales, 1998).

5. Philip Curtin, *Death by Migration: Europe's Encounter with the Tropical World in the Nineteenth Century* (New York: Cambridge University Press, 1989); *Disease and Empire: The Health of European Troops in the Conquest of Africa* (New York: Cambridge University Press, 1998).

6. Ken DeBevoise, *Agents of Apocalypse: Epidemic Disease in the Colonial Philippines* (Princeton: Princeton University Press, 1995).

Bankoff—Conservation and Colonialism

1. T. H. Watkins, "Father of the Forests," *American Heritage* 42, no. 1 (1991): pp. 86–98.

2. XII Philippines, Pinchot Papers, Box 640, File: Philippines, John Lydenberg's Account of Gifford Pinchot, Library of Congress, Washington, D.C.

3. The United States acquired the Philippines from Spain for twenty million dollars by means of the Treaty of Paris in 1898.

4. Stephen Fox, "Gifford Pinchot and His Place in the American Conservation Movement," *Theodore Roosevelt Association Journal* (summer 1987): pp. 7–10.

5. George Ahern to Gifford Pinchot, Manila, February 18, 1902, Pinchot Papers, Box 640, File: Philippine Island Trip Letters 1, Library of Congress; Gifford Pinchot to William Taft, April 6, 1901, Pinchot Papers, Box 640, File: 1902, No. 3, Library of Congress; Gifford Pinchot, *Breaking New Ground* (Washington, D.C., and Covelo, Calif.: Island Press, [1947] 1998), p. 213.

6. An account of his journey across Eurasia is given in his autobiography (Pinchot, *Breaking New Ground*, pp. 213–22).

7. Jacob van Leur, *Indonesian Trade and Society* (The Hague: W. Van Hoeve, 1955), p. 261.

8. Lecture on Forests and Forest Work in the Philippines, March 16, 1903, Yale Forest School, Pinchot Papers, Box 640, File: 1902, No. 9, Library of Congress.

9. Gifford Pinchot to James Pinchot, November 6, 1902, Pinchot Papers, Box 640, File: 1902, Library of Congress.

10. On Pinchot's itinerary around the islands, see Pinchot, *Breaking New Ground*, pp. 223–34; and Richard Tucker, *Insatiable Appetite: The United States and the Ecological Degradation of the Tropical World* (Berkeley: University of California Press, 2000), pp. 368–70.

11. Lecture on Forests and Forest Work in the Philippines, Second Half, March 16, 1903, Yale Forest School, Pinchot Papers, Box 640. File: 1902, No. 10, Library of Congress; Greg Bankoff, "One Island Too Many: Reappraising the Extent of Deforestation in the Philippines Prior to 1946," *Journal of Historical Geography* 33, no. 2 (2007): pp. 314–34.

12. XII Philippines.

13. Philippine Islands, Pinchot Papers, Box 640, File: Philippine Islands, pp. 12, 16, 26, 65, Library of Congress.

14. Lecture on Forests and Forest Work in the Philippines, Second Half.

15. Philippine Islands, p. 101.

16. XII Philippines.

17. Lecture on Forests and Forest Work in the Philippines, Second Half.

18. David Arnold, "Tropical Medicine before Manson," in David Arnold, ed., *Warm Climates and Western Medicine: The Emergence of Tropical Medicine, 1500–1930* (Amsterdam and Atlanta: Rodopi, 1996), pp. 7–8, 10.

19. Lecture on Forests and Forest Work in the Philippines.

20. Lecture on Forests and Forest Work in the Philippines, Second Half; Lecture on Forests and Forest Work in the Philippines.

21. G. van Wickle, Division of Forest Management, Forest District of Camarines, 1904, Pinchot Papers, Box 587, File: Forestry, Philippine Islands, Reports, Library of Congress.

22. Philippine Islands, p. 22; Lecture on Forests and Forest Work in the Philippines; Lecture on Forests and Forest Work in the Philippines, Second Half.

23. Greg Bankoff, *Cultures of Disaster: Society and Natural Hazard in the Philippines* (London: Routledge Curzon, 2003).

24. Donald Pisani, "Forests and Conservation, 1865–1890," in Char Miller, ed., *American Forests: Nature, Culture, and Politics* (Lawrence: University of Kansas Press, 1997), p. 21.

25. XII Philippines.

26. Reynaldo Ileto, "Hunger in Southern Tagalog, 1897–1898," in *Filipinos and Their Revolution: Event, Discourse, and Historiography* (Quezon City: Ateneo de Manila University Press, 1998), pp. 113–15; Marshall McLennan, *The Central Luzon Plain: Land and Society on the Inland Frontier* (Quezon City: Alemar-Phoenix, 1980), p. 169; Greg Bankoff, "Bestia Incognita: The Horse and Its History in the Philippines, 1880–1930," *Anthrozoös* 17, no. 1 (2004): pp. 3–25.

27. XII Philippines.

28. Ibid.; quote from Lecture on Forests and Forest Work in the Philippines.

29. XII Philippines.

30. Philippine Islands, pp. 52–53; Lecture on Forests and Forest Work in the Philippines; William Maule, Division of Forest Management, Forest District of Bataan and Zambales, 1904, Pinchot Papers, Box 587, File: Forestry, Philippine Islands, Reports, Library of Congress.

31. Lecture on Forests and Forest Work in the Philippines, Second Half.

32. Philippine Islands, pp. 27, 127; Ralph Bryant, Division of Forest Management, "Report of the Division of Forest Management for the Year 1903–04," Pinchot Papers, Box 587, File: Forestry, Philippine Islands, Reports, Library of Congress; Maule, Division of Forest Management, Forest District of Bataan and Zambales.

33. Philippine Islands, pp. 52–53, 56–57.

34. XII Philippines.

35. George Ahern to Gifford Pinchot, Washington, September 20, 1901, Pinchot Papers, Box 586, File: Forestry, Philippine Islands, Correspondence; XII Philippines; Lawrence Rakestraw, "George Patrick Ahern and the Philippine Bureau of Forestry, 1900–1914," *Pacific Northwest Quarterly* 58, no. 3 (1967): pp. 142–50; Dennis Roth, "Philippine Forests and Forestry, 1565–1920," in Richard Tucker and John Richards, eds., *Global Deforestation and the Nineteenth-Century World Economy* (Durham: Duke University Press, 1983), pp. 41–46; Tucker, *Insatiable Appetite*, pp. 367–71.

36. *Report of the Forestry Bureau of the Philippine Islands for the Year Ended September 1, 1903* (Washington, D.C.: Bureau of Insular Affairs, War Department, 1903), pp. 320, 515–16.

37. XII Philippines.

38. Ibid.; Henry Graves, "Confidential Report on the Condition of the Philippine Forest Service, 1905," Henry Graves Papers, Box 36/404, Manuscripts and Archives, Yale University Library, New Haven.

39. Graves, "Confidential Report."

40. Ibid.

41. XII Philippines.

42. Michael Williams, *Americans and Their Forests: A Historical Geography* (Cambridge: Cambridge University Press, 1992); Char Miller, *Gifford Pinchot and the Making of Modern Environmentalism* (Washington, D.C., Covelo; London: Island Press and Shearwater Books, 2001).

43. David Brody, "Building Empire: Architecture and American Imperialism in the Philippines," *Journal of Asian American Studies* 4, no.2 (2001): p. 131.

44. Williams, *Americans and Their Forests*, pp. 416–21.

45. Rakestraw, "George Patrick Ahern and the Philippine Bureau of Forestry," p. 144.

46. Stephen Fox, *The American Conservation Movement: John Muir and His Legacy* (Madison: University of Wisconsin Press, 1985).

47. Barry Walsh, "Gifford Pinchot, Conservationist," *Theodore Roosevelt Association Journal* 13, no. 3 (1987): pp. 3–7; Pinchot, *Breaking New Ground*, pp. 322–23.

48. Pinchot, *Breaking New Ground*, pp. 504–10.

49. George Ahern to Gifford Pinchot, Manila, February 28, 1902, Pinchot Papers, Box 640, File: Philippine Island Trip Letters 1, Library of Congress; Graves, "Confidential Report"; XII Philippines.

50. Lecture on Forests and Forest Work in the Philippines, Second Half.

51. Graves, "Confidential Report."

52. *Report of the Forestry Bureau of the Philippine Islands*, 315; Graves, "Confidential Report."

53. Graves, "Confidential Report."

54. Lecture on Forests and Forest Work in the Philippines, Second Half.

55. Rakestraw, "George Patrick Ahern and the Philippine Bureau of Forestry," p. 149.

56. XII Philippines. This passage is crossed out in Pinchot's notes but nevertheless reflects his thoughts even if he did not wish to make them public.

57. Williams, *Americans and Their Forests*, pp. 418–21; James Lewis, *The Forest Service and the Greatest Good: A Centennial History* (Durham: Forest History Society, 2005), pp. 42–55.

Doeppers—Manila's Imperial Makeover

1. Veena Talwar Oldenberg, *The Making of Colonial Lucknow* (Delhi: Oxford University Press, 1989).

2. Thomas S. Hines, *Burnham of Chicago: Architect and Planner* (Chicago: University of Chicago Press, 1979).

3. Daniel Burnham, "A Plan for the City of Manila," in U.S. War Department, Bureau of Insular Affairs, Philippine Commission, *Report of the Philippine Commission* (*RPC*), 1905 (Washington, D.C.: Government Printing Office, 1906).

4. See "Who Owns San Pedro Abad," *Philippines Herald*, April 16, 1921.

5. Hines, *Burnham of Chicago*, quote on p. 211; A. N. Rebori, "The Work of William E. Parsons in the Philippine Islands," *Architectural Record* 41 (April 1917): pp. 305–24, and 41 (May 1917): pp. 423–34.

6. Glenn Anthony May, *Battle for Batangas: A Philippine Province at War* (New Haven: Yale University Press, 1991), p. 165.

7. Warwick Anderson, *Colonial Pathologies: American Tropical Medicine, Race, and Hygiene in the Philippines* (Durham: Duke University Press, 2006).

8. Daniel F. Doeppers, "Feeding Manila in Peace and War, 1850–1945," manuscript.

9. Alvin J. Cox, George W. Heise, and V. Q. Gana, "Water Supplies in the Philippine Islands," *Philippine Journal of Science (PJS)* 9A, no. 4 (1914): pp. 273–74; "La trichina," *El Comercio*, June 10, 1881.

10. Xavier Heutz de Lemps, "Una 'urgencia' de ciento cincuenta años: La construccion de la traida de aguas de Manila (1733–1882)," read in ms., subsequently published in Denis Bocquet and Samuel Fettah, eds., *Réseaux techniques, modernisation urbaine, et conflits de pouvoir (XVIIIe. XXe. siècle)* (Rome: École Française de Rome, 2004).

11. Victor Heiser, *An American Doctor's Odyssey* (New York: Norton, 1936), p. 121; "Nuestro Grabados," *El Comercio*, July 29, 1882; Frank Lewis Minton, "How the 'Tigbalang' Fought the Waterworks," *American Chamber of Commerce Journal* 9 (April 1929): pp. 9, 14–15; RPC, 1902 pt. 1, p. 99.

12. See O. F. Williams, "Health of Manila," in *Reports of the Consuls of the United States*, 1899, vol. 60, no. 225, p. 295; Frederick H. Sawyer, *The Inhabitants of the Philippines* (London: Sampson Low, Marston and Co., 1900), p. 184; "Annual Report of the Municipal Board," in RPC, 1905, pt. 1, p. 494; Heiser, *An American Doctor's Odyssey*, pp. 111–30; and "Report of the Commission of Public Health," in RPC, 1903, pt. 2, p. 94.

13. Joseph A. Guthrie, "Some Observations While in the Philippines," *Journal of the Association of Military Surgeons* 13 (1903): p. 148; Ken De Bevoise, *Agents of the Apocalypse: Epidemic Disease in the Colonial Philippines* (Princeton: Princeton University Press, 1995).

14. See Warwick Anderson's chapter "American Military Medicine Faces West" in his *Colonial Pathologies*.

15. See Ira Klein, "Urban Development and Death: Bombay City, 1870–1914," *Modern Asian Studies* 20, no. 4 (1986): pp. 725–54.

16. Leopoldo A. Faustino et al., *Manila Water Supplies* (Philippines: Bureau of Science, Popular Bulletin, No. 9, 1931), pp. 14–15.

17. James J. Halsema, *E. J. Halsema, Colonial Engineer: A Biography* (Quezon City: New Day, 1991), pp. 30–31, 49–50, 331, nn. 23–24; *Manila Times*, Investors and Settlers edition, February 1910, p. 36.

18. Report by Paul C. Freer, Superintendent of Government Laboratories, March 14, 1904, in "Annual Report of the Municipal Board, 1903–04," pp. 162–64.

19. RPC, 1913, quotes on pp. 111 and 122. See also Cox, Heise, and Gana, "Water Supplies," pp. 274–85, 342–44; George W. Heise, "Notes on the Water Supply of the City of Manila" *PJS* (1916): pp. 1–13; Heiser, *An American Doctor's Odyssey*, pp. 121–32; "Report of the City of Manila," in RPC, 1901–2, vol. 1, p. 88; "Report of the City of Manila," in RPC, 1912, pp. 34–35.

20. George W. Heise, "Water Supplies in the Philippine Islands II," *PJS* 10A, no. 2 (1915): 149; U.S. War Department, Bureau of Insular Affairs, *Report of the Governor General of the Philippine Islands* (RGGPI), 1925 (Washington, D.C.: Government Printing Office, 1926), pp. 14–15; "Water Lack Serious," *Manila Daily Bulletin*, May 17, 1926; "The Typhoid Outbreak," *Philippines Herald*, January 12, 1927; "City Water Getting Low," *Manila Daily Bulletin*, May 15, 1929; "Annual Report of the Metropolitan Water District," in ms. RGGPI, 1928, pp. 8–11, and 1932, table 1; "Novaliches Dam, World's Largest Earth Barrier," *Manila Daily Bulletin*, June 14, 1929; Faustino et al., *Manila Water Supplies*; P. I. de Jesus and J. M. Ramos, "Effect of Filtration on the Sanitary Quality of the Water of the Metropolitan Water District" *PJS* 59, no. 4 (1936): pp. 455–71.

21. Heiser, *An American Doctor's Odyssey*; Anderson, *Colonial Pathologies*.

22. Heiser, *An American Doctor's Odyssey*, p. 169, quote on p. 104.

23. Ibid., quote on pp. 112–13; Thomas W. Jackson, "Sanitary Conditions and Needs in Provincial Towns," *PJS* 3B, no. 5 (1908): pp. 432–33.

24. Tomas Confesor, "To Mayor Posadas," *Critic* 1, no. 2 (1934): quote on p. 7; "Vegetables and Fruits Prohibited," *Manila Times*, January 14, 1908; *RPC*, 1913, pp. 111–12; Maria Luisa Camagay, *Working Women of Manila in the 19th Century* (Quezon City: University of the Philippines Press, 1995), pp. 34–37; "Hordes of Big Green Flies," *Tribune*, June 29, 1930, 5; "Colorum Markets Imperil Health of City Residents," *The News (Behind the News)*, June 25, 1939, p. 3.

McCook—"'The World Was My Garden"

1. A. Hunter Dupree, *Science in the Federal Government: A History of Policies and Activities* (Baltimore: Johns Hopkins University Press, 1957), pp. 155–56, 161–69.

2. See, for example, O. F. Cook, *Shade in Coffee Culture*, USDA Bulletin 25 (Washington, D.C.: Department of Agriculture, 1901); and O. F. Cook and G. N. Collins, *Economic Plants of Puerto Rico*, Contributions of the U.S. National Herbarium, no. 8, pt. 2 (Washington, D.C., Smithsonian Institution, 1902).

3. E. D. Merrill, *The Flora of Manila* (Manila: Bureau of Science, 1912); "Merrill, Prof. Elmer Drew," in Jacques Cattell, ed., *American Men of Science*, 7th ed (Lancaster, Pa.: The Science Press, 1944).

4. See, for example, Paul Standley, *Flora of the Panama Canal Zone*, Contributions of the U.S. National Herbarium, no. 27 (Washington, D.C.: Smithsonian Institution, 1928).

5. "Fairchild, Dr. David Grandison," in *American Men of Science*; David Fairchild, *The World Was My Garden: Travels of a Plant Explorer* (New York: Charles Scribner's Sons, 1938).

6. Frederic Rosengarten Jr., *Wilson Popenoe: Agricultural Explorer, Educator, and Friend of Latin America* (Lawai, Hawai'i: National Tropical Botanical Garden, 1991).

7. Philip Pauly, *Biologists and the Promise of American Life: From Meriwether Lewis to Alfred Kinsey* (Princeton: Princeton University Press, 2002), p. 88.

8. "Scientific Notes and News," *Science* 56, no. 1445 (September 1922): p. 275.

9. "Scientific Notes and News," *Science* 58, no. 1511 (December 1923): p. 491.

10. See "Zetek, James," in *American Men of Science*.

11. Pamela M. Henson, "Invading Arcadia: Women Scientists in the Field in Latin America," *Americas* 58, no. 4 (2002): pp. 577–600.

12. Richard A. Overfield, "Science Follows the Flag: The Office of Experiment Stations and American Expansion," *Agricultural History* 64 (spring 1990): pp. 31–35.

13. Barrett's career is summarized in "Barrett, Dr. Otis Warren," in *American Men of Science*.

14. On the environmental impact of American expansion, see Richard P. Tucker, *Insatiable Appetite: The United States and the Ecological Degradation of the Tropical World* (Berkeley: University of California Press, 2000).

15. Stuart McCook, "Global Rust Belt: *Hemileia vastatrix* and the Ecological Integration of World Coffee Production since 1850," *Journal of Global History* 1, no. 2 (2006): pp. 177–95.

16. Erwin F. Smith, "A Cuban Banana Disease," *Science* 31, no. 802 (May 13, 1910): p. 755; R. E. B. McKenney, "The Central American Banana Blight," *Science* 31, no. 802 (May 13, 1910): pp. 751–52; John Soluri, *Banana Cultures: Agriculture, Consumption, and Environmental Change in Honduras and the United States* (Austin: University of Texas Press, 2006), pp. 53–57, 70–73.

17. "The Tropical Plant Research Foundation," *Science* 59, no. 1538 (June 1924): x; Hugh H. Bennett and Robert V. Allison, *The Soils of Cuba* (Washington, D.C.: Tropical Plant Research Foundation, 1928); Tom Gill, *Tropical Forests of the Caribbean* (Washington, D.C.: Tropical Plant Research Foundation, 1931). For more on the TPRF, see Stuart McCook, *States of Nature: Science, Agriculture, and Environment in the Spanish Caribbean, 1760–1940* (Austin: University of Texas Press, 2002), chap. 5, conclusion.

18. Report reprinted in Carlos Chardón, "Graduate School of Tropical Agriculture," pt. 2, *Porto Rico Progress*, January 5, 1928, p. 7.

19. See "Merrill, Elmer Drew"; "Standley, Paul Carpenter"; and "Fairchild, Dr. David Grandison," all in *American Men of Science*.

Warren—Scientific Superman

1. James Hennessey, SJ, "The Manila Observatory," *Philippine Studies* 8 (1960): pp. 99–129, 107; W. C. Repetti, SJ, *The Manila Observatory* (Ann Arbor: Edward Brothers, 1948), pp. 16–17, 21; Miguel Saderra Maso, SJ, *Historia del Observatorio de Manila Fundado y Dirigido por los Padres de la Mision de la Compania de Jesus de Filipinas, 1865–1915* (Manila: E. C. McCullough, 1915), pp. 132–44.

2. R. de C. W., review of Jose Algué, *The Cyclones of the Far East*, in *Bulletin of the American Geographical Society* 36, no. 11 (1904): pp. 705–7.

3. Philip M. Finegan, "Manila Observatory," in *Catholic Encyclopedia*, http://www.newadvent.org/cathen/09601a.htm, accessed April 11, 2007; José Algué, SJ, *The Cyclones of the Far East* (Manila: Bureau of Public Printing, 1904), pp. 144–60.

4. Maso, *Historia del Observatorio de Manila*, pp. 132–44; Repetti, *The Manila Observatory*, pp. 14–24; Hennessey, "The Manila Observatory," pp. 106–8.

5. Repetti, *The Manila Observatory*, pp. 23–25; Maso, *Historia del Observatorio de Manila*, pp. 139–41.

6. Maso, *Historia del Observatorio de Manila*, p. 123; Repetti, *The Manila Observatory*, pp. 11–12.

7. Repetti, *The Manila Observatory*, pp. 24–25, 35–36.

8. *Reports of the Philippine Commission, the Civil Governor, and the Heads of the Executive Department of the Civil Government of the Philippine Islands (1900–1903)* (Washington, D.C.: Government Printing Office, 1904), p. 603.

9. Charlotte Benson, *The Economic Impact of Natural Disasters in the Philippines*, Working Papers, no. 99 (London: Overseas Development Institute, 1997), pp. 50–63.

10. Shiv Visvanathan, "On the Annals of the Laboratory State," in Ashis Nandy, ed., *Science, Hegemony, and Violence: A Requiem for Modernity* (Delhi: Oxford University Press, 1990), pp. 257–88, 279.

11. Ashis Nandy, "Introduction: Science as a Reason of State," in Ashis Nandy, ed., *Science, Hegemony, and Violence: A Requiem for Modernity* (Delhi: Oxford University Press, 1990), pp. 1–23.

12. Vandana Shiva, "Reductionist Science as Epistemological Violence," in Ashis Nandy, ed., *Science, Hegemony, and Violence a Requiem for Modernity* (Delhi: Oxford University Press, 1990), pp. 232–56.

13. *Reports of the Philippine Commission*, p. 174.

14. Repetti, *The Manila Observatory*, pp. 32–34, 37–38; Maso, *Historia del Observatorio de Manila*, pp. 161–69.

15. *Fourth Annual Report of the Philippine Commission, 1903*, pt. 2 (Washington, D.C.: Government Printing Office, 1904), p. 57.

16. "Remembering St. Louis, 1904: A World on Display and a Bontoc Eulogy," review of two documentary films, *A World on Display*, written and directed by Eric Breitbart and Mary Nance, narrated by Leona Luba, and *Bontoc Eulogy*, produced, written, directed and narrated by Marlon Fuentes, reviewed by Jim Zwick for H-Amstdy (H-Net American Studies), March 2, 1996, http://www.lib.berkeley.edu/MRC/Bontoc.html, accessed May 26, 2008.

17. Lewis E. Gleek, *The American Half Century, 1898–1946* (Quezon City: New Day, 1998), pp. 83–84.

18. William P. Wilson, "Philippine Trade and Industry on View," *American Monthly Review of Reviews* 28 (December 1903), http://www.boondocksnet.com/expos/wfe_philtrade 0312.html, accessed October 19, 2003, site no longer available.

19. "Report of the Director of the Weather Bureau," July 15, 1906, in *Annual Report of the Philippine Commission, 1906* (Washington, D.C.: Government Printing Office, 1907), app. G.

20. *Philippine Islands' Exhibit Board of Lady Managers of the Louisiana Purchase Commission: Report to the Louisiana Purchase Exposition Commission, 1905*, http://www.boonsdocknet.com/expos/wfe_1904_rblm_philippine.html, accessed October 19, 2003, site no longer available.

21. Maso, *Historia del Observatorio de Manila*, pp. 161–69; Repetti, *The Manila Observatory*, p. 25; Hennessey, "The Manila Observatory," p. 109.

22. *Report of the Philippine Commission to the President*, vol. 4 (Washington, D.C.: Government Printing Office, 1901), pp. 191–227.

23. "Federation and Meteorology: The Case of Meteorology, 1876–1908," Australian Science and Technology Heritage Centre, University of Melbourne, August 2001, http://www.austehc.unimelb.edu.au/fam/0038.html, accessed July 17, 2002.

24. *Report of the Philippine Commission to the President*, vol. 4, p. 339.

25. "Report of the Director of the Weather Bureau," August 31, 1905, in *Report of the Philippine Commission to the Secretary of War, 1905*, vol. 2 (Washington, D.C.: Government Printing Office, 1906), p. 100.

26. "Report of the Weather Bureau," 1912, in *Annual Report of the Governor General of the Philippine Islands* (Washington, D.C.: Government Printing Office, 1913).

27. Frank G. Haughwout, "How Strong Was the Wind?" *Philippine Magazine* 5 (May 1938): pp. 225–29.

28. Repetti, *The Manila Observatory*, p. 25.

29. W. Cameron Forbes, *The Philippine Islands* (Cambridge: Harvard University Press, 1945), pp. 246–47.

30. *Report of the Philippine Commission, 1903*, pt. 2 (Washington, D.C.: Government Printing Office, 1904), p. 56.

31. "Report of the Weather Bureau," in *Report of the Philippine Commission to the Secretary of War, 1906* (Washington, D.C.: Government Printing Office, 1907).

32. *Cosmos*, no. 1091, pp. 717–19, cited in *Report of the Philippine Commission to the Secretary of War, 1906*, vols. 8–13, p. 189.

33. "Report of the Weather Bureau," in *Annual Report of the Governor General Philippine Islands, 1923* (Washington, D.C.: Government Printing Office, 1925), p. 210.

34. Ibid., p. 259.

35. "Report of the Director of the Weather Bureau," August 31, 1905.

36. Robert F. Luce, "Brief History of Hydrographic Survey Work in the Philippine Archipelago," in *Manila Harbour Board Annual Report, 1934* (Manila: Government of the Philippine Islands, 1934), pp. 9–33, p. 33.

37. "Climatology," in *Report of the Philippine Commission to the President*, vol. 4, p. 125.

38. Ibid.

39. Algué, *Cyclones of the Far East*, pp. 11–17.

40. Maso, *Historia del Observatorio de Manila*, pp. 144–51.

41. "Codex of Resolutions Adopted at the International Meteorological Meetings, 1872–1907," London, 1907, http://www.bom.gov.au/bmrc/clfor/cfstaff/nnn/nnn_climate_quotes.htm, accessed September 3, 2002.

42. Nandy, "Introduction: Science as a Reason of State," p. 14.

43. William Boyce, *The Philippine Islands* (New York: Rand McNally, 1914), p. 35.

SURI—THE LIMITS OF AMERICAN EMPIRE

1. See Walter LaFeber, *The American Search for Opportunity, 1865–1913* (Cambridge: Cambridge University Press, 1993); Robert L. Beisner, *Dean Acheson: A Life in the Cold War* (New York: Oxford University Press, 2006); and Jeremi Suri, *Henry Kissinger and the American Century* (Cambridge, Mass.: Belknap, 2007).

2. Despite his own tendency to label the United States an empire, Williams recognized the importance of anti-imperial ideas in American intentions and actions. See William Appleman Williams, *The Tragedy of American Diplomacy* (New York: Norton, 1972), pp. 59–89.

3. Suri, *Henry Kissinger and the American Century*, quotations on pp. 144 and 162.

4. See Alexis de Tocqueville, *Democracy in America*, 2 vols. (New York: Knopf, 1994), especially vol. 1, chaps. 13, 14, 17, and 18. *Democracy in America* was originally published in French in 1835–40.

5. Bernard Bailyn, *The Ideological Origins of the American Revolution* (Cambridge: Harvard University Press, 1967).

6. See Thomas J. McCormick, *The China Market: America's Quest for Informal Empire, 1893–1901* (Chicago: Quadrangle, 1967); and Walter LaFeber, *The New Empire: An Interpretation of American Expansion* (Ithaca: Cornell University Press, 1963).

7. See Michael H. Hunt, *The Making of a Special Relationship: The United States and China to 1914* (New York: Columbia University Press, 1983); and Warren I. Cohen, *America's Response to China*, 4th ed. (New York: Columbia University Press, 2000).

8. Li Hongzhang was the most powerful Chinese foreign policy maker in the late nineteenth century. See Hunt, *The Making of a Special Relationship*.

9. See Erez Manela, *The Wilsonian Moment: Self-Determination and the International Origins of Anticolonial Nationalism* (New York: Oxford University Press, 2007); Vera Schwarcz, *The Chinese Enlightenment: Intellectuals and the Legacy of the May Fourth Movement of 1919* (Berkeley: University of California Press, 1986); and Chow Tse-Tsung, *The May Fourth Movement: Intellectual Revolution in Modern China* (Cambridge: Harvard University Press, 1960).

10. See Mark Philip Bradley, *Imagining Vietnam and America: The Making of Postcolonial Vietnam, 1919–1950* (Chapel Hill: University of North Carolina Press, 2000).

11. Russell F. Weigley, *The American Way of War: A History of United States Military Strategy and Policy* (New York: Macmillan, 1978).

12. See Jeremi Suri, "American Attitudes toward Revolution," in Alexander DeConde, Richard Dean Burns, and Fredrik Logevall, eds., *Encyclopedia of American Foreign Policy* (New York: Charles Scribner's Sons, 2001), 425–42; and Frank Ninkovich, *Modernity and Power: A History of the Domino Theory in the Twentieth Century* (Chicago: University of Chicago Press, 1994).

13. See, Weigley, *The American Way of War*.

14. On the American reconstruction of Japan and western Germany, see John W. Dower, *Embracing Defeat: Japan in the Wake of World War II* (New York: Norton, 1999); Thomas Alan Schwartz, *America's Germany: John J. McCloy and the Federal Republic of Germany* (Cambridge: Harvard University Press, 1991); and John Lewis Gaddis, *We Now Know: Rethinking Cold War History* (Oxford: Clarendon, 1997).

15. On this point, see Tony Smith, *America's Mission: The United States and the Worldwide Struggle for Democracy in the Twentieth Century* (Princeton: Princeton University Press, 1994).

16. See Geir Lundestad, "Empire by Invitation? The United States and Western Europe, 1945–1952," *Journal of Peace Research* 23 (September 1986): pp. 263–77.

17. William Appleman Williams, *Empire as a Way of Life: An Essay on the Causes and Character of America's Present Predicament along with a Few Thoughts about an Alternative* (New York: Oxford University Press, 1980), pp. 12–13.

18. See Julian E. Zelizer, *Thunder from the Right: The Politics of National Security in America since World War II* (New Haven: Yale University Press, 2008); Michael J. Hogan, *A Cross of Iron: Harry S. Truman and the Origins of the National Security State, 1945–54* (New York: Cambridge University Press, 1998); and Aaron L. Friedberg, *In the Shadow of the Garrison State: America's Anti-statism and Its Cold War Grand Strategy* (Princeton: Princeton University Press, 2000).

19. See Weigley, *The American Way of War*, pp. 192–477; and Suri, *Henry Kissinger and the American Century*, pp. 52–137.

Tomes—Crucibles, Capillaries, and Pentimenti

1. Charles S. Maier, *Among Empires: American Ascendancy and Its Predecessors* (Cambridge: Harvard University Press, 2006), p. 8. Among the big books on empire, three that attracted particular attention are Michael Hardt and Antonio Negri, *Empire* (Cambridge: Harvard University Press, 2000); Niall Ferguson, *Colossus: The Price of America's Empire* (New York: Penguin, 2004); and Cullen Murphy, *Are We Rome? The Fall of an Empire and the Fate of America* (New York: Houghton Mifflin, 2007).

2. Frederick Cooper and Ann Laura Stoler, eds, *Tensions of Empire: Colonial Cultures in a Bourgeois World* (Berkeley: University of California Press, 2007.)

3. Amy Kaplan, "'Left Alone with America': The Absence of Empire in the Study of American Culture," in Amy Kaplan and Donald E. Pease, eds., *Cultures of United States Imperialism* (Durham: Duke University Press, 1993), pp. 3–21; James A. Field Jr., "American Imperialism: The Worst Chapter in Almost Any Book," *American Historical Review* 83, no. 3 (1978): pp. 644–68.

4. John Milton Cooper, "Not Much of an Empire," paper read at the conference "Transitions and Transformations in the U.S. Imperial State: The Search for a New Synthesis, " University of Wisconsin–Madison, November 9–11, 2006.

5. Dipesh Chakrabarty, *Provincializing Europe: Postcolonial Thought and Historical Difference* (Princeton: Princeton University Press, 2000), p. 9.

6. Phillipa Levine, *Prostitution, Race, and Politics: Policing Venereal Disease in the British Empire* (New York: Routledge, 2003), p. 4.

7. Patricia Seed, *American Pentimento: The Invention of Indians and the Pursuit of Riches* (Minneapolis; University of Minnesota Press, 2001).

8. Ferguson, *Colossus*, p. 2.

9. Victoria de Grazia, *Irresistible Empire: America's Advance through Twentieth-Century Europe* (Cambridge, Mass.: Belknap, 2005).

10. Craig Calhoun, Frederick Cooper, and Kevin W. Moore, *The Lessons of Empire: Imperial Histories and American Power* (New York: New Press, 2006), p. 1. Note that, unlike Cooper and Stoler's *Tensions of Empire*, published in 1997, this more recent book includes several essays on New World empires.

Tyrrell—Empire in American History

1. "Dewey's Homeward Trip," *New York Times*, September 27, 1899, p. 3.

2. Louis Stanley Young, *Life and Heroic Deeds of Admiral Dewey* (Philadelphia: World Bible House, 1899), p. 446; "The Sculptors of the Dewey Reception in New York," *Scribner's*, December 26, 1899, p. 766.

3. "Dewey on the Filipinos," *New York Times*, September 27, 1899, p. 4.

4. "Dewey for Expansion," *New York Times*, October 5, 1899, p. 6. The United States also annexed Hawai'i as a territory (1898) and in the Treaty of Berlin acquired the islands that became American Samoa (1899). Moreover, Cuba was an American protectorate from 1898 to 1902.

5. "Dewey's Triumphal Arch," *New York Times*, July 30, 1899, p. 1. See also *New York Times*, September 28, 1899, p. 1.

6. Marjorie P. Balge, "The Dewey Arch: Sculpture or Architecture?" *Archives of American Art Journal* 23, no. 4 (1983): pp. 2–6, quoted at p. 6. See also "Not through His Own Arch," *New York Times*, October 5, 1899, pp. 6, 8. On film representations see Amy Kaplan, "The Birth of an Empire," *Proceedings of the Modern Language Association* 114 (October 1999): pp. 1068–79.

7. Quoted in Balge, "The Dewey Arch," p. 6. See also "Dubious Outlook for 'Dewey Arch' Fund," *New York Times,* April 21, 1900, p. 1.

8. http://www.andrewcusack.com/blog/2005/01/the_dewey_arch.php (accessed February 15, 2008); George P. Hall, "Madison Square with Dewey Arch," reproduced in Kenneth T. Jackson, ed., *The Encyclopedia of New York City* (New Haven: Yale University Press, 1995).

9. George Dewey, *Autobiography of George Dewey: Admiral of the Navy* (New York: Charles Scribner's Sons, [1913] 1916), p. 289.

10. Balge, "The Dewey Arch," p. 6; "Dubious Outlook for 'Dewey Arch' Fund."

11. Oscar Campomanes, "Body Count: The War and Its Consequences," in Angel Velasco Shaw and Luis H. Francia, eds., *Vestiges of War: The Philippine-American War and the Aftermath of an Imperial Dream, 1899–1999* (New York: New York University Press, 2002), pp. 134–36; James W. Loewen, *Lies across America: What Our Historic Sites Get Wrong* (New York: New Press, 1999), pp. 136–38; http://www.arlingtoncemetery.net/ussmaine.htm (accessed February 15, 2008); *New York Times,* June 1, 1913, p. 20; "Philippine Study Group of Minnesota Corrects the Misleading Philippine American War Plaque at the Minnesota State Capitol," http://www.crcworks.org/celebration.html (accessed December 1, 2007). The group successfully lobbied that a correction be added to a commemorative plaque claiming that the United States had entered the Philippines to liberate the Filipino people; the critics pointed out that most of the battles listed on the plaque were fought against Filipinos.

12. Irvin Molotsky, "Design for World War II Memorial Awaits Review, with Detractors," *New York Times,* July 17, 2000.

13. Campomanes, "Body Count," pp. 134–36.

14. Loewen, *Lies across America,* pp. 136–38.

15. Peter S. Onuf, *Jefferson's Empire: The Language of American Nationhood* (Charlottesville: University of Virginia Press, 2000); Dumas Malone and Basil Rauch, *Empire for Liberty: The Genesis and Growth of the United States of America,* 2 vols. (New York: Appleton-Century-Crofts, 1960), p. viii.

16. Samuel Flagg Bemis, *A Diplomatic History of the United States* (New York: Henry Holt, 1936), p. 467.

17. Louis A. Pérez Jr., *The War of 1898: The United States and Cuba in History and Historiography* (Chapel Hill: University of North Carolina Press, 1998), pp. 116–17.

18. For Rumsfeld's "Americans don't do empire" quote, see Bernard Porter, *Empire and Superempire: Britain, America, and the World* (New Haven: Yale University Press, 2006), 1. This exact expression does not appear in a transcript published in Niall Ferguson, *Colossus: The Rise and Fall of the American Empire* (London: Penguin, 2005), p. 1. See also Rumsfeld quoted in the *Progressive,* "Empire Snaps Back," June 2003, where the report is: "We don't seek empire," he snapped. "We're not imperialistic. We never have been. I can't imagine why you'd even ask the question." http://findarticles.com/p/articles/mi_m1295/is_6_67/ai_102750158 (accessed June 1, 2008).

19. For a review of these arguments see David Abernethy, *The Dynamics of Global Dominance: European Overseas Empires, 1415–1980* (New Haven: Yale University Press, 2000), pp. 19–20; Porter, *Empire and Superempire;* Charles S. Maier, *Among Empires: American Ascendancy and Its Predecessors* (Cambridge: Harvard University Press, 2006); and Ian Tyrrell, *Transnational Nation: United States History in Global Perspective since 1789* (Basingstoke: Palgrave Macmillan, 2007), chap. 10.

20. According to Arrighi, these features are highly characteristic of the American imperial moment. See Giovanni Arrighi, "The Three Hegemonies of Historical Capitalism," *Review* 8 (summer 1990): pp. 365–408.

21. Joseph S. Nye, *Soft Power: The Means to Success in World Politics* (New York: Public Affairs, 2004). Chinese interest in soft power was evident in several papers delivered at the conference "The United States after September 11: Changes and Continuities," October

20–21, 2007, Foreign Language Teaching and Research Press International Convention Center, Beijing.

22. Ian Tyrrell, "Prohibition, American Cultural Expansion, and the New Hegemony in the 1920s: An Interpretation," *Histoire Sociale/Social History* 27 (November 1994): pp. 413–45. On the concept of hegemony, see James Joll, *Gramsci* (London: Fontana/Collins, 1977), pp. 108–9; Antonio Gramsci, "Americanism and Fordism," in Quentin Hoare and Geoffrey Nowell Smith, eds., *Selections from the Prison Notebooks* (New York: International Publishers, 1971), pp. 279–318, 350; and T. L. Jackson Lears, "The Concept of Cultural Hegemony: Problems and Possibilities," *American Historical Review* 90 (June 1985): pp. 567–93.

23. "An Episcopal Diocese in the Philippines," *New York Times*, March 28, 1901, p. 8.

24. Alfred T. Mahan, "The Place of Force in International Relations," *North American Review* 195 (January 1912): p. 38.

25. Victoria de Grazia, *Irresistible Empire: America's Advance through Twentieth-Century Europe* (Cambridge: Harvard University Press, 2005).

26. Geir Lundestad, "Empire by Invitation? The United States and Western Europe, 1945–1952," *Journal of Peace Research* 23 (September 1986): pp. 263–77.

27. Michael Hardt and Antonio Negri, *Empire* (Cambridge: Harvard University Press, 2000).

28. Frederick Jackson Turner, "The Middle West," *International Monthly* 4 (December 1901): p. 794.

29. John Mack Faragher, ed., *Rereading Frederick Jackson Turner: "The Significance of the Frontier in American History" and Other Essays* (New York: Henry Holt, 1994), p. 9.

30. Albert Bushnell Hart, "The Next War," *New York Times Sunday Magazine*, February 8, 1920; Gary Marotta, "The Academic Mind and the Rise of U.S. Imperialism: Historians and Economists as Publicists for Ideas of Colonial Expansion," *American Journal of Economics and Sociology* 42 (April 1983): pp. 217–34; Albert Bushnell Hart and Cyrus F. Wicker, "The Caribbean Question: Discussion," *Proceedings of the Academy of Political Science in the City of New York* 7 (July 1917): pp. 231–40; Walter L. Williams, "United States Indian Policy and the Debate over Philippine Annexation: Implications for the Origins of American Imperialism," *Journal of American History* 66 (March 1980): pp. 810–31; Frederick Jackson Turner, "The Problem of the West," *Atlantic Monthly* 78 (September 1896): pp. 289–97.

31. Albert Bushnell Hart, "The Need for a Concord of Nations," *Annals of the American Academy of Political and Social Science* 96 (July 1921): pp. 161–65.

32. Leland H. Jenks, *Our Cuban Colony: A Study in Sugar* (New York: Vanguard, 1928).

33. Melvin M. Knight, *The Americans in Santo Domingo* (New York: Vanguard, 1928); J. Fred Rippy, *The Capitalists and Colombia* (New York: Vanguard, 1931). Other works include Margaret Marsh, *The Bankers in Bolivia: A Study in American Foreign Investment* (New York: Vanguard, 1928); Scott Nearing and Joseph Freeman, *Dollar Diplomacy* (London: George Allen and Unwin, 1926); Charles David Kepner Jr., *The Banana Empire: A Case Study of Economic Imperialism* (New York: Vanguard, 1935); and Bailey W. Diffie and Justine W. Diffie, *Porto Rico: A Broken Pledge* (New York: Vanguard, 1931). On Rippy see David Bushnell and John H. Coatsworth, "J. Fred Rippy (1892–1977)," *Hispanic American Historical Review* 68 (February 1988): pp. 103–4. On Knight see W. W. Borah, M. M. Davisson, and C. A. Mosk, "Melvin Moses Knight, Economics: Berkeley, 1887–1981, Professor Emeritus," http://content.cdlib.org/xtf/view?docId=hb967nb5k3&doc.view=content&chunk.id=div00029&toc.depth=1&brand=oac&anchor.id=0 (accessed February 14, 2008). On these studies and the Garland Fund that sponsored them see Emily S. Rosenberg, *Financial Missionaries to the World: The Politics and Culture of Dollar Diplomacy, 1900–1930* (Cambridge: Harvard University Press, 2003), pp. 144–46; and David M. Pletcher, "Caribbean 'Empire,' Planned and Improvised," *Diplomatic History* 14 (July 1990): pp. 447–48.

34. Mark Moberg, review of John Soluri, *Banana Cultures: Agriculture, Consumption, and*

Environmental Change in Honduras and the United States, American Historical Review 111 (October 2006): p. 1145.

35. Parker Thomas Moon, *Imperialism and World Politics* (New York: Macmillan, 1926), pp. 3–4, 456; Arthur Goddard, ed., *Harry Elmer Barnes, Learned Crusader: The New History in Action* (New York: Ralph Myles, 1968).

36. Earl A. Molander, "Historical Antecedents of Military-Industrial Criticism," *Military Affairs* 40 (April 1976): pp. 59–63; Charles Beard, *The Devil Theory of War: An Inquiry into the Nature of History and the Possibility of Keeping Out of War* (New York: Vanguard, 1936), pp. 28–29; H. W. Brands, *What America Owes the World: The Struggle for the Soul of Foreign Policy* (New York: Cambridge University Press, 1998), p. 121.

37. Ian Tyrrell, *Historians in Public: The Practice of American History, 1890–1970* (Chicago: University of Chicago Press, 2005), pp. 127–28; Mark T. Berger, "Civilising the South: The U.S. Rise to Hegemony in the Americas and the Roots of 'Latin American Studies,' 1898–1945," *Bulletin of Latin American Research* 12 (January 1993): p. 18; Van Gosse, *Where the Boys Are: Cuba, Cold War America, and the Making of a New Left* (London: Verso, 1993), pp. 13, 15–16; *New York Times*, April 13, 1937, p. 28.

38. See especially Dana G. Munro, *The United States and the Caribbean Area* (Boston: World Peace Foundation, 1934). For a survey of this and similar works see Pletcher, "Caribbean Empire," pp. 449–50.

39. William Appleman Williams, *The Tragedy of American Diplomacy*, rev. ed. (New York: Delta, [1959] 1961); William Appleman Williams, *Empire as a Way of Life* (New York: Oxford University Press, 1980); Andrew J. Bacevich, *American Empire: The Realities and Consequences of U.S. Diplomacy* (Cambridge: Harvard University Press, 2002), pp. 23–31. Other works associated with the Williams school included Thomas J. McCormick, *China Market: America's Quest for Informal Empire, 1893–1901* (Chicago: Quadrangle, 1967); and Walter LaFeber, *The New Empire: An Interpretation of American Expansion, 1860–1898* (Ithaca: Cornell University Press, 1963).

40. N. Gordon Levin Jr., "The Open Door Thesis Reconsidered," *Reviews in American History* 2 (December 1974): pp. 598–605; William H. Becker, "American Manufacturers and Foreign Markets, 1870–1900: Business Historians and the 'New Economic Determinists,'" *Business History Review* 47 (winter 1973): pp. 466–81; Mary Speck, "Closed-Door Imperialism: The Politics of Cuban-U.S. Trade, 1902–1933," *Hispanic American Historical Review* 85, no. 3 (2005): pp. 449–84; editorial comments by Barton Bernstein in Barton Bernstein and Allen J. Matusow, eds., *Twentieth-Century America: Recent Interpretations* (New York: Harcourt, Brace and World, 1969), p. 204.

41. Ronald Robinson and John Gallagher, "The Imperialism of Free Trade," *Economic History Review* 6, no. 1 (1953): pp. 1–15; Ronald Robinson and John Gallagher with Alice Denny, *Africa and the Victorians: The Official Mind of Imperialism* (London: Macmillan, 1961); D. C. M. Platt, *Latin America and British Trade, 1806–1914* (London: Adam and Charles Black, 1972).

42. Ernest May, *Imperial Democracy* (London: Macmillan, 1984), p. 259.

43. Paul M. Buhle and Edward Rice-Maximin, *William Appleman Williams: The Tragedy of Empire* (New York: Routledge, 1995), pp. xii, 158.

44. Studies critical of the Williams school dealt mostly with interpretations of the cold war phase of American foreign policy. See Robert James Maddox, *The New Left and the Origins of the Cold War* (Princeton: Princeton University Press, 1973); and Joseph Siracusa, *New Left Diplomatic Histories and Historians: The American Revisionists* (Port Washington, N.Y.: Kennikat, 1973). On Williams's *Contours of American History* see Oscar Handlin, *Truth in History* (Cambridge: Harvard University Press, 1979), p. 146. On the absences in Williams's work see Amy Kaplan, "'Left Alone with America': The Absence of Empire in the Study of American Culture," in Amy Kaplan and Donald E. Pease, eds., *Cultures of United States Imperialism*

(Durham: Duke University Press, 1993), pp. 13–14. For a recent assessment see Bacevich, *American Empire*, chap. 1.

45. Bacevich, *American Empire*, pp. 32–35; Buhle and Rice-Maximin, *William Appleman Williams*, pp. xii, 242.

46. Bacevich, *American Empire*, pp. 32–35.

47. But see the early William Herman Haas, ed., *The American Empire: A Study of the Outlying Territories of the United States* (Chicago: University of Chicago Press, 1940). Recent work includes Julian Go, "The Provinciality of American Empire: 'Liberal Exceptionalism' and U.S. Colonial Rule," *Comparative Studies in Society and History* 49, no. 1 (2007): pp. 74–108; Julian Go, "Chains of Empire, Projects of State: Colonial State-Building in Puerto Rico and the Philippines," *Comparative Studies in Society and History* 42, no. 2 (2000); and the essays in Julian Go and Anne Foster, eds., *The American Colonial State in the Philippines: Global Perspectives* (Durham: Duke University Press, 2003). Other relevant works include Laura Briggs, *Reproducing Empire: Race, Sex, Science, and U.S. Imperialism in Puerto Rico* (Berkeley: University of California Press, 2002); Eileen J. Suárez Findlay, *Imposing Decency: The Politics of Sexuality and Race in Puerto Rico, 1870–1920* (Durham: Duke University Press, 1999); Mary A. Renda, *Taking Haiti: Military Occupation and the Culture of U.S. Imperialism, 1915–1940* (Chapel Hill: University of North Carolina Press, 2001); and Paul A. Kramer, *The Blood of Government: Race, Empire, the United States, and the Philippines* (Chapel Hill: University of North Carolina Press, 2006).

48. D. K. Fieldhouse, *Economics and Empire, 1830–1914* (London: Macmillan, 1984).

49. Emily Eakin, "What Is the Next Big Idea? Buzz Is Growing for 'Empire,'" *New York Times*, July 7, 2001; Hardt and Negri, *Empire*.

50. Michael Parker, *The Kingdom of Character: The Student Volunteer Movement for Foreign Missions* (Lanham, Md.: American Society of Missiology and University Press of America, 1998), unpaginated introduction [p. 1]; Stephen L. Baldwin, *Foreign Missions of the Protestant Churches* (New York: Eaton and Mains, 1900), pp. 258–60. The latter gives figures taken from the 1898–99 official returns of the mission boards and reflects missionary numbers in 1898 when the returns were being gathered.

51. Ryan Dunch, "Beyond Cultural Imperialism: Cultural Theory, Christian Missions, and Global Modernity," *History and Theory* 41 (October 2002): pp. 301–25.

52. Paul Varg, "Motives in Protestant Missions, 1890–1917," *Church History* 23 (March 1954): p. 68.

53. Emily S. Rosenberg, *Spreading the American Dream: American Economic and Cultural Expansion, 1890–1945* (New York: Hill and Wang, 1982), p. 29; Parker, *Kingdom of Character*, p. 3.

54. Parker, *Kingdom of Character*, unpaginated introduction.

55. Arthur Tappan Pierson, *The Crisis of Missions; or, The Voice Out of the Cloud* (New York: Robert Carter and Brothers, 1886), pp. 64–65.

56. Bradley J. Longfield, *The Presbyterian Controversy: Fundamentalists, Modernists, and Moderates* (New York: Oxford University Press, 1991), p. 18.

57. John Mott, *The American Student Missionary Uprising; or, The History and Organization of the Student Volunteer Movement for Foreign Missions* (n.p., 1892), p. 11; John Pollock, "Studd, Charles Thomas (1860–1931)," in *Oxford Dictionary of National Biography* (Oxford: Oxford University Press, 2004).

58. This is not to endorse the idea of a psychic crisis of internal American origins as Richard Hofstadter does in "Cuba, the Philippines, and Manifest Destiny," in *The Paranoid Style in American Politics and Other Essays* (New York: Knopf, 1965), pp. 145–87.

59. *Washington Post*, December 14, 1898; Ian Tyrrell, "The Regulation of Alcohol and Other Drugs in a Colonial Context: United States Policy towards the Philippines, c. 1898–1910," paper presented at "Global Approaches: The Fourth International Conference on

the History of Drugs and Alcohol," August 10–12, 2007, University of Guelph, Guelph, Ontario.

60. Anne L. Foster, "Prohibition as Superiority: Policing Opium in South-East Asia, 1898–1925," *International History Review* 22, no. 2 (2000): pp. 253–73; Arnold H. Taylor, "American Confrontation with Opium Traffic in the Philippines," *Pacific Historical Review* 36 (August 1967): pp. 307–24, at p. 323; David F. Musto, *The American Disease: Origins of Narcotic Control*, 3d ed. (New York: Oxford University Press, 1999), p. 30.

61. For Taft see William Howard Taft, *The World-Wide Influence of the Y.M.C.A. Address by Hon. William Howard Taft Delivered at the Bedford Branch of the Young Men's Christian Association in Brooklyn, N.Y., on Sunday, December 21, 1913* (Brooklyn: YMCA, 1913), p. 23. For Root see *New York Times*, November 12, 1909, p. 4. For Mahan see Alfred Thayer Mahan, *The Harvest Within: Thoughts on the Life of the Christian* (Boston: Little Brown, 1909), pp. 118–24; and Greg Russell, "Alfred Thayer Mahan and American Geopolitics: The Conservatism and Realism of an Imperialist," *Geopolitics* 11 (spring 2006): pp. 119–40. For Roosevelt see Robert Bolt, "Theodore Roosevelt: Dutch Reformed Stalwart in the White House," *Theodore Roosevelt Association Journal* 17, no. 1 (1991): pp. 12–14; and Edward H. Cotton, *The Ideals of Theodore Roosevelt* (New York: D. Appleton, 1923), pp. 39–60, 137–76. For Wilson see *New York Times*, November 20, 1905, p. 5; and Wilson to John R. Mott, November 1, 1905, and Mott to Wilson, November 20, 1905, fl. 1760, box 100, John R. Mott Papers, Yale Divinity School Library.

62. See the extensive files in the Philippines' YMCA Administrative Reports, 1910–1912, for example, J. M. Groves, Report, August 18, 1910, box 5, Philippines, Administrative Reports, Krautz Family YMCA Archives, University of Minnesota; and memo, D. W. Egner (formerly private secretary to Philippine Islands director of health), May 25, 1908, fl. 2039–30, box 246, RG 350, Bureau of Insular Affairs Records, National Archives, College Park, Maryland. On Brent there is no adequate study to match the excellent Charles Henry Brent Papers, Manuscript Room, Library of Congress.

63. Homer C. Stuntz, *The Philippines and the Far East* (Cincinnati: Jennings and Pye; New York: Eaton and Mains, 1904), chap. 10; Kenton J. Clymer, "Religion and American Imperialism: Methodist Missionaries in the Philippine Islands, 1899–1913," *Pacific Historical Review* 49 (February 1980): pp. 29–50.

64. Obituary for Homer Stuntz, *New York Times*, June 4, 1924, p. 21; Clymer, "Religion and American Imperialism," pp. 29–50.

65. *New York Times*, August 6, 1906, p. 7.

66. Stuntz, *The Philippines and the Far East*, p. 508.

67. *New York Times*, August 6, 1906, p. 7. This globalism was a consistent message of the plethora of missionary expositions of all American Protestant denominations. "The World in Boston" Missionary Exposition of 1911 included pageants and other representations of the American missionary enterprise and its diverse targets. Later pageants moved to cities such as Providence (Rhode Island), Chicago, Baltimore, New York, and Cincinnati. See Julia C. Emery, *Century of Endeavor, 1821–1921: A Record of the First Hundred Years of the Domestic and Foreign Missionary Society of the Protestant Episcopal Church in the United States of America* (New York: Department of Missions, 1921), pp. 275–76; "Ten Thousand People to Portray Missionary Life," *New York Times Sunday Magazine*, January 22, 1911, 14; and Patricia R. Hill, *The World Their Household: The American Woman's Foreign Mission Movement and Cultural Transformation, 1870–1920* (Ann Arbor: University of Michigan Press, 1985), p. 161.

CONTRIBUTORS

PATRICIO N. ABINALES is professor at the Center for Southeast Asian Studies, Kyoto University, and co-author of *State and Society in the Philippines* (Rowman and Littlefield, 2005).

WARWICK ANDERSON is the University Research Professor at the University of Sydney and author of *Colonial Pathologies* (Duke, 2006).

GREG BANKOFF is professor of modern history at the University of Hull and author of *Cultures of Disaster* (Curzon, 2003).

AMÍLCAR ANTONIO BARRETO is associate professor of political science at Northeastern University and author of *Vieques, the Navy, and Puerto Rican Politics* (Florida, 2002).

CHRISTINA DUFFY BURNETT is associate professor of law at Columbia University and co-editor of *Foreign in a Domestic Sense* (Duke, 2001).

REBECA CAMPO is a doctoral student in the Psychology Department, Faculty of Social Sciences, University of Puerto Rico.

CHRISTOPHER CAPOZZOLA is associate professor of history at the Massachusetts Institute of Technology and author of *Uncle Sam Wants You: World War I and the Making of the Modern American Citizen* (Oxford, 2008).

MATTHEW CASEY is a graduate student in history at the University of Pittsburgh.

ANNA LEAH FIDELIS T. CASTAÑEDA is a student in the SJD program at Harvard University and author of "The Origins of Philippine Judicial Review," *Ateneo Law Journal* (2001).

CLARE CORBOULD is a lecturer in history at the University of Sydney and author of *Becoming African Americans, 1919–1939* (Harvard, forthcoming).

ALEJANDRO DE LA FUENTE is associate professor of history at the University of Pittsburgh and author of *A Nation for All* (North Carolina, 2001).

SOLSIRÉE DEL MORAL is assistant professor of history at Pennsylvania State University.

DANIEL F. DOEPPERS is professor emeritus of geography at the University of Wisconsin–Madison and co-editor of *Population and History* (Ateneo de Manila, 1998).

MARIOLA ESPINOSA is assistant professor of history at Southern Illinois University and author of *Epidemic Invasions* (Chicago, forthcoming).

ANNE L. FOSTER is assistant professor of U.S. diplomatic history at Indiana State University and author of *Projections of Power: The U.S. in Colonial Southeast Asia, 1919–1941* (Duke, forthcoming).

JOSEP M. FRADERA is *catedrático* of history at Pompeu Fabra University of Barcelona and author of *Colonias para después de un imperio* (Ediciones Bellaterra, 2005).

HUMBERTO GARCÍA-MUÑIZ is *investigador* at the Institute of Caribbean Studies, University of Puerto Rico (Río Piedras), and co-author of *La ayuda militar como negocio: Estados Unidos y el Caribe* (Ediciones Callejón, 2002).

JOSHUA GEDACHT is a graduate student in history at the University of Wisconsin–Madison.

RONA TAMIKO HALUALANI is associate professor of communications at San Jose State University and author of *In the Name of Hawaiians* (Minnesota, 2002).

KRISTIN HOGANSON is professor of history at the University of Illinois, Urbana-Champaign, and author of *Fighting for American Manhood* (Yale, 1998).

PAUL D. HUTCHCROFT is professor of political and social change at the Australian National University and author of *Booty Capitalism* (Cornell, 1998).

COURTNEY JOHNSON is assistant professor of Spanish and Portuguese at the University of Wisconsin–Madison and author of *Vernacular Empire: The Paradox of Hispanism in the Age of Imperialism* (forthcoming).

Contributors

PAUL A. KRAMER is associate professor of history at the University of Iowa and author of *The Blood of Government* (North Carolina, 2006).

BRIAN MCALLISTER LINN is professor of history at Texas A&M University and author of *The Philippine War, 1899–1902* (Kansas, 2002).

JANA K. LIPMAN is assistant professor of history at Tulane University and author of *Guantánamo: A Working-Class History between Empire and Revolution* (California, 2008).

OWEN J. LYNCH is an international environmental lawyer and co-author of *Whose Resources? Whose Common Good?* (Center for International Environmental Law, 2004).

GLENN ANTHONY MAY is professor of history at the University of Oregon and author of *Inventing a Hero* (Wisconsin, 1996).

STUART MCCOOK is associate professor of history at the University of Guelph, Canada, and author of *States of Nature* (Texas, 2002).

THOMAS MCCORMICK is professor emeritus of history at University of Wisconsin–Madison and author of *America's Half-Century* (Johns Hopkins, 1989).

ALFRED W. MCCOY is the J. R. W. Smail Professor of History at the University of Wisconsin–Madison and author of *A Question of Torture* (Henry Holt, 2006).

J. R. MCNEILL is professor of history at Georgetown University and author of *Something New Under the Sun* (W. W. Norton, 2000).

PABLO NAVARRO-RIVERA is associate professor of history and social sciences at Lesley University and author of *Universidad de Puerto Rico* (Ediciones Huracán, 2000).

ADAM NELSON is associate professor of educational policy studies and history at the University of Wisconsin–Madison and author of *The Elusive Ideal* (Chicago, 2005).

JOHN OHNESORGE is associate professor of law at the University of Wisconsin–Madison and author of "The Rule of Law" in the *Annual Review of Law and Social Science* (2007).

VICENTE L. RAFAEL is professor of history at the University of Washington–Seattle and author of *The Promise of the Foreign* (Duke, 2005).

Contributors

NATALIE J. RING is assistant professor of history at the University of Texas at Dallas and author of *The Paradox of the New South: The Problem with Region and Race* (Georgia, forthcoming).

JORGE RODRÍGUEZ BERUFF is *catedrático* in the Social Science Department of the University of Puerto Rico and author of *Política militar y dominación* (Ediciones Huracan, 1988).

MICHAEL SALMAN is associate professor of history at the University of California–Los Angeles and author of *The Embarrassment of Slavery* (California, 2001).

KELVIN SANTIAGO-VALLES is associate professor of sociology, Latin American and Caribbean studies, and Africana studies at Binghamton University, and author of *"Subject People" and Colonial Discourses* (State University of New York, 1994).

FRANCISCO A. SCARANO is professor of history at the University of Wisconsin–Madison and author of *Puerto Rico: Cinco siglos de historia*, 3rd ed. (McGraw-Hill Interamericana, 2008).

CHRISTOPHER SCHMIDT-NOWARA is Magis Professor of History at Fordham University and author of *The Conquest of History* (Pittsburgh, 2006).

GABRIELA SOTO LAVEAGA is assistant professor of history at the University of California, Santa Barbara, and author of *Jungle Laboratories: Mexicans, Identity, and the Global Quest for Hormones* (Duke, forthcoming).

JEREMI SURI is professor of history at the University of Wisconsin–Madison and author of *Henry Kissinger and the American Century* (Harvard, 2007).

PAUL S. SUTTER is associate professor of history at the University of Georgia–Athens and author of *Driven Wild* (Washington, 2002).

NANCY TOMES is professor and chair of history at the State University of New York–Stony Brook and author of *The Gospel of Germs* (Harvard, 1998).

IAN TYRRELL is Scientia Professor of History at the University of New South Wales and author of *Transnational Nation: The United States in Global Perspective since 1789* (Palgrave Macmillan, 2007).

JAMES FRANCIS WARREN is professor of Asian studies at Murdoch University in Australia and author of *Iranun and Balangingi* (Singapore University, 2001).

INDEX

Note: Italicized page numbers indicate illustrations and maps.

A. H. Clarke Company (Cleveland), 266
Abb, Madelfia A., 470
Abbas, Ackbar, 263–64, 270
Abernethy, David, 475
Abinales, Patricio N.: chapter, 410–20; mentioned, 394
academic disciplines, 133–34. *See also* anthropology; political science; social sciences; universities
Acheson, Dean, 523, 526
Adams, John Quincy, 64
advertisements: imported lingerie, *253*; Panama cruises, *317, 319*–20
Afghanistan: legal system of, 330; Soviet invasion of, 469; U.S. invasion and occupation of, 6, 79, 430, 532
Africa: British interests in, 44; crises in 1970s, 469; imperial partition of, 48; malaria work in, 323; state formation in, 615n41; as tropical, 298. *See also specific countries*
African-Americans: on annexations, 277; citizenship of, 198, 336, 338; on Cuban suffrage, 224; education of, 166; Filipinos compared with, 265; as pathogenic, 282–83; in Philippines, 199–200; racial discrimination against, 50–52, 89, 395, 441, 444–48. *See also* race in U.S.; racism and racial discrimination
Afro-Cubans: eliminating barriers for, 222–23; suffrage controversy and, 226–29; U.S. attitudes toward, 223–24. *See also* race in Cuba

agricultural products: bananas, 505; coffee, 40, 93, 505; corn, 132–33, 157–59; cotton, 40; hemp, 414; rice, 158; sandalwood, 242; timber, 479–88; tobacco, 42–43, 93; U.S. imports of, 251–52, 254–55, 256–58; vegetables (fresh), 496–98; wild yams, 275–76, 309–16. *See also* sugar industry
agriculture: diseases and pests of, 483, 505; imperial labor organization in, 40–41; industrial education programs for, 132–33, 157–59; invasive species concerns in, 502; management challenges in, 477, 499–507; migrant labor needed in, 208, 209; migration of farmers from, 132; progressives' encouragement of, 414; research programs in, 477, 499–507; sanitation concerns in, 496–98; slave-based labor in, 37–38; Spanish surveys of, 214. *See also* environmental management; plantations; tropical botany; tropical forestry
Aguinaldo, Emilio: advisor of, 345; army of, 461–62; capture of, 467; independence declared by, 202–3, *204*; penal colony tour of, 120
Ahern, George: forest management ideas of, 476, 479–80, 484, 486; as insular bureau chief, 487; Philippine tour of, 482–83
airplanes and aeroscience: airfield construction for, 441, 445, 448, 449–50, 455; in WWII, *435*

649

Alaska: annexation of, 360; appointed governor for, 438; organic law for, 54; Puerto Rican autonomy as model for, 149; treaty for, 337; U.S. purchase of, 49, 67
Albizu Campos, Pedro, 148
alcohol prohibition, 96. *See also* drug prohibition, U.S.
Alegría, Ricardo, 236
Alfonso XII (king of Spain), 90, 231
Algeria: dual regimes in, 61; scientific expeditions in, 476; as tropical, 298
Algué, José: Dewey's meeting with, 508; master plan of, 509, 512–14; meteorological work of, 477–78, 516–19; Spanish-to-U.S. transition under, 509–10; world's fair meteorological display by, 511–12
Alien Act (British, 1905), 198
Allee, Warder, 502
Allen, Henry T., 465
Allison, Robert, 506
Alvarez, Agustín, 459
Alvarez, Santiago, 350, 351–52
American: use of term, 173
American Civil War (1861–65): African-American citizenship after, 198; British relations after, 68; British view of, 66; commemoration of, 299, 541; economic aftermath of, 67; expansion and slavery issues in, 51–52; failure of Reconstruction after, 223, 224, 226, 382; Jeffersonian ideals and, 380–81
American Economic Association, 57–58
American Economic Review, 58
American Expeditionary Forces (AEF), 467
American imperial state: as aberration, 63–64; approaches to, 12–14, 33, 532–33; cartoons about, xvi–xvii, 36, 225; characteristics of, 7, 545–47; consensus created on, 188–90; continental component of, 39–40, 49–50, 64–66, 145, 274, 320–21, 398–401, 546; cultural hegemony of, 545–46, 551–54, 555; economic component of, 248–50; formal means of control, 72–73; formation process for, 13–14; health dimension of, 273–76; historiography of, 546–56; ignorance about, 544–45; informal means of control, 74–79;lacunae in discourse on, 530–31, 550; limits of, 523–31; map of, 22–23; as obfuscating label, 523–26; overseas component of, 66–73, 163–64; paradox of, 3–4; role of academic social science in, 178–79; selective memory of, 541–44, 554–56; soft power imperialism of, 175–78; structure of, 24–26, 177–78; transition to, 11–12, 88. *See also* commemorations; education; environmental management; globalization; Guam; Hawai'i; identity; imperial transitions; insular cases; Jeffersonianism; legal systems; military, U.S.; national security, U.S.; Panama Canal Zone; Philippines; policing; prisons and penal forms; public health; Puerto Rico; race; Wake Island
Americanization: centrality of, 22–23, 164–65; countermovements against, 131–32, 135–44, 145–50; definitions of, 140–41, 173; education as vehicle of, 22–23, 132, 146, 165–66, 172–74, 398–400; Islamic fundamentalism as response to, 527–28; progressivism linked to, 23–24; religion as vehicle of, 96, 132, 146, 399–400
American Journal of Tropical Medicine, 303
American Petroleum Producers in Mexico (APPM), 76
American Political Science Association (APSA), 134, 179, 181–83
American Revolution: global context of, 39; minuteman symbol of, 421, 422; as model for Philippines, 345–46; political development prior to, 379–80; as war for empire, 64
American Samoa: acquisition of, 639n4
American Sugar Refining Company, 354, 363
AMPR (Asociación de Maestros de Puerto Rico), 139, 578n11
Anderson, Benedict, 210, 262–63, 384
Anderson, Warwick: chapter, 277–87; mentioned, 273, 275, 493, 536, 537
Angelides, Phil, 430
Anglo-British empiricism, 35
Anglo-Saxonism: attitudes toward policing in, 212; racial formations underlying, 204, 234–37, 399–400; white poor people distinguished from, 299–300, 304–5, 306–8
Angola: marginalization of, 543
animism, 206
annexation: citizenship issues and, 332–33, 334–35, 606n2; Cuban suffrage in context

of, 227–28; DuBois on, 277, 287; expansionism via, 52, 65, 360–61. *See also* insular cases; *specific countries and states*
Año Terrible del '87 (terror campaign, 1887), 91–92
anthropology, 169, 230–31
Antigua: U.S. base in, 445
anti-imperialism: arguments of, 70, 72; constraints of, 524–25, 544–45, 638n2; definition of, 26; electoral politics and, 356–57; historiography of, 548–49; insular cases and, 363–64; mythology of, 63–64; organization for, 401; reports of atrocities and, 382
Antilles: French-U.S. agreement on, 446, 448; Spanish policy in, 47; in U.S. defense strategy, 434–35, 445, 446
anti-opium movement: assumptions about Chinese in, 97–98; criminalization of users in, 98–99; international efforts in, 95–96, 101–2, 103–4, 573n17; legacy of, 105; missionaries in, 85, 96–97, 99, 101
APPM (American Petroleum Producers in Mexico), 76
APSA (American Political Science Association), 134, 179, 181–83
Araneta, Gregory, 417
architecture, 15, 489–92
Arendt, Hannah, 4
Arielism, 148
Arlington National Cemetery, 541, 543
Armstrong, Richard, 196
Armstrong, Samuel Chapman, 134, 196
Armstrong v. United States, 56
Arnold, David, 482
Arrighi, Giovanni, 640n20
Arroyo, Gloria, 106–7, 114
Ascue, Andres, 121
Ashford, Bailey K., 16
Asia: British imperial turn to, 39, 43; consumer fascination with, 257; U.S. interests in, 67; weather information communicated to, 514–15. *See also specific countries*
Asian Exclusion Act (1924), 20
Asian studies, 186
Asociación de Maestros de Puerto Rico (or Asociación de Maestros Puertorriqueños, AMPR), 139, 578n11
assimilation: as one-way, 206; use of term, 173. *See also* Americanization

Associated Press, 210
Atkins, Edwin F., 503
Atlanta Constitution (newspaper), 252
Auburn prison model, 88, 90
Australia: British power sharing in, 44; New South Wales as British colony, 38
Austria: German takeover of, 434
authoritarianism: Spanish civil/military fusion of, 47; Western ideas underpinning, 330, 342–52
Autonomist Party (Puerto Rico), 233
autonomy: Cuban party for, 223, 229; local ideas of, 388; nationalism linked to, 147; political science recommendations for, 181–83; for Puerto Rico, 149, 233
Ayer, Edward E., 261–62, 264–65, 266

Bacardí Company, 454
Bacevich, Andrew J., 27, 469, 470, 549
Bailyn, Bernard, 379, 526
Balangiga massacre (Philippines, 1901), 397, 401, 471
Baldwin, Stephen L., 643n50
Balkans: conflicts in, 470; U.S. South compared with, 300
Bandholtz, Harry, 114–15
banditry (*bandolerismo*), 117
Bankoff, Greg: chapter, 479–88; mentioned, 476
Barbados: in U.S. defense strategy, 434–35
Barbour, Thomas, 502
Barceló, Antonio R., 438
Barker, Lewellys F., 303, 304, 306
Barnes, Harry Elmer, 547–48
Barreto, Amílcar Antonio: chapter, 145–50; mentioned, 132, 535
Barrett, Otis Warren, 504, 505
Barrows, David Prescott, 12, 152, 266, 368
Bataille, Georges, 349–50, 351, 352
Bates, John C., 402
Bates Treaty (1899), 402–3
Batista, Fulgencio, 458
Baylor, Ricardo, 456
Bayly, Christopher, 25
Beard, Charles, 548, 549
Beckett, Jeremy, 617n32
Belgium: in Congo, 31, 291
Bell, Genevieve, 166, 173
Bell, J. Franklin, 465–66, 467, 470
Bemis, Samuel Flagg, 64, 534
Bengal: EIC's operations in, 39

Bennett, Hugh Hammond, 321, 506
Bentham, Jeremy, 89–90
beri beri, 117
Bestor, Arthur, 51
Beveridge, Albert, 71
Bewley, Luther, 154, 157
Bibliographical Society of the Philippines, 268
Biggs, Hermann, 274–75, 283
Bingham, Hiram, 243
biomedical citizenship: concept of, 273, 278–81; transnational flow of, 286–87
birth control. *See* oral contraceptives
Black, Ruby, 437
Black Legend, 234, 237
blacks: expected racial amalgamation of, 195, 217–18, 219; as laborers for Panama Canal, 318. *See also* African-Americans; Afro-Cubans; race
Blaine, James G., 67, 184
Blair, Emma H., 21, 261–62, 265–66, 267
Blanco, Manuel, 501
Bliss, Tasker H.: administrative style of, 407, 413–14, 417; military reform ideas of, 394; on Muslim people, 411, 412; in WWI, 419
blood quantum concept, 246–47
Blue, Rupert, 283–84
Bodin, Jean, 342
Boer War (1899–1902), 68
Boletín Mercantil (periodical), 231
Bolivia: Spanish military move against, 42
Bolton, Edward, 413
Bolton, Herbert E., 186, 267
Bonifacio, Andres, 21
Bonwit Teller department store, 253, 254
books and manuscripts: collectors of, 264–65; forgeries of, 196, 261–62, 266–70; translations and mistranslations of, 265–66
Boot, Max, 28
borderlands concept, 278
botanical gardens, 474, 503, 507, 543
botany. *See* tropical botany
Bourne, Edward Gaylord, 265
Bowden v. Bidwell, 56
Boxer Rebellion (1901), 78, 177, 526, 556
Boys Reform School (E. San Millán, P.R.), 136–37
Brandes, E. W., 505
Brau, Rosalina, 450
Brau, Salvador, 93, 233–34, 235

Braudel, Fernand, 569n1, 570n2
Brazil: Portuguese in, 37, 39; slavery in, 40; as tropical, 298; U.S. *rapprochement* with, 184–85; WWII airfields in, 445
Brazilian Revolution (1893–94), 68, 72
Bremer, Paul, 471
Brent, Charles Henry, 101–2, 125, 554, 555, 573n17
British empire: agricultural plantations of, 38; cartoons about, 36; colonies, protectorates, and metropole distinguished in, 47–48; consumer imports in, 252; decline of, 68; decolonization in, 431; as definition and model of empire, 163, 534–35, 545; extent of, 3, 87, 88; governance structure of, 25, 35, 54–55, 59; Mexican Revolution involvement of, 76; opium smuggling and, 103–4; public health issues and, 290, 291; Puerto Rican invasion by, 232–33; representational hierarchy in, 45, 61–62; rise of, 38, 43; shift toward Asia in, 39, 43; slavery abolished in, 40–41; tropical geographic interests in, 298; U.S. as successor to, 27–28, 30; U.S. counter in Caribbean, 65–66; U.S. criticism of, 366–67. *See also* India
British Malaya: malaria work in, 323
Brown, Henry, 425
Brumbaugh, Martin G., 166, 169, 172, 173
Bruner, E. Murray, 82
Bryan, William Jennings, 357, 402, 417
Buck, Carrie, 276
Buck, Elizabeth, 241
Buckley, William F., Sr., 75
Bud Bagsak massacre (Philippines, 1913), 397, 407–8, 419, 463
Bud Dajo massacre (1906): cartoon about, 399; as deterrent, 416; events of, 120, 404–6; justification for, 406–7; precursors to, 402–4; as racialized violence, 393–94; transnational context of, 397–98; Wounded Knee massacre compared with, 397, 408–9
Buencamino, Felipe, 348
Bullard, Robert L., 464
Bundt, Thomas S., 449, 460, 466, 470–71
Burdett, Thomas F., 469
Bureau of Indian Affairs (U.S.), 398–401
Bureau of Insular Affairs (U.S.): citizenship issues and, 333–35; function of, 24; special

commissioner of, 57; world's fair display and, 511
Bureau of Land Management (U.S.), 320–21
Bureau of Plant Industry (U.S.), 499, 501–2
Bureau of Reclamation (U.S.), 320–21, 325
Burgess, J. W., 53–54, 55
Burgos, Jose, 269
Burnett, Christina Duffy: chapter, 332–41; mentioned, 217, 330–31
Burnham, Daniel, 15, 485, 490–91, 492, 498
Bush, George W.: on freedom, 31; imperialism of, 270, 389, 550; intelligence for, 269; Iraq invaded by, 6, 79, 389, 430, 471; State Department under, 28
Byron, George Gordon, Lord, 243

caciquism, 385–87
Cadena, Marisol de la, 142
Cailles, Juan, 463
Caldwell, Lynton, 377
California: disease epidemics in San Francisco, 282; navy interests in, 64–65; U.S. purchase of, 49
California Botanical Gardens, 507
California National Guard, 430
Cámara de Delegados (Puerto Rico), 235
Cambridge Seven, 552
Campo, Rebeca: chapter, 441–51; mentioned, 395
Campomanes, Oscar, 544
Canada: British power sharing in, 44; dominion status of, 66; indigenous and French subordinated in, 48; self-government in, 47; U.S. border with, 49
capitalism: in Cuba, 452–59; Hawaiian land use and, 241–44. *See also* consumption; economy
Capozzola, Christopher: introduction, 393–96; on U.S. territorial acquisition, 9
Caribbean Basin: British withdrawal from, 68; census counts of whites in, 215–16; fears of U.S. dominance in, 64; French and U.S. rivalries in, 395, 441–51; German threats to, 148–49, 443, 444; labor changes in, 44; sex tourism in, 276; slavery in, 40; as tropical, 298; U.S. counter to British in, 65–66; U.S. expansion into, 66–67, 72–74, 525; in U.S. defense strategy, 434–37, 438–40, 442, 444, 445. *See also specific countries*

Carlisle Indian Industrial School (Pa.): forced acculturation in, 165–67, 398–99; graduates of, *168*; legacy of, 172–74; model for, 134; outing program of, 171, 173–74, 586n39; Puerto Rican experiences at, 133, 169–72
Carnegie, Andrew, 69, 177
Carnegie Corporation, 24, 185
Carnegie Endowment for International Peace, 25
Carnegie Institution, 177, 178, 262, 267
Caroline Islands: typhoon early warnings for, 513, 516
Carriedo, Francisco, 493–94
Carroll, Henry K., 146, 213
Carter, Jimmy, 469
cartography: forestry management and, 487; in Netherlands, 107; weather-related, 516–17; world's fair display of, 511. *See also* geography
Case, James, 495, 498
Casey, Matthew: chapter, 220–29; mentioned, 193–94, 535
Cash, Wilbur J., 300
Castañeda, Anna Leah Fidelis T.: chapter, 365–74; mentioned, 330
Castro, Ramón de, 232–33
Catholic Church: Americanization via schools of, 132, 146; Cuban voting rights and, 227; education charged to, 163; glorified by Puerto Ricans, 147–48; social control linked to, 212–13; Spanish political regime linked to, 343–44. *See also* Algué, José
Cavalier de l'Etoile d'Anjoun, 450
CDC (Centers for Disease Control), 17, 326
censuses: adaptability of, 213–18; imperial transition context of, 211–13; of Spanish empire, 195, 210–11, 213–14
center and periphery concept, 60, 569n1
Centers for Disease Control (CDC), 17, 326
Central America: botanical publications on, 501; gunboat diplomacy in, 74, 178, 444; as tropical, 298; U.S. counter to British in, 65–66. *See also specific countries*
Central American Court of Justice, 185
Ceylon: hookworm campaigns in, 286
Chakrabarty, Dipesh, 534
Chalabi, Ahmad, 269–70
Chamberlain, Weston P., 285
Chandon, Claude, 448

Chapin, Charles V., 282
Chapman, Charles, 186
Chapman, Frank, 502
Chardón, Carlos, 506
Chardón Plan (1934), 143
Chassin, Henri Schueg, 454
Cherokee Nation v. Georgia (1831), 39–40, 50, 339
Chiang Kai-shek, 527
Chicago (Ill.): Columbian Exposition in, 490, 542; Field Museum of Natural History in, 262, 267–68, 507; Manila compared with, 490–91; Newberry Library in, 261, 262, 265, 267–68
Chicago Tribune, 401
Chile: health code for, 286
China: fake branded goods in, 263–64; informal U.S. imperialism in, 74, 77–78; missionaries and modernization in, 30; opening of, 66; opium prohibition struggle in, 85, 96–97, 101–2, 555; revolution and challenges in, 79, 527; soft power interests of, 545, 640–41n21; Spanish partnership with,37; territorial integrity of, 178; U.S. nation-building endeavors in, 526–27; vegetables imported from, 497; weather information communicated to, 514–15, 517
China Consortiums (bankers), 78
Chinese in Philippines: criminalizing behavior of, 98–99; excluded from immigration, 208; opium use and, 97–98, *100*; police extortion of, 111
cholera: decline of, 496; forestry management and, 483; Philippine epidemic of, 272, 494–95; prevention of, 284–85, 493, 494; Puerto Rico epidemic of, 213; riots due to, 494; sanitary food concerns and, 497; U.S. conquest of, 16
Chot, Robert, 448
Christianity: Americanization via, 399–400; conquest legitimated in, 344; cultural hegemony of, 546, 551–54, 555–56; Filipinos categorized by, 206; globalism in message of, 555–56, 644n67; Hawaiians introduced to, 196, 241–42, 243–44; ideas about sovereignty based in, 324–44; as justification for pacification, 402–4, 406–9, 411–14; natural law concept in, 348–49. *See also* Catholic Church; missionaries; Protestantism; religious beliefs

CIIS. *See* Carlisle Indian Industrial School (Pa.)
citizen: definition of, 336; as exclusive status, 340
citizenship: ambiguous meanings of, 335–38; "biomedical," 273, 278–81; duties of, 578n12; exclusions of, 526; National Guard and, 426, 429–30; reinvention of, 338–41. *See also* civil rights; voting and voting rights
citizenship in Philippines: denial of U.S., 356; distinctions in, 337; legal designation of, 332–33; Puerto Rico compared with, 340–41
citizenship in Puerto Rico: ambiguities of, 333–34, 335–38; identity constructed in, 141–43; imposed by U.S., 18, 20, 167, 198, 217, 333–35, 578n12; legal designation of, 332–33; local negotiations of empire in, 141–43; Philippines compared with, 340–41; project of building, 136–41; reinvention of, 338–41
civilian life and civil society: commercial collecting linked to, 264–65; in Cuba vs. Puerto Rico, 213
civilization and civilizing ideas: education linked to, 172–74, 412, 413–14; exposition displays of Filipino, 207; massacres and occupation justified in terms of, 398, 411–14; moral and bodily reform linked to, 278–86; of Philippine *ilustrados*, 202–3; public health linked to, 291; questions about citizenship and, 337–38; U.S. developmental goals of, 366–68. *See also* Americanization; Christianity; progressivism
civil rights: environmental management vs., 476; erasure of, 49–50; Hawaiian land use and, 239–41, 244–46; implications of insular cases for, 363–64; for representation, 45–46; uniformity vs. exceptionalism in colonies, 59–62. *See also* citizenship; voting and voting rights
Civil Rights Act (1875), 52
civil service: military power vs., 30, 543; in Philippines, 117, 368, 384, 386–87, 427; tasks of colonial, 24–25
class: citizenship-building project and, 136, 138–41; consumer imports as marker of, 255–58; Hawaiian social hierarchy and, 239–41; public health hygiene efforts and,

284–85; teachers' self-identity and, 141–43; yellow fever and, 289. *See also* race
Clausewitz, Karl von, 382
Clay, Henry, 51
Clay, Lucius, 529
Clayton-Bulwer Treaty (1850), 67
cleanliness, 276, 282, 303–4
Clemons, C. F., 429
Cleveland, Grover, 70, 72
Clifford, Bede Edmund Hugh, 445–46, 450
climate. *See* meteorology
clothing and fashion: feigning foreignness in, 258; in forced acculturation, 167; imports of, 251, 253, 254; worldviews linked to, 250
Club of Veterans (Cuba), 227
Coalición (Puerto Rican parties), 433, 436–38
Code of Raja Kalantiaw (forgery), 196, 261–62, 267
Código Narváez (Spanish prison code, 1848), 90
coercive tactics: information technologies linked to, 107, 108–10; innovative, seductive uses of, 83–84; rule by scandal as, 111–14
Cohen, Eliot, 28, 31
cold war: "empire" tainted by, 9; fears of communism in, 468; resurgence of interest in Philippine wars after, 470–71
Collier, Stephen J., 287
Coll y Toste, Cayetano, 216, 235
Colombia: agricultural advice for, 506; military assistance for, 67
colonial assemblies, 45–46. *See also* Philippine Assembly
colonialism: assimilation into liberal regime vs. exclusion of, 35; censuses in, 195, 210–19; focus on, 6–7; freedom for social experimentation in, 15; "geographies of intimacy" in, 275; "hard" aspects of rule, 11–12, 14; imperial production of knowledge in, 196, 260–70; Iwahig as experiment in, 124–26; Jeffersonianism in, 382–87; "laboratories of modernity" in, 5–6; maintaining control vs. rights in, 60–61; mediators of, 135–36; as mutually transformative, 180–81; racial state in, 204–8; "soft" aspects of governance, 3–4, 6; U.S. debate on, 69–72; U.S. rhetoric on, 366–68. *See also* American imperial state; empires; imperialism; transnational movement of ideas

colonization: definition of, 134
Columbian Exposition (Chicago, 1893), 490, 542
Columbia Teachers College, 157, 160
Columbus, Christopher, 21, 231–32, 236
commemorations: as critique of U.S. imperialism, 194, 220–29; of Dewey's victory, 541–43; reflections about empire in, 10; of Rizal, 21, 491; of Spanish period by Puerto Ricans, 147–48, 194–95, 230–37; of U.S. rule in Puerto Rico, 433–34; of U.S. wars, 541–43
commerce and trade: American empire based in, 261–62; in Cuba, 452–59; education linked to, 152–62; in Hawai'i, 241–44; imperial control of, 37–38; insular cases concerning, 362–63; yellow fever eradication critical to, 290, 291, 292–93, 295. *See also* agriculture; consumption; imports; Open Door policy
Commission on Pacific Islands and Porto Rico, 217
Commission to Revise and Compile the Laws of Porto Rico, 180
Commonwealth v. Alger (1851), 371–72
communism, 8, 28, 468, 548
Congo: Belgium in, 31, 291
Conley, Ray, 111–13, 114
Conrad, Joseph, 15
conservation movement: colonial opportunities in, 479–80; imperialism linked to, 321; preservationist vs. utilitarian, 486–87. *See also* environmental management
constitutional theory (U.S.): colonialism and, 330, 353–64; due process and equal protection in, 373–74; as flexible and constraining, 330, 365–74; National Guard international deployment and, 423–25; rational basis review in, 373; separation of powers in, 368–70. *See also* Constitution (U.S.); insular cases; U.S. Supreme Court
Constitution (Cuba, various years), 221–22, 229, 453
Constitution (Mexico, 1917), 76
Constitution (Philippines, 1898 and 1935), 346, 365–66, 372
Constitution (Puerto Rico), 147, 432
Constitution (Spain, 1812), 46–47, 61

Constitution (U.S.): on authority to raise and support armies, 424, 427; cartoon about, 359; as centralized federalism, 380; on citizenship, 52, 332–33, 335–36, 606n4; exclusion and exceptionality aspects of, 48–49; Fourteenth Amendment to, 52, 332–33, 338–40, 606n4; imperialism juxtaposed to, 177, 394; Indians subordinated in, 50; militia clause of, 423–25, 426; Philippine colonialism and, 353–64; territorial clause of, 54, 147; territorial governance and, 53–59. *See also* constitutional theory (U.S.); insular cases; U.S. Supreme Court

consumption: advertising for, 253; beginnings of, 197; imperial buy-in of, 248–50; informal empire of, 546–47; as marker of civilizational attainment, 255–58; provenance of objects for, 251–55; worldviews linked to, 249–50, 254–55, 258–59

convict labor: discipline and, 122–23; plantation work, 120; road building by, 91–92, 93, 119, 121. *See also* Iwahig Penal Colony (Philippines)

Cook, James, 238, 239, 243, 246
Cook, Orator Fuller, 500–501
Coolidge, Calvin, 20, 114
Cooper, Frederick, 533
Cooper, Henry A., 444
Corbould, Clare, 193–98
corn campaigns (Philippines): context of, 132–33; description of, 157–59
Cornell University, 165, 506
Corretjer, Juan Antonio, 164
cortisone production, 275–76, 309–16
Cosmos (periodical), 515
Costa Rica: botanical publications on, 501; hookworm campaigns in, 284
Coudert, Frederic R., Jr., 334–38
Coudert Brothers (law firm), 334–38
Council on Foreign Relations, 24, 25, 177, 178, 179
Courtwright, David, 96, 98
Cox, Robert, 426–27, 430
Cox v. Wood, 427, 430
Craig, Charles F., 285
Crame, Rafael, 104
Crane, Charles J., 464
craniometry, 90
criminal codes (Cuba), 222

criminalization: of daily activities, 93; of drug users, 98–99; of vagrancy, 212–13
criminal justice in Philippines. *See* Iwahig Penal Colony (Philippines)
criminology: rehabilitation idea in, 88–89; theoretical underpinnings of, 87, 90–91. *See also* prisons and penal forms
Critic (periodical), 497
Crone, Frank, 154, 159
Crowder, Enoch, 424–25
Crowther, Samuel, 299
Crystal Palace Exhibition (London, 1892), 257
Cuba: agricultural research in, 503, 504, 505, 506, 507; Autonomist regime in, 223, 229; constitutions of, 221–22, 229, 453; contract laborers from, 452–59; criminal codes of, 222; education in, 222–23; geography and economy of, 453–54; independence promised to, 72; missionaries in, 30; Puerto Rico compared with, 210, 213, 215, 219; Spanish atrocities in, 234; Spanish colonial changes in, 12, 222–23; Spanish political regime for, 46–47; Spanish prisons in, 91; Spanish reconcentration policy in, 293–94; Spanish work organization in, 41–42; suffrage controversy in, 194, 220–29; teachers in, 165; U.S. annexation of, 52, 65; U.S. attitudes toward, 71, 164; U.S. imperialism in, 47, 73, 74; U.S. neocolonial presence in, 452–59; U.S. strategy to acquire, 354–55; as U.S. protectorate, 639n4; wars of independence in, 56, 61, 294; workers' migration to base in, 456–57; yellow fever campaign in, 16, 274, 275, 288–96. *See also* Afro-Cubans; Guantánamo Bay (GTMO, Cuba); Havana (Cuba); legal systems in Cuba; public health in Cuba; race in Cuba; Spanish-Cuban-Philippine-American War (1898)
Cuba Libre (Cuban Liberation Army): principles of, 221–22; suffrage for, 226–27; U.S. attitudes toward, 223–24
Cuban American Sugar Company, 453
Cuban Communist Party, 457–58
Cuban Construction and Engineering Company, 495
Cuban Ministry of Justice, 458
Cuban Parliament, 223

Cuban Revolution (1868), 67
Cuba Sugar Club, 503
Cubí, Mariano, 90–91
Culion Leprosy Colony, 286
culture, U.S.: colonial influences on, 14; hegemony of, 545–46, 551–54, 555. *See also* Christianity; moral reform; progressivism
Cutter, Charles A., 111

Daniels, W. M., 59
Danish Virgin Islands. *See* Virgin Islands
"Dansalan declaration," 418–19
Dargo, George, 49
Davidson, Randall, 555
Davis, George W.: on census, 217–18, 219; on Mindanao and Moro Province, 402–3; Spanish appropriations of, 213; on Spanish colonial police, 84, 212
Davis, John W., 427
Dawes Act (General Allotment Act, 1887), 196
Day, William R., 608n40
Daza, Eugenio, 463
Deady, Timothy K., 471
El Debate (newspaper), 112–13
decentralization: applied to southern U.S., 381–82; state formation and, 378–81; Taft era in Philippines and, 382–87; undemocratic outcomes of, 389
decolonization: of British Caribbean colonies, 431; Haiti success in, 39, 61; as racial exclusion, 208–9
Deeks, William, 326
Degetau y González, Federico: citizenship questions of, 333–34; *Gonzales* case and, 334–35, 336–38; role of, 330–31
de la Fuente, Alejandro: chapter, 220–29; mentioned, 193–94, 535
DeLima v. Bidwell (1901), 56, 362
del Moral, Solsirée: chapter, 135–44; mentioned, 24, 131–32, 535
democracy and democratic ideals: American ideals of, 526–28; educational experiment in, 124–25; militarism juxtaposed to, 29, 31–32, 528–30, 531; paradoxes of, 127–28; prison reform experiment in, 118–19; slavery linked to, 40–41. *See also* freedom; Hamilton, Alexander; Jefferson, Thomas
Democratic Party (U.S.), 357, 381
Denby, Charles, 509

Denmark: Virgin Islands held by, 67
Destroyers for Bases agreement, 438, 445
Dewey, George: Algué's meeting with, 508; Manila Bay battle and, 106, 353–54, 355, 461; Root's correspondence with, 184–85; triumph of, 541–43, 555–56
Dewey, John, 96, 153
Dewey, Melville, 111
Diario de la Marina (newspaper), 226–27, 458
Díaz, Porfirio, 75
Dick, Charles, 423
Dick Act (1903), 423
diet: imports in U.S., 251–52, 254–55, 256–58; sanitary vegetables in, 496–98; U.S. attempt to change Philippine, 157–58
discrimination, custom vs. law, 51. *See also* racism and racial discrimination
La Discusión (newspaper), 226
disease: approaches to, 273–76; of local vs. colonial population, 289–90, 295; miasmatic theory of, 301, 302, 321–22; in Philippine prison, 117, 120, 121; Philippine Revolution perceived as, 348–49; racial degeneracy concept linked to, 139–40; sanitary food concerns and, 497–98; surveillance-oriented approach to, 275, 277–87; tropical discourse as evoking, 301–2, 321–25; vaccination campaigns and, 284; vector theory of, 323, 324. *See also* germ theory; medicine; public health; tropical medicine
diseases, specific: beri beri, 117; dysentery, 117, 494–95; enteritis, 290; leprosy, 279, 286, 483; meningitis, 290; pellagra, 303, 306; plague, 291, 497, 498; pneumonia, 290; syphilis, 276; tuberculosis, 290; typhoid, 282, 496. *See also* cholera; hookworms; malaria; yellow fever
Djerassi, Carl, 311, 312–14
Doeppers, Daniel F.: chapter, 489–98; mentioned, 477
dollar diplomacy concept, 5, 74
domestic policy: colonial expansion as influence on (or not), 28–32; Philippine precedents applied in, 15, 85–86, 95–96, 101–2. *See also* federal government, U.S.; transnational movement of ideas; *specific U.S. agencies and departments*
Dominican Republic: military interventions in, 18; U.S. attempt to annex, 67; U.S.

658   Index

Dominican Republic (*continued*)
  imperialism in, 73, 74; U.S. occupations of, 444
Dooley v. United States (1901), 56
Dorr v. O'Brien (1904), 611n52
Douglas, Stephen A., 51, 66
Downes v. Bidwell (1901), 180, 217, 362
Drake Winkleman Company, 459
Dred Scott case (1857), 52, 336, 338, 360
Drescher, Seymour, 41
Dreyfus, Alfred, 442
drug prohibition, U.S.: absence of, 101–2; cost of current war in, 86; criminalization of user in, 98–99; enforcement of, 102–4; missionaries' role in, 30, 96–97, 555; Philippine precedent applied to, 15, 85–86, 95–96, 105
Duany, Jorge, 169
DuBois, W. E. B., 277, 287
Duke Tobacco Trust, 177
Duncan, J. W., 406
Dunch, Ryan, 551
Dunne, Finley Peter, 363
du Pont de Nemours, Pierre Samuel, 134
Dupuy, R. E., 434
Durham Report (1838), 47
Durkheim, Émile, 329
Dutch empire: agricultural plantations of, 38; Puerto Rican invasion by, 233; U.S. criticism of, 366–67
dysentery, 117, 494–95

Earle, Franklin Sumner, 503
East India Company (EIC), 39, 43
Eaton, John, 165–66, 172
Éboué, Félix, 449
Echeverría, Luis, 315
economic development: in Moro Province, 414, 415, 416, 418; Open Door policy for, 78–79; post–Civil War, 67; post WWII, 546–47
economy: colonial in South, 306; expansion theory and, 69–72; free trade ideas in, 70, 71–72, 74–76; informal empire in, 74–79; plantation-based, 37–38, 40–42, 44; 1890s restructuring of, 68–69. *See also* consumption
education: Americanization fostered by, 22–23, 132, 146, 165–66, 172–74, 398–400; approaches to, 131–34; colonial policies in, 138–39; expansion of, 222–23; to overcome Islam, 412, 413–14. *See also* industrial education programs
education in Philippines: comprehensive study of, 157, 160; English in, 23; progressivism in, 24. *See also* industrial education programs
education in Puerto Rico: Americanization and English in, 23; centralization of, 164, 172–73; citizenship-building project in, 136–41; commissioners of, 146; identity construction and, 141–43; local negotiations of empire in, 143–44; progressivism in, 24; scholarships for study in U.S., 164, 166, 169, 585n14; Spanish language in, 147–48, 149; under Spanish rule, 163; subjects in, 140; teachers as mediators of, 135–36. *See also* Carlisle Indian Industrial School (Pa.); teachers (Puerto Rico)
education in U.S.: agricultural programs in, 158; Americanizing immigrant children via, 146; anti-imperialism and, 548–49; "civilizing" structures in, 172–74; colonial policy exchanges with, 131–34; corporate model of, 154; industrial programs in, 151–52, 153, 154; local control of, 14; of Native Hawaiians, 196; progressivism in, 23–24. *See also* Carlisle Indian Industrial School (Pa.); universities
Edward VII (king of England), xvi–xvii
Eggan, Fred, 262, 268–69
Egypt: scientific expeditions in, 476
EIC (East India Company), 39, 43
Eisenhower, Dwight D., 529
Eliot, Charles, 164
Eliot, George Fielding, 434–36
elites: co-optation of, 178; dialogue and collaboration with, 205–8; isolation of, 221, 222–23; mobilization of, 202–3; networking government and, 24–26, 177–78; suffrage controversy and, 226–29; U.S. favored by, 210. *See also* teachers (Puerto Rico)
Elkins, Stanley, 376, 378, 381
Elk v. Wilkins (1884), 336
Elmira Reformatory for Men and Boys, 88–89, 90, 91
El Salvador: crisis in 1970s, 469
Emergency Quota Act (1921), 20
Emerson, Haven, 284
empires: absolutist sovereignty as afterlife of, 342–52; applicability to U.S. (or not),

28–32; comparative approach to, 34–35, 441–42, 444–45, 545–47; continental vs. overseas expansion of, 4–5; definitions of, 6, 193, 538; differences among, 3, 5–6, 524–26; embrace of, 26; epistemology of, 196, 260–70; Eurocentric notion of, 534–35; experimental possibilities of, 83; formal vs. informal, 71–79; historiography of, 7–11, 199–200; liberal model of, 535–36; local negotiations of, 143–44; Philippine Revolution feared by, 348–49; political science discourse on, 181–83; race constructed in, 193–98, 199–209; remembered and forgotten, 541–56; use of term, 4, 532–33. *See also* colonialism; imperialism

empires project: description of, xiii–xv; structure of, 12–14

enemy: definitions of, 205

Engerman, Stanley, 40

English language: Americanization linked to, 22–23, 147, 164–65; forced use of, 167; hegemony of, 145–46; as legal language in Hawai'i, 245; statehood linked to, 149

Enlightenment: empire as conceived in, 34–35; Philippine Revolution ideals based in, 345–46, 348–49, 351–52

enteritis, 290

entomology: emergence of, 323–25; mosquitos that carry malaria (*Anopheles albimanus*), 284–86, 302, 323–26; mosquitos that carry yellow fever (*Aedes aegypti*), 16–17, 289, 295, 323–25; white ants (*anay*), 483

environmental management: approaches to, 476–78; components of, 475–76; definition of, 325–26. *See also* tropics

environmental management in Panama: disease and conquest in, 321–26; as ideal colonial project, 17, 275, 318–26

environmental management in Philippines: forestry in, 476, 479–88; meteorology in, 477–78, 508–19; public health and resource extraction linked to, 15–16; sanitation in, 477, 489, 492–98

environmental management in U.S.: colonial lens into, 485–86; core agencies in, 320–21; preservationist vs. utilitarian views of, 486–87

equality: Cuban constitution on, 221–22; demands for, 45–46; as ideal in Philippine Revolution, 345–46, 348–49; uniformity vs. exceptionalism in colonies, 59–62

Espinosa, Mariola: chapter, 288–96; mentioned, 274, 275, 536

Estación Experimental Agronómica (Cuba), 503, 507

Estrada, Joseph Ejercito, 114

eugenics: congressional policy based on, 20; criminology based on, 87; racial degeneracy concept in, 139–40; threats to, 110; U.S. southerners and, 276

Europe: American empire compared to, 63–64; colonies as laboratories for, 5–6; consumer imports in, 252; national rural police model of, 85; opium policies in, 101–2; revolution fears in, 348–49; scientific developments in, 274; tropical geography and disease discourse in, 298, 301; weather information communicated to, 514. *See also specific countries*

evangelization. *See* Christianity; missionaries

Evans, R. K., 429

exceptionalism: constitutional questions about territories and, 52–59; logic of, 53; selective American memory and, 541–44, 554–56; sovereign power to define, 324–44; in treatment of colonies vs. metropole, 44–52, 59–62; of U.S., 8, 29, 63–64; world context of, 4

Fabianism, 59

Fairchild, David, 321, 501, 502, 507

Fairchild Tropical Botanical Garden, 507

fakes, 263–64, 270. *See also* forgeries

Falklands/Malvinas: as British colony, 38

Fallon, Joseph A., 55

families and kinship relations: Hawaiian land use and, 239–41; in prison reform experiment, 123; rural-to-urban and nonnuclear shift of, 195

Farrington, Wallace, 429

Fast, Jonathan S., 355

Fauntleroy, P. C., 285

Faura, Federico, 508, 509

Federal Board for Vocational Education, 285

Federal Bureau of Investigation, 108, 537

federal government, U.S.: coercive social controls imposed by, 17; colonial influences on, 13–14; decentralization of,

660   Index

federal government, U.S. (*continued*) 375–77; Jefferson's opposition to centralized, 378–81; limits of, 83; Panama and extracontinental expansion of, 320–21, 325; public-private institutional nexus of, 24–26, 177–90; regulatory powers of, 369; Spanish bureaucracy in Philippines compared with, 367–68; surveillance limits on, 108. *See also specific agencies and departments*
Federalista Party (Philippines), 205, 207
federal plenary powers doctrine, 50
Ferguson, Niall, 4, 27, 535–36
Fernández, José, 456
Fernandez, Ramon, 111–12, 113
Fernández Duro, Cesáreo, 232
Ferrer, Ada, 226
Fewkes, Jesse Walter, 230
FFA (Future Farmers of America), 132
Fianza, Florencio, 106
Field Museum of Natural History (Chicago), 262, 267–68, 507
Fields, James, 534
Field Service Regulations (1905), 465
Filiberti, Edward J., 469, 470
Filipinos: African-Americans compared with, 265; as aliens, 607n16; categorization of, 206; citizenship questions and, 332–33; commercial competition concerns of, 372; excluded from U.S., 19, 208–9, 340; exposition displays of, 207; in Hawaiian National Guard, 429–30; hygienic moral and bodily reform of, 278–86; poor white southerners compared with, 304–5; Spanish social contract with, 346; in U.S. military, 428–29; use of term, 202–3; as Weather Bureau staff and volunteers, 509, 513, 518
Findlay, Eileen, 11, 212
Finlay, Carlos Juan, 16, 289, 324
Finley, John, 413
Florida: Spanish control of, 42
food supply. *See* diet
Foraker, Joseph, 334
Foraker Act (1900): centralized U.S. control under, 164, 210; debates on, 217; implementation of, 180, 216; limits of, 54; Puerto Rican response to, 234–36; transition to, 212; uncertainties about citizenship in, 334–35, 337. *See also* insular cases
Forbes, Alexander, 119

Forbes, William Cameron: on education, 367; on Iwahig judicial system, 123–24; Manila architecture and, 490–91; Manila water supply and, 495; prison reform under, 15, 119–20, 121, 122, 123, 127
Ford Foundation, 262, 267
Forest Law (1905), 485
forestry. *See* tropical forestry
Forestry Organic Law (1904), 484
forgeries: archiving and publication of, 261–62; collusion in, 269–70; exposure of, 268–69; imaginative acts in, 262–63; library's acquisitions of, 266–67; as symptom, 263–64
Formosa: weather information communicated to, 515
Forsythe, John, 251
Fortune (magazine), 309, 313
Foster, Anne L.: chapter, 95–105; mentioned, 85–86
Foucault, Michel, 88, 126
4-H movement, 158
Fourteen Points program, 527
Fox, Robert, 267–68
Fradera, Josep M.: chapter, 34–62; mentioned, 12, 211, 214–15, 533, 535, 538
France: China market interests of, 77; colonials in military of, 444; scientific expeditions of, 476; Vichy government in, 446, 448; WWII occupation of, 441. *See also* French empire
Francisco, Luzviminda B., 355
Franco, Francisco, 455
Franklin, Benjamin, 49
Frederick Snare Corporation, 452, 454–56, 457, 459
freedom: presidential rhetoric of, 31; sovereignty and experience of, 349–52; U.S. South in narrative of, 381–82. *See also* democracy and democratic ideals; liberty
free trade ideas, 70, 71–72, 74–76
French, Daniel Chester, 421
French empire: in Caribbean islands, 61, 441–44; colonial representation in, 45; decline of, 38, 39; in Indochina, 31, 61; public health issues and, 290, 291; regimes created in, 35; slavery in, 40, 41; tropical geographic interests in, 298; U.S. criticism of, 366–67; U.S. empire compared with, 441–42, 444–45

French Revolution (1789), 38, 345–46, 349–50
Friedman, M., 170, 171, 172
Fuller, Melville Weston, 371–72
Funston, Frederick, 464, 467, 468
Future Farmers of America (FFA), 132

Gaddis, John Lewis, 6
Gadsden, James, 49
Gadsden Purchase (1854), 237
Gall, Franz Josef, 90
Gallardo, José, 146
Gallardo, Silvino, 112–13
Gama, Vasco da, 543
Gamba, García, 93
gambling, 111–12
Gan Yong, 112–13
Garcia, Mauro, 268–69
García, Regino, 482
García Méndez, Miguel Angel, 438
García-Muñiz, Humberto: chapter, 441–51; mentioned, 395
Garnier, Matilde, 170–71
Garrison, Lindley, 425–26
Garrison, P. E., 285
gated communities, 319
Gates, John, 75
Gates, Merrill, 399–400
Gaulle, Charles de, 441, 449, 450
Gedacht, Joshua: chapter, 397–409; mentioned, 393–94
Géigel Polanco, Vicente, 148
General Allotment Act (Dawes Act, 1887), 196
General Federation of Women's Clubs, 256
Geographical and Statistical Institute (GSI, Spain), 215
geography: Cuban economy and, 453–54; imported goods as lessons of, 252–55; of Philippine wars, 412, 415–16, *481*; tropical disease and, 297–308. *See also* cartography; meteorology
George, William Reuben, 118–19
George Junior Republic reformatory (N.Y.), 118–19, 120, 124–25
Georgia (state): imperial rhetoric about, 300
Gerhardt, Charles H., 468
German empire: colonial authority in, 59; Mexican Revolution involvement of, 76; rise of, 88

Germany: British rivalry with, 67; China market interests of, 77; forest management in, 476; as protectorate, 55; submarines of, *443, 444, 445*; U.S. occupation and nation-building in, 529; WWII aggressions of, 28, 434, 438
germ theory: racialization of, 278–81; in sanitation and environmental management, 477, 489, 492–98; in tropical medicine, 289, 301, 302
Geronimo (chief), 400, 412
Ghost Dance, 400, 404. *See also* Wounded Knee massacre (1890)
Gibbon, Edward, 35
Gill, Tom, 506
Gillin, John R., 127
Gilmer, David J., 199–200, 205, 209
Ginsbaugh, Robert N., 469
Giraud, Henri, 441, 448–49
globalization: approaches to, 550; economic expansion in, 249; fake as symptom of, 263–64; informal empire compared with, 76; public health linked to, 301–2; shortcomings of, 79; U.S. as sole superpower in, 6, 10, 26–28, 188, 389, 470. *See also* transnational movement of ideas
global-racial regime, 87–88, 93, 570n2
Golay, Frank, 368
Gómez, Juan Gualberto, 592n42
Gómez, Máximo, 222
Gonzales v. Williams (1904), 332–33, 334–38, 340, 341
González, Isabel, 334–35
Good Housekeeping (magazine), 252, 254
Good Neighbor policy (1890), 67, 74, 452–53, 548
Gore, Robert, 433
Gorgas, William C., 16, 283, 323
Grandin, Greg, 142
Grant, Ulysses S., 320
Graves, Henry, 479–80, 484–85, 486, 487
Graves, William S., 467
Grazia, Victoria de, 14, 537, 546
Great Britain: China market interests of, 77; Destroyers for Bases agreement with, 438, 445; immigration fears in, 198; industrial revolution of, 88; missionaries from, 552; penology of, 89–90, 91; tropical medicine interests in, 290; U.S. postbellum relations with, 68. *See also* British empire

Greene, Jack P., 40
Gresham, Walter Q., 70
Grove, Richard, 476
Gruening, Ernest, 433, 438
GTMO. *See* Guantánamo Bay (GTMO, Cuba)
Guadeloupe: French regime in, 61, 442
Guam: agricultural research in, 503; citizenship questions in, 337; Filipino exile in, 345; U.S. imperialism in, 73; weather information communicated to, 514–15
guano islands, 606n8
Guantánamo Bay (GTMO, Cuba): Cuban contract workers of, 395–96, 452–59; military base of, 19, 73, 444, 545; as precedent for private contractors, 459
Guantánamo Sugar Company, 453–54
Guardia Civil and Guardia Rural (Spanish colonial police), 84, 85, 91, 92–93, 94
Guatemala: botanical publications on, 501
Gulf War (1991), 460, 470
gunboat diplomacy concept, 74, 178, 444, 448
Guomindang, 527
Guyana (earlier, British Guiana): U.S. base in, 445
Guyane: airfield construction in, 448–49; French African soldiers in, 444; French regime in, 441–42; French-U.S. agreement on, 446, 448; Puerto Rican civilian workers in, 395, 441, 449–51

habeas corpus, 363–64
Hagedorn, Herman, 412
Haiti: decolonization of, 39, 61; French defeat in, 442; as protectorate, 55; U.S. imperialism in, 18, 67, 73, 74; U.S. occupations of, 444; U.S. South compared with, 300
Haitian Revolution (1802), 290
Hall, Stuart, 238
Halualani, Rona Tamiko: chapter, 238–47; mentioned, 195, 196
Hamilton, Alexander, 376, 378, 380
Hamlin, Charles S., 57
Hampton Institute (Va.), 134, 165, 166, 196
handicraft production: commercial failure of, 161–62; industrial education program for, 159–61; U.S. consumption of, 255
Hanna, Mark, 71, 73, 403
Hardt, Michael, 27, 550

Harper's (magazine), 314
Harper's Weekly (magazine), xvi–xvii, 224, 322
Harriman, E. H., 75
Harrison, Benjamin A., 400
Harrison, Francis Burton, 102, 366–67, 427–28
Harrison Narcotics Act (1914), 15, 85, 102
Hart, Albert "Bushy" Bushnell, 300, 547, 549
Harvard Law Review (journal), 57
Harvard University: Arnold Arboretum at, 507; teacher training institutes of, 165; tropical medicine at, 285
Hatch Act (1887), 499
Havana (Cuba): attitudes toward GTMO in, 453–54; drainage works of, 495; infrastructure of, 455; yellow fever in, 288, 289, 292–93, 295, 323, 324
Havana Country Club, 455, 459
Havana Declaration (1940), 448
Havermeyer, Henry O., 354
Havermeyer Sugar Trust, 177
Hawai'i: agricultural research in, 503, 504; annexation of, 52, 360, 606n8, 639n4; as borderland, 278; cartoon about, 203; identity displaced in, 238–39; illegal overthrow of, 239, 243, 246; land use and property rights in, 195, 238–47; missionaries in, 196; organic law for, 54; population statistics of, 239; Puerto Rican autonomy as model for, 149; U.S. imperialism in, 73; U.S. interests in, 67
Hawaiian Homes Commission Act (HHCA, 1921), 246–47
Hawaiian National Guard, 429–30
Hawaiians: definition of, 246–47; excluded from land ownership, 195; kinship relations of, 239–41; land tenure system of, 241–44; (mis)recognition of, 238–39, 247; Native Americans compared with, 196; as private tenants, 244–46
Hawaiian Sugar Planters Association (HSPA), 503
Hay, James, 426
Hay, John: American influence and, 554; Open Door policy of, 178; power of, 523–26; Treaty of Paris negotiations and, 337–38
Hay-Pauncefote Treaty (1901), 68
Hechavarría, Venancio, 459

Heiser, Victor G.: background of, 496–97; cholera work of, 16; as industrial hygiene adviser, 285–86; penal colony tour of, 120; public health position of, 283–84; sanitary food concerns of, 497–98
Henry the Navigator (prince of Portugal), 543
Hepburn Board Report (1938), 436
Heritage Foundation, 24
Hester, E. D., 262, 268–69
heterogeneity, 46, 59–62
Heutz de Lemps, Xavier, 494
Hines, Thomas S., 491
Hispanic American Historical Review (journal), 21, 547
history: empire in American, 546–56; fraud and fabrication in, 262–64; Puerto Rican narratives of, 230–37; resources for, 264–67; taxonomy of race in transnational, 194, 199–209. *See also* commemorations
Hoar, George Frisbie, 356
Hobsbawm, Eric, 431, 432
Ho Chi Minh, 527
Hofstadter, Richard, 378, 643n58
Hoganson, Kristin: chapter, 248–59; mentioned, 14, 196, 197, 537
Holland. *See* Dutch empire; Netherlands
Hollander, J. H., 58
Holmes, Oliver Wendell, 276
Holmes, Oliver Wendell, Jr., 427, 430
Honduras: agricultural research in, 503; botanical publications on, 501; informal U.S. control of, 74
Hong Kong: founding of, 44; opium smuggling from, 103; vegetables imported from, 497; weather information communicated to, 514–15
hookworms: campaigns to eradicate, 284, 286, 303, 304, 305–6; clay-eating linked to, 304; as exotic in U.S., 303; poor afflicted with, 306; treatment for, 16; tropics linked to, 302
Hoover, J. Edgar, 537
House and Garden (magazine), 254
Howard, L. O., 321, 323
Howard, William Lee, 282–83
Hoy (periodical), 458
Hoyt, Henry M., 335, 336
humanitarian relief debates, 553
Huntington, Ellsworth, 297–98, 300, 303, 306

Huntington, Samuel P.: on Jeffersonianism, 377, 378–79; shortcomings of, 380, 381; on state formation, 150, 384
Hurley, Vic, 411–12
Hutchcroft, Paul D.: chapter, 375–89; mentioned, 331
hygiene: citizenship linked to, 281–82; education needed in, 283; enforcement of, 280–81; manufacturers' interest in, 285–86; racial context of, 278–79. *See also* public health; racial hygiene

ICC (Isthmian Canal Commission), 318, 326, 502
Ickes, Harold, 433, 437, 438
Ide, Henry C., 101
identity: approaches to, 193–98; construction of, 141–43; destruction of cultural, 164–65; of Hawaiians, 238–47; mestizo, 150, 236; of Puerto Ricans, 341; social-political context of, 238–39. *See also* Americanization; class; national identity; race
Ignatieff, Michael, 27
Igorot, Bontoc, *192*
Igorot people, 207
Ileto, Reynaldo, 263, 351
Illinois Convention (1820), 51
Illinois Department of Public Health, 283
illiteracy, 139–40
ilustrados (enlightened), 202–3, 207, 345, 346, 382
immigrants and immigration: agricultural needs for, 208, 209; Americanizing children of, 146; Chinese excluded from, 97–98; equality demanded by, 60–61; Filipinos excluded from, 19, 208–9, 340; in Hawai'i, 242–44, 246; medical screening of, 496–97; military subcontracts for, 456–57; to Moro Province, 414; as pathogenic, 282; public health issues and, 274, 275, 283; Puerto Ricans as, 148; Puerto Ricans excluded from, 334–38; race linked to policies of, 52, 197–98
Immigration Act (1917), 20, 208
Immigration Act (1924), 20, 197–98, 208
imperial information transfer, 3–4. *See also* information revolution; surveillance
imperialism: academic disciplines linked to, 176–77, 184–88; collector's interest linked to, 261–62, 264; consumption linked to,

imperialism (*continued*)
248–59; democratic ideals juxtaposed to, 29; expanding notions of, 175–76; "Great Debate" on, 70–72; immunity to, 63–64; Jesuit scientist linked to, 475, 508–19; post–WWII challenges to, 394–95; reciprocal aspects of, 13–14; as tourism, 318–20; "Triple Assault" in, 475; varieties of, 14–24, 78, 133, 178; visible in U.S. public health, 277–78. *See also* colonialism; empires; imperial transitions
imperial renewal rhetoric, 11–12
imperial transitions: censuses adapted in, 213–18; colonial appropriations in, 210–11; colonial logics of interior expansion applied to, 52–59; continuity from Spanish to U.S., 7, 12–13, 93–94, 211–13, 218–19; definition of, 34–35; exceptional treatment of colonies vs. metropole in, 44–52, 59–62; experimental possibilities of, 84; intersecting, coexisting empires in, 35–44; overview of, 11–12; penal reforms and policing in, 87–88; reflections on, 532–40. *See also* American imperial state; transnational movement of ideas
imports: as geographic lessons, 252–55; imperial sensibilities and, 249–50, 254–55, 258–59; post–Civil War increase in, 248–49, 594n1; as status markers, 255–58
indentured labor, 41, 44
Independent (newspaper), 228–29
India: British imperial structure in, 43–44, 47–48, 50, 73; British water system in, 495; cities under British in, 489, 492; consumer imports from, 252; decentralization in, 613n3; EIC's operations in, 39; forestry in, 487; malaria work in, 323; mutinies in, 48, 70; as tropical, 298
Indiana: industrial education program in, 153
Indian Citizenship Act (1924), 336
Indian Helper (CIIS periodical), 165–66
Indian peoples. *See* Native Americans
Indian Rights Association, 400–401
indigenous peoples: anthropologists' studies of, 230–31; "civilizing" process for, 172–74; distinctions among, 337–38; excluded from public, 372; forgeries by, 268–70; prehistoric Indians of Boriquén (Puerto Rico), 232, 233–34, 236; rights of possession over lands of, 49–50; role in

synthetic cortisone production, 275–76, 314–16; Spanish exploitation of, 37–38; world's fair display of, 511, 512. *See also* Filipinos; Hawaiians; Muslim people; Native Americans
Indochina: French in, 31, 61, 73; Vichy loyalty of, 448. *See also* Vietnam War
Indonesia: formal Dutch imperialism in, 73
industrial education programs: adviser for U.S., 285; basketry, 159–60; commercialization and standardization goals of, 152–53, 156; corn-growing program, 157–59; development of, 154–57; embroidery, 160–61; failure of, 161–62; imperial prioritization of, 151–52; lace making, 130; number of students in, 151; in U.S. vs. Philippines, 132–33. *See also* Carlisle Indian Industrial School (Pa.)
industrial hygiene, 285–86
information revolution: centralized processing in, 110–11; colonial laboratory for, 108–10; rationalized collection in, 107–8; slander and, 111–14. *See also* meteorology; surveillance
Institute for Research in Tropical America, 502
Institute of Chemistry (Mexico), 312, 604n24
Institute of Culture (Puerto Rico), 148
Insular Bureau of Forestry (Philippines): botanical publications of, 501; control of, 485–88; ideals underlying, 479–80; Pinchot's Philippine tour and, 480, *481*, 482–83; recommendations for reorganizing, 483–85
insular cases: on citizenship following flag or not, 55–56, 57, 180, 181, 217; decisions of, 362–64; *Gonzales* case in, 332–33, 334–38; National Guard deployment in context of, 425; questions in, 360–61; reinvention of U.S. citizenship and, 338–41; unincorporated territories concept in, 353, 373; use of term, 606–7n12
Insular Experiment Station (Puerto Rico), 503
International Peace Congress (The Hague, 1907), 184, 185
Intramuros (fortress), 490
Iran hostage crisis, 469
Iraq: Chalabi's information about, 269–70; Green Zone of, 492; legal system of, 330;

lessons from Philippine wars applied to, 461; U.S. invasion and occupation of, 6, 79, 389, 430, 471, 532. *See also* Gulf War (1991)
Irizarry, Luis, 433
Islam. *See* Muslim people
Islamic fundamentalism, 527–28. *See also* Muslim people
Isthmian Canal Commission (ICC), 318, 326, 502
Iwahig Penal Colony (Philippines): convict status and classification in, 119–21; discipline in, 121–23; as experiment in colonialism, 117, 124–26; judicial system of, 123–24; paradoxes of, 124, 127–28; self-governance in, 116, 118–19, 120, 121, 122–24, 125–26
Iwo Jima Monument, 541

Jackson, Andrew, 50
Jamaica: agricultural research in, 505; British financial assistance for, 44; GTMO contract workers from, 459; revolt in, 48, 61; U.S. base in, 445
Japan: China market interests of, 77; drug policy of, 98; empire of, 88; opening of, 66; as protectorate, 55; U.S. advisers for, 67; U.S. occupation and nation-building in, 529; weather information communicated to, 514–15, 517
Japanese-American war scare (1907), 466
Java: British occupation of, 43–44; crop diseases from, 505
Jay, John, 149–50
Jefferson, Thomas: continental expansion under, 64, 65, 427; on good government, 377; Hamilton's feud with, 376, 380; imperial aspects of, 39, 40, 49; social science proposal and, 134; Tocqueville compared with, 378–79
Jeffersonianism: applied to southern U.S., 381–82; approach to, 375–76, 613n3; global reach of, 389; optimism and decentralization in, 375, 376–77; state formation and, 378–81; Taft era in Philippines and, 382–87
Jenks, Jeremiah, 57
Jenks, Leland H., 547
Jessup, Philip C., 184–85
Jesus, Edilberto de, 42–43
Jim Crow laws, 52

Jocano, F. Landa, 267–68
Johns Hopkins University, 303
Johnson, Chalmers, 27
Johnson, Courtney: chapters, 3–33, 175–90; mentioned, 133, 213, 533, 536, 538, 539
Johnson, E. Finley, 113–14
Johnson, Hugh, 395
Johnson, Lyndon B., 525
Johnson-Reed Act (Immigration Act, 1924), 20, 197–98, 208
Johnston, John R., 505
Jones, Alfred Lewis, 290
Jones Act (1916): implementation of, 117; implications of, 544; limits of, 126, 149; passage of, 427; on Puerto Rican citizenship, 20, 217
Journal of American History, 9
Judge (periodical), 36, 225
judicial systems. *See* legal systems

Kame'eleihiwa, Lilikala, 239–40
Kamehameha I (king of Kanaka [Hawai'i]), 239–40, 242–43, 244
Kamehameha II (Liholiho, king of Kanaka [Hawai'i]), 240, 243
Kanaka (Hawaiian) language, 238–39
Kansas-Nebraska Act (1854), 51
Kaplan, Amy, 6, 10, 33, 273, 534
Katz, Frederich, 76
Kauaunui, Kehaulani, 196
Kautsky, Karl, 78
Kennedy, Paul, 27, 32
Kent, James, 133
Keopuolani (Hawaiian), 239–40
Kepner v. United States (1904), 611n52, 612n65
Kettner, James H., 339
"Kid Chicle" (Lino Rodríguez Grenot), 452–53, 456, 457–58, 459
kinship relations. *See* families and kinship relations
Kirim, Mohammed Jamalul, 402–3
Kissinger, Henry, 523, 525, 526
Knight, Melvin, 547
knowledge: American compendium of colonial, 21; consumption as producing, 197; imperial narrative of, 196, 260–70, 310–14
Kobbe, William A., 410
Korea: opening of, 67
Korean War, 459

Kramer, Paul A.: chapter, 199–209; mentioned, 193–94, 276
Kuleana Act (1850), 244–45

labor force: for agricultural work, 40–41, 208, 209; contract-regimen imposed on, 93; convicts as, 91–92, 93, 119, 120, 121, 122–23; exploitation of, 37–38, 40–42, 44; global-racial regime of, 87–88; indentured, 41, 44; for military, 395–96, 441, 449–51, 452–59; for Panama Canal, 318; responsibility for deaths of, 452–53, 456–59; for synthetic cortisone production, 275–76, 314–16; unfree and forced, 40–43, 213; U.S. consumers' attitudes toward, 255; yellow fever eradication critical to, 290, 293, 294. *See also* slaves and slavery
Laden, Osama bin, 528
LaFeber, Walter, 9, 32, 549, 558n14
Lakota people: Ghost Dance of, 400; massacre of, 393–94, 397, 398–401, 408–9
Lamb, Carroll H., 122, 123–24, 125, 127
LaMont, George D., 448
land and property ownership: Hawaiian land use (*'aina*) vs., 195, 239–47; in Moro Province, 417; Western ideal of, 242–44
Langhorne, George, 405
languages: centrality of, 173; of Hawaiians, 238–39. *See also* English language; Spanish language
Lansdale, Edward G., 468
"Large Policy" (1808), 65
Las Casas, Bartolomé de, 234
Latin America: co-optation of elites in, 178; political scientist's approach to, 179–81; reciprocity treaties with, 67; Root's tour of, 184, 185; U.S.-British differences over, 68. *See also specific countries*
Latin American studies, 179, 184–88
Laurel, Jose, 112
law and development efforts, 330
law and society movement, 329
Law of 1825 (Hawai'i), 243
Lawton, Henry W., 468
Layman's Missionary Movement (1906–8), 552
League of Nations, 547
Leahy, William D.: on battleships, 434; *Life*'s depiction of, 435; on Puerto Ricans, 148; Puerto Rico under, 432, 436–39

legal systems: approaches to, 329–31; clash of, 49–50; Hawaiian land use and, 243–46; racism in, 198. *See also* civil rights; land and property ownership; sovereignty; voting and voting rights
legal systems in Cuba: military subcontractor outside of, 454–56, 458; suffrage and equality in, 221–22; sugar companies outside of, 453–54
legal systems in Philippines: authoritarian sovereignty and, 330, 342–52; constitutional theory in, 369–74; documents of, 196; elections in, 383–84; forged document and, 196, 261–62, 267; instructions for, 363–64; Jeffersonianism and Taft era in, 382–87; New Deal ideas in, 330, 365–66, 374; in penal colony, 123–24; the public as notion in, 371–72; Spanish structure of, 368; U.S. constitutional theory and, 330, 353–64. *See also* Philippine Supreme Court
legal systems in Puerto Rico: citizenship ambiguities in, 332–41; criminal justice in, 92–93; Spanish structure of, 211–13; U.S. study of, 179–81
legal systems in U.S.: constitutional theory in, 330, 353–64; military subcontractor outside of, 456; racism in, 198. *See also* constitutional theory (U.S.); insular cases; U.S. Supreme Court
LeMay, Curtis, 529
Lemes, Lino, 459
Leopold II (king of Belgium), 291
Leopold, Richard W., 24, 29
leprosy, 279, 286, 483
LeRoy, James A., 266, 466
Leschohier, Alexander W., 311
Lessep, Ferdinand de, 442
Lete, Eduardo de, 264
Leur, Jacob van, 480
Levine, Philippa, 276, 534–35
Lewis, Merriwether, 476
liberalism, 60–61, 62
Liberia: agricultural adviser for, 504; Colonization Society in, 500; U.S. airfield in, 445
liberty: American ideal of, 526–28, 530; continental expansion in pursuit of, 63–64; Philippine ideal of, 345–46, 348–49. *See also* democracy and democratic ideals; freedom

libraries, 261, 262, 265
Lieber, Francis, 133
Life (magazine), 203, 313, 399, *405*, 435
Li Hongzhang, 527
Lili'uokalani (queen of Hawai'i), 243, 246
Lincoln, Abraham, 51, 378
Lindsay, Samuel McCune, 164
Linn, Brian McAllister: chapter, 460–72; mentioned, 396, 410, 528
Lipman, Jana K.: chapter, 452–59; mentioned, 395–96
Lipset, Seymour M., 149
literacy, 142–43, 152
Literary Digest (periodical), 359
"little brown brother": use of term, 206
Liverpool School of Tropical Medicine, 290
livestock diseases, 483
Lochner v. New York (1905), 373–74
Lodge, Henry Cabot, 50, 71
Loewen, James, 544
Lombardi, John, 214
Lombroso, Cesare, 90
London School of Economics, 59
Long, John D., 286, 541
Longfield, Bradley J., 552
Lopez, Sixto, 204
Louisiana: Spanish control of, 42; U.S. assimilation of, 49. *See also* New Orleans (La.)
Louisiana Purchase (1803), 39, 49, 64, 427, 442
Louisiana Purchase Exposition (St. Louis, 1904), 207, 230, 511–12
Love, Eric, 11
La Lucha (newspaper), 220, 221
Lundestad, Geir, 546
Luzon: U.S. imperialism in, 73
Lynch, Frank, 267–68
Lynch, Owen J.: chapter, 353–64; mentioned, 331

Mabini, Apolinario: background of, 345; on independence and natural law, 345–46, 348–49; on justice and reason, 343; photograph of, *347*; role of, 330–31
MacArthur, Arthur, 367, 464, 471
MacArthur, Douglas, 529
Macau: heritage of, 543
Machiavelli, Niccolo, 269–70
Mackie, John Milton, 300
Macleod, Roy, 309

Magellan, Ferdinand, 263, 264
Magoon, Charles E., 358–59, 361, 362
Magsaysay, Ramon, 468
Mahan, Alfred Thayer, 71, 393, 434, 442, 546, 554
Mahele (Division, 1848), 196, 244
Maier, Charles S., 6, 27–28, 532
malaria: in Cuba, 290; in Philippine prison, 117; prevention of, 121, 286, 323–25, 326; in San Jose, 15; tropics linked to, 302–3; U.S. campaign against, 284–85; U.S. conquest of, 16
Malcolm, George A., 113–14, 369–70, 371, 372
Manifest Destiny, 145, 163, 196
Manila: Carnival of, 156
Manila (Philippines): Bilibid Prison in, 116, 119–20, 121–22, 123, 124, 125; Botanical Gardens of, *474*; design and structure of, 15, 489–92; information technologies in, 109–10; Moro separatist movement and, 416–19; opium den in, *100*; politics of scandal in, 111–14; sanitation and environmental management in, 477, 489, 492–98; U.S. occupation of, 106, 109–10, 355, 461, 489
Manila Evangelical Union, 555
Manila Metropolitan Police, 109–13
Manila Weather Bureau and Observatory: cable and wireless communication of, 509, 513, 514–16; daily work of, 477–78, 516–19; master plan for, 509, 512–14; reorganization of, 508–9; Spanish-to-U.S. transition of, 509–10; weather maps of, 516–17; world's fair display of, 511–12
Manlapit, Pablo, 429
Manson, Patrick, 301
Manuel, E. Arsenio, 267–68
Mao Zedong, 527
Marcantonio, Vito, 437
Marco, Jose E.: acquisitions by, 262; collectors' interests and, 264; forgeries of, 268–69; library's acquisitions from, 266–67, 270
Marcos, Ferdinand E., 114
María Cristina (regent of Spain), 90
Marianas: typhoon early warnings for, 513, 515
Marker, Russell, 311
Marple, Allan D., 469
Marquardt, Walter W., 154, 159
Marsh, George Perkins, 321

Marshall, George, 529
Marshall, John, 40, 50, 51, 339
Marshall Plan, 546
Martínez, Providencia, 169–70
Martínez Nadal, Rafael, 437, 438
Martinique: French regime in, 61, 442
Marx, Karl, 375
Massachusetts: Minute Man statue in, 421; public health commission in, 284–85
Massachusetts Supreme Court, 371
massacres: Bud Bagsak, 397, 407–8, 419, 463; Bud Dajo, 120, 393–94, 397–98, 399, 402–9, 416; cartoon about, 399; Christianity as justification for, 402–4, 406–9, 411–14; implications of, 408–9; Moroland, 402–4, 407–8; Ponce, 395, 432, 433–34; as racialized violence, 393–94; Samar Island, 401–2, 406; terminology for, 463; transnational context of, 397–98; of U.S. soldiers (Bud Bagsak), 397, 401, 471; Wounded Knee, 398–401
Mauritius: British control of, 44
Maximilian (emperor of Mexico), 442
May, Ernest R., 8, 549
May, Glenn Anthony: chapter, 151–62; mentioned, 132, 263, 537
McClintock, Anne, 276
McCook, Stuart: chapter, 499–507; mentioned, 477, 537
McCormick, Thomas: chapter, 63–79; mentioned, 12–13, 32, 524, 533–34
McCoy, Alfred W.: chapters, 3–33, 83–86, 106–15; mentioned, 85, 533, 536–37, 538, 539
McDill, John R., 285
McEnery, Samuel D., 356
McFee, William, 319
McKinley, William: appointees of, 175, 177, 179, 185; assassination of, 108; attitudes of, 264, 549, 553; on Philippines, 21, 73, 264, 353–54, 363, 366, 368, 369, 461; as pragmatic expansionist, 71; Puerto Rico under, 146; reelection of, 205, 356–57; Sugar Trust and, 354–55, 358; Treaty of Paris negotiations under, 355–56
McKitrick, Eric, 376, 378, 381
McLaughlin, Allan J., 284–85
McNeill, J. R., 475–78, 536, 537
Mead, Elwood, 321
medicine: European vs. U.S. developments in, 274; as global form, 287; risk and containment perceptions in, 281–82; U.S. application of, 274–75. *See also* disease; germ theory; pharmaceuticals; tropical medicine
Meléndez-Muñoz, Miguel, 449
Meléndez-Utset, Juan, 441, *447*, 449–51
Mellon, Andrew, 75
meningitis, 290
mercenaries: definition of, 426
Merrill, E. D., 501, 507
Merritt, Wesley, 367, 471
Messersmith, George S., 455
meteorology: acclimatization concept in, 306; Algué's master plan of, 509, 512–14; cable and wireless communication in, 509, 513, 514–16; early warnings systems in, 475, 477–78, 514–19; economic value of, 510; instruments developed for, 511–12; pioneering text on, 508; on tropical vs. temperate climate, 297–99, 302, 307; weather map introduced in, 516–17; world's fair display of, 511–12
Mexican-American War (1846), 64–65, 293
Mexican Comisión Geográfico-Exploradora, 504
Mexican Revolution (1910): economic disruption of, 75–76; leftward legacy of, 76–77; U.S. National Guard and, 424–25
Mexico: 1877 conflict averted with, 66; cortisone production in, 275–76, 309–16; handicraft imports from, 255; Spanish military move against, 42; as tropical, 298; U.S. annexation of northern tier, 65; U.S. imperialism in, 74–77; U.S. occupation of Veracruz, 18, 76
Meyer, A. B., 264
Midway Island: U.S. interests in, 67
migrants and migration. *See* immigrants and immigration
Miles, Nelson A., 400–401, 404, 408
military, U.S.: approaches to, 393–96; Caribbean interventions of, 18–19, 26; democratizing role of, 528–30; education and training of, 449, 460, 466, 470–71, 529; episodic mobilization of, 5; expansion of, 32; Filipinos in, 428–29; history and policy in, 396; modern development of, 17; pre-WWII policy thinking in, 434–36; public debate on, 421–22; public health issues and, 277, 285; Puerto Rican crisis in 1930s and, 395, 431–40; Puerto

Ricans in, 395, 441, 444–48, 449–50; quinine use of, 290; reform ideas in, 394, 421–30; subcontracts of, 19, 452, 454–57; Total Force Policy on, 430; WWII civilian labor force for, 395–96, 441, 449–51, 452–59; WWI reshaping of, 15, 425–30. *See also* U.S. Army; U.S. Department of War; U.S. Marines; U.S. Military Information Division; U.S. Military Police; U.S. National Guard; U.S. Navy; *specific wars*
military-industrial-academic complex, 537. *See also* public-private connections
military operations other than war (MOOTW), 460–61
Mills, Richard W., 470
Milwaukee Public Health Department, 284
Mindanao. *See* Moro Province (Philippines)
Mindanao Herald (newsweekly), 406, 417
mines and mining, 75, 76, 115, 448
Minnesota: war memorials in, 543, 640n11
Minnesota National Guard, 430
Miramontes, Luis Ernesto, 312–13, 315
missionaries: colonial role of, 30, 32; conquest legitimated by, 344; cultural hegemony of, 546, 551–54, 555–56; in drug prohibition struggle, 85, 96–97, 99, 101; globalism in message of, 555–56, 644n67; in Hawai'i, 196, 241–42, 243–44; land surveys by, 245; political neutralization of, 345
Mississippi: sanitation in, 304
Missouri Compromise (1820), 51
Mitra, Ramon, Sr., 127
Monroe, Paul, 157, 160
Monroe Doctrine (1823): applied to Pacific Basin, 66–67; British acceptance of, 68, 72; components of, 49, 65; corollaries to, 68, 72; legitimation of, 26, 185; rights and obligations in, 181, 187; WWII French Caribbean under, 448
Montesino, Coronel Manuel, 90–91
Montesquieu, Baron de La Brède et de (Charles Louis de Secondat), 34
Moody, Dwight, 552
Moon, Parker T., 548
MOOTW (military operations other than war), 460–61
moral reform: civilizing ideas linked to, 278–86; colonial rhetoric of, 30, 31–32;

cultural hegemony of, 551–54. *See also* Christianity; progressivism
"Moral Uplift" program, 74
Moran, John, 294
Morant Bay Rebellion (1865), 48, 61
Morgan, J. P., 177
Morison, Samuel Eliot, 380
Morocco: Spanish prison in (Ceuta), 90
Moro Province (Philippines): Bud Dajo massacre in, 120, 393–94, 397–98, 399, 402–9, 416; campaigns against Muslims in, 462–63; economic development in, 414, 415, 416, 418; extended occupation of, 410–11; geography of, 412; Muslim resistance in, 414–16; Nacionalista networks in, 621n65; Pershing's assaults on, 403–4, 407–8; postcolonial era of, 420; religious diversity in, 410; Samar Island massacre, 401–2; separatist movement in, 416–19; studies of, 27, 469–70; transfer of power in, 418–19; U.S. administration in, 412–14. *See also* Muslim people
Morrill Land-Grant Act (1862), 499
Morris, Henry C., 134, 183
Morúa Delgado, Martín, 228, 592n42
Moses, Bernard: on American imperialism, 181–82, 183; institutional nexus created by, 187–88; positions of, 185–86; Root's relationship with, 133, 179
Mott, Lucretia, 118
Mozambique: agriculture director of, 504; marginalization of, 543
Muir, John, 485, 486
multiculturalism, 150
multilateralism, 79
El Mundo (newspaper), 229, 436–37
Munich Agreement (1938), 434
Munn v. Illinois (1877), 371–72
Muñoz Marín, Luis: government reform under, 439–40; politics of, 147, 433; teacher discourse and, 143; Tugwell's collaboration with, 432; Winship's removal and, 437–38
Muñoz Rivera, Luis, 170
Munro, Dana G., 548
Munson, Edward L., 285
Murphy, Marion Emerson, 454, 455
Musgrave, William E., 284
Muslim people: campaigns against, 462–63; massacres of, 120, 393–94, 397–98, 399, 402–9, 419–20; Moro separatist

Muslim people (*continued*)
movement and, 416–19; reconsidering resistance of, 414–16; suicide tactics of, 396, 403, 407; U.S. beliefs about, 206, 410, 411–12, 413–14. *See also* Moro Province (Philippines)

Nabuco, Joaquim, 184
Nacionalista Party (Philippines), 111, 386, 418, 621n65
NAFTA (North American Free Trade Agreement), 77
Nandy, Ashis, 604n9
Napoleon I (emperor of France), 107, 290
Napoleonic wars, 38–39
Nation (periodical), 224
National Association of Junior Republics, 125
National Association of Manufacturers (NAM), 285–86
National Coal Company (Philippines), 113–14
National Defense Act (1916), 426, 428, 429–30
National Geographic (magazine), 251, 256–57
National Guard (magazine), 425. *See also* U.S. National Guard
National Guard Association, 423
national identity: fiction and myth in, 269–70; us vs. them in, 150
national identity in Philippines: imaginative acts in, 262–63; racial formations resisted in, 204; U.S. appropriation of, 21
national identity in Puerto Rico: commemorating origins in, 147–48, 194–95, 230–37; U.S. collision with, 20–21
national identity in U.S.: Anglo-Protestantism of, 150; Civil War and South in, 298–99; consumer imports as marker of, 256; ideological tenets of, 31–32, 149–50; new kind of world leadership in, 176–77
nationalism: autonomy in, 147; mythology in, 147–48; paradox in perception of U.S., 149–50; politics of empire rejected in, 343. *See also* sovereignty
nationalism in Philippines: revolutionary sovereignty and, 345–49; Spanish political regime and, 343–44

nationalism in Puerto Rico: Americanization countered by, 147–48; citizenship and education in promoting, 131–32, 135–41; identity construction in, 141–43; local negotiations of empire in, 143–44; rise of, 148–50; teachers' role in, 132, 145–50
Nationalist Party (Puerto Rico), 432–34, 438–39
nationalization, 76–77, 372
National Origins Act (1924), 20
National Park Service (U.S.), 320–21
National Research Council (U.S.), 500, 502, 505–6
nationals (U.S. term): coining of, 335; definition of, 336–38, 340; immigration of, 208–9; legal designation as, 332–33; reinvention of citizenship and, 338–40; use of term, 198, 608n45. *See also* citizenship in Puerto Rico
national security, U.S.: academic research linked to, 176–77; Hawaii-Panama-Caribbean line in, 18–19, 434–37; Philippine experience as influence on, 17–18
nation-building concept, 526–27
Native Americans: anthropologists' studies of, 230–31; citizenship questions and, 336, 338–39, 606n4; as "domestic dependent nations," 39–40, 50, 339; equality demanded by, 61; exploited labor of, 37–38; forced acculturation of, 166–67, 171, 172, 398–400; as local independent communities, 56; massacre of, 393–94, 397, 398–401, 408–9; Muslim Moros compared with, 412; Puerto Ricans as, 167, 169; reservations viewed as colonies, 547; rights of possession over lands of, 49–50, 196
nativism, 208–9
Naturalization Act (1918), 429
natural resources: allocation powers over, 358–60; imperial exploitation of, 16, 37–38, 42. *See also* agriculture; conservation movement; environmental management; mines and mining; pharmaceuticals; tropical forestry; tropical botany
Navarro-Rivera, Pablo: chapter, 163–74; mentioned, 133
Negri, Antonio, 27, 550
Negrón de Montilla, Aida, 138
Nelson, Adam, 131–34

Netherlands: mapping of, 107. *See also* Dutch empire
Newberry Library (Chicago), 261, 262, 265, 267–68
New England Anti-Imperialist League, 401
New Orleans (La.): acquisition of, 64; disease in, 291–92; sanitation of, 304
New Republic (magazine), 300
New South Wales (Australia): as British colony, 38
New York: militia of, 423; reformatory in, 118–19, 120, 124–25; self-governing prison experiment in, 116, 118, 127
New York Botanical Gardens, 507
New York City: commemoration of Dewey's victory in, 542–43
New York City Department of Public Health, 274–75, 284
New York Commission on Prison Reform, 127
New York Times: on Bud Dajo massacre, 406; on convict self-government, 125–26; on corruption in Manila, 112–13; on Cuban suffrage, 224, 228; on Dewey's victory, 541, 542; on Winship in Puerto Rico, 433–34
New York Times Magazine, 27
New York Tribune, 254
New Zealand: British power sharing in, 44
NGOs. *See* nongovernmental organizations (NGOs)
Nicaragua: canal rights negotiations with, 67; crisis in 1970s, 469; informal U.S. control of, 74; U.S. counter to British in, 65–66
Nieves, Dolores, 171–72, 174
Nolan, Dennis E., 114–15
noncitizen national. *See* nationals (U.S. term)
nongovernmental organizations (NGOs): colonial role of, 30; cultural expansionism of, 146, 551–54; decentralization and local autonomy ideas of, 389; imperial roles of, 543–44; influences on, 280–81; policy forum and, 24; public-private institutional nexus of, 24–26, 177–90. *See also* missionaries
Normal School (Puerto Rico), 164–65
North Africa: Spanish prison in, 90
North American Free Trade Agreement (NAFTA), 77

North American Review (journal), 306
North Borneo: opium smuggling from, 103–4
Northwest Ordinance (1787), 40, 51, 360
Novak, William J., 338, 339
nullification movement, 381
Nuñez, Toribio, 89–90

Ochoa, Francisco, 457
Office of Experiment Stations (OES), 499
Office of Seed and Plant Introduction (OSPI), 501
Ohnesorge, John, 329–31
oil industry, 75–77
Oldenberg, Veena Talwar, 489
Olmsted, Frederick Law, Jr., 490
Olney, Richard, 72
Ong, Aihwa, 287
Open Door policy: as expansion strategy, 8–9; informal empire linked to, 56; internationalism as, 79; origins of, 178; U.S.-British use of, 66–67; U.S. version for China, 78, 524–25
open warfare concept, 17
opium trade: availability, 100, 102–4; investigative report on, 101; Japan's policy on, 98; licensed then banned, 85, 95–105; police raids and sting operations, 104, 111, 112–13; taxes on, 96, 99, 101. *See also* anti-opium movement
Opium Wars, 66, 77
oral contraceptives: discovery of, 309, 312–13; testing of, 275–76
Ordenanza General de Presidios del Reino (Spanish prison code, 1834), 90
Oregon: expansion into territory, 64, 65; U.S. purchase of, 49
Oregon Convention (1819), 64
O'Reilly, Alejandro, 214
O'Reilly, Gabriel, 160
Oren, Ido, 176–77
Orient: consumption of, 257; dualistic depiction of, 300. *See also* Asia
Ortiz de la Renta, Manuel, 136
Orton, William, 505–6
Osborne, Thomas Mott, 118–19, 126, 127, 128
Osmeña, Sergio, 372
Osuna, Juan José, 165, 169, 171, 173, 174
Otis, Elwell Stephen, 367, 402, 468, 469
Oulahan, Richard, 112–13

Outlook (magazine), 102
overproduction theory, 69

PAA (Pan American Airways), 441, 445, 448
Pacific Basin: U.S. imperialism in, 66–68, 72–73, 77–79, 525. *See also* meteorology; specific countries
Page, Walter Hines, 305–6
Pakistan: national identity of, 150
Palmer Raids (U.S.), 537
Panama: agricultural research in, 502–3, 505; botanical publications on, 501; climate and conquest of, 321–26; cruise line brochures on, 317, 319–20; health code for, 286; tourism in, 317, 318–20; U.S.-Colombian military and revolts in, 67. *See also* environmental management in Panama
Panama Canal: construction of, 123, 274, 317–18; economic benefits of, 78; expansionist function of, 72–73, 442, 444; French beginnings of, 296; military base and defense role of, 19, 434; Miraflores Locks of, 522; opening of, 18, 21; U.S. control of, 66–67, 68; U.S. West linked via, 320–21
Panama Canal Zone: cartoons about, 322; as de facto colony, 73; environmental management of, 17, 275, 283, 318–26; horticulturalist for, 504; as piece of U.S., 319; Puerto Rican soldiers in, 441, 445, 449; yellow fever in, 296, 317
Panama-Pacific International Exposition (San Francisco, 1915): basketry at, 160; Code of Kalantiaw at, 267; hookworm display at, 305; speakers at, 12, 21
Pan American Airways (PAA), 441, 445, 448
Pan-American conferences, 184–85, 186
Pan-Americanism: public-private institutional nexus of, 24–26, 177–90; reanimation of, 179, 548
Pan-American Sanitary Bureau, 286
Pan-American Sanitary Code (1923–24), 286
Pan American Union, 179, 185
Pan American World Airways, 19
Pardo de Tavera, T. H., 206
Parke-Davis laboratory (Detroit), 311
Parker, Michael, 552
Parsons, William E., 491, 498
Partido Revolucionario Institucional (PRI, Mexico), 76–77

Pastells, Pablo, 264
Paterno, Pedro, 348
Patronato Real (Royal Patronage of the Catholic Church), 343–44
Pavón, José María, 267, 268
Pease, Donald E., 10
Pedreira, Antonio, 148
pellagra, 303, 306
penal forms. *See* prisons and penal forms
Pennsylvania. *See* Carlisle Indian Industrial School (Pa.)
pentimenti concept, 535, 538
People of the Philippines v. Pomar, 373–74
Pepke v. United States (1901), 362–63
Pérez, Louis A., 222, 453
periphery. *See* center and periphery
Permanent Court of International Justice (The Hague), 185
Perpich, Rudy, 430
Perry, Matthew, 66
Pershing, John J.: administrative style of, 413, 417; British oil interests and, 76; immigration legislation and, 20; military reform ideas of, 394; Moroland assaults by, 403–4, 407–8, 419–20; post-Philippines career of, 408, 419–20, 467; on WWI tactics, 17–18
Peru: agricultural advice for, 506
Pétain, Philippe, 446
pharmaceuticals: quinine, 290; synthetic cortisone and contraceptives, 275–76, 309–16. *See also* drug prohibition, U.S.; opium trade
Philippine Assembly: establishment of, 117, 120, 207, 383, 385; Filipino control of, 612n18; Muslim "spokesmen" in, 419; National Guard established by, 427–28
Philippine Autonomy Act (1916), 612n18
Philippine Board of Control, 113
Philippine Bureau of Agriculture, 501, 504
Philippine Bureau of Education: commercialization and standardization goals of, 152–53, 159; corn campaign of, 132–33, 157–59; industrial programs of, 154–57, 159–61; sales department of, 156–57, 160, 161
Philippine Bureau of Health, 280, 282, 283–84, 496–97
Philippine Bureau of Public Works, 495

Philippine Bureau of Science, 503
Philippine Civil Service Act (1901), 384
Philippine College of Agriculture, 503
Philippine Commission: centralization bills of, 385; civil service principles of, 368, 384; constitution ignored by, 360–61; developmental goals of, 367–68; first, investigative group, 185–86, 204, 260; forestry laws of, 484, 485, 487; instructions for, 366, 382–83; insular cases concerning, 363–64; Manila architecture and, 490–91; Moro Province administration and, 412–13, 416–19; natural resource allocation and, 358–60; resistance suppressed by, 463; Spooner Amendment and, 357; weather service and, 509, 513
Philippine Craftsman (magazine), 155, 158, 159
Philippine Exposition (Madrid, 1887), 202
Philippine General Hospital, 284
Philippine Government Laboratories, 495
Philippine Independence Act (1934), 607n16
The Philippine Islands (comp.), 21, 261, 265–66
Philippine Islands Medical Association, 285
Philippine Journal of Science, 493
Philippine National Guard, 427–29, 430, 438
Philippine National Library, 261–62, 266–67
Philippine National Police, 106–7
Philippine Organic Act (1902), 54–55, 353, 363, 368, 612n18
Philippine Revolution, 202–3, 263, 345–52
Philippines: agricultural research in, 503, 507; annexation of, 52, 277; as borderland, 278; botanical publications on, 501–2; cartoon about, *203*; census of, 260; centralization of, 368; central-local relations in, 382–87; Chinese people in, 97–99, *100*, 111, 208; cholera epidemic in, *272*, 494–95; civil service in, 117, 368, 384, 386–87, 427; coercive, activist colonial rule in, 83–84; commonwealth period of (1935–46), 55; dam building in, 495, 496; decentralization of, 375–77; derecognition of, 204–5; drug prohibition in, 15, 85–86, 95–105; economic nationalism initiative in, 372; excluded from liberal U.S. framework, 47; GTMO contract workers from, 459; independence for, 18, 20, 126, 209, 340, 345–52, 544; Jeffersonianism and, 382–87; lingerie trade with, *253*, 254; natural resource extraction in, 16; patronage problems of, 384, 385–87, 414; production of knowledge about, 196, 260–70; the public notion in, 371–72; public welfare ideals and, 365–66; Puerto Rico compared with, 210; race in, 19, 199–209; religions in, 206, 207–8; Spanish bureaucracy and innovations in, 12, 365, 366, 367–68; in Spanish defensive strategy, 42–43; Spanish political regime for, 46–47, 343–44; "special provinces" of, 206; sugar mill bankruptcy and malaria in, 15; teachers in, 153, 155–56, 159, 206; U.S. bureaucratic goals and structure in, 24–25, 366–70; U.S. occupation and pacification of, 73, 182–83, 203–5, 283, 355–56; in U.S. defense strategy, 77–78; YMCA in, 554. *See also* Bud Dajo massacre (1906); citizenship in Philippines; education in Philippines; environmental management in Philippines; Filipinos; insular cases; Iwahig Penal Colony (Philippines); legal systems in Philippines; Manila (Philippines); meteorology; Moro Province (Philippines); national identity in Philippines; nationalism in Philippines; policing in Philippines; prisons and penal reforms in Philippines; public health in Philippines; Spanish-Cuban-Philippine-American War (1898)
Philippines Constabulary: establishment of, 109; Isabela Province company of, *82*; lessons of, for Vietnam War, 469; opium den raids by, 104; origins of, 15, 18; scaling back of, 416; sting operations and, 112; surveillance by, 86, 107, 110–11; U.S. backup for, 463; value of service in, *192*
Philippine Scouts, 117, 463, 469
Philippine Studies Program (Chicago), 262
Philippine Supreme Court: appeals to U.S. Supreme Court from, 611n52; colonial government legitimated by, 366; constitutional theory of, 369–70; legal approach of, 370–74; National Coal case before, 113–14
Philippine wars (1898–1913): atrocities in, 382; criticism of, 182–83; documents on, 465–66; emergence of, 542–43; geography and climate in, 415–16, *481*; in imperial transition context, 72, 74; lessons of, 17–18, 396, 460–61, 465–72; Manila

Philippine wars (*continued*)
fighting in, 492; medical issues and, 281–82, 283; military reform after, 422–25; Mindanao occupation in, 394, 410–20; number of casualties in, 463–64; phases in, 461–65; policing in context of, 106–15; race and, 204–5. *See also* massacres; Moro Province (Philippines); Spanish-Cuban-Philippine-American War (1898)

Philippine Weather Bureau. *See* Manila Weather Bureau and Observatory

Phillips, Thomas R., 446

Picó, Fernando, 211–12, 213

Pigafetta, Antonio, 264

Pinchot, Gifford: background of, 321; on conservation, 486; forest management ideas of, 15, 476, 479–80, 486–88; Philippine tour and recommendations of, 480, *481*, 482–85

Piñeiro, Jesús T., 432, 437

Pinzón, Martín Alonso, 232

plague, 291, 497, 498

plantations: agricultural management challenges of, 477, 499–507; contract-regimen for workers on, 93; economy based on, 37–38, 40–42, 44; hemp-growing, 414; latrine building on, 286; leases for Hawaiian, 246–47; mosquito control on, 326; penal colony compared with, 125–26; yellow fever eradication critical to, 294

Platt Amendment (1903), 55, 74, 293, 453

Plessy v. Ferguson (1896), 20, 50

Pocock, J. G. A., 270

Poland: German invasion of, 438

policing: approaches to, 83–86; in imperial transitions, 87–88; as legitimation tool, 114; of opium smuggling, 102–4. *See also* criminology; prisons and penal forms; surveillance

policing in Philippines: information technologies in, 109–10; as instrument of state power, 106–7; as laboratory, 14, 84, 107, 108–10, 114–15; powers of, 373; in Spanish rule, 84; vice prohibition and paramilitary actions linked in, 111–14. *See also* Philippines Constabulary

policing in Puerto Rico: in Spanish rule, 84, 87, 93, 212–13; in U.S. rule, 93–94. *See also* Guardia Civil and Guardia Rural (Spanish colonial police)

policing in U.S.: colonial laboratory for, 14, 84, 107, 108–10, 114–15; emergence in 1830–40s, 89; Spanish influenced by, 91

political parties: Cuba, 457–58; Mexico, 76–77; Philippines, 111, 205, 207, 386, 418, 621n65; Puerto Rico, 143, 233, 432–34, 436–40; U.S., 71–72, 357, 381, 548

political science: imperialism and colonialism linked to, 176–77, 181–83, 184; professionalization of, 188; Puerto Rico study based in, 179–81

Political Science Quarterly (journal), 53–54

politics: of commemoration, 147–48, 194–95, 230–37; consumption in context of, 249–50, 254–55; Jeffersonian-Hamiltonian differences on, 375–82; patronage-run, 384, 385–87, 414; power sharing in, 44; racial, 194, 199–209; of scandal, 111–14; as war by other means, 382–83

polity: definition of, 24

Polk, James, 64–65

Ponce de León, Juan: Columbus preferred over, 231–32; commemorations of, 21, 194; rehabilitated as symbol, 235–36, 237, 535

Ponce massacre (Puerto Rico, 1937), 395, 432, 433–34

poor people and poverty: as resistant to imperialism, 195; tropics linked to, 299–300, 304–5, 306–8. *See also* indigenous peoples

Popenoe, Wilson, 501–2

Popular Democratic Party (Partido Popular Democrático, Puerto Rico), 143, 432, 433, 437–39

Porto Rican Code Commission, 180

Portuguese empire: colonial representation in, 45; rise of, 35–36, 37; selective memory of, 543; trade promotion and resource exploitation of, 37–38

Posadas, Juan, 497

positivism. *See* rationality and order; social Darwinism

Post, Regis H., 235, 236, 237

postcolonial debate: components of, 26–32; emergence of, 10–11

Povedano, Diego Lope, 266–67, 268, 269

power: border crossings of, 201; centralization of, 213; definition of, 107; of imperial production of knowledge, 196, 260–70, 310–14; implications of smuggling for,

102–4; information revolution phase in, 107–8; institutions as naturalizing, 218–19; police as instrument of, 106–7, 114–15; political sharing of, 44; "soft," 545–46. *See also* colonialism; empires; imperialism

Prado, José, 171

Pratt, Richard Henry, 166–67, 171, 172, 173, 398–99

prisons and penal forms: approaches to, 83–86; "carceral continuum" in, 126; French penal colony and, 442; in Puerto Rico, 91–94, 136–37; theoretical underpinnings of, 87–89, 90–91. *See also* criminology; policing

prisons and penal forms in Philippines: as model for treatment of all Filipinos, 124–26; paradoxes of, 127–28; self-governance in, 15, 116

prisons and penal forms in U.S.: drug treatment vs. incarceration in, 99; impact of drug war on, 86; Iwahig as laboratory for, 116, 124–26; reforms in, 88–89; scandal linked to, 127, 128; work and discipline in, 118–19

progressivism: academia linked to, 183, 184–88; anti-imperialism linked to, 548–49; colonial opportunities in, 479–80; constitutional concerns in, 57–59, 425; foreign policy apparatus of, 176–77; as justification for pacification, 402–4, 406–9, 411–14; medical officer's interventionism and, 281–82; paradoxes of, 127–28; sanitary food concerns in, 496–97; Spanish colonialism juxtaposed to, 212. *See also* Americanization; Christianity; civilization and civilizing ideas

property ownership. *See* land and property ownership

protectionism, 70–72

Protestantism: Americanization via schools based in, 146; cultural hegemony of, 546, 551–54, 555–56; globalism in message of, 555–56, 644n67; gospel of hygiene in, 281–82. *See also* missionaries

PRRA (Puerto Rico Reconstruction Administration), 433, 439

public: definitions and exclusions of, 371–72

public discourse: on Bud Dajo massacre, 406–7, 416; coercive control of, 110; on economic expansion, 69; on empire and imperialism, 70–72, 356–57, 547–48; on foreign policy, 188–90; on governing territories and Constitution, 53–59; on Kid Chicle's death, 457–58; on national military force, 421–22; on Puerto Rico's status, 137–38

public health: approaches to, 273–76; cleanliness and, 276, 282, 303–4; colonial interests in, 288, 290–96; management of tropical nature in, 321–26; peculiarities of colonial nature in, 281–86; successes of, 475. *See also* disease; environmental management; medicine; tropical medicine

public health in Cuba: diseases critical in, 290; Wood's role in, 16; yellow fever concerns in, 288–96

public health in Philippines: centrality of, 15–16; code for, 286; environmental management of, 477, 489, 492–98; surveillance-oriented focus in, 275, 277–87; U.S. public health influenced by, 14, 273–74, 277–87

public health in U.S.: colonial influences on, 14, 273–74, 277–87; sanitation absent in South, 303–4; South as tropical area in, 297–308; southern neo-orientalism in, 276; tropical expertise in, 17; yellow fever concerns in, 291–93, 295

public-private connections: of government agencies, academia, and NGOs, 24–26, 177–90; of U.S. Navy and subcontracting company, 452, 454–56. *See also* environmental management; *specific foundations*

public works projects: Philippine bureau for, 495; in Puerto Rico, 91–92, 93, 433, 439. *See also* Panama Canal

Puerto Rican Bill (1900). *See* Foraker Act (1900)

Puerto Rican Department of Agriculture, 506

Puerto Rico: adapted to U.S. sphere, 47; agricultural research in, 503, 504, 505, 506, 507; annexation of, 52, 277, 333–34, 442; autonomy of, 149, 233; as borderland, 278; censuses in, 195, 210–19; coercive, activist colonial rule in, 83–84; current status of, 340–41; economic transition in, 395, 431–32, 439–40; formal U.S. imperialism in, 73; identity construction in, 141–43; insurgency in, 194–95, 210, 230–37; militarization in, 395; misspelled by U.S., 606n3; mythology of, 147–48; political and constitutional regression in,

Puerto Rico (*continued*)
54, 234–35; political crisis in 1930s, 395, 431–34, 436–40; political status debated, 137–38; population statistics, 216; prehistoric Indians of Boriquén, 232, 233–34, 236; prisons and penal forms in, 91–94, 136–37; public finances of, 58; public health in, 213, 303; public works projects in, 91–92, 93, 433, 439; racial regeneration project in, 139–41; rural-to-urban and nonnuclear shift of, 195; separatist campaign in, 147–48; Spanish regime and innovations in, 12, 46–47; Spanish to U.S. transition in, 211–13, 218–19; subaltern roles of, 395, 441, 444–51; tariff issues and, 362; transition to Commonwealth of (Estado Libre Asociado), 431–40; U.S. attitudes toward, 163–64, 234–35; U.S. bureaucratic structure in, 24–25; U.S. citizenship imposed on, 18, 20, 167, 198, 217, 578n12; U.S. studies of, 146, 179–81, 186–87; in U.S. defense strategy, 434–37, 438–40; WWII propaganda in, 392. *See also* citizenship in Puerto Rico; education in Puerto Rico; Foraker Act (1900); Jones Act (1916); legal systems in Puerto Rico; national identity in Puerto Rico; nationalism in Puerto Rico; policing in Puerto Rico; Ponce massacre (Puerto Rico, 1937); race in Puerto Rico; San Juan (Puerto Rico); teachers (Puerto Rico)

Puerto Rico Reconstruction Administration (PRRA), 433, 439

Puerto Rico Sugar Planters Association, 503

pulahanes religious cult, 401–2

quarantines, 292–93, 295
Quercy (French ship), 448
Quezon, Manuel, 111, 112–14, 418, 419

race: approaches to, 193–98, 199–200; black/white binary of, 194, 195, 197, 220–29; cartoons about, 225; census classification of, 215–19; centrality of, 277; construction of, 141–44; consumer imports as marker of, 255–58; definition of Hawaiians, 246–47; germ theories linked to, 278–81; heterogeneity in colonial societies, 46, 61–62; self-government based on, 47–48; taxonomy of, 205–8; transnational dynamics of, 199–209; tropical disease linked to, 303–4, 306–8; of U.S. prison population, 89. *See also* class; eugenics; racism and racial discrimination

race in Cuba: census classification of, 219; resistance to U.S. discrimination in, 20; suffrage controversy and, 194, 220–29. *See also* Afro-Cubans

race in Philippines: domestic politics of, 19; transnational dynamics of, 199–209

race in Puerto Rico: census classification of, 215–19; citizenship-building project and, 136, 138–41; identity construction and, 141–44; as sufficiently "white," 20; "whitening" of, 195, 217–18

race in U.S.: binary view of, 194, 220–29; centrality of, 19–20; Cuban views of, 223–24, 226. *See also* African-Americans; racism and racial discrimination; racism; whites

race science. *See* scientific racism
racial degeneracy concept, 139–44
racial hygiene: colonial public health model for, 284–85; colonial warfare and, 281–82; moral and bodily reform in, 278–80; NGOs influenced by concept, 280–81; social contact in, 282–83; transcultural flow of, 286–87
racialization process, 141–42
racism and racial discrimination: in anti-imperialism, 70; in "civilizing" process, 172–74; in cleanliness fetish, 276; consumption and, 197, 249–50, 258–59; in Cuban suffrage debate, 223–24, 225, 226; in forced acculturation, 167, 169; in foreign policy, 197, 275; forged documents in support of, 196; in imperialism, 71; inclusionary formation of, 205–9; in industrial education, 152; institutionalization of, 382; in legal systems, 198; Panama as model for, 319; in Puerto Rican commemorations, 194–95, 230–37; scientific justification for, 20, 48; Spanish use of, 46–47, 91; U.S. adoption of, 50–52; in U.S. military, 395, 441, 444–48; in U.S. prisons, 89; of whites vs. Americans in Philippines, 194, 199–209. *See also* violence

Rafael, Vicente L.: chapter, 342–52; mentioned, 263, 330–31

Raffles, Thomas Stamford, 44
railroads and railroad development, 75, 78, 320
Ramírez, Alejandro, 214
Ramírez Santibañez, José, 438
Rapenne, Jean, 449
rationality and order, 13, 35, 44, 176–77. *See also* environmental management; information revolution; surveillance; technologies of rule
Reconstruction (U.S.), 223, 224, 226, 382
Reed, Walter, 16, 294, 324
Reeves, William Pember, 59
Reglamento de Jornaleros (Puerto Rico, 1849–73), 213
Reinsch, Paul S.: as ambassador to China, 186; on colonial autonomy, 181–83; institutional nexus created by, 187–88; Root's relationship with, 133, 179
religious beliefs: bifurcation fostered in, 206, 207–8; of Hawaiian society, 241; in Philippines, 206, 207–8. *See also* Christianity; Muslim people
Renda, Mary, 11
"Report on Certain Economic Questions of the English and Dutch Colonies in the Orient" (report), 57–58
representational systems: hierarchies of, 45, 61–62
Republican Party (U.S.), 71–72, 357
Reserve Officers' Training Corps (ROTC), 449, 460
Rhode Island: public health officer in, 282
Rice, Condoleezza, 523
Richmond Planet (newspaper), 224, 226
Riggs, Francis Elisha, 433
rights. *See* civil rights; land and property ownership; voting and voting rights
Ring, Natalie J.: chapter, 297–308; mentioned, 276, 535
Rippy, J. Fred, 547
Rizal, José: attitude toward U.S., 202–3, 209; commemoration of, 21, 491; letters and artifacts of, 265; on virtue, 346
Robert, Georges, 446, 448
Robertson, James Alexander, 21, 261–62, 265–67, 270
Rochembeau Field (Guyane), 441, *447*, 449, 450
Rockefeller, John D., 75

Rockefeller Foundation: Heiser's career and, 498; hookworm campaign of, 303, 304, 305–6; influences on, 280; International Health Division of, 285, 286, 303, 305; Philippine studies funded by, 262, 267; tropical pathology catalogued by, 302; yellow fever campaign of, 326
Rockefeller Sanitary Commission, 305, 306
Rodman Board Report (1923), 436
Rodó, José E., 148
Rodriguez, Eulogio, 497–98
Rodríguez Beruff, Jorge: chapter, 431–40; mentioned, 395
Rodríguez Grenot, Lino "Kid Chicle," 452–53, 456, 457–58, 459
Roosevelt, Franklin Delano: on air power, 625n7; appointees of, 146; Cuban workers' complaints to, 456; on freedom, 31; Good Neighbor policy under, 548; as Hamiltonian, 378; New Deal ideas of, 395; Puerto Rican soldiers and, 446; Puerto Rico under, 148–49, 432–40; Vichy relations of, 448
Roosevelt, Theodore: appointees of, 177; attitudes of, 264; cartoons about, *xvi–xvii, 322*; China policy of, 178; circle of, 403, 555; on Dewey's victory, 541; on English language, 146; on freedom, 31; as imperial expansionist, 71, 264, 550; on militia law, 423; Monroe Doctrine corollary of, 68; on moral reform, 554; opium prohibition under, 101–2; peace in Philippines declared by, 462; Pershing rewarded by, 404; as police commissioner, 119; power of, 523–26; progressivism of, 394; sailors addressed by, 2
Root, Elihu: American Puerto Rico envisioned by, 217, 219; circle of, 177–78, *182*; on consumption and production, 69; habeas corpus ignored by, 364; imperial state constructed under, 25–26, 133, 175–76, 179, 188, 189; military reform ideas of, 17, 422–23, 424–25; on Monroe Doctrine, 187; on moral reform, 554; on natural resource allocation, 359–60; on Philippine government, 382; power of, 523–26; as pragmatic expansionist, 71; public-private institutional nexus fostered by, 177–90; Spooner Amendment and, 358, 361
Rose, Wickliffe, 306

Rosenberg, Emily, 551
Rosenkranz, George, 312, 604n24
Ross, E. A., 195
Ross, Ronald, 323
Rossiter, Clinton, 375
ROTC (Reserve Officers' Training Corps), 449, 460
Rowe, Henry S., 213
Rowe, Leo S.: on American imperial efforts, 181–82, 186–87; imperial understanding of, 179–81, 189; institutional nexus created by, 187–88; Pan-Americanism of, 184; positions of, 185; Root's relationship with, 133, 179
Roxas, Manuel, 113, 366
Rumsfeld, Donald, 471, 545, 640n18
Russell, Paul F., 286
Russia: China market interests of, 77; territories ceded by, 54. *See also* Soviet Union
Ryan, Carmelita S., 173

Sagra, Ramón de la, 90
Sahlins, Marshall, 242
Said, Edward, 146, 310
Saint Domingue. *See* Haiti
Saint Lucia: U.S. base in, 445
Salazar, Antonio de Oliveira, 543
Saldívar, José David, 278
Saleeby, Najeeb, 411
Salgado, Pedro, 456
Salman, Michael: chapters, 116–28, 260–70; mentioned, 84, 196
Samar Island (Philippines): account of fighting on, 465–66; massacre on, 401–2, 406
Sanchez, Ricardo, 471
sanitation. *See* environmental management; public health
San Juan (Puerto Rico): commemorations in, 231–34; prisons in, 91–92, 93; U.S. bombers over, 435; in U.S. defense strategy, 436
Santiago-Valles, Kelvin: chapter, 87–94; mentioned, 84–85
Saudi Arabia: as U.S. ally, 527–28
SCADTA (Sociedad Colombo Alemana de Transporte Aéreo), 445
Scarano, Francisco A.: chapters, 3–33, 210–19; mentioned, 195, 533, 536, 538, 539
Schapiro, Louis, 284

Schlesinger, Arthur M., Jr., 8, 28, 528–29, 558n14
Schmidt-Nowara, Christopher: chapter, 230–37; mentioned, 194–95, 535
Schmitt, Carl, 342
"School Week" (Puerto Rico), 136–37
Schurmann, Jacob, 185
Schurmann Commission. *See* Philippine Commission
Schwarzenegger, Arnold, 430
science: imperial narrative of, 309–16. *See also* entomology; environmental management; medicine; meteorology; tropical botany; tropical forestry; tropical medicine
scientific racism, 20, 48. *See also* eugenics
Scott, Hugh L., 400, 404–5, 619n16
Scott, James C., 107
Scott, Rebecca J., 50
Scott, William Henry, 263, 266–69, 270
Seed, Patricia, 535
Selective Service Act (1917), 426
Seligman, Edwin R. A., 57–58
Sellards, Andrew W., 285
Senegalese soldiers, 444
September 11 terrorist attacks, 532
Serbian ethnic cleansing, 28
Seven Years' War (1756–63), 39, 41, 214, 442
Seward, William H., 66
Sexton, William T., 467–68
sexuality and missionaries, 241–42, 243
Sharp, James Roger, 380–81
Shaw, Albert, 57
Shaw, Lemuel, 371
Shefter, Martin, 384
Siberian expedition (1918–20), 467
Sierra Club, 485, 486
Sierra Leone: British control of, 44
Signal Corps (U.S.), 108
Singapore: founding of, 44
Sing Sing prison (N.Y.), 116, 118, 127
Singson (Ilocano Chinese mestizo prisoner), 121–22
Sino-Japanese War (1894–95), 77
Skowronek, Stephen, 385, 387, 559n26
slaves and slavery: abolition of, 40–41; Jeffersonianism juxtaposed to, 376, 379, 380–82; in Puerto Rico, 212; repressing trade of, 44; spread of, 37–38, 42; U.S. divisions over, 51–52

Smith, Cornelius, 413
Smith, Erwin F., 505
Smith, Jacob H., 401–2
Smith, Richard W., 469
Smithsonian Institution, 169, 230, 499, 504
Smithsonian Tropical Research Institute (STRI), 325
smuggling, 102–4
Snare, Frederick, 452, 454–56, 457, 459
Snodgrass, John E., 286
social conjunctures concept, 570n2
social Darwinism, 87, 88–89, 90–91
social engineering concept, 110
socialism, 69, 548
Social Science Research Council, 127
social sciences: imperialism and colonialism linked to, 133, 176–79; professionalization of, 183, 188; proposal for discipline, 134; public-private institutional nexus of, 177–90. *See also* anthropology; Latin American studies; political science
Social Studies (journal), 548
Sociedad Colombo Alemana de Transporte Aéreo (SCADTA), 445
soft power concept, 545–46
Soil Conservation Service (USDA), 321
Soler, Bernardo, 450
Solis, Marcus, 429
Somalia: conflict in, 470
Sophie, Ulrich, 449
Soto Laveaga, Gabriela: chapter, 309–16; mentioned, 275–76
South Africa: British rule and segregation in, 48
South America: fears of U.S. dominance in, 64; as tropical, 298; U.S. airfield in, 445. *See also specific countries*
South Carolina: nullification movement in, 381
Southeast Asia: imperial governance in, 57–58; smuggling in, 102–4. *See also specific countries*
Southern Medical Journal, 303
sovereignty: definition of, 342; as following U.S. flag, 361; in law and development context, 330; in natural law, 346, 348–49; non-theological concept of, 350–52; revolutionary reappropriation of, 345–46, 348–49; Spanish Catholic version of, 343–44

Soviet Union: Afghanistan invaded by, 469; collapse of, 10, 470; fears of, 468. *See also* Russia
Spain: censuses in, 214, 215; Falangists of, 455; Filipino social contract with, 346; prisons and penal forms in, 89–91; territories ceded by, 53
Spanish-American War. *See* Spanish-Cuban-Philippine-American War (1898)
Spanish-Cuban-Philippine-American War (1898): American expansionism after, 26–27, 63–64, 145–46, 163–64; Battle of San Juan Hill in, 404; commemoration of, 10, 541–44, 640n11; communication technologies in, 109; Cuban suffrage in context of, 221; economic devastation of, 294; events of, 106, 203–4, 353; Latin American ill will after, 184–85; legacy of, 393–94, 396, 442, 444; public discourse on, 547–48; Puerto Rican narrative shift after, 234; racial formations in, 204; sanitation and medical developments in, 283–84; U.S. military development in, 17; yellow fever concerns in, 293. *See also* Philippine wars (1898–1913); Treaty of Paris (1898)
Spanish empire: archives of, 230, 235; censuses of, 195, 210–11, 213–18; colonial representation in, 45, 46–47; defensive strategy in, 42–43; displacement of, 21; education under, 163; exceptionalism among populations of, 61; forestry in, 476, 483–84; historical continuity from, 7, 12–13, 93–94, 211–13, 218–19; policing of, 84, 87, 91–93; political regime of, 46–47, 343–44; Puerto Rican commemoration of, 147–48, 194–95, 230–37; racial legacy of, 140–42, 194; racist exclusions of, 202; rise and fall of, 35–39; slavery in, 40; suffrage in, 221; trade promotion and resource exploitation of, 37–38, 42; U.S. appropriations from, 210–11; U.S. rhetoric in expelling, 11–12, 20–21, 65, 84, 212, 234, 237, 355; waterworks in, 493–94; work organization in, 41–42
Spanish language: academics' expertise in, 185–86; attempt to eliminate, 166, 167; celebrated in Puerto Rico, 147–48, 149, 236
Spate, O. H. K., 42
Spaulding, Oliver Lyman, 467

Spofford, Harriet Prescott, 254
Spooner, John C., 357–58
Spooner Amendment (1901), 357–60, 361
St. Florian, Friedrich, 543
St. Louis World's Fair (Louisiana Purchase Exposition, 1904), 207, 230, 511–12
Stahl, Agustín, 232
standardization, 152–53, 156, 159–60
Standley, Paul, 501, 507
Stanley, Peter W., 367
Stannard, David, 239
state formation: in Africa, 615n41; differences in, 5; Huntington on, 150, 384; Jeffersonian ideas and, 378–81; process of U.S., 13–14. *See also* national identity; nationalism
state power. *See* power
Statistical Commission (Spain), 215
Steinberg, David Joel, 382
Stepan, Nancy Leys, 140, 298
Stephens, H. Morse, 267
Stephenson, Gilbert Thomas, 51
Stiles, Charles Wardell, 303, 304
Stimson, Henry, 424–25
Stoler, Ann: on "geographies of intimacy," 275; on imperialism, 9, 10, 31, 533; on postcolonial debate, 26; on racial hygiene, 278
Storey, Moorfield, 401
Stowe, Harriet Beecher, 125
Stowe, Lyman Beecher, 125
Strobel, E. H., 57
Strong, Richard P., 285
Studd, Charles, 552
Student Volunteer Movement for Foreign Missions (SVM), 551, 552
Stuntz, Homer, 555–56
subjects: use of term, 363. *See also* nationals (U.S. term)
Suez Canal, 73, 318
suffrage. *See* voting and voting rights
sugar industry: alternative to work in, 453–54, 457; in Cuba, 294, 354–55, 453–54, 457; in French Caribbean, 442; in Hawai'i, 246; in Puerto Rico, 432; resource allocation debate and, 358, 362, 363; slave and unfree labor for, 37–38, 40–42, 44; tariffs and, 354–55; tropical agricultural research and, 503–4; viral disease of, 505. *See also* agriculture; plantations
Sugar Trust, 354–55, 358

supply and demand law, 69
Suri, Jeremi: chapter, 523–31; mentioned, 28–29, 30, 31–32, 538
Surinam: mining in, 448
Surlemont, Jules, 449, 450
surveillance: colonial experience translated to U.S., 536–37; in disease prevention, 275, 277–87; Philippine precedent in, 18, 85–86, 107, 109–10, 114–15; by Spanish colonials in Puerto Rico, 212; tools and techniques of, 107–8, 110–11; in yellow fever campaign, 295. *See also* information revolution; policing
Sutter, Paul S.: chapter, 317–26; mentioned, 274, 275, 276, 296, 537
SVM (Student Volunteer Movement) for Foreign Missions, 551, 552
Swope, Guy, 432, 439
Syntex Laboratories (Mexico), 309, 311, 312–14, 604n24
syphilis experiment, 276

Taft, William Howard: appointees of, 177; attitudes of, 206, 264; on Bud Dajo massacre, 406; Cuba under, 188; on decentralized government, 375; Jeffersonianism and, 382–87; Manila architecture and, 490–91; on moral reform, 554; on Moro Province, 417; on Muslim people, 411; National Guard deployment and, 424–25; on Philippine Commission, 185–86, 357; on Philippine judiciary, 370; Philippines under, 54–55, 110, 111, 471; photographs of, *182, 328*; on sanitary science, 283; Taylor's report suppressed by, 466; timber cutting question of, 358–60; visitors of, 480; Weather Bureau plan and, 512
Tagalog people: on *kalayaan,* 349, 350–52; "liberation" needed, 204
Tagliacozzo, Eric, 102–3
Taiwan: Japan's opium policy in, 98
Taliban, 28
Taney, Roger B., 198, 338, 360
tariffs: absent for Philippine embroidery, 161; Cuban sugar, 354–55; insular cases concerning, 362–63; Philippine agricultural exports, 620n35; Puerto Rican sugar, 362. *See also* taxes and taxation
Tausug people. *See* Bud Dajo massacre (1906); Muslim people

taxes and taxation: collection of forestry (Philippines), 485; in colony vs. metropole, 45–46, 47; constitutional questions about territories and, 54–55, 57–58; of opium trade in Philippines, 96, 99, 101; of tobacco, 42–43. *See also* tariffs
Taylor, Hannis, 427, 430
Taylor, John R. M., 464, 466
Taylor Grazing Act (1934), 320
teachers (Puerto Rico): citizenship-building project of, 136–41; goals of, 131–32; identity construction of, 141–43; as negotiating through imperialism, 143–44; recentering narrative on, 135–36; training of, 163, 164–65; U.S. teachers vs., 146
technological developments: cable and wireless communication, 509, 513, 514–16; cotton gin, 40; dam building, 495, 496; meteorological and seismic instruments, 511–12, 513–14; stereoscopy, 516
technologies of rule: blood quantam, 246–47; censuses, 195, 210–19; chemical discoveries, 314–16; commemoration narratives, 231–34; engineering projects, 317–18, 319–20; exported to U.S., 275; information tools, 107–10; land distribution, 195, 238–47; Western law, 330. *See also* education; legal systems; voting and voting rights
Teller, Henry, 354
Teller Amendment (1898), 72, 354–55
Tennessee Public Health Department, 303–4
Ten Years' War (1868–78), 222, 223
territorial incorporation doctrine, 334
territories: constitutional questions about, 53–59; as forerunners of states, 52–53; Northwest Ordinance on, 40, 51, 360; use of term, 163. *See also* nationals (U.S. term)
Texas: purchase of, 49, 64
Thompson, Wayne, 419
Tobago: racial discrimination in military stationed on, 445–46
Tocqueville, Alexis de: on American practicality, 376; Jefferson compared with, 377, 378–79; on liberty, 526, 530; limits of, 381
Tomb of the Unknown Soldier, 541
Tomes, Nancy: chapters, 273–76, 532–40; mentioned, 29, 30–31

Torres, Alberto, 457
torture: cartoon of, *405*; Spanish use of, 92; U.S. use of, 401–2, 462; use of term, 164
Total Force Policy, 430
tourism: consumer geographies in, 251–52; cruise line brochures on, 317, 319–20; empire as, 318–20; sex-focused, 276
TPRF (Tropical Plant Research Foundation), 505–6
trade. *See* commerce and trade
Transcontinental Treaty (1819), 64
transitions. *See* imperial transitions
transnational movement of ideas: approach to, 179–81; biomedical citizenship, 286–87; colonies as crucibles in, 533–40; economics, 248–50; education, 131–34; evaluation of, 523–26; forestry, 485–88; historiography, 230–31, 236–37; legal reform, 329–30; missionaries' role in, 551–54; public health, 273–74, 277–87, 326, 498; race, 193–98; racial politics in, 199–209; surveillance, 536–37; taxonomy of race, 194, 199–209; tropical inertia concept, 297–98; tropical studies, 300
Treaty of Berlin (1899), 639n4
Treaty of Guadalupe-Hidalgo (1848), 237
Treaty of Paris (1898): on civil rights of territories, 334, 337–38; commemoration of, 541–42; components of, 53, 234; legacy of, 393–94; negotiations of, 355–56; shortcomings of, 334, 360; social contract broken in, 346; tariff implications of, 362
Trinidad: racial discrimination in military stationed on, 445–46; U.S. base on, 445; in U.S. defense strategy, 434–35
Tripartismo (Puerto Rican parties), 438–39
Trocki, Carl A., 97
tropical botany: agricultural management approach to, 477, 499–500; economic usefulness of, 475; hunters and explorers of, 500–503; U.S. agricultural research applied to, 503–6; U.S. cosmopolitanism and, 506–7
tropical forestry: economic usefulness of, 475, 476; ideals underlying, 479–80; Pinchot's Philippine tour and recommendations on, 480, *481*, 482–85; preservationist vs. utilitarian, 486–87
tropicality concept, 482
tropical medicine: classification of, 302–5; colonial interests in, 288, 290–96;

tropical medicine (*continued*)
  forestry management and, 483; imperial geographies in, 297–308; professional mobility in, 283–86; quarantine officer in, 496–97; race linked to, 303–4, 306–8; racializing germ theories in, 278–81; terminology and specialization of, 301–2; training in, 285, 286, 303; vector theory in, 323, 324. *See also* disease; *specific diseases*
Tropical Plant Research Foundation (TPRF), 505–6
Tropic of Cancer, 3, 22, 33
tropics: agricultural research in, 477, 499–507; assumptions about, 297–99; disease evoked by, 321–26; dualistic depictions of, 299–300; forestry in, 476, 479–88; race and disease in, 302–8; racial discrimination in military stationed in, 445–46; tourism in, 317, 318–20. *See also* U.S. South; *specific countries*
Truman, Harry S., 149
tuberculosis, 290
Tugwell, Rexford G., 148, 432, 439–40, 446, 450
Tulane University, 285
Turner, Frederick Jackson, 547, 549
Turner, George, 358
Tuskegee Institute, 132, 134, 165, 166, 276
Tyack, David, 154
typhoid, 282, 496
Tyrrell, Ian: chapter, 541–56; mentioned, 28–29, 30, 32, 538

UFC. *See* United Fruit Company (UFC)
unfree and forced labor: imperial context of, 41; Spanish program of, 213; for tobacco crops, 42–43; voting denied for, 40. *See also* slaves and slavery
Unión Española (newspaper), 227
United Fruit Company (UFC): agricultural research of, 501, 503; former staff of, 452, 457–58, 459; mosquito control techniques of, 326; steamship line and tourism of, 319; towns of, 453, 456; wartime work compared with, 395
United States: airplane production in, 448; as backward, 533–34; colonial period of, 274; exceptionalism of, 8, 29, 63–64; Filipino attitudes toward, 202–3; Filipino social contract with, 346; frontier society of, 49–50, 63–64, 547; global power of, 6, 9, 10, 19, 26–32, 188, 389, 470; ideals identified with, 149–50; as military power, 528–30; multiple expansion processes in, 5–6; North-South division in, 50–52, 89; reunification of, 298–99; as revolutionary power, 526–28; role of Panama Canal in westward movement, 320–21; scientific expeditions of, 476; Southwest expansion of, 230, 237; state formation of, 378–81, 387–89; status in 1898, 13, 22–23, 559n26; weather information communicated to, 514. *See also* American Civil War (1861–65); American imperial state; American Revolution; Constitution (U.S.); drug prohibition, U.S.; education in U.S.; environmental management in U.S.; federal government, U.S.; legal systems in U.S.; military, U.S.; national identity in U.S.; national security, U.S.; policing in U.S.; prisons and penal forms in U.S.; public health in U.S.; race in U.S.; U.S. South; *specific states*
United States Steel Corporation, 177
universities: colonial service of professors in, 183, 184–88; as knowledge producing, 261; Philippine studies in, 262, 267–68; in public-private institutional nexus, 177–90; tropical medicine at, 284, 285. *See also* social sciences
University of California, 186, 284
University of Chicago, 262, 267–68
University of Puerto Rico, 164, 449
University of Wisconsin, 8–9, 186, 539, 548–49
Upjohn Pharmaceuticals, 312
Upton, Emory, 423–24
urban penalty concept, 493
Uruguay: health code for, 286
U.S. Agency for International Development, 388
U.S. Army: counterinsurgency terminology of, 460–61; education system of, 449, 460, 466, 468, 470–71; history and policy in, 396, 460–72; implications of colonial service in, 17–18; infrastructure construction of, 415–16; meteorological information for, 513; Mexico conflict and, 66, 76; Mindanao occupation of, 394, 410–20; Moro Province massacres by, 393–94, 397–409; Philippine pacification

by, 106–7, 108–10; yellow fever experiences of, 293, 294, 295. *See also* U.S. Army Medical Department; U.S. Military Information Division; U.S. Military Police

U.S. Army Medical Department: interventionism of, 281–82; sanitary developments of, 278, 283–84, 285; tropical medical training in, 303; yellow fever prevention by, 289

U.S. Board of Indian Commissioners, 399

U.S. Congress: act of sovereignty and options of, 53–54; army appropriations and colonial issues debated, 357–60; Hawaiian leases debated, 246–47; military reform debated, 423, 426; Philippine Commission's defiance of, 360; race science/eugenics policies of, 20; Treaty of Paris debated, 356

U.S. Department of Agriculture: challenges to, 325; meteorological information for, 510; plant quarantines by, 502; research of, 499–502; Soil Conservation Service of, 321; tropical research and, 503–7

U.S. Department of Education, 165

U.S. Department of Interior, Division of Territories and Island Possessions, 433

U.S. Department of State, 179, 608n45

U.S. Department of War: Bureau of Insular Affairs in, 24, 57, 333–35, 511; Division of Customs and Insular Affairs, report of, 361; expansion of feared and promoted, 70–71; on Guyane airfield, 449; Hawai'i National Guard and, 429–30; information technologies of, 108–10; meteorological information for, 510; National Guard deployment and, 424–25. *See also* Bureau of Insular Affairs (U.S.); military, U.S.; U.S. Army; U.S. Marines; U.S. National Guard; U.S. Navy; *specific wars*

U.S. Forest Service, 320–21, 325, 480, 488

U.S. Justice Department, 108

U.S. Marines, 18–19, 455, 471, 496, 541

U.S.-Mexico border, 278

U.S. Military Information Division, 17–18, 108–10, 115

U.S. Military Police, 18, 115

U.S. National Archives, 260

U.S. National Guard: federal control of, 426; founding of, 74; international deployment question about, 394, 423, 424–25; military reform efforts and, 422–25; public debate on, 421–22; WWI and, 425–30

U.S. National Herbarium, 499–500, 501

U.S. Navy: bases for, 18–19, 65, 74; expansion of, 71; fleet maneuvers in 1939, 436–37; "Great White Fleet" of, 2, 18; meteorological information for, 478, 509–19; Philippine occupation by, 203–4; pre-WWII thinking on, 434–35; WWII civilian labor force for, 395–96, 441, 449–51, 452–59. *See also* Guantánamo Bay (GTMO, Cuba)

U.S. Public Health Service: on animals and sanitation, 304; colonial service and, 278; leadership of, 283–84, 285; response to disease outbreaks, 286; tropical pathology catalogued by, 302

U.S. South: dualistic depictions of, 299–300; Jeffersonianism applied to, 377, 381–82; pathology of, 302–5; race and disease in, 306–8; tropical disease and, 301–2; as tropical space, 297–99, 305–6; yellow fever in, 291–93, 295. *See also* American Civil War (1861–65)

U.S. Supreme Court: affectation doctrine of, 371–72; appeals from Philippine Supreme Court to, 611n52; on citizenship for Puerto Ricans and Filipinos, 332–33; *Dred Scott* case and, 52, 336, 338, 360; on military deployment, 427, 430; on Native Americans, 39–40, 50; on racial segregation, 20, 49–50; rational basis review and, 373; on territories, 360; on women's sterilization, 276. *See also* insular cases

U.S. Volunteer Infantry, 199

USS *Charleston*, 184

USS *Connecticut*, 2

USS *General Alava*, 480, *481*, 484

USS *Houston*, 436

USS *Maine*, 543

USS *Missouri*, 522

USS *Olympia*, 508, 543

Valdezate, Zoraida, *168*, 169
Valle Atiles, Francisco del, 93
Van Deman, Ralph H., 114–15
Vanderbilt, Cornelius, 177
Varg, Paul, 551
Vaughan, H. W., 429
Vázquez Calzada, José L., 218

Veber, Rene, 448–49
Venezuelan Crisis (1895), 68, 72
Vietnam War, 430, 469, 527, 541, 549
El Vigilante (periodical), 457–58
Villa, Pancho, 408, 420
Villamor, Ignacio, 117
Villanueva y Jordá, Juan, 89
violence: conventional civilized vs. guerrilla savage, 204–5; Filipinos targeted in U.S., 208, 209; politics of recognition juxtaposed to, 201. *See also* massacres; torture; *specific wars*
Virginia: Hampton Institute in, 134, 165, 166, 196; women's sterilization in, 276
Virgin Islands: agricultural research in, 503; purchase of, 67, 444; in U.S. defense strategy, 434–35, 436
vocational training. *See* industrial education programs
Vogue (magazine), 253
voting and voting rights: Cuban controversy on, 194, 220–29; rejected for unfree, 40; southern obstruction of, 51

Wake Island: U.S. imperialism in, 73
Walker, William, 66
Wanamaker, John, 256
war: commemorations of, 541–43; as conventional civilized vs. guerrilla savage, 204–5; focus on "big," 460–61, 463, 466; individual character and, 464–65, 468; "open," 467; on terror, 389. *See also specific wars*
warding concept, 56
War of 1812, 65, 423
Warren, James Francis: chapter, 508–19; mentioned, 477
Washington, Booker T., 132, 166
Washington, George, 39, 49
Washington (D.C.): Manila compared with, 490–91
Washington Evening Star (newspaper), 401
Washington Star (newspaper), 407
water systems, 493–96. *See also* public health
Watson, Malcolm, 323
Webb, Beatrice, 59
Webb, Sydney, 59
Weber, Max, 107, 329
Webster, Noah, 145
Weigley, Russell, 528

Welsh, Herbert, 400–401
West, Kenneth W., 452, 457–58, 459
Westerberg, Carl F., 306
West India Improvement Company, 504
Westminster system, 45, 59
Westmoreland, William, 469
West Virginia: miners' uprising in, 115
White, Edward, 427
White, Frank, 152–55, 158, 159–60
White, John R., 120–22, 123, 127
White, Katherine Curtis, 195
whites: census classification and counts of, 215–19; poor whites vs. Anglo-Saxons, 299–300, 304–5, 306–8. *See also* race
white supremacy culture, 52, 194, 199–209
Wickersham, George, 424–25
wild yams, 275–76, 309–16
Wilkes Expedition (1838–42), 476
Willard, Frances E., 166
Williams, William Appleman: on anti-imperialism, 524, 638n2; diplomatic history of, 8, 32, 539; economic interpretation by, 548–49; on empire, 28, 530; references of, 558n14
Wilson, Woodrow: appointees of, 113, 186; defensive perimeter under, 18; election of, 207; idealism of, 79, 527, 547, 550; Kissinger on, 525; on moral reform, 554; Moro Province question and, 418; on Philippines and self-government, 279, 427–28; on prison reform and Filipinos, 119, 125–26; on threats to democracy, 528–29; WWI military and, 425–26
Winship, Blanton: criticism of, 432; military style of, 395, 433–34; on Puerto Ricans, 148; removed from governorship, 436–37
Winslow, Charles-Edward Amory, 282
Wisconsin School of U.S. Diplomatic History: legacy of, xv, 539; political context of, 8–9; sources used, 558n14. *See also* McCormick, Thomas; Williams, William Appleman
Wise, Hugh D., 465
Wolfowitz, Paul, 471
women: as consumers of imports, 249–50, 254–58; cosmopolitanism prized by, 197; Iwahig visits of, 121; oral contraceptives tested on, 275–76; organizations of, 256; sterilization of, 276
Wood, Leonard: administrative style of, 413–14, 417; Bud Dajo massacre and, 394,

397–98, 403–7, 408; criticism of, 470; on lessons of the Philippines, 396, 465; military reform ideas of, 394, 424; on Muslim people, 411, 415; postcolonial career of, 419; public health efforts of, 16; scandals surrounding, 111–14; suffrage controversy and, 226, 227, 228, 591n33
Wood, Osborne, 112
Woodward, C. Vann, 381–82
Woolsey, Thomas Dwight, 133
Worcester, Dean C., 185, 264, 509
Works Progress Administration, 439
World's Columbian Exposition (Chicago, 1893), 490, 542
World's Work (magazine), 305–6
World War I: effect of Philippine experience on fighting in, 17–18, 467; impact on herbaria, 502; military mobilization for, 15; National Guard and, 425–30; U.S. dominance after, 76
World War II: commemoration of, 541, 543–44; economic development after, 546–47; French and U.S. rivalries in Caribbean during, 395, 441–51; multilateralism after, 79; social movements disrupted in, 548; submarine warfare in, *443, 444, 445*; unconditional surrender in, 528; U.S. bombing and civilian casualties in, 529; U.S. military administration and, 394–95; U.S. propaganda in, *392*; U.S.–Puerto Rican relations in context of, 432, 434–37, 438–40
Wounded Knee massacre (1890): Bud Dajo massacre compared with, 397, 408–9; condemnation of, 400–401; events of, 398–400; as racialized violence, 393–94
Wright, Hamilton, 101

Yager, Arthur, 136
Yale Review, 57
yellow fever: cartoons about, *322*; as exotic in U.S., 303; locals little affected by, 289–90, 295; prevention of, 323–25, 326; in southern U.S., 291–93, 295; symptoms of, 288–89; U.S. conquest of, 16, 274, 275, 317; U.S. interests in eradicating, 290–96
Yellow Jack (film), 294
Yellowstone National Park, 320
yeoman farmer ideal. *See* Jeffersonianism
Young, Crawford, 615n41
Young Communist League (Cuba), 457
Young Men's Christian Association (YMCA), 551, 552, 554

Zetek, James, 502
Zinn, Howard, 33